Sales and Distribution Management

Text and Cases

THIRD EDITION

Krishna K. Havaldar
Director
Precision B2B Consultants,
Former Professor
Alliance University

Vasant M. Cavale
Management Consultant

Mc Graw Hill

McGraw Hill Education (India) Private Limited

Published by McGraw Hill Education (India) Private Limited,
Registered Office: Anjana Complex No: 5/90 A, Butt Road, St. Thomas Mount, Chennai – 600016, Tamil Nadu, India.

Sales and Distribution Management: Text and Cases, 3e

Tenth reprint 2024

Print Edition
ISBN-13: 978-93-5260-773-0
ISBN-10: 93-5260-773-2

eBook Edition
ISBN-13: 978-93-5260-774-7
ISBN-10: 93-5260-774-0

11 12 13 14 15 RAJ 28 27 26 25 24

Typeset at Text-O-Graphics, B-1/56, Aravali Apartment, Sector 34, Noida 201301 and printed and bound in India at Rajkamal Electric Press, Kundli, Haryana.

Visit us at: www.mheducation.co.in
Toll free in India: 1800 103 5875
Write to us at: support.india@mheducation.com
CIN: U80302TN2010PTC111532

Sales and Distribution Management

Text and Cases

THIRD EDITION

About the Authors

Krishna K. Havaldar is a Director of Precision B2B Consultants, in the areas of business-to-business (B2B) sales and marketing strategies and implementation. Earlier, he was a professor of Marketing at Alliance School of Business, Alliance University, Bengaluru. He has taught Sales and Distribution Management, Business (B2B) Marketing, Marketing of Services and Marketing Management. Prof Havaldar earned his postgraduate diploma in Business Administration from the Indian Institute of Management, Ahmedabad, and a degree in Electrical Engineering from Pune University.

He has a number of research publications and case studies to his credit. He was in top 10 percent of authors on Social Service Research Network (SSRN) by downloads during June 2017. Additionally, he is the author of a textbook on *Business (B2B) Marketing*, which is now in its fourth edition. He has also served as the Dean at the Xavier Institute of Management and Entrepreneurship (XIME), and as the Principal of RJS Institute of Management Studies, Bengaluru.

Before beginning his academic career, he had worked in the corporate sector for over 30 years at various positions of sales and marketing management, such as area sales manager, regional marketing manager, marketing manager, general manager, and vice-president. The list of companies includes Blue Star Ltd., Crompton Greaves Ltd., and Kirloskar Consultants.

Prof Havaldar is a life-member of Management Teachers Consortium (MTC) Global. He was presented with Excellence Awards for "Innovation in Teaching Pedagogy" and for "Outstanding Contribution to Management Education" by MTC Global. Presently, he devotes his leisure time to yoga, pranayama, meditation, and watching cricket—a passion which he has been carrying from his youthful days when he played cricket for Mumbai and West Zone schools, Pune University, and Ranji Trophy for Maharashtra Cricket Association.

Vasant M. Cavale is a management consultant (Network 7 Management Consultants) and has been teaching marketing and supply chain management courses at some of the leading business schools in India and abroad as a guest faculty. A graduate in Mechanical Engineering, he also holds a postgraduate diploma in Business Administration from the Indian Institute of Management, Ahmedabad.

Vasant Cavale worked for almost three decades in the marketing, sales, distribution and logistics departments of the Unilever Group at senior levels, both in India and overseas. He then worked with KPMG Management Consulting for three years as a Principal Consultant, Operations, where he facilitated setting up the supply chain management practice. He has handled a number of consulting assignments in various industry verticals in marketing, sales, distribution, SCM, performance improvement, cost reduction and people management in India and abroad. A member of The Institution of Engineers and Indian Institute of Materials Management, Vasant Cavale has also been involved in a number of training programs in many companies and industry groups in the subjects of his specialization.

His leisure interests include listening to music, watching movies, and reading. He is also associated with a couple of NGOs working for the underprivileged.

Dedicated to

My parents, late Smt. Sushila and late Shri Keshav Govind Havaldar,
my wife, Geeta, and children, Kiran and Shilpa, for their love and support

Krishna K. Havaldar

My parents, late Smt. Rukmini and late Shri NSR Cavale, and my wife, Meera

Vasant M. Cavale

Dedicated to

[illegible]

Krishna K. Havaldar

[illegible]

Vasant M. Cavale

Preface to the Third Edition

The third edition of *Sales and Distribution Management: Text and Cases* is aimed at adapting to the changing conditions prevailing in the market. Customers, nowadays, are using new technologies, such as the Internet, for collecting information on products and services, and making buying decisions. They now demand superior quality of products and services. The new developments in information and communication technologies are now changing the buying and selling practices. Many salespeople now use sales force automation programs, which help them to serve their customers in a more effective and efficient manner. Similarly, many sales managers, at various hierarchical levels, use computer technology to carry out sales management effectively. Asian, European, and the US trade agreements have made it less difficult for companies to sell products and services in different countries globally. In addition, competition in the domestic market from foreign competitors has increased substantially.

A major change happened in India on July 01, 2017 when the Government of India introduced the Goods and Services Tax (GST). As the tag says—One Nation, One Market, One Tax, this is of particular interest to all sales and distribution personnel in the country. The GST subsumes many of the taxes in force till July 1, 2017. Some of the several taxes subsumed by GST are:

- Central taxes like excise duty, additional excise duties, service tax, additional customs duty, and special additional duty of customs (SAD).
- State level taxes like VAT/sales tax, central sales tax, entertainment tax, octroi and entry tax, purchase tax, and luxury tax.

Some of the changes which will happen in the distribution front include:

- It will reduce the need for a large number of C&FAs and distribution centers which were set up primarily to avoid multiple taxation across states on the same set of goods.
- The GST will eliminate the need for hundreds of check-posts at state borders. This will result in avoiding goods trucks having to wait for hours at the check-posts in state borders. This will speed up deliveries of goods as transit time will get reduced substantially.

As an outcome of the changing conditions mentioned above, organizations have become even more market centric. It means that companies are using team selling approach for key customers instead of a single salesperson trying to respond to their important customers' needs. Logistics and retailing have seen marked changes in practices. Managers are required to manage multiple marketing channels such as telemarketing, online selling, and the company's salespeople.

This book will help managers to adapt to the changes that have been occurring and will continue to occur. The key features such as comprehensive coverage, easy-to-understand language adaptive reading, and application-oriented approach can be valuable to the readers of the book. It will benefit not only the students of management and commerce courses, but also aspiring managers, practicing managers, researchers, and sales professionals.

Major Revisions in This Edition

The third edition has been substantially revised to reflect many transformations in the market as stated earlier. While the whole book has been updated, the following topics have been added or expanded:

- Scope of sales management
- Strategic sales management
- Success factors in selling
- Selling challenges and skills
- Key accounts management
- Value of sales training
- Team and global compensation issues
- Sales force automation
- Use of social media theories in retail
- Favourable policy changes in retail in India
- Comparison of supermarkets and *kirana* stores
- Impact of technology on retail store operations
- Digital payment options
- Retail warehouse information systems
- FDI in retail in India
- Retail initiatives in rural India
- Features of online retail
- Online shopping for services
- Logistics support to e-tailing
- Cash and carry wholesale
- Payment methods for distributors
- Use of personal digital assistants
- Features of Competition Act 2002
- SAP sales and distribution module
- Convergence of supply chain and marketing
- Lean thinking in the supply chain
- Goods and Services Tax (GST)

Learning and Assessment Tools

The pedagogical format used for each chapter to make the learning easier includes:

Learning Objectives (LOs)

Learning objectives have been added to each chapter following outcomes based learning approach. It makes the study time more efficient and productive by emphasizing on the required development skills amongst students and to test the outcomes of the study of the course, as opposed to routine learning. This approach creates an ability to acquire knowledge and apply fundamental principles to analytical problems and applications.

Pedagogical Classification

The pedagogy is arranged as per levels of difficulty. All checkpoint problems are linked with Learning Objectives (LOs) and marked with Levels of Difficulty (LOD), to help assess the student's learning. This assessment of levels of difficulty is derived as per Bloom's Taxonomy.

E indicates Level 1 and Level 2, i.e. knowledge and comprehension based easy-to-solve problems.
M indicates Level 3 and Level 4, i.e. application and analysis based medium-to-difficult problems.
D indicates Level 5 and Level 6, i.e. synthesis and evaluation based very difficult problems.

Opening Vignettes

All chapters are introduced with an opening vignette, which typically consists of a company example dealing with many of the key issues to be discussed in the chapter. The opening vignette is meant to create students' interest in the topics to be covered and to illustrate the practicality of the chapter coverage.

Summary

A detailed chapter-end summary is provided in which each paragraph is linked to the learning objectives stated at the beginning of the chapter to recap the important learning outcomes.

Key Terms and Glossary

At the end of each chapter, key terms are stated to draw the attention of the students to their importance. The glossary for the chapters key terms is given at the end of the book. These key terms and the glossary are helpful for them in interview preparation.

Cases

The book has 48 short cases. These cases are given at the end of chapters that can be used for class discussion. In addition, there are 13 integrated cases at the end of the book, which can be used for students' group discussion and presentations, and for classroom discussion. These cases combine topics from various chapters and for identifying the chapters covered in a case, a case-chapter matrix is provided at the beginning of the integrated cases. The total number of cases in the book are 61.

Questions and Assignments for Students

At the end of each chapter, different questions are given which are categorized into conceptual, objective-type and application questions. These are carefully constructed to help both students and faculties. In addition, assignments for students are also provided.

Structure

The book is divided into two sections:

I. Sales Management, and
II. Distribution Management.

In **Section I**, Chapter 1 to Chapter 8, various aspects of sales management, including sales promotions, are dealt. Major topics covered in these chapters include the selling process, planning, sales forecasting, sales strategies, sales territories, sales organizations, staffing, training, motivating, compensating, evaluating, and controlling the salespeople.

In **Section II**, Chapter 9 to Chapter 16, distribution management is exhaustively covered. This section discusses the major topics such as the role of distribution in the marketing mix, classification of marketing channels, channel planning and design, selection, training and motivation of channel partners, managing channels and channel institutions like retailing and wholesaling.

Chapter 17 deals with international sales and distribution management and includes the various aspects of selling and distribution in global markets.

Web Supplement

An exhaustive Instructors' Teaching Supplement is updated which includes the following:

- PowerPoint slides
- Case notes
- Answers to chapter-end objective-type and application questions

Acknowledgments

Many individuals have contributed to the improvements in this edition. We wish to especially thank the following people:

- Prof B. S. Sachidanand, *Management Consultant and Trainer*
- Prof Mihir Dash, *Alliance University*
- Dr Shailendra Dasari, *Executive Director, Sathavahana Ispat Ltd.*
- Prof V. Harihara Subramanian, *Former Dean, Asian School of Business*
- Mr Sameer Gupta, *Director Sales, SS ABLE Advisory Private Ltd.*

We would like to thank our students for their contributions in the development of cases. We wish to recognize with grateful appreciation the efforts of the team at McGraw Hill Education (India), in shaping the third edition. In particular, we thank Ms Anuradha Kumar, Mr Hemant Jha, Mr Satinder S. Baveja, Ms Taranpreet Kaur, Ms. Navneeta Bisht, Ms Shalini Jha and Mr Suhaib Ali.

As always, a great deal of thanks goes to our wives, Geeta Havaldar and Meera Cavale, and our respective families for providing us time and support needed to prepare this edition.

KRISHNA K. HAVALDAR
(krishnahavaldar31@gmail.com)

VASANT M. CAVALE
(vasantcavale@gmail.com)

Publisher Note

McGraw Hill Education (India) invites suggestions and comments from you, all of which can be sent to *info.india@mheducation.com* (kindly mention the title and author name in the subject line).
Piracy-related issues may also be reported.

Preface to the First Edition

Rapid changes in communication and information technology, globalisation of business, increase in competition, and higher level of customer orientation have made sales and distribution management more important than ever. The market environment in the 21st century can be described as fast changing and dynamic.

The role of the salesperson is becoming larger. He or she is a professional who is not only selling products and services but also solving customer problems. The role of the sales and distribution managers is also changing. Today, these managers are looked at as corporate team leaders instead of persons who are in charge of the sales and distribution functions. They are expected to manage multiple channels and to coordinate sales and distribution functions, in order to achieve the goals and objectives of their organisations.

Purpose

The main purpose of this book is to fulfill the need to have *an integrated course on sales management and distribution management*, since most MBA or PGDM curriculums have sales and distribution management as a composite programme.

The primary aim of the book is to provide students of management with a firm foundation for understanding all main components of sales and distribution management. The book has a practical orientation, as it is written by authors who have worked as practising managers mostly in sales and distribution and between them have over 60 years of industry experience. The book, therefore, will be a useful resource to practising professionals in industry, training, and consultancy.

Structure

The text presents sales and distribution management concepts and practices in an easy-to-understand manner, with sufficient depth to develop a good understanding of the course.

The book has, roughly, two parts: (i) Sales Management, and (ii) Distribution Management.

Chapters 1 to 7 are on sales management and Chapters 8 to 15 are on distribution management. Chapter 16 is on international sales and distribution management.

Chapter 1 covers introduction to sales and distribution management, explaining the linkage of the two in a practical manner. In Chapter 2, we discuss personal selling with focus on preparation and process. Chapter 3 deals with planning, sales forecasting, and budgeting. Management of sales territories and quotas are presented in Chapter 4. The tasks of organising, staffing, training, motivating, compensating, leading, and controlling the salesforce are discussed in Chapters 5, 6, and 7.

The various aspects of distribution management are covered in Section 2, as follows.

Chapter 8 starts with the distribution management tasks in the context of the marketing mix and introduces the distribution function as a value-add to business. In Chapter 9, we discuss channel structures, functions and flows and channel relationships. Chapter 10 discusses about an important channel institution—Retailing and aspects relating to its operations and strategy. In Chapter 11, we do a similar analysis of another channel institution, namely, Wholesaling. This chapter also discusses specifics on distribution management.

Chapter 12 focuses on design and planning of channel systems and reviews the topics of vertical integration, outsourcing, non-store retailing and electronic channels. Management of channels including the important aspect of handling conflicts forms the major part of Chapter 13. In Chapter 14, we discuss channel information systems and points on channel implementation. The focus of Chapter 15 is on physical distribution including logistics, supply chain management and in particular, inventory management, transportation and warehousing. Finally, Chapter 16, similar to Chapter 1, integrates sales and distribution management, with a focus on international markets.

Pedagogy

The following pedagogical features are used for each chapter to stimulate learning:

Learning Objectives

Each chapter begins with Learning Objectives, which enable students to understand important points.

Chapter Summary

Each chapter closes with the summary of key points covered in the chapter.

Glossary of Key Terms

A glossary summarizing all key terms appears at the end of each chapter for handy reference.

Conceptual Questions

At the end of each chapter, conceptual questions are given to review key concepts and issues covered in the chapter.

Objective Type Questions

These questions, given at the end of each chapter, provide multiple choices for answers. Special attention was given during preparation of these questions because instructors desire such questions to assess students' competence in the subject accurately and fairly.

Application Questions

Application questions are supplied for each chapter, requiring students to apply what has been learnt in the chapter to a specific situation in sales and distribution management.

Cases for Analysis

Most chapters end with short cases. There are *23 short cases* at the end of chapters. These short cases provide an opportunity for students to apply the concepts to realistic and interesting sales and distribution management situations. The short cases can be used for class discussions or written assignments.

In addition, there are 11 longer and integrated cases at the end of the book. The longer cases, which integrate the concepts and issues in various chapters, are more appropriate for detailed analysis and class discussions, or presentations by individuals or student groups.

Teaching Supplements

An Instructor's Manual will be made available for instructors and will include the following teaching supplements:

- PowerPoint slides.
- Case notes.
- Answers to end-of-chapter questions.

KRISHNA K. HAVALDAR

VASANT M. CAVALE

Brief Contents

Contents

Section II : Distribution Management

Chapter 1

Introduction to Sales Management

LEARNING OBJECTIVES

After studying this chapter, you will be able to:

- **LO 1** Understand evolution and definition of sales management
- **LO 2** Explain the nature and importance of sales management
- **LO 3** Describe the levels of sales management positions
- **LO 4** Discuss the nature of personal selling
- **LO 5** Construct various aspects of strategic sales management and sales planning
- **LO 6** Identify emerging trends in sales management

On a Sunday afternoon in the month of April 2016, after a sumptuous lunch, Pradeep Dasgupta was relaxing in a happy frame of mind on an armchair. Pradeep was happy because only on the previous day, he received the delightful information of his promotion as the Regional Sales Manager-Eastern region, from his senior manager. Pradeep recalled his journey from the day he joined CGL company after successfully completing a degree in engineering.

He had decided to take up a career in sales and marketing, as he was interested in travelling and meeting people. He was also told by his college seniors that generally career growth is faster and compensation is better in sales and marketing, as compared to that in other roles, such as production and finance.

He was hired by CGL as a sales-trainee after tough rounds of written tests and interviews. He remembered how the company selected 10 sales trainees from over 100 applicants.

He knew that he would face intense competition in the corporate world and hence, he thought that he should continuously improve his knowledge and skills with positive attitude. After completion of a six-month sales-trainee program, Pradeep became a territory-sales representative to look after current and prospective customers located in South-Mumbai territory. He was required to call on the company's dealers to promote consumer durable products like fans, lamps and tubes. He resolved the dealers' issues, trained dealers' salespeople and encouraged the dealers to increase stocks and sales of the company's products. He also called on business customers to promote and sell industrial products, such as power transformers, High Tension (HT) and Low Tension (LT) switchgears and electric motors. His branch manager discussed with him the Key Result Areas (KRAs) to finalize his targets (or goals) in terms of sales volume, customer calls and communication skills. Pradeep exceeded the targets for the first two years and so, he was promoted as key accounts executive to look after five important accounts (i.e. important customers).

As a key accounts executive, his responsibility was to ensure that the company gets maximum share of business from these important customers, whose sales and profit potentials were high. Pradeep was an important member of a cross-functional team to implement key accounts programs. The objective of the team was to become the preferred or sole supplier to the key account, who was usually a business-to-business (B2B) customer. Here again, Pradeep, as a coordinator of the team, did a good relationship building task with excellent service to the key accounts. This resulted in getting highest share of business from the key accounts. After three years, on the position of key accounts executive, Pradeep was promoted and transferred to Indore branch, in Madhya Pradesh, as the branch manager. He was responsible to manage the branch, particularly the branch salespersons and support staff to achieve sales, profits, expenses, inventory and receivables targets or goals as well as customer satisfaction.

When Pradeep was working in Mumbai, he had successfully completed an online MBA program. This additional qualification helped him not only to get the branch manager position in the face of an intense competition within the organization, but also a better understanding on how to manage people and other resources. Pradeep worked hard and smart to consistently achieve the branch goals for the next four years. This had finally resulted in his promotion to eastern region as the regional sales manager. In addition, he was delighted to go back to his home town, Kolkata, amongst his relatives and friends.

From the viewpoint of an organization, sales management is an important function. Top management expects sales managers to achieve the objectives and goals of targeted (or budgeted) sales volume, provide profit contributions and effective customer service. What makes the achievement of sales managers' objectives difficult is that they have to adjust to the conditions, such as intense competition due to globalization, exceptionally demanding customers and fast changing technology. Sales managers need to have a professional approach with proper analysis of information about customers and competitors as well as development and implementation of effective sales strategies.

The opening vignette highlights how a sales trainee can rise to higher levels initially in sales positions and later in sales management positions with hard work and certain skills. In this chapter, we shall first understand evolution and definition of sales management and thereafter, we shall discuss the nature and importance of personal selling and sales management. We shall also look into the aspects of strategic sales management, sales planning and trends in sales management.

LO 1 Understand evolution and definition of sales management

EVOLUTION OF SALES MANAGEMENT

Before the industrial revolution, which began about 1760 A.D. in England, small-scale manufacturers had a commanding influence on the economy. Manufacturing received most of the attention, because that was the major problem. Goods were sold to nearby customers without any problem. After the industrial revolution in United Kingdom and the American Revolution in the United States, large-scale manufacturing organizations with huge quantities of goods started dominating the economy. Separate functional departments were established, which included manufacturing, finance and sales. Due to manufacturing of large quantities of goods, selling to nearby markets was not adequate and there was a need to expand the market. This was possible with the involvement of intermediaries such as wholesalers and retailers, selling the company's goods to consumers who were located far away from the manufacturing unit.

In the meantime, marketing activities like advertising and sales promotion, conducted by the manufacturer's sales department, became not only important, but also complex. It, therefore, became necessary to split the marketing function into sales function and other support functions like advertising, sales promotion, marketing research and market logistics (or physical distribution). This kind of typical organization, shown in Figure 1.1, is seen even today.

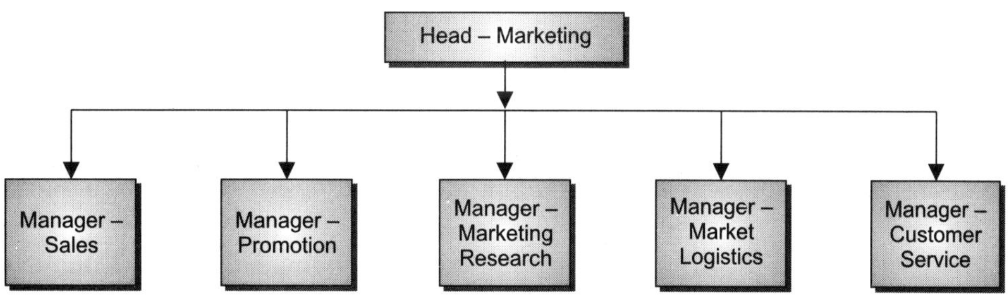

Fig. 1.1 **Typical Marketing Organization Structure**

It is important to understand that in spite of fragmentation of marketing functions, the sales department continues to occupy an important position even today, because it is the income (or revenue) generating function and no other function in an organization brings in income (or money).

WHAT IS SALES MANAGEMENT?

Sales management has been defined in many ways. One definition is:

"Sales management is the management of the personal selling part of a company's marketing plan."

Another most acceptable definition from American Marketing Association is:

"Sales management means the planning, direction and control of personal selling, including recruiting, selecting, equipping, assigning, routing, supervizing, paying and motivating as these tasks apply to the personal sales force."

However, this definition does not include evaluating and controlling sales force performance. Besides, the definition of American Marketing Association made sales management nearly same as "the management of sales force". This meaning of sales management is not in line with the broader responsibilities of modern sales managers. The responsibilities of modern sales managers, in addition to the above mentioned definition, are: (i) building sales force organization structure and territories; (ii) coordinating and communicating internally with other functions or departments of the company and externally with customers, intermediaries and agencies like advertising; and (iii) working as a member of strategic management team.

LO 2 Explain the nature and importance of sales management

NATURE OF SALES MANAGEMENT

The nature or characteristics of sales management can be explained by the following three ways:

(i) Its integration with marketing management
(ii) Scope of sales management
(iii) Role and skills of modern sales managers

Integration with Marketing Management

As sales management is a part of marketing management, sales planning should be integrated with marketing planning. A company's marketing team typically consists of two basic groups:

(i) Field selling (or personal selling) team
(ii) Headquarter marketing team

Field selling teams (or field sales force) remain in their territories/branches/regions contacting existing and prospective (new) customers. The headquarter based marketing team performs support and service functions or activities to assist field salespeople in their jobs. These headquarter based service and support functions are as follows:

- **Promotion/Marketing Communications** Consists of advertising, sales promotion, public relations, publicity, direct marketing and events/experiences.

○ **Marketing Research** Collecting and interpreting information on customers, competitors, products, markets and so on. For example, field salespeople need information on competitors' prices, discounts, payment terms and standard delivery time when they negotiate with customers for getting orders.

○ **Market Logistics** Physical distribution of finished goods including warehousing, inventory, transportation and order processing. For instance, a dealer of Mahindra automobiles resolved the problem of on-time delivery by keeping higher inventory of fast moving models and colors of vehicles.

○ **Customer Service** Pre-sales and post-sales services as well as delivery service to existing and prospective customers. For example, the problems related to post-sales service were resolved by the Mahindra dealer by assigning a service advisor to every vehicle when it came for service to the showroom.

○ **Coordination** Sometimes, there is a need to coordinate between customers, the company's salespeople and production or operations by employing inside salespeople. Increasing number of companies are employing inside salespeople to support customers and outside (or field) salespersons.

Figure 1.1 shows a typical marketing organization structure, which integrates sales and marketing functions. The support activities are either handled within the company or outsourced to specialists like marketing research agencies and advertising agencies. However, the real integration between sales and marketing teams would take place if there is a harmonious relationship that is built on the understanding of common goals and effective process of delivering intended service to the customers.

Scope of Sales Management

During the early period of gradual development of sales management, the scope of sales management was narrow. The main activities of sales management were recruiting, selecting, training, motivating and supervising salespeople. At the present period of time, sales management has much broader scope. In addition to the traditional activities as defined by American Marketing Association that is indicated earlier, sales managers are responsible for many more tasks. These include participating in strategic planning, forecasting sales, taking part in budgeting process, designing sales territories, developing sales force organization structure, coordinating internally with various departments or functions in the company and externally with customers and advertising agencies. Sales managers should ensure that all these tasks are effectively integrated.

The primary objective of sales management is to achieve the targeted or budgeted sales volume. Sales managers are also responsible to reach the goals of market share and sales growth. They are involved in the process of setting these objectives or targets. Whether these goals are achieved or not, depends not only on the performance of the sales team, but also on the quality of marketing decisions, the company's products and services as well as on marketing environment.

It is important to understand that jobs of first-level sales managers (for example, district, branch, or area sales managers) differ from other management jobs. These sales managers cannot directly supervise the work of the salespersons reporting to them on a daily basis, because many times the salespeople work away from the company offices to meet their business customers and intermediaries like distributors, dealers, and retailers. Thus, the scope of modern sales management extends from the management or administration of sales force to the various tasks described earlier. In addition, the top-level sales manager is a key member of the marketing team that makes several marketing decisions, such as pricing, marketing channels, promotion and market logistics.

Role and Skills of Modern Sales Managers

The role of a traditional sales manager has changed and hence, we will discuss the role of a modern sales manager. Instead of giving orders in an arrogant manner like a "boss", a modern sales manager behaves like a team leader with an ability to influence the salespeople towards achievement of objectives and treats them equally. Instead of salespeople coordinating with internal company departments or functions like advertising, sales promotion and shipping, the modern sales manager takes the responsibility of internal coordination. This helps salespersons to spend more time with their customers, understand customer needs clearly and give superior customer service.

Some of the important roles or functions of the modern sales managers are as follows:

- **Strategic Planning** The sales manager at the senior level is a part of the company's top management team for strategic planning. In particular, the modern sales managers' role is to develop long-term and short-term sales forecasts, to obtain information about changing needs of customers as well as strengths and weaknesses of competitors. These inputs from the senior sales manager are useful for evolving the company's strategic plans.

- **Coordination** In addition to managing the salespeople, the first-level sales manager has to coordinate with other functions or departments within the organization and also with customers, intermediaries like distributers, dealers and retailers. The first-level sales manager, like area sales manager, supports his salespeople; for example, coordinating with production planning and market logistics departments to ensure timely delivery of products to customers. The district or branch managers, who are also called first-level sales managers, conduct monthly or quarterly coordination meetings to discuss and resolve various issues with distributors or dealers.

- **Use of Technology** Modern sales managers use computers and technology more than the past sales managers. Enterprise Resource Planning (ERP) and Customer Relationship Management (CRM) software packages are used to ensure superior customer service and customer satisfaction than competitors in globally competitive markets.

- **Managing Multiple Channels** Besides the company's salespeople (i.e. personal selling channel), a modern sales manager manages other marketing (or distribution) channels, such as telemarketing (using the telephone), online selling through Internet, manufacturer's representatives (or the agents), and the intermediaries like distributors, wholesalers, dealers and retailers. Even in personal selling, the sales manager has options like team selling, independent sales representatives, key account executives and part-time salespeople.

Skills of a Sales Manager

A sales manager's job is complicated. It also varies widely from company to company and from consumer marketing to business marketing. Management thinkers propose a long list of skills, which can be summarized into three important skills: (i) people, (ii) managing and (iii) technical.

People Skills

The people skills include the sales manager's ability to motivate, lead, communicate, and coordinate effectively with the people around him. The ability to develop team-oriented relationships is important. With respect to salespeople, the first-level sales manager should understand the salespersons' individual needs and skills and carry out coaching or mentoring to improve their performance. In addition, the sales manager should be able to resolve conflicts between persons working with him.

Managing Skills

For managing the sales force, the sales manager should have administrative or managing skills like planning, organizing, controlling, and decision-making. These skills can be learnt by attending management development programs and also by observing or studying the behavior of successful and unsuccessful managers.

Technical Skills

These are specific tasks or functions such as training, selling, negotiating as well as the ability to use computers (or information technology skills) and problem-solving abilities in the specific industry discipline. Although sales skills alone do not necessarily make a good sales manager, some ability in selling is needed, as successful sales experience can help a sales manager resolve sales related problems faced by the salespeople.

IMPORTANCE OF SALES MANAGEMENT

Sales management is very important not only to a company but also to a student. A large number of people are employed in selling products and services to individual and household consumers, private and public sector companies as well as to institutions like hotels, restaurants and hospitals.

In this section, we will discuss the significance of sales management to both companies and students.

Importance to a Company

Sales management is the only function or department in an organization that brings in revenue. That is why sales management and financial results of a company are closely related. Financial results of a firm are stated in terms of sales (or sales revenue) and net profit (sales minus expenses). Thus, the financial results of an organization can be influenced to a large extent by the quality and performance of sales management.

The marketing effectiveness of a company depends not only on the development of the marketing plan, including sales strategy, but also on implementation of the plan and the strategy. Salespeople are responsible to carry out the sales strategy and hence, their selection, training, motivation, and compensation are key indicators to the performance of sales management and that of the organization. Perhaps, the only exceptions are companies that do not use personal selling (i.e. not selling the company's products and services through the company's salespeople), instead use the intermediaries like manufactures' representatives (or agents), distributors, wholesalers, dealers or retailers. Personal selling is less used in marketing of consumer goods and services, as compared to B2B (business-to-business) marketing, where the products and services are mainly sold through the company's salespeople.

Importance to a Student

Many students find their career opportunities in sales and sales management. This chapter discusses various types of sales positions, such as delivery salesperson, outside order taker salesperson, inside order taker salesperson, missionary salesperson and key account sales executive. There are also many sales management jobs available in today's business world, such as branch/area/district sales manager, regional/zonal/divisional sales manager, national/general sales manager and vice-president/director (sales). No other functions in management have so many positions available. In medium and large organizations, there are many sales management positions, but only a few managerial positions in finance, human resource, production or logistics. Generally, compensation is much higher for sales management positions than any other management areas. Normally, a good salesperson with some managerial potential can become first-level sales manager (see the next section on "levels of sales management positions" in this chapter) in about four to six years. For carrying out various activities of sales management, a fresh graduate would need knowledge of sales management. That is why, it is important for a student to study sales management.

LO 3 Describe the levels of sales management positions

LEVELS OF SALES MANAGEMENT POSITIONS

There are three levels of sales managers in the organization structure of many firms (i) Strategic or top-level managers, (ii) Tactical or middle-level managers, and (iii) Operational or first-level managers, as shown in Figure 1.2.

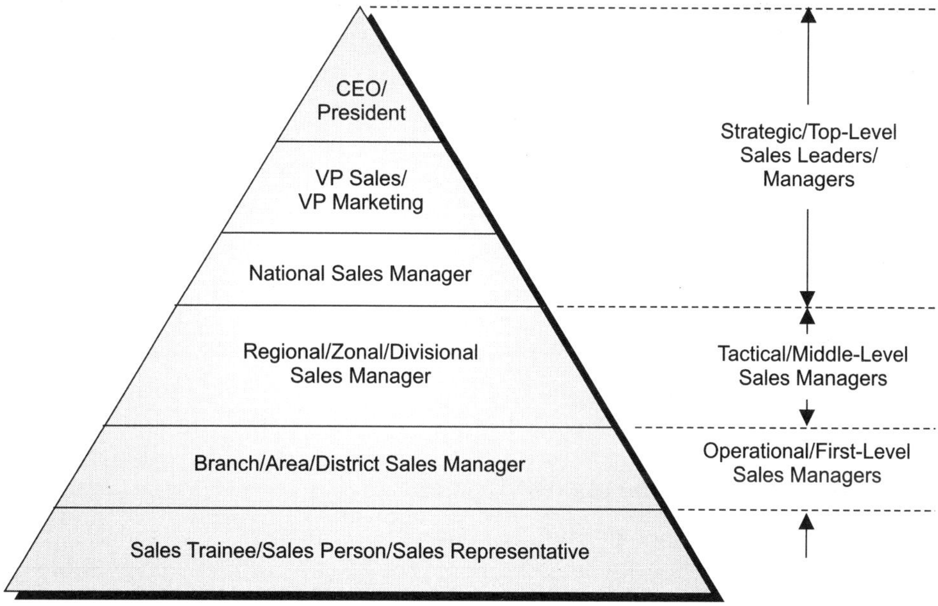

Fig. 1.2 Levels in Sales Management—Organization Hierarchy

Strategic (Top-level) Sales Managers

The highest level in sales management is often called director (sales), vice-president (sales), general manager (sales) or national sales manager. They are responsible for long-term (i.e. strategic) marketing and sales planning, including scanning external environment, setting long-term and short-term objectives and goals, developing strategies for achieving them, making decisions for implementing strategies and action plans and controlling the performance. They are also a part of top management team for the organization's strategic planning and coordination between various functional areas.

For example, after joining the company, the general manager (sales and marketing) of Steel Tubes Ltd. had set a strategic goal of becoming number one in terms of market share in precision steel tubes industry in three years from number three position. A market survey was undertaken to obtain information about the customers, competitors and external environment. Based on the findings of the market survey, a strategic marketing plan for the next three years and the marketing plan for one year was developed, discussed at the annual marketing conference, and finalized with a few changes. It was also the responsibility of the general manager (sales and marketing) to implement the marketing and sales plans through the branch and regional sales managers. Performance control was done by measuring the actual performance and reviewing the same against the goals or targets every quarter, when corrective actions were discussed and finalized for implementation.

Middle-level (Tactical) Sales Managers

These positions mostly carry the title of regional, zonal or divisional sales managers, whose major responsibilities are to manage several branches or districts reporting to them and also to implement the strategies and action plans approved by the top-management. In some companies, these positions are eliminated in order to make the organization flatter. Such organizations, sometimes, use cross-functional team selling for high sales potential customers.

For instance, GC Ltd. had four regional sales managers located at Delhi, Kolkata, Mumbai and Chennai, for a range of consumer durable and industrial products. Each Regional Sales Manager (RSM) had three to four branch managers reporting to him. The main responsibilities of the RSM were to: (i) allocate the regional sales and expenditure budgets to the respective branches, along with finalization of action plans for achieving the budgeted goals, after discussions with branch heads; (ii) implement marketing strategies and action plans; (iii) review branch performance every month and decide corrective actions; and (iv) suggest increments, promotions and training needs for all persons working in the region.

First-level (Operational) Sales Managers

This is the first level or entry-level position of sales management with titles such as branch sales managers, area sales managers, or district sales managers. They are directly responsible to achieve sales goals and objectives by providing day-to-day supervision to salespeople. They implement the strategies, procedures and rules decided by higher levels of management.

For example, as the branch manager of Ahmedabad office, A.R. Shah's sales performance for the year 2014–15 was above the yearly sales goal, but the profit contribution was below the target. The main reason was that the branch selling expenses were higher than the budget. After the analysis, it was found that six out of eight salespersons' travelling and lodging expenses were higher than the budgeted levels. During the performance review with the regional sales manager, Shah admitted that his supervision of salespersons was focused on achievement of sales targets, rather than the expenses of the salespeople. The regional sales manager pointed out that the branch manager's responsibility was not only to achieve the sales targets consistently but also to control the expenditure so as to achieve the profit contribution goal.

Staff Sales Management Positions

In most medium- and large-sized organizations, there are staff managerial positions, which provide assistance or help to the line sales managers and the salespeople. Sales training manager, customer service manager, or sales co-ordination manager are some of the examples of staff sales management positions. It is important to understand that these staff managers have an advisory role and that they do not have a line authority on line sales managers and the sales force.

LO 4 Discuss the nature of personal selling

NATURE OF PERSONAL SELLING

We know that personal selling is an important element of a company's promotional or communication mix. It is also called 'field selling' or 'selling through the company's salespeople'. Personal selling is defined as, "personal communication of information so as to persuade a prospective customer to buy a product, a service, or an idea that satisfies the needs of the buyer". The personal communication to a customer is usually done by a company's salesperson. The nature or characteristics of personal selling includes: (i) Transactional and relationship selling, (ii) Varying sales positions, and (iii) Sales as a career.

Transactional and Relationship Selling

Personal selling is mainly transaction-oriented because its purpose is to close a sale to a particular customer. The focus of the salesperson is to get the customer order or to close immediate one-time sale of the product or service. However, in the face of intense competition, companies at the present period of time are trying to improve their performance with high sales and profit potential customers by building a long-term supplier-customer relationship. The process by which a selling firm builds long-term relationships with key customers for the purpose of creating mutually satisfying relationships is called **relationship marketing** or **relationship selling** (since salespeople and sales managers play key roles in carrying out relationship marketing programs). Relationship marketing programs should be targeted toward customers with a high relationship orientation (i.e. need and desire for a relationship). Not all customers desire strong long-term relationship with suppliers. These customers perceive relationship marketing as unwanted hassle, extra cost, or waste of time. They prefer transaction oriented sellers who cut the price to get the sale. In relationship selling, the relationship between buying and selling firms is built on cooperation, commitment, communication and trust.

In addition, the relationship between a supplier and a customer is determined and controlled by a few major factors, as explained in Exhibit 1.1.

Varying Sales Positions / Sales Jobs

There are a wide variety of sales jobs or sales positions. These jobs differ in terms of degree of problem solving and requirements of selling simple to complex products and services. For instance, the job of a Britannia company's salesperson of taking orders for biscuits from wholesalers and large retailers is quite different than the job of a business development executive of Infosys selling an Enterprise Resource Planning (ERP) system to a bank. It is, therefore, useful to broadly classify the many types of sales jobs and place them into different categories:

- **Delivery Salesperson** The main responsibility of the salesperson is to deliver a product to household consumers or to business customers. Examples include delivery of milk and newspapers

Exhibit 1.1

Major drivers of customer relationships

Based on the empirical research from 1987 to 2004[1] representing different relationships, the major drivers of customer relationships are:

- **Conflicts** or disagreements between partners should be resolved amicably. If not, the relationship is damaged. Conflict has a major impact on the customer relationships, though it is a negative influence.
- **Competence or expertise** of a seller has the greatest positive impact of all the positive factors on a customer. Hence, a selling firm should focus on training its sales and service people in terms of their knowledge, skills, and attitude so that customers perceive the information provided by them in a more reliable and valuable way.
- **Communication** or the amount, frequency, and quality of information shared between a seller and a buyer has a significant positive effect on all aspects of relationship. It can help resolve disagreements, align objectives and expectations, and discover new value-creating opportunities.

In general, the most effective relationship marketing strategies are: (i) minimize conflict between a seller and a buyer; (ii) improve seller expertise; and (iii) ensure bilateral communication between a buyer and a seller.

to households as well as delivery of soft drinks and bread to retailers. Delivery salespeople also take orders from customers, but they do not engage in creative selling. Customer needs and the salesperson's good service as well as pleasant manners can lead to more sales.

❍ **Inside Order Takers** These salespeople mainly act as an inside order taker by responding to customer demands. There are two types of inside order takers. One type of salesperson stands behind the counter, like in a garment retail store. The salesperson gives service to the customer by responding to the customer's demands. Opportunities for creative selling are less. The second type of salesperson takes customer orders on telephone and also does outbound calling. This is called **telemarketing** (or teleselling). Examples include banks and credit card companies, who are the major users of telemarketing (or inside order takers) in India.

❍ **Outside Order Takers** These salespeople go out to the market and sell the company's products and services to the intermediaries like distributors, wholesalers, dealers, and retailers. For instance, the company's salespeople selling Fast Moving Consumer Goods (FMCGs) like soaps, detergents, and biscuits to distributors and wholesalers, whose sales representatives, in turn, sell the products to retailers. The company salespeople perform other tasks like setting up retailers' product displays, solving the problems of intermediaries and training intermediaries' salespersons. These salespeople do little creative selling.

- **Creative Sellers** These salespeople use imaginative ways to get orders; for example, selling tangible durable products like vacuum cleaners and refrigerators, as well as intangible services, such as insurance policies and educational courses. The salesperson should first clearly understand the prospective customer's needs or problems by asking questions. Thereafter, the salesperson shows how his product or service meets the customer's specific needs better than any other product or brand.

- **Consultative Sellers/New Business Sellers** These types of salespeople are experts in solving problems of business customers. They are creative and problem solvers who serve as consultants to their customers. For instance, a salesperson from a material handling company noticed a very long time taken by trucks from suppliers for unloading incoming materials in a passenger car manufacturing factory. He talked to the purchase executive of the car manufacturer and submitted an offer for Hydro-Electric equipment that would minimize the unloading time to five minutes from existing 15 minutes. The offer was accepted and the supplier fulfilled the promise. This resulted in the supplier getting orders for many such types of equipment not only from this factory but also from two more factories of the manufacturer who was benefited by substantial savings in the time, space and costs.

- **Key Account Sales Executive** A key account is an important customer who has a high sales and profit potential. A key account sales executive is given the responsibility to look after a few (typically three to five) number of such important customers. The supplier firm develops a Key Account Management (KAM) program with an objective of becoming a preferred or sole supplier to the key accounts. The KAM program includes complete understanding of the customer's business and needs, adopting relationship management approach, and using team selling method to deliver a solution that matches the key account's needs. For example, a manufacturer of precision steel tubes has key account teams focused on the manufacturers of two-wheelers and bicycles, who have high sales and profit potential. Each key account team has a key account sales executive as a team member to coordinate between selling and buying organizations.

- **Sales Support Salespeople** These salespeople support sales representatives with their specialized product knowledge to solve customers' technical problems. They are not responsible for selling a product or service. Sometimes, these sales support people are included as part of the sales teams selling to key accounts to provide technical information before the sales, during negotiations, or after the sales to solve customer problems. They are also involved in educating and training customers. Examples include industries such as steel, chemicals, and software services needing technical inputs from sales support engineers during negotiations between buying and selling organizations.

- **Missionary Salespeople** They are a type of sales support salespeople. They do not ask for orders, but provide product information and promote goodwill about the product and the manufacturer; for instance, medical representatives in pharmaceutical industry calling on doctors who write prescriptions when they are with their patients. Thereafter, the patients buy the drugs from a pharmacy.

It should be understood that the responsibilities of many salespersons may not clearly fall into one of the eight categories described above. It is the task of sales managers to determine the activities or responsibilities of the salespeople in their organizations.

Sales as a Career

As seen in Figure 1.2, the path to a career in sales management mostly starts with the position of a sales trainee or sales representative. We have also read about different types of sales positions from a delivery salesperson to a salesperson solving a customer's problems. Thus, there are a range of sales positions as well as a range of managerial positions in sales management.

Many people find their career opportunity in sales and marketing. Generally, sales offers more jobs than any other area of marketing, because each product or service has to be sold by a salesperson either to a household consumer, a manufacturing firm, an intermediary like a distributor or a retailer, an institution like a hospital or a college, or to a government organization like railways.

Rewards in Sales Career

Sales is also one of the most financially rewarding occupations. Sales career can hardly be boring, because it deals with people, whose wants or needs are ever-changing. It is one of the exciting and challenging careers. Even in a bad economic situation, a good salesperson is the last to be fired even if a company decides to cut back its employee strength.

Most companies develop attractive compensation plans for their salespeople in order to attract and retain good quality salespeople. After the initial training period of about 6 to 12 months, a new sales trainee typically gets a compensation package consisting of a fixed amount (i.e. a salary), a variable amount (i.e. a commission, profit sharing or bonus) and fringe benefits [for example, insurance, medical reimbursement, pension, Leave Travel Assistance (LTA)]. Generally, reimbursement of expenses, such as travelling, lodging and boarding is not considered as a part of the sales force compensation package. In case of team selling, where joint efforts are required from members of selling teams (derived from various departments such as sales, logistics, and customer service), some form of shared reward like a bonus is given for an outstanding performance.

In addition to financial rewards by way of attractive compensation, sales persons are given non-financial rewards such as recognition and promotion. These rewards help salespeople develop a feeling of self-esteem. **Personal satisfaction** is important in any career. Successful salespeople do get personal satisfaction because they give effective services to their customers and contribute to the success of their companies. Most salespeople sell in a competitive environment and good salespeople get personal satisfaction by winning orders from customers in a highly competitive market. Outside or field salespeople (unlike inside salespersons) are not restricted by the rigidity of an office, as they are able to travel, meet different kinds of people and face different situations. The variety and diversity of selling job make most salespeople enthusiastic.

More CEOs come from sales and marketing background than from any other functional areas. One of the major reasons for this is that salespeople understand the business from customers' perceptions and of all employees; they are closest to the customers. Hence, it is said that a sales career is one of the fastest routes to the top position in an organization.

Typically, a college graduate enters sales career as a sales trainee and then advances to a sales representative position. Depending on his performance, the career path may take positions of senior salesperson or key account executive to sales supervisor, area sales manager or district sales manager, which is the first-level sales manager's position. After this, the advances in career could be in the middle-level and top-level sales managers as shown in Figure 1.2.

However, if a person has completed a post-graduate diploma or degree program in management (PGDM/MBA), his growth in sales and marketing management would be faster as compared to a college graduate. After serving for a couple of years in the initial sales positions, the first important position can be a sales executive, marketing executive or area sales manager.

Salesperson to Sales Manager

In most companies, the path to a career in sales management starts from the position of a sales representative. Most companies want to have a person who is good in selling as well as in managing salespeople. However, the qualities required for a good sales manager are very much different from those needed by a salesperson. Most companies do consider top performing salespeople, when a vacancy for the first-level sales manager develops. Some of the important qualities to look for in selecting a person for the position of an area sales manager (i.e. the first-level sales manager) from a group of salespeople are as follows:

- Ability to be a team-player.
- Discipline in work habits like punctuality in attending meetings, customer appointments, and so on.
- Ability to manage a team and good communication skills.
- Selling skills—good in selling products, services, or ideas.
- Well balanced person with controlled self-esteem.

After the right person is selected for the position of a first-level sales manager, it is important that the selected person is given a short training on sales management. The person should be made aware of the changes that take place on promotion of a salesperson to sales manager. Some of these changes are as follows:

❍ **Changes in Goals and Objectives** A sales manager achieves the organization's or the territory's goals and objectives, but a salesperson tries to achieve personal goals of sales volume, sales calls, customer satisfaction, and so on.

❍ **Change in Responsibilities** The major responsibilities of a sales manager are sales administration work, including managing salespeople reporting to him. The major responsibility of a salesperson is selling.

- **Change in Views** A salesperson sees his job as completing certain activities given by his superior. However, a sales manager views his job as completing the activities pertaining to his territory effectively in order to achieve the goals or objectives of the sales territory, through his team.
- **Change in Skills Requirement** A salesperson needs to have selling, negotiation and communication skills. In addition to these skills, a sales manager must have managerial skills such as planning, directing, motivating, training and controlling the salespeople.
- **Change in Relationships** A salesperson needs to have a good relationship with customers, peers and superiors. When the salesperson gets promoted to the position of a sales manager, he has to develop new relationships with other managers, subordinates, who were his former peers and his new superiors.

Changing Role of Sales Force

In this section, we shall be discussing two extended roles of sales force–value creation for customers and value addition to the organization.

Value Creation for Customers

A cross-section of salespeople, sales managers and CEOs think that the purpose and role of the sales force are changing. The traditional role of the sales force has been to communicate the value of the selling firm's offering. In today's organizations, it is difficult for individuals and functions to survive and succeed unless they add or create value to the customer. What does "create value" mean? The basic and simplest equation of value is: **Value = Benefits – Cost**. This shows that there are two ways to create value. Either a company can create additional benefits or reduce the cost of the benefits it already provides.

For example, in consumer marketing, a marketing organization can create value by giving a wider choice of distribution channels from where an individual customer can buy a product. The different channels available to consumers for buying can be Internet, a retail store near his residence or a specialty store. In case of business marketing, the sales force can create value by clearly understanding the business customer's needs and offering a customized product or service to meet the specific needs.

Let us take the example of a software company, NM Technologies, which quotes for a software product to a pharmaceutical company. The salesperson of NM Technologies quotes $400,000, after finding out that the customer's labor cost will be reduced by $100,000 by using the software. Thus, he pitches for Return on Investment (ROI) of 25 percent (i.e. $100,000 savings per year divided by $400,000 cost of software). The competitor, AM Technologies quotes a price of $450,000, which would reduce the labor cost by $90,000. But the software offers additional benefits by which it would mark for attention overdue accounts receivables that will encourage the customer organization to take action to collect the receivables. This would result in a cash flow of about $250,000. The software also has a provision of reminding the company staff about refilling the stocks of the stockists on daily basis, which would increase the revenues by $300,000 and profits by $100,000 per year. Thus, AM Technologies' offering's benefits workout to increase in profits by $190,000 (i.e. $90,000 cost reduction + $100,000 profit increase). This makes ROI = $190,000 divided by $450,000 = 42 percent. In addition, the cash flow increase is $250,000. Compared to NM Technologies benefit of 25 percent ROI, AM Technologies benefits of 42 percent ROI and increased cash flow made the buying decision of the customer easy, due to superior value creation.

Earlier it was stated that there are two ways of creating value—to give more benefits or to reduce cost. The selling organization faces the question—which way is better? The answer depends on the customer. Some customers view the product as a commodity and want the benefits in terms of lowest price or cost. Many government organizations follow this buying strategy. Other type of customers want customized solutions and long-term (strategic) relationships with suppliers. These customers look for more benefits, such as reduction in raw material consumption, minimization of billing errors, better customer (i.e. the customer's customer) retention, revenue growth and brand enhancement. For creating these benefits, selling teams are needed, which are led by the sales leaders. These sales leaders, also called key accounts managers, get people together from various functional areas (a cross-functional team), that is, engaged with the customer team. Thus, relationships are built between the selling organization and the customer organization at various levels. This type of strategic value creation and relationships are very selective and typically restricted to a few large profit potential customers.

Value Addition to the Organization

The sales force must recognize that their focus is not only to collect orders but to generate a profit for the organization they work for. Many salespeople do not emphasize on profit. In the process of getting orders, large discounts are given, terms of payments are relaxed and delivery penalties are agreed. They get orders at any cost. This results in increased sales turnover but reduced profits.

Salespeople must understand that when they are selling several products of the company, they should know that different products have different contributions (to overheads and profits). In other words, they should sell more of those products which have high contributions, and should sell less other products which have low or poor contributions.

For instance, a steel component manufacturing company had two product categories (or product lines)—category 'A' had low contributions and category 'B' had medium to high contributions. The marketing head explained to the field sales force to book more orders for category 'B'. However, some salespeople focused more on category 'A' because it was easy to get orders to achieve the sales targets.

Many salespeople do not pay adequate attention to the terms of payments when they make an offer or during negotiations with customers. They give direct credit of 30, 45 or 90 days to customers who are not creditworthy. These salespeople do not understand that profits are realized only if 100 percent payments are received. If payments are not received from the customer, the profit remains on paper and gets added to 'debtors', but never realized. Salespeople should be very careful in giving credit to a customer. It should be given only after creditworthiness of the customer is established through accounts or finance department.

The above mentioned three issues—generations of profitable orders, selling high contribution products more and attention to terms of payments—would help the sales force to add value to the organization they work for.

LO 5 Construct various aspects of strategic sales management and sales planning

STRATEGIC SALES MANAGEMENT

Strategic planning (i.e. long-term planning) in an organization should be well integrated and properly coordinated. Strategic marketing plan should be consistent with the strategic plan of the company. Similarly, the strategic sales management plan should be decided based on the strategic marketing plan.

The aim of **strategic planning** is to develop the company's businesses, products, services and messages so that they achieve long-term objectives, such as sales growth and profits. Marketing plays an important role in strategic planning process. The marketing role includes assessing attractiveness of the company's products and services in the markets available to the firm, providing a customer orientation, and communicating the company's specific value advantages.

The **strategic marketing plan** includes selecting target markets and developing positioning strategy to meet the value requirements of the customers in each target market. Strategic marketing is a market driven process of strategy development. It takes into account the need to deliver superior customer value than its competitors. Strategic marketing also considers a constantly changing business environment. The focus of strategic marketing is on market targeting, strategic positioning, planning new products or services, and relationship strategies.

The **tactical marketing plan** identifies the marketing tactics or action plan, which includes product or service features, promotion or communication, pricing, marketing or distribution channels and customer service. These marketing activities are classified into four broad groups, which are called the four Ps of marketing: (i) product, (ii) price, (iii) promotion, and (iv) place (distribution).

Sales organizations need to strategically align their actions with the company's business and marketing strategies to create a more customer-oriented sales organization. Some of the important issues in **strategic sales management** are[2]:

- Development of strategic sales organization
- Strategic role of the selling function
- Choosing target customers and retaining them
- Role of sales force and customer relationship management strategy
- Designing sales territories and sales force deployment
- Long-term sales planning and forecasting

An in-depth examination of strategic sales management issues mentioned above is a subject of a textbook. Hence it has not been dealt with here. However, in the next section, we will deal with sales objectives, strategies and tactics, which are components of a sales plan.

SALES PLANNING

Sales managers are guided by strategic planning at the company level and at marketing level. While preparing a sales plan, which consists of sales objectives, sales strategies and tactics (or action plans), they should have a complete understanding of the process of sales planning. Figure 1.3 shows the relationship between objectives, strategies, and tactics.

Fig. 1.3 Relationship between Objectives, Strategies and Tactics

Sales Objectives

Objectives are the statements of intents and when they are quantified to specific and measureable targets with respect to time periods, they are called goals. For example, a company's sales objective is to have a good growth in sales. This sales objective is quantified to a sales goal of 15 percent growth in sales to be achieved during the next financial year.

The sales objectives and goals are derived from the company's marketing objectives and goals, which in turn depend on the company's objectives and goals. This concept is illustrated for an organization.

A company's goal is to increase net profits by five percent in 2014–15 over the net profits of 2013–14. Its marketing objective is to improve the market share and its sales goal is to achieve a sales growth of 15 percent in 2014–15 over the previous year of 2013–14.

Sales Strategies and Tactics

Strategies are ways of achieving the objectives. Tactics (or action plans) are the activities or the actions that should be carried out in order to implement the strategy. The sales strategies are mostly related to sales force strategies. We shall illustrate with examples to show the relationship between sales objectives, strategies and tactics.

Let us consider a company, which wants to achieve the sales objectives or goals of increasing the sales volume for its product–steel by 15 percent and reduce the selling expenses by 5 percent in the year 2015–16. The marketing strategies considered are:

- Enter export markets
- Penetrate the existing domestic markets
- Utilize existing sales force resource optimally
- Use effective and efficient marketing channels

From the marketing strategies, the sales strategies and the tactics were developed as shown in Table 1.1. The company's marketing head and regional sales managers worked out the marketing and sales strategies at the beginning of the financial year 2015–16. The sales force tactics (or action plans) were derived from the sales force strategies. The action plans should indicate who would take action and when. However, this is not shown in Table 1.1, as it would have made the table rather unwieldy.

Table 1.1 Sales force Objectives, Strategies and Tactics

Sales Objectives/Goals	Marketing Strategy	Sales force Strategy	Sales force Tactics (Action plans)
Increase in sales volume by 15 percent	• Enter export markets	• Identify the countries and the distributors	• Marketing or sales head to get relevant market information to decide selection of countries and the distributors
		• Sign sales agreements with the distributors	• Negotiate and sign agreements in 3–5 months
	• Penetrate the existing domestic markets	• Review and improve sales force training, motivation and sales incentives	• Train each salesperson in his deficient or weak areas • Effective supervision by field sales managers
		• Ensure all market segments are covered	• Link sales force incentives to segment-wise sales targets
Reduce selling expenses by 5 percent	• Utilize existing sales force resource optimally	• Use 'ABC Analysis' technique for customer visit plans and tele-marketing for prospective customers	• Focus company sales force selling to A class, (high potential) customers to increase its business share
	• Use effective and efficient channels	• Use Internet (online) selling and telemarketing, in addition to company sales force and intermediaries	• B and C class customers to be served by agents, dealers, telemarketing, and online selling

LO 6 Identify emerging trends in sales management

EMERGING TRENDS IN SALES MANAGEMENT

To be successful in a changing marketing environment, it is important that sales managers understand emerging trends in the following areas:

- Global perspective
- Revolution in technology
- Customer Relationship Management (CRM)
- Sales force diversity
- Sales Force Automation (SFA)
- Team selling approach
- Managing multi-channel marketing systems
- Ethical and social issues
- Sales Professionalism
- E-selling

Global Perspective

Global competition is intensifying. Domestic companies who never thought about foreign competitors suddenly find them in their backyards. Sales managers must manage their salespeople to meet international competition in their country and improve their company's personal selling efforts in other countries. Sales managers selling goods and services in the global market place face challenges such as differences in cultures, different languages, different requirements for buying, different styles of negotiation, and so on. Sales managers must also consider opportunities as many global markets are emerging and growing rapidly. A company need not be large to sell globally. Small- and medium-sized organizations can sell in global niche markets.

Some examples: Becher Company has 50 percent share of the world's oversized umbrella market. Steiner Optical Company has 80 percent share of the world's military field glasses market. Organizations that sell their products in global industries, such as cameras, mobile phones and aircraft engines need to compete on global basis to achieve economies of scale.

Global Account Management (GAM) is the term used by some companies to describe their management of large (key, major, or national) customers. These are important customers because they account for a large share of a selling firm's sales volume and profit. GAM includes the company's sales force operating in foreign countries. Multinational customer firms demand GAM structure from the selling firm. For example, Xerox uses a separate sales team for BMW, the German automobile manufacturer, who is its global customer. Xerox uses a GAM structure that includes various sales teams. Each sales team is devoted to a global customer.

Revolution in Technology

Digital revolution and the management of information have greatly increased the capabilities of consumers and marketing organizations. Buyers today can get information on products, compare suppliers' prices, and place orders on the Internet in a matter of seconds. They can access online a great amount of information about almost anything. Marketing organizations also have a new set of capabilities. Companies can collect more information about markets, customers, prospective customers and competitors by using the Internet. They can design websites and communicate information about the company, its products and services, and other things to the visitors. Marketers can customize their products and services according to the needs of individual customers. Companies can have two-way communications with prospective customers, existing customers, intermediaries and suppliers.

To compete effectively, salespeople and sales managers will have to adopt the latest technology. Some of the technological innovations for sales management are portable and desktop computers, cellular (mobile) phones, video-conferencing, and video-tape presentations. Technology can make some sales activities efficient and cost effective. Companies are setting up computer-based sales support systems to help salespeople in planning, executing and reporting on sales calls; in choosing the most prospective customers; in preparing quotations; in planning sales presentations; in entering, checking, and submitting orders with improved accuracy and in knowing updated information on inventory and delivery position.

Technological improvements in communication and shipping have made it easier for companies to market in other countries and also easier for customers to buy products and services from markets in other countries. In high-tech industries, technological leapfrogging strategy is practiced. For instance, Google used technological leapfrogging to overtake Yahoo to become market leader in search. In video-game market, first Nintendo, then Sega/Genesis, and thereafter, Sony's PlayStation have gained highest market share by introducing superior technology.

Customer Relationship Management

Combining relationship marketing with information technology has resulted in Customer Relationship Management (CRM) systems. Interestingly, the concept of relationship marketing came about earlier than CRM by bringing quality, customer service and marketing together[3]. Relationship marketing aims at building long-term, mutually satisfying relations with key party-customers, distributors, and suppliers in order to earn and retain their long-term preference and business. CRM enables companies to provide excellent real-time customer service by focusing on meeting the individual needs of each valued customer through the use of CRM software packages. CRM skill requires building a customer database and doing data-mining to detect trends, segments, and individual customer needs. Many companies have initiated CRM programs to expand relationships with existing customers, because getting new customers costs about five times more than the costs involved in retaining existing customers.

For example, at Bellary Iron Ores Pvt. Ltd., CRM system integrates sales, customer service, and market information from various sources with the help of software. It gives up-to-date information to the employees on each valued customer to enable them to give superior service. Both CRM and relationship marketing have the same aim of building mutually satisfying long-term relationships with valued customers. However, companies must find out which market segments and specific customers will respond profitably to relationship management.

CRM can be examined from strategic and organizational perspectives. From a strategic perspective, CRM is a process that identifies customers, creates customer knowledge, builds customer relationship, and shapes customers' perceptions of the company and its products. From an organizational perspective, the goal of CRM is to systematically select the right customers that fit the firm's generic competitive strategy (be it product leadership, cost leadership, or customer intimacy).[4]

CRM can be effective if salespeople support it and are willing to use it. Sales managers should, therefore, communicate its advantages to salespersons and ensure effective training to all employees on CRM system.

Sales Force Automation

Sales Force Automation (SFA) is typically a part of Customer Relationship Management (CRM). It has presented a technological help to salespeople as well as sales managers. SFA is defined as 'the application of computerised technologies to support salespeople and sales management in achieving their work related objectives'. There are many benefits of using SFA to salespeople, sales managers and senior management, including improved market share, sales revenue, and profitability. However, these benefits are possible only if salespeople adopt SFA technology.

Sales Force Diversity

The demographic characteristics of the sales force are changing and are becoming more varied. For example, more women are taking up careers in selling and sales management. In addition, today salespeople are more educated, with college degrees and some of them holding postgraduate degrees. Sales managers will have to manage a sales force consisting of women, more educated and less educated salespersons as well as senior salespeople. The needs or expectations of the varied sales force will be different and consequently, the motivational tools will not be the same.

In many instances, marketing, manufacture, and design of products take place in different countries. Even materials used are outsourced to some other countries. Salespersons have to link together business functions and customers located worldwide. In doing so, salespeople have to deal with legal and cultural constraints which differ substantially across the globe.

Team Selling Approach

The practice of team selling or a **selling team** is widely followed by most companies in recent years. Team selling approach is used when a company wants to build a long-term mutually beneficial relationship with major or key customers, who have high sales and profit potential. It is also used for selling a technically complex product or service to a prospective customer. The composition of the team may vary depending upon the customer's buying centre members but usually the selling team includes members from senior management, technical function, customer service department, and inside salesperson (who responds to the major customer's requirements by coordinating within the office) as well as a key accounts executive or a manufacturer's representative (or an agent, if needed). At Wipro Technologies, for example, which sells customized software services, the selling team consists of the business development executive, the technology expert, and the industry domain specialist. At 3M Corporation, selling teams include people from sales, management information systems and logistics.

There has been a trend in recent years to create large teams, which includes persons from both selling and buying firms to solve problems. For example, General Electric (GE) Company formed a cross-company large team with its customer Southern California Edison to minimize the downtime on its steam turbine generators. These cross-company teams are formed when the buying and selling firms enter into a partnering relationship.

An important point in the decision of a selling firm to use a sales team is to know the needs of the buyer and also to find whether the prospective business customer is using a buying team for purchase decisions. The major skills that are important to the successful performance of a sales team are willingness to cooperate, accepting the weaknesses or faults of others, appreciating the needs of others and communicating with others. Members of the sales team should be trained continuously to enhance the performance of the team. The increasing use of sales teams or cross-functional teams to win new and high potential customers as well as to service existing key accounts raises some important questions about the kind of incentives to be included in a compensation plan. If both group and individual incentives are used, which should be given higher weightage? These questions need to be addressed separately in sales research.

Managing Multi-channel Marketing Systems

A multi-channel marketing system, also called multiple sales channels or hybrid sales system, occurs when an organization uses two or more marketing (or distribution) channels to reach one or more customer segments. Major benefits of a multi-channel marketing system are: (i) lower channel cost (for instance, selling by use of phone instead of visits by salespersons to small sales potential customers); (ii) increased market coverage; and (iii) customized selling—selling technically complex products and services through the company's technical sales force and simple, low cost products through dealers. Earlier, Crompton Greaves, for example, used the company's sales engineers to sell technically complex products like power transformers and high-tension switchgears to state electricity boards and large manufacturing units, but sold ceiling and table fans as well as lamps and tubes through dealers to household consumers.

Multi-channels may also lead to conflicts and control problems, as two or more channels may compete for the same customer. A successful sales manager will have to effectively manage the conflicts between channel members by using various techniques like co-optation, exchanging persons, adopting super ordinate goals, diplomacy, mediation and arbitration. Many brick and mortar firms hesitated over whether to add an online channel. They felt that selling their products or services online would produce channel conflicts with their offline retailers. For instance, the store-based bookseller, Barnes and Noble, hesitated and delayed opening online site to challenge online seller Amazon.

Ethical and Social Issues

Sales managers have social and ethical responsibilities. Salespeople face ethical issues such as bribery, deception and high-pressure sales tactics. Giving payment or gift to get an order, misleading the customer by exaggerating the benefits of a product and using high-pressure sales tactics of committing wrong delivery schedules to a customer needing urgent deliveries of a raw material are the examples of unethical behavior of salespeople. Another example is of Enron company's salespeople who were accused of using wildly optimistic estimates for the forward price of commodities. This created the appearance that deals were profitable when actually they were losing money. Today sales managers have no choice but to ensure ethical standards from the sales force, otherwise they may be out of business or even land up in legal problems.

Contemporary sales managers understand the pluralistic nature of our society and the necessity of dealing equitably with various social groups. Adhering to social responsibility includes obeying the legal requirements, satisfying public expectations and participating in community development programs. In many companies, ethical, legal and social responsibilities are becoming important managerial functions. Top managers must be role models for employees. Companies must have a written document on code of conduct and it should be enforced by the top management.

Sales Professionalism

Today's top salespeople are largely made, not merely born. Selling has increased in complexity, because competition is more intense, customers are more sophisticated and products and services have become more technical. Success mostly comes to those salespersons who have a combination of natural ability and acquired skills. A study on what do buyers like most in a salesperson indicated qualities like reliability, credibility, professionalism, integrity and product knowledge as most valued[5]. The knowledge, skills and the right attitude to meet complex and competitive market conditions of today are acquired by a professional salesperson through intensive training and practice. Some of the successful organizations have their own centers for training and management development. Today's companies spend a lot of money each year to train salespeople in the art of selling and to make them professional. Sales professionalism is aptly defined as a customer-oriented approach that uses truthful and straight-forward ways to satisfy the long-term needs of both the customer and the selling firm. Another study of over 1000 customers by the HR Chally Group in 2002 indicated the following most important factors or characteristics of a professional salesperson:

- Provides service that solves problems and responds to customer needs.
- Has excellent product knowledge.
- Serves as an advocate for the customers within the selling firm.
- Keeps the customers up-to-date.

E-Selling

If a company converts its website from a promotional tool to a fully functional e-commerce operation, it can sell its products and services online (i.e. e-selling or selling on the Internet). Some of the e-commerce companies are Amazon, Flipkart and Snapdeal. More and more customers would expect selling companies to handle sales online. E-commerce means that the company or website offers to transact or facilitate the selling of products and services online. In e-marketing, a company's marketing efforts such as promotion and selling are done through the Internet. E-selling, which is a part of e-marketing, turns passive visitors on the company's website into active customers. E-selling can also build relationships with the company's target audience. For effective e-selling, a company should carefully select shopping-cart software and services. The company should also use a 'secure server' system and support customers before, during, and after they make a purchase. There has been a substantial increase in the use of e-selling or e-commerce by selling or marketing organizations. The main reasons include significant reduction in selling expenses and improvement in selling efficiency. For buyers, it takes less time to place orders on suppliers by the use of Internet for standard products and services.

For example, Samtec Company, a global manufacturer of electronic interconnects carries out online marketing or selling by creating a website. The company says that although online selling is a lot cheaper, it is far more difficult than selling through other channels. The main challenge is how to ensure that prospective customers visit the company's website. One of the strategies used by the company is to offer freebies to potential customers.

SUMMARY

LO 1

- We understood the evolution of sales management from 1760 Industrial Revolution in England to the important position it occupies today in a company.
- American Marketing Association has defined sales management as "planning, direction and control of personal selling, including recruitment, selecting, equipping, assigning, routing, supervizing, paying and motivating as these tasks apply to the personal sales force".

LO 2

- The nature of sales management can be explained by its integration with marketing management, scope of sales management, and role and skills of modern sales managers.
- The importance of sales management to a company can be described by emphasizing that it is the only function in an organization that brings in revenue. Sales management is also important to students, because there are many sales management jobs available for which knowledge of sales management is needed.

LO 3

- There are three levels of sales managers in the organizational hierarchy: (i) top-level (or strategic) managers, (ii) middle-level (or tactical) managers, and (iii) first-level (or operational) managers.

LO 4

- The nature of personal selling includes: (i) transactional and relationship selling; (ii) varying sales positions; and (iii) sales as a career. In transactional selling, the focus of the salesperson is to close one time sale of a product or service. In relationship selling, a selling firm builds long-term relationships with key customers for creating mutually satisfactory relationships.

LO 5

- Sales organizations need to strategically align their actions with the company's business and marketing strategies to create a more customer-oriented sales organization.
- When sales managers prepare a sales plan consisting of sales objectives, sales strategies and tactics (or action plans), they should have a complete understanding of the process of sales planning.

LO 6

- Some of the emerging trends in sales management are: global perspective, e-selling, revolution in technology, Customer Relationship Management (CRM), sales force diversity, team selling approach, managing multi-channel marketing systems, ethical and social issues, Sales Professionalism.

Key Terms

Glossaries of key terms are mentioned at the end of all chapters

Business selling
Creative selling
E-selling
Missionary salespeople
Partnering (or collaborative) relationship
Relationship marketing/Relationship selling
Response selling (or stimulus response selling)
Sales force automation
Sales management
Sales professionalism
Solution vendor
Team selling approach
Technical selling (or technical support salespeople)
Transactional selling
Value (or customer value)

Conceptual Questions

1. American Marketing Association's definition of sales management is nearly same as "the management of sales force". It is said that this definition is not in line with the broader responsibilities of modern sales managers. Do you agree with this view? Explain your answer with reasons. LO1 E
2. Explain why sales management is considered as an important function. LO2 M
3. Describe the difference in responsibilities between first-level and middle-level sales managers. LO3 D
4. How is relationship selling different from transaction oriented selling? LO4 M
5. Discuss how "outside order taker" sales position is different from "key account sales executive" position. LO4 D
6. Why is sales career considered exciting, challenging and a route to the top position in an organization? LO4 D
7. What changes will take place when a salesperson is promoted from a sales representative position to a first-level sales manager position? LO4 D

Note: Difficulty Level → E — Easy; M — Medium; D — Difficult

8. What are some of the important issues in strategic sales management? LO5 D
9. What are the components of a sales plan? Explain with an example the difference between a strategy and a tactic. LO5 M
10. How changes in technology help salespeople to perform various activities efficiently and in cost effective manner? LO6 D

Objective-Type Questions

Select the most appropriate response out of the various options available in each of the following questions:

1. Sales management has an important position in the organization because it is LO1 E
   (a) one of the oldest functions
   (b) closer to customers
   (c) the only income generating function
   (d) None of these
2. A company's marketing team typically consists of two groups; one is field (or personal) selling and the other is
   (a) advertising (b) sales promotion
   (c) marketing research (d) marketing LO2 E
3. Out of the three important skills for the success of a sales manager, the two are managing and technical skills. The third skill is
   (a) communication (b) negotiation
   (c) problem-solving (d) people LO2 M
4. Development of long-term marketing and sales strategies is the responsibility of
   (a) top-level sales/marketing managers (b) middle-level sales managers
   (c) first-level sales manager (d) None of these LO3 E
5. Companies often use transactional selling approach to.........number of customers.
   (a) few (b) large (c) medium (d) little LO4 M
6. Organizations many times use relationship selling approach to.........number of customers.
   (a) large (b) medium (c) few (d) many
7. Missionary salesperson's main responsibility is to
   (a) take order from customers (b) educate or give information to customers
   (c) solve customer's problems (d) respond to customer demand
8. Strategic sales management includes choosing target customers, development of sales organization and one of the following issues
   (a) sales promotion (b) advertising
   (c) consumer research (d) designing sales territories LO5 D
9. Team selling approach is typically used for
   (a) government companies (b) institutional customers
   (c) key customers (d) distributors LO6 D

Application Questions

1. Crompton Greaves Ltd. had a vacancy for the position of a divisional marketing manager at one of its product division headquarters. The company had a general policy of internal promotions whenever talents were available within the organization. For the vacant position, the company had 12 regional sales managers as candidates. Each of the four regions (North, East, West and South) had three regional sales managers—one each handling private sector industrial (or business) customers, government customers, and dealers. The products manufactured and marketed by this product division included industrial electric motors, switch-gear (electrical equipment used for starting electric motors) and domestic pump sets. What criteria would you suggest for selection, including major functions to be performed and important skills required for the position of Divisional Marketing Manager. LO3 D
2. Assume that you are a national sales manager. You will be opening a new branch for which you intend to promote one of the existing salespersons as a branch sales manager. What would be the criteria or qualities you look for in selecting a person for the position of branch sales manager? What kind of changes will take place in the position of the salesperson due to the promotion? LO4 D
3. Assume that you are a regional sales manager of Bajaj Auto Ltd. and you are asked by your general manager (sales and marketing) to submit your sales force strategy and tactics to achieve an increase in sales volume by 20 percent for the next financial year. What would be your response? LO5 M
4. Ashok Leyland Ltd., one of the leading manufacturers of commercial vehicles in India, was considered as a key account by MM Ltd., the manufacturer of material handling equipment. The general manager (sales and marketing) of MM Company formed a selling and servicing team which included the branch managers of Chennai (Tamil Nadu) and Bengaluru (Karnataka), one sales engineer and one service engineer from each of the two branches and overall coordination to be done by the general manager himself. The Chennai sales and service team looked after the Chennai manufacturing unit of Ashok Leyland. Similarly, the two adjacent plants at Hosur were provided post-sales service by the Bengaluru team. Although Hosur is in Tamil Nadu, Bengaluru city is nearer to the Hosur plants than Chennai city, and therefore, it was economical to serve the Hosur units of Ashok Leyland from Bengaluru. However, Ashok Leyland had a policy to purchase all high value items from their central purchasing office at Chennai by combining the requirements of all the manufacturing units. Negotiations with suppliers, including receipts of suppliers' quotations, were taking place at the central purchasing office at Chennai. Thereafter, purchase orders were released on successful suppliers, indicating the quantities and deliveries to be made by the suppliers to the various manufacturing units. Since the payments were released on completion of dispatches from the Chennai headquarter of Ashok Leyland, the invoices were raised by the suppliers on the Chennai office. This purchase process created a problem for MM Company. The branch manager of Bengaluru expressed his unhappiness with the general manager, indicating that although his branch was providing excellent service to Ashok Leyland, the credit for the entire sales was going to the Chennai branch. Besides, he wanted to know how his branch team will be compensated for their efforts in ensuring effective service to the key account. If you were the general manager, what would be your response? LO6 D

ASSIGNMENTS FOR STUDENTS

1. Talk to two sales managers from the same company. One sales manager should be at first level to whom salespersons report (i.e. branch/district/area sales managers) and the other sales manager should be at the top level to whom the first and/or second level sales managers report. Ask them about their responsibilities and Key Result Areas (KRAs). Describe in a report each of these two positions to highlight the difference.
2. Interview a salesperson from each of two different companies. Ask them about their responsibilities, sales targets, designations, and relationships with their customers. Compare the findings of the interviews with the sales positions and customer relationships described in the text. Prepare a report on this and submit it to your teacher.
3. Visit the website of sales and marketing management (www.salesandmarketing.com) and make a report on current issues of importance to sales management.

Reference Notes

1. Palmatier Robert W. et al., *Factors Influencing the Effectiveness of Relationship Marketing: A Meta Analysis*, Journal of Marketing, 7 October, pp. 136-53.
2. Cravens D.W., Meunier-Fitzhugh K.L., Piercy N.F., The Oxford Handbook of *Strategic Sales and Sales Management*, Oxford University Press, 2011.
3. Martin Christopher, Adrian Payne, and David Ballantyne, *Relationship Marketing: Bringing Quality, Customer Service, and Marketing Together*, Butterworth-Heinemann, Oxford, UK, 1991.
4. Thomas W. Leigh, *Customer Relationship Management and the Sales Force*, The Oxford Handbook of *Strategic Sales and Sales Management*, Oxford University Press, 2011, pp. 348–351.
5. *PAs examine the people who sell to them*, Sales & Marketing Management, 11 November, 1985, p. 39.

Additional Reference

- Christian P. Heida, Dartnell's 30th sales force compensation survey, Dartnell Corporations, Chicago, 1999, p. 171.

CASE 1.1

SM Equipment Pvt. Ltd.

Selection of a Branch Manager

Krishna Kumar, General Manager (Marketing) of SM Equipment Ltd., was in deep thought. He wanted to resolve the issue about the appointment of a branch manager for an important branch of Mumbai. The first point was whether to promote one of the experienced sales engineers with managerial ability from within the company, or to recruit a suitable candidate from outside. If he decides to promote someone from within the company, then question arises whom to select.

SM Equipment Company is a small-scale manufacturing company in private sector, manufacturing material handling equipment at Hosur in Tamil Nadu. Seventy percent of the company's sales of ₹100 million (about USD 1.5 million) came from specially designed and customized material handling equipment. The balance 30 percent sales were contributed by the standard products. Since the product is technical in nature, the company has been recruiting engineers in sales positions. Sales engineers are required to prepare quotations with technical specifications and negotiate techno-commercial issues with business buyers. Only in case of complex material handling projects, sales engineers asked for assistance from design engineers. The requirement of a branch manager at Mumbai had become necessary due to removal of the agent (i.e. manufacturer's representative). This was due to the agent's consistently poor performance in terms of sales, market share, and customer service (both pre-and post-sales). The Mumbai agent was given adequate time to improve the performance. However, when business customers from Mumbai started complaining bitterly about the service provided by the agent, the company had no other alternative but to give three months' notice for termination. This was done as per the agreement between the company and the agent.

Krishna Kumar had only three months not only for getting a branch manager, but also for recruiting five sales and service engineers each, with adequate number of support staff. In addition, he had to finalize a suitable and centrally located office place. Mumbai is known to have a high business potential with large number of factories and warehouses, where SM Equipment's products are required.

Krishna Kumar planned to release a recruitment advertisement in a leading newspaper, indicating the requirements of a branch manager, sales and service engineers, and office support staff. He thought of keeping the options open for selecting the branch manager from outside or within the company. After reviewing the files of the five senior sales engineers from Chennai, Bengaluru and Hyderabad branches, he shortlisted two persons –Pradeep Dasgupta and S. Nagaraj. Pradeep had done graduation in engineering and also had completed postgraduate diploma in business management from a leading management institute. He has been working with SM Equipment for the past six years. Pradeep initially worked as a sales trainee for one year and thereafter, as sales engineer for three years. Due to his good performance in achieving the sales targets, he was promoted as senior sales engineer two years ago. Pradeep is strong technically, but weak on people skills. Although he had completed a management program, his managerial abilities have not been tested so far. The other shortlisted person is Nagaraj, who had also obtained an engineering degree. Nagaraj has been with the company for eight years and like Pradeep, he also joined the company as a sales trainee. Nagaraj's performance has been very good, having exceeded the sales targets consistently. After working as sales engineer for three years, he was promoted as senior sales engineer. His human relations with customers as well as office colleagues have been good. His managerial skills are not known. Both Pradeep and Nagaraj have been loyal to the company. Krishna Kumar felt that they can be trusted to manage Mumbai branch, which is far away from the marketing head – office at Bengaluru and the factory at Hosur. He wondered whether he can trust a person who is recruited based on the newspaper advertisement, without knowing the person for a sufficient duration of time. Krishna Kumar, therefore, decides to consult his Managing Director soon. The selection of the branch manager position for Mumbai branch is critical and he has only three-months time to commence Mumbai branch operations.

Discussion Questions

1. Should the company select the branch manager for Mumbai from within or outside the organization? Justify your answer.
2. If the decision is to select the branch manager from within, whom would you select?

This case was prepared by Prof. Krishna K. Havaldar for classroom discussion.

CASE 1.2

DP Ltd.

Setting Things Right

Vasant Kulkarni, RSM (Eastern region) of DP Ltd., was lying on a bed in the company's guest house at Kolkata. Vasant came to Kolkata from Mumbai on transfer five days earlier. About a month back, Vasant was called by the General Manager (Sales), Ashok Advani, in Mumbai and was told, "Vasant you have been performing very well as the branch manager, Mumbai. The management has, therefore, decided to promote you to the next position of regional sales manager of Eastern region. Many congratulations to you." After a warm handshake with Ashok Advani, Vasant said, "Sir, many thanks for the promotion and the recognition of my efforts, but why am I transferred to eastern region of all the four regions?" Ashok smiled and said, "Well, basically to set things right! You see, the company has not been performing well in the Eastern region in terms of performance on sales and profits for the past three years. We thought that with your managerial abilities you can make a positive change in the performance of the Eastern region, and hence this transfer from Mumbai to Kolkata." All these matters came to Vasant's mind while lying in the bed.

DP Ltd. has been manufacturing and marketing consumer durable products such as fans and lighting since 1980. The company has three manufacturing units at Mumbai, Hyderabad, and Ludhiana. It's headquartered at Mumbai. The company is professionally managed. It has two divisions. Fan division manufactures ceiling, table, wall, pedestal and exhaust fans. The lighting division produces consumer lighting products such as CFL and LED lamps, home décor lighting, gate lighting and lighting accessories. The company's products are known for quality. It has a strong distribution network and good relationship with distributors and dealers.

Vasant had completed an MBA program from a leading management institute, after obtaining a degree in commerce. He realized that his role as regional sales manager would be different from his previous position as branch manager. In Mumbai, as a branch manager, salespeople were reporting to him. He was directly responsible to manage salespeople and achieve the goals in terms of sales, market share, and profit contribution for the branch. But now as regional sales manager, he is expected to manage the branches of eastern region viz., Kolkata, Patna, Bhubaneshwar, and Guwahati. He will be responsible to achieve the sales, market share, customer satisfaction and profit contribution targets for eastern region through the branch managers. In addition, Vasant was responsible to implement the company's marketing and sales strategies, coordinate with advertising and sales promotion agencies, organize training programs for salespeople and support staff, be a mentor to branch managers, allocate the eastern region's sales and expenditure budgets to the four branches, review the branch performance every month, and discuss and decide corrective actions to be taken.

Vasant thought that he was clear about his role and the tasks to be performed as a regional sales manager. However, he wondered what management concepts and techniques should he use to set things right, so that the performance of eastern region improves to the expectations of the management.

Discussion Question

1. If you were Vasant Kulkarni, what would you do and why?

This case is prepared by Prof. Krishna K. Havaldar for classroom discussion.

CASE 1.3

Kalyani Motors

Transition from a Salesperson to a Sales Manager

"Congratulations! You have been promoted as a team sales manager. Gear up for the next level where you will be contributing through others!" said Shekhar Narang, senior sales manager to the newly promoted team sales manager, Mohan Naidu, at Kalyani Motors. Now what? No new manager roadmap! Promotions always feel good—they generally come with more praise, more money and lots of expectations. But nobody advises you and gives you inside information on how to work with and manage others. In fact, much is learnt on the job. People are not born with the ability to lead others. It is a skill that has to be learnt.

Kalyani Motors is a prominent Maruti Suzuki dealership started in the year 2006. Exemplary team work and dedication by its entrepreneur resulted in rapid growth leading to establishment of its state-of-the-art workshop at Mysore road. Kalyani Motors has now gained reputation for its impeccable sales showrooms and service workshops and easy access to both rural and urban customers.

Mohan Naidu was an excellent salesperson consistently topping the charts on quarterly basis. He had risen from the ground level in the company. He was judged on a daily, weekly and monthly basis. Initially, he had difficulty in adjusting to the new sales environment at Kalyani Motors. He was basically a B.Com graduate with little knowledge about sales. He took up job since he belonged to a poor family and he was the sole bread winner. He was given a probation period of three months where he had to prove himself to the management at Kalyani Motors. Mohan was struggling to reach his sales targets. He was a very shy person by nature and unable to muster enough courage to speak to his manager.

After three months of joining, his manager Shekhar called him up to his cabin and said, "Listen! Mohan, we have been observing your performance for the last three months and we have noticed that you are not mingling well with your colleagues. If you are not interested in this job you are free to choose any other job. If you are not happy with your present job you can leave this company and do a favor for yourself. But if you are genuinely interested, we will offer you complete support for learning and development. Hence, I advice you to think about this and get back to me in a week's time". Mohan was feeling helpless. He didn't want to lose his job. He thought long and hard about his career and finally decided that he would change his attitude and fight out. The following week, he spoke to Shekhar and asked him to chart a career plan for him at Kalyani Motors. That helped Mohan in deciding his goals and framing a short-term and long-term growth strategy for himself at Kalyani Motors. Gradually, he also started liking his job and now he was enjoying the day-to-day challenges.

The salesmen at Kalyani Motors were judged on various parameters like sales targets, test drives, answering enquiries, evaluation of old vehicles, selling Maruti genuine parts and accessories and finally the customer satisfaction. Salesmen were also provided training at Kalyani Motors as well as at Maruti Suzuki Limited. The training was conducted 4 to 5 times in a year. To motivate the employees, there were contests like "best sales consultant", "best captain", "best manager - area-wise and region-wise".

The company also followed very high ethical standards. Any sort of unethical behavior was not tolerated and immediately dealt with. The managers would clearly declare during the initial days of new hires at Kalyani Motors – one bad apple spoils the bunch. The salespersons were also taught to target the potential customers according to their industrial backgrounds. For example, if the Information Technology (IT) industry was in recession, the salespeople would be asked and trained to get business from other industries like automobile and retail.

The transition from being a successful salesperson to a sales manager is often a tricky one to make. Whether it is because they find it hard to give up selling or feel that they have to show the team that they are the top salesperson, too many sales managers put their focus in the wrong direction. Early Greek mythology tells tales of sailors lured by Sirens. Their sweet music mesmerized the sailors and led them to believe that the illusion was reality. Ultimately, those sailors who blindly followed the tunes crashed their ships on the rocks and their boats sank. Sirens lure business executives and small business owners too. The song that the Sirens sing has one line—"promote my top salesperson, put six people underneath them and generate six times the sales". And like the sailors, many business executives and their companies have been led into harm's way.

Mohan had gone through the mill. Mohan has had more than 3 years of sales experience at Kalyani now. He was still not sure why he was promoted to the job of a team sales manager. He was pleasantly surprized but also slightly anxious about his new role. He looked through the window and felt nostalgic about his time at Kalyani Motors. He was looking back at his time spent at Kalyani Motors—the challenges he faced, his fears, his failures, his successes, what made him happy and what made him sad. There was a movie playing in his mind but only in the reverse order. He wanted to be a highly successful manager. He wanted to grow in his role and climb up the corporate ladder. At the same time, he also wanted to ensure that his subordinates do not go through the same trouble that he had gone through. He was genuinely interested in the learning and development of his people.

Discussion Questions

1. If you were Mohan's boss, what would you do to ensure Mohan's success as the team sales manager?
2. If you were the team sales manager, what would you do to develop the salespeople reporting to you?

This case was prepared under the guidance of Prof. Krishna K. Havaldar, by Mr. Mutahhir Khadri, an MBA student of Alliance Business Academy, Bengaluru, for classroom discussion.

Chapter 2

The Selling Process

LEARNING OBJECTIVES

After studying this chapter, you will be able to:

LO 1 Recognize the steps of the selling process

LO 2 Know the needs and methods of prospecting and qualifying

LO 3 Explain pre-approach steps, approach techniques and the buyer's needs

LO 4 Understand various methods of sales presentation, product demonstration and handling objections

LO 5 Determine the techniques of trial close and closing the sale and follow-up tasks

LO 6 Apply the success factors in selling

In United Machines Ltd., the selling process typically started with prospecting (i.e. searching and identifying potential customers). This was mostly done by the outside (or field) salespeople by requesting the existing customers to suggest the names of prospective customers. It was also done by the inside salespeople, who work within a company, by using the Internet and telephone. The prospective customers are then qualified by using criteria, such as their requirements for the company's products, their financial ability to buy, likelihood to buy in near future, and approximate value of their requirements. Based on these criteria, the prospective customers are placed in three groups: group 'A' (high value of requirements in near future); group 'B' (average value of requirements in near future); group 'C' (requirements after a long duration of time). Prospects in group 'A' are handed over to the company's sales engineers for converting them to the company's customers. Prospects in group 'B' are given to inside salespeople to communicate with them and obtain more information by using the Internet and telephone. Prospects in group 'C' are kept in a separate file for follow-up after some time.

Let us take an example of how United Machines followed the selling process to convert a prospective customer like AC Equipment Pvt. Ltd. into a customer. The process started with an inside salesperson, by using the Internet and telephone, identifying AC Equipment Pvt. Ltd., who wanted to set up an industrial compressor manufacturing unit in Mumbai. The prospective customer, AC Equipment, initially needed conventional metal forming and metal cutting machines, which were manufactured by United Machines. Since the requirements were in near future and of a large value, the sales manager of United Machines asked one of his experienced sales engineer, Atul Tandon, to make a preliminary visit. Atul gathered as much information as possible about AC Equipment from various sources like the Internet, trade journals and the Chamber of Commerce and Industry. He then called AC Equipment's purchase executive for an appointment for a meeting.

The first meeting between Atul and the purchase executive was positive. Atul collected a lot of information about the requirements of AC Equipment in terms of their production plan, type of machines needed, purchasing process, key buying committee members, etc. He then fixed his appointments with AC Equipment's technical persons, such as production manager, design engineer and maintenance manager to understand the technical specifications and other needs clearly. For these meetings, Atul was accompanied by his company's design head and production executive. Atul collected "Request for Quotation" (RFQ) letter from AC Equipment, who also sent such letters to other machine tools manufacturers. Atul prepared and submitted the quotation after discussions with his sales manager, design and production heads. Thereafter, a team consisting of two technical persons and the purchase manager of AC Equipment visited the manufacturing plants of all the machine tool manufacturers who had submitted their quotations. Subsequently, AC Equipment shortlisted three prospective suppliers of machines, including United Machines and called them for presentations, followed by negotiations.

United Machines had three members in their sales presentation team – the sales manager, the design head and Atul. Need-Satisfaction method was used for sales presentation, pointing out specially designed and customized machines to satisfy the specific needs of AC Equipment. Additional benefits offered were effective after-sales service (i.e. visit by the company's technicians within four hours of the receipt of a call or a message), free training of their maintenance staff, two-years' of free warranty service and special competitive prices. Negotiations took place in a positive manner with "both of us win" style.

After about two weeks, United Machines Ltd. received the order from AC Equipment valued at ₹65 lakh (about $100,000) for supply of metal forming and metal cutting machines, indicating the technical specifications and other terms. The sales manager congratulated Atul and other persons involved in the selling process. He asked Atul to check the order carefully for any discrepancies, visit the new customer and collect 30 percent advance payment that was agreed during the negotiation and mentioned in the order.

The opening vignette shows how the selling process was followed by United Machines Company. In this chapter, we shall discuss the steps involved in the selling process. Some exposure to selling is necessary for the students of sales management. To manage a sales force successfully, a sales manager should have adequate sales experience. For instance, if a salesperson, reporting to the branch sales manager approaches him for help in getting an order from a high-potential prospective customer, the branch sales manager should be able to solve the problem. Today's companies spend large amounts of money on sales training programs to train salespeople in the art of selling. If the training program is conducted by the branch sales manager or the area sales manager, he cannot do a good job without knowing how to sell.

LO 1 Recognize the steps of the selling process

STEPS IN THE SELLING PROCESS

Most sales training programs follow the major steps for effective sales (or selling) process. Salespeople carry out various activities to create sales and satisfy customers. These activities of salespeople are recognized as the steps of the selling process. However, there is no one method that can be used to close every sale. Not all types of selling activities pass through the eight steps of selling shown in Figure. 2.1. The steps in the selling process are suggested to work better in certain situations, based on experience. There is no magic formula to make a sale. However, it is widely believed that if a salesperson follows the suggested steps, the chances of success are greatly improved. The more prepared a salesperson is, the greater the chance of making a sale. Research confirms that in order to perform at satisfactory levels, salespersons should master basic selling abilities[1].

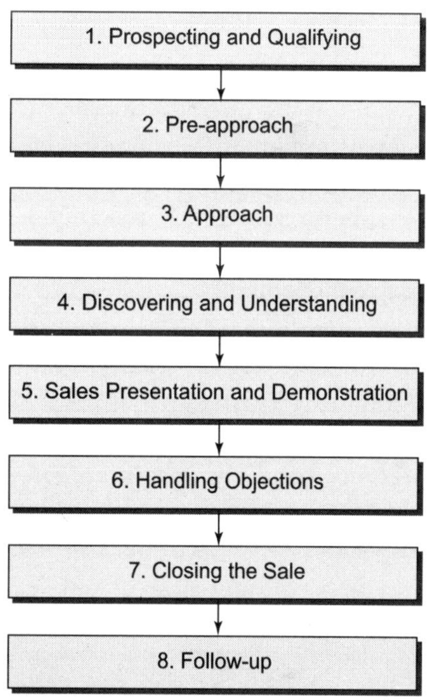

Fig. 2.1 Major Steps in the Selling Process

LO 2 **Know the needs and methods of prospecting and qualifying**

PROSPECTING

Prospecting is the process of identifying potential customers for the company's products and services. Regardless of how busy the salespeople are or how well they perform, if they want to achieve consistently good results in sales, they must do prospecting every day. This is important because there will always be a small percent of the customer base that will leave the company. The inflow and retention of prospects should be more than the outflow of customers.

A **prospect** is an individual, a family or an organization who has a need for the product or the service a salesperson is selling, has the ability to take a decision to buy and also the money to buy. A prospect is not the same as a **sales lead** (also called a lead or customer lead). A sales lead or a lead indicates the name and address of a person or a business firm who is a probable prospect (also called suspect). Once it is found through the Internet or telephone that the sales lead (i.e. suspect or probable prospect) need the company's product, has the money and has the ability to make a decision to buy, the sales lead becomes a prospect or prospective customer (also called potential customer). For example, the marketing head of a machine–tools manufacturing company, United Machines Ltd., gets mails from the German collaborator, with the subject title as "**Sales leads**".

In the mails, the German machine–tools manufacturing company, which has a tie-up with the Indian company, United Machines, gives information about the Indian executives who had visited their booths at some of the machine–tools trade shows and exhibitions at Hannover, Germany and other places. The information includes the names of the company executives, the firms' names and addresses, telephone numbers, e-mail IDs and the websites. The marketing professionals in United Machines then use the sales leads information to contact the probable prospects through e-mails and telephone to find if the company's products are needed and that the probable prospects have the required abilities to buy. If the answers to the above questions are affirmative, then the probable prospects or the sales leads becomes the prospects or the prospective customers.

Earlier most organizations had left the task of prospecting or identifying leads to their salespeople. Now, many companies' marketing professionals are undertaking the responsibility of identifying the leads. This enables salespeople to use their time on important selling activities, such as discovering and understanding prospective customers' needs, making sales presentations, handling customer objections and closing the sales.

Methods for Identifying Leads

To maintain a constant flow of new prospects, companies use various ways for identifying or generating leads (i.e. obtaining names and addresses of probable prospects). Some of the major methods are: consulting existing customers, referrals from external sources, referrals from internal company sources, use of Standard Industrial Classification (SIC) system, referring publications, networking by salespeople, cold canvassing and using World Wide Web. All these methods have been explained in detail as follows:

- **Consulting Existing Customers** This method is often used by salespeople when they are given the responsibility to generate their own sales leads[2]. Some customers hesitate to give referrals. Hence, it is important that salespeople build a good rapport or relationship with existing customers through effective customer service. This method is a convincing source of nearly two thirds of total sales leads[3].

- **Referrals from External Sources** Some organizations use external sources, such as suppliers, intermediaries, bankers, trade associations, Chambers of Commerce and commercial dot.com vendors. Many dot.com companies provide a list of leads for not too expensive fees. For instance, if one enters the keywords "sales leads" into "Google search", information of many sales leads companies appears. These companies sell leads by charging a reasonable amount.

- **Referrals from Internal Company Sources** Sales leads can be generated by company websites, trade shows, direct mail, company advertisements and telemarketing. A large number of people visit trade shows. The trade show participating companies enter the visitors' names, addresses and their interest in the registers kept in the booths. This information indicates the visitors' interest in the company's products and services. Companies also mail business letters with attachments to prospects, asking their interest in the company's products and services. Although the response rate for direct mail is low, it is a good information source from probable prospects. Company advertisements normally include a toll free number, which motivates prospects to respond. In inbound telemarketing, the prospect calls the company. This information about the prospect can be used by salespeople to make outbound calls to obtain more information. Outbound telemarketing (i.e. use of telephone) is also adopted by organizations to call prospects.

- **Standard Industrial Classification (SIC) System** It is a major secondary data source, which is used in industrial (or business) marketing. Each firm is assigned a four-digit number on the basis of its main line of business. For finding sales leads (or probable prospects), the company selling its products to a particular industry segment, say, pharmaceutical, finds the four–digit number of the pharmaceutical industry, viz. 3254. By referring to 3254 in International or Indian Standard Industrial Classification (ISIC) system, the company can discover names and addresses of a list of organisations that are included in the category 3254, their sales volumes, how many employees they have and so on. This list of firms is compared with the company's current list of customers. Thus, it provides an identification of the non–customer firms (i.e. probable prospects in each industry category). For example, a leading Information Technology (IT) company uses SIC system to identify and locate sales leads. Another related use of SIC is in estimation of market potential by using statistical series methods.

- **Publications** Newspapers, yellow pages, directories, trade journals, computer generated databases, commercial publications published by government and private publishers are the sources for identifying leads.

❍ **Networking by Salespeople** Salespeople become members of social organizations (e.g., Rotary and Lions clubs), civic organizations (e.g., Bangalore and Century clubs) and professional bodies (e.g., Management Teachers' Consortium and All India Management Association) to meet new people who may be potential customers or who may be able to provide leads. Salespersons may also communicate with friends, relatives and acquaintances to identify probable prospects or sales leads.

❍ **Cold Canvassing** It is a method in which a salesperson makes unannounced calls on companies that may need the products and services the salesperson sells. The support for this method is declining as it is time consuming and also costly. However, it may be effective for widely used consumer products and services as well as for office supplies in business-to-business selling.

❍ **World Wide Web** For searching and identifying leads, World Wide Web (WWW) can be used through its widely admired search engines. A lot of information is available for free through the use of popular search engines. For instance, "How to search on Google" gives a few tips to help find information. For complex searches, one can go to advanced Google search.

QUALIFYING

It is important that the lead is qualified to meet the necessary standards or conditions to receive further attention. The necessary conditions or criteria for the probable prospect or the lead to get qualified to the prospect or potential customer are as follows:

- The probable prospect has a need for the product or the service being sold.
- The probable prospect (could be an individual, a family or an organization) can afford (or has a financial capacity) to buy the product or the service.
- The lead or the probable prospect has an ability to make a decision.

Most companies contact the leads by phone or mail to find out the answers to the above mentioned criteria. In the past, the salespersons were expected to contact the leads or probable prospects. Today, the marketing departments in many companies undertake the tasks of prospecting and qualifying. This is done because cost of a salesperson has gone up substantially in terms of salary, incentives and travelling. Hence, salespeople are used for selling and relationship building with key prospective customers. The leads, after qualifying, are placed in three groups, i.e. (i) hot prospects, (ii) warm prospects, and (iii) cold prospects.

❍ **Hot Prospects** These prospects are likely to buy the company's products or services in the near future and are financially sound. Such prospects are handed over to the company's salespersons to convert them to the company's customers.

❍ **Warm Prospects** These groups of prospects are the fence sitters. They want to buy the company's products or services but are non-committal. These prospects are given to the company's telemarketing team for follow-up.

❍ **Cold Prospects** These prospects are likely to take a long-time to buy the company's products or services. They are indifferent and require a lot of efforts to be sold. Such prospects are kept in a pending list for future follow-up.

It is important that salespeople follow-up the hot prospects that are handed over to them, because a study[4] has found that generally salespeople get more than 80 percent of the buyers' business if they follow-up a sales enquiry, as compared to 40 percent share, if not followed-up. Sales managers should also advise the salespeople that usually it takes about four calls on an organizational prospect to convert an initial enquiry or lead into sales.

Process of Prospecting and Qualifying

Successful salespeople understand the importance of the process of prospecting and qualifying. They make use of the concept of the **sales-pipeline** or **sales-funnel**, as shown in Figure. 2.2.

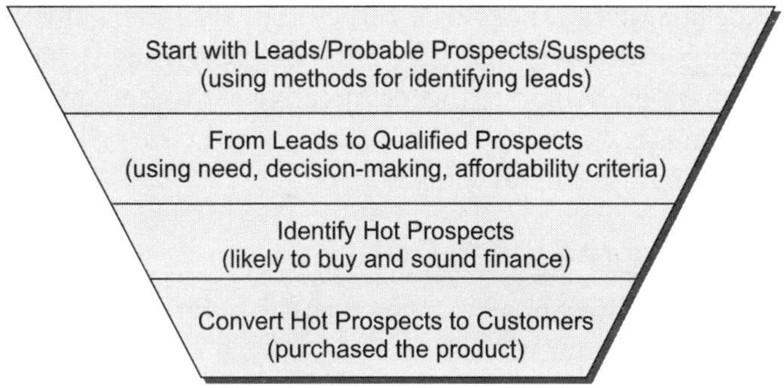

Fig. 2.2 Sales Funnel

The process of prospecting starts with the company identifying the names and addresses of the leads (also called suspects or probable prospects). The company uses a number of methods for identifying leads as explained in this chapter earlier.

The leads are then qualified by using the criteria of need for the product or service, ability to make a decision and affordability to buy. Out of the three groups (hot, warm and cold), hot prospects, who are likely to buy the company's products or services and have sound financial capacity have high probability of buying to become the company's customers. The process is called sales-funnel or sales-pipeline, because if a salesperson has 100 leads at a time, only about 50 become qualified prospects. From 50 qualified prospects, only about 20 are hot prospects. And finally about five prospects buy the company's products or services and become the company's customers. Successful salespeople always keep the sales-funnel full. For example, a leading software services company recruits management graduates in India to carryout prospecting and qualifying tasks using the Internet and phone. Thereafter, the qualified hot prospects are referred to the sales or business development executives located in the US and Europe for undertaking further steps in the selling process.

LO 3 Explain pre-approach steps, approach techniques and the buyer's needs

PRE-APPROACH

The pre-approach step generally includes two tasks: (i) information gathering in greater depth about the prospect by carrying out customer research, and (ii) planning the sales call on the prospect.

Information Gathering

The salesperson needs to collect as much information as possible about the prospect before visiting. The information to be collected from the prospective company includes the type of business, its products and services, purchasing practices, location of plants, names and background of people who make buying decisions, purchasing orientations and practices, the major problems or issues faced by the prospect and the industry in which it is operating and so on. The sources of obtaining the information about the prospect include the Internet or online information services, trade magazines, industrial directories, chambers of commerce, annual reports of companies, existing customers and suppliers and government publications. Information based on the in-depth research about the prospective customer makes the salesperson confident[5]. The more customer research the salesperson does, the more intelligent and informed he will sound when he finally approaches the prospect.

Planning the Sales Call

When a salesperson plans the sales call, before paying a visit to a prospective customer, he should consider four questions:

(i) Whom to see?
(ii) Where to go?
(iii) What are the call objectives?
(iv) How to approach the prospect?

If the marketing department of a company undertakes the activities of prospecting and qualifying, the name and address of the prospect is available with the salesperson. However, if the salesperson is required to find whom to see in a prospective customer organization, he should start as high up in the hierarchy as possible and reasonable. This means that in the customer research done earlier, it was necessary to find the most senior person at the location to which the salesperson wishes to sell. This is not necessarily the managing director or CEO of the firm, but may be the branch, district or general manager. The salesperson should find out who in the organization has the responsibility for purchasing the product or service that he is selling. This approach helps the salesperson to contact the right person. The salesperson should ensure that he has the contact address, telephone number and the right maps.

The next important task for the salesperson is to decide what objectives he would like to achieve for the particular call. Obviously, the ultimate objective is to get the order or close the sale, but this may not be feasible in the first call. As mentioned earlier, it takes, on an average, four calls on an organizational prospect to convert an initial enquiry into sales. The objective may be to get more information on the buyer's needs, buying criteria or knowing and meeting key buying decision-making people. The salesperson must set an objective for each of the sales calls.

The salesperson should also plan how he will approach the prospective buyer, and which method or technique of approach would be suitable for the particular prospect. If the objective of the sales call is to discover and understand the needs of the prospect, what kind of questions the salesperson should ask. Because salespeople can change their objectives, sales call plans and sales presentations for different types of customers (such as individuals, households, government organizations, private sector buyers) and with differing sales situations (like new purchase, repeat purchase, change in supplier), personal selling is referred to as **adaptive selling**[6].

APPROACH

After collecting the prospect's name and other relevant information, as mentioned earlier in pre-approach, the next step is to make an appointment to see the prospect. This is called the 'approach'. The approach (or meeting the buyer for the first time) takes a few minutes of a call, but it can make or break a sale. When a salesperson meets a potential customer for the first time, the first impression should be favorable[7]. The initial impression of a salesperson is based on his appearance, attitude and the opening line.

There are a few approach techniques. **Introductory approach** is mostly used by the salespersons as it is effective. In this approach, the salesperson states his name and the company name, preceded by a friendly and greeting smile and a firm handshake or 'Namaskar'. Most salespersons also present a business card. For example, "Good morning, Mr. Dasgupta, my name is Krishna Kumar from Crompton Greaves. I am here for 11 a.m. appointment". This is said with a friendly smile and a firm handshake. This is followed by a small talk that may be of particular interest to the prospect or new developments in the business. Anything will do to break the ice, but must not be stereotyped.

Another approach technique is to use an **opening benefit statement**. In this approach, the salesperson opens with a statement about how the product or service could help the buyer. For instance, a salesperson selling insurance policies may say, "By converting your existing insurance policy to our insurance plan, you can get ₹2,00,000 more coverage at the same premium that you are paying now". One more technique, called **product approach**, is used by salespeople if the product is new, unique or colorful. Some salespeople carry the new product or its cut-out in order to make a smooth transaction into the sales demonstration or presentation. For example, the salesperson hands over the new bottle of Pepsi to the retailer and waits for the retailer to begin the conversation. However, studies have shown that successful salespeople do not talk about their products, services, or the benefits of their solution until late in the sales call. The purpose of the approach is to gain the buyer's agreement to move forward to the next step of discovering and understanding the needs of the buyer.

DISCOVERING AND UNDERSTANDING BUYERS' NEEDS

Salespeople should know that individual consumers and business organizations buy products and services to satisfy their needs or to solve their problems. It is important, therefore, for salespersons to discover and understand their buyers' needs or problems. The best way to uncover and know the buyers' needs is by asking questions. Huthwait's research found that in successful sales calls it is the buyer who does most of the talking and not the salesperson.[8] Effective salespeople get customers to talk by asking smart questions. Companies like IBM and Xerox sponsored Huthwait's research of 35,000 sales calls, based on which SPIN model was developed, particularly for high-value business-to-business sales.

In **SPIN model**, there are four types of questions that salespeople can ask buyers to find, clarify, and understand their needs. These are situational questions, problem questions, implication question and need-payoff questions. Before asking questions, the salesperson must earn the right to ask questions by taking permission; for example, "In order to provide the right solution, do you mind if I ask you a few questions?"

Situational Questions

The questions that ask about the buyer's current situation are called situational questions to obtain information on how the customers may use their products. Examples are:

- How many people would occupy this conference hall which needs to be air conditioned?
- Who is involved in the buying decision for this product?
- How often do you carry out preventive maintenance of these machines?

Successful salespeople ask a few situational questions that are actually necessary. Research shows that senior buyers do not like answering factual questions. Hence, successful salespeople do their homework thoroughly at pre-approach stage and get required information from junior buyers.

To avoid asking unnecessary situational questions, salespersons should be sure that each question has a clear purpose. Also, the situational question should be related to the problem or the need the prospective buyer may have that the salesperson's product or service can resolve. The situational questions should be asked early in the sale so that salesperson can then move with ease into asking problem questions. Situational questions should not be asked on sensitive areas like conflict between different departments of buyers. If sensitive information is really required, it should be obtained indirectly and later in the sale when trust between the buyer and the seller has been established. Successful salespeople do not use SPIN questions in a rigid sequence. Hence, instead of asking many situational questions early in the sales call, they ask them when it makes sense to clarify and explore problems as they actually emerge. For example, the salesperson asks the potential buyer, "you said that employee turnover is a major problem for you. Can you tell me how do your compensation rates compare with your competitors?"

Problem Questions

These questions are used to discover problems, difficulties or dissatisfaction the customer is experiencing with the existing situation. Salespeople ask problem questions to uncover implied needs of the buyer. Examples are:

- Have you experienced any problems in servicing your machines?
- Have you had any difficulty controlling quality?
- Have you experienced any delays in getting those materials from your existing suppliers?
- How satisfied are you with the response time of your current service provider?

Salespeople should do their homework so as to first ask a few situational questions, which will set the context for asking the problem questions. If required, salespersons do follow-up by clarifying problem questions when the buyer starts to reveal problems, difficulties or dissatisfaction. Salespeople should be extremely cautious in asking problem questions in cases such as when the customer has made a decision recently in an area, when the buyer has a personal or emotional involvement or when the buyer is already using the salesperson's product or service.

A good method to plan problem questions is by thinking about the problems the salesperson's product or service can solve for a customer. Successful salespeople ask follow-up problem questions to clarify specific difficulties or problems that the buyer has identified. This can be done effectively by using the word-why? For example, when a buyer says, "I am not satisfied with our current supplier of steel", a good salesperson will ask, "Why are you not satisfied?" This gives the salesperson a better understanding of the buyer's dissatisfaction.

An effective salesperson explores or uncovers a problem from more than one way. This is done so that the salesperson can develop different needs if the buyer deflects the first one. For instance, "I can see why shortage of trained manpower is a problem for you in production. Would this issue be of concern to other functional areas like finance, marketing or logistics?"

Implication Questions

The implication questions ask the buyer about the implications, consequences or impact of the buyer's problem on its operations. Salespeople ask these questions to make the buyer think about the consequences of not solving the problem. Implication questions link a problem to other potential problems or consequences. Examples are:

- What impact the delays in receiving the components have on your production and customer satisfaction?
- Have these staff problems led you to lose any clients?
- What consequences the errors in your system have on your customers?

Successful salespersons plan implication questions before the sales calls, because they have to think implication questions by using their business and application knowledge. The purpose of the implication questions is to build the importance of a strong desire to buy the salesperson's product or service.

Salespeople should ask implication questions after problem questions, but before asking solution-value questions or need-payoff questions. This approach ensures that when the salesperson proposes a solution to the problem, the customer's interest will be high.

Need–Payoff Questions

Solution-value or need-payoff questions ask about the value, importance or usefulness of the solution to a problem uncovered earlier. Salespersons use these questions to increase the acceptability of their solutions. The purpose of these questions is to develop the buyer's desire for a solution. Need-payoff questions are positive and constructive, because they focus on the solutions. Examples are:

- If the rejection rate for this component at your quality inspection stage is reduced to less than one percent, how much money would that save you?
- By using our material handling equipment if you could save 2000 sq. ft. area in your warehouse, how much of saving would that mean?
- How important is it if the response time to your customers would improve by 50 percent?

By linking need-payoff questions to the buyer's responses or statements, the salesperson can prepare effective need-payoff questions. Also, if possible, the salesperson should use need-payoff questions that ask the buyer to identify clearly the benefits or pay-offs that are important to the buyer. Examples are:

- Wouldn't personal computers save time of your field or outside salespersons?
- You mentioned earlier that your management would like to minimize the inventory carrying cost of incoming materials. By supplying our components three times a day, linking to your factory's three shifts production timing, to ensure Just-In-Time (JIT) deliveries and excellent quality, wouldn't it achieve your management's needs?

In large- and medium-size organizations, the buying decisions are made by a group of people called 'purchase committees' or 'buying centers'. Hence, the salesperson's success in getting orders depend not just on how well he sells or convinces one buyer or purchase executive, but how well the buyer sells the salesperson's solution to other members of buying center. Need-payoff questions help the buyer to describe benefits to other members of the purchase committee. Thus, the buyer's confidence and enthusiasm in the salesperson's solution is increased.

The studies carried out by Neil Rackham[8] show that successful salespeople ask a few situational questions first. This is followed by problem (discovery) questions, implication questions, and need-payoff (or solution value) questions. Good salespeople use this sequence to ask questions to buyers. By following this process, successful salespeople uncover and understand the buyer's needs effectively.

LO 4 Understand various methods of sales presentations, product demonstration and handling of objections

THE SALES PRESENTATION

After understanding the customer's needs, the salesperson moves into the sales presentation. Although most presentations are oral, often business customers ask for written proposals, quotations or offers before oral presentations. A written **proposal or quotation** includes technical specifications of the product or service that meets customer's needs, price, terms of payments, delivery schedule, taxes and duties, proof of claims, additional benefits like service, training, guarantees that enhance the proposal.

The **objective** of the sales presentation is to persuade the customer that the product or service being sold will meet the customer's needs better than that of competitors.

Understanding Sales Presentation Methods

Salespeople must know the various methods (or approaches) used for making a sales presentation. These are: (i) Stimulus-response method (or canned presentation), (ii) Formula method (AIDA model or formula), (iii) Need-Satisfaction method (with FAB approach), (iv) Team selling method, and (v) Consultative selling method.

Stimulus-Response Method

It is also called ***canned approach,*** a memorized sales presentation or a prepared sales presentation. This method assumes that if a salesperson makes the right stimuli (e.g. sales presentation), he can get a favorable response from the prospect. The salesperson does most of the talking. Without knowing the needs of the prospect, the salesperson presents all the features of the product and then asks the prospect to buy the product. If the prospect does not agree to buy, another attempt is made to sell the product. This method is used by telemarketing people, door-to-door salespersons, and for training new salespeople. When canned sales presentation is prepared by the company's experienced people based on research, it can be useful to new salespeople. However, making the same presentation to all prospects or giving the same sales talk is not effective for sophisticated buyers or for creative selling situations. The major fault in this method is that the salesperson does not find out the needs of the prospect by asking him questions. The salesperson talks about the product features which may not be important to the buyer.

Formula Method

This method is also based on stimulus-response thinking and is also known as 'formulated approach' or 'mental states selling'. The salesperson assumes that most buyers can be led through mental states or steps in the buying process, and hence uses a well-known formula. It has four stages: (i) attention, (ii) interest, (iii) desire, and (iv) action (AIDA)[9].

❍ **Attention** The sales representative plans the sales talk by first getting the attention of the prospect by making a favorable statement about the prospect or the prospect's business. *Favorable first impression* is also created by formal dress, neatness, a genuine and warm smile, and a firm handshake (it should show warmth and not a test of strength!).

First impressions include body language, gesture, posture, handshake, smile, eye contact, manners, etiquette and greetings. It is very important that the salesperson's appearance and mannerisms are pleasant and courteous. A salesperson should build a rapport with the prospective customer with a sincere compliment or positive statement. Rapport-building leads to trusting relationship and feeling of comfort that eventually results in sales.

❍ **Interest** The salesperson leads the prospect's mind to the second stage of gaining an interest. In other words, the salesperson finds out which aspect(s) or factor(s) of the product or service appeals or attracts the prospect. Different methods are used by salespeople to uncover the prospect's interest or need. Some salespeople carry a sample of the product, or the product, if it is not bulky, for showing or demonstrating to a customer. Some other salespeople carry visual aids like CD, the product leaflet or the product photographs. Successful salespeople know that customers appreciate the things of interest and show interest in products and services that help to solve their problems or satisfy their specific needs.

❍ **Desire** The objective in this stage is to arouse a strong feeling in the prospect of wanting to have the product or the service that solves the prospect's problem. The salesperson continues with the sales presentation and demonstrates to the prospect how his product or service can solve the buyer's problem. In this process, the buyer may raise some objections, which need to be answered properly. We shall discuss how to overcome these objections subsequently in this chapter. Sometimes, salespeople face the problem of external interruptions like prospects getting phone calls. After the interruption, it is advisable that the salesperson quickly summarizes what has been said earlier before continuing with the sales presentation. The primary job of the salesperson is to ensure that the prospect's desire is fulfilled with his product or service.

❍ **Action** The action, in this stage, means buying action or closing the sale. Some sales people use trial close to test whether the prospect is ready to buy. If the prospect's answer to trial close question is favorable, then the salesperson asks for the order. If it is unfavorable, the salesperson continues with the presentation to fully convince the prospect about his proposal. We shall discuss more on trial close and closing the sale subsequently in this chapter.

The advantages of this method are that the salesperson has to plan the sales presentation and understand the customer's mental stages. The AIDA model is used throughout history. However, the AIDA's sales process has now changed (Figure 2.3) as also proposed by Shiv Khera in his book '*You Can Sell*' Westland Ltd., 2012, p.109.

From	To
A. Attention	Rapport
I. Interest	Need
D. Desire	Solution
A. Action	Close

Fig. 2.3 Change in the AIDA Model's Selling Process

Establishing rapport is now the priority of the salesperson in the first stage of getting the prospect's attention. In the second stage of gaining the prospect's interest, the focus of the salesperson is on understanding the buyer's needs or problems. In the third stage, the salesperson offers a compelling solution to the prospect's problem that arouses the prospect's feeling of wanting to have the product or service. In the last stage, the buying action takes place, when the salesperson uses the techniques of trial close and closes the sale.

Need-Satisfaction Method

This method is most challenging and a creative form of selling. It is an interactive sales presentation, which is different from the stimulus-response and the formula methods discussed earlier. The salesperson typically starts with 'uncovering and understanding the buyer's (or the prospect's) needs by asking situational, problem identification, implication, and need-payoff questions as described earlier in this chapter. Only after clearly understanding or investigating the needs or the problems of the buyer, the salesperson gives a written proposal (if the buyer wants it) or moves into sales presentation to show how his product or service can solve the buyer's problem. This is done in three ways: features, advantages and benefits.

❍ **Features** These are defined as facts, information or characteristics of the salesperson's product, service or market offering. For example, "Our ceiling fans have two ball bearings".

❍ **Advantages** The salesperson shows how the feature can help or give advantage to the prospect. For instance, "Because of the ball bearings, our ceiling fans hardly make any noise and have a longer life".

❍ **Benefits** The salesman then describes how the feature or advantage meets a clear and specific need expressed by the prospect earlier. When a prospect states the benefit, it becomes a powerful statement that can be used by the salesperson effectively for making a sale. To illustrate from the earlier example, "our ceiling fans can be effectively used in the class-rooms where noise level should be low, as needed by you". There is a very specific definition of benefits here, i.e. the benefits deal with specific needs mentioned by the buyer.

Table 2.1 gives some examples of products and services along with their FAB (Features, Advantages and Benefits).

Table 2.1 Examples of FAB Approach

Product/Service	Features	Advantages	Benefits
Domestic Pump sets	We have a special design for low voltage application.	Our pump sets can be used even when you have low voltage situations.	As mentioned by you, for your low voltage conditions, you can use our pump set.
Annual Maintenance Contract (AMC) for your computing system	We have 20 skilled technicians in your geographical area.	For this reason, you would get a fast response to a breakdown complaint.	We can give you a response within two hours, as desired by you.
Loading and unloading equipment	Our hydro-electric equipment is semi-automatic and customized.	Because of this, the time taken for loading and unloading your incoming and outgoing materials is minimum.	As required by you, our equipment takes less than 10 minutes to load or unload materials.

Most customers like this method and are willing to spend time to describe their needs. This method focuses on the customer, unlike stimulus response that focuses on the salesperson. The sales effectiveness of this method is much higher.

Team Selling Method

As discussed in Chapter 1, team selling is one of the latest developments in personal selling. Increasing number of organizations are using multi-person sales teams to deal with multi-person buying centre (or buying committees) of their customers[10]. Figure 2.4 shows an example of relationship between a sales team of selling firm and a buying center of a buying company. A salesperson (or key accounts executive) from the selling firm typically co-ordinates the selling activities of the sales team and a purchase executive or a materials executive of the buying firm typically coordinates the purchasing activities of the buying center. Individual members of the sales team and the buying center are from different functional areas and play one or more roles in the exchange process as shown in Figure 2.4.

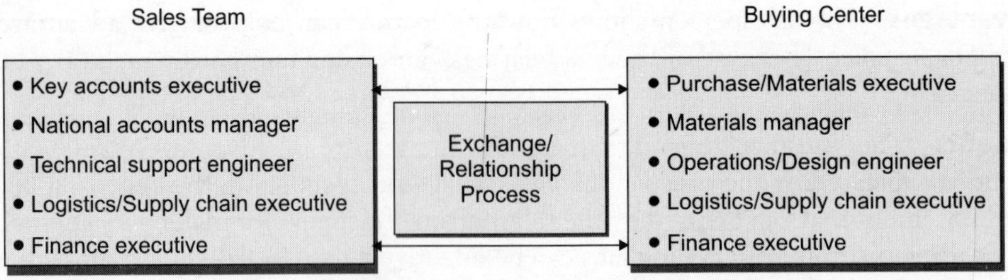

Fig. 2.4 Relationship Process between Sales Team and Buying Center Members

❍ **Strategic Issues** Team selling approach is not the best alternative in all selling situations. Since team selling is expensive, it should be used for key accounts (or customers), who have high sales and profit potential. It can also be used for complex selling situations, customized products and services, long-term contracts or new customers. Team selling should not be used for low sales and profit potential customers, who could be served by a salesperson with transactional selling approach. Similarly, routine (or repeat purchase) situations can be handled by a salesperson, without any need for a sales team. Generally, the decision to use sales teams depends on the needs of the buyer. If a customer uses a team of buying center members for purchasing products or services, then the marketing firm should use a sales team to match the functional areas and management levels of the buying firm. Companies like IBM, Xerox, HP, 3M, Wipro and Siemens use the team selling approach extensively. At IBM, for example, the sales team consists of client executive, systems engineer, consultant and product representative. The emphasis in team selling is on building a long-term relationship between selling and buying firms by focusing on the whole company and its capabilities, rather than just selling a product or a service.

❍ **Group Presentation** When a sales team makes the sales presentation to a group of decision-makers from the buying organization, it is called a 'group presentation'. Some of the guidelines for an effective group presentation are as follows:

- **Need-Analysis:** Before the group presentation, the salesperson or the key account executive should talk with all or most members of buying center (or purchase committee) to understand their needs or problems completely and what benefits they are looking for. Also, he should use the opportunity to build a rapport or a good relationship.
- **Introduction:** First part of the group presentation should include the company name, members of selling firm and their designations and a brief statement of the purpose or objectives of the presentation.
- **Convincing:** Mention, during the presentation, the company's experience, names of renowned customers, third-party certification of satisfaction and quality assurances.
- **Specific Benefits:** If the need-analysis was not done before the presentation, ask each buying team member the benefits they look for in the product or service they intend to buy. Then go through the presentation and show how the product or the service offered meets with each member's specific benefits.
- **Well Prepared:** At the end of the presentation, the selling team should answer questions from the buying team. The selling team should be so well prepared that all the questions

are answered well. The selling team should make each of its team members responsible to his area of specialization, such as technical, commercial, and so on.

Consultative Selling Method

Consultative selling is increasingly used as a professional selling process in the 21st century. This is also sometimes referred to as **problem-solving method**. Buyers have problems and they know that they do not have expertise to solve the problems. Buyers want solutions within their budget to achieve their strategic goals. Consultative salespeople or sales teams help customers not only in solving their problems or meeting the needs, but also to achieve the strategic goals of the customer. The salesperson uses the resources of the selling organization by seeking help from design, production/operations or any other persons or functions within or outside the organization, in order to solve the customer's problem. Salespeople understand the customer's strategic goals and work in a collaborative or partnering relationship with the customer to achieve the strategic goals and to solve the customer's problems. Many software suppliers, like Wipro and SAP, use consultative selling approach to solve their customer's business problems, such as enhancing business performance, setting up quality framework or creating value for their clients. For successful consultative selling, the requirements are as follows:

- Salespeople should have an in-depth knowledge of the customer's company, the customer's industry and carry out a detailed analysis of the customer's problems or needs.
- Salespeople should be aware of key members of the customer's buying center (or purchase committee) and get their acceptance of the needs/problems.
- Salespeople should prepare the proposal for solving the buyer's problems and thereafter, make the sales presentation, using team selling approach (described earlier in this chapter and in Chapter 1).
- Salespeople should use the selling firm's cross-functional expertise to provide solutions to the customer's business and technology related problems. If needed, external sources should be used by the sales team to become an expert on the customer's business and to solve the customer's problems.
- Salespeople should build long-term partnership with the customer, using relationship selling techniques.

How to Make an Effective Presentation?

For making an effective presentation, the following guidelines would be helpful:

❍ **Planning** As stated earlier in the section on pre-approach, it is important that the salesperson does planning, including setting objectives for each sales call and each presentation.

❍ **Use Technology** Salespeople should use the latest technology like virtual or Web- based and multimedia presentations as well as Instant Messaging (IM) for secret coordination between sales team members during presentations.

❍ **Adapt Presentation** The salesperson should customize his presentation tailored to the given situation and person(s).

❍ **Benefit Plan** Salespeople should use persuasive communication to create a visual picture in the prospect's mind of the benefits of the purchase.

❍ **Do Not Overload** The salesperson should avoid telling everything about the company, product and service. Only the information that is relevant should be presented, because the prospect can understand only limited information at a time.

❍ **Buyer's Language** The salesperson should use the language that is understood by the buyer. Salespeople should not use difficult words (or jargons), which are not understood by the customers.

❍ **Convincing** Salespeople must make the presentation convincing, by proving each point with the help of a third party proof. It is important that the prospect must believe in the statements made by the salesperson.

DEMONSTRATING THE PRODUCT

Demonstration is one of the important selling tools of a salesperson. Sales presentation can be improved by demonstration[11]. Demonstration proves the benefits of the product and reduces the risk of a wrong purchase to the buyer. That is the reason car salespeople allow prospective customers to test drive cars and many manufacturers' of industrial products arrange demonstration of their products in use.

Some of the benefits of using the demonstration as a tool for selling are as follows:

- Buyers' doubts or objections are cleared and their questions are answered. This improves a buyer's purchasing interest.
- It provides a good support in the selling process.
- It helps the salesperson to find out specific benefits for the prospective customer. The salesperson can then show how his product or service can satisfy those benefits.

Planning and Conducting Demonstration

The salesperson should do necessary planning by rehearsing the demonstration with colleagues, who act as buyers, to ask questions or raise objections. There should be a contingency plan in case of power failure or product break-down. The demonstration should be planned in two parts. In the first part, the salesperson should explain briefly the product features, advantages and benefits of the product (as described earlier in the use of FAB approach) and also how the product works. In the second part, the salesperson should show demonstration or actual working of the product. The salesperson should use simple language and avoid technical words or jargons, if possible. If jargons are necessary, the same should be explained in simple and commonly understood words.

The salesperson should also understand the purpose of demonstration—to obtain a sale or to lead for further discussions or negotiations. For achieving this purpose, the demonstration should be made interesting and the buyer should find it satisfying. Understanding the buyer's specific needs or specific benefits and showing how the product, that is demonstrated, satisfy the specific needs or benefits of the buyer are important parts to be kept in mind when the demonstration is conducted. At the end, the salesperson should summarize the important points, including the buyer's specific benefits and how these are met fully by the product. The salesperson should then use closing techniques to get the order or any action, like final negotiation or meeting, which will take the sale forward. Booklets and brochures can be left behind for customer reference.

Types of Demonstration

There are various types of product demonstration as listed below:

- Manufacturers of machines and equipment demonstrate their new products at exhibitions and trade-shows, which are organized by industry or trade associations, such as India Engineering Trade Fair in New Delhi.
- The salesperson may take his prospective customer to see some of his equipment already in use at another customer's premises. The salesperson has to ensure that this other customer should be completely satisfied with his product. Also, he has to take a special permission of the other customer for the visit of the prospective customer.
- Sometimes, a product demonstration is done by a salesperson by taking the equipment to the prospective customer's premises.
- One of the most common ways of product demonstration is by inviting the prospective customer to the selling firm's factory.
- Technical seminar is another type of a new product demonstration where a group of prospective customers are invited at a hotel or some other venue. Refreshment or lunch is generally provided in seminars.

MATCHING PRESENTATION METHODS WITH SALES SITUATIONS

The salesperson should understand the sales situation and then use a suitable method of presentation. This would make the sales presentation more effective, resulting in improved sales performance. Table 2.2 shows different methods of sales presentations and appropriate situations.

Table 2.2 Matching Sales Presentation Methods with Sales Situations

Sales Presentation Methods	Suitable Sales Situations
Stimulus-response method or canned presentation	Suitable when selling time is short and product is simple or non-technical. This method is used by salespeople with less experience, as it gives them more confidence. Used for door-to-door selling, telephone selling or sales training.
Formula method (AIDA model)	In straight re-buy or repeat purchase situation, when the customer is familiar with the product or service of the salesperson's company or when the salesperson is aware of the buyer's needs, this method is appropriate.
Need-satisfaction method (FAB approach)	Suitable for selling industrial products or consumer durable products, where the salesperson has to understand the prospect's needs first. It is a creative form of selling.
Consultative selling method	For selling high-cost technical products or value-added services like computer hardware and software solutions, and power transformers. Team selling approach and relationship selling techniques are used to create value for key customers. The sales team serves as consultants to their customers by identifying problems and finding effective solutions.

HANDLING OBJECTIONS

Objections, resistances or oppositions may typically take place during a sales presentation or when the salesperson asks for the order from the prospect. Objections should be welcomed because they show that the prospect has some interest and that if the objections can be answered satisfactorily, it would result in sales.

Two types of objections or resistances happen: psychological or hidden and logical, practical or real. **Psychological or hidden objections** include predetermined ideas or beliefs, preference for established brands, dislike for making decisions, and the prospect may not be the decision-maker but he does not want to let the salesperson know, anxiety or resistance to spend money. Logical or real objections are tangible such as quicker delivery schedule, high price, and product quality or product availability.

Handling Psychological/Hidden Objections

The best method of finding out hidden objections is to ask questions to the prospective customer so that he would keep talking. The salesperson asking questions to the prospect would also help the prospect in clarifying his thinking. Examples include:

- Would you mind sharing your objection?
- Why do you feel that way?
- What seems to be your concern?

However, the salesperson should never argue with or hurt the prospect, because this may lead to loss of the sale.

Handling Logical Objections

Some of the common methods of handling or overcoming the buyer objections are as follows:

- Ask question
- Turn an objection into a benefit
- Deny objections tactfully
- Show third-party certificate
- Offer compensation

Ask Questions

First listen to the buyer's objection carefully. Never interrupt, because nothing annoys a buyer more! Thereafter, clarify the objection by rephrasing it into a question and get the buyer's acceptance of the question. Let us take an example:

Buyer: "It seems price of your product is higher than your competitor."

Salesperson: "I accept your concern. Do you want to know why the price of my product is slightly higher than that of another supplier?"

Buyer: "Yes, that's what I want to know."

The salesperson then explains the benefits of his product to make it worth the price.

Turn an Objection into a Benefit

An experienced salesperson, with positive attitude and quick thinking can turn an objection into a benefit or a reason to buy. Consider the following:

Prospect: "The delivery period of four weeks for your equipment seems to be too long, as we need it in about two weeks, so that including installation and commissioning the project will have to be completed in five weeks from now."

Salesperson: "I appreciate your point, but this equipment is specially designed and manufactured to your specific needs. With four weeks delivery, we can do installation and commissioning in less than one week, so that overall it would be five weeks or earlier. Is that okay with you?"

Deny Objections Tactfully

Sometimes, objections are incomplete or not correct and in such situations salespeople should tactfully deny the objections indirectly. Consider the following example of indirect denial:

Buyer: "I don't want to buy your car, because a friend of mine told me that he had a lot of problems when he purchased your newly launched vehicle two years ago."

Salesperson: "Yes, I agree, two years ago when we launched our new brand of car, we had a few problems, but we solved all those problems within six months at our factory and also at our customers' premises free of cost. In the last one-and-half years our sales are highest, as compared to other brands and you can check with your friend now about the performance of the vehicle. If he gives you a good opinion, would you buy our car?"

The salesperson should not be arrogant or sarcastic when he denies incorrect objections.

Third Party Certificate

When the prospect expresses doubts about the product quality or performance, the salesperson uses some other customers' experience of using the product as a proof or testimony. However, the salesperson should get the prior approval from such customers. Sometimes, the prospect takes the initiative and asks the salesperson to give the names and telephone numbers of customers who have been using the product or service of the salesperson's organization. Favorable responses from such customers result in getting the order for the salesperson.

For instance, before buying six numbers of the equipment used for loading and unloading materials from trucks, ITPL, Bengaluru, not only visited the manufacturer's plant, but also went to Ashok Leyland's plants (the manufacturer's customer) at Hosur to see the performance of the equipment as well as to know the quality of service, including the availability of spare parts.

Compensation

Sometimes, the buyer has a valid objection, which makes the salesperson offer some kind of compensation or benefit to counterbalance the objection. For example, Reliance Industries were considering buying certain material handling equipment for the first time for their factories in Gujarat from a manufacturer, located in Karnataka. Reliance raised an objection to know how the manufacturer would ensure efficient warranty service and after-sales service. The manufacturer's senior marketing executive promised to station one service engineer at the customer's premises for one year and thereafter open a service center near Reliance Industries premises. This assurance satisfied the customer, who placed an order initially for a small value of material handling equipment with an assurance to place substantial value of orders subsequently if the concern for efficient after-sales service is taken care.

Handling Price Objections

One typical objection that almost always arises is price. The buyer who says "It cost too much" is pointing out that the value of the offered product is not worth the cost. It may be necessary for the salesperson to go back to the "SPIN model" (described earlier in this chapter) and ask some additional implication and need-payoff questions to increase the buyer's perception of the seriousness of the problem and the importance of a solution. If the buyer still feels that he cannot afford the product, then the salesperson should offer lower priced model and compare the same with the higher priced one. Another method of handling the price objection is to compare the price and value of competing alternatives. One other way of dealing with price objection is to break the price into the smallest possible units. For instance, "As said earlier, this equipment will last for 10 years at the cost of ₹10,000. See what you are getting for ₹1000 per year."

Handling Product/Service Objections

Sometimes the buyer doubts whether the product or service offered by the salesperson can solve the problem or meet the needs. In such a case, the salesperson should prove that the product will fulfill the need or solve the problem by using the following action plan: (i) demonstration of the product, (ii) testimonials, (iii) trial use, (iv) independent tests, (v) case histories, and(vi) expert opinion. In case the salesperson finds that his product cannot meet the specific need of the buyer, it is best to accept the same, but give special importance to the other needs the product can meet.

LO 5 Determine the techniques of trial close and closing the sale and follow-up tasks

TRIAL CLOSE AND CLOSING THE SALE

If the salesperson has answered the objections of the prospect satisfactorily, then this is the right time to close the sale. Closing the sale means asking for the order. A good salesperson, before closing does the trial close.

Trial Close

A trial close gives an indication to the salesperson as to how near he is to the actual close. A trial close asks the opinion of the prospect. It does not ask the decision of the prospect. The reason for using the trial close is that if the salesperson tries to close the sale by asking for the order after answering the objections, and if he gets the prospect's response as "no", it would be very difficult to change the prospect's mind. Trial closing is an effective way of getting feedback, whether the prospect liked the benefits offered by the product. It may also bring out the prospect's objections, if any. Trial close is an opinion of the buyer, whereas closing the sale is a buying decision of the buyer. Some examples of trial closes are:

- Which color do you prefer-yellow or green?
- Would you like to have this washing machine delivered tomorrow morning or evening?
- Out of the three models that are here, I think, you liked this model. Am I right?

If the prospect has responded favorably to the salesperson's trial close question, then the salesperson should know that it is time to close the sale. However, if the prospect's feedback or response to the trial question is negative, it means the feature, advantage or the benefit presented by the salesperson is not liked by the prospect. In such a case, the salesperson should go back to the presentation, instead of closing the sale, as shown in Figure 2.5.

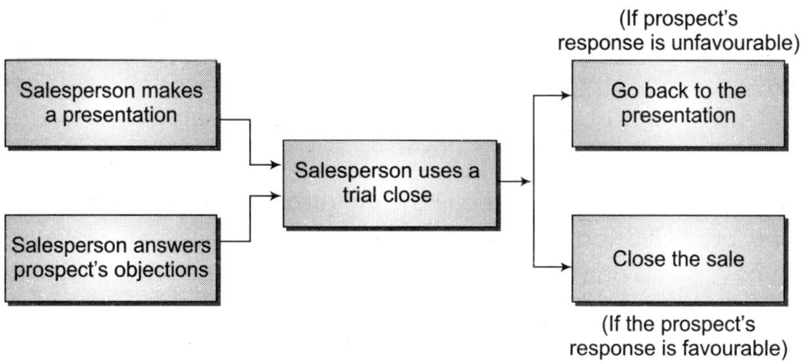

Fig. 2.5 Steps to be Followed by a Salesperson

Closing the sale means asking for the order. Closing is the process of helping the buyer to make a decision that will benefit him. When should a salesperson close the sale? The answer is when the buyer is ready in the mental buying process. Most of the time, prospective buyers give indications about their readiness to buy. Some of these **buying signals** are as follows:

❍ **Examines the Product** When a prospect examines the product carefully, the salesperson should use a trial close question such as "What is your opinion about this product?" If the answer from the prospect is positive, the salesperson should move on to close the sale.

❍ **Asks Another Person's Opinion** The prospect asks the opinion of another person—a colleague in office or a relative at home—"What do you think about this product?"

❍ **Asks Questions** Some of the questions the prospect may ask are: "When can you deliver this product? What is the price? What are your payment terms?" Sometimes, the salesperson asks another question in response to the prospect's buying signal question in order to better understand the prospect's needs or thoughts, such as "When do you want the delivery?", "How much quantity is required?" Or "What payment terms you want?"

❍ **Becomes Friendly** The prospect becomes friendly, once he mentally decides to buy. The anxiety or pressure of buying changes into relaxation. An ability to understand the prospect's buying signals correctly helps a salesperson decide when and how to close the sale. Although most of the time, the time to close the sale is after the presentation, it can also happen after trial close, during presentation or after answering the objections.

It is important for a salesperson to remember that when he asks for the order, he should remain quiet and not say anything. If the salesperson says something after asking for the order, the pressure on the prospect to make a decision goes off and may result in losing the sale.

CLOSING TECHNIQUES

Some successful salespeople always summarize the major benefits after the presentation, but before the close. Coming to a close without summarizing makes the presentation abrupt. A summary should be very brief indicating the major benefits flowing to the buyer. There are many closing techniques. Some of the major closing techniques are discussed below:

- **Alternative-choice Close** In this technique, the prospect is given a choice between two or more items or models and not between buying or not buying. For instance, "Which of the three models do you prefer?" By giving a choice, either the salesperson gets a "Yes, I prefer this model", or some kind of objections, which if satisfactorily handled, would enable to come closer to making the sale. This technique is effective, if used correctly.

- **Minor Points Close** This technique is similar to the alternative-choice close. It is sometimes easier for a prospect to decide on many minor points than to make a bigger decision on whether to buy or not to buy. By having the prospect make decisions on a product's minor points, the salesperson can cleverly lead into the decision to buy. For example, the salesperson may ask questions in quick succession, "If you buy this solar heater, which model would you prefer?", "How soon would you like it to be delivered?", or "Would you like to pay on installment basis?" With these kinds of minor point questions, the prospect typically develops a positive inclination towards buying the product.

- **Assumptive Close** In this method, the salesperson assumes that the sale is made. He then proceeds to ask questions to the prospect while preparing the bill or the order about the prospect's middle initials, spelling of names, home or office address, quantity desired and color. He then asks the prospect to sign the order, which is a sign of closing the sale.

- **Summary-of-benefits Close** This technique is very popular, because it is simple and straightforward. The steps involved are: (i) find out the important benefits of your product or service that appeal to the prospect's specific needs, (ii) summarize these benefits by using FAB (features, advantages, and benefits) approach and SELL sequence (Show the feature, Explain the advantage, Lead into the benefit, Let customer talk), and (iii) make a proposal. Consider the following illustration:

  The salesperson selling room air conditioning products could say, "Our air-conditioner has a high efficiency rating (feature), due to which it uses less electricity (advantage), which results in 15 percent saving in your electricity bill (benefit). That's good-isn't it?" (trial close). If the response is favorable, the salesman says, "When do you want the delivery-this week or next week?"

- **T-account or Balance Sheet Close** This technique is used by the salesperson when he takes a piece of paper and draws a large T on it. He places benefits of buying on the left side and drawbacks of buying on the right side, as shown in Figure 2.6.

In the illustration shown in Figure 2.6, the salesperson reviews the presentation with the prospect, writes down all the positive points or benefits on the left side of the T and all the negative points or drawbacks on the right side. He then says the following:

Benefits	Drawbacks
• Time saving • Less efforts • Easy installment payment • Immediate delivery	• More models

Fig. 2.6 T-Account or Balance-sheet Close

Salesperson: "Madam, this vacuum cleaner's high speed motor (feature) works very fast (advantage) and with less effort (advantage) and saves about 20 minutes in cleaning time (benefit). We will also give you immediate delivery (benefit) and easy installment payment scheme (benefit). Which of these benefits you like, you may kindly write on the left of T section, under "Benefits".

Prospect: "Yes, I like the benefits of time saving and easy installment payment."

Salesperson: "Ok, Now is there anything that you want us to improve?"

Prospect: "Yes, I want more choice to select from more models."

Salesperson: "Ok, please write that down, on the right side. Is there anything else, you would like to add?"

Prospect: "No."

The example shows that the product's benefits are more than the drawback. The salesperson should then use trial close and close the sale. A note of caution is that one drawback may be heavier than many benefits. This technique can be used as a back-up, if the summary-of-benefits close did not make the sale.

❍ **Special-offer Close** When a salesperson has done his best to close the sale, but the prospect is resisting, then the special-offer or special-deal may help close the sale. For instance, the salesperson might say, "If you buy this refrigerator today, I can give you a special discount of two percent."

❍ **Probability Close** This technique is used, when the prospect says, "I will think it over", or "I will let you know". The salesperson allows the real or hidden objections to come out by asking the prospect "please tell me the probability in percentage that next week when I call you back, you will take the decision of buying". If the probability is more than 50 percent for buying, the salesperson can convert the real objection to closing the sale, by using the various techniques described earlier. However, if the probability is less than 50 percent for buying, the chance of closing the sale is low. In such a case, return to the original position and start the selling process again.

❍ **Negotiation Close** Most salespeople close the sale after successful negotiations with buyers (or prospective customers). The attitude and style of negotiation of the salesperson determines the outcome of negotiation. The salesperson should have a positive and helpful attitude. Out of the various styles of negotiation, the salesperson should use 'both of us win' style. This style helps the salesperson and the selling organization to build a long-term mutually beneficial relationship with the buyer and the buying organization. It is, therefore, necessary that salespeople possess the skills of negotiation, which we will discuss later in this chapter.

Closing Techniques and Sales Situations

In order to understand better the suitable closing techniques to be used for different sales situations, a matrix is prepared, as shown in Figure 2.7.

Sales situations \ Closing Techniques	Negotiation	Probability	Special-offer	T-Account	Summary of benefits	Assumptive	Minor points	Alternative choice
Buyer is hostile	✓	✓						
Buyer is a friend	✓	✓				✓		
Buyer is unable to make a decision	✓	✓	✓	✓	✓		✓	✓
Buyer is selfish or greedy	✓	✓						
Buyer has certain opinion in advance	✓	✓		✓				
Buyer is an expert with a large ego	✓	✓		✓				

Fig. 2.7 Matrix on Closing Techniques and Sales Situations

Salespeople can review their customer profile to understand the sales situation, and use the appropriate closing technique based on the matrix shown in Figure 2.7. They should be well prepared before each sales call. This would result in superior sales performance and customer satisfaction.

FOLLOW-UP

Salespeople must understand that their job is not over after the receipt of the order. Successful sales people follow-up a number of related tasks, some of which are called customer service, as described in this section.

Check Customer Order

After getting the customer order, the salesperson should go through the same carefully to check if all the details such as delivery period, address of delivery, advance payment (if any) and so on are mentioned. If this checking is not done now, later on there may be delay due to the remark 'awaiting the information from the customer.'

Plan Follow-up Visit at the Time of Delivery

The salesperson should plan a follow-up call when the ordered equipment or the item is to be delivered. This visit includes checking if the product is received on time and without any damage in transit (if received in damaged condition, to arrange for insurance formalities), installation (if any), operating instructions and training the customer (if needed). This visit is very important because it will detect any problems or complaints, which the salesperson should solve to the customer's satisfaction. Consider the following example of handling customer's complaints promptly:

Crompton Greaves (old CGL company) launched its new table fan in Mumbai in 1973 with a lot of fanfare in a five-star hotel. On the next day of the launch, the company dealers complained about the improper oscillation of the new fan. The area sales manager and his salespeople, along with a team of technical people from the manufacturing unit of the company immediately swung into action, detected the minor fault and repaired all those fans with minor defect. This restored the confidence of the dealers to sell the new product, as the complaint was handled promptly.

Some buyers suffer from post-purchase anxiety (cognitive dissonance) about the wisdom of their purchase decision, particularly if there are problems on high value products or services. The follow-up visit of the salesperson assures the buyer and reduces the dissonance. For instance, many buyers of the newly launched 'Indica' car suffered post-purchase anxiety due to certain technical problems. However, immediate corrective actions from Tata Motors (Telco then) in solving these problems reduced the dissonance substantially.

Account Penetration

Successful salespeople know that there is still a lot of work to be done after making the sale. By contacting the customer after the sale, the salesperson lays the foundation of a positive business relationship. Account penetration means working and contacting people throughout the account (i.e. customer organization) and discussing about the selling firm's products and services. The successful account penetration depends on the knowledge of the customer organization's key buying center people, their buying situations and buying criteria.

Relationship Marketing

Today's salespeople work to build and maintain long-term, mutually beneficial partnerships with their key customers. Companies understand that it is much more expensive to gain new customers than it is to keep existing customers. Effective follow-up and customer service will help build loyal customers.

LO 6 Application of the success factors in selling

NEGOTIATION SKILLS

Salespeople should have certain skills and qualities to be effective in negotiation. Whether salespeople talk to one person or a group of people, there is a possibility of negotiation. In a few exchanges between buyers and sellers, there may not be much scope for negotiation as pricing and distribution are administered, such as purchase of petrol and diesel and travel by Indian Railways. However, much of business (or industrial) selling (i.e. from one business firm to another business firm or B2B selling), negotiated exchanges on prices, payment terms, delivery period and other aspects will take place.

Some of the major skills and qualities required by salespeople to be effective in negotiations are: planning, subject knowledge, listening, patience, communication, intelligence, clear thinking, integrity and trustworthiness[12].

When to Negotiate?

Negotiation is a proper procedure to be followed for making the sale when the following conditions or circumstances are present:

- The buyer puts certain conditions for buying to the seller. For instance, "If you will reduce the price of your product by 8 percent, I will buy".
- When the agreement between the buyer and seller will have to take place on several factors, such as price, delivery, quality and payment terms.
- When the product or service to be exchanged is customized to the requirement of the buyer and may take a long-time to execute the order.
- When there is a zone of agreement between the two parties and the final price is to be decided through bargaining.

Preparing for Negotiation with Customers

Successful salespeople prepare well for negotiations with customers by following the steps described as follows:

❍ **Planning** Gather information about competitors' prices, quality, service, share of business and so on. The selling firm's negotiators should also know the real needs of the customer, power or authority of the buying firm's negotiators, important buying factors of the firm or the industry. Some of the questions to be answered by the selling firm negotiators are:

- How flexible are the price, payment terms and delivery period?
- Are there any product features, training, or services that can be offered free as benefits, compared to the competitors?
- Which factors are not flexible?
- What are the limits beyond which we cannot make concessions?

❍ **Building Relationship** Much before the final negotiation, salespeople should use the available time to build an environment of trust, understanding and relationship with the customer. Without the rapport or good relationship, it would be difficult to collect the required information. Hence, a lot of formal and informal meetings are needed between the buyers and sellers, not only for building relationship, but also to collect the required information. A good relationship between the two parties eases the tension during the negotiation process.

❍ **Purpose** The purpose of negotiations could be several. It could be for increase in prices due to an increase in the cost of inputs such as excise duty, raw material, freight, and others or for getting higher share of business or for getting an entry into a high sales potential prospect or for getting payments against old/disputed bills. Whatever may be the purpose of negotiation, it helps salespeople to succeed, if they have a right approach or style of negotiation.

Styles of Negotiation

Theoretically, there are four different styles of negotiation. These are:

(i) I win, you lose
(ii) Both of us win
(iii) You win, I lose
(iv) Both of us lose

However in practice, styles (i) and (ii) are used usually, style (iii) is used sometimes and (iv) is rarely used.

Out of the four styles of negotiation, the style that is typically used for customers, suppliers, employees, and relatives is both of us win or win-win. Here, the negotiations are held for mutual satisfaction, and the focus is on development of genuine relationship based upon trust and understanding. This is achieved by the following guidelines:

- Much before the final negotiation, build an environment of trust and confidence.
- During the negotiation, be polite and humble, which would help the customer to communicate in easy manner.
- In the initial stage of negotiation, the focus should be on identifying and agreeing to the problems rather than solutions.
- Both sides should then work together, pooling their resources, ideas and sharing information to solve the problems stated earlier.
- Both sides should make concessions at regular frequency.
- Defensive posture, legalistic, or contractual approach should be avoided.

Salespeople should recognize, based on the following tips, if the prospect or the buyer uses 'I win, you lose' style:

- The buyer starts with tough demands or unreasonable offer.
- The buyer raises voice or makes emotional outbursts.
- The buyer does not reciprocate or is stingy to the concession made by the seller.
- The buyer ignores the time deadline.

Once the salesperson recognizes that the customer or the prospect is using this style against him, he should defend his position in the following manner:

- He should take equally strong position by presenting a clear but unemotional opposition to the prospect's demand.
- He must explain why he holds his position and seek the reason from the prospect for holding that position.
- He should stress on the consequences of a failure to resolve the issue. The purpose here is to move the other party from win-lose style to win-win style.

It may be difficult to remember the above points and how to use them. The solution to this difficulty is to practice. By practicing these points in role-playing exercises, negotiating skills can be improved.

Some Tips on Negotiation

- Observe the verbal and non-verbal language of the other party. The salesperson's own verbal and non-verbal signals should reflect positive attitude.

- Don't argue. Avoid rude and loud behavior.
- Be assertive, not aggressive. Assertiveness means firmness with politeness, whereas aggressiveness is firmness without politeness.
- Maintain eye contact without staring. Eye contact shows confidence and trust, whereas staring points out that the salesperson is daring and challenging.
- Stay focused on the topic of negotiation; don't go off-track. Keep asking questions to uncover the real anxiety or problem without being aggressive.
- Don't blame anyone because that makes the environment tense immediately.
- Avoid sarcasm.
- The salesperson should not reveal his weakness. For instance, if the salesperson has to achieve a target by the end of the month, he should not show his desperation.
- Don't make emotional decisions during negotiation that may have a problem carrying out later.

A good sales professional realizes that his ability to persuade the other person to his way of thinking should be used without offending.

SUCCESS FACTORS IN SELLING

Often a question is asked: 'Is selling an art or science?' The answer is: selling is both an art and science. Selling is an art because sales people deal with human beings who are often emotional, illogical and unpredictable. Also, successful salesperson has to use creative methods of selling and innovation with each prospect, which is an art of selling. Selling is a science because a good salesperson should follow the steps in the selling process discussed earlier in this chapter to increase the probability of making the sale. To take the secrecy out of selling we need to change selling from an art to a science.

To succeed in selling, a salesperson needs to develop a set of necessary skills and possess certain characteristics. These may be called success factors. A good sales professional should develop a set of skills viz., communication skills, listening skills and negotiation skills. We have already discussed negotiation skills earlier in this chapter. Before we deal with listening and communication skills, it should be understood that the selling process described earlier in this chapter must be followed. The probability of success in selling would be high if a salesperson carries on effectively with the selling process. We shall also discuss a set of characteristics that are required in a salesperson to ensure success in selling.

Communication Skills

Communication skills are important to sales managers as well as to salespeople. The sales manager continuously transmits information from the upper management to the salespeople and from the salespeople to the upper management. This communication should be correct, complete and at an appropriate time. In a sales situation, communication is transmission of verbal and nonverbal information and understanding between a salesperson and a buyer. Two-way communication is required to make a sale. Buyers generally react verbally and non-verbally to the salesperson's presentation. Modes of communication typically used in a sales presentation are words, visual aids, gestures and non-verbal communication.

Non-Verbal Communication

Acceptance and openness can be communicated through positive body language. Resistance and rejection can also be communicated with unpleasant body language. Non-verbal communication consists of posture, gestures, eye contact, facial expressions, and overall grooming. Some examples of body language or non-verbal communication are:

- Leaning forward shows interest.
- Facial expressions can show buying or rejection action.
- A buyer sitting with crossed arms or crossed legs shows a lack of openness.

Our non-verbal communication is driven by our subconscious. Hence, if there is a mismatch or contradiction between verbal and non-verbal communication, we should believe in non-verbal.

A brief description with examples of the various components of non-verbal communication has been provided here:

❍ **Eye Contact** Comfortable eye contact establishes sincerity and trust. Staring directly at the prospect could be taken as a rudeness or arrogance. Having shifty eyes can communicate cunningness or uneasiness. Looking at the ceiling or the fan shows non-caring attitude.

❍ **Posture** It refers to the way a person stands, sits and walks. A lazy or drooping way of standing or sitting and a protruding stomach can be interpreted as a lack of interest and tiredness.

❍ **Gestures** Yawning, playing with a pen or key chain and drawing absent-mindedly indicate indifference. If an oral communication uses right kind of gestures, it can enhance the effectiveness of what has been said.

❍ **Facial Expression** A smile represents friendliness. A stiff expression or tightening of jaw muscles is a symbol of opposition or hostility. Raising of eyebrows is an expression of disbelief.

❍ **Overall Grooming** It means professional or personal appearance, which is important to create a favorable first impression of a salesperson. Therefore, a salesperson should take due care of his appearance and dress. Generally, professionals dress conservatively in formal trousers and tie and not in casuals like jeans.

Verbal Communication

A salesperson must become aware of both verbal and non-verbal communication. A sales professional's tone should be pleasant and the pace of speech should be moderate—not too fast and not too slow. A good salesperson does not use vague words that have multiple meanings. Examples of such words are regularly, frequently and sometimes. These words are confusing, because the same words mean different things to different people, which become a hindrance in closing the sale. A salesperson should not use jargons and should use layman's language while talking to a prospective customer. Jargons can be used if the sales professional is talking to someone in his own profession. Successful sales professionals use positive and helpful phrases and questions as indicated next:

- What is your opinion about -----?
- Would you be comfortable with ------?
- What do you feel is the best way -----?
- Together I am sure we can --------

Listening Skills

In communication, there are two components: giving information and listening information. Both components are important but listening is more important than talking because it makes the other person feel significant. Salespersons are generally known to be good talkers. However, what separates successful salespeople from others is their ability or skills of listening[13]. That is why good salespeople speak less and listen more. Effective salespeople listen very attentively and actively to what is said and what is unsaid by analyzing both verbal and non-verbal communications. A prospective customer will speak if he/she is encouraged by the salesperson through his positive remarks and questions like "Can you add more details?" and "What you said is very interesting."

Successful companies send their salespeople to the sales training programs conducted by Dale Carnegie or Toast–masters because these training programs give special importance to listening along with effective speaking. Some of the important points for creating a positive environment for listening are:

- While listening, acknowledge and encourage the other person by nodding your head and occasionally saying "yes" or something to that effect.
- Maintain eye contact, without staring at the other person. Don't keep looking around the room or outside.
- Don't interrupt. It is bad manners.
- While listening, avoid creating distractions, such as playing with a pen or tapping your finger.

Characteristics of an Effective Salesperson

Though every selling position and situation is different, most sales managers agree that there are generally desirable characteristics for effective salespeople. These are briefly mentioned below:

- **Burning desire** or ego drive indicate a strong personal desire to succeed. Sales happen as a result of hard work and effort.
- Team selling is now the main method of selling to key customers. Hence, **cooperativeness** as a trait is considered important for a salesperson to work on teams.
- **ICT Savvy:** The salesperson must be able to work with electronic communication and technology. Salespeople need to be comfortable with information and communication technologies (ICT) so that they can use information and multimedia options effectively.
- **Empathy:** Empathy (i.e. the ability to understand and feel as the customer does) is an important characteristic that helps a salesperson to build relationship with customers.
- **Behavioral Factors:** Characteristics such as **positive attitude** or behavior and discipline are considered as vital for a salesperson. A positive attitude determines the success of a salesperson. The difference between a positive and a negative attitude can be **illustrated** by a very frequently used story of two salespersons who once went to Africa. Both salespersons went to sell shoes in different parts of Africa. They both saw people without shoes. One salesperson immediately sent a message to his manager saying 'There is no market for shoes here. No one wears shoes and therefore, I am coming back.' The other salesperson sent a message saying 'There is a huge market for shoes here. Nobody wear shoes and hence, we can make everyone wear them. Be ready for large sales.'

- **Discipline:** Another behavioral factor of an effective salesperson is discipline. It is defined as doing what ought to be done, when it is ought to be done, and whether we like it or not. Discipline is the quality that gives strength and courage to a salesperson to face big challenges.

Thus, the success factors in selling include effective use of the selling process, development of negotiation, communication and listening skills as well as possession of certain key characteristics as mentioned above.

SUMMARY

LO 1

- The eight steps of the selling process are: (i) prospecting and qualifying, (ii) pre-approach, (iii) approach, (iv) discovering and understanding needs, (v) sales presentation and demonstration, (vi) handling objections, (vii) closing the sale, and (viii) follow-up.

LO 2

- Prospecting is the process of identifying potential customers. Methods used for prospecting or identifying leads are: consulting existing customers, referrals from external sources, referrals from internal company sources, Standard Industrial Classification (SIC) system, publications, networking by salespeople, cold canvassing, and World Wide Web.
- Qualifying is the process of qualifying or meeting the necessary standards of the probable prospect or the lead. This is done by getting the lead meet certain standards, viz. (i) the lead or probable prospect has a need for the product or the service being sold, (ii) the lead has the needed financial capacity to buy, and (iii) the ability to make a decision.

LO 3

- The pre-approach step includes two tasks: information gathering about the prospect through customer research and planning the sales call on the prospect.
- The next stage of the selling process is called the approach, i.e. meeting the buyer for the first time. Out of the various approach techniques, introductory approach is mostly used by sales people.
- After approaching the buyer, the salesperson's next step is to discover and understand the buyer's needs or problems. For this, the salesperson asks smart questions by using "Spin Model", in which there are four types of questions, viz. situation questions, problem questions, implication questions and need-pay off questions.

LO 4

- Subsequent to understanding the customer's needs, the salesperson moves into oral sales presentation. Business customers often ask for written proposals or quotations before oral presentations. The various methods used for sales presentation are: (i) stimulus response (or canned presentation), (ii) formula method (or AIDA model), (iii) need-satisfaction (with FAB approach), (iv) team selling, and (v) consultative selling.
- Sales presentation can be improved by product demonstration, which can be used as an important selling tool. There are various types of product demonstration.

- Buyers' objections may take place during or after the sales presentations. Two types of objections happen: (i) psychological (or hidden), and (ii) logical (or practical). There are various ways of handling psychological and logical objections.

LO 5

- After the objections are answered satisfactorily, a successful salesperson uses trial close technique, before adopting closing techniques. In trial close, a salesperson asks the opinion of the prospect, whereas in closing techniques he asks for the prospect's decision of buying. There are many closing techniques which can be used depending on different sales situations.
- Successful salespeople carry on with the follow-up tasks after the receipt of the order from customers.

LO 6

- To succeed in selling, salespeople need to develop a set of skills (such as communication, listening, and negotiation) and possess certain characteristics. It must be understood that the selling process should be followed to improve the probability of success in selling.

Key Terms

Glossaries of key terms are mentioned at the end of all chapters

AIDA formula
Approach
Canned sales presentation
Closing
Consultative selling
Formula method
Non-verbal communication
Pre-approach
Prospecting
Qualifying
Standard Industrial Classification (SIC) system
Stimulus response method
Suspect
T-account close
Trial close

Conceptual Questions

1. Indicate the steps of the selling process. Why should salespeople follow the suggested steps of the selling process? LO1 E
2. What is prospecting? What are the different methods of identifying sales leads? LO2 E
3. What is cold canvassing? Why many companies are not supporting cold canvassing? LO2 M

Note: Difficulty Level → E — Easy; M — Medium; D — Difficult

4. What is the difference between a sales lead and a prospect? How are the probable prospects qualified? LO2 M
5. In what manner, the approach step is different than the pre-approach step? Describe briefly the approach techniques used by salespeople. LO3 E
6. How do salespeople discover and understand a prospect's needs? LO3 D
7. What are the different sales presentation methods? Which method would you recommend for a new washing machine? What are the benefits of using demonstration as a selling tool? LO4 D
8. Describe the methods used for handling buyers' objections. How would you handle if a buyer feels that the price of your refrigerator is high and he can't afford it? LO4 M
9. Explain the difference between a trial close and a close. Describe any two closing techniques. LO5 M
10. Discuss why a salesperson's job is not over even after getting an order. LO5 D
11. Explain the different success factors in selling. Why good sales people speak less and listen more? LO6 D

Objective Type Questions

Select the most appropriate response out of the various options available in each of the following questions:

1. Most sales training programs follow the steps of the selling process because
   (a) it is a standard process (b) it makes sales people comfortable
   (c) it improves the chances of success (d) none of these LO1 E
2. "Closing the sale" is the last step of the selling process. LO1 E
   Yes/No
3. A sales lead is also called a
   (a) consumer (b) business customer (c) suspect (d) client LO2 M
4. SPIN model, which is used for discovering and understanding buyers' needs, has four types of questions, viz. situation, problem, implication, and
   (a) formula (b) canned (c) approach (d) need-pay off LO3 M
5. Some of the commonly used methods of sales presentation are canned presentation, AIDA formula, team selling, consultative selling, and
   (a) questioning (b) product presentation
   (c) appreciation (d) need-satisfaction LO4 M
6. The legend for AIDA formula includes attention, interest, desire, and
   (a) arrangement (b) agreement (c) action (d) assistance LO4 E

7. The legend for FAB approach consists of features, advantages, and
   (a) betterment (b) benefits (c) bargaining (d) basics LO4 E
8. Trial close questions are used to check the prospect's
   (a) opinion (b) decision (c) ability (d) none of these LO5 M
9. Out of the different styles of negotiations, the one that is typically used for customers is
   (a) you win, I lose (b) I win, you lose
   (c) I win, you win (d) both of us lose LO5 D
10. The trait required in a salesperson for selection in a selling team is
   (a) integrity (b) cooperative (c) self-motivation (d) risk taker LO6 D

Application Questions

1. Need–satisfaction method of sales presentation is effective with the use of FAB approach. Identify a feature, an advantage and a benefit for the following products and services, assuming you are going to make sales presentation in your class: (a) a washing machine brand, (b) a passenger car brand, (c) an MBA program, and (d) a life insurance policy. LO4 M
2. **Experiential Exercises:** (a) Spend a day with a salesperson, selling products or services. Make a report on your experience, the selling process followed, the methods of sales presentation used, how the buyers' objections were handled and the closing techniques used; (b) For improving effectiveness of communication, ask each participant to make a presentation in the class for five minutes on any topic in the curriculum that is already taught or to be taught. Talk to each participant separately after the presentation to suggest improvements. Repeat the process to other participants and see the improvements in communication in each participant. LO1–6 M
3. **Team Exercise: A role play on sales presentation and negotiation:** The objective of this role play is to improve the sales presentation and negotiation skills. The role play needs three participants, volunteering to play the roles of Alok Banerjee, Ramesh Kulkarni, and Krishna Kumar. Each role player will read the situation and their respective brief only and reflect upon the role by going out of the class for 15 minutes (without interacting with other role players). During these 15 minutes, the instructor will ask another participant from the class to read out to other participants in the class the situation and the briefs given to the three role players. The instructor should ask the participants in the class to maintain silence during the role play, listen, observe and make notes about their individual views on the role play for discussion after the role play is over. There are three chairs, two chairs of Alok and Ramesh are next to each other and Krishna Kumar's chair is kept opposite and facing Alok's and Ramesh's chairs. First Alok and Ramesh return to the class, after 15 minutes and occupy their respective chairs. Krishna Kumar returns within two minutes, thereafter, introduces himself to Alok and Ramesh, and then starts talking to them. LO4&5 D

   The Situation: A multi-national company (MNC) had set up a new project in Mumbai. The company wanted an efficient system for handling their raw materials, work-in process and finished goods. The company appointed a technical consultant to advise them on the technical specifications and suitability of the suppliers. Based on the past experience of the MNC's operations in Kolkata, the company had shortlisted three leading suppliers of material handling equipment in India.

Supplier 'A' was located near Kolkata but the MNC did not have a good opinion about their after-sales service, although the quality of their equipment was good.

Supplier 'B' was located near Mumbai and the MNC did not have any experience of their quality of products and services.

Supplier 'C' was located near Bengaluru. The MNC was using their material handling equipment at their Kolkata factory. The quality of equipment of supplier 'C' was considered as satisfactory, and the perception about the service was excellent.

The executive of the MNC and their consultant (let us call them buyer) visited all the three suppliers, discussed their requirements and asked for quotation, along with the detailed technical proposal and drawings. After receiving these, the buyer had a second round of technical discussions to understand the three suppliers' technical offers and to get their clarifications on various technical matters.

The buyer then called all the three suppliers for final negotiations on commercial matters, such as prices, discounts, payment terms, warranty period, delivery period, transportation (freight) cost, transit insurance, installation and commissioning. E-mails were sent by the MNC to all the three suppliers to depute their senior managers for final negotiation and order finalization at Mumbai on 20 July 2016.

We shall now have a role play involving Alok Banerjee of the MNC, Ramesh Kulkarni of the consultant and Krishna Kumar of the supplier 'C'.

Brief for Alok Banerjee

He is responsible, as the project manager of the MNC, to get the delivery of the equipment in 8 weeks and to obtain a reliable system for material handling at a competitive price. The price difference between suppliers varies from equipment to equipment, but the overall cost of the project was ₹40 lakh (i.e. ₹4 million or about $60,000). For the supplier 'C', a discount or price reduction of about 7.5 percent on ₹40 lakh was needed to make the prices competitive in comparison to the prices of supplier 'B'. He also wanted to make sure about efficient after-sales service during the warranty period of one year and the subsequent period. Alok had a good relationship with the Kolkata branch manager of supplier 'C', since he was the production manager of Kolkata factory before his transfer to Mumbai as the project manager. Alok had met Krishna Kumar during his previous visit to the supplier's Bengaluru factory.

Brief for Ramesh Kulkarni

As the technical consultant to the MNC, Ramesh wanted to make sure that the best supplier gets the order for supplying, installing and servicing the material handling system. Since the consultant had an ISO 9000 certification, he was keen that the selected supplier had proper quality system, after-sales service system and technical specifications as per international standards. Ramesh knew that his role is to advise Alok, who is supposed to take the final decision on the supplier selection.

Brief for Krishna Kumar

Krishna Kumar is the General Manager (Sales and Marketing) of supplier 'C'. Before going for the final negotiation, he discussed with his company's managing director the lowest level of overall price of all equipment. The lowest acceptable total price could be ₹36 lakh (or in other words, a maximum discount of 10 percent could be given on the quoted price of ₹40 lakh). The delivery period of 8 weeks from the date of receipt of order, along with 10 percent advance payment was acceptable. If required, the cost of transportation and insurance could be absorbed by the company, although in the quotation it was charged to the customer. The payment terms, warranty period and installation charges, could be suitably negotiated. He had established a good relationship with Alok Banerjee directly during Alok's earlier visit to the Bengaluru factory. Krishna Kumar knew that the competitors were also trying hard to get this large value order, but he had the advantage of the satisfactory performance of its equipment at the MNC's Kolkata factory and the long-term relationship established through its Kolkata office.

ASSIGNMENTS FOR STUDENTS

1. Visit a first level sales manager (i.e. area, district or branch sales manager) to whom a group of salespersons report. Ask the sales manager if salespeople are trained to use a specific selling process. Which steps in the selling process does the company follow? Understand the entire selling process and make a report of your discussion with the sales manager.
2. Identify and interview two salespersons from different organizations. Ask them which approach techniques do they use when they meet prospective customers for the first time and what type of questions do they ask prospects to discover and understand their needs. Also find out from them which method of sales presentations do they normally use and the reasons for the same. Make a report comparing the findings of the two interviews.
3. Search the Internet to find a list of prospects for each of the following type of sales organizations.
   (i) a travel agency with a focus on business travelers.
   (ii) a manufacturer of air compressors used in factories.
   (iii) a manufacturer of industrial pump-sets.

Reference Notes

1. Mark P. Leach, et al., *The Role of Self-Regulation Training in Developing the Motivation Management Capabilities of Salespeople*, Journal of Personal Selling and Sales Management, Summer 2005, pp. 269–81.
2. Todd Natenberg, *Referrals: Your Key to Sales Success*, Selling, September 2004, p. 9.
3. Allen Lucas, *Leading Edge*, Sales and Marketing Management, June 1995, pp. 13–14.
4. Donath, et al., *When Prospect Calls*, Marketing Management Vol. 3, No.2,1994, pp. 26–37.

5. Quoted in Ginger Trumfio, *Opening Doors,* Sales and Marketing Management, May 1994, p. 81.
6. Spiro and Weitz, *Adaptive Selling Conceptualization, Measurement, and Nomological Validity,* Journal of Marketing Research, February 1990, pp. 61–69.
7. Weld F. Royal, *Unearthing Hard-to-Find Prospects,* Sales and Marketing Management, November 1995: p. 92.
8. Neil Rackham, *The Spin Selling Field book,* New York: McGraw Hill New York, 1996, pp. 8, 75–142.
9. E.K. Strong, *The Psychology of Selling,* New York: McGraw Hill New York,1925, p. 9.
10. Team Selling by Industry, Selling, January/February 1994. p. 46.
11. Kathleen Cholewka, *Ultimate Access,* Sales and Marketing Management, October 2001, p. 27.
12. Frank L. Acuff, *How to Negotiate Anything with Anyone Anywhere Around the World,* American Management Association, New York, 1993.
13. Don Beveridge, *Become a Good Listener,* Industrial Distribution, March 2000, p .82.

Additional References

- Heide, Dartnell's 30th Sales Force Compensation Survey, p. 162.
- Shiv Khera, *You Can Sell,* Rupa Publications India Pvt. Ltd., 2010, pp. 255–56.
- George Avlonitis and Despina A. Karayanni, *The Impact of Internet Use On Business-to-Business Marketing,* Industrial Marketing Management, Vol. 29, 2000, pp. 441–59.

CASE 2.1

Hindustan Hotel: Selling of Services

Hindustan Hotel promises a remarkable stay with its central location in the metropolitan city of Bengaluru. Flaunting a convenient location, the hotel is easily accessible to many tourist places. The hotel boasts of well-designed and fully-furnished rooms which provide a comfortable stay to the guests. Ample car parking space, spacious banquet hall and total air conditioning are some of the modern amenities that are provided at the hotel.

The lodging facilities have two categories, viz. Executive Deluxe and Executive Suite. The tariffs for executive deluxe are single bed ₹4,500 and double bed ₹5,250. Executive suite's tariff is ₹6,000. Marketing of the hotel's services is handled by a marketing manager. The selling function is taken care by a sales manager and four sales executives.

The sales manager with the help of inside company salespersons carry out prospecting and qualifying of potential customers. For this, they use the Internet, talk to the existing customers (i.e. the guests); advertise online and in business magazines as well as hire hoardings at key locations. Prospective customers with good business potential are then handed over to the sales executives. Bengaluru metropolitan is divided into four territories—north, east, west and south. The four sales territories were assigned to the four sales executives based on relative abilities of the sales executives.

On receiving the information about the prospects, the sales executives approach them and make sales presentations. They use AIDA (attention, interest, desire and action) formula for presentation. This formula was discussed in their training program. Thereafter, they handle the objections from the prospective customers and try to close the sales by using closing techniques. However, the business received by the sales executives has been 50 to 60 percent of their sales targets. This has resulted in a strained relationship between the sales executives and the sales manager.

Discussion Questions

1. Why the sales executives are unable to achieve the sales targets?
2. If you were the marketing manager what would you do and why?

This case was prepared under the guidance of Prof. Krishna K. Havaldar by Bala Ayyanar, an MBA student of Alliance Business Academy, Bengaluru, for classroom discussion.

CASE 2.2

RK Consultants—Selling Consultancy Services

When the mail from 2M-Hydraulics was received by Rahul Deshpande, the CEO of RK Consultants, he immediately talked on the intercom to his vice-president, Arun Pande, to personally handle this enquiry. "If you succeed to get this order and execute the same to the complete satisfaction of 2M-Hydraulics, it would open doors for many more orders in future," said the CEO.

"Yes, I agree with you, but for that I will have to fly to Ahmedabad immediately to meet the key people in 2M-Hydraulics and to understand clearly their needs, before submitting our proposal," responded Arun.

"Why not, go ahead, and let me know if you need any help from me," said Rahul and hung up. Arun looked at the website of 2M-Hydraulics and gathered information that the company had a technical tie-up with a German company and wanted to manufacture and market hydraulic valves, pumps, and other accessories in India. The company had decided on a distribution strategy of selling its products through dealers, who were expected to design, assemble, sale and service hydraulic power packs required for various applications for material movements. Arun spoke with Vikram Parikh, general manager of 2M-Hydraulics, and fixed an appointment to meet him.

Arun gathered information about market potential for Hydraulic components in major metros and cities, competition and requirements of 2M-Hydraulics. His doubt about "Can we get dealers in India performing so many tasks", was answered by the German manager, "If we can get them in Germany, why not in India?"

Arun came back to his office at Pune, discussed with Rahul and sent his proposal to Vikram Parikh. Within one week, Arun received a call from Parikh, asking him to come over to Ahmedabad for a presentation to a team of senior executives, to be followed by negotiation.

Discussion Questions

1. How was R K Consultants' approach to the customer's requirement?
2. If you were Arun Pande, which presentation method, negotiation style and closing technique would you use?

This case was prepared by Prof. Krishna K. Havaldar for classroom discussion.

Chapter 3

Strategic Planning, Sales Strategy, Sales Forecasting and Budgeting

LEARNING OBJECTIVES

After studying this chapter, you will be able to:

LO 1 Know strategic planning, the role of marketing and sales, and strategic issues

LO 2 Understand the development of marketing and sales strategies to ensure sales growth and also the selling challenges and skills

LO 3 Explain the types of sales forecast, basic terms used, forecasting approaches, sales forecasting methods, forecasting accuracy and selection of forecasting methods

LO 4 Organize the sales budget and know its purposes, money allocation methods and the budgeting process

Air-conditioning and Refrigeration Systems (ARS) Limited was established in the year 1990. According to its founder and CEO, Rohit Sharma, the company's mission is to fulfill the needs of its customers by offering superior value. To achieve this mission, ARS Ltd. has set up a strategic planning cell at its the corporate headquarters in Mumbai.

The General Manager, Strategic Planning, Mahesh Acharya, was asked in January 2015 to prepare a proposal to achieve the strategic objective of reaching the leadership position, i.e. achieving the highest market share in the air-conditioning and refrigeration industry in five-year period. With 15 percent market share, the company was at number two position. Blue Star company had established its leadership position with the highest turnover amongst the industry players.

ARS Ltd. has a wide product and service range, which includes central air-conditioning systems, room air conditioners, commercial refrigeration systems, cold storages and after-sales maintenance service for air-conditioning and refrigeration systems. The company has four state-of-the-art manufacturing plants, one each in North, East, West and South India.

Mahesh thought that he needed to talk to the marketing research manager and the marketing head in order to ensure that the various steps of the strategic planning process can be carried out effectively. He had no problem in getting acceptance from the marketing research manager to complete the tasks of scanning the external environment, analyzing the internal environment and forecasting the sales for the next five years on priority. The mail from the CEO to all the senior managers and the department heads regarding the strategic planning task had helped Mahesh to obtain cooperation from all managers.

Mahesh's next meeting with the marketing head, T. S. Krishnamurty, was important to understand what kind of marketing and sales strategies would help the company to achieve number one position in terms of market share. "We use differentiation strategy for our business", said Krishnamurty. "From this business strategy, we have developed our marketing strategy, which includes selection of target markets and development of a marketing mix. The sales strategy is developed for individual business customers, based on the company's marketing strategy", added Krishnamurty. Mahesh understood the broad statements on business strategy as well as marketing and sales strategies from the marketing head. He then responded thoughtfully, "You may please send me an email separately about the details of the strategies proposed by the sales and marketing functions. I am also interested to know the growth in sales that you will aim at in the next five years in order to achieve the number one position in the industry".

Krishnamurty smiled and responded slowly, "that is an interesting question and difficult to answer off the cuff! I will discuss with my sales and marketing team and thereafter, respond to the various issues. However, we will have to grow more than the air-conditioning and refrigeration industry's average growth of 20 percent. After receiving the sales forecast from the marketing research department, we shall prepare the sales unit volume and revenue budget in great detail".

Mahesh was satisfied with his discussions with the marketing head and the marketing research manager. He thought that he should continue to discuss the various aspects of strategic planning with other key managers and department heads such as finance, production and human resource department. Thereafter, Mahesh thought he would communicate the various steps and the timetable of the strategic planning process to all the department heads and managers.

The illustration of ARS Ltd. in the opening vignette highlights the importance of strategic planning, the role of sales and marketing, the significance of sales forecasting and sales strategy to achieve the sales budget. All these issues are discussed adequately in this chapter. In addition, this chapter covers topics like types and methods of sales forecasting, sales budget, money allocation methods and budgeting process.

LO 1 Know strategic planning, the role of marketing and sales, and strategic issues

STRATEGIC PLANNING

Strategic planning includes making decisions about the company's mission, long-term objectives, strategies and action plan. Senior managers are responsible for the development and implementation of a strategic plan. In most large, multi-product and multi-business organizations, planning is done at three organizational levels: (i) corporate strategic plans, (ii) divisional and/or business units' strategic plans, and (iii) product or functional plans, as shown in Figure 3.1.

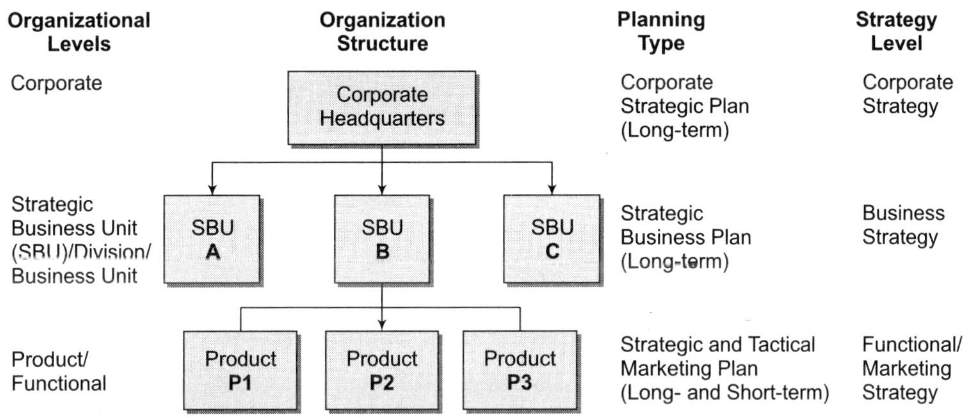

Fig. 3.1 Planning at Different Organizational Levels

The corporate headquarters is required to develop a **corporate strategic plan,** which guides the entire firm. Each business unit or Strategic Business Unit (SBU), out of the three SBUs shown in Figure 3.1, develops a **strategic business plan** to ensure a profitable future for that SBU. An SBU typically consists of multiple products (in Figure 3.1, SBU-'B' has three products, viz., P_1, P_2 and P_3). For example, Industrial systems SBU of CG Power and Industrial Solutions Limited have three products, viz., A.C. Motors, D.C. Motors and Alternators. Each product within a business unit develops a **strategic and tactical marketing plan** for achieving its objectives in its product market. The strategic (i.e. long-term) marketing plan includes selection of the target markets and the positioning or the value proposition that will be offered to the target customers. The **tactical** (or **short-term**) **marketing plan** determines product/service features, promotion/ marketing communications, pricing, marketing channels and customer service.

In Figure 3.1, under the strategy level, key decision areas for **corporate strategy** includes corporate mission, future growth directions and business portfolio. A separate **business strategy** is developed for each (SBU), which describes how the SBU plans to compete effectively in its industry. Since each SBU is composed of multiple products serving different markets, each product and market combination needs a clearly identified **marketing strategy**. Each marketing strategy includes the selection of target market segments and the development of a marketing mix (i.e. 4Ps).

Corporate Strategic Planning

Corporate strategic planning is developed at the company's headquarters to guide the whole organization. The planning process includes four steps of planning activities: (i) developing corporate mission and objectives, (ii) defining Strategic Business Units (SBUs), (iii) allocation of resources to SBUs, and (iv) developing corporate strategies to fill the strategic planning gap. The gap between desired sales and the expected sales over the same period is called the strategic planning gap. The corporate strategies used for filling the strategic planning gap are Ansoff's product-market expansion grid, integrative growth through backward, forward or horizontal integration within the firm's industry and diversification in an attractive new industry.

For effective planning and operations, a large multi-product or multi-business organization divides its major markets or products into SBUs. Each SBU has a separate business, a set of competitors and customers and a manager responsible for strategic planning and profits. The reasons for recognizing the firm's strategic units are to determine objectives and strategies and to allocate adequate funds to each SBU.

Business Unit (or SBU) Strategic Planning

Business unit's (or SBU's) strategic planning is done by the head of the business unit by developing long-term mission, objectives and strategies in the changing environment. The strategic planning process for each SBU includes the following eight steps:

1. Defining the business unit's mission.
2. Scanning the external environment (opportunities and threats analysis).
3. Analysis of the internal environment (assessment of strengths and weaknesses).
4. Developing long-term objectives and goals.
5. Formulating strategies for achieving the objectives and goals.
6. Preparing programs or action-plans from the strategies.
7. Implementing the strategies and action-plans.
8. Monitoring results and taking corrective actions.

Product or Functional Planning

Product or functional planning is done for each product within a business unit. It plans the specific procedures or systems required at lower levels of the organization. Functional managers normally develop plans for short periods of time (i.e. up to one year). They focus on routine tasks such as sales, production, material purchase, recruiting people, and dispatching goods. The functional plans like marketing, production, human resource and finance are developed by functional managers to carry out the routine tasks on day-to-day basis.

ROLE OF MARKETING AND SALES

As shown in Figure 3.1, in most large and multi-product organizations, strategies are developed at three organizational levels. These are: (i) corporate, (ii) business unit and (iii) functional.

Role of Marketing at Corporate Level

The role of marketing at corporate level is to provide information on competition and customer and advocate customer orientation, including the basic value of putting the customer first, as a part of long-term corporate strategy. Table 3.1 also shows the formal name as "corporate marketing."

Many organizations are adopting **analytic-driven** business decisions. It means, these companies analyze large chunks of raw data, find patterns and hidden insights for making critical business decisions. For instance, analysis of data about continuous changes taking place in customer needs and competitors' strengths and weaknesses are critical inputs for developing marketing and sales strategies.

Strategic planning (or strategic management) takes place at two levels of the firm: at corporate level and at SBU level. The third level is product or functional, which is a part of operations management. These are further discussed as under:

- **Strategic management** gives a direction to the firm and focuses on developing strategies to achieve long-term objectives and goals.
- **Operations management** maintains the direction given by strategic management and concentrates on day-to-day issues or activities like revenue, costs and profits. It includes all the functions such as finance, marketing, operations (or production) and human resource.

Table 3.1 **Role of Marketing and Sales in an Organization**[1]

Organizational Level	Role of Marketing and Sales	Formal Name
1. Corporate	• Provide information on competition and customer • Advocate customer orientation	Corporate marketing
2. Business Unit/SBU	• Provide competition and customer analysis. • Understand and forecast external environment. • Analyze competitive advantage. • Develop segmenting, targeting and positioning strategies.	Strategic marketing
3. Functional (i) Marketing	• Evolve and implement marketing-mix strategies and action plans to achieve marketing objectives. • Coordinate marketing related activities • Allocate resources	Marketing management
(ii) Sales	• Forecast short-term and long-term sales. • Develop and implement sales strategy.	Sales management

Role of Marketing at Business Unit Level

The role of marketing at business unit level is to: (i) understand and forecast external environment and carry out an analysis of customers and competitors, (ii) develop segmenting, targeting, and positioning strategies, and (iii) analyse competitive advantage. As shown in Table 3.1, it is in relationship with strategic management, or strategic planning; the marketing activity takes on strategic (long-term) nature and becomes strategic marketing. Strategic marketing focuses on long-term marketing strategies like selection of target markets, and positioning.

Role of Marketing at Functional Level

The role of marketing at functional level is to (i) develop marketing-mix strategies and action plan and implement them, (ii) coordinate marketing related activities and (iii) allocate resources. The marketing-mix consists of a marketing offer that is developed to appeal to a chosen target market segment. It includes a mixture of product, price, distribution (or place) and marketing communications (or promotion) strategies. The important part of development of a marketing-mix strategy is that it should satisfy the needs of the target markets better than that of competitors.

The role of sales function is to accurately forecast the sales of the company's products and services. The sales management also plays a key role in sales strategy development and implementation.

STRATEGIC ISSUES

Some of the major strategic issues that need brief discussion are: (i) strategic thinking process, and (ii) social selling.

Strategic Thinking Process

When a senior executive is faced with a situation that needs a strategic decision, such as selection of target markets, he unexpectedly meets with unknown areas. These unknown or uncertain areas can mostly be recorded accurately by asking strategic questions. Some of the examples of strategic questions are as follows[2]:

1. If an uncertain area is connected to the external environment, the strategic questions are: "Which external environmental factors will influence the company's performance?", and "How these external environmental factors will change over the next 5–7 years?"
2. If the unknown area is related to potential customers, the strategic questions are: "Who will be the company's potential customers in future?", and "Are there any market segments not being served adequately?"

Firms are required to conduct studies to obtain answers to the strategic questions. Thereafter, the managers can make effective decisions on strategic issues.

Most companies have formal planning manuals that state how the planning process is to be conducted.[3] The outcome of the planning process is mostly a formal written document that indicates the company's strategic intentions.

Social Selling

Social selling is the use of social media to interact directly with prospective customers, answer queries and offer the product or service that fulfills the buyer's needs. It is a dynamic process. Social selling is not only a new way of thinking, but is also a new way of working.[4]

One must accept the fact that today the customer has changed. For instance, a study by Forrester Research says that 91 percent of buyers of Information Technology (IT) products and services are now involved in social media. They make notes of online posts of various suppliers. A business-to-business selling firm uses social networks to find potential customers, connect to their needs and interests and thereafter, communicate with them in a suitable manner. The reliable supports of social selling are: participate, listen, communicate, connect, work jointly and close the sale.

Social selling should not be confused with social media marketing. There are some important differences which are as follows:

- The aim of social selling is to develop one-on-one relationships, whereas social media transmit one-to-many messages.
- Social selling pays attention to sales professionals, whereas social media focuses on marketing professionals.
- In social selling, sales and marketing come together to increase awareness, communicate with potential customers and convert them to prospective sales leads. However, in social media, marketing efforts in a firm are added to the sales process.

For example, IBM launched the social selling project in its cloud computing product division. The objective was to find the trends and issues being discussed in cloud computing. The company developed a social media program to train the salespeople to use LinkedIn and Twitter effectively. IBM also developed the social media toolkit that gave authority to each salesperson to join online discussions and answer queries. Each salesperson was supplied with a personalized digital page. This permitted the salespeople to offer suitable solutions. The results after six months confirmed the success of the pilot project. IBM received orders for the product during the quarter which was four times higher than during the same time year before.[5]

LO 2 **Understand the development of marketing and sales strategies to ensure sales growth and also the selling challenges and skills**

DEVELOPMENT OF MARKETING AND SALES STRATEGIES

We have seen earlier that each SBU is typically composed of multiple products serving different markets (Figure 3.1). Hence, each product and market combination needs a clearly identified marketing strategy. This marketing strategy must be in agreement with the business strategy. For instance, in the example described in the opening vignette, the firm ARS Ltd. uses differentiation strategy as its business strategy. The marketing strategy of the company should adopt product differentiation in relation to the competition instead of giving importance to low price.

Figure 3.2 shows the major parts of marketing strategy and the position of sales and personal selling strategies within the marketing communications (or promotional) strategy. Two important components of a **marketing strategy** of a firm are: (i) target market selection and positioning strategy, and (ii) development of marketing–mix (or the four Ps of marketing).

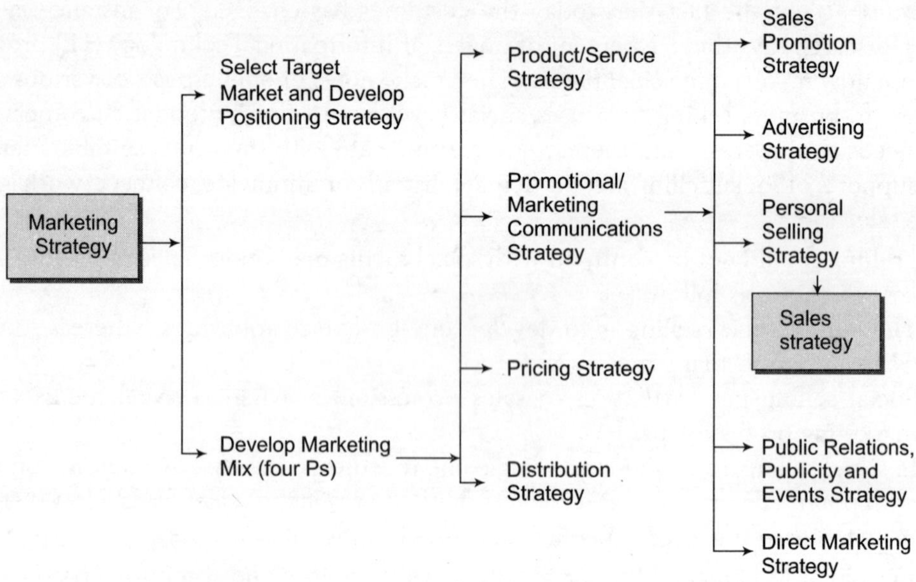

Fig. 3.2 **Marketing Strategy and Sales Strategy**[6]

In the target market strategy, a firm segments its markets by using segmentation variables. Thereafter, the firm evaluates the various segments and then, uses certain criteria to decide how many and which segments to target. For each chosen target market (segment), the company develops a market offering. This market offering is positioned in the minds of the target customers by delivering some key benefit(s). For example, Scorpio, a Sports-Utility Vehicle (SUV) by Mahindra and Mahindra is positioned as a vehicle that offers the luxury of a car and the thrill (or comfort) of an SUV. As mentioned earlier in this chapter, the target market selection and positioning strategy are a part of strategic (i.e. long-term) marketing plan.

The tactical (or short-term) marketing plan includes development of **marketing-mix,** which consists of a set of marketing tools the company uses to achieve its marketing objectives in the selected target markets. McCarthy classified these marketing tools into four broad groups, which he called the four Ps of marketing, viz. Product, Promotion, Pricing, and **Place.**[7] One of the important tasks for the head of marketing function is to prepare a marketing plan. The crucial part of the marketing plan is the development of a marketing mix that fulfils the needs of the target markets better than competitive offerings.

Out of the four strategies of the marketing mix, the marketing communications strategy consists of a mixture of several components. These are: sales promotion, advertising, personal selling, public relations, publicity, events and direct marketing. Many companies consider personal selling (i.e. selling through the company's salespeople), or advertising as the main tool. Other components, such as sales promotion, public relations, publicity, events and direct marketing are thought as supplemental tools. However, increasing number of firms have started adopting a new approach, known as **Integrated Marketing Communications (IMC).** IMC is a strategic integration of a variety of marketing communication tools, shown in Figure 3.2, in the most efficient and effective manner. The objectives of IMC are to select and use the most cost effective tools to achieve the desired marketing communications' objectives and to ensure a strong message with clarity, consistency and maximum impact.

A company's marketing strategy is implemented for individual customers through a **sales strategy**. For example, one of the target market segments of a precision steel tubes company is the two-wheeler manufacturers. All customers within the two-wheeler segment are not same in terms of needs, purchasing procedure, buying criteria, sizes of tubes, and so on. The company's sales professionals developed different sales strategies for Hero Motors, Bajaj Auto, TVS and others.

Why sales strategy is considered crucial by many companies? The reasons are as follows:

- In a competitive market, a company's sales and profit performance is highly influenced by its sales strategies for individual customers.
- A firm's decisions on sales force recruitment, selection, training, motivation, compensation, and performance evaluations are impacted by the sales strategies.

In the upcoming sections, we will discuss about the various components of sales strategy.

SALES STRATEGY

The company marketing strategy provides an overall game plan, but individual customer orders are won by having an effective sales strategy for each individual customer. Figure 3.3 shows four parts of an effective sales strategy[8]: (i) customer classification strategy, (ii) customer relationship strategy, (iii) selling methods, and (iv) marketing channel strategy.

Customer Classification Strategy[9]

Within a target market segment, the accounts or individual customers are classified into different customer groups. All customers within a target market segment are not the same. Some customers may have a good relationship with competitors, a few customers may have large sales potential and other customers may require medium or low value of the company's products or services. Hence, each customer is classified or categorized into one of the customer groups. Let us consider an example of a business marketing company.

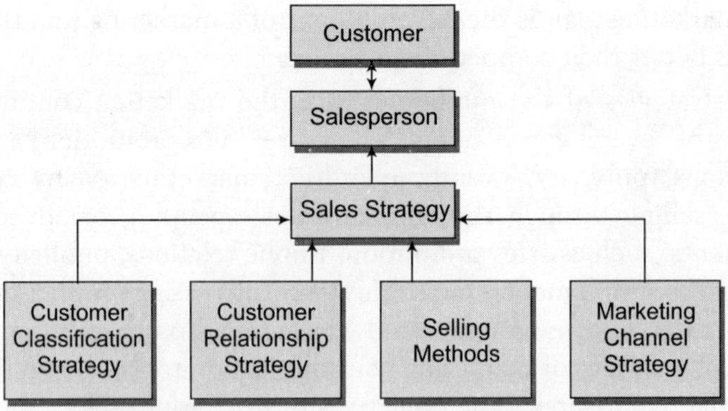

Fig. 3.3 Framework for a Sales Strategy

A compressor manufacturing and marketing company had targeted automotive market segment as one of the target segments. Within the automotive segment, it classified the customers into three different customer groups or customer segments:

- Class A: High sales and profit potential customers
- Class B: Medium sales and profit potential customers
- Class C: Low sales and profit potential customers, including customers who have good relationship with competitors

The company developed different marketing strategies for each of these customer groups, since their needs are different, as a part of strategic decisions. However, finally, the sales strategy is developed for each individual customer.

Customer Relationship Strategy

Buyers and sellers, particularly in business markets, have some kind of business (or working) relationships. These relationships have a range or spectrum. At the one end of the relationship range is a transactional relationship and at the other end, it is a partnering or collaborative relationship. In between these extremes are value added or solutions relationships, which are intermediate type of relationships. The company decides a customer relationship strategy for different customer groups as well as for each individual customer. For example, for Class A customers with high sales and profit potential, the company develops "collaborative relationship"; for Class B customers with medium sales and profit potential, the relationship to be developed is called "value-added"; and for low sales and profit potential customers, the company chooses to have "transactional relationship". We shall now briefly discuss characteristics of different customer relationship strategies.

❍ **Transactional Relationship** Transaction-oriented customers show less loyalty to a particular supplier. They switch suppliers for lower costs. Sales managers and salespeople would consider such customers for transactional relationship. In addition, the customers who have low sales and profit potential as well as those customers who have excellent relationship with competitors are the right customers for transactional relationship. Such customers are many and are offered standard products and services. The selling firm keeps its cost low and keeps the relationship on short-term basis. It is one-off relationship, where salesperson does not contact the customer after the order is executed.

A typical example of transactional relationship is a government customer, like Indian Railways, where the relationship is short-term. The selling firm is required to quote the lowest price against the tender enquiry and generally, sell standard products or services. Such customers typically do not expect superior quality of products or services from the suppliers. They are interested in the lowest price and availability of the product or service as per their specifications.

- **Value-added Relationship** These customers have medium sales and profit potential. The focus of salespeople is on complete understanding of present and future problems or needs of the customer, and offering better solutions or meeting those needs better than the competitors. For instance, a paint manufacturing company invited three material handling firms to offer solution to their material handling requirement for the newly built factory near Mumbai. The order was placed with the supplier who offered the best solution at competitive prices with effective pre-and post-sales services as per the requirements. The relationship between the buyer and the seller is medium- to long-term and can be called "partnering".

- **Collaborative Relationship** In a collaborative relationship between a buyer and a seller, the aim is to build long-term and mutually satisfying relationship with key customers in order to earn and retain their business.[10] The foundation of collaborative relationship is commitment and trust. Both the buyer and the seller should accept that the relationship is so important that it deserves maximum efforts to continue with it. The collaborative relationship includes joint problem solving, multiple connections and integration of business processes of the two companies. The products and services offered are customized. Even though the sales people want to select the customers with high sales and profit potential for collaborative relationships, it is equally important that such customers also wish to have a collaborative relationship with the supplier firms. Class A customers with high sales and profit potential are suitable for collaborative relationships.

Customers who are chosen for collaborative relationships are typically few in numbers and the cost of serving them is high. A good example of collaborative relationship is found in automotive industry, in which most two wheeler and four wheeler manufacturers have collaborative relationships with some selective vendors of components. Here, the buyers and sellers work closely together for mutual benefits. Their manufacturing processes are integrated to solve the problems related to costs, quality and availability. The aim of the selling firm is to become the preferred supplier.

Selling Methods

Salespeople should use different selling methods or selling approaches to suit different relationship strategies. The different methods of selling (or sales presentation methods) have been explained in detail in Chapter 2. These are: (i) stimulus response method, (ii) formula method, (iii) need-satisfaction method, (iv) team selling method, and (v) consultative selling method.

The selection of the selling method for a specific type of relationship is an important part of a sales strategy. To make this point more clear, let us consider the earlier example of compressor manufacturing company. The suitable selling method for Class A (major or key) customers, with whom the selling firm wants to have collaborative relationships, is team selling method and/or consultative selling method. For Class B (medium sales and profit potential) customers, with value-added relationships, the proper selling method would be need-satisfaction, or problem solving method. The third group of customers, classified as Class C and large in numbers, with transactional relationship strategy, should have typically stimulus response or formula method of selling. Sales managers and salespeople must understand that it is crucial to match selling methods with customer relationship strategies.

Salespeople should understand that the guidelines illustrated above in terms of matching the selling methods to relationship strategies are for specific groups of customers in a market segment. This is a strategic sales approach. However, certain amount of flexibility should be used while dealing with individual customers within a customer group. For instance, if there is a customer whose present sales and profit potential for the company's products/services is low, but has a potential to become Class B or Class A in near future, the salesperson should not hesitate in using need-satisfaction or consultative selling method that is proper for the customer.

Marketing Channel Strategy

Another issue in the sales strategy is to select an appropriate marketing channel (also called sales channel, distribution channel, or trade channel). A marketing channel is defined as a set of interdependent organizations involved in the process of making a product or service available for use or consumption. The various marketing channels available to firms for making a product or service available to customers are: (i) personal selling through the company salespeople, (ii) industrial distributors, dealers, wholesalers, or retailers, (iii) manufacturer's representatives, independent representatives or agents, (iv) telemarketing by using telephone, (v) Internet, and (vi) brokers and commission merchants. The description of the various channels is covered in Chapter 10 on Marketing Channels.

The selection of a suitable sales or marketing channel may be decided by a buyer or a seller. If the selling organization has made available the channel that suits the buying firm, the marketing channel facilitates the selling process. But, if the marketing channel provided by the selling firm is not convenient to the buyer, the selling firm may not make the sales. For example, Dell Computer company uses the telephone and the Internet as marketing channels all over the world. However, in India, these marketing channels are not suitable for many prospective customers who prefer the company salespeople or the dealers to demonstrate and discuss before buying computers. The company has realized subsequently the preference of the Indian customers and has added the company's salespeople and the dealers as new channels to the existing channels.

A manufacturer selling products and services may need different channels for different activities or functions. The company uses the Internet and the telephone as marketing channels for selling activities, specific transport carriers as delivery channels and local repair people as the service channel. Many selling firms use multiple channels to serve different target market segments. For example, an electrical equipment manufacturing company uses the company's salespeople to serve high potential corporate and government customers, i.e. the company's authorized dealers, to serve large number of small and medium-sized enterprises; the Internet is used to serve those buying firms who want to buy on online basis.

GROWTH IN SALES

Most companies' Chief Executive Officers (CEOs) or Chairman and Managing Directors (CMDs) desire that their company should become number one company in terms of sales in their respective industries. To achieve that position, they aim at sales growth more than the industry average growth. The responsibility of achieving higher growth in sales naturally falls on the head of sales and marketing function.

For example, the CMD of Material Handling Equipment (MHE) Pvt. Ltd. had strongly wished for achieving leadership position in the industry. However, the sales growth per year for initial period of seven years was about 15 percent on an average. This growth was not adequate to achieve the desired objective of becoming number one in terms of sales revenue. The CMD, therefore, hired an experienced person with MBA from a reputed management institute as General Manager (GM) – Sales and Marketing. The GM was given a goal of doubling the sales every year for the following two years. Surprised at the stiff target, the GM responded to the CMD, "I have not worked earlier in this industry, but you have been in this industry. If you are confident that the company can achieve 100 percent growth in sales, I will accept the target. Please give me two-months' time to carry out a study and prepare a proposed marketing plan, which I will implement after discussions with all concerned persons and finally approved by you." The CMD smiled and accepted the GM's suggestion with a warm handshake.

The GM then talked to his team consisting of sales and service engineers, who expressed their surprise that such a stiff target was accepted by him. They briefed him about the industry competition and the company's sales and service set up. The company had appointed agents at Chennai for Tamil Nadu state, Pune for Maharashtra state, and Hyderabad for Andhra Pradesh and Telangana states, to carry out sales and service activities. The company had its own sales and service engineers at its factory near Bengaluru to serve the customers in other states. The GM visited the three agents and their territories. He also met a few key customers to understand their perceptions about the company's products and services in comparison to the competition. After completing the study, he prepared a marketing plan in which the major strategies proposed were as follows:

- To strengthen the distribution network by opening the company's sales and service offices at high sales potential areas such as Mumbai, Coimbatore and Ahmedabad.
- To identify high sales potential (key) customers and form selling teams for them. These key customers to be visited once a week.
- To improve pre-sales and post-sales service to customers by conducting training programs once a quarter for the agents and the company's sales and service persons.
- To obtain ISO's quality certifications for production, installations and servicing of material handling equipment.

On getting approval to the marketing plan from the CMD, the GM implemented the plan. After completing implementation of the marketing plan, at the end of the first year, the company's sales went up from ₹3.20 crore (i.e. ₹32 million) to ₹5.88 crore (i.e. ₹58.80 million) showing a sales growth of 84 percent. At the end of the second year, the sales revenue was ₹11.17 crore (i.e. ₹111.70 million), which indicated a sales growth of about 90 percent. Although the sales growth in the two years was less than the target of 100 percent per year, it was substantially high compared to the previous years' average growth of 15 percent.

Sales and marketing managers use different strategies to achieve the objective of substantial sales growth, such as strengthening the distribution network, developing new products, improving customer service quality, backward integration, horizontal integration and diversification. The choice of strategies depends on the business situation faced by a company.

SELLING CHALLENGES

In Chapter 1, we stated that sales function is one of the most financially rewarding and one of the fastest routes to the top management. It is also one of the exciting and challenging careers. Today, selling has become more challenging job because (i) the buyer has more options, (ii) competition has become intense and complex, and (iii) customers are more knowledgeable due to the Internet and media. The customer is dependent on the seller's competence and character to sell the right product or service. Thus, the seller's honesty is put to test.

Salespersons' loyalties are sometimes torn between the customer demand and expectations of their sales manager. For instance, the customer demands credit for 30 days, but the sales manager denies the credit. Salespeople often experience serious disagreements between the customer and the selling company due to differences in requirements on various issues like pricing, delivery schedules and product specifications. Salespeople face such challenging situations, particularly when selling firms are not flexible.

Success of a company depends upon the achievement of the sales goal. The responsibility of generating sales revenue creates considerable pressure on salespeople. When the customer's requirements are in conflict with the selling firm's policies, the pressure or stress on salespeople increases. If the stress becomes excessive, it may result in harmful outcome. If the salespeople have the necessary support from the company, the required selling skills, the right traits and if they can carry on effectively with the selling process (described in Chapter 2), then they can contribute in the achievement of the organizational goals.

SELLING SKILLS

Earlier in Chapter 2, we have discussed the success factors in selling. It is rather difficult to generalize about the characteristics of a good salesperson and the selling skills required for success in selling because there are different types of sales jobs as indicated in Chapter 1. The characteristics and the selling skills would vary depending on the type of a given sales job. Despite this statement, let us consider the following selling skills and the traits or characteristics for success in most, if not for all, sales jobs. The characteristics are empathy, burning desire, team selling and technology savvy to be particularly important as described in Chapter 2 earlier. The absolutely necessary skills for success in selling are communication skills, listening skills, negotiation skills and problem-solving skills. Earlier in Chapter 2, we have discussed communication, listening and negotiation skills. We shall, therefore, discuss here problem-solving skills.

❍ **Problem-Solving Skills** Consultative salespeople or sales teams in business-to-business (B2B) selling situations create a value for their customers by solving the customers' problems. For example, a sales engineer from a material handling equipment manufacturing company noticed that unloading of components from heavy commercial vehicles (or trucks) was taking a long time in a passenger car manufacturing company. Not only the truck owners were unhappy about the long queues of trucks, but also the company's management was concerned as these trucks occupied a large portion of the factory area, apart from the truck drivers causing a lot of nuisance for the company employees. The sales engineer, after talking to the purchase executive, collected all the relevant information including the average time taken by a truck to unload incoming material. He called a design engineer from his factory and made a presentation to the buying centre members on how their equipment, called "Lift Table", could reduce the unloading time to about 30 percent of the time taken for unloading without their equipment. They also showed the third party certificates of their customers about the performance of the equipment. The buying centre members gave approval to the sales engineer to submit the quotation with technical and commercial details. The order was placed, after discussion, for one number lift table. The equipment was delivered and installed in five weeks from the date of the order. The trials showed a substantial reduction in the time of unloading of materials from the truck as per the claims of the supplier. The problem of long queue of trucks was resolved satisfactorily. The supplier firm received a repeat order for three number of the equipment.

Sometimes, a cooperative problem solving approach is adopted by having teams from buying and selling firms working jointly on problems like cost reduction or quality improvement. Such an approach leads to a strong relationship between the two organizations. The problem solving process typically includes the following steps: (i) identify or define the problem, (ii) create or develop alternative ways of solutions, (iii) select one of the alternatives as a solution, (iv) implement the selected solution, and (v) evaluate the solution.

LO 3 **Explain the types of sales forecast, basic terms used, forecasting approaches, sales forecasting methods, forecasting accuracy and selection of forecasting methods**

DEVELOPING SALES FORECAST

The purpose of a sales forecast is to plan the company's operations in an effective manner. The sales forecast is used by other functions, viz. (i) by the manufacturing or production for setting up the production capacity and planning the production, (ii) by the finance for raising cash for investment and operations as well as for profit planning, (iii) by the purchase of materials for planning the purchases, and (iv) by the human resource management for manpower planning. Thus, the sales forecast has a role as a forerunner to all planning activities in an organization. Accurate sales forecast is very important because all functions of a firm base their plans on the sales forecast. It is the responsibility of the sales and marketing managers to prepare an accurate sales forecast. If the sales forecast is not accurate, the plans based on it will be incorrect. No doubt, an accurate sales forecast can play an important role in the success of a company.

TYPES OF SALES FORECAST

The term "forecast" is generally used for prediction or estimation for a future period, such as weather forecast. A **sales forecast** is the estimated units or rupees (or dollars) of sales for a specific future time period based on an assumed marketing environment and a proposed marketing plan. Firms refer to a sales forecast by defining three factors: (i) the product level, (ii) the geographic area, and (iii) the time period. Figure 3.4 shows 90 different types (i.e. 6 × 3 × 5) of sales (or demand) forecast that can be made based on six different product levels, three separate time periods and five different geographical areas. It is, therefore, important that sales managers should specify the product level, the geographic area and the time period, when a sales forecast is communicated. For example, a company may plan a sales forecast for short-term (six months) for a particular product (or product line) for the four geographical regions to decide if the regional distributors are required.

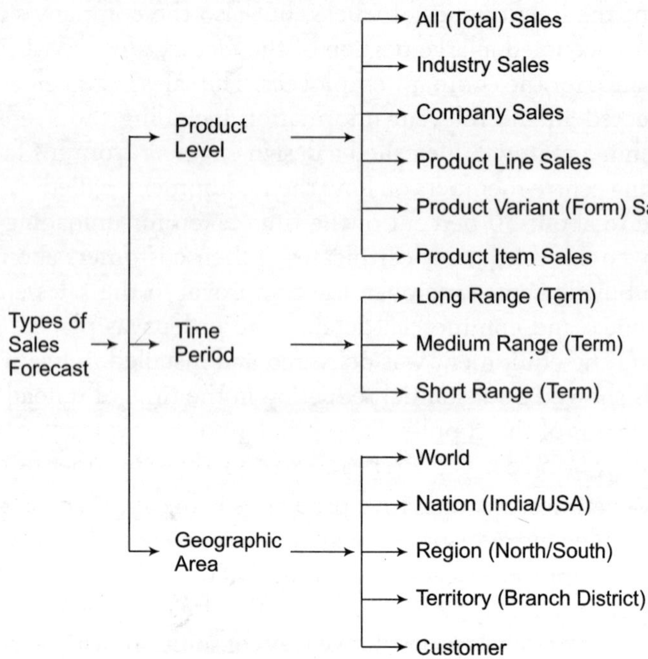

Fig. 3.4 Types of Sales Forecast

BASIC TERMS USED IN SALES FORECASTING

Before we discuss the approaches and the methods of sales forecasting, it is necessary to define and understand some of the basic terms used in forecasting the company sales or the customer demand. These terms are closely related, used loosely and therefore, can cause misunderstanding among academicians and managers.

Market Potential

It is the best possible (or maximum) estimated sales of a given product or service for the entire industry in a given geographic market for a specific period of time. For example, the market potential for Personal Computers (PCs) in India for the year 2016–17 is estimated to be 11 million numbers. Market potential is also called 'industry sales forecast'. The following four parts must be included for a complete definition of market potential as well as sales potential and sales forecast:

(i) Item marketed, such as a product or service.
(ii) Sales estimated in units or value (rupees or dollars).
(iii) Description of the market by a geographical area or type of customer, or both.
(iv) A specific time period, such as a particular year.

Market Forecast

It is the expected industry sales or market demand of a given product or service at one specific level of industry marketing expenditure, in a given geographical market, for a specific period of time. Market forecast is also called market size. For instance, the market forecast for smartphones in India for the calendar year 2017 is 174 million units.

Sales Potential (or Company Sales Potential)

It is the best possible (or maximum) estimated sales of a given product or service for a company in a given geographical area for a specific period of time. Sales potential is also defined as the maximum share (or percentage) of market potential that is expected to be achieved by a company. For instance, sales potential of ICICI Prudential is expected to be close to 10 percent of the gross premium collection of life insurance industry in India in coming years.

Sales Forecast (or Company Sales Forecast)

It is the estimated company sales of a given product or service, under a proposed marketing plan, in a given geographical market, for a specific period of time. There is a relationship between the company's sales forecast and the proposed marketing expenditure (or marketing plan). The sales forecast is the result of a proposed or assumed marketing expenditure plan. It means, the sales forecast would have to be revised, whenever changes are made in the marketing expenditure. A company may make a sales forecast for an entire product line (like detergent from Hindustan Lever) or a product item (such as, "Wheel" brand).

Sales potential and sales forecast are usually not the same. Sales potential is what a company would achieve under ideal conditions. Typically, the sales forecast is less than the sales potential, for different reasons, such as limited production facilities and/or inadequate financial resources.

FORECASTING APPROACHES

The two basic approaches for forecasting, as shown in Figures 3.5 and 3.6, are: (i) top-down (or break-down) approach, and (ii) bottom-up (or build-up) approach.

Top-Down or Break-Down Approach

In this approach, typically the company sales forecast is developed at the business unit (or SBU) level, by using suitable forecasting methods. The head of sales/marketing then breaks down the company sales forecast into regions, districts, territories, salespersons and individual customers' sales goals. The steps followed in this approach are shown in Figure 3.5.

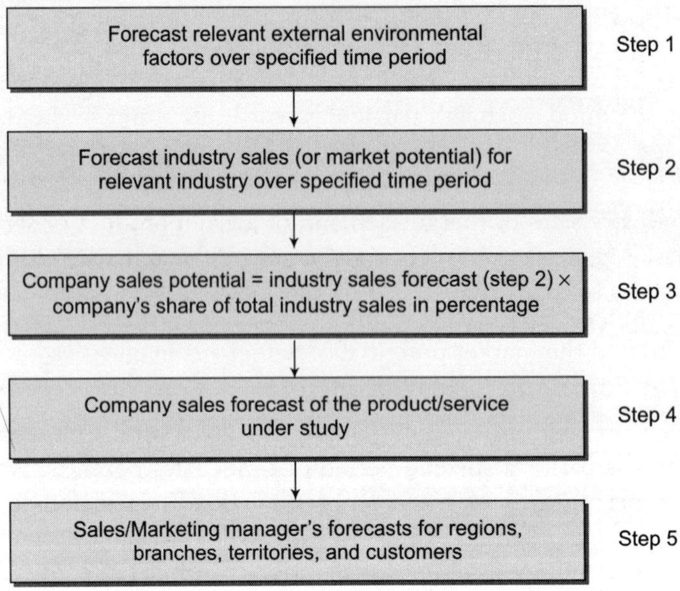

Fig. 3.5 Development of Top-Down Approach

The step 1 of Figure 3.5 includes external environmental factors such as political, economic, social/cultural, demographic and technological. A company should collect current and past information on those factors that are relevant to its business. The task involved is forecasting future trends, which is covered in the strategic marketing textbooks. The key steps in Figure 3.5 are step 2 and step 3. In step 2, some of the sales forecasting methods used for forecasting industry sales (or market demand) are: (i) executive opinion, (ii) regression analysis, (iii) moving averages, (iv) exponential smoothing, and (v) decomposition, which will be described subsequently in this chapter. In step 3, for estimating the company's share of the total industry sales, a number of factors must be considered, including the company's current market share, target customers and their perceptions about the company's performance on key factors like quality, service and price in comparison with that of the major competitors and the company's relationship with the major customers. With respect to step 4, the company sales forecast is usually lower than the company sales potential due to various reasons such as insufficient funds, increase in competition or shortage of raw material. The last step of breaking down the company sales forecast to different regions and territories is done based on market potential of different geographical areas. For this, two main methods are available: (i) market build-up method, primarily used by business marketers, and (ii) multiple-factor index method, mainly used by consumer marketers.

❍ **Market Build-up Method** The first step in this method is to identify existing and potential business buyers in the geographical territory. This information can be obtained from the state governments' industry departments. The second step is to find their potential purchases of the product under study. This data can be found based on a market survey to be conducted internally by the company or outsourced to a marketing research agency. The final step is to add-up the business potential of all the buying firms to obtain a fairly accurate estimate of market potential for the product or service for a specific geographic territory.

❍ **Multiple-Factor Index Method** For the consumer marketing company, the estimation of market potential for a geographical area is done not by identifying individuals and households, because they are very large in numbers. This method first identifies the factors that influence the sales of a product or service. Generally, there are more than one sales factor, such as population and income that influence sales. These factors are given certain weights, corresponding to the degree of sales opportunity.

Let us take an example of a company, manufacturing and marketing detergents all over India. The company wants to find the market potential of detergents in all cities, including Bengaluru. The major factors that influence the sales of detergents are population, personal income and retail sales, which are given weights of 0.4, 0.3, and 0.3, respectively. Suppose Bengaluru has 0.7 percent of India's population, 1 percent of India's disposable personal income and 0.9 percent of India's retail sales. The multi-factor buying index for Bengaluru would be:

$$0.4\ (0.7) + 0.3\ (1) + 0.3\ (0.9) = 0.85$$

Based on the Indian detergent industry forecast of ₹112 billion for the year 2012–13, the market potential for detergents for Bengaluru would be: 0.85 percent of ₹112 billion, i.e. equal to ₹0.95 billion for the year 2012–13.

Bottom-up or Build-up Approach

Bottom-up or build-up approach starts with the company's area or branch managers asking their salespersons to estimate or forecast the sales for individual customers in their respective territories, as shown in Figure 3.6.

Salespersons are given guidance by their respective area/branch sales managers on how to get information from the existing and potential customers on the estimated purchases of the company's products and services for the specified future time period. Each area or branch manager then adds the sales forecasts received from the salespersons, modifies the same wherever needed and sends the combined sales forecast figure for each product in units and value to his superior, that is, regional or zonal sales manager. Each regional/zonal manager adds the sales forecast received from the area or branch managers, modifies the same, if needed, and sends

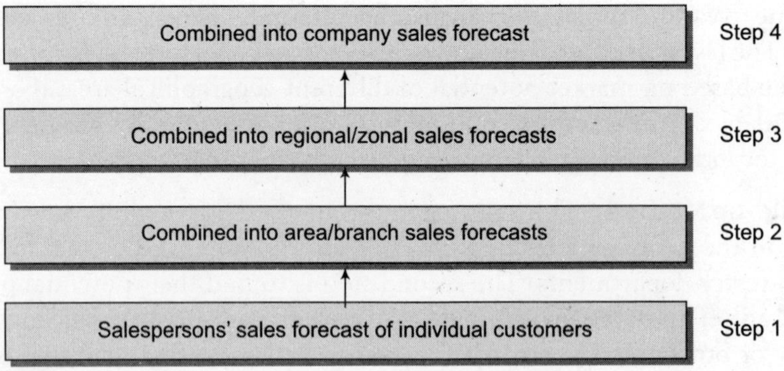

Fig. 3.6 Development of Bottom-up or Build-up Forecasting Approach

the regional sales forecast to the sales/marketing head. The head of sales/marketing repeats the process and presents his proposal to the CEO for discussion, modification and approval of the company's sales forecast.

The bottom-up approach requires some other sales forecasting methods, in addition to sales force composite, such as survey of buyers' intentions, Delphi and test marketing.

Some companies use both top-down and bottom-up approaches, in order to increase their confidence in the sales forecast. However, comparison of the two approaches indicates that top-down approach needs less time and cost, as it uses the data on forecast from the secondary sources like the planning commission report on market forecasts and indicators by the Centre for Industrial and Economic Research, New Delhi. The bottom-up approach is more accurate for short-term forecast (up to one year), as it is based on primary data collection, which means more cost and time. Firms may develop sales forecasts internally or buy forecasts from outside sources such as marketing research companies or specialized forecasting firms like Centre for Industrial and Economic Research, New Delhi. We shall now examine different methods of sales forecasting, keeping in mind that sales forecasting is the responsibility of the sales function.

SALES FORECASTING METHODS

As shown in Figure 3.7, sales forecasting methods or techniques can be classified as qualitative methods and quantitative methods.

Executive Opinion Method

This is an easily understandable and the most widely used method. It includes getting the opinions of senior executives of the company regarding future sales. The sales forecasts are made either by taking the average of all the executives' individual opinions or through discussion among the executives. Some executives' opinion may be supported by the use of forecasting methods and other executives may form their opinion based on experience and judgment. However, due care should be taken to ensure that the final sales forecast is not influenced by the opinion of the senior most executives more than other executives who may be more knowledgeable about the scientific methods of forecasting.

The advantages of this method are as follows:

- Forecasting can be done in a short time and without difficulty.
- Less expensive than other methods.
- Widely liked by mini, small and medium-sized (MSM) companies.

However, there are some disadvantages as well:

- Not based on systematic study.
- Influenced by personal opinions.
- Difficult to break-down the forecast into subunits (like regions, branches) of the company.

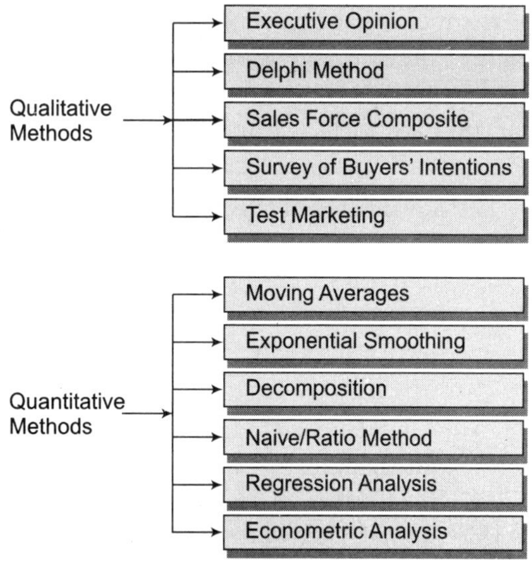

Fig. 3.7 Qualitative and Quantitative Forecasting Methods

Delphi Method

This method is similar to the executive opinion method and was developed by Rand Corporation. The difference is that the members of an expert panel do not meet or discuss in a committee. The procedure includes selection of a panel of experts from within and outside the company. The coordinator asks each expert separately to make a forecast on some matter. Each member of the expert panel submits in writing his forecast anonymously. The coordinator summarizes these forecasts into a report that is sent to each panel member. The experts are then asked to make another prediction separately on the same matter, with the knowledge of the summary of forecasts of other experts on the panel. This process is repeated until the panel of experts arrives at a consensus. The basic belief in this method is that the experts without any pressure or influence will develop a more accurate prediction of the future.[11] Thus, it is absolutely necessary to ensure that a high degree of expertise is represented on the panel.

The advantages of this method are:

- Objective forecast that is accurate.
- Useful for technology, new product and industry sales forecast.
- Both long- and short-term forecasting are possible.

However, the disadvantages are:

- Difficulty in getting a panel of experts.
- Break-down of forecast into products or territories is not possible.

Sales Force Composite Method

This method involves salespeople to estimate their future sales. It is an example of bottom-up approach and is also called a "grass-roots" approach. Each salesperson estimates in his territory how much quantity or value is existing and how much the potential customers will buy of each of the company's products and/or services that is required by them. This method is often used by B2B or business marketing companies. Sales representatives make the sales estimates in consultation with customers and/or sales supervisors based on their experience and understanding. The company sales forecast is made up (composite) of all the salespersons' sales forecasts.

The advantages of this method are:

- Forecasting is done by salespeople who are closest to the market and have better insight into sales trends than any other group in the company.
- Detailed sales estimates broken down by customer, product, sales representative and territory are possible.

The disadvantages of this method include:

- Sales forecasts are often pessimistic or optimistic, if salespeople are not trained in forecasting.
- If sales forecasts are used to set sales targets or quotas which are linked to incentive schemes, salespeople may deliberately underestimate the demand.
- Many salespersons are not interested in sales forecasting and prefer to spend time in the field meeting customers.

To encourage better forecasting, companies are adopting some of the following modifications to the earlier practices:

- Salespeople are given additional information, such as their past forecasts with actual sales, the company's assumptions on the business outlook during the forecasting period, major competitors' strategies, tactics, strengths and weaknesses, and the company's proposed marketing plan.
- The salesperson and the immediate sales supervisor work out the sales estimates independently. Then they meet and reconcile any differences in the figures. The same process is carried out between the sales supervisors and the territory manager and later on, between the territory managers and the sales manager.
- Conducting training programs for salespeople on the process and methods used for forecasting sales.

Salespersons' forecasts can be improved by using some of the modifications suggested above.

Survey of Buyers' Intentions Method

This method is sometimes called survey method, in which the information on customers' intentions on purchase of a product or service can be obtained through personal interviews, telephone surveys, e-mail surveys or other methods. It includes asking existing and potential customers about their likely purchases of the company's products and services for the forecast period. For instance, the question like the following is asked: Do you intend to buy a refrigerator within the next six months?

0.0	0.20	0.40	0.6	0.8	1.0
Not at all	Slight Possibility	Fair Possibility	Good Possibility	High Possibility	Certain Buying

The above is called a "purchase probability scale".[12] The customers are also asked other questions, such as product quality, features, price and service, which are all a part of the questionnaire. The information collected from the buyers help the company to make effective decisions not only in sales and marketing areas, but also on production, research and development.

Several research firms conduct periodic surveys of consumer buying intentions. They combine various bits of information into a consumer confidence measure. One such survey is done quarterly since December 2002 in India by *The Economic Times*, which measures the consumer optimism through Consumer Confidence Index (CCI).

Even though this method is grouped under qualitative methods, it can be classified as a quantitative method, when the respondents are selected based on probability sampling techniques and analysis is done with multivariate statistical tools.

The advantages of this method are:

- Useful in forecasting sales for industrial products, consumer durables and new products.
- It also finds customers' reasons for buying or not buying.
- Relatively inexpensive and fast, when only a few customers are involved (for example business buyers' survey).

The disadvantages of this method are:

- Sometimes buyers are unwilling to reveal their plans.
- Buyers are sometimes over optimistic.
- Expensive and time-consuming for consumer non-durable products where consumers are very large in number.

Test Marketing/Market Testing Method

This method is useful for forecasting the sales for a **new consumer product** which has no historical (or previous) sales figures. It can also be used for estimating sales for an established consumer product in a new territory. Not all firms undertake market testing. However, many companies think that market testing is useful not only for finding the market potential or sales forecast, but also for obtaining valuable information about customers and intermediaries. The major decisions to be taken by a company in market testing are: (i) How much amount should be spent on market testing? and (ii) Which method of market testing should be used? The answers to these questions depend on four factors: (a) the total project cost, (b) the degree of risk of failure for a new product as compared to a modified product, (c) the time pressure for launching the new product or brand, and (d) the cost of market testing.

For example, for a high-risk new product like a breakfast cereal which is to be launched nationally, the risk of failure is high. Hence, more amount needs to be spent on market testing to minimize the risk of failure. However, if a well-known company like Colgate wants to launch another brand of toothpaste, which is a modified product, the risk of failure and the amount to be spent for market testing would be much less.

The time and the amount of market testing may have to be minimized, if the firm is under time pressure because a competitor is about to launch its brand or the season is about to start. For instance, a company was about to launch a uniquely designed new table fan in Mumbai. The launch was scheduled in the last week of March. However, there was a delay in production and the fans were received from the company's factory to the finished goods warehouse in the first week of May. The marketing head had to skip the market testing as the summer season was almost over.

The major methods used for market testing of consumer products include: (i) Full-blown test markets, (ii) Controlled test marketing, and (iii) Simulated test marketing.

Full-Blown Test Markets

It consists of a company choosing a few (two to six) representative cities in which full promotion campaign is introduced, similar to what would be done in national marketing. The company's salespeople try to sell the new brand to the trade. The duration of the test market varies from a few months to one year, depending on the repurchase period of the new product. Buyer surveys are carried out to get information about consumer attitude, usage and satisfaction towards the new product. If the test markets show high trial and repurchase rates, the product should be launched nationally; if they show a high trial rate and a low purchase rate, the new product should be redesigned or dropped; if they show a low trial rate and a high repurchase rate, the product is acceptable, but more consumers should try it; if both trial and repurchase rates are low, the new product should be abandoned.

Controlled Test Marketing

The company with a new brand or product hires a research firm which gets a panel of stores that will carry the new product or brand for a fee at specified geographical locations. The research firm delivers the new product to the panel of stores, arranges promotions at the stores and measures the sales of the new product. The research firm also interviews sample consumers to get their perceptions on the new product. Both full-blown test markets and controlled test marketing expose the new product to the competitors. However, this does not happen in the case of simulated test marketing.

Simulated Test Marketing

In this method, about 30-40 consumers (or qualified shoppers) are selected, based on their brand familiarity and preferences in a particular product category, such as baby care and soft drink products. These shoppers are shown commercials or print advertisements of well-known products and also the new product, without any specific mention. These consumers are given a small amount of money and asked to buy any items in a store. The researcher of the company notes how many consumers buy the new brand and the competing brands. These consumers are interviewed to find reasons for buying or not buying. Those shoppers who did not buy the new brand are given a free sample. Some weeks later, after usage of the new brand, the consumers are interviewed on phone to find satisfaction levels, usage and repurchase intentions. This method gives moderately accurate results. The new brand is not exposed to the competitors. Also, the testing time and costs are much shorter than full-blown test.

Industrial-Product Market Testing

The methods used are alpha testing (i.e. testing within the company) and beta testing (i.e. testing with outside customers) for high cost and new technology products and services. For example, Infosys sent its new banking software product, Finnacle, to the experts for a thorough check-up to see if it was fit for the multi-billion dollar US market. The supplier of the new industrial product/service will ask the customers about their purchase intentions and other information after beta testing. Another method used for introducing a new industrial product or service is participating in the industry trade-shows or exhibitions.

The main advantages of these methods are:

- Their usefulness for forecasting the sales of new or modified products.
- In deciding whether a company should go ahead for a national launch of a new product, without spending a huge amount.

However, the disadvantages of these methods are:

- For some of the methods like full-blown test market and controlled test marketing, where there are possibilities of the information on new products going to competitors, there are chances of spoilage of the test marketing by competitors.
- If repurchase period is long, particularly for consumer durables, it is difficult for the company to wait to measure test results. In such cases, the company decides to introduce a new product in a small geographical area and subsequently roll out to other areas, in a planned manner.

Moving Averages Method

In this method, a company sales forecast is developed by calculating the average company sales for previous years. As shown in Table 3.2, a company's sales forecast was worked out by calculating moving averages for three and six year time periods.

The formula used is:

$$\text{Sales forecast for next year} = \frac{\text{Actual sales for past 3 or 6 years}}{\text{Number of years (3 or 6 years)}}$$

Another form of this technique is: $\text{Sales}_{t+1} = \frac{1}{n}(\text{sales}_t + \text{sales}_{t-1} + \cdots + \text{sales}_{t-n})$ where, sales_{t+1} is the sales forecast for the next period, sales_t is the sales in the present period, sales_{t-1} is the sales in the period immediately past, and so on.

Table 3.2 Moving Averages Method: An Example

		Moving Averages Forecast	
Year	Actual Sales	3 year	6 year
2010	840		
2011	880		
2012	864		
2013	832	861	
2014	862	858	
2015	948	852	
2016	956	880	871
2017 (forecast)		922	890

(Figures of Sales are in ₹ million)

When a forecast is developed for the next period, the sales in the oldest period are dropped from the average and replaced by the sales in the newest period and hence, the name "moving averages". If a company operates in a stable environment, a short two or three years' average may be most useful. However, if a firm is in an industry with cyclical variations, the moving average should use the data equal to the length of a cycle or a longer averaging period. Sales forecasts, using this method, are less accurate for products or services that experience sudden changes in sales or if there are major changes in the business environment due to unexpected entry of a strong competitor into the market.

The advantages of this method are:

- Relatively simple method.
- Easy to calculate.
- Widely used for short-term and medium-term sales forecasts.

The disadvantages of this method are as follows:

- Unable to predict a downturn or upturn in the market.
- Cannot predict long-term sales forecast accurately.
- Data is needed for products with stable sales histories.

Exponential Smoothing Method

This method is closely related to the moving average method for sales forecasting. By using the exponential smoothing equation, the forecaster can allow sales in certain periods to influence the sales forecast more than sales in other periods. The equation of exponential smoothing method is as follows:

Sales forecast for next year = (L) (actual sales this year) + (1 – L) (this year's sales forecast)

Another form of this technique: Sales_{t+1} = (L) Actual sales_t + (1– L) Forecasted sales_t.

where, (L) is a smoothing constant or probability weighing factor. Sales_{t+1} is forecasted sales. Actual and forecasted sales_t are in present period.

The forecaster decides the value of the smoothing constant based on: (i) review of sales data, (ii) knowledge and observation about the conditions in the forecasted period and conditions in previous period, and (iii) intuition. For instance, a smoothing constant (L) with a high value of (0.7) or (0.8) allows most recent periods of actual sales to influence sales forecast more than sales in earlier periods, whereas a smoothing constant with a low value of (0.2) or (0.3) allows earlier periods of actual sales to influence forecasted sales more than sales in recent periods. The smoothing constant (L) can range from something greater than zero to something less than 1.

Let us take the example of Table 3.2, and calculate the forecasted sales for the year 2017 by using the exponential smoothing method. The sales forecast for the year 2017 would be 0.2 × 956 + 0.8 × 880 = ₹895 million.

The advantages of this method are:

- Simple to operate.
- Forecaster's knowledge or understanding can be used in forecasting.
- Useful method when sales data have a trend or a seasonal pattern.
- Immediate response to an upturn or downturn in sales.
- Used by many firms.

The disadvantages of this method are:

- Smoothing constant is somewhat arbitrary.
- Long-term and new product forecasting is not possible.

Decomposition Method

In this method, the company's previous periods' sales data is broken down (or decomposed) into four major components, such as trend, cycle, seasonal and erratic events. These components are then recombined to produce the sales forecast.

Let us consider an example of this method by continuing from Table 3.2. Assume that various analysis have broken down (or decomposed) the previous sales data into the following components: A growth of three percent in sales is estimated due to the development in technology, capital formation and population (trend component). Increased terrorist activities are expected to reduce sales by 5 percent (erratic events component). A 10 percent reduction in sales is expected due to a recession in demand (cyclic component). The sales in the third quarter of the year are estimated to go up by 15 percent due to festive season, as compared to other three quarters (seasonal component). The forecaster would combine the different components, as under, in order to forecast sales for 2017.

Sales in 2016 was ₹956 million. The trend component shows that 2017 sales will be ₹985 million (956 × 1.03). The sales are reduced due to introduction of erratic event component to ₹936 million (985 × 0.95). The sales forecast changes further due to cyclic component of recession to ₹842 million (936 × 0.90). The annual sales forecast for 2017 is ₹842 million. The quarterly sales forecast would be ₹210 (842 ÷ 4) million, if seasonal component is not considered. But in practice, seasonal component like festive season in the third quarter would suggest 15 percent increase in sales forecast, that is ₹242 million (210 × 1.15) for the third quarter and a consistent sales forecast of ₹200 million (842 – 242 ÷ 3) each for other three quarters.

From the above example, we see that the trend, cyclic and erratic events are included in the calculation of annual sales forecast. However, the seasonal component is used for forecasting sales for a period of less than a year, like quarterly or monthly sales forecast. The major advantage of this method is that it is conceptually a sound method. However, the disadvantages of this method are:

- Difficult and complex statistical methods are needed to break down sales data into various components (software packages are available).
- Historical data is needed.

Naive or Ratio Method

Naive or ratio method is a time series method of forecasting, which is based on the assumption that what happened in the immediate past will continue to happen in the immediate future. The simple formula used is as follows:

$$\text{Sales forecast for next year} = \text{Actual sales of this year} \times \frac{\text{Actual sales of this year}}{\text{Actual sales of last year}}$$

Another form this method: $F_t = \left(\frac{Y_{t-1}}{Y_{t-2}}\right) Y_{t-1}$

where, F_t = Sales forecast for next year,

Y_{t-1} = actual sales of this year,

Y_{t-2} = Actual sales of last year.

> Let us continue with the example given in Table 3.2, and forecast the sales for the year 2017. Actual sales of the year 2016 is ₹956 million and that actual sales of last year (2015) was ₹948 million. The next year (2017) sales forecast would be (956 × 956/948) = ₹964 million.

The advantages of this method are:

- Simple to calculate.
- Requires less data.
- Accuracy is good for short-term forecast.

However, the method also has certain disadvantages such as:

- It cannot be used for forecasting sales for long-term periods and new products.
- Accuracy of sales forecast would be less, if past sales fluctuate considerably.

Regression Analysis

This is a statistical forecasting method that is highly suitable for forecasting the sales of established products or brands. Here, the company's sales is treated as dependent variable *y*. The company then identifies causal (cause and effect) relationship between the company sales and the independent variables (or predictors), which influence the sales. If there is only one independent variable (*x*), say, promotional expenditure, it is plotted on a graph of paired data of past sales and promotional expenditure. This is called **linear** (or **simple**) **regression**, with only one independent variable or predictor and different pattern of relationships, as shown in Figure 3.8.

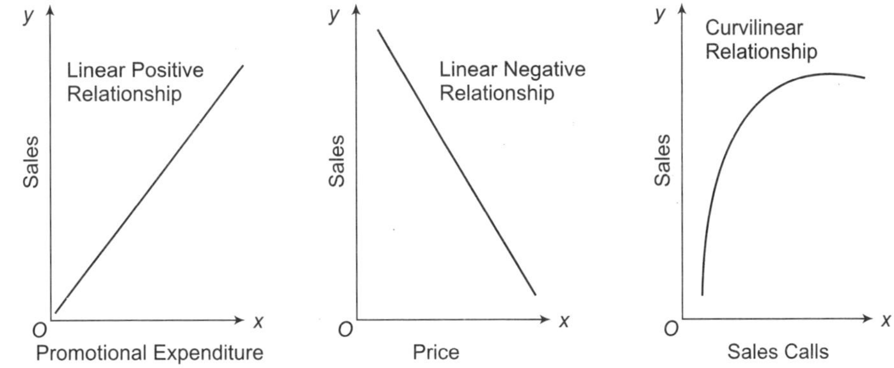

Fig. 3.8 Relationships in Regression Analysis

To show the relationship between paired data (x, y), called a scatter diagram, the simple method is to draw a freehand line on the plotted points, keeping in mind to minimize the distances of all the points from the line. This trend line can be extended to project sales in future periods. A more accurate method of finding the "best-fitting line" is to use the least-squares formula for a straight line, i.e. $y = a + bx$, where a is the intercept of the line on y-axis and b is the slope or trend of the line.

In practice, the company sales are influenced by several independent variables, such as price, promotional expenditure, and population. For example, population size, disposable income and age may be relevant predictors (or independent variables) for forecasting sales of pharmaceutical products. Another example is for forecasting the sales or demand for new passenger cars. The important predictors (or independent variables) are prices, disposable income, credit conditions, and stocks of passenger cars of different ages. To forecast the effect of several independent variables on the company sales, the method used is called Multiple Regression Analysis.

An Example of Multiple Regression Analysis

Let us consider an example of a company which wants to forecast the sales of trimmer and router bits (i.e. dependent variable) which is based on sales of wooden furniture, interior decoration, doors and window frames and wooden artifacts (i.e. independent variables). The sales data for the same is shown in Table 3.3.

Table 3.3 The Sales Data for the Dependent and Independent Variables in the Example

Year	Trimmer and Router Bits	Wooden Furniture	Interior Decoration	Doors and Window Frames	Wooden Artifacts
2011	123	23674	14564	2356	5345
2012	130	24532	17453	2541	5728
2013	138	26784	18245	2853	6024
2014	147	29342	21432	2914	6158
2015	155	31692	23127	3146	6324
2016	162	33457	25276	3256	6519
(Forecast) 2017	169.37	35320.30	27624.69	3369.85	6720.01

(Figures of sales are in ₹million)

Using multiple regression analysis, the sales of trimmer and router bits is expressed as a function of the sales of wooden furniture, interior decoration, doors and window frames and wooden artifacts as shown in Table 3.3.

Table 3.4 Regression Coefficients in the Example

	Coefficients				
	Non-standardized Coefficients		Standardized Coefficients		
Model	B	Std. Error	Beta	t	Sig.
1 (Constant)	23.633	1.882		12.559	.051
Sales of wooden furniture (FWF)	.002	.000	.549	37.074	.017
Sales of interior decoration (FID)	.001	.000	.228	16.825	.038
Sales of doors and window frames (FDWF)	.003	.001	.069	3.841	.162
Sales of wooden artifacts (FWA)	.006	.001	.162	9.739	.065

The sales forecast of trimmer and router bits (FTRB) can then be estimated using projections for the sales of wooden furniture, interior decoration, door and window frames and wooden artifacts. This can be obtained by using any sales forecasting method.

In this instance, the forecast of sales of wooden frame, interior decoration, door and window frames and wooden artifacts, are found by using the ratio method. This is given in the last line in Table 3.3. These figures are then used in the regression equation,

$$F_{TRB} = 23.633 + 0.002 \times F_{WF} + 0.001 \times F_{ID} + 0.003 \times F_{DWF} + 0.006 \times F_{WA}$$

to obtain a forecast for the sales of trimmer and router bits, as shown in the last line of Table 3.3.

The availability of computer software forecasting packages such as Statistical Analysis System (SAS) and Statistical Package for the Social Sciences (SPSS) has increased the usage of regression analysis in many companies.[13] The advantages of regression analysis are:

- High forecasting accuracy, if relationships between variables are stable.
- Objective method.
- Can predict turning points of the company's sales.

The disadvantages of regression analysis are:

- High degree of statistical competence needed.
- Can be expensive and time consuming.
- Not possible to forecast explanatory variables and products not having historical sales data.

Econometric Analysis[14]

In this method, many regression equations are built to forecast industry sales, general economic conditions or future events. The procedure followed is as follows:

First, find which predictors or independent variables influence sales and the relationships between sales and these predictors, as well as the interrelationships between the predictors. Thereafter, develop a number of regression equations representing these relationships. A forecast is prepared by solving these equations on a computer. The major advantage of this method is that highly accurate forecasts of economic conditions and industry sales are possible. The disadvantages are that a large volume of data is required representing the various predictors and statistical expertise is needed.

HOW TO IMPROVE FORECASTING ACCURACY?

Sales forecasting is an important and difficult task. It is, therefore, necessary to understand some guidelines that help in improving the accuracy of the sales forecast. These are: (i) use multiple forecasting methods, (ii) identify suitable methods and approaches, (iii) develop a few predictors, (iv) obtain a range of forecasts, and (v) use computer hardware and software tools.

Use Multiple Forecasting Methods and Approaches

Companies use two or three forecasting methods and both approaches to ensure high level of forecasting accuracy and to gain confidence. For example, an electrical equipment manufacturing company uses regression analysis (top-down approach) and sales force composite (bottom-up approach) methods to find if the sales forecast developed by the two methods and approaches are similar to each other. The regression analysis method has the top-down approach that is used at sales and marketing headquarter. The salesforce composite method has the bottom-up approach, involving all the salespeople and the field sales managers. In case the sales estimates of the two methods and approaches differ considerably, the company uses survey of buyer's intentions (bottom-up approach) or moving average method (top-down approach and a time series method). The final forecast is approved by the company's senior executives (executive opinion method: top-down approach).[15]

Identify Suitable Methods

The selection of a suitable forecasting method depends on the accuracy of the method, data requirements for forecasting, costs and time availability for forecasting. The forecaster should also keep in mind the advantages and disadvantages of each forecasting method, as mentioned earlier. Table 3.5 will give some guidelines to sales and marketing executives in selecting suitable forecasting methods.

Develop a Few Predictors

When the forecaster uses multiple regression analysis or econometric analysis, he should keep the number of independent variables or predictors as few as possible, because use of many predictors result in duplication of a few basic predictors like population and income. A good practice for the forecaster or marketer is to discuss the predictors that affect the sales of the company's products or services with the sales managers, salespersons and customers and thereafter, use these few predictors as independent variables.

Obtain a Range of Forecasts

Most forecasting firms prepare a range of sales forecasts, including minimum, intermediate and maximum estimates. The minimum sales estimates are based on the assumption of worst possible development and lowest market forecast for the product or service. The company also estimates the market potential (maximum possible sales estimates), assuming all helpful things to happen. Between the two extremes of minimum and maximum estimates, the forecaster makes suitable assumptions to calculate the intermediate sales forecast.

Guidelines for Selecting Suitable Sales Forecasting Methods

Table 3.5 gives guidelines to the sales managers and forecasters with information on time, cost, accuracy, application, strengths and weaknesses of the most sales forecasting methods.

Table 3.5 Guidelines for Selecting Suitable Sales Forecasting Methods

Forecasting Method	Time Required to Develop	Cost	Accuracy	Application	Strengths (Advantages)	Weaknesses (Disadvantages)
Executive opinion	Short (1 week) to medium (3–4 weeks)	Low	Fair	For short/medium term and new products	Quick forecast, less expensive	Subjective, no break-down*, unscientific
Delphi	Medium (3–4 weeks) to long (2–3 months)	Low to medium	Good	For long and short-term, technology, new product and industry forecast	Objective, e-mail facility helps quick exchanges, group approach	Getting real experts, break-down is difficult*, unscientific.
Sales force composite	Medium (2–3 weeks)	Medium	Fair to good (if trained)	For annual sales forecast for existing and new products/ services	Break-down* possible, use of insight of sales people	Less forecasting knowledge, optimistic or pessimistic estimates, sales persons' time spent on forecasting.
Survey of buyers' intentions	Long (3–6 months)	Medium to high	Good	For new and existing products/ services, industrial/ consumer durable products	Gives various information including customers, less cost and time, if customers are few.	Intentions may not result in buying; some buyers unwilling to reveal their intentions, expensive, if consumers are many.
Test marketing	Medium to long (2–12 months)	Medium to high	Good	For new or modified products	Minimizes cost or risk of national launch	Competitors may disturb

(Contd.)

Moving average	Short (few hours)	Low	Good for short-term and stable sales	For short- and medium-term sales and inventory, for large number of products	Simple and easy to calculate	Cannot predict downturn/upturn, historical data needed, less accurate for sudden sales changes
Exponential smoothing	Short (few hours)	Low	–Do–	–Do–	Simple, forecaster's knowledge used	–Do– Smoothing constant arbitrary
Decomposition	Short to medium (1–4 weeks)	Low to medium	Fair to good	For short-term Forecasting, software packages available	Conceptually sound	Complex, historical data needed, cannot predict upturn/downturn
Naive/Ratio	Short (few hours)	Low	Fair for short-term	For short-term forecasting	Simple to calculate	Less accurate, if past sales fluctuate
Regression analysis	Short (few hours) to medium (2–4 weeks)	Low to medium	Good	For the company sales forecast. Software packages available and essential	Objective method, can predict upturn/ down-turn	Technically complex, large historical data needed, need statistical competence
Econometric analysis	Medium to long	Medium to high	Good	For economic conditions and industry sales, Computer hardware and software essential	Simulation of economy, accuracy of causal relationships	Need expertise, large historical data needed

*Break-down means detailed sales estimates by territory, product and sales people.

Use Computer Hardware and Software Tools

Computers are playing an important role in sales forecasting. Personal computers (PCs) are used widely for sales forecasting, because they are fast and capable of storing and processing a large amount of data. There are number of software packages, as mentioned earlier, that are marketed for use in sales forecasting. Sales managers are increasingly using these software packages, as they are user friendly and helpful in avoiding manual calculations. Sales managers are realizing that they must overcome their computer phobia, as they find the computer an essential tool for sales forecasting.

LO 4 **Organize the sales budget and know its purposes, money allocation methods and the budgeting process**

SALES BUDGET

What is a sales budget? A sales budget consists of detailed estimates of expected volume of sales and selling expenditure. The sales volume part of the sales budget is based on the sales forecast.

The sales volume budget is generally set slightly lower than the sales forecast to avoid excessive risk. The accuracy of the sales budget is very important in the success or failure of the firm's total budget. This is because the sales budget is used mainly for planning the company's production, purchasing and cash flow.

The sales volume budget, which is derived from the sales forecast, is broken into (i) product-wise and size-wise or model-wise quantities, the average selling price per unit and resulting sales revenue, (ii) territory-wise quantities to be sold and sales revenue and (iii) salesperson-wise sales volume targets or quotas during yearly, quarterly and monthly budget period. Out of the three breaks of the sales volume budget mentioned above, (ii) and (iii) data are needed by the sales and marketing professionals, but other departments or functions need information on (i), i.e. each product-line and product item's estimated sales in quantities month-wise. For example, the sales budget for ceiling fan includes size-wise (32", 36", 42", 48", 56" and 60") sales forecast in numbers for each month for 12 months of the budget period. As mentioned earlier, the sales budget includes a detailed estimate of the sales volume as well as the selling expenditure.

The selling expenditure budget consists of the selling-expense budget and the sales department administrative budget. The selling-expense budget includes expenditures for personal selling activities, such as the salaries, commissions (or incentives) and other expenses for the salespeople. Any plans for increase in number of salespeople or technical service people during the budget period must also be included in this budget.

The administrative budget of the sales department should include the salaries of territory sales managers, sales supervisors, their secretaries and office staff. The budget should also include operating expenses like rent, power, supplies, office equipment and general overhead.

Thus, the national sales manager is responsible for preparing three detailed budgets: (i) the sales volume budget, (ii) the selling-expense budget, and (iii) the administrative budget of the sales department.

Purposes of the Sales Budget

The sales budget is the key factor for the successful performance of the sales department. There are many purposes or reasons of the sales budget, which include planning, coordination, and control.

Planning

The budgeting process in a company consists of profit planning based on forecasted sales minus the estimated cost of achieving the sales. The sales budget is the sales goal or a standard of performance at the company level. The company level sales goal is then broken down to detailed sales goals (or quotas) by products, territories and salespersons. Sales quotas or targets include sales volumes, selling expenses and key activities or tasks to be performed by the salespersons. Although the typical budget period is one year, the sales budget and quotas are prepared on quarterly and monthly basis. Once the sales budget and quotas are set up, the marketing, sales and branch managers start preparing plans or proposals for achieving the sales goals. Salespeople will then learn about their quotas or targets from their immediate managers and also how to achieve the same through an action plan.

Coordination

At the corporate level, the budget process is used for coordinating the activities of various functional areas. For example, the sales budget is finalized in a coordination meeting involving the functional heads like production, finance, marketing and human resource. During the operation of the budget, the production planning is done in consultation and coordination with sales and marketing functions. Within the marketing function, there is a need to coordinate the efforts and expenses of sales department with other support functions like advertising, sales promotion, customer service and marketing research. It is only through the coordinated efforts of all the functional areas, the sales budget can be achieved.

Control

A sales budget, as mentioned earlier, marks a standard of performance. In fact, the sales budget stated in terms of sales volume and selling expenses becomes a standard of performance, against which the actual performance is measured. Once the yearly sales budget at the company level and quotas at the marketing units (like territory, salesperson) level are finalized and broken down to quarterly and monthly goals, the same are measured against the actual performance. If the actual performance of a salesperson or a branch manager is found to be favorable during a monthly or quarterly budget review meeting, he/she is appreciated and suitably rewarded. However, if the performance is unfavorable with respect to the budgeted sales volume or selling expenses, the reasons are identified and corrective actions are initiated so that in the next review, improvement in the performance takes place. This process is called 'control', which is possible due to establishment of sales budget.

Methods Used for Allocation Of Money

Sales managers are required to decide expenditure levels for each item of selling expenses. The methods used for allocating money to each category or item of selling expenses are: (i) percentage of sales, (ii) executive judgment and (iii) objective and task.

Percentage of Sales Method

Sales and marketing managers use this method by multiplying the sales volume budget by various percentages of each category of expenses. For example, the sales manager may decide travel expenses for salespeople to be 0.3 percent of the budgeted sales revenue, advertising expenses to be one percent and sales promotion to be 0.8 percent of the budgeted sales volume. The sales manager may decide these percentages based on the past experience or on the basis of marketing and sales plans. These percentages are used during the monthly and quarterly evaluation of performance on sales volume and selling expenses for each sales territory manager and salesperson. The multiplication of the budgeted sales volume with the percentage of each expense category becomes the budgeted amount rupee (or dollar) for that category. The success of this method depends on the accuracy of the sales forecast, which is the responsibility of sales managers. To ensure that actual expenditure is close to the budgeted expense, the sales manager keeps his attention on the percentage budget for each expense category.

The Executive Judgment Method

Here, the sales manager uses his judgment to decide the budgeted selling expenses for each expense category. The judgment may be based on marketing and sales plans as well as opinions of senior sales executives.

The Objective and Task Method

The first step is to look at the sales volume objective to be achieved during the budget period (say one year). Then based on the marketing and sales strategies, the tasks or actions are decided that are required to be carried out in order to achieve the earlier stated sales objective. The third step is to estimate the costs of carrying out the tasks. The costs are then added up to find out whether the profit objective can be achieved. Review of sales revenue, cost and profit figures continues until the sales and marketing managers are satisfied with the sales and profit objectives, the tasks and the budgeted cost/expenditure of various items of selling expenses.

The Sales Budget Process

Most companies have certain processes or procedures for the preparation of sales budget. They have developed certain formats, worksheets, guidelines and time table for the preparation of the annual sales budgets. The steps generally followed for the sales budget process are mentioned in this section.

Review the Situation

The sales manager should review the past budget performance as well as the current and future (i.e. budget period) marketing environment. The review of past budget performance can help the sales manager to understand the deviations of the actual sales performance against the budget and the items or elements where the company showed favorable or unfavorable variances. Similarly, a review of the current and future forces of marketing environment such as customers, competitors, economy, technology, government policies and regulations would help the sales manager and the marketing manager to understand the changes taking place in the external environment. These review meetings of the sales and marketing key executives would help evolve guidelines and assumptions to be made for the budget period by all the field sales managers. If possible, the field sales managers and sales supervisors should also be involved in understanding the market situation. Ideally, this activity should start about 4–6 months prior to the commencement of the new accounting year.

Communication

The head of sales function should communicate in writing to all the field sales managers (such as area, branch, district and regional managers) about the budget preparation, including the formats, guidelines, assumptions and timetable. Each first-level field sales manager estimates the sales volume in units, the average selling price and the value for each product and service to be sold, along with the estimated selling expenses (consisting of salaries, commission and sales-force expenses like travel, lodging, food and entertainment to customers) and administrative budget (which includes salaries of sales managers, supervisors, office staff, operating expenses like rent, supplies, power, office equipment and general overhead).

Preparation of Subordinate Budgets

The subordinate budgets means the sales budgets prepared by the first-level sales managers, such as branch, area or district managers as well as the middle-level sales managers like regional, zonal or divisional sales managers. The first-level sales managers, in the companies which follow build-up or bottom-up approach in the budgeting process, are asked to estimate sales for each product item in terms of sales (in units), average price per unit and the resulting sales revenue. Branch or district managers can follow one or more suitable sales forecasting methods, such as moving average, exponential smoothing, naive/ratio or sales force composite. In the case of sales force composite method, as explained earlier in this chapter, the branch manager should give adequate training or guidance to the salespeople in the preparation of the sales budget for their respective territories. For preparing the sales expenditure budget, the branch manager can use either the percentage of sales method or the judgment method as described earlier in this chapter.

At the regional or zonal level, the sales budgets are prepared after receiving the branch-wise sales budgets from the respective first-level managers. The regional or zonal managers modify (if necessary) and add the respective branch or district sales budgets. They, thereafter, submit their sales budgets to the national sales manager or the marketing head.

Approval of the Sales Budget

In consultation with the marketing head, the national sales manager prepares two or three alternative proposals of the sales budget and makes a presentation to the top management of the company. After a detailed discussion on the alternative proposals, the sales budget finally gets approved by the top management.

Other Departments

The final sales budget is given to other departments or functions like production, finance, materials and human resource to prepare their budgets. Thereafter, the approved sales budget is broken down into each sales territory and into the quarterly and monthly periods. Only the sales budget has revenue and expenditure budgets, whereas all the other departments in the company have expenditure budgets. Accounts/Finance department prepares cash budget and profit budget, based on the sales revenue information given by the sales department and the expenditure budgets given by all the departments or functions. The budget preparation process has become more efficient with the use of computers.

SUMMARY

LO 1

- The strategic planning includes making decisions about the company's mission, long-term objectives, strategies and tactics or action plan. In most large, multi-product and multi-business companies, planning is done at three or four organizational levels: (i) corporate strategic plan, (ii) divisional and/or business unit's strategic plans and (iii) product or functional operational plan.

- The role of marketing and sales at the corporate level is to provide information on the customer and competition. At the business unit or SBU level, the role includes providing analysis of the customer and competition, forecasting external environment and analyzing the firm's competitive advantage. At the functional level of sales and marketing, the role is to evolve and implement the marketing – mix strategies and action plan, coordination, resource allocation, sales forecasting and developing and implementing the sales strategy.
- Some of the major strategic issues are strategic thinking and social selling.

LO 2

- The marketing strategy developed by a firm should be in agreement with its business strategy. Two important components of a company's marketing strategy are: (i) target market selection and positioning strategy and (ii) development of marketing – mix (or the four Ps of marketing).
- The marketing strategy of a company is implemented for individual customers through a sales strategy. An effective sales strategy has four parts: (i) customer classification strategy, (ii) customer relationship strategy, (iii) selling methods, and (iv) marketing channel strategy.
- The responsibility of achieving the management's desired growth falls on the head of sales and marketing function. Different strategies are used to achieve the objective of sales growth, such as strengthening the distribution network, developing new products, improving customer service quality, backward integration, horizontal integration and diversification.
- Today selling is becoming more challenging because the buyer has more options, competition has become intense and complex and customers are more knowledgeable due to the Internet and media. If salespeople get necessary support from their companies, have required selling skills and possess right traits, they can overcome the selling challenges and achieve the organizational goals. The required selling skills are: communications, listening, negotiation and problem-solving.

LO 3

- There are 90 different types of sales (or demand) forecasts that can be made based on six different product levels, three separate time periods and five different geographical areas (i.e. $6 \times 3 \times 5 = 90$). Hence, the sales manager should clearly specify the product level, the time period and geographical area when a sales forecast is communicated.
- Some of the basic terms used in forecasting the company sales or the customer demand are: market potential, market forecast, the company sales potential and the company sales forecast.
- There are two basic forecasting approaches: (i) top-down or break–down approach and (ii) bottom-up or build-up approach. Under each forecasting approaches, there are sales forecasting methods. The sales forecasting methods are classified as qualitative and quantitative methods. The qualitative methods are: executive opinion, Delphi, sales force composite, survey of buyers' intentions and test marketing. The quantitative methods are: moving average, exponential smoothing, decomposition, naïve/ratio, regression analysis and econometric analysis.

LO 4

- A sales budget consists of detailed estimates of expected sales volume and selling expenses. The sales budget is normally set slightly lower than the sales forecast to avoid excessive risk.

- The purposes of sales budget are: (i) preparation of a marketing plan to achieve sales goals, (ii) coordination of activities of various functional areas, and (iii) evaluation of actual performance against monthly and quarterly sales budgets and quotas (or targets) and taking corrective actions.
- The methods used for allocation of money to each item or category of selling expenses are: (i) percentage–of–sales, (ii) executive judgment and (iii) objective and task.
- The steps followed for the sales budget process are: (i) review of past, present and future situations, (ii) communication to all field sales managers, (iii) preparation of subordinate budgets by field sales managers, (iv) approval of the sales budget in consultation with the top management, (v) information about the final sales budget to other departments or functions such as production, finance, materials and human resource to prepare their budgets. Also, the sales budget is broken down into each territory and into the quarterly and monthly periods.

Key Terms

Glossaries of key terms are mentioned at the end of all chapters

Bottom-up approach
Decomposition
Delphi method
Econometric analysis
Executive opinion
Exponential smoothing
Integrated Marketing Communication (IMC)
Market forecast
Market potential
Moving averages method
Naive/ratio method
Objective and task method
Operations management
Regression analysis
Sales budget
Sales force composite method
Sales forecaster the company sales forecast
Sales potential or the company sales potential
Sales quota
Strategic Business Unit (SBU)
Strategic planning
Survey of buyer's intentions
Test marketing
Top-down (or break-down) approach

Conceptual Questions

1. What is meant by 'strategic planning'? What is the role of sales and marketing managers in an organization? LO1 E
2. What is 'social selling'? Is it same as social media marketing? LO1 M

Note: Difficulty Level ⟶ E — Easy; M — Medium; D — Difficult

3. Explain the difference between a marketing strategy and a sales strategy. Describe the components of a sales strategy. LO2 D
4. What are the strategy options available to firms who want to achieve the desired sales growth objectives? LO2 D
5. Differentiate between a market forecast and a sales forecast. What factors should be indicated by a sales manager while communicating on a sales' forecast? LO3 M
6. Compare the top-down and bottom-up approaches and indicate the examples of sales forecasting methods that are used under each of the two approaches. LO3 D
7. Describe any one of the qualitative methods and also one of the quantitative methods of sales forecasting and indicate their respective advantages and disadvantages. LO3 D
8. Why is the sales forecasting accuracy important to a company? What should be the guidelines to be followed by a sales manager to ensure forecasting accuracy? LO3 D
9. What is a 'sales budget'? What are the purposes of the sales budget? LO4 M
10. Which methods should be used for allocating money to various items of selling expenditure budget? Explain the typical process followed by a company to prepare its sales budget. LO4 M

Objective Type Questions

Select the most appropriate response out of the various options available in each of the following questions:

1. In most large, multi-product and multi-business firms the strategic planning is done at, apart from the corporate level
   (a) product level (b) business unit level
   (c) functional level (d) None of the above levels LO1 E
2. The role of marketing in a large and multi-business company at the corporate level is to, apart from providing information on customers and competitors
   (a) develop marketing strategy (b) develop competitive advantage strategy
   (c) advocate customer orientation (d) develop sales strategy LO1 E
3. Is the social selling same as the social media marketing?
   (a) Yes (b) No (c) Don't know LO1 M
4. The sales strategy for each specific customer has four parts, viz. classification of accounts, relationship strategy, selling methods and
   (a) pricing strategy (b) product strategy
   (c) promotion strategy (d) marketing channel strategy LO2 D
5. Sales budgets are generally set slightly ________ with respect to the sales forecasts
   (a) lower (b) higher (c) the same LO4 E

6. To achieve the sales growth objective, the options available to a firm include strengthening distribution network, backward and horizontal integration and one of the following
   (a) new product development (b) integrated marketing communications
   (c) marketing research (d) None of these **LO2 M**

7. Both the top-down and bottom-up approaches aim at calculating
   (a) market potential (b) sales potential
   (c) company sales forecast (d) None of these **LO3 M**

8. For forecasting the demand for a new product, the forecasting methods available are executive opinion, Delphi, sales force composite, test marketing and
   (a) regression analysis (b) moving averages
   (c) survey of buyers' intentions (d) exponential smoothing **LO3 D**

9. Software forecasting packages are available for regression analysis, econometric analysis and one of the following forecasting methods
   (a) naïve method (b) moving averages method
   (c) test marketing method (d) decomposition method **LO3 M**

10. The sales forecasting methods suitable for a long-term forecasting are regression analysis, econometric analysis and
   (a) Delphi (b) moving averages
   (c) sales force composite (d) survey of buyers' intentions **LO3 D**

11. The method of sales forecasting that gives a detailed break-down of the sales forecast by products and territories is, apart from the survey of buyers' intentions
   (a) exponential smoothing (b) regression analysis
   (c) Delphi method (d) sales force composite **LO3 M**

12. A sales budget consists of estimates of
   (a) sales volume (b) selling expenses
   (c) sales administration costs (d) All of these (e) None of these **LO4 M**

Application Questions

1. Suggest a marketing strategy and a sales strategy for a courier service company operating in the domestic market. Make suitable assumptions, if needed. **LO2 M**

2. Develop a sales forecast, based on the data given below, for the year 2017. Use any two methods of sales forecasting and give reasons for selecting the methods.

Year	Actual Sales	
2011	550	
2012	625	
2013	690	
2014	750	
2015	825	
2016	915	907 (Forecast)
2017	?	

LO3 M

3. ABC company's foods division launched into toffee segment in December 2016. The market size for toffee in India in 2015–2016 was at ₹4200 million and it was growing at 10 percent annually. Which sales forecasting method(s) would you suggest to the company and why? **LO3 D**

4. World Semiconductor Trade Statistics (WSTS) group forecasted global chip or (semiconductor) sales to grow at 19.4 percent for 2004 in October 2003. However, the chip sales grew by 28.4 percent in 2004 to $213.6 billion, due to strong demand for PCs, cell phones, DVD recorders and other electronics products. WSTS had forecasted global chip sales to rise by 8.5 percent in 2005 and then shrink to 0.7 percent in 2006. Why there were wide fluctuations in the sales forecast for semiconductor industry? Which method of sales forecasting would you suggest to WSTS? **LO3 D**

5. You are appointed as a branch manager by Crocodile Products at Pune, India, for selling Crocodile brand of shirts, trousers, T-shirts, innerwear and accessories. This is a new branch, covering western parts of Maharashtra state. For allocation of the expenditure budget for Pune branch for each item of the selling expenses, which method would you use and why? Explain the process to be followed. **LO4 M**

ASSIGNMENTS FOR STUDENTS

1. Use the Internet to select two companies whose marketing headquarters are in your city. Conduct in-depth interviews with the head of sales/marketing function of each organization to find the following:
   (a) Role of sales and marketing in the corporate strategy development.
   (b) How sales strategy is linked to marketing strategy?
   (c) Which strategies are used to achieve the objectives of sales growth?
   (d) What are the selling challenges and how these are met?
   Compare and contrast the findings of the two companies and submit a report to your teacher.
2. Develop a new consumer product or service idea. Prepare an estimate of market potential for the same by using census data available on the internet.
3. Contact a company's senior sales manager and talk to him about the following issues:
   (a) How the company's sales budget is determined? What process is followed for the same?
   (b) What method is used for allocating marketing expenditure to various marketing elements like advertising, sales promotion, marketing research, customer service and so on?

Reference Notes

1. Krishna K. Havaldar, *Business Marketing*, 4th ed., Chennai, Tamil Nadu, McGraw Hill Education (India) , 2014, p. 409.
2. Vithala R. Rao and Joel H. Steckel, *Analysis for Strategic Marketing*, Pearson Education, 2006, p. 12.
3. Hopkins David S., *The Marketing Plan*, New York.

4. Chamaria Apurva, *You Are the Key-Unlocking Doors through Social Selling,* Bloomsbury, 2015, pp.17-20.
5. http://www.slidesshare.net/rajeshdgr8/social-media-sales-strategy-ibm
6. Thomas N. Ingram, *et al., Sales Management—Analysis and Decision Making,* 4th ed., Thomson Learning, 2001, p. 73.
7. E. Jerome McCarthy, *Basic Marketing--A Managerial Approach,* 12th ed., (Homewood, IL = Irwin, 1996).
8. Thomas N. Ingram, *et al., Sales Management—Analysis and Decision Making,* 4th ed., Thomson Learning, 2001, p. 81.
9. Malcolm Campbell, *The New Sales Force,* Selling Power, July-Aug,1999, p. 51.
10. Evert Gummesson, *Total Relationship Marketing,* Boston: Butterworth-Heinemann, 1999.
11. Brockhaus William L. and John F. Mickelsen, *An Analysis of Prior Delphi Applications and Some Observations on its Future Applicability,* Technological and Social Change 10,1977, pp. 103-110.
12. Mark Barash, *Eliciting Accurate Sales Forecasts from Market Experts,* Journal of Business Forecasting, Fall 1994, p. 24.
13. Wittink Dick R., *The Application of Regression Analysis,* Allyn and Bacon Publisher, 1988
14. Gujarati Damodar, *Essentials of Econometrics,* fourth edition, Boston: McGraw Hill, 1998.
15. Benito E. Flores and Edna M. White, *A Framework for the Combination of Forecasts,* Journal of the Academy of Marketing Science, Fall 1988, p. 95.

Additional Reference

- Anne T. Coughlan, et al., *Marketing Channels,* 6th ed., Prentice Hall, 2001, pp. 2-3.

CASE 3.1

AG Refrigerators Ltd.

"The company's sales forecast for the year 2016–17 will be 8,80,000 numbers of refrigerators" said Satish Kumar, General Manager (Sales) of AG Refrigerators, in the budget meeting held on January 20, 2016 at the company's headquarters at Bengaluru.

"In addition to the company's total sales budget, the marketing function will need the information about the market segments, the share of household and institutional customers as well as that of rural and urban markets. Production function would like to know the quantities required by the various types of refrigerators like frost-free and direct-cool refrigerators as well as the different sizes from 55 liters to 310 liters. These figures are absolutely essential for working out marketing and production plans, and thereafter, overall company's budget for the year 2016–17", intervened Vinod Dhavan, President, AG Refrigerators, before the Vice-President (Sales and Marketing) could say anything.

Satish Kumar responded, "Yes, sir. We can estimate the break-up of the total sales budget for refrigerators into the product types and sizes as well as market segments, but we have to first decide whether our sales budget would be equal to or lower than the sales forecast."

"I think, before we take that decision, we would like to know how accurate is your sales forecast and which forecasting methods have you used," asked the Vice President (Sales and Marketing).

"Well, the method used by us was moving averages and the accuracy of our sales forecasting is good for short-term forecasting with stable market conditions and availability of historical data", said the confident looking Satish Kumar.

Discussion Questions

1. By using the moving averages method would Satish Kumar get the break-up of the sales forecast into the product types, sizes, and market segments? Justify your answer.
2. Should the company's sales budget be lower, higher or equal to the sales forecast and why?
3. Do you agree with the sales forecasting method used by Satish Kumar? Give reasons.
4. What should the company do to improve the forecasting accuracy?

This case was prepared by Prof. Krishna K. Havaldar for classroom discussion.

CASE 3.2

KR Cash and Carry Pvt. Ltd.

Pradeep Dasgupta, General Manager (Sales and Marketing) of KR Cash and Carry Pvt. Ltd., was highly concerned to find a drop in sales for the past three months from January to March, 2016 and no growth in sales for the year 2015–16. He wondered if this was due to the attrition of the salespersons in the past six months. In the last monthly performance review meeting on March 8, 2016, he did ask the three sales supervisors, to whom the salespersons report, to analyze the situation and come up with their suggestions in the April performance review meeting.

KR Cash and Carry Pvt. Ltd. (KRCC) is a wholesaler who procures food and non-food goods from the manufactures and sells the same to the small retailers, businesses and institutions on mostly cash and carry basis. Basically, the company is doing business-to-business (i.e. B2B) selling. As a leading wholesaler, the territory covered by its salespeople is the entire city of Kolkata. Pradeep has segmented the market on the basis of "type of customer". The three market segments are small retailers, small businesses, such as hotels, restaurants and caterers and institutions like schools, colleges and hospitals. Each market segment is manned by a group of salespersons and headed by a sales supervisor. The salespersons are asked to follow certain guidelines such as visiting at least 10 customers a day, submitting a sales report in the standard format every day, and communicating the information about availability of the products, prices and special offers to their respective customers. The salespeople treated all customers alike, without any classification. They maintained a transactional relationship with their customers. The salespersons used the standard AIDA (attention, interest, desire and action) formula for making the sales presentation to their customers.

In the meantime, Pradeep received a call from the company's Managing Director, expressing displeasure on the stagnating sales for the year 2015–16 and the declining sales of the last quarter. Pradeep was told by the Managing Director to be ready for a performance review meeting in the next week. Thereafter, Pradeep called an urgent meeting of the three sales supervisors to know the reasons for the poor sales performance and about the attrition of the salespersons. He also asked the sales supervisors to give suggestions for improvement.

The sales supervisors gave the following reasons:

- The salespeople feel that they are not paid adequately as compared to their efforts.
- The salespersons are not given the updates on the prices and availability of the company's products.

- For those institutional and business customers who do not buy on cash and carry basis, there are many instances of delayed deliveries.

The suggestions from the sales supervisors for improvement can be summarized as follows:

- To motivate salespeople the management should increase their salaries every year during festive season and make adequate reimbursement on travel, food and medical expenses. In addition, there should be employee engagement activities to make work life more interesting.
- The company should develop a mobile application so that information on changes in the prices and availability of products can be obtained through the salespersons' smart phones.
- The delivery service to the business customers can be improved by adding a few delivery vehicles and training the employees of the logistics department.

Pradeep was doubtful about some of the reasons and suggestions given by the sales supervisors. He thought that all aspects of the stagnating growth in sales have not been dealt with. Pradeep wondered how to make his presentation to the Managing Director comprehensive.

Discussion Questions

1. Should Pradeep accept all the reasons and suggestions given by the sales supervisors and make his presentation to the Managing Director accordingly?
2. What other strategies and actions would you suggest to substantially improve the growth in sales?

This case was prepared by Prof. Krishna K. Havaldar based on the case data provided by Akshath Kotian, Chandrika S., Gokul U., and Amin Ansari, MBA students of Alliance Ascent College, Alliance University, Bengaluru.

CASE 3.3

LeafCo Pvt. Ltd.

LeafCo Pvt. Ltd. is a medium-scale agro-business unit situated just outside Jamshedpur, Jharkhand, India. It produces three special grades of leaf pulp, all which are sold to local small-scale manufactures, who produce leaf-paper containers, leaf-paper bags and leaf-paper packing materials for the nearby markets in Jamshedpur and Ranchi. Grade A is primarily used in the production of leaf-paper food containers, grade B is used in the production of leaf-paper bags and leaf-paper packing materials and grade C is primarily used in the production of leaf-paper packing materials. The by-products of its pulp production processes are sold to local small farmers as fertilizer.

The quarterly sales figures of LeafCo of the different grades of leaf-pulp and quarterly sales figures of different leaf-pulp products are given in the accompanying Table 1.

The Jharkhand government has recently announced a policy promoting eco-friendly products. For this reason, the marketing manager of LeafCo expects the market for leaf-paper products to grow at twice or even thrice the current growth rate, and expects that LeafCo's customers will expand their marketing operations to other nearby markets, such as Bokaro and Dhanbad.

Table 1 Sales Figures of the Leaf-Paper and Leaf-Paper Products

Quarter/Year	Grade A Sales (1000 Metric Tons)	Grade B Sales (1000 Metric Tons)	Grade C Sales (1000 Metric Tons)	Leaf-Paper Food Containers (1000 Units)	Leaf-Paper Packaging Materials (1000 Units)	Leaf-Paper Bags (1000 Units)
Q1_2001	9.021	8.005	4.085	25773	27234	105642
Q2_2001	8.944	8.162	4.041	25554	26939	109356
Q3_2001	9.072	8.419	4.218	25920	28121	112132
Q4_2001	8.964	8.880	4.411	25612	29405	118797
Q1_2002	9.034	8.755	4.330	25811	28864	117379
Q2_2002	9.171	9.193	4.500	26204	29998	123861
Q3_2002	9.255	9.435	4.734	26444	31563	125576
Q4_2002	9.191	9.832	5.044	26261	33627	129395
Q1_2003	9.031	10.056	5.258	25803	35052	131018
Q2_2003	8.940	10.226	5.242	25544	34949	134626
Q3_2003	8.938	10.455	5.427	25538	36183	136740
Q4_2003	8.904	10.803	5.482	25440	36547	142967
Q1_2004	9.013	10.791	5.585	25752	37233	141359
Q2_2004	9.052	10.826	5.497	25864	36647	143230
Q3_2004	9.209	10.677	5.474	26312	36492	140550
Q4_2004	9.149	11.011	5.596	26141	37306	145617
Q1_2005	9.247	11.116	5.692	26419	37948	146419
Q2_2005	9.368	11.280	5.686	26767	37904	149787
Q3_2005	9.524	11.651	5.572	27213	37148	158721
Q4_2005	9.809	11.816	5.839	28027	38925	158476
Q1_2006	9.678	12.355	6.209	27650	41394	164321
Q2_2006	9.582	12.434	6.502	27377	43345	161990
Q3_2006	9.749	12.880	6.954	27855	46363	164864
Q4_2006	9.626	13.279	7.192	27502	47945	169698
Q1_2007	9.790	13.552	7.593	27972	50621	169796
Q2_2007	9.817	13.699	7.588	28785	50584	172809
Q3_2007	9.918	14.539	8.105	28337	54036	182718

On the other hand, the operations-cum-finance manager is less enthusiastic about the growth potential of the market, pointing out that their customers are small-scale units, so that they would face serious capacity constraints and logistic difficulties, if they tried to expand into other markets. He suggests a more cautious approach to forecast the demand.

Discussion Question

1. Use appropriate assumptions and techniques to forecast the quarterly demand of the three grades of leaf-pulp for the next two years, and justify the same.

This case was prepared by Prof. Mihir Dash of Alliance University for classroom discussion. It has been reproduced with his permission.

Chapter 4

Management of Sales Territories and Quotas

LEARNING OBJECTIVES

After studying this chapter, you will be able to:

- **LO 1** Define a sales territory and explain the reasons for setting up sales territories
- **LO 2** Describe the procedure for designing a sales territory
- **LO 3** Utilize the knowledge of Information Technology (IT) for designing sales territories
- **LO 4** Discuss sales quotas and their importance
- **LO 5** Explain the types of sales quotas and methods for setting sales quotas
- **LO 6** Plan the administration of sales quotas

When T. S. Krishnamurthy, General Manager (Sales and Marketing) of a new company, Saragam Aluminium Ltd., was preparing the marketing plan, he thought of focusing the company's marketing efforts initially on the four southern states of India. This was a logical decision because the manufacturing unit was located in southern India at Anekal, near Bengaluru, and the marketing and company headquarters were also located at Bengaluru. He thought that the logistics as well as sales and serving expenses would be less in southern region as compared to the expenses in other regions. Also, initially, for a new company like Saragam Aluminium, the production would be less than 500 metric tons per month, against the installed capacity of 1000 metric tons of aluminium extrusions per month. Krishnamurthy was informed by the company's Managing Director that the installation of extrusion presses and other equipment would be completed by June 2015 and that the production would commence from July 2015. Initial production would be about 150–200 metric tons per month, which would go up to 300–350 metric tons in one year and about 500 metric tons by the end of second year.

The major market segments for aluminium extrusions are building and construction industry (60 percent) with the main application being door and window frames. The automotive industry (for engine mounts, radiator frames and other applications), telecom industry (for telecom equipment) and solar power sector (for solar panels and mounting systems) are the other major market segments. The industrial applications account for the balance 40 percent of the total market size of 300,000 metric tons of aluminium extrusions. The industry is fragmented with 60 manufacturers of aluminium extrusions.

In order to improve the market coverage and control the selling expenses, Krishnamurthy decided to set up sales territories. For this, cities were used as control units. Based on 2011 census, there were three tier-1 cities and 16 tier-2 cities in the five southern states of India. Cities were classified based on their population. The market potential of southern region was estimated at 25 percent of all India market potential (or market size) of 300,000 metric tons of aluminium extrusions. This worked out to 75,000 metric tons.

Saragam Aluminium's sales potential was estimated at 4 percent of 75,000 metric tons, i.e. 3,000 metric tons for one year. However, for the accounting year 2015–16, since the company's production commenced in July 2015, for 9 months period, the company's sales potential was estimated at 2,250 metric tons. Krishnamurthy then calculated sales potential of each control unit by using the concept of multi-factor index, which is based on factors like population and income that influence sales of aluminium extrusions. Each tier-1 and tier-2 city has different multi-factor index depending on its population and disposable personal income. Thus, the sales potential of each city was estimated by multiplying the sales potential of the company by each city's multiple-factor index. Thereafter, Krishnamurthy estimated how much volume of aluminium extrusion each salesperson should sell so as to ensure profitable operation. Since this was a new company, there was no data available for the past sales, cost and profit contribution. Krishnamurthy, therefore, used his judgment to come up with a figure of 50 metric tons per month or 450 metric tons for 9 months' period of 2015–16 of sales goal or quota per salesperson. The sales territories were then made by collectively considering adjoining or nearby cities until the sales potential of each territory were equal or greater than the expected sales volume from each salesperson.

The next decision to be made by Krishnamurthy was the number of salespeople needed to achieve the sales volume goal. The most appropriate method for the new company to calculate the sales force size, as per Krishnamurthy, was sales potential (or break-down). The following formula was used:

$$N = \frac{S}{P}(1 + T)$$

where,

N = The number of salespeople needed or the sales force size

S = The annual sales forecast for the company = 3,000 metric tons
P = The estimated productivity of the average salesperson = 50 metric tons per month × 12 month = 600 metric tons
T = The estimated percentage of annual salespeople turnover = 20 percent

Therefore, $N = \frac{3000}{600}(1 + 0.20) = 6$ salespeople

Thus, company hired and trained six salespeople. They were assigned to the sales territories determined earlier based on the ability index of the salespersons and their social background. The ability index included factors like product and market knowledge as well as communication and selling skills of the salespersons. The social background included the salespersons' fluency of the local languages and whether they lived in urban or rural environment.

Thereafter, the sales goals or sales quotas for each salesperson were discussed and finalized by the sales manager to whom all the six salespersons reported. The sales quotas or targets included a combination of three elements, viz. the sales volume in metric tons and rupees; the selling expenses like travelling, lodging, food, customer entertainment and development of new customers (this was an important task since business development of aluminium extrusions involved industrial applications in automotive, telecom, solar power, and other industries). Yearly sales quotas were broken down to monthly and quarterly targets for the purposes of reviewing the performance and taking corrective actions, wherever required.

The illustration of Saragam Aluminium Ltd. in the opening vignette indicates some of the issues involved in the management of sales territories and quotas. There are issues such as definition of sales territory, reasons for setting up sales territories, procedure adopted for designing sales territories and use of information technology for designing sales territories. In addition, there are also some more issues such as importance and types of sales quotas, methods for setting sales quotas and administration of sales quotas. All these issues are discussed in this chapter.

LO 1 Define a sales territory and explain the reasons for setting up sales territories

DEFINING A SALES TERRITORY

A sales territory consists of existing and potential customers assigned to a salesperson. The territory may or may not have geographical boundaries. However, generally, a salesperson is assigned to a geographical area consisting of present and potential customers. For instance, a salesperson is asked to look after the customers located in Mumbai territory.

The basic concept of a sales territory is that a territory or a market is made up of present and potential customers, rather than a geographical area. Hence, in defining a sales territory, the keyword is customers, instead of geographical area. For example, in selling life insurance policies, salespeople sell mainly to relatives, friends or known people, without thinking of their geographical locations. Similarly, small companies do not use geographical divisions. Such examples of not using geographical territories are very few. In most companies, it is beneficial to assign salespeople to geographical territories, consisting of present and potential customers.

In many companies, salespeople are assigned to sales territories that are not properly designed. A research has found that more than 50 percent sales territories are not designed correctly, resulting in lower sales[1]. It is, therefore, an important task of a national sales manager, who is responsible for supervising regional or zonal sales managers, to design sales territories properly. The national sales manager or the head of a sales function is also responsible to increase or decrease the number of sales territories as well as to change the geographical boundaries of sales territories. Another research has shown that firms with correctly designed sales territories have higher sales volume, more productive salespeople and better market share[2].

REASONS OR BENEFITS FOR SETTING UP SALES TERRITORIES

There are many reasons for setting up and subsequently reviewing or revising sales territories[3]. Some of the major reasons or benefits for companies to establish sales territories are: (i) increased market (or customer) coverage, (ii) reduced selling expenses, (iii) better sales force performance evaluation, (iv) improved customer relationship, (v) increased salespeople's effectiveness, (vi) improved coordination, and (vii) benefited salespeople and company. All these benefits have been explained in detail in this section.

Increased Market or Customer Coverage

A well-designed sales territory allows salespeople to spend sufficient time with present and potential customers. The salesperson can identify and classify customers based on their sales potential. Proper market or customer coverage is possible, if the company sets up the territories intelligently and assigns its salespeople carefully. Sales territories should be large enough to ensure reasonable workloads to salespeople, but small enough to see that all existing customers and prospects are visited adequately as needed by the customers. The field sales managers can control the activities of salespeople, if the sales territories are set up properly. Well-designed sales territories allow salespeople to cover existing and potential customers economically and adequately.

Reduced Selling Expenses

By setting-up well designed sales territories salespeople spend less time on the road, fewer nights away from home, resulting in less cost of travelling and less expenses on lodging and food. Not only the selling expenses are reduced, but the sales volume goes up as the salesperson spends more time with the customers. The result is reduction of selling expenses as a percentage of sales revenue. With no geographical sales territories, the salespeople would crisscross each other as they travel to and from their customers, spending more time and money in travelling. With proper sales territories, there is a reduction in the selling expenses of the salespeople.

Better Sales Force Performance Evaluation

The sales manager can evaluate the performance of each salesperson in a better way, when the salesperson is assigned to a specific sales territory. Each sales territory's market potential can be estimated. Sales quotas (or sales goal) for each salesperson can be decided on the basis of the company's share of the market potential of the territory. With the use of computers, the actual sales performance can be measured on a weekly, monthly, quarterly and yearly basis, and the same can be compared with the respective sales goals of the salesperson. The performance evaluation of the salesperson assigned to a specific sales territory can be done not only with respect to sales, but also in terms of selling expenses, customer service, customer satisfaction levels, as the salesperson's responsibilities can be clearly defined.

Improved Customer Relationship

When the salesperson spends adequate time with the present and the potential customers to understand their problems (or needs) thoroughly and to find solutions to their problems or satisfy their needs, their relationships improve. The customer relationship is developed over a long period of interactions between the salesperson and the buyer. These interactions and regular visits are possible because each salesperson is assigned to a group of customers. Some salespeople develop collaborative or partnering relationships with a few high sales and profit potential customers, for mutual benefits of the buying and the selling firms. The selling firm becomes a sole or preferred supplier, as a result of a long-term, mutually beneficial relationship between the buying and the selling firm. The salesperson is the basic building block of such a partnering or collaborative relationship.

Increased Salespeople's Effectiveness

When the sales territory is properly designed, the salesperson's workload is reasonable and the conflicts are minimum as specific customers are assigned to them. A salesperson is responsible to maintain good relationship with specific customers. All these positive factors contribute to improve the salesperson's performance and effectiveness in terms of consistently achieving and exceeding the sales goals or quotas.

Improved Coordination

The company's sales performance improves substantially, if the salesperson is involved in coordinating the various elements of marketing communications (or promotion). For instance, distribution of sales promotion materials [like coupons, point-of-purchase (POP) displays, and samples] to retailers, ensuring adequate stocks of brands or products at retail stores before a major advertising campaign and training retailers' salespersons. Integrated Marketing Communications (IMC) concept can be effectively implemented by coordinating the promotional activities through the salespeople to the retailers and customers in various sales territories. Other activities like marketing research, telemarketing, and use of the Internet can also be carried out in the sales territories, which will help salespeople improve their performance.

Benefited Salespeople and Company

Proper territory design and effective allocation of salespeople to territories will result in improved sales force performance, which in turn benefits the company. When the company's sales revenue increases and the selling expenses are controlled, there is a marked improvement in the profits. Thus, the company is benefited due to improvement in the top-line (sales revenue) and the bottom-line (net profits). When the performance of salespeople improves, they are rewarded through good increments, incentives and in some cases, promotions. Due to the benefits received by the sales force as well as the company, the overall working environment improves.

REASONS FOR NOT SETTING-UP SALES TERRITORIES

In spite of earlier mentioned reasons or benefits of setting-up sales territories, there are certain situations when sales territories are not required. Some of the reasons for not setting up sales territories are: (i) a small company with one or few salesperson(s) selling in a local market may not need to set up sales territories, (ii) personal contacts or relationships is the basis for making the sales, such as life insurance policies and network marketing, (iii) the salespeople are not motivated due to restrictions of sales territories and (iv) the company management may not be aware of the advantages or benefits of developing sales territories or may not know how to set up sales territories. However, setting up sales territories and assigning salespeople effectively is the best way to manage a market.

LO 2 Describe the procedure for designing a sales territory

PROCEDURE FOR DESIGNING SALES TERRITORIES

The design of sales territories is very important to salespeople and the company management, as the performance on sales and profits is linked to the well-designed sales territories. The ideal objectives in territory design are to have equal opportunity (or sales potential) and equal salespeople workload for all sales territories. Typically, these objectives are difficult to achieve in practice, although sales managers do make great efforts to achieve the same. Any differences in the sales potential and the workload of salespeople in different territories, which remain at the end, can be taken care of when sales quotas or sales goals are set up for salespeople and sales territories. This will be discussed later in this chapter. Figure 4.1 shows the steps involved in designing the sales territories.

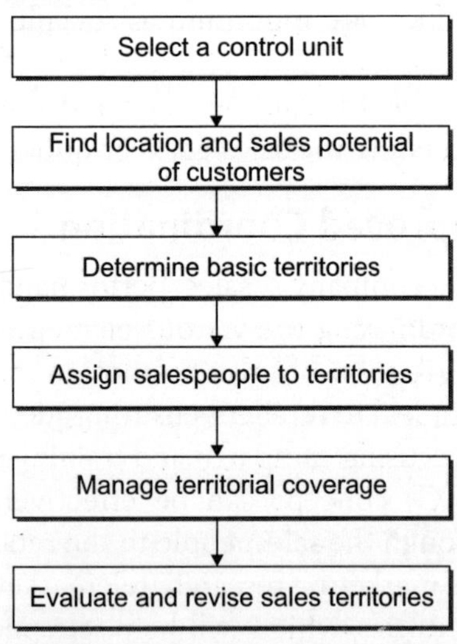

Fig. 4.1 Procedure for Designing Sales Territories

Select a Control Unit

The first step in territory design is to select a geographical territorial base, called 'control unit', that will be used in the territory analysis. Commonly used control units are states, metropolitan areas, cities, districts, towns and pin-code areas. In general, the sales manager should select the smallest control unit. There are two reasons for this: (i) the control units' market potential and the company's sales potential should be possible to calculate and (ii) adjustments (i.e. additions or deletions) of the control units should be possible when tentative territory boundaries are modified to make final territories. For example, if a company wants to delete one control unit (say, Hosur city) from Chennai territory and add it to Bengaluru territory, for minimizing the cost and time of contacting customers, it can be done if the control unit is small (such as city, town or district). Brief descriptions of the above mentioned control units, as applicable to Indian situations, are as follows:

- **States** A few companies may consider building their sales territories around states, by selecting the same as a geographical control unit. This is done if a company has a few salespeople for covering the entire national market with a selective distribution strategy. The states differ in terms of population, area, purchasing power and industrial development. The largest state, namely, Uttar Pradesh, has a population (as per 2011 Census) of 199 million and the smallest state, i.e. Sikkim, has a population of 0.6 million. Most companies would not consider the states as a control unit, because many states have large areas and adjustments of territories will be very difficult, for any specific reasons like minimization of time and cost of travelling of salespeople.

- **Metropolitan Clusters** These are also called 'metropolitan areas' with large populations in urban and suburban areas. They have a large number of households with high levels of buying incomes and retail sales. These are concentrated markets for many consumer and industrial products. The information on market forecast of metropolitan areas is also available[4]. According to McKinsey report of October 2014, 49 metropolitan clusters will account for about 77 percent of India's incremental GDP from 2012 to 2025[5]. However, metropolitan clusters/areas are too large for consideration of control units.

- **Cities/Town/Districts** The administrative set up varies from one country to another. In USA, cities and postal zip-code areas are used as control units. However, in India, the administrative set up consists of districts, tehsils/talukas, towns and villages. It is possible to get statistical market data for various products at town and district levels. But below the district level (tehsil/taluka and village), it is difficult to get statistical market data. Hence, in India, district, cities or towns can be used as a control unit. Socio-economic statistical data of 620 districts of India is available on the Internet based on Census of India, 2011.

Find Location and Sales Potential of Customers

The next step is to find the location and the sales potential (or business potential) of the present and prospective customers within each control unit. Location information of present customers should be available from the company's sales database. However, the information on prospective customers can be obtained not only from the company's salespeople, but also from outside sources like telephone directories and industry associations. For industrial products and services, where often there are a few buyers, identification of business (or B2B) customers is desirable and possible. However, for consumer products and services, it is unnecessary and expensive to carry out identification of final consumers.

After the present and potential customers are identified in business (or B2B) marketing, the company should estimate the total sales potential of all customers in each geographical control unit. For this, services of either a marketing research agency or the company's salespeople can be used. Each present and potential customer can be contacted with a questionnaire to obtain information about the requirements of the selling company's products and services at present and in future and also other information on competition, buying criteria, etc. Sales potential of each control unit is then estimated by summing up the sales potential of present and potential customers.

After the sales potential of control units are calculated, it is necessary to classify the customers based on their sales and/or profits potential. One of the commonly used methods is called ABC analysis. In this method, all the customers are entered in the reverse order of their sales potential, by first entering the name of the customer whose sales potential is the highest. Then the name of the customer with second highest sales potential is entered. This process is repeated till the names and sales potential figures of all the customers are entered. The total sales potential is calculated by adding the sales potential of all the customers. 'A' customers are those whose sales potential add up to 70 percent of the total sales potential. Next group of customers whose sales potential add up to 20 percent are classified as 'B' and the balance 10 percent sales potential is accounted as 'C' customers.

Determine Basic Territories

The third step in designing sales territories is to decide the basic or fundamental territories. This can be done by using either the build-up method or the breakdown method. The build-up method equalizes the workload of salespeople and is commonly used by the manufacturers of industrial products and services or by the companies that want selective distribution strategy. Breakdown method equalizes the sales potential of territories and is popularly used by manufacturers of consumer products and services or by firms that want to adopt intensive distribution strategy. We shall first discuss the build-up method and then the breakdown method.

Build-up Method

In this method, the basic territories are set up by building-up from the control units. The objective to be achieved is to equalize the workload of salespeople. The procedure followed is shown in Figure 4.2 and is explained as follows:

1. **Decide Call Frequencies:** It means how many times a customer should be visited by the company's salesperson per year. The factors that influence call frequency are the customer's sales and profits potential, cost of visiting the customer, buying behavior of the customer and the nature of the product or service offered. The optimum call

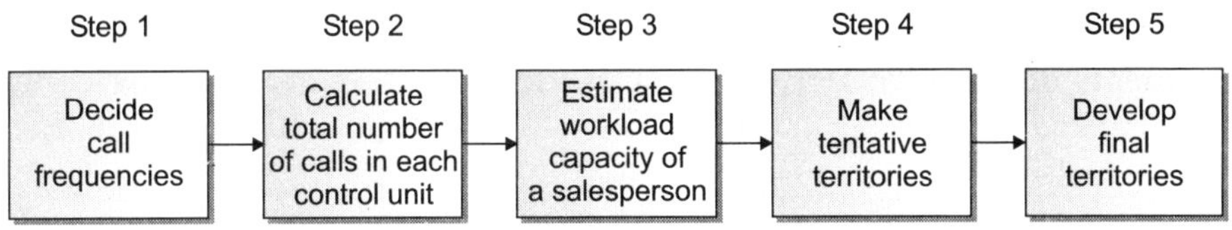

Fig. 4.2 **Build-up Method of Territorial Design**

frequencies, for different types of customers, can be decided by using computer software or by managerial judgment. Let us consider an example shown in Table 4.1. The call frequencies for type A customers, with high sales and profit potential, are four times a month and for B and C types of customers, with medium and low sales and profit potential respectively, the call frequencies are twice and once a month respectively.

2. **Calculate the total number of calls in each control unit:** In the example shown in Table 4.1, the total number of sales calls needed in districts X and Y, which are the control units, are 552 and 720 respectively. This is done by multiplying call frequency per month by number of customers and 12 months.

Table 4.1 **An Example of Call Frequency and Customer Visits**

Customer Type	Call Frequency per Month	District-X		District-Y	
		No. of Customers	No. of Calls per Year	No. of Customers	No. of Calls per Year
A	4	3	144	4	192
B	2	7	168	8	192
C	1	20	240	28	336
	Total	30	552	40	720

3. **Estimate workload capacity of a salesperson:** A salesperson's normal workload capacity is estimated by multiplying the average number of calls a salesperson can make in a working day by the number of working days in a year. For instance, the average number of calls a salesperson makes in a day works out to five, based on the average travel time of 30 minutes per call, the average length of one hour for each call and eight hours per day working. If the number of working days in a year (after accounting for leave and holidays) is 250, then the estimated workload capacity for the salesperson per year works out to be 1250 calls (250 × 5).

4. **Make the tentative territories:** In this step, the company should group (or gather) adjoining control units (which share their borders) until yearly number of calls needed in those control units equals the total number of calls a salesperson can make (i.e. workload of a salesperson). In example shown in Table 4.1, districts X and Y together need (552 + 720) 1272 visits (or calls) per year, which is almost equal to 1250 calls of normal workload of a salesperson.

5. **Develop the final territories:** In cases where workloads of salespersons are not equalized, adjustments of tentative territories are made by adding or removing certain control units. The objective is to achieve equalized workload for each salesperson. Before a sales manager finalizes the sales territory design, he should discuss with the salespeople, who are familiar with the customers and the territories. This may bring out certain logical changes, which need to be carried out before making the final sales territories.

Breakdown Method

As mentioned earlier, this is another method of territory design that is used by companies who have decided to have intensive distribution strategy, mostly for selling consumer products. The objective is to equalize the sales potential of territories. The procedure (or the steps followed) for implementing this method is shown in Figure 4.3.

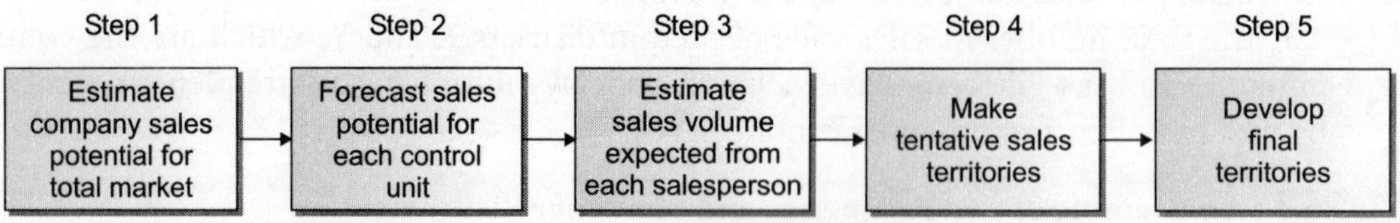

Fig. 4.3 Breakdown Method of Territorial Design

1. **Estimate the company sales potential for total market:** The first step in the procedure is to estimate the company sales potential (or the company sales forecast) for its total market by using the sales forecasting methods, discussed in Chapter 3.
2. **Forecast sales potential of each control unit:** In order to forecast or estimate the sales potential of each control unit, the sales manager multiplies the total sales potential of the company by a multiple factor index of each control unit. The concept of multiple factor index has been discussed earlier in Chapter 3. Thus, the total sales potential of the company is broken down to the individual control units.
3. **Estimate the sales volume expected from each salesperson:** Here the sales manager must estimate how much each salesperson must sell, in order to ensure profitable operation. For this, the sales manager studies the past sales as well as the cost and profitability analysis, as shown in the following example.

   Example: The direct selling cost of each salesperson for next year is estimated as ₹600,000. The cost of goods sold is estimated at 60 percent of sales and the expected profit contribution at 15 percent of sales. Then, the minimum sales expected from each salesperson is calculated as follows:

   Profit contribution = Sales – Cost of sales – Direct selling cost of each salesperson

   $$0.15x = x - 0.6x - 600{,}000$$

   where, x = minimum sales from each salesperson

   Solving the above equation, x = ₹24,00,000

   After accounting for the indirect costs and using his judgment, the sales manager decides the sales per salesperson to be little over twice the above sales figure, at ₹50,00,000 (or ₹5 million) per annum.

4. **Make tentative sales territories:** In this step, the sales manager makes tentative territories by combining adjoining control units (which share a border) until the sales potential of each territory is equal to or greater than the expected sales volume from each salesperson. Continuing with the example discussed above, the sales potential of each territory should be equal to or greater than ₹50,00,000 (or ₹5 million). Care should be taken to ensure that the boundaries of the each territory exist together with the borders of the control units.
5. **Develop final territories:** The tentative territories need to be adjusted due to special considerations such as geographical locations of customers or unequal sales potential of some territories. The adjustments are done by moving specific customers or control units from one territory to another territory. The objective is to achieve equal sales potential of territories.

Assign Salespeople to Territories

Once the sales territories are designed, the sales manager is ready to assign or allocate individual salespeople to each territory. In designing the sales territories, we assumed that the salespeople have equal selling abilities and that each salesperson would perform equally well in any territory. However, these assumptions are not realistic. The assumptions are used only for territorial design purpose, but cannot be accepted when salespeople are assigned to sales territories.

In a sales force, salespersons are not the same in their selling abilities and effectiveness. They vary in experience, selling skills, initiative, age and physical conditions. Sales performance may also be influenced by factors like social and cultural characteristics of the customers. Therefore, in assigning salespeople to territories, the sales manager should consider two criteria: (i) relative ability of salespeople, and (ii) salesperson's effectiveness in a territory.

❍ **Relative Ability of Salespeople** A sales manager should evaluate the relative abilities of salespeople based on key factors, such as product and market knowledge, past performance in achieving sales quotas (or goals), ability in verbal and written communications and selling skills. By either giving different weights, depending on importance, the sales manager evaluates each salesperson on relative ability and decides an ability index with maximum score of 1 for weights and 10 for evaluation, as shown in Table 4.2. The relative abilities of salespeople are then linked to sales potentials of various territories.

Table 4.2 Evaluation of Relative Ability of a Salesperson

Evaluation Factors	Weights (A)	Evaluation (B)	Salesperson's Ability Index Score: (A) × (B)
Product knowledge	0.15	9.0	1.35
Market knowledge	0.10	8.0	0.80
Past sales performance	0.40	10.0	4.00
Communication skills	0.15	8.0	1.20
Selling skills	0.20	9.0	1.80
	1.00		9.15

It should be understood that the weights (i.e. importance) of the evaluation factors may vary from company to company and the evaluation factors may also differ, depending upon the product and customer characteristics. In the example shown in Table 4.2, the "ability index" of the salesperson is 9.15. Similarly, the ability index of other salespersons should be worked out, keeping in mind that the salespersons' scores are based on relative evaluations and not absolute evaluations.

❍ **Salesperson's Effectiveness in a Territory** The sales manager should judge the effectiveness of a salesperson by comparing the salesperson's social, cultural and physical characteristics with those of the territory[6]. For instance, the salesperson who was born and brought up in urban environment of Mumbai or Delhi will find it very difficult to deal with customers from rural territory. It would also help if the salesperson is familiar with the local language and customs of the territory. The objective of the sales manager in matching salespeople to territories is to maximize the sales and profit potential of territories. This objective is achieved by making the salesperson comfortable with the customers in the territory and the customers comfortable with the salesperson. Thus, the decision on assigning salespeople to territories should also be based on salesperson's considerations. The salesperson's considerations include personal relationship between salespeople and customers. The existing excellent relationships between the salesperson and customers should not be disturbed by the sales manager while carrying out the task of assigning or deploying salespeople to territories.

Manage Territorial Coverage

After designing sales territories and assigning salespeople to different sales territories, the next task of the sales manager is the management of territorial coverage or in other words, how each salesperson should cover the assigned sales territory. This task consists of three activities: (i) planning of efficient routes for salespeople, (ii) scheduling the salespeople's time, and (iii) using time management tools.

Planning of Efficient Routes for Salespeople

Planning of efficient routes for salespeople is a managerial activity. Often sales managers initially train salespeople in route planning and subsequently ask them to prepare their own route plans. Routing is a travel plan or pattern used by a salesperson for making customer calls in a territory. Studies indicate that left to their own routing method, salespeople spend one-third of their daily working hours travelling. Thus, most salespeople are unable to plan efficient routes.

The main advantages of routing are: (i) reduction in travel time and cost by excluding backtracking and criss-crossing by salespeople in their territory, (ii) improvement in territory coverage, as salespeople reduce their travel time and increase selling time.

There are, however, certain objections to routing. Some sales managers are of the opinion that routing reduces salespeople's flexibility and initiative, particularly when customers' needs change and market conditions vary. This objection can be overcome by using computers for updating the route plans.

❍ **Procedure for Setting up a Routing Plan** The first step in setting up a routing plan is to identify the present and prospective customers on a territory map. Next, each customer should be classified into high, medium or low sales potential and call frequency for each class of customer to be decided. For instance, high potential customers are to be visited four times a month, medium potential customers twice a month, and low potential customers once a month. The route plan should be built around locations of high potential customers. Generally, medium and low potential customers will fall into place near high potential customers, with a few exceptions. Prospective customers should be allowed some time. Some of the commonly used routing patterns are shown in Figure 4.4.

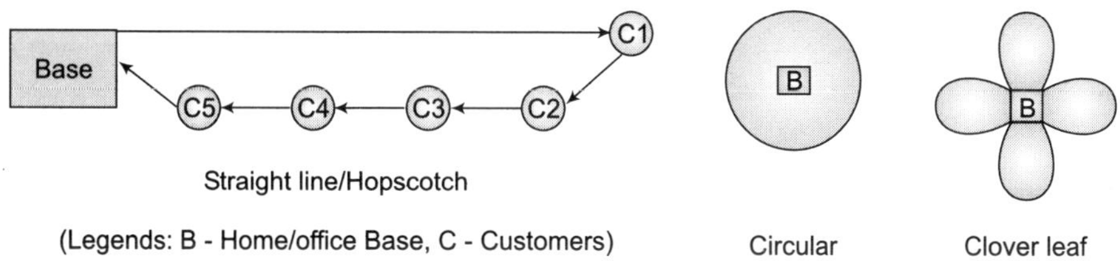

Fig. 4.4 Common Routing Patterns

In straight line route pattern, the salesperson starts from office or home base and makes sales calls in one direction. This can be combined with hopscotch pattern, in which the salesperson starts early and drives to the farthest point from home or office base before making the first call. Thereafter, he makes sales calls on customers on the way back to home/office. This process is repeated in different directions so that the salesperson starts from office/home in the morning and returns in the evening. The important factor to remember is the travel time, which should be minimized. In circular route pattern, the salesperson starts from his base and moves in a circle, making sales calls, ending back at the office/home. In clover leaf pattern, the first route covers a part of the territory, the next trip of the salesperson covers the adjoining circle and this is continued until the entire territory is covered.

Computerized mathematical models have been developed to help the sales manager decide the route that will minimize the travel cost or maximize the selling time[7].

❍ **Application and Importance of Routing** The degree of importance to the application of routing depends on two factors: (i) the nature of the product and (ii) the type of the job of salespeople. For example, for Fast Moving Consumer Goods (FMCGs) like soft drinks, bread and grocery products, which are sold to retailers, there is a need for frequent servicing and therefore, a route plan is absolutely necessary. Similarly, driver-cum-salesperson type of jobs should have proper route plans, since if the calls are not made regularly, the company can lose important retailers. However, the sales jobs with creative selling to find solutions to difficult problems such as inventory control and superior customer service may need a flexible route plan. In general, application of routing is important for all companies, but for some companies one should be flexible in its implementation[9].

Scheduling the Salespersons' Time

Scheduling is planning a salesperson's specific time of visits to customers. Scheduling the salesperson's time should be considered as the time allocation problem. Studies have shown that the best salespersons are those who manage their time effectively.

❍ **Allocation of Time** The sales manager must first decide and communicate the major activities or duties of the salesperson and the amount of time that should be allocated to each activity. Although the activities or tasks vary from company to company, generally these are classified into the following areas, along with the time spent, as shown in Table 4.3[10].

Table 4.3 How Salespeople Spend Their Time

Salespeople's Tasks	Time Spent (percentage)
Administrative tasks	15
Service calls	13
Face-to-face selling	32
Waiting/Travelling	21
Telephone selling	19
Total	100

It is interesting to note that 19 percent time is spent by a salesperson on the telephone. Many companies are using telephone selling in order to reduce the cost of selling. The tool that is used widely to help the salesperson to understand how they spend their time is called "time and activity analysis". The salesperson records the time spent on various activities over a period of two weeks. The sales manager and the salesperson then discuss and decide how to increase the time spent on major activities like face-to-face and telephone selling.

❍ **Customer Calls** Companies often communicate the norms of visits to existing customers and prospects to their salespeople. This is done because, if left to their own wish, many salespeople will spend most of the time with the present customers, who are known to them. However, the company wants business from new customers also. For instance, CG Power and Industrial Solutions Limited asked its sales engineers to spend 80 percent of their time with the present customers and 20 percent of their time with prospects, with a guideline that they should stop visiting the prospect after four unsuccessful calls.

A study has found that some salespeople spend too much time selling to small and less profitable present customers, when they should be putting more efforts on selling to large and more profitable customers[11]. Companies, therefore, specify call norms for existing customers, depending upon their sales and profit potentials. A real-life example of a regional sales manager, who was transferred from western region to eastern region in India, is worth mentioning here. The sales were stagnant in eastern region and one of the decisions taken by the regional sales manager was to ask the salespeople to find sales potential of the existing business customers for the company's products and then to make four sales calls a month to high sales potential customers, two calls a month to medium sales potential customers and only one call a month to low sales potential customers. He also guided the salespeople on route plans. The sales of eastern region jumped up substantially for four successive years, due to a number of decisions taken by the regional sales manager on territory coverage, motivational issues and training of salespeople.

Time Management Tools for Salespeople

There are many supports available to help salespeople manage their time more efficiently and productively. These are: (i) use of computers, mobile communication equipment and other high-tech equipment and (ii) inside salespeople.

❍ **High-Tech Equipment** Desktop and laptop PCs, CDs, automatic dialers, e-mails, fax machines, telephonic-conferences, videophones and smart phones are the time management tools that are available to salespersons and sales managers.

In particular, in some companies salespeople have laptop computers that they carry as they travel around their territories. The main objective of having high-tech equipment is to help salespeople make more efficient use of their time. Salespeople use their laptop computers to enter and transmit their visit reports and customer orders, get information on inventory and delivery status, access a customer's file to get up-to-date information before making the sales call, exchange messages with customers and sales managers, and make sales presentations to customers.

❍ **Inside Salespeople** To reduce time demands on their outside salespeople, many companies are increasingly using inside salespeople, who remain within the organization[12]. There are three types of inside salespeople: (i) sales assistants to provide clerical support for the outside salespersons, such as delivery follow-up with production, confirmation of customer appointments, responding to customers' questions and so on; (ii) technical support people to give technical information and respond to customers' technical questions; and (iii) telemarketers to find new sales leads, qualify them and refer high and medium sales potential prospects to outside salespersons and low potential prospects to the company's intermediaries. Outside salespeople, who travel outside the company, are then free to spend more time selling to the existing key customers, getting orders from prospects and building long-term relationships with key customers.

Time Management Tools for Sales Managers

The same high-tech equipment, such as laptop computers, smartphones and others (as stated above for salespeople) are available to sales managers to help make more efficient use of their time. Most sales managers use e-mails to communicate with their salespeople.

Computerized support systems like CRM (Customer Relationship Management) and ERP (Enterprise Resource Planning) are used by many companies for effective use of management resources including time and to improve the efficiency of an enterprise. The direct benefits of an ERP system are: (i) business integration, (ii) flexibility and (iii) better analysis and planning capabilities. Although ERP software packages are designed for various areas of business performance improvements such as finance, manufacturing, inventory reduction and so on, we shall consider a few examples related to sales and marketing.

> Coverking Company, a manufacturer and distributor of customized automotive accessories, wanted to achieve a growth rate of 30 percent. However, it had a problem that most of its over 500,000 orders for customized car covers, floor mats and other accessories were received by phone, due to which there was a delay in order entry. The company wanted to reduce the time it spent on order entry, without compromising on customer service. The solution to the problem was found in ERP package of Bann IV, along with other Microsoft software programs, operating systems and databases. Customers could enter orders from any computer equipped with web browser and check inventory via the Internet. The system provided customers a comprehensive menu of order options. Users could select a product, fabric, color, etc., to place a customized order in a fraction of time required for a phone order. Apart from a remote order entry solution, the ERP system reduced the turnaround time for manufacturing customized products by 25 percent. Overall the company had a saving of about $200,000 annually.

> Another example is about the problem of manual billing process and resulting delays and errors, faced by Alcone Company, which also wanted to provide greater information access to its staff. The company decided on ERP system from PeopleSoft Select, with operating system and database from Microsoft, to solve the problem. After implementation, the billing process was automated, resulting in increased billing, improved efficiency and tremendous savings in time and effort. The ERP system paid for itself within two years.

Increasing number of companies are using CRM (Customer Relationship Management) software to integrate sales, marketing and customer service functions and to give all customer interacting persons and departments access to share customer data in real time. Many banks were the first ones to use CRM systems.

In addition to using high-tech equipment and support systems, sales managers should also practice a few simple rules for effective time management which are as follows:

- Make plans—for each day and each week.
- Make or take phone calls twice—before lunch and at the end of the day. Learn to be brief.
- Read and reply e-mails/fax messages once or twice in a day.
- Interruptions from the boss and customers have to be responded. Unnecessary interruptions from others need to be minimized by politely saying "no".
- Prioritize the activities/tasks in terms of importance and urgency, based on ABC analysis of activities.
- Concentrate efforts on major (or 'A' type of) activities/tasks during prime hours when we work most effectively.
- Learn to delegate routine and less important tasks or activities to others.

We all, including the sales force and sales managers, have one thing in common—a 24-hour day. It is how we use our time that makes the difference.

Evaluate and Revise Sales Territories

Evaluation of sales territories is done by first setting up qualitative and quantitative goals, performance standards or quotas. For example, monthly, quarterly and yearly sales goals, number of calls to be made to 'A', 'B' and 'C' type of customers located in each sales territory and customer service or customer satisfaction index or rating are some of the goals for salespeople. The second step in the evaluation process is the measurement of the actual performance of the salesperson assigned to the sales territory. The information on the actual performance of each territory is furnished routinely to sales managers and salespersons through the computers by many companies. The third step is to compare the actual performance with the goals or the performance standards for each territory on monthly, quarterly and yearly basis. If the goals are met, the field sales manager appreciates the salesperson and recommends him for appropriate increments or rewards. However, if some or all the goals are not achieved, corrective actions, including new action plans, are discussed by the sales manager with the sales person. These action plans are developed for the sales territory and the same are implemented by the salesperson.

Revising Sales Territories

Studies have found that more than half (55 percent) of all sales territories need to be revised or realigned because they are either very large or very small[13]. It is, therefore, necessary that sales managers review their sales territories periodically — at least once a year. However, care should be taken by sales managers to make sure that poor performance of sales territories is due to incorrect territory design or alignment and not due to other reasons, such as ineffective supervision, incorrect incentive scheme and compensation plan.

A question that is frequently asked is: "How to know that the existing territories need revision?" Some of the answers to this question are:

1. Sometimes, the selling time and activities change substantially. For instance, a material handling company found that their customers started demanding customized equipment, instead of standard equipment. The company's sales engineers had to spend more time to understand clearly the needs of the customers and to give pre-sales service. These additional activities resulted in the company's sales engineers requiring more time to get orders. Hence, the company made the territories smaller and recruited new sales engineers giving each salesperson more time to sell.

2. In many companies, the sales territories are overlapping, resulting in inefficiencies and higher costs. This situation should be corrected by revising the territories.

3. When the sales potential of a territory grows faster than expected, the salesperson assigned to this territory exceeds his sales goals substantially without covering the territory adequately. The salesperson may get high incentives and appreciation from the company's management. However, the company is losing its market share to the competitors. In this situation, there is a need to measure the sales potential of different territories and revise the sales territories by equalizing the sales potential or the workload of salespersons.

Another question that comes to mind is: "Why in many companies the sales territories are not balanced?" There are two main reasons for this situation. First, the company's management asks the first level sales managers, viz. area/branch/district sales managers to design or revise the sales territories that are located within their respective branches. Generally, these sales managers are very busy with other tasks and hence, they do not spend adequate time and efforts in designing their sales territories. The second reason is that many sales managers are not aware of the basic concepts of equalizing sales potential of sales territories and equalizing workload of salespersons. They also do not know that their sales performance can go up substantially, if their sales territories are balanced with equalized sales potential or equalized workload of salespeople.

For revising the sales territories, sales managers can follow the same procedure as shown in Figure 4.1 for designing sales territories. Companies should periodically evaluate and revise their sales territories in order to respond effectively to the changing market conditions.

LO 3 Utilize the knowledge of Information Technology (IT) for designing sales territories

USE OF INFORMATION TECHNOLOGY FOR DESIGNING SALES TERRITORIES[14]

Instead of using the earlier described build-up or break-down methods, Information Technology (IT) is used to determine sales territories. IT firms have developed a software, called "geographic information system (GIS)".

GIS[14] is not only quicker but also deals with all aspects of design of sales territories. The output of the software depends upon the data that is put into the computer. The data includes the satellite images or aerial photographs of the territories, customer locations, frequency of sales calls, sales potential of control units and so on. The GIS output is presented in an easy-to-understand graphic or map form.

The hardware required for the GIS system includes a standard laptop or desktop computer working on a Windows operating system and a color printer of good quality. A person operating GIS system must be properly trained. For example, a company which is in the business of renting cars, uses a GIS software to review and revise many of its sales territories. The performance of the company's salespersons improved substantially in terms of achievement of sales goals and productivity as a result of using the software, instead of the earlier method of manually plotting and analyzing sales territories.

Global Positioning System (GPS)[15]

This gadget communicates with satellites to find the exact position and give direction to clearly identified geographical locations. By only entering the address of a prospective customer, a sales person is supplied with directions on how to reach there. This direction also includes which highway to drive on and the fastest route around unexpected road construction. GPS devices are particularly useful for salespersons who travel on unfamiliar and large sales territories. Also, sales managers can use GPS gadgets to follow the movement of their salespersons. This can help to find if salespersons are covering their sales territories efficiently. The prices and features of GPS devices vary greatly. The complete navigation system with automated computer voice is available at the high price.

LO 4 Discuss sales quotas and their importance

SALES QUOTAS

In the previous chapter, we discussed the sales forecast and the sales budget. The next logical step for a company is to set up the sales goals or sales quotas, for marketing (or sales) units, such as regions, sales territories, salespersons, distributors and dealers. We shall now discuss the various parts of sales quotas, which are often tied to sales force motivation and compensation.

What are Sales Quotas?

Sales quotas are sales goals (or performance standards) set by a company for its marketing units for a certain period of time. The marketing unit includes a sales region, a sales territory, a branch office, a salesperson, a distributor or a dealer. Sales quotas (also called quotas) can be set on sales volume (rupees or dollar sales, and unit volume), selling expense, profit margin, selling and non-selling activities, customer satisfaction or some combination. For example, each salesperson is given a sales volume goal and a selling expense budget as a sales quota for the year 2016–17. Annual sales quotas for each marketing unit are broken down to quarterly and monthly quotas.

Sales quotas are developed from the annual marketing plan of the company. After preparing the sales forecast, the company decides its annual sales budget, which includes the company's goals for sales volume and selling expenses. The company sales budget is then broken down to sales quotas for regions, branches and sales territories. Thereafter, each branch or area sales manager decides for his territory's quota for the salesperson, distributors and dealers, who are attached to the territory. How a branch or area sales manager sets the sales quotas for the marketing units reporting to him, will be discussed subsequently in this chapter.

IMPORTANCE/PURPOSES OF SALES QUOTAS

Importance, purposes or objectives of sales quotas are: (i) providing performance standards, (ii) controlling performance, (iii) motivating people, and (iv) identifying strengths and weaknesses.

Providing Performance Standards

A sales quota provides to the sales manager a tool to measure the performance of the salesperson. A quota also provides a goal (or a target) to the salesperson. Hence, a quota is a performance standard, against which the actual performance is compared to understand whether the salesperson is performing well or not. Even salespersons cannot be sure about their performance being satisfactory, without measurement of actual performance against standards like sales quotas. For example, a branch manager of a consumer durable marketing company sets sales quotas for his salespersons in terms of sales volume and selling expenses per annum. The yearly quota is further broken down to quarterly and monthly quotas for each salesperson. The branch manager uses these quotas as performance standards for each salesperson and measures the actual performance to compare with the quotas on monthly, quarterly and yearly basis. A study has found that 92 percent of the companies use quotas as a performance standard for salespeople[16].

Controlling Performance

By setting quotas for salespersons' selling and non-selling activities, sales volume, and selling expenses, the sales manager is controlling the performance of salespeople. For instance, when an activity quota of eight calls per day on retail units or four calls per day on business customers is set, the salespeople know that they have to make those many number of calls. The sales manager is indirectly monitoring or controlling the activities of salespeople by setting quotas. Similarly, to check wasteful expenditure on customer entertainment, lodging and meals, expense quotas are set as a percentage of sales. For example, in one company, expense quota for selling expenses (which included travelling, customer entertainment, lodging and meals) was 0.5 percent of sales. The company reimbursed sales expenses only up to 0.5 percent of sales. This helped to limit the selling expenses. The sales manager has the power to influence and direct the behavior of salespeople reporting to him. By setting quotas on sales volume, the sales manager directs the efforts or activities of salespeople towards the achievement of performance on sales. For example, a company wanted its salespeople to spend more time with customers, so the sales manager sets a quota of five calls a day for each sales person[17].

If the actual performance of the salesperson is favorable in comparison to the quota, the sales manager should appreciate and reward the salesperson suitably. However, if the salesperson's performance is unfavorable consistently over a period of time, the sales manager should find out the reasons for the poor performance by talking to the salesperson and the customers and reviewing the sales analysis and the sales reports of the salesperson. Only after understanding the reasons or causes of the poor performance, corrective actions, such as training in deficient areas, counseling the salesperson or reviewing marketing strategies can be carried out by the sales manager. This is how the sales manager controls the performance of the salespeople.

Motivating People

Most salespeople are motivated by money[18]. Quotas directly influence salespeople's motivational levels and amount of energy[19]. Sales force compensation is often tied to the extent or degree of achievement of sales quotas. The financial compensation includes salaries, commissions and/or bonuses (which are also called incentives). The incentives, in most companies, are linked to the quotas. If salespeople believe that the quotas are achievable, they will put extra efforts to achieve the quotas and earn the rewards of incentive payments or recognition. Motivation of the salespeople is also linked to the setting of quotas. Sales managers should not set sales quotas that are too high and non-attainable. At the same time, they should not set easily attainable quotas. In both these situations, motivation of salespeople declines.

Sales contests are the additional motivating factors for special selling efforts of salespersons. The performance during the period of the sales contest is linked to quotas set for individual salespersons. Typically, special quotas are set for sales contests in order to create enthusiasm among salespeople, resulting in superior performance. The incentives or rewards for achieving special quotas during the sales contests are also attractive, in terms of winning trips abroad, e.g. Australia, Singapore, Malaysia, Thailand or Sri Lanka. Sales contests motivate average salespersons to turn in above average performances.

Identifying Strengths and Weaknesses

When the actual sales performance is compared with the respective quotas of different territories and salespersons, the sales manager can identify successful and unsuccessful performers. Further, analysis of causes of poor performance of some sales territories may reveal that the salespersons have not put in adequate efforts, the sales quotas were not set correctly or the supervision by area sales managers was not good. This analysis helps identify weaknesses as well as strengths of the company in comparison to its competitors. Talking to customers helps in the analysis because the customers' perceptions are important in understanding the reasons for the company's strengths and weaknesses. Sales managers should, therefore, not only review the actual performance of salespeople with their quotas on regular basis, but also talk to the key customers formally as well as informally.

LO 5 Explain the types of sales quotas and methods for setting sales quotas

TYPES OF SALES QUOTAS

Companies set many types of quotas. The most common types of quotas are: (i) sales volume, (ii) gross margin or profit contribution, (iii) expenses, (iv) activities, and (v) combination.

Sales Volume Quotas

The sales volume quota is the most widely used type of sales quota because it is simple to understand and calculate. Most companies set sales volume quotas for individual salespersons, distributors, retailers, geographical areas or product lines, for a specific period of time. For effective control, it is proper to set sales volume quotas for the smaller selling unit. For instance, instead of setting quotas for regions (such as North, East, West and South), it is better to set quotas for branches or districts within a region. Similar approach is used for setting sales volume quotas for products for specific time periods. For example, the management can achieve better direction and control by setting quotas for individual product items and brands, instead of setting it for entire product lines. Similarly, annual sales volume quotas are broken down to quarterly and monthly quotas. Generally, companies establish sales quotas for all those items for which they make a sales budget. Companies set sales volume quotas in rupees or dollars sales volume, unit sales volume, and/or point sales volume.

❍ **Rupees/Dollars Sales Volume Quotas** When salespeople are required to sell many products, it is easier to manage if quotas are set in rupees or dollars rather than in units of product. For instance, in Crompton Greaves when the organization structure was changed from product division to customer segment orientation, the salespersons handling business customers were required to sell all 31 products of the company and their sales targets or quotas were expressed in rupees lakhs (or millions) per year, which were further broken down to quarterly and monthly quotas. Another reason for using rupees sales volume quotas is that it allows an analysis of selling expenses to sales, expressed in percentages or ratios.

❍ **Unit Sales Volume Quotas** Companies set sales volume quotas in units (numbers, tons or liters) of products in three different situations. One situation is when salespeople are selling a few products. For example, a company, which markets only two products, viz. ERW and CEW precision steel tubes to business customers, has set sales quotas for branch managers and salespersons in rupees as well as in metric tons (MTs). The second situation is when prices of the product fluctuate rapidly, resulting in salespeople achieving the rupee sales quotas easily due to increase in prices. The third situation is when the price of each product or service is very high and it is easy to understand unit sales quotas. For instance, a company, manufacturing power transformers, sets sales volume quotas in numbers for its regions and sales engineers, because the average price of each power transformer is ₹20 million.

❍ **Point Sales Volume Quotas** Some companies use sales volume quotas that are conveyed in 'points'. It is used in a situation when the company wants to improve its profitability, by asking salespeople to sell more those products that relatively contribute more to the profits. For example, a company had two products, product A's contribution to profit was two times that of product B. In order to improve the profitability, the company sets sales volume quotas in points, by assigning two points for each metric ton sales of product A and one point for each metric ton sales of product B. Salespeople could achieve their sales quotas in points easily by selling product A more than product B. This also helped the company to achieve its profitability goal.

Sales volume alone does not show the effectiveness and productivity of a sales person. It does not point out the selling expenses, profit contribution and important non-selling activities of the salesperson. Hence, the sales managers use other types of quotas, goals or targets. Companies set goals or quotas to control gross margin or profit contribution and expenses of various marketing (or sales) units, such as districts, branches, regions, salespeople and products.

Gross-Margin or Profit Contribution Quotas

Gross margin quota is decided by subtracting 'cost of goods sold' from sales volume. The cost of goods sold information is given by the company's manufacturing department, which tells how much it costs to manufacture the product. The problem of gross margin quota is that sales managers and salespersons have no control on the cost of manufacturing and hence, they are not responsible for gross margins. Some companies, therefore, decide profit contribution quotas by subtracting the cost of goods sold and the salespeople's direct selling expenses from the sales volume as shown in Table 4.4. Direct selling expenses of salespeople include apart from their salaries, travelling, lodging, boarding and customer entertainment. The problem of profit contribution quotas is that some salesperson may reduce necessary expenses like travelling, which may have a negative effective on sales. This can be seen in the case of the salesperson, Sunil, as shown in an example of Ludhiana branch in Table 4.4. However, profit contribution as a percent of sales is more in case of Sunil as compared with other two salespersons. Companies use profit contribution quotas to convey to field sales managers and salespeople that profits are more important than sales volume and that they should focus on profitable sales.

Table 4.4 An Example of Profit Contribution Comparison of Salespersons

	Salesperson-Ashok	Salesperson-Sunil	Salesperson-Mahindra	Total Ludhiana Branch
Sales (₹)	4,10,08,000	3,85,15,000	4,60,07,000	12,55,30,000
Cost of Sales (₹)	3,07,56,000	2,88,86,250	3,45,05,250	9,41,47,500
Gross Margin (75%) (₹)	1,02,52,000	96,28,750	1,15,01,750	3,13,82,500
Salary (₹)	1,24,000	1,15,000	1,40,000	3,79,000
Direct Selling Expenses (₹)	3,90,000	3,10,000	4,70,000	11,70,000
Total Selling Expenses (₹)	5,14,000	4,25,000	6,10,000	15,49,000
Profit Contribution (₹)	97,38,000	92,03,750	1,08,91,750	2,98,33,500
Profit Contribution/Sales (%)	23.7	23.9	23.6	23.7

Expense Quotas

Companies are trying to control rapidly increasing costs of selling, such as travelling, lodging and food. The objective of setting expense quotas is to control the costs of marketing (or sales) units, such as sales territories and salespeople. Often expense quotas are used along with sales volume quotas, so that selling expenses are kept in line with sales volume. Therefore, expense quotas are stated as percentages of sales, so that salespeople give attention both to sales volume and the costs of achieving it. In some companies, other or direct selling expenses such as travelling, lodging, food and customer entertainment have a quota of 2 percent of sales.

Such a uniform setting of expense quota as a percentage of sales has a problem as there are variations in territories in terms of degree of concentration of customers, resulting in variations in travelling, lodging and boarding expenses of salespersons. There are also differences in product mixes required by customers as well as market potential and abilities of salespersons. It is, therefore, advisable to administer the expense quotas intelligently and with flexibility. Sales managers should convey to salespeople that expense quotas are meant to make them cost conscious, allowing all reasonable expenditures and not allowing anyone to make money dishonestly.

Activity Quotas

Many companies set activity quotas so as to direct salespeople to carry out important job related activities. These activities are useful for achieving performance goals or targets of salespeople. The process of deciding activity quotas includes: (i) defining the important activities, (ii) finding out the time required for carrying out these activities, (iii) deciding the priorities to be given among the various activities, and (iv) deciding the quotas or frequency for important activities. Table 4.5 shows an example of how a company selling lighting products to household and business customers determines activity quotas for its salespersons.

Table 4.5 Activity Quotas for a Lighting Products Company

Activities of a Salesperson	Time Required	Priority (Importance)	Quotas (Frequency)
*Calling on present business customers classified into A, B, C	For A = 60 minutes B = 30 minutes C = 15/20 minutes	1 4 8	4 calls per month 2 calls per month 1 call per month
*Calling on 'hot' prospects	30–60 minutes	3	5 calls in two month
*Calling on retailers	20–30 minutes	2	Avg. 2 calls per month
*Payment collection from payment overdue customers	15 minutes	5	Avg. 1 call per month
*Obtaining and reporting market information	*Info. Gathering: 10 minutes per customer *Reporting = 30 minutes each week	6 7	During sales calls 4 times a month

It should be understood that activity quotas are set when salespeople not only have to carry out selling activities, but also important non-selling activities. Some of the important non-selling activities are payment collection from customers, getting and reporting market information. One problem faced by sales managers is how to ensure salespeople perform their activities effectively. To solve this problem, the method used is to combine activity quotas with sales volume and expense quotas which leads us to combination quotas.

Combination Quotas

Companies set combination quotas or goals when they want to control sales force performance on both key selling and non-selling activities. Combination quotas typically use 'points' as a common measure to overcome the problem of different measures used by various quotas discussed earlier. Because performances against combination quotas are computed as percentages, these quotas are known as point systems. Here the points are the percentage points. Table 4.6 illustrates how points system is used in combination quotas.

Table 4.6 **Evaluation of salespeople with combination quotas**

Type of Quota	Quota	Actual	Percent Quota	Weight	% Quota × Weight
	For Salesperson: Srinivas				
Sales Volume (₹)	4,50,000,00	4,27,50,000	95	3	285
Selling Expenses (₹)	4,50,000	4,95,000	90	1	90
New Customers (Nos)	24	29	120	2	240
				6	615
	Total Point Score = $\frac{615}{6}$ **= 102.5**				
	For Salesperson: Pradeep				
Sales Volume (₹)	4,25,000,00	4,46,25,000	105	3	315
Selling Expenses (₹)	4,25,000	4,46,250	95	1	95
New Customers (Nos)	30	24	80	2	160
				6	570
	Total Point Score = $\frac{570}{6}$ **= 95**				

In Table 4.6, the selling expense quota is one percent of sales volume quota. Although Pradeep exceeded his sales volume quota, because he could not develop new customers to the extent of the quota, his total point score was less than 100. In case of Srinivas, the total point score exceeded 100, although he achieved 95 percent of sales volume quota. This makes combination quotas difficult for salespeople to understand. To overcome this problem, actual performance should be continuously monitored and discussed with salespersons with respect to the quotas and with the help of personal computers. The sales manager should also supervise on regular basis to ensure that some smart salespersons do not try to beat the system in any ways.

Another application of the combination quotas is to evaluate salespeople's performance in selling various products of the company. The company decides weights for various products based on profitability of each product. Each salesperson has a sales volume quota for each product. Similar process, as shown in Table 4.6, is followed to calculate the performance of each salesperson by calculating the total point score.

Sales managers should not use too many types of quotas or too many products in the combination quotas system, because it will confuse the salespeople. The focus should be on a few items of quotas or products that are important to the company.

METHODS FOR SETTING SALES VOLUME QUOTAS

Sales volume quotas or other types of quotas are set by companies by using several methods. The quotas are set based on: (i) territorial sales potential, (ii) past sales experience, (iii) total market estimates, (iv) executive judgment, (v) salespeople's estimates and (vi) compensation plan.

Territorial Sales Potential

This method is commonly used by large firms for setting sales quotas. The procedure used includes first estimating the market potential (or industry sales forecast) for a product line for a geographical area, using sales forecasting methods discussed earlier in Chapter 3. The second step is to estimate the multiple factor index, as explained earlier in Chapter 3, for each sales territory or geographical area. Next, the expected industry sales in each territory (also called 'territorial sales potential') is obtained by multiplying the industry sales forecast by multiple factor index. Finally, the company's estimated market share in the territory is considered out of the territory market potential in order to come up with sales volume quota for the territory. For example, estimated market potential (or industry sales forecast) for skin care products in India is ₹13.50 billion. The multiple factor index, using population and buying power, of Mumbai is estimated at 1.5. Then expected industry sales for skincare products in Mumbai is ₹202.5 million (13.50b × 0.015). Further considering the company's estimated market share of 20 percent, the sales volume quota for Mumbai's salespersons would be ₹40.50 million (202.5 × 0.20).

Past Sales Experience

Some companies consider past sales only for setting sales volume quotas. They take the past year's sales for each geographical sales territory, add an arbitrary percentage and decide the figures as sales volume quotas. Another alternative method is to take an average of previous three or five years' sales of each territory, add a percentage by which the market is expected to grow and thus, set sales quota for each territory. This method is better than the earlier method, because it considers the importance of the sales trend. The advantages in this method are that quota setting calculations are simple and costs of administration are low. However, there are several disadvantages.

Companies that use this method only for setting sales quotas assume that future sales are related to past sales. This assumption may not always be correct. Besides, if past sales were achieved by poor market coverage, the past mistakes will be carried on in future without any correction. Also, it ignores changes in sales potential of territories. Hence, companies should not consider past sales as the only method for deciding the territory sales quotas. It should be considered as one of the many methods for determining sales quotas.

Total Market Estimates

This method is used by small- and medium-size firms who do not have data, money and people to determine sales potential for individual sales territories. Such companies set quotas for sales territories based on the following year's total market estimates (also called market potential or industry sales forecast) as described in Chapter 3. They then decide the company's estimated market share for the following year from the total market estimate to arrive at the company sales forecast. The next step is to find out each territory's percentage share of the total company sales in the previous year. For instance, if a territory's past year's sales were seven percent of the total company sales, then the territory's sales quota would be seven percent of the total company sales forecast for the next year.

However, if the company is new and there is no information on past sales, the management first determines the market potential (or total market estimate) for its product. The company then estimates what portion (or share) of the market it could achieve in the first year. Thus, the company sales forecast is calculated by multiplying market potential by estimated market share. Thereafter, the company sales forecast (or sales budget) is broken-down to individual territories by multiplying it with multiple factor index for each territory. This procedure is used by new companies for setting sales volume quotas for its newly established territories.

Executive Judgment

Sometimes companies use executive judgment method only for deciding sales volume quotas, when the company is new, the product and territories are new or very little market information is available. In these situations, senior executives or managers use their judgment, based on their past experience to predict not only the company sales, but also sales quotas for territories. However, the quality of the judgment may not be good without any reference to quantitative market information, such as sales potential, population and market share. For instance, managing director of a material handling company asked its newly appointed vice-president (marketing) to double the previous year's actual sales to decide the company sales budget as well as sales volume quotas of several territories for the years 1994–95 and 1995–96. This decision was taken based on the discussion the managing director had with the chairman in the absence of market information. Although the territorial sales performance varied as compared to sales quotas, the company managed to achieve its sales budget. However, when the management again decided to double the sales budget and sales quotas for the year 1996–97, it failed to achieve its sales goals because of the recession in the economy. Based on this and several other examples, it can be said that the executive judgment method should be used along with other methods, but it should not be the only method used for deciding sales budget and sales volume quotas.

Salespeople's Estimates

Some companies ask their own salespersons to set their own sales quotas in situations, such as starting a field sales operation and expanding sales into new geographic regions or territories. The reason for this decision is that the salespersons are closer to their territories than management, and therefore, can do a better job. Asking salespeople to set their own quotas happens rarely, because salespeople either overestimate their abilities to set very high sales quotas or set too low sales quotas to earn high commissions or incentives. Salespersons' morale becomes down when they find that they could not achieve their own sales quotas, which were set too high[20]. When sales quotas are set too low, salespeople are not motivated to put forth maximum selling efforts. If quotas are set unrealistically high or low, either by the salespeople or by the management, it can cause dissatisfaction and low sale force morale. To ensure effective quotas, increasing number of sales managers discuss sales quotas with their salespeople. Sales managers use forecasting methods, past sales figures and combine these with the inputs from salespeople, before coming up with final sales quotas[21].

Compensation Plan

Some companies set quotas to fit with their sales compensation plan. For instance, the sales quota for this year is based on the past year's actual sales. If the last year's sales was ₹12 million, the sales quota for this year is set at ₹12 million and the salesperson is paid commission of a percentage of sales achieved over the quota of ₹12 million. Another method which is preferred by salespeople and used by some companies is based on salary plus commission plan. For example, the company wants to pay a monthly salary of ₹15,000 plus a commission of three percent on all monthly sales over ₹500,000. The sales quota of ₹500,000 is set in such a way that it is very difficult for the salesperson to exceed a total compensation of ₹30,000 (₹15,000 salary *plus* ₹15,000 incentive) per month. The objective of the companies who use this method is that the salespersons should receive the projected amounts of compensation. These companies do not give any thought to sales potential of territories and past sales. Although compensation plan is often tied to the degree of quota achievement, sales volume quota should not be based on the compensation plan alone, because that would "put the cart before the horse".

LO 6 Plan the administration of sales quotas

ADMINISTRATION OF SALES QUOTAS

For effective administration of sales quota, the company's sales department should: (i) set realistic quotas, (ii) understand problems in setting quotas, (iii) ensure salespeople understand quotas, (iv) know marketing environment and (v) make sure flexibility in administration.

Set Realistic Quotas

Some companies, like Xerox, believe in setting high quotas that most salespeople find difficult to achieve, but are attainable by a few salesperson with extra efforts. Some other companies, like 3M, set modest quotas that majority of the sales force can achieve, so that salespeople would accept quotas as fair and attainable. However, a general view is that the salesperson's quotas should be at least equal to the last year's sales plus a percentage of the difference between the territory's market potential and last year's sales. When sales quotas are related to territory sales potential, they are considered as accurate and realistic. If salespeople feel that the quotas are unrealistic, they will not be motivated. A fair quota involves a proper blend of sales potential and previous sales experience. Good quotas are fair, accurate and attainable. For improving accuracy, set quotas for shorter periods so that periodic adjustments can be made.

Understand Problems in Setting Quotas

Underestimation and overestimation of territory sales potential, based on which the sales quotas are set, create problems. For instance, if the company underestimates its sales potential, the salespeople will easily achieve their quotas and the company will pay incentive amounts more than required. On the contrary, if the company overestimates its sales potentials, the salespersons will find it very difficult to achieve their quotas, which may lead to demotivation and dissatisfaction. This problem can be solved by making the quotas realistic as suggested earlier.

Another problem is faced by the company if it launches many new products into the market. Existing salespersons have to spend more time and efforts for introducing new products and thus, do not get adequate time to achieve quotas for the established products. A possible solution is to recruit new salespeople in order to increase the size of sales force.

One more problem is faced by the company whose salespeople have to deal with a large number of products and customers. If quotas are set for each product, the salespeople may not achieve quotas for many products and also may not satisfy all the customers. The salespeople may get frustrated and may even quit the job. In such a situation, the salespeople should be allowed to focus on the major customers and products in order to maximize sales and profits.

Ensure Salespeople Understand Quotas

The company management must ensure that the salespeople understand the purposes or objectives of sales quotas. Salespeople should also understand quota setting procedure. This is important because if the salespersons understand the process of setting quotas, they feel the quotas are fair, accurate and achievable. If salespeople do not understand how the quotas are set, they feel bitter and suspicious. There are methods available to help salespeople understand quotas. These are:

- **Participation in Quota-Setting** By allowing salespersons to take part in the process of quota-setting, not only the understanding of salespeople about quotas increase, but also their questions are answered properly and salespersons' inputs can be used in quota setting. The salespeople will be more inclined to accept the sales quotas, if they are involved in its development.

- **Continuous Feedback** Sales managers should give continuous feedback to salespeople on their performance in relation to quotas and what should be done by salespeople to improve their performance. This requires frequent meetings between the sales manager and salespeople as well as regular reports. Sales management should communicate to salespeople that sales quota performance will be considered in their salary reviews and promotions.

Know Relationship between Quota Selection and Marketing Environment

Successful companies select the type of quota that is important to them based on the marketing environment and the company objectives. As mentioned earlier in the combination quotas, companies should have a few number of quotas, generally not more than three. If salespeople have too many quotas, their efforts and energy get scattered and they get confused. The following illustrations would help to understand how successful companies select a few quotas that have relationships with marketing environment and sales situations:

- When the company has many new salespeople, it is proper to have one or two activity quotas to ensure that salespeople do the right things.

- When the company's products are in growth stage of product life cycle or in a high growth economy, the quotas should be on percentage growth in sales or growth in market share.
- When the company's product or service is in maturity stage, the sales growth will be limited, and profit contribution quotas would be important for salespeople and territories.
- When the company's objective is to increase sales from existing customers, the quotas for salespeople should include sales growth and customer satisfaction or customer service.

Make Sure Flexibility in Administering Quotas

Any major changes in market demand or the company's strategies or policies must be looked into and the quotas should be changed suitably. For example, if the company increases its prices by 10 percent, due to an increase in the cost of raw materials and other inputs, the sales quotas have to be suitably adjusted. However, small changes in the market conditions, which do not have much impact on the company sales, can be ignored.

COMPANIES NOT USING QUOTAS

Some companies do not use sales quotas for different reasons. Companies such as Nortel and Siegel think that sales quotas drive salespeople to achieve sales volume, ignoring customer service and customer satisfaction, which have long-term impact of repeat business[22]. These companies should use more number of parameters for evaluating and rewarding salespeople. Some other companies have difficulties in setting accurate quotas by combining various factors like territorial sales potential, salespersons' abilities and territory coverage difficulty. Some sales managers do not use the words sales quotas, but prefer to use the words 'sales goals' or 'sales objectives'. These sales managers use quotas, but under different names. Many executives prefer not to use sales quotas, if it means basing them on "guesstimates". Some sales managers do not use sales quotas because quotas place too much emphasis upon making sales. This may be a correct criticism of sales volume quotas, but not of all quotas.

In a situation, when a product or service is in short supply, sales quotas are not suitable. This is called sellers' market. Thus, sales quotas are proper in buyers' markets. Any organization that decides not to use quotas should have forceful reasons, because if they do not have sales quotas or goals, they cannot achieve the company goals and objectives.

SUMMARY

LO 1

- A sales territory consists of existing and potential customers located within a given geographical area and assigned to a salesperson.

- The major reasons for setting up sales territories are: (i) increased customer coverage, (ii) to control selling expenses, (iii) helps evaluate of the salespersons' performance, (iv) improve customer relations, (v) increased effectiveness of salespersons, (vi) improved coordination and (vii) benefited salespeople and the company.

LO 2

- The procedure for designing sales territories include the following steps: (i) select a control unit, (ii) find location and sales potential of customers, (iii) decide basic territories, (iv) assign salespeople to territories, (v) manage territorial coverage and (vi) evaluate and revise territories.

LO 3

- Sales managers are increasingly using computer hardware and software to design their sales territories. The software that is used is known as "Geographic Information System" (GIS).

LO 4

- Sales quotas are sales goals or performance standards set by a company for its marketing units for a certain period of time. A marketing unit includes a sales region, a sales territory, a branch office, a salesperson, a distributor or a dealer.
- The importance or objectives of sales quotas include: (i) providing performance standards, (ii) controlling performance, (iii) motivating people and (iv) identifying strengths and weaknesses.

LO 5

- Companies set many types of quotas. The most common types of quotas are: (i) sales volume, (ii) gross margin or profit contribution, (iii) expenses, (iv) activities and (e) combination.
- Methods for setting sales volume quotas are: (i) territorial sales potential, (ii) past sales experience, (iii) total market estimates, (iv) executive judgment, (v) salespeople's estimation, and (vi) compensation plan.

LO 6

- For effective administration of sales quotas, the company's sales department should: (i) set realistic quotas, (ii) understand problems in setting quotas, (iii) ensure salespeople understand quotas, (iv) make sure flexibility in administration and (v) know relationship between quotas selection and marketing environment.
- Some companies do not use sales quotas. These companies should have forceful reasons, because if they do not have sales quotas, they may not achieve the company goals.

Key Terms

Glossaries of key terms are mentioned at the end of all chapters

- Activity quotas
- Breakdown method
- Build-up method
- Combination quotas
- Control unit
- Expense quotas
- Inside salespeople
- Profit contribution quotas
- Routing
- Sales quotas or quotas
- Sales territory
- Sales-volume quotas
- Scheduling

Conceptual Questions

1. What is a 'sales territor'y? What are the reasons for companies to establish sales territories? Why a company may not want to have sales territories? **LO1 M**
2. Briefly describe the procedure used for designing sales territories. **LO2 D**
3. What are the major differences between build-up and break-down methods, which are used for deciding basic sales territories? **LO2 M**
4. What criteria or factors should a sales manager consider while assigning salespeople to territories? **LO2 M**
5. What are the advantages and disadvantages of routing and what is the procedure for setting up a routing plan? **LO2 M**
6. What are the time management tools available to salespeople for managing their time more efficiently and productively? **LO2 E**
7. How can a sales manager use information technology for designing sales territories? **LO3 M**
8. What are sales quotas and why it is important for a sales manager to set quotas for salespeople? **LO4 M**
9. Describe briefly the common types of quotas set by companies for salespeople. **LO5 E**
10. Explain the methods used by companies for setting sales quotas. **LO5 M**
11. What factors should sales managers consider to ensure effective administration of sales quotas? **LO6 M**

Note: Difficulty Level → **E** — Easy; **M** — Medium; **D** — Difficult

Objective Type Questions

Select the most appropriate response out of the various options available in each of the following questions:

1. In defining a sales territory, the keyword is
   (a) sales (b) customer (c) geographic area (d) none of these **LO1 M**

2. Effective territory design and allocation of salespeople to territories result in
   (a) improved sales force performance (b) improved company performance
   (c) both of the above (d) none of the above **LO2 E**

3. In designing sales territories, the sales manager should start the process by selecting a geographical control unit that is
   (a) small (b) large (c) medium (d) any size **LO2 E**

4. Basic territories can be determined by using
   (a) build-up method (b) break-down method
   (c) both the above methods (d) any one of the two methods **LO2 M**

5. In build-up method, companies try to
   (a) equalize the sales potential of territories
   (b) equalize the workload of salespeople
   (c) equalize both sales potential of territories and workload of salespeople
   (d) none of the above **LO2 M**

6. In assigning salespeople to territories, the sales manager should consider two criteria, viz. relative ability and the effectiveness of the salesperson by comparing the salesperson's
   (a) social characteristics (b) cultural characteristics
   (c) physical characteristics (d) all the above, with those of the territory **LO2 M**

7. Some of the commonly used routing patterns are straight line, hopscotch, cloverleaf and
   (a) rectangular (b) square (c) circular (d) hexagonal **LO2 E**

8. Many companies are increasingly using inside salespeople to
   (a) reduce time demands on their outside salespeople
   (b) give market information to other departments internally
   (c) improve their internal working
   (d) None of the above reasons **LO2 M**

9. The information technology software used for designing sales territories is called
   (a) GPS (b) GIS (c) MIS (d) none of these **LO3 M**

10. Some companies use point sales volume quotas, instead of rupees or unit sales volume quotas, in order to improve the performance on
    (a) sales volume (b) selling expenses (c) profitability (d) market share **LO5 D**

11. Sales quotas are not suitable in:
   (a) buyers' markets
   (b) sellers' markets
   (c) competitive markets
   (d) none of these

   LO6 D

Application Questions

1. Assume you are appointed as a head of marketing of Saragam Aluminium Company, which is a new company, manufacturing and marketing aluminum extruded products, such as door, window and partition aluminum frames, heat sinks for electronic equipment and electrical control panels. Customers include households and business organizations. The factory is located in Hosur district of Tamil Nadu, about 38 kilometers from Bengaluru. You have discussed with your CEO to initially focus sales and distribution efforts in southern region, consisting of Karnataka, Tamil Nadu, Andhra Pradesh, Telangana and Kerala. You are required to design sales territories to cover the five southern states. Describe how you would go about your task. LO2 M
2. In the above example, the next task is to assign salespeople to territories. What major criteria would you keep in mind in assigning salespersons to different territories? LO2 M
3. One of the salespersons in the above mentioned Saragam Aluminum Company, who is given the territory of Kerala state, comes to you for help. He is having two problems: (i) how to cover the entire state with varying market potentials of different cities and districts, and (ii) how to prepare his route plan and scheduling of customer visits, considering his major tasks of presales service, face-to-face selling, sending weekly reports including market information, collection of payments from dealers as well as business customers and telephone selling. What guidelines would you give to help your salesperson? LO2 D
4. The marketing strategy of Steel Tubes Ltd. (STL) was to focus on selling CEW (Cold drawn Electric Welded) tubes more than ERW (Electric Resistance Welded) tubes. This product strategy was determined due to very low profits of the company. What would you suggest, as a consultant, to the company when the types of quotas for salespeople are developed in order to show in a suitable manner the company's need for improvement in profitability? (*Note*: Profitability of CEW tube was about twice that of ERW tube). LO5 M
5. A company wants to control its sales force performance on both selling and non-selling activities. The major factors contributing to the selling performance are sales volume (in Rupees) and average number of sales calls per day. The major non-selling factor is the payment collection from customers. Design a suitable sales quota system and show it with an example. You may make suitable assumptions, if needed. LO5 M
6. Your company had introduced a sales quota system in the previous year, based on sales territory potential. When you were reviewing the performance of salespeople, you noticed that some salespeople could easily achieve their sales quotas as the sales potentials of their territories were underestimated and for some other salespeople exactly reverse had happened. What suggestions would you make to your senior sales manager to make sales quotas realistic for the salespeople for the present year? LO6 D

7. Assume you are a branch manager of a company, which has recently introduced a sales quota system that is linked to the incentive scheme for the salespeople. However, the salespeople have complained about the frequent short supply of some products which have affected their quarterly incentive payments. As the branch manager what would you do? LO6 D

ASSIGNMENTS FOR STUDENTS

1. Visit the website of 'Geographic Information System' (GIS), www.gis.com and find out how a GIS system can help a sales organization to design and realign its sales territories. Thereafter, search the Internet for other competing products. Compare the features and prices of competing GIS software products and suggest the most suitable system for a large FMCG company like Hindustan Unilever.
2. Select a life insurance company and a pharmaceutical company. Visit these companies to find out the following:
   (a) When did the company revise its sales territories?
   (b) What were the reasons for the same?
   (c) Did the company use GIS software for designing the sales territories? If yes, what was the process followed for the use of GIS system? If no, what were the reasons?
3. Identify three different organizations. First company should be a marketing consumer products, the second firm should be into marketing industrial products (i.e. doing B2B marketing) and the third company should be carrying out marketing of services. Contact the first level sales manager (e.g. area, district or branch sales manager) from each of the three companies. Request them to explain answers to the following questions:
   (a) What types of sales quotas (or goals) are used by the company for its salespeople?
   (b) What methods were used for setting sales quotas?
   (c) Did the company face any problems in administering sales quotas? If yes, how these problems were resolved? If no, the reasons for the same.

Reference Notes

1. Sinha Prabhakant and Zoltners, Andris A., *Sales Force Decision Models: Insights from 25 years of Implementation*, Part 2 Interfaces 31, no.3, May-June 2001, pp. S8-S44.
2. Artur Baldauf, David W. Cravens, and Nigel F. Piercy, *Examining Business Strategy, Sales Management, and Salesperson Antecedents of Sales Organization Effectiveness*, Journal of Personal Selling & Sales Management, Spring 2001, pp.109-22.
3. Zoltners Andris A.and Lorimer Sally E., *Sales Territory Alignment: An Overlooked Productivity Tool*, Journal of Personal Selling and Sales Management, Summer 2000, pp. 139-50.

4. http://www.indiastat.com for statistical information on market forecast, administrative setup, etc., accessed on 03-01-2010.
5. http://www.mckinsey.com/global-themes/asia-pacific/understanding-indias-economic-geography, accessed on 17-04-2016.
6. Anderson, Hair, and Bush, *Professional Sales Management*, 2nd ed., McGraw Hill Education, 1988.
7. 15a http://www.gis.com is a website that gives this information, accessed on 05-01-2010.
8. *The DCI-SFA Show Preview Guide*, a supplement to Sales and Marketing Management, March 1998, pp.1–41.
9. Blackshear Thomas and Plank Richard E., *The impact of adoptive selling on sales effectiveness within the pharmaceutical industry*, Journal of Marketing Theory and Practice, Summer 1994, pp. 106–25.
10. *How Salespeople Spend Their Time*, Sales and Marketing Management, Feb. 26, 1990, p. 81.
11. Bommer Michael R.W., O'Neil Brain F., and Sethna Beheruz N., *A Methodology for Optimising Selling Time of Salespersons*, Journal of Marketing Theory and Practice, Spring 1994, pp. 61–75.
12. Narus James A. and Anderson James C., *Industrial Distributor Selling: The Roles of Outside and Inside Salespersons*, Industrial Marketing Management 15, 1986, pp. 55–62.
13. Sinha and Zoltners, *Sales-Force Decision Models: Insights from 25 years of Implementation*", Part 2 Interfaces 31, no. 3, May-June 2001, pp. S8–S44.
14. Spiro Rosann, Rich Greg, Stanton William, *Management of a Sales Force*, McGraw Hill Education, Indian Edition, 12th ed., 2015, p. 395.
15. *Gadget of the Month*, Financial Management, September 2001, p. 53.
16. The Alexander Group, *Sales Compensation Trends Survey*, 2004, p. 2.
17. Andy Cohen, *Moving Out*, Sales and Marketing Management, January 1996, pp. 24–25.
18. *What Motivates U.S. Salespeople*? American Salesman, February 1994, pp. 25–30.
19. Arnott Nancy, *Leading Edge*, Sales & Marketing Management, July 1994, p. 11
20. Wotruba Thomas R. and Thurlow Michael L., *Sales Force Participation in Quota Setting and Sales Forecast*, Journal of Marketing, April 1976, pp. 11–16.
21. John Apple, *Fasten up Your Salespeople*, Business Week, April 15, 1996, p. 118.
22. Peter Burrows, *The Era of Efficiency*, Business Week, June 18, 2001, p. 92.

Additional Reference

- Rasmussen Erika, *Protecting Your Turf*, Sales and Marketing Management, March 1998, p. 90.

CASE 4.1

CG Engineering Ltd.: Achieving Quotas

Ashok Desai was transferred on promotion from western region, where he worked as area sales manager of CG Engineering Company to eastern region as regional sales manager. This happened suddenly one fine day. He was told by the company's general manager (sales) that he was promoted and transferred from western region to eastern region "to set things right", as eastern region was not performing well in terms of sales and profits. CG Engineering was manufacturing and marketing electrical engineering products such as transformers, electric motors and switchgears to business customers in India. It had four regional offices at Delhi, Kolkata, Mumbai, and Chennai.

Ashok's main responsibilities were to manage effectively 11 sales engineers reporting to him and achieve the sales volume and profit contribution quotas. For Ashok, who was transferred from western region to eastern region, not only the business customers but also the company's sales team were new. The sales engineers were compensated based on fixed salary and perquisites like house rent allowance and medical reimbursement. There was no incentive scheme. From business potential point of view, the major states in eastern region were West Bengal, Bihar, Assam and Orissa. Ashok observed that the sales engineers were not covering the eastern region market adequately and were not following any system of routing and scheduling. He also thought that salespeople were spending more time in travelling and less time in selling activities. After talking to sales engineers individually, he got an impression that most of them were not motivated, as they were not given adequate freedom of operations and recognition, whenever they received good orders. Ashok thought that there was a good scope for applying what he had learnt at the management institute and achieve superior results as expected by the general manager (sales).

Discussion Question

1. If you were Ashok, what would you do to achieve the sales volume and profit contribution quotas?

This case was prepared by Prof. Krishna K. Havaldar for classroom discussion.

CASE 4.2

MM Marketing Pvt. Ltd.: Designing Territories and Setting Quotas

Krishna Kumar, the marketing manager of MM Marketing was thinking how to go about designing sales territories, assigning salespeople to the territories and setting sales quotas, particularly as the product was new. The new product, called Swishflow fan was a unique kind of a table fan with an attractive air-conditioner like looks. Considering the initial production capacity of only 100,000 numbers in the first year, Krishna Kumar decided to market the product at the beginning in major cities of Maharashtra and Gujarat states. The marketing and sales headquarters was located at Mumbai. The target customers were households as well as commercial organizations, who could use this product as a table-fan and also as a wall-mounted fan.

Krishna Kumar thought that the sales territory design should include geographical areas with high market potential for achieving the sales budget of 100,000 numbers in the first year and a growth of 50 percent per year for the subsequent four years. He calculated the size of the sales force by using the sales potential method as seven numbers. Krishna Kumar was of the view that the sales quotas should include sales volume, selling expense and also number of sales calls per day, in order to have a proper control on salespeople. He wondered how to design the sales territories, what should be the criteria for assigning salespersons to the sales territories and how to set the sales quotas considering the factors mentioned above.

Discussion Question

1. If you were Krishna Kumar, how would you respond to the questions posed in the case?

This case was prepared by Prof. Krishna K. Havaldar for classroom discussion.

CASE 4.3

Guhring India Pvt. Ltd.: Territory Coverage and Time Management

Pradeep Joshi, sales and service engineer, north Karnataka region of Guhring India is under tremendous pressure from his zonal manager (South) to cover Karwar district and Goa state in addition to the four districts in Karnataka state. Pradeep is finding it very difficult to cover adequately the existing four districts, viz. Belagavi (old name: Belgaum), Dharwad-Hubbali (old name: Dharwar- Hubali), Shivamogga (old name: Shimoga) and Koppal. There are 30 business customers in Belagavi district and 25 business customers in other three districts. Pradeep is responsible to achieve a sales volume goal or quota and effective pre-sales and post-sales technical service to the existing and prospective business customers.

Guhring India Pvt. Ltd is a 100 percent owned subsidiary of Guhring KG, which has its headquarters at Albstadt, Germany. Guhring is a leading manufacturer of high quality rotary precision cutting tools. The main business activities of the company are trading of standard tools, manufacture of custom made tools and related services. With its rich experience of 118 years, Guhring is renowned worldwide for its quality precision manufacturing and outstanding tool performance. It operates 70 manufacturing plants around the globe. The company was incorporated in India in 1997. The manufacturing plant and the headquarters are located at Bommasandra Industrial area, near Bengaluru. Guhring India has three zonal sales and service offices at Gurgaon, Haryana state for North India; at Pune, Maharashtra state for Western part of India and at Kanchipuram,Tamil Nadu state for South India.

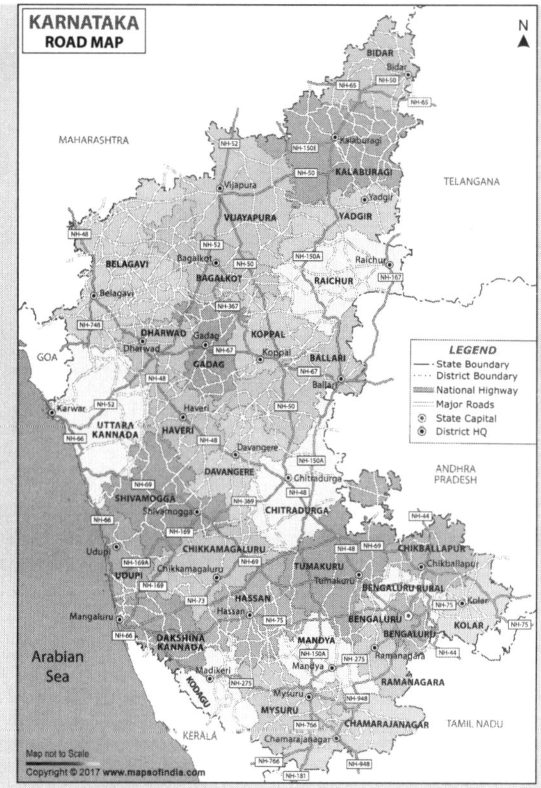

Road map of Karnataka State

Pradeep strongly felt a need to talk to his manager. He, therefore, talked to his south zone manager on his mobile phone, "Sir, good morning. I would like to talk to you about my sales territory. Sir, please try to understand that even after working for 12–14 hours a day and six days a week I am unable to visit all the 55 business customers in a month. How can I do justice to the additional business customers located in Karwar district and entire Goa state?" Krishnamurty, the zonal manager (south), responded "Pradeep, what you are saying needs some discussion. Tell me, are you following any route plan and customer visit schedule?" "No Sir, I do not follow any specific plan. I visit customers based on their needs and spend about two weeks in Belagavi, where we have 30 customers and balance two weeks in other three districts with about 25 customers." said Pradeep. "Well I now know why you are facing the problems of coverage of your sales territory and time management. Since, you have joined our company recently, I have not been able to discuss with you how to do the routing and scheduling as well as time management. I will visit your territory in the last week of this month and explain to you about these issues. In the meantime, you get a road map of Karnataka state," responded Krishnamurty and disconnected the call.

Discussion Question

1. If you were Krishnamurty, how would you resolve Pradeep's problem?

This case was prepared by Prof. Krishna K. Havaldar based on the case data obtained by Pavan Kumar, an MBA student of Alliance Business Academy, Bengaluru, for classroom discussion.

Chapter 5

Organizing and Staffing the Sales Force

LEARNING OBJECTIVES

After studying this chapter, you will be able to:

LO 1 Know the purposes of a sales organization and classify the basic types of sales organizational structures

LO 2 Explain specialization in sales organizations, categorize key accounts, and create a sales organization for key accounts

LO 3 Determine the size of the sales force and describe the sales force staffing process

LO 4 Carry out recruitment and selection of the salespeople

LO 5 Organize hiring and socialization of the salespeople

After developing a marketing plan, which included amongst other elements, marketing objectives and strategies, Suresh Kumar wondered what kind of sales organization the company should have to implement the marketing plan. Suresh Kumar was hired Marketing Manager by MM Textiles Ltd., a textile machinery manufacturing company, for launching and marketing a number of new consumer durable products, like a table fan with a unique design and a water purification unit. As the company, SM Private Ltd., a subsidiary of MM Textiles Ltd., was new, Suresh Kumar was happy to have an opportunity to carry out all the marketing tasks from the very beginning.

Suresh was hired in July 2011 for launch of a uniquely designed new fan, Pavan, in March 2012 in Mumbai, India. He had adequate time to develop and implement the marketing plan. As the company was new with only one product in the beginning, Suresh thought of adopting a line sales organization with salespeople reporting to him directly. He himself would perform both sales and other marketing functions. The size of the sales force calculated, based on sales potential method, was five. In order to determine the job specifications for the salespeople to be recruited, Suresh conducted a job analysis and then prepared the job description. The job specifications for the sales people included the basic education of graduation, minimum two years of selling experience (as he did not have enough time and manpower to train fresh sales trainees), and traits of empathy (i.e. ability to feel as the customer does), team player, and selling ability.

Since it was a new company, Suresh could not use internal recruitment sources. He placed an advertisement in the *Times of India*'s Mumbai edition. A large number of applications were received, many of them not matching the job specifications mentioned in the advertisement. Suresh had to carry out the screening of the resumes. He shortlisted 20 candidates for an initial interview and tests. Suresh Kumar himself conducted the initial interviews and used outside experts to carry out aptitude and personality tests. He further shortlisted 10 applicants after the initial interviews and tests. These candidates were then interviewed by the Director of the company to finally select five applicants for the position of sales representative. As the company's HR manager was stationed at their factory at Baroda, in Gujarat, Suresh carried out the activities of making the job offer and getting the acceptance of the same by the candidates. Thereafter, it was the responsibility of Suresh Kumar to take care of induction and socialization of the newly recruited salespersons.

The opening vignette illustrates how a marketing manager determines a sales organization, size of the sales force, and the staffing process. After an organization decides its sales goals and strategies, the implementation of strategies and action plans takes place through the sales organization. This chapter deals with the types of sales organizations, size and staffing process of the sales force as well as managing key accounts. The staffing process consists of planning, recruiting, selecting, hiring, and socialization of the sales force.

LO 1 **Know the purposes of a sales organization and classify the basic types of sales organizational structures**

PURPOSES OF A SALES ORGANIZATION

An organization structure defines relationship among jobs and amongst the people in a company. The aim is to arrange the tasks or jobs in such a manner that the people involved can perform effectively and efficiently and act together rather than perform individually. An organization structure is a tool that managers use to employ resources for getting things done.

A sales organization structure should be evolved in such a way as to assist the sales manager and salespersons to carry out the required tasks efficiently and effectively. It gives a framework showing what tasks or activities are performed by whom in the sales organization. The purposes of a sales organisation[1] are: (i) determining a degree of centralization, (ii) allowing a degree of specialization, (iii) defining line and staff positions, (iv) showing a market orientation, (v) achieving an effective co-ordination, and (vi) ensuring a reasonable span of control. These are discussed in this section.

Determining the Degree of Centralization

A centralized structure has authority and responsibility placed at higher levels of management. In a decentralized organization, the responsibility and authority for carrying out tasks are delegated to lower-level managers. No company is totally centralized or decentralized. In many companies some activities like purchase of high value items and pricing decisions are centralized to minimize costs, and some activities like evaluating and controlling salespeople are decentralized for better control and communication. However, most companies have either a centralized or decentralized orientation. A decentralized sales organization structure helps decision-making at lower levels, resulting in faster customer service. However, care should be taken that some people at lower levels do not misuse the authority and are trained adequately in decision-making. **For instance**, in an equipment manufacturing company, after-sales technical service is decentralized to branch sales offices to ensure effective customer service, but training of branch service persons is centralized for better quality and less costs.

Allowing the Degree of Specialization

A general approach is that each salesperson carries out all selling activities and each sales manager performs all sales management tasks. However, this generalist approach becomes less effective as the number of salespeople and complexity of the company's products and/or markets grow. Hence, some degree of specialization is required, so that individuals can concentrate on a few activities. For example, some salespeople may sell only some products or may visit specific types of customers, such as government, institution or trade, and some managers may focus on obtaining market information or training salespeople. By focusing on a few tasks, individuals can become experts on those activities, resulting in better performance of the organization. There is a trend towards specialization. The question is whether a company should go for geographic, product, market, or functional specialization? We shall discuss this later in this chapter.

Defining Line and Staff Positions

Sales management positions are grouped into line or staff. Line positions in sales management have line authority, which means people in management positions have formal authority or power to direct and control immediate subordinates. Line sales managers have responsibility and authority to direct and control subordinates reporting to them. Line sales managers are involved in performing sales management activities and are responsible for achieving certain sales targets or goals. Staff management positions have staff authority, which means advising or recommending roles in their respective areas of specialization or expertise. **For instance**, training manager and marketing research manager have advisory responsibility and not sales generating responsibility. We shall discuss about line and staff organizations later when we discuss basic types of sales organizations.

Showing Market Orientation

When markets are varied and complex, the company gives an adequate response by having a market orientated organization structure. Present and potential customers fall into many market segments, such as consumer (e.g., individuals and households) and business (e.g., OEMs, institutions, government). Each market oriented sales team develops suitable sales strategy for the segment it serves. As the sales organization is market-based, each market-oriented sales team can adapt its selling strategy to respond to the changing market conditions. **For instance**, if an original equipment manufacturer (OEM) buyer prefers to deal with suppliers on online basis, the company with market-oriented organization structure will quickly make all the products and services available on the Internet, and conduct business electronically. If the customer is a government organization like railways, the dealing salesperson should be familiar with the tendering process and policies like buying from the lowest price bidder.

Achieving Effective Coordination

In principle, all functions in the organization should interact harmoniously in order to achieve the firm's objectives. However, in practice, inter-departmental relations are not harmonious and have rivalries and distrust. In a typical organization, each function has a potential impact on customer satisfaction, and hence all the departments need to "think customer" and work together to satisfy customer needs and expectations. It is, therefore, necessary to have effective co-ordination between sales and other marketing units as well as sales and other non-marketing departments such as finance, production, and other functions. One of the ways to have an effective co-ordination is to have regular meetings with other functions or departments. Such meetings help to understand each other's viewpoint, which becomes the basis for effective coordination. Other means of achieving coordination are training programs and effective supervision.

Ensuring a Reasonable Span of Control

A span of control refers to the number of individuals who report to each sales manager. For instance, if a sales manager's span of control is ten, it means he or she has ten subordinates to supervise. A general guideline is that the span of control should be six or eight. However, the recent trend is towards a flat organization structure, which means reducing the number of organizational (or hierarchy) levels, in order to get closer to the customer. Flat organization structures are used to achieve decentralization, whereas tall structures are more suitable for centralized organizations. Span of control depends on the job descriptions of subordinates as well as abilities of subordinates and sales managers. The above mentioned purposes of sales organization are useful when designing a new sales organization or revising the existing organization structure.

BASIC TYPES OF SALES ORGANIZATIONAL STRUCTURES

Many factors influence the structure of the sales organizations. Organizational planners should know major influencing factors, such as customers, competitors, products, company's personnel, company size and marketing channels. The four basic types of organizational structures are: (i) line sales organization, (ii) line and staff sales organization, (iii) functional sales organization, and (iv) horizontal organization. We shall now discuss the main characteristics, advantages, and disadvantages of each type of sales organization.

Line Sales Organization

It is the simplest sales organization structure. All managers, from top sales manager to middle level managers, have line authority.

As discussed earlier, line authority means people in management positions have formal authority to direct and control immediate subordinates. Line managers are responsible to achieve certain sales targets or goals. Figure 5.1 shows a typical line sales organization.

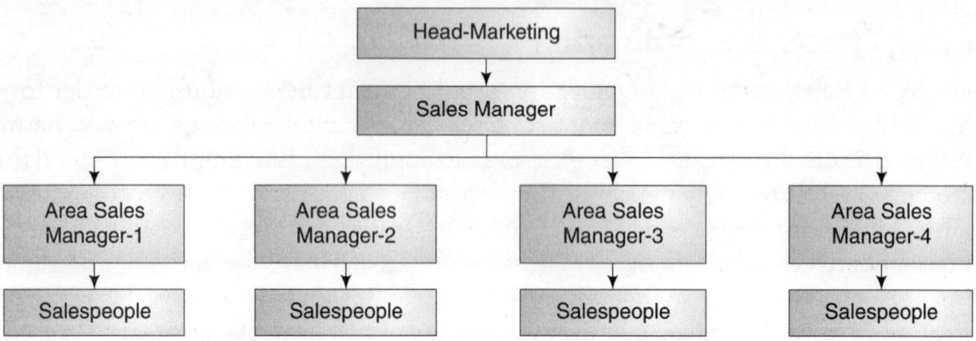

Fig. 5.1 Line Sales Organization Structure

This organization structure is widely used in small firms and in companies having a small number of salespeople. The *advantages* of line sales organization are clear authority and responsibility, quick decision-making, and low cost. However, the *disadvantages* are that too much depends on the head of sales, who has no support from subordinates with specialized knowledge and skills, such as advertising, sales promotion, and marketing research. The sales head does not have adequate time to do planning and analysis. As the organization grows, the line sales managers are overburdened, and in turn make them ineffective. At this point, a growing organization should consider changing over to line and staff sales organization structure, or any other suitable structure.

Line and Staff Sales Organization

In this type of organization structure, a group of specialists are made available to the sales or marketing head. These specialists, called staff, are experts in certain support activities such as marketing research, sales training, advertising or communications, and marketing services. Staff managers have the role of advising or assisting line sales managers. Staff managers like marketing research manager and communications or promotional manager do not have the authority to issue directives to salespeople, who report to line sales managers such as area sales managers or branch sales managers. However, staff managers have line authority over their own staff people. Figure 5.2 represents a typical line and staff organization structure.

Line and staff organization structure is likely to be used in medium- and large-sized companies when (i) number of customers is large, (ii) market coverage is national or regional, (iii) sales force size is large, and (iv) many products/services are sold. The advantages of this structure are:

- Better marketing decisions due to assistance from specialists staff such as promotional manager and marketing research manager who are experts in their respective areas.
- Better sales performance, as sales managers can focus their efforts on selling function.
- Top sales and marketing managers can concentrate on planning, coordination, human resource, and control aspects, as their detailed work became less.

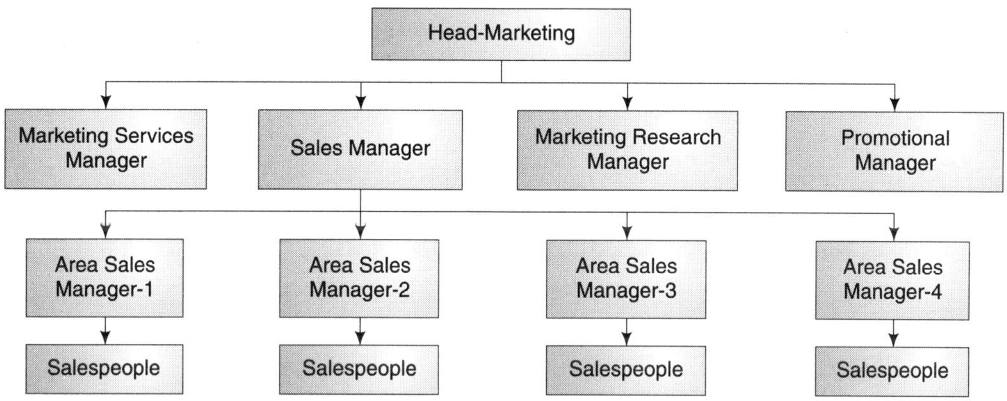

Fig. 5.2 Line and Staff Sales Organization Structure

The disadvantages of this structure include:

- Higher cost and coordination work.
- Slower decision-making.
- Conflict may arise if staff managers take line authority instead of staying in an advisory role.

Functional Sales Organization

In this sales organization, the principle of specialization is fully used. Each staff specialist manager, such as marketing research manager and promotion manager, has line authority (or functional authority) of his function over salespeople. **For example**, marketing research manager can directly issue instructions to all salespeople to obtain certain market information. As shown in Figure 5.3, salespeople receive instructions from four different managers on different aspects of their work.

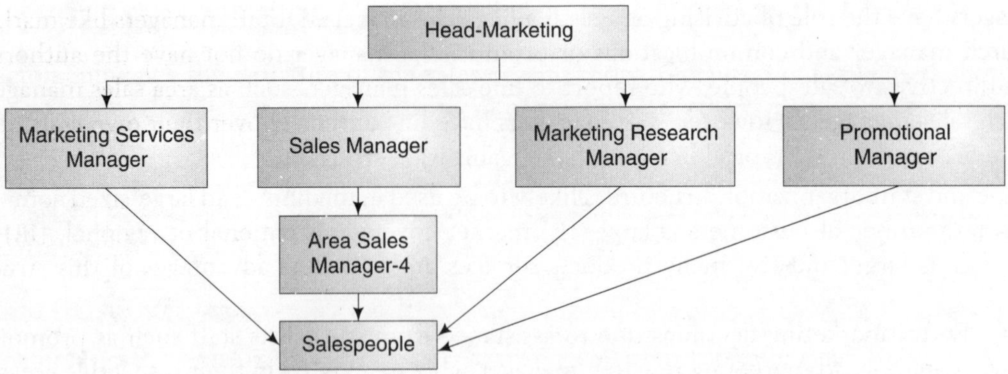

Fig. 5.3 Functional Sales Organization Structure

A few large-sized companies, with many products and/or market segments may use functional sales organization structure, with a modification of limiting the number of staff managers who may use the functional line authority. The advantages of qualified specialists guiding the sales force and high degree of division of labor get nullified by confusion and frustration of salespeople, who have to respond to several bosses. The main advantage of a functional sales organization is its administrative simplicity. However, its effectiveness is reduced as the company's products and market segments increase. Besides, the marketing head has a very difficult task of coordinating the competing functional heads who report to him. Hence, functional sales organization may be used in modified version, but in its pure form, it is not suitable.

Horizontal Sales Organization

This organization structure removes management (hierarchy) levels and also departmental boundaries[2]. The support functions like strategic planning, human resources, and finance are looked after by a small team of senior executives. All other people in the organization are the members of cross-functional teams, which perform many core processes like product design, sales, and production or operations. These teams also work with customer teams to solve the customer's problems. Companies like Motorola and General Electric, who are establishing long-term partnering relationships with their key customers and gaining greater customer responsiveness and efficiencies, have been adopting the horizontal organization structure, as shown in Figure 5.4.

The advantages are reduction in supervision, unnecessary tasks, and costs, and substantial improvement in efficiency, and customer responses with enthusiasm.

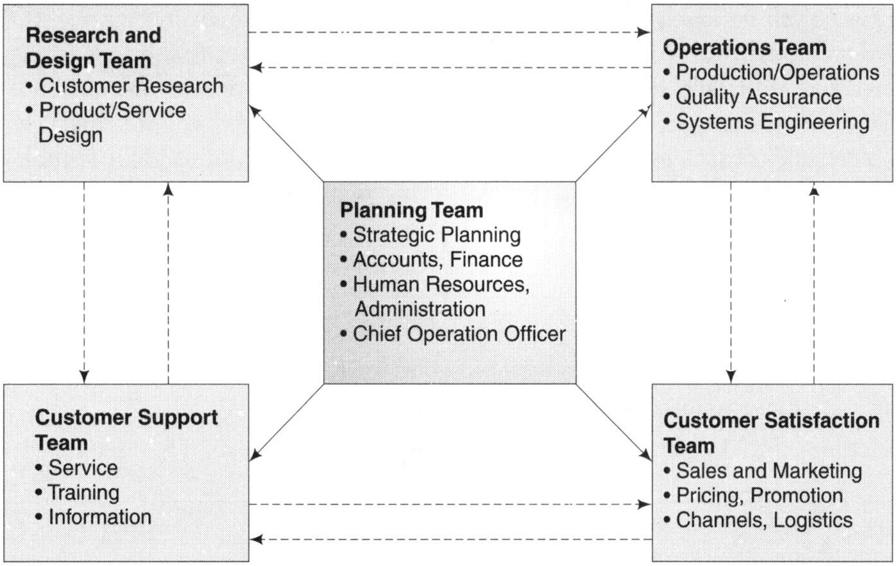

Fig. 5.4 **Horizontal Organization**

LO 2 **Explain specialization in sales organizations, categorize key accounts, and create a sales organization for key accounts**

SPECIALIZATION IN SALES ORGANIZATIONS

Generally many medium- and large-sized companies expand one of the basic sales organization structures discussed earlier in some specialized design, in order to increase the effectiveness of their sales force. The bases of this specialization are factors such as: (i) geography, (ii) product, (iii) market, (iv) functional, and (v) a combination of these factors.

The question arises as to what criteria a company should use in order to select one of the several specializations mentioned above. The criteria or factors to be used are: (i) meeting customer needs, (ii) nature and number of products, (iii) abilities of the sales force, and (iv) sales costs. Based on these criteria, a company decides to divide its sales force into groups in order to increase the effectiveness of the sales efforts.

Geographic Specialization

Many large companies, selling in national markets, organize their sales operations along geographic specialization. Typically, each salesperson is assigned a geographic area, and is made responsible for all selling activities to all customers within the assigned area. A reasonable number of salespeople are placed under a territory manager. The territory sales manager is generally called a branch, area, district, or regional sales manager. Companies with large number of salespeople, often have two or three levels of territorial sales managers, as shown in Figure 5.5. There is a trend towards regionalization and localization. The national market is subdivided into regional markets based on ethnic and demographic segmentation, with different promotional strategies for each region. Many companies now have local marketing managers (or area market managers) to support local sales efforts at regional and district levels in high sales volume markets. These area market managers help the company's marketing plan and strategies to adjust to the local needs. They prepare regional and district plans for selling all the products of the company.

The advantages of geographic specialization are as follows:

- Better market coverage
- Better control over sales force
- Superior customer service
- Quick response to local conditions and competition.

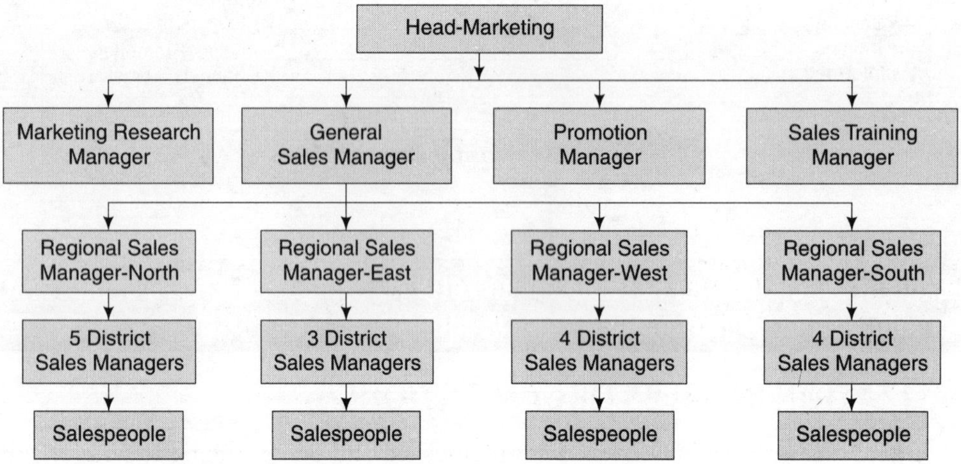

Fig. 5.5 Geographic (Specialization) Sales Organization

The disadvantage is that generally geographic specialization has a limited specialization of marketing tasks. This means each district sales manager is made responsible to work on local sales promotion, advertising, and information collection, in addition to managing sales people reporting to him. Therefore, a geographic sales organization is often combined with market or product sales organization.

For example, Cambell Soup Company changed its sales organization from product specialization basis to geographic specialization basis in order to achieve the objectives of better service to retailers, lower selling cost, and simplifying its sales operations. Earlier the company had five different product divisions with five divisional managers, along with respective sales managers, and salespeople. This resulted in five Campbell salespeople calling on retail stores who were dissatisfied with the service. The revised sales organization helped the company achieve its objectives as stated above.

Product Specialization

Product specialization is useful when the company has a large number of products and/or brands. There are two types of product specialization: (i) sales organization with product managers (or divisional marketing managers with responsibility for a group of products) as staff specialists, and (ii) sales organization with product specialized sales force. Figure 5.6 (b) shows the company having two groups of products – product group A and product group B. Each divisional marketing manager (usually called product manager) has the responsibility for planning and implementing a marketing plan for each group of products. They have no line authority over the field sales managers and the sales force. They can only recommend or request to the regional sales managers. Each salesperson sells all the products of groups A and B, as there is no specialization by product at sales people level.

In Figure 5.6 (a), salespeople in each group sell only the products included in that group. The regional and district sales managers are line managers and have no staff assistance. The advantage of this organization is that each product gets a specialized attention from the salespeople and territory sales managers. But the main disadvantage of Figure 5.6 (a) is that more than one salesperson from the company calls on the same customer, resulting in customer dissatisfaction and increase in selling cost. Organization structure in Figure 5.6 (b) corrects the problem of duplicate calls on a customer, but its weakness is the lack of product specialization by salespeople.

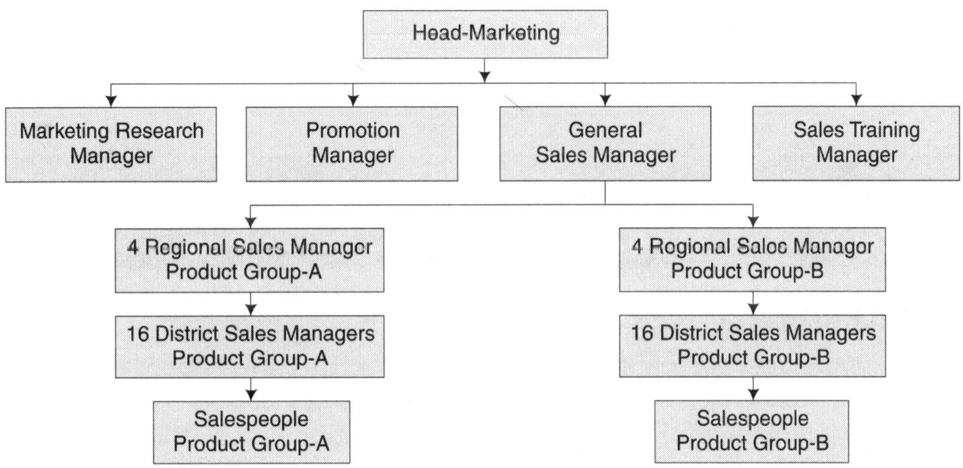

Fig. 5.6(a) **Sales Organization with Product Specialized Salesforce**

Fast moving consumer goods (FMCGs) companies like Proctor and Gamble use the product staff specialization [Figure 5.6(b)] organization to ensure adequate attention to product lines and brands at the planning level. The product managers develop a cost-effective marketing mix strategy for each product and brand, and react quickly to changes in market place. The trend is to move from product or brand driven organization (like Pepsodent toothpaste) to category management (like any toothpaste category) to customer-need management (mouth care). Thus, the focus of the organization is on a basic customer need[3].

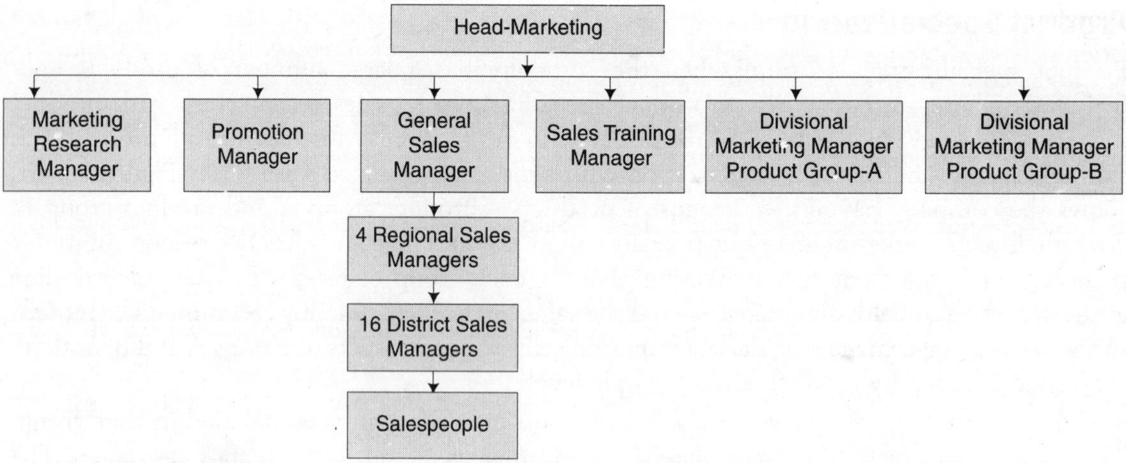

Fig. 5.6(b) Sales Organization with Product Managers (or Divisional Marketing Managers) as Staff Specialists

Many consumer goods companies like Proctor and Gamble and Pillsbury, and some service organizations, such as large commercial banks, use sales organizations with product, brand, or divisional marketing managers, who support specific product groups [see Figure 5.6(b)]. Each product or brand manager is responsible for ensuring effective planning, coordination, development, promotion, and achievement of objectives for the respective product group or the brand. Some other companies, which have wide range of products, like 3M Corporation, uses sales organization with product specialization sales force [see Figure. 5.6(a)]. In 3M, separate groups of salespeople sell different group of products, such as healthcare, safety and security, home and leisure, displays and graphics, and so on.

Market Specialization

An increasing important type of specialization is market specialization. Market specialized sales organization is desirable when customers are classified by specific types, user industry, or by channel of distribution[4]. Figure 5.7 shows a sales organization structure with market specialization. In this structure, salespeople carry out all the selling activities for all products but for certain specific customer groups. These customer groups, such as government, commercial, and dealers have different buying practices and preferences. The use of market specialization in sales organization structure is increasing in recent years, while the use of product specialization has been reducing.

The advantage of market specialization is that sales and marketing efforts are organized to meet the needs of specific customer groups. This is consistent with the customer orientation or market-centered philosophy of the company. There are several examples of companies reorganizing along market specialization. Crompton Greaves, which had product groups orientation, changed over to customer type sales organization as shown in Figure 5.7. Similarly, Xerox switched from product-oriented sales organization to a market-oriented structure. Other examples of companies that have already changed over to the market specialization sales organizations are IBM[5], General Electric, and Hewlett–Packard.

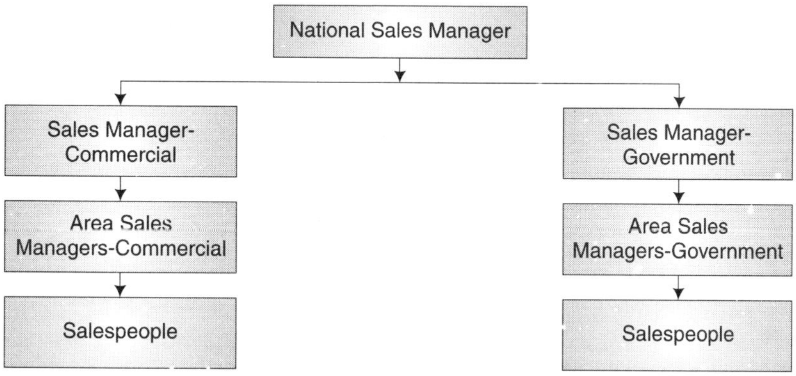

Fig. 5.7 Sales Organization with Market Specialization

There are some disadvantages of market specialization structure such as duplication of territory coverage (different salespersons working in the same territory but covering separate customer groups) and higher selling costs.

Combination Sales Organization

So far we have assumed that a company organizes its sales force by using one of the bases of specialization, such as geography, product, market, or functional, as discussed earlier in this chapter. Table 5.1 summarizes what has been discussed previously by comparing the advantages and disadvantages of different sales organization structures. From Table 5.1, it can be seen that the strengths of one organization structure are the weaknesses of other sales organization structures. Due to this reason, many companies use combination or hybrid sales organization structures that include many specialization organization structures discussed earlier. These companies minimize the disadvantages and maximize the advantages shown in Table 5.1. An example of combination or hybrid sales organizations is shown in Figure 5.8. This sales organization structure combines geographic and market specializations, by first dividing the total domestic market into four regions, viz., North, East, West, and South. Thereafter, each region is further segmented in to specific customer groups such as government, commercial, and dealer. The basis of specialization will vary from company to company, but some kind of specialization is needed for firms to remain competitive.

Table 5.1 Comparison of Different Structures of Sales Organizations

Sales Organizations	Advantages	Disadvantages
Functional	• Simple to administer • Qualified specialists guide salespeople • High degree of division of labor	• Difficult task of coordination of functional heads. • Sales force confused due to many bosses • Geographic/Customer duplication
Geographic	• Better market coverage • Better sales force control • Superior customer service • Quick response to local issues • No geographic/customer duplication	• Limited specialization of marketing tasks • Support of area market managers is needed to territory or district sales managers.
Product	• Each product gets attention from salespeople/territory managers • Product managers develop cost effective marketing strategy for each product or brand	• High cost • Geographic or customer duplication resulting in customer dissatisfaction
Market	• Customer needs are better met • Market-centered philosophy implemented	• High cost • Geographic duplication with different salespeople working in the same territory

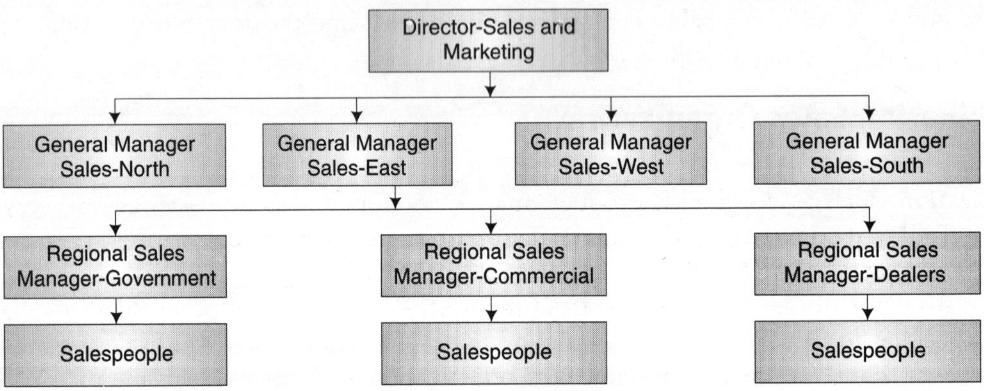

Fig. 5.8 Combination/Hybrid Sales Organization

MANAGEMENT OF KEY ACCOUNTS

Key accounts (also called major accounts, house accounts, national accounts, strategic accounts or global accounts) are customers who buy large volume of the company's products or services and are profitable. These are important accounts or customers to whom special attention is given by the companies. Some key accounts have one geographic location and hence, the supplier finds that such customers are easy to serve and these are called **major accounts**. On the contrary, there are other types of key accounts who have several geographic locations and are therefore, difficult or complex to serve. These are called **national accounts.** For example, Bosch Company at Bengaluru which manufactures auto components has many key accounts. Some of them like Maruti Suzuki India Limited until 2006 had factory only at Gurgaon in North India. It was a major account. Since 2007, it has manufacturing facilities at two locations—Gurgaon and Manesar—and hence, can be termed by Bosch Company as a national account. Another key account of Bosch company is Ashok Leyland, which has manufacturing plants at several locations like Chennai and Hosur, and hence it is categorized as a national account.

Identification of Key Accounts

For identifying key, national, or major customers, companies use the following criteria: (i) the customer should purchase a large volume of the supplier company's products or services in terms of sales volume (in rupees or dollars), which may be a large share of the supplier company's total sales; (ii) the customer should buy more profitable products or services; (iii) the customer may require a high level of service at one or several geographic locations; (iv) the customer may be price-sensitive; and (v) the customer may desire a long-term (strategic) partnering or collaborative relationship with the supplier firm. For applying these criteria, the supplier firm should first measure sales and profit potential of customers. Thereafter, customers' expectations of services, prices and relationships should be understood. Key customers can then be identified.

Managing Key Accounts

The management of key accounts may vary from company to company, but there are certain similarities in their operations:

1. *The objective* of the key account management is to become the preferred or sole supplier to the key account (or important customer). This will provide substantial sales and profits to the supplier firm.
2. *The strategies* used to achieve the objective are:
   - Appoint a *key account manager* to lead a cross-functional team consisting of key account sales executive, technical support person, logistics executive (for a national account with several geographic locations), and an inside salesperson. This is called *team-selling*. The team carries out a number of tasks, such as developing and growing customer business, providing excellent customer service, and ensuring long-term collaborative relationship at various levels in the customer organization.
   - Depending upon the key customer's needs, provide added value, special price advantage, special warranty service (if required) and customized products or services with quality better than competitors. **For instance**, MM Company considered TVS Motor Company, in Tamil Nadu, as a key account for its material handling equipment. MM Company had a team-selling approach to achieve its objective of becoming a preferred supplier. Since TVS Motor Company had factories at Hosur (Tamil Nadu), a village near Mysore (Karnataka), and a village in Solan district (Himachal Pradesh), MM Company's selling team consisted of key account executives and branch managers of Bengaluru and Delhi branches (to serve TVS

Motor Company's three factories), a senior design engineer, a senior technical service engineer, and a logistic executive. The team was headed by the marketing head. MM Company clearly understood TVS Motor Company's material handling requirements at their factories, offered customized equipment at competitive prices, extended warranty service to 24 months (instead of standard warranty of 12 months), gave free training to the technical staff, and carried out prompt after-sales-service including easy availability of spare parts. Collaborative relationship was developed at junior, middle, and senior levels between the two organizations. This resulted into 80 percent share of business of material handling equipment from TVS Motor Company to MM Company.

Creating a Sales Organization for Key Accounts

Companies need to create or develop a separate sales organization structure for major or key accounts. We shall discuss the various alternatives available for the same hereunder.

Alternative Sales Organizations for Key Customers

Many companies have developed separate organization structures and marketing programs for key customers (or accounts).

These large customers are very important to the selling organization, because they account for a large share of the selling organization's sales volume and profits. There is a definite need for close co-ordination not only within the selling firm, but also between the buying and selling firms. This cannot be handled by the normal salesperson. Therefore, companies use the following alternative organizational methods for dealing effectively with their key customers[6]: (i) creating a key account management team, (ii) using existing territory sales managers, or (iii) creating a separate division of sales force.

❍ **Creating a Key Account Management Team** This sales organization structure is offered to key accounts that have multiple divisions or factories at many locations. These customers need uniform pricing and coordinated service for all their divisions. To meet these needs, the selling firm has a key account manager (KAM), who supervises the existing field salespeople calling on customer divisions within their territories. For example, Xerox company's key account managers work with local branch salespeople for key customers on both national and branch levels[7]. Similarly, key accounts managers of 3M Company work with local salespersons around the world on corporate strategic accounts (or key customers)[8].

❍ **Using Existing Territory Sales Managers** Some companies ask their existing territory (or branch) managers to take the responsibility of looking after key customers located in their respective territories. This method may be acceptable if there are a few key accounts which have single locations, so that coordination between different territories or branches is not required.

However, territorial manager's time spent on servicing key accounts may affect the quality of their sales force management.

❍ **Creating a Separate Division of Sales Force** Some companies have "key accounts programs", consisting of cross-functional people who handle all aspects of relationships with large accounts. The company's largest accounts get a "strategic account management team", consisting of cross-functional people, who are permanently assigned to one customer. **For instance**, Proctor and Gamble stationed a strategic account management team in 1992 to work with Walmart at Bentonville. If a company has several such large accounts, it may create a separate division of the sales force. Some apparel manufactures who produce and sell private-label clothing for large chains like Sears and J S Pemny, have used this method. The sales organization structure integrates sales, marketing, and manufacturing activities that affect the key accounts. Another method is to create a separate sales force for serving key accounts. **For instance**, Hewlett–Packard[9] has a separate sales force to look after major or key accounts. There are other groups of salespeople who handle distributors and smaller customers. Benefits of key account management are: (i) increased market share, (ii) enhanced customer satisfaction, (iii) superior sales and profit performance.

LO 3 **Determine the size of the sales force and describe the sales force staffing process**

SIZE OF THE SALES FORCE

Once a company decides its sales organization structure, it is ready to determine the size of the sales force. How many salespeople are required to meet the company's sales volume and profit objectives is a key decision. It is also a difficult decision because the competition level, demand for the company's products and services, and nature of customer segments vary across different sales territories. Salespeople are the company's very productive and expensive assets. If the company has less than optimum size of sales force, there will be a loss of sales and profits, and if it has more than the required numbers, there will be an increase in sales and costs and reduction in the profits. The methods available to determine optimum sales force size are: (i) workload, (ii) sales potential (or breakdown), and (iii) incremental.

Workload Method

The assumptions made in this method are that all salespeople will have equal workload, and that the total workload in covering the market includes number of present and prospective customers, customers' sales volume potential, and travel time. The company first calculates the total work load necessary to cover the entire market and then divides it by the work time available to each salesperson, thus calculating the total number of salespeople needed. The steps involved in this method are explained as under with an example from B2B (business to business) sales, i.e. selling from one selling firm to many buying companies.

1. Classify Present and Prospective Customers According to Their Sales Potential

Suppose the company estimates 500 numbers Class A (large sales potential) and 1000 numbers Class B (medium sales potential) customers to be covered by the company's salespeople in the entire nation. Business customers with small sales potential (Class C) will be looked after by telemarketing people or the company's dealers.

2. Decide Time Required Per Sales Call and Desired Call Frequencies for each Customer Class

Assume that both present and prospective business customers require the same time per sales call and the same call frequencies per year, the decisions are as follows:

Class A: 60 minutes per call × 36 calls a year = 36 hours/year per customer

Class B: 30 minutes per call × 12 calls a year = 06 hours/year per customer

3. Calculate the Total Workload Necessary to Cover the Entire Market

In the above example, this calculation is as follows:

Class A: 500 business Customers × 36 hours/year	=	18000 hours
Class B: 1000 business Customers × 06 hours/year	=	6000 hours
Total	=	24000 hours

4. Decide the Total Work Time Available per Salesperson

Suppose the company decides that salespeople should work 40 hours per week, 45 weeks per year (allowing seven weeks for casual and earned leave and holidays), then each salesperson has 1800 hours/year (40 hours/week × 45 weeks per year) for selling, non-selling activities (such as collecting information on customers and competitors, preparing and sending sales reports, etc.), and travel time.

5. Divide the Total Work Time Available by Different Activities Per Salesperson

Suppose the management decides that salespeople should divide their work time as follows:

Selling activities:	40 percent	=	720 hours
Non-selling activities:	30 percent	=	540 hours
Travelling:	30 percent	=	540 hours
Total	100 percent	=	1800 hours

6. Calculate the Total Number of Salespeople Needed

This is done by dividing the total workload to cover the entire market by the total selling time available per salesperson:

$$\frac{24000}{720} = 33.3, \text{ i.e. 33 salespeople needed}$$

Workload method is relatively simple to apply with managerial judgment. The method is also conceptually sound, as the size of sales force is based on the selling efforts needed. It can be adopted for all types of selling situations. However, the method needs accurate information on prospective customers and sales potential of existing and prospective customers. The method also needs changes since the call frequency for the prospective customers are generally higher than that of existing customers. A weakness of the workload approach is that it disregards profits and costs involved with serving customers. Another fault can be traced to the assumption that all salespeople have the same work load. Does it also mean that they will utilize their time with equal efficiency?

Sales Potential Method

In this method, the sales manager estimates the productivity of the average salesperson with average performance and forecasts the sales volume of the company. The method also considers the anticipated sales force turnover in terms of resignations, retirements, and promotions. The basic formula is:

$$N = \frac{S}{P}(1 + T)$$

where, N = Number of salespeople needed, or size of the sales force

S = Annual sales forecast for the company

P = Estimated productivity of the average salesperson

T = Estimated percentage of annual sales force turnover

For example, if the firm's sales forecast is ₹50 million for next year, the annual sales volume productivity for the average salesperson is ₹2 million, and anticipated annual sales force turnover is 20 percent; the calculation is,

$$N = \frac{50,000,000}{2,000,000}(1 + 0.20) = 25 \times 1.20 = 30 \text{ salespeople}$$

The sales force size = 30 salespeople

The advantages of this method are that it is simple and straight forward. However, this method is conceptually weak, as its calculations show that sales forecast decides the number of salespeople. Another limitation is that it does not include the lead time needed for recruitment and training the salespeople to the desired level of sales productivity. In spite of the method's limitations, it is often used for deciding sales force's size.

Incremental Method

This method is based on marginal-analysis theory of economics. Its basic concept is that profits will increase when additional salespeople are added, only if the incremental sales revenues exceed the incremental costs. In other words, this method suggests that a salesperson should only be added when the additional revenue from the salesperson is more than the cost of the additional salesperson.

To illustrate this method, we shall consider an example of a company whose total sales volume varies directly with the number of salespeople working in the market. Costs of goods sold (cost of manufacturing) remain almost constant at 60 percent of sales. The company's salespersons receive a salary of ₹1,20,000 each year plus commission of 6 percent on their sales volume. In addition, each salesperson gets travel and food allowance of ₹6,000 per month, that is ₹72,000 per year. At present, the company has 30 salespeople and sales manager wants to decide whether or not to add more salespeople. The sales manager estimates the increases in sales volume, costs of goods sold, selling costs, and profit contribution as shown in Table 5.2.

Table 5.2 Example of Incremental Method

Number of Salesperson (A)	Sales Volume (₹) (B)	Cost of Goods (₹) (C)	Gross Margin (₹) (D) = (B) – (C)	Salaries (₹) (E)	Commissions (₹) (F)	Travel & Food Allowance (₹) (G)	Profit Contribution (₹) (H) = D – (E + F + G)
31	12,00,000	720,000	480,000	1,20,000	72,000	72,000	216,000
32	960,000	576,000	384,000	1,20,000	57,600	72,000	134,400
33	768,000	460,800	307,200	1,20,000	46,080	72,000	69,120
34	614,400	368,640	245,760	1,20,000	36,864	72,000	16,896
35	491,520	294,912	196,608	1,20,000	29,491	72,000	–24,883

From Table 5.2, the sales manager can add four more salespersons to the existing 30 salespeople, because adding 4th salesperson (number 34) brings an additional profit contribution of ₹16,896, but adding 5th salesperson (number 35), produces a negative profit contribution of ₹24,883. Thus, the optimum size of sales force in this example is 34. Table 5.2 shows sales volume going down with addition of more salespersons because these figures are based on the sales response function developed by the company's marketing research department.

This method is conceptually accurate, as it quantifies important relationships between sales force size, sales volume, costs, and profits. But sometimes it is also difficult to apply in practice, since the needed historical data are not always available. In addition, the method requires a company to develop a sales response function to describe the relationship between salesperson's effort and resulting sales volume. Not many firms have the research ability to develop sales response function. Thus, this method cannot be used for new companies where historical data and research experience are not possible.

STAFFING THE SALES FORCE

Proper staffing of the sales force is very important as it has a strong impact on a company's sales performance and profits[10]. The sales force is involved in carrying out the company's strategic marketing plan. One cannot over-emphasize how critical it is to choose the right salespeople. The full costs of unsuccessful recruitment, selection and training are probably very difficult to estimate. In one study, it is estimated that it costs anywhere from 50 to 150 percent of an employee's salary to replace that person[11]. It is clearly seen that *sales force staffing, which includes planning, recruitment, selection, hiring, and socialization, is among the most challenging and important responsibilities of sales management.*

Sales Force Staffing Process

Sales force staffing process consists of five major stages:

1. Planning the recruitment and selection process.
2. Recruiting sufficient number of applicants.
3. Selecting the most suitable applicants.
4. Hiring those applicants who have been selected.
5. Socialization of the new recruits into the organization.

Figure 5.9 shows the above mentioned major stages, which are further broken down into related tasks. We shall discuss each stage.

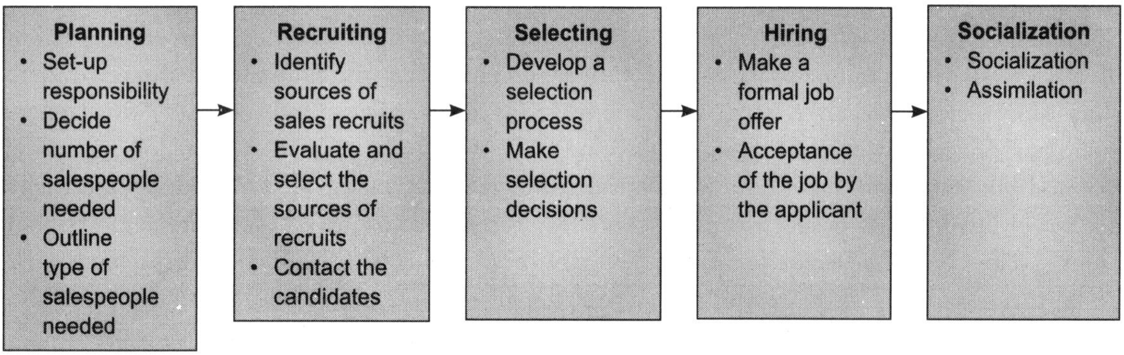

Fig. 5.9 Five Stages of Sales Force Staffing Process

The Planning Stage

As shown in Figure 5.9, the first activity in the planning stage is to set up the responsibility for the various stages and activities of the staffing process. The second task is to decide the number of salespeople needed. The third activity of determining the type of salespeople needed includes three tasks: (i) conduct job analysis, (ii) prepare job description, and (iii) develop job qualifications (or specifications) that a sales recruit should have. We shall now discuss each of the three activities included in the planning stage.

❍ **Setting-up Responsibility** The company management must decide who will be responsible for the various stages and activities of staffing process. The decisions may vary from company to company, depending on the size and culture of the organization. In a small organization, most of the staffing decisions are made by the head of the organization. However, in a medium or large size company, the responsibility of identifying and selecting the sources, contacting the candidates, developing a selection process, socialization and assimilation are typically given to human resource department managers. The sales managers at middle and senior management levels are generally responsible for activities such as deciding the number and type of people needed, selecting, and making the job offers to the salespeople.

Proper coordination is required between sales, marketing, and human resource department executives. **For instance**, in a large engineering company, the responsibility of hiring sales engineers was given to the regional general managers of four regions – North, East, West, and South. The regional general manager–East, asked the human resource manager–East, to take the responsibility of all the activities of recruiting sales engineers, except for deciding the number and type of sales people needed, selection, and making the job offer. The last four activities were the responsibility of the regional marketing managers and the regional general manager. Regional marketing managers were asked to co-operate with the regional human resource manager in the various activities of staffing process.

❍ **Deciding the Number of Salespeople Needed** The decision on how many salespeople are needed by the company is an important part of planning. It forces the various regional and branch sales managers to plan their manpower requirements well in advance, before the beginning of a new financial year. This helps the human resource (HR) department to program the various stages of staffing process. Senior management of the company should also review any changes in their marketing strategy and its impact on the number of salespeople. **For instance,** a company decided to close its branch at Sonepat in North India, since two major customers stopped buying its products due to backward integration (making those products internally instead of buying from outside sources). This resulted in two excess salespeople from Sonepat branch. The company decided to open two new branches at Faridabad (in North India) and Pune (in Western India), to exploit the increased market demand from automotive industry.

For calculating the number of salespeople needed, each territory sales manager should consider the following points:

- Decide the optimum sales force size by using one or (preferably) more of the three (workload, sales potential, and incremental) methods. These methods are discussed earlier in this chapter.
- Add number of promotions, retirements, transfers out, terminations, resignations expected from the existing salespeople.
- Subtract expected transfers into the branch and the existing salespeople.
- Make a total of new salespeople needed, as shown in Figure 5.10, and submit it to the senior sales manager.

Optimum Salesforce Size	Add Promotions	Add Retirements and Transfers out	Add Terminations, Resignations	Subtract Transfers in and existing Salespeople	Total new Salespersons needed
25	2	2	1	23	7

Fig. 5.10 Example of Number of Salesperson Needed

After receiving the information on the number of salespersons needed from each territory sales manager, the national sales manager calculates the total number of new salespersons to be hired. What is also important is that this planning of number of salespeople needed should be done 5 to 6 months in advance of new financial year, so as to allow adequate time for recruitment, selection, hiring, assimilation, and training of a new sales persons.

❍ **Outline the Type of Salespeople Needed** As a part of planning stage, a company should prepare a detailed job analysis, job description, and specifications of the salespeople needed. This will be useful for making decisions on selection, promotion, and training of salespersons. The steps involved in the process of developing a profile or outline of the type of salespeople, as shown in Figure 5.11, are: (i) job analysis, (ii) job description, and (iii) job qualifications or specifications.

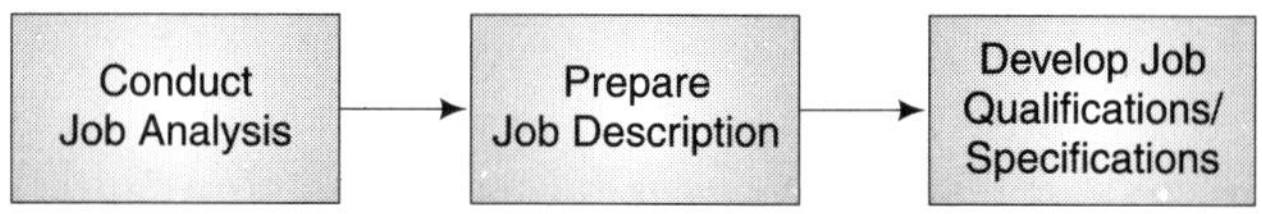

Fig. 5.11 Process of Developing Sales Force Profile/Outline

New companies will have to go through the three steps represented in Figure 5.11. Even existing firms need to review these steps from time to time to ensure that the job specifications represent the current activities and responsibilities of salespeople.

Conducting Job Analysis A job analysis is systematic collection of information on a particular sales job. It includes deciding the job's objectives and how to achieve them. The procedure followed for conducting job analysis involves developing the duties (i.e., tasks required as a part of salesperson's job), such as understanding customer needs and making sales presentation. For this, salespersons, customers, and sales managers should be interviewed. A structured questionnaire should be used to collect relevant information on importance of various tasks ; what kind of knowledge and skills are needed by the salesperson to perform the job well, type of customers, such as individuals, business, or institutional, and so on.

The person conducting the job analysis may be a person from the sales team, or human resource department, or an outside consultant. This person should also spend time making customer calls with some salespeople, interviewing them, observing, and recording the various tasks performed and time taken by the salesperson.

Preparing Job Description Companies use job analysis to develop job description. Job descriptions are formal, written statements describing detailed account of the job. Most well-prepared job descriptions generally cover the following points:

- **Title of the Job:** A complete description so that there is no uncertainty. This is particularly important in an organization having many types of sales jobs. Some of the examples of sales titles are sales representative, marketing representative, and sales engineer.
- **Reporting Relationship:** To whom should the salesperson report. **For instance**, the reporting manager of a sales representative may be the branch manager, district manager, area sales manager, or sales/marketing manager.
- **Types of Products and Services to be Sold:** For example, office equipment like photocopiers, fax and multifunctional devices, courier services, and software services.
- **Types of Customers to be Visited:** For instance, commercial or purchase managers in business organizations.

- **Duties and Responsibilities:** For instance, visit planning, selling activities, customer service, market information collection and communication, call report preparation, payment collection from customers, and customer relationship.
- **Job Demands:** Mental and physical demands of the job, such as travelling, achievements of sales and other targets.
- **Key Result Areas (KRAs):** Achieving sales goals, maintaining goad customer relationship, and submitting market information reports.
- **Location and Geographical Area to be Covered:** The present location of the place of work and the geographical area to be covered by the salesperson (which may change in future). For example, the location of the job is at Bengaluru and the area to be covered is Bengaluru city.

A job description is almost certainly the most important tool that is used in managing the sales force – for instance, in recruiting, selecting, training, compensating, and evaluating the salespeople. It is, therefore, important that the job description should be in writing and in great detail.

Developing Job Qualifications/Specifications Duties and responsibilities mentioned in the job description should be used to decide job qualifications, or job specifications (also called hiring specifications). A sales recruit should have certain traits (or characteristics) to perform well on the job. However, determining the job qualifications or specifications is probably the most difficult part of the entire staffing process. This is because there are no generally accepted traits and abilities of salespeople for success across various selling positions. Many studies have attempted to determine which qualifications are most important for a sales position. A few studies are mentioned below:

Charles Garfield, in his study of super achievers concluded that super sales performers show the following traits: (i) risk taking, (ii) powerful sense of mission, (iii) problem-solving bent, (iv) care for the customer, and (v) careful call planning[12]. Mayer and Greenberg offered one of the shortest lists of traits. They concluded that the effective salesperson has two basic qualities: (i) empathy (the ability to feel as the customer does) and (ii) ego drive (a strong personal need to make the sale)[13]. Avlonitis and Karayanni concluded in their study that the salesperson of the future must be able to work with electronic communications and technology[14]. A study of 26 of the leading corporations, including General Electric and AT&T, found that the "ability to work in a team" was a job requirement[15].

For managing key accounts (i.e., major customers) many firms use team selling approach. Some of the important characteristics of the team salesperson are adaptability, and the ability to put the team's objectives above their own. There is no single satisfactory method available for every company for deciding the qualifications (or specifications) needed for selecting its salespeople. This is because, there are many types of sales jobs and there is a corresponding variance in job qualifications for different sales jobs. However, some of the methods used for developing job specifications are as follows:

- **Study Job Description:** Some companies develop job specifications based on the carefully prepared job description statements. This is particularly a useful method for the new company, which does not have personnel histories of past salespeople.

- **Analyze Personnel Histories of Salespersons:** A large company, which is in business for a many years, can decide the job specifications of its salespeople by analyzing the personnel histories of its present and past salespeople. The procedure is to analyze various traits (or characteristics) of good and poor performing salespersons to find out if there are certain characteristics that are present in good (performing) salespersons and absent in poor (performing) salespeople. The traits of the good sales persons are then used to develop job specifications (or a job profile) of the type of salesperson the company is seeking. **For instance**, based on an analysis of its current sales consultants, Accenture company discovered that students with part-time jobs and extracurricular activities were more likely to succeed than those with higher grade-point averages[16].
- **Ask Customers:** One more method is to ask customers. Most customers say they want the salesperson to be knowledgeable, reliable, helpful, and honest. Based on these methods, each company should develop its own job specifications, including sales experience, education, skills, and personality traits for selecting salespeople.

After deciding the number and type of salespeople needed by the company, the next stage is recruiting.

LO 4 Carry out recruitment and selection of the salespeople

RECRUITING THE SALES FORCE

This stage includes: (i) finding or identifying the sources of sales recruits, (ii) evaluating and selecting the recruiting sources, and (iii) contacting candidates through the selected source(s).

Recruiting includes activities to get individuals who will apply for the job. The *general purpose of recruitment* is to provide a pool of qualified job candidates from where a company selects the right persons. This means recruitment activities do not include the selection of people. If a company wants to recruit a large number of salespeople, recruiting and selection processes should be done continuously. To maximize the chances of finding the right person, some companies take two specific actions: (i) for selecting one right salesperson, they get 20 applicants, and (ii) they offer the benefits that sales recruits want[17]. Sales managers and human resource executives should update their information on government employment regulations on a continuous basis. **Examples** are: Equal Pay Act of 1963 and Equal Employment Opportunity Act of 1972 in USA, and Equal Remuneration Act of 1976 in India.

Identifying the Sources of Recruiting Salespeople

For identifying or locating prospective candidates, companies use internal and external sources. Internal recruitment sources come from inside the company. They include: (i) employee referral programs, (ii) current employees, and (iii) promotions and transfers. The external sources of recruitment include: (i) advertisements, (ii) the Internet, (iii) educational institutions, (iv) employment agencies, (v) other companies (competitors, customers, non-competitors), and (vi) job fairs.

Internal Sources

❍ **Employee Referral Programs** Basically a referral is a recommendation (or the action of referring) by one individual that another person can be hired for a position. The employee referral program includes the company employees referring or recommending known persons for hiring for sales positions. This is now one of the most popular methods of locating sales recruits because it is very effective, relatively quick, and less expensive compared to other recruiting methods like advertising and employment agencies. In the employee referral scheme (or program), many companies like Microsoft and Southwest Airlines have incentive schemes to give monetary rewards to employees who provide successful referrals. The successful referral means the person referred is hired and meets initial performance goals. Talent crunch across the sector is prompting both MNCs (multi-national companies) and Indian companies to turn to their employees to fill in vacancies, for a price. Existing salespeople and purchase executives within the company are good sources for referral programs in identifying prospective sales candidates. The major disadvantage of using the employee referral scheme is that the company may not get enough of them and therefore, the company uses other sources as well.

❍ **Current Employees** This is a source of job recruitment in two ways: (i) current employees can recommend friends and relatives to the company, and (ii) they also can be candidates by applying for the sales job[18]. Many organizations like to recruit within their own companies because (i) the cost of recruitment is less, (ii) it improves employee morale, and (iii) the management is able to evaluate the applicant's potential as a salesperson. **For example**, General Motors normally recruits from within the organization.

❍ **Promotions and Transfers** Internal promotions and transfers generally result after the company announces sales job openings through newsletters, in meetings, or on the bulletin board. One study found that employees of the company who were internally transferred to the sales positions gave more long-term profits than salespersons from any other source[19]. This is possible because these employees are already familiar with the company's products and policies. Internal promotions to sales managers' positions can minimize the company's time and cost.

External Sources

❍ **Advertisements** By advertising in newspapers and trade journals for sales jobs, a company can produce a large pool of applicants in a short time. Advertising is generally less expensive on a cost-per-applicant basis. However, a large number of applicants who respond to newspaper advertisements, may not be qualified for the job, due to below average quality of many applicants. A company can be more selective by advertising in trade publications or through the Internet instead of a daily newspaper. However, in case of trade magazines, lead time to place an advertisement in the next issue is much longer (typically 6 to 8 weeks) than in newspapers. To ensure an advertisement's effectiveness, the following points are useful:

- Add restrictions (like bachelor's degree) to avoid receiving too many unqualified applicants.
- Advertise on a Sunday for a classified advertisement.

- More information in the advertisement about job specifications helps in screening applicants
- When speed of response is important, use classified newspaper advertising or online advertising.
- Use business publications like *Economic Times* for recruiting persons with business experience.
- Focus on prospective candidates' needs and interests, instead of too much of the company information.
- Use the advertisement as a unique sales proposal to motivate candidates to reply.
- A recruitment advertisement must attract attention and have credibility.
- Provide phone, e-mail id, website, fax numbers, and mailing address.
- Answer enquiries immediately before they cool off.

The information usually included in recruitment advertisements are: (i) company name, (ii) product or service, (iii) territory, (iv) hiring qualifications, and (v) how to contact.

❍ **The Internet** Many companies use their own websites to approach the applicants for various positions including sales. The *advantages* of this web-based recruiting are very low cost and time of getting applicants resumes. However, the company has to bear the cost of screening a large number of resumes to find the applicants who qualify for the sales position. Many companies use the Internet recruiting websites, such as www.monster.com, www.naukri.com, www.salesheads.com, and www.jobsearch.com. As a large number of job seekers accessing the Internet are college students, advertising on bulletin boards or in job banks will help in reaching the college market. Potential applicants can post their CVs on these sites so that firms can call them for interviews.

❍ **Educational Institutions** Large companies such as Hindustan Unilever, Wipro, and ICICI Bank use colleges and universities as a popular source for sales recruits. Small firms are less likely to recruit in college campuses because many graduates prefer large and well-known companies, who have extensive training programs and company benefits. Some companies offer internship programs to college students during vacation periods and students with good performance are offered jobs upon graduation. Companies not only find educational institutions as a cost effective source, but also that college students usually can be hired in shorter time and at lower salaries than experienced salespersons[20]. Often companies searching for future managers, look at educational institutions for position of sales recruits. Recruiters have an important role in attracting students for sales jobs. In order to do an effective recruiting job, recruiters should focus on job satisfaction, salary, opportunities for job advancement, and company's financial stability. Campuses of educational institutions have placement centers which contact companies for recruitment.

❍ **Employment Agencies** A commonly used source is the private employment agencies. They usually work from a job description provided by the human resource managers or sales managers. They can be asked to do initial screening of candidates. Private employment agencies have become human resource (HR) consultants. These agencies charge fees, usually ranging from 10 to 20 percent of the first year earnings of the person hired through the agency. The employer's cost for the employment agency's fees is offset by the savings in the advertising and initial screening tasks done by the agency. Professionalism of private employment agencies varies to a great extent, but there are good agencies who give useful services to companies by referring qualified candidates.

In India, the government has established employment exchanges in many cities. Unemployed persons register their names and submit their CVs to these exchanges. Companies collect candidates' details from the employment exchanges and call them for interviews.

❍ **Other Companies (Competitors, Customers, Non-Competitors)** A salesperson recruited from a competitor knows the products and markets well, has selling experience, and requires little training. However, such a salesperson may ask high salary and it may be difficult for such a salesperson to make adjustments in the new organization. Besides, some sales managers consider the practice of hiring competitors' salesperson as unethical, as the salesperson may use confidential information of the former employer. Also, such salespeople may not show loyalty to the recruiting organization. However, if the applicant has sound reasons for switching companies, it may be a good decision to get the competitor's salesperson.

Customers' purchase executives have some knowledge of the abilities of salespeople who call on them. Hiring a good employee of a customer has disadvantages and this should be done, if it is a must, tactfully without losing the customer. Some companies welcome back former employees who have left.

Salesperson working for non-competing firms is another source, if they are selling similar or related products or selling to the same markets. These salespersons have selling experience and need relatively less training. A firm that hires from other company must find out why the applicant is interested in changing the job and why they want to work for the hiring firm. Although it is difficult to determine the real reasons, good sales managers should be able to form some ideas to arrive at effective decisions.

❍ **Job Fairs** Many employers are brought at one location for recruiting with the arrangements of job fairs. Candidates visit the booths of the employers they are interested in. The employer may also ask a particular candidate for a meeting, based on the candidate's resume received earlier. Generally job fairs are held in the evening hours or on Sundays, so that presently employed salespeople can attend them. This problem will not arise for virtual job fairs on the Internet.

Evaluation and Selection of Recruiting Sources

After identifying the sources of recruiting salespeople, a company selects those sources that are effective based on the past database. This database is built over a number of years, as per the evaluation format shown in Table 5.3. However, for a new company, selection of the recruiting source depends on its cost.

Table 5.3 Evaluation of Recruiting Sources

Recruiting Sources	Number of Recruits	Number Hired	Number Retained (After 2 years)	Percentage Retained (After 2 years)	Cost of Recruiting	Performance Rating (After 2 years)	Special Remarks (if any)
Employee Referral							
Current Employees							
Promotions and Transfers							
Advertisements							
The Internet							
Educational Institutions							
Employment Agencies							
Other companies (a) competitors (b) customers (c) non-competing firms							
Job Fairs							

The focus in the evaluation of recruiting sources is on three factors: (i) performance rating of the sales force (excellent, very good, average, and poor) at the end of the two years of working, (ii) percentage retained (after 2 years working with the organization), and (iii) the cost of recruiting, which should include the total cost of recruiting, including travel, hotel, proportionate salary, and so on. Once the data is built over a period of one year, it can be used for the subsequent years for selecting the most effective source of recruiting at the least cost. However, this data needs to be updated every year to ensure continuous improvement in the recruiting stage.

Contacting Candidates

Once a company selects the sources of recruiting salespeople, contacting the candidates is done by human resource department.

SELECTING THE SALES FORCE

Earlier in sales force staffing process in Figure 5.9, after the recruiting stage the selection stage was shown, consisting of the following two activities: First, the company should develop a procedure or process and tools for measuring applicants against the job specifications or qualifications that were developed in the planning stage. The second activity is to make the decision on selection.

We shall first identify the major selection tools, which are used by companies for selecting salespeople.

The Selection Process

The selection process consists of a number of steps through which applicants pass. These steps are like filters. At any of these steps, an applicant may be dropped from further consideration.

The major steps in the selection process are shown in Figure 5.12. The selection tools used by companies for selecting the salespeople are: (i) screening resumes, (ii) application blank, (iii) initial interview, (iv) intensive interview, (v) testing, (vi) reference check, and (vii) physical examination. These tools are placed on the steps in the selection process as shown in Figure 5.12.

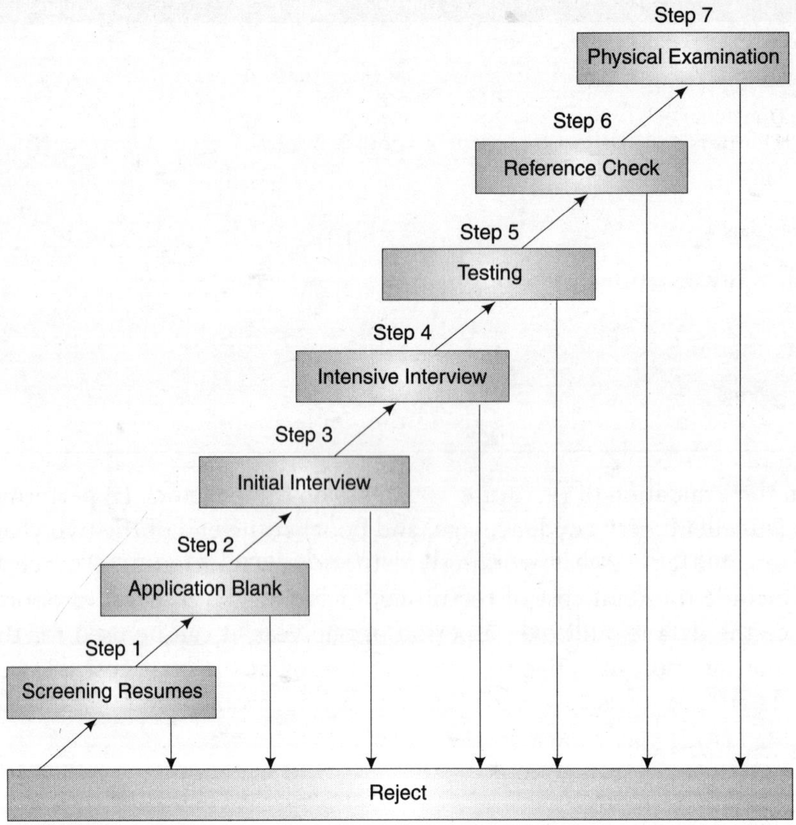

Fig. 5.12 Major Steps or Tools in Selection Process of Salespeople

Companies using multiple-step selection process differ in terms of the number of tools used and their order of inclusion. No matter which tool is used first—screening resumes, application blank, or initial interview—generally the least costly tool should be used first. Research on selection of tools/methods have shown that psychological tests have the highest predictive validity for evaluating an applicant's future job performance. However, personal interviews, the most widely used selection tool, have the least predictive validity of job performance. The selection process and tools are only to help in sound executive judgment and are not substitute for it. Let us discuss the various selection tools.

Screening Resumes

This tool is used when a company receives a large number of resumes, based on the recruitment sources like newspaper advertisements or campuses of educational institutions. To eliminate unqualified applicants, initial screening of resumes is done by the human resource or sales managers, based on comparison of the applicant's curriculum vitae (CV) with job specifications (or qualifications) that was developed earlier in the planning stage. This tool need not be used, if initial screening of resumes was done earlier by human resource (HR) consultants or somebody else.

Application Blank

It is one of the widely used selection tools. Application blank, which is also called formal application form, or personnel history record, is a convenient and methodical method of collecting relevant information from the applicant. The applicant may be asked to fill the application form/application blank. The relevant information in the application blank may include education, work experience (or employment history), physical and personal characteristics, membership of social and business organizations, positions held in organizations, records of earnings, reasons for leaving each previous job, hobbies and other interests. However, questions such as age, religion, or marital status should be asked only if such questions are in accordance with local laws and regulations. The format of the application blank or application form differs from company to company. There are some *advantages* of using the application form as a selection tool. These are: (i) comparison of many applicants is made easy because the information of each candidate is presented in the same order, (ii) the interviewer asks questions to investigate closely the information such as job experiences and education given in the application blank during the interview sessions, (iii) the application blank can be designed to comply with the legal and regulatory requirements of the local government, and (iv) it gives relevant information required by the company, but not mentioned in the applicant's resume or curriculum vitae (CV).

Personal Interviews

The purpose of a personal interview is to decide a person's fitness for a job. The interview takes place between a recruiter and an applicant to see if a match exists between what the company is offering the applicant and what the applicant is offering the company. Another purpose of interviewing is to get more information about the facts stated in the application blank. **For instance**, if an applicant has changed many jobs at short intervals and has stated the reasons for changing jobs as "better prospects", the recruiter may ask the applicant to explain what is meant by better prospects. Interviews are the most widely used selection tool. Studies have found that interviews can be good predictors of success in sales job because sales job requires skills similar to those on show in the interview[21]. However, in many cases, interviews are not as effective as they could be. This is because the interviewing process depends primarily on the behavior of the interviewer and many interviewers do not know how to interview an applicant effectively, and also how to interpret an applicant's responses. Many interviewers talk too much, listen too little, and ask wrong questions. Companies should, therefore, conduct workshops to improve interviewing skills at various levels of management. A properly conducted interview is a good predictor of the candidate's performance and should be used in the selection process. Some companies conduct interviews not only of the applicant, but also of the applicant's spouse[22]. This is done to ensure that the spouse supports the away-from home life style of the salesperson.

Interview Structure

Although sales managers agree that interviews have a great effect on the selection process, there is not much agreement on how structured the interview should be. The interview structure (or types of interviews) varies from the totally structured (patterned or guided) interviews at one end to the unstructured (non-directed or informal) interviews at the other end. The third type of interview is called semi-structured.

- **Structured Interview** Managers may use the structured interview for initial screening, but it is not suitable for getting an in-depth look at the candidate. In *structured or guided interviews*, all the applicants are asked the same questions and their responses are noted. This type of interviews are useful when one or several interviewers see different candidates and based on evaluation rank the candidates and also when many junior sales executives are involved in the selection process, but do not know what questions to ask. The structured interviews are criticized as being rigid. This is not always true, since some trained interviewers do make some changes without reducing the merit of the structured form.

- **Unstructured (or Non-directed) Interview** In this type of interview, generally the interviewer begins by asking a few open-ended questions like "tell me about yourself" or "tell me about your family". The interviewer gets the applicant talking on subjects such as school and college activities, achievements in life, work experience, and so on. The interviewer does a very little talking (about 10 to 20 percent), adequate to keep the conversation moving forward. The basic concept is that the applicant's traits or characteristics are discovered if the applicant is encouraged to speak freely. It takes a highly skilled interviewer to use non-directed (or unstructured) type of interview effectively. Even applicants in many cases are not comfortable with this method of interviewing. Research has clearly shown that unstructured interview type is not accurate in predicting the job performance of salespeople[23]. However, some human resource experts say that this interview technique produces insight into an applicant's attitudes, personality, and interests. The main disadvantage is that the company may face difficulty in getting a skilled interviewer.

- **Semi-structured Interview** Many companies today use *semi-structured interview type*, which is somewhere between the structured and the unstructured type interview. This type of interview allows a two-way flow of information between the applicant and the interviewer. In most cases, only a few main questions are pre-planned and for the balance period of time, there is an adequate flexibility for the interviewer to move from general questions like economic environment to specific questions on product and selling process. Many companies use semi-structured interview type to pay particular attention to the applicant's behavior and the performance.

- **Behavior and Performance based Interviews** Studies have found that these techniques of interviews are better predictors of subsequent success of applicants than other types of interviews. Behavior-based interviews are based on the theory that what a person has done in the past is indicative of what that person will do in future. The interviewer asks behavior-based questions to the applicant, such as "Give me an example of how did you overcome a customer objection" or "Tell me what closing techniques did you use in your previous selling job?" However, if the candidate did not have any previous selling experience, the questions are asked about intended behavior like how the applicant would behave in a job–related situation? The **examples** of these types of questions are: "How would you deal with a customer who is not sure about the benefits of your product, as compared with the other products in the market?" or "How would you convince a customer to buy your product, when the price of your product is higher than that of your competitor?" The basic concept is that salespeople's behavioral intentions are related to their subsequent behavior.

A Performance-based interview asks applicants to perform exercises simulating selling situations. **For instance**, the company gives applicants one of the products in advance for making presentation during the interview. These simulations of selling activities are useful in evaluating candidates based on their selling skills.

Initial Interviews

These are used to clarify questions about applicants' job qualifications, such as graduation level grades or marks and type of products and services sold in previous jobs. The interviewer makes preliminary judgment whether a similarity exists between the job specifications and the applicant's characteristics. The purpose of initial interviewing is eliminating unqualified candidates. The candidate's questions about the company and the job are also answered. Some companies conduct initial interviewing by asking questions over the phone or using computer-assisted interviewing. In the computer-assisted interview, **for example**, applicants are shown a video with three alternative scenarios for helping a customer and then applicants are asked to select the best one. The computer indicates applicants' strengths, weaknesses, and other areas that need further investigation. The initial or preliminary small interview is short about 15–20 minutes. It can be handled by a junior human resource or district sales manager.

Intensive Interviews

To get an in-depth view of the candidate, one or more intensive interviews are conducted. In many cases, intensive interviews include many managers conducting interviews in a particular order. To achieve depth and usefulness, when several managers conduct interviews in sequence, proper planning and co-ordination is required. In intensive interviews, many interviewers use semi-structured interview format that is based on the applicant's behavior and performance, as discussed earlier. However, a few interviewers use stress interview technique as a part of intensive interview.

- **Stress interview** In this technique, the interviewer deliberately places the applicant under stress, to find how the applicant might cope with the stress when selling. **For instance**, the applicant may be handed an object such as a pen or mobile phone and asked to sell it to the interviewer. In some stress interviews, the interviewer may ask a number of rapid questions, even before the applicant could reply. This puts the applicant under stress. In another method of stress interview, the interviewer intentionally becomes aggressive, or rude in questioning to see the reaction of the applicant. This method of interviewing has been used in the past, but is not often used these days because the candidates get irritated and less interested in the job. Besides, there is a little correlation between how a person handles stress in an interview and stress on the job, as found in some studies.

Testing

Many firms use tests as an additional means of improving their selection decisions. The purpose of testing is to decide whether applicants have certain traits or characteristics that lead to success in sales job. This results in improved performance and lower sales force turnover. Selected tests are designed to measure aptitude, intelligence, knowledge, personality and interest of salespeople.

Aptitude Tests measure a person's aptitude for selling, learning ability and social aptitude. Examples of aptitude tests are: (i) general sales aptitude test, (ii) sales aptitude checklist. **Intelligence tests** measure mental intelligence or intelligence quotient (IQ) which includes memory, inductive learning and word fluency. Examples are: (i) Wonderlic Personnel test, (ii) Otis test of mental ability. **Knowledge Tests** measure knowledge of applicants on subjects like marketing terms, product, and information technology (IT). **Personality Tests** measure traits or characteristics, such as extrovert, self-confidence, and empathy that are needed for a particular sales job. Some examples of these tests are: (i) Edwards Personal Preference Schedule (EPPS), (ii) Gorden Personal Profile. **Interest tests** measure the level of interest in a sales career. Examples are: (i) Kuder Occupational Interest Survey, (ii) Strong-Campbell Interest Inventory.

Those companies who have had success with tests suggest that tests are useful for identifying a candidate's strengths and weaknesses. In addition, tests reveal candidates who have key traits that are connected with successful salespersons[24]. The main problem with testing is that tests are sometimes misused because managers do not understand that all applicants who fall within a range of scores are equally qualified for the job. Many sales managers use tests due to the requirement of their headquarter office.

Another problem to look out for in testing is that few applicants can fake their responses, particularly for personality tests. Tests must have reliability (i.e. consistency of test results) and validity (i.e. the test measures what it claims to measure) otherwise they cannot be used successfully. One more issue is that tests are sometimes used as the sole deciding factor. If an applicant has done well in interviews and reference checks, but his test scores are low, management may not hire this person.

Tests can be useful selection tools, if the following suggestions are followed:

- Sales managers should not attempt to design tests. This responsibility should be given to human resource department and experts in testing.
- Use tests as a part of selection process, but do not make hiring decision based only on test results.
- If psychological tests (including personality and intelligence tests) are used, be sure to meet legal aspects of testing.
- Select a test that minimizes the applicants' ability to anticipate desired responses.
- Tests can identify areas for further close investigation, if they are administered and interpreted before final intensive interview.

Companies like Gillette, Proctor & Gamble, and IBM give high weights (importance) to test scores in their overall selection process.

Reference Check

The applicants who have successfully come out of screening resumes, application blank, interviews, and testing, may then become the subjects of a reference check, or background investigation. Referees are the names of persons from whom information can be obtained on an applicant's ability and character. In conducting reference checks or background investigation, it is advisable to request job-related information only.

A company may check an applicant's references by e-mail, letter, telephone, or personal visit. Each method has some limitations. A personal visit may take too much time when a reference is located at a distance. Some references do not give any information to a stranger on telephone. A letter or e-mail is, therefore, used, but it has a problem. The problem is that most firms are very cautious about giving out meaningful information in writing about former employees. This is because of fear of being sued for defamation or a company policy of limiting the information of past employees. In spite of these limitations, a reference check makes sure the true identity of an applicant and may confirm his employment history.

Most candidates list as references only those persons who are certain to give them a positive reference. In order to get a more unbiased information of the candidate, a company can ask reference names of other people (not listed by the applicant) who would be familiar with the applicant's work, such as the candidate's former employers, former customers, and past teachers. Questions that could be asked to a previous customer are: "Was the person efficient and dependable?" or "How would you rank this person compared to other salespeople who call on you?" When talking with an applicant's previous employer, questions that could be asked are: "Would you rehire this person, if there is a possibility?" or "Why did the applicant leave?"

Background investigations are also carried out by some investigating agencies, which specialize in pre-employment investigative interviews with former employers, and co-workers of applicants. Reference checks or background investigations are very important because some applicants tell lies about their past job responsibilities, past salaries, and educational records.

Physical Examination

Most companies want their prospective employees to undergo physical examinations because good health is important to a sales person's success. The objective is to find any physical problem that may prevent the job performance of an applicant. A company should have a policy about drug testing and drug use for its sales people and its sales managers. If a drug testing program is in place in an organization, all applicants are required to be tested. Sometimes, the costs of physical examinations and medical tests are high and therefore, they are given towards the end of the selection process. However, increasing number of companies are asking applicants to complete the forms dealing with their health without seeing a medical doctor.

Assessment Centers

These are centralized units established within companies to evaluate qualified applicants in all aspects. Some companies use assessment centers as a tool of selection process. These centers are setup to conduct simulated exercises, such as role-playing, business games, case analysis, and individual presentation for the purposes of not only selection, but also promotion or development. Participants' performance is evaluated by trained executives within the company or outside experts.

Although the costs of assessment centers are somewhat high, the quality of people selected through assessment centers go up substantially[25]. Increasing number of companies, such as Wipro, Infosys, Ford Motor Company, and Indian Oil Corporation have set up assessment centers.

Selection Decision

When all the steps of the selection process have been completed, one thing is yet to be completed and that is selection decision–which applicants are to be selected? For making a selection decision, the sales manager should decide the important job specifications which are necessary for performing the duties of the sales job. When selecting the salespersons for rural markets in India, the company should decide the selection criteria, such as willingness to work in rural areas, knowledge of local language, and cultural congruence to adapt to rural environment and ethos. These criteria are different for urban markets[26]. The sales manager should then evaluate each applicant's qualifications and potential in relation to the selection criteria. Sometimes the sales manager has to decide about whether an applicant's strength in one selection criterion can compensate for a weakness in another criterion, whether the applicant should meet certain minimum levels against each criterion, so as to be successful[27]. After evaluating the available candidates, the company makes a list of the candidates according to the preference.

LO 5 Organize hiring and socialization of the salespeople

HIRING STAGE

The hiring process should be implemented properly so as to give a positive impression of the company to the candidates, who look for good work environment, where people are made to feel important. There are two activities in the hiring stage: (i) the company making the job offer and (ii) acceptance of the job offer by the applicant.

The Company Making the Job Offer

The key contents of a job offer are designation, responsibilities, and compensation.

The details of compensation to sales force will be covered in chapter 6. The job offer for salespersons includes any or all of the following: (i) salary, (ii) performance-based incentives, (iii) company vehicle (two or four wheelers), (iv) house-rent allowance, (v) medical expense reimbursement, and any other fringe benefits. Some companies even offer reimbursement of relocation expenses to the new employee for moving residence from one place to another. The job offer or the appointment letter also includes, as a part of terms of service, probationary (i.e. training and testing) period, the last day of joining duty, designation (or job title), the reporting manager, and the place of work. The job responsibilities and key result areas (KRAs), derived from job specifications, are also included in the job offer. While communicating with selected salespersons, sales managers or human resource managers do the selling to get these salespeople join the company. Some companies like IBM, even go to the extent of paying bonus to the salesperson who has highly sought-after skills and qualifications[28]. Some firms show consideration of helping the potential employee's spouse find a job. This becomes an important factor for the candidate to accept one company's offer over another.

Acceptance of the Job Offer by the Applicant

In some companies, job offers are made by the human resource manager, and in some other firms the offers are made by the sales manager to whom the candidate will be reporting. Often, the job offers are first made over the telephone and only after the telephone offer is accepted by the candidate, a formal letter is sent. A fairly large number of candidates who are offered a job do not accept it. One reason is that the candidate finds the job not suitable according to his or her requirements. Another reason is that the candidate has received another company's offer and the other company continues to follow till the candidate accepts the offer. When initial job offers are made on telephone, the sales manager should tell the candidate how much time will be allowed for job acceptance and also give options to the candidate to negotiate on some terms, if they want to. Some managers prefer to make job offers in person, instead of over the telephone. This puts pressure on the candidate to respond immediately by signing the duplicate copy of the job letter. The wording of the formal letter of appointment should be done carefully since it is a contract between the company and the candidate.

SOCIALIZATION

After hiring the candidate, socialization and assimilation activities are involved, which complete the staffing process. Socialization is the process through which the new salespersons learn values, norms, attitudes, and behavior of people who are already working in the organization. It also introduces the new salespeople to the job and to their work environment. If the company is not successful in socializing new salespeople, they may soon leave the company. On the other hand, successful socialization of new salespeople helps them to adjust to the new job, resulting in job satisfaction and improved performance. Socialization process begins before the new recruit accepts the job offer and continues until the salesperson is fully assimilated into the company culture. Socialization is achieved through the salesperson's interactions with other people in the organization.

Many companies, like Proctor & Gamble and Ford Motor, who hire college graduates for sales positions, offer summer internships to college students. These internships permit students to learn about the organization before making a commitment, and help the companies to assess if the students can do the job well and also whether they fit into the company's culture. Several other companies start communicating with applicants, when initial contact is made, by distributing booklets or leaflets of the company to the applicants, which describe information about the company and its operations. In addition, the sales manager answers the questions of the applicants. Some firms show applicants videotapes or films about the company's mission, shared values, employee benefits, and the information about the job[29]. The more the applicants understand about the company and its culture, the more effective their decision of accepting the offer will be. Besides, the more information applicants get during the recruitment and selection process, the assimilation into the organization will be smoother.

Assimilation is the second stage of socialization process. It starts when the applicant accepts the job offer. The newly hired employees must become familiar with the people working in the organization, understand the norms and values of the company, and learn how to perform various activities of the sales job. In many companies, a lot of this information is covered in the initial training programs for new recruits.

The first few days are particularly difficult for new recruits. The sales managers should give as much time as possible to the new salespersons. A good method is that the sales manager should spend some time with the new salesperson at the beginning of each day, give relevant information and reading material, and answer questions. The organization structure should be explained to the new salesperson with reporting relationships. The new salesperson should be introduced to other employees reporting to the same boss. Present employees should be given the background information on the new salesperson so that they converse on some common matters. Introduction to other employees should be such that the new employee has a short chat with each of them. This orientation or assimilation of a new salesperson is an important part of a sales manager's job. Sales managers should set the performance standards for new salespeople and set right kind of examples for salespeople.

An effective socialization and assimilation process can help:

- Increase job satisfaction and performance of the salesperson.
- Reduce turnover of people and cost to the company.
- Give positive image of the company and the job.
- Minimize job related uneasiness for the salesperson.

A new salesperson should be socially integrated into the new environment. If a newly hired salesperson comes to a new city, there are problems, such as locating a new home and arranging for his children's school admissions. The sales manager in such situations should help the new salesperson by making suggestions about schools, real estate agents, doctors, and shopping areas. New salespersons spend a lot of time with their co-workers in the office and develop personal relationships with them, from which they derive a great deal of satisfaction. In order to retain new salespeople, companies must have socialization and assimilation processes in place.

SUMMARY

LO 1

- The purposes of a sales organization include degree of centralization, degree of specialization, line and staff positions, marketing orientation, effective coordination, and span of control.
- Sales organization can be classified into four basic types: (i) line sales organization, (ii) line and staff sales organization, (iii) functional sales organization, and (iv) horizontal organization.

LO 2

- Generally, many medium and large-sized organizations expand one of the basic sales organization structures into a specialized design, for increasing the effectiveness of their sales force. The bases of specialization are: (i) geographic specialization, (ii) product specialization, (iii) market specialization, (iv) functional specialization, and (v) combination.
- Many firms have developed separate organization structures and marketing programs for key accounts (or major customers). Management of major, key, or national accounts is very important to a supplier firm as it provides substantial sales and profits. Identification and, management of key accounts are the areas that need special attention.

LO 3

- After deciding the sales organization structure, the company is ready to determine the size of the sales force. For this, there are three methods available: (i) workload, (ii) sales potential or break-down, and (iii) incremental method.
- Proper staffing of the sales force is very important as it has a strong impact on the performance of the company. Sales force staffing process consists of five major stages (or phases): (i) planning, (ii) recruiting, (iii) selecting, (iv) hiring, and (v) socialization. The planning stage includes three steps: (i) establishing responsibilities, (ii) deciding the number of salespeople needed, and (iii) outlining the type of salespeople needed. The process of outlining or profiling of needed salespersons consists of three steps: (i) conducting job analysis, (ii) preparing job description, and (iii) developing job specifications or qualifications.

LO 4

- After the planning stage, the recruitment stage follows with a purpose of providing a pool of job candidates from various internal and external sources. Companies evaluate the various sources and select those sources which are effective.
- The next stage of staffing process is the selection process, which includes a number of steps or tools: (i) screening resumes, (ii) application blank, (iii) initial interview, (iv) intensive interview, (v) testing, (vi) reference check, and (vii) physical examination.

LO 5

- After the selection process is completed, there are two activities in the hiring stage: (i) the company making the offer, and (ii) the applicant accepting the job offer. The socialization process starts before the new salesperson accepts the job offer and it continues until the new salesperson is assimilated into the company culture. Effective socialization and assimilation (which is the second stage of socialization) process can help the company to improve performance and job satisfaction of the salesperson, reduce cost and turnover of people, give positive image of the company and minimize the salesperson's job related uneasiness.

Key Terms

Glossaries of key terms are mentioned at the end of all chapters

Application blank
Assessment center
Assimilation
Employee referral program/scheme
Hiring
Incremental method
Job analysis
Job description
Job qualifications/specifications
Key accounts
Line position or line authority
Recruitment
Reference check
Selection process
Socialization
Span of control
Staffing
Staff position or staff authority
Workload method

Conceptual Questions

1. What are the basic purposes of a sales organization? Explain any one of those purposes. LO1 M
2. Why is the line sales organization not suited to a large organization? Which type of basic organization structure would you recommend for a large company operating globally and trying gaining greater customer responsiveness and efficiencies? LO1 D
3. What type of specialized organization structure would you suggest to a large company having several products and services and many market segments in order to increase the effectiveness of its salespeople? LO2 M
4. Why have many companies developed separate organization structures and marketing programs for key accounts? What alternative organizational methods are available for sales managers for dealing effectively with key customers? LO2 D
5. What are the methods used to determine optimum size of the sales force? Explain any one of these methods. LO3 M
6. What are the major stages in the sales force staffing process? Which activity or part is considered by sales manager as the most difficult in the entire staffing process and why? LO3 D
7. Describe the relationship between conducting a job analysis, preparing a job description, and developing job qualifications or specifications. LO3 M

Note: Difficulty Level → E — Easy; M — Medium; D — Difficult

8. Mention the various internal and external sources used by companies for locating or identifying the prospective candidates. Why are employee referral programs or schemes becoming one of the most popular methods of locating sales recruits? LO4 M

9. Why are interviews most widely used selection tools? Mention the various types of interviews and which type of interview would you use in the final round of sales force selection? LO4 M

10. Why is increasing number of companies using assessment centers as a tool of selection process? LO4 D

11. Describe the importance of socialization and assimilation. LO5 E

Objective Type Questions

Select the most appropriate response out of the various options available in each of the following questions:

1. A sales manager in line position has an authority over the immediate subordinates to
   (a) recruit and select (b) direct and control
   (c) recommend and plan (d) none of these LO1 M

2. In a flat organization structure the span of control, as compared to a hierarchical organization structure, is
   (a) more (b) less (c) same (d) none of these LO1 E

3. Line sales organization structure is most suitable for
   (a) small-size organizations (b) medium-size organizations
   (c) large-size organizations (d) none of these LO1 M

4. In the horizontal sales organization, most people in the organization are members of
   (a) management teams (b) departmental teams
   (c) functional teams (d) cross-functional teams LO1 D

5. A company can avoid geographical or customer duplication in one of the following sales organizations:
   (a) functional (b) geographical (c) product (d) market/customer LO2 D

6. Key accounts are also referred as
   (a) major accounts (b) corporate accounts
   (c) house accounts (d) all of these LO2 M

7. One of the assumptions made in workload method for calculating the sales force size is that
   (a) work load of salespeople are unequal
   (b) work load of salespeople are equal
   (c) potential of territories are same
   (d) potential of territories are different LO3 M

8. For new companies, who do not have personal histories of salespeople, job specifications can be developed from
(a) study of job description
(b) study of many past researches
(c) asking customers
(d) all of these
(e) none of these
LO3 M

9. Studies have found that one of the following types of interviews is far superior for predicting subsequent success of applicants than other types of interviews
(a) structured interviews
(b) unstructured interviews
(c) semi-structured interviews
(d) behavioral and performance based interviews
(e) stress interviews
LO4 M

10. Increasing number of companies are using assessment centers as a tool of selection process because
(a) they conduct simulated exercises
(b) use outside experts in addition to company executives
(c) it is a recent trend
(d) quality of people selected is high
LO4 M

11. An effective socialization process can help:
(a) job satisfaction and performance of the salesperson
(b) reduce salesperson turnover
(c) give positive image of the company and the job
(d) all of these
LO5 M

Application Questions

1. What kind of organizational specialization within a sales department do you recommend for each of the following companies?
(a) A textile machinery manufacturing company diversifying into a consumer durable product, such as a uniquely designed table fan that can be used by household consumers and business customers initially in western India.
(b) A strategic business unit (SBU) (or a business unit) of a large company with wide range of products, such as room air-conditioners, packaged air-conditioners, central air-conditioning plants, water-coolers, refrigerators, and cold-storage plants, selling to households, factories, commercial establishments like hotels, theatres, hospitals, and government organizations all over the nation.
LO2 D

2. In a newly established company, manufacturing and marketing aluminium extruded products, such as door, window, and partition frames; heat sinks for electronic products like computers and printers, and other industrial applications, the sales and marketing manager decided to initially sell the products in southern markets of Karnataka, Andhra Pradesh, Telangana, Tamil Nadu, and Kerala, as its factory was located near Bengaluru. The company appointed two salespersons for Karnataka, and one each for Tamil Nadu, Andhra Pradesh, Telangana, and Kerala for selling its products to dealers and business customers. The sales manager was aware that having six salespersons to cover the entire southern market was
LO3 M

inadequate. However, he was not sure how to calculate the size of sales force. If you were the consultant, what would you suggest?

3. As an organization, your college or institute has a specific organizational structure. Obtain a copy of it or draw it. Is it a specialized organization structure? What is the degree of specialization? Is the span of control adequate? Assuming you would like your college to function effectively, what changes to the current organizational structure do you suggest? Give reasons for suggesting changes or no changes to the existing organization. **LO1 D**
4. Some nationalized banks recruit only experienced persons or promote people from within the organization. Some others like ICICI Bank and IDBI recruit extensively from management institutes. Explain the differences in sources of recruits used by these financial organizations selling essentially the same kind of financial services and products. Compare the advantages and disadvantages of different sources of recruits. **LO4 M**
5. Some sales and human resource managers think that reference check is not an effective selection tool. What are your views on this? Why is this selection tool used by most companies, despite its few stated drawbacks? **LO4 M**

ASSIGNMENTS FOR STUDENTS

1. A group of students are required to visit the marketing / sales offices of a company that sells consumer products and a firm that sells industrial products. Compare the sales organization structure, the type of specialization, hierarchy levels, span of control, and how the organization structure contributes towards customer service. Make a report and submit the same to the teacher.
2. There are many Internet sites that provide services for getting a job. Visit any three recruiting websites (e.g., www.monster.com, www.naukari.com) and report what services each one provides (in addition to job listings).
3. Interview two sales managers from two different companies. Request them to explain the staffing process followed by them. Compare the same with what is described in the text book. Make a report and submit it to your teacher.

Reference Notes

1. Ruekert, Walker, Jr, and Roering, *The Organization of Marketing Activities: A Contingency Theory of Structure and Performance*, Journal of Marketing, Winter 1985, p. 13.
2. John A. Byrne, *The Horizontal Corporation*, Business Week, December 20, 1993, pp. 76–81.

3. Rober Dewar and Don Shultz, *The Product Manager: An Idea whose Time has Gone*, Marketing Communications, May 1998, pp. 28–35.

4. Chad Kaydo, *Reorganizing a Sales Force*, Sales & Marketing Management, March 2000, p. 90.

5. Geoffrey Brewer, *Brain Power*, Sales & Marketing Management, May 1997, pp. 39–41.

6. Sanjit Sengupta, Robert E. Krapfel, and Michael A. Pusateri, *An Empirical Investigation of Key Account Salesperson Effectiveness*, Journal of Personal Selling & Sales Management, Fall 2000, p. 253.

7. Kerry J. Rottenberger-Murtha, *The Lean and the Green*, Sales & Marketing Management, February 1993, pp. 68–71.

8. Erika Rasmusson, *3M's Big Strategy for Big Accounts*, Sales & Marketing Management, September 2000, pp. 92–98.

9. Daniel S. Levine, *Justice Served*, Sales and Marketing Management, May 1995, pp. 53–58.

10. Rene Darmon, *Where do the Best Sales Force Profit Producers Come From?*, Journal of Personal Selling and Sales Management, 3 (Summer 1993), p. 17.

11. Chad Kaydo, *Overturning Turnover*, Sales and Marketing Management, 149 (November 1997), p. 50.

12. Charles Garfield, *What Makes a Top Performer?*, Sales & Marketing Management, May 1989; *What Makes a Super Salesperson?*, Sales & Marketing Management, August 1984, p. 86.

13. David Mayer and Herber M. Greenberg, *What Makes a Good Salesman?*, Harvard Business Review, July–August 1964, pp. 119–25.

14. George Avlonitis and Despina A. Karayanni, *The Impact of Internet use on Business-to-Business Marketing*, Industrial Marketing Management, 29 (2000), pp. 441–59.

15. Geoffrey Brewer, *Brain Power*, Sales & Marketing Management, May 1997, pp. 39–48.

16. Nina Munk and Suzanne Oliver, Think Fast, Forbes, March 24, 1997, pp. 146–51.

17. Erin Strout, *How to Win Today's Recruiting War*, Sales & Marketing Management, March 2000, p. 85.

18. Erin Stront, *Finding Your Company's Top Talent*, Sales & Marketing Management, May 2000, p. 113.

19. Darmon R.Y., *Where do the Best Sales Force Profit Producers Come From?*, Journal of Personal Selling & Sales Management, Vol. 13, Issue 3, 1993, pp. 17-29.

20. Audrey Bottjen, *The Benefits of College Recruiting*, Sales & Marketing Management, April 2001, p. 11.

21. E James Randall and Cindy H. Randall, *Review of Salesperson Selection Techniques and Criteria: A Managerial Approach*, International Journal of Research in Marketing, 1990, pp. 81–95.

22. James M. Comer and Alen J. Dubinsky, *Managing the Successful Sales Force*, (Lexington, MA: Lexington Books, 1985), pp. 5–25.

23. George F. Dreher and Thomas W. Dougherty, *Human Resource Strategy: A Behavioral Perspective for the General Manager*, (Boston: McGraw-Hill Higher Education, 2001), p. 107.

24. Ron Panko, *Getting Testy about Sales Screening Tests*, Best's Review-Life-Health Insurance Edition 98, December 1997.

25. Randall, Cooke, and Smith, *A Successful Application of the Assessment Centre Concept to the Salesperson Selection Process*, Journal of Personal Selling and Sales Management, 5(May 1985), p. 53.

26. Prof. Staju Jacob, *Hiring Salespersons for Rural Markets,* Indian Business Academy, Bangalore, India.

27. W.E. Patton III and Ronald King, *The Use of Human Judgment Models in Sales Force Selection Decisions,* Journal of Personal Selling and Sales Management, 12 (Spring 1992), p. 1.

28. Michele Marchetti, *The New Gold Rush,* Sales and Marketing Management, 150 (September 1998), p. 42.

29. Ginger Trumifio, *Recruiting Goes High Tech,* Sales & Marketing Management, April 1995, pp. 42–44.

Additional References

- Shapire and Moriarty, *National Account Management: Emerging Insights,* Cambridge, Mass: Marketing Science Institute, 1982.
- Christopher J. Bachler, *Resume Fraud: Lies, Omissions, and Exaggerations,* Personnel Journal, 74(June 1995), p. 50.

CASE 5.1

SEL Company—Modification in Sales Organization Structure

"It is becoming almost impossible to keep track of products and sales policies of 31 different products from six product divisions," said UK Gupta, regional sales manager (industries) of Eastern region of SEL Company. The modified market-oriented organization structure was in operation for over a year, and the sales engineers as well as the regional sales managers, handling business customers, were finding it very difficult to remember technical specifications, pricing policies, and customer benefit points of so many products. In the modified sales organization structure, all the 31 products of the company were sold by the three groups of salespeople – one group serving business (private sector) customers, the second group selling to dealers who thereafter sold company products to micro and small-sized customers, and the third group of salespersons looked after government customers like state electricity boards and railways. It was interesting to note that the private sector business customers needed more number of SEL's products than the other two groups.

This geographical and market combination sales organization structure was implemented from the earlier geographical and product based sales organization structure on the recommendation of a professor from a management institute. "In fact," said Gupta, "the earlier geographic and product-based organization was much better, as sales engineers looked after only five or six products and therefore became experts to give correct technical advice to customers." However the problem in the earlier organization structure was that some customers were getting irritated with two or three sales engineers calling on them from different product divisions of the company.

Both types of organization structures were having some merits and a few drawbacks. However, despite these problems faced by the sales engineers, the sales and profit performance of all the four regions showed marked improvement. The question was whether other factors, such as general improvement in the economy, the company's marketing strategies, and the competitors' performance have contributed to the increased sales and profits or was it due to the modification in the sales organization structure.

Discussion Questions

1. Was the decision to modify the organization structure right? Justify your answer.
2. Are there any other alternative sales organization structures available to the company?
3. If you were the general manager of eastern region to whom UK Gupta reported, how would you respond to his problem?

This case was prepared by Prof. Krishna K. Havaldar for classroom discussion.

CASE 5.2

Airflow Ltd.—Hiring Salespeople

"Why 4 out of 10 salespersons left within 6 months of joining the company?", asked the marketing director to the sales manager, Sunil Kumar, of Airflow Ltd. "I think, there may be something wrong with our staffing process," responded Sunil Kumar, without knowing the real reasons for the turnover of salespeople.

Airflow Ltd. started manufacturing and marketing consumer durable products like table fans for household consumers and business customers in 2013. The marketing office was located in Mumbai, the commercial capital of India. Airflow was a newly established company and for its first year of operations, the company decided to recruit ten salespersons to cover major metros and cities of Maharashtra state. The staffing process included deciding the job qualifications of salespersons. The administration manager was asked to place the advertisements in the local newspapers. The resumes of applicants were forwarded to Sunil Kumar, who screened the same and sent interview calls to about 25 applicants. The initial interviews were conducted by Sunil Kumar and the final interviews of the short-listed applicants by the marketing director. The selected candidates were issued the appointment letters. Some of the candidates had a problem of finding suitable residence, but the company policy did not provide any consideration for the same. Sunil Kumar conducted one-week training program and generally guided the new salespersons, who reported to him directly.

There was a delay in the receipt of the new fan from the factory, located at Baroda in Gujarat. During this period of three months, Sunil Kumar was asked to conduct market surveys and to look after the marketing communications function of the entire group of companies. He asked the salespersons to collect market information on various prospective new products like water purifiers and power tillers in which the group was considering the possibilities of future investments.

During this period, 4 salespersons suddenly stopped coming to work, after collecting their salaries of the previous working months.

Discussion Questions

1. What might be the reasons of 4 out of 10 salespersons leaving the company within 6 months of joining?
2. What improvements do you suggest in the staffing process followed by the company?
3. Was Sunil Kumar right in getting market surveys done by the new salespersons?

This case was prepared by Prof. Krishna K. Havaldar for classroom discussion.

Chapter 6

Training, Motivating, Compensating, and Leading the Sales Force

LEARNING OBJECTIVES

After studying this chapter, you will be able to:

LO 1 Know the value of sales training and understand the sales training process

LO 2 Explain what is motivation, its importance, and the theories of motivation; select the motivational tools, and outline the guidelines for motivating salespeople

LO 3 Understand the objectives of a compensation plan, design an effective compensation plan, and classify the types of compensation plan

LO 4 Discuss sales leadership and supervision; analyze leadership characteristics, styles, and skills to determine leadership effectiveness; describe how to supervise salespeople

Power Controls Ltd. (PCL) is one of the leading manufacturers of modular-type power switchboards, control panels, and bus ducts. It is located at one of the leading Indian cities, viz., Hyderabad. The company was incorporated in the year 1985 with a commitment to a world-class customer experience. PCL's quality policy of customer delight is backed up by its ISO 9001-2000 and ISO 9001-2008 certifications of quality. The company markets its products to market segments like steel, automotive, paper, cement, and building construction. Its business customers include Wipro, Taj Hotels, Hewlett Packard, Grasim, TCS, and many more. To improve customer satisfaction, teamwork, and performance of individual employees, the company has set up an effective training centre. It has well-qualified and experienced trainers for constantly honing the skills of all employees.

The objectives and contents of training programs for new sales trainees are broader and different from those for experienced salespersons. For example, for new salespersons the content of the training programs includes knowledge of the company, the products, the customers, and the competitors, as well as selling and presentation skills. Whereas for experienced salespersons the training programs are specific, depending on the training needs – like, negotiating skills or product knowledge for a new product. The company uses different methods of training to suit a specific training program and also to improve attention and interest of the trainees. The different methods of training used by the company include lecture, demonstration, role playing, case studies, simulation games, online training, audio cassettes, films, and on-the-job training. Most of the training takes place at the company's centralised training centre. However, sometimes the company uses video conferencing to minimise travel and lodging costs of salespeople. Most of the trainers are available internally, but sometimes outside training specialists are involved in the sales training programs. The company evaluates its training programs to improve the design and implementation of its future training programs.

Depending on the needs of the salespersons, the customers, and the company, the sales manager of the company selects the tools of motivational mix. It includes both financial and non-financial rewards, such as salary and commission (financial tools) and promotion, recognition, job enrichment, accomplishment award, and effective supervision (non-financial rewards). Thus, the company offers several motivational tools, which help to meet the needs of each salesperson. This makes the company's motivational program effective.

The company's compensation plan for the salespeople is developed to achieve the objectives of attracting and retaining quality salespeople, controlling the activities of salespeople, and making the plan fair or just. The type of compensation plan selected by the company is called combination plan, which includes a fixed component of salary and variable components of commission and performance bonus. The fixed component of salary is about 60 percent of the total compensation and is adequate to take care of the salespeople's living expenses. The variable component of commission is linked to the performance goals of sales volume and selling expenses. The performance bonus (i.e., one time lump sum payment) is linked to the performance on development of new customers. The other bonus is paid to all the employees irrespective of their performance, once a year, as per the Government's Bonus Act. Thus, the compensation plan for the salespeople is effective in terms of achieving its objectives.

The senior sales and marketing management team demonstrated their excellent leadership quality by consistently achieving the company objectives in terms of sales volumes, profit contribution, and customer service.

As the above opening vignette illustrates, successful companies give importance to training, motivation, and compensation to its salespeople and also to other employees. Today's salespeople must be prepared to meet the demands of value-conscious customers. Superior quality of service and products would ensure customer delight. Effective training, motivation, and compensation can help to meet the challenges from customers and competitors. In this chapter, first the value of sales training and its process is discussed. Then various aspects of motivation and compensation of salespeople are explained. And finally the characteristics, styles, and skills of sales leadership as well as sales force supervision are discussed.

LO 1 Know the value of sales training and understand the sales training process

VALUE OF SALES TRAINING

Most sales managers recognize that sales training is important for the success of salespeople. Research has shown that sales training leads to selling effectiveness, improved customer relations, and higher retention of salespeople[1].The value of sales training is clearly understood at Intel, which states that increases in sales from its sales force are due to its heavy investment in sales training[2]. Another company, Nabisco, found its sales increased rapidly above the usual level after sales training. In addition, the company stated that its investment in sales training resulted in improved teamwork, morale, and customer satisfaction[3].

Many companies view sales training as an important means for protecting their investments in their salespeople[4]. The U.S. companies give more than 30 hours per year training to the average salesperson[5]. Time and money invested in sales training vary depending on the types of sales (e.g., consumer products or services, industrial products or services), experience of the salespersons, and size of the firm. Table 6.1 shows an average time invested for training a salesperson per year[6].

Table 6.1 Time Invested in Sales Training

Type of Sales	Training Period for New Salespersons per Year (Months)	Continuing Training for Experienced Salespersons (Hours per Year)
Consumer products	3.4	35.8
Consumer services	3.3	33.9
Industrial products	4.8	31.6
Industrial services	4.8	30.8
Office products	3.8	41.8
Office services	3.2	33.3

Note: Time shown are averages.

When a company invests time and money for training salespersons, the sales manager is also required to spend time in planning and implementing the training program. Sales managers should take care to ensure that time and money are spent properly. However, customers often feel that the salespeople who serve them are not effective. Even salespersons who have undertaken training have been sad because their hopes are not fulfilled[7]. Thus, it is clearly seen that many sales training programs are not effective. There are three major reasons for this. First, the training needs of salespeople are not estimated completely with every detail. Second, the customer's opinion or liking is not considered. Third, after the sales training programs, reinforcement or follow-up trainings are not done.

It should be understood that training cannot solve all the problems. For example, if a company's sales are low, it may be due to unsatisfactory quality of the product, wrong marketing strategy or reduction in market demand. However, if the sales training is correctly designed, implemented, and reinforced, it can result in improved performance of salespeople and better customer relations.

UNDERSTANDING THE SALES TRAINING PROCESS

Successful sales training programs follow three phases, viz. (i) identifying who should be trained and their training needs, (ii) designing and executing a training program, and (iii) evaluation and reinforcement of a training program. This is shown in Figure 6.1.

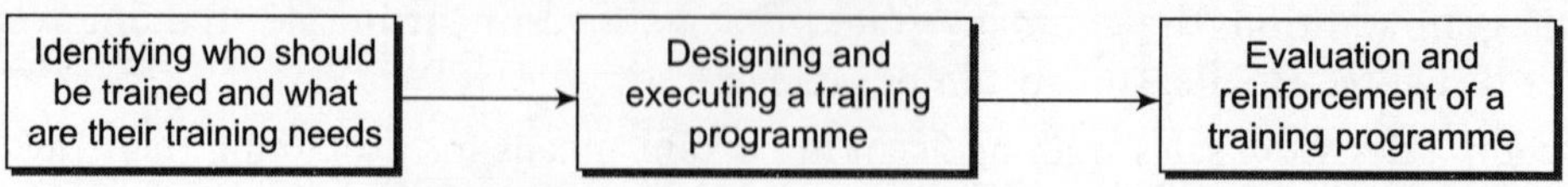

Fig. 6. 1 **The Sales Training Process**

Identifying Who Should Be Trained

Most companies identify not only their newly hired salespersons, but also the company's existing or experienced salespeople, sales representatives of their intermediaries, and the company's sales managers.

Newly Hired Salespersons

Table 6.1 shown earlier gives information about an average time invested by companies for training new salespersons per year. However, the training period for new hires varies from two to six months. For industrial or technical products and services, the time and costs are more than consumer products and services.

Existing Salespersons

Experienced or existing salespersons can benefit from refresher courses or continual training. The amount of training depends on the training objectives and needs. There is also a trade-off between the gains from training and the lost sales and customer service due to the salesperson's absence from the field. No doubt, benefits from training will be greater in the long-term view than any short-term losses. The time required for training existing salespersons may vary from one to four days.

Intermediaries' Sales Representatives

Sometimes companies train the sales representatives of their intermediaries, such as dealers, distributors, manufacturers' representatives (or agents). For technically complex products, manufacturing firms train their customers' or users' employees. This reduces the customers' complaints and equipment downtime.

Sales Managers

It is important to give training to the company's sales managers by providing training within the firm or send then to outside management programs conducted by the Indian Institutes of Management (IIMs) and others.

IDENTIFYING TRAINING NEEDS

The purpose of identifying or assessing the training needs is to understand the specific objectives of training for individual salesperson, such as improving product knowledge, selling techniques, or relationship building. However, often the need for sales training becomes obvious only after knowing the declining sales force performance. Instead of reacting to solve the problems of sales force performance, the role of sales training should be to prevent problems on a proactive basis. Capability gaps arise when the salespeople do not have the required knowledge, skills, or capabilities to become successful on the job. Sales training exists to overcome deficiencies and to make salespeople continuously successful.

Sales managers should identify the training needs for both newly hired sales trainees, and experienced (regular or existing) salespeople. For example, new salespeople may need training in sales techniques, whereas experienced salespersons may need training in negotiating skills. In addition, some companies, who use the team selling approach for major customers, the training needs of the selling teams should be considered.

Methods Used for Identifying Training Needs

Some of the methods used to decide the training needs are: (i) sales manager's observation, (ii) sales force survey, (iii) customer survey, (iv) performance testing, (v) job description, and (vi) sales force audit.

Sales Manager's Observation

Field sales managers spend a lot of time in the field working with the salespeople. These first level sales managers observe the need for a particular sales training, based on the specific difficulties (or deficiencies) of the salesperson. The sales manager tries to find the salesperson's difficulties by going into the field and talking to and customers.

Sales Force Survey

To identify the training needs of the salespeople, it is important to conduct sales force survey, as an independent activity or combined with other sales activities like sales reports. However, if field sales managers and their salespeople disagree on the training needs, it is better to discover this disagreement and find a solution before designing the sales training program.

Customer Survey

It is very much recommended for some companies, where personal selling is the key element of their sales and marketing strategy, to conduct customer survey to identify sales training needs. The customer survey also helps to understand customer expectations, the company's salespeople's competencies, as compared to that of competitors' salespeople in the same industry. This practice is followed at 3M[8].

Performance Testing

Some companies test knowledge and skills of salespeople by conducting performance testing of salespersons on a regular basis. Sales trainers evaluate the performance of salespersons on presentation skills, product knowledge, customer relationship management, and so on, to determine training needs.

Job Description

In Chapter 5, it was mentioned that job description statement would be useful not only for recruitment and selection, but also for sales training and evaluation of sales force. Job description mentions clearly the responsibilities, and the key tasks or key result areas (KRAs) of the salespeople. It is, therefore, a logical tool to be used in assessing the training needs, particularly by a new company.

Sales Force Audit

As a part of marketing audit or sales audit, some companies use sales force audit for assessing training needs of salespeople. Generally conducted once a year, the sales force audit asks questions on the training programs: about its adequacy, contribution, and revision.

Popular Sales Training Needs

Although the needs of sales force training differ across companies and over the periods of time, there are some training needs that are popular. These are: (i) product knowledge, (ii) customer knowledge, (iii) competitive knowledge, (iv) selling skills, and (v) company knowledge.

Product Knowledge

Usually product knowledge is the frequently covered topic in sales training programs. It includes advantages, applications, and limitations. If the product or service is technically complex, more time is spent in giving the detailed knowledge. When the company develops a new product or carries out major modifications of the existing product, training on new product is needed even for experienced salespeople.

Customer Knowledge

The sales training may include relevant information about the company's customers, such as types of customers (like household consumers, government customers, institutional customers), knowledge of customers' businesses, customer needs, buying motives, buying orientations and procedures, sales potential, and so on. Some companies classify their customers into A, B, and C based on their sales potential and then train their salespeople to carry out routing and scheduling plan. For international or foreign customers, the training programs should include cultural differences and business practices followed in foreign countries. Salespeople should be trained to develop partnering relationships with key customers by clearly understanding the customer's problems and solving them better than competitors.

Competitive Knowledge

Knowledge of competitors' products or services in terms of strengths, weaknesses, strategies, and tactics as well as prices, discounts, payment terms is very important for salespeople to plan the sales strategy. Competitors' knowledge would help a salesperson during a sales presentation, overcoming customer objections, negotiation, and finally closing the sale.

Selling Skills

One study points out that over 30 percent of time is spent on sales techniques or selling skills out of the total time spent in sales training programs[9]. Many salespeople are not competent in selling skills and hence, they need training on "how to sell". There are many common shortcomings (like lack of sales strategies for individual customers, ineffective questioning and listening skills, giving benefits before understanding the customer needs) which can be removed by a good training program. Training in customer relationship building methods for retaining current customers, and negotiation skills are now considered as very important for training by most sales managers and salespeople[10].

Company Knowledge

New sales trainees should be told about the company's vision, mission values, objectives, organization structure, policies and selling practices. The general policies may include personnel policies like canteen facilities and leave policies. Selling practices may include number of sales calls per day, how to handle returns from customers, expense account, sales reports, and so on. Channels of communication and how to contact key people in the organization structure are important for new salespeople. It is also necessary for the trainees to understand the history and any other relevant background information that helps to develop a sense of pride about the company.

DESIGNING AND EXECUTING A SALES TRAINING PROGRAM

After the first phase of identifying the training needs of the people to be trained, the second phase of designing and executing the sales training program is considered. There are five decisions a sales manager has to take while designing and executing a sales training program. These decisions are summed up to the popularly known one word called ACMEE (aims, content, methods, execution, and evaluation) as shown in Figure 6.2.

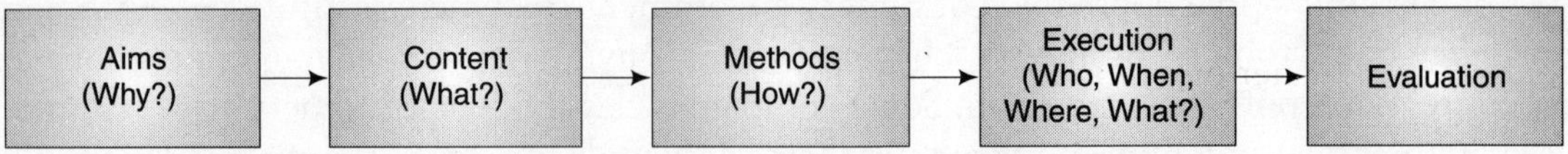

Fig. 6.2 ACMEE Decisions for Designing a Sales Training Program

The first three parts of ACMEE decisions relate to the design aspects of the sales training program. This consists of aims (or objectives), content, and methods of the training program. The last two parts represent execution and evaluation, as shown in Figure 6.2.

Designing the Sales Training Program

We shall discuss each of these phases or steps, so as to understand these steps clearly and in more detail.

Aims/Objectives of Sales Training (Why is Sales Training Needed?)

The first step in designing the sales training program is to decide the specific aims or objectives. Although sales training needs and objectives vary from company to company, some of the common objectives are mentioned below:

- Orienting new salespeople to the sales job.
- Increase sales productivity.
- Improve the performance of the salespeople.
- Increase sales, profits, or both.
- Lower sales force turnover.
- Improve customer relations.
- Introduce new products, markets, and promotional programs.
- Create positive attitudes and improve sales force morale.
- Prepare new salespeople for assignment to a sales territory.
- Improve teamwork and cooperative efforts.

Some of the above objectives are interrelated. For example, if sales productivity goes up, it will increase the sales and profits of the company. The **benefits** of setting aims or objectives for sales training are as follows:

- Objectives help to describe the expectations of sales training.
- Written objectives may get budget support from top management.
- Training objectives can be used for measuring effectiveness of training.
- Specific training objectives become an effective communication tool to communicate with all those who are involved in the training program.

Content of Training Program (What should be the Content of Sales Training?)

The **content of the initial training for new sales trainees** will be broader and different from the content of refresher or continuing training for experienced salespersons. Usually the contents or the topics of the training program for new salespeople for initial training will include: (i) company knowledge, (ii) product knowledge and application, (iii) customer knowledge, (iv) competitor knowledge, (v) the selling process, and (vi) selling skills or sales techniques. These topics have been covered earlier under popular sales training needs. Some companies may add some more topics such as negotiating skills, communication and listening skills, sales presentation skills, customer relationship building skills, team-selling skills, time and territory management skills, computer-assisted selling skills, knowledge of ethical and legal issues in selling and knowledge of commercial terms and conditions. All the above topics may not be covered in every training program. In fact, the contents of the training will depend upon the objectives or aims of the sales training program.

The **content of continuing training program for existing or experienced salespersons** will be more specific, depending on the training needs and objectives. For example, if the company wants to launch a new product, or introduce a change in the sales organization structure, a sales training program is organized for the existing salespeople with specific content or topic of product knowledge and application for the new product or benefits of the revised organization structure. Many companies who sell their products and services to business customers, particularly government firms, the knowledge of commercial terms and conditions, such as terms of payment, bank guarantees, penalty against delivery failure, excise duty, central sales tax, and value added tax (VAT) is very useful to salespeople. The proposed goods and services tax (GST) will subsume 17 indirect taxes including central excise duty, state value-added tax, octroi, entry tax, etc. It is likely to be introduced in India from July 1, 2017.

Many companies are paying particular attention to building long-term mutually satisfactory **relationships with key customers.** Salespeople are trained to identify the key accounts (i.e., important customers), who have high sales and profit potential. The strategies used to manage the key accounts are also discussed with experienced salespersons. One of the strategies used is the **team selling approach.** Some salespeople work as a part of a sales team. Some of the skills that are important to the successful performance of a sales team are: placing team success above individual success, willingness to cooperate, keeping others informed, and accepting the shortcomings of others. The topics of the training programs include building sensitivity and trust among teammates.

Time and territory management, including routing and scheduling are important to salespeople because if used properly it can greatly improve the productivity of salespersons. Territory management is the responsibility of the first level sales manager, but he/she can guide or train salespeople to use time management tools like smart phones and laptop PCs as well as how to plan efficient routes and schedule customer visits, as described in chapter 4 earlier.

Ethical and legal issues in selling need to be discussed with salespeople as one of the topics to avoid litigations on product liability, making false claims about the company's products and services, and giving bribes or costly gifts to customers. These aspects are discussed further in Chapter 7.

Sales Training Methods (How will the Sales Training be Conducted?)

These training methods are required to suit a specific training program. In fact, the use of several different methods in a training program helps to improve attention and interest of the trainees, and makes the learning process better. Training methods are grouped into five categories, as shown in Figure 6.3. These are: (i) class room/conference training, (ii) behavioral learning/ simulations, (iii) online training, (iv) absorption training, and (v) on-the-job training (OJT). The selection of different methods for a specific training program depends upon how well the topic and the audience are combined.

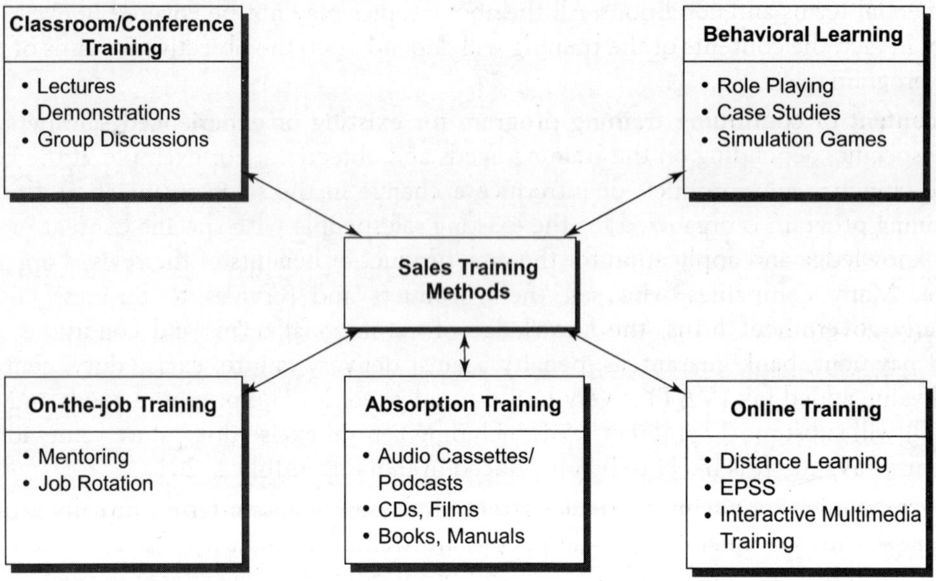

Fig. 6.3 Methods Used in Sales Training Programs

Classroom/Conference Training

The methods used in the classroom or conference setting are lectures, demonstrations, and group discussions. These are further explained as follows:

- **Lecture** This method is used by the trainers to give greater information in a short time to a relatively large number of participants. Because lectures usually do not generate active participation of the trainees, it leads to boredom and therefore, lecture sessions should be short and placed between other activities. Lecture sessions can be successful by use of visual support like power point presentation and by involving the audience through thought provoking questions. Company information, basic product knowledge, customer and competitive information, and a basic outline of a subject can be presented by the lecture method. For example, Merck's pharmaceutical's medical representatives spend 90 percent of their training in the classroom, where they are taught through lectures on the scientific principles of medicines[11].

❍ **Demonstration** A good method to teach product knowledge is to demonstrate the operation and use of the product. For example, Whirlpool Corporation used an unusual type of demonstration, by asking newly hired salespeople to live for two months in a house that was equipped with its appliances. The salespeople learnt about the company products by using these appliances in their daily lives[12]. Videotapes are also used for demonstration of selling skill and products knowledge. Business marketing companies manufacturing technically complex products or equipment like furnaces and machine tools demonstrate their products to prospective customers at their factories, where customers can see not only the product in working condition, but also the manufacturing process and quality control measures. Trade shows and exhibitions are also used by manufacturers to demonstrate their products in working conditions.

❍ **Group Discussion** A simple form of group discussion is one in which the trainer leads the discussion and encourages participation from the salespersons. If experienced salespersons are present in the group, their exchange of ideas and thoughts would be useful to newly hired salespersons. However, group discussions are not useful if the sales trainees are so inexperienced that they cannot contribute. Other forms of discussions are case studies and panel discussion. Trainees are given cases on business situations to study and then the trainer leads the class discussion to analyze the case and solve the problems described in the case. A panel discussion consists of a small group of people brought together to discuss a specific topic of interest to salespersons such as customer relationship and customer centric approach. After each panel member makes a brief presentation on the given topic, the participants ask questions to the panel members. This results in useful discussion on the given topic. Some companies use innovative games to train their salespeople[13]. For example, each salesperson is asked to read a particular book before a group of salespeople meet for presentation and discussion. The discussion moves them quickly from academic to business situations, resulting in a lot of learning.

Behavioral Learning

The methods that focus on behavioral learning or simulation are role playing, case-studies, and business games. In these methods, either trainees' behavioral mistakes are corrected or desirable behavior is described.

❍ **Role Playing** It is a very popular method for teaching the selling skills. In role play, the trainer presents a frequently faced and realistic sales situation to the sales trainees. Separate briefs are given to role playing individuals to help them develop their roles. Normally, one sales trainee plays the role of a salesperson and another sales trainee acts as a purchaser. The role playing is videotaped or performed live for a group of trainee participants, who then do critical assessment of the role play. An effective role playing method is to first ask the person who has played the role of the salesperson to express his views and thereafter, ask the views from the trainee participants[14]. Then, the trainer should assess positive points of the role play performance and suggest the areas of improvement. In role playing, trainees learn the importance of being knowledgeable about the customer, competitors, company, product, and industry. They also learn that a good role-playing session is learning by doing. The trainer should make clear to participants to take criticism in the right way. Companies like Johnson & Johnson, DuPont, Coca-Cola, and many other firms use role playing not only for teaching selling skills, but also for teaching some growth-related skills such as creativity, emotional intelligence, and adaptability[15].

❍ **Case Studies** A case is a narration of a business situation. Cases try to represent real life businesses or sales situations. Cases should be linked to learning objectives, such as understanding the training needs of salespeople or sales forecasting methods to make it an effective learning. Case studies are beneficial to salespeople for better understanding of sales and marketing concepts, problems and strategies. Small cases of one or two pages may be given to trainees for reading and analyzing in advance, preferably as an overnight home work. One method of case teaching is open discussion, in which the trainer steers the class discussion towards learning objectives. Another method is called group exercise in which trainees discuss the case in a group of 6 to 8 participants and prepare themselves to make presentations. The instructor/trainer may pick trainees from each group at random for presentation. After the presentations, the instructor summarizes the case keeping in mind the learning objectives.

Cases are written with different approaches. One approach is to describe the business situation and the problem(s) faced by the company without giving any solution(s). At the end of the case, the questions are asked to the trainees or the students to analyze the case and find appropriate solutions. Another approach in case studies is to describe the business situation, the problem(s) faced by the company, and how the company solved the problem(s). The questions at end of the case, ask trainees/participants to comment on the decisions or actions taken by the company and how they would have solved the problem. If the case is given to the trainees in advance for reading and participation, the trainer may need 30 to 60 minutes for classroom discussion.

Major **benefits** of case study method are: (i) it improves analytical skills and problem-solving, (ii) the trainees' understanding of business situations increases, (iii) the trainees learn to apply the theoretical concepts to the practical business situations described in the case. The major **drawbacks** are: (a) the trainees may face difficulties in selecting the right concepts for application to solve the problems described in the case, (b) if the participants or trainees do not put adequate efforts towards reading and preparation of cases at home before classroom discussions; they are not benefited by the case method.

❍ **Simulation Games** These are pre-programmed computer packages, and are based on real life sales situations. These games help in learning impact of decision-making, by allowing sales trainees to make decisions either in their own or customer's organizations. Trainees make decisions on sales forecast, pricing, advertising, size of orders and the like. Thereafter, the trainees are given feedback regarding the outcomes of their decisions. Business games generate a lot of enthusiasm due to competitive game playing. However, they do take a lot of time for generating decisions and for making the whole process effective.

For example, a firm called AchieveGlobal developed a CD simulation to teach salespeople how to be successful[16]. It teaches trainees how to apply need-satisfaction selling method. Many companies use simulation CDs as well as the simulation games that are available through the Internet.

On-the-job Training

The most important and frequently used method of training salespeople is on-the-job training (OJT). Eighty-four percent companies surveyed use on-the-job training[17]. In this method, a new or junior salesperson is assigned to a senior sales supervisor, or a senior salesperson. Generally, the new salesperson accompanies the senior salesperson for some period of time to observe the senior making several sales calls, which include the activities like sales presentations, overcoming customer objections, and closing the sales. Later, the new salesperson makes sales calls, initially on easier customers; while the senior salesperson or supervisor, accompanying the new salespersons, observes and coaches. The supervisor and the new salesperson discuss each of those sales calls. The supervisor then advises the new salesperson how he could have done the call more effectively. OJT puts the sales trainee or the new salesperson in a more practical sales situation than any of the other method. IBM and Boeing get some of their best training results when they pair a seasoned veteran with a beginner[18]. It is important that the sales supervisor or the senior salesperson maintains a positive attitude during on-the-job training, so that the trainee imbibes positive attitude, even if the sale is not made. Normally, OJT is used as the final stage of the sales training program. This method is most suitable when a salesperson is to be trained in a very short time. OJT can also be used for the experienced salesperson, when he is accompanied by his field sales manager, who makes valuable suggestions for improvement, after they leave the customer's office.

- **Mentoring** It is a type of on-the-job training used by many companies. Mentors usually provide the new employees advice and support, as well as information about the corporate culture. In some companies field sales managers or senior salespersons serve as mentors. Junior salespersons are assigned to them. Companies like GE Capital, IBM, and Boeing get their top-ranked salespeople by senior salespersons mentoring junior salespersons[19].

- **Job Rotation** The sales trainee or new salesperson work in different jobs for short stints. For instance, in a fast moving consumer goods (FMCG) company, a new salesperson, as a part of OJT, is asked to work for two months each in a retail shop, company logistics department, and field selling function with a senior salesperson. This makes the new salesperson aware of the working of different departments of the company. In some companies, job rotation is used to groom salespeople for management positions. In some other companies, salespeople work in different territories of the market to get a better understanding of the marketing environment.

Online Training

Many companies are turning to online training as it takes 50 percent less time and costs 30 to 60 percent less than other methods of training[20]. In addition to saving in cost and reaching employees in distant global locations, salespeople can opt for training online when it is convenient to them, without losing selling time. Many times the online training pays particular attention to basic skills and knowledge, such as product, company, and competitors' information. Face-to-face training (such as role play or on-the-job training) can then be used for teaching and doing the selling repeatedly to improve the selling skills. In addition, online training reach information to salespeople at great speed. However, some salespersons may postpone online training lessons or even may not do them. Such problems can be resolved by setting time limits for finishing the lessons and penalizing or rewarding depending upon the progress made by salespeople.

- **Electronic Performance Support System (EPSS)** It improves on the traditional computer based training by making the information available to the salesperson immediately and in a personalized manner. In this system, employees can obtain information from tutorials whenever they need. Salespeople have access to a large amount of data as and when they require. The data or information needed by salespeople may include product specifications; customer information, like buying criteria and key buying committee members; competitors' prices; and so on. For all these information, the salesperson has to only click for immediate access, instead of asking someone else for help. That is why EPSS is called just-in-time training.

- **Interactive Multimedia Training** It is quicker, less costly, and more effective than the conventional employee education. It is used for retraining salespeople, who can repeat or skip the material as desired. By combining written work, pictures, sound, animation, and video the multimedia tool increases the quality of training. When salespeople are asked to take more responsibilities like prospecting, after-sales-service, and customer relationship building, they need retraining. Interactive multimedia has become known as an effective method for retraining salespeople. This method of training is interactive by which, based on the requirements of the sales trainees, the training material can be adjusted and delivered. This technology is also available to small firms.

- **Distance Learning** It is defined as the education of students who may not always be physically present at the school/college. These courses are conducted either hybrid, blended or 100 percent whole instructions. A number of other terms (viz., e-learning, online learning, distributed learning) are used which approximately have the same meaning as distance learning. Salespeople who want to progress further in their career into sales or marketing management would like to adopt distance education route to obtain a degree or diploma in management education. This method is like a personal training approach.

Mail correspondence, which is the oldest form of distance education, is an asynchronous delivery technology. Similarly e-mail, video and audio recordings, print materials, voice mail and fax are other forms of delivery. Many courses offered by both open universities and campus based institutions use periodic sessions of day teaching to supplement the session delivered at distance (e.g., through e-mail). This type of mixed distance and campus based education has recently come to be called **"blended learning" or "hybrid learning"**.

Distance learning can also use interactive radio instruction (IRI), interactive audio instruction (IAI), online virtual worlds, digital games, webinar, and webcasts, all of which are referred to as **e-learning**. The widespread use of computers and the internet have made distance learning faster and easier. Respected universities, such as Harvard and Stanford, and institutions, like Indian Institute of Management, Ahmedabad, and Bengaluru, offer degrees and diplomas in management education. Enrolment for online courses has been seen to increase with the advancement in technology. Massive open online courses (MOOCs) offering large-scale interactive participation and open access through the World Wide Web (WWW) are recent developments in distance education.

Absorption Training

It includes supplying audio cassettes or podcasts, product manuals, books, and CDs to salespeople, who read (or absorb) these materials without any urgent doubts and comments. This method is useful in introducing basic materials like the product manual and the company sales policies that are to be covered in more detail at a later date or to reinforce earlier training.

❍ **Audio Cassettes/Podcasts** These are supplied to salespeople, so that driving time can be used as training time[21]. This is one of the methods of absorption training and is used increasingly by many companies. Topics covered in the audio cassettes include humorous skits that teach valuable sales techniques, time management, and motivational speeches. Similarly, podcasts that cover a wide range of topics which are downloaded on to iPods, CDs or some other MP3 players, are provided by companies like IBM and General Motors to their salespeople[22].

Selecting an Appropriate Training Method

Sales managers and sales trainers do face a problem of selecting appropriate sales training methods out of several methods discussed earlier. Generally active learning is more effective than passive learning, as shown in Table 6.2. For example, role playing, case studies, and on-the-job training methods represent active learning, whereas audio cassettes, books, and lectures are passive learning methods.

Table 6.2 What People Remember[23]

People Generally Remember
• 10% of what they read
• 20% of what they hear
• 30% of what they see
• 50% of what they hear and see
• 70% of what they say
• 90% of what they say as they do a thing

One more part to be considered at the time of selecting a suitable training method is to know whether the particular method should be used for training a group of trainees or an individual salesperson. For example, if a company hires a group of 10 sales trainees, the training methods which can be used for them are shown in Table 6.3. Whereas, for training an individual salesperson the training methods available are different, as indicated in Table 6.3.

Finally, selection of the appropriate training methods mainly depend upon whichever methods effectively convey the contents of the training program as well as achieve the objectives or aims of the training, keeping in view the budgeted expenditure.

Table 6.3 Training Methods

Group Training Methods	Individual Training Methods
• Lecture	• Distance learning/online training
• Demonstration	• Demonstration
• Group discussion	• EPSS
• Role playing	• Interactive multimedia
• Case studies	• Audio cassettes/podcasts
• Simulation games	• CDs, books, manuals
• Sensitivity analysis	• On-the-Job
• Films	• Job rotation

Executing a Sales Training Program–Organizational Decisions for Sales Training

In Figure 6.2 shown earlier, the execution step of ACMEE (the first E) requires making certain important decisions.

Answers to the following questions will indicate the decisions:

- Who will be the trainees?
- Who will conduct the training?
- When should the training take place and for what duration?
- Where should the training be done? And where will be the venue of the training?
- What will be the budgeted expenditure for the training?
- What are the instructional materials to be used for the training?
- What are the aids required for the training?
- Is the time-table prepared for the training program?

Who will be the Trainees?

Usually the trainees include new and existing salespeople, intermediaries or their salespeople, and sales managers.

❍ **New and Existing Salespeople** It is understood that initial sales training is required for newly hired salespeople. However, continuing sales training for the existing salespersons is not very clear. Usually companies are benefited by giving priority for training those salespeople who find difficulties to achieve their sales goals. In addition, whenever there are changes in the company's product-mix, market segments, or organization structure, retraining programs are needed for existing sales force to effectively handle the new developments.

❍ **Intermediaries** Sometimes it is necessary for the company to train its intermediaries, such as distributors, dealers, and manufacturer's representatives. These intermediaries or their salespeople need training in product and market knowledge as well as in certain skills like selling and negotiating.

❍ **Sales Managers** Although the focus of our discussion in this chapter is on training salespeople, companies are aware that sales managers also need training. Some companies like Ford Motors, Genentech, and Wipro have talent development programs that provide management training to junior and middle level managers.

Who Will Conduct the Training?

Usually there are three sources of sales trainers: (i) line sales personnel, (ii) staff trainers, and (iii) outside training specialists. Any one or combination of the above sales trainers can be used. However, it is common for a company to use all the three sources, each for different purposes.

❍ **Line Sales Personnel** Senior salespersons, branch or regional sales managers, and sales managers, who have line responsibilities are usually the main trainers of the company's salespeople. These trainers bring in to the training program years of sales experience, which helps trainees to relate to them. The management should select those line sales personnel who have both sales and teaching abilities. The main advantage of having line sales personnel is that they carry more authority and can establish better rapport with the sales trainees. To get a line salesperson with both sales and teaching abilities may be difficult, in which case the person can be trained. The inclination of most companies is to train their own sales trainers than recruit outsiders.

❍ **Staff Trainers** Large companies can hire a specialized staff training officer/manager to conduct training programs. Small companies may not afford the cost. Generally, it is recommended that personnel or HR department should not be given the responsibility of conducting sales training program, although they may be involved in handling physical arrangements or giving information on personnel policies. The advantage is that the specialized staff trainer can attend to the details of sales training program in a more professional manner than others.

❍ **Outside Training Specialists** In large companies, outside training specialists are involved in sales training programs for bringing in new ideas and training methods. However, some small and medium sized firms allow the outside training specialists to conduct the training of their salespeople. Some outside training firms administer an entire training program, whereas others may specialize in a very narrow field, like training pharmaceutical sales representatives, or training sales engineers in business-to-business selling. Many firms hire outside specialists to conduct a part of a sales training program. Most of outside specialists or experts are true professionals putting on a good show. They help to maximize the benefits of sales training programs.

When Should the Training Take Place?

Most sales managers assert that newly hired trainees should receive formal group training before placing them in field selling. Experience shows that training groups smaller than 15 are costly, while those larger than 40 are less effective in terms of learning. Timing of initial sales training program depends upon the size of the sales trainees and the company's plan.

The need for training does not end with completion of the initial sales training program for newly hired salespeople. Salespeople periodically need refresher or continuing training. In Tata Iron and Steel Company (TISCO), for example, every employee (including salespeople) is required to undertake a training program of minimum 10 days each year. The ongoing educational program, called Learning for Excellence in Advice and Professionalism (LEAP), includes web and classroom courses and a series of workshops for salespeople at different stages of their professional development[24]. Continuing sales training for experienced salespeople are often scheduled for off-pack selling periods.

Where should the Training be Conducted?

The decision on the location of sales training includes two alternatives: centralized training and decentralized training. Many companies overcome the disadvantages of using either centralized or decentralized training by designing a training program that includes both.

Centralized Training

Training at a central location is called centralized training, which is typically held at the home/head office, at the manufacturing plant or at a resort. Some large companies that hire many salespeople and other employees have central training facilities. For example, Infosys has its training facility at Mysore. Centralized training places have excellent facilities and equipment as well as highly skilled people to teach. Another advantage is that trainees can see the manufacturing facilities and meet top executives of the company. Trainees are away from home and can focus on learning. However, two major disadvantages of centralized training are that they are expensive due to the cost of travel, meals and facilities, and the time at central location is limited. These disadvantages can be overcome by organizing video conferencing.

Decentralized Training

It can take place at a branch, regional office, or the hotel room. The advantages are lower cost when compared with centralized training, and branch managers getting opportunity to conduct training programs to prove their organizing qualities. Unless directed by senior managers, execution of decentralized training programs is often less effective. However, as video conferences are becoming more popular, many companies are having the advantages of an effective centralized training facility without spending on travel cost of salespeople. In such cases, trainees in all the branches can participate in the training program conducted from a central training facility. Retraining programs for experienced salespeople are held at centralized or decentralized locations.

What would be the Budgeted Expenditure?

After going through the various steps of assessing the training needs, deciding aims (or objectives) of the training program, determining the content of the training program, selecting the sales training methods, and taking organizational decisions like who will be the trainees, who will conduct training, when should the training take place and where should the training be done, the training manager should now consolidate all the stages of the sales training process into a written document, mentioning the estimated expenditure for conducting the training program. It is necessary to get the approval from the top management for the budgeted (or estimated) expenditure. Top management should not only give the approval for the budgeted expenditure, but also give direction and encouragement for conducting the sales training program. Successful sales managers have positive attitude and recognize that sales training is very important for their success.

What are the Instructional Materials to be used?

Instructional materials such as manuals and company publications are provided to the trainees as study guides during the training program and also as references later.

Manuals

These contain cases, directions for role playing sessions, sales policies, the company systems, and related reading materials. Instead of cluttering the manual with information of hardly any value, a careful selection of items should be done for inclusion.

Company Publications

Printed materials such as the company's product brochures or leaflets, technical and trade books are included. These publications serve later as references.

What are the Training Aids Required?

A training aid is an extra support device that is capable of sight and/or sound stimuli. The blackboard or whiteboard is the most used device that adds visual to vocal appeal. In addition, sound system (or mike), overhead projector, screen, and personal computer (PC) are required for audio-visual presentations. Sales training films are available commercially. A company can produce tailor-made films to suit its requirements. For role playing session, a company can use a record player to record and play back the discussion between a buyer and a seller.

Implementation of the Organizational Decisions

Someone in the organization should take the responsibility for the entire process of sales training, starting from identifying the sales training needs, designing and executing the sales training program, and evaluating and reinforcing the same, as shown in Figure 6.1 earlier. The person who is given the responsibility of the entire sales training process is usually the sales training manager or the sales trainer. Ideally, the sales trainer should have a vision, energy, and persistence to plan or design on both short-term and long-term basis. The sales trainer should have experience in selling, having been promoted through the ranks. This helps the sales trainer to understand the sales process, management of the company's salespeople, and the culture of the organization.

Implementation of a sales training program is the most tedious part of the sales training process. Preparation of training time table, arranging internal and external trainers, making travel arrangements of participants, arranging the conference hall and the teaching aids (like multi-media projector, sound system), and many other items. It is important to pay attention to the details in order to ensure successful execution of the sales training process. Preparation of a list of all activities helps in proper implementation of the training program.

The actual performance or execution of the training program as per the time table may not take more time as compared to the other stages or steps described earlier. An effective sales trainer makes a final check on all the activities of the list one or two days prior to commencement of the training program. This is a good practice, as it gives sufficient time to take corrective actions on some activities (like one of the trainer unable to take his/her session due to some personal emergency). As the training program gets going, the sales trainer should monitor the progress of the trainees. Feedback from the sales trainees should be obtained before, during and at the end of the program on various issues, including effectiveness of the trainers, and the arrangements of the training program.

EVALUATION OF SALES TRAINING PROGRAM

The evaluation decision (the second E in ACMEE) pays particular attention to measurement or evaluation of effectiveness of sales training program. It is difficult to evaluate a sales training program. This difficulty arises because it is hard to decide which future sales performance variations are due to sales training. There are other factors, such as environmental (like economic condition, changes in competitive strategies and tactics), motivation of the salespeople, changes in the company's marketing and sales strategies, which may influence sales and profit performance of the company more or less than the sales training. There are no analytical techniques available for clear isolation of the influence of these factors.

In spite of the above stated difficulty, most companies measure the effectiveness of sales training to evaluate whether present expenditures on sales training are worthwhile, and to improve the design and implementation of future sales training programs. In evaluation, the company must decide "what outcomes will be measured", "how these outcomes will be measured", and "when to measure these outcomes". These outcomes fall into the following four categories: reactions, learning, behavior, and results[25], as shown in Table 6.4.

Table 6.4 Framework for Sales Training Evaluation

Outcomes to Measure	What to Measure? (Specific Items to Measure)	How to Measure? (Data Collection Methods Used)	When to Measure (Information Measurement Methods Used)
Reactions– Participants' perceptions/reactions	• Training objectives • achieved? Training worthwhile?	• Questionnaires • Interviews	• After the training
Learning– Knowledge, skills or Attitudes learnt	• Knowledge • Skills, or • Attitudes	• Tests • Interviews	• After the training Tests/Interviews • Before and After Tests
Behavior– Change in Behavior	• Trainee's Change of Behavior	• Observation by Supervisor/Customers • Self-assessment by Trainees	• After training, over one year
Results– Performance results; Benefits more than cost of training?	• Sales • Profits • Customer Satisfaction	• Company data • Managerial Judgement • Market Survey	• After training, Quarterly Yearly

Reactions

These outcomes point out the participants' perceptions or reactions. Whether the sales training achieved the objectives and whether the training was worthwhile. Reactions of the sales trainees, their supervisors, or the training staff can be measured by interviewing them or asking them to complete questionnaires. Their reactions can be measured after the completion of the training.

Learning

This outcome measures how much knowledge, skills, or attitudes were learnt or absorbed by the sales trainees. The information collection methods used are tests or interviews of the sales trainees. There may be "before" and "after" tests or tests and interviews taken "after" the training is completed.

Behavior

The outcome here measures whether there was a change in the trainee's behavior. The assessment of the trainee's change of behavior is conducted by the immediate supervisor, who can observe the trainee after the sales training, over a period of one year. The measurement may also include self-assessment by the trainee or observation by customers.

Results

These are the most important outcomes. They point out whether the outcome of training has improved performance results, and whether the benefits of training were more than the costs. The measures used to assess the final results are: sales, profits, customer satisfaction, number of new customers, and market penetration. The methods used to collect the relevant data or information on results are: company data (on sales, profits, number of new customers), market survey (for customer satisfaction), and immediate supervisor's or manager's judgment. These results can be measured every quarter for one year, after the training.

It is suggested that both financial and non-financial effectiveness should be evaluated[26]. Table 6.4 summarizes the evaluation of sales training in a framework, based on what is described above. Many successful companies calculated "return on investment" (ROI) on training investments. **For instance,** IBM measures training investments in the same manner as any other investment.

Reinforcement to Sales Training

Most salespeople would not change their behavior after a training program, unless there is some reinforcement to the sales training. According to one study, four or five coaching reinforcements are needed in sixteen-week period after the sales training, otherwise salespeople's learning will become less powerful by 80 percent[27]. In another study, Xerox Company found most of its salespersons continued to hold only 13 percent of what they learned in training programs after 30 days. Yet, in many companies, follow-up or reinforcement trainings are not done because of various reasons, such as sales managers do not have time, they do not give importance to this activity, or they are not recognized or rewarded for their efforts[28]. The training methods often used to reinforce the training are: (i) refresher training which includes continuous training to overcome deficiencies of experienced salespeople and also retraining for salespersons whose job requirements have changed due to changes in sales territories or their promotion, (ii) senior salespeople or sales managers coaching new salespersons, and (iii) web-based or online methods to reinforce formal training sessions. Companies must have some type of reinforcement training, after the formal sales training, as a part of the sales training process. For example, Boston Scientific Corporation makes arrangements for reinforcement or follow-up sessions in various cities around the world[29].

LO 2 **Explain what is motivation, its importance, and the theories of motivation; select the motivational tools, and outline the guidelines for motivating salespeople**

MOTIVATING THE SALESPEOPLE

Some salespeople are ambitious and self-starters. They put forth their efforts without any special training or incentives from the management. However, the majority of salespeople need encouragement, training, and motivation. The first level branch/district sales manager's performance depends upon the composite performance of the salespeople. That is why they are interested to know the factors influencing salespeople to achieve desired performance. "How do I motivate my salespeople?" is one of the most common questions asked by sales managers. To answer this question satisfactorily, a sales manager should understand what is motivation and its importance, learn the relevance of theories of motivation to motivate the sales force, and select an effective combination of motivational tools.

What is Motivation?

Motivation is originally derived from the Latin word "*movere*", which means "to move". The desire to spend effort to fulfill a need is motivation. In a sales job, motivation is the amount of efforts the salesperson makes to complete various activities of the sales job. **Examples** of these activities are: meeting prospective customers, identifying their needs, making sales presentations, overcoming their objections and closing the sales. Further studies on motivation conclude that the most commonly used definition of motivation includes three dimensions: intensity, persistence, and direction[30], as shown in Figure 6.4.

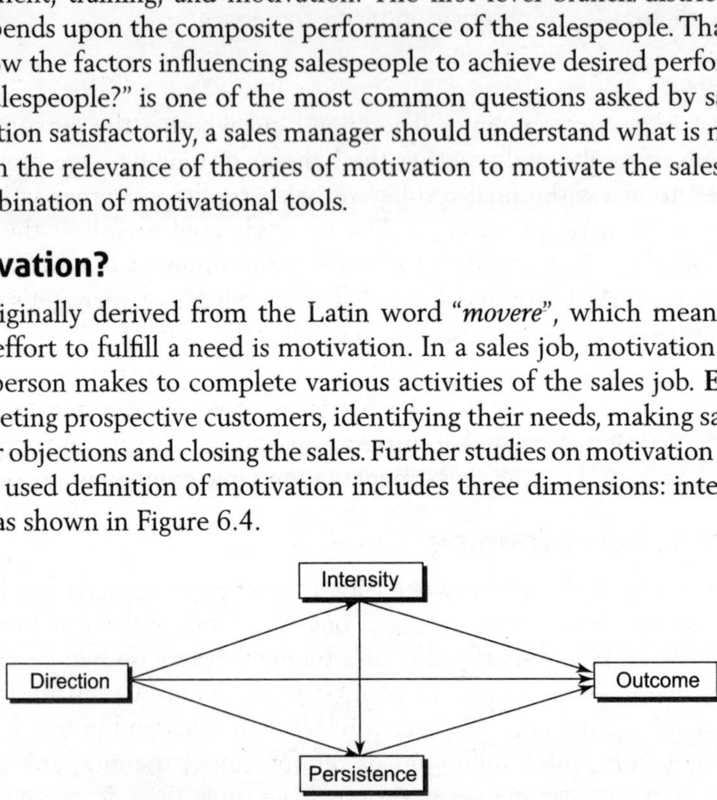

Fig. 6.4 **Dimensions of Sales Motivation**

Intensity refers to the amount of physical and mental efforts the salesperson spends on a given task. **Persistence** describes how long the salesperson continues to put forth effort. **Direction** suggests the salesperson's choice of actions among various job activities. For instance, a salesperson decides to concentrate on a key high sales and profit potential customer (which is the direction). The salesperson increases the number of sales calls on this customer from 2 to 4 per month (which is intensity), until the salesperson gets the first order (persistence). Figure 6.4 shows the dimensions of sales motivation, in which the direction (or choice of action) of the salesperson has an effect on the intensity and persistence. Similarly, intensity makes a difference to persistence, that is, how long a salesperson continues to do a particular task. Salespeople are often required to perform many selling and non-selling activities. It is therefore, important that salespeople focus their efforts in the direction which is in line with the company's strategic plan. The direction of the salesperson's effort is, therefore, as important as the intensity and persistence of that effort. These concepts are supported by studies, which indicate that larger levels of effort or intensity are not necessarily connected with greater levels of outcome or performance[31]. That is why in Figure 6.4 the outcome or performance of a salesperson is influenced by all the three dimensions: direction, intensity, and persistence.

Motivation can also be looked at as intrinsic or extrinsic. If salespeople consider their job as essentially rewarding (or providing satisfaction), they are **intrinsically motivated**. However, if salespersons are motivated by the rewards given by their organization, such as financial incentives and recognition, they are **extrinsically motivated**[32]. Although a salesperson's overall motivation can include both intrinsic and extrinsic motivation, some salesperson will seek intrinsic rewards (such as challenging work, feelings of personal worth and a sense of accomplishment), other salespeople will prefer extrinsic rewards (such as salary, fringe benefits, and promotion). We shall discuss these motivational tools or methods later in this chapter.

IMPORTANCE OF MOTIVATION

It has been estimated that about 10 to 15 percent of salespeople are self-motivated, requiring little external incentives. They are ambitious and self-starters. However, the majority of salespeople are not adequately motivated, requiring encouragement and incentives from the management. The company management recognizes the importance of sales management and salespeople because the financial performance of the company depends upon the achievement of sales volume objective, which is the primary responsibility of the sales management. Sales managers find the task of motivating salespeople difficult and important due to the following factors: (i) changes in marketing environment, (ii) conflicting company objectives, (iii) unusual nature of the sales job, and (iv) separate motivational package.

Changes in Marketing Environment

Marketing environmental factors, such as demographic, economic, technological, politic-legal, and socio-cultural, change continuously. Sales managers find it difficult to develop an effective mix of motivational methods for salespeople in the changing marketing environment. The incentive scheme may become ineffective due to the recession in the economy, or a change in technology. For example, a technology change from jelly-filled telecom cables to fiber-optic cables will make selling jelly-filled cables very difficult as business customers recognize the huge benefits of fiber-optic cables.

Conflicting Company Objectives

Salespeople are required to achieve the company objectives and goals, such as sales volume, profit contribution and customer satisfaction. Sometimes these objectives conflict with each other. For instance, a customer is satisfied if the salesperson confirms matching the competitors' price with the company's price. However, the company management is unable to do so, because by bringing down the company's price to the level of the competitor's price, the company can not achieve the profit objective (in fact, it will make a huge loss). The salesperson is frustrated that after putting a great amount of efforts, the order from the customer is lost to a competitor and he is unable to achieve the sales quota and the incentive. With widely varying objectives, developing an effective motivational mix is difficult.

Unusual Nature of the Sales Job

This is an important factor. Salespeople usually work alone and their working hours are long and irregular. They are often away from home causing them to miss many special parts of family life. They have an inferior status in relation to the purchase officers. While many customers are polite and considerate in their business dealings with salespeople, some buyers are bad mannered and difficult to deal with. Salespeople often face hostile competing salespersons who compete for the same business. In many cases, salespeople do not have the authority to do what is needed to get a business, and therefore, they sometimes lose large orders for which they had worked very hard to get. These conditions cause salespeople to become dissatisfied. As a result, salespeople usually need more motivation than other employees do to reach the expected performance levels.

Separate Motivational Package

Salespeople have individual characteristics like strengths, weaknesses, goals, and problems that influence their motivations. Most desirably, the firm should evolve a different motivational package for each salesperson. However, this approach will have practical problems in a company. A solution to this problem is to develop a motivational mix that is relevant for all salespeople, and it should also appeal to the different individual needs. For instance, newer salespeople are sensitive to the achievement of sales quotas and financial incentives. More established and go-getter salespeople look for promotions and recognition.

RELEVANCE OF MOTIVATIONAL THEORIES TO SALESPEOPLE

Motivation has been researched for many years. We shall discuss those motivational theories that are relevant to the motivation of salespeople. Some of these theories or behavioral concepts in motivation are: (i) Maslow's hierarchy of needs theory, (ii) Hertzberg's dual-factor theory,

(iii) Vroom's expectancy theory, and (iv) Churchill, Ford and Walker model of sales force motivation. Also, if a sales manager understands some of the behavioral concepts that have an effect on salespeople's motivation, it will be easier to develop an effective motivational mix.

Maslow's Hierarchy of Needs Theory

Abraham H. Maslow proposed five levels of needs that every individual seeks to satisfy[33]. These basic needs are shown in Figure 6.5. Maslow argued that the needs form a hierarchy. When no needs are fulfilled (or realized), a person focuses on his or her physiological needs, such as food, shelter, clothing, and health care. When physiological needs are achieved, safety needs become important factors such as job security, safety, income security of human behavior. When these are satisfied, social needs (like friendship, belongingness, acceptance) become important and so on up the hierarchy. Until the more basic needs of physiological and safety needs are well satisfied, the higher order needs will not be aroused. However, sometimes it may happen that a lower level need, like job security, which was previously satisfied, may become unfulfilled (due to the loss of job). In such cases, lower level needs happen before the higher-level needs.

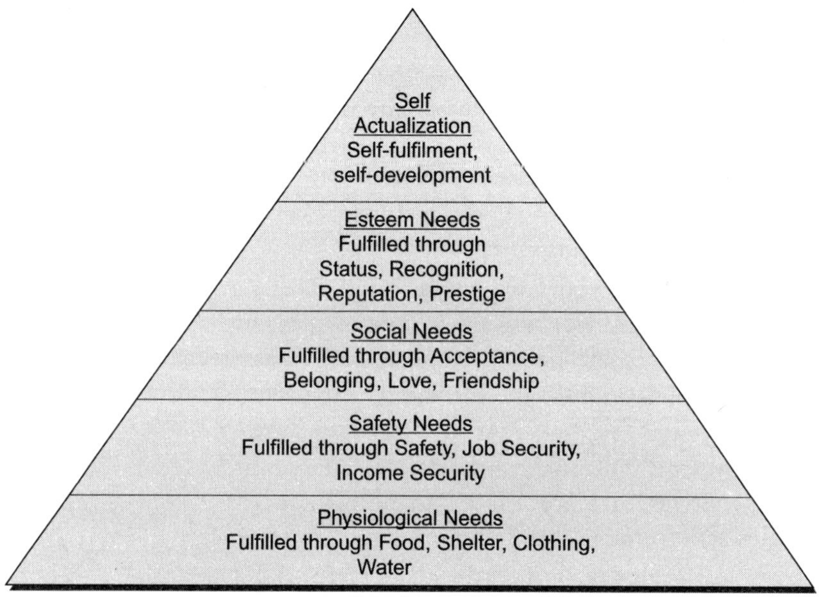

Fig. 6.5 Maslow's Hierarchy of Needs

This theory has a relevance to sales force motivation. Different salespersons will have different needs, and therefore, what may act as a motivator for one salesperson may not be effective with another. A sales manager can take suitable managerial actions only after an accurate assessment of the needs of individual salespersons. For example, if the salesperson's physiological needs are not satisfied, the sales manager should offer an acceptable income and benefits package because money and financial rewards can buy the products and services to satisfy these needs. Another salesperson may look for job security and for satisfying that need, the sales manager should remove the fear of failure by guiding the salesperson to perform well to achieve the sales goals. For fulfilling social needs, a sales manager arranges sales meetings and social functions, sets up selling teams for key customers and mentoring programs. For satisfying esteem needs, some of the actions the sales manager takes are promotions, public recognition of achievements, and appreciation letters. Self-actualization needs are rarely identified at the level of salespeople, but if it is found, a sales manager may consider special assignments with higher authority and responsibility like mentoring new salespersons.

Hertzberg's Two-Factor Theory

A theory of motivation developed by Frederick Hertzberg is called dual-factor theory, in which sources of dissatisfaction and satisfaction are grouped into two groups: hygiene factors and motivation factors[34]. Examples of hygiene factors are working environment, security, type of supervision, interpersonal relationships, salary, fringe benefits, and company policies. They are called hygiene factors because they deal with the condition of the work environment, and not the work itself. Absence of hygiene factors can cause job dissatisfaction, but presence of these factors does not lead to job satisfaction. Fulfilling the hygiene factors would bring up motivation to a theoretical zero level, or a neutral point, but would not result in a positive motivation.

If positive motivations were to be achieved, attention would have to be given to motivation factors. These include recognition, responsibility, achievement, challenge, opportunities for growth, and the interest value of the work. These factors are part of the job (or work). For the person to feel motivated these motivational factors must be present. When motivation factors are fulfilled, it leads to job satisfaction.

Dual-factor theory has two important conclusions that can be drawn: (i) The sales management should provide good enough working environment, sensible supervision, job security, and reasonable compensation to salespeople to prevent job dissatisfaction. (ii) The management should also provide opportunities for growth, recognition, and responsibility to motivate salespersons.

Pay can be both hygiene and a motivation factor. Salary is included as hygiene factor, whereas commissions or incentives that are related to performance are considered as the automatic recognition to sales achievement and therefore, a motivation factor.

A salesperson's achievement is directly observable as higher sales (except in missionary selling) is a motivational factor. Similarly, a sales manager can give higher degree of responsibility (and therefore motivation) to salespeople by giving authority to offer discounts, preparation of route plans, and scheduling sales calls to customers. A study with a group of salespeople showed that greater responsibility given to salespeople by such changes resulted in higher sales success[35].

Vroom's Expectancy Theory

This theory assumes that a person's motivation to make efforts depends upon his expectations for success. Vroom based his theory on three concepts: expectancy, instrumentality, and valence[36].

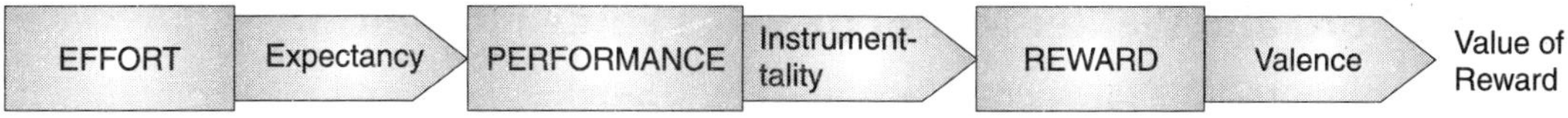

Fig. 6.6 Vroom's Expectancy Theory of Motivation

Expectancy

This concept refers to the person's perception of the relationship between effort and performance. It points out to what extent a person expects (or hopes) that increased efforts will lead to superior performance. The relevance of the concept to sales situations is presented in Figure 6.6. Examples of efforts of a salesperson include more sales calls on customers and longer working hours. Superior performance in sales situations means increase in sales, higher level of customer satisfaction, and increase in number of new customers.

Instrumentality

This concept refers to the person's perception of the relationship between performance and reward. It shows the degree to which a salesperson believes that higher performance will lead to some kind of reward. For instance, the reward may be increase in salary, recognition, or promotion.

Valence

This concept describes the value placed on a particular reward by a salesperson. For instance, if the reward is the recognition given to the salesperson by the sales manager, it may not carry much value to the salesperson. For some other salesperson recognition may be a great value.

To understand the theory better, let us consider an example. If a salesperson believes that by working harder, he will achieve higher sales (meaning high expectancy) and that higher sales will lead to increased incentive (or commission) payment (meaning high instrumentality) and increased incentive payment is very important (high valence), then a high level of motivation should happen. Of course, different salespersons have different valences (values) for the same reward. Some salespeople who have a large family to support may value increased salary or commission, while for younger and more educated salespersons promotion may be more valuable.

Sales managers should, therefore, communicate clearly to the salespeople the performance standards (or sales quotas) which are derived from the company objectives and goals. Another important point that comes out of this theory is that the sales quotas (or sales targets) should be such that salespeople should perceive these targets as achievable (high expectancy), otherwise the first link shown in Figure 6.6 will be cut off. The expectancy theory, as presented in Figure 6.6, is a diagnostic framework or tool that can be used for analyzing problems related to salesperson's motivation. For example, does the company's reward structure provide what salespeople want?

Churchill, Ford and Walker Model of Sales Force Motivation

The problem of motivating salespeople is studied by Churchill, Ford, and Walker[37]. They have developed a model, as shown in Figure 6.7.

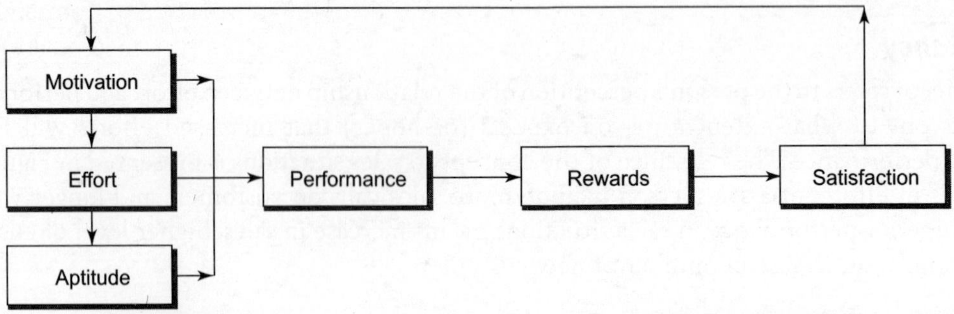

Fig. 6.7 **Model of Sales Force Motivation and Performance**

The model in Figure 6.7 points out that a salesperson's performance depends on three factors: degree of motivation, efforts, and aptitude. A higher degree of motivation, efforts, and aptitude will lead to a greater performance. Greater performance will lead to greater rewards (like higher pay, financial incentive, and recognition). Greater rewards will lead to higher satisfaction level. Higher satisfaction will reinforce motivation. This model is derived from Vroom's expectancy theory.

Sales managers should convince salespeople that they can sell more by putting more efforts. They should arrange training programs to improve the abilities of salespeople. The salespersons' job satisfaction declines if: (i) expectations of their superiors are not clear, and (ii) conflicting demands from the company and its customers are not resolved. Sales managers have an important role to play in all these areas.

Sales managers should convince salespeople that rewards for superior performance are worth the extra efforts. This point suggests that the sales manager should give rewards that are valued by the salespeople and should try to sell the reward's worth to the salespeople. However, if the rewards are set arbitrarily or are too small or of wrong type, then the linkage between performance and rewards are weakened.

The researchers went on to measure the importance of different rewards. The reward with highest value (No. 1) was pay (money or finance), No. 2 was promotion, No. 3 was personal growth, and No. 4 was sense of accomplishment (or achievement). The least valued rewards were liking, respect, security, and recognition. However, the importance of motivators (or value of rewards) varied with demographic characteristics of salespeople. Financial rewards were mostly valued by older salespeople with large families. Younger, unmarried, better educated salespeople with small families prefer higher order rewards, such as personal growth, promotion, respect, and sense of accomplishment.

SELECTING AN EFFECTIVE MIX OF MOTIVATIONAL TOOLS

For designing an effective motivational mix (or an optimal reward system) the sales manager should first know each salesperson and understand his specific needs. In addition, it is important to establish the performance goals of each salesperson, against which the actual performance can be measured. The motivational package (or mix), which consists of various motivational tools or methods, should have some components that can be made to fit to the individual salesperson's needs. As most successful salespeople have the best opportunities to leave the company for more attractive jobs, views of the salespersons regarding the reward system or motivational tools as well as their personal goals and needs must be understood. The sales manager must also understand the company management's point of view. In recent years, the customer needs have become more important than salespeople's needs in deciding the sales force reward system (or motivational mix). Meeting the needs of customers, salespeople, and the company management is a challenging task for a sales manager. A compromise between differing interests becomes necessary for designing or selecting a mix of motivational tools.

Motivational tools or methods are usually divided into two broad categories: financial rewards, and non-financial rewards, which are summarized in Table 6.5.

Table 6.5 Motivational Tools in the Motivational Mix

Financial Rewards/Tools	Non-Financial Rewards/Tools
• Financial compensation plan	• Promotional opportunity
–Salary	• Sense of accomplishment
–Commission	• Personal growth opportunities
–Performance bonus	• Recognition
–Fringe benefits	• Job security
–Combination	• Sales meetings
• Sales contests	• Sales training programs
• Team compensation	• Job enrichment
• Global compensation issues	• Effective supervision
	• Praise and encouragement

Financial Rewards

The financial rewards include: (i) financial compensation plan, (ii) sales contests, (iii) team compensation, and (iv) global compensation issues. Compensation is defined as financial and non-financial methods of rewards for the salespeople.

Financial Compensation Plan

Most companies use financial compensation plan to motivate salespeople. Financial compensation includes: (i) current spendable income (such as salary, commission, and bonus), (ii) deferred income (like retirement pension pay, provident fund, or gratuity payment), and (iii) various insurance plans, which provide income when needed, and fringe benefits. We shall focus on current spendable income, because it is relevant to sales force reward or motivation system. The other two components of financial compensation are a part of the overall company policy that is applicable to all employees. A study found that salespeople prefer salary raises and commission or incentives over any other type of motivational reward[38]. The financial compensation plan for salespeople will be discussed subsequently in this chapter.

Sales Contest

Sales contests are short-term selling campaigns offering incentives like prizes or awards which can be an effective motivational tool if they are carefully and properly designed. A sales contest should have a specific purpose, such as increase short-term sales volume; sell more profitable product mix; or getting new customers. The design of the sales contest should consider the following points: (i) each salesperson has an equal opportunity to win, (ii) the basis of awards be for improvement over current performance, and (iii) select "open-ended contest", in which unlimited number of salespersons can win, by offering awards or prizes to all salespersons showing improvement. Prizes should be attractive, each consisting of cash prizes, merchandise, or travel. Studies have found that noncash prizes like merchandise and travel are more effective than cash prizes for motivating salespeople[39]. At least 10 percent of the contest budget should be spent on promotion, so that there is an excitement in the company. Care should be taken to ensure that salespersons do not use undesirable methods, such as storing orders, overselling, and using pressure tactics. One of the ways to overcome the problem of salespeople using undesirable methods is not to announce the contest period in advance. Differences in cultural aspects and expectations of overseas salespeople should be understood, before designing sales contest program for them. Although, there are no set guidelines on contest duration, most sales contests run from one to four months.

Team Compensation

Team selling strategy is becoming important, particularly in B2B selling. For example, M.M. Material Handling company's selling teams include members from sales, design, finance, and customer service functions. Many companies are, therefore, adjusting their compensation plans to recognize the importance of team performance. Designing a compensation plan for a selling team can be a challenging task; salespeople who are used to get commissions on their individual efforts may not like team-based compensation. In addition, it is difficult to determine an individual member's contribution to overall team performance. Given these challenges, several guidelines should be followed in designing a team-based compensation plan. These are: (i) Companies should be ready to try out new ideas to find the right compensation plan for sales terms. (ii) There should be discussion among team members. (iii) Inputs from the team members are important to ensure teams' succeed. (iv) Reward both individual and team performance by having a balance between individually based and team-based compensations. This means, the majority of compensations of a salesperson is in salary form, and performance bonus and commission are a part of team compensation. (v) Team members of a selling team should evaluate their fellow members' contributions to the overall performance of the team. This will highlight how each team member contributes to the performance of the team. Team compensation can build motivation and can lead selling teams to higher performance levels.

Global Compensation Issues

It is difficult to standardize compensation packages for salespeople living outside their native country. Cultural factors have strong influence on compensation of salespeople. For example, in Southeast Asia straight salaries are considered as more necessary and proper than compensation packages involving variable commission. In Japan, bonuses or commissions are paid based on the performance of the entire sales force, whereas in the United States, the compensation of salespeople is influenced more by the variable element of commission that is linked to the individual salesperson's performance. These practices are connected to cultural norms. For instance, individualism is rewarded in the United States, whereas in many other countries collectivism or group orientation is valued. Sales managers and human resource executives involved in finalization of compensation packages for salespeople living around the globe need to know the living costs, taxes, government regulations and cultural aspects prevailing in those countries.

In many other situations, sales representation in other countries is obtained through a network of distributors, dealers, or manufacturer's agents. These situations are not difficult to deal with. Normal decisions such as discounts on the company's price list or commissions on net sales can resolve the issues after due negotiations. The difficulty arises, as discussed earlier, when compensation packages are to be decided for expatriate salespeople.

Non-Financial Rewards

It is easily seen that salespeople are motivated by both financial and non-financial incentives. Examples of non-financial incentives are shown in Table 6.5. These incentives or rewards are discussed in this section.

Promotion

Changes in titles or promotions are ranked high among younger and better educated salespersons[40]. If promotion is tied to sales performance, the company should have two routes for promotion. One route follows promotion to a managerial position, where managerial skills are required. The second route of promotion is created to reward the outstanding sales performance. An example of such a promotional path is:

Salesperson → Senior Salesperson → Key Account Executive

Promotion provides a salesperson a higher responsibility and authority. The feeling of higher responsibility has a motivating effect on the salesperson as it makes him feel that he is a key person in the company.

Sense of Accomplishment

A sense of accomplishment cannot be handed over to the salesperson from the company. A sense of accomplishment comes out from the salesperson's mind, and therefore, a company can only facilitate the process by which it develops. A sense of accomplishment is an intrinsic motivation and it is considered as one of the important rewards by salespeople. The question is: "How can a firm facilitate a sense of accomplishment in the sales force?" The answer is to take the following steps: (i) to communicate to the salespeople the important role they play in achieving the organizational objectives and goals by generating the sales revenue (nobody else in the company does this), ensuring customer satisfaction, and contributing to the growth and profitability of the organization; (ii) to identify individual salespersons who have achieved superior performance through high level of efforts and to establish the link: efforts → performance → reward; (iii) to make the management by objectives (MBO) as a standard management practice; and (iv) to strengthen the sense of accomplishment by communicating to salespeople how some salespersons have been achieving their sales goals (or quotas) consistently year after year.

Personal Growth Opportunities

Many salespeople rank opportunities for personal growth high in the list of sales force rewards. Many well-known companies have policies to encourage salespeople's participation in seminars, workshops, and distance learning programs. For example, companies like Dell, Symphony Services, Sasken Technologies have policies by which employees can attend seminars and workshops on topics of their choice. Some companies display their training programs, during the process of staffing the salespeople, as an opportunity for personal growth.

Recognition

Most sales managers realize that they must pay more attention to the individual salesperson's higher-order needs, such as recognition, appreciation, and admiration. Most salespersons take pleasure in getting public recognition of their successful achievement. Both informal and formal recognition are a part of sales force motivational mix.

Informal recognition is usually delivered in private conversation or correspondence between a sales manager and a salesperson. However, it is a good managerial behavior to appreciate the salesperson in a public ceremony, involving senior managers. Formal recognition programs are generally based on individual or group accomplishments, indicating superior performance. These programs suggest public recognition for accomplishment in the presence of peers and seniors in the company and include a symbolic award of lasting psychological value, such as certificates and plaques. Formal recognition programs have been popular in sales organizations. Examples are: Life Insurance Corporation of India has a formal reward program, called "crorepati" agent. All top salespeople make great efforts to be named a member of the President's Club at Xerox Corporation[41], and GTE Company introduces its top performers into the "Winner's Circle". Another outstanding way to recognize top performing salespeople is to nominate them for awards by industry associations.

Job Security

It is generally valued by older salespeople who are nearing retirement age, but is the least-valued reward among younger salespeople. In today's business situations, with high degree of mergers, acquisitions, and downsizing of organizations, it is becoming very difficult for companies to offer job security as a motivating factor. It is widely perceived that government organizations offer job security, which is difficult for private sector companies to offer.

Sales Meetings

Most companies use sales meetings for motivational and communication purposes. Regularly held sales meetings provide salespeople a break from routine, a chance to meet with senior managers of the company and also other salespeople, and to identify with a larger group. Sales meetings are not only an important tool for motivation, but also an important tool for communication and education.

It is important to carefully plan and conduct a sales meeting. A sales manager can use the ACMEE (aims, content, method execution, and evaluation) approach to ensure that the sales meeting is well-planned and effectively conducted. **Aims** or objectives of the sales meeting should be clear. Although the general purposes are to communicate and motivate salespeople, specific aim is needed. Examples are: (i) improving time management, (ii) introducing a new product or service, (iii) communicating changes in marketing or sales strategies. **Content** of a sales meeting is derived from the specific aims. For instance, if the aim is to introduce a new product, content may include product demonstration, specifications, applications, and benefits compared to the existing products in the market. **Methods** used depend upon the aim, the content, the time available, and the place of the meeting. For local meetings at district or branch offices, typically group discussion is used. Regional and national meetings may use a mix of several methods, as discussed earlier in sales training. **Execution** decisions include meeting place and time, speakers, room arrangement, audiovisual equipment, provision of materials like pads and pens, refreshments, timing of breaks, and so on. **Evaluation** is often neglected, but it is important. Participants' feedback is essential in a sales meeting evaluation form.

Sales meetings are held at national, regional, and local levels. National conventions are usually held once a year and may include a select group of top performers to meet with and hear top executives of the company as well as to receive awards for their superior performance. Regional conventions have a work-oriented agenda, such as finalization of territory sales quotas, review of territory performance and discussion on regional problems. Local meetings are held weekly or monthly at the district or branch offices, when salespeople discuss their sales problems, top performers are given due recognition, and training programs are held on specific topics. Many companies are realizing the benefits of video conferences and are using them to inform and motivate the entire sales force of the company at one time, instead of conducting national sales meeting which have substantial costs[42].

Sales Training Programs

As discussed earlier in this chapter, a good sales training program increases the performance of salespeople and therefore improves their sense of self-esteem. It reduces their survival fear. Salespeople, who are in the same training program, have increased social linkage with each other. A feeling of belongingness is developed among the salespersons.

Job Enrichment

It is an outcome of Hertzberg's two-factor theory on motivation. Job enrichment gives a salesperson more responsibility, autonomy, variety of tasks, and growth opportunities. It gives the salesperson more decision-making, planning, and controlling powers. For example, if the sales manager decides to pass on his discretionary powers of discounts to some of the experienced and capable salespeople, that would motivate the salespersons. In addition, the sales manager authorizes these salespersons to make their call plans and routing plans. Such actions on job enrichment would show improvement in job performance, as seen in a study of AT&T's sales representatives[43]. Another example of job enrichment is when a company asks a senior salesperson to do on-the-job training to a new sales trainee.

Effective Supervision

It is the day-to-day control of the salespersons under normal working conditions. The objective of supervision is to improve the performance of salespersons. One of the tasks of the first level sales manager, to achieve the above mentioned objective, is to motivate the salesperson. For motivating salespersons through effective supervision, it is important for sales managers to understand the personal needs and aspirations of each salesperson reporting to them. Companies having decentralized sales organizations assign the supervision of sales force responsibility to branch or district managers, who are first level sales managers. For effective supervision, these managers are expected to spend adequate time with their salespersons.

Branch, district or area sales managers, who have the responsibilities of supervising salespeople, bring about working relations with salespersons for purposes of providing motivation, correcting shortcomings, making salespersons understand their responsibilities, communicating the company policies, helping to solve sales-related as well as personal problems, evaluating performance, and continuing sales training. These first level sales managers not only manage salespeople, with above mentioned activities, but also manage the company's branch warehouse, provide customer service, communicate with the sales and marketing regional and head offices, and carry out any other branch/district related work. Hence, it is difficult for them to give adequate time to supervision of salespeople. However, it is important that they spend adequate time with salespeople, because effective supervision improves the job performances of salespersons.

Praise and Encouragement

An area or branch sales manager can motivate his or her salespersons without great effort and cost by praising and encouragement. A word of appreciation like "well done," or "good efforts" in written or verbal communications from a sales manager to a salesperson is a very effective way of motivation that is least expensive. Salespeople get some orders from customers and also don't get a few orders. In situations when salespersons don't get orders, despite trying very hard, a word from the sales manager acknowledging the hard work would go a long way.

GUIDELINES FOR MOTIVATING SALESPEOPLE

Sales managers should understand that almost everything they do will influence sales force motivation. Some guidelines for motivating salespeople, described as follows in brief, would help sales managers:

Difference Between Can't Do and Won't Do

What appears as a motivational problem (i.e., won't do) of a salesperson may be a competency or ability problem (i.e., can't do). Most salespersons won't do activities that they can't do. In other words, sales performance depends on both ability and motivation (i.e., efforts). It is important to know that motivation—the desire to exert effort—is not the only requirement for successful sales performance. Salespeople must have the ability to perform as well as the motivation to do the sales job.

Include Individual Needs into Motivational Programs

Motivation is a complex process. At the heart of the complexity of motivation is the concept of individual needs. Using one motivational program to motivate all salespeople may not be effective. It is also not practical to design different motivational programs for each salesperson. What are the alternatives available to sales managers to resolve this problem?

One alternative is to provide something for everyone. That is, to include individual needs of salespersons into the motivational program. The second alternative is called sales force segmentation in which the sales force is segmented, or divided, into several groups based on their designations or selling experience. Thereafter, a suitable motivational mix can be designed for each group of salespeople to meet the needs of each group[44]. Another method is to offer several motivational packages and let each salesperson choose any one of those packages. The basic idea is that individual consideration should be kept in mind when motivating and rewarding the salespeople.

Plateaus Salespeople

An important problem faced by most first level sales managers is how to motivate a plateau salesperson, who has almost stopped improving and developing, following a period of progress. Plateaus salespeople are usually around 40–50 years of age, performed well in the past, but not performing up to the expectations at present. They have developed a good relationship with a few major customers and therefore, it is difficult to terminate them. The main reasons of this situation are less chances of promotion, perceptions of unfair treatment, and lack interest or enthusiasm.

The symptoms of this state are the sickness, absenteeism, less working hours, lack of energy and enthusiasm, sloppy work, resistance to changes, and not keeping up-to-date with new products and technologies. The sales manager should recognize the symptoms and work on a number of alternative solutions. First, the sales manager should discuss the situation with the plateau salesperson and set some performance standards. If the performance does not improve, the sales manager should consider the following imaginative solutions: training or coaching new salespersons, developing a new territory, market surveys for new products, collecting competitive information, or change in the territory and customers.

Proactive Approach and Good Communications

Sales managers should control potential problems in motivation by identifying and removing them. This can be done by regularly communicating with salespeople, praising good performance, including suitable recognition programs, and discussing less than expected performance with salespersons in a constructive manner. Sales managers should listen carefully to salespeople, respond to them promptly, and set a good example. Above all, good communication should exist between the sales manager and each salesperson. For the salesperson, existence of good communications means freedom to talk business and personal problems with the sales manager. Similarly for the sales manager, it means ease in talking with the salesperson and providing assistance in resolving any problems faced by the salesperson.

LO 3 **Understand the objectives of a compensation plan, design an effective compensation plan, and classify the types of compensation plan**

COMPENSATING THE SALES FORCE

As discussed earlier in this chapter, among the various elements in the motivational mix, financial compensation or pay is given the highest importance for motivating salespeople. It is, therefore, a widely used method or tool for motivating salespeople. Companies should review their compensation plans once a year to make certain that the compensation plans are in line with the changes in marketing environment and the company's strategies. The structure of the sales force compensation, as discussed briefly earlier in this chapter, is as follows:

1. **Financial compensation**, which includes (a) **Direct payment** of money (or current spendable income), such as salary, commission, and bonus; and (b) **Indirect payment,** which includes fringe benefits (or perquisites), such as retirement plans, medical reimbursement, and leave travel assistance (LTA). It also includes various insurance plans that are financed by the company.
2. **Non-Financial compensation** was shown in Table 6.5 and discussed earlier. Hence, our discussions will focus on financial compensation. We shall first discuss the objectives of a good compensation plan and thereafter, take up the steps in designing a sales compensation plan.

OBJECTIVES OF A COMPENSATION PLAN

A good compensation plan should consider objectives from the company's viewpoint and also the salesperson's viewpoint. Sales managers should recognize that some of the management objectives may conflict with the salesperson's objectives. We first consider objectives from the company's viewpoint.

The Company's Viewpoint

The company wants to attract, retain, and motivate competent salespeople. A good compensation plan should attract and keep top-quality salespeople. It should also motivate salespersons to reach and exceed their sales goals. In a study of sales and marketing executives, 70 percent reported that their compensation plans were effective or very effective in motivating the salespeople[45].

To Control Salespeople's Activities

The compensation plan should offer incentives to control and direct several key activities of salespeople, such as selling more high profit-contribution products, payment collection, and customer relationship building. Of course these key tasks will vary from company to company. For instance, in a precision steel tubes manufacturing company, the company paid a higher rate of commission to salespersons who sold more quantities of high-contribution product, viz., CDW tubes. Also, bonus was paid to the salespersons who achieved the monthly payment collection targets.

To Attract and Retain Quality Salespeople

If the company's compensation plan is good, competent salespersons will come to work in the firm. A sound compensation plan helps to retain good salespeople. An innovative compensation plan helps to improve productivity of salespersons.

To Be Flexible

A good compensation plan should be flexible to adapt to new products, new territory, and differing territory sales potential. Some companies use individualized compensation plans, in which each salesperson is allowed to choose the percentage of his or her compensation as fixed (i.e., straight salary) and the percentage that is variable (i.e., commission based)[46].

The Salesperson's Viewpoint

We now consider the objectives of a compensation plan from the salesperson's viewpoint.

To Have Regular and Incentive Income

The salesperson wants the compensation plan to provide a regular income every month that is fixed and secured against any problems or emergencies. If the salesperson is sick and cannot work for a period of time, or if the sales are down due to various factors, he/she should get some fixed salary to take care of living expenses. This is important because if salespersons are worried about how to meet living expenses, then they cannot concentrate on doing their job well. An extra reward, in addition to fixed income, should be included in the compensation plan to produce above average performance.

To Have a Simple Plan

The compensation plan should be simple for salespeople to understand easily. They should be able to calculate their own incomes. Even most company managements prefer to have a simple compensation plan. This objective may be in conflict with the objective of flexibility, indicated earlier. A compensation plan that is simple may not be flexible.

To Have a Fair Payment Plan

The compensation plan should ensure fair or just payment to all salespeople. This can be done by selecting those factors which can be measured and controlled by salespeople. The plan should not penalize salespeople because of factors beyond their control. For instance, a factor like "customer satisfaction" can be influenced by several reasons, including product quality and delayed deliveries.

DESIGNING AN EFFECTIVE SALES COMPENSATION PLAN

Designing or devising a new sales compensation plan or revising an existing plan consists of a number of steps, as shown in Figure 6.8. This is a systematic approach that assures an effective compensation plan.

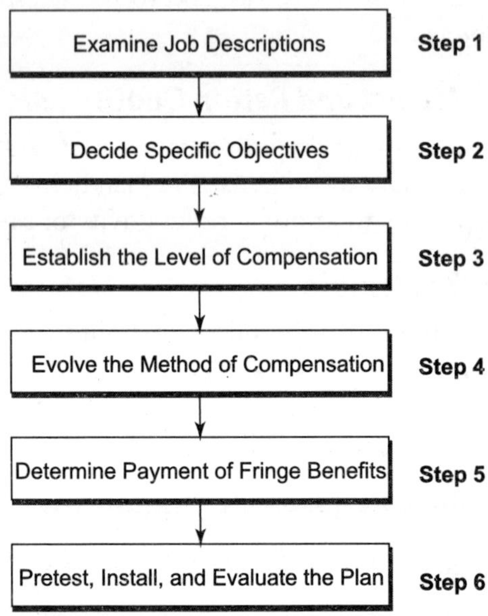

Fig. 6.8 **Steps in Designing an Effective Sales Compensation Plan**

Examine Job Descriptions

The first step is to examine the existing job descriptions[47], which were prepared earlier in the staffing process, for all sales positions[48]. There are various sales positions, such as missionary salespeople, outside order takers, delivery salespersons, consultative sellers, creative sellers, and key account sales executive. Each of these positions needs a separate job description, with detailed job responsibilities and key performance standards, to decide how much the company should pay. If there are no written sales job descriptions, they are now prepared. If the job descriptions are outdated or incomplete, they need to be revised.

Decide Specific Objectives

An effective compensation plan should have specific objectives for the salespeople. These sales force objectives should be derived from the company's sales and marketing objectives. Also, sales managers should include those specific objectives over which salespeople have maximum control, such as number of sales calls to be made to "A" and "B" class customers, selling expenses, and new customers to be developed. Achievement of objectives like customer satisfaction and sales volume depend on various factors, such as product quality, pricing policy, after-sales services (if needed) in relation to competitors and therefore, salespeople have some control but not maximum control. Besides, the specific objectives should be those that can be measured by the company, like selling expenses, sales volume, and number of sales calls made, number of new customers developed, and sales reports sent. Examples of specific objectives are as follows:

- Increase sales volume of high profit contribution products by 20 percent.
- Develop minimum 10 new customers in one year.
- Make four sales calls to "A" class customers per month.
- Incur selling expenses of less than two percent of sales revenue.

Establish the Level of Compensation

It is an important task to decide levels of pay for various sales positions. A level of pay or compensation means the average pay or money earned by the salespeople per year (or per month). The level or amount of compensation or pay should be competitive to attract and retain good quality salespeople. Firms decide the level of compensation based on the following factors:

- the levels of pay for similar sales positions in the industry and community.
- the levels of pay for comparable jobs in the company, and
- education, experience, and skills required to do the sales job.

When the information on the average levels of compensation in the industry and community is obtained, it should be checked if indirect pay or benefits, such as pension and insurance, are included or not[49]. The company should also consider the cost of living in different metros, cities, and towns. In some companies, company-wide job evaluation programs are done, which are used to establish compensation levels for sales positions.

The annual pay or income levels vary to a large extent between industries, within the same industry, and sometimes within the same company. The supply/demand balance varies across communities and industries. In high growth industries, and main cities like Mumbai and Bengaluru, demand exceeds supply and therefore, the pay levels are high. Another factor driving pay levels is industry profitability. High-profit industries can afford to pay more and low profit industries pay less.

Sales jobs also differ widely, as we have seen earlier. Compensation levels are higher for more difficult jobs, like selling CNC (computerized numerically controlled) machines. While deciding levels of pay, companies should decide a range of pay, instead of a specific average pay. The income range states clearly what salespeople can earn, depending on their performance as well as the company's performance.

Evolve the Method of Compensation

One of the key tasks in designing an effective sales compensation plan is to develop the compensation method by which the salespeople will be paid. The most widely used elements of compensation are: (i) salaries, (ii) commissions, (iii) bonuses, and (iv) indirect monetary benefits, such as paid vacation (or leave travel assistance), sickness (or medical reimbursement), pensions, accident and life insurance, which are also called **fringe benefits,** perquisites, or perks. Usually, (v) expense allowances or reimbursements, which include travel, lodging, dining, and customer entertainment, are not included in the compensation.

TYPES OF COMPENSATION PLANS

If we do not consider the "fringe benefits" and "expense reimbursement" from the elements of compensation since they are not used alone, there are only three basic types of compensations:

(i) Straight salary,
(ii) Straight commission, and
(iii) Combination of salary, commission, and/or bonus.

Only about 32 percent of all firms use either a straight salary or straight commission method. Balance 68 percent of all companies use a combination method to pay their salespeople[50]. However, there are large variations among industries. For example, most electrical equipment companies prefer "straight salary plans", whereas real estate industry firm mostly use "straight commission plans".

Straight-Salary Plan

In a straight-salary compensation plan, salary is a fixed sum representing total payments received by a salesperson for his services. The payments of salary are at regular intervals of usually monthly or weekly. It is the simplest compensation plan. This plan is more common among industrial-goods firms than among consumer-goods companies. However, its importance has been declining.

Advantages of a Straight-Salary Plan

- It provides salespeople a secure income, since their living expenses will be covered. This may make recruitment of salespeople easy.
- It helps to develop a sense of loyalty to the company, resulting in lower turnover of salespeople.
- It makes salespeople willing to perform non-selling activities, such as payment collection from customers, obtaining and reporting market information. Changing salespeople's territories is less problematic.
- It helps to increase customer loyalty, as salespeople have less incentive to overstock customers.
- From the company's viewpoint, it is simple and economical to administer and easy to budget. For the company's management, it provides strong financial control over salespeople.

Disadvantages of a Straight-Salary Plan

- It provides little financial incentive to salespeople to exert more efforts and to improve performance.
- Fixed salaries may be a burden to new firms or to those firms which are in declining profitability phase, since salaries represent fixed overhead.
- May lead to average, but not outstanding performance.
- Differences in salaries among salespersons are in many cases due to seniority on the job instead of merit.

Many disadvantages or weaknesses of the straight-salary plan are minimized through good sales administration. Each salesperson's performance is regularly reviewed and salaries are paid based on the performance.

A straight-salary plan is best suited to the following situations:

- For sales trainees, who are involved in learning about the job, until training is completed.
- For missionary sales activities, involved in spreading information widely instead of asking for order.
- When the company wants to introduce a new line of products or enter a new geographical territory.

Straight-Commission Plan

Unlike straight-salary plans, straight-commission (or commission only) plans offer strong financial incentives in order to ensure superior performance. Straight-commission plans are diametrically opposite to straight-salary plans. In contrast to the straight-salary plan, which is a fixed payment for a unit of time, a commission is a payment for the performance of a unit of work. This plan is based on the assumption that salespeople should be paid according to their productivity.

The sales manager has to decide on the following factors in developing a straight-commission plan:

❍ **Commission Base** The base on which the salesperson's performance is measured and commission will be paid. The most popular commission base is sales volume. For example, sales in Rupees (or Dollars) or units (or numbers) of the product. However, companies are gradually adopting profitability-based commission plans, in order to improve sales force productivity.

❍ **Commission Rate** It is the rate to be paid per unit, usually expressed as a percentage of sales or gross profit. Commission rates vary to a large extent, and it is a very difficult decision to decide the suitable rate. The commission rate, the percentage paid to the salesperson, may be a constant rate over the compensation period. A progressive commission rate increases as salespersons reach pre-stated targets. A regressive rate decreases at some pre-decided point. Regressive rate may be suitable when the first order is difficult to get but reorders are easy. For example, getting the first order from an original equipment manufacturer (OEM) is very difficult, but subsequent orders are considered as routine.

○ **Commission Start** The starting point for the commission payment, that is, after selling the first unit or after reaching the sales quota or target.

There are two classifications of the straight-commission plans: (i) straight commission with salespeople paying their own travelling, lodging and boarding expenses, (ii) straight commission with the company paying travelling and other expenses.

○ **Commission Payout** It is the time when the commissions are paid. Some companies pay commission to salespeople after the customer is billed for the order and the payment is received, and not after the order is obtained. Many companies pay 50 percent of commission after the customer is billed and the balance commission is paid after the receipt of 100 percent payment from the customer.

Advantages of a Straight-Commission Plan

- It gives strong financial incentive (or motivation) to the salespeople to work hard and improve the sales volume.
- It attracts high performers and removes ineffective salespersons.
- It controls selling costs, as the commission is a variable cost which is incurred only when a sales is made.
- It requires less supervision from the sales manager.
- It has flexibility, since commission rates can be revised for different products, so that salespeople are encouraged to sell more those products with the highest profit contribution.

Disadvantages of a Straight-Commission Plan

- The focus is on getting the sales rather than building long-term customer relationship. These salespersons use high-pressure tactics which results in loss of customer goodwill.
- Less control of the sales manager on the non-selling activities (such as collecting and reporting customers' and competitors' information) to be performed by the salespersons.
- Little loyalty of salespeople to the company, which may lead the salespeople on commission to leave the company if sales drop or business environment becomes worse.
- If commissions are not limited by a cap on the money earned, then salespeople may earn more than their managers, who would resent this outcome and the salespeople may not respond to directions from such managers.
- Salespeople put greater efforts on the easy-to-sell and low-profit contribution product items and neglect difficult-to-sell and high-profit contribution items. If the company management tries to correct this by using differential commission rates, it increases record-keeping expenses.

A straight commission plan is best suited to the following situations:

- In certain industries like manufacturers of furniture and office equipment and insurance, the major responsibility of the salespeople is to get orders. Other non-selling activities like getting payments and market information are not important.

- The direct-sales industry, including Tupperware, Amway, and Avon, pays by straight-commission to a large number of salespeople, who are called independent distributors.
- Wholesalers, who have limited working capital, pay their salespeople by straight-commission. Similarly, manufacturers' representatives (also called agents) are paid by straight-commission.

Combination Plan

A combination plan combines salary and incentive. In other words, it is a judicious blending of salary, commission and bonus. With an effective combination plan, the company's management tries to obtain both motivation and control of salespeople. There are three types of combination compensation plans that are used by most companies: (i) Salary plus commission, (ii) Salary plus bonus, and (iii) Salary plus commission plus bonus.

Effective combination plans offer a balance of incentive, control, and flexibility to reward important sales force activities. However, the most difficult part of structuring the combination plans is to decide the salary (fixed component) and incentive (variable component of commission and bonus) mix. In other words, to decide the relative amounts to be paid to salespeople in salary, commission, and bonus. The incentive portion of combination plans (i.e. commission and/or bonus) has been increasing over the past 20 years and is now around 40 percent. The balance 60 percent is salary to offer regular income to salespeople. However, the salary and incentive mix for a company depends on the sales and marketing objectives of the company as well as the nature of its selling activities. For example, if the company's short-term objective is to increase its sales and profits substantially then the incentive portion should be greater. The salary part should be larger if the company is dependent heavily on advertising, customer service, and team selling to achieve sales volume objective.

Earlier we have discussed commission, but not bonus. A **bonus** or a **performance bonus** is a lump sum amount paid for an above-average performance to an individual or group. Typically, bonuses are used to direct salespeople's efforts towards short-term objectives, such as adding new customers, introducing new products, or collecting overdue outstanding payments from customers. Bonuses may be offered in the form of cash, merchandise, or free travel.

In India, there is a practice of companies paying bonus to all its employees during festival period for celebration. "The payment of Bonus (Amendment) Act 2015", applies to every factory and establishment that employs 20 or more persons. All employees earning up to ₹21,000 are eligible to receive statutory bonus.

Because of its nature, a bonus cannot be used alone, but is used strictly as supplementary to a salary or commission. The bonus is an extra financial incentive to the salesperson for achieving good results.

Salary Plus Commission Plan

This plan achieves the balance between the fixed (salary) and variable (commission) elements of a salesperson's pay. Some companies link the variable portion of a salesperson's pay to the achievement of goals like customer satisfaction and customer retention. For instance, IBM partly rewards salespeople on the basis of customer satisfaction as measured by customer surveys[51]. This plan is most suitable when the company wants to get increased sales as well as superior customer service or customer satisfaction. Though there is no general agreement, a fair compensation mix is 60 percent salary (fixed element) and 40 percent commission (variable element). Salary plus commission plan is used by many companies because it has the merits of a salary plus adjustability of a commission.

Salary Plus Bonus Plan

Usually this plan is used by the companies who want to control selling and non-selling activities of the salespeople with a larger portion of fixed element of salary (i.e., more than 60 percent), and still present some incentive to achieve either a short-term or a long-term objective. For example, short-term objectives could be introducing new products, minimizing slow moving stocks, or developing new customers. The long-term (strategic) objectives may be achieving a higher level of customer satisfaction and customer retention. Some companies use bonuses to reward team performance of sales teams. If the team goals are achieved particularly for major or key customers, then all the members of the team are paid bonus.

Salary Plus Commission Plus Bonus Plan

Some companies use all the three elements, viz., salary, commission, and bonus in their compensation plans. This plan allows a company an adequate control of salespeople's activities, an incentive to increase sales to the expected level, and a bonus to achieve specific objectives like developing new customers and introducing new products. For instance, Siebel Systems pays a base salary plus commission plus a quarterly bonus based on customer satisfaction surveys to each salesperson[52]. This plan is also suitable for companies who sell seasonal products like fans and air conditioners, which have high inventory during off-season and low inventory during the peak season. The companies can minimize the inventory imbalances by using the incentive scheme, consisting of commission and bonus.

Advantages of a Combination Compensation Plan

- The company management can have a control over the activities of salespeople.
- Management has flexibility to reward the desirable activities of salespeople.
- Feeling of security for salespeople as fixed salaries take care of living costs. In addition, salespeople have financial incentives to earn more by producing superior performance. This has a favorable effect on the moral of salespeople.
- Bonuses can be added to a salary base to encourage, such activities as selling excess inventory, introducing new products, and obtaining new customers.
- Different combination plans can be developed for sales trainees, senior salespersons, and key account executives. This helps in having better cooperation between sales managers and salespeople.

Disadvantages of a Combination Compensation Plan

- The plan is more complex and difficult to administer. The administration costs are high.
- If too many short-term and fire-fighting type objectives, such as liquidating excess inventory and collecting overdue payments are achieved, more important long-term objectives like customer satisfaction and customer centric approach may be delayed.
- This plan may not achieve the desired objectives if not carefully planned, implemented, and understood clearly by salespeople.

Determine Payment of Fringe Benefits

Indirect payment plan is also called 'fringe benefits'. These are medical reimbursements and payments, group life insurance, travel insurance, accident insurance, retirement benefits (like gratuity and pension plan), social security (or provident fund), profit sharing, stock options, paid vacations (or leave travel concessions), and so on. Fringe benefits help satisfy safety and security needs, although some (such as payment of social club fees and automobile) contribute to fulfillment of higher-order needs like esteem. They help prevent job dissatisfaction, but do not add to job satisfaction. Fringe benefits are not motivating factors. Most companies provide some of these benefits in order to remain competitive with other companies in the industry or community. Indirect payments or benefits help in attracting applicants. These benefits give a degree of security to salespeople and make them loyal to the company. However, fringe benefits do not have direct relationships to job performance.

Pretest, Administer, and Evaluate the Compensation Plan

These are explained briefly in this section.

Pretesting

Before a new (or proposed) compensation plan is adopted, the company should pretest it. Pretesting the proposed compensation plan is a simulation exercise that can be done on a computer. However, to understand how much harder the salespeople would work and to know its impact on sales force activities, some companies pretest the proposed compensation plan on one or more branch sales offices for adequate duration of 6 to 12 months in order to evaluate to what extent the company's sales and marketing objectives are achieved. Pretesting should be done with the involvement of all concerned people like salespersons, sales managers, human resource, and finance executives.

Administering

The company should introduce the proposed or new compensation plan to salespeople carefully. The new compensation plan should be announced well in advance of the date of implementation. If the proposed compensation plan is announced at a national or regional sales meeting, the company should explain the reasons for changing the previous plan. Each salesperson should even be asked to calculate the salary, and incentives at the various sales levels. The company should either conduct pretesting in one or more branch sales offices, as mentioned earlier, or carry out field-testing of the plan in a few district sales offices, under actual selling conditions for about 6 to 12 months. These tests would help the company to make some changes in the proposed plan, based on the feedback from salespeople and the results obtained. As the companies are changing their compensation plans frequently and compensation plans are becoming more complex, some companies like Johnson & Johnson, and Hewlett Packard are outsourcing the administration of their compensation plans. Some of the companies that provide these services are Oracle, Synergy, and Trilogy[53].

Evaluating

After the new plan is established, it should be evaluated on quarterly, half-yearly or yearly basis. Whether the objectives of the compensation plan have been achieved or not is the main question to be answered. If it has achieved the objectives, the plan can continue. If the objectives of the plan are not achieved, the management of the company has to determine if the reasons are related to the compensation plan, in which case some changes need to be carried out. Some companies audit their compensation plans annually. This is a good practice, as it makes certain that the compensation plan is in line with the company's strategic plan.

LO 4 **Discuss sales leadership and supervision; analyze leadership characteristics, styles, and skills to determine leadership effectiveness; describe how to supervise salespeople**

LEADERSHIP AND SUPERVISION OF A SALES FORCE

Leadership is absolutely necessary to a sales manager's effectiveness. Sales managers not only supervise but also lead. That brings us to a point to understand the difference between sales force leadership and supervision. Leadership is the ability to influence other people towards the achievement of specific goals and objectives. Research indicates that leadership ability can be learned[54]. Leadership is a people oriented action, which is different than administrative or problem-solving activities. Sales leadership requires that sales managers equip and empower the salespeople. They should understand each salesperson's needs and at the same time develop teamwork.

Supervision is directing of the day-to-day activities of the salespeople. Supervision is a part of leadership. Leadership requires more foresight and intuition than supervision, because supervision deals more with maintenance and improvement of the existing state, whereas leadership in most cases requires review of objectives and activities of the sales force. We shall now briefly discuss the difference between leaders and managers.

A manager achieves organizational goals and objectives in an effective and efficient manner through planning, organizing, staffing, directing, and controlling the organizational resources. Leading is a part of the manager's function. Leaders have an emotional influence on people. Leaders have a vision of the future. They convey that vision to others and stimulate them to realize it[55].

LEADERSHIP EFFECTIVENESS

Effectiveness of a leader depends on three factors: (i) personal characteristics or traits, (ii) leadership style or behavior, and (iii) leadership skills. An effective leader achieves planned results consistently. In case of sales management, an effective sales manager achieves the sales goals and objectives consistently. We shall first discuss personal characteristics of a leader, and then dwell on leadership styles and skills.

Personal Characteristics of a Leader

Some of the most important personal characteristics of an effective leader are: visionary, honesty, energetic, self-starter, and decisive. However, no one has been able to identify the exact personality traits that make an effective sales management leader.

Visionary

A leader should be a person with imaginative and original ideas about the future. He must create an inspiring vision and set direction. Effective leaders inspire people to achieve more than they have ever dreamt.

Honesty

Ethical or honest leaders inspire people not just through words but also by means of actions. If the leader makes honesty and ethical behavior a key value, his team will follow suit. Without integrity or honesty, no leader will survive for a long time.

Energetic

Effective leaders have great physical and mental powers. They have adequate strength and vitality to manage a great variety of activities and relationships. Energetic people are generally highly enthusiastic about the work or cause.

Self-Starter

Leaders must be self-starters. They take initiative and act before other people do. They have the ability to act independently and with a new approach.

Decisive

Leaders are regularly called on to make decisions that impact the organization and the people they lead. Effective leaders have the ability to make decisions quickly and confidently.

Leadership Styles

The combination of behaviors that a manager uses is known as the manager's leadership style. A manager's behavior should be in agreement with different styles of leadership. We shall look at different styles of leadership, such as: (i) transformational leadership, (ii) transactional leadership, and (iii) situational leadership.

Transformational Leadership

Transformational leaders transform (or change) the basic values, beliefs, and attitudes of followers such that the followers are willing to perform at levels above and beyond expectations. They act as change agents. Such persons are charismatic, inspirational, and driven by a sense of mission. They use two-way communication. Behavior of transformational leaders that are relevant to sales managers include team building, leading by example, creating a vision, and giving an individualized attention.

- **Team Building** Transformational leaders build teamwork by encouraging followers to work together towards a common goal. In team selling, it is important for sales managers to build an effective team. This is done by identifying a common goal, asking team members to help each other, and recognizing the importance of non-salespeople like engineers, production people and others.

- **Leading by Example** Transformation leaders lead by example. Their behavior is in line with the goals and values of the organization. They (sales managers) show high level of honesty and work ethic, which inspires their subordinates (salespeople) also to be honest and work hard. In a sales situation, these sales managers demonstrate proper selling techniques, so that salespeople learn how to handle the sales calls. Transformational leaders give a professional impression with their neat appearance and ethical values. They are effective role models.

- **Creating a Vision** The sales manager, who is a transformational leader, first understands the company's overall vision and mission statements, breaks down the same into the sales objectives that are understood by the salespeople. In only 20 percent companies, sales managers create meaningful mission in this manner[56].

- **Giving an Individualized Attention** Sales managers, as transformational leaders, give individual attention to each salesperson, by understanding each salesperson's needs, feelings, background, family, hobbies, and so on. This is a difficult and time consuming but an important activity. This helps the sales manager to solve salesperson's problems. Salespeople will respond positively to such sales managers who care for their subordinates.

Transactional Leadership

Transactional leadership is considered same as supervision. In other words, transactional leadership usually describes those supervisory tasks that relate to the day-to-day activities and control of the salespeople. Sales managers, who have transactional style of leadership, give verbal feedback to their salespeople in terms of appreciation and criticism. For instance, the sales manager admires the salesperson when he or she gets a large order, but the same salesperson gets a scolding if there is a delay in submitting a quotation to a customer. Transactional leaders are task oriented. They concentrate on getting the work done. These leaders usually have one way communication of telling salespeople about the company rules, policies and procedures. They are good supervisors and have a working relationship with salespeople.

Situational Leadership

What makes a sales manager an effective leader? Which leadership style should a sales manager adopt? The answer is the situational leadership. It means the sales manager who has an ability to use the leadership style (i.e., either transformational or transactional) that fits the current situation and the individual salesperson. For example, in a crisis situation, in which the company does not have adequate orders due to demand recession, the sales manager should clearly communicate the objectives and strategy to the salespeople and demonstrate how to get orders in such a situation. This, in other words, is leading by example, which is transformational leadership. In another situation for a newly hired and inexperienced salesperson, the sales manager uses transactional leadership by using one-way communication, explaining how the sales process is followed.

Yet another situation is how the sales manager should motivate a long experienced salesperson whose performance is below expectation. The sales manager should first talk to the salesperson individually (i.e., individualized attention), understand his needs or problems, ask the salesperson how he can contribute to the achievement of common goals and objectives of the territory (i.e., team building). That may include training new salespeople, or developing a new territory. Then depending on the salesman's strengths and interest motivate him to take up an activity that would contribute to the improvement of his and the territory's performance.

All these examples indicate appropriate behavior of the leader in different situations.

Leadership Skills

The skill areas for effective sales management leaders include communication skills, problem-solving skills, and interpersonal skills. However, no one has been able to identify a magic combination of skills that ensures leadership.

Communication Skills

An effective leader must have good spoken and written communication skills. The sales manager communicates information from higher level managers to the salespeople and from the salespersons to the upper management. Effective sales managers deliver clear and timely information through a suitable media, or interpersonal communications.

Problem-Solving Skills

Effective leaders should anticipate potential problems, diagnose the same, and make suitable decisions. There are examples of leadership crises that could have been avoided by anticipation of a potential problem. For instance, an area sales manager, who was transferred to a new territory to improve the declining sales, diagnosed the problem after getting feedback from the customers and salespeople that customer service needed improvement, salespeople needed motivation, and competitors' information was insufficient. The area sales manager decided to spend half of his time in the field with salespeople to guide them on their selling skills; ensure improvement in customer service by ensuring that salespeople take actions on pre-sales, during-sales, and post-sales services; and inform senior management about the accurate information on competitors' pricing policies and product strategies to get appropriate decisions. Effective sales managers spend large amount of time in identifying specific problems, diagnosing the nature of the problem by examining the symptoms, and selecting an appropriate response to match the situation.

Interpersonal Skills

Effective sales managers have good working relationship with their salespeople. They understand each salesperson as an individual, find out the needs and aspirations of each salesperson and motivate them to perform well to achieve the sales goals. Effective leaders also establish good relationship with their superiors and peers. They are dependent more on reasoning than on authority.

SUPERVISING SALESPEOPLE

As mentioned earlier, supervision is a part of leadership, and it includes directing and controlling of the day-to-day activities of salespeople. There are variations on how closely a sales supervisor or first-level sales manager should supervise salespeople. Usually salespeople who are paid on commission basis receive less supervision in comparison with salespeople who are compensated by salaries. The objective of supervision is to improve the job performances of salespeople. The manager with supervisory responsibilities establishes working relations with salespeople. A sales manager uses a combination of methods to supervise or interact with salespeople. These are direct supervisory methods and indirect supervisory methods.

Direct Supervisory Methods

These include telecommunications, sales meetings, personal contacts, and coaching.

Telecommunications

Many sales managers use telephone, e-mails, voice mails, fax messages, and computer-based support systems. Companies such as Hewlett–Packard, Procter & Gamble, and IBM give each of their salespersons a laptop for carrying out various activities, such as report writing, call planning, accessing customer information, submitting quotations, corresponding with customers, entering and monitoring customer orders, and so on. By using the computerized-support system, these companies have reported improvement in accuracy, productivity, and management effectiveness.

Sales Meetings

As discussed earlier in this chapter, sales meetings are used by the sales managers to communicate information on any change in policies and procedures, to arrange for training programs, and to inspire or motivate salespeople to achieve sales quotas or targets.

Personal Contacts

The sales manager visits customers with each salesperson for various reasons, such as calling on a specific customer to handle a particular problem, training a salesperson, team selling effort, and getting market information. The sales manager discusses strengths and weaknesses of the salesperson after the sales call[57].

Coaching

In the role of coaching, a sales manager concentrates on the continuous development of a salesperson. Coaching is intensively teaching or training a salesperson on-the-job through instruction, demonstration, and practice. Successful coaching takes place when there is trust and respect between the sales manager and the salesperson. The major part of a coaching session is the joint sales call, when the sales manager and the salesperson visit a customer. After the meeting with the customer, the sales manager discusses the salesperson's areas of improvement. With regular coaching sessions, the sales manager can improve selling skills, develop positive attitudes and work habits, and help the salesperson to be more efficient and effective.

Indirect Supervisory Methods

Many companies use the following methods, which can have effective supervisory control as they work towards the company goals and objectives. These are: sales reports, compensation plans, sales analysis, and expense accounts/reports.

Sales Reports

The salesperson's activities can be monitored and evaluated as a supervisory tool by using sales reports. In addition, the data on the customer and competitors given in the sales reports is used for the company's marketing information system. Usually sales reports include information about the calls made (against the call norms), orders obtained, new customers developed, competitive activities, customer problems and needs, and so on. Salespeople are also required to submit a call plan, which gives the details of their plans of customer visits for the upcoming period. The call plan makes a salesperson plan the activities as per the company norms of calling on various classes of customers, including time to be spent on new customers. Many companies consider sales reporting activity as one of the main responsibilities of salespeople and therefore, salespeople are evaluated and rewarded based on salespeople providing timely and accurate information in their sales reports.

Compensation Plan

As discussed earlier in this chapter, it is one of the most important methods that encourages salespeople to carry out those activities that will maximize their income. In other words, the compensation plan directs the activities of salespeople, and influences the efforts and time spent by salespeople on various activities.

Sales Analysis

By using the sales analysis report, which is discussed in Chapter 7, the sales manager can evaluate the performance of each salesperson by comparing what was sold and how much was sold with the sales quotas or targets. Thereafter, the sales manager can guide or help those salespeople who need help in achieving their sales targets or quotas.

Expense Accounts/Reports

Expense reports or expense accounts indicate how much money was spent by salespeople on travelling, lodging, meals, entertainment, as compared to the company policies on various expense items. It helps to keep control on selling expenses. Many sales managers are flexible on expense accounts as long as the additional selling expenses have produced increased sales and profitability.

SUMMARY

LO 1

- Research has shown that if sales training is correctly designed, implemented and reinforced, it can result in improved performance of salespeople, higher retention of salespeople, and better customer relations.
- The sales training process consists of: (i) identifying who should be trained and their training needs, (ii) designing and executing a training program, and (iii) evaluation and reinforcement of a training program.

LO 2

- The desire to spend effort to fulfill a need is motivation. In a sales job, motivation is amount of efforts the salesperson makes to complete various activities of the sales job.
- The company management recognizes the importance of sales management and salespeople because the financial performance of the company depends upon the achievement of sales volume objective, which is the primary responsibility of the sales management.
- Some of the theories of motivation are: (i) Maslow's hierarchy of needs theory, (ii) Hertzberg's dual-factor theory, (iii) Vroom's expectancy theory, and (iv) Churchill, Ford, and Walker model.
- Motivational tools or methods are divided into two broad categories: (i) Financial rewards, consisting of (a) financial compensation plan (which includes salary, commission, performance bonus, and fringe benefits), (b) sales contests, (c) team compensation, and (d) global compensation issues; (ii) Non-financial rewards consisting of (a) promotional opportunity, (b) sense of accomplishment, (c) personal growth opportunities, (d) recognition, (e) job security, (f) sales meetings, (g) sales training programs, (h) job enrichment, (i) effective supervision, and (j) praise and encouragement.
- Some guidelines for motivating salespeople are: (i) sales performance depends on ability and efforts (or motivation) of salespeople, (ii) motivational programs should consider individual salesperson's needs, (iii) know how to motivate plateau salespeople, and (iv) have proactive approach and good communications with salespersons.

LO 3

- A good compensation plan for salespeople should consider the objectives from the company's as well as salespersons' viewpoints. The objectives from the company's perspective includes controlling salespersons' activities, attracting and retaining competent salespeople, ensuring flexibility, and remaining competitive. The objectivities of the compensation plan from salespeople's viewpoint are having regular and incentive income, having simple to understand, and fair payment plan.

- Steps in designing an effective sales compensation plan consist of: (i) examining job descriptions, (ii) deciding specific objectives, (iii) setting up levels of compensation, (iv) developing the compensation mix, (v) determining indirect payment plan, and (vi) pretesting, administering and evaluating the compensation plan.

LO 4

- Sales leadership requires sales managers to understand each salesperson's needs and at the same time develop teamwork. Supervision is directing of the day-to-day activities of the salespeople. Supervision is a part of sales leadership.
- Effective leadership depends on a combination of the leader's personal characteristics, styles, and skills. Personal characteristics or traits include the leader's honesty, vision, initiative, energy, and decisiveness. Effective leaders need communication, interpersonal and problem-solving skills. Leadership styles are transactional, transformational, and situational. Effective sales manager should have situational leadership style, which means the manager should adopt either transformational or transactional style depending on the needs of the situation and the individual salesperson. The first level sales managers generally supervise salespeople. They should use both direct and indirect methods for supervising salespeople.

Key Terms

Glossaries of key terms are mentioned at the end of all chapters

Absorption training
Bonus
Business games
Capability gap
Compensation
Compensation mix
EPSS (Electronic Performance Support System)
Expectancy theory
Hertzberg's dual-factor theory
Instrumentality
Leadership
Maslow's hierarchy of needs
Motivation
Motivational mix
Plateau salesperson
Refresher training
Sales analysis
Situational leadership
Supervision
Transactional leadership
Transformational leadership
Valence

Conceptual Questions

1. Why should the training needs of salespersons be assessed? What are the methods used for identifying the training needs of salespeople? LO1 E
2. Describe briefly the steps involved in designing and executing a sales training program. LO1 M
3. How would you stimulate a sales manager to organize reinforcement program for new salespeople after their formal sales training program? LO1 M
4. What are the purposes of evaluation and reinforcement of sales training? What is refresher training? LO1 E
5. What is the meaning of motivation? Why is the task of motivating salespeople difficult and important for sales managers? LO2 E
6. Explain any one of the theories of motivation and its relevance to sales force motivation. LO2 M
7. "If you pay a salesperson enough, you will have a well-motivated salesperson". Comment. LO2 D
8. What factors should be considered by a sales manager before designing (or selecting) a mix of motivational tools? What are the different motivational methods or tools that are available to sales managers? LO2 M
9. What is the structure of sales force compensation? Which objectives should be considered for effective compensation plan? LO3 D
10. Explain briefly the steps involved in designing an effective compensation plan. LO3 M
11. Which compensation plan allows an organization the most control on salespeople and which plan is better for obtaining high sales? Why? LO3 M
12. Define 'leadership'. Explain the factors on which effective leadership is dependent. LO4 D
13. What is 'sales supervision'? Which methods are used to supervise salespeople? LO4 M

Objective Type Questions

Select the most appropriate response out of the various options available in each of the following questions:

1. Job description statement of sales force is useful for
   (a) recruitment process (b) selection process
   (c) sales training (d) compensation and evaluation of salespeople
   LO1 E

Note: Difficulty Level → E — Easy; M — Medium; D — Difficult

(e) All of these (f) None of these

2. The most important and frequently used method of training salespeople is
(a) lectures (b) demonstrations (c) case studies (d) on-the-job training
(e) online training LO1 M

3. One of the factors used when sales managers select suitable training methods is based on a study, the findings of which states that people generally remember most of what they
(a) read (b) hear (c) see (d) hear and see
(e) say (f) say as they do LO1 M

4. Motivation is originally derived from the
(a) Persian word (b) French word (c) Latin word (d) Greek word
(e) Sanskrit word LO2 D

5. Churchill, Ford, and Walker model of sales force motivation was derived from
(a) Maslow's hierarchy of needs theory (b) Vroom's expectancy theory
(c) Hertzberg's dual-factor theory (d) None of these LO2 E

6. The concept of instrumentality in expectancy theory refers to
(a) the salesperson's perception of the relationship between performance and reward
(b) the salesperson's perception of the relationship between effort and performance
(c) value placed on a particular reward by the salesperson
(d) All of these (e) None of these LO2 D

7. Sales contests are
(a) long-term (b) medium-term
(c) short-term incentive programs LO2 E

8. The first step in designing an effective sales compensation plan is
(a) set up specific objectives (b) examine the existing job descriptions
(c) decide levels of pay or compensation (d) decide indirect payment plan LO3 M

9. Which of the following leadership style would you recommend to sales managers as most effective?
(a) Situational leadership (b) Transactional leadership
(c) Transformational leadership (d) None of these LO4 M

Application Questions

1. If you are appointed as a sales trainer for a consumer products strategic business unit (SBU) of a large multi-national company with 100 salespeople, how would you decide their specific training needs? LO1 E

2. As a regional sales manager (South), you have decided to promote one of the existing salespersons for the position of branch sales manager for a new branch at Coimbatore in Tamil Nadu state. What kind of training would you conduct for this salesperson? LO1 M

3. If you were an area sales manager, how would you motivate the following salespersons reporting to you?
   (i) A high performing salesperson, whose morale is down because he did not get an expected promotion as a marketing executive, although he has been consistently exceeding his sales targets (or quotas) for the past four years. The main responsibilities of marketing executives are selling to a few key accounts, and coaching some sales trainees on the job. LO2 M
   (ii) An older salesperson whose performance has been below expectations for the past few years, although he had performed well in the past. He seems to have lost enthusiasm, although he has developed excellent relationship with a few key accounts, from whom the company gets good sales volume. LO2 M
4. Assume you have joined a company as a sales manager for hydraulic products and services. This company was recently selected as authorized distributor for Bosch India hydraulic products. As a distributor, your company is required to perform various tasks, such as prospecting, promoting, preparing technical offers, negotiating and getting orders, executing orders, collecting payments, giving pre- and post-sales services, and maintaining excellent customer relationship. Your company is required to operate in Mumbai territory (including New Mumbai). Develop a compensation plan for your salespeople, including financial and non-financial compensation methods. LO3 E
5. Suppose you are faced with the following problems as a sales manager: (i) salespeople are not spending adequate time to develop new customers, and (ii) salespeople are selling profitable products less than non-profitable and easy-to-sell products to achieve their sales volume quotas. Suggest a compensation plan that can be used to solve these problems. LO3 M
6. Choose an individual who is considered to be a great leader (e.g., Mahatma Gandhi, N.R. Narayana Murthy). Use the internet and library resources to examine this individual to determine what makes (or made) this person such a good leader. Explain this leader's traits or characteristics, leadership skills, and leadership style. What have you learnt from this leader that could help you to be a better leader? LO4 M
7. As a branch sales manager for STI Ltd., Sunil has 10 salespersons reporting to him. Sunil is a good transactional leader, but is not a transformational leader. Is this problematic? Why? LO4 D

ASSIGNMENTS FOR STUDENTS

1. Identify a company which conducts sales training programs regularly. Talk to the first level sales manager (i.e., area, district, or branch sales manager). Understand the whole process of sales training including reinforcement followed by the company. Prepare a written report describing the training process and adding your suggestions for improvements based on the inputs from the text book.

2. Select three salespersons who have undergone a training program. Talk to them to find out their training needs, whether their needs were fulfilled or not after the training program, and the reasons for the same. Submit your report with your observation.
3. Identify two salespersons from different companies. Conduct an in-depth interview with each salesperson separately to find their views on the kind of financial and non-financial motivational tools used by their respective companies. Compare the motivational tools used by the two firms and give your suggestions for improvements.
4. Select 10 salespersons from different companies and ask them what portion (or percentage) of their financial compensation is fixed (i.e., salary) and what portion (or percentage) is variable (i.e., commission and/or performance bonus) out of the total financial compensation. What are their views on their firm's financial compensation policy? Are they paid any fringe benefits (or perquisites)? Submit your report based on the information collected from the salespersons and indicate your comments.

Reference Notes

1. Mark P. Leach and Annie H. Liu, "Investigating Relationships among Sales Training Evaluation Methods", *Journal of Personal Selling and Sales Management*, Fall 2003: pp. 327–39.
2. Melanie Berger, "Intel", *Sales and Marketing Management*, 149 (October 1997): p. 56.
3. Robert Klein, "Nabisco Sales Soar after Sales Training", *Marketing News*, 31(January 1997): p. 23.
4. Christen P. Heide, *Dartnell's 30th Sales Force Compensation Survey*, (Chicago: The Dartnell Corporation, 1999).
5. Sarah Lorge, "Getting into Their Heads", *Sales and Marketing Management*, 150 (February 1998): p. 58.
6. Robert C. Erffimeyer and Dale A. Johnson, "Future of Sales Training: Making Choices among Six Distance Education Methods", *Journal of Business and Industrial Marketing*, 12 (Summer 1997): p. 185.
7. Mark McMaster, "Is Your Training a Waste of Money?", *Sales and Marketing Management*, (January 2001): pp. 42–48.
8. William Keenan, Jr, "Getting Customers into the Act", *Sales and Marketing Management*, (February 1995): p. 58.
9. Honeycutt, Howe, and Ingram, "Shortcomings of Sales Training Programs", *Industrial Marketing Management* 22 (1993): p. 117.
10. Gillian Flynn, "The Nuts and Bolts of Valuing Training", *Workforce* 77 (November 1998): p. 80.
11. Elana Harris, "Best at Sales Training", *Sales and Marketing Management*, (July 2000): p. 68
12. Betsy Cummings, "Welcome to the Real Whirled", *Sales and Marketing Management*, (February 2001): pp. 88–89.

13. Paradigm Learning, www.paradigmlearning.com/products, March 20, 2002.
14. Thomas N. Ingram, "Guidelines for Maximizing Role-Play Activities", in *Proceedings, National Conference in Sales Management*, (Dallas, TX, 1990).
15. Julia Chang, "Born to Sell?", *Sales and Marketing Management*, (July 2003): pp. 34–37.
16. Dan E. Hupp, "Selling beyond Quota: Adult Edutainment", *Training & Development*, 52 (August 1998): p. 61
17. Heide, *Dartnell's 30th Sales force Compensation Survey*, p.141.
18. Dobbs, "Training on the Fly", *Sales and Marketing Management*, (Nov. 2000): p. 96.
19. The HR Chally Group, "The Customer-Selected World Class Sales Excellence Ten-Year Research Reports", 2003, p. 59.
20. Malcom Fleschner, "Business Class", *Selling Power*, (September 2001): p. 133.
21. Andy Cohen, "Staying in Touch", *Sales and Marketing Management*, (April 1994): p. 35.
22. The HR Chally Group, "The Customer-Selected World Class Sales Excellence Ten-Year Research Reports", p. 56.
23. William Scholz, "Communication in the Business Organization", Englewood Cliffs, N.J.: Pearson Education, 1962, p. 86.
24. Elana Harris, "Best at Sales Training", *Sales and Marketing Management*, (July 2000): p. 68.
25. Donald Kirkpatrick, "Evaluating Training Programs: The Four Levels", (New York: Berret-Koehler, 1992).
26. Honeycutt, Karande, Attia, and Maurer, "A Utility Based Framework for Evaluating the Financial Impact of Sales force Training", *Journal of Personal Selling & Sales Management*, (Summer 2001): pp. 229–38.
27. Sarah Lorge, "Getting into Their Heads", *Sales and Marketing Management*, 150 (February 1998): p. 58
28. Neil Rackham and Richard Ruff, "Managing Major Sales", (New York: Harper Business, 1991), p. 130.
29. Slade Sohmer, "Emerging as a Global Success", *Sales and Marketing Management*, (May 2000): p. 125.
30. Walker, Churchill, and Ford, "Where do we go from Here? Selected Conceptual and Empirical Issues Concerning the Motivation and Performance of the Industrial Sales force, in Critical Issues in Sales Management", College of Business Administration, University of Oregon, 1979: p. 25; Ruth Kanfer, "Motivation Theory and Industrial Organizational Psychology" in *Handbook of Industrial and Organizational Psychology* (Palo Alto, CA: Consulting Psychologists Press, 1990), pp. 75–170.
31. Jeffrey K. Sagar and Mark W. Johnston, "Antecedents and Outcomes of Organizational Commitment: A Study of Salespeople", *Journal of Personal Selling and Sales Management*, 9(Spring 1989): p. 30.
32. Thomas N. Ingram, Ken S. Lee, and Steven J. Skinner, "Empirical Assessment of Salesperson Motivation, Commitment and Job Outcomes", *Journal of Personal selling and Sales management* 9(Fall 1989): p. 25.

33. Abraham H. Maslow, *Motivation and Personality*, 2nd ed. (New York: Harper & Row, 1970), chapters 3–7.
34. Frederick Hertzberg, Bernard Mausner, and Barbara B. Snyderman, *Motivation to Work*, 2nd ed. (New York: John Wiley & Sons, 1959).
35. Paul W.J., Robertson K.G., and Hertzberg F., "Job Enrichment Pays Off", *Harvard Business Review*, (March–April 1969) pp.1-29.
36. Vroom V.H. *Work and Motivation*, John Wiley, New York, 1964.
37. Churchill Jr, G.A., Ford N.M., Walker Jr. O.C., "Motivation and Performance of Industrial Selling", *Journal of Marketing Research*, 14(May 1977): p. 2.
38. Libby Estell, "Economic Incentives," *Sales and Marketing Management*, (October 2001): p. 54.
39. Julia Chang, "Trophy Value", *Sales and Marketing Management*, (October 2004): pp. 24–29.
40. Cron, Dubinsky, and Michaels, "The Influence of Career Stages on Components of Salesperson Motivation", *Journal of Marketing*, 52 (January 1988): p. 78.
41. Leslie Brennan, "Sales Secrets of the Incentive Stars", *Sales and Marketing Management*, (April 1990): pp. 92–100.
42. "HowAvonRingsTheirChimes",*SalesandMarketingManagement*,(November1986):pp.117–118.
43. W.J. Paul, et al, "Job Enrichment Pays Off", *Harvard Business Review*, (March–April 1969): p. 78.
44. Thomas N. Ingram and Danny N. Bellinger, "Motivational Segments in the Sales Force", *California Management Review* 24 (Spring 1982): pp. 81–88.
45. "Does Your Sales Compensation Plan Motivate Your Salespeople?", *Sales & Marketing Executive Report*, (March 5, 1997): p. 1.
46. Andy Cohen, "What Keeps You Up at Night?", *Sales and Marketing Management*, (February 2000): pp. 46–47.
47. Please see Chapter 5, for job descriptions of salespeople.
48. Please see Chapter 1, for various types of sales jobs or positions.
49. Christen P. Heide, *Dartnell's 30th Sales Force Compensation Survey*, (Chicago: Dartnell Corporation, 1999), p. 49.
50. Heide, *Datnell's 30th Sales force Compensation Survey*, pp. 42–43.
51. "What Salespeople are Paid", *Sales and Marketing Management*, (February 1995): pp. 30–31.
52. Eilene Zimmerman, "Quota Busters", *Sales and Marketing Management*, (January 2001): p. 59.
53. Peter Kurlander and Jan Blackburn, "Sales Compensation Software: A Practical Guide", *Compensation & Benefits Review*, (September/October 1999): pp. 54–62.
54. Paul Hunting, "Developing Natural Leadership", *British Journal of Administrative Management*, (May/June 2001): pp. 28–29.
55. Charles M. Futrell, "Sales Management: Teamwork, Leadership, and Technology", Thomson Asia Pvt. Ltd., Singapore, 2003, p. 332
56. Betsy Cummings, "Getting Reps to Live Your Mission", *Sales and Marketing Management*, (October 2001): pp. 15.
57. Rex C. Houze, "Effective Sales Management", *American Salesman*, (May 1995): pp. 3–5.

CASE 6.1

CG Ltd.

"It seems our branch managers, marketing executives, and senior sales engineers need training on sales forecasting, as I find their actual sales figures are way off their sales forecasts for the past two years", said D.S. Kulkarni, general manager-eastern region, CG Ltd., to U.N. Gupta, regional human resource manager, east.

"Yes Sir, we can plan a training program in eastern region at our Kolkata office, but let me first talk to the participants to understand their needs", responded Gupta. Thereafter, Gupta swung into action and spoke with the 2 branch managers, one each at Patna and Guwahati, as well as with the four marketing executives and 10 senior sales engineers. Gupta also spoke with the 3 regional marketing managers of eastern region, who looked after different groups of customers, such as industries, dealers, and government.

"All participants are interested in the training program with focus on sales forecasting topic, but some of them also want negotiating skills, team selling, and selling skills topics to be included. Besides, regional marketing managers (RMMs) are unable to spare the participants for training for more than two days, as otherwise the customer service will suffer", informed Gupta to Kulkarni.

"Well, that's good. You arrange the training program for two days on a Friday and Saturday or Saturday and Sunday, after finding out who will be the trainers, the quality of the trainers (internal and external), methods and content of training, training aids, expenditure estimate, and place of training. Remember this training program is for senior sales engineers, marketing executives, and branch managers, and therefore, it is important that every aspect of training should be of good quality", responded Kulkarni.

Gupta knew that one of the regional marketing managers, Pradeep Dasgupta, was a product of Indian Institute of Management, Ahmedabad, and was a visiting faculty to IIM, Kolkata. Gupta requested Pradeep to help him find good trainers for the training program to be conducted within 2 or 3 weeks at the company's conference hall at Kolkata.

Pradeep arranged a marketing faculty, Prof. R. Dholakia from IIM, Kolkata, for sales forecasting and team selling topics, and thought he himself would take the topics of selling and negotiating skills. Each topic was scheduled for 3 hours with a break of 15 minutes after 90 minutes.

Prof. Dholakia used multi-media presentation to explain the theoretical background of the subject, followed by case method of studies. Pradeep used role-playing method effectively for selling and negotiating skills. The feedback of participants after the training program gave overall rating of 4 on a 5-point scale, with some individual comments of sales forecasting session being too theoretical.

Discussion Questions

1. Has the company followed a proper process for the training program? Justify your answer.
2. What type of training was done by the company? Do you have any suggestions for improvement?

This case was prepared by Prof. Krishna K. Havaldar for classroom discussion.

CASE 6.2

STI Ltd.

"Sir, I think, we need to have an incentive scheme for our field salespeople, so as to motivate them to put more than normal effort. This will help us to increase our market share and also make it possible for us to become number one player from number three position that we are currently at. We had declared in our last annual marketing conference that we would become the leader in the Precision Steel Tube industry in three years. I believe we have to start working on that goal. Do you agree, Sir?", asked Krishna Kumar, the newly appointed head of sales and marketing, to the Executive Director of STI Ltd, B.G. Gururaja Rao.

"I agree to the extent that we have to work on our long-term goal of becoming the leader in terms of market share. That does not mean that we have to work without considering the impact on the company's profitability. So far, in last 15 years of our company's operations, sales and other functional employees have been paid a fixed salary, fringe benefits, and once a year bonus (as per government regulation on bonus). Why should we pay incentives to only salespeople? Why not consider people in production, which is also a line function? What about other support functions like accounts, administration, and human resource? We need extra efforts from all employees, not only salespeople. If we try to motivate salespeople by paying commission on achieving their sales targets, other employees and particularly shop-floor workers and supervisors will demand extra money by some kind of incentive scheme. If we deny incentive payments to other employees, they will not only get demotivated, but may even go on a strike. Besides, the profit contribution per unit of our product sold is very low and any increase in cost due to incentive payments without substantial increase in sales volume will wipe out the thin profitability of our company. We have to consider the various factors before we take a decision on the incentive scheme for salespeople. I hope you understand this", responded Gururaja Rao.

"Yes, Sir, I suggest we discuss this subject later in our monthly budget review meeting, when other managers and also our chairman and managing director will be present. In the meantime, I will also apply my mind and prepare a specific proposal, which I will discuss with you before the budget review meeting", said Krishna Kumar and thereafter, left for his office.

Discussion Questions

1. Do you think this company needs an incentive scheme for motivating their salespeople? Give reasons.
2. Suggest a suitable compensation plan for the salespeople, including both financial and non-financial rewards. Justify your answer.

This case was prepared by Prof. Krishna K. Havaldar for classroom discussion.

CASE 6.3

CD Products Ltd.

"We are transferring you from Mumbai to Chennai as the branch manager with immediate effect. Our Chennai branch has not been performing well in terms of sales and profits for the past two years. We want you to improve the branch performance. How soon can you go to Chennai?" asked Keshav Apte, general manager (sales) to T.S. Krishnamurthy, branch manager, Mumbai. Krishnamurthy was taken aback! "How soon do you want me to go to Chennai, Sir?", Krishnamurthy asked Apte, hiding his surprise at this sudden development. "Say, in 24 hours." Apte responded. "Sir, may I tell you tomorrow about how soon I can go after talking to my parents and wife?", Krishnamurthy pleaded to his boss, Apte. "Okay, let me know tomorrow. Remember, this matter is urgent", said Apte with all seriousness that was visible on his face.

On the following day, Krishnamurthy informed his boss Apte that he would go to Chennai in 48 hours. "I will go first and will take my family later after 3 to 4 weeks once my accommodation is finalized. Is that okay, Sir?", asked Krishnamurthy. "Yes, that is fine. You take the help of our administration staff for your flight booking from Mumbai to Chennai and for a suitable accommodation at Chennai. You are one of our effective managers and I wish you success in your work at Chennai. I am confident you will stand up to our expectations with superior performance of Chennai branch." With these words and a broad smile Apte shook Krishnamurthy's hands. Krishnamurthy thanked his boss for the kind words and left for his office.

CD Products Company was manufacturing and marketing consumer durable products, such as ceiling, table, and exhaust fans, domestic pump sets, and lighting products. All the products had good reputation in the market for quality. The company had 12 branches spread all over India. Each branch was headed by a branch manager. All the branch managers reported to the general manager (sales), whose office was located at the company's headquarters at Mumbai.

Even before Krishnamurthy reached Chennai, the Chennai branch manager, Jairam, had left for Kolkata, where he was transferred as the branch manager. Krishnamurthy was, therefore, introduced to all the staff of Chennai branch by the branch HR head. Chennai branch had 2 senior sales representatives, 6 junior sales representatives, 2 sales trainees, and 3 support staff. Krishnamurthy thought that before he made any changes in the system and the functioning of the branch, he should talk to each person of the branch to understand his or her background, needs, and aspirations. He also wanted to meet the major dealers, institutional, and business customers.

After meeting individually all the staff, Krishnamurthy called all of them for a team-meeting. He was surprised to find many of them including the senior sales representatives coming late for the meeting. When questioned, they responded that traffic jams had delayed their arrival. Krishnamurthy explained to the staff that he would hold once a month meetings with all the staff and once a week meetings with all the salespersons. This would help in two-way communications, understanding the problems, taking timely corrective actions, reviewing the branch performance, building the teamwork, and team spirit.

Krishnamurthy found during his visits to dealers, institutional, and business customers that salespersons lacked product knowledge, competitive information, communication, and negotiation skills. Salespersons told him that unlike the competitors' salespeople, they did not get any commission, which had a demotivating effect on them. Salespeople also indicated that there were no personal growth opportunities for them and hence, turnover of salespersons was over 20 percent. They said that they never received any encouragement and recognition whenever they obtained good orders. They informed Krishnamurthy that the earlier branch manager hardly visited the dealers and business customers. They complained that Jairam did not guide them in resolving the dealers' problems, preparing routing plan and scheduling of customer/dealer visits.

Krishnamurthy received useful feedback from the dealers and business customers. They said that the quality of the company's products was good, better than many competitors' products, but the customer service was not up to their expectations. The product deliveries were generally delayed. No special help was received when the dealers' customers sometimes asked for urgent supplies. The branch manager rarely visited and salespersons' visits were irregular. Hence, their problems remained unresolved for a long time. Unlike their competitors, they never had a dealer meeting with the company's branch manager.

After listening to the branch salespeople, dealers, and business customers, Krishnamurthy wondered what actions he could take and for which decisions he had to talk to the general manager (sales) in order to motivate his salespeople as well as the dealers.

Discussion Questions

1. For which decisions Krishnamurthy need to talk to the general manager (sales) and why?
2. Which motivational tools can be used by Krishnamurthy without anyone's permission?
3. What care should Krishnamurthy take while implementing the various motivational methods?

This case was prepared by Prof. Krishna K. Havaldar for classroom discussion.

Chapter 7

Evaluating and Controlling the Salespeople

LEARNING OBJECTIVES

After studying this chapter, you will be able to:

LO 1 Know the characteristics and control of salespeople's expenses

LO 2 Discuss marketing and sales audits for evaluating a sales organization's effectiveness

LO 3 Carry out sales, marketing cost, profitability, and productivity analyses for evaluating the effectiveness of a sales organization

LO 4 Examine purposes and procedure for evaluating and controlling performance of the salespeople

LO 5 Know the use of sales force automation tools for performance evaluation and social media as a selling vehicle

LO 6 Find ethical, social and legal responsibilities of sales managers and salespeople

Sunil Nair, General Manager, Sales and Marketing, is in deep thought about consistent low profitability of BG Steel Tubes Ltd. For the past three years that he has been with the company as the head of sales and marketing, the net profit to sales has been hovering around two percent. Sunil wondered if there is a need to review the effectiveness of the sales organization as well as the current performance evaluation system of the salespeople, so as to identify strong and weak areas from grass-root levels of the company.

At present, salespeople at branches are given only sales targets or quotas. Their performance is evaluated based on the actual sales of steel tubes in quantity (tons) and value (Rupees) against the sales quotas (in tons and Rupees). The focus is only on sales volume. Direct selling expenses of salespersons like salaries, travelling, lodging, food, and customer entertainment are not controlled because targets or quotas for the selling expenses are not set. Also, Sunil thought that salespeople should be made aware about the products which contribute more to the profits and therefore, should be sold more compared to the products that contribute less to the profitability. In other words, salespeople should be evaluated on their performance on not only sales volume, but also on selling expenses and contribution to profitability.

Sunil thought that the same consideration need to be shown to the branch managers, who are evaluated at present based on their performance on sales volume. The sales analysis gives information on each branch's actual sales for every month as well as its comparison with the sales target or quota. It also gives information on the actual and targeted (or budgeted) sales on cumulative basis up to the particular month. The sales analysis alone cannot show a complete performance evaluation of the company's branches. In addition Sunil opined, the branch selling expenses and profit contribution should be analyzed every month or quarter, so that corrective actions can be initiated wherever needed. If each branch performs well with respect to its profitability, the probability of achieving profitability goals at the company level would be much higher.

Sunil has more ideas which he would like to implement after a thorough discussion with other functional managers and top management. One idea is to carry out marketing and sales audits which would help to find out opportunities and problems as well as indicate action plan for performance improvement. Another idea is that the company should use the sales force automation (SFA) software, which is typically a part of customer relationship management (CRM). The SFA can make the performance evaluation of salespeople easier and faster. One more idea Sunil wants to explore is the use of social media as a selling vehicle.

Sunil now feels confident that if the top management approves his proposals or ideas and his colleagues in the company support the implementation of the same, the company can improve its performance on profits substantially.

The opening vignette above shows how a company's sales and marketing head thinks about various ways to evaluate the performance of salespeople and the branches, analyze the problems, take corrective actions to improve the company's performance. In this chapter, we will discuss not only the issues mentioned in the opening vignette, but also some other issues like ethical, social, and legal responsibilities of sales managers and salespeople.

LO 1. Know the characteristics and control of salespeople's expenses

SALES FORCE EXPENSES

Some companies allow full reimbursement to their **salespeople** for legitimate sales expenses incurred while on the job. Typical reimbursement of sales force expenses include: (i) travel, (ii) food, (iii) lodging, (iv) entertainment of customers, and (v) telephone. Many companies introduce tight controls on these expenses to ensure proper spending by the **salespeople**. Companies have a system of expense plans that reimburses **salespeople** for their food, lodging, travel, customer entertainment and any other legitimate expenses incurred while on the job.

The characteristics (or quality levels) for deciding an effective expense plan are:

- It should *be fair to the salesperson*. The expense plan should pay for all business activities carried out as per the requirement of the company. The salesperson should neither gain nor lose.
- The expense plan should be *fair to the company*. It should be affordable to the company and should not allow padding of expenses by the salespeople.
- An effective expense plan should be *simple to understand and easy* to administer. Expense reports or forms should not have unnecessary details.
- It should be *clear enough* to prevent misunderstanding between sales managers and salespeople. Sales managers should explain the plan to the salespeople in detail.
- The expense plan should allow differences in travel expenses among different territories. For instance, cost of travel may be high in "A" class cities as compared to "B" class cities.
- The reimbursement of expenses should be done *without much delay*, or make an advance payment as "tour advance" to salespersons.

Ways of Controlling Expenses

Companies follow different policies or ways for reimbursement of sales expenses incurred by salespeople. For controlling the selling expenses, there are four types of expense plans: (i) the salesperson pays all expenses, (ii) the company pays all expenses (also called, unlimited payment plan), (iii) the company partially pays expenses (or limited-payment plan), and (iv) combination plan.

The Salesperson Pays all Expenses

Usually, salespeople who are compensated by straight commission, pay all the selling expenses incurred by them. Some companies prefer to pay a little higher commission rate so that their salespeople pay all the selling expenses. From the company's viewpoint the advantages are that the plan is simple and there are no costs of administration. The disadvantages are that the company has little control over the salesperson's activities, and salesperson may not effectively carry out non-selling activities like obtaining market information and sending sales reports, as the salesperson will only focus on selling activities. Besides, the salesperson tries to minimize the selling expenses, such as not travelling long distances to call on and entertain prospective customers.

From the salesperson's view point, this plan helps the salesperson get some income tax advantage, as he is paying his own expenses. Other advantages for the salesperson are that he does not have to explain the selling expenses to the company and he has a freedom of operation.

The Company Pays all Expenses (Unlimited Payment Plan)

It is the often-used expense plan by companies. In this plan, the company reimburses salespeople for all business related expenses they incur while on company business. There is no limit on sales expenses, however salespeople are required to submit details of their expenses for approval by their sales manager.

The main advantage of this plan is that the company management has a good control over the salesperson's activities. There are no problems due to geographical differences in costs of travel or food. It gives freedom to the salesperson from psychological anxiety about the money to be spent on travel or customer entertainment for making the sale.

The major disadvantages are that it allows some salespeople to spend more than what is reasonable and to make money by padding their expenses. This may lead to disagreements between the sales manager and the salespeople. However, this plan should reduce the number of disagreements.

The Company Partially Pays Expenses (Limited-Payment Plan)

This plan has two methods. One method is to give the salesperson a lump sum (or a flat sum) for a period of time, such as a day or week. For instance, the company may allow ₹2,000 for room and food each day the salesperson stays away from home overnight, or allows not more than ₹200 for lunch, if the salesperson can be home each night.

The second method is to set a limit on the amount to be reimbursed for each expense item. For example, the company may pay up to ₹200 for lunch or dinner, ₹1,500 for lodging, and ₹100 for breakfast. The company may allow monthly expenses on mobile phone communication, vehicle parking, etc. The company management may set the same limits in all territories or may set different limits for class "A" and "B" cities to account for geographical cost differentials. This plan is suitable when salespeople have routine and repetitive travel routes.

The main advantages of this plan are in budget planning as the selling expenses can be more accurately estimated and also the disputes between sales managers and salespeople are less, since the limits of expenses are known in advance. Management can control salespeople's activities by allowing or disallowing certain items of expenses.

However, the plan has certain disadvantages. Management requires more time to establish the limits of expenses and also to administer the plan. The plan can be inflexible. A salesperson may incur some unusual expense (for example, customer entertainment), which he could not escape without losing the customer. If the entertainment is not an allowable expense, the salesperson may not be reimbursed. High performing salespeople may not like such limits on expenses.

However, some companies avoid such problems by allowing unusual expenses if salespeople give an explanatory note. This plan cannot prevent salespeople making money by padding the expenses up to the allowable limits.

Combination Plan (Expense-Quota Plan)

By combining the limited and unlimited plans, advantages of both plans can be obtained to develop a flexible method. For example, the company may set limits on some items like food and lodging, but no limit on travel cost, which allows a salesperson to visit a distant customer location. Another method followed by companies under expense-quota plan is that the management studies individual sales territories, estimates sales volume and selling expenses over a specified period, and sets an expense quota. For instance, the sales manager can decide an expense-quota of ₹8,000 for a month because the expected monthly sales is ₹4,00,000. This enables the company management to allow salespeople a monthly expense account not to exceed two percent of their net sales. The advantages of the expense-quota plans are that management has some control on selling expenses and salespeople have some flexibility within total expense budget.

LO 2 **Discuss marketing and sales audits for evaluating a sales organization's effectiveness**

MARKETING AUDIT

Although the term audit is most often used to refer to financial audits (i.e. inspection of an organization's accounts) carried out by accounting firms, the audit concept is extended to other functions in recent years.

A marketing audit is a comprehensive, periodic, and systematic examination of a company's marketing plan, environment, objectives, strategies, tactics, performance, organization, and people with a view to find out opportunities and problems, and recommend an action plan to improve the company's marketing performance. It also evaluates the long-term business growth alternatives of the company.

As per a study[1], an average US Corporation loses half of its customers in five years, half of its employees in four years, and half of its investors in less than one year. This indicates some weaknesses. Organizations that become aware of their weaknesses must carry out a thorough study that is called a marketing audit. A complete marketing audit is a large project that is time-consuming, problematic, and costly. But the rewards can be substantial.

A marketing audit covers a company's total marketing system. The audit concept can be applied to a company's major functions within the marketing management. For example, a company can audit the sales function, or the marketing research department. Often outside sources, like management consulting firms, are employed to carry out the marketing audit to ensure unbiased approach.

SALES AUDIT

A sales audit is a comprehensive, systematic, diagnostic, and prescriptive tool[2]. The purpose of a sales audit is to assess whether a firm's sales management process is adequate, to give direction for performance improvement, and to recommend the needed changes.

Sales audit is a good method for evaluating the effectiveness of a sales organization. Because auditing should be objective, it should be conducted by someone from outside the sales organization. This could be someone from another functional area within the firm or an outside consulting firm. However, members of the sales organization should participate actively, as most of the information is provided by sales managers and salespeople.

The sales audit is an expensive and time-consuming process, but the benefits are much more than monetary and time costs. Marketing and sales audits should be conducted on regular basis, so that the company can identify and correct potential problems before they become troublesome.

The Evaluation Process of a Marketing/Sales Audit

Whether it is a marketing audit or a sales audit, the evaluation process is the same. It consists of three stages, as shown in Figure 7.1.

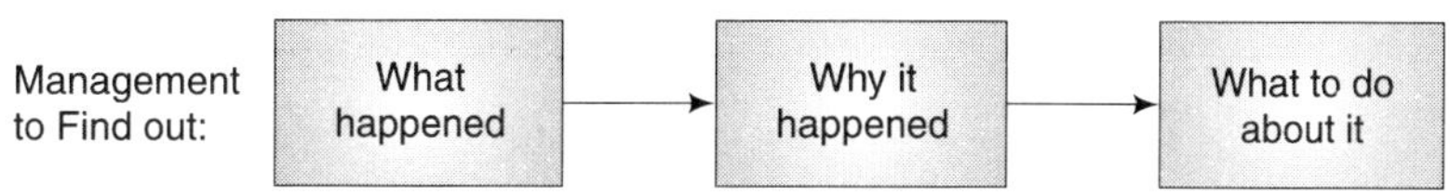

Fig. 7.1 The Evaluation Process of Marketing/Sales Audit

It is the responsibility of the company's management to find the following:

What Happened

The company should get the information by comparing the actual performance with the goals or targets. This will show favorable or unfavorable variations. For instance, if the actual performance on sales at the end of first quarter of the year 2016 is ₹90 million against a sales goal of ₹100 million, it shows a negative or unfavorable variance of ₹10 million.

Why It Happened

This stage is more difficult and time consuming. What specific factors have contributed to the negative variance? There are many factors, including environment, competition, marketing mix elements, salespeople, and sales managers. Which of these factors have contributed, for example, for the negative variance mentioned in stage 1?

What to Do about It

In this stage, the corrective actions are decided and implemented to solve the problems, overcome the harmful conditions, or leverage the favorable conditions. For example, if the customer service is not as per the customer expectations, first find what kind of service needs improvement – presales, during sales, or post-sales – and then implement suitable corrective actions.

Since a full marketing audit is costly and takes a long time many companies evaluate different elements of marketing. For instance, one company may analyze its sales volumes only, but another firm may decide to analyze sales, marketing cost, and profitability. We shall, therefore, discuss analysis of sales volume (or sales analysis) first, and later, marketing costs, profitability as well as productivity analyses.

LO 3 **Carry out sales, marketing cost, profitability, and productivity analyses for evaluating the effectiveness of a sales organization**

EVALUATION OF EFFECTIVENESS OF A SALES ORGANIZATION

Sales organizations have many goals and objectives. Therefore, many factors need to be analyzed to evaluate the effectiveness of a sales organization. (Here, the effectiveness means an organization that gives expected or targeted results consistently). Figure 7.2 shows four types of analyses that are usually needed to develop a comprehensive model for evaluation of a sales organization. These are: (i) sales analysis, (ii) marketing cost analysis, (iii) profitability analysis, and (iv) productivity analysis.

Each type of analysis can be done in different ways. For example, sales analysis can be done by total sales, sales by territory, sales by products, sales by customers, and sales by salesperson. Actual sales can be compared with sales quotas (or sales goals/targets), sales of previous periods, or sales of competitors. Sales analysis should be done at different levels of the sales organization, such as regions, branches, districts, and territories. Many companies, in a study, use sales analysis for evaluating their sales organizations, but few companies use reports on marketing cost, profit contribution, net profit or return on assets analyses[3].

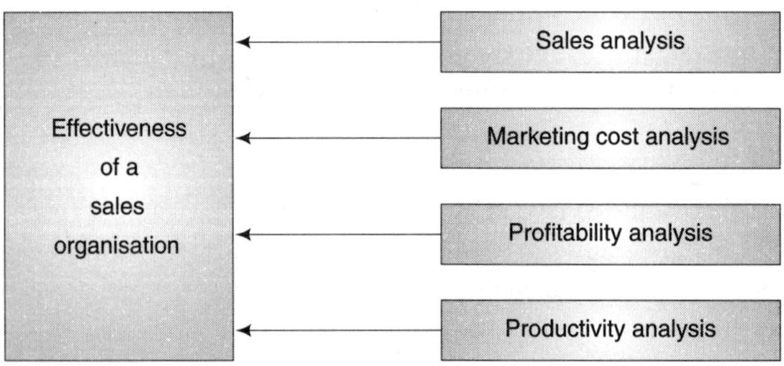

Fig. 7.2 **Effectiveness Model of a Sales Organization**

Sales Analysis

Sales analysis (or sales volume analysis) is an important element for evaluating the effectiveness of a sales organization, because the purpose of a sales organization is to generate sales. Sales managers use sales analysis to evaluate current performance, take corrective actions, and do future planning.

Sales analysis is described as a detailed inspection of a company's sales data, which includes collecting, classifying, comparing, and drawing conclusions. All companies collect sales data in the form of customer sales invoices or cash register receipts, which are needed for maintaining their accounting records.

Definition of what is meant by a sale is necessary before starting a sales analysis. The company must decide when a sale takes place – whether at the time an order is received, shipped (and invoiced), or paid for. Most companies define a sale when an order is shipped or transported and invoiced. The sales organization should develop an information system based on whatever definition of sale is decided.

Another point companies have to decide is whether to concentrate on sales value (e.g., Rupees or Dollars), or sales units (e.g., tons or numbers). It is often useful to include both sales value and units in a sales analysis, because each one gives different type of evaluative information.

Framework for Sales Analysis

There are many alternatives available to a company for analyzing Sales Volume of a sales organization as shown in Figure 7.3. These alternatives are grouped in three important decision areas: (i) all levels in the sales organization, (ii) different type of sales, and (iii) different type of analysis.

All Levels in the Sales Organization

Sales analyses should be done at all levels in the sales organization. There are two reasons for this: (i) **for evaluation and control purposes**, sales managers at various levels need sales analyses. At higher levels, that is national sales managers and regional sales managers, sales analysis is needed not only at their levels but also at the next level(s) below for evaluation and control, and (ii) **for identifying problems** (or strengths and weaknesses), companies use a *hierarchical sales analysis*. This includes evaluation of sales performance from the company level down to the last level. **For instance**, the sales analysis is first done at total organization level, by comparing the actual sales with the sales budget of the company, both in value (Rupees or Dollars) and units (numbers, tons, or liters). If the actual sales performance of the company is not up to the budgeted level, the sales analysis of the next level, say, regional level is done to identify which region(s) are having problems in reaching their sales quotas.

Next, sales analyses are done for all the branches (or districts) reporting to those problematic (or weak) region(s). This would identify low sales in specific branches. Further sales analyses are done for all territories in those low sales branches. This would point out territories which are not achieving their sales quotas. Further analysis is needed to find out why these territories are

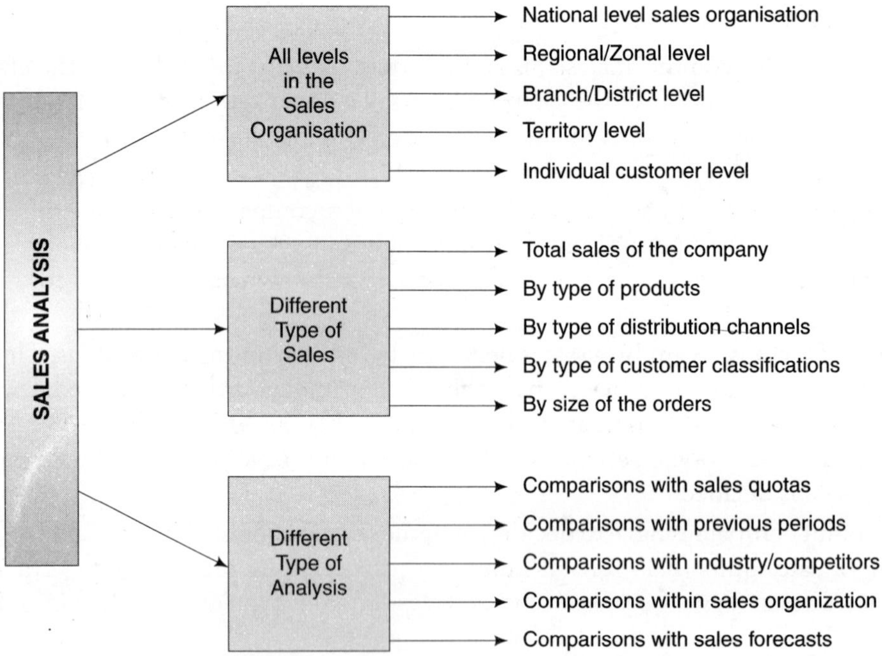

Fig. 7.3 **A Framework for Sales Analysis**

not achieving their sales quotas by carrying out analyses of customers in the territories, talking to customers, salespersons, and the branch manager(s). Corrective actions can then be taken to increase sales from these problematic territories. Thus, the hierarchical sales analysis method is a systematic way to carry out a sales analysis, to identify strengths and weaknesses (or problems) in the sales organization.

Different Type of Sales

Analyses of different type of sales, shown in Figure 7.3, at different organizational levels definitely increases the sales manager's ability to discover problem (or weak) areas in the company's sales performance. But it makes the evaluation process confusing. A better way is to extend the hierarchical sales analysis, by focusing different type of sales on to the problematic territories. This would help understand the sales problems of the territories completely, by knowing which products and customer types are having low sales as compared to the sales quotas. Additional analysis would be needed for these products and customers to find out why sales are low and what needs to be done to improve sales performance.

Different Type of Analysis

In Figure 7.3, different types of analyses are mentioned. Out of these, comparisons of actual with sale quotas are widely used by companies because it gives interesting information. Comparisons of actual performance with sales forecast or sales budget are done at the company level. Based on the company sales budget, sales quotas are set at regional, branch or district, and territory levels. Some examples are presented to show how comparisons are done between sales quotas and actual sales in Tables 7.1 to 7.4. Table 7.1 explains the performance of different branches. Table 7.2 shows sales analysis by product lines for a consumer durable products company. Table 7.3 indicates sales analysis by customer classification. Table 7.4 is a composite measure of sales effectiveness, sales growth, and market share. In Table 7.4, an effectiveness index can be calculated by dividing the (actual) sales by the sales quota and multiplying by 100. This index helps to compare the sales effectiveness at different organizational levels. As shown in an example in Table 7.4, sales growth of this year over last year's sales is another useful analysis for the four regions of the company. Market share analysis is also done for the four regions of the company by dividing the (actual) sales by the industry sales and multiplying by 100.

Table 7.1 Sales Analysis by Branches

Regions	Sales Quota	Actual Sales	Difference (+/–)	Performance (% of Quota)
Delhi	400	376	–24	94
Kolkata	300	273	–27	91
Mumbai	410	418	08	102
Chennai	390	402	12	103
Total	1500	1469	–31	98

Table 7.2 Sales Analysis by Product Lines

Product Line	Sales Quota	Actual Sales	Difference (+/–)	Performance (% of Quota)
Ceiling Fans	425	415	–10	98
Table Fans	240	264	24	110
Exhaust Fans	175	190	15	109
Lamps and Accessories	360	353	–07	98
Total	1200	1222	22	102

Table 7.3 Sales Analysis by Customer Classification

Class of Customers	Sales Quota	Actual Sales	Difference (+/–)	Performance (% of Quota)
Class 'A'	970	922	–48	95
Class 'B'	315	343	28	109
Class 'C'	215	210	–05	98
Total	1500	1475	–25	98

(**Note:** All figures in above tables are in ₹ million)

Table 7.4 Different Types of Sales Analysis

	Northern Region	Eastern Region	Western Region	Southern Region
Sales (₹ million)	23	22	28.5	27
Sales Quota (₹ million)	25	20	30	25
Effectiveness Index	92	110	95	108
Sales Last Year (₹ million)	22.5	19	28	24
Sales Growth (%)	2	16	2	13
Industry Sales (₹ million)	250	200	300	250
Market Share (%)	9	11	10	11

Often, a sales analysis alone does not give complete information for evaluating effectiveness of a sales organization. The benefits of extending the sales analysis to marketing cost and profitability analysis are very much recognized. However, the most widely used measure of evaluation of a sales organization continues to be sales analysis.

Marketing Cost and Profitability Analysis

While sales analysis is useful as one of the elements for evaluating the effectiveness of a sales organization, for comprehensive evaluation other elements like marketing cost analysis and profitability analysis should also be considered, as shown in Figure 7.2 earlier in this chapter.

A marketing cost analysis is a study of a company's marketing costs. The purpose of marketing cost analysis is to determine the profitability of sales (or marketing) units, like market segments, sales territories, and products. This is done by subtracting the marketing costs from the sales revenue, associated with the particular sales unit. Marketing cost analysis is a managerial tool that is used for planning and control of a company's future operations. Often, an analysis of past financial events helps as a guide for future operations. **For example**, a study on a bank's cost and profitability found that 30 percent of the bank's branches were unprofitable, and 60 percent of their customers generate losses[4]. For carrying out a proper marketing cost analysis, the company must have an account classification system.

Companies need to measure the profitability of their territories, customer groups (or market segments), products, distribution channels, and customers. This information will help the management to decide whether any sales and marketing activities or products should be expanded, reduced, or eliminated in future.

Procedure for Marketing Cost and Profitability Analysis

The procedure followed for conducting a marketing cost and profitability analysis for a sales organization includes the following steps: (i) state the purpose of the analysis, (ii) identify functional (or activity) expenses, (iii) convert (or change) natural accounting expenses into functional expenses, (iv) allocate functional expenses to market segments, products, or other marketing/sales units, and (v) prepare the profitability of the marketing/sales units.

State the Purpose of the Analysis

Before starting the marketing cost and profitability analysis, the sales manager should decide the purpose. Whether the purpose is to find the profitability of sales territories, market segments, products, branch offices, or sales representatives? Depending upon the answer, the marketing costs are classified as either direct or indirect costs. For instance, a salesperson's salary is a direct cost with respect to an allocated territory, but an indirect cost with regard to various products or customer groups. By stating the specific purpose of the analysis, the costs can be classified.

Identify Functional (or Activity) Expenses

Each company should prepare a list of major activities (or functional) marketing costs that are relevant to its own marketing program. A manufacturer of material handling equipment, for example, performs different activities compared to a retail chain. However, a typical list of marketing cost, as shown in Figure 7.4, includes personal selling expenses, advertising and sales promotion expenses, order processing expenses, packing and delivery expenses, warehousing and inventory expenses, and administration expenses. Administration expenses consist of costs of sales offices, including salaries of sales managers and staff, travelling, and office maintenance costs. Order processing expenses include costs of processing customer's purchase orders and billing.

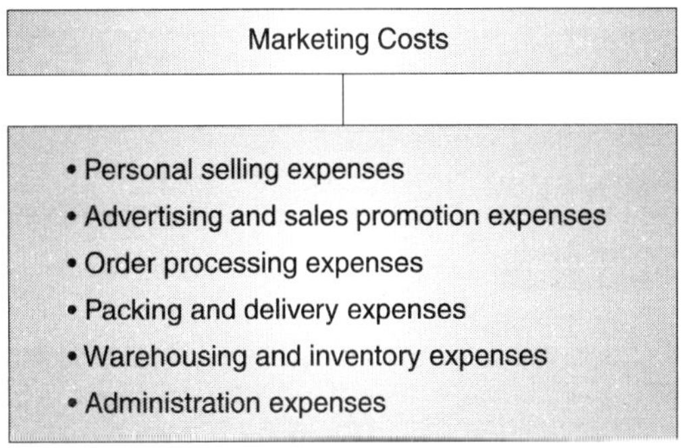

Fig. 7.4 Major Functional/Activity Expenses List

Convert Natural Accounting Expenses into Functional Expenses

In typical accounting records, expenses are classified according to the object of expenditure. The natural (or traditional) ledger accounts may classify marketing expenses as office rent, sales salaries, and advertising costs. However, for an effective marketing cost analysis these accounting expenses are converted (or changed) into functional (or activity) expenses. A more accountable method for allocating costs is **activity-based costing (ABC)**, which allocates costs to marketing/sales units on the basis of how the units actually spend or cause these costs (or expenses). Costs are gathered and then allocated to the units by suitable factors that drive costs up or down[5].

We shall take an example of Saragam Aluminum Company's simplified profit and loss statement, presented in Table 7.5. We take each natural expense and allocate it to various activities (or functions). Salaries are dispersed to the functional areas where the recipients work, as shown in Table 7.6.

Travel expenses include food and entertainment expenses incurred in personal selling and are therefore allocated to personal selling expenses. Similarly, entire natural expenses on advertising and sales promotion are allocated to the functional expenses of advertising and sales promotion. However, the expenses on supplies and telephone are allocated to each function (or activity group) that incurs this expense. Rent is allocated to the various functions in proportion to the floor space used by them. Allocations of natural expenses to functional expenses are shown in Table 7.6.

Table 7.5 Saragam Aluminium Company's Profit and Loss Statement

Sales		₹75,00,000
Less cost of goods sold		₹52,00,000
Gross margin		₹23,00,000
Less sales expenses		
Salaries	₹11,00,000	
Rent	₹3,50,000	
Supplies and telephone	₹1,50,000	
Travel	₹1,20,000	
Advertising and sales promotion	₹80,000	
Total sales expenses		₹18,00,000
Net profit		₹5,00,000

Table 7.6 Saragam Aluminium Company: Natural Expenses Allocated to Functional Expenses

Natural Expenses	Total	Functional Expenses				
		Personal Selling	Advertising and Sales Promotions	Warehousing & Inventory	Order Processing	Administration
Salaries	11,00,000	6,00,000	1,50,000	1,00,000	1,00,000	1,50,000
Rent	3,50,000	100,000	40,000	1,40,000	35,000	35,000
Supplies and telephone	1,50,000	40,000	25,000	35,000	30,000	20,000
Travel	1,20,000	1,20,000	--	--	--	--
Advertising and sales promotion	80,000	--	80,000	--	--	--
Total	18,00,000	8,60,000	2,95,000	2,75,000	1,65,000	2,05,000

(**Note:** All figures are in Rupees)

Allocate Functional Expenses to Marketing Units

To find the marketing costs and profitability of marketing units, such as branches, regions, market segments, products, or channels, the functional expenses should be allocated to the marketing unit under study. There are several bases for allocating functional expenses to different marketing units, which are presented in Table 7.7. Before we present cost allocation, let us first differentiate between direct and indirect expenses.

Direct expenses are incurred with respect to a single unit of sales or marketing operation. Hence, they can be allocated to a particular marketing unit (e.g., market segment, product, or sales territory). For example, personal selling expenses can be directly allocated to sales territories, if a territory cost analysis is being done and each salesperson has a territory. Here, personal selling expenses include the salesperson's salary, commission, travel, food, and customer entertainment. Costs of local newspaper advertisements and point-of-purchase (POP) materials can be charged to a sales territory.

Indirect costs are shared by more than one marketing unit and hence, allocation problems happen with these costs. For instance, if a product cost analysis is done, personal selling expense are allocated based on selling time given by a salesperson to each product. In a cost analysis for market segment or customer group, the personal selling expenses may be distributed based on the number of sales calls on each customer group. In case of indirect costs, some costs are partially indirect and some are totally indirect, For example, administration costs, including salary and office staff cost of general manager (sales), are totally indirect. Methods used for allocation are: (i) divide administration costs equally among territories, products, or market segments, (ii) allocate the indirect administration costs in the same proportion as the total direct costs. Both methods are easy to do, but can be inaccurate.

Table 7.7 **Bases of Allocation of Functional Expenses to Marketing Units**

Function	Bases of Allocation of Expenses
Personal selling	• Direct to sales territories for a territory cost analysis • Selling time given to each product for product cost analysis and for market segment cost analysis, number of sales calls to each customer group or market segment
Advertising	• Direct or by circulation of media to sales territories • Direct or media space given to each product and market segment
Sales promotion	• Direct or equal charges to marketing units
Warehousing and Inventory	• Physical unit of goods handled, shipment, or orders received (applicable to all marketing units)
Order processing	• Number of customer orders (applicable for all marketing units)
Administration	• Equal charges among territories, products, or market segments, or in proportion to direct costs of marketing units

Prepare Profitability of Marketing Units

Profitability analysis of marketing units (i.e. regions, branches, channels, products, or market segments) can be developed by preparing profit and loss (or income and expense) statements for marketing units. However, the question comes how to allocate indirect or shared expenses to various marketing units. There are two approaches of allocating marketing costs for profitability analysis: (i) full-cost (or net profit) approach, and (ii) contribution (or profit contribution) approach.

In the **full-cost approach,** all marketing expenses, both direct and indirect, are allocated to the marketing unit under study. By allocating all marketing costs, the company is trying to find the net profit of each marketing unit. This is presented in Table 7.8. In the **contribution approach,** only the direct expenses are allocated to each marketing unit, for which profitability analysis is being done. The indirect or shared expenses are not included. After deducting the direct costs from the gross margin, the amount that remains is the contribution of the marketing unit to cover the overhead (indirect) expenses and a profit. An example, which includes both approaches, is shown in Table 7.9.

Table 7.8 Full-Cost versus Contribution Approaches

Full-Cost Approach	Contribution Approach
Sales	Sales
Minus : Cost of goods sold = Gross margin	Minus : Cost of goods sold = Gross margin
Minus: Direct expenses	Minus: Direct expenses
Minus: Allocated Indirect expenses = Net profit	= Contribution (available to cover overhead expense and profit)

The example presented in Table 7.9 uses full-cost approach for evaluating the profitability of western region and the contribution approach for assessing the profitability of the three branches within the western region. The profitability calculations of branches include branch sales, cost of goods sold and branch direct selling expenses. This generates profit contribution for each branch. The profitability calculations for the western region include branch selling expenses, western region direct selling expenses (that are not allocated to the branches), and allocated portion of indirect expenses. This gives a net profit figure for the profitability evaluation of the region.

Table 7.9 Example of Profitability Analysis

	Full Cost Approach Western Region	Contribution Approach		
		Branch A	Branch B	Branch C
Sales	400	150	130	120
Less cost of goods sold	300	112.5	97.5	90
Gross margin	100.0	37.5	32.5	30
Less branch direct selling expenses	12.7	4.5	4.2	4
Less west region direct selling expenses	12.0	--	--	--
Profit contribution	75.3	33.00	28.3	26
Less allocated indirect expenses	36.3	--	--	--
Net profit	39.0			

(**Note:** All figures are in Rupees million)

There is a considerable argument over the relative merits of contribution and full-cost approaches. Supporters of full-cost approach state that the purpose of a marketing cost study is to decide the net profitability of the marketing unit under study. They think that contribution approach does not satisfy this purpose. Besides, full-cost supporters think that a contribution approach may be misleading, because a product or market segment may show a positive contribution, but after deducting allocated indirect expenses, the product or market segment may show a loss.

Supporters of contribution approach argue that it is very difficult to arrive at a satisfactory procedure for allocating the indirect costs. Therefore, contribution approach is more objective in evaluating the profitability of a marketing unit. Further, these advocates point out that a full-cost approach may show that a product or a branch has a net loss, whereas, this marketing unit may be contributing positively to the overhead costs.

In reality, both approaches are useful in marketing costs and profitability analyses. A full-cost approach is useful when making a long-term study of the profitability of different products or market segments. The contribution approach is useful for short-term marketing decisions, such as evaluation of profitability of branches and regions, when only direct costs are allocated to them. Branch and regional managers are responsible for direct expenses incurred by them and are not responsible for indirect expenses, over which they have no control. There seems to be a trend towards the contribution approach, for a short-term analysis.

Productivity Analysis

Productivity analysis is useful for complete evaluation of effectiveness of sales organizations. Productivity is usually measured by ratios between outputs and inputs. For example, sales per salesperson are used by many companies as a measure of productivity. There are other productivity ratios, such as selling expenses per salesperson, sales calls per salesperson, and quotations submitted per salesperson. One main benefit of these productivity ratios is that they can be compared directly across the sales organization levels (e.g., sales branches) within the company and also with other sales organizations. For instance, productivity analysis between different branches within a sales organization shows specific areas of high and low productivity.

The productivity analysis gives useful information that is not available with sales, marketing cost, and profitability analyses done earlier. Sales profitability and productivity are interconnected. Profitability analysis has a financial view, whereas productivity analysis has a more managerial orientation. Improvement in sales productivity should get converted into increase in profitability.

Companies are using some of the following methods that are focused on increase in sales and internal cost cutting, for improving the productivity:

- Hiring independent sales agents (also called manufacturer's representatives), who are paid on a straight commission basis.
- Reducing the size of the sales force.
- Relying on the internet, telephone, direct mail, and video conferencing to reach customers.
- Increasing participation in trade shows or exhibitions to present the products to a large number of potential customers within a short duration.
- Using the latest communications and computer technology to help the selling process.
- Removing or minimizing unprofitable products and sales territories by doing cost-benefit analysis periodically.

Return on Assets Managed (ROAM)

It includes some elements of productivity by comparing profits and asset investments. The formula for calculating ROAM is:

$$ROAM = (Profit\ contribution/Sales) \times (Sales/Assets\ managed)$$

Here, the profit contribution can be either a net profit figure from a full-cost approach or profit contribution from a contribution approach. Assets managed usually include inventory, accounts receivables or any other assets at each sales organizational level.

LO 4 Examine purposes and procedure for evaluating and controlling performance of the salespeople

EVALUATING AND CONTROLLING THE PERFORMANCE OF SALESPEOPLE

One of the most important responsibilities of sales managers is to evaluate the performance of their salespeople. However, performance evaluation process is time consuming. It is also a difficult process, particularly for the sales manager who has to tell poor-performing salespersons how and why their performance is not up to the expectations.

We shall first look at the purposes or objectives of evaluating the sales force performance, and thereafter, discuss the procedure and different methods of sales force evaluation.

Purposes of Sales Force Performance Evaluation and Control

The basic objective of the performance evaluation of salespersons is to determine how these salespersons have performed. The outcome of sales force performance review can be used for other sales force management purposes[6] such as to:

- Improve the salesperson's performance.
- Decide the appropriate increment in pay and incentive payment based on the actual performance of the salesperson.
- Identify the salespeople who may be promoted.
- Determine the training needs of the individual salesperson and the entire sales force.
- Identify the salespersons whose services may be terminated, after giving adequate chances for improvement.
- Motivate salespeople through adequate recognition and reward for good performance.
- Find out their strengths and weaknesses.

The salesperson's performance appraisal should be carefully developed and implemented in order to make available information needed for several purposes mentioned above. For example, if the purpose of performance evaluation is to identify salespersons for promotion to the first level of sales management positions (such as district or branch sales managers), then the performance evaluation should focus on those criteria that are relevant to the effectiveness as a sales manager. This should be done in addition to the current performance as a salesperson. The same points that are mentioned above are also applicable when we talk about the importance and the objectives of performance evaluation of salespeople.

Procedure for Evaluating and Controlling Sales force Performance

The steps involved in the procedure or system of sales force evaluation and control are presented in Figure 7.5.

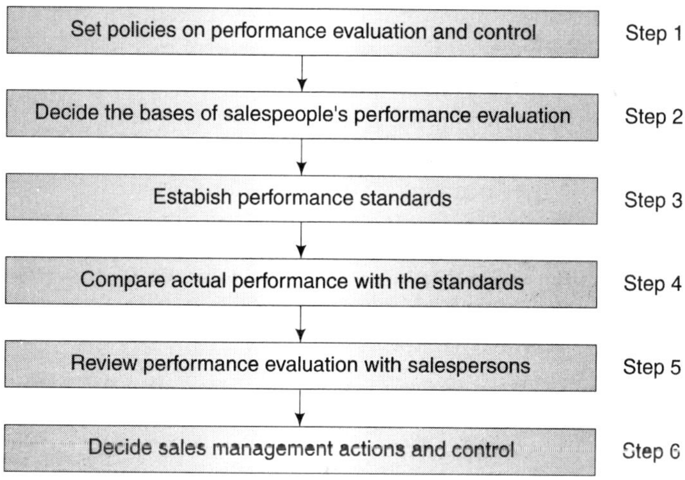

Fig. 7.5 Salesforce Performance Evaluation and Control Procedure

Step 1 – Set Policies on Performance Evaluation and Control

Before evaluating the performance, the company management should establish the basic policies. Several studies have generated information on general policies followed by most sales organizations[7]. Some of these policies are as follows:

- **Frequency of Evaluation** Some sales organizations evaluate salespeople's performance once a year, although most firms conduct evaluations six-monthly or quarterly[8]. Quarterly performance reviews help in frequent communications and performance improvement. For instance, IBM India has abolished the company's previous yearly appraisal assessment methodology. In the new checkpoint appraisal system, employees will be subjected to four yearly reviews, replacing the previous system of one annual review[9].

- **Who Conducts Evaluation?** Most salespersons' performance evaluations are conducted by the field sales manager (that is, a district or branch manager) who supervises the salespersons. In some firms, in addition, the manager above the field sales manager is also involved in the salesperson's performance evaluation.

- **Assessment Techniques** Increasing number of companies are using a popular assessment technique, known as **360-degree feedback**[10], involving multiple raters, including first level sales managers, internal and external customers, team members (in team selling situations), and salespeople themselves. In other words, it involves getting evaluative feedback from an employee, his or her peers, subordinates, superiors, and customers. It is particularly effective in team selling situations. Advantages of this method are that it helps to understand customers' needs, improve performance and discover obstacles to success.

❍ **Management by Objectives (MBO)** In some companies, the sales manager and the salesperson discuss and agree on the salesperson's specific objectives or goals. They also develop an action plan, based on the sales strategy, for the achievement of the objectives or performance standards. Involvement of salespeople in setting their performance standards or quotas increases their commitment and responsibility[11]. The sales manager and the salesperson review actual performance against objectives periodically and take corrective actions, if needed. This method is very common and comprehensive for setting goals or performance standards for salespeople. Setting the right objectives or performance standards is important for the success of the MBO method.

❍ **Sources of Information** Most firms use several sources of information for evaluating the salespersons' performance. The most important source is sales report, which includes work plans (or call plans), call reports, expense reports, new business reports, lost business reports, local business, and economic condition reports. In addition, field sales managers' calls, prospect and customer files, customer letters and complaints, customer surveys, and company records are some of the common sources of information. Today many companies use computers for collecting, analyzing, and reporting information that is useful for evaluation.

Some other policies, such as bases of evaluation and review of sales force performance will be covered when we discuss step 2 and step 5 respectively of Figure 7.5.

Step 2 – Decide Bases of Salespeople's Performance Evaluation

Before deciding on bases or criteria for performance evaluation of salespeople, a sales organization should decide whether it will give importance to: (i) outcome (or results) based viewpoint, (ii) behavior (or activity/effort) based viewpoint, or (iii) both outcome and behavior-based measures, when evaluating salespeople's performance. Once this general category, out of the three alternatives, is selected, the company can then select the specific criteria or bases for evaluating salespeople.

❍ **Outcome/Result-Based Viewpoint** This perspective concentrates on the salesperson's results with little direction or supervision by the sales manager. Outcome or output bases use quantitative criteria, and therefore, they minimize biases and subjectivity of evaluators. They are also relatively easy to measure. Examples are: sales volume achieved and number of orders received.

However, since this viewpoint considers "results only", it may not give an equal base to compare the performance of one salesperson with that of another salesperson. This is because the salesperson who is assigned a high sales potential territory can achieve the sales goals or quotas easily, compared to another salesperson whose territory sales potential is average or low and therefore, finds it difficult to achieve the sales quotas. Another reason may be the difference in competitors' efforts in different territories. Due to such uncontrollable factors, salespersons' results-based performance may get affected.

❍ **Behavior/Activity/Effort-Based Viewpoint** This perspective focuses on the salesperson's behavior and characteristics, with substantial direction and supervision of the first level sales manager. It uses both quantitative criteria (like number of calls made per day) and qualitative criteria (like product knowledge and customer relations) for evaluating the salesperson's performance. The likely consequences of giving more importance to behavior-based (as compared to outcome-based) viewpoint are mentioned below with reference to the findings of a study[12]:

- The salespeople will be more customer-oriented, team-oriented, and professionally competent.
- The salespeople will be more committed to the company.
- The salespeople are more likely to accept authority, participate in decision-making, and welcome management performance reviews.
- The more innovative and supportive the culture is likely to be.
- The salespeople will perform better on both selling and non-selling activities.
- The salespeople will perform better on outcome performance criteria (like achieving sales volume quotas).
- The sales organization will perform better on sales organization effectiveness criteria (such as, sales volume, profitability, and customer satisfaction).
- The salespeople's job satisfaction will be greater.

The above-mentioned findings give strong support for inclusion of some behavior-based criteria. If these are not included and only outcome or result-based criteria are considered, as done by some sales organizations, then salespeople may focus on short-term results (like sales volume) and long-term objectives (like customer relationships) may suffer.

❍ **Both Outcome-Based and Behavior-Based Viewpoints** One logical conclusion from this discussion is that sales organizations should use both outcome-based and behavior-based criteria when evaluating performance of salespeople. The research mentioned earlier, points out that some companies use a hybrid approach (of using both outcome-based and behavior-based viewpoints) for controlling the sales force. The hybrid approach has given importance to quantitative results, attitudes, efforts (or activities), and supervision. Another research by the same researchers has shown that an evaluation system that gives importance to the behavior criteria more than the outcome or results criteria, has many positive effects on the salesperson's overall performance[13].

❍ **Criteria/Bases for Salespeople's Performance Evaluation** For a comprehensive evaluation of salespeople's performance, companies should use as many bases as possible. In other words, companies should use multiple criteria, as the typical salesperson's job is multidimensional. Salespeople usually sell various products or services to several customers and carry out many selling and non-selling activities.

Although specific bases or criteria for salespeople's performance evaluation for a company depend upon the company's viewpoint on performance evaluation and the selling situation, the selection is made from a list of: (i) quantitative result bases, (ii) quantitative behavioral bases, and (iii) qualitative behavioral/activity bases, shown in Table 7.10. Whichever bases a company may choose from this list, it is important that the company communicates the same to salespeople in the beginning of the financial year, so that they know and understand the bases or criteria for achieving the expected performance.

Table 7.10 Criteria/Bases for Salespeople's Performance Evaluation

Quantitative Result/Output Criteria/Bases	Quantitative Behavioural/Activity Criteria/Bases	Qualitative Behavioural/Effort/ Activity Criteria/Bases
• **Sales volume** (a) In value (Rupees/Dollars) (b) In units (numbers, tonnes) (c) To previous year's sales (d) As a percentage of quota and market potential (market share) (e) By products and customer groups • **Accounts (Customers)** (a) Number of new accounts (b) Number of lost accounts • **Orders** (a) Orders are divided by calls (b) Sales are divided by orders • **Profit margin by products,** Customer groups	• **Customer calls** (a) Number of customer calls (b) Number of calls per day (c) Number of calls per customer • **Nonselling Activities** (a) Number of reports sent (b) Number of days worked (c) Selling and nonselling time (d) Number of customer complaints (e) E-mails/letters to prospects (f) Dealer meetings held (g) Service calls made (h) Overdue payments collected • **Direct selling expense** (a) as a percentage of sales (b) as a percentage of quota	• **Personal efforts/skills** (a) Communication skills (b) Selling skills (c) Team player (d) Time management (e) Planning ability • **Knowledge** (a) Product (b) Competition and customers (c) Pricing (d) Company policies • **Customer relation/goodwill generation** • **Personality and attitudes** (a) Cooperation (b) Enthusiasm, Resourcefulness (c) Initiative and aggressiveness (d) Punctuality **Appearance and health**

Step 3 – Establish Performance Standards

Performance standards are generally called sales quotas, which we discussed earlier in Chapter 4. Some companies call them as sales objectives, sales goals or sales targets. Setting performance standards is a difficult, but an important task. Salespeople's actual performance is measured against the performance standards.

Performance standards for quantitative output or results have a close relationship with the company's sales forecast or sales budget and quotas for territories, regions, branches, products, and salespeople. This is because the sales quotas are derived from the company's sales budget, which depends on the company's sales forecast. As said earlier, performance standards are same as sales quotas. However, performance standards for qualitative and quantitative behavioral or activity criteria are difficult to set. For this, companies either carry out "time and duty analysis" of sales jobs or use executive judgment.

Sales managers must ensure that performance standards are fair and reasonable. They should not be too high or too low. If these guidelines are not followed then salespeople will not be motivated and it will have harmful effect on the sales performance. After the standards of performance are established, it is equally important to communicate the same to the salespeople. This will remove misunderstandings about the performance standards against which the actual performance of salespersons are compared.

Step 4 – Compare Actual Performance with Standards

In this step, the individual salesperson's actual performance is measured and then compared with the predetermined performance standards. Sales managers can use different methods for measuring the performance of salespeople. Periodically, sales managers are required to evaluate the performance of each salesperson in a permanent record for the benefit of the salesperson in tracking his progress and also for review by other sales and marketing managers. For this, various types of rating forms or evaluation methods are used.

❍ **Performance Evaluation Methods** Companies use different forms or methods for evaluating salespeople. Some of the commonly used forms are: (i) graphic rating, (ii) ranking, (iii) behaviorally anchored rating scale (BARS), (iv) management by objectives (MBO), and (v) descriptive statements. Sales managers are supplied with these evaluation or appraisal forms for evaluating each salesperson. No one method or form provides a perfect evaluation. Therefore, it is necessary to understand the strengths and weaknesses of each method so that some of these methods can be combined to produce an effective evaluation system for a sales organization.

Graphic Rating This method is most commonly used in sales organizations. It is particularly useful in evaluating salespeople's qualitative behavioral or efforts related criteria. A **semantic differential** type of graphic rating scale uses opposite adjectives on a five or seven point scale. Numerical values are assigned to each level and the manager can check any one of them. The example in Figure 7.6 presents several qualitative behavioral criteria used for evaluating the salespeople. After the sales manager checks level of all performance criteria, individual scores are totaled to arrive at an overall performance evaluation score for each salesperson. Graphic rating scale has many positive characteristics, such as comparability (that is, it is possible to compare results of individual salespeople), job relatedness (that is, it can be designed to meet the needs of each sales organization), practicality (that is, it is easy to understand and implement in a short time), and standardization (that is, measurement instrument and evaluation process are similar throughout the sales organization).

The reliability and the validity of this scale should be checked or assessed continually. The main disadvantage of this method is that it is not capable of detecting differences adequately in performance of individual salespeople or among the performances on different criteria for the same salesperson. For instance, some sales managers are lenient in their evaluation, and may give all salespeople ratings around the average or around the higher level. Also, some managers are subject to a "halo effect", which means their evaluation on one criterion affect their ratings on other criteria. The advantages of graphic rating scale clearly exceed the disadvantages. However, care should be taken to reduce the biases of sales managers.

Selling skills	Excellent	7	6	5	4	3	2	1	Poor
Team player	Superior	7	6	5	4	3	2	1	Inferior
Product Knowledge	Excellent	7	6	5	4	3	2	1	Poor
Attitude	Positive	7	6	5	4	3	2	1	Negative
Customer relations	Excellent	7	6	5	4	3	2	1	Poor
Time management	Superior	7	6	5	4	3	2	1	Inferior

Fig. 7.6 Example of Graphic Rating Scales

Ranking This method ranks all salespeople according to the relative performance on a performance criterion. The advantages of ranking method are that it forces discrimination in performance of salespeople on each criterion, and provides a standardized approach to evaluation. However, it has many disadvantages. It is not useful for decision-making. It has less practicality and it is difficult to assess differences between ranks.

Besides, information obtained from graphic rating scale can be transformed into rankings, but ranking data cannot be translated into graphic rating scale. Ranking method is therefore suggested only as an addition to other evaluation methods. For example, in G.E, sales managers are required to state the top 20 percent and bottom 10 percent of salespeople. The top salespersons get bonuses but the bottom salespeople are dismissed.

Behaviorally Anchored Rating Scales (BARS) Also referred as behavioral expectation scales, this method links salesperson's behavior with specific results, as shown in the Figure 7.7. This method is a repetitive process and allows different sales managers to arrive at more consistent and objective evaluations, since the rating scales have similar interpretations.
Constructing a sales-oriented BARS include four steps[14]:

- **Identify Decisive Events:** Some sales managers, salespeople, and customers are asked to describe specific events of effective and ineffective sales performance behavior. When any of the above persons identify decisive events, the person is asked to give an actual example. These decisive events are then condensed into a smaller number of performance categories
- **Improve Decisive Events into Behavior Anchor Statements:** The sales managers and salespeople who are developing this system improve the decisive events into a still smaller set of behavioral statements of seven to twelve, which are described in general terms. The behavioral statements are then given to another well-informed group of salespeople, who are asked to assign an appropriate performance dimensions to the behavioral anchor statements. A behavioral statement is usually retained for the final BARS if 60 percent or more of the second sales group assigns it to the same performance dimension as the first group did.
- **Rate the Effectiveness of the Behavioral Statements:** The second group of salespeople is asked to rate the behavior statements as to how accurately they describe the performance dimension.

Performance result: Cooperation with Other Sales Team Members

Performance Categories and Definition of the Dimension	Scale	Behavioral Anchor statements
	10	
Very High : This indicates a strong willingness to cooperate with other members of the sales team	9	Could be expected to cooperate when help or assistance is requested by other team members.
	8	Could be expected to go out of his or her way to help the team achieve its goals.
	7	
Moderate : This indicates an average amount of cooperation and willingness to be part of the sales team	6	Could be expected to occasionally support the team members with field sales problems.
	5	
	4	Could be expected to contribute half-heartedly to the team effort to achieve goals.
	3	
	2	Could be expected not to care much about the team and its members.
Very Low : This indicates an opposition and nonteam oriented effort, which hurts group performance	1	
	0	Could be expected to oppose members of the team and act against the team goals.

Fig. 7.7 **Example of Behaviourally Anchored Rating Scales (BARS)**

- **Select the Behavioral Anchor Statements for the Performance Dimension:** Finally, five to seven behavioral anchor statements are selected for performance dimensions with vertical scales. Generally, a proper BARS takes time to develop over a period of time.

In the example in Figure 7.7, six behavioral anchor statements have been assigned numbers on a 10-point rating scale to show the linkages between behavior and the results. BARS can be used to evaluate individual salespersons. The main advantage of this method is on job relatedness, as a given selling situation relates directly to the job of salespeople. It gives the salesperson specific direction for improvement, such as what is expected from him to achieve a high rating. It also makes the sales manager free from performance evaluation worry. BARS method is more logical and reliable. It also reduces rating mistakes.

Management by objectives (MBO) The most common and comprehensive goal setting and results-based evaluation method is the MBO method, which is discussed briefly earlier in this chapter. Steps followed in a typical MBO method are as follows: (i) the sales manager and the salesperson discuss and set specific objectives or sales quotas for the salesperson for a specific time period, (ii) they also prepare an action plan for the achievement of the objectives, (iii) they review actual performance periodically against the stated objectives, sales quotas, or performance standards and take corrective actions.

MBO should include a procedure for setting objectives or quotas, particularly keeping in view the various criteria or bases presented in Table 7.11. This ensures that objectives include quantitative result-based and quantitative behavioral-based criteria. The individual sales quotas (or performance standards) can be assigned weights to show their relative importance. These can be combined to produce an overall index, as shown in an example in Table 7.11. The example illustrates the evaluation of performance for one salesperson on four performance criteria or bases, which combine quantitative results and efforts. The unequal weights show the difference in importance given by the company to various bases. The overall performance of the salesperson is arrived at by dividing total of weighted performance index by total of weights, which is equal to 102.5. Before this, weighted performance index for each performance criteria is calculated by multiplying the performance index with the respective weight. Use of quotas in MBO gives a very useful method for evaluating salesperson's performance. It also indicates the areas where the performance is good or poor.

Table 7.11 Example of MBO Performance Evaluation

Performance Criteria/Bases	Objective/ Quota	Weight	Actual Performance	Performance Index	Weighted Performance Index
• Sales volume	₹72,00,000	4	₹80,00,000	111	444
• Number of new accounts	24	3	20	83	249
• Number of calls per day	6	2	7	116	232
• Number of reports sent	24	1	24	100	100
	Total	10			1025
• Overall performance					102.5

Descriptive Statements In this method of performance evaluation, sales managers are required to write either a short or detailed description of each salesperson's performance on specific criteria. These criteria or bases vary from company to company, but some of the commonly used criterias are: goal attainment, selling ability, territorial management, job/product knowledge, and customer relations. Another method, used by some organizations, includes writing a profile about the individual salesperson's specific performance, abilities, and potential.

Problems or disadvantages of descriptive statements method are many. First, there is a subjectivity of evaluation both in writing and interpreting descriptive statements. Second, some evaluators may not be good or capable writers, resulting in misinterpretations of performance evaluations. Third problem is that many managers are too severe, lenient or neutral in their descriptions of performance, resulting in biased evaluation. Another problem sales managers may face in accurately evaluating salespeople if the number of salespeople to be assessed is large. This method should be used either with some form of graphic rating scale or when the number of salespeople to be evaluated is less and that evaluators are well-trained.

In summary, as said earlier, combining different methods is a good approach to maximize the strengths and minimize the weaknesses that are present in these methods.

Step 5 – Review Performance Evaluation with Salespeople

Once the salesperson's performance has been evaluated, the sales manager should conduct performance review or appraisal session with the salesperson. This is a very challenging part of the sales manager's job, because it can be a very sensitive occasion. It is difficult to point out the salesperson's weaknesses or failures to meet the standards. The sales manager should contact the salesperson and set a time and place for the performance review meeting. Before the meeting, the salesperson should be asked to review his or her job description and the past performance, by using the company's evaluation form. It is important that both the salesperson and the sales manager should consider performance review as a positive method, which helps the salesperson to solve existing problems and perform better in future. Thus, both should have a positive attitude towards the review. Research has indicated that usually salespeople evaluate themselves better than their manager does. The following guidelines are useful when reviewing performance:

- First, performance criteria or bases should be discussed.
- The salesperson should be asked to review his own performance.
- The sales manager should present his view on the salesperson's performance, by first highlighting good qualities of the salesperson. Corrective actions on weak areas should also be discussed.
- Mutual agreement on the performance must be established.
- If disagreements or serious differences of opinion occur, the sales manager should carefully explain the reasons to the salesperson.

The sales manager should review the evaluation of each criterion, by first reviewing the high ratings of the salesperson and then going down to other ratings. The sales manager and the salesperson should together find out the reasons for the performance variations as compared with performance standards. The manager should then summarize the total performance evaluation. Thereafter, the sales manager and the salesperson should develop mutually agreed objectives and action plan for the future period.

Immediately after the review session is over, the sales manager should write a letter to the salesperson re-stating the performance evaluation results and the objectives for the future period. A copy of this letter should be sent to the sales manager's immediate boss. In today's litigious society, it is important to document such reviews.

Step 6 – Decide Sales Management Actions and Control

The performance evaluation procedure followed so far gives a very important information about performance of salespeople. It is the responsibility of the sales management to use this information for improving the performance of individual salespeople, sales teams, and the operations of the sales organization. Another use of the performance information is to identify problem areas, find the causes of the problem, and decide sales management actions to solve the problems. These steps are discussed in this section.

❍ **Identify the Problem Areas** A sales manager should review the performance of each salesperson against each performance criterion. The manager should then summarize the results across all salespeople who are supervised by him. This shows whether there are common areas of low performance. For instance, if most salespeople are not meeting their sales quotas, the situation is different than when only one or two salespeople are not achieving their sales quotas.

❍ **Find Causes** Next to identifying the problems, such as poor performance areas, the sales managers should work backward to find the causes of the unsatisfactory performance. For example, if the problem is that some salespeople have not achieved their sales quotas, then the sales manager should review with salespeople all factors that contribute to the achievement of sales quotas. Some of these factors that may cause poor sales performance could be less sales calls made, poor coverage of market/customers, and superior performance of competitors on important areas of product quality, service, or pricing. Talking to customers often helps to find causes of the unsatisfactory performance.

❍ **Decide Sales Management Actions** Next to finding the causes of poor performance, the sales manager should decide a suitable action to minimize or remove the cause of the problem, so that in future the salesperson's performance will improve. The sales manager's action, for example, may be to train salespersons on selling and negotiating skills, redesign sales territories, suggest for review of the compensation plan, or recommend for review of the company's sales and marketing strategies.

The problems may affect many salespeople or one individual salesperson. The basic approach in deciding the actions of sales management remain the same. In fact, in many companies step 5 of the performance review is combined with step 6 of sales management actions. The sales manager, during the performance review meeting, should also highlight good performance areas, appreciate the salesperson for the good performance, and reward him suitably.

LO 5 **Know the use of sales force automation tools for performance evaluation and social media as a selling vehicle**

SALES FORCE AUTOMATION

Since the beginning of 1990s, sales force automation (SFA) has presented technological help to sales managers and salespeople. SFA is typically a part of a customer relationship management (CRM) system. It is often used by business-to-business (b2b) marketing organizations. SFA software, marketed by solutions providers, helps salespeople and sales managers to manage various aspects of sales administration efficiently and effectively.

Sales force automation (SFA) is defined as[15]: "SFA is the application of computerized technologies to support salespeople and sales management in the achievement of their work-related objectives."

Important technological components of SFA are computer hardware and software. Hardware includes desktop, laptop, or handheld smart phones, and contact or call centre telephony technology. Software consists of both "point" solutions and integrated solutions. "Point" solutions software are designed to give help in one area of sales management. The integrated packages are devoted to sales force applications only. In addition, the integrated packages can be included into comprehensive CRM systems, which operate over sales, service, and marketing areas.

The SFA Ecosystem

The SFA ecosystem includes: (i) SFA solutions providers, (ii) hardware and infrastructure suppliers, and (iii) service providers.

SFA Solutions Providers

There are different types of SFA solutions providers. Some solutions providers are SFA specialists, who concentrate and become expert in a particular function or activity within SFA. **For instance**, product configurator is a software-based application engine that allows a company to configure a complex product or service based on pre-defined rules. Sometimes, prospective customers interact directly with configurators. For example, Dell computer website permits customers to build their own personal computers (PCs).

There are vendors, such as Siebel and sales force.com, who offer CRM suites that include SFA modules. Another type of vendors offer enterprise suites which have a full range of IT solutions, including customer relationship management (CRM) that consists of SFA modules.

Hardware and Infrastructure Vendors

Inside salespeople and sales managers use desktop or laptop computers from hardware suppliers. But outside or field salespeople often need hand-held devices or laptop computers. For the field salespersons, mobile or wireless solutions are needed. SFA applications should be supported by hardware and infrastructure to take care of increased number of users.

Service Providers

Service providers are needed for modifying a selling process, changing an organization structure, planning a training program for salespeople or conducting customer analysis. Service providers can help achieve success for SFA project and also can contribute to the project cost to a large extent.

SFA Software Functionality

SFA applications offer a range of functions. Some of these functions are described here:

Account (or Customer) Management

This software offers a total view of the customer details including customer contacts, enquiries received, quotations submitted, orders received, shipments made, payments received and pending, and unresolved issues. Salespeople and sales managers find the customer information very usefull.

Lead Management

It allows sales leads to be allocated to salespeople based on territory, product expertise or other variables. It helps fair workload distribution to a sales team. Lead management permits companies to create, allocate, and monitor sales leads, which give information about prospective or potential customers. The objective to be achieved is to convert the lead (or sales lead) into a qualified prospect and thereafter, to a customer.

Territory Management

This software helps manager to establish, modify, and balance sales territories so that salespeople have equal sales potential or equal workloads. It reduces the travel time of salespeople as well as cost of selling. It improves customer coverage and productivity of salespeople.

There are many more SFA applications that are a generic set of sales related functions. SFA software is also available for industry specific applications. For example, Siebel offers customized solutions for over 12 different industries, e.g., defense, transportation and aerospace. Similarly, SAP has applications for over two dozen industry contexts.

Benefits from SFA

There are many advantages of using SFA. Although the primary benefit from SFA is improved efficiency, different stakeholders have differing appeals.

- **Salespeople**: Higher conversion rates from enquiries to orders, superior sales performance, higher customer satisfaction rating, and higher level of compensation.
- **Sales managers**: Improved salesperson productivity, reduced selling costs, improved customer relations, and correct reporting.
- **Senior management**: Increased market share and sales revenue, and improved profitability.

None of the above benefits are likely to be received by a company if its salespeople do not adopt the technology. Adoption is possible if salespeople find the SFA easy to use and useful. Salespeople should also get adequate training to learn the system. The value of the SFA depends on the salespeople's ability and willingness to regularly enter the data about customers, competitors, expenses, orders received and so on. Above all, senior management support for SFA is absolutely necessary.

USE OF SOCIAL MEDIA

Before we discuss how should we use social media, let us see what does the term "social media" means[16]. Social media refers to platforms like Twitter, Facebook, LinkedIn, Google Plus, where people can come and communicate with each other, regardless of their locations. Research indicated that the number of social network users worldwide was over two billions in 2016. This would open new areas for sales professionals to concentrate their communications towards existing and prospective customers. They can communicate with people without meeting them. This means they can interact with current and prospective customers in lesser time. Then why are some people not using social media? Some of the common reasons are:

- Having no time for social media.
- Unfamiliar with how to use social media

- Feel too old for social media
- Social media seems overwhelming.
- Risk of sharing the wrong information.
- On social media, mistakes get magnified.

The answer to all these problems can be given by answering one question:

How should we use social media? Should we spend time on it? Or should we invest in it?

Our competitors may be developing a relationship with our current and prospective customers. They may be participating in the social selling process. Sales professionals and business organizations, who use social media, are likely to be more satisfied with the outcome than casual users. Sales and marketing professional communicate with their target clients and prospects on regular basis and hence they are getting substantial growth in sales.

Social media is changing the business rules by cutting across value chain elements of marketing – viz., sales, customer service, marketing, and other business areas. This has not happened with traditional marketing.

Use of social media to interact directly with the prospect until the prospect is ready to buy is called **social selling.** A social seller uses social media to find potential customers, relate to their needs and interests and "engage" or attract their attention in a proper way. These communications not only create sales leads, but also build a relationship.

Benefits of Social Media

Some of the major benefits of social media are: (i) real-time communication, (ii) improved visibility, and (iii) increased customer relationship and loyalty.

Real-time Communication

There is an increased communication prospective between customers and the company that enables two-way movement of ideas, views, and opinions. It gives an opportunity to the company to enter and promote its products and services. For instance, a customer may be dissatisfied about the performance of a product or service. He or she may post the information on a social media platform like Twitter, Facebook, or LinkedIn. The company may respond by suggesting ways to resolve the problem. This real-time communication may help the company to connect with the prospective customer.

Improved Visibility

Once a salesperson involves himself on social platforms by sharing his views, ideas, and suggestions, people have knowledge about the salesperson and his company. This gives visibility to the salesperson and his company.

Increased Customer Relationship and Loyalty

The salesperson's involvement or engagement with prospects help create interest and desire to buying action. Once these prospects get converted to become the company's customers, they will advocate the company's products or brands to their friends and relatives online and offline. Thus, the use of social media results in increased customer relationship and loyalty.

Compared to the traditional sales channels like distributors, wholesalers, and retailers, social selling is cheaper and more exciting. Typically, prospective customers look for social platforms like Twitter, Facebook, LinkedIn, Google Plus, and You Tube for references. Hence, a social seller should get connected to these platforms. This allows the seller to share valuable information like case studies, reports, and videos with the prospects and build relationships. Out of all social network or platforms, LinkedIn is increasingly used as a platform for social selling. Social selling is a very good tool for salespeople.

LO 6 **Find ethical, social and legal responsibilities of sales managers and salespeople**

ETHICAL, SOCIAL, AND LEGAL RESPONSIBILITIES OF SALES PERSONNEL

An organization consists of individuals. These individuals' ethical values help shape those of the organization. *The Oxford Dictionary* defines **ethics** as "the moral principles" that govern the behavior of a person or group. **Business ethics** deal largely with the relationship between business practices and the moral concepts of right and wrong. Most individuals have their own personal ethics, which shows what they will and will not do. But as soon as a person becomes a salesperson or sales manager, he must think what is good for the company too.

Business Ethics and Sales Management

Sales managers have ethical responsibilities with respect to their own actions and the actions of their salespeople. Often sales managers face ethical dilemmas in carrying out various sales management tasks like getting orders from government customers, pricing decisions, hiring salespersons, evaluating salespeople, and so on. Sales managers are also responsible to set up, communicate, and enforce the ethical standards to their salespeople. A survey of sales managers found that 49 percent of the sales managers said their salespeople lied on a sales call and that 22 percent said their salespeople have sold products their customers didn't need. 58 percent of the sales managers surveyed said that they have found salespersons cheating on an expense bill[17]. If sales managers ignore the unethical behavior and activities of their salespeople, the consequences will be serious viz., lawsuits, fines, and imprisonment. It may also result in loss of reputation and customers.

Ethical Situations Involving Salespeople and Sales Managers

Occasionally salespeople and sales managers may be involved in some of the following ethical situations:

Dealing with the Company

Damaged-merchandise credit is an example of ethical problem involving salespeople and sales managers. A salesperson or sales manager may give credit to a customer for damaged merchandise when no damage has taken place. Another example is when changing the job, a manager may want to take key customers to the new employer who is also the company's competitor. As mentioned earlier, there are many situations involving salespeople cheating on expense bills.

Dealing with Customers

Here the main ethical issues involve gifts, information, and entertainment, as explained below:

❍ **Gifts** Giving gifts to customers, particularly at the time of New Year or a festival season, is a traditional business practice. But, today it is under close examination. A ₹200 worth gift to a ₹2 million a year customer may be merely a gift, but is it acceptable for a pharmaceutical company to invite its doctor-customers to Jamaica for an all-expense-paid seminar? Salespeople should follow some guidelines to avoid gift giving that is unethical or in bad taste:

- Follow your company's policy on gift giving
- Keep the value of gifts low
- Do not give gifts to customers' spouses
- Never give gift before a customer does business with the firm
- Walk away from the business if the customer pushes for something that exceeds these guidelines

❍ **Misrepresentation** Salespeople sometimes misrepresent by exaggerating the capabilities of their products or services and making false statements just to close a sale. Knowingly, sometimes salespeople sell a higher priced product when lower priced product would have satisfied the customer need. For example, pharmaceutical salespeople were pushing higher priced calcium channel blockers for high blood pressure when cheaper diuretics and beta blockers were equally effective[18].

❍ **Entertainment** Business entertainment is a part of sales promotion. Some salespeople spend this money on customers who have less business potential. Some useful guidelines have been developed on this subject:

- Keep the entertainment suitable to the customer and its business potential.
- Be careful to customer's feelings toward types of entertainment.
- Entertain to develop long-term business relationship and not for one order.

Establish a Code of Ethics

Sales managers and salespeople must understand that ethical behavior is not only morally right, but also sound over a long-term point of view. Higher levels of ethical behavior have been noticed in companies where codes of ethics are established and enforced[19]. The code of ethics adopted by the American Marketing Association is a good example. Other examples are Boeing company's "Business Conduct Guidelines" and Norton company's "Policy on Business Ethics". A code of ethics can contribute to the general ethical climate of an organization, if it is endorsed and enforced by the top management. A code of ethics becomes an effective means of guiding behavior only if it is enforced, otherwise, it is meaningless.

Social Responsibilities

The "concept of corporate social responsibility" (CSR) means distinguishing right from wrong and doing the right. Social responsibility is management's obligation to make decisions and take actions that will help in the welfare and interests of society and the company.

A firm's main social responsibilities are to its eight major stakeholders, consisting of customers, community, creditors, government, owners, managers, employees, and suppliers. These stakeholders can be remembered by using the acronym **CCC GOMES**. A company has four main social responsibilities to its eight major stakeholders. These are ethical, legal, economic, and voluntary.

Ethical Responsibilities

Ethical responsibilities include dealing with stakeholders with reasonableness and impartiality. Unethical behavior takes place when decisions enable an individual or the company to gain at the expense of society. Society demands ethical standards from the company management.

Legal Responsibilities

Modern societies lay down laws and regulations that organizations are expected to follow. Organizations are expected to fulfill their economic goals within the legal requirements imposed by local municipal councils, state legislators, and central or federal regulatory agencies[20].

Economic Responsibilities

A company's economic responsibility is to produce and market the goods and services that the society wants and to maximize profits for its owners and shareholders. Often some companies work only to maximize profits. No doubt, profits are required to stay in business and to expand. Many people will be affected, if companies go out of business.

Voluntary Responsibilities

A company's desire to make social contributions on purely voluntary basis, including philanthropic contributions that offer no monetary return to the company. Examples are contributions towards earthquake and tsunami disaster relief fund from many organizations and individuals in India in 2004–2005. This is the highest criterion of social responsibility because it goes beyond societal expectations to contribute to the society's welfare. Some companies make use of social audit to assess how they are performing in achieving social goals. A social audit is defined as a systematic evaluation of the company's activities that have a social impact.

Legal Responsibilities and Sales Management

Government laws and regulations enacted by local, state, or central (federal) levels, have an impact on the company's sales and marketing department, particularly in pricing, advertising, and personal selling areas.

❍ **Price Discrimination** It is unlawful for a seller to discriminate in price among different customers when the discrimination has a harmful effect on competition. It is also unlawful for a buyer knowingly to induce or receive a discriminatory price. In order to ensure equality of opportunity for all, sellers are required to treat similar buyers equally with respect to price and terms of sale. For example, if a company is selling a product to trade segment, it should give the same trade discounts, volume discounts, and cash discounts to all the dealers. This is based on Competition Act, 2003, in India.

❍ **Price Fixing** It is unlawful (under Competition Act, 2003) for competitors to agree to fix prices or form "price cartels". Even the informal exchange of price information with competitors or discussions of pricing policies at trade association meetings have been found illegal by the courts.

❍ **Consumer Protection** It is illegal, under Consumer Protection Act 1986, (Indian legislation), to make false or misleading claims about a product or service. The seller may also be sued for any damages or personal injuries, arising out of a customer's misuse of the product due to misleading claims of the seller.

Bribes

Payment of money or giving gifts to gain or retain a customer is illegal (under Indian Contracts Act 1872, and Sale of Goods Act, 1930). Using bribes to get information about competitors is also illegal. Bribery continues to put salespeople and sales managers to ethical test. "Everyone is doing it" is not a valid excuse if given by a salesperson. Penalties are given to those found guilty of taking or giving bribes.

Problems Related to the Internet and Telemarketing

Rapid growth of Internet (or online) marketing and telemarketing have given rise to some new problems, which have ethical overtones. Some legislation are needed about the practices of sending unsolicited promotional material to prospects via e-mail and telephoning people at home, particularly at night.

Sales managers must accept responsibility for ensuring that salespeople avoid violations of local, state, or central laws. Every member of a sales organization must remain up to date on all regulations and laws that affect selling activities. In addition, the company management must make a determined effort to create an ethical climate within the organization to serve organizational and customer objectives.

SUMMARY

LO 1

- Selling expenses include travel, food, lodging, telephone, and customer entertainment. Most companies have sales force expense plans to control selling expenses. These are: (i) salesperson pays all expenses, (ii) the company pays all expenses, (iii) the company partially pays expenses, and (iv) combination plan.

LO 2

- A marketing audit is a comprehensive periodic, and systematic examination of a company's marketing plan, environment, objectives, strategies, tactics, performance, organization, and people with a view to find out opportunities and problems, and recommend an action plan to improve the company's marketing performance.
- A sales audit is a comprehensive, systematic, and prescriptive tool with a purpose to assess whether a company's sales management process is adequate to give direction for improvement of sales performance.

LO 3

- For evaluating the effectiveness of a sales organization, it is necessary to carry out: (i) sales analysis, (ii) marketing cost analysis, (iii) profitability analysis, and (iv) productivity analysis.
- Sales analysis is a detailed inspection of a company's sales data, which includes collecting, classifying, comparing, and drawing conclusions. There are different types of sales analysis a company can carry out. Some of the common types of sales analysis include sales analysis by branches, products, and customer class.
- For comprehensive evaluation of effectiveness of a sales organization, marketing cost and profitability analysis should also be carried out. The purpose of marketing cost analysis is to determine the profitability of marketing or sales units, such as sales territories, products, and market segments. This is done by subtracting the marketing costs from the sales revenue, associated with the particular sales unit.
- Productivity analysis is useful for comparing productivity ratios across the sales organization, levels (e.g., branches) within the company and also with other sales organizations. Productivity is usually measured by ratios between outputs and inputs. Examples are sales per salesperson, selling expenses per salesperson or sales calls per salesperson.

LO 4

- The main purpose or objective of the performance evaluation and control of salespeople is to determine how the salespeople have performed. Some of the other major purposes are to decide the increments, promotions, training needs, and rewards for good performance as well as areas of performance improvements.
- The procedure for evaluating and controlling sales force performance includes the following steps: (i) set policies on performance evaluation and control, (ii) decide the bases of salespeople's performance evaluation, (iii) establish performance standards, (iv) compare the actual performance with standards, (v) review performance evaluation with salespersons, (vi) decide sales management actions and control.

LO 5

- Sales force automation (SFA) is the application of computerized technologies to support salespeople and sales management in the achievement of their work-related objectives. The SFA ecosystem includes (i) SFA solutions providers, (ii) hardware and infrastructure suppliers, and (iii) service providers.

- Social media refers to platforms like Twitter, Facebook, LinkedIn, Google Plus, where people can communicate with each other, regardless of their locations. Use of social media to interact directly with the prospect until the prospect is ready to buy is called 'social selling'.

LO 6

- Salespeople and sales managers have ethical, social, and legal responsibilities. A code of ethics can contribute to the general ethical climate of a company. A company has for major social responsibilities, viz., ethical, legal, economic, and voluntary to its stakeholders. Sales managers must ensure that salespeople avoid violations of local, state, or central laws. Sales personnel must remain up to date on all regulations and laws pertaining to selling activities.

Key Terms

Glossaries of key terms are mentioned at the end of all chapters

Behaviorally anchored rating scales (BARS)
Contribution approach
360-Degree feedback
Ethics/Business ethics
Expense plan
Full-cost approach
Management by objectives (MBO)
Marketing audit
Marketing cost analysis
Productivity analysis
Profitability
Return on assets managed (ROAM)
Sales Analysis
Sales audit
Social responsibility

Conceptual Questions

1. Compare the various types of expense plans for controlling the selling expenses of salespeople. Mention the main advantage and disadvantage of each type. LO1 M
2. How marketing and sales audits help in improving the performance of marketing and sales functions? LO2 M
3. What is 'sales analysis'? How hierarchical sales analysis is used for identifying problems? LO3 D
4. What is the purpose of marketing cost analysis? How activity-based costing (ABC) is used in marketing cost and profitability analysis? LO3 D

Note: Difficulty Level ⟶ E — Easy; M — Medium; D — Difficult

5. What is the difference between a full-cost approach and a contribution approach for profitability analysis? Discuss their relative merits and demerits. LO3 D
6. Describe briefly the steps involved for evaluating and controlling sales force performance. LO4 D
7. Explain the steps followed in a typical management by objectives (MBO) evaluation method. How 360-degree feedback evaluation technique is different from MBO method? LO4 M
8. What is 'sales force automation (SFA)'? Why is increasing number of companies using SFA? Describe how companies use social media as a selling vehicle? LO5 M
9. What is 'business ethics'? Describe ethical situations involving salespeople and sales managers. How can general ethical climate be improved in a firm? LO6 M
10. What are the main social responsibilities of a company to its stakeholders? Explain the areas in sales and marketing functions where government laws may have an impact. LO6 M

Objective Type Questions

Select the most appropriate response out of the various options available in each of the following questions:

1. The sales force expense plan, which has the least administrative expense for a company, is one of the following types
   (a) the salesperson pays all the expenses
   (b) the company pays all the expenses
   (c) the company partially pays expenses
   (d) combination plan LO1 E
2. The main purpose of a sales audit is
   (a) to study the sales management process
   (b) to understand the problems of the sales function
   (c) to improve the sales performance
   (d) none of the above LO2 M
3. Evaluation of effectiveness of a sales organization is done by carrying out
   (a) sales analysis (b) cost and profitability analysis
   (c) productivity analysis (d) all of these
   (e) none of these LO3 M
4. Most companies define a sale when an order is:
   (a) received (b) shipped (or transported)
   (c) shipped and invoiced (d) paid for LO3 M

5. The purpose of marketing cost analysis is to determine:
   (a) costs (b) profitability
   (c) sales (d) all of these LO3 M

6. For making a long-term study of profitability of different products and market segments, the most appropriate approach is:
   (a) full-cost method (b) contribution method
   (c) both the methods (d) none of these LO4 M

7. The most commonly used evaluation method by sales organization for evaluating salespeople is:
   (a) descriptive statements (b) management by objectives (MBO)
   (c) graphic rating scales (d) ranking
   (e) behaviorally anchored rating scale (BARS) LO4 M

8. Sales force automation (SFA) helps salespeople to manage various aspects of
   (a) distribution management (b) sales administration
   (c) pricing (d) product management LO5 M

9. Price discrimination and price fixing are considered as unlawful under one of the following Indian laws:
   (a) Consumer Protection Act, 1986 (b) Competition Act, 2003
   (c) Indian Contracts Act, 1872 (d) Sale of Goods Act, 1930 LO6 D

Application Questions

1. As a measure to cut the costs, in order to improve dwindling profits, the head of sales and marketing sends a communication to all sales managers at all levels to cut the selling costs by ten percent without affecting the sales volume quotas. As an example, he says if a sales manager wants to visit a territory outside the home-town, he should take an overnight train instead of going by a flight. This measure is temporary, till the company's profitability improves. How would you convey this measure to your salespeople and make them accept it? LO1 M

2. Conduct a sales analysis to evaluate the effectiveness of the following mentioned branches.

	Branch 'A'	Branch 'B'	Branch 'C'	Branch 'D'
Sales	32.85	39.55	38.23	23.85
Sales quotas	33.90	38.80	36.20	25.50
Sales last year	29.50	33.75	31.50	21.22
Industry Sales	103.25	132.0	108.50	84.00

(Note: All figures are in ₹ Million) LO3 M

3. "Why is your performance disappointing?", asked Vijay Dhavan, district sales manager, to Ashok after looking at the computer statement of his district's performance. The four territories are by

and large similar in market potential and competition. Vijay, therefore, set monthly quotas for the four territories by dividing the district quotas equally to the four territories as follows:

Monthly Performance Analysis: Month – December 2015, District – Bijapur.

Performance Criteria	Quota	Alok	Suresh	Ashok	Pradeep
Net sales product 'A'	₹2,00,000	2,10,000	2,05,000	1,58,000	1,95,000
Net sales product 'B'	₹3,00,000	3,20,000	3,01,000	2,78,000	3,10,000
Net sales total	₹5,00,000	5,30,000	5,06,000	4,36,000	5,05,000
Number of new customers	2	3	2	1	2
Number of Calls	140	170	150	125	145
Sales expenses	₹5000	5300	5100	4800	4900

i. How is Vijay's district performance analyzed?
ii. What actions should Vijay take?

4. You are a sales and marketing manager and you have just launched a new unique kind of table fan in the market, which you have found to have a basic design defect on oscillation mechanism. In the meeting with the CEO of the company, in the presence of production and marketing heads, you have pleaded to stop selling, rectify the defect, and thereafter, produce and sell the fan in the market. The CEO does not agree and insists you should continue selling, production to continue producing and rectifying the defect in the meantime. Your marketing head does not say anything. You think it is not ethical to sell a defective product. What will you do? **LO6 M**

ASSIGNMENTS FOR STUDENTS

1. Meet a senior sales manager to whom first level sales managers (e.g. district/branch/area sales managers) report. Ask him how the performance of the districts/branches is evaluated in terms of sales, selling expenses and profit contributions. Compare it with what you have learnt in the textbook. Make a report and submit it to your teacher.
2. Contact two salespersons from two different companies. Ask them the following questions: (i) How their performance is evaluated? (ii) What criteria are used for evaluation? (iii) Are they satisfied with the evaluation process? Why? (iv) Does the evaluation help them to improve their performance?
3. Visit the sales force automation website *www.salesforce.com* and find out how salespeople and sales managers are benefited from using this website. Find other competing software products for similar application.
4. Talk to two salespersons and ask them about ethical issues, such as bribes, false promises, wrong information, faced by them as a part of their job, and how they have dealt with these issues. How differently could these issues be handled?

Reference Notes

1. Frederick Reichheld, *The Loyalty Effect*, Harvard Business School Press, Boston, 1996.
2. Alan J. Dubinsky and Richard W. Hansen, *The Sales Force Management Audit*, California Management Review, Winter 1981, p. 86.
3. Morris, Davis, Allen, Avila, and Chapman, *Assessing the Relationships among Performance Measures, Managerial Practices, Satisfaction When Evaluating the Salesforce: A Replication and Extension*, Journal of Personal Selling and Sales Management, 11, Summer 1991, p. 25.
4. The MAC Group, *Distribution: A Competitive Weapon*, Cambridge, MA: MAC Group, 1985, p. 20.
5. Thomas Stevenson, Frank Barnes, and Sharon Stevenson, *Activity-Based Costing: An Emerging Tool for Industrial Marketing Decision Makers*, Journal of Business and Industrial Marketing, 8, 1993, p. 40.
6. Jan P. Muczyk and Myron Gable, *Managing Sales Performance through a Comprehensive Performance Appraisal System*, Journal of Personal Selling and Sales Management, May 1987, p. 41.
7. Jackson, Schlacter, and Wolfe, *Examining the Bases Utilized for Evaluating Salespeople's Performance*, Journal of Personal Selling and Sales Management, 15, Fall 1995, p. 57. Michael H. Morris and Sean R. Aten, *Sales Force Performance Appraisal: Contemporary Issues and Practices*, in Progress in Marketing Thought, MS: Southern Marketing Association, 1990, p. 413.
8. Linda S. Pettijohn, R.Stephen Parker, Charles E. Pettijhon and John L.Kent, *Performance Appraisals: Usage, Criteria, and Observations*, Journal of Management Development, 20(9) (2001), pp. 754–71.
9. *Good Bye Annual Appraisals, IBM says Hello to Checkpoint*, in Economic Times, Bengaluru, February 3, 2016.
10. Brent Green, *Listening to Leaders: Feedback on 360-Degree Feedback One Year Later*, Organization Development Journal, Spring 2002, pp. 8–16.
11. J. Taylor Sims, *Industrial Sales Management: A Case for MBO*, Industrial Marketing Management, 6(1977), pp. 44–45.
12. Erin Anderson and Richard L. Oliver, *Perspectives on Behavior-Based versus Outcome-Based Sales Control Systems*, Journal of Marketing, 51, October 1987, p. 76.
13. Erin Anderson and Richard L. Oliver, *Behaviour- and Outcome-Based Sales Control Systems: Evidence and Consequences of Pure-Form and Hybrid Governance*, Journal of Personal Selling and Sales Management, Fall 1995), pp. 1–16.
14. A. Benton Cocanougher and John M. Ivaneevich, *BARS Performance Rating for Sales Force Personnel*, Journal of Marketing, July 1978, p. 87.
15. Francis Buttle, *Customer Relationship Management-Concepts and Technologies*, Elsevier, 2009, pp. 395–410.
16. Apurva Chamaria with Gavrav Kakkar, *You are the Key*, Bloomsbury Publishing, India, 2015, pp. 48–53.

17. Erin Stout, *Are your Salespeople Ripping You off?*, Sale and Marketing Management, February 2001, p. 59.

18. Catherine Arnst, *Is Good Marketing Bad Medicine ?*, Business Week (*www.business–week.com*), April 13, 1998.

19. Charles H.Schwepker Jr., *Ethical Climate's Relationship to Job Satisfaction*, Journal of Business Research, October 2001, p. 40.

20. James Srodes, *Corporations Discover It's Good to Be Good*, Business and Society Review, Summer 1990, pp. 57–60.

CASE 7.1

GTI Company Ltd.

Analysis of Sales Volume

"Can you tell us why your sales volume performance is lower by ten percent in comparison to the sales budget at the end of first quarter?", asked the CEO of GTI company to the general manager (sales and marketing) in the monthly budget review meeting.

"Yes, Sir. It is due to the recession in bicycle industry, which is one of our target market segments." responded the GM.

"Have you analyzed whether the actual sales are less than the budget only because of bicycle segment or any other market segments and which regions, branches, salespersons, and customers have contributed to the negative sales variance?" persisted the CEO, showing anxiety on his face, as he looked to the general manager.

At this point, the finance manager intervened and said, "I think, our computerized sales analysis gives sufficient data to find which regions and branches have contributed to the negative performance. However, it does not give information on the performance of salespeople and customer-wise sales data, because the information on quotas of salespersons and codification of customers has not been given by the field sales managers so far."

"Yes, I agree with the finance manager and based on the sales analysis, I have analyzed to find northern region, particularly Ludhiana and Sonepat branches have not performed well. Most bicycle manufacturers are located in Ludhiana and Sonepat. I spoke with the concerned branch managers, who have informed me about the recession in bicycle industry," said GM (sales and marketing).

"Well, why the information on recession was not discussed three months ago, when we finalized the yearly budget, and what corrective actions are you taking to make up for the lost sales in the next three quarters?", asked the CEO.

"We overlooked the point on changes in the marketing environment, when we discussed the company sales forecast, and we shall come up with our proposal on the corrective actions in next two weeks from now," responded the general manager (sales and marketing).

Discussion Questions

1. If you were the GM (sales and marketing), how would you identify the areas for corrective actions?
2. What corrective actions would you suggest to make up for the lost sales in the next quarter?

This case was prepared by Prof. Krishna K. Havaldar for classroom discussion.

CASE 7.2

KKN India Ltd.

Sales Force Performance Evaluation

"My salespeople should get maximum annual increments because western region sales have given a maximum sales growth of 25 percent against the total company's sales growth of 15 percent. Besides, western region has contributed 35 percent of the total company sales," said Suresh Deshpande, regional sales manager (western region) to the general manager (sales), K.V. Apte.

"Well, I do appreciate that your salespersons' performance have been exceptional and they should be suitably rewarded. But that does not mean salespeople from other regions are not performing well. The overall market potential index and growth of western region are much higher as compared to other regions. For instance, eastern region's market potential index is 16 percent of all India, and its growth is limited. That affects the sales performance of eastern region. The salespeople in eastern region do work hard, but the results are not as good as western region", responded Apte.

"But, Sir, I am only talking on behalf of my region and my salespeople. I am not aware of market conditions of other regions. Our performance evaluation method compares the actual sales of this year with the previous year's sales, and the market potential of various territories were not considered when the sales quotas were established. The sales force performance evaluation only measures the sales results, but not the efforts of the salespeople. If efforts are not measured, how can anybody say that particular salespeople are spending adequate efforts in the right direction? Perhaps, there is a need to review our sales force performance evaluation system. But, as per our present system of evaluation of salespeople, my salespersons have shown a good performance over the previous year and should, therefore, get appropriate increments in their salaries. I am giving you their individual performance evaluation papers with a request to approve maximum possible increments to them," advocated Suresh for his salespeople.

"Okay, I will look into this matter. I would like to see how would you perform, if you were transferred to eastern region", said Apte with a smile and moved over to the conference room for a meeting.

Discussion Questions

1. Do you agree to Suresh's point of view? Justify your answer.
2. What improvements would you suggest to the existing system of performance evaluation of the salespeople of this company?

This case was prepared by Prof. Krishna K. Havaldar for classroom discussion.

CASE 7.3

SHB Bank: Fraud Control Unit

Karan Singh was a fresher with a computer engineering degree and also an MBA. He was campus recruited for SHB bank as the Business Development Manager.

SHB bank was an MNC bank with its headquarters in London. It has been in India for more than 80 years. According to the norms of the bank, every fresh recruit has to undergo a compulsory training and an online examination before joining his/her respective job position.

Karan was trained for seven days and after that there were seven online tests that were to be cleared before joining the job. Due to a viral attack he missed 3 days of his training. In these days he missed the training on the procedures and norms that had to be followed when dealing with customers. He completed the other days training and gave all the tests and cleared them, with the help of a colleague. The job profile assigned to him was that of a Business Development Manager, in which he had to source new financials for the bank.

Karan was put in the team of Mukesh Desai, an aggressive sales manager. Desai was known to be a tough taskmaster but he was the best at work. The team under him consisted of six members of which Karan was the latest and the freshest. The routine for work followed by Desai was that the team had to report in the morning and then for the review of the day in the evening. The monthly targets were divided into weekly basis and a clear route map for achieving the same had to be presented by the team. Desai was good at his work of getting the work done and numbers were his mantra. He was supportive but wanted the team to demand it if needed. Silence for him was that everything was in place.

Karan joined the team. The first month went smoothly in getting accustomed to the system. All his teammates were supportive but competitive. From his third month he was assigned targets. He could not meet the same and this continued for another two months. Desai now demanded an explanation which Karan couldn't provide. He was asked to prepare for his prospects for the following day and then leave for the day's work, and this made him work for 12 hours a day. The pressure was immense. The common meetings scared him a lot as he did not have convincing reasons for not meeting his targets. Karan was afraid of his boss. His teammates always supported him and tried helping him but they also had their own targets and so everyone had to be on their own.

The pressure grew as time passed and Karan had become desperate to crack a deal. And one day during a cold calling session he came across a customer who wanted to invest money. His name was Mathews. He wanted to open a current account since he had a small business setup. This was a hot prospect for Karan. He was desperate for the deal and even the customer wanted it to be done as soon as possible. Within two days all documentation happened and the account was logged in. Karan was satisfied on his achievement.

After a month Karan was asked to be present in FCU. The FCU was the "fraud control unit" which ensured that no fraud occurred with the inward financials. They verified all the documents. FCU asked Karan to provide an explanation for the submission of the source of funds coming into the account of Mathews. Karan had no clue what was wrong. The bank had found that Mathews was having a huge cash inflow and outflow through his account and this further induced the bank to find the source. It was found that the international money was flowing in. A small business of his could not have a legitimate source for bringing in such huge amounts.

An income tax raid froze Mathews account and proved that he was actually trying to convert his black money through the veil of the business. The bank had the rule that every customer should be very genuine and it was the sourcing person's responsibility to ensure that in the first place. All the documents should be verified and checked by the sourcing person against the originals. And the desperateness of getting the account had made Karan compromise the procedure. Rather he was not very clear on what he missed. FCU asked Karan to give a written explanation for his ignorance. Karan did not know what to do and whom to approach. Whom could he rely on? Would his boss support him? Or would this be a reason for humiliation in his team? Would his team support him?

Discussion Questions

1. Critically evaluate Karan as a sales person and Desai as a boss?
2. Whom should Karan approach and what could be possible solution for the issue?

This case was prepared by Prof. Krishna K. Havaldar based on the case data provided by Lanna Lalithan, alumnus of MBA program of SBS-ABA, Bengaluru, for classroom discussion.

CASE 7.4

Intel Pentium Chip Flaw

Over the last 20 years, technology has been growing at a rate that, before these times, had been unimaginable. Even a monopolistic company like Intel, which has many people working and testing every product, can have major technological problems. In late 1994, reports were surfacing that the latest Intel Pentium microprocessor chip was flawed. At that time, over 80 percent of the world's personal computers used this chip.

Apparently, flaws in complicated microprocessors were considered common. Many of these flaws were compensated or handled by software and were undetectable by the user. However the flaw discovered in the Pentium chip in 1994 was detected by the users. A flaw in the floating point unit (FPU) resulted in incorrect answers when double precision arithmetic calculations were performed.

The issue started when Intel released a Pentium processor with a rounding error, which occurred during a division instruction. This rounding error didn't occur every time the instruction was executed, just once in 27,000 years, or so they thought. Intel knew the problem but decided to release the product into the customers' hands anyway. There were a number of factors that they considered before deciding it was acceptable to release this flawed processor to the public. One factor involved in this decision was that since the instruction had such a small rounding error along with it occurring once in a great while, they thought it would go unnoticed. Intel's plan was to release the chip and just fix the flaw on the future processors. This action would make Intel a great deal of profit, no one would find out, and once the processors sold out, the rectified ones would be released and everything will be normal. The only problem with this idea was that Thomas R. Nicely, mathematics' professor, found about the error. Nicely contacted Intel about the problem but Intel ignored him and denied to accept it as a problem. After much research, Nicely was sure of his findings, and *Electrical Engineering Times* published it. Intel initially denied the problem until the glitch in the processor was widely known. Intel then accepted the glitch, but said that this problem was insignificant and would not affect the users.

Most people did not accept this statement. More people started looking into this issue and found out that this rounding error happened much more frequently than Intel anticipated. For most typical users, it was noticed, on an average, every 24 days. Intel was not able to get away with not having to throw away all of the flawed processors and taking $475 million expense to replace each and every chip.

About the Company

Intel has grown significantly for the past 40 plus years and has become a major player in the semiconductor industry. They created the first commercial microprocessor in 1971 and now are leading manufacturers of CPUs in the world.

Intel is the world's largest semiconductor chip maker, based on revenue. The company is the inventor of the x86 series of microprocessors, the processors found in most personal computers. Intel was founded on July 18, 1968, as Integrated Electronics Corporation and is based in Santa Clara, California, USA. Intel also makes motherboard chipsets, network cards and ICs, flash memory, graphic chips, embedded processors, and other devices related to communications and computing.

Intel's customers include:

- Original equipment manufacturers (OEMs) and original design manufacturers (ODMs), who make computer systems, cellular handsets, handheld computing devices, and telecommunications and networking communications equipment;
- PC and network communications products users (including individuals, large and small businesses, and service providers) who buy PC components and board-level products, as well as networking and communications products, through distributors, resellers, and OEM channels throughout the world; and
- Other manufacturers, including makers of a wide range of industrial and communications equipment.

Impact on Intel

Intel's initial reaction towards the detection of defects in Pentium directly hurt Intel's reputation. At this time there were a very few major processor companies and Intel was by far the largest. Their reputation was that they were the best and they would do anything to stay the best. This really took a hit when users found out that they produced and released a flawed processor knowing that it did not work 100 percent of the time. This made people to think that it could be the downfall of Intel and this caused many people to sell their stocks. Over a two-week period Intel's stock dropped by 5 percent, which was a major drop for just a short period of time. Intel had to incur heavy losses in terms of cost incurred on various factors like fixing of flaw, replacement of chips, etc. The problem was so bad that IBM halted shipments on all of their computers that contained the Pentium processor.

Impact on Intel Customers

The mistake done by Intel hurt the reputation of the companies and people involved with the flawed chip. The resellers who sold these flawed chips as well as the businesses and people that used these computers for mathematical use were also affected by these chips. There were many different OEMs (Original Equipment Manufacturers) of these Pentium chips at the time such as Dell, Gateway, Hewlett Packard and Compaq, but the main OEM of the chip was IBM. All these companies faced a decline in reputation with their customers and decline in sales and stock price. IBM's stock fell $1.25, Dell's stock fell $3.31, Gateway's stock fell $1.62, Hewlett Packard's stock fell $2.75 and Compaq's stock fell $.87 by close of that day.

Parties which were Affected

There were numerous parties which were also affected by the Intel's release of the processor in the market. The first demographic included the businesses that use computers to deal with numbers in their day-to-day activities. Examples of this were accounting firms, where customers trust the firm to do their taxes and other finances. This could be a major issue if the results from their programs were not right. Other fields in the business divisions were medical and research facilities that use computers to keep records of the patients, or use programs that are number-intensive and need to be accurate. The other party which was affected comprised of individuals using computers for their personal usage. They used computers for calculations, spreadsheets, finances, school work, etc.

References

http://www.emery.com/1e/pentium.htm
http://en.wikipedia.org/wiki/Intel_Corporation

Discussion Questions

1. How did Intel handle the situation arising out of flawed Pentium chip?
2. How differently could it have dealt with the problem?

This case was prepared under the guidance of Prof. Krishna K. Havaldar by Megha Goel and Megha Sharma, MBA students of Alliance Business Academy, Bengaluru, for classroom discussion.

Chapter 8

Sales Promotion

LEARNING OBJECTIVES

After studying this chapter, you will be able to:

LO 1 Know definition of Sales Promotion and reasons for importance of sales promotion

LO 2 List the benefits, drawbacks and objectives of sales promotion

LO 3 Describe different types of sales promotions

LO 4 Discuss the effects of sales promotions on sales and profits

LO 5 Integrate sales promotion with other elements of communication-mix

LO 6 Check evaluation of sales promotion

Murli Bhasin, General Manager of DP Ltd., made up his mind to launch the new table/pedestal fan "Breezy" in the financial capital of India, Mumbai. The plan is to launch the new product in Mumbai and after six months, roll out to other markets. Bhasin had earlier discussed and planned full-page advertisements in all the major newspapers in Mumbai. As the launch date of Breezy is planned on March 15, the release date for the advertisements is also scheduled on the same date. The marketing plan that was developed earlier, based on the findings of the marketing research and the internal discussions, included integrated marketing communications (IMC) plan.

The IMC plan enabled the company to combine and integrate different promotional or communication components, such as advertising, sales promotion, public relations, personal selling and direct marketing. It provides clarity and consistency of messages, maximum impact on target markets, and cost effectiveness. Based on the IMC plan, the company's marketing team decided to use newspaper advertisements, supported by the outdoor advertising (viz., billboards or hoardings) placed along the road sides.

Whereas advertising offers a long-term image and awareness for the new product, sales promotion offers an incentive to buy the product. Among all the available communication elements, sales promotion is the only method to motivate consumers, traders, and the salespeople at the same time in carrying out sales. Out of the various sales promotion tools that are available, the marketing team selected the following tools—one each for consumers, traders, and dealer salespersons.

- **Consumer Contest** The objectives to be achieved are: (i) to create an interest or excitement and brand awareness, (ii) to build traffic at retail stores, (iii) to encourage brand purchase, and (iv) to attract new customers. Consumers are invited to compete on the basis of their knowledge, skills, or creativity. Participants are required to write a slogan, fill-up the entry form and submit the same to a panel of judges, who will select the best entries. Attractive prizes are given to the selected participants.
- **Display or Promotional Allowance** For this sales promotion, the objectives are (i) to encourage trade to promote the company's new product and (ii) to provide special display at the point-of-purchase. This allowance is given to the dealers for arranging desired display and promotion of the company's products. The allowance is usually a fixed amount per table fan or a percentage deduction from the list price for merchandise ordered during the promotional period.
- **Push Money** The objective here is to motivate the dealers' salespeople to sell more of the company's brand of table fan. In this method of sales promotion, the company pays a fixed amount (say, ₹50 per table/pedestal/wall-mounted fan) to the dealers' salespersons for selling "Breezy" table fans. This payment is known as push money or spiffs.

Personal selling (i.e. selling through the company's salespeople) is also included in the IMC plan. The company must secure distribution, motivate dealers to stock and promote the company's products.

Murli Bhasin called up his sales manager and communication manager to review implementation of the IMC plan, so that the launching of the new table/pedestal/wall-mounted "Breezy" fan would be smooth.

As discussed in the opening vignette, advertising alone is not always adequate to ensure that the company's communications about its products reach consumers. Companies also use sales promotion tools or methods targeted at consumers, intermediaries, and salespeople to distribute their products and to stimulate sales. Most successful companies' integrated marketing communications (IMC) plans include consumer/business sales promotions as well as trade and sales force sales promotions that are coordinated or integrated with advertising, direct marketing, public relations/publicity, and personal selling.

In this chapter, we examine the definition and reasons for increasing importance of sales promotion. We explore the objectives, benefits, and drawbacks of sales promotion. We classify the different types of sales promotions. We also discuss the effects of sales promotions on sales and profits. Thereafter, we will consider how sales promotion can be integrated with the other elements of the communication-mix through integrated marketing communications. Lastly, we check evaluation of sales promotion.

LO 1 Know definition of sales promotion and reasons for importance of sales promotion

DEFINITION OF SALES PROMOTION

As often happens with definitions, there is no single definition of sales promotion that is universally accepted by all. Different experts and bodies have defined sales promotion in different ways. Some selected definitions are given below in order to get an insight into the subject.

According to the *American Marketing Association*, "In a specific sense, sales promotion includes those sales activities that supplement both personal selling and advertising and coordinate them and help to make them effective, such as displays, shows and expositions, demonstrations and other non-recurrent selling efforts, not in the ordinary routine."

As per the definition given by the *Institute of Sales Promotion, UK*, "Sales promotion comprises that range of techniques used to attain sales/marketing objectives in a cost effective manner by adding value to a product or service either to intermediaries or end users normally but not exclusively within a defined time period."

Don E. Schultz and William A. Robinson define it as: "Sales promotion is the direct inducement or incentive to the sales force, the distributor or the consumer, with the primary objective of creating an immediate sale."

According to Philip Kotler, "Sales promotion, a key ingredient in marketing campaigns, consists of a diverse collection of incentive tools, mostly short-term, designed to stimulate quicker and/or greater purchase of particular products or services by consumers or the trade.

From the above definitions, we can conclude that the aim of sales promotion is to achieve sales/marketing objectives that are immediate or short-term. Traditionally, sales promotion is seen as an activity that is not repeated often. However, due to high degree of competition, repeated sales promotion activities have become necessary in some product categories. Sales promotions are done often in current competitive market conditions. Many times, sales promotion is described as **extra-purchase-value (EPV)** and **below-the-line-selling**[1]. It is said that while advertising presents a reason to buy, sales promotion offers an incentive to buy. Sales promotion is a different element in the promotion or communication-mix. It is not only important but also a very effective tool of marketing.

IMPORTANCE OF SALES PROMOTION

Role and importance of sales promotion in a company's integrated marketing communications (IMC) program have increased substantially over the past decade. Not only has the total amount of money spent on sales promotion gone up, but the percentage of promotional or communication budget allocated to sales promotion has grown as well. Some of the major reasons for increasing importance of sales promotion are: (i) growing power of retailers, (ii) many managers focus on short-term sales, (iii) increasing competition, and (iv) consumers' price sensitivity.

Growing Power of Retailers

In recent years, there has been transfer of power from the manufacturers to retailers. Grocery store industry has combined into larger retail chains with greater buying power. These large retail chains put pressure on manufacturers to provide more discounts and allowances. In addition, sophisticated in-store computer systems and optical checkout scanners have enabled retailers to gain access to important and useful data on which products or brands sell. Retailers use this data to demand more discounts and allowances from the manufacturers of lagging brands. Besides, the shelf-space in any retail store is limited and all manufacturers want prime shelf-space in the retailer's showroom. Retailers demand display or merchandise allowances from manufacturers to gain desired shelf-space.

Managers' Focus on Short-Term Sales

The sales managers are under pressure to achieve monthly, quarterly, and yearly sales goals. Salespersons as well as branch or area sales managers receive requests from retailers and wholesalers for additional discounts and allowances. Area or branch sales managers may then put pressure on brand, product, or marketing managers to use sales promotion tools to help them achieve sales volume targets. Compared to any other promotional or communication component, sales promotion is a more effective method to create short-term sales. Hence, many marketing and brand managers depend on sales promotions directed at the consumers, the trade, and the salespeople to achieve short-term sales goals.

Increasing Competition

In Indian business environment, a rapid change is taking place from the "seller's market" to the "buyer's market". This means, the competition is increasing and marketers have to attract and retain customers by uncovering and meeting target customers' needs better than competition. To gain and/or maintain a competitive advantage, manufacturers create innovative sales promotions based on the needs of consumers and intermediaries.

Consumers' Price Sensitivity

Consumers have become more sensitive about prices. Marketers are making more use of sales promotion in their marketing plans because consumers respond positively to the price reductions provided in it. The main reason for increased sensitivity to sales promotion is that they save money in an environment of growing inflation. Another reason is that consumers have become used to sales promotion due to frequent sales promotions carried out by marketers. Some studies have found that up to 70 percent of purchase decisions are made by consumers in the retail stores, where consumers are likely to respond to sales promotions.

LO 2 List the benefits, drawbacks and objectives of sales promotion

BENEFITS AND DRAWBACKS OF SALES PROMOTION

Marketers or sellers use sales promotion methods or tools because they give certain benefits as well as drawbacks to manufacturers, consumers, and traders.

Benefits to Manufacturers

Price Differentiation

By using sales promotion techniques or tools like coupons and discounts, manufacturers can introduce difference in prices of its products and services in particular cities and towns. Manufacturers can also offer price reductions for its products to customers who visit their stalls in trade shows and exhibitions. Farris and Quelch found in their study that manufacturers use sales promotion methods to adjust fluctuations in demand and supply situations, without making any changes in the price-lists of products[2].

Inducing Trial

Manufacturers or selling firms use sales promotion tools to induce trial for new products for prospective customers by lowering the costs of perceived risk[3]. In most cases, a seller gives a free sample to the prospect to induce initial product trial. **For example**, a fruit-seller selling grapes asks the consumer to taste a grape.

Increase in Sales Volume

Compared to any other communication-mix components, sales promotion tools are more effective in giving higher short-term sales volume. When firms are under pressure to increase sales, particularly in the third and fourth quarters of a year, due to shortfalls in actual sales compared to the sales budgeted (or targeted), sales promotions are helpful. It would be possible for companies to measure the impact of sales promotions on sales volume and profit.

Building a Database

Some sales promotion techniques like coupons, consumer contests, and sweepstakes require consumers to provide their demographic profile like name, address, education, and occupation, which can be used for building a database that is useful for direct marketing program.

Easy to Design and Implement, and Less Expensive

Sales promotion methods are relatively easy to design and implement as well as less expensive compared to other promotional elements such as advertising and public relations. Hence, even smaller companies can use sales promotion tools effectively without much help from advertising agencies.

Useful for Small Players

Small manufacturers use sales promotion to increase their market share, in comparison to a product category leader who is interested in the entire product category growth, and has a large advertising budget[4].

Benefits to Consumers

Loyalists versus Switchers

Research has shown that loyal consumers would buy the product even if the price is high, while brand switching consumers (or switchers) would only buy, if the prices are reduced due to sales promotion. Sales promotion tools using price concessions ensure that switchers pay lower prices than loyal consumers[5]. Consumers who switch brands based on sales promotional deals think themselves smart and intelligent.

Price-Sensitive Customers

Due to uncontrolled inflation, customers have generally become more price sensitive. Some consumers look or wait for attractive sales promotional offers from manufactures before buying durable products like color televisions, washing machines, and refrigerators. Marketers use sales promotional tools to reach price-sensitive customers, who may switch brands to get benefits from price concessions[6].

Benefits to Traders

Forward Buying

Many retailers and wholesalers do forward buying. It means buying more quantity or stocking up a product during the sales promotion (or deal) period and reselling it to consumers once the deal or sales promotion period has ended.

New Product Introduction

Retailers or dealers are aware that due to sales promotions more customers get exposed to new products or brands. Some of these customers may buy new brands. Hence, traders consider it less risky to keep stock of new products or brands, which are linked to sales promotions.

Increased Store Traffic

Sales promotional tools used for traders help in increasing visits by customers to the retail stores. Increased customer traffic to the store increases the sales and profits. Some of the large retailers have become so powerful that they demand trade promotions from the manufacturer at the cost of advertising and consumer promotion[7].

Drawbacks to Manufacturers

Reduction in Brand Value

When a manufacturer uses sales promotion techniques too often for a brand, the consumer devalues the brand. Dominant brands should not be on sales promotion for more than 30 percent of the time[8]. Otherwise, there is a risk of decreasing brand loyalty. Hence, manufacturers offer sales promotional deals less frequently for brand leaders. Increasing expenditure on sales promotion has decreasing effect on brand image.

Dilution of Quality Image

For a high-involvement product category like color television continuous sales promotion by a manufacturer could have a negative effect on its quality image. Consumers may perceive that a particular brand is not selling well as the quality may not be good and hence promotional deals are offered. Thus, there is a dilution of the quality image of the brand.

Drawbacks to Consumers

Consumers are Confused

In high-involvement product categories like color television, washing machines or refrigerators when almost all brands offer promotional deals, consumers' perception is that all brands are in the same quality range. The decision-making in selecting a particular brand becomes difficult. Consumers believe that the list price of a product is a fiction. They are not sure of a brand's value. In other words, consumers are confused.

Drawbacks to Traders

Traders become Price-Sensitive

Frequent use of trade promotional tools by manufacturers make traders more price sensitive. A few large retailers demand trade promotions from manufacturers. Forward buying of excessive stocks on quantity discounts can lead to diversion of some of these stocks to non-deal areas.

Increased Competition

Retailers and dealers face increased competition from other intermediaries. They experience pressure from manufacturers for carrying new items and higher level of inventory, promoting different brands by displaying the same, and price reduction as well as "pushing" certain products or brands.

SALES PROMOTION OBJECTIVES

Marketers have different objectives for consumer-oriented sales promotion and trade-oriented sales promotion.

Objectives of Consumer-Oriented Sales Promotions

To Increase Sales

Sales promotions help to increase sales or defend market share for established brands. One way to do this is by giving incentives like a coupon, bonus pack, or price deal to consumers who switch from competing brands.

To encourage Trial and Repurchase

Many new products fail within the first year due to lack of promotional support needed either to encourage initial trial by consumers or to induce repurchase. Initial trial can be increased through sales promotion methods like sampling. The success of a new product or brand also depends on repeat purchase after trial. Sales promotion tools such as coupons or refund offers are often used with a sample to encourage repeat purchase after trial.

To Support Integrated Marketing Communications

Many firms are using integrated marketing communications (IMC) approach. Sales promotion supports the IMC approach for a company or brand.

To Target Specific Segments

Sales promotion tools such as contests, events and samplings are effective to reach specific market segments.

Objectives of Trade-Oriented Sales Promotions

To Encourage Retailers/Dealers to Display

An important objective of trade sales promotion is to encourage retailers or dealers to participate in displays and promotion of a brand. Displays perform services such as reminders to consumers, encourage unplanned purchases and increase sales.

To Support New Product Promotion

Manufactures recognize the limited availability of shelf space in retail stores. They use trade sales promotions to encourage retailers to stock and promote new products or brands.

To Build Channel Partners' Inventories

Manufacturers often build inventories of intermediaries by using trade promotions. This will ensure that channel partners will push products or brands that have high inventory levels. This will also result in intermediaries not running out of stocks of such products.

LO 3 Describe different types of sales promotions

TYPES OF SALES PROMOTIONS

Manufacturers use different types of sales promotions that are directed at consumers, the trade, business customers, and the sales force. These are called consumer promotions, trade promotions, business promotions, sales force promotions. We shall discuss each type of these sales promotions in greater details.

Consumer Promotions

Consumer promotions (also called consumer sales promotions) are directed at consumers. The broad objectives of consumer promotions have been discussed earlier in this chapter.

Consumer promotions should be tied into the integrated marketing communications (IMC) plan so as to make them effective. **For instance**, advertising has a long-term effect in terms of creating awareness and interest, whereas consumer promotions have a short-term effect on consumers. Some of the major tools of consumer promotions are shown in Figure 8.1.

- Samples or sampling
- Coupons or couponing
- Premiums or gifts
- Contests and sweepstakes (or prizes)
- Refunds and rebates
- Price-off or price-cut
- Bonus-packs
- Frequency programs
- Event sponsorship or event marketing
- Point-of-Purchase (POP) displays

Fig. 8.1 Major Consumer Promotion Tools

Samples (or Sampling)

Sampling can be a successful way to stimulate trials and increase sales[9]. 71 percent of consumers in one study said they would try a new product if they liked a sample. Sampling tool is used to encourage consumers to try a new product. Generally, samples are provided free of charge. In business markets also, firms sometimes provide samples of products to prospective customers. Samples are distributed in various ways. Some of the common ways of distributing samples are as follows.

- **In-Store Sampling:** Samples are distributed at the retail stores by setting up booths or tables.
- **Direct or Door-to-Door Sampling:** Samples are distributed at the residences of consumers and are either sent by post or delivered directly. In business marketing, salespeople deliver samples directly to their prospective customers. This method permits selective sample distribution, which is an advantage to the marketer.
- **Response Sampling:** Samples are made available to individuals, households, or business firms, who respond to a media offer made by the marketer on television, a magazine, a journal or the Internet.
- **Media Sampling:** Sample is included in the media outlet. **For instance**, a small sample of detergent can be included in a magazine advertisement in the blister pack attached with a page.

- **Selective Sampling:** Samples are distributed at a site, such as a trade show or sporting event.

The main benefit of sampling is that it is a very effective way to persuade consumers to try a new product. Another benefit is that consumers experience the product or the brand directly, thereby gaining more recognition of its advantages.

The major disadvantage of sampling is that it is one of the most expensive methods of consumer promotion. Another possible disadvantage is that some products need a longer time for consumers to judge. This may require supplying larger quantity to consumers, which manufacturers may not afford. Sampling is effective when it introduces a new product. Samples also help promote a current product to a new market or to new prospective customers. **For example**, free samples of "Promise" toothpaste were distributed to about 100,000 homes in Delhi. Within three months, a tracking study indicated that Promise toothpaste had achieved 17 percent trial rate, a repeat purchase rate of 22 percent, and a market share of 12 percent in Delhi city[10]. Criteria for effective sampling are: (i) low unit value, (ii) short purchase cycle, and (iii) divisible products broken in to small sample sizes. That is why manufacturers of packaged-products like food, cosmetics, health care, and toiletries are main users of sampling.

Coupons (or Couponing)

A coupon is a price reduction offer, generally in the form of a certificate, to a consumer. A coupon can be redeemed or exchanged for a price-off, a gift or a discount on the subsequent purchase. Some of the most preferred methods of distributing coupons are: (i) print media, that is inserting coupons in advertisements in newspapers and magazines, (ii) direct mail, (iii) enclosing in other products or attaching to them (also described as "on/in-package"), and (iv) through retailers.

❍ **Types of Coupons** Some of the major types of coupons are: (i) instant redemption coupon, (ii) bounce-back coupons, (iii) scanner-delivered coupons, (iv) cross-ruff coupons and (v) response offer coupons.

In an **instant redemption coupon,** as the name suggests, the consumer can immediately redeem the coupon (i.e. exchange the coupon for goods or money) while making the purchase. These coupons are placed on/in-packages (i.e. on the outside or inside of the package) and are distributed often in retail shops. The instant redemption coupons are used for purchase of additional packages of a product and for trial purchases of a new brand. The *main advantages* are that customers can use them immediately, the manufacturer has virtually no distribution costs, and redemption rate is high.

In case of **bounce-back coupons,** coupons are placed inside packages so that customers can not redeem them immediately. The objective of this type of coupon is to encourage the customer for repeat purchase of the product, since the coupon placed inside the package offers a price reduction.

Scanner-delivered coupons are issued at the cash register in a retail shop. These coupons are caused when a product item is scanned. Typically when the competitors' product item is scanned, the company's coupon is issued to the consumer. This approach encourages brand switching. **For example**, Coca-Cola™ gave coupon for Diet Coke™ to everyone buying Coke™ at certain supermarkets.

In **cross-ruffing,** a coupon for one product is placed on the package of another product. Cross-ruff coupons should be on products that fit together normally and that these products are purchased and consumed or used at the same time. For instance, Britannia Industries may place a coupon for butter on a package of bread. Companies with wide products lines often use these coupons.

Response offer coupons are issued on requests made by customers. Customers' requests may be received by phone or mail. Coupons are then distributed through e-mails or sales representatives. Response offer coupons are used for both household and business customers. **For example**, furniture suppliers may use response offer coupons for household and business customers, either based on their requests or invite them to make the purchase.

There are many *advantages* of coupons. Coupons can help in persuading consumers to try an existing or a new product. Coupons encourage repeat purchase of brands by regular consumers, new users or infrequent users. A large number of prospective customers can be reached with coupons in a short time. Coupons encourage brand switching. Manufacturers of existing products can make use of coupons to pre-empt a competitor introducing a new product in the market. This strategy can be used by manufacturers of toilet soaps, tooth paste, razor blades, and shaving cream.

One of the *disadvantages* of use of coupons is that imitation can take place when coupons are copied and sent to the manufacturers for reimbursement. Coupon frauds can also occur when coupons are redeemed through a fraudulent retail shop that does not exist. Sometimes, wrong redemption of coupons happens because of the error by the sales clerk who does not check the size of the product properly and allows the discount for another size of the product. Since an average supermarket redeems a large number of coupons, there are possibilities of mistakes, imitations, and frauds.

❍ **Key Factors** Let us now consider the important factors that make coupons as an attractive tool of consumer promotion. First factor is that the coupons should be for the preferred brand or the brand that is readily recalled by consumers. Consumers find coupons for such brands more attractive than coupons for unknown brands[11]. The second key factor is the face value of the coupon. If the coupon face value is higher, it is more attractive to consumers, who are more likely to redeem it. Third is the distribution method. Consumers prefer distribution of coupons through newspaper "free standing inserts" (FSI), which allow them to choose coupons in privacy of their homes. Consumers generally do not like distribution of coupons in the store, as they don't want to make decisions on choice of coupons while shopping.

Many retailers develop stronger relationships with those manufactures who use coupons as consumer promotional tool. This is because the coupons bring more consumers into the retail store which results in higher sales volume. Besides, the coupons have no direct cost to the retailer.

Premiums (or Gifts)

A premium (or a gift) is a reward given to the consumer for purchasing a product or service. When a company offers a premium, the consumer pays full price for the product. The premium may be free or available at a price lower than the usual market price. If a manufacturer selects the right type of premium, it can improve the brand image. The major types of premium are: (i) in/on-package, (ii) free-in-the-mail,(iii) self-liquidating, and (iv) store or manufacturer premiums.

- **In/on-Package Premiums** These are often free small gifts that are hidden inside the package so that the consumer must buy the particular brand or product to find out which gift or premium the package has. Sometimes, the gift is fixed on the package, such as an attractive pet jar free with the pack of Bru Coffee – Chicory mixture, as shown in Figure 8.2. These premiums (or gifts) are related to the product. **Examples** are toothbrush with toothpaste, blades with razor.

Fig. 8.2

- **Free in-the-Mail Premiums** These gifts are received by the consumer after the proof of purchase are mailed to the manufacturer. Sometimes more than one purchase is required to receive the free gift. The disadvantage is that in-the-mail premiums do not offer immediate reward to the purchaser.

- **Self-Liquidation Premiums** In this type of premium, consumers pay some or all of the cost of the premium, including shipping and handling. The manufacturer offers a gift for a particular amount to be paid by the consumer along with the proof of purchase of the product. It is called self-liquidating premium because the consumer pays the amount towards the costs of the premium and mailing. The drawback in this premium is that it has a very low redemption rate.

- **Store or Manufacturer Premium** These gifts are given by either the manufacturer or the retail store when the customer purchases a product. **For example**, the new Boost brand (a trade mark of Glaxo SmithKline Consumer Healthcare Ltd.) offered a free skipping rope along with a price reduction of ₹7 for a 500 g jar at M.R.P. (maximum retail price) of ₹135.00 and the photograph with a signature of the brand endorser, Sachin Tendulkar, as shown in Figure 8.3.

Fig. 8.3

The advantages are that premiums are good methods of adding value to a product or a brand. They strengthen the image of the brand. Premiums can attract new consumers and can give "thank you" message to the existing customers. If the premium is selected with care, it is often more appealing to consumers than a discount.

To make premium program more effective, the premium or the gift should match the target audience. **For instance**, the Boost sales promotion program offered a free skipping rope to its target audience—the school going children. The second important point to be taken care of is that the premium should be tied to the company's product. In Figure 8.2, it is shown that a free and attractive pet jar was tied to the Hindustan Unilever's Bru brand of Coffee – Chicory mixture. The third point to make a premium program successful is that the quality of the gift should be good and consumers strongly want to have it. Premium programs should be integrated with other elements of integrated marketing communications (IMC).

The drawbacks of premium programs are their high cost and short lifespans. Some companies have huge stocks of unused premiums in their warehouses because either the premium item is not liked by consumers or the redemption rate is very low. If the premium is not liked by usual consumers, it may reduce the product sales. High cost of a premium may not increase profits, but can strengthen the brand image.

Contests and Sweepstakes (or Prizes)

The success of contests and sweepstakes depend on how attractive are the prizes. Both are used in consumer markets and business markets. Target audience participates in the contests or sweepstakes if they perceive that the prizes are desirable. Prizes may include a trip abroad, substantial cash prizes or a car. Contests and sweepstakes create enthusiasm and excitement in consumers due to the "instant-millionaire syndrome".

Contests normally require participants to buy the product and send the product wrapper or barcode as a proof of purchase. The participants are required to perform some activity, such as completion of a sentence or a slogan, which may say: "I like the product or brand 'x' because ..." A panel of judges selects the winners based on who provides the most appropriate answers. An **example** of a consumer contest was from British Airways in which first the advertisement on the contest was released in mainline daily newspapers in main cities like Delhi, Mumbai, Kolkata, Chennai, Bengaluru, and Hyderabad on the day of the contest. The participant had to watch the TV commercial that evening and answer a series of five questions based on the commercial. Then the participant had to complete the statement: "I like the British Airways Commercial because ..." and send the entry within a week. The winner of the contest received two free tickets to London.

In **sweepstakes**, participants do not have to purchase the product. Companies are permitted to restrict consumers to one entry per visit to the store. The chances of winning sweepstakes are based on probability factor. Entrants need to submit their names and addresses for the prize drawing. Official entry forms as well as hand-written entries are permitted. Winners are decided by selecting names at random for prizes from entry forms.

The problems linked to contests and sweepstakes are on their effectiveness and high level of expenditure. Consumers get many gambling opportunities such as state lotteries, casinos, and the internet gambling. As a result, contests and sweepstakes offering prizes may not be exciting or interesting. Expenditures connected to contests and sweepstakes include supportive advertising, POP (point-of-purchase) displays, contest-related materials, and prizes. Failure to incur the expenditure may minimize the chance of success.

Factors that contribute to the success of contests and sweepstakes are: (i) instant prize to winners, (ii) highly rewarding and exciting if well planned and executed, and (iii) effective integration of contests and sweepstakes with advertising, POP displays, and other communication elements, as a part of integrated marketing communications.

Refunds and Rebates

Refunds and rebates provide price reduction after purchase by the manufacturer to consumers or business customers. The consumer sends the proof of purchase for the product or service to the manufacturer who then refunds a part of the purchase price.

A **refund** offers a price reduction on "soft goods", such as food or clothing. Generally, value of refunds is small. **For example**, a computer magazine, *Chip*, offered a refund of ₹350 on enrolling for one year. **Rebates** are widely used for consumer durables like automobiles, televisions, and computers, which are "hard goods". Rebates can also be given on services like software services. Rebates are normally larger in value because they are given on major ticket items. However, the *Random House Dictionary* defines a refund as repayment of total money paid for purchase and a rebate as a repayment or return of only part of the money paid for purchase. In marketing, both these terms are used interchangeably. Refunds and rebates can be used to introduce new products, reward loyal consumers, increase purchase frequency, and encourage brand switching.

A study of consumer perceptions found perceived difficulties linked to the redemption process followed in rebates[12]. Consumers do not want to save cash receipts and proofs of purchase, fill out forms, and mail in the offer. Another study has found that many retailers have become unhappy with rebates due to the burden and expense of administering them[13].

To make refunds and rebates effective, the manufacturer should make the refund or rebate program visible to consumers through a promotional or advertising campaign. Also the refund and rebate should be perceived by consumers as reward for purchase. **For example**, Maruti Suzuki announced a gift cheque of ₹30,000 as a loyalty reward on purchase of a Maruti Esteem car, if the family already owned any other Maruti car. The offer was valid for a month only.

Price-offs (or Price-Cut)

It offers a temporary price reduction to consumers. Typically price-offs are marked on the product packages and are in the range from 10 to 50 percent off on the regular price. The price reduction comes out of the manufacturer's profit margin, not the retailer's.

Fig. 8.4

If price-offs are given by the manufacturer, it ensures that the price reduction reaches the consumer rather than the retailer. Price-offs normally stimulate sales of the existing product and encourage consumers to purchase larger quantities. Price discounts or price-offs are communicated to the consumers through advertisements in newspapers, magazines and television as well as at the point-of-purchase. One example of price-off is shown in Figure 8.4 from NEERU's ladies wear, including saris, in an advertisement, with up to 50 percent off that appeared in a popular magazine.

Price-off programs may increase the sales, but it can hurt long-term profits[14]. Hence, firms should not depend too much on price-offs to increase sales. Besides, too many price-off offers can damage the company's image and may encourage consumers to become more price sensitive.

To make price-off programs more effective, it is better to give price-off on product items which have higher mark-ups or contributions to profits. The objective of the price-off program should be to get new customers. The main advantage of a price-off offer is that consumers get immediate reward of a saving in money, unlike other sales promotional tools such as rebates, contests, and sweepstakes, where they have to wait for the reward. The advantage to the manufacturer is the flexibility in selecting the market area and the product item in which the discount offer will be given. The disadvantage is that if competitors announce a similar discount offer, it will trigger a price war. Another disadvantage is that price discount can make customers suspicious about the quality of the product.

Bonus-Packs

A bonus-pack (also known as price-pack) offers the consumer an extra amount of a product at the regular price by providing extra units. This gives the consumer more value for money. For instance, AXE Denim brand offered a bonus pack with 30 percent extra lather shaving cream to consumers at the regular price of ₹55.00, as shown in Figure 8.5.

Fig. 8.5

The brand AXE Denim was introduced by Hindustan Unilever Ltd. (HUL).

Advantages of a bonus pack are as follows:

- It provides more value to consumers, in a direct way and hence, it can have a strong influence on the purchase decision of the consumer.
- It can prevent a competitor's promotion of a new brand.
- It rewards customer loyalty by offering them free merchandise.

Some studies have shown that consumers are doubtful about offers of bonus packs[15]. When the bonus is large (**for example**, two shirts for the price of one shirt), consumers perceive that the price was first increased to make up for the additional quantity. When the bonus is relatively small (**for instance**, three shirts for the price of two shirts), consumers think the bonus was not attractive enough. Another problem is that bonus packs normally need additional shelf space for which retailers do not get any extra profit margins. However, retailers are benefited as bonus packs may result in larger purchase orders through the retail outlet[16]. Bonus packs are generally popular with consumers because they get additional product at the same price.

Frequency (or Loyalty) Programs

Frequency, loyalty, or continuity programs are one of the most popular sales promotion tools. The program is designed to motivate consumers to make repeat purchases. This is particularly suitable for products and services where consumers see little difference between brands. The airline industry has a little brand loyalty. To gain loyalty of existing customers, American Airline was one of the first major companies to introduce frequent-flyer program in 1981. The customer, in this program, earns certain points on each flight, which can be used for a free upgrade or a free ticket. Since then frequency programs have become common in various product and service categories, such as hospitality, travel, and retailing. Many retailers have loyalty programs that offer consumers a chance to accumulate points that can be redeemed for rewards. The focus is to build retail store loyalty by rewarding frequent shoppers.

❍ **Reasons (or Objectives) of Frequency Programs** There are a number of reasons why frequency programs are popular. These are: (i) to develop loyalty among the existing customers. Many marketers understand the importance of retaining the existing customers and building relationship with them, (ii) to develop databases consisting of useful information about their customers' characteristics, needs, and locations. These databases can be used for cross-selling (i.e. selling other products and services) to existing customers, (iii) to match or preempt the competitor's frequency program. This helps to retain the existing customer, which is cheaper than getting a new customer.

Frequency programs from companies vary from simple to complex. Generally successful programs are simple to understand and use. Loyalty programs do not appeal to those customers who want immediate rewards. Also, these programs lack excitement, which consumers experience in contests and sweepstakes.

Event Marketing or Event Sponsorship

Event marketing and event sponsorship have become popular in recent years as consumer-oriented sales promotions. Although these two terms are often used interchangeably, there is a difference between them.

Event marketing takes place when a company or brand is linked to a specific event. This includes some type of the company's physical presence, such as a booth or display at the event. Marketers do event marketing by associating their products or services with some popular events like a sporting event, a musical concert or festival. Companies like General Motors and Philip Morris spend huge money on event marketing in USA. In India, the Times of India group pioneered "Femina Miss India Contest" and "Lakme Fashion Week", which are some of the examples of event marketing.

In the **event sponsorship**, a company develops sponsorship relationship with a specific event. The company provides financial support to the event and in return gets the right to display a brand name, an advertising message, or a logo. By sponsoring an event, the company gets the opportunity to do free publicity. It can also improve the company's image. **For instance**, Sahara Group in India was the sponsor of Indian Cricket team for several years. The brand "Sahara" was displayed prominently on the players' attire whenever the Indian cricket team played international matches in all forms (i.e. Test, one-day, and T20) of cricket matches.

To ensure a successful event sponsorship, a company should take the following steps.

- Develop an integrated marketing communication (IMC) program.
- Decide marketing, communication and sponsoring event's objectives.
- Select the event that matches with the target market segments.

- Use the event to place the company name, logo, and product or service information in the brochure and advertisements for the event.
- Distribute samples or let the consumer experience the product or service at the event.
- Evaluate if the event objectives are achieved and also the investment in the event.

❍ **Event Marketing Agencies** Due to increasing popularity of event marketing, event marketing agencies have come up to plan, execute, and evaluate events. Agencies like Nimbus and Madison have specialized in sports events, and Wizcraft International in glamorous events such as film awards and beauty contests.

Point-of-Purchase (POP) Displays

POP displays take place at the point-of-purchase or point-of-sale in retail stores at a place where they will be noticed. POP displays are the important promotional tools because they are the last chance for the manufacturer to reach the consumer[17]. The reasons for doing POP displays are to attract attention, inform, persuade, and remind consumers about certain brands.

Point-of-Purchase materials, displays or advertising include posters, danglers, banners, stand-up racks, brand logos, product dispensers and the like. POP displays are effective for increasing sales. Studies have shown that 70 percent of the decisions about the brands for all products are made in the retail store. In many instances, POP displays influence the buying decision, including impulse or unplanned purchases.

The major users of POP display materials are apparel, food, and sporting goods retailers. Retailers prefer POP displays that provide information and educate consumers. Retailers are generally not interested in promoting a few brands, but instead want to increase the total sales and profits of the retail store. Hence, sometimes retailers do not use POP materials supplied by manufacturers by giving reasons like inappropriate for the store, incorrect size, or poorly built displays. This may result in a waste of money for the manufacturer. It is, therefore, necessary that manufacturers should consider retailers' preferences on POP displays. In addition, POP displays should be integrated with current advertising and promotional messages. Manufacturers should also try to develop customized, reusable, and easy to stock POP displays.

Effectiveness of POP displays should be measured. One such method is to tie-up the POP display with a point-of-sale (POS) cash register. Retail stores measure sales before and during a POP display program. This method helps both the manufacturers and the retailers to test market and identify the POP display that has the highest impact on the sales.

Trade Promotions

The trade promotions (or trade sales promotions) are directed at resellers, such as distributors, wholesalers, dealers, and retailers. Trade promotions are a part of "push strategy" of the manufacturer. Studies have shown that manufacturers spend more funds on trade promotions than consumer promotions[18]. Many manufacturers want to reduce expenditures on trade promotions, but they are unable to do so because of resistance from resellers, pressures from their competitors as well as from their own sales managers, and the effect on sales and profits. In fact, the growing power of large retailers has increased the ability of retailers to demand more trade promotion, which is at the cost of consumer promotion and advertising[19]. Manufacturers hope to obtain some benefits or achieve various objectives by offering trade promotions to resellers. We have earlier, in this chapter, discussed the objectives, benefits, and drawbacks with respect to trade sales promotions.

Challenges in Managing Trade Promotions

Manufacturers often face a number of difficulties with trade promotions. First, many retailers and wholesalers do **forward buying**, that is buying large quantities and stocking up during the promotional (or lower price) period and reselling the same after the manufacturer's promotional period. Second, retailers and wholesalers do **diverting**, i.e. buying more quantities of products by taking advantage of the low price promotional deal and then selling some of the products purchased at low price to stores or intermediaries outside the deal area. Third, sometimes retailers do not do certain things that they agreed to do. Despite these challenges, trade promotions have importance in the present market context.

Types of Trade Promotions

Manufacturers use a variety of trade promotional tools for persuading resellers. We shall discuss major types of trade promotions. These are shown in Figure 8.6.

Trade allowances
Trade contests
Trade incentives
Training programs
Trade shows
Cooperative advertising

Fig. 8.6 Major Trade Promotion Tools

❍ **Trade Allowances** One of the major types of trade promotion is called trade allowances that are offered to wholesalers and retailers as financial incentives in order to encourage them to purchase, promote or display the manufacturer's products. The types of trade allowances are: (i) off-invoice allowance, (ii) slotting allowance, (iii) promotional allowances, (iv) drop-ship allowance, and (v) exit fees.

Off-Invoice Allowance (or buying allowance) It is a discount offered to channel members in the form of an off-invoice allowance. Off-invoice allowances are offered on each case ordered by resellers or a percentage is deducted from the invoice. A buying allowance, which is tied with the purchase of certain minimum quantity of the product, can also take the form of free goods. The reseller gets extra cases free with the purchase of specific number of cases. **For instance**, one free case for every ten cases purchased. Buying allowance, off-invoice allowance, or free goods forms of trade promotions are used commonly for a number of reasons. They are effective way in giving support to intermediaries to purchase the manufacturer's products. They are easy to understand and implement. The manufacturer expects wholesalers and retailers to pass the price reduction to consumers, resulting in higher sales.

Slotting Allowance This allowance is paid by the manufacturer to retailers to handle the new product. Slotting allowance or fees are also called **stocking allowance, introductory allowance,** or **street money**. Retailers and manufacturers have different view points on the slotting allowance, which is demanded by retailers from manufacturers for agreeing to handle a new product.

Retailers justify charging slotting fees based on the following points. First, retailers argue about the additional costs they have to incur for accommodating new products. These costs include inventory carrying, redesigning or rearranging store shelves, entering new products into their computers, and training or briefing store employees on the new products[20]. Many new product introductions fail and hence, retailers make a loss on the investment on the new products. Second, adding a new product means reducing the shelf space allocated to other product or deleting another product. Third, slotting fees force manufacturers to carry out test marketing. This step would reduce the number of new products introduced each year and thereby reducing the number of new product failures.

Manufacturers feel that slotting fees are unfair and too high. Small manufacturers cannot afford to pay slotting fees. The findings of a study on slotting fees pointed out that slotting fees lead to higher retail prices, are applied in an unjust manner, and place small companies in a situation of disadvantage[21].

Promotional Allowances In many cases, manufacturers give retailers (or dealers) allowances or discounts for participating in advertising and sales support activities. Also called **display or advertising allowances or merchandising allowances,** these allowances are given for advertising the manufacturer's products or brands in the local newspapers, arranging special displays, and carrying out promotional programs in the retail store. Most manufacturers mention in the agreements with retailers, dealers, or distributors regarding the activities to be performed to be able to receive the promotional or merchandising allowances. These allowances are given as discount (or deduction) from the list (or basic) price or a fixed amount per case during the specific promotional period.

Drop-Ship Allowance This allowance is paid by the manufacturer to retailers for bypassing a wholesaler or a distributor when orders are placed. Retailers are expected to pass the savings to customers by lowering the prices, instead of keeping a larger margin. By dispatching goods directly, the manufacturer may develop a stronger relationship with the retailer, but this may result in unsatisfactory relationships with the wholesaler or the distributor. Hence, drop-ship allowance should be handled with care.

Exit Fees Manufacturers pay exit fees to retailers to remove a product item from retailer's shelves (or inventory). This is often done when the manufacturer wants to introduce a new model or a new size of an existing product. **For instance**, Crompton Greaves introduced a new size 36'' ceiling fan to the existing sizes from 42'' to 60'', which were already in the retailer's inventory. The risk of introducing a new size is lower than that of a new product. Hence, instead of charging a slotting allowance, the retailer asks for exit fees. In order to accommodate a new size of an existing product, the retailer has to remove one of the existing product items from the inventory.

❍ **Trade Contests** Manufacturers achieve sales goals by using trade contests which are directed towards salespeople of retailers, distributors or wholesalers. Monetary rewards are given to the salespeople for selling the manufacturer's products. These payments are also known as **spiffs** or **push money**. Sometimes the contest prizes or rewards are valuable merchandise such as televisions, washing machines, or stereos, which are given for selling the manufacturer's brand over competing brands. Trade contests work well if they are restricted to exclusive dealers like in two- and four-wheeler automobile industry.

- **Trade Incentive** It includes cash payments to the retailers' salespeople. **For example**, a manufacturer of washing machine may offer ₹400 per washing machine to salespersons who sell the manufacturer's brand instead of brands of other manufacturers. Many retailers or dealers do not allow their salespeople to participate in the manufacturer-sponsored contests because they want their salespeople to sell the brand that meets the customer's needs, rather than pushing the brand that serves the salesperson's personal interest.

- **Training Programs** Manufacturers often conduct sales training programs for salespersons of retailers or dealers. These training programs are conducted at the locations of retailers to provide information about the product features and advantages over competitors' brands, particularly for high-value products like computers, washing machines, and cars. Because of additional knowledge of the manufacturer's brand, the retail salespeople are more likely to sell the manufacturer's brand instead of other competitors' brands. These training sessions are conducted by the manufacturer's trainers for salespeople of retailers, dealers, and distributors.

Many manufacturers ask their own salespersons to provide sales training to retail salespersons as they meet retail sales staff during their regular sales visits to retailers or dealers. The training includes updating retail sales staff on changes in product-mix, benefits or advantages over competitors' products, selling tips and other relevant information. Some manufacturers provide video cassettes, product brochures, and other relevant materials to retailers' salespeople, who can use the information to answer customers' queries.

- **Trade Shows** Trade shows, trade fairs, and exhibitions are an important form of sales promotion. Many industry associations make arrangements for trade shows and exhibitions every year. For example, Indian Machine Tools Manufacturers' Association (IMTMA), and Indian Electrical and Electronic Manufacturers' Association (IEEMA) hold annual trade shows in India. Worldwide, over 5,000 trade shows or trade fairs take place each year with about 100 million people visiting the same. National and international trade shows are attended by thousands of buyers. International companies attending Indian trade shows have increased in recent years. As international attendees are often senior executives with authority to make decisions on purchases, more meeting spaces and conference centers are made available at the international trade show[22]. Trade shows are particularly important for business marketing companies.

Manufacturers or suppliers participating in trade shows buy the required space to set up their booths, arrange displays and demonstrations of their products. Trade show participants expect several *benefits* such as identifying prospective customers, generating sales leads, introducing new products, meeting existing customers, booking orders, and gathering competitive information. A study has shown that trade shows generate product awareness and can have a measurable economic return[23].

Marketers of consumer products also have stalls in local trade fairs and trade shows in order to increase their sales. **For instance**, manufacturers of household furniture, tiles, bathroom fittings, and furnishing have booths in "inside-outside" exhibitions, which are held every year. Consumers visit these exhibitions or trade fairs in large numbers as they become opportunities for family outings. The social aspect of trade shows is that some companies use them to entertain key customers and develop relationships with important intermediaries.

Because there are a large number of trade shows, a manufacturer should select a trade show based on two criteria. One criterion is whether the trade show fits with the firm's objectives and the second is whether the trade show attendees match with the profile of the manufacturer's customers. One approach is to talk to the manufacturer's customers to know which trade shows they visit.

❍ **Cooperative Advertising** In cooperative advertising the cost of advertising is shared by more than one company. There are three types of cooperative advertising: (i) horizontal cooperative advertising, (ii) vertical cooperative advertising, and (iii) ingredient-sponsored cooperative advertising. Only the vertical cooperative advertising is the trade oriented promotion.

Horizontal Cooperative Advertising It is sponsored by a group of retailers or other firms who provide certain products or services to the market. *For instance,* dealers or retailers located along the same road near each other sometimes give a part of their promotional budgets to cooperative advertising fund.

Vertical Cooperative Advertising It is the trade-oriented promotion. Here the manufacturer reimburses the retailer a percentage (generally 50/50 basis) of the advertising costs connected with advertising the manufacturer's products in the retailer's advertisements for local markets. However, the retailer should follow certain guidelines regarding cooperative advertising issued by the manufacturer in order to receive the reimbursement. These guidelines may include size, content, and format of the advertisement and that competing products should not be included in the ads. Some manufacturers prepare the ad material themselves and give the same to the retailer for placing in the local media. To find out the correctness of the retailer's claim on reimbursement, the manufacturer asks for the proof of ads. Use of the internet for keeping track of cooperative advertising process has increased[24]. Manufacturers or their advertising agencies have been using the internet to make it possible for retailers to know the guidelines of cooperative ads, to submit claims online, and to download the manufacturer's logos and formats.

Both manufacturers and retailers are benefited from cooperative advertising due to additional advertising at reduced costs. Most cooperative ads are linked to retailers' purchases. Cooperative ads appear often in various media for consumers as well as for business customers.

Ingredient-Sponsored Cooperative Advertising This is encouraged by the manufacturers of raw materials and component parts. The main purpose of ingredient-sponsored cooperative advertising is to help in successful promotion of the customer's end product which includes the manufacturer's raw material and/or component parts. Many raw materials or components suppliers use this type of cooperative advertising. One of the most successful and **well-known example** is the **Intel inside** theme-based cooperative advertising program. Intel offered a cooperative fund to all PC makers that place the Intel logo on their computers. The accrued co-operative fund could be used to pay up to 66 percent of the cost of a print advertisement or 50 percent of the cost of a broadcast ad. About 1400 PC makers, including the top 10 PC makers took advantage of the Intel co-operative advertising programme[25].

Business Promotions

In business marketing or business-to-business marketing, the *objectives* of using sales or business promotion tools are: (i) gathering sales (or business) leads, (ii) rewarding business customers, (iii) impressing customers, (iv) establishing contacts with prospective customers, (v) building long-term relationships with key customers, and (vi) introducing new products.

Major business promotion tools (or methods) are shown in Figure 8.7.

- Trade shows (or exhibitions)
- Promotional novelties (or gifts)
- Seminars
- Demonstration
- Catalogs

Fig. 8.7 Major Business Promotion Tools

Trade Shows or Exhibitions

We have discussed earlier about trade shows in trade promotions and the same is applicable here in business promotion.

Promotional Novelties/Specialty Advertising/Gift

Promotional novelties or products, also known as specialty advertising or gifts, are useful items bearing an advertising message and/or the brand name of the product or the company. It is given free. Promotional products are used to introduce new products, thank a customer for support, or strengthen the name of the company, its product or service.

Specialty advertising or promotional gifts include writing instruments (like pens, pencils, highlighters), apparels (such as T-shirts, golf shirts), calendars, and so on. These gifts are distributed by salespeople, via direct mail campaigns or at trade shows. Specialty gifts should be unique and of good quality so as to strengthen business relationships and communications with existing and prospective customers. A study has shown that inclusion of a specialty gift item in a thank-you letter can improve customers' attitudes towards a company's sales representatives by 34 percent and towards the company by 52 percent[26]. A major advantage of specialty advertising or promotional novelties is its ability to supplement other integrated marketing communications (IMC) programs, such as personal selling, trade shows, and direct-mail effectively due to its low cost and repeat exposures. Another advantage is that it creates goodwill in the customers. However, a poorly designed promotional gift may affect the company's image.

Seminars

Business marketers conduct technical (or educational) seminars for buying companies about state-of-the-art developments. Major advantages of conducting technical seminars are creating a favorable image about the company and establishing contacts with technical people (from design, research and development, production, maintenance, and quality control functions) who are not only the buying centre (or purchase committee) members but also key influential members in buying committees in customer firms.

Typically in seminars, audio-visual presentations are made by the technical experts of the selling firm. This is followed by a discussion or question-answer session on technical matters. The participants, who are the technical people from buying companies, are thereafter invited for a meal or refreshment.

Demonstration

Product demonstration in business marketing is done at the trade shows, during sales presentations, at the supplier's manufacturing unit, at the third-party, the existing customer's premises or in demonstration advertising. A product or service demonstration is particularly effective when the prospective industrial buyer is buying a high-cost equipment or machine for the first time (i.e., new purchase situation). In demonstration, a product or service is shown in actual use. This can be very effective in convincing the prospective customers about the benefits and performance of the product. Sometimes TV is used as a medium to demonstrate a product in action. Demonstration advertising is planned to give an example of the benefits of the product or service by showing it in actual use.

Catalogs

Apart from the traditional hard copies, Catalogs are now available on the internet. By putting the Catalogs online, marketers save substantial printing and mailing costs. In addition, selling firms have better access to consumers and business customers as well as global customers. Many direct marketing firms have found that combining catalogs and websites can be an effective way to sell.

Catalogs are of either general or specific type. A general catalogue is used by companies who have extensive product categories and product items. It contains brief information about all products of the company. A specific type catalog or leaflet contains detailed information about the specific products in which a particular group of customers are interested. Catalogs should include information that buyers need, such as product specifications, applications, performance data, drawings, service requirements, and prices. There are some websites that facilitate e-commerce by publishing e-catalogs. **For example**, indiainfo.com has e-catalogs for products like books, toys, watches, jewelry, apparel, and so on.

Maintaining and updating mailing list or customer data-base is important for all marketing companies who want to distribute their product catalogs. Sales persons and trade shows are the other methods of distributing catalogs. Catalogs may themselves have to be updated to reflect the changes in the suppliers' products and services.

Sales Force Promotions

When sales promotional activities are directed at the salespeople, it is called sales force sales promotions or sales force promotions. The main objective of sales force promotions is to improve the performance of the sales force. Other objectives are: (i) to increase sales volume, (ii) reduce the selling cost, (iii) promote new products, (iv) book more orders, (v) develop prospective customers' list, and (vi) build up morale and enthusiasm.

Some of the major tools or methods of sales force promotions are shown in Figure 8.8.

- Sales contests
- Incentive schemes
- Sales meetings
- Training programs
- Sales manuals

Fig. 8.8 Major Sales Force Promotion Tools

Sales Contests

These contests are meant for the company sales people, who are asked to increase the sales volume over their sales quotas (or targets) in order to win prizes. These prizes could be substantial cash rewards, paid vacations (or trips) within or outside the country, medals or merit certificates. Sales contests are typically held for a short-period of about three months or one quarter. Salespeople get a share of excitement when the contest is well planned and executed. The success of a contest depends largely on the selection of prizes and prize structure. Designing a contest requires a long lead time. However, the contest should be announced to the sales people just a few days before the start of the contest to prevent any manipulations by salespeople.

Incentive Schemes

Most companies have incentive schemes for their salespeople. Incentive schemes are meant to encourage salespeople to put in more efforts so as to increase their actual sales more than their respective sales targets or goals. The incentive scheme is a part of the variable component of their compensation package, which is about 20 to 40 percent of the total compensation package. The other component is the fixed salary of the salesperson which is paid without any linkage to the performance. The incentive scheme is linked to the performance of the salesperson who is paid extra money if he exceeds the sales targets.

Sales Meetings

A sales meeting is an important method for communication, education, and motivation. Sales meetings are held at district, branch, or regional levels. Generally, sales meetings provide a social occasion for the salespeople to identify with a larger group, to meet and talk with senior executives of the company, and give a break from routine jobs. Successful branch, district, or area managers regularly hold sales meetings for salespeople to motivate them.

Training Programs

One of the objectives of training programs is to improve the sales force productivity. Today, new salespersons (or sales trainees) spend a few weeks to several months in training. For industrial products marketing firms, the training period is on an average 28 weeks; companies that market services, it is 12 weeks; and for consumer products selling firms, the training period is 4 weeks. Training is given not only to new sales trainees, but also to experienced salespersons in their areas of deficiencies like negotiating skills, product knowledge, or managing customer relationship. **For example**, at IBM initial sales training is given to new sales persons, and continuing training is given every year to experienced salespeople. Since the main purpose of many training programs is to teach sales trainees to sell or improve current selling skills, the training program's content includes selling skills and product knowledge as major topics.

Sales Manuals

Depending on the type of products manufactured and marketed by the company, sales manual may be short or long. **For instance**, a company manufacturing technical product like electrical switchgear, the sales manual may go up to many pages. Sales manual normally include product specifications, applications, manufacturing and quality control processes, technical drawings, and so on. This information is useful to sales people during sales presentations and negotiations with customers. Salespeople do receive updated information on various aspects over a period of time for inclusion in the sales manuals.

LO 4 Discuss the effects of sales promotions on sales and profits

EFFECT OF SALES PROMOTION ON SALES AND PROFITS

The effect of sales promotion on sales can be understood from the fact that many sales and marketing professionals when faced with the problem of stagnating sales or lower than targeted sales use sales promotion tools to achieve the desired sales volume. Studies have also found that up to 70 percent of purchase decisions are made in retail stores, where consumers are likely to respond to sales promotion methods[27]. Consumers are becoming more responsive to sales promotion offers from manufacturers and retailers because they save money.

Sales promotion motivates consumers with attractive offers of coupons, refunds, or price-offs that save money. Sales promotion also provides financial incentives to intermediaries like wholesalers and retailers to stock and promote a manufacturer's products. By providing incentives through sales promotion tools to consumers and traders, manufacturers aim at speeding up the selling process and increasing sales volume[28]. Many firms' integrated marketing communication (IMC) programs include consumer, trade, business, and sales force sales promotions that are integrated with advertising, direct marketing, personal selling, publicity and public relations. Effects of sales promotions on sales can also be explored by analyzing the following four factors: (i) increased purchase of a product category, (ii) quick or delayed purchase, (iii) brand switching, and (iv) repeat purchasing.

Increased Product Category Purchase

Some sales promotion tools raise the level of demand by creating new occasions for purchase. Purchase of a product category goes up sharply in certain situations. **For example**, an appealing display of "Milkmaid", a condensed milk brand, and a free recipe book given on purchase of two packs, increased the consumption rate of the product. Consumers are persuaded to try different recipes. In some other cases, a purchase occasion is created if a sales promotion offer lowers the price of the product below the customer's price limit. Examples of high-involvement products such as automobiles, washing machines, and refrigerators can be given for the purchase occasion.

Quick or Delayed Purchase

In certain situations, consumers delay their purchase of a product (say, washing machine) because of forthcoming sales promotions. In another situation, the consumer advances the purchase of the passenger car because of a sales promotion, though the intention was to buy it after three months. In situations when consumers buy more than their immediate requirement of, say, detergent due to sales promotion, such acceleration in buying extra quantity not only increases sales of the brand, but also results in stockpiling by consumers.

Brand Switching

When the sales promotion of a brand encourages consumers to buy the brand instead of buying the one they bought on earlier purchase occasions, it is called "aggressive switching". In the second type of sales promotion effect, known as "defensive switching", the aim is to retain the customer by encouraging her to buy the same brand as was bought on earlier purchase occasions, instead of switching to an another brand. When a retailer uses sales promotion tools to promote his retail store, consumers may respond byswitching to the store that is promoting instead of the regular store.

Sales promotions offering discounts or price-offs influence consumers to purchase the brand. However, the decision of the consumer to buy discounted brand would depend on three factors: (i) importance the consumer gives to the price compared to the quality, (ii) the quantity of discount, and (iii) the consumer's attitude towards price. Such sales promotions offering discounts may also encourage some customers to buy an otherwise expensive brand, which they could not afford on normal basic or list price. Studies have found that sales promotions induce substantial brand switching[29].

Repeat Purchasing

When a consumer purchases a product or brand on sales promotion, repeat purchase of the brand depends on the satisfaction of the customer. **For instance**, when a buyer purchased Siemens washing machine on an attractive sales promotion offer and was satisfied with its performance, it is possible that the next time, when there is a requirement, he would buy the same brand again. In case of low-involvement (i.e. low-cost and frequently purchased) products, like detergent and salt, consumers make repeat purchases because of habit. However, in case of high-involvement (i.e. costly and high level of engagement) products, such as passenger car and house, the consumer makes an evaluation after experiencing the performance. If the evaluation is positive repeat purchase is possible.

Incremental Sales and Profits

A study has found that trade sales promotions generate incremental sales, but can be unprofitable to the manufacturer on a per-event basis[30]. Another study shows that industry profit increases if manufacturers adopt a product category–management perspective, because price competition is lessoned[31]. The price competition results appear to be applicable to trade promotions. An interesting aspect of rebates, a consumer sales promotion tool, is slippage, which means the consumer purchasing a product that has a rebate available but failing to turn in the rebate. Slippage rates are found to be high. Slippage is a source of profit for manufacturers, because the presence of the rebate can attract customers who, after purchasing, do not bother to mail in the rebate. One aspect of sales promotions that reduces the profitability is the tendency to attract customers who would have bought the product anyway. Database marketing offers a solution by using a customer data file to target promotions to the most desirable customers. In a study, the researchers examine a coupon whose face value can be customized to each household. Their results suggest that the customized coupon is more profitable than a blanket-mailed coupon. They also found that information on consumers' previous choices is more useful than demographics alone[32]. Studies have suggested strong potential for database marketing and customized sales promotions. This appears to be a sure way to increase the company's profits. Studies have found that sales promotion is not necessarily profitable to manufacturers in all situations, but it is certainly effective at generating sales.

LO 5 Integrate sales promotion with other elements of communication-mix

INTEGRATION OF SALES PROMOTION WITH COMMUNICATION-MIX ELEMENTS

Many marketers used traditional method of treating the various marketing and communications elements as virtually separate activities, with different budgets and different objectives. These marketers did not recognize that the wide range of marketing communication-mix elements (such as advertising, sales promotion, public relations, personal selling, and direct marketing) must be coordinated or integrated to communicate effectively and consistently to target markets. During 1980s, many companies came to see the need for strategic integration of their promotional (or communication) tools. These companies started moving towards integrated marketing communications (IMC), which includes integrating the various communication-mix elements and other marketing activities that communicate with the firms' customers. The first definition of IMC, developed by American Association of Advertising Agencies, states:

"A concept of marketing communications planning that recognizes that added value of a comprehensive plan that evaluates the strategic roles of a variety of communications disciplines—for example, general advertising, direct response, sales promotion, and public relations—and combines these disciplines to provide clarity, consistency and maximum communications impact."

The move toward integrated marketing communications is one of the most important marketing developments that occurred during the 1990s. The IMC approach is being adopted by large, medium, and small companies. The major changes taking place in marketing due to acceptance of IMC approach are as follows:

- More marketing budget allocation is made to sales promotion rather than media advertising so that overall cost effectiveness can be achieved.

- Companies are turning to targeted communication tools such as the internet, sales promotion, event sponsorship and direct mail.
- Many companies are using computers to build databases with customers' profiles, their purchase details, and other relevant information in order to determine target customers and communication tools.

Proper integration of advertising, sales promotion, and personal selling is needed for the company to get the most out of its communication budget. **For instance**, advertising in mass media is required many times to inform consumers about sales promotional offers such as coupons, contest entry forms, or price-offs. Consumers are more likely to respond positively to a price-off offer or to redeem a coupon for a brand they are aware of due to advertisements than a brand they are not familiar with. Similarly, when sales promotion tools like sampling or couponing are used for new product trials, alongwith media advertisements, it results in use of the new product for a long period of time[33]. The opposite is also true, that the effectiveness of an advertisement can be increased by a company by using a sales promotion tool like a premium (gift) offer or a coupon. A **good example** of coordination between sales promotion and advertising campaign is of British Airways, which had advertised in mainline daily newspapers about a consumer contest, alongwith TV commercials, with the objectives of generating quick awareness of British Airways and stimulating consumer involvement with the airline.

Studies have found that combining advertising and personal selling has resulted in reduced costs, improved coverage, and increased the probability of a sale. A study by Theodore Levitt showed that sales representatives from well-known companies are better received by prospective customers than those from companies that do not spend on advertising to create awareness[34]. In another study, it was found that selling cost were 20 to 28 percent lower if the prospective buyer had received or seen an advertising message before the salesperson's arrival[35].

Sales promotion and personal selling also support each other. For instance, salespeople deliver many sales promotion tools such as free samples, coupons, or premiums to retailers. Point-of-purchase (POP) materials are delivered by salespersons to retailers to ensure these are used properly. When a new product or a brand is launched by a company, it should be ensured by the sales force that sufficient stocks are available with the retailers. If not, it creates a wrong perception in the minds of prospective customers. **For example**, when a company launched a new *atta* (wheat flour) brand in the Indian market, the advertisement in the newspapers mentioned that any person who carries the newspaper advertisement to a retailer would get 1 kg of *atta* free. However, when the company's sales force did not ensure adequate stocks of the new brand of *atta* at the retail stores, it resulted in many prospective consumers going back empty handed with dissatisfied feelings.

Some sales promotion tools, such as sales contests, sales meetings and sales training programs are directed at the company's sales force. There are incentive schemes to motivate salespeople to put more efforts so as to achieve the sales goals. Thus, without effective coordination or integration among not only sales promotions, advertising and the sales force, but also other components of integrated marketing communications, consistent achievements of sales targets and cost effectiveness would not be possible.

LO 6 Check evaluation of sales promotion

EVALUATION OF SALES PROMOTION

Evaluation of sales promotion is done by measuring the results and comparing the same with the objectives that are set earlier. If the sales promotion objectives are directly related to sales, it is easy to evaluate by measuring sales before, during, and after the sales promotion. However, if the objectives of sales promotion are not directly related to sales, such as to entice switchers, or help non-users for trial, evaluation is difficult. The sales promotion can be evaluated at three stages: (i) pre-testing, (ii) concurrent testing, and (iii) post-testing.

Pre-Testing

It is done by using focus groups and consumer panels. Pre-testing is done to find out perceptions of consumers in terms of risk and value (i.e. benefits less cost) of a product. **For example**, a consumer considers whether it would be worth buying an unknown brand of shirt at 50 percent discount. Is it risky buying an unfamiliar brand? Another method of evaluation is called **portfolio test**, in which portfolio of different sales promotions is prepared, shown to a group of consumers, and their responses are recorded in writing. One more approach is called **ballot method**, in which different sales promotions are prepared with illustrations and the same are mailed to a list of consumers, who are asked to vote for the most liked sales promotion and return the ballot to the company.

Responses of intermediaries are also evaluated before finalizing a sales promotion program. The company executives visit retailers and wholesalers and seek their views on the proposed sales promotion program. This approach is useful to get the support of intermediaries.

Concurrent Testing

In this testing, sales data is collected on weekly or monthly basis when the sales promotion is in progress. If the sales promotion tool used is coupon distribution, then the data collected is for coupons redeemed. The advantage is that based on the sales data obtained on weekly/monthly basis, the company can extend the period of sales promotion, if needed.

Post-Testing

A company can find out awareness and attitude of consumers as well as purchases made by using one of the methods of data collection, after the sales promotion period is over. The data collection methods that can be used are telephone interviews, mailing of questionnaires or personal interviews of consumers.

In order to find the impact of the sales promotion on the sales of a brand or product, sales figures are obtained before the sales promotion (i.e. pre-promotion) sales at the end of the promotion period and one month after the sale promotion has ended. These sales figures are compared with the sales promotion objective to find if the objective is achieved. Let us take **an example** of bonus back sales promotion program of the brand AXE lather shaving cream (Figure 8.5 shown earlier). Assume that the company's objective was to increase sales by

40 percent in the sales promotion period over the pre-promotion sales of x million rupees. If the sales go up by of $1.4x$, the sales promotion objective is achieved. However, it is highly possible that after the sales promotion period is over the sales would come down.

SUMMARY

LO 1

- The most suitable out of the various definitions of sales promotion is: "It is a key part of marketing campaigns, consisting of varied incentive tools, mostly short-term, designed to stimulate quicker and/or greater purchase of particular products or services by customers or the traders."
- The major reasons for importance of sales promotion are: increasing influence of retailers, managers' focus on short-term sales, increasing competition, and consumers' price sensitivity.

LO 2

- The objectives of consumer-oriented sales promotions are: to increase sales, to encourage trial and repurchase, and to target specific segments. Whereas, the objectives of trade-oriented sales promotions are: to encourage retailers to display products or brands, to support new product promotion, and to build intermediaries' inventories.
- Major benefits of sales promotion to manufactures are: increase in sales, trial for new products, and price differentiation. Major benefits to traders are: forward buying and increased visits by consumers, and main benefit to consumers is money saving due to price concessions.
- Major drawbacks to manufacturers are: reduction in brand value and dilution of quality image. Major drawbacks to traders include increased competition and traders becoming more price sensitive. Drawback to consumers is that they are not sure of value of various brands, as they are confused.

LO 3

- Manufactures use different types of sales promotions that are directed at consumers, traders, business customers, and the salespeople. These are called consumer promotions, trade promotions, business promotions, and sales force promotions.

LO 4

- Effects of sales promotions on sales can be explored by analyzing four factors, viz., increased product category purchase, quick or delayed purchase, brand switching, and repeat purchasing. Studies have found that sales promotion is not necessarily profitable to manufacturers in all situations, but it is certainly effective at generating sales.

LO 5

- Instead of traditional method of treating sales promotion and other elements of communication-mix separately, many marketers started adopting integrated marketing communications (IMC) concept, in which a variety of communications elements are combined to provide clarity, consistency, maximum communications impact, and cost effectiveness.

LO 6

- Evaluation of sales promotion is done by measuring the results and comparing the same with the objectives that are set earlier. Sales promotion can be evaluated at three stages, viz., pre-testing, concurrent testing, and post-testing.

Key Terms

Glossaries of key terms are mentioned at the end of all chapters

Bonus pack
Bounce-back coupons
Contest
Cooperative advertising
Coupons
Cross-ruff coupons
Event marketing
Event sponsorship
Forward buying
Frequency program
Ingredient sponsored cooperative advertising
Point-of-Purchase (POP) promotion
Premium
Rebate
Sales contest
Sales promotion
Specialty advertising/Promotional novelties
Samples (or Sampling)
Self-liquidating premium
Sweepstakes
Trade promotions

Conceptual Questions

1. How is 'sales promotion' defined? What are the reasons for the importance of sales promotion? LO1 M
2. Explain the major objectives, drawbacks, and benefits of sales promotion to manufacturers. LO2 M
3. What is 'consumer promotion'? Mention some of the major tools of consumer promotions. LO3 E

Note: Difficulty Level → E — Easy; M — Medium; D — Difficult

4. Why are samples used as a tool of consumer promotion? What are its major advantages and disadvantages? LO3 M
5. What is 'a premium'? What are the major types of premiums companies use? LO3 M
6. Is refund different from rebate? What are the major problems or difficulties associated with refunds and rebates? LO3 E
7. What is a 'bonus pack'? What are the advantages of using a bonus pack? LO3 E
8. Why is point-of-purchase (POP) display an important promotional tool? Why do retailers sometimes not use POP materials? What should manufacturers do to correct the situation? LO3 M
9. Why are trade promotions a part of push strategy of manufacturers? What are the major tools of trade promotions? LO3 D
10. What is a slotting allowance or fee? What are the views of retailers and manufacturers on the slotting allowance? LO3 M
11. What are the objectives of using sales promotion in business marketing? What are the major business promotional tools? LO3 M
12. Discuss the effects of sales promotions on sales and profits of a manufacturing firm. LO4 M
13. Explain how companies are benefited by integrating various elements of communication-mix. LO5 D
14. Discuss how sales promotions can be evaluated at pre-testing, concurrent testing and post-testing stages. LO6 D

Objective Type Questions

Select the most appropriate response out of the various options available in each of the following questions:

1. Sales promotion is one of the elements of communication-mix used by companies. Other elements are advertising, personal selling, public relations, publicity, and
   (a) consumer marketing (b) business marketing
   (c) direct marketing (d) international marketing LO5 M
2. Compared to any other component of communication-mix sales promotion is more effective in achieving
   (a) short-term sales (b) medium-term sales
   (c) long-term sales LO2 E
3. Bounce-back coupons are placed
   (a) inside packages (b) outside packages
   (c) neither inside nor outside packages (d) both inside and outside packages LO3 D

4. Premium, a consumer sales promotional tool, offers to consumers
   (a) price reduction (b) gifts
   (c) contests (d) none of these
   LO3 M

5. Rebates are price reductions offered by manufacturers for
   (a) hard goods (b) soft goods (c) all types of goods
   LO3 E

6. Frequency program is also referred to as
   (a) occurring program (b) loyalty program
   (c) bonus program (d) modulation program
   LO3 E

7. Event marketing and event sponsorship are
   (a) same (b) different
   LO3 E

8. Trade promotions are a part of
   (a) push strategy (b) pull strategy
   (c) pull and push strategy (d) none of these
   LO3 M

9. Sales promotion is effective in generating
   (a) profits (b) sales (c) both (a) and (b) (d) none of these
   LO4 E

10. Integration of sales promotion and other elements of communication-mix helps in providing clarity, consistency, high communication impact, and
    (a) profitability (b) cost effectiveness
    (c) competitive advantage (d) none of these
    LO5 M

11. If the objectives of sales promotion are not directly related to sales, then evaluation becomes
    (a) difficult (b) easy (c) neither easy nor different
    LO6 M

Application Questions

1. Assume that you are working for a medium-sized company, manufacturing and marketing detergents and toilet soaps. At the end of second quarter, your company's sales performance was not satisfactory. The sales were around ten percent lower than the budgeted sales. Your marketing head calls for a meeting to discuss the sales performance and corrective steps for the balance two quarters. What would be your suggestions? LO3 D LO4 D LO5 D
2. A company is launching a new washing machine in the Indian market. You are one of the marketing executives recruited by the company. What would be your suggestions on: (i) break-up of the promotional budget into various elements of promotional or communication-mix, (ii) sales promotional tools to be used, and (iii) integration of different communication-mix elements (make suitable assumptions, if needed)? LO3 M LO5 M
3. You are the head of a business marketing company, manufacturing and marketing electric motors to OEM customers, government firms, and small-scale buyers. What sales promotional tools would you use to increase short-term sales? Justify your decision. LO3 M

4. A company wants to introduce a new brand of table salt. Which sales promotional tools would you recommend in addition to advertising campaign? Give reasons. LO3 M

ASSIGNMENTS FOR STUDENTS

1. Talk to two of your friends. Find out if they have purchased any products or services based on sales promotions. Do they associate price discounts or price concessions offered by sales promotions with the quality of the products or services? What are their views on sales promotions?
2. Visit two retail stores and observe the product displays. Talk to the retail store manager or owner and find the impact of sales promotion practices on (i) consumer foot-falls, (ii) consumer buying behavior, and (iii) the store's sales.
3. Identify two executives from pharmaceutical firms. Find what kind of sales promotions are offered to medical practitioners and drug stores.

Reference Notes

1. Kazmi S.H.H. and Batra S.K., *Advertising and Sales Promotion*, Second Edition, p. 451. The term "above the line" refers to advertising carried out through the mass media of print, television, radio, and outdoor. "Below the line" describes all other forms of communications, such as sales promotion, direct marketing, public relations, and event marketing.
2. Paul W. Farris and John A. Quelch, *In Defense of Price Promotion*, Sloan Management Review (Fall 1987), pp. 63–69.
3. Blattberg Robert C., Gary D. Eppen, and Joshua Lieberman (1981), *A Theoretical and Empirical Evaluation of Price Deals for Consumer Nondurables*, Journal of Marketing, 45(1), pp.116–29.
4. F. Kent Mitchel, *Advertising/Promotion Budgets: How did we get Here, and what do we do Now?*, Journal of Consumer Marketing (Fall 1985), pp. 405–447.
5. Narasimhan Chakravarthi (1988), *Competitive Promotional Strategies*, Journal of Business 61(4), pp. 427–49. Raju Jagmohan S., V. Srinivasan, and Rajiv Lal (1990), *The Effects of Brand Loyalty on Competitive Price Promotional Strategies*, Management Science 36(3), pp. 276–304.
6. Varian Hal R. (1980), *A Model of Sales*, American Economic Review, 70 (4), pp. 651–59.
7. Paul W. Farris and Kusum L. Ailwadi, *Retail Power: Monster or Mouse?*, Journal of Retailing (Winter 1992), pp. 351–69.
8. Robert C. Blattberg and Scott A. Neslin, *Sales Promotion: Concepts, Methods, and Strategies* (Upper Saddle River, NJ: Prentice Hall, 1990). This text provides a comprehensive and analytical treatment on sales promotion.

9. Clarie Mahoney, *Because it's Worth It,* Soap, Perfumery and Cosmetics, 72(7) (July 1999), pp. 61–64.
10. Pran Choudhury, Ricky Elliott, and Alan Toop, *Successful Sales Promotion,* (Orient Longman Limited,1992), pp. 24–25.
11. Kapil Bawa and S.S. Srinivasan, *Coupon Attractiveness and Coupon Proneness: A Framework for Modeling Coupon Redemption,* Journal of Marketing Research, 34(4) (Nov.1997), pp. 517–25.
12. Peter Tat, William A. Cunningham III, and Emin Babakus, *Consumer Perceptions of Rebates,* Journal of Advertising Research, 28(4) (August/September 1988), pp. 45–50.
13. Martha Graves, "Mail-In Rebates Stirring Shopper, Retailer Backlash", *Los Angeles Times,* January 11, 1989, Pt. IV, p.1.
14. Mike Ogden, *Price-Based Promotions May Hurt Your Bottom Line,* Washington Business Journal, 18(6) (June 18, 1999), p. 54.
15. Beng Soo Ong and Foo Nin Ho, *Consumer Perceptions of Bonus Packs: An Exploratory Analysis,* Journal of Consumer Marketing, 14(2–3) (1997), pp. 102–12.
16. Larry J. Seibert, *Are Bonus Packs Profitable for Retailers?* Chain Store Age, 72(12) (December 1996), pp. 116–18.
17. Matthew Martinez and Mercedes M Cardona, *Study Shows POP Gaining Ground as Medium,* Advertising Age, 68(47) (November 24,1997), p. 43.
18. Jack J, Kasulis, *Managing Trade Promotions in the Context of Market Power,* Journal of the Academy of Marketing Science, 27(3) (Summer 1999), pp. 320–32.
19. Paul W. Farris and Kusum L. Ailawadi, *Retail Power: Monster or Mouse?* Journal of Retailing (Winter 1992), pp. 351–69.
20. William L. Wilkie, Debran M. Desrochers, and Gregorey T. Gundlach, *Marketing Research and Public Policy: The Case of Slotting Fees,* Journal of Marketing and Public Policy, 21(2) (Fall 2002), pp. 275–88.
21. Paul N. Bloom, Gregory T. Gundlach, and Joseph P. Cannon, *Slotting Allowances and Fees: Schools of Thought and Views of Practicing Managers,* Journal of Marketing, 64 (April 2000), pp. 92–108.
22. Mathew Flamm, *Alien Influences,* Crains New York Business, 15(46) (November 15, 1999), pp. 35–36.
23. Srinath Gopalkrishna, Gary L. Lilien, Jerome D. Williams, and Ian K. Sequeria, *Do Trade Shows Pay Off?,* Journal of Marketing, 59 (July 1995), pp. 75–83.
24. Dana Blankenhorn, *Memphis Company Solves Co-op. Ad. Accounting Problem Online,* Advertising Age's Business Marketing, 83(12) (December 1998), pp. 3–4.
25. Bradly Johnson, *IBM Moves Back to Intel Co-op. Deal,* Advertising Age, 68(10) (March 10, 1997), p. 4.
26. M.J. Caballero and J.B. Hunt, "Smiling Jack: Measuring Goodwill", Unpublished research report from the center for Professional Selling, Baylor University, 1989.
27. "1996 Trend Report", Actmedia, Inc., Anaheim, CA.

28. Scott A.Nielson, John Quelch, and Caroline Henderson, "Consumer Promotions and the Acceleration of Product Purchases", in *Research on Sales Promotion: Collected Papers*, Katherine E. Jocz (ed.) (Cambride, MA: Marketing Science Institute, 1984).

29. Gupta Sunil, *Impact of Sales Promotions on When, What and How Much to Buy*, Journal of Marketing Research 25(4), (November1988), pp.342–55.

30. Blattberg Robert C. and Scott A. Neslin (1993), "Sales Promotion Models", *Handbook in Operations Research and Management Science*, Marketing edition.

31. Zenor Michael J. *The Profit Benefits of Category Management*, Journal of Marketing Research 31(2) (May1994), pp. 202–13.

32. Rossi Peter E., Robert E. McCulloch, and Greg M. Allenby, *The Value of Purchase History Data in Target Marketing*, Marketing Science 15 (4) (1996), pp. 321–40.

33. Edwin L. Artzt, *The Lifeblood of Brands*, Advertising Age, (November 4, 1991), p. 32.

34. Theodore Levitt, *Communications and Advertising Selling*, Journal of Marketing, 31(April 1967), pp.15–21.

35. John E. Morrill, *Industrial Advertising Pays Off*, Harvard Business Review, (March/April 1970), p. 4.

CASE 8.1

Healthy World

After introducing popcorn and Sundrop cooking oil, ITC Agrotech launched wheat flour (*atta*) under the brand name Healthy World. US-based food products firm, Conagra, has 51 percent stake in ITC Agrotech. The vice president of the company says, "We took an Indian perspective out of the Conagra portfolio, with relevance to the local palate... Healthy World marks our entry into mass market products."

Priced at ₹18.50 for a 1 kg pack of *atta*, Healthy World comes in packs ranging from 500 gm to 5 kg. ITC Agrotech claims that it spent nearly one year on R&D before launching Healthy World, benchmarking it against national players in the branded *atta* category like Annapurna from Hindustan Unilever Limited and Pillsbury. There are several regional brands too. Parameters such as softness, taste, color and texture preferences are said to have been looked into in detail before finalizing the variant. "Our research revealed that the preferences in the North and South India differ distinctly across almost all parameters of *atta*. While creamy to white color and finer size is preferred in the south, the north consumer is more discerning as far as taste goes", informs the marketing manager.

Consumers in the south are more receptive to branded *atta*, but the north leads in consumption, where average monthly household consumption is 27 kg as against just 3 kg in the south.

Conagra claims to be the largest miller in the US. ITC Agro took over the *atta* manufacturing portion of a partner in Chennai to streamline it in line with its parent company's manufacturing process. What will also help ITC Agro is the fact that it has established itself as a health conscious manufacturer with Sundrop. The distribution network is already in place. In fact, the Healthy

World plans to leverage this with the image of the boy somersaulting (The Sundrop trademark) with the proclamation – "from the makers of Sundrop".

The branded *atta* market is estimated to be in excess of ₹350 crore (i.e., ₹3500 million or $ 53 million), with category advertising spend of about ₹20–25 crore (₹200–250 million or $ 3–3.8 million). The theme line of Healthy World says, "More Health. More Energy".

Discussion Questions

1. Develop a sales promotion plan to encourage continued consumption of Healthy World in North India.
2. How would you make your sales promotion competition proof?
3. How would you evaluate the results of this promotion?

Source: A&M, March 31, 2000.

CASE 8.2

Pizza Hut

Pizza Hut has a sense of occasion, of being there at the right time. Be it a heart-shaped pizza on Valentine's Day or a special sales promotion during the cricket World Cup, Pizza Hut is on the ball-with eye catching promotions. In the summer of 2000, in New Delhi, Pizza Hut launched its innovative Pizza Pooch menu as well as a Birthday Party package exclusively for kids in the 6–10 years age group. Senior marketing manager of Tricon Restaurant International said, "There is a specific reason to cater to this segment. Though, at this age children are under their parents' guidance, they perceive themselves to be teenagers and have the ability to choose or demand a particular brand of their own choice".

The $20 billion Tricon Restaurants that owns Pizza Hut, Taco Bell, and Kentucky Fried Chicken (KFC) has nearly 29,000 outlets globally. The large number of Pizza Hut outlets is in Paris, followed by Moscow and Hong Kong. Pizza Hut started itself in several cities and it also has a 100 percent vegetarian restaurant in Ahmedabad.

Innovative sales promotional activities and a popular logo have helped Pizza Hut expand. The senior marketing manager said, "Our focus is just not on offering a great pizza but also on providing excitement and good customer service." The manager further emphasized on the customer focused operations and intensive research done to identify customer needs and satisfaction. Besides, Pizza Hut conducted in-house research on psychographics of the Indian consumer that led to the use of cartoon characters in campaigns. The Indian Market Research Bureau (IMRB) also carries out regular surprise checks at the different outlets to monitor the quality of service. Moreover, a regular test, CHAMPS (Cleanliness, Hospitality, Accuracy of order, Maintenance, Product quality and Speed of service) is conducted in-house.

The company says that its Pizza Pooch birthday package is full of fun and excitement. What is unique in the package is the normal price of ₹125 per child that offers much more than only goodies in the main menu. The birthday party includes a well-decorated area within the Pizza

Hut outlet with several gifts for the children. Moreover, the party is conducted by a trained host with lots of games, prizes, and a special gift for the birthday child. Pizza Hut, better known as a family restaurant, takes the onus of relieving parents of the cumbersome job of clearing up the mess after the kiddies have enjoyed themselves thoroughly.

The Pizza Pooch menu, on the other hand, includes a wholesome meal and a gift for the child. The menu has been intricately designed with pictorial games. A free set of crayons is provided to keep the children occupied while their parents dine. The campaigns created by HTA are eye-catching with cartoon characters on the mailers, hoardings and print advertisements where the cartoon characters are aimed at matching the varying moods of kids. The birthday party concept is not entirely original – local fast food major Nirula's has been doing it for years, as does KFC.

Discussion Questions

1. What factors, in your opinion, are favorable to make the Pizza Hut sales promotion successful?
2. Suggest two sales promotions to attract girls to Pizza Hut. Give your reasons for suggesting specific promotions.

Source: A&M, August 15, 2000.

Chapter 9

Introduction to Distribution Management

LEARNING OBJECTIVES

After studying this chapter, you will be able to:

- **LO 1** Identify the role of distribution management in the marketing mix
- **LO 2** Explain the requirements of distribution channels
- **LO 3** Know the introduction to distribution channel strategy
- **LO 4** Describe the various types of distribution channels
- **LO 5** Discuss the different levels of intensity in distribution effort
- **LO 6** Understand the relationship between sales management and distribution management

Comfort Consumer Appliances Co.

Rajesh, CEO and George, Head of Marketing of Hyderabad based Comfort Consumer Appliances Co. (CCAC) were discussing the distribution efforts required to make a success of their new product–Air Coolers developed with an imported technology and a brand name Breeze. This was the first product in the company with many more to follow and hence, necessary to make a success of it.

Details of the product were as follows:

Product:

- Air coolers in 3 sizes meant for household consumers. Brand name: Breeze
- Competition: 5 major companies in the market including well-known brand names like Symphony and Kenstar

Price: Kept the same as the number 1 brand in the market

Promotion: Company decided to highlight the special technology of the cooler which meant that it would consume 20 percent less power than all the existing brands. This was the USP of Breeze.

The discussions between the CEO and the Head of Marketing centered around the place part of the marketing mix–the distribution effort required. Some of the points which were debated were as follows:

- CCAC wanted to confine the initial efforts to the two states of Telangana and Andhra Pradesh. Within these 2 states, George suggested that they would concentrate on the major towns. Some of the alternatives discussed were:
  - Appoint company salesmen to sell directly to major retailers in each town
  - Sell to consumer appliances wholesalers and dealers in smaller towns. These outlets would be multi-brand outlets. This may require Breeze to have better margins/commissions to succeed.
  - Sell only online through well-known e-commerce sites.

Companies cannot physically reach their hundreds or even more number of customers/consumers directly and hence, need to use the medium of distribution channels. The members of the distribution channels could be C&FAs, CSAs, distributors, dealers, stockists, agents, wholesalers and retailers. A combination of direct company distribution and a set of channel members are used by companies depending on their products and the markets they service. Distribution channels provide the right situation for time, place and possession utilities for the company products in relation to its consumers.

This chapter will also provide us the learning about how distribution management is an integral part of sales management.

LO 1 Identify the role of distribution management in the marketing mix

ROLE OF DISTRIBUTION IN MARKETING MIX

As we have already discussed, the 4Ps of the marketing mix include product, price, place and promotion. Distribution management deals with the 'place' part of the marketing mix. In the next few chapters, we will discuss one major aspect of the distribution management process, which is the role and relevance of distribution channels in helping the 'place' aspect of the marketing mix.

Distribution Management

This aspect of the marketing function provides place, time and possession utility to the customer. If a consumer wants to buy a tube of Colgate toothpaste, the distribution management in the company ensures that the toothpaste is made available to this consumer at a retail shop close to his residence—thus, providing the 'place' utility. If this consumer wants to buy this particular pack of toothpaste at 8 p.m. on a Tuesday, the company in particular ensures that the tube is available at the retail counter at this chosen time of the consumer—thus, providing the 'time' utility. When the consumer goes to the retail shop to buy the tube, he can pay for it and take it home whereby he becomes the owner of the tube of the toothpaste and thus, the 'possession' utility has also been provided for.

In this entire exercise, the consumer has had no direct dealing with the company whose brand of toothpaste is his choice. He has only dealt with the retailer close to his home. How the company has made sure that he gets the tube of toothpaste at the shop closest to his home when he wants it, is the role that the distribution management function of the company has played; this will be discussed in the next few chapters.

The situation would be somewhat similar even in the cases when a consumer wants to buy a refrigerator or medicines or an industrial buyer plans to buy a motor or a generator.

Definition of Distribution Management

- The management of all activities which facilitates movement and coordination of supply and demand in the creation of time and place utility in goods.
- The art and science of determining requirements, acquiring them, distributing them and finally maintaining them in an operationally ready condition for their entire lives.
- Broad range of activities concerned with the efficient movement of finished products from the end of the production line to the consumer and in some cases it also includes the movement of raw materials from the source of supply to the beginning of the production line.

We read about the role manufacturing and services sectors play in the growth of the GDP of any country. The manufacturing sector cannot contribute to the growth without the support of the distribution systems in operation to help the manufacturing sector reach the goods and services to the end user. Like other sectors of the economy that have been influenced by globalisation and information technology, distribution sector has also undergone a lot of changes.

In the past, companies undertook such distribution related operations and many companies believed that distribution could be best performed by them. This required them to build and maintain a huge sales force. But as markets expanded with the population, companies started realizing that direct distribution to an extended clientele was unmanageable and also quite expensive. Hence, they started looking for intermediaries who could do this job better.

Today, with the development of an excellent network of intermediaries, there is no need for companies to perform these functions themselves. The intermediaries are able to perform these functions and deliver benefits at a lower cost than if the company were to do it by itself.

Intermediaries, as the name implies, are a link between the manufacturer and his customers. Their primary job is to re-distribute the products of the company in a manner that it reaches the ultimate consumer and gets used. Irrespective of whether one is trying to sell consumer products, technical equipment and machinery, paints and varnishes or computer hardware, the role of intermediaries today has become indispensable. It is only the degree of 'intermediation' which can vary between industries and groups of customers.

Physical distribution also includes the aspects of transportation, storage and inventory management. Some aspects of physical distribution and logistics will be dealt with in Chapter 16.

> **Reality Bite**
>
> ***Customer support centers being outsourced by e-commerce companies***
> Channel partners are working with e-commerce companies to provide them with information technology support. The principal company can then focus on customer service and sales. The channel partner would set up a call center to provide this support. Economic Times (May 30, 2015) reports that companies like Flipkart and Amazon are using such channel partners.

LO 2 Explain the requirements of distribution channels

NEED FOR DISTRIBUTION CHANNELS

We saw earlier how a consumer is able to buy a tube of his favorite toothpaste at 8 pm on a Tuesday from a shop close to his home. However, the question of how this tube was made available at a time and place convenient to the consumer by the company was not answered. In this particular example, it is likely that the toothpaste would have been manufactured in one of the plants of Colgate and delivered to a Carrying & Forwarding Agent (C&FA) of the company who would have then sold the goods (physically moved the goods to the distributor on the advice of the company and collected the sales proceeds by a pre-signed cheque) to a distributor of the company. The distributor would have had a beat plan drawn up with the help of the company whereby he would be visiting the retailer close to the consumer's home every Friday. As the distributor had sold the tube of toothpaste (along with many other products of the same company) to the retailer on a Friday, the consumer was able to buy his chosen product when he needed it.

There are three intermediaries who have performed various activities relating to the distribution function in this example—the C&FA, the distributor and the retailer. It is also likely that the retailer would have run short of some stocks on the previous Monday and when he went to buy some items from the nearest wholesaler, he also bought some tubes of Colgate toothpaste. This would add one more intermediary into the system.

Apart from the above, there could be some transporters, stores personnel, labour and others who have also participated in the distribution operation that made the product available to the consumer when and where he wanted it.

For this simple example of a tube of toothpaste, the company could reach the ultimate consumer by several routes:

- Direct from the company, if it runs a house-to-house campaign.
- Direct from the company, if it has put up a stall in a consumer product exhibition to promote its products.

- The company delivers the product in bulk to a C&FA or a distribution centre, which breaks bulk and gives it to distributors. The distributor sells convenient lot sizes to the retailers from where the consumer buys it.
- The distributor could sell the product to a wholesaler who then sells it to the retailer from where the consumer picks up his pack of toothpaste.

The channel or set of intermediaries help the process of 'exchange' of the product or service at a certain margin to themselves.

Intermediaries help in the smooth flow of goods and services. This intervention is necessary as there is a difference between the assortment of goods and services generated by the producer and the assortment demanded by the consumer. The difference results from the fact that producers typically produce a large number of limited variety of goods, whereas consumers usually desire only a limited quantity of a wide variety of goods.

Distribution channels are required as the companies by themselves cannot directly reach and sell the products to their millions of consumers as could be seen in the toothpaste example narrated earlier.

Whether selling products or services, marketing channel decisions play a role of long-term importance in ensuring the presence and success of a company in the marketplace. Presence ensures that the product gets wide distribution and it reaches out to the maximum number of customers and prospects. The success is ensured when a distribution network performs this function more effectively than any other competitor network.

Intermediaries or channel members are normally expected to perform the following functions:

1. To accumulate the right kind of goods, aggregating and sorting to meet consumer needs at the point of purchase.
    - Food World outlets would know what consumers in their catchment area are looking to buy when they visit a FW outlet and hence, would stock up at least all these items, besides a host of other related products to take care of the 'impulse' nature of many customer purchases.
2. To believe in routine and simplified transactions and work with large number of products (at the wholesaler and retailer level), so that the distribution costs could get minimized.
    - Investing in the infrastructure and the operating expenses by a channel member will get dispersed over the large number of products (volume) he is able to handle quickly.
3. To provide information both to the sellers and the buyers to help them manage their business better.
    - The corner shop, which may be a small retailer, influences the buying decisions of his customers by recommending to them the 'best value for money' products. He also talks to company representatives about the products which sell better and which promotions were or were not successful.
4. To buy a large variety of goods and can compare costs and prices and make the right recommendations to their customers.

- For example, an electronic goods dealer can give the right advice to a customer if he asks for it before deciding on buying a color TV.

5. To be aware of the environment in which they operate and hence, isolate the companies from the direct impact of these local conditions.
   - A food retailer would choose the right kind of food products to stock and sell so that in case food Inspectors take samples under the FSSAI Act, the sample would pass tests and there is no backlash on the producer.
   - Similarly, a chemist would alert the company about any drugs which are getting close to their expiry date so that the company can replace these with fresh stocks.
6. To reduce the number of touch points. The company will not be able to meet the demands of thousands of its consumers directly and hence, needs intermediation.
   - For example, if an FMCG company were to directly carry out the distribution effort, it would need to contact thousands of dispersed retailers and wholesalers to sell its product.

Even if a company were to eliminate some of the intermediaries, the functions performed by them cannot be eliminated and must be carried out by some entity or the other. An intermediary is any channel member other than the manufacturer or the end user.

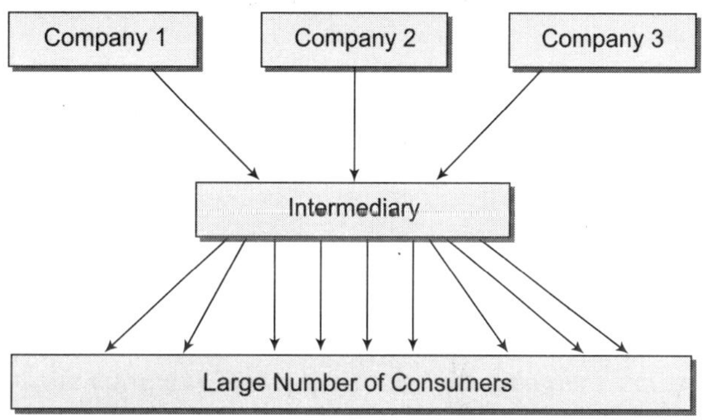

Fig. 9.1 Role of an Intermediary

The most popular and obvious argument in favor of having the intermediaries is—manufacturers produce large quantities of a limited number of goods whereas a consumer would buy small quantities of a large number of goods. For example, the monthly grocery list of a housewife would have 30 to 40 items spanning across at least 12 companies besides various non-branded items also—only the channel members can aggregate all these products and service the customer.

Placing goods or services where they are needed and when they are needed is the job of distribution channels. The route between producers and consumers that goods companies take to reach their end-users or customers is called marketing channels, trade channels or distribution channels.

Some well-known definitions are as follows:

1. Marketing channels are the distribution networks through which producer's products flow to the market. **—Cundiff, Still and Govoni**
2. Marketing channel may be defined as the external contractual organization which management operates to achieve its distribution objective. **—Bert Rosenbloom**
3. A distribution channel is a set of **interdependent** organizations involved in the process of making a product or service available for use or consumption by the customer or industrial user. **—Kotler and Armstrong**

Are Intermediaries Necessary?

The question most often asked is if distribution intermediaries are really required? The answer to this would be, not always, as sometimes the commitment of the intermediary and his need for an excellent distribution effort may not be of the same intensity as that of the company.

- With the advent of the Internet, examples of aggregators like Flipkart, Snapdeal, Amazon and Dell which directly deal with the consumers, are plenty.
- The example of Bata India is a case in point. Bata has set up a distribution network of hundreds of its own outlets where it sells its branded footwear directly to the consumers. In fact, Bata consumers do not think of any other way of buying their favorite footwear.
- Another well-known company is Eureka Forbes which does not have any physical stocks of its products in any place for consumers to access. Instead, the company's sales people call on their prospects at their homes, introduce the product, demonstrate its effectiveness and sell the products directly.

Normally, in case of technically complicated products, the company may want to handle the distribution themselves as they cannot expect the intermediary to learn as much and as well about the product as their salesperson. Also, the intermediary in this case may not be able to handle questions about the product as effectively.

- A company dealing in medical equipment would be a case in point. The medical diagnostic equipment sold by the company has a large capacity and are imported and quite expensive. The customers for this equipment are hospitals, nursing homes and major diagnostic laboratories. The company sells the equipment through its own technically qualified salespeople. The distributors are meant only to 'finance' the expensive equipment bought by the customers who may get a month's credit to pay for the products.

However, cost is a major consideration for a company wanting to handle the distribution function by itself. If the distribution objective is to reach hundreds of outlets with the product, it may be more cost-effective to use a channel member. Moreover, it can also be said that distribution is also a specialised function and best when left to the experts whose core competence is to reach the product to the millions of consumers, hence, the role of wholesalers and retailers. Experience shows that the cost efficiency and effectiveness of indirect distribution (use of channel members) is higher than in the case of direct distribution (use of company channels of distribution).

How Do Distribution Channels Add Value to the Marketing Mix?

Most companies use a combination of direct and indirect distribution modes. The choice of this combination and the contribution of each set is determined by:

- The nature of the company and its products
- The nature and dispersal of the company customers
- The business goals of the company
- The market expectation of credit. This is an important factor. There is the classic example of Brooke Bond India which shifted to the distributor system partly because

the company's 'direct distribution system' could not handle credit. Some details of this example are given later in this chapter.

- The company's capabilities and strengths
- Speed with which a company wants to increase its sales and coverage of the market. The established channels have the strength of providing the fast penetration into the market
- Nature of competition and how it operates
- Company's market shares. A small company with a low market share may not have the clout to get the interest of the channel members. It is a common complaint that many small companies do not get the type of 'stockists' they want but have to settle for whatever is available.

The above factors help decide the ratio between direct distribution and outsourcing the balance of the distribution activities. The marketing strategy of a company decides how much revenue would be generated from consumer sales and how much from the institutional business. Contribution to the total business from each segment decides the choice of the channel. Choice of the distribution network is a company-level, long-term decision and not just the decision of the sales function.

For example, most Fast Moving Consumer Goods companies in India use conventional distribution channels of C&FAs, distributors, wholesalers and retailers for their mass customer base but still use the direct channel of company sales people and dispatches from their factories for 'institutional' buyers like star hotels, hospitals and big industrial establishments. Some institutions, like the Canteen Stores Department (CSD), refuse to deal with the intermediaries and are willing to transact business only directly with the company.

Similarly major hospitals, which buy medical diagnostic equipment (worth millions) deal only with the company and do not want intermediaries to be part of the process.

Discrepancies and Distribution Channels

One of the well-known researchers and authors on channel management, Wroe Alderson (Factors governing the development of Marketing Channels—Marketing Channels in Manufactured Products edited by Richard M Clewett, Homewood, IL, Richard Irwin 1954, pp. 5–22) is credited with the concept that distribution channel members take care of four discrepancies that exist in the market place:

(i) Spatial discrepancy
(ii) Temporal discrepancy
(iii) Need to break bulk
(iv) Need to provide assortment

The fifth discrepancy not covered above, but relevant in the Indian context is that of financial support. Each of these aspects is briefly described in Table 9.1:

Table 9.1 Role of Distribution Channels

Discrepancy Character	Spatial	Temporal	Break Bulk	Assortment	Financial Support
	Helps reduce the distance between the producer and the consumer	Helps speed up in meeting the requirement of the consumer	Reduces large quantities into acceptable lot sizes for the consumer	Provides variety to the consumer to choose from	Helps fund the activities of the product to the consumer

Note: Temporal: helps reduce time (speed up) in meeting the requirement of the consumer

Spatial Discrepancy

As the name indicates, this discrepancy occurs due to the 'space' or distance between the production point of a product or service and its consumption point. The product has to be 'carried' between the two points. This is best done by an intermediary whose job is transportation.

Complexity is added by the scattered nature of the consumers and that the process of reaching these consumers should also be cost effective.

- For example, HUL makes Pears soap at one location in India from where it gets distributed all over the country and even overseas.
- Intermediaries involved: C&FA, transporters, distributors, wholesalers and retailers.

Temporal Discrepancy

This refers to the time difference between the production point and the time at which the product may get bought or consumed. All products meant for consumption in hundreds of locations can only be made in a limited number of production points. This means that the products have to be made and stored at many locations closer to the points of consumption. This requires a lot of effort to forecast the demand in different locations and planning to get the stocks to those locations so that the products are available when the consumer wants them.

- The most striking example is of Maruti Udyog which has just two plants in Gurgaon and Manesar in contrast to the hundreds of its consumers all over the country where the cars are to be made available. The problem of arranging spares for these cars is even more complex.
- Intermediaries involved: Dealers and transporters.

Need for Breaking the Bulk

To minimize the production costs, products have to be made in large quantities or in 'bulk'. However, consumption of these products is in smaller quantities. There is, therefore, a need to break the bulk into consumable quantities. For example, a tube of 200 gram toothpaste may come in a case with 240 packs but when it is sold to a retailer, the distributor may have to sell in dozens and hence, has to break the case to sell. Similarly, the company may send full truck loads of an assortment of goods to the C&FA where the bulk is broken down into smaller loads meant for the distributors. At the retail level, the consumer may buy only one pack of the product. The payments for the products happen in the reverse order. The consumer pays for one pack of 200 grams toothpaste, the retailer buys 2 dozens and pays for it and the distributor may buy several cases and pay for it. The C&FA collects payments from all the distributors served by him for the quantities sold to them and remits to the company.

- The obvious example is of Colgate which makes toothpaste in bulk quantities and may use a host of intermediaries to break bulk and reach the end user.
- Intermediaries involved: C&FAs, transporters, distributors, wholesalers and retailers.

India is the ultimate example in breaking bulk. It is only in our country that you can buy one stick of a cigarette, one toffee or one tablet of Anacin.

Need for Assortment

The same company may make one set of products in one plant and another set of products in another plant located far away. At the consumer level, when they visit their favorite retailer, they expect all the products of the company to be available. This aggregation of arranging for the entire assortment is done by the channel members. Even for the same kind of product, like toilet soap, the consumer may want to look at various brands before deciding on his purchase. Hence, the retailer is forced to keep different brands.

- An example of this is the auto component manufacturer MICO which makes fuel injection equipment, spark plugs and so on in two to three different plants in India both for the original equipment manufacturers and the after market. For the after market, they need to provide the assortment at the retail end.
- Intermediaries involved: Distributors, stockists and retailers.

Wroe Alderson (Dynamic Marketing Behaviour by Wroe Alderson) has highlighted the above four discrepancies where the need for intermediaries is inevitable. In the Indian context, there is one more discrepancy which the channel partners take care of. This is the need to provide financial support.

Need for Financial Support

In India, most companies are reluctant to sell on credit or give limited credit to their distributors. The market, however, demands a lot more credit. The channel partner takes on this responsibility and is partially compensated for this cost in the margin or mark-up which the company provides him. The channel partner, for example, may sell a product on 30 days credit to the customer but the company may give him only a week's credit.

Many companies operate only with stockists who finance the purchase of the product but do not undertake any re-distribution. It is for the company salesmen to meet the customer and sell the stockists' stock to the market.

- An example of this is the medical diagnostics industry where the equipment are bought by the distributor but the hospital to whom the distributor sells pays him only after 60 days of delivery.
- Intermediaries involved: Distributors, stockists and wholesalers.

To summarize, distribution channels perform some of these functions:

- Collection of information about customers, competitors and any other entities which can affect a company's marketing efforts.
- Provide for storage and physical movement of the goods.
- They place orders with the manufacturers of the goods for delivery to end users or other customers.
- They canvass the sales of the products they handle through effective communication. They do the actual 'selling'.
- They are the link for transfer of ownership of the goods from one party (the manufacturer) to another (the end user).
- The ownership and possession can be smooth and does not affect the end-user.
- They finance the inventories after the goods leave the manufacturer till they reach the end-user.
- They also provide credit facilities to their buyers. They help the manufacturer to effectively run trade and consumer promotions.

HOW DOES DISTRIBUTION ADD VALUE?

The distribution function using the network of the channel partners adds value to the selling function by providing time, place and possession utility to the consumer. As described earlier, time utility is making the product available when a consumer wants it. Place utility is making the product available where he wants it. Possession utility is provided when the consumer can buy the product and the ownership gets transferred to him at a time and place convenient to him or her. For providing the possession utility, the channels simplify the transactions by maintaining contacts with their upstream partners which could be the C&FA or even the company. The downstream channels involved here are the distributors, wholesalers and the retailers (upstream channel members are closer to the producer and downstream channel members are closer to the consumers). The transactions involved could be order taking, order communication, order processing, delivery of the goods and collection of payments. In coordination with the upstream partners, the downstream channel partners take care of all these transactions.

In addition, the channel provides the additional benefits of providing service associated with the product.

- For example, if one were to buy a color television, in addition to selling the TV to the consumer, the dealer may provide the services of delivering it to the home of the buyer and helping him install the set and run the programmes for him so that the TV becomes immediately useful to the buyer.
- Examples of cars, washing machines and the like are all with this additional support which extends beyond time, place and possession utilities.
- In the case of all industrial products, the service extends to help in installation, running it and making the customer understand as to how he or she can run the equipment at peak capacity. It also includes providing guidance on routine maintenance so that the machine does not breakdown. This is also true in the case of IT hardware.

- In the case of a re-seller who is permitted to sell an IT software, he has to help run the software parallel to the existing legacy software for the customer to get accustomed to the new software.

The value provided by the intermediaries is a direct result of the distribution strategy of the company which is primarily guided by the customer service policy and the intensity of competition.

LO 3 Know the introduction to distribution channel strategy

INTRODUCTION TO DISTRIBUTION CHANNEL STRATEGY

The company's marketing strategy is part of the overall business plan of the company and its corporate strategy. Distribution, being part of the marketing effort, forms a critical part of the marketing strategy. It is critical because the distribution channel strategy cannot be frequently changed as it requires building a network based on sound and long-term relationships.

The overall strategy and direction for the company is spelt out in its corporate strategy. The marketing strategy outlines how this overall company strategy will be achieved using the company products and its distribution network. Organizing and managing the distribution function forms the part of the distribution strategy.

The distribution strategy could be looking at some of these factors:

- Defining customer service levels. This is the most critical factor in designing the channel strategy. The customer service level is what the customer is most interested in and hence, requires extra care in defining.
- Defining the distribution objectives to achieve these service levels.
- Outlining the steps or activities required to achieve the distribution channel objectives.
- Deciding on the structure of the network to implement these activities to achieve the distribution objectives. These could be a combination of inside resources like the sales personnel and the outside resources like C&FAs, distributors and others.
- A clearly defined policy and procedure for the network to carry out its daily activities to achieve the objectives. Most companies cover this through an operations manual for the field operations so that there is no ambiguity or difference in interpretation.
- Stating the key performance indicators. This is only to check that the strategy is working well. This has to be worked out separately for each channel member.
- Understanding the critical success factors to make the distribution strategy effective.

We will discuss briefly each of the elements of the distribution strategy.

Customer Service Levels

The nature of the industry in which the company is operating, its products and services, its market share and the nature of competition help define the level of customer service the firm can promise its customers. Sometimes, the affordability also dictates the service level. Companies could even think in terms of categorising their customers into A, B and C categories (Pareto's Law) to decide different levels of service.

- Category A customers, who contribute the maximum to the company volumes and revenue, will obviously get special treatment. A consumer product company could take extra care of its distributors. An automobile company takes extra care of the defence services who may contribute to maximum sales of its trucks.
- B category customers are the next set of customers who contribute regularly but in moderate levels to the business. They get second priority in service but are important as they have potential to become A category.
- C category customers are low contributors and may not even be regular. They can be handled as part of the routine marketing plans.

The extent of competition could also decide the level of service to be provided. The firm may increase the service levels in a prominent market where its share of the market is to be improved. Service levels could be in terms of number of distributors servicing the market, frequency of visits to the customers both by the channel partners and the company sales personnel, ready availability of stocks to service the market, and so on. Once the service levels are decided, the distribution objectives can be set.

Setting Distribution Objectives

Apart from the firm's decision on the service levels to be provided, the customers also have certain expectations from the company and its channel partners. For example, retailers selling HUL products would want the company and its distributors to service them in such a way that they hold minimum stocks and at the same time never run out of stocks. The distribution objectives to be worked out by HUL in this case would take care of this requirement of the customers also. The distribution objectives clearly spell out as to what is expected out of the network in ensuring the desired levels of customer service to meet the expectations of its customers. The expectations could only be in terms of the time, place and possession utilities as well as the period of credit which the company may be willing to offer its customers.

Set of Activities

This part of the distribution strategy defines the manner in which the company and its channel partners go about implementing the customer service objectives set earlier. This task is normally performed jointly by the company sales personnel along with the channel partners. Some of these steps could be:

- Periodic (normally monthly) geographical sales forecasts.
- Arranging for dispatch of the products from the plants or C&FAs to a point closest to the market — normally the distributor point based on some pre-agreed stock norms. The agreed levels of inventory at different points in the network are to be maintained.
- Developing beat plans for market coverage.
- Developing journey and beat plans for service engineers.
- Market visits to sell the products.
- Collection of sales proceeds.

- Carrying out promotional activities.
- Calling regularly on A category customers to build long-term relationships.

It is necessary to clearly define these steps at this stage of the distribution strategy so that the company can also decide who has to perform each step defined here. Obviously some of the steps are to be taken by the company sales personnel and the others by the channel partners.

The Distribution Organization

Having established the service levels to be provided, the distribution objectives and the steps and activities to achieve the objectives, the firm has to now determine as to who will do what. This step will help define the organization structure to support the entire strategy. Decision points here could be:

- Extent of in-company support (own sales team) and outsourcing (use of channel partners). The planning of inventory, arranging for dispatches, credit management and collection of sales proceeds are activities normally done by the company personnel. This is accomplished by the salespeople and the logistics function.
- Like it was mentioned earlier, this is also based on 'affordability'. Own sales team may mean higher fixed costs whereas a bigger outsourced network may mean higher variable costs, if the volume goes up. Normally, the channel partners are compensated based on percentage of sales value. Firms also operate on a mark-up system about which we will discuss later. Either way, it indirectly affects the margins of the company.
- Selecting the channel partners including C&FAs and distributors, stockists or agents. This 'establishes' the channel that cannot be easily and frequently changed. The strategy also defines the guidelines and rules for selection and appointment of partners.
- Setting clear objectives for each of the channel partners and systems to monitor the activities and measure the performance of the channel partners.
- Ensuring the correct and agreed level of financial investments by the channel partners in the company business. For example, leading companies specify the size of the warehouse which the distributor should have, the number of vans he should operate to cover the market, the number of sales and back office people he has to employ, his beat plans and the amount of credit he is expected to give in the market.

Policy and Procedure

It is expected that the company sales personnel and its channel partners understand what is expected of them and discharge their roles and responsibilities faithfully. But as the salespeople may change and the network is so vast with a large number of channel partners, not all of them may understand the policy and implementation guidelines in the same manner. Hence, companies clearly define policy and implementation guidelines. Normally this is in the form of Operating manuals which are in the custody of the salespeople. The operations manual is capable of answering any query on procedure which the sales people or the channel partners may have on what action is to be taken in a given situation. The operations manual **(Standard Operating Procedure – SOP)** is an important tool to manage the distribution organization.

Apart from routine procedure, policy guidelines are also required on:

- System for redressal of complaints from the channel partners.
- System for settling disputes.
- Any additional payments to the channel members.For example, in difficult territories or for covering rural markets, the firm may decide to subsidise the freight costs for carrying the goods to these markets for sometime till the volumes pick up.
- Coverage of institutional business and service levels to be extended.

Key Performance Indicators (KPIs)

The effectiveness of the strategy can only be judged, if the company has agreed on certain measurement criteria with its channel partners. It is obvious that these KPIs will all revolve around the promised service levels to the customers. If the service levels as perceived by the customer are being consistently achieved, the strategy and the implementation plans are working well. Some of the most popular KPIs are listed below:

- Consistent achievement of targets by product groups, periods and territories.
- Achievement of market shares.
- Achievement of profitability.
- Zero complaints from the customers.
- No stock returns.
- Ability to handle emergencies and sudden spurts in demand.
- Balanced sales achievements rather than period/month-end sales skews.
- Market coverage with ready stocks.
- Excellent management of accounts receivables.
- Minimize sales losses on account of stock-outs.
- Minimize damages to products.

Critical Success Factors (CSFs)

Like any strategy, the distribution strategy also will be successful if it has the support and backing of the top management of the company. This can be achieved by involving them in the formulation of the strategy. Some of the CSFs are outlined below:

- Clear, transparent and unambiguous policy and procedure.
- Serious commitment of the channel partners.
- Fair dealing of the company with all its partners. No undue favors to some of them at the cost of the others.
- Clearly defined customer service policy.
- High levels of integrity to be demonstrated by all the channel members.
- Equitable distribution in times of shortage of a product.
- Compensation to channel partners on special promotional activity should be prompt and not delayed.

LO 4 Describe the various types of distribution channels

AN OVERVIEW OF DISTRIBUTION CHANNELS

A distribution channel is a group of people and firms involved in the transfer of title or ownership as the product moves from the producer to the ultimate consumer.

The American Marketing Association describes a distribution channel as the structure of intra-company organization units and extra-company agents, dealers, wholesalers and retailers through which a commodity, product or service is marketed.

Distribution channels are nothing but intermediaries or middlemen between the producer and the consumer. Further distribution channels:

- Are there as the producers cannot reach all their consumers.
- Multiply reach and provide efficiency to the marketing process.
- Facilitate smooth flow and create time, place and possession utilities.
- Have the core competence and the reach which the company may not have and they can do this entire process more cost effectively.
- Provide contact, experience, specialization and scales of operation.

Distribution channels can broadly be classified as:

❍ **Sales Channel** which has the functions of motivating buyers, sharing information between the consumer and the company, negotiating fair bargains for the consumer and financing the transactions.

- A distributor for Nestle would perform all these functions for the company by dealing with the retailers and wholesalers who stock and sell the company products.
- A franchisee for Pepsi would act in a similar manner.

❍ **Delivery Channel** which is only meant for physical transactions.

- This is the primary job of a Carrying & Forwarding Agent. A C&FA for Marico would ensure that the orders received from the company for the company distributors would be physically delivered to them on time in full. The C&FA would also receive and stock the company products for distribution.

❍ **Service Channel** which performs after sales service like a Maruti service station.

- A franchisee for HP would help its customers either service or repair the PCs or other hardware bought by the customers from HP.

We will discuss more about different types of distribution channels in later chapters but try and get an overview here. Distribution channels normally include the following:

- Company owned Distribution Centres (DCs) or Carrying & Forwarding Agents (C&FAs) or Consignment Selling Agents (CSAs)
- Distributors, dealers, stockists, value added resellers and agents—who could be exclusive or shared.
- Wholesalers who stock and sell a variety of products including that of competition.

- Retailers who are the ultimate and direct connect with the end user or consumer.
- For industrial products, the company's own sales force and marketing team could also serve as a part of the channel system.

Each channel member has unique characteristics and serves some objectives for the companies doing business in a given market or geography. We will look at the brief profile of each of them here:

C&FAs and CSAs

This category is known as facilitators. Carrying and Forwarding Agents are basically transporters who act as a mid- way point between the company and its distributors. Their role is to collect the products from the company plant and store them in a central location for breaking bulk and dispatching to the distributors against indents from the company. C&FAs take physical possession of the goods but do not pay for it. The goods in the C&FA warehouse still belong to the company. In India, before the introduction of Goods and Services Tax (GST), the sales tax rules were so difficult that it was required that companies with a national distribution had to keep one distribution centre of their own or at least one C&FA in each state; with the introduction of GST, the need/number of C&FAs may reduce.

Consignment Selling Agents act as C&FAs but also sell the goods to the market and then remit the value of the goods sold to the company. C&FAs or CSAs are on contract with the company.

Distributors, Dealers, Stockists, Agents

This set of channel members are also known as stockists, agents and guarantors depending on the extent of re-distribution undertaken by them for the companies they represent. Agents do not invest in the company's products. All belong to the same category of company outsourcing to help distribute products to retailers. Some characteristics of distributors are:

- They are required to invest in the product by buying it from the company.
- They are on commission, margin or mark-ups.
- They may or may not get credit from the company. They, however, give credit to their customers who are wholesalers or retailers.
- Commission or margin is a percentage of the price at which they buy the product from the company.

Mark-up is still a percentage but based on the selling price to the customer/retailer.

Distributors work in the markets and redistribute the stocks to the customers—wholesalers and retailers. Stockists may just invest in the products but expect the company to sell the products to the customers. Agents, dealers are only helping distribution with their contacts in the market place either with wholesalers/retailers or institutions. Distributors may be exclusive for the company or shared with others. Normally they sign some kind of an agreement or contract with the firm. We will learn more about them in Chapter 11.

Wholesalers

They normally operate out of the main markets in a city. They deal with a large number of companies' products and packs. They have their own shops in busy trading areas. They depend on large volumes of business as their margins are quite low. In some cases, it is known that wholesalers manage their margins on some products just by selling empty cases or cartons in which the products are received. Their features are:

- They choose and decide what products they will sell.
- They are not on contract with any company.
- Their customers are other wholesalers, retailers and institutions.
- They negotiate about 15 days credit from the distributors and special privileges on giving purchase requests more than once a week even though the beat plan of the distributor may give them one visit a week.
- They extend credit terms to their loyal customers.

With the increase in the number of supermarkets, the role of wholesalers is getting diluted. We will learn more about wholesalers in Chapter 12.

Retailers

They are the shopkeepers who set up shops in the market place to cater to the needs of hundreds of consumers. If the retailer is located in a busy part of the market where the consumer traffic is large, he can command a lot of profitable terms from the distributors and companies—like credit, promotions, renting display space and so on. Anyway, the retailer makes the highest margins in the entire supply chain. Retailers extend credit to only about 25 percent of their customers. They have also started home delivery to their regular customers close to their outlet.

Value added resellers purchase the incomplete product or kit and add value by assembling it and selling to the customer depending on his specifications. Examples could be of personal computers or even bicycles. We will discuss retailing in more detail in Chapter 11.

Understand Different Kinds of Distribution Networks*

In this section, we will discuss different kinds of distribution networks.

Consumer Products

1. Direct from the producer to the consumer—it is normally used in the following situations:
   - Where small quantities are only produced.
   - For markets and products where enough channel support is not forthcoming.
   - For limited number of buyers—useful for industrial products.
   - Where customers are located in groups or clusters like in industrial estates (B2B).
   - If the cost of channel systems (indirect) is higher than going direct.

* These examples should be considered as illustrations only and not as recommendations on how the channel needs to be set up.

- If the products are perishable.
- Where products require demonstration, lengthy negotiations etc. before the sales and extensive after sales service (Eureka Forbes vacuum cleaners is a good example).
- Ideal for most services—from producer direct to end user.

2. Producer to the retailer and on to the consumer (consumer durables is an example)
   - Product requires intensive distribution.
   - The retailers can give good promotional support and support for installation and commissioning.
   - The product range is limited.
3. Producer to the distributor/wholesaler to the retailer to the consumer
   - Product requires intensive distribution like a soap or shampoo which has to be made available in every outlet selling such products.
   - The coverage of the markets gets financed by the middlemen to a great extent.
4. Producer to one intermediary to end user: short channel ideal for services.

Reality Bite

Companies tap 'affiliate marketing platforms' to increase reach

In its edition dated March 2, 2015, *Business India* has described Affiliate marketing platforms as discount coupon and cashback websites to help online customers save money. Some of the e-commerce products being handled by these firms are: electronics, fashion, food and travel.

Some of the companies already in operation in this space include: coupondunia.in, cuponation, pennyful.in, cashkaro.com and mydala.com.

The publication has further described how these companies work:

- They give a discount coupon code of a product on an e-commerce website to an interested online shopper. Consumer uses it during check-out to avail the discount.
- This gives the e-commerce site a customer and if a sale is registered on its site, the portal gives a pre-decided commission to the affiliate marketing site. Here, the platform is working as a distribution channel for the e-commerce site.
- Cashback websites go a step further and claim to pass on 70–90 percent of the commission received from the e-commerce portal to the online shopper which is deposited in his bank account.

Industrial Products

As industrial products are generally technical in nature and mostly B2B, the channels need to be shorter. The simplest network would be direct from the producer to the customer as shown on the extreme right in Figure 9.2. Apart from the company selling directly to the customer, a company may use an industrial distributor (someone who sells industrial products but does not stock competition goods) or use agents to reach such industrial distributors in remote locations (for example, motors and pumps, for hardware supplies etc.).

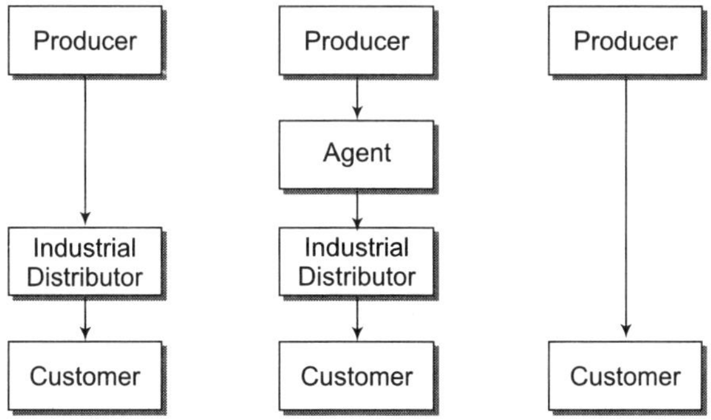

Fig. 9.2 **Distribution Channels for Industrial Products**

Consumer Products

The channel system in consumer products is the most evolved. Consumers are millions in number and companies can use every possible route to reach them. Hence, the network could have all the channel members mentioned in Chapter 10—C&FAs, distributors/dealers/stockists, wholesalers and retailers. Some configuration examples are shown below (for example, all FMCG products.)

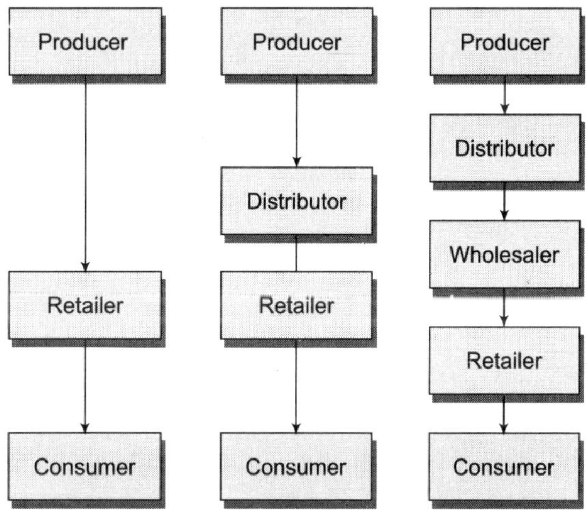

Fig. 9.3 **Distribution Channels for Consumer Products**

Consumer Durables

The network here can be similar to that of consumer products (FMCG) except that durables also need to be 'maintained' in a properly operating condition throughout their life. For this, the producer has to rely on service back-up which could be run by the company itself (through its distributors or dealers) or through a franchise route. Unlike FMCG products, durables may not have exclusive distributors or dealers. However, companies can run their own retail outlets (for example, Videocon, LG, Samsung, etc.).

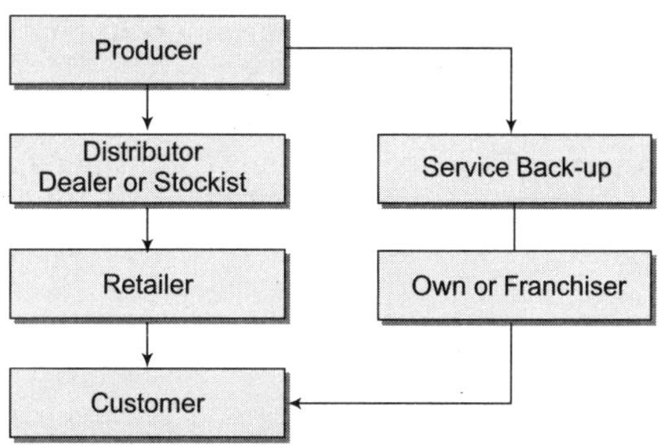

Fig. 9.4 **Distribution Channels for Consumer Durables**

Reality Bite

Mumbai based firm ties up with Amazon for rural India

Vakrangee is a Mumbai based firm operating 12,500 kiosks and wants to increase the count of these centers to 50,000. These centers operate as ATMs and e-governance kiosks. *Economic Times* in its issue dated August 5, 2015, states that Vakrangee is working with Amazon to facilitate online payments in rural India. For Amazon, the tie-up would mean marketing, sales and pick-up services through these V-centers to service rural India.

Pharmaceutical Products

In the case of pharmaceutical products or medicines, apart from distributors (who could be exclusive) companies also use dealers and stockists in smaller towns. Even in pharma, there are independent wholesalers who provide the reach to chemists. An additional factor in the pharma channel is the doctors who are required to 'prescribe' the medicines for the chemists to sell them to the consumers.

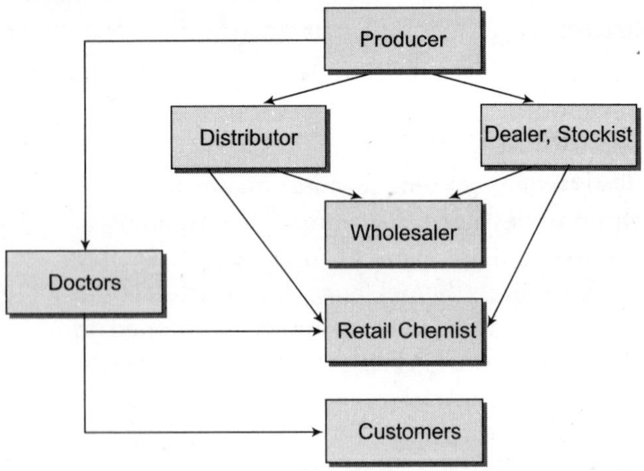

Fig. 9.5 Distribution Channels for Pharmaceutical Products

Textiles/Paper, etc.

In the case of products from the process industries like paper and textiles, the network is quite simple and straightforward with its components of distributors (major cities), dealers and stockists (in smaller towns). If the producer is located far away from the customers (for example, textile producers in Surat selling sarees to customers in South India), the producer uses a local guarantor who is a middleman who 'guarantees' payment to the producer from the customer. Of course, the direct company retail outlets are not shown in Figure. 9.6 (for example, Reliance Vimal, Bombay Dyeing, etc.).

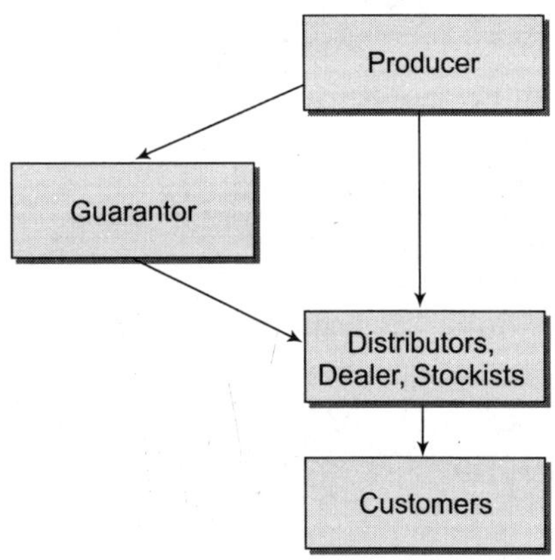

Fig. 9.6 Distribution Channels for Process Products

Chemicals and Fertilizers

The channel network in the case of chemicals and fertilizers, as shown in Figure 9.7 is quite simple. Apart from the regular distributors/dealers/stockists, there could be additional channel members like wholesalers in feeder markets where the farmers may be buying most of their agricultural-inputs.

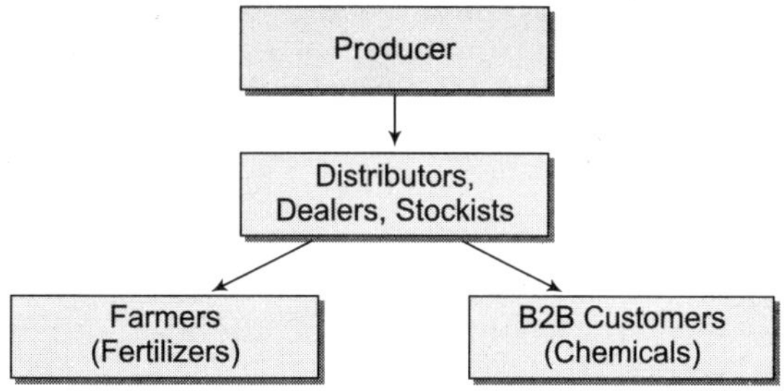

Fig. 9.7 Distribution Channels for Chemicals and Fertilizers

Automotive and Engineering

The network of channels for the original equipment (cars, two-wheelers etc.) follows the conventional system of using dealers who are exclusive. For OEM customers in the engineering industry, the sales could be direct from the company through its salespeople to customers. In addition, the vehicles need to be maintained at their peak potential. Maintenance and servicing can be done by company own dealers or authorized service centres (also outsourced) in towns where there may be no dealers. The dealers who service the vehicles and the ASC have both got to have support for spares and servicing. See Figure 9.8.

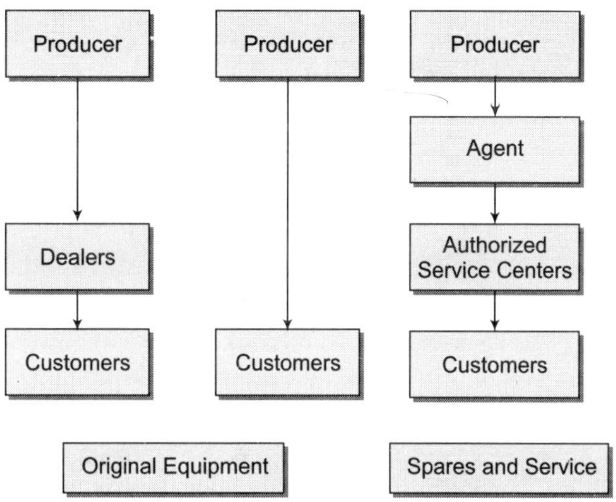

Fig. 9.8 Distribution Channels for Automotive and Engineering

Services

As would be explained in Chapter 14, the channel network for services is normally the shortest. There would be at most one intermediary in the channel system. This channel partner would be an agent or a franchisee.

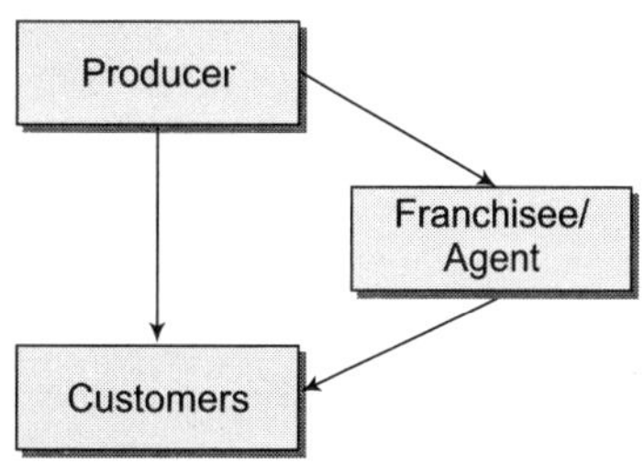

Fig. 9.9 Distribution Channels for Service

Cellular Services

In the mobile phone industry, the producer has to cater to a large number of customers very similar to the consumer products industry. The producer has to support his customers through a combination of hardware (the handsets), software (the content of the mobile) and the services (keeping the mobile working through the network). All these facilities are provided through a combination of appointed dealers or franchisees and the company sales team itself. One of the ways this is done by the company sales team is to focus on the B2B business (for example, corporate clients) and the individual customer business through the channel partners.

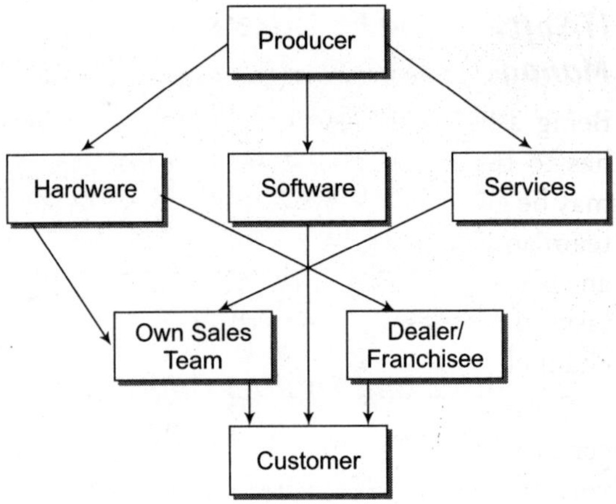

Fig. 9.10 Distribution Channels for Cellular Services

IT hardware

The network here has a combination of own sales team (for high-value customers) and the channel partners like dealers/re-sellers to service a larger number of smaller customers. At times, the hardware companies also use channels called 'Value-added Resellers' (VARS) / **system integrators** who do not just sell the 'boxes' but also make the hardware ready to use by putting in some software packages as part of the sales deal. Just like in other technical products, the sales channel has to be backed up by a service channel which could be own or outsourced.

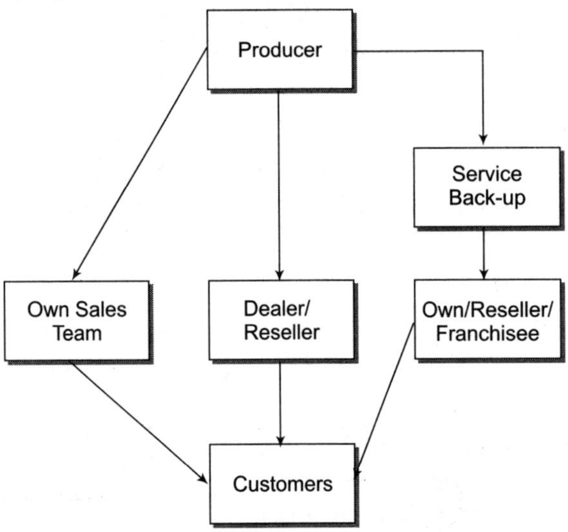

Fig. 9.11 Distribution Channels for IT Hardware

IT Software/Services and Management Consulting

Being services selling, the channel network has to be necessarily short. The selling part may be given to sales or business development team and the implementation can be done by an execution team. Only routine, repetitive tasks, if any, would be outsourced to suitable channel partners.

Some illustrations of how channel networks can be set up and operated for various industry verticals, have been mentioned above, there could be variations in the suggested illustrations depending on the company, its products, customers and competition.

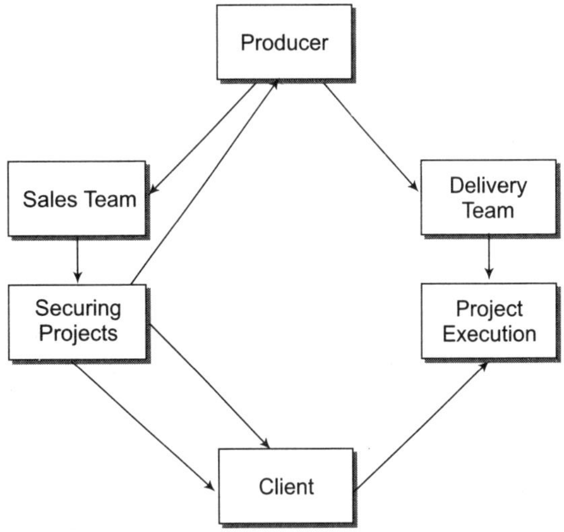

Fig. 9.12 **Distribution Channels for IT Software/Services and Management Consulting**

Distribution Channels for Rural Markets

Almost three fourths of India's population or approximately 850 million (census 2011) people live in rural areas, which lack basic infrastructure such as roads, transportation, electricity, water, health and education. The rural market size is estimated at ₹240,000 crore (2015) and with estimated growth of between 8-10 percent per year.

Rural India has enormous potential for business for any company—it has over 71 percent of the total households in the country spread over 6,42,000 villages. Many companies like Hindustan Unilever, Colgate, Gillette and Philips have been effectively reaching the rural consumers for many years now. Coca Cola seems to be growing at over 35 percent in rural markets compared to their growth rate of 25 percent in urban areas—this in spite of Coke covering only about 25 percent of the total rural market.

Even for FMCG products of daily use, the penetration levels in rural markets are quite low primarily for three reasons: different lifestyles, low income levels and inadequate infrastructure. However, there is good news for marketers: income levels are growing, the aspirations of rural consumers to have all that their urban counterparts have is on the rise. Efforts by the government and several other agencies to improve infrastructure—primarily access—are proving useful. Independent agencies run media vans that show movies in distant villages and run product promotions and demonstrations during breaks.

Two well-known initiatives of companies to provide 'reach' for their products to rural consumers and also facilitate movement of agricultural produce to urban markets are: HUL Shakti and ITC e-Choupal. More on these initiatives are mentioned in Chapter 14.

Other rural initiatives include:

- Efforts by the mobile services provider Reliance Infocom set out to get its network to about 400,000 villages (or 50 percent of the rural population).

- Godrej Aadhaar plans to set up over 1000 stores to benefit rural consumers.
- Amul, LG, LIC, BSNL and Hero Honda are some of the other companies which have made inroads into rural India.
- Some of these initiatives are based on: (i) partnering with self-help groups in rural India, (ii) internet-based rural kiosks/hubs, and (iii) direct selling.

Some characteristics of rural markets are as follows:

- About 17 percent of villages account for 50 percent of the rural population and 60 percent of rural income.
- Access to most markets is either difficult or does not exist. Weekly shandies (haats) and feeder markets provide indirect access and are being exploited.
- While there is access to at least a community television in every village, electricity is a major problem.
- The rural consumer understands colors and symbols more than brand names.
- The retail outlets are small. There are at most two to four outlets in a small village.
- The retailer stocks only one brand in a category, they cannot invest in more brands.
- The brands the retailer stocks are the ones which sell the most or the ones to which he has got the best access. This clearly shows that the retailer can be persuaded to stock a brand, if the company or its channel visits his store to sell the product.

Mass-based consumer products companies are the first ones to make efforts to reach the rural consumer through a maze of different channels. As access is difficult, many local regional brands have been cropping up—some of these are fake, counterfeits of major and well-known national brands.

Selling Agricultural Equipment to Rural Farmers: Some Thoughts

The range of equipment which can benefit the farmer is quite wide—ranging from hand-held farm tools to high-end farming equipment like harvesters, tractors and others like computers and telecom equipment.

A notable characteristic of rural agriculture is the large proportion of small land holdings. The pattern of land holdings in rural India is:

- 80 percent of the land covering about 700 million farmers is of a size 2 hectares or less.
- Another 15 percent of the land holding covering about 5 million farmers is between 2 and 5 hectares.
- Only 5 percent of the land held by 0.5 million farmers is above 5 hectares in size.

Obviously, it is the 0.5 percent of the farmers who can afford productive farm equipment.

Any distribution network has to take care of the wide variance in farming conditions within India's agricultural regions and a diversity of farming methods and crop portfolios. This situation creates a complex marketing challenge which is not at all uniform. Developing a distribution channel strategy under these circumstances is difficult, if the segments are not clearly identified and understood and a specific value proposition is developed for each. The focus of distribution channels is dictated by the reach, capability and the support of the available infrastructure.

The safest bet to reach industrial equipment to farmers is:

- Use channel partners in feeder markets—dealers of seeds, fertilizers are a good bet.
- Use these dealers and company sales people to set up stalls and promote in shandies.
- Use agricultural support staff to give demonstrations in the farms.
- Give free equipment to opinion makers—leading farmers in the villages.

LO 5 Discuss the different levels of intensity in distribution effort

DIFFERENT LEVELS OF INTENSITY IN DISTRIBUTION

This determines the intensity of desired distribution after a firm has decided on the most appropriate channels of distribution. In a way, the intensity denotes the service level that the organization provides to its customers. There are three types of distribution intensity: (i) Intensive distribution, (ii) Selective distribution, and (iii) Exclusive distribution.

A brief explanation of the three different patterns of distribution is as follows:

Intensive Distribution

This strategy is to make sure that the product is made available in as many outlets as possible so that anywhere the consumer goes, he or she should be able to get the product of his choice.

If HUL is proud of the fact that its products are available in 3 million outlets, it can be the best example of intensive distribution. This system helps increase coverage and hence, sales and is most suitable for FMCG products.

Automobile manufacturers would prefer this intensity of distribution for their spare parts.

Selective Distribution

It is obvious that in this case only a few selected outlets will be permitted to keep the company products. The outlets are carefully selected by the company in line with the image it wants to project about itself and its exclusive products. This may be dictated by the value of the product. For example, if one is shopping for Tanishq jewelery, it would be available in a few selected outlets only. Selective distribution gives the advantage of making the product available in outlets that matter the most and keeping distribution costs lower. These outlets may sell competing companies' brands also

Exclusive Distribution

This is more selective than the earlier example. Only one outlet in a market may keep the product. In addition, the outlets set up by companies for their own products could also be counted among these. Example is of Bata outlets or Titan showrooms.

The producer is interested in keeping a close watch and control on the distribution of his products. It requires a good relationship between the producer and the reseller. Examples include exclusive women's apparel and electronic appliances. These outlets will sell a single company's brands only and no competing companies' brands.

Intensity of distribution will feature again in Chapter 15 when we discuss Channel Implementation.

Characteristics of Channel Intensity

As mentioned in the section above, these are the choices available to companies to choose their channel distribution strategy. A summary is as follows:

- **Intensive** It ensures widespread coverage, volumes and availability. As final consumers are very large in number, provides convenience to them. However, the channel control is not easy. Large numbers of channel partners are required.
- **Selective** It ensures a good image, moderate market coverage and limited channel control. The numbers of users are also limited but they are brand conscious. This system will not provide a niche positioning. This system can be managed with a moderate number of channel members.
- **Exclusive** It helps create a premium and prestigious image for the product. Prices can be stable and margins kept high. Good channel control and loyalty are possible. Companies can focus on major or key accounts. Sales potential is limited. Limited number of channel partners will do.

LO 6 **Understand the relationship between sales management and distribution management**

RELATIONSHIP BETWEEN SALES MANAGEMENT AND DISTRIBUTION MANAGEMENT

In Chapter 1, we have tried to understand the importance of sales management to a company, the skills required by sales managers and the way salespeople go about setting objectives and a strategy and plan of action to achieve the objectives. We will now try and understand the relationship between sales management and distribution management and see how the two are always interlinked.

Distribution management serves the primary function of ensuring that the product or service is made available to the consumer within an arm's length of his desire. Distribution management takes care of the availability (physical distribution) and the visibility. It provides 'time', 'place' and 'possession' utility to the consumer. It is the sales manager who decides the organization which is responsible for the distribution effort. Normally, this organization is a combination of the company's own sales force and a set of marketing channels.

Distribution is an integral part of sales management. It is the heartbeat of sales management. Either sales management or distribution management cannot exist, operate or perform without each other. While sales management may plan the strategy and the operational details to achieve revenue, growth and market shares, it is the distribution part which executes these plans, of course, under the guidance of the sales managers. Planning and execution is a team effort between sales managers and the distribution channels.

Table 9.2 Sharing Responsibilities: Sales and Distribution working together

Sales Management Task	Distribution Management Role
Achievement of volume and market shares	Physical movement and storage of products closest to the markets Ensuring high shelf visibility Keeping high stock pressure at all selling points
Coverage of markets and outlets	Follow beat plan/call plan designed by sales management using 'milk-run' principles Making each customer call productive Extending required level of credit
Width and depth of distribution	Push all products, brands, packs in each outlet Sell more than competition Ensure high visibility Focus on slow movers
Managing institutional business and key accounts	Getting orders and execution Extending credit as necessary Keeping high stock pressure to avoid entry of competition
Competition tracking and action to protect market shares	Regular oral and confirmed reports Follow up on competition Promotions and sales incentives for corrective action
Market feedback and reporting	Both for own products and competition Report on good practices of other non-competing companies
Finished goods inventory management at C&FAs and distributors	Retain stocks up-to norms Order at the replenishment level Disposal of damaged stocks
Managing distribution channels – recruitment, development, evaluation and exit, if necessary	Each channel member has to manage his downstream channels Contracted channel members like distributors have a special role Conducting training programmes and example setting sessions
Handling customer and consumer complaints	First level of interface with the customers and hence, prompt action is expected Bring to the notice of sales management, if problem persists Quickly remove complaint/damaged stocks from the market
Implementing marketing plans – product launches, consumer and trade promotions, merchandising	Ensure wide and equitable distribution Ensure high visibility Make every promotion a success in terms of set objectives Ensure success of new product or pack launches
Participation in promotional events	Organise and participate in exhibitions, fairs and melas Take initiative to support sales management Spend on the event and then claim re-imbursement
Local advertising – wall sites, hoardings, shop boards	Direct responsibility of the distribution channels Productive use of Rupee spends Spend on the task and then claim re-imbursement
Cost effective operations	Ensure each task assigned by sales gets maximum results
Interface with other functions in the company	Through sales managers only
Recruitment, training, development and evaluation of the sales-force	Follow guidelines for own sales-force management

As we said earlier, distribution management has the responsibility of physical movement and storage also. The only sensible and cost effective alternative of getting all these tasks accomplished is through sound distribution management with the help of marketing channels.

Distribution Channels

The distribution channels to be managed by sales management could be a combination of:

- **Own Sales Force** Recruited and trained to manage key accounts and the distribution channels
- **C&FAs or Depots** To break bulk. Depots are the company own warehouses. C&FAs are carrying and forwarding agents who are primarily transporters with own or hired warehouses. They break bulk and send company goods to its distributors, dealers or stockists based on dispatch orders given by the salespeople. C&FAs work on a commission.
- **Distributors, Dealers, Agents and Stockists** The backbone of the distribution system. They are the people who buy the goods from the company and sell it to the customers like wholesalers, retailers and institutions. They may be exclusive to the company like contracted distributors or also work for other companies like dealers and stockists. All these channel partners work on a mark-up.
- **Transporters and Warehouse Operators** These channel members ensure physical movement and safekeeping of the goods. These channel members are usually managed by the logistics function and not sales management. They could be either on contract or hired, as necessary. Today there are a number of logistics service providers who take the entire responsibility of distributing the goods from the factory gate of the company to all its customers including collection of sales proceeds.
- **Independent Wholesalers in the Market** They are already operating in the markets and sell a variety of complementary goods like groceries, plumbing equipment, electrical accessories, spare parts or food items. They are not bound on contract with any company. They operate on low margins but high volumes.
- **Independent Retailers in the Market** More relevant for consumer goods and pharmaceutical products. They could be the corner store or a modern retail format. Retailers are the most pampered lot in the entire distribution network as they are closest to the end user or consumer.

Distribution management can also be done by the company itself. Most companies today outsource the distribution effort as it is possible to find competent distribution channels to perform the functions.

Distribution channels can be in-house or outsourced. Experience has taught sales management that it is more cost and effort effective to outsource the distribution function.

Examples of own distribution channels include Eureka Forbes and Bata.

Exhibit 9.1

Eureka Forbes

The company products line vacuum cleaners, water filters etc were meant for everyday use by the housewife. At the same time, these products had been carefully created by the company to take advantage of simple technology to help the housewife to do her daily household chores. The products could be effectively sold by demonstrating the way they should be used and to highlight the end results. In order to do this, right from the start the company decided to sell and distribute these products directly through their own sales people. This model being effectively followed to sell products in millions of Indian homes even though these products are also being made available on a limited scale in chosen retail outlets.

Exhibit 9.2

Bata India

This company is another classic example of using direct distribution to sell footwear. The company decided to set up hundreds of their own outlets (the by now familiar Bata shop as the consumer identifies them) all over the country manned by company employees to sell the products to the walk-in consumers. This network has very effectively served the company and its consumers for many decades now. Later the company started giving the Bata franchise to private outlets in smaller towns. These outlets are distinguished from the company ones as they are known as BSC (Bata Shoe Company) outlets.

There are hundreds of examples of outsourced distribution like Maruti, LG and Nestle.

It has been seen that more intense the distribution required (like for a consumer product company), the better it is to use a host of distribution channels. Exclusive distribution may be more effective, if it is done by the company itself. Of course, this is only an indicator and should not be taken as a rule of distribution management.

How Sales Managers and Distribution Channels Work Together

Sales management and the distribution function together take certain actions to ensure that the customer service objectives of the company are fully met. Some of these action points are as follows:

- **Demand Management** A critical step in getting sales volumes and earning revenues. Both sales managers and their channel members help this activity through forecasts, obtaining business and securing orders to meet set volume targets.

- **Supply Management** This is the major responsibility of the distribution channel working under the guidance of the sales management.

- The company depot or the carrying and forwarding agent on contract with the company receives the orders from the field force and processes them for dispatch to the primary customers of the company—distributors or institutions. They also collect the value of the sales made. This is the primary sales.
- The distributor/dealer/stockist/agent receives orders from his customers (traders or institutions) either directly or through the salespeople and processes them for dispatch. They collect the value of the sales made. This is the secondary sales.
- Both the C&FA and the distributor provide storage space for safe keeping of the goods till they are sold out.
- The C&FA and the distributor may use own transport vehicles or hired transport to move the goods from their premises to that of the customers.
- The wholesaler or the retailer is the most important channel partner for mass based consumer products. He is the one directly in touch with the end users. He makes sure that he buys the products, stocks them, displays them and sells them to the end users.

All the above activities are possible only under the supervision of the salespeople. None of the channel partners (particularly, the ones on contract with the company) acts without the knowledge and support of the company sales managers. There has to be a continuous and regular coordination between the sales management and the distribution channels to generate demand and manage it in a cost effective manner every day.

Sales Operations Planning

The planning of the sales operations is always done jointly by the sales managers and the channel members. Some of the points in the operations planning exercise are highlighted here:

- List of markets to be covered and the schedule—the company would like to be represented in full strength in all potential markets and outlets.
- Market share objectives to be achieved and how—built into the secondary sales targets agreed with the channel partners.
- Tracking competition in order to always do better than them.
- Designing coverage beat plans/call plans using a milk run concept—how many outlets to be covered in a day, frequency of calls on an outlet and when a call is to be made. The milk run concept makes sure that there is no crisscrossing in the coverage—the calls are made in a sequence.
- Ensuring highest call productivity—every call has to be made to give results.
- Market working methods and tools—whether to cover the markets with ready stocks or book orders and deliver stocks later, how to run the call, how much credit to extend and to whom.
- Sales promotion efforts—could include the power of the sales call or the consumer and trade promotions occasionally run by the company.
- New product/pack launches—each such event has important milestones in volume sales, placement of the products and merchandising to be achieved. These are agreed with the channel partners and then it is their responsibility to achieve the same.

- Shelf space maximization and merchandising—most relevant to consumer products. The intention is to occupy the best shelves fully, giving little chances for competition to be present. This also means utilization of costly point-of-purchase (POP) materials effectively in the market place. The shelf space to be achieved in each outlet should at least be in proportion to the market share enjoyed by the company in the particular market.
- Reports and records—include those required by the company and those required for statutory purposes (government rules). All reports and records have to be timely and accurate.

To summarize, sales management and distribution management are two sides of the same coin and are inseparable. Sales management plans operations (with inputs from the channels) and sales management and distribution channels execute these plans. They have a tremendous influence on each other's working and work together to deliver the highest levels of customer service.

The Government of India has introduced the Goods and Services Tax (GST) from July 1, 2017 which has focus of One Nation, One Tax. The tax borders between the states are not relevant any more. Many states have already closed the check posts between states. As a result, companies may reduce the number of Carrying and Forwarding Agents (C&FAs) compared to before the introduction of GST.

SUMMARY

LO 1

- Companies cannot physically reach their hundreds or even more number of customers/ consumers directly and hence, have to use the medium of distribution channels. The members of the distribution channels could be C&FAs, CSAs, distributors, dealers, stockists, agents, wholesalers and retailers. A combination of direct company distribution and a set of channel members is used by companies depending on their products and the markets they service.

LO 2

- Distribution channels provide the right situation for time, place and possession utilities for the company products in relation to its consumers. These are called spatial and temporal discrepancy correction. In addition, channel members help in breaking bulk of the products produced in huge volumes into consumer friendly sizes, support the assortment of a variety of products in consumer friendly doses. Another important role of the distribution channel is to provide financial support to the marketing effort to maintain healthy inventory levels and credit in the market place.
- Distribution channels could be classified as sales channel, service channel or delivery channel depending on what is expected of the channel by the firm. Companies can also decide the intensity of the distribution effort required for their products depending on the nature of the product and the competition. The intensity could be intensive, selective or exclusive.

LO 3

- A distribution strategy would look at some of these factors:
  - Defining customer service levels.
  - Defining the distribution objectives to achieve these service levels.
  - Outlining the steps or activities required to achieve the distribution channel objectives.
  - Deciding on the structure of the network to implement these activities to achieve the distribution objectives. These could be a combination of inside resources like the sales personnel and the outside resources like C&FAs and distributors.
  - Clearly defined policy and procedure for the network to carry out its daily activities to achieve the objectives.
  - Stating the key performance indicators. This is only to check that the strategy is working well.
  - Understanding the critical success factors to make the distribution strategy effective.

LO 4

- The types of channels used depend on the industry, the products and the customers. The channels could vary directly from the company to its customers or consumers to a multiple number of intermediaries between the company and its customers/consumers.
- Developing distribution networks for rural markets in India has been difficult in the past as access to these markets has been lacking. Today's rural consumers have the benefit of improved income levels and aspirations. The Government has invested hugely in developing infrastructure so that access to rural markets improves. Most product companies are using this progress to reach the rural consumer through existing and new kinds of channels.

LO 5

- Distribution is an integral part of sales management. It is the heartbeat of sales management. Either sales management or distribution management cannot exist, operate or perform without each other. While sales management may plan the strategy and the operational details to achieve revenue, growth and market shares, it is the distribution part which 'executes' these plans, of course, under the guidance of the sales managers. Planning and execution is a team effort between sales managers and the distribution channels. Distribution management has a major role in all the tasks performed by sales management and the extent of this involvement depends on the level of the distribution channel in the overall distribution hierarchy.
- Distribution management has the responsibility of physical movement and storage also. The only sensible and cost effective alternative of getting all these tasks accomplished is through sound distribution management with the help of marketing channels. Distribution channels could be a combination of own sales force, C&FAs, distributors/stockists, transporters, warehouse operators and independent wholesalers and retailers.
- There has to be a continuous and regular coordination between the sales management and the distribution channels to generate demand and manage it in a cost effective manner every day. Sales management and distribution channels management are two sides of the same coin.

Key Terms

Glossaries of key terms are mentioned at the end of all chapters

Assortment
Break bulk
C&FA
Customer service
Distribution channel
Distribution management
Distribution objectives
Distributor
Exclusive distribution
Financial support
Intensive distribution
Intermediaries
Marketing channels
Place utility
Possession utility
Re-distribution
Retailer
Selective distribution
Spatial discrepancy
Temporal discrepancy
Time utility
Wholesaler

Conceptual Questions

1. Discuss the role of distribution management in the marketing mix. LO1 E
2. Why are distribution channels required? What role do they play in the marketing of products? LO2 E
3. What are the steps to be taken to decide on a distribution strategy? LO3 M
4. Explain all the functions of intermediaries. LO2 E
5. What are the five discrepancies that the channel members take care of and how do they do it? LO2 E
6. How does distribution add value to the marketing effort? LO2 M
7. Explain in detail the distribution objectives for a FMCG company. LO2 M
8. Explain the key performance indicators for evaluating a distribution strategy. LO3 M
9. What are the critical success factors for making the distribution strategy effective? LO3 D
10. Explain in detail the different kinds of channel partners. LO4 E
11. Explain briefly the three patterns of distribution and in what situations are they relevant. LO5 M
12. Enumerate some of the principles for developing distribution for rural markets. LO3 M

Note: Difficulty Level → E — Easy; M — Medium; D — Difficult

13. Explain the possible distribution network for industrial products. LO3 E
14. What are some of the unique examples of developing rural distribution? LO3 M
15. Describe how sales managers and distribution channels work together in planning the sales operations. LO6 M
16. Under what circumstances can a company sales team work independently of distribution channels? Explain with some examples. LO6 D
17. List down the various kinds of channel members and their roles in ensuring effective distribution. LO4 M

Objective Type Questions

Select the most appropriate response out of the various options available in each of the following questions:

1. The distribution function provides the consumer place, time and __________ utility.
   (a) possession (b) ownership (c) exchange (d) supply LO1 E
2. An intermediary is a critical link between the manufacturer and his __________.
   (a) suppliers (b) customers (c) distributors (d) competitors LO1 E
3. __________ is major consideration for a company to handle the distribution function by itself.
   (a) Experience (b) Competence (c) Cost (d) Confidence LO2 E
4. The distance between the production point of a product and its consumption point is known as __________ discrepancy.
   (a) temporal (b) location (c) mileage (d) spatial LO2 E
5. __________ is the process of converting products made in large quantities to small lot sizes suitable for customers.
   (a) Aggregation (b) Breaking up (c) Breaking bulk (d) Re-packing LO2 E
6. __________ provides a variety of products for the customer to choose from.
   (a) Merchandising (b) Assortment
   (c) Retailer (d) Wholesaler LO2 E
7. Making the product available to the customer when he wants it is known as __________ utility.
   (a) time (b) possession (c) prompt (d) fast LO2 E
8. __________ distribution ensures that a product is available in a large number of outlets.
   (a) Regular (b) Intensive (c) Consistent (d) Daily LO6 E
9. Making the product available to customers in just one outlet in a market is known as __________ distribution.
   (a) selective (b) unique (c) exclusive (d) creative LO5 E

10. A channel partner who stocks and sells a company's products without buying them is known as a __________.
(a) distributor (b) transporter (c) wholesaler (d) C&FA **LO2 E**

11. Perishable products would benefit from __________ distribution from producer to consumer.
(a) direct (b) fast (c) regular (d) consistent **LO5 M**

12. ______________ distribution ensures widespread coverage, volumes and availability.
(a) intensive (b) selective (c) regular (d) steady **LO5 E**

13. A premium and prestigious image for the product can be created by __________ distribution.
(a) exclusive (b) intensive (c) selective (d) quick **LO5 E**

Application Questions

1. Please draw up the outline of a distribution strategy for a company selling electrical equipment. **LO3 M**

2. Sharp edge is a company making razor blades. They want to enter the market in Hyderabad and AP. Harish Malhotra, their marketing manager, is of the opinion that razor blades need selective distribution by a direct company distribution network. Discuss the merits of this suggestion and give the right direction to Harish. **LO5 M**

3. Mr. Cool is a brand of high end cooling glasses. How would you go about making a distribution plan for this brand? Is exclusive distribution the right answer? **LO5 D**

4. Rajan, the regional sales manager of Hercules Motorcycles Ltd., has just completed the monthly meeting in his office with his six dealers of Chennai. Rajan is quite upset as the meeting did not go as well as planned. The problem started with the targets for the next month he gave to the dealers. None of them was willing to accept it saying that the targets were too stiff and not achievable. The dealers were also not convinced about the ability of the proposed promotional support for the month helping them achieve the targets. The problem is compounded as 25 percent of the margins to the dealers are directly linked to achieving their monthly targets. **LO6 D**

   This is the third month running that Rajan is facing the target issue with the dealers. Rajan strongly believes that Hercules and its sales management understands the company needs, the competition and the prospects better and hence, they can decide the targets for the dealers.

   The dealers have been missing the targets in the previous two months also. In month 1, only 2 dealers beat the targets and in month 2 only one dealer could meet his target. Month 3 targets just given to them are even stiffer as Rajan is under pressure from his VP-marketing to make up some of the losses of the previous two months. He is planning to meet five of his Bangalore dealers the next week and is sure to face a similar problem there also.

   How do you think Rajan should tackle the situation to ensure targets are met? Can you suggest a system of sales planning for the future so that Rajan does not get into this situation again?

ASSIGNMENTS FOR STUDENTS

1. Meet any distributor, dealer or a channel partner of any company. Check with them about: (a) expectations of the company from them, and (b) their expectations from their principal company.
2. Study the current distribution network of Patanjali products. Develop a channel strategy ideal for them.
3. Surf the Internet and select any product or service. Identify three companies in the same category. Track their complete distribution network and the roles of the players in this network.

Reference Notes

1. William F Schoell, *Marketing—Contemporary Practice & Concepts*.
2. Bert Rosenbloom, *Marketing Channels—A Management View*.
3. DJ Bowersox and MB Cooper, *Strategic Marketing—Channel Management*.
4. VS Ramaswamy and S Namakumari, *Marketing Management—the Indian Context*.
5. Wroe Alderson, *Factors Governing the development of Marketing Channels—Marketing Channels, in Industrial Products*, edited by Richard M. Clewett, Homewood, Ilinois Richard D. Irwin, 1954, pp. 5–22.
6. R V Badi and N V Badi, *Rural Marketing*, Himalaya Publishing House, chapters 5 and 23.
7. Y Ramkishen, *New Perspectives in Rural and Agricultural Marketing*, Jaico Publishing House, Chapter 8.

CASE 9.1

Modern Motors – Selecting Suitable Channel Partners

Modern Motors (MM) makes electrical equipment like motors, pumps, small transformers, generating sets etc., it has been doing business for the last 10 years and has an established brand name known for quality. It has a factory located close to Bengaluru.

MM sells its products under the brand name Modern in the 4 southern states of Karnataka, Tamil Nadu, Kerala and Andhra Pradesh. In Karnataka and Tamil Nadu, it has a dealer network and in the other 2 states it sells its products through wholesalers of electrical products. Karnataka and Tamil Nadu account for 70 percent of the business and the other 2 states account for the balance 30 percent.

When MM first started the business in Karnataka and Tamil Nadu, they found it difficult to find channel partners being a new company. They recruited a set of 10 salespeople (5 in each state) and started selling directly to retailers, wholesalers and some business customers. The salesmen became experts in selling MM products and the company started doing well.

When MM entered the markets of Andhra Pradesh and Kerala, they recruited about 2 salesmen each in these two states and started selling to wholesalers only. They expected that the wholesalers would make efforts to further distribute the goods to the rest of the market which they did to some extent.

At the time of this review, they had two 'kinds' of channels in operation.

Business was growing and the current distribution network seemed to have limited reach and bandwidth. Secondly, MM felt the need for a more robust distribution network in Andhra Pradesh and Kerala. One alternative was to recruit more salesmen.

After 5 years of successful operation with salesmen as the focus of the distribution effort, the company decided to use outside sources a lot more formally. They decided to recruit dealers in Karnataka and Tamil Nadu. They could not find many businessmen who were willing to become dealers. They made an offer to some of their own salesmen to become dealers which they agreed. They finally made two kinds of dealers: (i) salesmen who became dealers (ii) market businessmen who became dealers. The terms and conditions of all dealers were the same. This practice has been on for 5 years.

The experience of MM with the two kinds of dealers, both of whom are giving good results has been different:

- The salesmen turned dealers were very knowledgeable about the markets, customers, competition and the products. They, however, had a 'know-all' attitude.
- The businessmen dealers had the primary focus on their profitability.
- Both kinds of dealers 'resisted' any kind of company policy changes.

MM wanted to build a strong distribution network in the states of AP and Kerala instead of just relying on the wholesalers to provide the 'reach' for their products with the relevant markets/customers. MM had the following options:

1. Continue with the wholesalers being serviced by the company salesmen.
2. Appoint dealers in all prominent and potential markets. For this, they could:
    a. Appoint company salesmen as dealers. They did not have enough numbers.
    b. Appoint market businessmen (maybe some of the wholesalers) as dealers.
    c. Have a combination of the two sets of dealers.
    d. Have only market businessmen appointed as dealers.

Discussion Questions

1. Can we help them decide the course of action with a clear rationale?
2. What are the pros and cons of continuing to work with wholesalers only?
3. If the decision is to appoint dealers, what should be the MM expectations from them?

This case has been prepared by V M Cavale for only classroom discussion.

Chapter 10

Marketing Channels

LEARNING OBJECTIVES

After studying this chapter, you will be able to:

- **LO 1** Understand the meaning of Marketing channels
- **LO 2** Explain the concept of channel flows
- **LO 3** Learn about the evolution of Marketing channels
- **LO 4** Discuss what channels are expected to deliver
- **LO 5** Describe prominent marketing a channel systems
- **LO 6** Evaluate costs and margins of the distribution system

Natural Products Company (NPC) is based in Coorg, Karnataka. It was established to take advantage of the natural ingredients available in this part of Karnataka to develop natural products without any harmful chemical ingredients. The marketing office of the company was in Mysore. Ramesh was the Head of Sales and Marketing at NPC.

The product to be marketed was a shampoo which was extensively test marketed in various geographies and received good acceptance and willingness to buy scores from consumers. The shampoo was also tested in well-known labs and endorsed by doctors to certify the natural ingredients. Three pack sizes were developed – sachets of ₹5 and ₹10, and bottles of 25 mL, 50 mL and 100 mL. The packaging design was colorful and elegant. Pricing of the shampoo packs was dictated by the prices of major competitors and was in line with consumer expectations.

For distribution, the company obviously was looking at intensive distribution efforts. They decided to launch the shampoo in Bangalore, Mysore and only 8 other towns in Karnataka.

Ramesh was involved in discussing the distribution organization structure with two Assistant Sales Managers (ASMs) selected for Karnataka. Ramesh and his two ASMs had a reasonably good experience of the FMCG industry. Some of the alternatives on the distribution structure which were discussed were as follows:

- Follow the *C&FA* > *distributors* > *wholesalers/retailers* route like all FMCG companies. Would we be able to get exclusive distributors?
- Should we appoint dealers/stockists in smaller towns—they will all be dealing in multiple shampoo brands—how do we make them pay attention to our shampoo?
- Can we recruit company salesmen and do direct distribution to wholesalers and retailers and keep the distribution structure simple to start with? Should we focus only on modern retailers with these salespeople?
- Should we make the proposition even simpler by selling only on e-commerce sites? Will not NPC then become just another seller?

In this chapter, we will learn about the types of marketing channels and the functions they perform in order to deliver the expected customer service. Further marketing channels can be classified into different systems based on the structure of the channels required to meet customer needs. We will also look at channel costs and how channel partners can sustain their business while delivering expected customer service levels.

LO 1 Understand the meaning of Marketing Channels

MARKETING CHANNEL

Channel Definition

Marketing channels are defined as internal (own salesforce) or external (all kinds of channel partners) contractual organizations that management operates to achieve its distribution objectives (reaching the product or service to the consumers/end-users/customers).

What is the Role of Producer and End User in Marketing Channels?

The manufacturer is the creator of the product or service and can also be the originator of the service. For example, if one leg of the distribution network is the company sales and service network, then the manufacturer also provides the customer service output. In the case of financial institutions like banks and insurance companies, the product and service roles of the producer are performed by him giving the impression that he is also a channel member. Reaching the product or service from the producer to a consumer direct could also be an example of direct distribution.

At times, the end-users behave like channel members when they buy larger quantities than required for regular or immediate consumption and hence, perform the flows of physical possession, ownership and financial flows. They are almost acting like retailers in this case. The consumers may buy these larger quantities at a time for various reasons like: (i) the manufacturer is offering a bargain on the product which normally is not available, and (ii) the product/commodity is available at the best price as it is a seasonal product (like food grains, edible oil or spices, for example). In fact, manufacturers are eager to make such attractive offers so that:

- the consumer stocks up and this prevents entry of a competitor brand into the consumer household
- having bought higher quantities than immediately required, there is a tendency to consume more than normal.

Manufacturers or end-users cannot be considered as part of the marketing channel. It is appropriate to only call the intermediaries as the marketing or distribution channel members and understand their role properly.

Channel Formats Possible

The wide variety of channel formats possible has been always sorted into four categories based on who drives the channel. These four categories are: (i) producer driven, (ii) seller driven, (iii) service driven, and (iv) other formats. We shall briefly discuss some of the most common formats in Table 10.1.

Table 10.1 Examples of Channel Formats

Producer Driven	Seller Driven	Service Driven	Others
Company owned retail outlets	Existing retailers, wholesalers	Carrying and Forwarding agents	Multi-level marketing
Licensed outlets	Franchisees	Transporters	Co-operative societies
Consignment selling agents	Modern store formats	Warehouse owners	Kiosks
Brokers	Specialty stores	Couriers	Vending machines
Franchisees	Discount stores	Credit card companies	Gift makers
Distributors	Agents, dealers, stockists	Financial institutions	TV home shopping networks, catalogue shopping
	Door-to-door salespeople	3P logistics service providers	Internet based sellers, exhibitions, trade shows, database marketing

Reality Bite

Top retailers being used as brand icons

Economic Times (June 27, 2015) has written as to how Vodafone is using top retailers in Rajasthan, many of whom are kirana stores to promote its brand. Vodafone provides these retailers a cut-out of the store owner clad in a dhoti and pagdi and holding a placard about Vodafone to be placed in the entrance to the store.

Producer Driven

In this case, the manufacturer produces and tries to reach the product directly to his customers. It could be a high technology product like a generator made to customer specifications or a product, like petrol, sold to consumers through company owned outlets. Examples could include:

- **Company Owned Retail Outlets** Petrol pumps, Bata shoes, Reliance mobiles or a large number of branded garment retail stores. Titan and Tanishq watches and jewellery stores are other examples.
- **Licensed Outlets** The company gives exclusive rights to some retail outlets to sell their products to consumers, for example, Bata outlet. Similarly in Karnataka, there are a number of licensed retail outlets for the Karnataka Milk Marketing Federation (KMMF), known as Nandini outlets, who sell all the milk products of KMMF.
- **Consignment Selling Agents (CSAs)** The company passes on the physical stocks to the intermediary, who pays the company only after the products have been sold. Most Indian companies selling mass based products use CSAs in North-East India, as most of the states, except Assam, are difficult to reach and volumes may not support a C&FA in each of these states.
- **Franchisees** Product and merchandising are decided by the company and the franchisee has to buy from the company to sell. Companies like Bata (under the BSC brand) and Kids Kemp Toys operate through franchises in smaller markets. This is also true for branded pizza parlors. Franchisees could also be a part of the producer based channel formats and work directly under the company.
- **Brokers** The intermediary contacts the user and sells the product on behalf of the company without taking any physical possession of the goods. He takes a commission when the sale is consummated. Such brokers are used by paper manufacturers, textile companies and for selling shares.

Vending machines, used mostly for beverages (soft drink companies call them fountains), are another example of a producer reaching his consumers directly. The bank ATMs can be considered in the same format.

Seller Driven

The company making the products uses wholesalers and retailers in the final stage to reach their consumers or end-users. This is the format used by most of the consumer product and pharmaceutical companies where the number of consumers to be reached is in thousands and it can only be possible to do this through hundreds of retailers. Some of the retailer based systems are:

- **Existing Retailers** These people are established in the markets and are used by all companies trying to reach the end-users. Food retailers are also part of this system. Convenience stores set up in each locality, which may deal with a limited number of merchandise like milk, eggs and bread, are also examples of existing retailers. The most common formats of such retailers in India are the *paanwalas* at every street corner and the scores of provision stores.
- **Department Stores and Supermarkets** These are examples of much bigger retailers who not only sell a large number of branded products but also sell other grocery, stationery and clothing items. Many of them, even in India, have started selling their own brands also.
- **Specialty Stores** These are retailers who sell one type of merchandise only. For example, the large number of branded furniture stores, Tanishq jewellery outlets and Shoppers Stop.
- **Discount Stores** As the name suggests, these stores sell the same products and brands as the supermarkets but at much lower prices using the power of volume buying and lower overheads. One well known example is the Subhiksha brand of discount stores in Chennai and in Bangalore. (Subhiksha has since closed down.)

Others may include existing wholesalers in the market, who deal with a variety of goods and companies, and the door-to-door salespeople or *pheriwalas* who may sell vegetables, carpets, steel utensils, etc.

Service Driven

All kinds of transporters provide service on contract for companies to reach their ultimate customers. They are the people who facilitate the distribution. These are the most common and best category of service based channel formats.

Similarly, all the providers of warehouse space also help store the products closer to consumer markets and reach them with minimum waiting time. These could be public warehouses like the ones run by the state warehousing corporations or the private warehouses and cold storages.

The C&FA has become an integral part of the distribution channel network in India. They are on contract and provide both time and place utility, both storage and transport. They were set up by mass consumer product companies to overcome the state sales tax laws but have now become critical to the operations of many companies.

- **3P (Third Party)** Logistics service providers take care of the entire distribution from the gate of the factory to the retailer. They are contracted by companies who wish to outsource this entire distribution task. Couriers are similar to C&FA agents but handle much smaller packets.

Exhibit 10.1

Coffee Chains

India is seeing a lot of growth in a new category of channel directly in touch with the consumers. These are the coffee chains which you see in large numbers in the major cities and also percolating to the smaller towns. Café Coffee Day is the pioneer in this new channel directed at the youth as an experience and a place to hang-out. Presently Café Coffee Day, Star Bucks, Barista and Coffee World are in operation. Many more like Gloria Jean, Mr Bean Coffee Junction, etc., have also arrived.

Other Formats

- **Multi-level Marketing Systems** The sales agent sells the company products and also recruits other sales agents to keep the chain getting stronger. His income is a combination of the commission on what he sells and what the agents he has recruited sell. The best example is that of Amway. Other companies operating on this system are Tupperware, Modicare and Herbalife.

- **Co-operative Societies** These were set up particularly in rural India to help farmers. These co-operatives are formed by the farmers themselves and have a number of outlets set up closer to the farmers' location dealing in agricultural inputs, daily use products and sometimes, may also help sell the agricultural produce. The Agricultural Produce Marketing Committees set up in each state are a good example of co-operatives helping sell agricultural produce. In urban areas also, employees of companies get together and set up their own co-operatives.

The hundreds of telephone kiosks that dot the entire country is another example of a format with a limited objective.

Vending machines for tea, coffee, soft drinks and even contraceptives reach the consumers directly. This has been discussed more in Chapter 12.

Companies are also setting up computer based kiosks for giving information useful and relevant to consumers. One example of this is the computer kiosks set up by the Railways to give reservation and seat availability information to prospective travellers. E-Chaupal of ITC is another format of a successful computer based format. This has been explained in detail in Chapter 13.

Gift and souvenir producers make products suitable for gifting by companies and also put the company logo for identification and customizing the gifts.

Television home shopping is also catching up in India, if one were to go by the number of tele-shopping networks which keep advertising on TV.

Catalogue shopping formats are also available though they have not yet caught the interest of consumers in India.

The Internet is getting a popular channel for doing business. While in countries like US, the use of Internet is widespread, in India also, the growth of this format has been extended beyond books, gifts and air/train travel and cinema tickets. B2B marketing on the Internet has also had better response till date in India. We will discuss more of this in a later chapter.

Exhibitions, fairs and other trade shows are another format for companies to sell directly to consumers. These are very popular in India. The *shandies, haats and melas* in rural India are of a similar genre.

Database marketing is becoming popular with time share companies, credit card selling and insurance companies. Mailing is the medium used by these companies to contact prospects.

Channel Levels

The number of channel members decides the level of the channel in operation.

A **zero-level channel** denotes a direct distribution set-up where the product or service is provided to the end-user directly by the company.

The channel manager has to create a fine balance between ensuring the desired level of service output and the cost at which this will be delivered. The slightest miss in this balance is an invitation to competition to move in.

A **one-level channel** consists of one intermediary. For example, the company may sell to the retailer who further sells to the consumers. The best example is the case of the Canteen Stores Department which buys directly from companies and sells to hundreds of service personnel who are its customers, through its own over 3000 outlets. The other example is of large format retailers like Big Bazaar and Food World.

A **two-level channel** would have two intermediaries. This is the most common for all FMCG (consumer goods) companies in India who have their own distributors who sell to retailers who service the consumers.

Some of the channel members are also part of the reverse logistics process whereby something from the consumers has to go back to the producer. The most common example of this is the empty soft drink bottles that the soft drink makers want to get back from the market. This could also be called 'backward channels'.

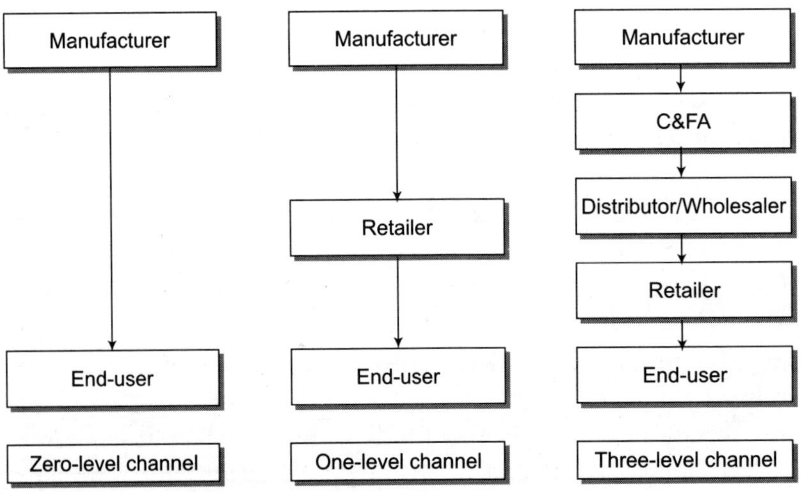

Fig. 10.1 Examples of Channel Levels

Service Channels

In the case of product marketing, well-established channel members can be recruited for a fee. In the case of selling services like health, education, banking insurance and others, the concerned companies have to establish their own unique channels for distribution of their service to the largest number of end-users.

To illustrate, a bank may set up hundreds of its own branches closest to the prospects and in addition, may recruit independent agents to get the customers to walk into the branches. A consulting company may use one team for business development and another team of its own to execute the projects brought in by the business development team. Even professional entertainers may have to use various channels to promote themselves.

An orchestra may use mass media, events and websites to promote their service to prospects. A magician may target his communication to schools and places where birthdays of children are organized.

LO 2 Explain the concept of channel flows

CONCEPT OF CHANNEL FLOWS

In the introductory chapter on distribution, we saw the functions performed by marketing channels. Let us briefly look at the summary of these functions to understand the functions and flows of marketing channels as a starting point for the discussions in this chapter.

The company or firm has to make efforts to get details about its prospective customers, existing competitors and other market forces. The more detailed this information, the better it is.

Once the potential customers have been identified, the company has to plan to communicate effectively with them to persuade them to buy the company products or services.

The prices and other terms by which the customers can take possession of the company products are decided and made transparent. There should be no ambiguity on this factor.

The channel partners facilitate change of title of the products from the manufacturer to the end-users or consumers. They place orders on the manufacturers, buy the products and pass it on to the customers (distributors, wholesalers and retailers).

Many of the channel partners like the distributors, wholesalers and retailers not only take physical possession of the goods, they also pay for it. They are responsible for the stock or inventory holdings in their possession.

The channel partners, who take physical possession of the goods like the Carrying and Forwarding Agents (C&FAs), are also taking responsibility for the safe keeping of the goods in their possession on behalf of the manufacturer. They take some amount of risk in this task. Similarly, all channel partners who buy and keep the product to reach to the end-users are also taking risks of storage, losses, price fluctuations, and so on. The channel partner is expected to assume this risk, if he has to be in business with his principals.

The channel partners take responsibility for safe keeping and storage of the products till they move to the next stage. Movement of the goods to the next stage is also the responsibility of the channel member. For example, the C&FA is responsible for storage of the products and transport to the distributors after getting their orders. The channel members take the responsibility for the required storage and transportation.

The company may or may not sell the products to the channel partner on credit. But in order to face the competitive market situation, most of the times the channel partner has to extend credit to his customers. A consumer product company distributor extends credit to about 50 percent of the wholesalers/retailers covered by him in the market.

The channel partners help transfer of ownership from one party to another and take care of all the documentation, insurance (sometimes for very high value items) and statutory requirements [like sales tax/value added tax /and soon Goods and Services tax (GST)].

All these functions recognize three kinds of flows: (i) forward, (ii) backward, and (iii) both.

(i) ***Forward flow:*** These are from the company to the customers, basically goods and services.

(ii) ***Backward flow:*** These are from the customers to the company, mostly the value of the goods or services bought by the customers. Sometimes, this may also be the goods returned from the markets or meant for reuse (like soft drink bottles).

(iii) ***Both ways flow:*** Which is mostly, information.

The above three kinds of flows are further broken down into five flows which are as follows:

1. Physical flow of goods
2. Title flow of goods (includes negotiation, ownership and risk sharing)
3. Payment flow for goods (financing and payment)
4. Information flow about the goods, orders placed, orders executed, and so on
5. Promotion flow about the trade and consumer promotions

The channel partners or members are involved in various degrees in all these flows.

Some marketing practitioners make a distinction in physical flows as physical possession and ownership. For example, a C&FA is used for only storing the goods and breaking bulk. He does not pay for the goods but only holds it on behalf of the company—physical possession. A distributor, however, has to buy the goods from the company for redistribution to customers in his territory. He gets physical possession as well as the ownership of the goods. For the physical flows, the costs involved are of transport, storage and inventory carrying. Ownership is the same as change in title to the goods.

Between the physical flows and the title (ownership) flows, there is always an element of negotiation of prices and other terms of the physical exchange of the goods for cash or other means of payment. Between the title transfer and payment, there is also an element of risk. For example, a producer may give a price guarantee to his distributor to protect him against price drops after the distributor has bought the goods at a certain price. (For example, this may happen in the edible oils business where prices are volatile).

Transfer of title can also happen with some credit terms so that the buying channel member need not have to pay for the goods immediately.

It is obvious from the above discussion that for every flow in the channel, there is an element of cost involved. Channel partnerships work extremely well only if there is no ambiguity as to who pays for these costs. The channel manager lists all the tasks to be performed by the different channel members and is also aware of who is incurring what costs to keep the entire network working effectively. This will help him measure the cost effectiveness of the network to deliver the expected and accepted level of customer service.

What about Information?

All the activities and tasks performed by the channel members can only be effective if the transactions at each stage are covered by the correct, accurate and immediate information of the company, the channel members and the customers. The flow of information keeps the channel performing, evaluating situations and taking corrective action in time.

Information flows are most of the times taken for granted and hence, do not feature separately in the list of channel flows. Normally, the information flows are in the nature of reports and records which could be verbal or written. Some of the examples of the information flows are given below:

- One-time information to the channel members on the features of the company products or services and the customers who need to be provided the products or services by the channel partners. Apart from the product features, the one-time information also includes the prices, margins and any promotional and merchandising support.
- The inventory levels to be held by the distribution centres are to be informed to the C&FAs.
- The *frequency of stock* receipts at the C&FAs, the production centres from where they would be received.
- The indents or orders from the distributors would be conveyed to the C&FA by the salespeople almost daily.
- Once a month, the distributors may be given the targets they have to achieve for the month. This would be by value and volume, by pack size or SKU. Information is to be conveyed by the sales force on the targets to the distributors and later the performance on target by the distributors to their salespeople.
- During the month, the distributors would convey their orders to the salespeople. These orders would be in line with the targets to be achieved.
- In the market, while visiting the customers or retail outlets, the distributor gives the information about the company products, competition, prices, any promotional offers on hand, and so on.
- The invoices generated by the C&FA on the distributor and the cash memos given by the distributor to his customers are also examples of information.

The channel flow is ideally to be handled by the most competent channel member in terms of who can deliver best services at the lowest cost. While modifying the channel network, it is likely that some of the channel members may get eliminated but the flows handled by them cannot be removed and have to be handled by someone else. We will discuss briefly the role of some prominent channel partners in each of these flows.

The manufacturer himself, though not a direct part of the channel of distribution, is involved in the flows of physical possession (till it is passed on to the next stage of the distribution centre, C&FA or a direct customer), ownership (till the value of the goods are realized), risk sharing, negotiations (with his own customers on the terms of sale), information and arranging for suitable promotions for the product to reach its ultimate user.

The C&FA or distribution centre is only concerned with physical (storage and breaking bulk), information (status of stock levels and orders received and being processed), title flow (pass on the goods to the distributors based on their orders) and payment flows (most C&FAs in the FMCG sector have blank signed cheques given by the distributors which they fill up and remit into the company account as soon as goods are dispatched to the distributor).

The company distributor is involved in all the five flows. He takes physical possession of the goods for selling on to the retailers. He buys goods from the company through its distribution centre or the C&FA and hence, takes title of the goods (ownership). As he has bought the goods and paid for it, he is involved in the payment flow. He is in constant touch with the company through orders and reports, which is the information flow. He gets involved in the promotional activities to support the product or brand along with the company and this is part of the promotion flows.

Very similar to the distributors, the wholesalers and retailers are also involved in all the five flows though their role in two of the flows—information and promotions—is rather limited. In the case of information, most of it is what is verbally conveyed to the distributor or company salesman at the time of their visit to the outlet. Sometimes, it may take the form of passing on a written consumer complaint to the distributor. The promotion role is even more limited to passing on the consumer offers given by the company to its consumers and providing space in the outlet for display-of-point of sale promotional materials. Participation in merchandizing the company products and display contests could also be part of this promotion flow support (Table 10.2).

Table 10.2 **Channel Partners and their Involvement in Flows**

Manufacturer	C&FA or Distribution Centre	Distributor or Dealer	Wholesaler or Retailer
Physical	Physical	Physical	Physical
Title/ownership	Title	Title/ownership	Title/ownership
Information	Information	Information	Information
Risk sharing	Payment	Payment	Payment
Promotions	Order processing	Negotiation	Negotiation
		Risk sharing	Risk sharing
		Promotions	Promotions
		Order placement	Order placement

Reality Bite

Brick and mortar stores benefit online sellers

It has been a well-established fact that a majority of online customers would have browsed in B&M stores before buying products online. *Economic Times* (July 09, 2015) has highlighted the value of showrooms for online sellers. The showrooms are set up to help create an image for the online sellers

Relationship of Flows to Service Levels

Channel design depends on the product, the customers, and what competition has to offer. The purpose of the channel is of course to maximize customer service. At the same time, there is a cost associated with the channel system and this should be affordable to the company. Designing the flows of the channel virtually reflects the design of the channel itself. In addition, the place and physical possession flows are important as the consumer would want the product at place and time which suits him. Surely for a consumer wanting a 200-gram pack of toothpaste, would want it in a retail outlet close to his place of residence, at a time convenient to him and in a 200-gram pack only.

The nature of the product dictates the flows required in the channel system. For example, for any consumer product, breaking bulk and assortment could be serious requirements. On the other hand, for a high-value engineering product, reduced waiting time and direct promotions would be more relevant.

In all cases, the ownership flow is relevant as otherwise the ownership of the product has to flow directly from the producer to the consumer. This situation is the exact opposite when the company is making high-value capital machinery. The number of channel partners and the flows also increase with the intensity of distribution being sought by the firm. All the flows, therefore, directly impact the service levels of the company.

Exhibit 10.2

Growth of Electronic Channels

A growing channel for consumer contacts is the Internet and e-commerce transactions. The Internet and Online Association of India is very optimistic of this channel growing exponentially for both B2B and B2C transactions. The metros like Mumbai, Delhi and Chennai, are ahead in the use of the Internet for buying and selling. Some of the goods sought by consumers on the net are books, railway and air tickets, electronic gadgets, music, movie tickets, hotel bookings, apparel, gifts, etc.

Each channel member performs only some of the channel flows. The channel flows performed by all the channel members put together help deliver the customer service output. For example:

- the producer (not necessarily a channel member) is responsible for physical possession, ownership, promotions, finance and risk sharing.
- the distributor or stockist performs the flows of physical possession, promotions, negotiation (for price discounts), financing (inventory and market credit), ordering (on producer), order processing (from wholesalers and retailers) and payments.
- banks, financial institutions and credit card companies may be involved in finance and risk sharing.
- Institutional buyers deal in negotiation (of terms), physical possession, ownership, ordering, finance and payment.

Reality Bite

PDS does not seem to be delivering desired level of customer service

The PDS or ration system is meant to primarily deliver essential commodities like food grains, sugar and kerosene to the most needy among the country's population. Despite the high spending on the PDS infrastructure, this goal does not seem to be reached in nearly 50 percent of the intended beneficiaries, says *Business India* in its edition dated March 30, 2014. One of the reasons for this seems to be the deliberate siphoning off in the system. This is an example of an elaborate, well-intentioned and planned distribution network not delivering what it is meant for.

LO 3 Learn about the evolution of Marketing Channels

EVOLUTION OF MARKETING CHANNELS

Marketing channels make exchanges possible between the one who has something to offer to the other who is in need of that something—exchange of products, services or even information. The use of the word "marketing channel" seems to have started to describe the trade intermediaries who connect companies and the users of their products.

These "exchange relationships" have evolved with the maturity of markets and development of technology. To quote marketing experts—marketing channels are enduring but flexible systems. For example, the relationships in the network today with the use of the Internet are far different from all the routine relationships in a network from the company, its Carrying and Forwarding Agent (C&FA), distributor, a wholesaler and a retailer.

A summary of the major the milestones in the evolution of marketing channels is as follows:

- In the past, all the products were those which were produced on the agricultural farms and it was necessary to have the points of production to be close to the points of consumption. The farmer would obviously sell his produce within the limits of his physical reach.

- The Industrial revolution (1760-1820: transition from hand production methods to machines) changed the way producers started looking at providing reach to their customers/consumers. Industrialization also resulted in urbanization. While industrialization required movement of raw materials and means of making production happen—machinery and equipment etc., these added new dimensions to distribution—creating an assortment, transportation etc., which brought traders into the system.
- After the Second World War (1939-1945), the US economy ended up with huge stockpiles of inventory which needed to be marketed in order to release valuable working capital. The concept of branding had become apparent as economies of scale ensured high levels of production and inventories. Distribution, by then, was relevant only for the 'place' part of the marketing mix.
- The effort put on 'selling' spawned a host of independent intermediaries in the form of wholesalers and retailers. (In the US, two of the pioneering retailers were Marshall Field in Chicago and John Wanamaker in Philadelphia).
- Two major developments in the US also impacted the distribution networks—the automobile and the highway systems. It was then possible to move merchandise to previously inaccessible locations. At this point, American citizens seemed to be moving to suburbs and retailers also started moving to these locations—suburban shopping centres and later malls got developed.
- The early 1950s are credited with laying the foundation of the marketing concept which meant each channel member had to work towards meeting the needs of his customers. The 'pull' concept was taking shape. Gathering and using customer information became the norm.
- The next stage was into 'relationship' marketing which meant mere transactions were not enough—relationships were required to be built for long-lasting and strong business results. Sophisticated databases and interactive technologies became a big support to pursue this strategy.

These are just some of the steps in the trail of distribution evolution. An excellent example from a strong distribution network is given below.

Reality Bite

A successful workplace and service provider-Regus

Regus India is a subsidiary of a world's leading workplace and service provider. *Business India* (June 21, 2015) states that Regus is operating successfully in over 100 countries and 2300 locations. In India, it is present in about 14 cities and 60 business centers. It is planning to also provide such space and services in tier 2 and tier 3 cities.

Exhibit 10.3

HUL for Lux Toilet Soap

This example has been taken from one of the best known FMCG companies in India and may reflect the way distribution in the entire Indian market behaved over the years. After all, HUL is still recognized as having one of the best distribution networks of any company in India.

HUL has an intensive distribution network which ensures that Lux is available in every outlet at all times. This effort includes demand generation activities, building good trade relationships and incentivizing retailers to stock and sell more Lux every day. The distribution network for Lux is a very good example of how the network has evolved over many years.

In the first stage, the company used to collect bulk orders directly from the wholesalers in the markets. About one-third of the orders were also booked from the large retailers in the market. Company salesmen used to aggregate these orders and send an indent for the quantities required to the HO. The goods were sent to the company salesmen who used to collect them and distribute to the wholesalers and major retailers. They also used to collect cash on delivery which was remitted to the company.

In the 1940s, the company went one step further to provide quality products and services to its consumers. The company appointed one wholesaler in each market as a registered wholesaler and a focal point for the company goods. The purpose of the registered wholesaler was to store the goods after having paid for it (financing). The company salesmen would sell the goods in the market and distribute them through distribution units provided by the company. The registered wholesaler was paid a commission of 1 percent of sales. This system increased the 'reach' for the company.

The next stage was introduction of the system of re-distribution stockist (RD) who replaced the registered wholesaler. The RD was required to provide warehousing, distribution units and buy the goods from the company. The company was keen that the distributor was serviced regularly by supplying company products to him. This led to the establishment of company depots in strategic locations. The depot was meant to keep inventory closer to the location of the re-distribution stockists so that stocks could be rushed to them quickly—the depots were stock points which helped in trans-shipment and breaking bulk. Eventually, the company outsourced this responsibility to Carrying and Forwarding Agents (C&FAs). The C&FA system helped reduce cost of freight, reduced time to market and improved customer service. A C&FA would also help avoid the 4 percent prevailing central sales tax.

The next stage in the evolution of the distribution network in HUL was the IT enabling of the network. The primary objective of the IT system was to ensure quick replenishment of stocks to the re-distributors. The RDs were connected to the company through an internet-based system known as RSNet—online interaction on distributor orders, information sharing and keeping track of information. For example, it was possible to know at the end of every day, the pack-wise, brand-wise sales and stock levels for each distributor for that day. The RSNet system while improving customer service at all sales points, also helped in ensuring visibility of the products. RSNet was a part of the bigger Project Leap which was the focus of the entire supply chain.

LO 4 Discuss what channels are expected to deliver

WHAT IS THE CHANNEL EXPECTED TO DELIVER?

While the channel is used by the firm to reach the end-users of its product or service, the end-user or consumer expects that the channel will deliver some service output of interest to him. Some of these expectations include:

- Variety of products to suit a person's needs at one place. A housewife shopping for groceries will expect the retail outlet of her convenience to stock all her needs for the month.
- The channel member or outlet has to be located close to the location of the consumer. The housewife in the earlier example would want all her monthly grocery items in the retail outlet closest to her place of residence. If Maruti claims that they have service stations even in the remotest parts of the country, they are claiming more spatial convenience for car owners than any other car company.
- Speed of delivery is another important expectation. The product or service should be available when the consumer wants it. He is not willing to wait for it. The waiting time should preferably be nil every time he decides to buy something.
- The product should be available in different lot sizes to suit the consumer. The channel member, for example, cannot stipulate that the consumer should buy four packs of his favorite brand of toothpaste every time. If he wants only one pack, he should be able to buy it every time.
- In addition, channel members like retailers provide more benefits to the consumer like home delivery, credit till pay day and well packed staple food items.

Providing all these services to consumers may cost additional amount but most consumers are willing to pay for the convenience. However, with intense competition among channel members, most of these services are being provided to consumers at no additional cost.

To summarize, the channel delivers the following to support customer service:

- Bulk breaking or facility for the customer to buy quantities suitable for his use. This is most relevant in consumer products and pharmaceuticals.
- Place utility, also referred to as spatial convenience—facility for the consumer to buy the product at a place of his convenience.
- Minimum cycle time, also called waiting time—facility for the customer to buy the product as soon as he realizes his need for it, he does not want to wait for it.
- Assortment facility, facility for the consumer to buy a variety of goods at the same place and same time.
- In the case of consumer durables or technical products meant for business users,

Table 10.3 Expectations of Customers from the Channels

Expectations from Channels
Variety and assortment in one location
Breaking bulk—availability in preferred lot sizes
Close to customer/consumer location
Speed of delivery—no waiting time
Any additional services
Support for installation
After sales service support
Financing support

the channel also provides four additional facilities. These are: (i) installation support, (ii) after sales support, (iii) training of personnel, and (iv) finance (Table 10.3).

- Support for installation and getting the product ready for use. For example, a consumer buying a refrigerator would like the company dealer to deliver the fridge at his residence, connect it properly and demonstrate that it is working well before leaving the customer place.
- After sales support—normally given free for about a year and then the customer has to pay for it by signing an Annual Maintenance Contract (AMC). For example, most car makers allow three services on new cars up to a running of 10,000 km or 3 months free.
- The customer personnel, who will operate the equipment, are trained by the company technicians on how to run, operate and maintain the equipment.
- Financing support either a loan arranged through a bank or facility to pay in instalments. This is true for most consumer durables and automobiles today.

However, in order for the channel partner to provide these services, there are certain policy decisions with which the company or firm has to take the support of the channel partner. These policies could relate to:

- Clear pricing—the MRP on consumer packs is a good example of this. Of course, the retailer is free to sell the goods below the MRP; discount stores do this.
- Making the terms of sale clear—cash on delivery or credit for 15 days, for example, policy on damaged stocks returns is another such policy that needs to be clearly defined. The terms, of course, could vary with the size of the channel partner and his contribution to the company business.

Even the delivery frequency needs to be defined. For example, most FMCG companies may deliver thrice a week to major wholesalers, whereas to retailers it may be only once a week. Pharmaceutical companies may serve major hospitals as and when they place their orders which may mean even three times a day. In the case of consumer products, it is to be specified if the channel member (like a distributor) has to cover the market with ready stocks or he can book orders in the market and deliver the goods later.

The territory is assigned to the channel partner, like a distributor for coverage. This avoids channel conflict and also ensures regularity of coverage of the customers on agreed frequency. However, the Monopolies & Restrictive Trade Practices (MRTP) Act does not permit formally assigning territories to distributors/agents/stockists. (The MRTP Act has been replaced by the Competition Act, 2002 from September 1, 2009. You will study more on this in a later chapter.)

Table 10.4 Channel Policies Summary

List of Channel Policies
Clear and transparent pricing
Clear terms of sale for channel members
Defined delivery frequency
Assigned territory and beat plans
Payment terms—cash or credit and how much
Permitted minimum margins
Additional support when required
Complaint handling system

The margins and other facilities the company will provide the distributor for help in doing its business in the defined territory. Most of these relate to financial responsibilities—payment terms (most FMCG companies use blank pre-signed cheques), credit, margins, and distribution subsidies (some companies pay a part of the distribution costs for covering rural markets). If not a policy, there should be clear guidelines (may be even in writing) to the channel partners on problem solving and complaint handling procedure.

Marketing support to the channel members like advertising, point of purchase materials, merchandising support, trade and consumer promotions do not form part of any policy shared with the channel members but are planned and executed as required.

Summary of Channel Functions

- Physical distribution—reaches the product or service to the user.
- Keeps contact with the company customers including handling customer complaints.
- Helps build long-term relationships—relevant for selling in B2B.
- Market feedback to a company—on company products, promotions, pricing and competition activities.
- Company rules, terms, promotions, etc., are communicated to the customers.
- Negotiates prices with the company and its customers.
- Understand market trends and keeps the company informed.
- Matches terms and conditions to suit customers.
- Handles risks for price fluctuations.
- Handles final stage product assembly—for example, bicycles.
- Finances credit into the market and inventory holdings.
- Provides after sales service.

LO 5 Describe prominent marketing a channel systems

PROMINENT MARKETING CHANNEL SYSTEMS

We have seen that companies use a variety of channel partners depending on the business they are in and the level of customer service they are striving for. The various channel partners can be grouped into three channel systems: (i) Vertical marketing systems, (ii) Horizontal marketing systems and (iii) Multi-channel marketing systems.

We will look at each of these systems in brief here.

Vertical Marketing Systems

This is at variance with a conventional marketing channel system of a producer, distributor and retailer. Each of these channel members including the company acts independently and tries to run a profitable business. If all these entities were to act together as one team to provide service to the end-user, it would be called a 'vertical marketing system'. All the members of the marketing network co-operate and work together. Various parties like producers, wholesalers and retailers act as an integrated system to avoid conflicts. This coming together improves operating efficiency and marketing effectiveness. They benefit from size and bargaining power and reduce duplication in efforts.

Vertical marketing systems are of three types: (i) corporate, (ii) administered, and (iii) contractual.

Corporate VMS

Successive stages of production and distribution are handled by one entity. This gives a high degree of control over the channel for the company. Large retailers like Food World and Shoppers Stop are increasing the level of own products and brands in their stores to get this kind of leverage. The company would like to do this in order to ensure that it has a direct control on the distribution of its products.

To further illustrate, this could also be ideal for a company selling precious medical diagnostic equipment. As such equipment are very expensive and highly sensitive to use, the company would keep a tight control on the distribution and use of such products to protect its reputation.

One broad example of corporate VMS is the airline services providing services at value for money prices. Other examples of corporate VMS could be Bata, Bombay Dyeing, Raymond, Titan, Sears and Goodyear.

Administered VMS

Here the ownership of the different distribution channels is not with one entity rather one entity is of a certain size and it influences that it can control other channel partners. Most manufacturers of large market share products like HUL or Nestle can dictate terms to retailers, for example, on stock levels, shelf space allocation to them and prominence of displays.

One large entity usually coordinates the distribution activities and gains market power by dominating the channel. This power could be exercised in gaining shelf space, special displays, commanding pricing policies and promotional strategies.

Other examples include Pepsi, Coca Cola and Gillette. All these companies have very strong brands established over a long period and enjoy a strong consumer franchise. The channel members associated with these companies, including the wholesalers and retailers in the market place, are proud to stock and sell their products and would, therefore, be willing to listen and act on the company demands which they would not extend to lesser known companies/brands.

Contractual VMS

Contractual VMS are convenient arrangements between channel members when they get together to obtain economies of scale or use favorable opportunities to increase their sales. These could take the form of operating promotions together. These are rightly called "value-added partnerships".

Contractual VMS can take the form of franchisees, retailer co-operatives or wholesaler sponsored chains. Some examples are given below:

- Wholesaler sponsored value chains like Kemp Toys. It could be a chain of retailers to build standardized selling practices and gain from buying economies.
- Retailer co-operatives like Janta Bazaar, Apna Bazaar and others where a business entity is built to get economies of scale.
- Manufacturer sponsored retail franchise like car dealers of Maruti and Hyundai.
- Manufacturer sponsored wholesaler franchise like soft drink bottlers who buy the concentrate from Pepsi or Coca Cola.

There could also be a link to one part of the distribution organization—a franchise organization, like for some pizza brands. Service firm sponsored retailer franchise like Starbucks, Cafe-Coffee Day, McDonalds and Pizza Hut where a distribution network is franchised.

Horizontal Marketing Systems

This system operates between two or more totally unrelated companies but the arrangement of working together provides benefits to both. They can then exploit the marketing opportunity better by this tie-up. This is a highly opportunistic arrangement and could be short or long-term. Each company sees the strength of the other which it can exploit to its advantage. It is obviously a mutually beneficial arrangement.

Examples could be of supermarkets having ATMs of leading banks in their premises or Café Coffee Day outlets at airports. Retail outlets in petrol pumps are other examples.

Recently, one would have heard of the efforts of companies trying to work with each other to benefit from distribution synergies. The thinking seems to have emanated from the FMCG companies like HUL and Colgate which are known for their widespread and intensive distribution reach. They look at distributing non-competing mass consumption products which do not have a strong distribution presence for a fee. This will help the other company to increase its reach and also help the service provider company to share its distribution costs.

Multi-channel Marketing Systems

This system is adopted by companies which use two or more marketing channels to reach different customer segments. Most FMCG companies, for example, have a different set of channels to service the retail trade and institutional customers.

This system has the benefits of:

- Far better coverage of the market and its various segments by using the most appropriate means of reaching each segment.
- Adding a new channel to reduce the costs of distribution. For example, a company may decide to get orders on phone from customers located far away rather than sending the salesperson or distributor. However, this may not reduce the cost of physically reaching the customer which can also be overcome by specifying purchase lot sizes or reducing frequency of deliveries.

Large high potential customers, companies could build in a customized channel. For example, some companies use their own salespeople to call on big customers and collect orders even though they may get the products delivered by the distributor. Some consumer product companies get sales orders from the Canteen Stores Department through their own salespeople and may deliver it directly from their factory or in the case of smaller CSD units, through their nearest distributor. Even the price and other terms are negotiated by the company personnel only.

Multi-channel distribution is used in situations where:

- The same product is sold to different market segments.
- Unrelated products are sold in the same market—like HUL selling detergents and ice creams in the same market.
- The size of buyers varies—selling tea to retailers and big hotels. This could also be seen in the case of pharmaceutical companies who can have three different sets of salespeople calling on: (i) doctors who prescribe the products, (ii) chemists who stock and sell the products direct to the end-users who come with doctors' prescriptions, and (iii) hospitals and nursing homes which use the products to treat their patients.
- Geographic concentration of potential consumers varies—like in urban and rural markets.
- The reach is difficult for certain segments—like selling in Ladakh or the North Eastern states.

Managing the additional channels is not always simple, as we will see in Chapter 14 when we will discuss channel conflicts.

LO 6 Evaluate costs and margins of the distribution system

COSTS AND MARGINS IN DISTRIBUTION SYSTEMS

Each channel member in a system has to incur some cost to ensure distribution up to the customer level. The costs include the capital investment (distribution vans, for example) and working capital (as in market credit, inventory cost, etc.) and operating expenses (salaries and incentives for people, utility expenses etc.).

The company for which the channel partner works will ensure a margin or more likely a mark-up from which the channel member has to deduct his expenses to arrive at his margins.

Channel members are never happy talking about the margins they are making. Companies would do better to talk about ROI rather than margins. This has also been explained in Chapter 11.

Costs can be estimated for channel partners who are on a contract or similar formal relationship with a company like C&FAs, distributors, dealers etc. For independent channel partners like wholesalers and retailers, their costs can only be estimated (anyway it is not uniform among them).

Two examples are explained as follows:

Carrying and Forwarding Agent (C&FA)

Costs incurred:

- Storage/warehousing
- Handling of goods—loading and unloading
- Warehouse operating costs—utilities and communication
- Labour costs

Companies normally give about 1 to 2 percent margin to the C&FA on the total value of the goods handled.

Distributor

Cost incurred:

- Interest cost of inventory
- Cost of credit extended in the market
- Operating expenses for distribution units—vans, etc.
- Manpower cost
- Cost of utilities, communication, etc.

Companies in the FMCG industry normally give a mark-up of about 5 percent. After meeting all costs, the distributor is able to get an ROI between 25 percent and 30 percent. In industrial goods, the mark-up could be up to 10 percent and the ROI between 35 percent and 50 percent.

Wholesalers normally manage with a margin of 1 percent on their turnover as they rely on large volumes.

There have been several opinions of how much margins retailers make—the estimates vary between 20 percent for chemists or general stores to 50–60 percent for food retailers. The retailer makes the largest margins in the entire distribution network.

Exhibit 10.4

Eureka Forbes—Direct Distribution Success Story

Eureka Forbes has pioneered the concept of direct sales in India and has become one of the largest direct sales organizations across the globe.

The company bagged Asia's Most Admired Knowledge Enterprise (MAKE) Award for 2005, among 27 finalists from 8 countries in Asia. More recently, it signed up with Lux International of Switzerland for direct sales in Europe.

Eureka Forbes, a ₹550 crore company today, is the leader in water purification systems, vacuum cleaners and air purifiers. Known to be aggressive in sales, with a penchant for influencing purchase decisions at home, EF pioneered the concept of direct sales in India. The Managing Director, S L Goklaney, says, "Today, we are one of the largest direct sales organizations across the globe. One reason for the success has been our belief in the vision to provide happy, healthy and pollution free environment that is built on trust and lasting relationships with our customers."

In water purifiers, the company commands a 64 percent market share and in vacuum cleaners it has 80 percent market share. The uniqueness with EF has been its marketing strategy. The company has about 7000 sales personnel on its payrolls, operating from over 92 cities and 450 smaller towns, through franchised direct operations. S K Palekar, Senior VP Marketing and Knowledge Management, says, "We have consciously avoided taking the dealer route. Our method of selling is based on value and depth, unlike a dealer who sells on price."

The company claims a strike rate of one out of every four sales calls culminating into sales. It has also got a strong retail network of 20,000 outlets to tap the walk-in customer, who has seen the product's plus points when the company representative called home earlier.

The top management of EF emphasizes that, "The flanking strategy helps the company in getting the customers missed out on the first call. We are not makers of transactions but builders of relationships. When the consumer durables industry went through a slowdown a couple of years ago, we grew at 12–15 percent CAGR over a five year period."

One time sale is a strict NO at Eureka Forbes. The company has a strong service network of 900 plus personnel across the country with Mumbai alone having about 70 service centers; and 80 percent of their customers are within 3 km radius of their service centers.

"According to the senior management team, with India having 210 million households, and since we have barely managed to touch 4.2 million of them, the world is our oyster".

— *Business India*, November 20, 2005

This is a good example of a direct distribution network sustained over a long period of time. As the products happen to be of direct help and use for the housewife, the direct company salesmen network has been effective in the demonstration effect of selling. The salesman teaches the housewife how to use the gadget and also highlights the ensuing results.

SUMMARY

LO 1

- A marketing channel is either a company owned or contracted organization that helps provide the reach for the company product or service to its customers or end-users. Channels get classified based on formats driving them like producer, seller or service provider.

LO 2

- The marketing channels are expected to perform a number of functions. These functions recognize three kinds of flows:
  - *Forward flow*: From the company to the customers, basically goods and services

  - *Backward flow*: From the customers to the company, mostly the value of the goods or services bought by the customers.
  - *Both ways flow*: Which is mostly information
- These flows are further explained in terms of physical possession, title, payments, information and promotions.
- All the flows cannot be performed by any single channel partner unless the company is willing to carry out all the tasks. Hence, there is a need for a set of intermediaries to perform each of these flows.
- The channel flows lead to customer service levels. Again each of the channel partners has a different role varying by degrees in generating the customer service levels.

LO 3

- Marketing channels support the exchange relationships between companies and the users of their products. Major economic developments in countries have evolved channels into supporting systems for these economic activities.

LO 4

- The service deliverable of the channel systems could be bulk breaking, place utility, reduced waiting time, assortment facility, installation and after sales support, and financial help. Of course, delivering this service output has a cost attached to it as the channel partner has also to be remunerated for the channel flow he performs. It is the responsibility of the sales manager to ensure that the cost is optimized in terms of customer service levels.

LO 5

- Marketing channel systems are basically classified into:
  - Vertical marketing systems: System where various channel entities band together to deliver service to the customer. VMS is of three types: (i) Administered—one channel leader influences and controls the other channel partners, (ii) Corporate—successive stages of production and distribution handled by one entity, and (iii) Contractual—channel members agree to work as a team by having convenient arrangements with each other and make use of favorable opportunities and economies of scale.
  - Horizontal marketing systems: Two or more unrelated companies working together to benefit both.
  - Multi-channel marketing systems: System where a company uses two or more channels to reach different customer segments.
- The origin of marketing channels in rural areas started with the efforts made by farmers to reach their produce to the consumption centres. The evolution of marketing channels only got strengthened after the industrial revolution and when the companies discovered the benefits of economies of scale in production. In the US, the coming of automobiles and the creation of major highways seem to have spawned the idea of major organised retailers outside major cities.

LO 6

- Channel costs include costs of investment in infrastructure and the operating expenses and working capital. Companies prefer to talk about ROI with their channel partners than talking about margins they make from the business of distribution.

Key Terms

Glossaries of key terms are mentioned at the end of all chapters

Administered VMS
Channel formats
Contractual VMS
Corporate VMS
Financial flow
Horizontal marketing system
Information flow
Multi-channel marketing system
Payment flow
Physical flow
Promotion flow
Service deliverables
Title flow
Vertical Marketing Systems (VMS)
Zero channel level

Conceptual Questions

1. Enumerate the functions performed by marketing channels. LO4 E
2. List the channel flows with a brief explanation of each of them. LO2 M
3. What are the possible channel formats? Explain their characteristics? LO2 M
4. Explain the various channel levels with examples. LO4 E
5. Describe the prominent channel systems with examples. LO5 M
6. Trace some of the major steps in the evolution of channel systems. LO3 E
7. Summarize some of the costs which a distributor will consider for understanding his profitability. LO6 M
8. List some of the major functions of distribution channels. LO4 E

Objective Type Questions

Select the most appropriate response out of the various options available in each of the following questions:

1. Ownership flow in a channel means transfer of __________ goods.
   (a) title (b) storage (c) value (d) consumption LO2 E

Note: Difficulty Level → E — Easy; M — Medium; D — Difficult

2. Physical possession flow deals with __________ and transportation in a channel system.
   (a) receipt (b) billing (c) storage (d) accounting **LO2 E**

3. A C&FA or distribution centre is only concerned with __________, information and title flows.
   (a) storage (b) physical (c) ownership (d) financial **LO2 E**

4. The number of channel partners and flows increases with the __________ of the distribution planned.
   (a) depth (b) intensity (c) width (d) nature **LO2 E**

5. A zero level channel denotes a __________ distribution set up.
   (a) direct (b) own (c) dedicated (d) indirect **LO2 E**

6. Bulk breaking is the facility provided by the channel to the customer to buy in convenient __________ for her use.
   (a) lots (b) sizes (c) discounts (d) quantities **LO4 E**

7. A vertical marketing system is one in which all the members of the marketing network __________ and work together.
   (a) plan (b) co-operate (c) compete (d) collaborate **LO5 E**

8. A multi-channel marketing system uses two or more marketing channels to reach __________ customer segments.
   (a) different (b) many (c) similar (d) convenient **LO5 E**

9. A contractual VMS is a convenient arrangement between __________.
   (a) companies (b) competitors
   (c) channel members (d) customers **LO5 E**

10. A corporate VMS is a system in which successive stages of production and __________ are handled by the same entity.
    (a) distribution (b) marketing (c) branding (d) selling **LO5 E**

11. Channel members facilitate __________ relationships.
    (a) exchange (b) profitable (c) long-term (d) strong **LO4 E**

12. Channel member ________is a fair measure of the financial performance of a channel.
    (a) sales (b) margins (c) profits (d) contribution **LO6 E**

Application Questions

1. Explain the channel flows required for a company selling electric motors and pumps and identify the channel intermediaries who can best perform these flows. **LO2 M**

2. The Marketing Manager of Growmore Fertilizers is looking for companies for developing a horizontal marketing system together. You are to advise him on the type of companies which most suitably meet his needs and why. **LO5 D**

3. Lovely Textiles is planning to set up a direct distribution network to sell its fabrics. What advice would you give them and why? LO4 M

4. Prime Mover Products: channel partner role in relationships—

   Prime Mover is one of the largest makers of Product Life Cycle management (PLM) products. PM had one primary channel partner known as Full Circle (FC) for one part of the world. Ultramarine was a major customer of PM and had implemented their PLM solution and was quite happy with the solution. Ultramarine was eager to upgrade the solution and approached FC to give a proposal. FC informed PM regional office of this request. The PM Regional Manager suggested that they give a joint proposal but FC refused. FC got the approval of PM to independently give the proposal to Ultramarine. The Regional Manager was eager to try and get this business from Ultramarine directly and hence, submitted another proposal for the same requirement.

   Ultramarine was confused. They had two proposals—one from the principal (PM) and the other from their channel partner (FC). Ultramarine also found that the proposal from FC was technically superior of the two. Ultramarine informed FC that the principal PM had also submitted a proposal for the same job.

   You represent Full Circle, the trusted and crucial channel partner of PM. What would you do in this situation in order to execute the job while keeping your relationships with your principal (PM) and key customer (Ultramarine) intact? LO4 D

ASSIGNMENTS FOR STUDENTS

1. Select any product in a retail outlet in any product group: (i) FMCG, (ii) consumer electronics and (iii) consumer durables. For this selected product, trace the flow: (a) physical, (b) collection, and (c) information.
2. Meet 2 channel partners of any company: (i) C&FA, (ii) distributor/dealer. See if you can see their signed contract with their principal company. What are their obligations? What can they expect in return from the principal company?
3. Try and work out the costs incurred, margin earned and the ROI for the following types of channel partner by meeting them. (i) FMCG distributor, (ii) a pharma company distributor, and (iii) an automobile dealer.

Reference Notes

1. *E-commerce set to touch Rs 1200 crore,* Business India, July 31, 2005, p. 18.
2. *Happening Times,* Business India, Nov 20, 2005, p. 92.

3. Bert Rosenbloom, *Marketing Channels—A Management View*, The Dryden Press.
4. Badi and Badi, *Rural Marketing*, Himalaya Publishing House, Chapters 5 and 23.
5. Ramkishen Y, *New Perspectives in Rural and Agricultural Marketing*, Jaico Publishing House, Chapter 8.
6. *Marketing Channels—A Management View*, Bert Rosenbloom, The Dryden Press.

CASE 10.1

Research One Ltd. (ROL)

The Team Meeting

JFK, the CEO of Research One Ltd. (ROL) had called for an urgent meeting of the sales team and the delivery team to build some guidelines for future projects and make any changes required in the sales and delivery process. The meeting was to discuss the following major issues and find suitable solutions:

- Understanding customer needs correctly before making a proposal.
- Getting the delivery team to clearly understand the scope of work before starting the implementation.
- How could the delivery team get involved in developing the Scope of Work (SOW) so that at the end of the project, the customer would be delighted with the delivery of the solution?
- ROL had a benchmark realization per project hour of $150. They were not getting anywhere near this figure. What could be done to achieve this?

In the one-day interactive workshop called by the CEO, the teams had to come out with actionable solutions.

The Company

ROL is a Knowledge Services Company based on an offshore model. It assists clients to make focused strategic decisions. It provides customized market research, business intelligence reports and media services.

ROL believes in understanding client requirements and delivering results, which assist the client in making key decisions. It pairs up as a strategic partner in resolving client's issues through an effective Account Management Function (provide customized solutions depending on the changing expectations/business conditions) led jointly by Sales and Delivery Lead which enables them to act as a consultant.

The Company has made steady progress and has been able to achieve sales growth of over 30 percent, in 2009 vis-à-vis 2008. Majority of its clients are US based and belong to a range of industry verticals including industrial, consumer and retail, technology and telecom, media and automotive.

Consistent Growth

ROL has been in business for over 7 years and has grown from just 14 people in 2002 to 400 in 2009. Its revenues have grown five times since inception from $4 million to $20 million and along with this, the sales staff has increased from 6 to 60 including onsite/offsite account managers. The account managers are not only responsible for maintaining key accounts but also in delivering and presenting the research projects to assist in effective delivery and solution building.

When the company started, the onsite sales team along with the assistance of the sales support team used to pitch to clients. The delivery team provided a Subject Matter Expert (SME) in providing nuances of how ROL's capability could assist them in developing effective solutions to their issues.

Delivery Model

The process of initiating a research project is outlined as follows:

- The sales support team provides the information on the proposed project to the onsite sales team who then interact with the client.
- After this first interaction, the onsite sales team talks to the delivery team to develop a proposal.
- The proposal is sent to the client for approval on the scope and deliverables of interest to the client.
- After the client approves the proposal (with modifications, if any), the onsite sales lead sends a Research Request Form (RRF) to the delivery team.
- The delivery team has to now work with the client to deliver the project as defined by the Scope of Work (SOW) in the client approved proposal.

The negotiations with the client to finalize the project was initially done by the sales team along with an SME. Later, the role evolved and was managed by the account manager.

Providing Customer Delight

The delivery team was consistently delivering customer satisfaction and decided to focus on customer delight in future. This meant extensive research efforts beyond the SOW. This additional input resulted in a lower realization per project hour from the earlier $150 to recent $40.

At times, the lower realization was also due to inadequate attention paid by the onsite sales team in properly identifying the SOW or the client not pointing out the exact requirements even at the time of 'kick-off' meeting with the delivery team. The deliverables in such cases also went beyond the SOW.

Existing Project Delivery Flow

The situation demands answers to the questions given below

Discussion Questions

1. What system should the onsite sales team put in place to ensure that the client requirements are clearly understood and mentioned in the SOW?
2. At the time of kick-off meeting, what precautions should the delivery team take to re-confirm that the SOW is exactly what the client is looking for in terms of deliverables?
3. How can the delivery team help in developing the SOW so that Research One is seen as delivering customer delight?
4. What more needs to be done to ensure that the realization per project hour is closer to the benchmark $150?

This case study has been prepared by V M Cavale with the help of Adarsh Arun Halwe, a student of TAPMI – CEE, for only classroom discussion.

Chapter 11

Channel Institutions: Retailing

LEARNING OBJECTIVES

After studying this chapter, you will be able to:

- **LO 1** Understand retail and relationships in retail
- **LO 2** Explain the theories in retail
- **LO 3** Review global and Indian retail scenc and trends
- **LO 4** Identify the types of retailers, trade and retail formats, and retail categories
- **LO 5** Describe the retail management strategies
- **LO 6** Discuss retail operations, performance measures, retail in rural India and FDI in retail
- **LO 7** Outline franchising and e-tailing

Sunrise Stores

Sunrise Stores (SS) is a well-known retail store in a major tier-two city located in a prominent residential area. Sunrise has been operating in the same location for over 36 years. It is presently owned and managed by Gopal, who inherited the store from his father.

Over the years, Sunrise has grown manifold thanks to many of their regular customers. Two supermarkets have sprung 3 km away but they couldn't sway Sunrise's customers.

Sunrise deals in all house-hold goods, groceries, food grains, frozen foods, etc., but not fruits and vegetables. Some of the factors which customers like about Sunrise are:

- Availability of choice of products/brands/pack-sizes. If a particular product is asked for regularly, but is not available in Sunrise, Gopal will make the efforts to get it for customers.
- Fair prices, assured good quality
- Personalized touch—in spite of having three employees, Gopal likes to attend to customers himself also
- Credit facilities and home deliveries to select regular customers
- Correct implementation of any company promotions on brands
- Goods can be returned if customers are not happy with the quality.

Gopal estimates that his store has over 6000 SKUs and about 300 regular customers. He normally sells on cash but in the last one year, Sunrise has started accepting credit/debit card payments.

All the financial accounts of the store are maintained manually by Gopal himself; he is proud of his ability to keep correct updated accounts and he pays all taxes promptly. Many of his vendors have appreciated his efforts on book keeping. However, Gopal is not willing to share any of Sunrise Stores financial information with anyone.

A month ago, Gopal had a visit from Patrick, a software engineer from a company called Retail Mantra which provides IT enabled solutions for small enterprises including independent retailers. After learning about the operations of Sunrise, Patrick said that Retail Mantra can help Sunrise streamline its business by offering the following IT solutions:

- A cash register based system for billing, accounts receivable and sales
- A POS system for stock management and control and financial book keeping
- A customized POS solution for automation of purchases and payments.

The meeting was a preliminary one. Even costs and benefits were not discussed. Patrick promised to come back in 10 days with some live examples on how these systems have helped retailers like Sunrise.

Gopal is in a dilemma whether he should opt for such a simple system to IT enable most of his routine operations that would give him enough free time for enhancing sales and customer service.

LO 1 Understand retail and relationships in retail

INTRODUCTION TO RETAIL AND RELATIONSHIPS

According to the English dictionary, *retail* is derived from the term *retaillier*, which seems to be a French word meaning "to break bulk". In broad terms, that is what a retailer does very well. To illustrate, the retailer buys a carton/case/box of Britannia Tiger biscuits from the distributor, but sells a packs of 100 g, and not the whole carton, to the consumer. The term retailer also implies that he deals directly with the end-user or consumer. Being the last link in the distribution channel by which the manufacturer reaches the end-user consumer, the retailer has more knowledge of the customer's wants and needs and can influence the end user's buying decisions.

Some of the other characteristics of retail trade are:

- The order sizes tend to be small but many.
- The retailer caters to a wide variety of customers and hence has to keep a large assortment of goods.
- A lot of the buying in the retail outlet could be on impulse, and hence managing inventory is critical.
- Retail store service personnel (in smaller stores) and the goods displayed (in major stores) are an important element of the selling process.
- The retailer's strengths are in ensuring "availability" and "visibility" of the product he sells – true for the corner grocer or the supermarket.
- The targeted customer mix decides the elements of the "marketing mix" which the retailer has to develop to optimize his investment. The elements of the marketing mix so designed, gives the "image" to the store.

Any business entity selling to consumers is "retailing". The goods may be sold in a shop, in person in the home of the consumer, on the street, by mail, on the Internet, telephone, or a vending machine. Even renting products to an end user is retailing. Order sizes in retail tend to be small but more frequent. Shops into retail consider their location as the most critical part of doing business. Sellers online consider delivery as the most critical part of doing business. With the growth of Internet on mobiles, the scope for online retailing has enhanced considerably.

Retailers focus on location, type of customers targeted, the product offering, customer communication, promotions, and scope for increasing footfalls and stickiness as some of the factors in designing their marketing strategies. Franchising and electronic retailing are more specialized forms of retail.

DEFINITION OF RETAILING

Any business entity selling products and services to consumers is "retailing". The goods may be sold in a shop, in person, by mail, on the Internet, telephone or a vending machine. It could be sold on the street or in the home of the consumer. Just as for products, retail also has a life cycle. Newer forms of retail come up to replace the old—this is faster in the western world, but not so much in India.

Retailing includes all the activities involved in selling or renting consumer products and services directly to ultimate consumers for their personal or home consumption. Ultimate consumers make most of their purchases in retail stores, which are independent of the producer.

A study of consumer buying habits found that only about 35 percent of supermarket purchases were specifically planned. The rest included impulse purchases, substitutions of one brand for another, and generally planned purchases for which consumers had no specific brand in mind. These decisions can be greatly influenced by the quality of the retailers' merchandising efforts.

How do consumers decide which retailer to buy from?

A consumer selects a retailer based on the following factors:

- Price (value offered, credit, special discounts)
- Location (convenience, parking, safety, stores nearby)
- Product selection (width and depth of assortment, brands, quality)
- Special services (home delivery, special orders, gift wrap, valet parking)
- Helpful salespeople (courteous, knowledgeable, fast check-out)
- Fairness in dealings (honesty, return privileges)
- What does the retailer do to ensure stickiness in his customers?

Functions of retailing include:

- Performing marketing functions that enable them to make available a wide variety of products to the consumers.
- Helping create time, place, and possession utilities.
- Adding form utility such as when a clothing retailer alters a trouser to fit a customer.
- A retailer's services also help create an image for the products he sells.

Retailers add value to products through:

- The services they offer such as credit, delivery, extended store hours.
- The personnel they hire who help identify and solve customer problems.
- The store's location, perhaps near other stores or in a bazaar to facilitate comparison shopping.

A retail firm can be classified according to:

- Form of ownership—sole ownership, partnership, corporation, consumer co-operatives.
- Operational structure—independent, chain, franchise.
- Service and price orientation—full service, limited service, self-service, normal margin, discounter, off-price.
- Merchandise offering—general, mass or specialty. Merchandise width refers to the number of non-competing product lines offered for sale. Merchandise depth refers to the number of brands, models or styles carried for each product category.
- Where the sale takes place—in the store or non-store.

We have dealt with types of retailers in detail later in this chapter under the section "Trading/Retail Formats and Types of Retail". Still it is worth mentioning some kinds of retailers as listed in Table 11.1.

Every business publication today proclaims that retailing is the fastest growing industry across the world.

Retailing today has to constantly re-invent itself in new ways to thrive. While deciding strategy and the distribution systems, the retailer has to take into account the "bottom-up" pressure exerted by the consumer. The customer decides whether the retailer is good for him or not based on what "new items" the retailer can offer him both in terms of the range of products and the bundled services. The retailer has to, therefore, constantly innovate to keep the "stickiness" of his customers intact.

Table 11.1

Type of Retailer	Characteristics
Speciality Store (Crossword)	Narrow product line with deep assortment—apparel, furniture, books
Departmental Store	Several product lines in different departments – Shoppers Stop, Big Bazaar
Supermarket (Big Bazaar)	Large, low-cost, low-margin, high volume, self-service operation with a wide offering
Convenience Store (*Kirana* Store) (Aishwarya Kirana)	Small stores located in residential areas, open long hours all days of the week—limited variety of fast moving products like groceries, food
Discount Store	Standard merchandise sold at lower prices for low margins
Corporate Chains	More outlets commonly owned and controlled by one firm like Reliance Retail
Voluntary Chain	Wholesaler sponsored group of independent retailers
Retailer Co-ops	Independent retailers with central buying operations and common promotions
Consumer Co-ops	Co-operative societies of groups of consumers operating their own stores—farmers, industrial workers, and so on
Franchise Organization (Café Coffee Day)	Contractual arrangement between the producer and retailers—selling the producer's products exclusively

Retailers can at times be wholesalers but the reverse may not be possible. Retailers focus on the cost side and the demand side of the businesses.

- They need to be profitable with optimum inventory. The inventory turnover has to be high even if the margins are low so that the profitability is ensured.
- The second goal is to provide optimum service levels to the shoppers compared to competition.

Traditional retail (the grocer in your locality) believes in high margins as his volumes are limited. His costs are also well contained and he can provide personalized services to his customers.

The modern retailer believes in large volumes at low margins. He also tries to control his costs but does not provide personalized services. In either case, the model followed has to end up "profitable" for the enterprise.

- The retailer gets his merchandise from the company or its distributor or even a wholesaler and sells it in sizes suitable to his customers.
- He has to decide the assortment/range/portfolio of the products that he will stock.
- He has to decide the kind of services that he will provide from his outlet.
- He has to finalize the delivery model that he will follow for meeting the requirements of his customers.
- The pattern of payments he is willing to accept for selling the products to the customers.

Retailers can be classified based on their size, location, range of products handled, and ownership profile. Most of the time when marketers talk about a Point-of-Sale (POS) or Point of Purchase (PPP), they are referring to a retail point.

In the marketing mix, the retail point is covered by the "p of Place". Not only is the retail shop the point where the purchase interaction takes place between the retailer and his customers, it is the most important point where the customer gets all his information about scores of companies and their products. The most critical channel flows of the retailer are physical and information, even though the retailer is responsible for all the channel flows identified in Chapter 9.

The information flow at the retailer point is two way. While the retailer is the source of all information about the company products to the consumers, he is also an important point of feedback from the consumers to the companies whose products he sells. This information to the companies also bestows on the retailer some influence on the company decisions in terms of pricing, packaging, promotions, and the entire product strategy. The retailer is also an important information source to companies on all their major competitors.

Challenges for Retailers

Given below are some of the major challenges faced by retailers:

- Customer satisfaction
- Ability to acquire the right products
- Product presentation
- Traffic building
- Layout
- Location
- Keeping pace with technology

THE RETAILER AS A SALESMAN

For all mass based consumers products like FMCG products, over the counter medicines, consumables like electric bulbs, batteries, and even for consumer durables like radios, refrigerators, televisions, and washing machines, the retailer is an influential salesman at the most critical point of purchase. Most consumers, who may get confused by the wide choice of products available, will finally buy one product based on the retailer's recommendation. Even when a product of the consumer's choice is not available, the retailer will not let the consumer go empty handed but would recommend an alternative product, which most of the times the consumer will accept as he trusts the retailer. The retailer is thus, an effective salesman for a large number of companies whose products he stocks and sells in his shop/enterprise.

The influence of the retailer in rural markets is even more. Most rural consumers get influenced by the retailer's recommendation and buy only those products that he suggests. In many cases, the consumer has a running account of his purchases (the cumulative credit extended) with the retailer and has no choice but to buy the product suggested by the retailer. Rural retailers normally stock a limited number of items and expect high margins from these as they extend credit to more customers than their urban counterparts.

Companies cannot ignore the power of the retailer in influencing the buying decisions of the customer. As the direct contact with the end user, the retailer can positively help the company by becoming its POS salesman. It is no surprise, therefore, to see in the market place, the number of ways in which companies keep wooing the retailers.

Example of an Innovative Retailer

Phone-in Drive-Through Market, US: A customer orders groceries by telephone from the store's 4000-item-catalog. Three hours later, he can pull into the pick-up lane outside the market's cavernous warehouse where his groceries will be waiting on a six-foot high shopping cart (in the interim, the perishables have been properly refrigerated). In two minutes, he can pick up, pay for and haul off the groceries without getting out of his car. In this new-fangled supermarket, parking problems and check-out-lines are a thing of the past.

LO 2 Explain the theories in retail

THEORIES IN RETAIL

Marketing experts have classified retail theories into two broad categories as:

• Cyclical Theories	(i) Wheel of Retailing (ii) Accordion
• Evolutionary Theories	(i) Dialectic Process (ii) Natural Selection

These retail theories are explained briefly below:

Wheel of Retailing

This theory was proposed by Malcomb Mcnair (1958) and enumerates the way in which retail organizations change during their lifetime. This is described below in brief:

- A retail outlet starts with low prices, margins and simplicity. With time, in order to improve the footfalls and stickiness, the outlet would add additional services for its customers. This would add cost to the business.
- In the second stage, the outlet has higher prices, margins and a better image. In order to keep the customers happy, more services need to be added.
- There is an escalation of the second stage into the third stage where the retailer has built a "premium" image.
- This creates a gap in the market which gets filled by an entirely new outlet which starts at stage 1 of low prices, margins and simplicity.

A summary of the theory is given below:

Stage 1	Innovative Stage	Low price, low service, limited product offering
Stage 2	Traditional Stage	Improved product offering, better service and higher prices
Stage 3	Mature Stage	Increased competition, lower returns on investment, premium pricing possible

Retail Accordion Theory

This theory is proposed by Hollander and has also been described as general-specific-general theory (also called a cyclical theory). It explains that an outlet which starts as a general retailer grows into a specialized retailer and in course of time, becomes even a bigger general retailer. The examples of retail outlets in these phases are general broad-based outlets with a wide assortment moving to narrow based outlets with a specialized assortment and then on to the broad-based assortment again.

Theory of Natural Selection

The evolution of retail stores is influenced by the environmental factors like economic, demographic, legal, political, and technological. Retailers who successfully adapt to these factors are more successful.

The Dialectic Process Theory

This theory explains the reaction of a retailer to the actions of its competitors. The theory says that retailers mutually adapt from their "opposites" as in competitors. Any challenge by a competitor, by introduction of differential advantages, is countered by the retailer by a similar action, reducing the impact of the competitor and this process goes on.

In Conflictual Theory, this conflict between a retailer and its competitors is also likely to result in a new retail format.

There is also the concept of Retail Life Cycle, which is described as follows:

Retail Life Cycle (based on the Wheel of Retailing)

This theory looks at retail similar to the product life cycle. The stages explained by the retail life cycle include four stages which retail experts say can be clearly identified. These four stages are: (i) innovation (at the launch, online, value retail, etc.), (ii) quick growth (factory outlets, fixed price stores), (iii) maturity (consolidation—convenience, fast food, supermarkets), and (iv) decline (general stores, catalog retailers).

Some of these features are summarized as follows:

Innovation	Differentiated service in the product, format. Limited competition, good growth, reasonable profits—at the launch, online, value retail
Accelerated growth	Sales grow fast, competition emerges, some retailers become leaders and will invest more. Cost pressure on all retailers. Factory outlets, fixed price stores
Maturity	Severe competition, growth rates slow down. Retailers change strategy, formats and product offering—convenience, fast food, supermarkets
Decline	Some retailers lose competitive advantage, growth negative, costs increase and profits go down—general stores, catalog retailers

Experts also explain retail in terms of a business model. The components of the model include the challenges of new information, improved communication technology, shorter PLCs, global markets and tougher competition. The business model also includes the components of products and services offered, pricing policy, communication for consumer reach and size, appearance and store locations.

LO 3 Review global and Indian retail scene and trends

THE GLOBAL RETAILING SCENE

The retail world globally is well organized and in most developed countries is controlled by major companies. It is estimated that the global business in retail is worth US $6.6 trillion. In the developing countries, the retail trade is mostly unorganized. The size of the retail market varies from $2325 billion in the US to $180 billion in India. Of this, the share of organized retail is 85 percent in the US and about 5 percent in India. China has 20 percent and Taiwan is big at 80 percent.

US Retail Industry

Estimated size in Billion USD:
2014: 4632, 2015: 4785, 2016: 4952 and 2017 (est): 5125 or over 5 trillion dollars. Average growth rate: 4.5 percent per annum.

Sources: informationvine.com, emarketer.com, plunkettresearch.com, credencys.com, businesswire.com, thebalance.com; accessed on 27 May 2017

The retail sector is considered as part of the service sector and in countries where organized retail is strong, the contribution of the service sector to the GDP is very high. At the same time, the employment potential of the retail sector is also high. (It is estimated that 2 million retail outlets in the US employ about 22 million people). One can deduce from this that the retail sector plays a major role in the growth of the economy of any country. Globally, organized retail is becoming powerful over its suppliers and the producers of goods are taking action to protect their turf.

Retailers Dictate Terms

At one time, the packaged goods manufacturers were calling the shots in the retail sector. Today, with modern organized retail, the retailer is gaining an upper hand. Even with the limited growth of organized retail in India, the few modern retailers negotiate and get the most favorable terms from their consumer goods suppliers, which are themselves big companies like HUL, Nestle, Colgate, and Marico. Modern retailers get quantity discounts, sell shelf, and display space and get special discounts on promotional stocks. They also put conditions for stocking and selling new products.

Some of the reasons for the growth of the power of the retailer over the manufacturer particularly in the Western countries are:

- Consumer product margins for the retailer are low and in order to get higher volumes they need to get a share from others and hence the situation has become very competitive. This creates an enormous pressure on retailers to perform well. They need to spend more money on the stores to get footfalls.
- Retailers have to run business models which are result oriented and highly cost effective. Competition does not permit them to increase prices. Hence they have to make all efforts to reduce costs. Without the support of the suppliers, they cannot reduce costs, unless they reduce customer service. They look for economies of scale while working out terms with their suppliers.
- Merchandisers in retail are also in charge of buying. The profitability of the retailer is decided to a great extent at the stage of buying itself. Buyers influence the service levels, revenue, profitability, quality, and competitiveness. Naturally, they have to put pressure on their vendors to achieve these.
- The number of new products introduction is becoming unmanageable. The new products could be innovations, line extensions or substitutes. Even though store sizes have also increased substantially, they cannot accommodate all the new entrants and hence have to be choosy—which again gives them enormous power over their suppliers. Moreover, the manufacturer cannot guarantee the success of the new product. Only the past history of success with the company can give them a fair chance that the retailer will keep their current new product. Again in the US, retailers charge a penalty to companies whose products do not succeed.
- New developments in information technology are helping retailers to:
    - analyze what are their fast moving and most profitable products/brands/packs,
    - identify which are their profitable store locations,
    - recognize who are their most loyal and good customers. Each store can have the daily data of the average and the individual "shopping basket size" of all their customers for that day in addition to the composition of that shopping basket. They can tailor their promotions to suit these profitable units. Naturally the other products, brands, and SKUs get less priority, thus affecting the business of those vendors.
    - manage inventory, better—we will discuss about "efficient consumer response" in Chapter 13.

Retailers have several different formats to compete with—both brick and mortar, and click and mortar. For example, traditional corner/grocery stores in India still dominate the scene.

In order to overcome the difficulties, which the manufacturers face as a result of the increased power of retailers over them, they have started offering additional benefits to continue to be in the good books of the retailers. Some of these benefits are listed below:

- Hiring specific shelves for displays. The practice can be seen in all major cities in India even with small retailers.
- Selling with discounts on quantity purchases (known as QPS).

- A fee to be paid to the retailer if the product does not do well.
- Sharing of press advertising expenses featuring the store and the manufacturer brands.
- Payments for displays and shelf space—widespread in India also.
- Guaranteed taking back of slow moving or damaged stocks—again prevalent in the Indian context.

Except for the failure fees, which is not relevant in the Indian context, most of the consumer product companies follow all the practices listed above when dealing with modern organized retail in India as well. In India, the unsold stocks may be just returned to the producer.

Retailers' Own Brands/Private Labels

Modern retailers in the Western countries, particularly in Europe, have resorted very strongly to keep their own developed brands to compete with the better known company brands on their shelves. This practice is catching up—Shoppers Stop, Big Bazaar, and Nilgiris are already into developing and selling their own brands. We will see some examples later in the chapter.

Retailers' own brands have some inherent advantages:

- They are as good as the major brands but are priced less as they have cost advantages.
- They provide higher margins to the retailer.
- If successful, they give better bargaining power to the retailers. They can demand better terms from the national company brands.
- The task of merchandising becomes simpler.

Manufacturers' Response to Growing Retail Strength

Most of these responses are what has happened in the US where the retail power is evident. Some of these responses may be relevant in the Indian context some years down the line when the Indian organized retail grows big and influential.

- Manufacturers are taking the help of new technologies to manage organized retail better. Two such technologies are EDI (electronic data interchange) and VMI (vendor managed inventory) to manage the physical possession and ordering flows.
- Producers are putting less reliance on higher discounts to get better sales. Price cut promotions result in excess stocking during the promotions and hampers the planning at the supplier level. Suppliers plan to reduce frequent price cuts and use the savings for other customer driven promotions.
- Developing and introducing new products and pack sizes—pertinent in Indian context also. Of course, convincing the retailer to stock additional products, brands, or SKUs is not an easy exercise. Anyway it will take some time to copy and introduce the new product—this may at least give a six-month window to establish the new product.
- In the apparel industry, manufacturers use their own outlets to showcase their own brands, keep in direct touch with consumers, and counter the pressure from the major retailers. Some of these outlets are also meant to sell seconds and export surplus items.

Exhibit 11.1

Malls in India

There are about 105 malls in India with a total space of about 49 million sq. ft.

The top three most expensive retail locations in the world (rental per sq. ft. of real estate) are: (i) New York Upper 5th Avenue, (ii) Hong Kong Causeway, and (iii) Avenue des Champs Elysees, Paris

Ten most expensive retail locations in India (ET Retail—Cushman and Wakefield—main streets across the world):

1. Khan Market, Delhi—monthly rental ₹1250 per sq. ft.—world 28
2. Connaught Place, Delhi—₹850 per sq. ft.
3. DLF Galleria, Gurgaon—₹800 per sq. ft.
4. Linking Road, Bandra, Mumbai—₹760 per sq. ft. (F&B, apparel); (no space)
5. South extension, Delhi—₹700 per sq. ft.
6. Colaba Causeway, Mumbai—₹625 per sq. ft. (limited space)
7. Park Street, Kolkata—₹500 per sq. ft.
8. Greater Kailash 1, Delhi—₹460 per sq. ft.
9. Camac Street, Kolkata—₹450 per sq. ft.
10. Kemps Corner, Mumbai—₹425 per sq. ft.

Sources: www.wlivenews.com/top-10-biggest-shopping-malls-in-india.htm; http://www.rediff.com/money/slide-show/slide-show-1-indias-biggest-malls/20130424.htm; www.thehindubusinessline.com/specials/india-file/the-mall...20/article8807777.ece;accessed on 22 May 2017.

Retail Relationships

A successful retailer builds strong relationships both with his suppliers and his customers. Supplier relationships help in getting the products at the best bargains. A part of the benefits of good buying can be passed on to customers to gain competitive advantage and ensure "stickiness". Customer satisfaction is a result of total customer experience and not just price or assortment that the retailer has to offer.

Total customer value = product value (part of the assortment/offering) + service value (additional facilities like credit for example) + image value (pride associated with shopping with the retailer). To get this total customer value, the customer pays a total cost comprising of monetary cost (price paid for the product), time cost (time spent on shopping), psychic cost and energy cost (effort put into shopping).

In order to consistently deliver a value proposition to consumers, a retailer tries to make sure of the following:

- Customer delivered value should be what the customer thinks is right
- The value delivery has to be consistent
- The retailer should have a system in place to measure customer satisfaction
- Customers should be clear on the value proposition the retailer has planned for them—retailer communication should take care of this

- The positioning of the retailer with the "value delivery" focus should be in line with the intended target market.

Exhibit 11.2

Indian Retail Market Expected to Double in Subsequent Five Years

Overall retail market: 12 percent per annum; modern trade: 20 percent per annum; traditional: 10 percent per annum
2015: $ 600 billion; 2020: $ 1 trillion
Modern trade—2015: $ 60 billion; 2020: $ 180 billion
e-commerce—2015: $ 15 billion; 2020: $ 60 to 70 billion
Modern—supermarkets, hypermarkets and organized retail outlets
Traditional—smaller grocery stores
Some economic indicators:

- Average HH income—2010: $ 6393 2020: $ 18,448
- Urbanization—31 to 40 percent
- Nuclear HH—200 million
- Consumption spend per capita—25 to 50 percent
- Attitudinal shift in younger generation—75 percent
- People buying online—35 million of 100 million in 2 years

Sources: http://www.livemint.com/Industry/5Xu8P8GltZk8XEsz7Xk74O/Indian-retail-market-to-double-in-next-5-years-report.html, accessed on 22 May 2017; http://image-src.bcg.com/Retail-2020-Feb-2015-India_tcm21-28775.pdf, accessed on 22 May 2017.

THE RETAIL SCENE IN INDIA

It is estimated that there are over 12 million retail outlets of various sizes and varieties in India, most of them being in the unorganized sector. This works out to over 10 outlets per 1000 population. The unorganized sector, which has scores of independent, small stores, contributes to about 93 percent of the retail business. The average per capita space for retail in India is 2 sq. ft. compared to about 15 sq. ft. in the US—clearly denoting that the retail outlets are dispersed and very small. This is in line with the population of India itself, which is dispersed. Moreover, nearly three fourths of the population is rural, in hundreds of small villages that cannot support bigger retail formats. The estimated size of the unorganized retail market in India is ₹5,83,000 crore.

Comparison of B&M Stores with Global

Retail experts have compared some simple metrics (sales over space, gross margins and rentals) in India with global numbers and these are given below:

Sales per sq. ft.—India: ₹1500 to 2000; International: ₹8000 to 12000
Gross margins—7 to 8 percent lower in India
Rentals—Surprisingly 1.5 to 3 percent higher in India

Some Salient Features of Retail in India

Traditional retail in India is widely dispersed into thousands of small retail outlets servicing a limited trading area. Moreover, since nearly three-fourths of the population is in rural India, the number of outlets is also large.

Organized retail still forms only 4 to 7 percent of the total retail trade in India but is steadily growing. It is estimated that the retail sector in India is the second biggest employer after agriculture and currently provides livelihood to about 7 to 8 percent of the adults. In the next 10 years, about one million new jobs are likely to be created in the retail sector. This emphasizes the importance of developing the organized retail sector.

Share of Organized Retail (Percentage of Total)

In the western economies, US (85 percent), UK, Germany and France, the contribution of organized retail is close to 80 percent. Only Taiwan matches this number. South Africa and Japan have contributions of around 70 percent from organized retail. About 50 percent of the total is organized in countries like Brazil, Malaysia and Thailand. In India, organized retail contributes about 8 percent to the total and is still less than China and South Korea at about 20 percent.

Some modern retail formats existing in India are given in Table 11.2.

Table 11.2 Modern Retail Formats in India (2003)

(Figures are number of outlets in 2003)

Name	Number	Name	Number	Name	Number
Supermarkets		Samaviyka	10	**Discount store chain:**	
Apna Bazar	114	Triveny	10	Subhiksha (closed)	87
Foodworld	72	Vesta	10	Margin Free	87
Trinethra	51	**Hypermarkets**		**Convenience chain:**	
KendriyaBhandar	36	Big Bazaar	6	BPCL In & Out	79
Amudham	27	Giant	1	Convenio	15
Sabka Bazar	21	**Department chain:**		HP Speedmart	14
Arambagh	18	Shoppers Stop	11	Akbarallys	8
Maratha stores	18	Pantaloon	8	Club HP	8
Nilgiris	16	Westside	8	**Health & Pharmacy chain:**	
Adanis	15	Ebony	6	Apollo	85
Sahakari Bhandar	15	**Grocery chain:**		Raj Rajya Sahakari	36
Supplyco	13	Raj RajyaSahakari	6	Health & Glow	14
Janatha Bazar	12	Five Star	5	Himalaya Ayurvedic	13
Basco	10	Shreyas	5	Medicine Shoppe	9

Source: *Business World Marketing White-book*, 2005, p. 289 – reproduced with permission.

One of the arguments used in support of the fact that the percentage of contribution of organized retail in India to the total retail business is still very low is that Indians prefer to buy fresh food and hence depend on traditional small outlets. This argument does not hold when we look at figures below giving the percentage average monthly expenditure on fresh food in many countries (in some of whom the organized retail is flourishing well):

Australia	49	Taiwan	54	Malaysia	44
New Zealand	38	Korea	48	Thailand	45
Japan	62	China	57	Philippines	47
Hong Kong	52	Singapore	53	Indonesia	47
Vietnam	57	Sri Lanka	40	India	42

Source: Business World Marketing White-book, 2005, p. 269 – reproduced with permission.

Salient Retail Numbers

The information is selected from the Business World Marketing White-book, 2009–10.

Table 11.3 **The Retail Evolution**

Pre 1980s	Mid 1980s	Early 1990s	Late 1990s	2000 onwards
Weekly markets	**Super markets**	**Departmental stores**	**Shopping malls**	**Hypermarkets**
Food and grocery Clothing Cosmetics Consumer durables	Food and grocery Other household	Apparel and accessories Consumer durables Home furniture and furnishings	Food and grocery Apparel and accessories Consumer durables Home furniture and furnishings	Food and grocery Apparel and accessories Consumer durables
Neighborhood *Kirana* stores				
Food and grocery Other household				
Government supported shops				
Wheat, rice and sugar Kerosene oil Khadi clothing Other household				

Source: *Technopak*, p. 270 – reproduced with permission

Table 11.4 Commitment among Shoppers

Kind of Shopper	Critical Needs	Commitment Drivers
Traditional Format	Polite, courteous staff Availability of store staff Wide range of products, brands Fresh, high-quality stocks Reasonable prices Availability in all pack sizes	Quality stocks, at reasonable prices Polite and courteous store staff
Modern Format	Polite, courteous store staff Fresh, high-quality stocks Availability of latest products, brands	Availability of latest products, brands Freshness of stocks Modern shopping experience

Source: *Technopak*, p. 287 – reproduced with permission.

Table 11.5 Shopper Segments

Kind of Shopper	Features	Percentage of Total
Experiential	Shopping for food and groceries – look for new products, brands and stores	24
Active	Find food and grocery shopping a highly pleasurable experience. Gives freedom from their daily routine and chores.	13
Dutiful	Food and grocery shopping is a necessity and duty. They do it responsibly and efficiently.	18
Status	Food and grocery shopping is done to acquire the latest and the best. Need to get recognized and enhance status. Want to feel sophisticated and classy.	12
Pragmatic	Systematic and well planned food and grocery buying. Look for well-known brands and have complete knowledge.	16
Reassurance seekers	Food and grocery shopping helps unwind, relax and feel reassured. Help overcome stress and feel comfortable.	17

Source: *Technopak*, p. 287 – reproduced with permission.

Average time spent by Indian literate youth in minutes per day:

- TV – 97
- Internet – 70
- Radio – 61
- Magazines – 44
- Newspaper – 32

Table 11.6 Hierarchy of Factors for Evaluation of a Modern Format

1.	Freshness of products stocked
2.	Cleanliness/hygiene of products stocked
3.	Availability of wide range of products and brands
4.	Availability of products in different pack sizes
5.	Ready stock availability of products

Source: *Technopak*, p. 298 – reproduced with permission.

Organized retail could have manufacturers' retail stores, chain stores, or single large stores. Four product categories dominate organized retail—clothing, food, consumer durables and books and music, in that order. The fastest growth in organized retail is in food, followed by books and music, consumer durables and clothing, in that order.

It is only in the last decade or so that consumers in urban India are looking for convenience in shopping. They now want their entire needs to be met in one outlet and this has given rise to the growth of organized sector—supermarkets and malls. The organized sector still contributes only about 7 percent of the retail business in India. Apart from convenience, the consumer looks towards organized retail to provide lower prices (economies of scale—example, Pantaloons, Big Bazaar), good ambience of shopping and scope for "look and feel" of the merchandise. The Indian consumer looks for "Value for Money", and the large formats are able to provide this.

Some actions proposed are likely to support retail in improving customer service. Some examples are given below.

Favorable Policy Changes: (Proposed by Some States)

- Retail enterprises to remain open 365 days
- Function between 5 am to 11 pm
- Remain open between 11 pm to 5 am for logistics and supplies
- Additional 50 percent FSI in space for retail development
- Women employees to work till 10 pm with safety measures in place

Private Label Brands in India

Private label brands exist in Indian retail also. Westside, Benzer, Globus, Pantaloons and Shoppers Stop have all developed a high percentage of revenues from their own brands. As can be seen from the retailers mentioned, most of the retailer owned brands still happen to be only in apparel.

A summary of the retail formats which exist in India in the organized sector is given below:

- Sponsored by companies or corporate groups
- Large format stores like supermarkets, departmental stores and now hypermarkets
- The focus of these stores is on ambience and making shopping a pleasure
- Some of them use the latest technology for customer care and supply chain management
- Capable of employing large numbers of people
- Effectively manage operating costs

- Offer consumers value for money

Even within organized retail, different formats could mean a different value proposition for the consumers. Some examples are given below:

- Supermarkets by definition normally deal with food and household products and offer convenience to the consumers (Food World, Big Bazaar)
- Departmental stores offer a much wider variety—focus is more on apparel kind of goods where the consumer has choice (Shoppers Stop)
- Hypermarkets and discount stores where the focus is on best prices in large stores with a wide choice (Big Bazaar)
- There could also be specialty stores with a single product category but extensive choice (Reebok)

Unorganized retail continues to dominate the scene and will be there for a long time. The consumer is familiar with its format and feels comfortable dealing with it. Some of its salient features are:

- All outlets are owned either by individuals or families.
- Formats include *kirana* (grocery) stores, *pan/beedi* stores, chemists, pavement vendors and general stores.
- Would probably employ 95 percent of the people who are in retail.
- Provide personalized service and convenience. Many of them specialize in home delivery of small orders also.
- Maintain running accounts of regular consumers' purchases and collect money once a month.
- Open for very long hours.
- Do not find the need for use of technology.

Summary of Points Made by Jean Paul Thill, CEO of KPMG (EMEA) on FDI in Retail in India

- Globalization brings the prices down for consumers, but it threatens jobs too. I believe there is space for the organized retailers as well as the unorganized retailers in India.
- I do not know of any other economy that has one foot in the 21st century—India has a world class IT industry—and the other in the 19th century, as in the case of retail. Indian retail industry has a number of intermediaries, which makes things very expensive for consumers. Modernizing and globalizing retail is also important for extending the benefits of economic growth to the more than 600 million farmers in India, as investment is required in storage and timely delivery of fruits and vegetables.
- India is of continental dimensions and our advice to retail MNCs is to start reasonably small with two or three hypermarkets close to the city center with adequate parking facilities and gradually expand to the outskirts.

Source: KPMG India.

Real estate space available for organized retail is getting saturated in the metros and tier 1 cities in India and is now looking at tier 2 cities for expansion. Unlike in the west, where the large store formats are located in the outskirts of cities or the suburbs (the consumer has a car and is willing to travel the extra distance to do his or her shopping), in urban India, the consumer wants the additional convenience of the large format store to be located in the heart of the business or residential district. This is creating tremendous pressure on real estate to find such spaces in the heart of the cities, which are already congested. This is forcing retailers to either limit the size of their stores or look for tier 2 cities for expansion. Again, depending on the space available and the location, large organized retailers may have to look at 3 or 4 different formats for their stores.

Unlike in the west where the organized retail may account for upwards of 50 percent of the total retail business, in India, for a long time, the unorganized retail (usually referred to as the "mom-and-pop" stores) will continue to exist and share the retail pie. The smaller retail outlets will always provide the service based on personal relations and physical closeness to consumer's homes. Moreover, most of these stores provide "credit" to their regular customers who may be about 25 percent of their total consumer base (they keep a running account of the purchases by the consumer and take the payment once a month when the consumer gets his salary).

Top Retail Companies in India 2016

1. Reliance Retail Ltd. – 2621 stores, 200 cities, 12.5 million sq. ft.
2. Reliance Trends – 200 stores, 1.5 lakh garments per day
3. Reliance Digital – 1100 stores (RR largest by revenue)
4. Future Retail Ltd. – 570 stores, ₹12000 crore revenue, 12.5 million sq. ft.
5. Aditya Fashion and Retail (formerly Pantaloons) – 130 stores, 200 brands
6. Shoppers Stop – 72 departmental stores
7. Trent Ltd. – Westside, Star Bazaar, Landmark, Fashion Yatra
8. V Mart Retail Ltd. (2013) – 69 stores, 51 cities, 5.58 lakh sq. ft.

Source: Wells Invest.in – June 23, 2016.

Trends in Retailing in India

There are a number of factors that are supporting the growth of organized retail in India. These can be summed up as follows:

- The consumer has come of age and asks for what he needs. He no longer easily accepts what the retailer recommends.
- Income levels are rising and with it the requirement of variety and willingness to pay the price if the "value" is right.
- The explosion of communication channels like TV, cable, DTH and mobiles has a tremendous influence on the product choices expected.
- Increased literacy in both urban and rural areas makes the consumer more conscious of his bargaining power.
- Growing number of nuclear families in urban areas.
- The increased influence of the retailer through the product offering and the additional facilities he provides.

- Rural markets and consumers want whatever is available in urban areas and are willing to pay the price for it.
- Better organized supply chains both by the supplier companies and the retailers with a large number of outlets in different locations.
- The effort on infrastructure created by the government—roads, communication facilities, and so on.
- The advantages of bargaining with bigger volumes—economies of scale.
- Entry of the corporate sector in retailing.
- The influence of foreign players on the retail sector will only grow with the opening of FDI.
- Entrepreneurs willing to look at investments in the retail sector.
- Emergence of the "store" as a brand.
- The advantages for retailing from the use of information technology.

Some of the trends in retailing already existing in the western world are also likely to be replicated in India soon. For example:

- New retail formats keep coming up.
  - Examples include ATMs at bus stations, convenience stores at petrol pumps and beverage vending machines everywhere.
- New retail forms also get quickly replicated and lose their novelty.
  - Food and groceries retailers like Nilgiris, which were unique at one time, are no longer so.
- Growth of IT has helped growth of non-store retailing. (More details later in this chapter).
- Competition is very severe between different kinds of stores—all of them are trying to woo the same consumer.
  - The Food World outlet could be competing against the corner grocer.
- Broad categories of retailers are of two varieties—mass merchandisers (like Big Bazaar, or convenience stores) or speciality retailers (like leading jewelers, Reebok stores).
- Leading modern retail formats with all-under-one-roof policy are still the preferred destination for shoppers.
  - The huge rush when Big Bazaar announces their discount sales is a clear indication of this.
- The modern retailers are professionally managed and operated as many of them are corporates.
- Technology is becoming a critical and competitive tool.
- Modern retail is not just a place for buying goods, but also a place to meet other people and socialize.
  - It is not surprising to hear young people say, "Let us meet in the Forum Mall coffee shop at 4 p.m."

Projected Trends

It is learnt that India has the largest number of retail outlets of any country in the world. From the street corner *paanwala* to the modern retail outlets, everyone exists in the same market and has got their own set of loyal customers. Some of the salient numbers (have since gone up substantially) on retail as given by McKinsey Consulting (retail report 2015) are as follows:

Country	Population	Retail Business
USA	263 million	$ 2500 billion
China	1.3 billion	$ 350 billion
India	1 billion	$ 200 billion

It is obvious that there is a tremendous potential for retail industry in India to grow considering the factors earlier narrated.

Organized Retailing in India

The average retailer/grocer around the corner in India gives his customers all the benefits of assortment, lot size, home delivery, credit and order acceptance on telephone also and is difficult to beat in terms of service by any modern retail format. In the case of the local retailer, the consumer has to buy standing on one side of the shop and normally outside the shop, and shopping does not provide the ambience of a modern retail format. Moreover, the average retailer has got fixed prices for what he is selling whereas the modern retailer enjoys benefits of scale and can give discounts on prices. The traditional retail outlets will continue to exist in India along with the modern retail formats.

In urban areas, where the consumer is hard pressed for time, it is more convenient to drive to a major retailer like Food World or Big Bazaar and buy all the goods which a consumer wants all under one roof. Most modern retail formats are developing in big malls in the cities and these malls also have entertainment and food courts. Shopping here is therefore no longer a chore but a pleasant outing for the family. Urban consumers prefer this to the mom-and-pop stores. There is, therefore, a lot of potential for modern big retail formats. It is not just the high end customer who prefers these supermarkets but the urban middle class is using these in large numbers.

Some salient numbers give the picture in terms of the future of the retailing industry in India:

- India has got the world's second largest consumer market after China.
- The retail industry provides tremendous employment opportunities—currently around 7 percent of the total employable adult population. Considering that this figure is 20 percent for the US, the scope for growth is wide open.
- In urban areas, the number of retail outlets is expected to be growing at the rate of 8 to 10 percent and in other smaller towns at 4 to 5 percent.

- The supplier base is growing as the consumer is becoming more demanding. It is possible to even access imported goods. Even in consumer products some of the MNC companies are trying to get their foreign brands into India.
- Real estate is a scarce commodity. It is becoming quite difficult to access large retail spaces in urban areas even at exorbitant prices. This is forcing organized retailers to start looking at secondary towns for expansion. It is to be understood that the potential for organized retail in urban India is still not fulfilled.
- Modern retail is coming out of its "lifestyle" image. Compared to the Shoppers Stop, Globus, and Pantaloons' kind of outlets in the past (which primarily denoted lifestyles and confined to garments and accessories), the Nilgiris, Subhikshas, Big Bazaars and Food Worlds have changed this concept. Hence the interest of the middle class urban consumer to shop at these modern retailers.

LO 4 Identify the types of retailers, trade and retail formats, and retail categories

TRADING/RETAIL FORMATS AND TYPES OF RETAIL

Retailing is the process of reaching out to customers through suitable formats to provide a choice of product offerings providing value for the money they spend and in a pleasing ambience so that the consumer keeps getting back to the same store again and again. The format is obviously the physical features of the store and the service it provides. Retailers use the format to distinguish themselves from each other. The format could include the location of the store, its size, layout/design, the range of offerings and also the service.

Retail formats are defined by location, merchandise offered, size, price of goods and any special offers to the consumers. It is only the modern organized retailers who have given the consumer newer formats. For ages, the only format known to the Indian consumer has been the small shopkeeper nearest to his place of residence. The consumer has been concerned with the location which has to be close by rather than what is the physical characteristics of the store he frequents. The storekeeper also started extending the convenience of home delivery, payment once a month and hence the physical format did not matter to the consumer. Modern retail formats have added to the pleasure of shopping through their formats.

Retail Formats Possible:

A. General Merchandise
   1. Departmental stores—width and depth of products by department
   2. Full line discounter—high volume, low cost, fast turnover, low prices
   3. Specialty stores—limited number of specialized products
   4. Off-price retailer—branded merchandise at everyday low price, no service

5. Variety store—deep assortment of inexpensive goods—stationery, gift items
6. Factory outlet—manufacturer owned stores

B. Food Retailers
   1. Conventional store—limited assortment, local retailers
   2. Conventional supermarket—large departmental stores specializing in food
   3. Food based superstore—large retailer including bakery, sea food and non-food
   4. Combination store—food and non-food for a one-stop experience—high impulse
   5. Su percenters/hypermarket—super store + discount store—40 percent of non-food—example: Walmart

C. Non-Store Retailing
   1. Direct marketing—interactive, non-personal media, telemarketing, direct mail, etc.
   2. Direct selling—at home or office
   3. Vending machines—sales through machines
   4. Catalog marketing—mail order business
   5. Telemarketing

D. Non-Conventional Channels
   1. Electronic /Internet/e-tailing
   2. Airport retailing
   3. Franchising—means privilege or freedom

For the consumer, he now has the choice of shopping using a store format which is a physical entity or a non-store format which could be through the Internet or through a catalog. In the physical store format he has the benefit of getting a look and feel of the product he is buying and assisted by a store salesman. The physical store format therefore provides more satisfaction to the consumers.

We will briefly discuss the various store formats possible. From the definitions given below it should be evident that this format classification is more relevant in the western context and such clear distinctions are still not made in Indian retail.

Location Formats: Categorized by where the store is located in relation to the customer using it. The physical situation of the store defines the format here.

Merchandise based Formats: As the name indicates, the category is based on what products the retail format offers to the consumers. They could be ranging from highly specialized to those dealing in large assortment.

Size based Formats: This classification is based on the total space available in the store for the consumer to browse and do all the activities which the store provides for. The merchandise, the facilities, and the variety varies with the size. Real estate prices in urban India are a major factor in deciding the size of retail formats.

Price based Formats: The pricing strategies of these stores are different from the normal retail stores in any market to attract their customers. Their main attraction is obviously the low prices they offer regularly or occasionally (like a silk saree sale conducted in a marriage hall for one week).

Concession Based: This is almost like franchising where the store brand is common among various contracted parties running the individual stores. The smaller concessionaire complements the offerings of the major store while using the strength of the major retailer brand. The major retailer is also careful in selecting the concessionaire partner. For example, a retail mall or Big Bazaar may choose Café Coffee Day as the concessionaire to operate in its premises.

Ownership based Formats: This classification is based on who owns and runs the store. It could be owned by individuals, a company or a cooperative for example.

Whatever format the retailer starts with, it is so designed that it is possible to increase the number of outlets in the same format and in various geographic locations whether within a city or in different cities. If the format is successful, it should be replicable in other locations also. The initial choice of the format by the modern retailer is based on:

- The location (city or town) and the number of outlets in that location the retailer wants to operate in.
- The ownership of the retail chain. The owners may decide to operate in a certain format in line with their experience of the retail trade. For example, Nilgiris, which started as a store for fresh dairy products, has stuck mostly to food items as this is the strength of the owners' family.
- What the retail chain wants to stock and sell. Most retail formats specialize in textiles or garments and accessories.
- The manageable size of the stores based on the average expected footfalls per day.
- The intention on pricing by the retailer—whether his focus is on discounts or full pricing.
- The capability of the owners to run all the stores by themselves or if they intend to outsource the store brand to others to operate.

Irrespective of the initially chosen format, this should be replicable as already suggested. The reasons for wanting to expand are given below:

- Long-term profitability may be based on getting a minimum number of stores operating in a location (city or town) or even across the cities.
- Creates more shopping opportunities to the consumers and if the format is successful in one location, once expanded, can give satisfaction to larger number of customers.
- Can experiment with various formats and get consumers to try out and become a part of the regular business. For example, Fabmall, which started as an online store format also

introduced brick and mortar stores under the FabMart brand which was later sold out to a retail chain.

For the same retailer, different formats can help compare and contrast and, therefore, improve all formats (for example, Reliance Retail).

Shoppers Stop Expands: Recently published reports indicate that the retailer has had a make-over and added additional products and international brands in the stores. Shoppers Stop plans to add about 18 stores in the next three years.

Types of Retailers

Retailers have been classified below based on the conventional understanding of retail practices and most of these categories are relevant in the Indian context:

- Conventional retailers—try to avoid price competition.
- General stores—carry anything which can be sold in a reasonable volume.
- Single line or limited line stores—specialize in certain line of related products (men's clothing).

Expanded assortment and service

- Speciality shop—sell special types of products (sporting goods).
- Department stores—combine many limited line stores and specialty shops.

Mass merchandising retailers

- Supermarkets—large stores specializing in grocery with self-service and wide assortment.
- Catalog showroom retailers—sell several lines out of a catalog and display showroom with back-up inventories.
- Discount houses—offer a wide assortment at substantial price cuts.
- Mass merchandisers—large self-service stores with many departments that focus on low margins but high turnover.
- Hypermarkets—very large stores that try to carry not only food and drug items but all goods and services that the consumer purchases routinely.

Some retailers focus on added convenience

- Convenience (food) stores—limited line food stores offering convenience and not assortment (milk, bread and RTE snacks).
- Automatic vending—selling and delivering products through machines.
- Door-to-door selling directly at the consumer's home.
- Telephone and direct mail retailing.

A more detailed classification of retail stores as prevalent in the western context is given below. Some of these categories do not exist in India and may not even make a presence. It is, however, necessary to know these details in the context of how retail has developed elsewhere. Where relevant, Indian examples have been given in Table 11.7.

Table 11.7

Type of Retailer	Brief Description
Chain store	Retail stores could be in multiple locations but easily recognizable by the store design, brand name/logo, common merchandising plan and the same customer service and promotional strategies.
High street (western term)	Stores located in busy shopping areas. These necessarily have to be small (not more than 2000 sq. ft), limited assortment of merchandise, no parking facilities.
Destination (western term)	These stores have to attract the customers with large size, good bargains, ample parking space and wide variety to choose from but located in a particular part of the city which takes some effort to reach. Megamart may be a good example.
Convenience store	This is the store around the corner that meets all the daily needs of consumers close to it, is open almost 18 hours in a day. These stores have the provision of home delivery at short notice. Also called provision or *kirana* stores.
Family store	Is defined as an apparel store which caters to the entire family.
Speciality store	Deals with a large variety of a limited range of goods. Bata shops and Titan showrooms are good examples. They could be company owned or franchised.
Departmental store	Normally of a size of over 10,000 sq. ft and keeping various goods in different sections (departments) and stocking over 25,000 SKUs. Food World could be a departmental store.
Supermarket	Similar to the above but at times on a smaller scale. Foodworld outlets in some cases can be considered as an example also.
Emporium (used by government or export firms)	Usually promoted for selling a particular category of products. This is very similar to a speciality store. Most state governments operate these to promote their handicrafts. Examples – Rajasthali, Mriganayani, Cauvery, Poompuhar and the like.
Superstore	Is considered as bigger than a supermarket but operating on a single floor. Experts say that a superstore stocks a wide variety of food and other items. It may also have a chemist, bakery or florist on its premises.
Shopping mall	These are growing rapidly in India. These are a number of different retail stores organized in one premises, which is several stories high and with ample parking facilities. It may even include entertainment and food stalls. Independent retailers pay for the space in the malls which are usually over 200,000 sq. ft.
Shopping center (any market)	Is a collection of retail outlets of typically the same size of around 800–1000 sq. ft. Each of these retailers have leased the store premises from the same owner. There are hundreds of these in urban India.
Hypermarket	Is considered more than 200,000 sq. ft. but one retailer brand. It stocks almost everything including groceries, food, non-food, textiles, garments, footwear, and stationery. Hypercity and The Big Bazaar Giant store in Hyderabad are such hypermarkets.
Discount store	These retail outlets buy in bulk from producers on low negotiated prices and can offer discounts of up to 20 percent on the listed consumer price to the consumers.
Every day low price (EDLP)	These are discounted stores in the western countries who announce low prices every day on some select merchandise.
Category killer (western term)	This is a speciality store with a large assortment at very low prices. They offer the best price in the market and hence are a threat to all other retailers. This again is not a regular feature of Indian markets.

Factory outlet	Most of the garment and footwear manufacturers have these outlets. They would be selling either regular goods or in many cases "seconds" or "export surplus" materials. These used to be earlier in the factory premises but can now be seen across cities. Examples include Bombay Dyeing, Reebok, Arvind Brands.
Warehouse	This store is temporary and is run by individual parties for a limited period "sale". They normally engage a huge space like a marriage hall to conduct this sale.
Single price denomination	All the items in the store are priced at one or two attractive, low prices. The dollar stores are making their appearance in urban India also.
Stop-over store	This is a store within another like the grocery and food stores seen in petrol stations.
Kiosks	Is a small independent unit which can be located in busy places like airports, and bus stations and normally sells soft drinks, cigarettes, beverages and is open on three sides to handle the rush of customers. There could also be kiosks to just give information. One is reminded of the "May I Help You" kiosks you see in major railway stations.
Vending machines	Dispense fixed quantities of products for fixed prices. Self-operated by the consumer—beverages, magazines, chocolates.
Independent store	Owned by a single person or one or two partners. All the hundreds of retail stores in India come under this category whether they are grocers, chemists or ration shops.
Franchise	The store brand is common but operated by many persons on behalf of the main retailer. Some of the Titan showrooms, and Kids Kemp Toy stores are under this format.
Hawkers	Visit residential localities with their merchandise and sell house–to-house with almost fresh stocks every day. A common Indian phenomenon.

RETAIL FOCUS ON CATEGORIES

Category has been defined as the "basic unit" for making merchandising and buying decisions by a retailer. It can be broadly described as the product lines carried by the retailer—like men's apparel, women's apparel, kids wear, etc. The category in the stores is as classified by the retailer and may not be common among similar retailers. The consumer's buying behavior is a clear indicator for defining the categories by a retailer.

Category management focuses on three parameters:

(i) Efficient introduction of new products into the stores
(ii) Running product promotions effectively
(iii) Optimum store assortment (the best product mix), reflecting trading area (catchment area from where the store's customers come), and customer needs.

Customer needs are obviously influenced by:

- Characteristics of the consumers: age, occupation, location, economic status, etc.
- Buying pattern of consumers in products, brands, variants, pack sizes preferred, etc.
- How much time do consumers spend on shopping?
- Do sales promotions, low prices, etc., induce consumers to buy more?
- Frequency of purchases by product categories

For some categories, consumer studies by experts have shown clear patterns, for example:

- For staples the penetration is high as also the frequency of purchase
- For niche products the penetration and frequency of purchases may be low

These patterns of consumer buying will decide the route for category management.

Category Lifecycles

A trend generates high sales for a short period of time. Fashions last longer (many seasons) but the sale in each season is likely to be different. Basic products (also called staples) reflect continuous demand over a long period of time. Seasonal products are only relevant in the appropriate seasons.

Category Types

Routine categories: Customers use the retailer as the preferred vendor for these items—milk, bread, soft drinks from the closest convenience store, for example.

Destination category: This is the customer's first choice for specific products—buying drapes from Drapes Avenue.

Season categories: The retailer is well-known for selling seasonal merchandise—buying mangoes in season from horticultural outlets.

Convenience categories: Cigarettes from *paanwallas*.

Retail experts have created further sub-categories in products like: transaction categories—products frequently purchased on impulse like soft drinks, traffic builders—products with high market share like milk or bread, cash generators—products with high stock turns and margins like seasonal fruits, image creating products—unique image projection like high-end watches, and excitement creators—high impulse products like video games for kids.

Category Management

In major retail organisations, individual category managers are responsible for their business and its profitability. This means several category managers compete for the limited resources and have to make their "part of the business" profitable. Category management drives the "success" of the retailer and his dependents like his suppliers.

Some of the relevant points on managing categories are highlighted here:

- Should reflect the trading area of operation
- The survey of the trading area before setting up the store would have thrown up enough pointers to have decided the categories being offered
- Should be stocked on the shelves in an appealing manner as if the consumers had arranged it themselves
- The classification should clearly reflect the consumer preferences and the placing in the stores should demonstrate this well
- For the same categories between two retailers, the category management should show the differentiation between the two.
- The categories in the store have to be made available and visible to ensure multiple purchases and drive "impulse" buying
- The decisions on category management need to be dynamic to reflect changing customer needs

- The major goal of category management is creating unique customer value and thereby ensuring stickiness (the customers should keep coming back to the store for their purchases).
- Ideally all the categories should end up profitable through the manner in which they are managed.

Merchandize Buying Rules

Selection of Vendor

Price, quality, reliability, time for processing of orders, time for delivery from the time of order placement, terms and conditions offered (delivery time, credit, after sales support, etc.), advertising and promotion support, ethics in doing business and any exclusive rights provided to the buyer.

Selection of Merchandise

Quality inspection by sampling, negotiated terms, order and delivery times, inventory holding rules, re-ordering costs, etc.

Building Competitive Advantage

In order to build competitive advantage, a retailer has to focus on the following areas:

- Location convenient to the maximum number of target customers
- Customer service to build relationships—in order to increase the "stickiness". Retailers have started building databases of their customers so that they can track preferences and design store promotions of interest to the maximum number of customers
- Strong vendor relationships—to get preferential treatment
- Ability to manage information—about consumer preferences, trends, competition, regulations
- People management—as it is one of the three assets with which the retailer works. The people should feel ownership of their stores and this should reflect in their interactions with customers
- Managing merchandize—most important aspect—what to buy and how to make it available and visible in the store
- Overall store management—ambience, easy access to merchandise, quick check-outs, help in buying decisions, etc.

THE ROLE OF THE RETAILER

The retailer is able to provide the service to the customers by the following:

(i) merchandising,
(ii) service,
(iii) format used, and
(iv) communication process used.

These aspects are used in a combination and any one of these factors alone cannot help in successful retailing. These aspects of retail management are discussed briefly below:

The Versatile ATM (Automated Teller Machine)

A bank ATM is a good example of the bank providing service to the customer 24×7. Apart from cash dispensing, today, ATMs deliver a host of other services which are outlined as follows:

- Withdrawing cash and checking balance in the account
- Monitoring the status of cheques issued
- Filing a request for a cheque book or an account statement
- Deposit cheques and cash
- Paying utility bills
- Pay fees of some educational institutions or make donations to some temple trusts, etc.

Merchandising

The definition of merchandising is – "a set of activities involved in acquiring goods and services and making them available at the places, times and prices and the quantity that enable a retailer to reach his goals." As you can see, this definition encompasses almost all the aspects of retail management. The focus is on acquiring the goods and storing them so that any consumer can access them at a time, place, and quantity convenient to her. The consumer has, however, no direct influence on the price factor.

Merchandising directly affects the revenue and profitability of the store. Merchandising also takes into account the assortment of the goods and the quality. The merchandiser is the most important person in a modern retail store. Some of the factors influencing the merchandising policy of the store are:

- The aims and objectives of the retailer
- The demographic characteristics of the population the store is expected to serve
- The level of customer service the retailer is willing to provide
- Presence of competition in the location
- Width and depth of the assortment the retailer wants to provide
- Any other services (like home delivery, monthly running account) which the retailer wants to provide

Merchandise Planning

Merchandise planning and control relates to merchandise variety and assortment. Variety has been defined as the different kinds of goods (men's apparel, ladies garments) to be carried, or services offered. Assortment decisions relate to range of choice (like brands, styles, models, colors, sizes).

One of the critical factors taken into account by merchandise planners is the stock turnover ratio. It is the cost of merchandise sold divided by the average inventory value at cost. The steps in merchandise budgeting include planning the stock levels at the beginning of the month by SKU, any stock losses, purchases for the month, and profitability for the month.

Merchandising Strategy

A retailer following a wide merchandising strategy will stock different categories. For example, it may stock grocery, stationery, apparel, household appliances, books, and electronic items. It will be positioned as a one-stop shop for the customer. Retailers following this strategy will attract high customer traffic and high loyalty. This strategy attracts customers who want to reduce their shopping trips. Giant hypermarket in Hyderabad and all Big Bazaar outlets are good illustrations of this strategy.

In a deep assortment strategy, the focus is on stocking a wide variety from a specific product group. Exclusive shops like that of Reliance Footprint, Bata, or Titan are typical examples. A deep merchandising strategy will involve stocking all the varieties of brands, at all price points, and a wide choice within the category. Customers wanting to buy a specific product (like watches) would only go to these shops.

Some of the factors which impact the width and depth of the goods stored are:

- The company's strategic objectives in terms of its prospects, the service levels it wants to extend to them and the profitability target it has set for itself.
- Expectations of the customers from the store. Local tastes and income levels affect what and how people buy.
- The space availability. Obviously the wide strategy requires more space than the deep one.
- Relationships with the suppliers.
- Availability of trained personnel.
- Type of product being sold. For mass based consumer products a wide merchandising strategy is preferred. For a sophisticated item like cell phones, a deep merchandising strategy would be better.

Table 11.8 Comparison of Wide and Deep Strategies

Wide Strategy	Deep Strategy
Loyal customer base easily built up	Takes longer to build a loyal base but lasts longer
Attracts a lot of impulse buyers	Depends on planned buying only
Depends on volume sales	Depends on niche business opportunities
Size of each bill generated by a customer to be maximized	Wanting to sell more modern and upgraded product versions
Lower margins	Higher margins
Cross merchandising – related products stacked together on nearby shelves	
Requires more space	Requires less space
Suitable for mass based consumer products	Preferred for niche products.

Category Management

This is the management of the retail business by looking at the performance of categories of products rather than the brands or models comprising the category.

Each category of products in the store can be treated as a strategic business unit (SBU) and its profitability can be maximized.

For each category, depending on its off-take, the shelf space, the fill rates and the display efforts are clearly defined to achieve a targeted level of profitability.

- Some examples of categories could be foods, detergents and soaps, personal care products, kitchen ware, cosmetics, jewelry, stationery, footwear.
- The classification of a category is always done on the way the customers perceive the grouping.

The Merchandising Function

A retailer takes care of the purchase, storage, display and sales of the goods. The merchandising decision is based on the requirements of the prospective customers. The strategy, once decided will more or less remain consistent till the lifetime of the retailer or store.

The merchandising manager has the following functions to perform:

- Making the products available in the store so that at no point a customer goes back without buying his requirement as there was a stock-out.
- Making the products available in variety and assortment that the customer is accustomed to.
- Taking the right decisions of introduction of new products and packs.
- Getting the products at the right prices and taking advantage of all promotions that companies are willing to offer. This is part of the planning process.
- Planning the shelf and other space to be allocated for the display of the goods in the store.
- Making sure that all the products get the display they deserve so that the customer does not miss any product he wants to buy. Visibility of the products in the store is the job of the merchandising manager.

The steps to be taken in a merchandise planning process are listed below (as you can see, the steps are similar to operating a storage point/unit in a factory or a distribution warehouse):

- Start with the sales plan—this is the sales forecast by Stock Keeping Unit. This is done taking into account the past data and using some simple statistical techniques.
- Estimate the write-offs (covered by credit notes for losses) likely for the period—this is the estimate of any goods that may not get sold and must be heavily discounted or written off. The reasons for this could be damages, and pilferage. This is a regular feature though very small, but has to be taken into account in the planning process.
- Develop an inventory holding plan—for the beginning and the end of the planning period. This stocking norm can be based on a ABC analysis. This is purely a management decision to ensure that there are no stock-outs or excess stocks.
- Plan the merchandise required—is done using a simple formula: total merchandise needed = sales plan + likely reductions or write-offs + closing inventory planned. This plan is the level of investment in inventory required for the period under review.
- Calculate the purchases required—again based on a simple calculation: purchase quantity required = merchandise plan – opening inventory for the period.

- Once the goods are in, define the mark-up by SKU in line with the profitability target. This is done every time a new set of goods is received at the store. The MRP if not already marked on the pack is a combination of cost of goods sold, operating expenses, reductions likely, and the expected net profit from the SKU.

The retailer keeps track of two merchandising ratios to judge his performance. These are: (i) stock turnover ratio and (ii) gross margin return on inventory.

In essence, the merchandising manager manages both the front end of the store (which is exposed to the customers) and the back office operations (which is exposed to the suppliers). For providing both the availability and variety in the retail operations, the retailer incurs costs of holding inventory. The merchandising function has to ensure that this cost is also optimized. The manager works with a clear budget.

To decide on the quantity of the stocks to be held by each SKU (both in the store and the back store) the merchandising manager can use the principle of ABC analysis. The permitted stock levels of different SKUs are never the same. For example, a store will not hold the same level of stocks of a toothpaste of 200 g, 100 g and 50 g. The store cannot go wrong by increasing the availability and assortment in the A category items.

The merchandising manager has to take a decision on:

- Products to be sold
- Variety of each category
- Pack sizes and SKUs
- Price points of the products
- Quantity of each product, category, SKU to be carried at any point of time and the relevant price points.

Financial Aspects of Merchandising

Financial control of merchandising monitors—the financial investment in merchandise over any period of measurement. It helps in defining the quantity of inventory to be permitted for each category or department of the retail operations. The most important aspect of financial control in any retail operation is the stock and inventory valuation and accounting. This aspect can be measured by store to get an idea of individual store profitability. The complexity involved can be gauged by the fact that a store which may have more than 10,000 SKUs (it is estimated that food and grocery retailers carry about 10,000 SKUs and fashion and lifestyle stores carry about 60,000 SKUs) most of whom have been purchased many times at different prices but all stocked and selling in the stores. One can imagine if all the stock valuation and accounting has to be done manually. Fortunately for most modern retailers, the power of computers reduces the burden of accounting and valuation.

Private (retailer own brands) have cost advantages over national brands. These cost advantages are in manufacturer margins, overheads, and taxes. For the same retailer margin, they can be up to 25 percent cheaper than national brands.

Foreign Auto-retailers interested in the Indian Market

Global automobile dealers are in touch with Indian auto companies to set up retail chains. Some examples: AutoNation (USA), Al-Futtain Group, Bahwan (Middle East) and Inchcape (UK) are talking to Honda, BMW, Mercedes, and Volkswagen. The focus of the international dealerships is to guarantee volumes and margins (gross margins of 12 to 15 percent are expected compared to 2 to 3 percent for local dealers).

- Auto Nation has 272 dealerships worldwide for 37 manufacturer brands.
- Inchcape UK represents Toyota, BMW, Mercedes, Audi, Honda, Chevrolet, and Volkswagen.

Customer Service

Implications of customer service can be as broad as the retailer chooses them to be. The basic function of retailer is to provide the goods most likely to be bought by his prospective customers at a place and time when the customer wants them. In addition, he should ensure that his goods are of a good quality and affordable by the customers.

Some of the factors affecting the customer service are:

- The location of store and its working hours. The extreme example is of Mustafa stores in Singapore located in "Little India" and open 24 hours.
- The assortment of the goods—the width and depth as mentioned earlier.
- The prices at which the goods are made available. Unless it is a "lifestyle" kind of store, the competitors in the area are a key determinant of the prices.
- Help and assistance within the store to support the selection of the goods by the customer. This could either be the sales staff or the way the goods are displayed and the prices announced on the shelves.

The above are the basic customer service elements expected of any retailer. In addition, the "value add" could be in terms of more services like:

- Free demonstrations of the product, help in installation. At times it could even be a simple thing like providing batteries free along with a transistor or a film roll with a camera. These add-ons could be peculiar to the store and not necessarily what is prescribed by the manufacturer.
- Within the store premises, there could be additional facilities like a coffee shop, ATM, and a beauty parlor. The strength of most of the shopping malls coming up in India is in many choices being available under one roof, thus making shopping a pleasure.
- The store may even provide services like accepting orders on phone, home delivery, a credit account for the customer, transport to the stores, and so on. Majority of the independent grocery outlets in any locality are doing well on the strength of these kinds of services provided to their "regular" customers.

Customer Service Needs

Every customer who is a prospective buyer in a retail outlet has expectations of the store in terms of basic needs to be fulfilled (sometimes called the qualifying needs) and add-ons, which the particular store may provide (also called determining needs). This part sets the store apart from others in the marketplace.

The basic requirements ensure that the customer at least visits the store. The add-ons ensure stickiness with the store. The retailer has to provide for both these needs of the customer. To illustrate, a basic need would be to ensure good displays giving the details about the products without having to ask any staff.

The add-ons could mean providing gift wrapping, loyalty points and rewards. After sometime the add-ons become basic services and the retailer has to think of new add-ons to keep his competitive edge. Retailing is an open marketing concept and it is easy for competition to understand how a retailer operates and copy good practices in no time.

Nielsen Consumer Audit Expands Scope

Nielsen is one of the leading consumer and retail audit firms operating in India. It has all the major FMCG companies on its client list. Based on the feedback it has been getting from its customers, Nielsen has decided to increase the number of retail stores where the audit is done from about 17,000 to about 25,000. The increase in number helps increase the depth and the state-wise coverage. From now, Nielsen is also going to rope in some semi-wholesalers in the store audit panel.

Planning Customer Convenience

The retailers' choice of service levels determines the attractiveness of the retailer to his target market. As in any distribution channel, the service levels are directly related to the channel flows which the retailer participates in and a summary is given below:

- The planning starts with the store ambience. While shopping may still be an inevitable chore, the retailer can make the experience "pleasant" by creating the right ambience—brightly lit, well displayed, clearly marked aisles and shelves, ready product information, etc.
- While manufacturers make their products in large batch lot sizes, the consumers may want to buy just one unit of the product. The retailer facilitates this operation. Retailers, however, may encourage consumers to buy bigger lots by giving promotions.
- The retailer has to be careful in planning the layout of the store in such a way that the consumer can find the product of his choice easily. With both men and women working, the time saved in searching of products of their choice is important. This searching time gets reduced with the spatial convenience the store provides – plenty of shelves, clearly visible displays and boards announcing the product categories.
- Customers expect their products to be available in their store of choice at all times. They cannot wait to get the product even the next day. Traditional retailers in India have the habit of rushing their person to another shop and getting the product instead of letting go of their regular customers. Delivery time also includes the time spent in the check-out counters. Once the customer has selected his goods, he would like to pay the bill

quickly and get out of the store. An example of a no-waiting retail outlet is the vending machine.

- Variety and assortment are normally used in place of each other but there is a subtle difference. Variety is the different classes of goods making up the product offering or the breadth/width of product lines. Assortment is the depth of product brands or models offered within each generic product category. For the customer, both are equally relevant. This function is the critical role played by the buyers in the retail organisation.
- Focus on the customer starts with the in-store sales personnel who assist the customer in his purchases. Another customer service example is providing shopping carts/baskets within the store.

The most important factor in a retailer as far as a consumer is concerned is convenience. Convenience includes elements like getting all the products in less time, faster checkouts and ever helpful store staff. This may not strictly apply in the context of the Indian consumer who is willing to spend the time to get the best bargain. However Indian consumers do associate organized retail with self-service.

The two most important factors necessary for a retail store are obviously the range of goods on offer and the customer service dimensions of the store. In addition, there are certain factors which determine the personality of the store or what is called the trade format. The trade or retail format distinguishes one retailer from another. The elements of the trade/retail format are:

- The store ambience—modern retail outlets are not only a place for the customer to buy a product of his choice, but a place where he enjoys doing it. Modern retail makes shopping a pleasure and it is the store ambience that makes this possible. It takes a lot of thought, money and effort to create the right ambience.
- We discussed in other chapters about the importance of time for the customer. He would like to enjoy his shopping experience without having to waste too much time on the actual purchase activity in the store. To illustrate, a housewife who comes to buy her monthly groceries in Food World would like to pick up the goods on her shopping list in the least possible time. The saving in time is what gives some retail stores the name of convenience stores. The interiors of such stores are of a practical design to reduce the time for search and pick up of the goods. They are well lighted and functional in their approach to store design.

The store ambience and the interior design meant to reduce the shopping time can contribute as differentiators to the retailer strategy.

- Location is often stressed as a very important factor in developing the trade format of a retailer. Most of the modern retail outlets are located in the busiest shopping centers. With soaring real estate prices, some of the stores are forced to move to suburban locations.
- The physical characteristics of the retail store are also factors to be considered as part of the trade format. These include location, the external appearance (modern retail stores have the same external facade in every location), the interior designs, the arrangement of the shelves and the goods, and the arrangement of the departments as all these influence the footfalls for the store and become part of the store positioning strategy.

Cook and Walters (D Cook and D Walters, *Retail Marketing Theory & Practice*, Prentice Hall, USA, 1991), retail management experts have identified two kinds of shoppers for whom the trade formats are designed. One is the task focused shopper and the other is the leisure shopper.

The task focused shopper visits the store to buy specific things he has already planned for. The housewife visiting Food World to buy groceries is a case in point. For her, the importance in the format is "convenience" and minimum time to pick up the goods on her list. The store format should be pleasing and the goods should be easily and quickly accessible. For her, the shopping is a "chore" and a "task".

The leisure shopper is more interested in the ambience and the environment within the store. For him, shopping is a pleasure. He has plenty of time and has come to the store or the shopping mall to generally have a good time. Incidentally, he may also do some shopping. Lifestyle stores could be a good example. Modern shopping malls have cinema theatres, food courts, bowling alleys to attract the young leisure shopper. The influence of the type of shopper on the trade format can be seen from the chart below:

Table 11.9 Influence of Type of Shopper on Trade Format

Task Focused Shopper	Leisure Shopper
Convenient Location	Exclusive goods
Proximity to other similar stores	Wide choice
Correct merchandise selection	High-end image
High availability	Good ambience
Competitive prices	High level of visual merchandising
Fast customer check-out	Additional facilities
Good product visibility	Theme displays
Customer advice support	Departmental focus
	Customer advice support
Example: grocery shopping	Example: apparel shopping

Source: Cook & Walters

There is also another categorization of the goods from the point of consumers' effort required in acquiring them. This categorization is in three ways defined briefly below:

- Low value goods—are those where the probable gain from shopping and making comparisons is small compared to the time, effort and mental discomfort involved in the search (example: toothpaste).
- High value goods—are those where the probable gain from shopping and making comparisons is large compared to the time, effort, and mental discomfort involved in the search (example: refrigerator).
- Specialty goods—are clearly distinguished by brand preferences (example: Maruti Zen car).

Trading area is defined as the "catchment" area from which most of the customers of a retail store are expected to come from. For a general store, the customers come from within a short distance. Their necessities are of a specific nature like groceries or medicine for which they do not want to travel long distances.

- The grocery or general store or chemist around the corner is the most common type of a store where the locality in which it is situated becomes the primary trading area.
  For specialty stores, the trading areas can be very large. Customers do not mind traveling long distances to buy from these stores.
- V B Bakery in Bengaluru was a famous bakery located in south Bengaluru, but used to get customers from all over Bengaluru as their products had become so famous by sheer word of mouth.
- MTR is a restaurant again in Bengaluru which has become famous all over the world. Customers travel long distances to dine here.
- If you want to buy a Mont Blanc Pen in Bengaluru, you either go to William Penn or Leela Galeria.
- Shoppers Stop is a specialty apparel store and has a wide trading area.

Trading area increases with the size of the store and the variety it offers. If a new store opens in any location, the trading area of existing stores shrinks. It is, however, a known fact that consumers are attracted to retail stores which are closer to them and more attractive than others in that location.

India's Largest Mall

India's largest mall, the Mantri Square, opened in Bengaluru in March 2010. It has a size of 919,516 sq. ft. of space. It overtakes in size the Ambience Mall of Gurgaon with a space of 873,000 sq ft. Mantri Square is considered as a regional mall only and not a super mall which has to have at least 11 lakh sq. ft of space. Mantri Square is about one-fourth in size compared to the world's biggest mall, The Dubai Mall (3,770,000 sq. ft.).

Planning the Retail Format

This has already been covered earlier in the chapter. Some salient points are stressed here as relevant to retail planning.

- The "format" denotes the kind of store it is. The format is again the choice of the retailer based on his long term strategy. Once the format is decided, it is quite difficult to change as the customers then start recognizing the store by its format. The format gives the image to the store.
- Similarly Nilgiris in the South started as an offshoot of a dairy farm and was known for its milk and food products. Even today, when the stores have grown enormously, Nilgiris is well known as a food retailer. This is the format chosen by the retailer and well known to customers.
- Kids Kemp started as a toy retailer and graduated into an apparel retailer in its Kemp Fort avatar.

- The same retailer follows different formats in different locations. (MK Ahmed in Bangalore has simple MK Ahmed Stores in some areas and supermarkets under the MK Retail brand name in other areas).
- Large modern retailers prefer sticking to the same format in every location.

Medical Diagnostics Chains Plan to Expand by Acquisitions

Medical diagnostic chains like Super Religare Labs, Piramal Diagnostics, Dr Lal Pathlabs, etc., are planning to expand their operations by acquiring stand-alone pathological laboratories which dominate the market. It is estimated that the medical diagnostics (pathological labs) and imaging (X-rays etc.) market in India is worth over $1 billion. Organized players have a share of about 10 percent of this. It is the stand-alone private labs which hold the balance share. The major chains plan to acquire the smaller labs and hope to increase their share of the market to around 25 percent in the next three years.

Customer Communication

Communication refers to the manner in which the retailer makes himself known to his prospective customers. This communication, initially, may take the form of press advertisements, hand bills, and the like. Later on, the customers themselves communicate about the stores by word of mouth. If customers are happy with the stores and its services they recommend the store to others.

The retailer also has to communicate to his customers about any special events and promotions in the newspapers. We keep seeing full page advertisements almost every week from Big Bazaar or Food World about the promotions the stores are running presently. Crossword Book Store for example, invites eminent authors to come and speak about their books and invite the general public for these lectures and sell a lot of books on that day.

Communication basically is used by the retailer to:

- Announce the opening of the retail store
- Tell customers about the promotions running
- Inform customers about any additional facilities introduced in the store.

Communication forms the fourth part of the retailer strategy after positioning, merchandising and customer service. It is meant to create a "preferred image" of the store in the minds of the customers. The communication is supposed to create the "perception" of the store in the eyes of the customer. The communication strategy to a large extent is focused on the intended catchment or trading area of the store. The communication can have a long term objective of "brand building" of the store or a short term objective could be to announce a "promotion". Both of the objectives converge around creating more store traffic.

The store exterior is a means of good communication. Give-aways within the store could be another means which will get quickly carried by word-of-mouth to other customers.

The choice of media for the communication has also got to be localized to regional TV, local print media, radio, and hoardings. Retailers use mailers with newspapers effectively.

Big Bazaar has been using special pages with local newspapers to communicate major promotions to their customers and prospects.

The retailer expects instant results out of communication—Big Bazaar would like the consumers to rush to the store as soon as the promotion is announced. Moreover, the communication is usually about short term events and has a very limited response time. Most of the communication from retailers seems to be giving importance to lower or more attractive prices. For example, most of the "sales" advertisements in newspapers are about selling regular or branded items at attractive discounts.

The other feature of a retailer communication is that it does not normally feature one product or brand but a host of products about which the retailer wants to tell the customers. This kind of advertising would be frowned upon by a producer. Reverting to the Big Bazaar example, it features dozens of items in all product categories in which the retailer has something to offer to his customers.

A cardinal rule to be followed in store promotion is that there should always be some excitement or event happening in the store or there is a chance that consumers may forget the store—they have so many other attractions in the market. It is for the store manager to keep creating these exciting programmes revolving around his store so that consumers keep coming in hordes, and when they come, the store has so much to offer that it converts them into buyers. Some examples of this excitement creation are given below:

- Kemp Fort used to have a "fashion show" with local models every evening to get shoppers to the store before they went home from work.
- Crossword book store invites leading authors to talk about their newly released books in the store. The book gets sold in large numbers on that day (the author normally autographs each buy) but the store traffic creates a large impulse buying.
- All the pizza parlors run special combo offers to attract families.
- Food Bazaar has regular discounted sales periods.
- Retailers have special offers for frequent buyers or loyalty cards. Shoppers Stop has a regular campaign running on this.
- A percentage off on buying a certain amount like ₹2000 or ₹3000 on any day. Or all such buyers could be part of a lucky draw for the day with exciting prizes.

Special merchandising and display efforts and store decorations during festival days like Diwali or Christmas have become a common feature of most modern retail stores.

LO 5 Describe the retail management strategies

RETAIL MANAGEMENT STRATEGIES

Experts have identified some basic rules for formulating strategy in retail management:

Market Focus	Format Selected	Appropriate Strategy
Existing	Current	Market penetration
Existing	New	Format development
New	Existing	Market expansion
New	New	Diversification

From the customer's point of view, the following expectations of the consumer in terms of his/her convenience are to be kept in mind while framing the retail strategy:

- Access to the store: location, hours of operation, parking, and all aspects within the store which make the buying experience fast
- Access within the store: the ability to search for products without too much difficulty
- Possession utility: making goods available and visible any time the consumer decides to do his shopping
- Quick transactions: speed of completing the purchasing process

Source: Seiders, Berry and Gresham

Steps in Retail Strategy

1. Developing a mission statement of the organization: clearly defines the purpose of the firm and motivates the promoters and employees. This section also mentions the product categories that the retailer will deal in.
2. The ownership pattern has to be decided next as in any business.
3. The objectives of the retailer are to be clearly stated: long- and short-term goals in terms of who the customers that the retailer is targeting are, and what this retailer would provide for them. Apart from sales, service, market shares, etc., the objectives could also define the profit targets. The objectives are to be in line with the mission defined earlier.
4. Segmentation and positioning of the retailer is the next step. Segmentation is the decision on the kind of customers the retailer wants to service. Positioning is the manner in which the retailer would like to present himself to the customers—the "image" he would like to create about his business in the minds of his customers—for example if he is a discount retailer.
5. Develop the overall strategy for operating the business. Some of the points to be covered here include the location of the stores, the merchandise offered, the communication process about the stores, etc., (the elements of the marketing mix). The strategy also highlights how the business plans to manage environmental factors like legal, social, cultural and technological.
6. Plan the routine activities of the stores in terms of timings, the store layout, and check-out.
7. Next step defines the control mechanisms that will be put in place—these would relate to the merchandise carried, the inventory norms, the pricing system, the methods of handling any leakages, etc.

8. Last step is to define the parameters for measuring the performance of the stores and the frequency. As we shall see later, the performance measure of "retail" is in terms of the productivity of its inventory, space, and the people employed.

Retail Strategies

It is obvious that the retailer develops his strategy based on a number of factors. Some of these factors are:

- The markets and customers he is targeting
- The location of the store or stores
- The store "image" to be created in the minds of the prospects
- The store design aspects

> **Importance of Location in Retailing**
>
> Published reports say that India Gate in Delhi is the biggest point for retailing ice cream in India followed by Marina Beach, Chennai. More than 200 push cart vendors fight for their share in this location which accounts for a total ice cream business of about ₹4 lakh ($ 9000) daily in the season. This location accounts for almost 11 percent of ice cream sales in Delhi!

- The merchandise to be offered
- The type of store personnel to be recruited and what is expected of them
- The promotions to be run to build footfalls initially and stickiness later on
- The supplier handling systems including credit and other terms
- The terms offered to prospects and customers

Before we look at the possible strategies in retail, it is necessary to understand the key drivers of a retail business. These are:

- The number of footfalls each day into the store—the number of people visiting the store. In the case of a street corner store, the visitors come with a clear purpose of wanting to purchase something. In the case of modern store formats, the visitors could also include people who have just come to browse around and may not even buy anything.
- The number of footfalls converted into a purchase—this is relevant for all modern store formats. If the consumer has come with an objective of buying something, he can be persuaded to buy a lot more things. If the visitor has just come to browse, he should get attracted with the merchandise and the way it is displayed, to buy something.
- Increase the depth of purchases of each customer—it is the purpose of the retail outlet to get a maximum share of the customer's wallet before he leaves the outlet. This is true for both traditional outlets and modern retail stores. In the traditional outlet, the shopkeeper persuades the customer to buy a few additional things which had not been planned. In the case of modern store formats, the wide range, the loudly announced prices and the merchandising efforts should create this selling effort.

- Retention of the customers—once they have shopped in a retail outlet, they should keep coming back and also "recommend" the outlet to their friends and acquaintances. In the case of the traditional retail outlet this is achieved by the proximity to the consumer home and the "relationship" which the retailer develops with his customers. In the case of modern retail outlets this has to be achieved by the wide range of products available under one roof, the attractive prices, the excellent ambience and all the other services (food courts, entertainment), which makes shopping a pleasant experience.

Dell Modifies Business Model

The most famous business model of selling customized PCs on the Internet has been the highlight of Dell Computers for a long time. In 2009, Dell bought over Perot Systems which is more of a services and systems consulting company. Dell is now focusing on developing a lot more of its business by providing IT services apart from the core business of selling PCs. One such example was the huge contract signed in 2009 by Dell India with Max Healthcare. From a hardware seller, Dell is now into IT services also.

The modern store format has the additional task of getting customers and retaining them in different geographies where the consumers may not even think alike.

The retail strategy is therefore to be based on effectively achieving these objectives. Some of the broad strategies which are possible to relate to:

- having a range of products but with some differentiation which can be the "signature" of the particular retailer. The differentiation can be in terms of the product related benefits or the store related benefits like additional services provided—like home delivery.
- having an efficient operation which gives the customers what they want with the least effort on their part. Easy to access product shelves, clearly marked pricing, faster check outs could be some of these facilities
- building long term relationships with customers like "frequent buyer cards". Such card holders can then get additional benefits every time they buy something of a certain value from the store.

The common grocery store in any locality started differentiating itself from others by selling cleaned and packed grocery items.

Creating a differentiation in the product offerings, though difficult, can be a long-term competitive advantage to the retail chain. Most of the apparel retailers try to create this differential by selling a large number of brands created in their store name or store labels. Park Avenue of Raymond, Pantaloons, and Shoppers Stop have all successfully attempted this strategy.

The differentiation can also be created by a different pricing strategy. The pricing can be premium but indicating high value, reasonable pricing with good value, or low pricing and high value for money. As you can see, any pricing strategy has to focus on giving value to the consumer.

Using Oil Company Outlets to Reach Small Towns

This is a good example of a kitchen appliance manufacturer who is using the presence of leading petrol/diesel companies to reach into smaller towns. Stovekraft, which makes LPG stoves, has tied up in a co-branding effort with major oil companies Indian Oil Corporation, HPCL, and BPCL to reach its stoves into the smaller towns. It is estimated that Stovekraft has a 20 percent market share of LPG stoves in India. The company has also created a presence in retail with over 18 company owned/franchisee outlets in Bangalore for Pigeon cookware and over 65 stores in South India for their hobs and chimneys brand Gilma. This is an example of a successful horizontal marketing channel system.

Positioning Strategy

This is the identity that the store develops for itself in terms of what it has to offer the customers. This positioning, once defined, cannot be easily changed. The positioning is defined only by two things—the product range being offered and the value add of the store itself. The product range can be wide or narrow. The value add can be high or low. Some examples:

- The Lifestyle brand of stores can be termed as offering a wide range with a high value add.
- A Tanishq jewelry store could be an example of a limited range with high value add.
- A Bata shop would be offering a limited range (footwear) with a limited value add (it is functional).
- A Food World outlet offers a wide range of goods but with limited value add.

International Retailers Reducing SKUs

Supermarket chains are reported to be reducing many product choices, variants and pack sizes from their shelves. This has affected both branded and own label goods according to a survey in late 2009. The most affected goods are in the categories of pet-care products, alcohol, cleaning goods, and fresh fish. This is forcing companies also to prune their product lines.

- Asda has been delisting all second and third ranked brands of some products.
- Unilever plans to offer fewer pack sizes and brand variants in the UK from its 2500 SKUs in food and cleaning products sold in UK supermarkets. The idea is to strip out unnecessary complexity from its supply chain to improve customer service.
- Heinz plans to cut 20 percent of its lines

Product Differentiation Strategy

Star Bazaar to Sell TESCO Products

Trent, which is the retail arm of the Tata Group, operates the Star Bazaar retail outlets. Star Bazaar has started selling about 60 private label brands of TESCO (UK) in its hypermarket outlets. TESCO is the third largest retailer in the world and is the wholesale partner of Trent. Some of the proposed products are shampoos, biscuits and baby diapers.

Here the entire strategy is built around the products that the store or chain deals in. These could be national brands or the store's own private labels. In the case of the product differentiation strategy, there could be some scope for change over a period of time:

- Feature exclusive national brands that are not available at competing retailers. This is highly unlikely as the national brands would want a wider exposure and not likely to make it exclusive for some stores. The national brands could however be choosy on the kind of outlets they want to feature their brands in.
- Feature mostly private labels—Westside.
- Feature big specially planned merchandising events. Kemp Fort which started as a kids toy mega store used to have a lot of specially designed events like fashion shows which were distinctive to these stores only.
- Specialty stores follow the principle of exclusivity in the product they offer—Tanishq jewelry.

Operational Superiority

It is another strategy which the retailer can follow to provide long lasting value to the customer. This requires the retailer to clearly define his processes and streamline them to deliver value to the customer. There should not be any waste of effort or resources. For example, while providing a large assortment and ensuring zero stock-outs, the retailer has still got to have the optimum inventory levels. Similarly, while a large number of check-out counters will reduce the waiting time for the customers, this has to be correctly worked out to avoid employing extra personnel.

The operational efficiency is reflected in the clock like manner in which the retail outlets operate and this becomes noticeable by the customers. This visible operational efficiency then becomes a hallmark of the retailer. Pizza parlors are known to advertise that they would deliver the pizza within 30 minutes of an order or would return the money if not delivered in that time period.

The customer service strategy has to be developed so that it creates the "stickiness" in the customers. With the help of the information technology applications, retailers can collect a lot of personal data on their customers, their purchase patterns and their preferences. An analysis of this information can give the retailers enough information to develop suitable customer loyalty programmes to create the desired stickiness and repeat visits, continued patronage, and business. The focus is now on creating customer delight and not just customer satisfaction.

A Modern Pathology Laboratory: (ET)

One good example of an industry leader in the pathology lab space is that of Thyrocare Technologies Ltd. which is a ISO 9001–2000 certified laboratory with over 20,000 customer service centers in India. Thyrocare claims to have capabilities to process over 50,000 investigations in a day. It has a big, central lab in Mumbai. Some unique features of Thyrocare operations are:

- Uses bar coding technology for accurate processing of samples
- Uses air cargo logistics for incoming specimens from across the country
- Uses the power of the web for delivering electronic reports the next day across the country
- The focus of Thyrocare is on quality, cost, speed, and reach

Credit Terms Depend on the Brand Strength

Major retail chains treat national brand companies differently from the smaller players who also contribute to the success of the retail chain business. While national brands may give modern trade a credit period of at best 21 days for payment of bills, smaller suppliers have no such luck. They are at the mercy of the big retail chain whose customers they need. Smaller suppliers may have to give credit of up to 60 days. The retail chain is likely to sell their products within 15 days and get the use of the working capital for another 45 days to generate higher returns for the retail chain!

Store Location

The location of the stores could be used as an effective strategy to get the competitive advantage. Here the early movers get the advantage. Smaller and specialized retailers can afford the real estate costs in the main market places. Big, modern retail formats requiring much larger space, may not always be possible to be located in the main markets. Most retailers are getting located in old buildings that get demolished to make way for multi-storied retailers in all major cities. Many retailers like Shoppers Stop find it convenient to become part of large malls getting developed. A good location is obviously a major competitive advantage as the higher costs could be easily made up by larger footfalls.

New Locations for Fast Food Companies

Passenger transit locations in India like train stations, airports, bus stations, etc., where everyday millions of consumers pass through, have become the focus locations for fast food retail chains.

Consumers are willing to pay more for recognized brands as they promise value for money. Some of the examples are:

- McDonalds plans to set up 40 outlets in transit locations. It is already present in airports and railway stations of some major cities.
- Café Coffee Day which presently operates in all major airports is now targeting the smaller airports also.
- Kamat Restaurants can be seen along many major highways.
- Rajdhani, the Gujarati restaurant chain is tying up with HPCL for opening outlets at HP petrol pumps.
- Nirulas has opened 10 Express kiosks at Delhi and around and plan to increase the number to 100.

Rise in Commodity Prices Force Small Biscuit Manufacturers to Cut Retailer Margins

The last thing that any retailer wants any company to do is to cut his retail margin. However, in the face of rising commodity prices in early 2010 (in particular sugar), small biscuit companies, which hold nearly 50 percent share of the $ 1.4 billion Indian biscuit market, have been forced to cut retail margins from about 15 percent to about 13 percent. These companies have created a retail presence based on the strength of their retail margins which are much higher than the big players, but have now got to cut this as they cannot increase prices. Smaller companies do not also have the muscle of heavy advertising or promotions. Neither can they reduce the weight of the biscuits. They are forced to resort to a measure which can affect their sales.

For the city or town to be chosen for the store location, enough data is readily available on the potential value of major markets for the retailer to decide which towns to enter or to be present in. Most major retailers would like to saturate their presence in one city or town before expanding to other locations. For example, Shoppers Stop concentrated on Mumbai for quite some time before moving to other cities. Similarly Food World outlets were concentrated in Bangalore, Hyderabad, and Chennai to establish a sound presence among the customers in these cities.

Factors in Development of Strategy

Some salient points to be remembered in developing a retail strategy are given here:

- The background and experience of the promoter.
- The products and merchandise to be sold in the stores. Apparently textile companies can expect to be more successful retailing apparel.
- The profile of the potential customers. This applies more to the specialized stores. Food retailers should be aware of the local food preferences when setting up their outlets. In some South Indian towns with a large proportion of vegetarians it may not be easy to establish a McDonalds or a KFC outlet.
- The location depends to a large extent on the availability of real estate to suit the size of the proposed outlets.
- Availability of good suppliers is not an issue as most branded product companies would be delighted to do business with a retailer who can create large footfalls. It is only when the store wants to create its own brands that it has to worry about sourcing. If international MNC retailers like Walmart and Tesco can source products globally, this is not a major problem to be overcome.
- Profitability in organized retail is still estimated at low levels in India. Large, consistent volumes gathered from a large number of outlets may still be the only way of achieving decent profitability.

Service with New Features

In 2009, the Ministry of Communication implemented a major task of re-branding India Post. The modernization of post offices was taken up with a lot of enthusiasm and strict deadlines. Senior officers were required to be present in post offices to improve service to the common man. A set of "change leaders" was assigned the task of educating and training staff on the aspects of "service with a smile". This is a good example of standardization of services and at a higher standard than before.

LO 6 Discuss retail operations, performance measures, retail in rural India and FDI in retail

RETAIL PERFORMANCE MEASURES

Kiosks are Turning Out to be Prominent in Shopping Malls

The trend in high rent shopping malls is to set up kiosks of 60–100 sq. ft size normally to sell different kinds of stuff like candies, flowers, fast foods/snacks, toys, bangles etc. Kiosks are becoming successful as they depend on the footfalls into the mall. Kiosks make economic sense as the rental normally does not exceed 15 percent of sales.

We will discuss briefly here about some of the measures by which retailers evaluate their performance.

- *Gross margin return on inventory investment (GMROI):* Gross margin percentage multiplied by the ratio of sales to inventory. The advantage of this measure is that it combines both inventory control and profitability and can be used for companies, markets, individual stores, departments, products and even SKUs.
  Examples: A gross margin of 50 percent sales to inventory ratio of say 4 = GMROI of 200 percent.
- *Gross margin per full time equivalent employee (GMROL):* Retailers plan to optimize this ratio. Retailers have to use all their resources to maximize this ratio.
- *Gross margin per square foot (GMROS):* This is a measurement of how well the floor and other space in the store is being utilised.

Other Retail Performance Measures

- Return on equity (as true for any business)
- Return on assets
- Return on sales (similar to GMROI)
- Sales per transaction
- Hourly customer traffic (measures footfalls)
- Shrinkage to sales ratio
- Customers served per full time equivalent employee
- Value of purchases per buyer

ASPECTS OF STORE DESIGN

There are two important considerations in store design: functional and social. The functional aspects relate to convenience of the shopper and include protection, placement, easy access, information, and displays of the merchandise. The social aspects take into consideration the ambience, the image and attractiveness. Together the two aspects define the "character" of the retail store. The store design is a combination of the exterior and the interior of the store. One cannot easily miss the store designs like McDonalds or KFC anywhere in the world. We have similar examples in India of Café Coffee Day, Foto Flash and Food World.

Within the store, the products could be grouped in many ways depending on – functional products depending on end usage (all kitchen related items could be together, all grocery items are to be together), the impulse purchase considerations (most easily visible and attractive displays), by customer segments (men's toiletries in one place, women's apparel in another place) or based on storage considerations (consumer durables need a special place). In terms of displays, it is generally the practice to put all fast moving items at an eye level of the customer on the shelves so that it is easy for the customer to pick it up and it is easy for the store staff to replenish the shelves. The slow moving items are normally kept in the lower shelves. Brand managers of companies would want their new products or slow movers to be kept at an eye level on the shelves. In addition, some stores practice the placement of the slow movers on the left end of the shelf and the fast movers on the right end of the shelf (closer to the right hand of consumers).

Mobile payment options for Consumers: Mobile wallet is a virtual mobile based wallet where one can store cash for making mobile, online or off-line payments.

Some mobile payment options:

1	Airtel Money	11	MobiKwik
2	Citi Masterpass	12	MomoeXpress
3	Citrus Pay	13	MoneyOnMobile
4	Ezetap	14	Mswipe
5	FreeCharge	15	Ola Money
6	HDFC PayZapp	16	Oxigen
7	Pockets by ICICI Bank	17	PayMate
8	JioMoney	18	Paytm
9	JUSPAY	19	PayUmoney
10	LIME	20	State Bank Buddy

Digital Payment Options – Some Data

- India has the record of being the second highest in APAC region for digital payment options
- 40 percent of respondents of the survey used smart phone wallets
- Purchases pattern: mobile recharge 60 percent, travel services 52 percent, utility payments 58 percent and online shopping 58 percent

Source: ACI Survey.

Some salient points in store operations are given below:

- The product assortment strategy, the buying, sources, policies and practices are all decided by the buyers or merchandise managers.

- All the stores in a retail chain need not carry all the items. About two-thirds of the items may be common, but the balance one third is different and based on the local customer preferences.
- Merchandise managers are offered nearly 100 new items every week (it seems that this figure is more like 250 to 300 in the west) and they reject about 70 percent of them. The criteria for acceptance include—consumer demand and acceptance, supporting strong advertising and promotions and good financial incentives.
- The service mix on offer to customers includes:
    - Pre-purchase—advertising, displays, shelf space arrangements, shopping hours and any telephone or other requests acceptance.
    - Post-purchase—quick check-outs, gift wrapping, goods returns policy, alterations, installation help, and so on.
    - Other services which could include information, payment by cheques, facilities for parking, food courts, child rooms and the like.
- The vendors may help the retailer in advertising and promotions in many ways like:
    - Sharing the retailers' advertising costs for their products.
    - Delivering stocks just in time—vendor managed inventory.
    - Help in developing computer systems which are linked to the vendor so that he is aware as soon as his product moves out of the shelf.
    - Point of sale aids to attract customers.
    - Sponsorship of in-store selling promotions.

Role of Digital Wallets in a Cashless Economy

- RBI says customers can store up to ₹20,000 in a digital wallet
- Digital wallet company FreeCharge has tied up with IOC, BPCL and HPCL—pay at petrol pumps by scanning QR code. LPG users—QR codes carried by delivery boys
- Citibank + Paytm – wallet add money scheme
- FreeCharge – wallet on delivery (WOD) for instant payments
- Find something nearby – Paytm has a nearby feature – search for the nearest Paytm enabled stores
- Creating virtual cards for online transactions—debit card with a pre-set spending limit introduced by HDFC, KMB, SBI, Axis, ICICI—with an expiry date
- Eat, buy now, pay later with Simpl—used by Bookmyshow, Fassos, Freshmenu, Zipgo, Zimmber. A Simpl app on smartphone. Payment using Simpl
- Paytm has 15 crore users. Will add on 50 crore Jan Dhan customers even without mobiles
- MobiKwik has introduced virtual and physical cards—even if merchant does not use MB – card mapped to wallet balance.

Sources: Economic Times Bureau. cashlessindia.gov.in, www.globallogic.com, razorpay.com, National Payments Corporation of India website accessed on 31 May 2017.

Table 11.11 **Digital Payment Options**

S. No.	Option	Features
1.	M-Wallets	Payment mode via smartphones. Easy payments to vendors. SBI Buddy, HDFC PayZapp, ICICI Pocket, Paytm, MobiKwik—in all 40 licences.
2.	NEFT & RTGS	One-to-one and B2B funds transfer. Operate only during banking hours.
3.	Immediate Payment Service	Real time electronic funds transfer system using mobiles. Operates 24x7x365
4.	Plastic money	750 million cards—about 400 million regular users—250–300 million debit cards primarily for cash withdrawal in ATMs—27 million credit cards—transaction fees 2–20 percent—annual interest on card dues 36 to 40 percent
5.	Mobile banking	Access and operate bank account via bank app or browser
6	Unified payments interface (UPI)	Interconnects banks to help transfer funds—sender and receiver need a UPI identity (about 30 banks)
7	Aadhar enabled payments system	Complete payment using biometric authentication
8	Bharat Interface for Money (BHIM)	UPI based service to enable money transfer using just a mobile number
9	Unstructured supplementary service data	GSM based system to help money transfer for feature phone users

Sources: Shelley Singh, *Economic Times*, January 05, 2017, cashlessindia.gov.in, www.globallogic.com, razorpay.com, National Payments Corporation of India website accessed on 31 May 2017.

Table 11.12 **What People Used**

Payment System	Volume (million)	Value (₹ crore)
UPI	0.1	40
Mobile banking	2.2	4790
Plastic cards	8.8	1490
RTGS	0.4	468150
NEFT	6.5	65310
IMPS	1.8	1580
USSD	0.09	0.72

Source: RBI, December 29, 2016.

Efficient Consumer Response (ECR)

Efficient Consumer Response originated in the US when major grocery retailers felt the threat from alternate retail formats like discount stores, hypermarkets, etc., which offered specific highly discounted goods. ECR was developed as a grocery industry supply chain support system. The objective was to deliver better value to grocery customers by eliminating non-value adding costs and inefficiencies. ECR supports the "pull" system.

How does ECR Work?

ECR captures customer demand information at the point-of-sale in the store to generate replenishment orders on the vendor (it therefore "pulls" the product based on consumer off-takes).

ECR develops a responsive consumer-driven supply chain. Companies/their distributors and the customers (retailers) work together to maximize customer satisfaction and minimize cost of the supply chain. The technology used is that of e-commerce. Any SKU moved out of a store shelf by a consumer is immediately registered in the vendor system. The vendor can aggregate all such off-take during the day and replenish the quantities by the store the immediate next day. The retailer has only got to keep minimum inventory as the vendor is almost "on call" 24×7. P&G and Walmart have been credited with the use of ECR for the first time in the retail industry. Experts believe that ECR is a modification of the Quick Response Logistics or the Just-in-Time system used in the manufacturing sector.

ECR also helps in efficient store assortment, product introduction, running product promotions and product replenishment.

Retail Warehouse Information Systems

- Inventory management, stock-outs, opportunity loss, slow processing, improper display of products, no proper customer relationship, lack of customer experience
- Stage 1: Ease of transaction—impulse buying, mode of payment. Speed of transaction – scanning, billing, inventory tracking and tracing
- Information Systems Retail Value Chain: Manufacturer >> storage warehouse>> carrier >> supplier >> retailer >> customer
    - Supplier to manufacturer—shipment orders
    - Retailer to company HQ—sales data

Use of IT for

- CRM—acquiring and retaining customers
- Security—shrinkage control
- Managing e-payments
- Online shopping facilitation

Benefits of Point of Sale

Inventory control, invoicing/receiving, interface with accounting, reports, enforced accuracy, integrated customer care handling, general ledger, AP, AR, support for tax audit

Some Retail Systems

- Hand-held POS systems
- Customer data base

- RFID—electronic tagging
- Planogram for product layout
- Magic mirrors—depict appearance in any outfit without having to wear it

FOREIGN DIRECT INVESTMENT (FDI) IN RETAIL IN INDIA

The growing trend in organized retail is attracting the interest of global players. However, the government of India till recently did not permit foreign direct investment (FDI) in the retail industry. Foreign players had to take the route of franchising to operate in India. Even then, well known foreign retail brands like Marks and Spencer, all the footwear brands (Reebok, Adidas, Nike, and others), McDonalds, and Swarovski are already in India.

A large number of MNC retailers have been showing interest in investing in the retail industry in India. While this may help improve the standard of retailing, it creates intense competition and gives the benefit of world class retailing formats to the Indian consumer; it also affects the Indian retail industry which is still largely unorganized. There is a tremendous resistance to FDI in retail in India from the industry itself. The government of India did not permit FDI in retail till recently. It was only permitting foreign wholesalers to operate in the trading space. The well-known example is of Metro AG from Germany which operates two "cash-and-carry" outlets for retailers in Bangalore.

The Government of India permits franchisees of the foreign retailers like KFC, McDonalds, Tag Heuer, Swatch to operate in India. It is essentially an Indian partner operating the stores to the international standards of the foreign partner. Some foreign brands likely to make a foray into India are: Ferragamo, Hermes, Prada, Armani, Chanel and Gucci, Gap, Zara, Ralph Lauren, Old Navy, and Banana Republic.

FDI is the channel for getting foreign capital into the country. FDI is allowed in different sectors in different percentages approved by the Government. As the retail sector is growing fast, it has ample scope for FDI.

The GOI has recently in a slew of its reform statements, announced up to 51 percent FDI in multi-brand retail and 100 percent in single-brand retail. The GOI mandate on FDI in retail also prescribes that an organized retail outlet may be set up only in cities with a population of more than 10 lakh as per 2011 census. Governments in states and union territories are free to make their own policies within these guidelines.

Some of the rules prevailing are summarized below:

- Single brand retailing—100 percent FDI with certain favorable conditions
- Multi-brand retailing—51 percent FDI permitted
- Cash and Carry Wholesale—100 percent FDI permitted

FDI in Retail – Milestones

2006

- FDI of 100 percent in C&C wholesale—automatic route
- FDI of 51 percent with Government approval (FIPB) in retail

2010

- July 2010—seeking opinions of all stakeholders for allowing FDI in multi-brand retail—49 percent suggested—no decision taken

2012

- 100 percent FDI in single brand retail (January 2012), 51 percent multi-brand (September)
- Single brand 49 percent automatic route—beyond needs Government approval—one brand sold internationally
- Beyond 51 percent: 30 percent local sourcing from SMEs (max investment: $ 1million)
- Multi-brand: $100 million investment: 50 percent in back-end infra like manufacturing, processing, packing, design, distribution, logistics, QC, storage etc. + 30 percent local sourcing

2015:

- Single brand retail—global technology brands like Sony and Apple to open fully owned stores. 30 percent local sourcing from date of first store + online trading

2016:

- 100 percent FDI in market-place formats of e-commerce
- Defined market place and inventory led models of e-commerce
- Discount limits defined
- Sourcing—not more than 25 percent from one vendor
- Inventory based model—kept out of 100 percent FDI
- 100 percent FDI in multi-brand processed food retailing—sourced and manufactured in India (Walmart, Ikea) —approval from Foreign Investment Promotion Board (FIPB)
- Single brand retail and food retail in e-commerce—three years for brands like Apple and Leco—no sourcing norms
- Relaxed sourcing norm: another five years—state of the art and cutting edge technology

Sources: India retailing.com, June 23, 2016; www.makeinindia.com, Hindustan Times, India Brand Equity Foundation accessed on 31 May 2017.

Retailing Initiatives in Rural India

Some of the features of rural India include the process of reaching 642,000 villages, about two thirds of which are still not easily accessible.

Some of features of rural markets are:

- Dispersed population and trade, large number of small markets, poor road connectivity
- Low density of shops per village, poor storage systems, poor visibility and product display, poor reach of media and hence communication.
- Estimated that nearly 50 percent of rural population prefers buying from the weekly shanties/*haats*

- Rural retailers stock mostly local and regional brands with higher margins and longer credit periods.

There are various means used by companies and other businesses to reach rural markets and consumers. Some of these methods are given below:

- Wholesalers in feeder markets are used to provide reach into villages; used the hub and spoke model to provide the reach.
- Company vans carrying goods with a journey cycle and with ready stocks, conduct both sales and promotions, are quite effective but expensive.
- Mobile traders are mostly unorganized, deliver daily need products directly to the homes, may use bicycles, mopeds or hand carts, have a deep reach, good rapport with customers but may also sell fakes.
- The oldest marketing channel happens to be the weekly shandies or *haats*.
- Some corporates have tied up with women self-help groups in villages to provide distribution for their brands; HUL Project Shakti is an example. Companies also use syndicated distributor models with 2 or more companies running distribution vans into the villages.

The rural retail market size is estimated as (₹ crore): 2010: 180,000 and 2015: 240,000

Some major companies running significant retail outlets in rural India include:

Table 11.13

Godrej Aadhaar	*Khushiyonka, khushhalika.* Managed by Godrej Agrovet and provides crop advisory services, water testing, crop finance, products. 24 outlets each outlet covering 20 villages.
ITC Chaupal Sagar	An extension of the e-choupal system. Rural malls created. Each mall spread over 5 acres, costing about ₹4 crore. Proposed in 15 states with about 1000 rural malls.
DSCL Hariyali Kisan Bazar	302 outlets in 8 states providing all agricultural services and most of the products required in rural. They have qualified agronomists working 24x7 and helping 10 million farmers covering 30 million acres.

Support for Retail in Rural India

- Market research firm Nielsen expects India's rural FMCG market to reach a size of US$ 100 billion by 2025 (from $20 Billion in 2018). McKinsey Global Institute forecasts the annual real income per household in rural India to rise to 3.6 percent. This is a clear indication that rural retail is expected to flourish in the next few years. It is estimated that rural India accounts for about 40 percent of the FMCG business in India.
- Besides the growth of the FMCG sector, the government of India has taken a number of initiatives to strengthen the rural sector and the rural consumer.
- There are a number of initiatives being taken by various agencies which will help rural consumers. Some examples are given below:
    - The Ministry of Rural Development is expecting to achieve its annual targeted length of 48,812 kilometers of rural roads by March 31, 2017 under the Pradhan Mantri Gram SadakYojana (PMGSY).

- The National Bank for Agriculture and Rural Development (NABARD) plans to provide around 200,000 point-of-sale (POS) machines in 100,000 villages and distribute RuPay cards to over 34 million farmers across India, to enable farmers to undertake cashless transactions.
- The Ministry of Textiles has signed memorandum of understanding (MoU) with 20 e-commerce companies, aimed at providing a platform to artisans and weavers in different handloom and handicraft clusters across the country to help them sell their products directly to the consumer.
- The Ministry of New and Renewable Energy (MNRE) has an annual target of setting up one lakh family size biogas plants to the states and union territories for FY 2016–17.

- The allocation to the Mahatma Gandhi National Rural Employment Guarantee Act (MGNREGA) has been ₹48,000 crore (US$ 7.2 billion) in the year 2017–18, which is the highest ever allocated amount
- In the Union Budget 2017–18, the Government of India mentioned that it is on course to achieve 100 percent village electrification by May 1, 2018

Franchising Route for Global Brands

Franchising India Holdings Ltd, a franchising solutions company, estimates the following about the franchise industry in India: one lakh franchises with a market size of $ 7.2 billion growing at the rate of 38 percent per annum. *Business India* (November 1, 2009) states that by 2013, it is expected to reach a size of $ 20 billion. There are 1200 franchise concepts in India providing employment to about 9.5 lakh people. The ROI from the business ranges from 15 to 20 percent. Some of the companies which are getting into licensing/franchising arrangements in India are: Ford Motor Company for toys, apparel and auto accessories and California Pizza Kitchen (15 restaurants over the next 10 years). Franchise India launched the Franchise India Program 2009 which was a year round program for guiding international brands for doing business in India.

LO 7 Outline franchising and e-tailing

FRANCHISING AND E-TAILING

There are 4 types of franchise operations: wholesaler sponsored, retailer sponsored, manufacturer sponsored, and service company sponsored:

- Wholesaler sponsored voluntary chains—like the example of the franchised stores of Kemp Fort for toys.
- Retailer sponsored cooperative chains—Janata Bazaars, Delhi Super Baazar and all cooperative society stores.
- Manufacturer sponsored franchising systems—soft drink majors sponsor bottlers to buy concentrate, produce beverages and sell to retailers. Auto companies sponsor auto dealers.

- Service company sponsored franchising systems—financial institutions sponsor firms to sell mutual funds, etc.

The franchisor is the firm which wants to sell its products or services. The franchisee is the firm or group of individuals who are willing to sell the products or services on behalf of the franchisor.

Top 10 Best E-Com Websites in India

1. eBay.in – high end products, good quality, reasonable price
2. Indiatimes Shopping
3. Askme Bazaar
4. ShopClues
5. Myntra (Blr)
6. Amazon.in
7. Paytm
8. Snapdeal
9. Jabong
10. Flipkart

Sources: Techin Asia, May 30, 2016—Vinod Kardam; www.digit.in, (top 50), walkthroughindia.com, companiesinindia.net, www.thetoptens.com accessed on 31 May 2017.

How Does the System Work?

- The franchisor gives advice and help to the franchisees.
    - Finding a good location, blueprints for the shop or store, financial, marketing and management assistance.
- Franchisees own the business but must adhere to the franchisor's requirements on merchandising and operations to preserve uniformity and control.
- Benefits to franchisee:
    - Quick recognition among potential customers
    - Management training provided by the franchisor
    - Franchisor may buy ingredients, supplies and parts and sell to the franchisee at lower prices than the market
    - Financial assistance where required
    - Promotional aids, in-store displays and the like
- Benefits to franchisor:
    - Expansion is possible much faster
    - Local franchisee pays lower rates for advertising than a national firm
    - Owners of the franchisee are motivated to work more than just employees
    - All local taxes and licenses are responsibility of the franchisees

Electronic Retailing or e-Tailing

Electronic retailing, as the name suggests, is shopping on the Internet without the consumer having to visit a physical store. With the increased use of the Internet by the average Indian, the scope for electronic shopping is growing.

Retailing on the Internet/e-Tailing

In Internet retailing the seller and the buyer meet through the interactive electronic network of the World Wide Web. There are some advantages to the producer of selling his product or service on the net:

- Creates a favorable image for the company
- Reaches geographically dispersed consumers anywhere in the world
- Provides all information about the product, choices available, price comparisons, answers to queries, details of loyalty programs, etc.
- Promotion of new products or services and use demonstrations to highlight features

Retailing on the Internet—Some Salient Points

There are some salient points of retailing through Internet. They are:

- Assortment can be unlimited—depending on the ability of the retailer to physically deliver the products
- Items are not on hold—someone has to deliver the product and it involves delays and costs
- On the net, a consumer cannot touch or feel the product
- Better information makes the consumer a better shopper
- Internet makes it easier to do comparison shopping and to compare prices from different sellers
- The consumer has to plan ahead when he buys on the Internet.

Business India (Ferbaury 12, 2006) states that the government is planning to set up one lakh information kiosks across six lakh villages, apart from building a state-wide information network including introducing internal protocol television (IPTV) in Mumbai and Chennai, setting up server farms to host Indian websites and an Indian language translation web browser to increase Internet usage in the country over the next three years. The info kiosks would be common service centers and would enable villages to access services like weather reports and commodity data.

Library Online

This is a first ever example of its kind in India and is already quite well known. This is a book lending library online. The name is Librarywala.com. The growth in the use of the Internet in the cities, rise in literacy rates, increase in incomes and consumers looking for convenience were all factors which influenced the setting up of this library. But as consumer tastes were vast, setting up an inventory of a vast range of books proved a challenge. Information contained online includes the name of the author, number of pages and reviews received from readers of the book.

Table 11.14 Top 10 E-Commerce Companies in India 2016

S. No.	Company	Details
1	mjunction	Started by Tata Steel + SAIL in 2001. Largest e-market place for steel in the world. Transactions up to 2015 – ₹350 thousand crore GMV $ 9.7 billion
2	Flipkart	Blr2007. 40 million products in 80+ product categories, 8 million shipments per month, 75 million registered users, 10 million daily page visits, 85000 sellers, 17 state-of-the-art warehouses, acquired Myntra in 2014. GMV $ 7.5 billion
3	Snapdeal	Market place model from 2010. 12 million+ products, 1.5 lakh sellers, 5000 cities GMV $ 4.3 billion
4	Amazon India	World's largest cloud service provider. GMV $ 1.995 billion
5	MakeMyTrip	Online travel from 2000. GMV $ 1.648 billion
6	Paytm	From 2010—owned by One 97 Communications. 100 million registered users, 60 million orders per month GMV $ 1.16 billion
7	Myntra	Blr in 2007. 1000 brands, 1.5 lakh products, delivery in 9000 locations, delivery app only model in 2015. $ 0.8 billion
8	ShopClues	Started in 2011. 12000 merchants, 2 lakh+ retail products. GMV $ 0.4 billion
9	Infibeam	Ahmedabad 2007. GMV $ 0.33 billion
10	IRCTC	Run by the Indian Railways. Ticketing, Tourism, Catering—serves 13 million passengers each day. GMV 0.225 billion

Sources: mbaskool.com; www.digit.in, (top 50), walkthroughindia.com, companiesinindia.net, www.thetoptens.com accessed on 31 May 2017.

Advantages of online retail

- Fast, easy
- Money saving
- Interesting shopping experience
- 24×7 shopping
- Shopping with coupons to get discounts
- Shopping from home
- Rich product availability

Disadvantages of online retail

- No product touch and feel
- Delays in shipping
- Shipping charges extra
- Risk of card misuse

Online shopping sites in India (some of these have been detailed in Table 11.14)

1. Amazon
2. Flipkart
3. Snapdeal
4. Paytm
5. eBay
6. Jabong
7. Myntra
8. ShopClues
9. Pepperfry
10. HomeShop18
11. Nearbuy
12. Zovi
13. Infibeam
14. FirstCry
15. Indiatimes
16. Lenskart
17. Croma Inc
18. Koovs
19. American Swan
20. ZoomIn

Some examples of online shopping for services are given Table 11.15.

Table 11.15 Examples of Online Shopping for Services

Service Sought	Examples
Travel	MakeMyTrip, Thomas Cook India, TicketGoose, Booking.com, Expedia Travel, Travelguru.com, Cleartrip, Yatra.com, Travel ChaCha, Ezeego1
Matrimonial	Shaadi.com, Jeevansathi.com, SimplyMarry, M4Marry.com, Kerala Matrimony, etc.
Insurance comparison	Insuring India, Apnapaisa.com, Policy Tiger, PolicyBazaar, BankBazaar, MyInsuranceClub.com, QuickBima, Easypolicy
Hotel booking comparison—Techulator	Booking.com, Agoda.com, TripAdvisor, HotelsCombined, trivago.in, Hotels-Scanner.com, Hotels.com India, HotelsCompare.co.in, Goibibo, ixigo
Cabs (India travel blog)	Uber, Ola cabs, Meru Cabs, Easy Cabs, Savaari, TABcabs, Megacabs, Wings Radio Cabs, Cel Cabs
Medicines (Indian CEO)	mChemist.com, Netmeds.com, MeraPharmacy, www.mediartlifesciences.com, BuyDrug.in, MedPlusMart, Apollo Pharmacy
Food (digital and mobile apps)	Foodpanda, Just Eat, TastyKhana, TravelKhana, Domino's Pizza, FoodMingo, Faasos, Zomato, TimesCity, Burrp
Movie tickets	BookMyShow, Ticketplease, Ticketnew, Big Cinemas, Cinemax
Learning (O-L education, Upwork)	Coursera, Lynda.com, Udemy, Udacity, Khan Academy, Codecademy, Bloc, iversity, Skillshare, General Assembly
Banking (Top10Wala.In)	ICICI Bank, Corporation Bank, State Bank of India, HDFC Bank, IDBI Bank, Axis Bank, Citibank India,
Shopping (Top 10—Insider)	Flipkart, Jabong, Snapdeal, Myntra, HomeShop18, Amazon, Tata CliQ, Pepperfry
Mobile wallets (Social Beat)	Paytm, Momoe, PayUmoney, MobiKwik.com, Citrus Pay, State Bank Buddy, Citi Master, ICICI Pocket, HDFC Chillr, LIME
Leisure Travel (World Blaze 2016)	MakeMyTrip, Cox & Kings, Thomas Cook India, Yatra.com, Travelguru.com, Cleartrip, SOTC India, Goibibo, Expedia Travel, HelloTravel
Doctor's appointment	Kare4u—for booking

Jobs (World Blaze 2017)	Naukri.com, LinkedIn, Shine.com, TimesJobs, Monster India, iimjobs, Glassdoor, FreeJobAlert.Com, Careesma, JobStreet.com
Grocery (grabon)	Bigbasket, Grofers, ZopNow, Godrej Nature's Basket, Reliance SMART, Amazon Groceries, BazaarCart, Naturally Yours
Payment Gateways	CCAvenue, PayZippy, DirecPay, EBS, ICICI PaySeal, PayU

The number of Internet users in India, currently close to 40 million, is expected to top the 100 million mark by 2007, various studies suggest. Seven out of every 10 Indians surf the net from the country's more than 100,000 cyber cafes. The number of these cafes is projected to rise to 2.62 lakh by 2010. Internet usage in India is growing more in depth than in spread, a study by JuxtConsult has revealed.

Just like in physical retailing, the challenge is to get consumers to the online store (equivalent to the footfalls in the physical store) and getting them to buy the products. Consumers have to be convinced of the advantages of shopping online which are: (i) there is no geographical boundaries—a consumer in Amritsar can shop for something which an e-store in Chennai is offering, (ii) there are no time restrictions—the shopping is 24×7, (iii) and the payment is online—there is no need to even handle cash.

Some Unique Examples of Selling on the Internet

TV Channels for Viewing (*Business India*, February 21, 2010)

The web site *www.viewmy.tv* provides a user-friendly interface to access more than 2500 free TV channels across 100 countries. This is considered one of the finest aggregation services and one of the earliest social networking services. The channels have been classified under: sports, culture, knowledge, cinema, news, education, etc. The site depends entirely on advertising revenues.

Site for Selecting Right Education Choices (*Business India*, February 21,2010)

A campus and education network which includes comprehensive information on educational institutes, courses offered, campus reviews posted by students and alumni is known as *www.minglebox.com*. Minglebox is one of the largest education portals in the country. It also covers updated information on admissions, notifications, deadlines for exams, online guidance and counselling facilities.

Selecting a Music Band of Choice (*Business India*, September 20, 2009)

This is a website where a person can know and hear about different band groups, download and buy their music, check out musical events and interact with the artistes. The band groups can upload their profiles, share and sell music, announce events and sell tickets.

A Website for Entrepreneurs (*Business India*, April 04, 2010)

Entrepreneurs can get advice, information and assistance for their businesses on a free-to-use American web site known as *www.startupnation.com*. For budding entrepreneurs, it has a lot of tips and step-by-step guides. The support is provided on the site by people who have "already been there, done that".

Card Game Rummy Online (*Business India*, April 04, 2010)

A site launched in early 2009 provides the online version of the popular card game "rummy". The game is played in a knock-out format on the net.

Shifting to a Different DTH Service Provider could be a Reality Soon (*Business* India, April 04, 2010)

Even if a set-top box and dish may have been purchased by one service provider, a consumer may soon be able to shift to another service provider without having to pay additional charges. Plans are afoot to soon introduce the "technical interoperability" provisions.

Keeping Track of Car Servicing (*Business India*, March 21, 2010)

KPIT Cummins Infosystems Ltd and the DSK Group recently launched in Pune an online service to help consumers plan, and monitor and track the servicing of their cars. The web site *www.clickservicessmile.com* caters to 4-wheeler owners at present. The site enables users to view their cars getting serviced, access information on the exact faults of their vehicle, the amount to be paid, rates for car parts and other details. Once registered, the web site acts as a source of vehicle history, information and maintenance schedules.

Learning to do Homework on the Net (*Business India*, November 15, 2009)

Here is an example of a unique effort on the Internet to run a coaching and tutoring institute. The name of the site is www.studentoffortune.com. It is a home tutoring market place. A student with a problem with his lesson raises it on the site and offers to pay a certain fees for its solution. Any other student or teacher accessing the site, can offer a solution at the offered price. If no help comes at the price, the student can raise the bid.

Online Retailers

Some of the steps in developing an online retail format are given briefly here:

- Creating an online store. The starting point is the store front with a distinct identity and image giving the "look and feel" of a store.
- The store front will have enough "browsing" options to take the consumer to the merchandise on offer along with all features, pricing and how to order instructions. In this part of the presentation, there should be no ambiguity. In this part of the store, the visual appeal is properly built up.
- Electronic space being almost unlimited, online merchandising can display vast number of brand packs. The customer, if he wants, can browse through all these hundreds of items before making the buying decision.
- The other advantage of online retailing is the ability to analyse the enormous quantity of data that it generates. This data can be analysed to find out as to who visited the online store, what all did they see, what did they buy and how many times. This data can be used to suggest the right merchandise which would interest the buyer the next time he visits the site. Amazon.com uses this data very effectively to suggest the books of interest to the visitor (based on past data about the visitor) every time someone logs on to their website.

- Carrying a large assortment online does not mean any inventory costs. The website or the e-retailer should only make arrangements to deliver the goods bought online in the promised time to the customers so that the "stickiness" can be kept up.
- As online shopping has some advantages in the costs, it should be possible to offer prices online which are more competitive than brick-and-mortar stores.

Disadvantages of Online Retailing

- Modern organized retail excites the customer because of the pleasant ambience it creates for shopping. This ambience cannot be created online particularly if the customer is shopping online either from his work place or his residence.
- Modern retail formats make the shopping experience also entertaining. The online format cannot support this part of shopping. Moreover, if the customer is shopping in a modern mall, he has access to food courts and multiplexes offering him his favorite entertainment. This can never be replicated online.
- In the physical shopping process, there is a major see, touch and feel factor which adds value to the customer purchase process. This is absent in the online version.
- In the online version, there is no one to assist the customer in his purchases. This impersonal shopping may not be liked by most customers.
- Most urban customers even are still reluctant to make payments using their credit cards online due to confidentiality and security reasons. They fear that their credit card details may get misused elsewhere.

Distribution Systems for E-Commerce Sites

Product/service delivery options available for e-commerce retailers as per Phoenixx:

- Create own logistics division—heavy investment but complete control. Also requires a lot of warehouse space. Customer faith will be high. Example: e-Kart of Flipkart
- Entrust all the responsibilities to a third party—reasonable rates, stable track record, low volumes, high billing
- Most common—work jointly with a 3P service provider

E-commerce companies consider that logistics defines their success. They consider speed of delivery as important as the quality of products they sell on their sites. Their demand from delivery companies is more reach, and faster shipping at lower costs.

Some salient numbers are:

- The e-commerce market in India will be worth about $220 billion by 2025 says Bank of America's Merryl Lynch
- The size of the logistics market in India by 2020 is expected to be about $300 billion according to research agency Novonous, with a CAGR of 12.7 percent

Notable developments in 2015:

- A number of start-ups came into the logistics space and investing in them
- Snapdeal—hyper-local route to ensure delivery of packages to customers within one hour of placing the order—Snapdeal Instant

- Snapdeal also introduced 4 hour deliveries with card payments and also reverse pick-ups in just 90 minutes
- The company's own fulfillment centers handled 60 percent of the orders for shipment
- Amazon increased their fulfillment centers to 21 across India with 5 million cubic feet space—considered the largest network in India
- Flipkart tied up with their partner stores to act as alternative delivery channels, so that customers can pick up their shipments at their convenience.
- Some aspects of automation technology were applied to the logistics arms of the e-commerce companies—better data analytics to forecast customer demand more accurately, picking and moving packages to designated delivery points and making all warehouses processes quicker and smoother.
- Paytm introduced e-fulfillment centers and return processing centers.
- ShopClues developed technology to integrate with 90 percent of their logistics service providers to ensure faster tracking and information flow between merchants and customers
- Flipkart has an algorithm on routing which makes delivery and pick-up more accurate and fast. Flipkart's investment in MapmyIndia has helped the company on this requirement.
- Amazon India has engaged with an NGO in a pilot project of rural delivery network in Tier III and IV towns, through logistics firm Connect India E-Commerce Pvt. Ltd., incorporated by founders of BASIX group

Delivery Vehicle tracking focus in 2015:

- Amazon introduced fast and reliable Internet connectivity across devices to use technology for better vehicle tracking.
- In September 2015, Paytm invested in logistics solution provider LogiNext to strengthen its supply chain.
- LogiNext–which caters to Paytm, Myntra and Amazon among others MapmyIndia even provides "heat maps" for giving information on those areas where maximum delays are happening.
- LogiNext also works with cold chain logistics service providers for delivering perishables. Temperature and other settings required for a particular product could be set by an app by the delivery boys.
- Flipkart invested in Blackbuck for capturing data on vehicle utilization and movement.
- Inadequate mobile coverage in many areas makes vehicle tracking difficult.

More developments in 2016 (as per Infobharati.com):

- Flipkart announced an investment of $2.5 billion in logistics requirements over the next 5 years
- Snapdeal made acquisitions in the technology and logistics sectors. It also tied up with logistics service provider gojavas—all to reduce delivery times by 70 percent

- The huge investment of the GOI on infrastructure projects and a lot of it on roads is going to help improve deliveries for the e-commerce companies
- Logistics service providers who are tying up with e-commerce majors include LogiNext, GreyOrange, Roadrunnr and Delhivery.

Top 10 Courier companies for e-commerce delivery:

- Blue Dart Express
- DHL Express
- DTDC India
- The Professional Couriers
- UPS
- FedEx
- FirstFlight
- Aramex
- GATI Ltd.
- ExpressIt Delivery

India Post is emerging as a leading courier service provider also. Some salient features of the couriers as highlighted by Phoenixx are mentioned in Table 11.16.

Table 11.16 Salient Features of Courier Service Providers

Name	Salient Features
India Post	Highest coverage, maximum reliability. Affordable costs. About ₹30/90 per 500g
FedEx	Excellent delivery service, fairly competitive. Limited coverage + international. ₹32/72 per kg
FirstFlight	220 countries, 4500 pin codes in India. ₹35/500g
DTDC India	Delivering value to 10,000 pin codes, 240 countries.
Aramex	Delivery unlimited, 2872 pin codes, ₹60/500g, untimely + losses
gojavas	Delivering million smiles, competitive prices, 2010 pin codes, ₹22/500g
DHL Express	Global, steep prices, ₹600/500g
Ecom Express	Affordable, 1500 pin codes, ₹22/500g
Blue Dart Express	Good service, slightly expensive, ₹55 to 75/500g
ShipRocket	Software solution used by DHL Express, Aramex, FirstFlight, Ecom Express, DTDC India—serves 12000 pincodes

Logistic Support to E-retailing

Developing a website for B2C business in retailing is probably the simplest part. Once the online store is attractive enough to get the visitors, the possibility of conversions to the purchase of goods is quite high if the offerings are exciting. The sale can get successfully consummated only if the delivery of the product is made to the customers. Fulfilment of the online orders is the most important and critical part of the e-retailing business. Once the customer places the order online, he expects almost immediate delivery which of course is not possible. Most online retailers promise delivery within 24 hours within the same city and between 48 to 72 hours for upcountry deliveries. Even to meet these deadlines, the logistics support has to be effective. The logistics part is normally done through well-known and efficient couriers. Most of the goods sold online can be transported through couriers.

IT in Retail

Zensar Technologies plans to become a leader in retail IT solutions in both domestic and global markets. It has recently acquired Seacom Technology's intellectual property rights for the latter's point of sale (POS) products as well as its existing customers. Seacom is a leader in the Indian market for POS solutions that are mission-critical solutions designed especially for a hypermarket scenario to ensure smooth and uninterrupted flow of the voluminous billing process. Seacom's Smart Shop range of POS solutions for the food and grocery retail sector is already in use in most of the major hypermarkets in India.

Receipt of Payment Against Orders (Payment Gateway)

This again is the difficult part of doing the business. Most retailers prefer only cash on delivery. Customers may be reluctant to pay through their credit cards and not all of them may have credit cards. Most retailers prefer if the payment is made in advance using credit cards. Cheques cannot be accepted due to delays in payment and possible bouncing. The ideal mode of payment is cash. At the time of delivery if the customer is asked for cash, there could be some problems like:

- The person present and receiving the goods may not be the one placing the order and may ask that the courier should come later to collect the cash.
- The person placing the order may not accept all the goods fully. What happens if some of the goods are returned?
- It could happen that the order may not be accepted as the customer has changed his mind or bought the product elsewhere in the meantime.
- Would the courier be willing to accept cash from the customers? How would the courier pay it back to the retailer?
- How would the courier handle returned goods?

The challenges of online retailers lie in utilizing the unique aspects of the Internet:

- Nearly infinite "real estate"
- No constraints of operational timings or geographical boundaries
- The interactive ability to reach customers in their personal spaces – be it home or office
- Comparatively miniscule cost
- Consumers feel the advantages of home delivery, time savings, virtual showrooms (greetings/gifts) are open 24×7 and products can even be delivered on a future specific date.

Flight and train bookings are the biggest contributors to the growth in online shopping besides direct purchases. Some popular items on the online shopper's list are: books, electronics, tickets, apparel, and gift items.

For distribution, a hub and spoke model seems the most suitable – where there is a local network of distributors.

Biggest hurdle is broadband connectivity. E-commerce market led by: Japan – sales last year of $38.4 billion, South Korea $6.3 billion, and China and Taiwan each $1.1 billion.

Future could be in mobile shopping—in October 2004, there were 44.5 million mobile users and growing at 1.5 million per month.

Digital payments, highlighted earlier in this chapter, offer an excellent solution.

SUMMARY

LO 1

- Any business entity selling to consumers is "retailing". The goods may be sold in a shop, in person, by mail, on the Internet, telephone, or a vending machine. It could be sold in a shop, on the street, or in the home of the consumer. Some of the other characteristics of retail trade are:
  - The order sizes tend to be small but many.
  - The retailer caters to a wide variety of customers and hence has to keep a large assortment of goods.
  - A lot of the buying in the retail outlet could be on impulse and hence managing inventory is critical.
  - Retail store service personnel (in smaller stores) and the goods displayed (in major stores) are an important element of the selling process.
  - The targeted customer mix decides the elements of the "marketing mix" which the retailer has to develop to optimize his investment. The elements of the marketing mix so designed, gives the "image" to the store.
- Retailing includes all the activities involved in selling or renting consumer products and services directly to ultimate consumers for their personal or home consumption. A consumer selects a retailer based on several factors like price, location of the store, the merchandise selection available, the help salespeople give in the store, any special services provided and fairness in dealings.

LO 2

- Marketing experts have developed a number of theories on retail like: Wheel of Retailing (evolution of retail), Accordion Theory (general-specific-general transformation of retail outlets), Natural Selection (another treatise on evolution) and Retail Life Cycle (similar to a product life cycle).

LO 3

- It is learnt that India has the largest number of retail outlets of any country in the world. From the street corner *paanwalla* to the modern retail outlets, everyone exists in the same market and have got their own set of loyal customers.
- Today, with modern organized retail, the retailer is gaining an upper hand. Even with the limited growth of organized retail in India, the few modern retailers negotiate and get the most favorable terms from their consumer goods suppliers. Organized retail still forms only 4 to 7 percent of the total retail trade in India but is steadily growing.

LO 4

- The "format" is obviously the physical features of the store and the service it provides. Retailers use the format to distinguish themselves from each other. The retailer is able to provide the service to the customers by the following: merchandising, the service, the format used, and the communication process used. These aspects are used in a combination and any one of these factors alone cannot help in successful retailing.

LO 5

- It is obvious that the retailer develops his marketing strategy based on a number of factors. Some of these factors are:
  - The markets and customers he is targeting
  - The location of the store or stores
  - The store "image" to be created in the minds of the prospects
  - The store design aspects
  - The merchandise to be offered
  - The type of store personnel to be recruited and what is expected of them
  - The promotions to be run to build footfalls initially and stickiness later on
  - The supplier handling systems including credit and other terms
  - The terms offered to prospects and customers
- In framing the retail strategy, the retailer uses a suitable combination of markets, formats and product offerings. The focus is on meeting the "needs" of the consumer at his "convenience". The steps in the retail strategy are the same as in any other marketing activity starting from the mission, objectives, segmentation, positioning, building a strategy, and operational details and finally measuring the performance for continuous improvement.
- In major retail organizations, individual category managers are responsible for their business and its profitability. This means several category managers compete for the limited resources and have to make their "part of the business" profitable. Category management drives the "success" of the retailer and his dependents like his suppliers.

LO 6

- Retail performance measures include the gross margin return on inventory investment and the gross margin per full time equivalent employee.
- A successful retailer builds strong relationships both with his suppliers and his customers. The retailer likes strong relationships with his suppliers so that he can get the best bargains in favor of his customers. In order to consistently deliver a value proposition to consumers, a retailer tries to make a number of operational improvements.

LO 5

- The chapter also highlights some of the unique retail initiatives taken for rural markets and the electronic channels – the Internet.
- Electronic retailing, as the name suggests, is shopping on the Internet without the consumer having to visit a physical store. With the increased use of the Internet by the average Indian, the scope for electronic shopping is growing.

- It is only in Jan 2006 that the government of India has permitted up to 51 percent foreign direct investment (FDI) in single brand businesses in India. The brand should be one but it can cover any number of products.
- Retail is today the fastest growing industry in India and is critical to the success of a large number of consumer products.

Key Terms

Glossaries of key terms are mentioned at the end of all chapters

Assortment
Accordion theory
Browsing
Category
Convenience store
Customer loyalty programme
Customer value
Department store
Determining needs
Discount store
Electronic data interchange (EDI)
Electronic retailing
Footfalls
Foreign direct investment (FDI)
Franchise arrangement
Functional aspects
Gross margin return on inventory
High-value goods
Leisure shopper
Low-value goods
Merchandise depth
Merchandise width
Merchandising
Payment gateway
Positioning
Qualifying needs
Retailing
Segmentation
Shopping basket
Social aspects
Speciality store
Stickiness
Stock turnover ratio
Store ambience
Supermarket
Task focused shopper
Theory of natural selection
Trading area
Trading or retail format
Variety
Vendor managed inventory (VMI)
Wheel of retailing

Conceptual Questions

1. What are the functions of a retailer? How do these functions fit into the marketing mix for a retailer? LO1 M
2. What are the major retail formats in India? What are the characteristics of each of them? LO4 D
3. There is an argument that modern retail formats can never match the customer service flexibility of the corner grocery store. Discuss. LO4 D

Note: Difficulty Level → E — Easy; M — Medium; D — Difficult

4. What are some of the promotions which a retailer can organize to:
   a. Increase footfalls to his store?
   b. Ensure stickiness of his customers?
   c. Increase the size of the average shopping basket? LO6 M
5. Under what circumstances can a retailer extend credit to his customers? In such a case, what should be his collection model? LO5 M
6. Can large retail chains become distributors for FMCG companies? How? LO5 D
7. What is 'merchandising'? How does the store manager prepare his merchandising plan? LO5 M
8. How can a store enlarge its trading area? LO5 M
9. Please list down all the points to be considered for developing a retail strategy. LO5 D
10. Can franchising be used as a route by a retail chain before establishing its own stores? In such a case, what happens to the franchisees? LO7 M
11. Briefly explain some of the theories which have been developed on retail. LO2 M
12. How does retail have a life cycle of its own? LO2 D
13. To develop a value proposition for his customers and ensure long-term relationships, what are some of the steps which a retailer can take? LO6 M
14. Highlight some of the factors which a consumer thinks is creating convenience for him in retail. LO3 M
15. What are the factors to be considered for effective management of categories? LO3 M
16. What are the areas in which a retailer builds competitive advantage? LO5 M
17. List down some of the important retail performance measures. LO6 E
18. What are some of the initiatives which have been taken in retail for rural markets? LO6 M

Objective Type Questions

Select the most appropriate response out of the various options available in each of the following questions:

1. In retail, order sizes tend to be small, but ___________.
   (a) regular (b) consistent (c) occasional (d) many LO1 E
2. A store selling standard merchandise at low prices and for low margins is known as a ___________ store.
   (a) convenience (b) mom and pop (c) discount (d) grocery LO1 E
3. A franchisee sells a producer's products ___________.
   (a) regularly (b) exclusively (c) occasionally (d) wholesale LO7 E
4. Modern retailing systems are characterized by low margins, high inventory turnover, and ___________ service levels.
   (a) minimal (b) maximum (c) excellent (d) poor LO3 E

5. FDI is permitted up to __________ percent in single brand businesses in India.
(a) 45 (b) 49 (c) 53 (d) 51 LO6 E
6. Merchandise planning relates to merchandise variety and __________.
(a) choice (b) depth (c) assortment (d) width LO5 E
7. The merchandising function also __________ the cost of holding inventory.
(a) minimizes (b) optimizes (c) controls (d) manages LO5 M
8. Providing convenience to the shopper is the __________ aspect of store design.
(a) functional (b) pre-requisite (c) optional (d) financial LO5 M
9. In electronic retailing, a consumer cannot touch or __________ the product.
(a) evaluate (b) reject (c) see (d) feel LO7 E
10. Electronic retailing facilitates __________ shopping.
(a) home (b) comparison (c) any-time (d) regular LO7 E
11. Supplier relationships in retail are meant to get the best __________ for customers.
(a) bargains (b) prices (c) service (d) treatment LO5 E
12. Customer relationships are meant to add a competitive advantage and should result in ______.
(a) stickiness (b) footfalls (c) profits (d) revenues LO5 D
13. Customer value for a retailer is measured as a sum of the product, service, and ________ value.
(a) image (b) delivered (c) loyalty (d) profit LO6 M
14. The appropriate strategy for existing markets in the current retailer format would be market __________.
(a) penetration (b) entry (c) saturation (d) consolidation LO5 M
15. The retailer is used as the preferred vendor for __________ category items.
(a) routine (b) special (c) food (d) durables LO4 M
16. Category management reflects the __________ area of the retailer.
(a) trading (b) influence (c) coverage (d) allotted LO4 M
17. __________ creates the most important competitive advantage for a retailer.
(a) location (b) price (c) discount (d) promotion LO6 E

Application Questions

1. All-in-One is a large (2500 sq. ft.), well established individual retailer in a prominent Delhi locality. He has a regular clientele of hundreds of local citizens. Recently two major national retail chains have opened supermarkets in the same locality. Sushil Arora, owner of All-in-One is worried. Should he enhance the value added services from his store (reducing his profitability) ***or*** should he sell out to a third retail chain which also plans to enter the same area? What should he do and why? LO5 D

2. CF Retail (customer friendly) is a prominent 12-year-old retail chain with 18 outlets in a major Indian metro. They have a combined retail space of over 80,000 sq. ft and the outlets are very popular. CFRetail has come to know that a major retail chain from the USA is planning to get into this metro but is holding on because of FDI regulations. CFRetail wants to approach this retail chain to establish a Joint Venture (JV). This JV would avoid competition and with

the international store brand name, make CFRetail even stronger. As a marketing Manager of CFRetail, you are required to develop a convincing presentation to some of the US chain board members who are visiting India Develop this presentation. **LO4 M**

3. Aroma Teas is a well-known branded tea company in central India. Both their leaf and dust tea brands are quite popular. Recently, a marketing consultant has advised them to set up a large number of vending machines to dispense their brand's liquid tea. The marketing consultant believes that this will increase trials, usage and market share of Aroma. Do you agree? What research should the company do before getting into this? Develop a marketing plan for implementation of this idea. **LO3 M**

4. Tasty Snack Foods: issues for setting up a retail stall in an exhibition—Tasty was a newly set up snack foods company in a major metro. The owner Mr. Sanjay had a business family background and was well educated. After doing enough research, he had decided to venture into the snack food business.

   Three months after Tasty was started there was a major consumer products exhibition in the metro where Tasty had started operations. The exhibition was a popular annual event running for three days. On the advice of a close friend, Sanjay decided to hire a stall in the exhibition to get good exposure for the new snack food brand. While planning as to how to make the stall successful, Sanjay was trying to answer the following questions:
   - The stall would be manned by people without much selling experience. How many people were required to run the stall?
   - Even he had inadequate knowledge of the selling process in a stall like the one being set up.
   - How to make the stall presentable and ensure footfalls?
   - What was the inventory required to start the stall?
   - How to decide the price of the snack products in the stall? Should it be different from the retail market?

   As Tasty was a new and small company, they could not hire an agency with experience to set up and run the stall for them.

   Can we help Sanjay to resolve his dilemma? **LO5 D**

5. Vibgyor Paints: increasing market share in retail—Vibgyor Paints was a licensee producer and distributor of major paint companies from the UK. They were having serious problems in their Protective Coating products in the country X where their market share was around 5 percent. Protective Coating portfolio was important for Vibgyor Paints as it contributed to 25 percent of the sales in the country under review.

   Mr. David Johnson, who was the National Sales Manager of Vibgyor Paints in country X had done a reasonable amount of analysis in trying to find the causes for this poor performance in spite of being present in the country for over 3 years now and having a license from some of the world's well-known brands. David came to the conclusion that the problem was at the retail end of the market. Some of these issues were:
   - Large fluctuations in demand – forecasting could not be accurate
   - Vibgyor Paints was a relatively new entrant and had to be content with small volumes
   - There was a large color variance in demand
   - At times, Vibgyor Paints could not quickly meet the demands also

   Vibgyor Paints Protective Coating brand was relatively less known in the market. There were two major brands which dominated the retail market – Rainbow in premium and National in the popular segment. Vibgyor Paints has been making all distribution efforts to make its brands available and visible in the retail segment.

David was pondering the question of how to get retailers to take more interest in Vibgyor Paints Protective Coating products and help him increase his market shares. What should he do?

LO5 D

ASSIGNMENTS FOR STUDENTS

1. Visit a *kirana* store. Look around the store. Make a note of all the product categories held. Study the number of brands, number of SKUs, size of the store, estimated value of the inventory held, number of vendors dealt with, replenishment cycle, book keeping, records, licences, etc. Just try and understand the complexity of setting up and running a *kirana* store.
2. Go to a KFC of MacDonald franchise store. Meet the owner. Ask him details about: (i) what the franchisor expects from him? (ii) what does he get in return from the franchisor? How much business volume does he generate daily? Are there any worries, concerns, pain points in operating the franchise for a leading brand?
3. Remember the last time you ordered and received any product online. Try and collect all the information to track the product from its point of origin to your doorstep. Does the same process get reversed if you were to return an unsatisfactory product? How does the payment flow from you to the online retailer and then to his vendor?
4. Visit a modern retail store. List down all the efforts made by the store on 'merchandising'. Understand the nature of the tasks involved, the frequency of action, and the persons responsible to the tasks. Draw up the broad objectives of these merchandising efforts and how are the results measured.

Reference Notes

1. William F Schoell, *Marketing: Contemporary Practices and Concepts*, (Allyn & Bacon), Chapter 13, pp. 362–393.
2. WD Perrault Jr & EJ McCarthy, *Basic Marketing: A Global Managerial Approach*, (Irwin McGraw Hill), Chapter 13, pp. 348–365.
3. DJ Bowersox, MB Cooper, *Strategic Management: Channel Management*,(McGraw Hill), Chapter 2, p. 46.
4. Maureen Guirdhom, "Chapter 1", *Marketing: The Management of Distribution Channels*, (Pergamon Press), pp. 3–24.
5. C Glenn Walters, "Chapter 5",*Marketing Channels*, (Goodyear Publishing), pp. 114–145.
6. *Malls in India*, Business India, November 20, 2005, p. 10.

7. *Business World Marketing,* (WhiteBook), 2005.
8. ORG Marg and ETIG: ET Knowledge Series: Changing Gears – Retailing in India – Survey, May 2003.
9. *Eye on FDI,* Business India, November 20, 2005, pp. 42.
10. *Online Shopping: The Growing Market Place,* Business India, July 31, 2005, p. 29.
11. Neelam Mathews, *India's Retail Rush,* Chain Store Age, August 01, 1999, p. 52.
12. Karl Haller, "The End of E-Retailing", *E.-Retail Intelligence Update,* (Price Waterhouse Coopers), February 2000.
13. SW Norton, *An Empirical Look at Franchising as an Organisation Form,* Journal of Business, 1988, pp. 197–218.
14. Rajiv D Pant, *Motivation of Franchising: Rhetoric vs Reality,* International Small Business Journal, Winter 1995, pp 10–32.
15. D Cook & D Walters, *Retail Marketing Theory and Practice,* (USA: Prentice Hall), 1991.
16. *Details on Internet Usage,* Business India, January 01, January 29, and February 12, 2006.
17. KSA Technopak India website and Proceeds of Retail Summits.
18. *Western Union Expands,* Business India, January 15, 2006.
19. *The Loot: Multi-branded Discount Store,* Business India, November 06, 2005.
20. *Retail Boom,* Business India, April 09, 2006.
21. *Nilkamal Plastics,* Business India, January 29, 2006.
22. *IT in Retail,* Business India, March 26, 2006.
23. Website of KPMG India.
24. Retail Management – Functional Principles & Practices, Gibson, G. Vedaman (Jaico).
25. Learning in Retail Management from the Symbiosis Center for Distance Learning.

CASE 11.1

Chaitanya Retail

The retail market size in India is consistently growing and even the organized sector (including e-commerce) is benefiting. Most retailers (including the small grocery shops) understand the basic concepts of retailing: customer orientation, coordinated efforts between vendors, retailers and customers, value-driven approaches of retailers and a clear goal-oriented effort every day.

Chaitanya is an ayurvedic retail store in a major metro. It serves a major ayurvedic producer in India and deals with over 3000 SKUs of that company.

Some salient features of Chaitanya Retail are:

- Located for seven years in a good location
- The store is near a residential area and a shopping mall
- It has over 200 sq. ft. of space and employs two people
- It carries about ₹3 lakhs of inventory on an average

- It replaces inventory on an average about ₹1 lakh every week. It does not extend any credit to its customers though it gets about a week's credit from its principal.
- Average sales per day is about ₹35,000 with about 50 customers and an average bill amount of ₹700. About 35 percent of the daily sales is by credit cards and the balance is by cash.
- The owner, Suresh has invested about ₹30 lakh in the business. His working capital requirements are about ₹11 lakh per month and operating expenses about ₹50,000 per month.
- The store provides information about ayurvedic doctors for reference by its customers. It periodically takes ads in the local newspapers
- There is a daily scheduled visit by doctors for consultation

Suresh has got an opportunity to start a store in an adjacent locality where a ready premises of 300 sq. ft is available for an monthly rental of ₹30,000. The scope for business in the new locality is at least 50 percent more than the current store. Investment required would be proportionately higher and so would the monthly operating expenses. Suresh could manage the new store and can rely on his assistant Shekhar to operate the existing store with help from Suresh.

Suresh has made a preliminary survey of the new locality and is quite satisfied that it has the expected potential for business. The location of the proposed new store is also quite ideal.

Discussion Question

1. You need to advise Suresh if it is worthwhile to start the new store. You can make any suitable assumptions.

This case has been prepared by Prof. Vasant Cavale for only classroom discussion.

CASE 11.2

Santosh Kirana

Santosh Kirana is a local retail store in the village Narsingarh situated 40 km from a major town. It is one out of three *kirana* stores in Narsingarh. The village has a population of 632 (about 120 HH) as per the last census. Santosh is the biggest of the three outlets in the village and is more centrally located and popular.

Being just 40 km from the town, Narsingarh has the benefit of most branded company distributors and dealers visiting the village to sell their products. Narsingarh has a Public Health Center, a small post office and the branch of a District Co-operative Bank. On Sundays, the village hosts a traditional *haat* primarily for fruits and vegetables. On *haat* days, there is an additional number of customers from other nearby villages who also visit Santosh Kirana for their purchases of the week.

Features of Santosh Kirana

The store is located in the house of the owner Bansi Bhaiyya. The store area is about 150 sq. ft. It stocks and sells all daily needs household goods and kitchen items including wheat, pulses and *atta*. Santosh Kirana stocks only one or two prominent brands in each product category. Bansi estimates that he has about 300 SKUs in all. Bansi knows every villager and has developed good relations with all of them. He does consignment selling and extends credit to chosen customers.

Most company products are delivered at his doorstep. Once or twice a month, Bansi visits the town to buy food grains.

The Issue for Discussion

Recently the distributor and company salesman of Natura, a company making and selling natural products visited Narsingarh village. They also met Bansi Bhaiyya in Santosh Kirana.

The Natura company people explained the unique features of the company Natura and its products. In particular, the company salesman highlighted the efforts of the company to create high awareness levels of the company and its products to the entire population of the country. He spoke about the high decibel, sustained advertising campaign on various TV channels. The salesman and distributor also said that the company products were receiving an excellent response all around as evident from the well-publicized reports on the sales achievements of the company. They wanted Santosh to stock and sell Natura company products. They said they would put up a new name board for Santosh Kirana highlighting some of their popular products.

The company representatives of Natura also informed Bansi about some of the other features of their business including:

- Quality features of the products and value for money for the consumer
- Price advantages to consumers, price to retailers, MRP, retailer margins, etc.
- Promotions support
- Distributor visit scheduled once a week. Prompt on-the-spot delivery of products
- Company credit and return policies

Bansi was very impressed with the sales pitch of Natura. He was not sure if he should add Natura products to his portfolio. It meant additional working capital, space constraints to be managed and additional selling efforts required. He told the Natura people he needed one week time to decide.

Discussion Questions

1. If you are Bansi, what will be your decision on the proposal of Natura and the reasoning behind your decision?
2. If you are the Natura company salesman, how will you persuade Santosh Kirana to stock/ display/ sell your company products? If Santosh Kirana introduces Natura products, the other two retail outlets in Narsingarh may automatically follow suit.

This case has been prepared by Prof. Vasant Cavale for only classroom discussion.

CASE 11.3

Prabhat General Stores

Prabhat was a popular grocery shop in a prominent locality in a major city. It has been in existence for nearly 30 years in the same location. The shop has a size of nearly 1000 sq. ft. which is an asset for this locality. The locality has grown exponentially in the last one decade and many modern apartment complexes have also come up. It is to the credit of Prabhat that it has been able to add many of these new residents as their regular customers.

Prabhat gives credit to some loyal customers. It also has a delivery boy who makes home deliveries to homes using a moped.

Prabhat keeps more than 3000 SKUs and meets all the monthly needs of its customers. The shop also keeps additional brands and SKUs whenever consumers suggest such additions. Prabhat also has excellent relations with company distributors and manages reasonable credit from them. They buy food-grains from the main *mandi* market located about 4 km from their shop. Such purchases are made by the owner Ghanshyam himself once every week.

The Proposal

One of the largest e-commerce companies, Market-one ,was trying to improve its delivery process for its grocery/home needs products so that it could be the chosen supplier of such products to housewives at their homes. In order to develop the last mile connectivity, Market-one decided to tie up with prominent local *kirana* shops to make deliveries of orders booked online. Market-one wanted to provide consumers instant and convenient access.

Market-one would offer a commission to these *kirana* partners for their efforts. They would also pay a small charge for physical deliveries but within four hours of getting the orders.

Market-one approached Prabhat with this proposal and suggested that they become a delivery partner for Market-one on the terms briefly explained above. Prabhat found the proposal of Market-one quite attractive and signed up with them. The area assigned to Prabhat was almost the same catchment area from where Prabhat's current household customers were coming but this would help Prabhat increase the number of customers. The initial estimate of number of orders to be handled per day and the expected volume was also indicated to Prabhat by Market-one and seemed quite attractive. Market-one would pay the commission and freight subsidy once a week based on the details of deliveries made each week and confirmed by Prabhat.

The Experience

After being a service provider for Market-one for about 10 weeks, Prabhat had some issues which they could not handle and were thinking seriously about continuing the arrangement. The three prominent issues were:

- The list of orders booked on- line and the physical inventory available with Prabhat did not match. This meant incomplete orders and customer complaints.
- The weekly payments were always delayed and required constant follow-up with Market-one.
- The number of daily orders being received were not anywhere close to the promises made

Discussion Questions

1. Can you guide Prabhat on the future course of action?
2. Should Prabhat continue to handle the Market-one business or give it up? Why?
3. What suggestions can Ghanshyam give to Market-one to improve its business and also benefit Prabhat in the process?

This case has been prepared by Prof. Vasant Cavale for only classroom discussion.

Chapter 12

Channel Institutions: Wholesaling

LEARNING OBJECTIVES

After studying this chapter, you will be able to:

- **LO 1** Understand the functions of a wholesaler
- **LO 2** Identify the various classes of wholesalers
- **LO 3** Explain strategic issues in wholesale
- **LO 4** Learn about cash and carry wholesale
- **LO 5** Analyze the limitations of wholesaling
- **LO 6** Evaluate the important type of wholesaler—the distributor

Raja Oil Depot (ROD) is a well-known wholesaler in the main market of a major city in India. The current owner, Raja Dorai, belongs to the third generation of the family who had initially set up this shop. ROD started as an edible oil wholesaler many years back. Since then it has grown into a general trader in food grains, oil, grocery items and general merchandise.

Raja caters to over 200 retailers in and close to the main market. Another 100 retailers from different parts of the city are also his customers. Raja has made a name for quality goods, fair dealings and honest practices. He has developed a computerized billing and accounting system and pays all taxes correctly. Customers who are in the main market and place orders for over ₹10,000 at a time get door deliveries through a three-wheeler owned by ROD. Some of the prominent retailers also get selective credit on a consignment basis.

Raja has developed an excellent reputation among businessmen in the market. ROD has earned the respect of over 40 branded companies who orders supplies from them. Some of the functions which Raja claims that ROD performs are:

- Deals with branded products of about 40 companies—stock and sale—with negotiated credit and discount terms.
- Breaking bulk to customer friendly lot sizes—branded goods, grocery items and food grains (including grading and packing).
- Stocking of an assortment of goods for customer convenience.
- Storage and protection of inventory.
- Transport of goods to selected customers on specific order value.
- Financing of inventory and selective extension of credit.
- Collect and disseminate market information to needy vendors.

Recently, ROD has been approached by an ASM of Acme Products (AP) with an offer of becoming their distributor in the main market. Acme has promised that ROD will be the exclusive distributor for all the products of AP in this market.

The ASM of AP has outlined the following duties of a distributor of AP and the expectations of the company from the distributor:

- Achieving secondary sales targets as specified by the company.
- Investment in infrastructure—warehouse for stocking, vehicles for secondary distribution, office equipment etc.
- Working capital requirement for inventory and credit.
- Merchandising in the retail stores including running company planned promotions.
- Recruit manpower—back office and salespeople.
- Coverage of markets as per company advised beat plans and coverage of new markets and key accounts.
- Compulsory statutory compliance.
- Separate wholesale and distributor points.

Raja Dorai asked for some time from the ASM to think on the proposal. He was not sure whether he should accept this offer of AP and become their distributor. He was worried that it would affect his wholesale business adversely. He did not know how he could handle both businesses (distributor for AP and wholesaler) at the same time.

Wholesalers are required in the channel hierarchy for the simple reason that in a widespread economy like that of India, consumers can only be reached by hundreds of retailers and reaching out to so many retailers is not possible for a company. As we will see, wholesalers are of two kinds: (i) freelance wholesalers and (ii) company-contracted wholesalers like distributors or dealers. Wholesalers operate a cost effective re-distribution network as they believe in low margins but large volumes. Wholesalers tend to focus on particular product categories for their business.

Distributors, who are one form of wholesalers, normally operate exclusively for one company and take care of its re-distribution to retailers both urban and rural, and also institutional business. Distributors hold company inventory closer to the markets and extend credit to their customers.

In the previous chapter, we studied about the most critical channel institution that interacts directly with the end user or consumer—the retailer. This chapter will be devoted to the channel members who are one rung above in the hierarchy to retailers—the wholesalers.

The two major forms of wholesaling system are:

(i) Operating through well-established freelance wholesalers in the market who work with dozens of companies.
(ii) Operating with distributors, dealers, stockists and agents who have been contracted by the company to work for it.

Wholesalers operate on large volumes but with chosen groups of products. For example, a food or grocery wholesaler is different from a pharmaceutical wholesaler or an automobile spare parts distributor. The wholesale business can be done by self-appointed wholesalers, company channel members or even the manufacturer who may sell to other manufacturers. Wholesale business is mostly Business-to-Business (B2B), i.e. between businesses and institutions. In many markets, the wholesaler may also sell to consumers directly like a wholesaler in a rural market.

Definition of a Wholesaler

There are various definitions of a wholesaler. Some of them are given below:

> Wholesalers buy and resell merchandise to retailers and other merchants and to industrial, institutional and commercial users, but do not sell in significant amounts to ultimate consumers.
>
> —*Cundiff & Still*

> The wholesaler, or the wholesale trader, is a trader, who purchases goods in large quantities from manufacturers and resells to retailers in small quantities.
>
> —*S E Thomas*

> A person or firm that buys merchandise and resells it either to retailers for subsequent resale to the consumer or to a business firm for industrial and business use is called a wholesaler.
>
> —*Mason & Rath*

> Wholesaling is concerned with the activities of those persons or establishments that sell to retailers and other merchants, and/or industrial, institutional and commercial users, but that do not sell in large amounts to final consumers.
>
> —*US Bureau of Census*

Wholesale businesses sell physical inputs and products to other businesses. Wholesaling is closely associated with tangible goods. These entities create value add by providing the channel flow services.

Channel members who support the service industries do not handle any goods but only services. However, as no tangibles are involved, they cannot strictly be considered as wholesalers when they are operating in the service industries.

Wholesalers, whether freelance or working for companies, operate on the principle of optimum results for their efforts, have thin margins, are expected to minimize errors in operation and maximize service (effectiveness), and minimise operating costs (efficiency). They buy the goods for resale, maintain inventory, take risks of price changes, negotiate terms with the companies, procure orders, deliver them and even extend credit to their customers.

Features of Freelance Wholesalers in India

Following are the characteristics of freelance wholesalers in India:

- Freelance are usually located in the main markets. They operate out of their wholesalers shops only.
- They handle a large assortment of similar products. For example, there could be grocery wholesalers, cement wholesalers, electrical fittings, construction materials or pharmaceutical wholesalers.
- They do not work for any particular company but sell the fast moving products and brands.
- They operate on thin margins. For example, a cigarette distributor may just depend on the outer cartons sales for his margin.
- They try to negotiate quantity discounts from the companies selling to them. For competitive reasons, they may even sell the goods by passing on the entire discount to retailers.
- In major markets, if the company operates at a high discount on prices, the wholesalers tend to sell below company prices and upset the company sales.
- They keep a running account of the purchases made by their customers. They rarely let a customer go away without selling him the full list of the goods he comes to buy.
- It has also been noticed that wholesalers in secondary markets and rural areas get easily tempted to stock and sell infringements and counterfeits of well-known brands.
- Another characteristic of some wholesalers, which gives a bad name to the entire category, is their preference of avoiding paying local taxes.

Wholesalers Deliver Value

It is obvious that wholesalers sell mainly to resellers or to businesses who consume the goods. They buy from many producers, stock the goods in centralised locations and sell to scores of their customers who may be widely dispersed.

- Wholesalers/distributors keep goods in hand that the customers need and make them accessible. Their customers can rely on their inventory.
- Though they always operate on low margins and high turnover, at times, they get together to bargain for better terms—example of distributors in Kerala getting together.
- They normally pass on benefits of discounts or incentives to their customers.

There are some basic differences between wholesalers and retailers:

- Wholesalers are less bothered about the location, ambience or promotions. Their main focus is to be in the main market and extend favorable prices and selective credit to their customers.
- They deal with other businessmen and not consumers (exceptions being the rural market as highlighted earlier).
- They deal with a specific group of products only.
- Their trading area is much larger than the retailers' trading area.
- They deal in much larger individual transactions both with their suppliers and their customers.
- Their margins are lower but made up with much higher volumes.

LO 1 Understand the functions of a wholesaler

FUNCTIONS OF WHOLESALERS

A summary of the functions of wholesalers is given below. However, it is to be noted that the degree of these functions varies between freelance wholesalers, company distributors, and stockists or agents.

- Sales and promotion of chosen company products.
- Buying the assortment of goods to be handled.
- Breaking bulk to suit customer requirements.
- Storage and protection of the goods till they are sold out.
- Grading and packing of goods like commodities.
- Transportation of the goods to the customers.
- Financing the purchase of the goods and extension of credit to the customers.
- Bearing the risks associated with the business.
- Collecting and disseminating market information to suppliers and customers.

Exhibit 12.1

Sharing Distribution Networks

A recently noticed trend is that some companies share their distribution networks with other companies selling non-competing products. Which is a win-win situation for both. The company sharing its established network is able to get more mileage for the costs which it is incurring on the network and the company utilizing the network has an established channel without the pain of starting from scratch. Some of the well-known examples of such a synergy are: Godrej & Boyce and HMT watches, ITC e-Choupal selling TVS motorcycles, ICICI general insurance products, FMCG products like Colgate, Marico and Duncans.

Wholesaling Functions for Producer Suppliers

The wholesaling functions for producer suppliers are as follows:

- Order collection and marketing agency for the producer: The wholesaler collects orders from a large number of small retailers and distributes the goods in small lots which are uneconomical for the producer to do.
- The manufacturer is able to produce on a large scale as the wholesaler places truckload or container load orders goods.
- Wholesaler places orders in advance; which ensures a great deal of sales certainty to the producer who need not keep elaborate inventory or have stocks left behind.
- The manufacturer can, thus, focus on quality and quantity to be produced.
- The wholesaler is in touch with the market and understands its pulse extremely well and as a source of information on the latest consumer trends, he reduces the need for market research from the manufacturer.
- Wholesaler helps in maintaining price stability—buys and sells even when the prices are high or low—keeps providing a constant stream of customers.

A summary of the functions is shown in Table 12.1 (these functions apply to distributors also):

Table 12.1 **Wholesaling Functions for a Producer Supplier**

Functions	How Do They Do It
Selling	• Act as extension of the producers' sales force • Seek out supply sources and reduce the producers' need for sales personnel
Stocking	• Reduce producers' need for carrying large inventories and invest in warehousing
Financing	• Reduce warehousing costs • Reduce producers' commitment to working capital • Producers' also receive payment for goods even before they are sold to ultimate users • Better screening of credit applicants—reduces bad debts
Market information	• Closer contact with final buyers gives better information and reduces need for market research
Risk reduction	• Credit sales to their customers • Risk of owning title to the products • Risk of carrying inventory • Order in advance and help to even out production scheduling

Wholesaling Functions for Retailers and Other Customers

- A retailer does not have the financial resources or the space to keep the full assortment of products required by his customers at all times. He is aware that the wholesaler is like a reservoir from where he can draw his requirements quite frequently.
- By getting the stocks when required, the retailer manages his own inventory well, thereby reducing the risks of carrying extra stock.

- Wholesalers deliver goods promptly—there is no waiting time. His customers need not place orders in advance and wait for deliveries.
- Wholesaler delivers the best value for the goods handled by him.
- The retailer gets information about new products, promotions and the like in advance from the wholesalers. He can, therefore, plan his purchases better.
- The freelance wholesaler usually handles the goods of a large number of manufacturers. A wholesaler is, therefore, a one-stop-shop for the retailer who does not have to contact various manufacturers to get the variety of goods needed.
- Distributors also sell directly to retailers but their call frequency is defined and if the retailer does not buy from his distributor, he has to wait his turn till the next visit. The freelance wholesaler fills this gap by supplying goods as and when required.
- The wholesaler normally sells to important retail customers on credit. This is a major benefit. The retailer can manage his scarce working capital better.

A summary of the functions is shown in Table 12.2 (these functions apply to distributors also).

Table 12.2 Wholesaling Functions for a Retailer

Functions	How Do They Do It
Buying	• Forecast customer product requirements • Buy products to meet those requirements • Have sales representatives to call on customers
Stocking	• Carry inventory so that customers can operate with smaller inventories • Help customers buy right quantities—not excess or deficient • Share with customers the economies of operating bigger warehouses
Market information	• Provide information about producers and their products • Provide information about markets to producers • Detect developing trends in various industries • Keep customers informed of competitive developments
Financing	• Sell on credit • Carry inventory • Reduce customer commitments on warehousing space
Risk reduction	• Customer tie-up in inventory is reduced • Small customers also can buy on credit (but not from producers)
Relationship	• Own and transfer title to products without customers having to negotiate with the companies • Customers can spend more time on selling than on buying
Aggregation	• Aggregate quantity and assortment of products • Buying in bulk reduces freight costs • Frequent and speedy delivery reduces investment in inventory

LO 2 Identify the various classes of wholesalers

CLASSIFICATION OF WHOLESALERS

Wholesalers can be classified based on the products they do business in, the trading area covered by them and the nature of the marketing functions performed by them. In the next two sections, we cover a brief description of the type of wholesalers who operate in the markets—the first section is a broad classification and the second is more specific classification. It is to be noted that many of these classifications do not exist in the Indian context.

Wholesalers have been traditionally classified into various categories depending on the range of functions they perform. A broad classification is given below and some of these terms are explained later.

- Full service—Stocking, selling, offering credit, delivery and any other types of business assistance are all provided; company distributors are a good example.
- Limited service—The name indicates that the range of services is limited; examples include cash and carry (Metro type), truck w/s, drop shippers, rack jobbers (some of these terms are non-existent in the Indian context), mail order houses, etc.
- Merchant wholesalers—Independent businesses which include distributors, jobbers, etc.
- Brokers and agents—Obviously, these people bring the buyer and seller together and they rarely handle the goods themselves and get a commission out of all transactions.
- Miscellaneous—Include agricultural produce business, petroleum bulk handlers and auction companies.

Some of the categories covered under each of the major classifications are given in Table 12.3 with a brief explanation of each category.

Table 12.3 Types of Wholesalers with Explanations

Wholesaler	Brief Explanation
Full Service	
General merchandise	Stock a wide assortment of unrelated product lines—drugs, hardware, electrical supplies, auto equipment, nonperishable foods, detergents and cosmetics
General line	Carry one or two product lines but in depth—drugs, grocery and hardware
Speciality	One particular line of products like health foods, sea foods, etc.
Rack jobbers (Western)	Stock displays of products not normally carried by retailers. Regularly call on retailers to restock the racks and shelves and take back slow-moving and damaged stocks.
Voluntary chains (Western)	Most common in grocery retailing. The wholesaler combines the requirements of the retailer members and gets quantity discounts.
Producer cooperatives	Most common in agricultural products (APMC Yards in India). These are set up by farmers to buy and sell in large quantities.

(Contd.)

Limited Service	
Cash & carry	Usually stock a limited number of products, mostly staples and fast turnover items. Customers tend to be small retailers and goods are sold to them in cash only. Example: Metro Cash & Carry, Best Price Wholesale.
Drop shippers (Western)	Deal in bulky products. Take orders from their customers and pass these on to the manufacturers. Buy in their own name, arrange transport and even extend credit. They do not store, handle or deliver the products, thereby keeping operating costs low. Deal in full loads only.
Truck wholesalers	Operate rolling warehouses. Sell a limited line of products directly from their trucks to their customers. Wholesalers operating in different shandies and distributors covering rural markets on a beat plan are good examples.
Mail order	Send catalog to customers—small retailers and small industrial users. Sell based on catalog.
Retailer cooperatives	Most commonly found in grocery retailing. Independent retailers form such groups to get quantity purchase discounts.
Manufacturer's agents	An independent wholesaling middleman who sells on a commission basis for several manufacturers of related, but non-competing products. Example, Speciality foods, furniture, electrical equipment, plumbing supplies, etc.
Commission agents	Physical control of their principals' products, provides storage, and negotiates sales between principals and buyers. The commission house enjoys broad powers such as prices, methods and terms of sale although it must obey its principals' instructions. Agricultural marketing—food grains and livestock.
Selling agents	Handles competing product lines, operate nationally, handles entire range and marketing tasks for their principals.
Auction companies	Sales made to the highest bidder. Charge a fixed fee or commission for their services. An auction company uses the auction method of catalog and competitive bidding by prospective buyers in order to sell its principal's products. Used cars, livestock, tobacco, fruits and vegetables.
Merchandise brokers	Bring buyers and sellers together but do not physically handle the products.

A manufacturer's agent:

- Extends contractual relationship with his principals.
- Handles sales for each of his principals within an exclusive territory.
- Represents non-competing but related products.
- Possesses limited authority on prices and terms of sale.
- Is used when a manufacturer finds own salesmen uneconomical or when he cannot afford it.

These agents, important in the marketing of industrial goods and hardware, are technically qualified to sell such items.

A selling agent operates on an extended contractual basis, negotiates all sales of a specified line of merchandise or the entire output of his principal and usually has full authority with regard to prices, terms and other conditions of sale.

Resident buyer represents buyers only. Specializing in buying for retailers, he receives his compensation as a fee or commission basis. The resident buyer operates in lines like furniture and apparel, where there are well-defined 'market centres' to which retailers ordinarily travel to make their selection. An Indian exporter of carpets or handicrafts, for example, could have a resident buyer overseas.

WHOLESALERS—KEY TASKS

We have discussed the functions of wholesalers. We can now look at the key tasks they execute in order to discharge their responsibilities. These are discussed in detail in this section.

Assembling or Aggregating the Goods

At the beginning of the assembling or aggregating stage, the wholesaler is very clear on the requirements of his set of customers—retailers and any business institutions. He knows the type, quality and quantity of the goods his customers need and hence, is able to place orders to his suppliers who are normally producers or even other wholesalers.

In the case of a distributor working for a company or number of companies, his work is better cut out. His customers are defined by the market coverage plan advised to him by the company. He has past history of the buying pattern of these regular customers and is able to place a near accurate order on the company for what he needs at pre-determined intervals (also defined by the company). At times, the orders are collected from the distributor by the company salesperson or by the C&FA over phone. In all the cases, the wholesaler buys the goods from his principals.

Warehousing of the Goods

After the wholesaler or distributor has bought the goods from the company, protection of the goods becomes his responsibility. He has to make sure that he has adequate and safe storage space for the quantities bought. The warehouse premises may be his own or rented. Depending on the value of the goods, the wholesaler may even insure the goods. If the goods have to be stored in temperature-controlled conditions, the wholesaler or distributor has to provide for the cold storage facilities. The goods have to be protected against weather conditions and also in a manner that they do not get spoilt or damaged as the cost of such losses will have to be incurred the wholesaler.

Order Booking and Execution

The wholesaler has to book orders from his customers on a regular schedule to sell the goods already bought. In the case of a wholesaler operating out of a shop in the market, the customers (retailers, other wholesalers) come to his shop to buy the goods. He has to use his selling skills to ensure that they buy all their requirements from his shop only. He may set his own revenue target to be achieved every day or week or month.

In the case of a company distributor, he or his sales staff has to visit each customer and book orders that can be delivered with ready stocks or later as per the schedule. The order booking is also done as per a beat plan by which the distributor works his markets.

Transportation of the Goods

The freelance wholesaler rarely delivers the goods to the doorstep of his customers. The customers normally come to his shop, place orders and collect the goods and take them back. In the case of a company distributor, however, he has to deliver the goods to the customer premises. In all cases of wholesalers, they do deliver the goods to their industrial and institutional customers.

Financing of the Business

The wholesaler has to provide finance for buying the goods he wants to sell. Sometimes, companies extend credit facilities to a wholesaler or a distributor. If the freelance wholesaler is buying from another wholesaler (like a company distributor or a bigger wholesaler), he may get the goods on credit terms. The wholesaler is, however, expected to extend credit to his customers who could be other wholesalers, retailers or institutions.

Risk Bearing

The wholesaler has already paid for the stocks he is trying to sell. As he owns the stock, he is responsible for any losses incurred on the stocks while in his possession. There is also a partial risk of bad debts on credit extended to customers.

Grading and Packing

The wholesaler breaks bulk and sells to his customers in smaller lot sizes. For this, he may have to do some re-packing. In the case of commodity type products like agricultural products he also does the cleaning and grading of the goods. For example, a rice wholesaler buying from different rice mills will grade the rice, price it differently and then sell it to his customers. In the process, the wholesaler will also clean the rice of external contaminants.

Providing Market Information

A wholesaler is a two-way communicator of valuable information. He informs his retail customers of various types of goods available, competition, promotions in force and so on. To his suppliers, he provides information gathered from the retailers about the consumer's reaction/response to the company products.

In the case of company distributors, the information is collected by the company through structured report formats. The wholesaler is an important source of competitors' information particularly on prices, promotions. A list of major wholesale markets in India is given in Table 12.4.

Table 12.4 Some Major Wholesale Markets in India

S. No.	Name of Wholesaler	Features
1	Chawri Bazar, near Jama Masjid, Delhi	Major products: paper, brass and copper Started in 1948 as the first hardware wholesale market in Delhi.
2	Abdul Gani Textile market, Erode, TN	Popular name: Gani market. 1000 shops with 300 permanent shops; daily footfall 10,000–30,000 (festive season); largest selling product Bharani Jamakallams (light carpets)
3	Golden Rock Shandy, Market Square, Trichy, TN	Started in 1926 as a weekly shandy on Sundays selling household essentials. Products—consumables, metalware, pots, clothing, furniture, meat, fish, poultry, livestock and electronic goods. Claims regular 30,000 customers—also retail.
4	Mahatma Gandhi Market, Trichy, TN	Popular as Gandhi market; began in 1867 as Fort wholesale farmers' market, expanded in 1927.
5	Gudimalkapur market, Hyderabad	For vegetables. Also includes a Jambagh flower market.
6	Khari Baoli market, near Red Fort, Delhi	It is a wholesale grocery market. It is Asia's largest spices wholesale market also selling nuts, herbs, food products, rice and tea; started in 17th century. Shops known by serial numbers like chawal wala 13, 21 Number ki dookan, masale wala 33 etc. Some prominent sections: Spices, Gadodia market, non-branded consumer goods, Sadar Bazar, wholesale engineering goods, GB Road and wholesale herbs, Katara Tambaku.
7	Rice Bazar, Thrissur, Kerala	200-year old rice wholesale market.
8	Sadar Bazar, Delhi	Largest wholesale market for household items in Delhi. Some products include toys, imitation jewelry, stationery, den of FMCG counterfeit goods (cosmetics) and authentic Indian food. Smaller markets within include: Pratap market, Swadeshi market (art jewelry), Teliwara timber market. Negatives: over congestion, power cuts, lack of sanitation, improper roads and traffic jams.
9	Mahatma JyotibaPhule Mandal (Crawford market), opp. Mumbai Police HQ	Established in 1905 by first Municipal Commissioner of Mumbai, Alfred Crawford. Wholesale fruit, vegetable and poultry market. Built in 1869 designed by British architect, William Emerson, 22,500 sq m.
10	Koyambedu wholesale market complex, Chennai	One of Asia's largest perishable goods market. Spread over 295 acres, 1,000 wholesale and 2,000 retail shops. Product categories include fruits and vegetables, flower, textiles and food grains. Estimated 1 lakh visitors daily, and 1,500 lorries and heavy vehicles each day. 400 vehicles parking. Bio-methanation plant to generate power from fruits and vegetables waste.

LO 3 Explain strategic issues in wholesale

STRATEGIC ISSUES IN WHOLESALING

For a wholesaler, there are primarily two strategic questions to be answered:

- Whom to sell to?
- How to sell to them?

The answer to the first question is in terms of the 'target' market the wholesaler has to address. The second question is answered by the 'marketing mix' the wholesaler will use to reach his target market. One important influencer of all his strategic decisions is the nature of competition the wholesaler has to overcome.

Selecting Target Markets

This will comprise the group of customers for focus to contribute to a substantial part of the wholesaler business. Some of the factors on which this decision can be based are as follows:

- Location of the wholesaler—normally in the main market in the town.
- Size and composition of the markets—size of the retailers and their characteristics (what they expect from a wholesaler).
- The trading area which the wholesaler can look at—distance of likely customers from his location.
- Purchasing habits of likely customers—for example, is it a market driven by credit?
- Nature of competition from other similar wholesalers.

Once the wholesaler has answers to these questions, he can decide on the marketing mix he should be working with to be successful.

Marketing Mix

The discussion here will be confined to the original 4Ps—Product, Price, Promotions and Place. Again, the points given below apply more to freelance wholesalers and not to company contracted distributors, dealers, etc., who are more controlled by the company they work for and need not independently make many of these decisions.

Product Decisions

A wholesaler would normally decide a range of product categories in which he will transact business and stick to it. If it can be specialised like a cigarette wholesaler, a pharma wholesaler or a food grain wholesaler, the complexity is minimized. Having decided the product category, the wholesaler has to make sure that it is profitable as he operates on thin margins. He would plan to operate on lowest levels of inventory as a major means of ensuring profitability. A limited assortment of profitable products is what the wholesaler would prefer.

Pricing Decisions

As highlighted earlier, the wholesaler works on quite thin margins (1–2 percent of sales even) and has to decide prices accordingly. Most of the time, it is the competition in the market which determines how much price he can charge. On top of it, his customers would also expect him to extend the credit. The wholesaler has to negotiate his own prices and discounts very carefully with his suppliers who are companies or their distributors. The wholesaler has to meet his costs of establishment, inventory, transporting, breaking bulk, etc., and still be profitable.

Promotions

The simplest promotion a wholesaler understands and runs is to give the best prices to his customers. The wholesaler normally passes on all the benefits he has been able to successfully negotiate and get, and retains only the barest minimum margins for himself. When manufacturing companies run product sales promotions for consumers, the wholesaler would like to bargain and get the highest quantities so that his customers can benefit. In trade promotions, however, the wholesaler would like to buy at the highest slabs available.

Place

This decision has already been taken care of when the wholesaler decided on his location in the first place. He can only service the customers in the trading area in which he operates.

MAJOR WHOLESALING DECISIONS

Some of the operational decisions arising out of the primary strategy as outlined above are given in this section.

Which Markets to Operate in?

The focus has shifted from achieving large volumes at low margins to getting profitable volumes even though margins in wholesaling continue to be low as freelance wholesalers have to be very competitive to get business. However, distributors and other agents who work for companies have more steady margins dictated by sheer availability (it is not easy to get good distributors or stockists). However, distributor margins are also defined by the industry and the competition.

Manpower

This is not a major issue for freelance wholesalers who operate out of their own shops. All the buying, which is the critical part of the operation, is done either by the owner getting the goods from bigger wholesalers or *mandis* or buying it from company salespeople or distributors who call on the wholesalers. In the case of company distributors who are charged with the responsibility of re-distribution, the staff recruitment is critical and has to be done to suit the company requirements. The frontline staff (salesmen) should be able to visit the markets, sell the goods and collect the sales proceeds. The back office or clerical staff has to manage the inventory, keep records and submit regular reports. A certain skill level in the manpower is expected. If the distributor happens to be an industrial distributor, he has to get people with the right technical skills and knowledge.

Which Product to Sell?

Product-related decisions could be related to width and depth of the merchandise, the purchasing policies and additional service offerings, if any. The width and depth of the goods is influenced by the profile of the customers he is catering to and the financial resources he has to manage for the merchandise. Purchasing, as mentioned earlier, is the responsibility of the owner who makes sure that he gets the best bargains in pricing, so that he can deliver the best value to his customers.

Service offerings are more relevant to company distributors and stockists who may provide vans for market coverage or even cover additional rural markets. It could also mean providing servicing of equipment in the case of industrial distributors.

Promotional Support

The most common form of promotion is the passing on the price benefits to the customers. Personal selling with own sales staff has now become a part of the distributor functions and is no longer considered as a promotion effort.

Credit and Collections

Nowadays, extending credit has become a competitive necessity to retain customers. However, the wholesaler/distributor/stockist is very selective about who he will extend the credit to. In the case of institutional buyers, a fixed period of credit is always part of the contract. Credit for retail is linked to the volume of business they contribute.

Image and Customer Perception

Wholesalers who sell at the best and lowest prices and were earlier not associated with good quality. However, these notions have changed. While they continue to give good prices, they also deal with quality products. Company distributors have the rub-off advantage of imbibing the image of the company they are working for. No wonder, distributors are always keen to work for companies like HUL, Nestle, Colgate, ITC, etc.

Warehouse Location and Design

The location of the freelance wholesaler has to be in the heart of the business district to provide easy access to all his local and Mofussil customers. The distributor location is decided by the company. The freelance wholesaler is not worried about the design of his warehouse. However, the company distributor has to follow norms specified by the company.

Inventory Control

There has to be a fine balance between keeping optimal level of stocks and getting the benefits of quantity purchases. Most wholesalers manage this by instinct and past experience. In the case of distributors, the company decides the level of inventory to be carried. For most FMCG, pharma and auto spares companies, the distributors are required to carry two to three weeks of sales as inventory.

So far in this chapter we have tried to understand the characteristics of all kinds of wholesalers and how they operate and deliver customer satisfaction. Later, we will look in little more detail at one category of wholesalers who are the most common in business—company appointed distributors or dealers.

LO 4 Learn about cash and carry wholesale

CASH AND CARRY WHOLESALE

Cash and Carry (C&C) Wholesale is a unique concept in wholesaling and is thought to have been conceptualized by Mr Lawrence Batley in the US. Some of the well-known definitions of C&C wholesale are given below:

1. Cash and Carry is a form of trade in which goods are sold from a wholesale warehouse operated either on a self-service basis or on the basis of samples (the customer selects goods from an electronic catalog or selects from specimen articles). Customers (retailers, companies, hotels, restaurants) buy in cash on the spot and carry away the goods.
2. There are significant differences between "classical" sales at the **wholesale** stage and the **cash and carry** wholesaler. These differences are based, in particular, on the fact that customers of the **cash and carry** wholesaler arrange the transport of the goods themselves and pay for the goods in cash and not on credit (European Union Trade Commission).

In the US, Cash and Carry Wholesale started with food product wholesalers and has now moved on to many more product categories but with the primary focus on food and grocery retail. Some of the well-known examples from the US are: Sam's Wholesale Club (from Walmart) with about 115 stores and Smart and Final with almost the same number of stores.

The C&C wholesalers are becoming a key supplement for operators who need emergency replenishment of food items, groceries, paper goods and other dining-room or kitchen products that run out between scheduled distributor visits.

Cash & Carry is no longer a shopping place for just the independent traders and retailers. C&C wholesalers are expanding beyond selling food items, office equipment and plasticware—into agricultural produce, frozen food, dairy products, meat, baked goods and bakery equipment—directly impacting the business of distributors who have been focusing on large orders and planned service schedules to maximize their efficiency.

As much as 100 percent Foreign Direct Investment (FDI) is permitted in the Cash and Carry format in India.

Establishment of C&C wholesalers can directly impact the business of independent wholesalers for the following reasons:

- The C&C wholesaler buys in big quantities and can influence the discounts he gets as well as the terms of the trade (like credit, etc.) with companies.
- Companies may sell directly to C&C wholesalers in place of routing it through their distributors and the saving in distributor margin may get passed on to the C&C wholesaler.
- Most C&C wholesalers gradually introduce their own brands of products at prices lower than national brands.

- The C&C wholesaler can guarantee the quality of the goods unlike a conventional wholesaler.

There are three disadvantages for a retailer buying from a C&C wholesaler compared to his regular wholesaler:

- The retailer does not get credit. He has to buy on cash. His regular wholesaler may give him credit.
- The retailer has to travel some distance to go to the C&C wholesaler from where he has to bring back the goods by himself. The regular wholesaler may be located in the same market as the retailer. C&C wholesalers like Metro AG are now sending salespeople to retailers to collect orders and also tying up with logistics service providers to make deliveries to the retailers.
- All transactions are documented and the retailer cannot 'avoid' paying taxes on his business.

There are two good examples of Cash and Carry formats operating in India now—Metro AG and Best Price Modern Wholesale collaboration between Bharti Retail and Walmart). The two formats are described briefly in subsequent paragraphs.

Exhibit 12.2

METRO Cash & Carry

METRO Cash & Carry started operating in 1964 with the opening of the first wholesale outlet in Germany. METRO is now present in over 30 countries and over 500 locations handling more than 50,000 products.

"As worldwide no. 1 in self-serve wholesale, we systematically address the needs of our customers. In keeping with our motto 'From professionals for professionals,' we offer an extensive range of high-quality food and non-food products at competitive prices. With efficient logistics and a business concept that can be adapted flexibly to the requirements of diverse markets and locations, we are actively setting the stage for sustainable growth."

—Thomas M. Hübner, CEO METRO Cash & Carry

Mission Statement of Metro is reproduced here:

"METRO is a Cash & Carry self-service wholesaler for businesses and professionals. METRO provides quality products and business solutions at the lowest possible prices."

METRO C&C in India

METRO Cash & Carry entered the Indian market in 2003 with two distribution centers in Bengaluru. The company currently operates 23 wholesale distribution centres across the cities of Bengaluru, Hyderabad, Mumbai, New Delhi, Kolkata, Ludhiana, Jaipur, Jalandhar, Zirakpur, Amritsar, Vijayawada, Indore, Surat and Lucknow.

METRO Cash and Carry India offers a line of food and non-food products under its exclusive *Own Brands* category, to meet the needs of its business customers. Customers find an assortment of over 1,100 high quality products under METRO's *Own Brand* labels, ranging from groceries and commodities, dairy, bakery and frozen products to detergents, toiletries, stationery, household products, apparel, footwear, linens, furnishings, tableware, luggage and appliances.

Sourced directly from Small and Medium Enterprises (SMEs) across the country, these products offer a distinct price advantage for customers without compromising on range or quality. With METRO's inputs, SMEs are able to research and analyse market requirements and manufacture goods that stand up to stringent production specifications, rigorous quality audits and product tests.

List of METRO's Own Brands

- ARO—basic daily use products
- HoReCa Select—for hotels, restaurants and caterers
- Fine Food—fine foods and VFM
- Tarrington House—home products
- Tailor & Son—clothing
- Fairline—non-food
- Authentic—basic fashion
- Lambertazzi—travel goods
- Sigma—office goods

Customers

Traders, resellers, self-employed, corporates and SMEs, hotels, restaurants, caterers and canteens are some of the customers of METRO.

METRO highlights some of the advantages of buying from them as follows:

- Quality products are sold at the best prices possible. METRO promises great value for money.
- Almost all products required by the trader are available in one place—over 18,000 items.
- Traders need not tie up money in inventory—they can buy their requirements whenever they want. Products are replenished on shelves within 15 minutes of getting sold out.
- The store has extended working hours—16 hours and 7 days a week.
- The store relies on modern storage technologies including a cold storage.
- The store provides adequate parking space for the customer vehicles.
- There is a customer service team available in the store for any help or advice.
- The fortnightly catalog lists a host of promotions. If necessary, the store can send e-mails or alerts on mobiles.
- Traders get clear invoices for all purchases.

Exhibit 12.3

Bharti Walmart Best Price Modern Wholesale

Bharti (India's largest private telecom operator) and Walmart (the world's largest retailer) had tied up together to open Bharti Walmart—Best Price Wholesale, a Cash and Carry wholesale business. The first outlet opened in Amritsar, Punjab in 2009.

Bharti Walmart worked closely with local suppliers to develop one of the best supply chains in India in terms of sustainability and efficiency. Best Price Modern Wholesale offered an assortment of around 6,000 items, including food and non-food items, which are available at competitive wholesale prices, allowing retailers and business owners to lower their cost of operations. Over 90 percent of these goods and services are sourced locally, thereby helping keep costs to a minimum. This model will help in the growth of the local economy and creating job opportunities. The vendors are a mix of farmers, manufacturers and private labels.

The first store in Amritsar was spread over 50,000 sq. ft. and cost about $7 million. About 30,000 customers and 800 suppliers locally signed up to do business with BWM.

Some of the unique features of BWM are listed below:

- The store boasts a 'Mera Kirana' and a Business Solutions Center to guide small and medium retailers on best practices in assortment planning, layout, displays, backroom management, store hygiene, customer retention techniques and accounting.
- 'My Partner' program which conducts seminars on 'taxation' for traders.
- Live demonstrations and food safety and hygiene programs for hotels, restaurants and caterers.
- BWM promises best prices with unmatched convenience, choice, quality and hygiene.
- BWM has also adopted four local schools meant for underprivileged children—a good example of corporate social responsibility.

Earlier in 2010, BWM organized a Best Price Rice Mela in Amritsar for all its customers. Leading rice brand makers like Dawat, Hello, Amira and Tilda showcased their range of products to selected 200 customers of BWM. The Mela highlighted some of best practices in retailing of rice for the benefit of the customers.

Reality Bite

Cash and Carry Wholesalers in India

As of 2016, there are an estimated 89 stores of 4 companies operating in the C&C wholesale space in India. These comprise of 21 from Walmart Best Price Wholesale, 22 from Metro, 6 from Booker UK and 40 from Reliance Markets. They contribute about 3 percent of the FMCG business in India. Carrefour France which had 5 wholesale stores exited the market as they could not deal with the regulatory framework.

It is estimated that the total wholesale industry in India handles about ₹6.4 trillion of business and contributes to about 6.3 percent of the nation's GDP. The wholesale business is estimated to be growing at 8 percent per annum with C&C growing faster at about 12 percent per annum.

LO 5 Analyze the limitations of wholesaling

LIMITATIONS OF WHOLESALERS

While wholesalers are an important link in the marketing channel, they also have some drawbacks that are mentioned briefly below:

- The goods made by the manufacturers are to reach the ultimate users in the intended manner. As an intermediary, the wholesaler may not at times (during product shortages) give the correct information to the manufacturer or the retailers/institutional customers. Many a times, the wholesaler (including a distributor) may not ensure equitable distribution of the goods. Wholesalers in textiles and paper industry (like guarantors) do not like the manufacturers and customers to ever meet—they like to keep them apart.
- Addition of the wholesalers into the channel network may add to the costs, which get reflected in the prices paid by the end customers. This is clearly reflected in the food-grains, fruits and vegetables business in India where the farm gate prices are very low while the consumer prices are very high and all the difference is due to the margins earned by the middlemen.
- Wholesalers tend to corner all the goods and hence, influence the pricing of the goods to retailers and consumers. In most speculative businesses, for example edible oil, this practice is prevalent.
- Consumers have no say on pricing and quality in a wholesaler dominated system.

TRENDS IN WHOLESALING

Electronic commerce and use of the Internet throw up following challenges for wholesalers and distributors:

- If the company has a good delivery system across various markets, it can eliminate wholesalers.
- It has encouraged the formation of various trading exchanges particularly for commodities where wholesalers had a major role.
- This has also helped grow third party logistics service providers willing to handle the products from the factory gate to the retailers.

Some patterns in wholesaling practices are as follows:

- Progressively wholesalers are becoming more concerned about their customers and are using technology providing for better service.
- Adopting selective distribution policy to maintain profitability (this does not apply to company distributors).
- Modernizing their warehouses and physical handling facilities.
- Internet exchanges are putting pressure on wholesalers whose primary role is providing information to bring buyers and sellers together.
- Wholesalers spend a lot of time in developing markets and resist moves of suppliers and customers to cut them out.
- Profit margins are low—between 1 percent and 2 percent.

Exhibit 12.4

Agricultural Produce Market Committee (APMC)

An Agricultural Produce Market Committee (APMC) is a marketing board established by a state government in India. The APMC is meant to ensure that: (i) the farmers are not exploited by intermediaries and (ii) the entire farm produce is brought to a market yard and sold at a proper price through an auction.

Each state which operates APMC markets, geographically divides the state and markets (*mandis*) are established at different places within the state. The traders in these markets need a license to operate in the market. Retailers and food processing companies cannot buy directly from the farmers.

Some of the features of the APMC (*mandi*) are: (i) helps a contract farming model; (ii) creates a special market for perishables; (iii) even farmers can set up such markets with a license to operate; (iv) clearly defined and implemented licensing norms; (v) a single market fee for the entire market; and (vi) revenue from the APMC is used to improve its infrastructure.

Some issues relating to the APMC are: (i) delayed payments to the farmers by the wholesale traders; (ii) incomplete payments; (iii) sales receipts not given by traders to the farmers affect their availing loans from banks.

There are an estimated 2,500 primary markets and about 5,000 sub-markets in India.

Source: APMC Model Act 2003, State Agricultural Marketing Boards, Arthapedia, National Common Market in Agricultural Commodities, National Agricultural Market.

FUTURE OF WHOLESALERS IN INDIA

The wholesaler is the most likely middleman who is targeted by companies and customers alike for getting eliminated. While companies have clearly defined roles for their own distributors, the freelance wholesaler (who is always the friend of the company that gives him the biggest margins) is the one who does not have friends in companies or customers. But with the widespread geography of India and 75 percent of the population being in the rural areas, the freelance wholesaler is going to be a part of the trading scene for a very long time.

Some of the actions companies are taking to eliminate the wholesaler are:

- Coverage focus on retailers and institutions through their distributors.
- Using major modern retail formats as wholesalers.
- More outlets like Metro (Cash & Carry) to be encouraged.
- Enforcing strict price control so that the wholesaler cannot sell below the company price.

The freelance wholesalers have also a number of factors in their favor to continue operations:

- Companies still have limitations in their coverage which has to be made up by the wholesalers.
- There are hundreds of small companies who cannot afford own distribution networks and depend entirely on the wholesalers.

- In food grains, fruits and vegetables, there are hardly any organized distribution networks. Only wholesalers can help move goods from the farm gate to the consumers.
- Even big companies need wholesalers to get big sales volumes.
- Wholesalers extend credit to their customers—companies will never be able to match this.
- Retailers have no choice but to visit wholesale markets/*mandis* to purchase food grains, cereals, pulses and in the process, the wholesaler is able to sell them a lot more goods.

LO 6 Evaluate the important type of wholesaler—the distributor

DISTRIBUTORS/DEALERS/STOCKISTS

A distributor is a wholesaler nominated by a company to exclusively re-distribute the company products to all retailers and institutions in a designated territory. He does not deal in competitor's products. Examples are:

- A redistribution stockist for HUL.
- A distributor for Philips lighting division.
- A distributor for L&T engineering division.

A dealer has a similar role of a distributor but has two differences: (i) he may not have a clearly defined territory and sells both in the market and from his shop, and (ii) he may deal with competitive products also. Examples are:

- A dealer for an edible oil company.
- A dealer for garment brands.
- A car dealer would be an exception as he could be exclusive but still sells only from his showroom.

A stockist may be working for one company and may have a pre-designated territory but he does not re-distribute the stocks. He sells them to customers who visit his shop. Examples are:

- A stockist for paper products.
- A stockist for automobile spares.

All three categories extend credit selectively to some of their customers.

Distributor Management

We will discuss here the aspects of distributor management for an FMCG company—right from the stage of defining the requirement of a distributor to the stage of a distributor exit. It is to be noted that the management of distributors is not much different for other industry verticals.

A distributor is a person appointed by a company who has responsibilities for:

- Buying adequate quantities of all the products and pack-sizes of the company for re-distribution.
- Ensuring full market coverage of all the customers in the territory assigned to him.
- Helping finance the operations. While the distributor normally buys by paying for the goods immediately, it is necessary for him to extend credit to his customers. He has to bear the cost of this credit.

- Maintaining the inventory of the company products at his end. As these stocks have already been paid for, he bears the inventory cost also.
- Assisting the company in all its promotional efforts whether directed towards the trade or the end consumers.

The distributor has the capacity to maximize the sales and distribution of the company products in the marketplace.

Need for a Distributor

A distributor may be required under three circumstances: (i) for entering a new town, (ii) for additional coverage in the same town, and (iii) for replacing an existing distributor.

When entering a new town with a distributor network, it is necessary to first assess the potential for the company business to decide if the town can sustain a full-fledged distributor and the number of distributors required. The town profiling is, therefore, done for the chosen town including the potential and the current competitors and their channels operating in the town.

Once the potential is understood and it is clear that the town can support one or more distributors, it is necessary to estimate the cost of servicing the market. The cost of servicing the market is to be seen in relation to the likely benefit of serving that market using distributors. The cost elements to be considered are:

- Logistics cost of serving the market.
- The number of outlets to be covered—wholesale, retail and institutions.
- Frequency of visits required for the market and the outlets.
- Sales revenue likely from each visit.
- Whether the markets are to be covered with ready stocks or orders can be booked for later delivery.
- The likely collections during each visit—this takes into account the credit to be extended.

Expectations from the Distributor

This is to be defined right at the beginning so that the prospective candidates can be advised and secondly to get the right kind of distributor. The expectations are:

- Achieving sales targets in volume, value and brand packs.
- Financial commitment for inventory and credit to be extended in the market.
- Investment in infrastructure—storage space and vehicles for distribution.
- Manpower—for selling and handling the office records and reports.
- Distribution capabilities—market and outlet coverage with productive calls as per a pre-designated beat plan.
- Developing new markets and new accounts.
- Managing key accounts and institutional business.
- Merchandising and displays in the market (most important for FMCG and pharmaceutical products).

- Secondary sales efforts and tracking. Primary sales is what the distributor buys from the company. Secondary sales is what the distributor sells in the market to customers and is more important.
- Effectively handling promotions and schemes initiated by the company. The promotions have to help achieve the targets set for them by the company.
- Managing damaged stocks.
- Organizing and participating in promotional events.
- New products and pack-sizes launch—assisting the company.
- Handling consumer quality complaints.
- Handling statutory requirements on behalf of the company.
- Payments and remittances to the company in time.

After having identified the need for a distributor in a market, the salespeople have to go about taking action to find the right distributors. Most companies would prefer that they get the best distributors possible and they get exclusive distributors (no company would want that their distributor handles any competitive product).

For a new company, getting exclusive distributors in most major markets would not be possible as all of such prospective distributors would already be working for other major FMCG companies. The company would have to compromise and get a distributor who is dealing with non-competing products or persuade a prominent freelance wholesaler to take up its distributorship.

Selection of Distributors

The distributor recruitment and selection process is quite tedious and involves the following steps:

- Based on company requirements, identifying two or three prospects for each appointment necessary.
- Background check on each short-listed candidate. This has to be done discreetly by salespeople talking to dealers and retailers in the market.
- Meeting the prospects, explaining to them what is required and finding out their interest levels. While talking to the prospects, it is also necessary to get more information about themselves directly. A checklist for collecting such information is always necessary so that no relevant point is missed out. The salespeople have to speak the truth about the company products and the potential for business. For well-known companies and brands like HUL, Colgate or Nestle, more prospects would be eager to work for the company and there may be no need to talk about the company.
- After getting all this information, the salespeople have to shortlist one or two final candidates with whom the dialogue can continue.
- The final selection could be made on qualitative and quantitative factors. The qualitative factors could be willingness/eagerness, confidence in himself and the company products, willingness to spend time in the market by the owner himself, willingness to abide by the company rules, keeping the image of the company intact and so on. The quantitative factors could be calculated approximately as shown in Table 12.5.

Table 12.5 Quantitative Factors for the Selection of Distributors

Parameters	Rating (1 to 5)	Weightage (%)	Score
Financial status		50	
Market standing or goodwill		15	
Infrastructure		10	
Location in the town		10	
Present businesses		5	
Market coverage capability		5	
Involvement in the business, influence, innovativeness, market friendliness		5	
TOTAL		100	

The candidate with the highest score will get selected. The entire selection exercise has to be done by the salespeople without any bias as this is a long-term decision for the company.

Security Deposit

Most companies take a security deposit from the distributor before appointing him. The security deposit has to be paid as a demand draft or a bank guarantee. The quantum of the security deposit is a maximum of two weeks of the expected sales value. The security deposit is to protect the company against any payment defaults by the distributor.

Payment by the Distributor

The distributor is required to keep about ten pre-signed blank cheques with the company. Every time the company or its C&FA dispatches goods to the distributor, the value of the goods is immediately entered in one of the cheques and deposited into the bank account of the company. When the number of blank cheques of any distributor comes down to about two, he is required to send a fresh set of another 10 blank cheques. If any payment of the distributor through his cheque bounces, he is required to remit the value immediately by Demand Draft (DD) and the next two orders dispatched to him also needs to be paid by demand drafts. After completing the three normal orders by payment through DDs, the salespeople may permit his purchases through cheques again. The second time a cheque of the distributor bounces, he can be terminated.

Reality Bite

Payment Systems in India

- Electronic clearing services—credit transactions
- Electronic clearing services—debit transactions
- Credit and debit cards
- Real Time Gross Settlement (RTGS)
- National Electronic Funds Transfer (NEFT)
- Immediate Payment Services (IMPS)

(Contd.)

Payment Methods for Distributors

Method	Brief description
Real Time Gross Settlement (RTGS)	RBI network facilitates bank-to-bank transfer on gross basis. Fastest money transfer—no waiting time. Final and irrevocable settlement. Remitting and receiving banks should have core banking. Minimal charges. RTGS for large value >2 lakh needs IFSC—11 digits—on cheque leaves. About 1,15,000 bank branches.
National Electronic Funds Transfer (NEFT)	Individuals / firms / corporates to any individual / firm / corporate can electronically transfer funds—one bank branch to another. Hourly batches of transactions. Wide network of banks. About 1,17,000 bank branches.
National Electronic Clearing Services (NECS) – Credit	Can be used for payments from company to its distributors. One-to-many facility for large value or bulk payments. Receiver's account is credited with the payment by the party making the payment. Periodic payments—monthly, half yearly, yearly, etc.
National Electronic Clearing Services (NECS) – Debit	Can be used for payments from distributors to company. Small value payments from individuals to companies. Payment through banks / corporates/Govt. Depts. Telephone and electricity bills, card payments, etc. Not very popular.
Immediate Payment Services (IMPS)	Initiative of National Payments Corporation of India. Bank account to bank account. Mobile banking app can be used with a MMID (mobile money identifier)—7 digit code. Sender enters MMID of receiver and amount of transfer—instant credit. Money transfer also using receiver's IFSC code.
Bharat Bill Payment System (BBPS)	Uses a network of agents with multiple payment modes. Instant confirmation of payment—still in implementation stage.

Sources: RBI.org.in, Payments and Settlement Systems Act 2007, RBI Procedural Guidelines.

Credit to be Extended by the Distributor

In most markets, due to the intense competition between companies, the distributor has to extend some credit to his customers—the retailers and the institutions. The average credit period could be 15 days for the retailers and 30 days for the institutions. Extending this credit and collection of the payments is the responsibility of the distributor and the company, while encouraging this practice or even insisting on it, does not finance this activity. As a thumb-rule, if the distributor is covering 100 percent of the outlets in the market (which he is expected to do, anyway) he would extend credit to about 50 percent of the outlets or about 60 percent of his revenue from the market. The extent of credit depends on the strength of the company products and the competition prevailing. The average number of days for sales in credit in the market is about 15 days. Salespeople keep track of this while visiting the distributor and his markets.

If the distributor is not extending the kind of credit required, it is likely that the coverage is not 100 percent and he may be avoiding some outlets. The salespeople are required to take corrective action on this while working the markets with the distributor.

Investment in Inventory

The distributor is required to always maintain a certain level of the company goods in inventory. Normally, in the FMCG industry, this level of inventory is about two weeks of saleable physical stocks (not including stocks on order). The term 'saleable' is important as any damaged stock is not to be considered for this inventory norm. The inventory has to be held in all brands/ packs and not just in fast moving lines. The salespeople should constantly monitor this inventory holding and not let it go down for any reason.

Investment in Infrastructure

The distributor has to invest in a storage space (rented or own warehouse) with a capacity for at least one month of average sales, manpower—for selling and collections and keeping the accounts and suitable vehicles to operate in the markets. The entire infrastructure is to be built up at the start of the operations and not in instalments.

Distributors tend to tell the salespeople that they would start the operations with some minimum support and build up as required over a period of time as the sales improves. This is not a good practice as the ideal build up never happens and when volumes go up, servicing the market becomes a problem.

The distributor is required to have his own salesmen for covering the market. Again, the tendency to rely on company salespeople to generate secondary sales for the distributor should be seriously discouraged. Generating secondary sales is the responsibility of the distributor salesmen and the company salesforce helps increase volumes or handle difficult customers and markets.

It is necessary to tell the distributor right in the beginning if the distributor or his salesman has to cover the markets with ready stocks or if he can book orders and then deliver them separately. Accordingly, he will have to put in vehicles to cover the markets. It is always a good practice to cover the markets with ready stocks. If the stocks are delivered on the spot, the retailer will not be able to have 'second thoughts' on what he wants to buy.

The company should insist that the distributor should have a personal computer for keeping all records and generating reports. The office person has to be trained in using the PC.

Manpower

The distributor should also have adequate number of salespeople to cover the market as per the agreed beat plan. These salesmen are in the payroll of the distributor but selected by the company salespeople along with the distributor.

Reality Bite

Modern retailers are also becoming distributors for FMCG products. They have the advantage of higher volumes and with a number of outlets in major cities, are able to create hundreds of consumer interfaces. FMCG companies want to exploit this strength by appointing them as distributors and making supplies directly. The companies can pass on some of the savings in the costs incurred on normal distributors to these retailers. Moreover, the company is directly aware of the off-takes in these outlets to help them plan their own efforts better. A separate sales team can service these outlets.

A thumb-rule for deciding on the number of salesmen takes into consideration:

(i) Frequency of coverage of the outlets—some of the major outlets may have to be covered twice a week, most of the outlets once a week and smaller and rural outlets may be once in a fortnight.

(ii) An average of 40 outlets should be called on every day by the salespeople.

(iii) Whether the coverage is with ready stocks.

It is expected that at least 90 percent of the calls for the day are productive—some sales is done in each outlet.

For running the office, keeping records, generating reports and banking, one person may be sufficient. The distributor also needs helpers along with the salesmen for physical delivery of stocks in the market and help in merchandising.

The company could use a simple rating system to evaluate the infrastructure likely to be provided by the distributor. This is shown in Table 12.6.

Table 12.6 **Rating System for the Distributor**

Assessment parameter	Weightage (%)
Warehouse capacity as required for the volume to be handled	30
Manpower—sales and office	20
Distribution and delivery vehicles	20
Computer support	20
Communication systems	10
Total	**100**

Coverage of Markets

The 'territory' of the distributor is defined by the company along with the distributor. Once the territory is defined, the number of outlets to be covered in the territory would be known. At the rate of 40 outlets per day and the frequency of visit, the total number of days required to cover the entire market once is available.

A beat plan is then drawn up. The beat plan decides the day, frequency and the market to be visited and the number of outlets to be covered each day. The distributor salespeople are required to cover every single outlet as per the beat plan and make each call 'productive'. The distributor is not permitted to sell from his shop, as this practice, if permitted, can affect market coverage.

The distributor is required to cover attached markets/villages and this will be specified while assigning the territory to the distributor. For covering interior markets (rural), the company may initially (for about 6 months till the sales stabilizes) provide cost sharing support for distribution. It is expected that the distributor himself (the owner or proprietor of the distributor firm) visits the markets regularly with his salesmen at least twice a week, not just for the collection of payments but to actually sell the company products.

Developing Rural Markets

The distributor is expected to develop all interior markets within about 20–25 kilometres of radius of his location. Some of these markets may not initially be on the beat plan of the distributor, but as his business stabilizes and his salespeople are able to work the markets better, he would start looking at these additional markets within the time allotted by him for his territory coverage. At times, the first visit to these markets is initiated by the company salespeople. For example, HUL used Operation Harvest to seed rural markets. While covering these additional markets, the distributor has to take care that none of these markets are already on the beat plan of an adjacent distributor.

Outlet Coverage

As already mentioned, each outlet has to be a productive call every time. In addition, for each outlet covered, there are three important tasks to be performed:

- Width of distribution—The number of brands/packs of the company sold to the outlets and stocked by them.
- The depth of the distribution—The stock pressure maintained. If the outlet is visited once a week, at any point of time the outlet should have at least 10 days to two weeks stock for sales.
- Merchandising—In each outlet, the distributor has to ensure getting the maximum shelf space for the company products, well displayed products, first-in first-out to be followed, good utilization of point-of-sale material, and proper care to protect the products from any damage.

New Accounts

In every market, new outlets keep getting opened regularly. The distributor salesmen have to keep track of these and automatically cover them without being prompted by the company salespeople every time. If the number of new outlets is more, or a big supermarket comes in, there may be a revision required in the beat plan itself which the company salespeople can be requested to take care of.

Institutional Accounts

Institutions are outlets that buy the company products for their own consumption or use. The distributor is expected to also cover all the institutional accounts in his area and sell them their requirements. Selling to institutions is quite time consuming as it involves meeting the right people, getting the orders, delivering the goods and finally collecting the payments. Normally, the institutions are tackled directly by the owner or the proprietor of the distributor firm as sales also depends on developing sound relationships.

Secondary Sales Effort and Tracking

A secondary sale is the sale that the distributor makes to his customers—both retailers and institutions with or without the direct involvement of the company sales personnel.

The secondary sale is the right measurement of how well the company products are accepted in the market and determine the market share of the products and is critical to be measured regularly. Salespeople cannot feel happy on the volume they have achieved by selling to the distributor—the primary sales. The distributor will buy more only if the secondary sales happen regularly.

The simple formula for calculating the secondary sales of a distributor for any month is: opening stocks at the beginning of the month PLUS purchases during the month MINUS the closing stocks at the end of the month. Most FMCG companies track secondary sales carefully.

Competition Tracking

The distributor is in the best position to inform the company about all the current and proposed activities of the competitors in the marketplace. His main information comes from his customers—the large number of retail outlets he services. Apart from informing the company through monthly reports, the distributor who is constantly in touch with the salesmen and supervisors of the company conveys a lot of information, by phone, to the company. Of course, all the information is to be taken with a pinch of salt as the distributor is likely to exaggerate the information relating to competitor's prices, discounts and so on. Salespeople verify this information from what other distributors tell them as well as their own understanding from their market visits. It is naturally expected that the competitors are also equally well informed as the primary source is always the retailer.

Handling Product Promotions

The company keeps operating a variety of promotions on its products to sustain and grow market shares. Some of these promotions could be:

- Trade promotions like ₹'*x*' off per case, '*y*' free on a case of '*z*', or quantity purchase schemes where, if the retailer buys a certain number of cases in a specified time period, he may get a table fan free and so on. Purpose of trade schemes is to keep up stock pressure at the retailer.
- Consumer promotions are meant to induce trials and could be free offers or Rupees off on some products/packs.
- Merchandising schemes or display schemes or contests on particular brands to create a stir in the market and attract more consumers to the brand on display. These could be used for a brand launch, brand facing severe competition or for a brand showing signs of being tired.

All the product promotions have to be implemented by the distributor and his salesmen with support from the company sales and marketing people. The distributor is clearly advised by the salespeople on the rationale and objectives of the promotion and the critical success factors. It is the sole responsibility of the distributor to implement the promotion to get the maximum mileage. If the promotion involves money transactions like a price off per case, the distributor has to have the proof of expenditure which can be claimed from the company later.

The distributor is required to give a formal report in the format given by the company as to how well he implemented the scheme and the results which were obtained. If the distributor wants to operate on a scheme of his own (like a cash discount on case lots of a product/pack), he has to get the permission of the company before implementing such schemes even though he is paying for it on his own. The purpose of the permission is to ensure that the scheme in one territory should not affect an adjacent territory. At times, the salespeople may even suggest that he run such a scheme to reduce excess stocks held by the distributor.

Managing Damaged Stocks

In spite of the best handling of the company products and proper stacking, at times, some of the stocks may get damaged. Occasionally, with the permission of the company sales personnel, the distributor may have to take back damaged stocks from influential retailers in the market. There could also be instances of consumer complaint that require stocks to be taken back.

All such damaged stocks are a cost to the company and have to be carefully handled by the distributor to reduce the losses. The distributor can either destroy or dispose off at reduced prices all such stocks after getting the permission of the sales personnel of the company. He will then claim reimbursement of the loss in the normal route.

Attending to Consumer Complaints

The retailer is the first point of contact for the consumer who has any complaint against a company product. The retailer normally uses his judgement on the genuineness of the complaint, takes back the offending pack and gives a fresh pack to the consumer. But the retailer has to get a written complaint from the consumer along with the customer's address. The distributor, when he visits this retailer, has to get the written complaint and the offending pack from the retailer (as a rule complaint packets should never be left in the market longer than necessary), and gives him a fresh pack to replace what he has given to the consumer. The distributor passes on the offending pack and the written complaint to the company salespeople for further action. He claims for the value of the free packs in the normal course. The distributor educates his retailers so that there is no delay or argument in attending to genuine consumer complaints.

Organizing and Participating in Promotional Events

Some of the promotional events, in which the distributor takes initiative and participates wholeheartedly on behalf of the company, could be:

- Putting up stalls in local exhibitions, *melas*, fairs or important events to sell and promote the company products.
- Organizing promotional sales in chosen retail counters.
- Organizing special merchandising efforts on new product or pack launches.
- Organizing home-to-home selling campaigns.

The distributor organizes all these events under the guidance of the company salespeople. In many of them, the company salespeople also participate fully. The total cost of such events is paid by the company. But the distributor, as an influential local person, is responsible to make all these events highly successful. Costs of these promotional events are incurred by the distributor and reimbursed by the company.

Reimbursement of the Cost of Promotions to the Distributor

Most trade promotions run by the company and operated in the market are initially paid by the distributor. For example, if there is a ₹20 off per case on a branded tea run by the company, for all purchases in case lots by the retailers, the distributor extends the discount at ₹20 per case in the cash memos he gives to the retailers. He collects ₹20 per case less on the sales made in this particular brand/pack size. If he has sold 200 cases in this trade promotion, he would have deducted a total of ₹4,000 in the cash memos. He has to be reimbursed this amount by the company. The distributor is permitted to claim this discount while submitting his monthly accounts to the company and send duplicate copies of all cash memos (in this case totalling ₹4,000) to the company with his claim. The salespeople will verify the claim and give him a rebate of ₹4,000 in the next invoice sent to him and write out a cheque for the invoice amount less ₹4,000. It may take the company about 15 days to sanction the amount already spent by the distributor. This means for about twenty one days in all the distributor has invested in the promotions run by the company. This is a part of the distributor investment. Salespeople managing the distributor have the right to verify in the market, if the promotion is properly being extended by the distributor to his customers.

New Product/Pack Launch

The company invites the distributors by area or region for a new product/pack launch meeting to make them aware of the reasons for the launch and the objectives to be achieved. The purpose of getting the distributors involved in these launch meetings is to ensure that they implement the launch in their own territories in a textbook fashion. Apart from the effort in the market in making the new product/pack available in each outlet, first class merchandising and visibility, the distributor is also required to give oral and written reports on the effectiveness of the launch and competitors' reaction during all such launches. The field force of the company will assist the distributor in all major markets. The distributor is required to keep the efforts on the launched product/pack at a very high level till the time it reaches stable sales levels (retailers start asking for more stocks to sell).

Motivational Tools for Distributors

The various ways in which companies motivate their channel partners are covered in Chapter 13. However, it is necessary to list some of the motivational tools here which are used by the companies to get the maximum out of the distributors.

- Visits of the company field force to 'work' the markets with the distributor and his salesmen to maximise sales, support promotions and set examples.
- Secondary sales target achieving incentives—most common and popular.
- Quantity purchase discounts on primary sales meant for the distributor.
- Sales contests with attractive prizes in kind for making a success of new product launches or slow moving packs.
- Extending credit to the distributors. To be used only selectively in very difficult markets. This practice is very difficult to get out of, if introduced once.

- Distribution cost subsidy for covering interior and difficult markets—again to be used very selectively and for a specific time period only.
- Secondary sales contests for distributor salesmen.
- Inviting distributors for important company meetings, for example, launch meetings.

Categorization of Distributors

The company salesforce has to manage all the distributors equally well irrespective of the size of the distributor. But the salespeople may not be able to spend equal time with all distributors nor is it practical. A number of companies are resorting to classifying distributors into A, B and C categories to decide the priorities between the distributors. The ABC classification is done by the classic Pareto Principle. For example, A distributors would together account for 20 percent in number but may contribute 70 percent of the business. For a number of FMCG companies, distributors in the four main metro cities of India would contribute to 60 percent of their business.

The support activities of the company, which may vary between the three categories of distributors, are:

- Frequency of visits by company sales personnel.
- Help in retail coverage and generating secondary sales.
- Support on schemes and promotions.
- Conducting distributor meets—obviously the venue of such meetings would be the location of A class distributors.
- Arranging merchandising, in-store selling and home to home efforts.
- Focus on institutional business.
- Participation in events for brand promotion.
- Ensuring a reasonable Return on Investment (ROI).
- Help in developing interior/rural markets.
- Training and development of distributor manpower.
- Developing computer support.
- Security deposit to be collected.
- Credit to be extended, if any.
- Keeping retailer cards updated.

Performance Evaluation of Distributors

This is to be done by the salespeople every six months and should be totally transparent to the distributors. The parameters for assessment and the weightage of each should be known to the distributors—there should be no surprises or after-thoughts. Some of these parameters for evaluation are shown in Table 12.7.

Table 12.7 depicts only an example. The parameters and the weightages need to be decided specifically for the company. The ratings could be: excellent-5, good-4, average-3, below average-2 and poor-1. Any distributor who scores less than-3 will be on notice. Even if the distributor is scoring 3, he would be warned to pull up within a specific period in the parameter where he has scored badly.

Table 12.7 Parameters for Distributor Evaluation

S No.	Criteria	Weightage (%)	Score	Aggregate Score
1.	Infrastructure – IT support – Storage Space – Manpower – Communication	10		
2.	Coverage – Outlets – Territory – Productivity	20		
3.	Secondary sales (volume)	60		
4.	Handling promos and events	5		
5.	Stock levels (volume)	5		

Some of the other parameters that can be considered are:

- Efforts on new products and packs
- Performance on institutional business
- Adding and developing new markets and outlets
- Handling market complaints
- Feedback from retailers on service levels
- Timely submission of reports

Distributor Margins

Most companies pass on the distributor margin in the form of a mark-up. The company sells to the distributor at price '*x*'. He is permitted to sell to his customers at price '*y*' defined by the company. The difference between x and y is his margin. The gross margin is normally about 5 percent and the net margin the distributor can make is about 2 to 3 percent.

Distributor Return on Investment

Most FMCG companies expect their distributors to achieve an ROI of about 30 percent. If the ROI is not achieved, the company helps the distributor to improve secondary sales or even add some more markets to him. If the ROI exceeds 30 percent, the company gives him additional tasks to bring down the ROI to 30 percent. Some of these additional tasks could be:

- Increase in interior or rural coverage
- Increase in the frequency of calls
- Targeting more institutional business
- Recruitment of additional salesmen
- Increased focus on merchandising
- More IT support to be provided

Examples for calculating a distributor ROI are given below:

Method 1: Dealer A		
Year turnover: (₹ lakh) (All product groups of company)	24.92	
Investment (₹ lakh) (Infrastructure, Investment, credit)	2.98	
No. of investment turns/year	= (24.92/2.98) = 8.36	(A)
Yearly Income: (₹ lakh) (Commission, Incentives)	1.39	
Yearly Expenses: (₹ lakh)	0.43	
Net income from company business: (₹lakh)	0.96	
Net income as % of turnover:	(0.96 × 100/24.92) = 3.85%	(B)
Dealer ROI = (A) × (B) = 8.36 × 3.85 = 32.2%		
Method 2: (Same Dealer A)		
Investment (₹ lakh) (Infrastructure, Investment, Credit)	2.98	
Net income from company business: (₹lakh)	0.96	
ROI = Income/ Investment = 0.96 × 100 / 2.98 = 32.2%		

Reports/Records of the Distributor

The distributor has to keep some records for the sake of the company and for the statutory (law of the land) purposes. He is also required to regularly submit the reports to the company as per their advice. A sample list of such records and reports is given below:

Records:

- Secondary sales achieved by pack-size in volume and value (daily).
- Stock level by pack-size at the end of each day.
- Sales tax and other registration certificates for the business.
- Copies of all invoices for stock receipts from the company.
- Copies of all cash memos for secondary sales made.
- Originals of any other statutory certificates to be displayed on the premises.
- Bank pass book and list of cheques issued to the company.

Reports (frequency not indicated here):

- Daily secondary sales report
- Daily stock report
- Damaged stock report
- Report on all promotions and schemes
- New product/pack launch report
- Primary sales report and remittances
- Claims made and approved by the company
- Disposal of damaged stocks

Statutory Compliance

There are a number of laws to be complied with by the distributor for doing business. It is the responsibility of the distributor to comply with all these laws and indemnify the company he works with against any legal hassles. This would be clearly stated in the written agreement he has to execute with the company.

Distributor Profile Database

The company on its part has to compile and keep updated a database containing the brief profile of all its distributors. This profiling has to be a one-time exercise and the updating can be done twice a year. This database is very valuable for field managers for implementing any promotions and product launches. The profile will contain the basic essential details of every distributor.

Distributor Exit

The purpose of carefully selecting and appointing a distributor for a territory is to ensure that the distributor keeps the business relationship going for a long time. It is, however, possible that in some circumstances, the company may have to part with the distributor. At times, for personal reasons the distributor may not want to continue the business. In either case, the exit procedure should be properly worked out so that the parting does not result in any legal disputes later on. Most of the times, the distributor exit is handled orally between the field salespeople and the distributor, all dues are properly settled and a no dues letter is given to the distributor and a similar letter (on the appropriate letter head) obtained from the distributor.

The above paragraphs briefly described the manner in which a formal wholesaler—the distributor—is managed by a company.

Exhibit 12.5

Distribution Channels for Software

The different kinds of channels available for selling software are:
Vendors to:

- Distributors
- Value-added resellers
- System integrators

Distributors act between the vendors and the value-added resellers and system integrators. They handle procurement and payment between the vendors and the VARs. A distributor's customer base includes the vendor's resellers and SIs.

Functions of the distributor

- Operate warehouses across the country to store and deliver hardware products and software media—work on economies of scale to deliver products more efficiently than vendors.

- Handling the logistics of all transactions with customers—getting the unit—hardware or a box of software to the customer.
- Host network operations centers for training customer staff in the use of the hardware or the software.
- Educate resellers about new products from vendors—pre-sales training, road shows and demos for resellers on behalf of vendors.
- Services relating to the procurement process—contract negotiation, marketing for resellers/SIs and warranties.

Channel flow followed

Vendor to distributor, distributor to resellers/SIs, reseller/SI to end customer. New systems of distribution are being developed by software vendors—Managed Service Providers (MSPs) and Software-as-a-Service (SaaS). Experts feel that even with these innovations, the role of distributors may not get diminished. They will continue as their essential function will remain as that of provider of greater efficiency and scale between vendors and resellers/Sis.

Exhibit 12.6

Managing Distributor Salesmen

From a combination of different sources, some salient points on how six major FMCG companies manage their distributor salesmen have been put together. A summary is given below:

- Company salespeople are involved in the staffing of the distributor salespeople.
- The minimum qualification has to be 12th standard pass. Quite a few salesmen are diploma holders and a select few are graduates.
- Their experience may vary between 1 to 3 years.
- The salesmen are paid a combination of fixed salary and a variable component. The average for these companies was: fixed ₹9,500 per month and variable ₹2,500 pm = total ₹12,000 pm.
- The incentives could be a combination of the achievement of targets in number of bills cut, number of lines sold per day, achievement of secondary sales target, use of PDA, focus brands and coverage efficiency. In all these companies, the monthly secondary targets achievements varied from 95 percent to 98 percent.
- Some of the other numbers for the 6 companies (average per day per salesman) are:
    - Required number of sales calls per day (outlets to be covered)—40
    - Number of productive calls per day—16 (only 40 percent—seems quite low)
    - Average number of lines (SKUs) sold per day—varies between 90 to 160
    - Average sales value per month—₹8 lakh

Note: These numbers are only indicative and do not suggest any standard practice

Use of Personal Digital Assistants

In order to keep a close track of the distributor salesmen and to reduce their paperwork/reporting, all the companies provide the salesmen with hand-held devices. These are normally smartphones with Android operating systems.

Some of the data which these Personal Digital Assistants (PDAs) contain or capture from the market are indicated below:

- Companies call these field information systems by different names like Vajra, Smart Dust, On-track, Blaze, etc.
- Selection of routes, beat plans, call plans and targets.
- Performance: overview, target achievement, value and quantity by SKU and product category.
- Any specific objectives—coverage on the launch of a new product, etc.
- Any schemes/promotions for the day—the salesmen have to synchronize every morning to get the latest updates.
- Customer dashboard: date, order booked, payments collected and any stock returns.
- Mode of payment
- Credit status
- Price to retailer by SKU and total value of the bill
- Inventory held by the retailer/wholesaler
- Some of the PDAs also have:
    - A bar code scanner
    - Selected training PPTs
    - Recent commercials
    - Help with field surveys

These devices are also used to compile data about competitors.

SUMMARY

LO 1

- Wholesalers are required in the channel hierarchy for the simple reason that in a widespread economy like India, consumers can only be reached by hundreds of retailers and reaching out to these hundreds of retailers is not possible for a company. Hence, the need for the wholesaling system. Wholesaling system can take two forms:
    - Operating through well-established freelance wholesalers in the market who work with dozens of companies.
    - Operating with distributors, stockists and agents who have been contracted by a company to work for it.
- Wholesalers operate on large volumes but with chosen groups of products.
- Wholesaling is concerned with the activities of those people or establishments that sell to retailers and other merchants, and/or industrial, institutional and commercial users, but that do not sell in large amounts to final consumers.

- Wholesale businesses sell physical inputs and products to other businesses. Wholesaling is closely associated with tangible goods. These entities create value addition through providing the channel flow services.
- Functions of wholesalers include:
  - Sales and promotion of chosen company products.
  - Buying the assortment of goods to be handled.
  - Breaking bulk to suit customer requirements.
  - Storage and protection of the goods till they are sold out.
  - Grading and packing of goods like commodities.
  - Transportation of the goods to the customers.
  - Financing the buying of the goods and extension of credit to customers.
  - Bearing the risks associated with the business—price volatile products.
  - Collecting and disseminating market information to suppliers and customers.

LO 2

- Wholesalers can be classified based on the products they do business in, the trading area covered by them, and the nature of the marketing functions performed by them.

LO 3

- Wholesaling decisions include which markets to operate in, manpower to be used, what products to sell, promotional effort, credit and collections, image and customer perception to be created and the warehouse location and design.
- The future of wholesalers in India, either freelance or contracted, seems to be bright even though attempts are made to reduce intermediaries.

LO 4

- Cash and Carry (C&C) is a form of trade in which goods are sold from a wholesale warehouse operated either on a self-service basis or on the basis of samples (the customer selects goods from an electronic catalog or selects from specimen articles). Customers (retailers, companies, hotels, restaurants) buy on cash on the spot and carry away the goods.
- The C&C wholesaler creates advantages over normal wholesalers through effective negotiations with companies on the terms of business. The C&C wholesaler also develops his own products for sale to the customers.
- There are two good examples of C&C wholesalers who have started operations in India—Metro C&C from Germany and Bharti Walmart Best Price Modern Wholesale.
- Selecting target markets, the products, the marketing mix are some of the key decisions for a wholesaler to plan his strategy.

LO 5

- Wholesalers, out of self-interest at times, are prone to negative practices like withholding information from companies serving them, not ensuring equitable distribution of products in short supply or buying more during trade promotions and undercutting the company prices. In a wholesale dominated system, consumers have little say in pricing and quality. In spite of all this, companies are not able to reduce the role of wholesalers in a dispersed geography like India because they play a major role in re-distribution.

LO 6

- A distributor is a wholesaler nominated by a company to exclusively re-distribute the company products to all retailers and institutions in a designated territory. He does not deal in competitor's products. The management of distributors is well streamlined by the companies they work with.

Key Terms

Glossaries of key terms are mentioned at the end of all chapters

Brokers and agents
Cash and carry wholesale
Dealer
Distribution depth
Distribution width
Distributor
Equitable distribution
Full-service wholesaler
Key accounts
Limited-service wholesaler
Mail-order wholesalers
Manufacturer's agents
Merchandising
Productive call
Rack jobbers
Risk bearing
Secondary sales
Security deposits
Selling agents
Speciality wholesaler
Stockist
Territory
Truck wholesaler
Wholesaler

Conceptual Questions

1. Explain the different channel flows performed by wholesalers. LO1 E
2. What are the functions of a wholesaler? How does it differ between the manufacturer suppliers from whom they buy the goods to the retailers and institutions to whom they sell the goods? LO1 M
3. Does the concept of wholesaling apply to service industries? If not, why not? LO1 M
4. Explain the difference in operations between wholesalers and retailers. LO1 D
5. There is a strong argument in favor of wholesalers that they help in filling up all gaps in distribution of essential products. Do you agree? How do the wholesalers do this? LO3 M

Note: Difficulty Level ⟶ E — Easy; M — Medium; D — Difficult

6. Do you believe wholesalers corner all the goods when they are in short supply and influence the pricing? If so, how do you think companies overcome this situation? LO3 M
7. What are the expectations of a company from its distributors and how do the distributors discharge these responsibilities? How does the company ensure that the distributors deliver the expectations? LO6 M
8. What are the characteristics to be checked before appointment of a distributor? LO6 M
9. Explain the importance of secondary sales and how is it measured? LO6 M
10. Explain the system of performance evaluation of distributors. LO6 M
11. "The distributor ROI is a good measure of the success of a distributor". Discuss this proposition. LO6 D
12. Do you think the future of wholesaling in India is bright? If not, what is likely to happen? LO5 M
13. What are some of the advantages and disadvantages of cash and carry wholesalers? LO4 M
14. How does C&C wholesale differ in operations from conventional wholesalers? LO4 D
15. Explain some of the unique features of Metro C&C. LO4 E
16. What are some of the features of Bharti Walmart Best Price Wholesale on sourcing their products? LO4 M

Objective Type Questions

Select the most appropriate response out of the various options available in each of the following questions:

1. Wholesalers operate with a chosen group of products but expect _________ volumes from them.
   (a) large (b) regular (c) minimum (d) consistent LO1 E
2. Wholesaling is always associated with _________ goods.
   (a) tangible (b) consumer (c) bulky (d) industrial LO1 E
3. Secondary sales, is the sales made by the distributor to _________ covered by him.
   (a) outlets (b) institutions (c) wholesalers (d) retailers LO6 E
4. A distributor is required to keep track of competition activities and also attend promptly to customer _________.
   (a) complaints (b) questions (c) orders (d) requirements LO6 E
5. Width of distribution refers to the _________ number of brands and packs sold in any outlet.
   (a) maximum (b) minimum (c) large (d) regular LO6 E
6. _________ is a reasonable measure of how well a distributor is doing in his role.
   (a) ROI (b) Margin (c) Profits (d) Revenue LO6 M

7. A __________ wholesaler sells a limited range of fast moving goods to his customers on cash.
(a) Cash& carry (b) Full service (c) Freelance (d) Rural LO1 E

8. A __________ facilitates selling and buying operations without taking title to the goods.
(a) Broker (b) Agent (c) Distributor (d) Stockist LO2 E

9. A wholesaler places orders in __________ on his suppliers.
(a) advance (b) bulk (c) truckloads (d) batches LO1 E

10. The most common form of promotion adopted by a wholesaler is passing on __________ benefits to his customers.
(a) price (b) margin (c) promotion (d) credit LO3 E

11. In C&C, customers have to buy the goods on the spot by paying cash and __________ away the goods.
(a) carry (b) transport (c) pack (d) sell LO4 E

12. C&C wholesalers can affect the business of independent wholesalers and also __________.
(a) distributors (b) retailers (c) dealers (d) customers LO4 E

Application Questions

1. Ashok is the General Sales Manager of Bright Detergents which has just entered the market with an excellent new brand (proven in lab tests and test marketing). He is looking for distributors in Mumbai. His initial visit to the markets is very disappointing as most of the prominent traders are already distributors for the existing majors. He has to be satisfied with second rung of prospective distributors. Ashok strongly feels that using the top 100 wholesalers in Mumbai to stock and sell Bright Detergents is a better proposition than selecting distributors. Do you agree? Can you guide Ashok in the right direction? He intends to make Bright the third biggest detergent brand in Mumbai in two years' time. LO2 M

2. The sales and marketing team of Modern Motors (MM) is getting into the classic debate of whether they should go for a distribution network or continue with their current distribution through wholesalers selling electrical goods. MM is in the business of making electrical goods with electric motors dominating their business. MM operates only in the states of Tamil Nadu and Karnataka through freelance wholesalers. Their business has grown from ₹15 crore some years back to ₹32 crore now. The top management feels that they should contract distributors for their growing business. The sales and marketing team is divided in its opinion. Some of their competitors use distributors and some use freelance wholesalers. Please advise the MM sales team with a clear and logically thought out decision. LO3 D

3. Please calculate the ROI for Classic Distributors who are distributors for a FMCG company. The relevant figures are given below (all figures in ₹lakh): LO6 E
   - Yearly turnover : 42.30
   - Investment : 5.90
   - Yearly income : 4.65
   - Yearly expenses : 1.70

Do you think this ROI is reasonable/low/high?

If you are the sales manager of the FMCG company in charge of Classic, what action will you take after knowing this ROI?

4. Refresh Confectionery is a market leader in hard boiled sweets. It has 5 different products, 7 brands and about 37 SKUs. It has 47 stockists in AP. So far, the company salespeople and stockists were being incentivised based on the primary sales to the stockists. LO6 D Manoj has recently joined Refresh as a General Sales Manager. He has come to Refresh from a major FMCG company and strongly believes in developing a distribution network and measuring secondary sales. How do you think Manoj should go about implementing his intentions?

5. High Pressure Pumps Inc.: getting more out of independent channels—

   HPPI is a leading manufacturer of pumps for industrial use and counts a large number of companies in the industry verticals of manufacturing, chemicals, LO6 D oil, gas etc. as its valued customers. HPPI undertakes assembly, sales and service of these high-quality pumps.

   The industry strongly depends on well-established dealers who are basically trading companies to reach the end users. These trading companies are well established and influential in helping the end user on the brand of pump most suitable for his needs.

   The issue under consideration is as follows:

   Most customers have bought the HPPI pumps from the dealer/trading company. When a problem arises with the product, the dealer is not able to solve it and escalates it to the company. This results in two issues for HPPI: (i) loss of brand image and (ii) customer irritation as the company takes time to solve this problem.

   The company cannot avoid using such trading companies as channels. Competition also works closely with these influential trading companies as channel partners.

   What are some of the action points to manage these 'independent' channels and also solve these customer relationship problems?

ASSIGNMENTS FOR STUDENTS

1. Visit a wholesaler in your city. Specify which product category he focuses on. Spend enough time to learn all about his operations like products, packs, brands, purchase methods, classification of customers, customer numbers, credit policies (buying and selling), handling damaged stocks, margin levels, operating expenses etc. Write a complete profile of this wholesaler.

2. An Agricultural Produce Market Committee (APMC) is a wholesale market set up primarily for dealing in food grains (a *mandi*). Visit an APMC in your city, meet a wholesaler in the APMC and understand his complete operations. Write a brief note on this wholesaler.

3. Visit any company contracted distributor in your city. Understand his operations end-to-end—purchase from vendors till sales to customers. Calculate his ROI. List his unique features. Arrive at a score for his level of customer satisfaction.
4. Compare and contrast the operating systems of 3 contracted channel partners: (i) A FMCG distributor (ii) An automobile dealer (iii) A consumer durable dealer. Calculate each of their ROI in full detail.

Reference Notes

1. Schoell William F., *Marketing—Contemporary Practices and Concepts*, pp. 398–421.
2. Bowersox and Cooper, *Strategic Management—Channel Management*, McGraw Hill Education, pp. 40–45.
3. Guirdhom Maureen, *Marketing—The Management of Distribution Channels*, Pergamon Press, pp. 24–40.
4. Walters Glenn C., *Marketing Channels*, Goodyear Publishing, pp. 114–145.
5. Jha and Singh, *Marketing Management—An Indian perspective*, Himalaya Publishing House, pp. 340–349.
6. Bose, Biplab S., *Handbook of Marketing management*, pp. 691–698.
7. *Sales and Distribution Management*, ICFAI Press.

CASE 12.1

Sona Agency: Biscuit Wholesaler

Sona Agency (SA) is a leading wholesaler in a tier 2 city. It deals with food products and is well established in the market. A leading biscuit company is supported by SA very well. SA has been selling this leading company's products for the last 20 years. It sells bread (2 varieties), biscuits (10 varieties) and cakes (4 varieties).

Some of the salient features of this wholesaler are:

- Purchases company products every three days.
- Pays in advance by DD or RTGS—gets a 2 percent discount on such purchases.
- Extends 15 days credit to his customers who are mostly retailers and restaurants.

- SA has the following regular customers: bakeries— 16 retail and 2 corporates—both of which have manufacturing plants in the city in which SA operates. Besides this, there are many smaller retailers who are also customers of SA.
- Estimated daily sales—₹2 lakh of which about 10 percent only is walk-in.
- Employs five people including two salesmen.
- Working capital needs—₹8 lakh per month (seems very low). Inventory average at any point of time is ₹5 lakh.
- Operating expenses ₹30,000 per month.
- Margin 4–10 percent and ROI about 30 percent—the wholesaler is reluctant to talk about this.
- Product expiry dates: bread 3–4 days, biscuits 6 months and cakes 3 months—the company takes back such stocks.
- VAT on goods 15 percent. Wholesaler holds both TIN and CST certificates.
- Gives up to 10 percent discounts on cash purchases by customers.
- Has an inventory storage space of 2000 sq. ft.

Issues being faced by SA

At the time of the review of this wholesaler, he claimed to be facing the following problems:

- Managing credit was becoming an issue. On the one hand, there was pressure from the company salespeople to sell more of their products and on the other hand, the customers used to delay payments for the supplies made. Many customers pay only after 20 days.
- Even though SA is required to keep only about 5 days of company stock (SA buys twice a week), at times the stock levels in biscuits exceeds 10 days and this affects the working capital and the ROI of SA.
- It is difficult to retain the trained manpower both in the back office and the field salespeople. SA had established strong systems to manage its business and this knowledge helped the staff to quickly change jobs by leaving SA.

Discussion Questions

1. Can we help SA by developing the framework for better management of credit by them without the principal company losing any business?
2. Develop a system for management of SA inventory so that it does not exceed an average of 7 days from the current 10 days.
3. Please give some tips to SA to help them retain the trained manpower without too much additional cost.

Chapter 13

Designing Channel Systems

LEARNING OBJECTIVES

After studying this chapter, you will be able to:

LO 1 Understand the concept of customer needs and define channel objectives

LO 2 Learn about channel design and planning process

LO 3 Illustrate different channel alternatives and how they meet the customer needs

LO 4 Identify the method of evaluating various channel alternatives including current intermediaries (when the channel system needs modification)

LO 5 Explain how channel partners are selected, trained, and kept motivated

LO 6 Understand some rules for channel design implementation

LO 7 Summarize the principles of vertical integration and electronic channels

Health Care Products, India, (HCPI), is a new company in the healthcare and lifestyle wellness products. The parent company of HPCI in the US is a global leader in these product categories. The company focus is on mothers, children and infants.

HCPI planned to enter the Indian market with a unique product. It is a low-cost infant warmer used for vulnerable babies born premature and of low weight. Normally, such babies are put in an incubator for a limited number of days till they gain weight and get close to normal weight. Use of such incubators in hospitals and nursing homes is quite expensive for the parents of the babies.

After years of extended research, HCPI has developed this unique instant warmer branded as "Warmhug" and priced about 10 percent of the cost incurred on using an incubator. This product is a boon to mothers of premature babies and will become popular due to its simplicity in usage. The Warmhug baby warmer looks like a small sleeping bag and is easy to handle and transport.

The company has created a robust sales organization in India. The sales set-up includes:

- Sales Relationship Managers to build strong ties with doctors, hospitals, and nursing homes
- The relationship managers have the support of product usage trainers to work directly with customers
- A 24×7 helpline to handle customer queries.

HCPI has also developed an efficient back office department to register and manage customer orders.

Mr Balaji, the national sales Manager (a 15-year veteran in the pharma and healthcare business) was delighted with the efforts so far. He was confident that with the sales organization and the supporting order management system, HCPI was ready to flood the market with Warmhug.

The market reality came as a shock to Balaji. He was not able to get "dealers" for the product, Warmhug. Even though salespeople met prospective dealers and tried to convince them about the US parent company of HCPI and the wide range of international products in its repertoire, dealers were still not interested.

Balaji was also not sure how to educate customers (mothers in the select set) on how to use the product. Mothers (in a simple market research conducted by HCPI) seemed reluctant to depend on an unknown product to protect their precious new-born.

Balaji was thinking seriously of the most effective channel network to be created and developed for HCPI in India.

Designing and setting up a channel system starts by clearly defining the customer service objectives the channel system is expected to achieve. Customer service gets defined by the nature of the product being offered and the market/customer being serviced. Competitor's channel systems also influence the decision.

Picking up from various channel alternatives possibly is based on the ideal fit, the cost implications and the ease of availability of channel partners.

The role of each channel partner gets clearly defined at this stage. Once the channels are clearly defined, the process of selecting them, training them and keeping them continuously motivated are all put in place.

Companies can always decide on having own networks for distribution or outsourcing them. Electronic channels are also a strong option available now.

LO 1 Understand the concept of customer needs and define channel objectives

CUSTOMER NEEDS AND CHANNEL OBJECTIVES

We have seen in earlier chapters that there are a number of factors that determine the nature of the distribution channels that are required in different situations. Some of these factors need to be recollected here:

- Nature of the product or service being distributed
- Expectations from the system.
- Deliverables of the system
- Location and nature of the customers
- Nature of competition and its distribution systems
- Intensity of distribution required
- Nature of the markets being targeted

To summarize, the channel system gets built around the local opportunities, conditions and requirements. A marketing channel is expected to add value to the product passing through it (Table 13.1). To start the channel design process, it is necessary to understand the various factors which will impact the channel design so that these can be kept in mind while arriving at the final channel design. As the final channel design is almost a permanent one, it is necessary to ensure that all the relevant factors are taken into account.

Table 13.1 **Summary of Channel Design Factors**

Channel Design Factors
Product mix and nature of product
Marketing mix elements
Width and depth of market/outlet coverage planned
Long term commitments to channel partners
Level of customer service planned
Cost affordable on the channel system
Channel control requirements of the company

The channel system is a bridge between the manufacturer and the ultimate customer of the products or services offered by the company. While deciding on the most suitable channel alternatives the company would, therefore, consider its product mix and marketing mix (types of products or services, the price, promotional support and width and depth of coverage planned), long-term commitments required from the channel partners, level of customer services the company is willing to deliver, the factors requiring control of the channel and the affordable cost.

LO 2 Learn about channel design and planning process

CHANNEL DESIGN AND PLANNING PROCESS

Designing a suitable channel system will require defining the customer needs, clarifying the channel objectives, looking at alternative systems which can meet these objectives, cost of the channel, and finally evaluating the various alternatives to hone in on the ideal channel system. The channel system has to be a combination of the revenue generation or the commercial part and the physical delivery of the goods or services or the logistics/supply chain part. In some industries like engineering goods and textiles, the sales part may be one entity and the delivery may be another. There may even be a third entity which is responsible for servicing. The number of authorized service centres of automobile companies is the third kind of entity. Even the responsibility for the installation of the equipment may rest with a third entity. The channel design has to pay attention to all links in reaching the product from the manufacturer to the end-user.

The process of design of the channel system answers some of these questions:

- What activities are the channel members required to perform? Which of these activities is to be performed by which channel partner?
- How is the performance of these activities going to help the company achieve its customer satisfaction objectives?
- The number of channel members required in the network and of each category—for example how many C&FAs, distributors, agents or stockists do we need?
- How do we define the relationship between these various channel entities?
- Are the roles and responsibilities of the various channel partners clearly defined so that there is no ambiguity and they can perform their roles without constant reminders?
- Are all the channel members also clear on how they would get compensated for their services?
- Is the compensation plan fair to all the categories in relation to the tasks they have to perform?
- Are the channel members aware of how their performance is going to be judged, by whom and at what frequency? What is the risk of performance being not up to the target?

The channel design and planning process is very similar to any other marketing task and has to start with segmentation—putting customers in similar groups based on their needs. The second step is positioning—creating the right channel system to meet these customer needs. A channel system may not be able to service all segments of customers and has to "focus" on the ones it will address. At the development stage, one defines the roles and responsibilities of the channel members prior to actual implementation. Conflicts may arise and need to get resolved after implementation.

Variables which Affect the Channel Structure

The variables which affect the channel structure are as follows:

Market Related

This is the summary of the consumer needs which is aggregated at the market level and is of first relevance to the design of channels.

Product Related

Physical characteristics of the products like size, weight, unit value, perishability, etc., influence the channel structure. Customized products require smaller channel length and so do services. Mass-based, customised products require lengthier channels with many levels.

Company Related

Channel design is also based on the size of the company, its products, financial strength (affordability) and managerial capabilities. Larger companies obviously can exercise more power on the channel system.

Intermediary Related

The channel structure also depends on what kind of channels are likely to be available, how much would it cost to run them and what services are they capable of offering.

Environment Related

This is not in the control of the company which is trying to build a channel system. Some of these environmental factors include social, cultural, legal, economic, and technological framework of the geography where the system is being set up.

More details are explained in Chapter 17 on International Sales and Distribution Management.

Stages in Channel Planning

The various stages in channel planning have been illustrated in Figure 13.1.

The stages in the channel planning process follow similar lines as most important marketing tasks. This is a four stage process which has a clear focus on the customer segments being addressed by the company designing the system.

Fig. 13.1 **Stages in Channel Planning**

Segmentation Stage

As the name indicates, it is the clusters of customers on the basis of what each segment expects out of the channel. For example, in a pharma company there could be three segments of customers: (i) the doctors who endorse particular brands of medicines, (ii) the chemists who stock and sell a large number of company-branded medicines, and (iii) the hospitals and nursing homes which buy the medicines for use to treat their patients. Each of these segments has got a different requirement from the company channel servicing it. This stage gives an idea of the type of channel partners the sales manager should be looking for to develop the channel system.

Positioning Stage

It defines the channel element which is required to service each of the segments. Each potential customer segment has a different expectation from the distribution channel and the sales manager has to decide which channel partner is ideal to meet these expectations and how many of them are required. At this stage, the number and type of intermediaries is decided. The sales manager also defines the service objectives and flows which each of the channel elements is required to perform. At this stage, an image of the channel system gets formed in the minds of customers who will use it.

Focus Stage

In the focus stage, the sales manager decides only the segments that need to be addressed. It may be expensive or impractical to target all the segments. Apart from cost there could be constraints imposed by the environment, the managerial talent pool available and the competitive scenario. In the pharma illustration, which was discussed earlier, the company may decide that they will focus only on (i) doctors in all A category towns, (ii) chemists located in the main markets of these A category towns, and (iii) only big government and private hospitals in these towns.

Developing the Right Channel Alternative

If the channel system being established is new, at this stage the sales manager could work out the best possible alternatives. One yardstick for this could be to carefully study the systems followed by successful existing competitors. Even the channel partners of competitors may be willing to share some information on good practices followed by their principals.

If there is an existing channel, which needs to be modified, the sales manager will have to undertake the exercise of finding the gaps between the ideal and the existing channels and understand how these gaps could be minimized.

Reality Bites: Banks Want Rural* Kirana *Stores as Channel Partners

Banks are looking at rural *kirana* (grocery) stores to help them increase their "reach", as the rural (*kirana*) shopkeeper has good information about the financial status of most of his customers. RBI guidelines from 2009 allow banks to work with *kirana* stores, chemists, PCO operators, retired teachers and petrol pump owners to extend their reach to rural consumers. Banks can permit *kirana* stores to extend a loan of up to ₹25,000 per borrower for a fee they will get from the bank. This opens up a new channel for banks and the potential is large.

Defining the Customer Needs

Customer needs are defined by the desired customer service levels expected out of the channel system. As seen elsewhere, the service levels desired by the customers relate to: lot size, waiting time, variety and assortment, spatial convenience, and service support (more so for technical products).

Briefly, each of these service levels is described here:

- **Lot Size** It is the most convenient size of the product that the customer can buy at a time. For example, this could be 200 g of a toothpaste pack or 2 kg pack of wheat flour or a 10 HP motor with accessories.

- **Waiting Time** It obviously refers to the time elapsed between the desire in the customer to buy the product and the time when he can actually buy it. The waiting time for any consumer product is almost zero—the customer will not want to wait to buy a 200 g pack of his favourite brand of toothpaste. However, the same customer may be willing to wait one week to buy his brand of refrigerator in the size and color he desires. Waiting time may most of the time, therefore, depend on the value of the product being sought.

- **Choice to the Consumer** The company has to offer the customer a variety of products to choose from. For example, HUL has a bouquet of toilet soaps and shampoos for the consumer. At the retailer level he may offer the consumer an assortment of different company brands in toilet soaps and shampoos, for the same product the customer may want to look at alternative brands in the same outlet. Similarly, when the customer goes out to buy a particular product he may want to look at buying other products of a similar nature. For example, a housewife wanting to buy the groceries for the month would like to buy all the items on her list in one go and in one outlet without having to come again to buy a few items or going to another outlet for some of the items. The channel system is required to provide this assortment.

- **Place Utility** It is most of the times directly influenced by the intensity of the distribution being followed by the company. For consumer products, obviously, the distribution has to be highly intensive as the consumer would like to buy his products from an outlet closest to his residence, and it is the duty of the channel system to provide the product in this outlet. The other example of place utility, which comes to mind, is that of Maruti service stations available in the remotest corners of India.

Example of a Service Channel

From early 1990s, Maruti has worked on providing a network of service centers across the country to be close to the Maruti 800 owners. Even in the remotest corners there is a Maruti service station. The focus was on creating a sense of total dependability. This in turn gave a tremendous franchise for the brand sales. Could the Maruti car owner ask for better reassurance than this?

- **Service Support** Service back-up is all the add-ons that the channel can help provide. In case of industrial products, it could be the after sales support for maintenance and repairs. This service starts with help in installation and training of the company personnel in operating the machinery or equipment. In the case of consumer durables, it could mean things like credit, home delivery, free installation and regular service follow-up.

The channel design takes into account all these service deliverables desired by the customer. Providing more would add to the costs and may have to come out of the price the customer pays for the product. The customer is willing to pay for the additional services only to a certain extent. The channel designer has the delicate task of making all the service deliverables available at a cost affordable to the customer and to the channel designer.

A customer-oriented channel is an efficient balancing of service levels with the cost of providing that service. Some of the examples of channel systems are provided in Table 13.2.

Table 13.2 Examples of Channel Systems

Product Category	Likely Channel Network
Industrial/ Technology	Company direct marketing to customers. Channel partners for specific distribution tasks
FMCG	Large network of channel partners, wholesalers and retailers to reach thousands of dispersed end users
Fertilizers, pesticides, seeds	Rural based system of feeder markets, channel partners and wholesalers
Pharmaceutical	Segment specific channel partners and retail chemists
Construction materials	Relevant distributors, wholesalers and retailers
Travel support	General Sales Agents, tour operators and Internet
Banking and Insurance	Authorized agents, Internet

Defining Channel Objectives

Channel objectives are simply what the channel system is expected to do to support customer service. These objectives can be set in terms of the customer service deliverables mentioned earlier. Once the objectives are clearly stated, it is expected that the system will carry out all the activities required to achieve the service levels at the least cost. For the same product or service, the service levels required may vary between segments of customers for the product or service. A one-time customer has to be treated differently from a major industrial unit, which can be a long-term source of business. Either of them cannot be neglected, but have to be treated differently. For each of these segments, the firm requires to develop the most appropriate channel support. It is not necessary that the firm may choose to service all the segments. For example, for a consumer product there could be the consumer segment (retail) which needs to be serviced through a combination of distributor/wholesaler/retailer whereas there could be an institutional segment (a 5-star hotel) which may get serviced by the company directly through its sales force.

Channel objectives are dictated by the product characteristics also. Some examples are as follows:

- Industrial products require direct marketing by the company.
- Consumer products, which need to be made available in large number of outlets to suit the equally large number of end users, require the firm to exploit the channels available in the market place like distributors, wholesalers, and retailers.
- A company selling frozen desserts and ice creams has to look for a channel system that has a cold chain.
- A company selling seeds would like a channel design with a focus on rural distribution—outlets, stockists interested in fertilizers.

- Multi-level marketing companies depend on distributors who in turn recruit more distributors.

Obviously, one size that fits all kind of channel systems is not available. While the system design takes into account the strengths and weaknesses of the various channel members available, it also has to consider what the competitor is doing—after all, no firm would like to give the competitor any advantage in reaching the customer better or faster.

The status of the economy at any point of time may also determine the choice of channel partners. In a depressed economy, speed of reaching the customer is of the essence and since costs have to be kept under control, the channel system would be short. Even legal aspects may have a role in the channel design. For example, the legal requirements force petroleum companies to follow a clearly defined channel system only—they do not have much flexibility. Similarly, the MRTP Act does not permit assigning territories to distributors—the Competition Act will now apply.

MRTP Act Replaced by the Competition Act

Current Status of MRTP Act: this Act is not in force in India currently as it was repealed and replaced by the Competition Act 2002 with effect from September 1, 2009. The MRTP Commission was replaced by Competition Commission of India.

Provisions of the Competition Act, 2002

No enterprise or association of enterprises or person or association of persons shall enter into any agreement in respect of production, supply, distribution, storage, acquisition or control of goods or provision of services, which causes or is likely to cause an appreciable adverse effect on competition within India.

Any agreement entered into between enterprises or associations of enterprises or persons or associations of persons or between any person and enterprise or practice carried on, or decision taken by, any association of enterprises or association of persons, including cartels, engaged in identical or similar trade of goods or provision of services, which:

- directly or indirectly determines purchase or sale prices;
- limits or controls production, supply, markets, technical development, investment or provision of services;
- shares the market or source of production or provision of services by way of allocation of geographical area of market, or type of goods or services, or number of customers in the market or any other similar way; and
- directly or indirectly results in bid rigging or collusive bidding, shall be presumed to have an appreciable adverse effect on competition.

Provided that nothing contained in this sub-section shall apply to any agreement entered into by way of joint ventures if such agreement increases efficiency in production, supply, distribution, storage, acquisition or control of goods or provision of services.

LO 3 Illustrate different channel alternatives and how they meet the customer needs

CHANNEL ALTERNATIVES AND MEETING CUSTOMER NEEDS

A company looks at alternatives for its distribution channel after it has decided on the targeted customers and the customer service deliverables it desires from its channel partners to reach these customers. At the time of deciding on the alternatives, the company will scan for:

- **Business Intermediaries Currently Available in the Market** Consumer product and pharma companies can also target any distributors, all wholesalers and retailers already operating in the market, to support their product distribution.

- **The Number and Type of Intermediaries Required** This is based on the customer expectations, the service levels the company is willing to deliver and the intensity of distribution desired. If the metro city based major retailers want delivery of goods twice a week, the number of distributors or their salesmen required would automatically go up.

- **Any New Channel Members that Need to be Specially Developed** If an engineering company has developed a highly sophisticated testing equipment, which requires a sound technical knowledge to explain, demonstrate, and operate, the company may select and train a set of exclusive distributors and their salesmen rather than picking up existing technical product distributors.

- **Roles of Each of the Channel Members** As already emphasized earlier in this chapter, each channel partner has a specific role to play in reaching the product to the end user. A C&F agent has a different role than a distributor or a retailer. The company will naturally specify these roles to the respective channel members to avoid any confusion or conflict.

Cost of the Channel System

The cost of the distribution channel ultimately gets reflected in the price the end user or consumer of the product or service has to pay. Balancing the level of customer service required and the cost willing to be spent by the company on the distribution system is an important responsibility of sales management. Cost elements of the channel network include:

- Margins of the channel partners
- Cost of transportation of goods between the company and the end-user
- Cost of order booking and execution
- Cost of stock returns/date expired stocks taken back from the market
- Cost of any reverse logistics required—for example, getting empties back.

Current Intermediaries

As business activity has grown over the years, a number of intermediaries or ready channel partners are already in operation and can be utilized. Some of these intermediaries are:

- **Distributors or Redistribution Stockists** They could already be working for some companies but would welcome business from new firms not directly in competition with their existing company portfolios. This is the most common and ready resource available.

❍ **Carrying and Forwarding Agents** They provide services of breaking bulk, warehousing, and transport. Most leading transporters act as C&FAs. Their services also get extended to collection of sales proceeds for despatches made against distributor orders.

❍ **Logistics Service Providers** These are one step ahead of the C&FAs. They will be willing to undertake all the distribution activities once the goods or finished products are handed over to them at the factory gate.

❍ **Manufacturers' Agents, Stockists, Guarantors** These are businessmen who provide the financial support to sell goods in the marketplace. They provide the credit support to companies who do not want to give credit directly to their customers or distributors.

❍ **Financing Agencies** These could be banks or similar institutions who finance the channel partners and even the customers. To illustrate, banks may finance the car dealers and also give soft loans to car buyers. They could finance the builders, and at the same time give low interest housing loans to apartment buyers.

All the above intermediaries work on commission, discounts or mark-ups and have some kind of a contractual arrangement with the companies they are working for. Unless specifically contracted as such, they are not exclusive to a company.

❍ **Wholesalers, Semi-Wholesalers** These are traders who are based in the market place and buy and sell a variety of goods either to consumers or retailers. The company distributors may extend credit to them, and they in turn extend credit to their customers.

❍ **Retailers** The least denomination traders in the market place. They are the direct interface for business with the ultimate customers or end users of the products. They are not exclusive to any company.

❍ **Service Centers** Are meant for servicing any equipment or consumer durable. These could be authorized by the company or could even be freelance. If authorized by the companies, they can be expected to carry genuine spare parts. The concept of authorized service centres is most common in the automobile sector.

All these intermediaries normally make their margin, based on the difference between the price at which they buy from the company and the maximum retail price marked on the product. For service centers, they charge for the spare parts based on company price lists but the labor charges are negotiated with the customers.

The best channel for distribution is the distribution directly done by the company sales force. These salespeople are assigned clear territories and are expected to contact all the prospective customers in their assigned area and sell them the company products or services and arrange physical delivery.

Companies try to search and develop innovative distribution channels. The often quoted example is of Nirma Chemical Works, which when it first introduced the Nirma detergent powder, used the existing wholesale channels in the country quite effectively without setting up any exclusive distribution network of its own. At the time, Nirma was challenging well established companies like HUL which already had an excellent distribution network.

At times, a company may choose an unconventional channel as it may find it difficult or expensive to work with existing channel networks. Again the example of Eureka Forbes water filters and vacuum cleaners, which uses mostly a direct sales force, comes to mind. Motorola, for their high end mobile phone, Moto G, Motorola decided to use an online channel, Flipkart only.

Number of Intermediaries

Even after the company is clear on the distribution channels it wants to operate, it has to finalise the numbers of each category of intermediary. The numbers should be adequate for expected coverage of the target markets but at the same time should not be too much to dilute the effort and add to the costs. Companies normally err on the safe side. They start with some distributors in all critical markets and after experience add on more numbers. Too many distributors could mean that they keep stepping into each other's markets frequently. An edible oil company had the habit of increasing the number of distributors in a town whenever existing distributors did not perform well. They thought that the new distributors would recover any lost sales, but the situation in fact became even more difficult. They learnt a lesson the hard way and corrected themselves.

It is not easy to get rid of channel partners. It is also not a sign of good business to "sack" any channel partner. The company gets "marked" by the trade.

The number of intermediaries is a careful balance between the need to ensure full coverage of the markets/outlets and ensuring that there are not so many intermediaries that none of them is making money selling the product.

The main consideration to decide the number of intermediaries is the "intensity" of distribution which the company desires. As seen in Chapter 9, the distribution could be exclusive, selective or intensive. Exclusive is when the channel system has been set up for use by the company only. Selective is when the company chooses to use only a limited set of intermediaries to keep its distribution tight and well controlled. In the case of intensive distribution, the objective is to spread the availability to reach the maximum number of dispersed customers where the customer universe itself is very large.

Hybrid Channels

Companies which use multiple channels are those with a hybrid channel structure. The term "hybrid" means that some parts of the channel are managed by the company itself and some others are handled by intermediaries.

The most common example of a hybrid channel is when the company sells its products or services directly online through the Internet and also through the regular retailers. Another example would be where the company uses its own sales team to sell to key accounts but uses the channel partners to sell to all other customers (for example, an FMCG company selling direct to modern trade and using distributors to sell to the rest of the trade—wholesalers/retailers).

Similarly, most companies in the B2B domain sell directly to key accounts but use channel intermediaries to sell to smaller accounts. Some of the examples of hybrid channels are as follows:

- Mobile phone operators having own outlets and also retail channels

- Most textiles companies like Bombay Dyeing, Reliance, Raymond, etc., have own outlets as well as other retailers
- Airlines sell tickets directly at their counters or through channels on the Internet (e.g., makemytrip.com) or even travel agents
- IT hardware sold directly as well as through re-sellers

Hybrid channel structure has the following advantages:

- It increases the "reach" through own efforts as well as exploiting the local strengths and relationships of channel partners
- For key accounts, the producer wants to exert his influence on the price and terms and conditions of sale—for example, the company may not give credit to its distributor but may extend credit to a direct key customer
- It creates a healthy competition between the company direct sales channel and the intermediaries. This can also mean setting best practice benchmarks for the channel partners
- It tries and limits the dependence of the producer on the channel partners
- Market feedback will be more authentic as the company is also in touch with some of the customers

LO 4 **Identify the method of evaluating various channel alternatives including current intermediaries (when the channel system needs modification)**

EVALUATION OF MAJOR ALTERNATIVES

It is necessary to decide on the criteria before evaluating the alternatives. The common criteria for evaluation are: cost factors, ability to control, adaptability to changing circumstances and range of products and the volume the channel is capable of handling. Briefly the factors are described in this section.

Cost

A company may already have a sales force in place, which can be expanded if necessary. It is necessary to first determine if the sales force is capable of handling the entire range of products for distribution for today's volume and for the future growth. If the sales force is capable of this, and the company is willing to incur the cost to run the sales force, this is the best alternative to select. Of course, own sales force is suitable only in cases of exclusive or selective distribution. In case the distribution has to be much wider like in the case of intensive distribution, all channel systems may not run for the same cost for the desired service levels. If possible, the costs of the different channel systems at different volumes are to be estimated and compared. Obviously, the system with the lowest cost would be preferred.

Ability to Manage and Control

The distribution network, though contracted like the C&FAs and distributors is still considered an extended arm of the company to reach its customers and end users of its products effectively.

Such contracted partners have certain obligations to the company to run the network. The operating guidelines are decided by the company and the channel partners are to abide by these rules.

Some of the operating rules decided by companies and followed by the channel partners are:

- Width and depth of coverage of the markets
- Frequency of coverage
- Call rates per day and productivity of calls
- Working the markets with ready stocks or by booking orders for deliveries later
- Extent of credit to be extended in the market
- Efforts required on displays and merchandizing
- Attention to new product distribution
- Participation in exhibitions, fairs, *melas* and *shandies* to promote the products
- After-sales service support for consumer durables
- Servicing support for automobiles
- Distributors' own salesmen for selling
- Minimum stocks of products to be held at any point of time

In order to ensure proper operations, the company may train the personnel of the channel partner. In addition, the company also provides suitable product literature to educate the channel partner and his people about the company products and selling techniques.

Adaptability

The channel system must not only be suitable to handle the current sales volumes, but also make efforts to grow the volumes and support it at the same level of commitment and involvement. The channel should be capable of handling the distribution in some of these changed circumstances:

- Addition, elimination of products
- Additional service support required
- New territory coverage—for example, covering rural markets for FMCG products, agricultural inputs, tractors, pump-sets, seeds, and fertilizers
- New institutional business leads
- Price increases and adverse consumer reactions
- Rationing of stock due to limited availability

Range and Volume to be Handled

This is a basic requirement of the channel system. This is the ability to handle larger range of products and volumes. Of course this directly benefits the channel partner as he is compensated directly in relation to the volume of business he generates. In an FMCG environment, this also makes the market working for the salespeople and the distributors difficult as in each outlet, they need to talk about "*x*" number of brands and "*y*" number of stock keeping units (SKUs).

Ideal Channel Structure

The ideal channel structure has to be optimal in terms of customer service delivery and the costs associated with it. A summary of different scenarios is provided here.

A C&F agent or wholesaler is the ideal channel choice for bulk breaking, whereas, if intensive distribution is desired, one looks at a large number of retailers.

For industrial and engineering goods, the company may look at its own technically qualified sales people to support dealers whose primary function would be to finance inventory and credit.

All this of course, assumes that outsourcing the distribution effort is more cost effective for the company. Besides, using the core competence of the channel partners is also an important consideration.

LO 5 Explain how channel partners are selected, trained, and kept motivated

SELECTING CHANNEL PARTNERS

In an emerging economy like India, where most international companies have established themselves in all product categories, if a new company were to start looking for partners to set up their distribution network, it would be really difficult. For example, most of the successful C&FAs and distributors would have aligned themselves with an already existing and now successful company. The difficulty would be felt more in the urban markets.

The company would have gone through the steps of identifying the customer needs to be fulfilled, the kinds of channel systems which are available and evaluated them on the basis of some of the criteria suggested above. Now the company is ready to recruit the right kind of partners and this is when they come across the problems of finding the right partners.

The process of recruitment could include placing advertisements in the press or getting the salespeople to visit the markets and speak to the promising candidates. At times, existing channel partners also give good references of prospective candidates in other towns. Poaching from competition is not considered an ethical practice. The obligations of channel partners have been provided in Table 13.3.

Table 13.3 Obligations of Channel Partners

Obligations of Channel Partners
Market coverage
Development of new markets
Development of new key accounts
Holding inventory
Extending credit to the market
Proper implementation of promotions
Key Account management
Technical advice and support
Service support
Complaint handling
Market feedback and reporting

The table summarizes some of the main tasks required to be performed particularly by contracted channel partners. It is expected that the firm appointing the channel partners would explain these obligations to the prospective channel partners before they are appointed so that they are clear as to what is expected of them.

Given below are two examples from the consumer products industry on the parameters which are examined before appointing channel members—a C&FA and a distributor.

For companies like FMCG and pharmaceuticals, only some of the channel partners like C&FAs and distributors can be recruited. The other channel members like wholesalers, retailers and chemists already exist in the market and automatically become part of the network. There is no effort required in selecting these channel members. The effort is only in persuading them to stock and sell the company products.

If the same search for a dealer is being made by an automobile maker, he would look for these additional qualifications in the prospective dealer:

- A good sized showroom in a leading market with an excellent frontage.
- The promoter dealer has to be an engineer who understands automobiles.
- The dealer is required to have qualified engineers and mechanics.
- Test ride vehicles and facilities.
- A technically superior servicing station.
- Enough clout and influence with the transport authorities to process customer documentation fast.

Exhibit 13.1

Carrying and Forwarding Agent (C&FA)

The primary requirement of a C&FA should be that he is a Transporter with good warehousing facilities. The C&FA is normally selected to operate in territories or a state in which he is located.

The responsibilities of a C&FA include: (i) receipts of goods, (ii) storage and care, (iii) order receipts from salespeople, (iv) order processing, (v) dispatch with correct documentation, (vi) record keeping, (vii) sales and stock reports, (viii) collection of sales proceeds from distributors, and (ix) managing secondary transport for dispatches.

Parameter of Selection	Criteria for Selection
Location of the party	In or close to a main market of the company
Location of the warehouse	Close to a major market
	Outside octroi limits
	Should have proper road/transport access
	Labour availability

	Utilities support Connected by phone
Past experience	As a C&FA for a similar company As a transporter should have access to a good warehouse
History of past business	Should have handled similar but non-competing companies Ability to maintain confidentiality of transactions
Financial strength	To handle all operating expenses till re-imbursement Insurance
IT capability	Adequate own hardware Trained staff to handle simple programmes and reporting formats
Flexibility	In operating hours daily To handle peak loads
Transportation facilities	Reliability and consistency in sourcing of vehicles Additional volumes to be handled at short notice
Attitude, commitment	To be of the highest order/positive Willing to expand business Disciplined

Exhibit 13.2

Distributor

The explanation below could apply to any company which might appoint distributors to provide reach in product categories like soaps, tea, hair oil, branded *atta*, etc.,—mostly in the FMCG space.

A distributor also known as a redistribution stockist does just that. He buys the company products from the company C&FA and re-distributes (sells) it to all the wholesalers, retailers, and institutions from where the final consumer or end users buy it or where it may get consumed (in an institution). The distributor "invests" in the product and ensures that it reaches closest to the point where the end user buys the product and hence has got a major responsibility within the distribution network. He is, therefore, selected based on a larger number of parameters as can be seen here:

Parameter of Selection	Criteria for Selection
Size of the channel partner	Current business portfolio Financial strength/asset ownership including personal assets of partners
Own sales force	Number of sales people Qualifications, background, experience

Current business	Products handled, volume handled Should be of similar products but non-competitive Product quality, compatibility and complimentary
Reputation	Leadership in the market Integrity, fairness in dealings
Market coverage	Territory/intensity Regularity, reliability Relationship, productivity Beat plan adherence Value of Institutional business handled, if any
Credit extended in the market	Percentage of outlets Percentage of current business Bad debts, if any
Stock distribution	Ready stocks or order booking
Infrastructure availability	Warehouse Distribution vans Hardware/personal computers/connectivity
Sales performance	On current business Awards, prizes, certificates won on performance
Management of the business	Educational background, Qualifications of partners Direct involvement in the business
Market working	Efforts on merchandising, displays
Handling sales promotions	Past experience
Inventory management	Adherence to stock norms recommended by the company

- Capable showroom salespeople who understand the minutest feature of their products.

If a company were looking at building a distribution network to penetrate rural markets with agricultural inputs like fertilizers, seeds and insecticides they would prefer to look at wholesalers in feeder markets where most farmers would be coming for their purchases. The major requirement of such distributors would be to finance the farmers for the inputs and wait patiently till the harvest to realize their payments.

For each category of product or service one can think of, the characteristics required of all the channel members can be clearly listed down.

Channel Design

ACER India—An Excellent Example of Building a Distribution Network

- Products: desktop and laptop PCs, tablets, servers, storage devices, displays, LED, LCD and Plasma TVs, smart-phones, peripherals

(*Contd.*)

- Both consumer and corporate sales
- Shift from enterprise biz model to consumer model
- JV with Wipro: enterprises focused company. Acer: customer focused company
- ACER consumer segments: large B2B institutions, insurance, government, and infrastructure

Action:

1. Best in class distributors brought in: Ingram, Redington
2. They had their own dealers
3. Resellers for distribution in smaller geographies

Channel segmentation:

1. Distributors—retail oriented—IT specialty stores—ACER branding
2. Exclusive Acer retail in Acer malls
3. MBOs—Acer points
4. Support—merchandizing, promotions, training of sales personnel

Source: Company published information.

Factors Influencing Channel Selection

The three most important factors influencing channel selection are: (i) nature of the product or service and the relevant markets, (ii) the company characteristics and (iii) the kind of channel partners who are likely to be available.

Product and Market Factors

The product customer combination influences channel selection to a large extent. For example, selling shampoo in urban markets compared to selling fertilizers to farmers. Some of these are as follows:

- The nature of the product—for example, a consumer product or an industrial product
- The number of customers and their frequency of purchase
- Cost of the product/its price
- Level of customer service required as decided by the customers/market
- Is the product simple (soap) or technically complex (generator)?
- What is the geographical concentration of the market? Are there recognizable clusters of customers (industrial estates) or consumers (segments)?

Company Characteristics

The company can decide for itself how it wants to reach its customers. For example, when Nirma was first launched, the company chose to work with independent wholesalers.

Some of these are as follows:

- Financial resources of the company and affordability of the channel to be selected
- Degree of control the company wants to exercise on its channels
- Degree of risk the company wants the channel to share
- Management abilities—ability to manage the channel partners to effectively deliver promised levels of customer service

Channel Considerations

This depends mostly on what is available for quick implementation and achieving the customer service goals. Some of these are as follows:

- Level of service capabilities of the proposed partners
- Availability of middlemen
- Attitude of intermediaries towards company policies

At times, it may also be required to look at environmental factors like competition, socio-cultural factors, and economic and technological factors.

Channel Design: Six Factors to Consider (Example from a Packaged Foods Company)

1. *Nature of the Product:* perishability, size and weight, unit value of product. Standardization, technical nature of products, product lines.
2. *Nature of the Market*: number of buyers, industrial or consumer, size of order, geographic concentration of the market, buying habits of customers.
3. *Nature of Middlemen*: cost of distribution of goods, availability of desired middlemen, suitable marketing policies for middlemen, services provided by m/m, ensuring greater volume of sales, reputation and financial soundness.
4. *Nature and Size of the Manufacturing Unit*: manufacturer's reputation and financial stability, ability and experience of the undertaking, desire for control of channel, industrial conventions, and services provided by the manufacturer.
5. *Government Regulations and Policies.*
6. *Existing Competition and Their Product Reach Capabilities.*

Change of Channel Members

Any change in the selected channel members is quite rare unless the company is not satisfied with the performance of a partner. Changing channel partners is not a pleasant experience, and if done often, it results in the company not getting good partners willing to work with it. However, there may be major changes in the structure of a company which may warrant a change in its distribution network.

Exhibit 13.3

Major Distribution Revamp—Brooke Bond Lipton

Till the mid-1990s, Brooke Bond India Ltd. (BBIL) and Lipton India Ltd. (LIL) were independent companies and fierce competitors in the market place. By then both companies were wholly owned subsidiaries of Unilever PLC. Unilever saw synergies in the merger of the two companies—hence, Brooke Bond Lipton came into existence.

One of the major areas needing integration was the distribution network as till then each company was following a different distribution strategy. More details are given as follows:

(*Contd.*)

Situation Before

Parameter	Brooke Bond India Ltd. (BBIL)	Lipton India Ltd. (LIL)
Products	Packet tea, bulk tea, Instant Coffee, Roast and Ground coffee	Packet tea, bulk tea, Edible Fats and Dairy
Distribution system (approximate)	C&FAs—35 Distributors—300 Direct salesmen—1200 Supervisors—150	C&FAs—40 Distributors—1500 Salesmen—600 Supervisors—120
Distribution focus	Volume from retailing	Volume from wholesalers
Collection of sales proceeds	Cash sales—no credit	Immediate payment from distributors, but they extended credit to the market
Market working	With ready stocks and own salesmen	Mostly order booking through distributors
Total volume	X tons per year	0.5 X tons per year
Planning cycle	Weekly	Weekly
Salesmen unions	All India Federation	Local unions
Sales managers	30 ASMs located in the field closer to their territories	28 ASMs in 4 Branch HQrs
Branch managers	6	4
General manager—sales	1	1
Production	Own factories + 3P units	Own factories + 3P units

Action points on distribution integration:

- All C&FAs were not required. The stronger, more experienced C&FAs only retained. Ability to handle additional bigger volumes.
- Distributors retained from the territories where the respective company had higher market shares. Financial strengths and reputation along with market coverage history were also reviewed.
- For new distributors, it was a Greenfield selection. In the South, they were to have abilities to sell coffee also.
- Salesmen ideally should have been based on one salesman to manage 10 to 12 distributors. This would have meant a drastic reduction. However, a more lenient view was taken and surplus salesmen were separated.
- Surplus supervisors and ASMs were also separated.
- Branch managers were about five in excess. These were given new responsibilities away from sales.
- Both the GSMs were retained with one having responsibility for the north and east and the other for west, central and south regions.
- The entire distribution integration took six months to complete.

Situation After

Distribution element	Number	Distribution element	Number
C&FAs	40	Supervisors	150
Distributors	2300	ASMs	30
Salesmen	600	Branch managers	5

Training Channel Members

This starts at the time the channel member is recruited and continues right through the time that the channel member is associated with the company. The training is done for the channel member owners and their staff.

Training assumes a lot of importance since the market views the channel member as the company and the intermediary has to maintain a high and right profile for the company he represents.

Training could include:

- On the job field training to the channel salespeople on the way to work in the markets and achieve sales, collect payments and ensure the right kind of merchandizing.
- Classroom training to the distributor and his staff on the company products, the competition and ways of tackling competition to gain market shares.
- Special meetings for launch of new products and the manner in which these need to be launched. At times, there is also an orientation programme before major promotions are launched.
- Training on submitting reports and maintaining records.
- Statutory requirements.
- Care of the company products in the custody of the channel member—the C&FA or the distributor.
- In the case of technical products, the training has to be on all technical specifications and developing the skills to answer customer queries.
- For technical and industrial products, the personnel have to be trained on recognition of specifications, installation procedure, repair and maintenance and how to give effective demonstrations to prospects.
- Servicing of engineering products including automobiles.

It is clear that training is an ongoing process as the markets in which companies operate are not static and customer expectations keep increasing.

Strategic Factors in Channel Design: Example from an Auto-Ancillary Products Company

Product	Environment	Strategic
Product / service characteristics	Market characteristics	Product positioning
Ancillary services	Customer expectations	Market coverage intensity
Complementary products	Competitor channels	
After sales care	Channel characteristics	

(Contd.)

Factors Affecting Channel Choice

- Understanding the ultimate users
- How they prefer to purchase merchandise: where, when, why, how

Example of a High-End Electronic Device

- Purchased only a from a well-established, reputable dealer
- Only after considerable shopping to compare price and merchandise characteristics
- Willing to get some inconvenience (time and distance to locate the most acceptable brand)
- After extended dialogue with all interested parties—dealer, users, purchasers
- Purchase may be postponed
- Only from a dealer equipped to render prompt and reasonable product service

Channel Objectives

- Growth in sales—existing or new market
- Maintenance/Improvement of market share
- Achieve a pattern of time, place and possession utilities
- Create an efficient channel

Motivating Channel Partners

Companies operate with ambitious volume and growth targets which require extra efforts on the part of the company sales force and their channel partners to achieve. The channel members need to be kept highly motivated to deliver results consistently. The channel members need to be constantly reminded that they are partners of the company in ensuring that the end users are always fully satisfied.

Motivating channel members includes efforts in designing capacity building programmes, training, promotions support, marketing research and of course working along with the company sales personnel. The starting point is the understanding of the requirements and needs of the intermediaries and what can influence them to perform at the peak of their potential in delivering customer satisfaction.

Based on the power format suggested by French & Raven (John R French Jr & Bertram Raven—*The Bases of Social Power in Studies in Social Power* edited by Dorwin Cartright, University of Michigan, 1959, pp. 150–166), given below is the list of some of the powers which can be used on intermediaries to make them effective:

- Referent Power
- Expert Power
- Legitimate Power
- Reward Power
- Coercive Power
- Support Power
- Competition Power

French and Raven have defined only the five power bases of: reward, coercive, legitimate, expert and reference. Support and competition power have been added by the authors.

These persuasive powers are explained in a little more detail ahead:

Referent Power

This power emanates out of the eminent position that the company holds in the industry. This power generates instant recognition and respect and any intermediary associated with this kind of an organisation will automatically get a favourable rub-off of this image. Companies like Microsoft, Infosys, HUL, Telco, Colgate have this referent power in the businesses in which they operate.

Expert Power

This implies that the company has some special knowledge that is value adding to the channel partner. This support could take the form of specialised knowledge on developing business in which the company may train the sales personnel of the distributors. Without this training support, the intermediary would not be able to perform well. The disadvantage of this kind of power is that it has got limited utility unless the company keeps developing valuable knowledge, which can continue to add value to the intermediary. Companies like Maruti, LG, and Samsung have developed this kind of expertise power which is recognized by the industry in which they operate.

Legitimate Power

This is enforcing any task expected of the intermediary as per the agreement or contract signed with the company. The company has the right to get this work out of the channel partner and the intermediary has the responsibility to deliver this expectation. For example, if HUL and other such consumer product companies expect the distributor to maintain a stock level of two weeks' sales of the company products, the distributor has an obligation to do so. The contract could also stipulate the number of salesmen the distributor is required to employ to ensure certain coverage of the markets as agreed with the company. FMCG companies clearly specify the number of outlets to be covered by the distributor each day, the frequency of calls, and even the percentage of productive calls expected (which has to be close to 100 anyway).

Reward Power

As the name implies, companies provide incentives to the channel partners to perform additional tasks at specific points of time. This power is the most persuasive but cannot be used to an extent where it may become a habit or get taken for granted. Money motivation cannot be used every time for every new task the intermediary is expected to perform. Example of a reward power is when a new product is launched and the distributor is paid an incentive if he is able to achieve the placement of the new product in 100 percent of the outlets covered by him within four weeks of the launch.

In the case of rewards, it should be made clear to the partner that it is for a specific duration and for a specific task only after which it may be withdrawn so that there is no resentment once the period is over.

Coercive Power

This is the power of a "threat" used by the company to put a defaulting channel partner back on track. The threat could be taking away some support or even discontinuing the channel partnership if the partner does not do something which the company wants him to do as part of the requirement to sell more of the product. For example, a consumer product company may have an order from a major customer who wants a credit of 15 days. The company has to persuade the distributor to extend this credit to the customer and may use such coercive tactics to do so.

Most big companies which have well-established distributors use this tactic occasionally. The distributor considers it a prestige to be a partner of the company and would be more than willing to make some sacrifices to keep the business. His dependence of the company is very high.

This power has to be used only in exceptional cases as otherwise the partner may not like it and may use it against the company at some other time.

Support Power

The company using the channel partners for distribution of its goods and services has the ability to give additional support to the channel partners to help increase volumes. This support could be in the form of promotions on the product (both trade related and consumer related) and subsidies (like bearing a part of the distribution cost, cost of auxiliary salesmen employed by the distributor to increase coverage, etc.). The company can use this support selectively to encourage the more effective partners by giving them additional support to perform even better. This will also alert the less performing partners to do better in the hope of getting some of this kind of encouragement.

Sometimes this power can take the form of "spot cash" awards, which senior sales management, while on a field sales trip can give in appreciation of a good sales effort by the distributor or his salesman.

Competition Power

This is not to be confused with the competition faced by the firm in the market. It is the method of generating "rivalry" among channel partners so that they try to "compete" on performing better than their peers. Sometimes this may be openly organized sales contests with targets on volume and other parameters or it could be the constant comparisons which sales managers do in their meetings with the channel partners, when they rate the performance of all their partners and rank them in order of good performance.

Developing motivating programs by companies is to ensure co-operation of the channel partners so that the company objectives of better customer service can be achieved. The intermediary is also eager to develop a long-term relationship with his principals. Motivation could be positive incentives like better margins, special promotions, subsidies on distribution expenses, sharing the credit cost, sales contests, or merchandizing support. At times the motivation has to be negative in terms of cutting down on some of the benefits to force the distributor to fall in line with the company operating norms—these should always be used sparingly as they impact long term relationships.

Better managed companies use the medium of the contract or the agreement with the distributor to spell out the obligations and the benefits. The obligations could relate to market coverage, developing new markets, inventory levels to be held, level of credit to be extended, development of key accounts, key account management, complaint handling, technical advice and services, and market feedback and reporting. The benefits could be the compensation plan including margins, subsidies, and incentives (occasional). If the intermediary is clear on these things, the relationship can flourish.

For multilevel marketing companies like Amway, Modicare, and Tupperware, the relationship between the company and its distributors is the main source of motivation in keeping the distributor with the company and keep recruiting more distributors and getting sales. The relationship is strengthened by various kinds of promotions, sales meetings and experience sharing by the most successful distributors.

Managing the channel partners is a major responsibility of sales management in every company. This "managing" has to result in a long term relationship where the channel partner considers himself as an integral part of the company business and positively contributes to growth. Sales management decides on the obligations of the channel system and the benefits. Sales management has to gradually develop their channel partners into the thinking that the income earned by the partner is from making the business grow. The partner has to share the responsibility for growth along with the company he works with.

Evaluating Channel Members

The performance and success of the company business depends on the effectiveness of its distribution channel. It is therefore necessary for the company to constantly keep reviewing the performance of the channel partners to ensure the highest standards of performance and help them improve where required. The evaluation will be against targets on sales quota achievement, average level of inventory held, percentage of volume achieved by extending credit, productive calls per day, number of servicing complaints attended to, and so on.

Evaluation can be done by answering some simple questions about the channel system in use:

- Does the system deliver the targeted customer service levels as defined by the company?
- The performance of all the partners in the channel network has to be cost effective for their defined roles on flows and customer service deliverables targets. Is this really happening?
- Is the channel system operating at the lowest total cost possible for the given service level?
- Are all the channel members performing at the peak of their potential and delivering high quality and timely outputs?
- Does the system have a good performance measurement procedure in place and is this transparent to all the channel partners?
- Do the channel members feel that the company they are working for is fair and equitable in the remuneration and return on investment allowed for their services?
- Does the system have the capability of motivating low performers into putting efforts to the best of their potential and capability?
- Is the system capable of taking action on complaints quickly and correcting itself for better performance in the future?

Leading companies like Nestle, Coca Cola, Colgate, and HUL in the FMCG sector not only evaluate the performance of their distributors on monthly results but also keep tracking their return on investment (ROI). They assure a 30 percent ROI to the distributors and in case the distributor is making a ROI in excess of this, they would give additional tasks—like rural van coverage for example to bring the ROI in line with the promised 30 percent. It could also happen that intense competition is coming in the way of the distributor achieving his ROI in spite of his best efforts. In such a case the company may design special product promotions for a limited duration to support the efforts of the distributors.

While the evaluation process is meant to help improve the performance of the channel partners through counselling, retraining, and motivating, in extreme cases it may also be required to terminate a partner. This alternative would be used in exceptional cases only.

Performance evaluation of the channel partner is done on the same tasks which have been agreed with him at the time of his appointment. The specific targets, for each of the tasks, are decided on a periodical basis. For example, targets on volume and outlet productivity could be for even a week or a month. Targets relating to increasing market shares, outlet coverage could be for a longer period like six months. The performance is measured at the appropriate time periods for which the targets have been set. The company could even give weightages for each of the parameters of measurement and work out the weighted average score of the channel partner to decide his level of performance. We will read more on this in Chapter 14.

Evaluation of Effectiveness of Channel Systems

A summary of the points (the points are of such a general nature that a combination of them can be used while judging the channels for any product or service) in evaluation of channel effectiveness is given as follows:

- Volume generated by each channel partner
- Profit contribution of each channel partner
- How aggressively is the channel pushing the company product?
- How exclusive is the channel? (this applies more to dealers and stockists who may not be exclusive)
- Does the channel partner send in his orders for goods on time and in adequate quantities to meet his quota? The mix of products in the orders placed should cover the full product portfolio and not just the fast movers
- Does the channel partner support the promotional and advertising efforts of the principal? (more relevant for B2B scenario)
- The channel should be doing business for the principal in an ethical manner only
- Extent of customer relationships being built by the intermediary even without the direct intervention of the principal

Modifying an Existing Channel Network

Most of the points covered in the discussion so far in this chapter apply equally well to modifying an existing channel system. The steps to be taken are summarized here:

- The service deliverables that the channel has to offer are listed down in as much detail as possible. For an existing channel this list is already available. But as we have set out to modify the existing channel obviously there are service levels which the current system may not be delivering.
- Service cannot be at any cost. We have agreed that service has to be at an optimum cost. We need to define the level at which each of the deliverables is to be delivered to the customers. The customer will define this and what competitors are doing will help us refine this.
- The service level objectives have to be drilled down into the activities which the channel is expected to perform to achieve those objectives. These activities are the channel flows and are to be clearly defined so that the channel partner has no confusion on what is expected of him.
- We have also seen earlier that all activities cannot be performed by the same channel member. Secondly, the company would like to outsource some of the activities to its channel partners who are better qualified to do the job. Once it is decided as to who in the channel system will do which of the activities, it is necessary to work out the cost of performing these tasks. This step will help us determine the best service level which can be provided at an optimum or minimum cost.
- Now the channel structure is possible to define with a set of channel partners who are expected to do set tasks to deliver the customer service at the optimum or minimum cost.

Now the ideal channel structure as arrived at is to be compared with the existing channel network to identify the gaps. Bridging these gaps gives us the new channel system. When comparing the ideal and the existing criteria to be used, one needs to include efficiency, effectiveness, capacity, agility, consistency, reliability and integrity.

- The new channel system is then put in place with clearly defined key performance indicators to measure its performance at periodical intervals.
- This exercise can also be carried out at the comparison stage by comparing the ideal channel structure with the channel network being operated by other companies in a similar kind of business. Comparisons with competition or other companies in the same industry are required when the company is looking for a Greenfield distribution system.
- The comparison does, however, give information relating to: (i) tasks performed by various partners in the system and any problems faced by them, (ii) the inter-relationships between the channel partners, (iii) estimate of the service levels delivered by the channel members and the cost incurred, and (iv) an idea of the kind of motivational tools being employed to keep the channel members performing at the peak of their potential. The steps to modify an existing channel system are summarized in Figure 13.2.

The process follows the logical steps of identifying the desired service output, the activities necessary to achieve this output and the cost of providing the agreed service output. The objective of the channel network may be possible to achieve with the "ideal" network or channel structure. It is obvious that any gaps with the existing channel system will need to be plugged in the new design.

CHANNEL DESIGN COMPARISON FACTORS

We have already seen the criteria for comparing two channel systems as being efficiency, effectiveness, capacity, agility, consistency, reliability and integrity. It is necessary to quickly understand what each of these terms mean in the context of distribution channels:

- *Efficiency*: The standard definition of input vs. output applies here also. The measure is the effort required to achieve a desired service level. The inputs could relate to the number of people involved, the inventory support, the financial implications like credit.
- *Effectiveness*: This is the analysis of how well the channel system meets its objectives. If one of the objectives of the channel network is to achieve 100 percent on time, in full deliveries, the number of times this is achieved over the total number of deliveries can be measured and would indicate the effectiveness of the system. For an existing system this data is readily available. For a new channel design this can only be estimated.

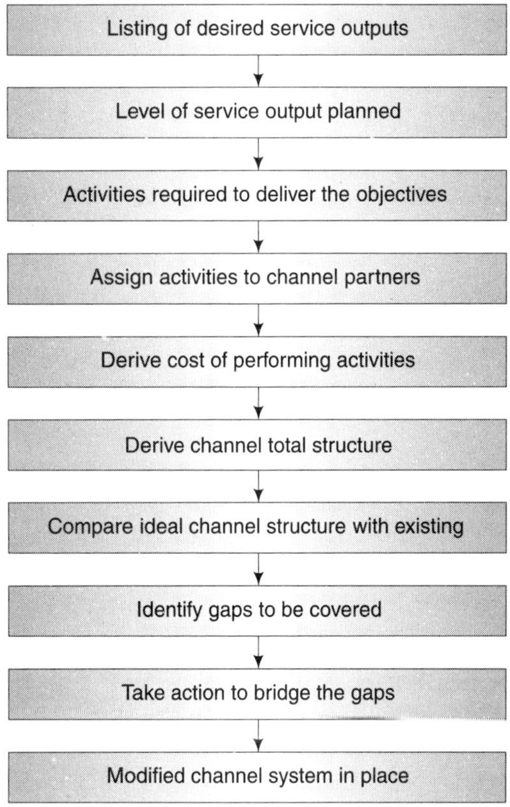

Fig. 13.2 Steps to Modify an Existing Channel System

- *Capacity*: The purpose of this factor is obvious. If the channel has been designed for a current volume of business handling a specific number of customers, it should still be effective when, for example, the volume doubles and the number of customers goes up by another 50 percent. Similarly when the demand for the company products suddenly goes up at the end of the month or during a festive season, the channel system should still work well. The system should have the capacity to tackle short term shocks and also manage long term growths equally effectively.
- *Agility*: This is the ability to handle changing demand patterns (because of the nature of the product or the impact of competition), new customers, new products, or pack sizes. For example, a C&FA is expected to handle very high volume changes at the end of each month and should be prepared to handle this rush. A pharma company or a high technology company may keep introducing innovative products often and would expect the channel partners to take it in their stride and continue a first class performance on service levels.

- *Consistency*: The channel network should deliver the same level of service day after day or month after month without fail. This keeps the customer satisfaction levels at a high level and will not allow customers to stray and hence is an important factor in the working of the channel network.
- *Reliability*: This is measure of the commitment on performance of obligations and the certainty with which the commitment is met. This factor allows the company to make promises on delivery to customers which it knows will be met by the channel system. This factor gives the company confidence in the system delivering as per promises. Many Indian companies have realised the seriousness of reliability in the context of exports.
- *Integrity*: A channel system may have all the qualities described above, but it still has to do business in a fair and above-board manner. At no stage is it expected to indulge in any practices which may have the slightest nature of irregularity. Any such actions can reflect badly on the organisation for which the channel partner is working. For example, successful companies would not want their distributors getting business even from major accounts by any means other than prescribed honest methods. They also insist that the records and registers maintained by the channel partners on account of doing business with the company to always reflect the truth and being open to scrutiny from any government agency at any time.

LO 6 Understand some rules for channel design implementation

CHANNEL DESIGN IMPLEMENTATION

After a detailed analysis of the business requirements (the nature of the products or services being distributed), the customer needs (what the customers expect from the extended arm of the company, which is the distribution channel), the channel objectives, the channel alternatives possible for a set of customer service needs, the current intermediaries (this is relevant when we are trying to modify the channel system), evaluation of alternatives and finally the selection of the most suitable channel design, it is time to draw up an implementation plan. This is outlined below:

Probiking is direct bike retail initiative from Bajaj Auto for its complete range of high end bikes through a well-planned network of state-of-the-art den type bike showrooms in all metros, major tier-2 and tier-3 towns. These showrooms are a showcase of Bajaj Technology & Products where consumers can understand, feel and experience through self-interactive displays like Tech centre, Interactive design station (IDS) & Unique Dynamometer.

It offers differentiated buying experience to consumers through various touch and feel points in a cozy environment.

- While Tech centre offers at-a-glance understanding of technology and products.
- IDS facilitates Probikers' to access detailed product information, key in personal details, generate quotations and fire a print out.

(contd.)

- Dynamometer offers excellent indoor bike riding experience where all bike performance characteristics like Acceleration, Speed, Torque, Power & Decelerations, etc. can be tested. Bajaj Auto had also planned to launch the Kawasaki Ninja 250R.

Probiking currently offers high end Bajaj bikes in the range 200–220 cc which will get upgraded to higher cubic capacities and also add international bikes like KHI. The entire retail process is focused & customer centric and there are arrangements for delivering bikes right at customers' door step in specialized vans.

Sources: Company publication such as http://www.bajajauto.com/about_probiking.asp; http://www.bajajauto.com/probiking_store.asp; accessed on 22 May 2017.

The criteria for appointing the channel partners are first specified so that a prospect wanting to work with the company in any part of the channel network is aware of the expectations of the company. The criteria have been defined in two examples earlier in this chapter (of a C&FA and a Distributor). Some basic criteria could be: (i) previous experience, (ii) investment capabilities, (iii) storage space made available, (iv) selling manpower, and (v) transport facilities available.

Document the channel objectives for the company salespeople and all the channel partners to understand and act upon. There should be no ambiguity on this. The purpose of the channel members could vary between a pizza delivery requirement and that for delivering life-saving drugs.

The profile of the customers who are being serviced by the channel partners is to be clearly understood. This profile is based on what is relevant for the channel. For example, if the channel is dealing with fertilizers, it is necessary to understand the farmers who are the end users and their requirement from the channel in terms of seasonal availability, and easy payment terms. The company selling fertilizers has to get the channel network to understand the profile of the farmers it is catering to.

List all the elements of the customer service levels which will be delivered by the system. This listing will also help determine the key performance indicators when the channel has to be evaluated. If a company is selling cars, it has to define the expectations of the car buyers from the channel in terms of ability to choose from a range, education on technical details as relevant to the buyer and the after sales service support for repairs and maintenance.

After defining the service objectives it is necessary to list down all the tasks which will help achieve these objectives. The tasks are listed in the right sequence in which they are to be performed. For example, if the service objective is to deliver consumer goods to the retailer at a frequency of a week (to avoid stock-outs) the activities which are to be listed are: (i) the number of outlets to be covered, (ii) the time taken by the distribution unit in each outlet, (iii) the number of outlets to be covered in a day, (iv) the means of reaching the outlets with the ready stocks, (v) the most suitable day to visit the particular market and the detailed beat plan for the distribution unit. It also highlights the reports and records that have to be completed at the end of each working day.

While designing a new channel network, we saw how it is necessary to compare with existing channels of competition to get some benchmark good practices, which can be adopted. For existing channel modification, it is necessary to study the existing channel in terms of how it is delivering the customer service needs and the gaps which need to be filled up. After all, a differentiation in terms of better customer service delivery can give a competitive advantage. For example, if a PC manufacturer has a waiting time of two weeks to deliver a PC to a prospect and there are certain characteristics of its channel network which results in this logistical waiting time, a new channel can be built keeping this in mind and reducing the waiting time to just one week and create a competitive advantage.

The customer service objectives are delivered by a set of channel partners who together form the channel network. This could be the C&FA, the distributors, wholesalers and retailers supported by the company sales force. Each of these partners has a definite role to play in delivering the customer service objectives. The tasks/activities listed above have to be listed down by channel partner. For example, for a pharmaceutical company, the C&FA has the role of storage, breaking bulk and secondary transport to the distributor whereas the distributor has to sell and deliver the medical supplies to institutions like hospitals, doctors and retail chemists. The tasks to be performed by each of them are different.

There is a cost associated with each activity and this has to be worked out so that the salespeople who manage the channel network can work with a clear budget. Service cannot be expected at any cost—the affordability is finite. Companies have now started using activity based costing (ABC) for this purpose. Development of the budget for the year is important so that the commercial performance of the system can be tracked during the year.

Each channel partner has to be clear on: (i) roles and responsibilities, (ii) how this role is expected to be discharged—steps or activities required to be performed, (iii) cost of each activity, and (iv) what can the channel partner expect from the company as remuneration, subsidies and reimbursement of out of pocket expenses for the specified role. Most progressive companies not only define the remuneration but also tell the channel partners the return on investment (ROI) percentage they can expect while working for the company. For example, a 25–30 percent ROI is considered quite good for a distributor of a consumer product company.

The channel partner is also informed well in advance that his performance will be measured by the company at regular intervals, normally twice a year. The key performance indicators are also made known to the channel partner so that there is no ambiguity on what is expected and how the evaluation will be done. The performance measures could be relating to: (i) discipline in following the beat plan, (ii) number of outlets to be covered each day by the distribution unit, (iii) percentage of productive outlets, (iv) percentage outlets extended credit, (v) stock levels held by the distributor, (vi) volume achieved against target, and so on.

Apart from following the tasks and activities given by the company, the channel partners are also required to submit a lot of reports to the company and also maintain a number of records of transactions to keep updating the transactions and also for statutory purposes. The list of reports and records are to be very clearly spelt out for each channel partner at the start of the operations. Of course, during the course of the operations, the need could always arise for adding/deleting some of these reports/records. Figure 13.3 illustrates the steps involved in channel design implementation.

The sequence of steps has been clearly defined in the figure below starting with the criteria of appointing channel partners, the profile of the customers to be serviced, clearly defined customer service objectives, define the tasks to be performed (after getting an idea of best practices from competition) and the channel structure which can best perform these functions at a budgeted cost.

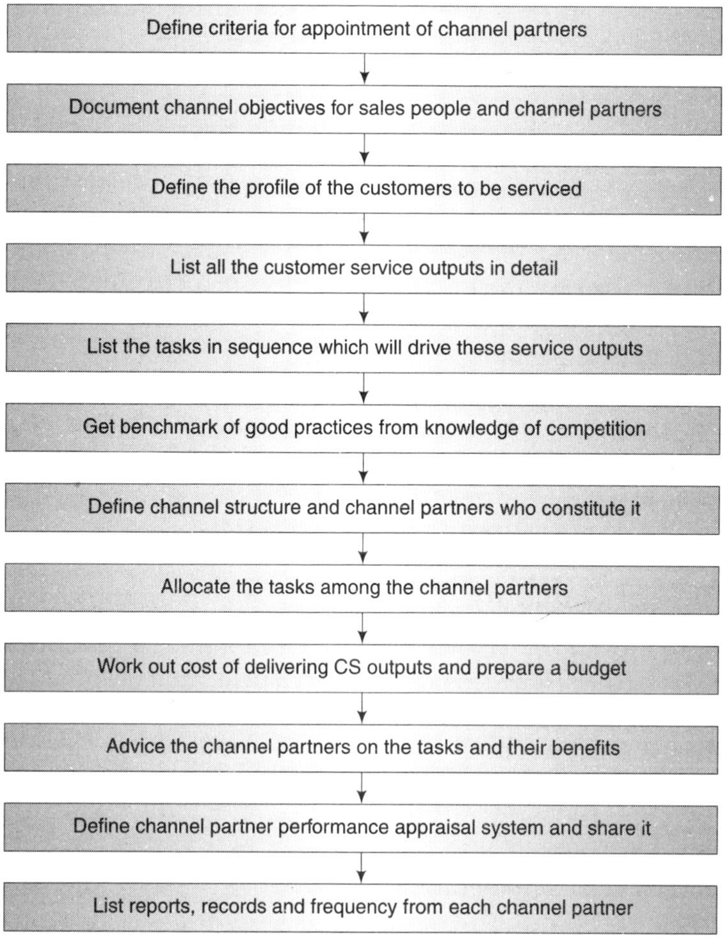

Fig. 13.3 Steps Involved in Channel Design Implementation

LO 7 Summarize the principles of vertical integration and electronic channels

VERTICAL INTEGRATION—OWNING THE CHANNEL

At the time of setting up a new channel network, there are two broad options. One option is for the company to set up its own network which is called vertical integration. The second option is to set up a channel network outside the company by appointing separate channel partners which would then be called outsourcing. Some factors to decide either of these options have been discussed here.

The discussion should answer the questions relating to the distribution channels:

- Whether the same organisation should do the work of production, branding and distribution; which firm is best suited to do the distribution even if the consumer is willing to pay for the channel flows and if the distribution task should be outsourced?
- These questions challenge the fundamentals of marketing channels. If we have agreed that reaching thousands of customers/consumers directly by the company is difficult or nearly impossible, the need for intermediaries is automatically established.
- The integration could be for the manufacturer to also do the distribution (downstream integration) or the channel member to also market the products (upstream integration).
- Downstream integration for the manufacturer would be where the producer of the products also undertakes the distribution of its products. The manufacturer will then have to make sales, fulfill orders, offer credit to customers and deliver the goods—all these through its own people and organisation.
- Upstream integration for the channel member would be for him to make the products, brand them, and sell them. The instances of dealer own brand/retailer own brand/in-house brands of major retailers, are examples of this.

In both the above cases if one organization does all the work from production to marketing to distribution, it is said that the channel is vertically integrated.

Own the Channel or Outsource?

If the firm decides to own its marketing channels it will influence its distribution and also its manufacturing practices. The prospects and customers also identify the producer by his marketing channels and in their minds create an 'image' of the manufacturer. The choice once made is almost permanent and cannot be changed and resources would get committed.

The above "image" is obviously different for the manufacturer who has outsourced his distribution to conventionally recognized channel partners.

Brooke Bond India and Vertical Integration

Brooke Bond India Ltd. was the classic example of a company which practiced the Vertical Integration (direct distribution system) for over six decades till the mid-90s. Brooke Bond was the market leader in branded packet tea, roast and ground coffee, and instant coffee.

It used to have hundreds of depots in the country each of them manned by a company salesman. At its peak it had over 1,500 sales depots and 165 sub-depots (called *chota* depots) and about 1,600 salesmen. The additional salesmen were required to take over the operations of the depot when the permanent salesman went on leave.

The direct distribution network used to cover over 5 lakh outlets, nearly 20 percent of which were in rural India. The network covered nearly 60,000 tea shops which were direct consumption points for the tea, coffee and instant coffee which were the products of the company.

(contd.)

By the 1990s, when the competition had intensified, the direct distribution had two distinct disadvantages compared to competition (Lipton, Tata, and Nestle) which were all operating through distributors. These disadvantages were:

- All company distributors were selling on 15 to 20 days credit to the wholesalers and retailers. BB, which had a direct distribution through its own salesmen, was selling only on cash and for operating reasons, could not extend credit.
- BB salesmen were all unionized under an employees' federation. At times of disagreement with the company, the employees tended to work to rule at times disrupting the sales. The company did not have alternative distribution channels.

By that time, both BB and Lipton, the two giants in the beverages industry, had both become a part of Unilever PLC, which for synergy reasons, merged the two companies. As Lipton already had a distributor channel in operation, and in view of the above disadvantages of the BB direct distribution, the combined company Brooke Bond Lipton shifted entirely to the distributor channels. A large number of salesmen were rendered redundant and separated.

If the company decides to own its channels for whatever reasons, it is necessary that this important aspect of the company's operations should be planned carefully starting with defining the objectives, the flows to be performed and all concerned being aware of what is expected of each of them.

A classic example of an integrated organisation is Bata India which has been successfully running its distribution through own outlets for many decades now.

How Much of Vertical Integration?

The degree of distribution varies from outsourcing the entire marketing channel functions at one end (market contracting), to partly taking on some of the flows (part vertical integration) to the other extreme of doing all the work by the firm itself—the vertical integration end of the sequence.

In the distribution outsourcing model, the channel partner does the distribution function using its resources of people, money and taking the necessary risks. The channel partner is responsible for the loss or gain from its business and the firm tries to exert the necessary control to get its objectives achieved in a cost effective manner. Again it is a question of exploiting the core competence of the channel partners, which is distribution.

The channel partners will work on a commission which is generally a mark-up on the company price to the channel partner. Outsourcing shifts all costs and most of the risks to the third party on contract.

In the part vertical integration all the costs and responsibilities are shared between the firm and the contracted channel partners. The benefits also get shared. Companies do operate a combination of channel partners and own sales people to manage them. This model could also be used for retail distribution and selling to Institutions.

This mode is practiced by companies which are into selective distribution, franchising, etc.

In the vertical integration mode, the company has to perform all the functions taking full responsibility for the distribution effort. It has to put in its resources of money, people and taking on all the risks of this part of the business also. While the gain or loss is totally in its hands, it also has total control over the operations. The major argument in today's context against vertical integration is that distribution may not be the "core competence" of the company and is best left to the "experts" who can be expected to do the job better.

Some of the issues relating to this "continuum" of operations are as follows:

- The cost of manpower to run the operations by the firm is substantial. Moreover, the company may not be able to get the right manpower at an affordable cost. Hiring a limited number of people by the channel partner locally is easier than for a company to recruit a large number of the right kind of people from various locations nationally.
- The number of people to be managed would be quite large for a national firm. Company personnel work with some rules and this may reduce their effectiveness or not get the company the benefit of their full potential. A large field force would also need more supervisors. A local channel partner is able to keep the working of his own people more flexible as the laws are more accommodative of his practices.
- Vertical integration provides the control over the distribution function but may not give the expected benefits. Better control of the operations seems to be the only argument strongly in favour of vertical integration.

Why Vertical Integration?

VI is justified if the efficiency of the operations get enhanced as a result of this action. Efficiency, obviously, is the ratio of the results obtained divided by the resources employed to achieve these results. What this means is that revenues should increase more than costs.

In reality, owning the distribution function by the company itself is never an easy proposition. This brings us to the topic of outsourcing distribution.

Vertical integration seems to have worked well in some of these situations:

- The company products and brands are highly technology driven and need highly trained and skilled manpower to explain and sell. (Medical diagnostic equipment)
- The competition being faced is low and market shares are high and it is cost effective to use own distribution networks. (Eureka Forbes)
- The number of customers to be serviced is small. (Earth moving equipment)
- It is not easy to forecast sales accurately and hence revenue commitments cannot be made to channel partners. (IT industry)
- The products may need specialized handling (LPG distribution or cold chain products)
- If the company is an ancillary unit to a bigger organisation (A supplier to Maruti).
- The company is not able to get good and reliable channel partners.

Some of these reasons may also apply to channel members who may want to integrate upstream and produce the products they want to sell (Organized retailers).

Outsourcing Distribution

Outsourcing is employing existing channel partners like wholesalers and retailers or developing partners like C&F agents and distributors.

A 3P marketing channel has certain inherent advantages compared to the company doing the operations on their own. These advantages are:

- Core competence—their main job is distribution and hence there is a focus. They are best suited to do this job. This focus enhances their effectiveness.
- Motivation—as they are independent, they are eligible to get all the benefits of their operations. The profitability motive is sufficient to drive them to perform to the best of their ability. The channel partner is primarily a businessman and is in business to make money.
- Flexibility in operations—they are not bound by the strict rules of operation which a firm has to follow. Moreover all the persons employed by him are multi-skilled and can stand in for each other.
  - For example, a C&FA may keep his warehouse working till midnight in an emergency, whereas a company warehouse is run by its employees who may demand overtime to do the extra hours.
  - Another example: a distributor may decide the best frequency of making calls on his customers. While he may call on "A" category customers thrice a week (including once by himself), he may call on a "C" category customers only once a week.
- His operations are smaller and hence better managed and controlled. If the distributor works for many non-competing companies, he is able to share his overheads among all these operations and gain from economies of scale.
- Local strengths—he can manage his customers and environment better as he has built up relationships over a period of time. His ability to cover the market is higher as he understands well how the market and the outlets operate. Examples of the distributor knowledge of institutional customers in his territory are well known.
- Independent operations—he is answerable to himself to start with and if he is abiding by the rules set by the company, he can do well. Entry and exit barriers are low but the stronger channel partners survive almost indefinitely. Distributors feel proud that they are working for major companies for generations. It is very difficult, for example, to get a good distributor in a market today. Retailers and freelance wholesalers are even independent of any single company.
- Threat of replacement—the 3P operator knows that if he does not perform well, he can be replaced. He makes sure that his performance is of the high standard expected of him.
- High local knowledge—he knows his territory and its nuances extremely well and can keep a sharp look-out for his competitor's activities.

Outsourcing distribution is the most common situation in most industries. Companies have realized that the contracted channel members can do a better job of distribution in a more cost effective manner. The company would do well in sticking to its core competencies of production and branding.

Non-Store Retailing and Electronic Channels

In this section, we will be discussing non-store retailing and electronic channels in detail.

Non-Store Retailing

Non-store retailing is the selling of goods and services outside the confines of a retail facility. It is a generic term describing retailing taking place outside of shops and stores (that is, off the premises of fixed retail locations and of markets stands).

- The non-store distribution channel can be divided into direct selling (off-premises sales) and distance selling, the latter including all forms of electronic commerce.
- Distance selling includes mail order, catalogue sales, telephone solicitations and automated vending.
- Electronic commerce includes online shopping, Internet trading platforms, travel portals, global distribution systems and teleshopping.
- Direct selling includes party sales and all forms of selling in consumers' homes and offices, including even garage sales.

Non-store retailing is sometimes also labelled "home shopping". The non-store distribution channel is marked by low entry thresholds. Compared to store retailing that requires a retail outlet, inventory, cash flow to hire staff and advertising, non-store retail start-ups usually have to invest little to reach out to potential buyers of the goods and services they offer. Non-store retailing is therefore not only used by established brick and mortar business retailers who develop an online bricks and clicks business model presence, but also by the individual pure play, often him- or herself a consumer, to create an e-shop or to run sales parties. The rise of social media helps to connect sellers to potential buyers.

Selling Door-to-Door

All households in India are exposed to the dozens of *pheriwalas*/hawkers who come shouting about their wares on every street. They may be selling bread, fruits and vegetables, flowers, ice cream, plastic ware, or even carpets. Even the *raddiwala* who buys old newspapers at your doorstep is in this category. These hawkers develop their own beat plan and visit the localities and sell their wares on cash. They normally buy and sell only such quantities which they are able to dispose of on the same day.

At times these hawkers may even be selling services like repairs of locks, umbrellas and footwear or cleaning wells or sharpening kitchen knives.

The other kinds of door-to-door selling are the milkman and the newspaper boy.

At times, in order to support a new product launch, a company may even use a planned effort at selling door-to-door to get consumers to try its new product.

Vending Machines

This is another good example of non-store retailing. Vending machines are used for beverages, soft drinks (they call them fountains), condoms, and even magazines. They can work 24×7, they require little space, they can be placed in places with high people traffic and do not even need a person to man them. ATMs at banks are another example of vending.

Tele-Shopping

With very high viewing levels of television in India, tele-shopping is gaining a lot of ground. Most of the products sold through these networks relate to either the kitchen or health related. They use the medium of the TV to demonstrate the results from the use of these products and accept orders by phone and deliver the product and collect the payment at your door-step.

Marketing through Catalogs

This is a concept almost non-existent in India. The retailer (like Sears Roebuck, for example) regularly publishes catalogs of goods he is selling along with prices. The consumer can browse through these catalogs (normally seen on flights or in furniture shops) and then order the goods to be delivered directly to him by the retailer and paid for by him.

Some characteristics of catalog marketing are:

- A catalog is meant to break bulk as it sells in consumer friendly lot sizes
- It varies between product groups
- Earlier it had a wide variety and assortment of general merchandise. It is tending towards a deep assortment of a narrow range of specialty goods.
- Giving the consumer the spatial convenience of shopping from home.
- There is always a waiting time to get the goods delivered varying between 4 days to 15 days. Overnight deliveries are rare and very expensive.
- The consumer cannot touch, feel, or try the goods before buying.
- Women are more likely to do catalog shopping than men.
- Apparel is the most common item of catalog shopping. Some of the other products are food, home products, books, computers and music.

Apart from the convenience, consumers believe that in catalog shopping, the type of merchandise is unique and the prices are fair.

In catalog marketing, the product has to be available before the order, there may be product returns, the catalog has to be updated at quite a cost to cover all the latest products, inventory has to be carefully managed and the tasks of physical distribution have to be well planned. This is not an easy business to be in. In spite of all this effort, the company has to still build strong relationships with its customers so that they provide long term business. Catalog marketing has no "impulse" buyers.

Even in the West, where catalog marketing is most prevalent, companies are known to follow a multiple channel strategy. They have brick-and-mortar stores along with the catalogs. These stores could even be used for delivery of the goods to the consumers. A good example is that of Bloomingdales.

Selling Direct

Direct selling is the company reaching the product directly to the consumer of the product. The focus here is on personal selling.

Some examples of direct selling organizations are: Amway, Tupperware, Herbalife, Modicare, Avon and Mary Kay.

Each distributor in a direct selling organisation recruits more such distributors. Hence this model is also called multi-level marketing.

The distributors (also known as consultants, advisors or just sales people) are not company employees but only on contract to canvas business among consumers and sell the company products. They are distributors also because they buy the goods from the company and sell it to consumers after adding their mark-up.

The distributor's earnings depend on:

- The mark-up they get on the products they buy from the company and sell direct to the consumers.
- A commission is also paid on each such sale made by the distributor.
- A commission is also paid on the sales made by all the additional distributors recruited by each distributor.

Some companies have used the successful model of the direct selling organisation to develop what are known as "pyramid" schemes. Here the distributors have to pay a fixed fee to the company to become distributors. They also get rewarded for recruiting more distributors who pay the fixed fees in return for becoming distributors. The focus seems to have been wrongly shifted from product sales to recruiting more distributors and the company earning more revenues from the fees charged.

In the case of the organized and legitimate direct selling organizations, the distributor has to initially buy a small "starter kit" of the company products which he is required to sell. The distributor has to necessarily sell the products to his friends and acquaintances and this creates a wrong image of the direct selling effort. Direct selling does not seem to have worked well in India so far even for the very well-known companies from the US.

Another good example of direct selling in the Indian context where the model is totally different is the Eureka Forbes company which sells household cleaning and water purifying equipment direct to consumers through its own employee salesmen.

Use of Electronic Channels

Electronic channels are those which use the Internet to sell goods to the consumers directly. The consumer buys his requirements online. The channel can be B2C (for consumers) or B2B (for businesses).

The size of the market depends on the size of the population which has access to computers and more so access to the Internet. For more details on electronic retailing, please also refer to Chapter 11.

Electronic channels as selling tools are dependent on the following:

- Access of consumers to computers
- Access of consumers to the Internet
- The arrangements made by the companies to market their goods on the Internet
- The ability or ease for the consumer to pay for the goods bought by him on the Internet
- The ability of the producer of the goods to deliver the goods to the online buyers with the least waiting time

All these hold equally well for B2C or B2B.

Business to business (B2B) transactions on the Internet, happen mostly through exchanges, which bring the producers and the customers together on the net. Most successful exchanges deal in commodities.

The advantages of online buying are obvious and some of these are:

- Buying is possible 24×7 (anytime of the day or night and on any day of the week)
- May still take less time than going to a store and buying
- Good value for money in terms of pricing and other promotions
- Access to a wide assortment of goods.

Electronic channels effectively perform the channel flows of breaking bulk, spatial convenience and reducing waiting and delivery time (the consumer can utilise his time for other things once the online order has been placed), providing wide variety and assortment and good customer service at the doorstep of the consumer. In addition, there are a number of websites coming up which help the consumer in comparative shopping.

Reality Bite

Internet Usage in India

Total population (estimate 2016)—132.7 crore
Internet users in India (estimate 2016)—46.2 crore
Share of India population—34.8 percent penetration
Share of world Internet users—13.5 percent

Source: Internet and Mobile Association of India

Online Banking

ATMs, credit cards, debit cards, electronic clearance service (ECS), mobile banking, NEFT, payment system indicators, POS terminals, RTGS

- Online banking, also known as Internet banking, e-banking or virtual banking, is an electronic payment system that enables customers of a bank or other financial institution to conduct a range of financial transactions through the financial institution's website.
- To access a financial institution's online banking facility, a customer with Internet access would need to register with the institution for the service, and set up a password and other credentials for customer verification.
- The customer visits the financial institution's secure website, and enters the online banking facility using the customer number and credentials previously set up. The types of financial transactions which a customer may transact through online banking are determined by the financial institution, but usually includes obtaining account balances, a list of the recent transactions, electronic bill payments and funds transfers between a customer's or another's accounts.

Internet marketing channels available for all companies:

- SEO: search engine optimisation
- PPC: pay per click campaign

(Contd.)

- Social media
- Affiliate
- Shopping channels
- Mobile marketing
- Video marketing
- eDM: e-mail direct marketing
- Online PR: article content marketing
- Display advertising
- Directory review sites (Yelp)

Companies are now offering after sales services also online. For example, it is possible to track the status of the order also online.

Some of the concerns of using electronic channels/online for buying products continue to be:

- Security concerns on using credit card numbers on the net for making payments
- Product returns are not easily done
- Stock-out of the product
- Delivery delays even after agreed waiting times
- Consumers may not be willing to pay for shipping or handling
- Consumers not sure if they are getting a good bargain in terms of pricing

Other applications of the use of the Internet are in Electronic Data Interchange (EDI), Vendor Managed Inventory (VMI) and Continuous Replenishment Programs (CRP). [More on these in Chapter 16]

- EDI—the use of the Internet by a company and its suppliers to exchange information and data
- VMI—the system of suppliers keeping inventory on behalf of their customers and supplying regular quantities as per an agreed schedule
- CRP—use of electronic scanners on retail display shelves to relay information to suppliers about the selling of their products so that they could replenish stocks to the retailer to replace on the shelves.

Use of electronic channels also affects costs in the following situations:

- Most of the physical handling and logistics have to be outsourced to couriers or third party logistics service providers. This is quite expensive as individual small orders of consumers have to be executed till their door-step.
- Generating sales from an Internet requires a lot of persuasion and attractive offers which may cost the company more than offline.
- Prices get customized often and the consumer always expects lower prices online. Airline ticket sales are a good example (makemytrip.com)
- Exchanges in B2B help the company to negotiate with a number of sellers and then get the best bargains. This may reduce the margins of the online sellers.
- Additional inventory (with uncertainty of sales) may have to be maintained to avoid stock-outs after the online orders have been received.

- Making secure payments on the net may be more costly.

There could also be some channel conflicts as a result of electronic transactions:

- The consumer may get full details from a brick-and-mortar store and then buy online. The marketing effort of the physical store is wasted. The reverse could also happen.
- The online channel may eat into the sales of longer established channels of the same company like distributors and retailers.
- If the online channel offers a better bargain to the consumer than the physical store, it could create even more difficulties.
- If the physical store has to deliver the goods booked online, they may get lower margins and may not be always willing to perform this task.

Some of these causes of channel conflict can be avoided if the online and offline products are different (not a very practical proposition), the prices on both are the same and the physical channels are compensated in some manner for the "loss" of sales to their electronic counterparts.

SUMMARY

LO 1/LO 2

- The nature of the distribution channels that are required in different situations varies with a number of factors. Some of these factors need to be recollected here:
  - Nature of the product or service being distributed
  - The expectations from the system
  - Location and nature of the customers
  - Nature of competition and its distribution systems
  - Intensity of distribution required
  - Nature of the markets being targeted
- In summary, the channel system gets built around the local opportunities, conditions and requirements.

LO 3/LO 4

- The channel design takes into account all these service deliverables desired by the customer. The channel designer has the delicate task of making all the service deliverables available at a cost affordable to the customer.
- At the time of deciding on the channel alternatives, the company will scan for:
  - Business intermediaries currently available in the market
  - The number and type of intermediaries required
  - Any new channel members which need to be specially developed
  - Roles of each of the channel members
- Cost elements of the channel network include:
  - Margins of the channel partners
  - Cost of transportation of goods between the company and the end user
  - Cost of order booking and execution

LO 5

- The main consideration to decide the number of intermediaries is the "intensity" of distribution which the company desires.
- The common criteria for evaluation of channel alternatives are: cost factors, ability to control, adaptability to changing circumstances and range of products and the volume the channel is capable of handling.

LO 6

- Factors influencing the selection of channels are the nature of the products, markets, the company characteristics and the type of channel partners most suitable.
- Similarly for defining the channel structure, the variables which play a role relate to the markets/customers, the company, its products, kinds of intermediaries in the industry and the environment including competition. One of the channel structures to be used could be a "hybrid" one using company resources partly and partly outsourcing the distribution.
- Training of channel partners includes on-the-job market working, class room sessions for the channel sales people on company products and services, selling techniques, benefits selling, overcoming objections, new product launches, reports and record keeping, ensuring statutory compliances, technical details, and servicing for engineering products. Training is an ongoing process as markets are not static and customer needs keep changing.
- Motivating channel members can be done by using the company's power of referent power, expertise, legitimate power, reward and coercion.
- The factors normally considered for looking at alternative channel designs are scanning each channel design in terms of its efficiency, effectiveness, capacity, agility, consistency, reliability and integrity all in the context of delivering customer service levels.

LO 7

- The degree of distribution varies from outsourcing the entire marketing channel functions (market contracting), to partly taking on some of the flows (part vertical integration) to the other extreme of doing all the work by the firm itself—the vertical integration end of the continuum.
- VI is justified if the efficiency of the operations gets enhanced as a result of this action. Efficiency obviously is the ratio of the results obtained divided by the resources employed to achieve these results.
- Outsourcing is, employing existing channel partners like wholesalers and retailers or developing partners like C&F agents and distributors.
- A 3P marketing channel has certain inherent advantages compared to the company doing the operations on their own.
- Non-store retailing includes selling through catalogues, other forms of direct selling, and through electronic channels both for consumer (B2C) and industrial goods (B2B). As the name suggests, the goods are sold to the consumers/customers without the need for brick-and-mortar stores.
- Direct selling is the company reaching the product directly to the consumer using the product. The focus here is on "personal" selling.
- Electronic channels are those which use the Internet to sell goods to the consumers directly. The consumer buys his requirements online. The channel can be B2C (for consumers) or B2B (for businesses).

Key Terms

Glossaries of key terms are mentioned at the end of all chapters

Agility
Assortment
Capacity
Catalogue marketing
Channel system
Coercive power
Competition power
Consistency
Continuous replenishment program (CRP)
Direct selling
Effectiveness
Efficiency
Electronic channels
Electronic data interchange (EDI)
Expert power
Hybrid channels
Integrity
Intermediary
Legitimate power
Lot size
Referent power
Reliability
Reward power
Spatial convenience
Support power
Vendor managed inventory (VMI)
Vertical Integration
Waiting time

Conceptual Questions

1. List the service outputs desired by customers and explain how a channel network delivers these requirements. LO1 E
2. How does a company decide on the number of intermediaries required in its channel network? LO5 D
3. What are the parameters used to evaluate channel alternatives? LO4 M
4. Explain the various methods used by companies to train their channel partners. LO6 M
5. What are the factors that decide the nature of distribution channels required in a given situation? LO1 E
6. What are different methods available to companies to motivate their channel partners? LO6 M
7. What are the factors normally considered for evaluating alternative channel designs? LO4 M
8. Under what circumstances is it worthwhile for a company to own its distribution channels? LO7 M
9. Multi-level marketing channels can succeed with proper training and lower prices of popular products. Do you agree? Why? If not, why not? LO7 D

Note: Difficulty Level ⟶ E — Easy; M — Medium; D — Difficult

10. What are the factors which are critical for the success of electronic channels? LO7 E
11. Explain the factors which influence channel selection. LO6 E
12. Define some of the company characteristics which need to be taken into account for selecting the right kind of channels. LO6 M
13. Enumerate the various parameters which can be used to determine channel effectiveness. LO4 M
14. Explain the term "hybrid" channels with examples. LO5 M

Objective Type Questions

Select the most appropriate response out of the various options available in each of the following questions:

1. The channel system is a __________ between the manufacturer and the ultimate customer of the product.
   (a) bridge (b) contact (c) negotiator (d) hindrance LO1 E
2. Providing incentives to channel partners for them to perform better or perform additional tasks is known as __________ power.
   (a) promotion (b) reward (c) persuasion (d) remuneration LO1 E
3. __________ is continued successful performance at higher volumes of business.
   (a) growth (b) discipline (c) loyalty (d) capacity LO1 E
4. All entities operating in a channel system are known as __________ .
   (a) distributors (b) stockists (c) Intermediaries (d) agents LO1 E
5. _______ power emanates out of the eminent position that the company holds in the industry.
   (a) reward (b) referent (c) leadership (d) stable LO1 E
6. If the channel network delivers the same targeted level of service always, it is considered __________ .
   (a) consistent (b) efficient (c) effective (d) useful LO2 E
7. Time elapsed between customer desire to buy a product and actual buying is called __________ __________.
   (a) thinking time (b) deciding time (c) waiting time (d) free time LO2 E
8. Ability of the channel system to handle changing demand patterns is called __________ .
   (a) consistency (b) diligence (c) stability (d) flexibility LO2 E
9. Facilitating the customer to buy her desired product from an outlet of her choice is known as ____________________ .
   (a) spatial convenience (b) lot sizing
   (c) convenience shopping (d) perfect distribution LO2 E

10. Spatial convenience is most influenced by the ________ of distribution being followed by the company.
(a) correct (b) intensity (c) method (d) channel LO2 E

11. A ________ integrated company undertakes all activities relating to production, marketing and distribution.
(a) vertically (b) horizontally (c) fully (d) completely LO7 M

12. Electronic channels use the ________ to transact business.
(a) telephones (b) Internet
(c) catalogues (d) databases LO7 M

13. The ________ of customers and their frequency of purchase also defines the kind of channel to be selected.
(a) number (b) kind (c) nature (d) size LO6 E

14. While selecting channels, the company has to consider the ________ and the degree of control required.
(a) affordability (b) suitability (c) reach (d) experience LO6 M

15. The use of multiple channels to reach different customer segments is also known as ________ channels.
(a) hybrid (b) complex (c) combined (d) distribution LO5 E

Application Questions

1. Define the customer service outputs expected out of a channel system set up to sell tractors. LO1 E
2. Shine-well Lighting Systems is a company making electric bulbs and tube-lights. Design a suitable channel network for Shine-well. LO3 M
3. Talk-more Telecom is a mobile telephone company which ranks No. 3 in the industry. They are trying to evaluate their current channel systems. What factors should they consider for this evaluation? LO4 M
4. Please develop a suitable motivation plan for the distributors of a sewing machine company which is losing market shares. LO6 M
5. Read-well Books is a new book store idea. The owner, Mr Abhishek, who is an MBA from the US, wants to create an Amazon in India. What are the factors he has to consider to decide on this idea? Should he have an online store or should he establish a chain of brick-and-mortar stores? Can you help him take a decision with sound reasons? LO4 D
6. Modern Motors Ltd: How is a dealer to be selected?

   Modern Motors makes electrical goods. It is a leader in electrical motors. MML has an established distributor network in two states. It sells through electrical goods wholesalers in two more states. Current distributors: 3 in state 1 and 2 in state 2. The current turnover of MML is ₹32 crore (about $ 6 million).

Ten years back when scouting for distributors, MML found it difficult to get good distributors. They appointed ex-employees as distributors: state 1—2, and state 2—1. Other distributors were regular businessmen.

MML is now in the process of streamlining their distribution efforts in the remaining two states. They have had a "mixed" experience with two kinds of distributors (those who were ex-employees and those who were businessmen).

Ex-Employee Distributors

- They are charged up, eager, growing.
- Understand products, customers, markets and competition very well—react fast.
- Do not listen to advice. Have a "know-all" attitude.

Businessmen Distributors

- They are less professional—not pro-active to develop new business.
- Primary motive is profitability.

Both the types of distributors resist changes to operating requirements.

MML competition follows similar patterns while recruiting distributors.

MML wants to formally enter the markets of the two additional states. They plan to have a regular distribution network by appointing distributors.

MML wants to decide on the following:

- Should they continue with wholesalers only in these two states?
- Should they start selecting and appointing distributors?
- Should the distributors be selected from ex-employees or from market businessmen (some of whom may be the current wholesalers)?

Can we help them decide? LO3 D

ASSIGNMENTS FOR STUDENTS

1. This exercise requires that you meet any distributor of a FMCG company to understand how the company recruited him. What were the factors they considered? What were the questions they asked? In his opinion, what was the weightage of the various parameters on which he got selected? In short, get a first-hand knowledge of the selection process for channel partners adopted by the principal company.
2. Meet any automobile dealer and his sales and service people. Get to know from them the training methods adopted by their principal company for the dealer and his support team. What is the frequency of such formal training? How much of this happens at the dealer point and on what topics? How has the dealer and his support staff benefited from the training programs of the previous year?
3. The motivational methods adopted by companies for their channel partners is to be understood as part of this exercise. You could meet a distributor or dealer of a prominent company and get to know from him as to what were some of the methods by which his

principal company keeps his interest levels at a peak in the business to deliver superior customer service. Which of these methods gives the best results according to the channel partner and why?

4. Surf the Internet to study any new company which has set up a distribution network and understand how they went about the task.
5. The Internet would provide you several examples of companies who decided to go the route on vertical integration of "owning" the channel. Compare and contrast at least three of these examples and summarize your learning from this exercise.

Reference Notes

1. Bert Rosenbloom, *Marketing Channels—A Management View*, Chapter 6 (pp. 213–252) and Chapter 8 (pp. 281–303).
2. DJ Bowersox and MB Cooper, *Strategic Marketing*, Chapter 5 (pp. 145–167), Chapter 6 (pp. 170–190), Chapter 8 (pp. 225–244).
3. M Guirdhom, *Marketing: The Management of Distribution Channels*, pp. 40–68.
4. CG Walters, *Marketing Channels*, Chapter 6, pp. 146–169.
5. Louis P Bucklin, *A Theory of Distribution Channel Structure*, IBER Special Publications, Berkeley, 1966.
6. V Kasturirangan, MAJ Menezes, EP Maier, *Channel Selection for New Industrial Products: A Framework, Method & Applications*, Journal of Marketing, July, 1992.
7. Milind Lele, *Matching your Channel to your Product Life Cycle*, Business Marketing, December, 1986.
8. R Wise & P Baumgartner, *Go Downstream: The New Profit Imperative in Manufacturing*, HBR, September–October, 1999, pp. 133–141.
9. JA Narus and JC Anderson, *Re-Thinking Distribution*, HBR, July–August, 1996, pp. 112–120.
10. E Malmborg, *Improve Customer Information: A Key to Catalogue Success*, Direct Marketing, June, 1999.
11. W Alderson, *Dynamic Marketing Behaviour*, RD Irwin, 1965.
12. J F Gaski, *The Theory of Power and Conflict in Channels of Distribution*, Journal of Marketing, 1984, p. 10.
13. *4Ps, Festering Success and Value*, November, 2005, p. 30.
14. *Multiplexes Encourage Online Bookings*, Business India, November, 2005, p. 20.
15. *India-Centric Plans*, Business India, December, 2005, p. 12.
16. *Going Pro*, Business India, November, 2005, p. 107.

CASE 13.1

Snow White Paper Company (2)

Snow White (SW) Paper Company is located in an agricultural belt about 300 kilometres from a metro city. It makes writing and printing paper. Its primary raw material is wheat straw. Last year, the company had a turnover of ₹134 crore on a volume of 45,000 tonnes of paper. While preparing the business plan for the current year, the top management was concerned with the following distribution issue which they want "you" to help resolve:

Problem: Finished Goods Distribution

The paper industry is dominated by selling agents who bring the manufacturer like Snow White and the buyers like printing/publishing companies, note book makers, etc. together. The manufacturer sells the paper to the end-user customer on the advice of the "selling agent". The agents make a commission of about 2 percent on all transactions.

Some other points relevant to the distribution of paper are as follows:

- Snow White depends on about 110 agents to canvass business for it from the users.
- The company also sells about 23 percent of its paper directly to some government organizations.
- The agent arranges for the buyer to pay the company for its product by advance demand draft. It is expected that the agent provides the credit support to the buyer.
- Agents are not exclusive for Snow White and work for other paper mills also and normally play the mills against each other. They have a grip on the business and are reluctant to put the mill directly in touch with the buyers.
- There is always an uncertainty on the orders and the price which would be obtained on the orders—the company cannot plan its profits properly nor offer the best service to the end users so that they always ask for Snow White.

Discussion Questions

1. A company needs to know its customer base and their yearly requirements in order to decide the price, plan quantities, and the profitability. If SW does not know who is buying their products, which variety and in what quantity, how can they plan their sales and profitability? Nor can SW develop loyal customers who assure regular sales.
2. How can you help Snow White to become less dependent on the selling agents and plan its sales and profitability better? How can they plan their customer service efforts?

Chapter 14

Channel Management

LEARNING OBJECTIVES

After studying this chapter, you will be able to:

LO 1 Understand how and why channel conflicts occur

LO 2 Outline ways of managing channel conflict

LO 3 Discuss about channel practices followed to resolve conflicts

LO 4 Identify some principles of channel management and channel policy

LO 5 Comprehend the way in which services use marketing channels

LO 6 Learn about some unique distribution channels

Sticky Adhesives (SA) is a top manufacturer of tile adhesives, joint fillers. It is present in many countries and has over 35 production units.

Some of the products of SA are mostly construction industry related adhesives and water proofing materials like:

- Tile and stone fixing adhesives
- Joint fillers-grouts
- Epoxies, masonry mortars, water proofing materials, chemicals and admixtures, wall levelling plastics.

Problem

The problem relates to one metro city with two exclusive distributors covering two territories with six salesmen between them. The distributors are meant to call on: (i) retailers and (ii) contractors / builders through their sales team. There are 1000 potential customers in that metro city.

Issues concerning distribution

- Poor coverage of customers by the distributors—retailers complain about poor attention/service
- There is an irregular follow-up with customers
- Lack of awareness of SA products among many potential retailers
- Unattended complaints on stock-outs
- SA extends only 15 days credit against 30 days given by competition
- There is a negative word-of-mouth publicity by retailers

In an informal survey of 250 outlets by the company, it was shocking to note that only 27 were aware of SA water proofing materials (one of their important products).

Impact of the Problem

Sales loss, new outlets not added, existing customers switching to competition brands and brand image loss.

The ASM, Mr Jai has spoken to the distributors earlier on this, but the situation has not improved. With proper coverage and regular sales, the distributors can easily make a ROI upwards of 40 percent on SA products.

In the previous chapter, we studied the aspects of channel design. In this chapter, we will try and understand some of the aspects of management of the channel system. Channel management is in three broad phases: (i) Use of power bases, (ii) Identifying and resolving channel conflicts, and (iii) Channel coordination

In the next few sections, we will discuss each of these aspects of channel management.

In the previous chapter, in the context of motivation of channels, we discussed the five power bases in marketing channels as enumerated by French & Raven. Here, we will see how these power bases are used in the context of implementing and managing channels.

The channel system consists of a number of players who are not all equally motivated to implement the ideal channel design as their expectations from the channel differ. It is the efficient use of the power bases that brings diverse channel partners in line for the implementation and effectiveness of the channel.

LO 1 Understand how and why channel conflicts occur

WHAT IS CHANNEL CONFLICT?

Channel conflict is a situation of discord or disagreement between channel members from the same marketing channel system. Conflict always has negative connotations and is driven more by feelings than facts.

Conflict is considered part of any social system. A channel system which brings together disparate entities to form a working relationship is also a social system. In such a system, if one entity in the relationship is behaving in a certain way or doing some things which will directly affect the performance, of another entity, or come in the way of its goals, a situation of "conflict" arises.

Conflict could be the result of: (i) each channel member wanting to pursue his own goals, (ii) each wants to retain his independence, and (iii) there are limited resources, which all of them want to utilize in the pursuit of their goals.

Conflict is a situation where one channel member perceives the behavior of another channel member to be impeding the attainment of its goals or its effective functioning. One school of thought believes that some functional conflict is necessary as only then will the channel perform effectively. Some features of conflicts:

- It is initially latent and does not affect the working of the channel members.
- It is not possible to detect till it reaches a level of disruption.

Stages of Conflict

Experts believe that conflicts can occur in four stages in any channel partnership. These are latent, perceived, felt and manifest. Each stage is progressively more severe than the earlier one. A brief description follows:

Latent

Some amount of discord exists but does not seem to be affecting the working of the channel partners nor affecting the achievement of the customer service objectives.

Perceived

This is the stage where the discord becomes noticeable and the channel partners become aware of the opposition. Even at this stage, the channel members take the situation in their stride and go about their tasks in a business-like manner. There is still no cause for worry, but the opposition has to be recognized.

These types of conflicts are also called: (i) attitudinal conflict where there are disagreements on roles, expectations, perceptions and communications with each other and (ii) structural conflicts which may relate to goals not matching, independence and lack of resources.

Felt

Here we are reaching the stage of worry, concern and alarm. Here the parties are trying to outsmart each other. This stage is also known as affective conflict as the channel gets affected by the discord between the players. Channel members feel upset that the other parties do not value their 'feelings' of discontent. The cause of the discord may not always be economical but also imputed to personal motives. This stage of the conflict has to be effectively managed and not let to escalate.

Manifest

This is the last stage where the conflict has escalated to a level which reflects the open antagonistic behavior of the channel partners who have a "dispute". There is an open confrontation. It could take the forms of openly opposing the initiatives taken by the other party thereby affecting the performance of the channel system. At this stage the resolution of the conflict may require an outside intervention. Even after the resolution of the conflict, it may permanently alter the chemistry of the channel system.

Reasons for Channel Conflict

There are many reasons for channel conflict. Some of these are listed below:

- Roles not defined properly. Roles can be called the expected behavior from the channel member.
- Resource scarcity—allocation between channel members of valuable resources seems unfair to some of them.
- Differences in perception on the business environment. Use of point-of-sale materials is an example. Another example is that of quantum of credit to be extended.
- Channel members have certain expectations from each other for the future also. If these expectations do not seem to be materializing, conflicts could occur.
- Decision domain disagreements—confusion of which channel member has to take decisions on which aspects of the operation. An industrial distributor may feel that price quote to a big account is his choice. The principal company may not agree.
- Goal incompatibility—the channel partners do not agree on objectives.
- Communication difficulties—misunderstanding or misinterpretation of routine business communication. Most such problems occur in the way business development is to be done.

As there are a number of channel members operating in marketing channel systems and each of them has different responsibilities, many of which are common tasks, there is always the chance of conflict. Some conflicts are easy to resolve and some are more difficult. Let us try and understand some of the reasons for conflict between channel partners.

Goal Incompatibility

The objectives of the company and its distributors may not always match. In situations of intense competition, the company would like the distributor to enhance his inputs to his customers like:

- Increase frequency of market visits.
- Provide a sales force for full market and outlet coverage.
- Extend more credit.
- Part with some of his margin to offer discounts and sell more.
- Keep more stocks.
- Work markets with ready stocks.

All these inputs may increase the sales of the company products but will reduce the profitability of the distributor. There is a clear goal incompatibility here between the firm and its channel partner.

Unclear Role Definition

The company appoints a channel partner to canvass business from all industrial prospects in the designated territory of the dealer. At times, in order to bag big orders from key accounts, the company may send its sales manager to directly call on these accounts and get business on negotiated terms. This will upset the dealer who is confused—he is not clear about his role. This conflict relates to role definition for the channel member. The example can be of engineering products, where companies have dealers, dealers cum service partners and service agencies all operating in major markets. There is a constant confusion as to who is to do what.

New Channel Partner

Addition of any new channel partner also causes channel conflict. A major pharma company may appoint a separate distributor to canvass business from hospitals and nursing homes leaving the existing, financially not so strong distributor with only chemist calls. This would create immediate conflict.

Target Fixing Exercise

Most frequent conflicts arise between the company field force and the channel partners as the field force tends to give inconsistent instructions to dealers. The monthly target fixing exercise is a constant source of conflict. It seems that the salespeople of the company always feel that the distributor can do much more than he normally does and hence fix optimistic targets. If the distributor incentives are linked to his achieving targets, there is an immediate source of conflict.

Extension of Credit

Extension of credit to customers is another problem area. The distributor thinks that he is more knowledgeable of his customers and knows whom to extend credit to. At times, the salespeople may force him to extend credit to an apparently big customer not knowing his past credit record. The distributor feels that the company is dictating terms on how he should run his business and resists.

Multiple Distributors

Companies cannot legally define the territories of their distributors. At times, when there are more than two distributors in the same town, there is the problem of selling in each other's designated territories and this is a constant source of conflict. One dealer may even offer better terms to the customer in the other territory than his own, creating a further conflict among the customers also.

Difference in Perception

The marketing and salespeople in the company are always optimistic of the sales volumes as they have been planning for it. They try to 'force' this enthusiasm on the distributors or stockists to persuade them to stock more. The distributors may want to watch the results before committing more working capital. The conflict of perception arises between them.

Loss of Opportunity

In the case of exclusive dealers or distributors of companies, their fortunes are dependent on the company products doing well. They do not have a choice to look at alternatives. If the business of the company does not do well and the dealer sees other good opportunities passing him by, he gets concerned. This loss of opportunity could be a conflict.

Clash of Interest

As clash of interest is conflict, it can occur between different channel partners whenever some of them feel that they have been denied certain benefits compared to another channel member. Most of the time, the conflicts can arise with the set of channel members on contract with the company in some manner like the sales force, the distributors, C&FAs and others. These conflicts can be managed and controlled. Conflicts with the trade partners like freelance wholesalers and retailers may not be easy to resolve and the concerned trade partners may stop doing business with the company.

Channel Conflict in Hybrid Channels

Hybrid channels have already been explained in Chapter 13.

There are some areas where channel conflict can arise in hybrid channels. Some of these are as follows:

- A company agrees to a credit sale to the key account for payment after 60 days. The distributor is asked to make this sale but gets only 30 days from the company.
- The company's salespeople sell to the key account and agree on delivery twice a week, which the distributor may not like as his distribution cost is affected.
- The price agreed by the company for a direct sale customer is lower than that for the rest of the customers serviced through the channel. This is the most common cause of conflict between the brick and mortar and the electronic sales on the internet.
- Company's salespeople make the sale and collect the payment whereas the distributor is only to deliver the product to the customer.

Types of Channel Conflict

Type of Conflict	What Happens?
Hybrid channels	Producers and retailers selling to the same customers
Horizontal conflict	Occurs between channels at same level—like distributors who stray into each other's designated territory
Vertical conflict	Channels at two different levels get into this kind of conflict. Frequently it is a domain or perception conflict. For example, a C&FA who despatches more goods to a distributor.

Examples of Channel Conflict

Channel conflict arises out of discord/disagreement either between the channel principal and the channels or between channel members themselves. Some examples of the differences which can arise are given as follows:

Difference Arising Out of	Example
Understanding of objectives	Producers think of long-term profits but channels look at short-term gains.
Customer service goals	Producers deal with key accounts directly and agree on delivery to three different locations which may not be acceptable to the channel partner.

(Contd.)

Difference Arising Out of	Example
Product focus	Channels prefer to invest in and sell only fast moving products. A manufacturer is interested in selling the entire product range including slow movers.
Perception	Keeping a specified inventory by the channel partner is insisted on by the producer so that market opportunities are not lost. Channel member would like to buy just-in-time.
Compensation or margins	Margins never seem to be adequate to the channel partners. Companies should focus on ROI and not just on margins.
Domain—territory coverage	Channel partners stray into others' territory or service their customers.

Competition and Conflict

It is necessary to understand the difference between the two terms. Competition is any behavior which is objective or target driven. It is always indirect and impersonal. Competition is healthy. Conflict is direct behavior and is opposing in nature. It is more personal. Conflict could be damaging.

Channel conflict is generated when the actions of any channel member come in the way of the entire channel achieving its objectives. It has been seen that channel conflicts occur basically for three reasons:

- Goal conflict—the understanding of the objectives of various channel members is different.
- Domain conflict—the channel members understand their responsibilities and authorities differently.
- Perception conflict—the channel member's understanding of the marketplace is different and hence the actions they propose do not match.

In all these cases, there is a mismatch in the way the channel members act and this can result in conflict and affect the achievement of the overall goals of the channel. The sales managers, who manage the channel, need to first identify the sources of the channel conflict and then take action to resolve the channel conflict.

The channel manager could use one or a combination of the channel powers mentioned later to resolve the channel conflicts.

Example of a Major Telecom Operator

Problem

- Fake sales of SIM cards by field sales executives—SIM cards opened, activated, not used further
- High cost of rural coverage
- Low ARPU—average revenue per user in rural and not picking up

Solution

- Separate urban and rural agents to enrol subscribers
- Key Performance Indicators given to field sales executives and agents: (i) number of SMS activated (ii) period of activation—minimum 2 months survival period (iii) SIM renewals to match SIMs in operation except genuine drop-outs

(Contd.)

- Incentives for meeting KPIs in rural
- SMS tracking of FSEs, daily reports, training
- Rural retailers identified
- *Chottu* (small) recharge cards—₹10, 20, 30

Results

- Fake SIM card sales came down
- Productivity of FSEs and agents improved

LO 2 Outline ways of managing channel conflict

WAYS OF MANAGING CHANNEL CONFLICT

Companies need to make efforts to quickly resolve channel conflicts before they seriously impact customer service. With the experience of handling different kinds of channel conflicts which may occur, various ways of containing and managing channel conflict effectively have been developed. We will discuss these methods here.

Channel Coordination

While channel conflict exists as long as channels are in operation, the sales manager has to ensure that the channel system he is operating is well coordinated. What does this mean?

A channel system is said to be well coordinated if each channel member understands his role correctly and performs it to help the entire system to achieve its customer services objectives.

In a coordinated channel, therefore,

- the interests of all the channel members are protected
- the actions of all channel members are in line with the overall objectives of the channel
- the channel flows are streamlined to deliver the customer service objectives as desired by the end customers

Channel coordination is an ongoing effort keeping in mind the customer requirements, the way the markets and competition behave and the strengths and weaknesses of the channel partners.

In the next few sections we will discuss the aspects of channel power, channel conflict and channel coordination in more detail.

Use of Channel Power

Power is a part of any channel network. All channels consist of a number of players who are dependent on each other and it is the power equations between them that keep them working together to achieve the channel objectives.

We have seen in the previous chapter that there are basically five types of power—reward, coercion, referent, legalistic, and expert power (French and Raven). The other two aspects of power—competition, and support are not discussed here. The extent of dependence of one part of the channel on the other part decides the most appropriate power base that operates. We need to understand some aspects of this dependence of channel members in detail.

Example of a company selling *paan* masala products

Problem

Distributors meant to sell to wholesalers and retailers in designated markets. They used to sell in excess quantities to wholesalers who tend to hoard the fast moving products and create an artificial shortage in the market.

This resulted in:

- Wholesalers selling at higher prices to retailers reducing their margins
- Retailers started selling above MRP to consumers stating that there was a product shortage
- Hoarding resulted in product quality deterioration

Solution

Company created a limited number of super-distributors who could be better managed with the limited number of salespeople employed.

Most of the earlier distributors became sub-distributors under these SDs. They did not mind as the product had a good demand in the market. All channel partners were given specific targets and stock supplies to match these and not more.

Focus was shifted to retail distribution with closer supervision. Penalty of losing the channel partnership if any irregularities noticed acted as a deterrent.

Managing International Distribution Channels: Clara Lu, Trade Decko—Expert View 1

1. Choosing the right market for the company products—will benefit the company. Prior research required—ability to communicate in a foreign language clearly.
2. Local logistical concerns to be understood—decide between local retailers or online. In either case, physical reach to be defined.
3. For selling online to international markets—ship goods overseas direct to the customers—insurance, lost goods and international freight.
4. Distribution to international retailers—delivery, collection of payments, communication, lack of transparency are some issues to be understood and managed.
5. Managing multiple currencies and risk of currency fluctuations to be managed. Companies have started using cloud-based inventory management and sales management systems. Companies also have the advantage of advanced international shipping services.

Power is defined as "the ability to influence the actions of channel members". This has to be understood as:

- Some channel members have the ability to influence others in the channel system.
- This influence is necessary for the overall better performance of the system in delivering customer service levels.
- The channel members who are being 'influenced' are willing to act in situations when they normally would not have acted in that manner.
- "Power" is the instrument of such an influence.

Power normally gives a feeling of one party exploiting another to its own advantage. Exercising power in any situation is misunderstood as force or pressure. However, in the context of managing distribution channels, it should be taken in a value adding sense even if the type of power exercised is coercion.

One example is the need for company distributors to extend credit to retailers in the market place. While companies do not extend credit to their distributors, they insist that the distributor extend credit in the market. While this may look like use of pressure tactics, in the interest of the distributor and the company business, the distributor falls in line with this instruction.

For example, in the past bicycle manufacturers used to almost give the complete bicycle to the dealer to sell. The dealer only had to add a few optional accessories of interest to the buyer and then sell it to him. The situation has changed today. Most of what the dealer gets is sub-assemblies of the bicycle in boxes. He has to assemble the full basic bicycle at his end before selling it to the buyer. The optional accessories are in addition. Some of the older dealers may not take kindly to this additional "work" they have to do to sell a bicycle. The consumer gets a feeling of a "customized" bicycle and feels happy that the bicycle has been built to his specifications. If the bicycle manufacturer is a market leader, the dealer would reluctantly agree to this condition as he wants to retain this important and prestigious dealership.

Some of the situations where the exercise of power becomes necessary are:

- All the channel members are dependent on each other to deliver the customers the service they expect.
- Helping the entire channel system gives the feeling to some of the channel partners that others may be making more margins at their cost. There is no ready willingness to fall in line with the system objectives.
- Each channel member is in business to maximize his own profits. He is less worried about the profitability of the whole channel system from the manufacturer to the end consumer. He feels total system profitability does not benefit him.

This focus on individual profitability affects the thinking on cost factors like inventory holding, extending credit or running promotions as these are partly financed by channel margins and are all areas where the channel members do not have the same thinking.

In any relationship there is an element of dependence. This dependence benefits the partners. Where it does not help, they start looking for other partners. Channel members' dependence on each other is based on the benefits (usefulness) they can derive from the dependence and whether there are alternatives possible (indispensability) in case any dependence becomes less beneficial at any time.

Channel members (for example distributors) consider themselves important (that the company is dependent on them) and powerful, but this perception of power has not much value if the company can find alternatives (other distributors willing to work for them) to replace them. Here, both the factors of usefulness and indispensability are at work.

A good example of two companies once again getting together to share resources and channels of distribution is that of the Gujarat Co-op Milk Marketing Federation (owners of Amul brand) and the National Dairy Development Board (owners of the Safal brand). This cooperative strategy has always been the strength of the milk sector.

Exhibit 14.1

AMUL: Streamlining Receipts and Payment Systems

- 54 sales offices, 6000 dealers, 1 million retailers, 3.5 million milk producers and 1 billion customers
- Milk purchase from farmers: paid at POD: 80 percent in cash
- Distributors / retailers paid by post-paid cheques + limited electronic payments
- Branch level collection and reconciliation of accounts became complicated – massive administration overheads + high operating costs + risks of bounced cheques

Solution

- Tied up with BNP Paribas: (i) for improving cheque clearing process (ii) facilitate electronic payments (iii) distributor to use mobile banking (iv) facilitate direct debit
- BNP Paribas: (i) outsourcing cheque management (ii) e-receipt solutions—reconciliation (iii) inter-bank mobile payment device (iv) direct debits through NACH: National Automated Clearing House

Results

- Improved collection process
- Improved operational efficiency and control—collection speeded

Source: Company published information.

There are some simple methods of assessing the usefulness (beneficial nature) and the indispensability (alternatives not possible). Usefulness would be the list of benefits one channel partner provides to its principal (or the reverse also). Indispensability would be to look at the competition which may be willing to take the position of the channel partner. A combination of the usefulness and the sense of indispensability is the effect of the dependability and a starting point for deciding the appropriate power source to be used in the relationship.

How does one decide about the existence of such dependence?

- How important is the business of the principal to the channel member? This could be measured by the percentage contribution to the business of the channel partner (for example, 100 percent revenue of an exclusive distributor would be from the company using him and hence he is 100 percent dependent on the company to continue to be in business).
- The channel member has always been the best channel partner possible. If the company finds that the alternatives it can consider to replace the distributor in the market are all inferior to him, the company becomes more dependent on him. Of course, no company would embark on this exercise if the existing partner is doing so well.
- Consistent good performance of the company in the past. If the distributor finds that the company products are continuously doing well in the market, his dependence on the company gets stronger. For example, you only have to talk to a Maruti dealer or a HUL distributor to understand this.

- All new product and pack launches in the past have been successfully (in terms of results) handled by the channel member. The company cannot afford to even antagonize such a partner.
- The customers—wholesalers, retailers and institutions depend entirely on the channel partner (a distributor for example) to work in their best interests even within the working parameters specified by the company. Such a channel partner is indispensable for the company and its customers as well.

Example of a Direct Marketer Tupperware: Channel Conflict Issues

Tupperware is a multi-national company selling storage and containment products—kitchen and home—directly to its consumer through their sales consultants.

Products

Plastic bowls, storage containers, SS cookware, fine cutlery

In some countries, lifetime guarantee given but not permitted in India. Direct marketing to consumer by TW consultants who are rewarded free products based on sales.

TW member of Indian Direct Selling Association (IDSA)—cannot use online stores of e-commerce. The company is not permitted to use any other channels also.

Problem

Some consultants, salespeople and of TW started selling on online sites and retail outlets—offered at discounts of 40 percent, whereas consultants given only 24 percent. Consultants felt betrayed.

This practice violated IDSA guidelines. Violation of code of conduct cases filed. Sales consultants started giving up their support to this business.

Solution

- Errant partners were fired.
- Advised e-commerce sites not to accept TW products for sale.
- Government requested to issue clear guidelines.

Source: Company published information

Five Sources of Power

These have been identified by French and Raven as: rewards, coercion, expertise, legitimacy and reference.

Briefly, each of these is described below:

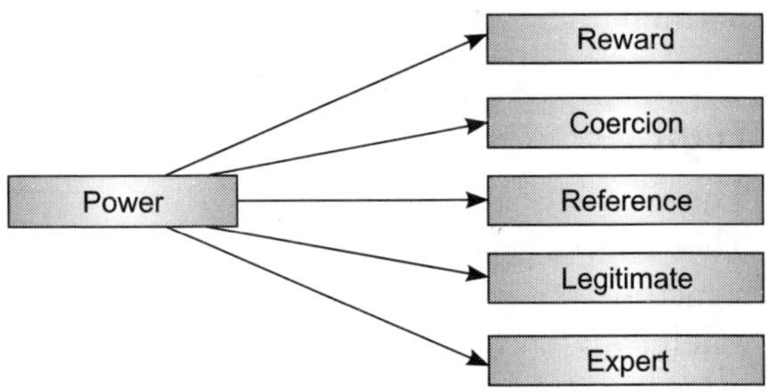

Fig 14.1 **The Five Sources of Power**

Rewards

Reward is a benefit given to a channel member for him to conform his behavior in line with the system. The reward could be financial or otherwise (recognition, for example). These could be:

- Incentives on achieving sales targets,
- Best distributor award in the annual sales conference.

The reward power is the most popular in the administration of marketing channels. However, it should not be used too often as otherwise it will be taken for granted and expected always.

Coercion

Coercion power is the hint of punishment for the channel member if he does not fall in line with the requirements of the channel principal. This disincentive could again be economical or non-economical. This could be:

- Withholding of incentive payments if the infrastructure promised by an industrial distributor is not built up.
- Pushing the distributor on purchases through demand drafts against earlier permission to purchase on cheques.

Use of coercive power even once in the channel system develops distrust in the channel partners and the relationship may never be strong again. Of course, if the channel partners have the maturity to understand the necessity of the principal having to resort to the use of this power, the one instance can also strengthen the relationship.

Expertise

Expert power is based on the special knowledge that the channel principal may have which is of particular benefit to the channel partners. For example:

- HUL has spent a lot of time and effort to develop an efficient supply chain system to reach the products faster to the markets at optimum cost. Distributors of HUL naturally would value this expertise.
- Handling institutional business and modern retail formats requires special knowledge of these customers. Companies, which have developed this knowledge over time, will help the customers and their channel partners like C&FAs.

It is obvious that expert power gets developed over a period of time and may require investments in time, effort and even financial terms. Only the results obtained will convince the channel partners of the "expertise". The channel partners develop trust in the expertise. Secondly, any particular aspect of the expertise is not permanent. After some time, the channel partners take them for granted and expect more of it. The channel principal has to make efforts to keep renewing the expertise continuously.

Legitimacy

The name suggests it all. This power emanates from contracts or agreements usually in writing. These contracts clearly define the parameters of behavior and action expected from each of the signatories to the contract and gives rights for them to enforce the behavior or action in case of a default. For example:

- The contract may stipulate that the distributor will cover the markets with ready stocks.
- The contract may state that for an industrial distributor he will give a 30-day credit period for collection of payments from all orders above a certain rupee value.

The source of legitimate power started from operating norms and values. Norms and values develop historically and become standards of behavior, which are expected even if not given in writing. For example, if the market gets a 15-day credit historically, it is expected that a new company entering the market will honor this practice. Over time, when the channels became larger with more channel partners, it was necessary to standardize some of these practices by clearly stating them in the form of contracts. If HUL has over 4000 distributors they have to be working on a standard contract rather than the varieties of traditions that may be prevailing in all the markets in which they operate. Again, it was a known practice in Brooke Bond that no credit was to be extended to the market and all sales was only against cash. This was an unwritten rule but strictly followed and became an operating norm in due course. Legitimate power is the most objective of all the powers between the channel partners.

Reference

This power stems from sheer association. A principal may be considered as the industry gold standard and the channel partners associated with this principal feel proud to be part of his distribution organisation and may exhibit behavior and actions which in the normal course cannot be expected of them. For example:

- Nestle has a reputation of giving the highest value brands to its consumers. If Nestle were to scout for a distributor in a new market, there would be several good prospects who would want to work with the company.

Exhibit 14.2

Reducing Reach for Cost Effective Distribution

Tasty Ice Creams is reviewing its distribution network in a particular geography. The break-up by category in this geography was impulse small packs 60 percent, large family packs 30 percent and parlors just 5 percent. Tasty operated premium ice cream parlors and had developed over 300 flavors.

At the time of the review, Tasty had franchisees running these 127 ice cream parlors in about 70 A, B and, C category towns. Each parlor was in size between 1500–1800 sq. ft. This operation had resulted in high overhead and logistics costs and forced Tasty to sell ice creams at high prices. It was clear that Tasty could not do well with this kind of arrangement.

Tasty decided to revise its distribution strategy and took the following action:

- It eliminated its network of parlors from all C category towns. They dropped the number of towns to about 40 and parlors to about 120 franchisees.
- Store sizes were reduced to about 300 sq.ft.
- They decided to get into institutional business by getting key account customers like star hotels. This segment started yielding about 30 percent of this business.
- They created all parlors in A grade cities into high ambience stores. All other stores were converted into ice cream kiosks.
- Tasty started selling pre-packed cups in organized retail shops. This included shop-in-shop counters.
- Results were very encouraging—sales improved, costs dropped and the business became profitable.

- If Vijay Sales has established itself as an outstanding consumer durables retail chain, even well-known international brands like LG or Samsung would want to be present heavily in Vijay Sales outlets.

Referent power helps in companies being selective in the channel partners they would like to work with. It gives the dominant channel partner with the right reputation, the choice of choosing his partners. Again, this referent power can only be developed over a long period of time with a lot of hard work.

In reality, the powers do not operate in isolation but in combinations to get more impact for the influencer. The power bases are also classified as coercive (coercive and reward) and non-coercive (legitimate, reference and expert). If any channel member or principal is able to provide all the five power bases to its channel partners, it is the ideal channel, but difficult to achieve. Once the power bases on offer by competition seem better, the channel partners start looking elsewhere for better bargains.

Countervailing Power

It is not that the channel principal or one of the channel partners has the power advantage over the others in the channel. Many times, the channel member may have some influence on the principal also. The typical example of a distributor and his company comes to mind. While the company may have legitimate, reward, coercive, referent and even expert power over its distributors who are to abide by its regulations, even the distributor, in the market in which he operates can have referent and expert powers over his own customers and this is equally valuable to the company. Again it boils down to the question of interdependence of channel members. This power is aptly called countervailing power.

The role of this dependence in channel relationships is very critical as it reduces confrontation and improves cooperation for the overall good performance of the channel system. In this context, experts use the terms fairness, solidarity, no exploitation, no blocking and equitable opportunities as some of the characteristics of such harmonious relationships.

However, the picture is not always rosy. At times, the relationships seem to exploit the weaker partners. We have seen the fate of ancillary units set up in support of major public sector enterprises close to them and having them as the only customers. The ancillaries did well as long as the principal did well. Their resources were tied up with the production for their principals only. The relationship was one of interdependence as narrated above with both the principals and the channel partners having power bases of their own. When the business of the principals started declining, it affected the ancillaries even more than it did the principals. They were not prepared for any other business and were stranded. Many of them had to just close shop when orders started drying up. This is one of the reasons that distributors shy away from being exclusive for any single company unless it is a company like HUL, P&G, Nestle, L&T or Maruti.

To summarize, channel members take time to build power. Once having acquired the power, they would do well to use it carefully to support their objectives and also protect themselves against unnecessary conflict.

Relationship Marketing and Distribution Channels

Barton AWeitz (University of Florida) and Sandy A Jap (MIT), Journal of the Academy of Marketing Sciences, fall 1995—Expert View 2

Three control mechanisms include:

1. ***Authoritative:*** One party in the relationship uses its position or power to control the other party; imbalance in resources.
2. ***Contractual:*** Agreement defines responsibilities; incentive based on performance; territory exclusivity (franchisees), activities, policies, procedure, rewards.
3. ***Normative:*** Shared set of implicit principles or norms.

Norms = firm's organizational culture; shared beliefs of employees

Bilateral = accepted by both

- Unilateral or bilateral control: Either one or both parties
- Use of multiple control mechanisms

Steps in Managing Channel Conflict

There are four steps to be taken to manage conflicts. These are enumerated as under:

- Understanding the nature of the conflict and measuring its intensity
- Tracing the source of the conflict
- Finding out the consequences of the conflict
- Strategy and action plan for resolution

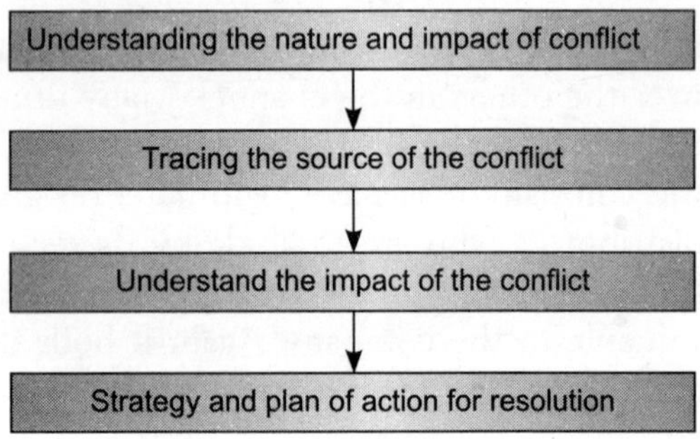

Fig. 14.2 Four Stages for Conflict Resolution

Nature and Impact of Conflict

This step starts with identifying that a conflict exists and then understanding how serious the conflict is. There could be several steps in this process:

- To list down the major issues which have arisen between the parties concerned for the last 3 to 6 months and could be a source for concern. In a company–distributor relationship, some of these issues could be infrastructure provided by the distributor, his coverage, credit extension and the settlement of claims by the company.
- Some of these issues are not serious and can be routine, and get tackled routinely. There may only be a time delay. It would be necessary to rank the issues in terms of their importance to the relationship and the achievement of the joint goals. The ranking can be from very important to trivial.
- All issues are not likely to arise at the same time or even with the same frequency. Apart from listing the issues and prioritizing them in order of importance, it is also necessary to check how frequently have these issues surfaced in the review period and what are the views of both parties on the issues. If coverage by a distributor is an important issue and it has been brought to the notice of the distributor by the salespeople four times in the last 6 months, it is a major and urgent issue.

- The next step would be to assess the perception of each party on the issue and how strongly each feels about what is being expected from him about the issue. Here we are trying to assess the seriousness of the conflict to decide the kind of solution which is likely to work. In the example given above, if the distributor feels that his coverage of the markets is adequate but the company feels otherwise, there is a mismatch that needs to be addressed.
- The last step is an inventory of all the issues ranked in importance, frequency of occurrence and the views of the parties concerned on what really seems to be the problem.

This final list is to enable developing a way out of the situation giving more importance to the serious issues which may become "manifest" conflicts if not resolved now.

Tracing the Source of the Conflict

Some of the causes of conflict could be broadly identified as:

- The objectives set by the channel members for themselves may not match the overall requirement of the channel system—clash of goals.
- Channel members may "read" the business/market situation differently.
- The channel members understanding of their domain areas where they feel they have the independence of operations.

Some of the methods used to find out if conflicts exist include:

- Checking with channel members at regular intervals about what they think of each other's performance.
- What in their opinion are some of the irritants of the system? How successfully have these been tackled in the past?
- Salespeople continuously assess the performance of the channel members and can sense latent conflicts. They also keep making efforts to resolve these early.

❍ **Clash of Goals** Clash of goals or goal divergence seems to be the most common. For example, the distributor may feel that he has done a good job if he has covered all the potential outlets in his territory and sold fast moving products to them. This goal is at variance with the channel principal (the company) who feels that he has to cover all outlets (not just potential ones) and sell all products at each outlet (not just fast moving goods). The objective of the distributor here may be to maximize his profitability whereas the objective of the principal is 100 percent coverage and distribution.

❍ **Different Perceptions** Apart from the clash on goals there is also the situation of the perception of aspects of doing business starting with the targets. The perception could vary between the channel members about their role in the channel system, product features, the customers, and the competition. This could be because of the relative difference in attention they pay to the aspects of the business. The distributor would look at the customers more closely and may not have a clear idea of the way the products have been developed. His perception is from selling to the customers' angle and the manufacturer, while wanting the attention from customers would also focus on the products he has so carefully developed. The manufacturer is very clear on what he expects the product to do. A good process of constant communication between the channel partners can help handle the situation better.

❍ **Unclear Domain** The third area of discord mentioned earlier was the definition of the domain as perceived by each channel principal and his channel members. Some members may feel that some others are not pulling their weight in the achievement of the channel objectives. In industrial products, after-sales service support becomes one such bone of contention. Some of the company dealers believe that servicing of the equipment is the responsibility of the company and the dealer only has to sell the product to the customer and train him how to use it. The company may think that the dealer is also required to service the products post-sale and the dealer has to develop the infrastructure and the expertise for this. It is also a fact that in order to overcome the possible domain conflict on such an important issue, the company sets up a parallel chain of authorized service centres. Even if the dealer agrees to take the responsibility for the servicing domain, there could still be the discord on how much spares the dealer has to carry or whether he should carry them at all.

❍ **Market Domain Conflicts** The conflict regarding who should cover what markets is the most frequent among channel members and keeps getting resolved and surfacing regularly. The conflict could be between:

- similar channel members in the same system,
- between the channel principal and his channel partners,
- channel members at different levels in the same system, and
- channels outside the regular system.

Let us briefly look at each of these:

Similar Channel Members This conflict arises between channel members with similar roles and responsibilities. This is also known as horizontal channel conflict. For example, let us look at a company which is operating a set of five distributors in a city each of whom has been given some territories to cover. The usual problem is that some of the distributors stray into each other's territories to sell products. Or, at times, a wholesaler in one territory visits a distributor in another territory and buys the goods. The problem gets compounded if the non-designated distributor gives some kind of discount on the sales.

Channel Principal and his Channel Members Again, this is a common occurrence. The company salespeople, who meet a major key prospect in the territory of the distributor, would promise some additional benefits to get the business from the prospect and convert him into a key account. This benefit would normally not be available for the distributor to that extent. The problem gets compounded if the salespeople promise the big customer a 15-day credit and the distributor has to supply the products on these credit terms. This problem can also arise with multiple channels in the same markets—like distributors for retail selling and company salespeople for institutional business.

The other serious area of discord happens when a company introduces a new distributor in a territory, which already has a few distributors. The existing distributors feel capable of covering all the markets and institutions, but the company feels that they need an additional distributor to take care of the additional potential. The concern gets worse if the new distributor territory is carved out with new areas and some cuts in the areas of existing distributors.

The third area of conflict arises if the company has a different set of distributors for different sets of products and all of them call on the same wholesalers and retailers to sell their products. Each distributor would like to maximize the sales for his products. The retailer has limited funds from which he has to buy all the company products. If the distributor visiting him first takes away a major chunk of the funds, the sales of other products of the same company brought by another distributor of the same company, may suffer. Conversely, if the retailer has a problem with a distributor of one set of products, he may not cooperate with other distributors of the company also (for no fault of theirs). This is also called multi-channel conflict.

It could also happen that the company sells the products from its own exclusive outlet in a market with other outlets also stocking the company products. Even if the company sells on an electronic channel, there could be competition between the company channels and the others. The company uses these multiple channels to increase the coverage and market shares.

Channel Members at Different Levels Here, the channel members are working for the same products in the same territory. In their eagerness to get business, some of them may act in a manner that hurts the other channel member. The common example is that of wholesalers who buy large quantities on discounts and then sell the same products undercutting the company prices. The distributor who has sold the large quantity to a wholesaler in his territory finds that in the next week, the wholesaler is re-selling the goods to the retailers in the same territory at a price at which the distributor cannot sell. Unscrupulous salespeople at times encourage such a practice to achieve their targets in one period. This is also known as Vertical Channel conflict.

The most common problem between distributors and C&FAs relates to the products the C&FA dispatches to the distributor. At times, the C&FA does not have a particular product indented by the distributor, and in order to ensure a full truck load dispatch, after checking with the salespeople, the C&FA loads the additional quantities of a product the distributor did not even order. The C&FA immediately deposits the distributor's cheque into the company account. This becomes a major issue.

Channel Members Outside the System This problem can also arise with channel members at different levels as explained above. At times, the distributor has a major wholesaler in his territory who may not be buying from him (it could be that the wholesaler was also a prospective distributor, but did not get selected and has decided not to buy from the official distributor). Such a wholesaler may buy from another major territory nearby and sell at discounted prices in the territory of the designated distributor. If the wholesaler buys from a cash-and-carry outlet like Metro, he can still create problems on retail distribution. In pharmaceutical distribution you hear about discounted goods from major hospital chemist shops getting into the market at lower prices than permitted.

The grey market used to be a major source of imported electronic goods in India till some years back. These outlets used to eat into the genuine sales of good electronic brands produced in the country. With liberalization, this problem has almost vanished.

How Conflicts Escalate

It is a known fact that as long as a set of diverse business people operate in a channel system, there is bound to be some conflict. Like it was mentioned earlier, it is acceptable to have such conflicts as long as they are in the early stages of latent and perceived conflicts and do not escalate into manifest conflicts. It is also a known fact that when a conflict has escalated into a dispute, which has got resolved amicably, there is always an element of "distrust" which is built into the system. It is never known when this shimmering discontent and mistrust of fellow channel members may ignite into another problem. It is, therefore, ideal to identify the conflicts at the earlier two stages and resolve them.

One of the ways channel members use to control each other is to use the power of coercion. Coercion is nothing but a channel principal for example, telling his channel partner—"you better do what I say or otherwise . . . " The first reaction from the target is always one of retaliation. Retaliation transforms to action depending on the 'independence' of the target.

Anyway, like it was mentioned earlier, coercion as a power tool has to be used only in exceptions as it is not best for developing channel relationships. Channel systems work well with good relationships between the members in the long run. The power of coercion can be used effectively only when the channel partner using this power on another is himself doing an excellent job of what is expected of him and is a role model.

Developing a Distribution Channel Strategy: Ian Linton, Studio D—Expert View 3

Choice of channels: each channel gives different options to deal with prospects and customers; strategy must also incorporate the right level of control and support.

Reach: provide existing coverage of the territories; Internet is a choice in areas where a physical distribution network does not exist.

Cost: comparison of direct and indirect cost; resources for processing, stockholding, delivery, invoicing and customer service need to be kept in mind.

Contribution: access to additional customer base with no additional S&M costs; distributors and dealers provide the local market knowledge.

Support: modify performance and identify support needs. Marketing support programs for different channels—advertising and marketing campaigns to drive business to your channel partners. Training programs for channel partners and their salespeople are required at regular intervals.

Customer Service: large customers or key accounts—direct by company salespeople; channel partners to deal with a large number of small customers.

Managing Channel Conflict

As long as companies do business with channel partners who are anyway outsiders, and not part of the company, channel conflicts keep happening. It may not be possible to ever create a situation of no conflict at all. It should, however, be possible to resolve conflicts so that relationships between channel partners develop for their mutual benefit. Some of the ways of managing conflict are:

- At times of adversity or difficulty which the firm and its channel partners are facing (like a dominant competitor who is suddenly very active), they tend to unite together with a common purpose and goal of defeating the adversary and retaining their market shares. This collective goal setting could be a good way of managing conflict even in normal circumstances. The targets or goals can be planned and agreed mutually with a clear reasoning why they need to be achieved.

- Participation in the planning process is sometimes extended formally to the channel partners. They then feel that they have been a "partner" in the decision-making and are more likely to abide by it. For example, when a new product/brand or pack is launched, the distributors are invited for a launch meeting to tell them more about the launch and its objectives. During this meeting their views are sought and together with them, spot targets are set for each of them to be achieved in the first few months of the launch.
- A number of companies make their management trainees to work in the business of the channel partner as part of the training process. This creates a confidence in the channel member and also gives an opportunity for the company to understand how the channel partner operates. For example, a management trainee in an automobile company may work in the dealer showroom and service centre as part of his training.
- If the conflict does not get resolved easily, the company will then have to resort to: (i) diplomacy or relationship, (ii) mediation by a third party, and (iii) arbitration. The last resort to resolve a dispute (conflict has now escalated into a dispute) is of course a legal recourse.

Focussed management of Industrial Channels: Mark Harvey—Expert View 4

Systematic Approach to Channel Optimization:

1. Identify the most profitable customer segments.
2. Select the strongest channel partners to serve these segments
3. Determine and implement the most optimum mix of marketing programs on which to focus limited resources
4. Fully exploit the internal channels of internet, direct sales force and the key account teams

Legal and Ethical Issues

Laws always safeguard the interests of the weaker partner in any dispute. The company dealers and distributors have protection under the law. While the company and its channel partners may want go the legal way only as a last resort, it is necessary to know some of the legal issues (earlier covered by the MRTP Act) and what they suggest by way of conflict resolution:

- Use of exclusive dealers by companies is not permitted. The company cannot bind the distributor from doing any business of his choice.
- Similarly, the company cannot formally designate the "territory" to be covered by a contracted channel member. This protects both the company (who can appoint more dealers in the same area) and the channel member who can sell in geography of his capability.
- Full-line forcing is not legally permitted. The company cannot force the dealer or a retailer that if he wants a popular product, he has to also buy a slow moving product.

- Termination of contracted distributors for poor performance is not easy even when it is mentioned in the contract/agreement. The cause has to be clearly established. Non-performance cannot be easily proved if the dealer challenges the target and the target setting process itself.

Most of these are also not permitted by the Competition Act 2002 which has replaced the MRTP Act.

Building Channel Relationships

Companies need to build long term strategic relationships with their channel partners for the benefit of both and reducing the likelihood of channel conflicts. As seen in an earlier chapter, one of the most effective ways of building long lasting and useful relationships with channel partners is to keep them motivated. Some of these motivational tools used by channel systems for motivation and avoiding channel conflicts are:

- For retailers, payments for shelf display space (Indian companies do this very effectively)
- Higher trade discounts than competition
- Higher margins for better distribution efforts measured in terms of coverage, distribution and productive calls
- Strong advertising, merchandizing and promotional support
- Support of field salespeople—particularly in achieving secondary sales
- Challenging sales targets and joint planning to achieve them
- Protect channel members' territories
- Develop high quality, innovative and distinctive products
- Assure unrestricted stock returns—quite a risky proposition
- Provide sales training to distributor salesmen
- Offer financial assistance—subsidies on distribution to new markets or rural markets
- Provide logistical support
- Channel members get a share of the margins on direct sales to institutions
- Online ordering facility
- Providing market research support—help with information which can make their selling effort easier
- Generate customer leads and pass on to channel partners
- Communicate promptly all crucial marketing related decisions
- Get the channel partners to give useful suggestions and implement some of them
- Capacity building in the channel members—training of channel members could be one such effort (Example: Operation Dronacharya of HUL to train salesmen of distributors)
- Incentives on sales and merchandizing achievements

Analyzing the Effects of Channel Management: Ian Linton, Studio D—Expert View 5

1. Enhancing the results from the channel by applying appropriate marketing, financial and training resources.
2. Measurement indices used for channel effectiveness: market share changes, sales volume achieved by each channel category, cost of reaching the market and level of customer satisfaction.

3. Market share to be measured at regular intervals like every 6 months
4. Cost of operations to be measured as cost + channel margins
5. Sales is measured in terms of growth by different channel categories
6. Customer satisfaction based on quality of services as perceived by customers

Principles of Channel Management

Channel management is in four steps:

1. The planning effort—setting the objectives.
2. The organization structure to deliver the customer service objectives—the people and the channel members and a clear definition of responsibilities.
3. Ability to control the channel—measuring progress towards the objectives and making course corrections.
4. Measuring performance for constant improvement. Performance is measured against a standard which is discussed and agreed by all concerned, capable of achievement with reasonable effort and time, focus on results and not on the manner of achieving results, flexible—has to take account of changing circumstances like competition, in line with the objectives of the firm—corporate objectives are the starting point for marketing objectives, is expressed in physical units (volume) or monetary terms (rupees).

Example of By-passing Intermediaries

It is the food companies like HUL, Tata Spices, Pepsi, ITC (remember e-Chaupal), etc. which started the practice first for sourcing their requirements of farm produce like fruits, vegetables, wheat and spices direct from the farmers bypassing the middlemen who used to take away the lion's share of margins with very little value addition. With middlemen there was also no assurance of consistent good quality. This good practice seems to only be growing with companies like Reliance, Godrej, and Bharti's Field Fresh also joining the bandwagon to go direct to the farmers for buying their requirements. These companies are also into guiding the farmers on getting better yields from their farm landholdings.

Disintermediation Suggested in Food Grains Distribution

In the early months of 2010, the prices of food grains in India had gone up, seriously affecting consumers. The Food Corporation of India (FCI) acquires the food grains from farmers by paying a Minimum Support Price (decided by the Government) to them and then the FCI sells the grain in bulk to the states at a price which is MSP plus storage and transportation costs. The states sell the food grains to traders through an auction system. The prices are likely to increase as a result of this process. It is being suggested that the food grains should be sold directly to government supermarkets like Kendriya Bhandars, Apna Bazaars and the Public Distribution System (ration shops) cutting out the traders and their margins. This revised distribution policy is expected to have a favorable price impact for consumers.

Channel Control

A word about control of the channels is to be discussed here. Some of the methods used to control channel members are:

- Signing a contract/agreement enforceable by law. The purpose is more to standardize procedure on products to be handled, territory and customers to be covered (Beat Plans), inventory to be maintained, market working norms, support which would be provided and payment terms.
- We have already seen the effect of using power bases to manage and control channel members. The use of power is guided by the degree of dependence of the channel members on each other.
- There is also a structure which is put in place to ensure controls. This structure includes reports, records and working within budgets for cost control.
- Lastly, the best way to ensure control is for the field managers of the company to work closely with the channel partners in the "market-place".

Channel control is required to optimize the performance of the channel system as the resources are better utilized and there is an element of compliance and cooperation between the channel members.

Experts (Bucklin's theory of channel control—"A Theory of Channel Control" by LP Bucklin, *Journal of Marketing,* 1973, pp. 37–47) mention a "zone of indifference" where compliance is complete and the channel members are willing to accept orders from the channel principal without questioning it. They accept the authority of the channel principal. The compliance continues till the benefits exceed the sacrifices the channel members may have to make for the compliance. Once the tolerance level is crossed (benefits do not any longer justify the sacrifices), the control weakens and conflicts arise. At this stage, increased control only induces the channel members subject to this control to look for more lucrative opportunities outside the current channel system.

It is necessary to understand as to who is a channel leader or channel principal. Obviously, he is the most influential of the channel members. In the case of a contracted channel, the channel principal is the manufacturer who has appointed the distributors. It is normally the largest player with the assets or the highest sales.

Channel leader is the organization which:

- decides the objectives of the channel,
- has to put together the resources to achieve the objectives,
- builds the channel system from scratch, and
- coordinates the activities of all the channel members.

Service within Reach

This is a good example of a firm which provides the services of a personal assistant on call. The firm is called Big Help. In the words of the founder, Mr Suresh Paryani—"we take away all the daily hassles that consume time and energy and let our customers concentrate on what is really important". The cost of the service is ₹4000 per month (about $90) and an assistant is assigned to the customer. The customers call up the designated assistants each time they want some work to be done. Each assistant handles five customers. Most common tasks performed include documentation, research, and coordination. The service started from March 2010 in Mumbai.

Vertical Management Systems (VMS)

In Chapter 10, we had discussed different kinds of management systems including VMS. A vertical management system does help in the control and management of channel systems. VMS is a network of vertically aligned and coordinated entities which work together as a system. This definition fits in a marketing channel quite well.

In an administered VMS:

- The channel members plan the distribution tasks together through the use of partnerships and alliances.
- The manufacturer or channel principal has a major influence on the rest of the channel members.
- The channel relationships are also formalized in contracts if necessary.

We have also seen that in a contractual VMS, there are different kinds of channel systems which are possible like:

- Retailer cooperative organisations—synergy through group buying, group advertising, record keeping and so on.
- Wholesaler sponsored voluntary chains—mutual cooperation for providing a range of services to members.
- Franchise systems—help expand reach without adding too much to costs.

Maximum control on the channel system is possible through a corporate VMS as the company owns and operates organisations in the distribution system. The implications for the channel here are:

- High level of control possible on the entire channel.
- Entry into desired markets is easier as the channel belongs to the firm.
- Control over how the product is sold at different levels.
- Protection of company and product reputations.

The disadvantages of a corporate VMS are in requiring large number of employees to manage the system and the higher levels of inventories required.

LO 3 Discuss about channel practices followed to resolve conflicts

PRACTICES FOLLOWED FOR CONFLICT RESOLUTION

The business has to go on successfully. If conflicts happen, they have to be accepted and resolved so that the channel continues to deliver superior customer service. There are several ways companies have developed, with experience, to resolve channel conflicts.

Conflict solutions can be standardized in environments where the principal is operating with channel members on contract to ensure fairness and equity. In instances where the conflict arises between channel partners who are not bound by contracts or agreements of any kind, the conflict resolution is guided by best past practice. Some of the channel conflict resolution methods are described in this section.

Examples include joint membership of trade associations, distributor councils, personnel exchange between channel partners and if none of this works, going to a third party mediator or arbitrator. Let us see if some of these methods work in the Indian context:

- Joint membership of trade associations could exist in engineering kind of industries where a principal and his channel partners may both be members of a chamber of commerce, but this may not be the right medium to help them resolve their conflicts.
- Distributor councils sound more like distributor unions in the Indian context and companies may never encourage this. We have seen the example of distributor associations in Kerala boycotting the sales of many FMCG company products to bargain for better margins. Obviously this kind of association is used as a medium of coercive power.
- Personnel exchange between channel partners can and does happen in the IT hardware, engineering, automobile industries where company personnel work with the distributors to develop selling skills and servicing capabilities. The distributor personnel may also get trained on the shop floor of the principals.
- Mediation can also be done through trade associations.
- The final stage of arbitration has a legal connotation and is the last resort.

All the above solutions can work in situations where there are contracted channel partners and not with independent channel members. For disputes with independent channel members like wholesalers, dealers, agents or even retailers, the problem has to be solved on a case to case basis by a dialogue between the parties to the discord.

Some of the other methods used for resolution of channel conflicts are:

- Sharing of information between channel partners can avoid conflicts. The risk is that normally confidential information may have to be shared.
- Exchanging personnel between channel partners.
- Working together for sharing of responsibility—the two channel members establish a separate channel between them to route information, support and any other requests to be made on each other. It is like a permanent third party mediator on the premises.
- Use of third parties for mediation or arbitration—only when the situation has gone out of control of the channel members involved.
- Clear rules of conduct to help build good relationships. The norms for behavior get established over a period of time. Following these rules by both parties helps prevent conflicts.
- Use of incentives and rewards—the most popular of all the conflict resolution methods is to offer financial or economic incentives. To make it a more negotiated settlement, the payments can be agreed to be paid on a certain performance agreed as part of the conflict resolution.
- Joint goal setting by the channel principal and its channel members. There is some risk in this approach as no channel member will voluntarily accept stretch targets.

- Direct interaction between channel members for joint problem solving. This happens all the time under the supervision of the salespeople managing the channel.

Styles of Conflict Resolution

Kenneth W Thomas has spelt out five kinds of conflict resolution styles (*Conflict and Conflict Management—Handbook of Industrial and Organizational Psychology*, edited by M D Dunnette, 1976).

They are explained further as under:

- Accommodation: a situation of complete surrender. One party helps the other achieve its goals without being worried about its own goals. Obviously this method strengthens the relationship. The emphasis is on full cooperation and could result in the other party also becoming flexible in its approach. If not handled properly, it could result in exploitation of the benevolent situation. On the other extreme, it can lead to exploitation of the party willing to be accommodative.
- Collaboration or problem solving: this route tries to maximize the benefit for both parties while finding a solution to the dispute—a win-win approach. This approach requires a lot of time and effort to succeed. Both sides should be prepared to share sensitive information for this approach to work.
- Compromise: a solution where both parties agree to give up some of their requirements and find a mid-way solution. Can only work with small and not so serious conflicts.
- Competition or aggression: this means being concerned about one's own goals without any thought for the others—a purely selfish style. Long term results could only be detrimental to the system.
- Avoidance: used by weak channel members. This can only happen where the relationship is not of much importance and the problem is postponed or discussion is avoided. As there is no serious effort on getting anything done, conflict is avoided.

The styles are a combination of assertiveness and being cooperative.

Example

At times, two competing companies enter into pacts called "co-opetition" or "controlled competition". This is to make sure that the suppliers, etc. do not exploit them both at the cost to the customer. This co-opetition could take the forms of joint purchase negotiations, sharing market information and vendor development. Recently one came across such an example between two automobile majors.

LO 4 Identify some principles of channel management and channel policy

CHANNEL POLICIES

Some of the aspects of channel management covered here have already been highlighted in Chapter 12 under Distributor Management. Some of these policies have been discussed here in the context of the entire marketing channels and not just "contracted" channel partners. The major aspects of channel policies relate to: (i) which markets to service, (ii) the customer coverage within these markets, (iii) pricing, (iv) product line to be handled, (v) selection of the right channel, (vi) termination of a channel membership and (vii) ownership of the channel. Let us discuss each of these aspects in this section.

Markets to be Serviced

Sales policy of any company whether selling FMCG, industrial products or services dictates that all markets with potential for doing business need to be serviced. Resource limitations prevent the same level of servicing for all markets. The sales manager "prioritises" his markets and devotes maximum channel power in the most potential markets.

For industrial products, the customers are normally located in clusters and it is easier to decide the market coverage for the dealers. In the case of consumer products and pharmaceutical products, the markets are spread widely including a vast rural market. For these kind of products, the frequency of market coverage is decided based on the importance or potential of the market and the prevalent competition. In either case, what competition does, decides the kind of market coverage most of the times. The market coverage plan is reflected in the beat plan of the channel partner.

Companies make sure that there is no overlap of markets between their contracted channel members like distributors, stockists, dealers or agents (as otherwise, this could be the primary reason for channel conflict).

Independent wholesalers and retailers normally service the market in which they are located. Except for institutions in the market they service, their entire sales happen from their own outlets—their customers come to them for purchases.

Customer Coverage

This is the second part of the beat plan. After deciding the list of markets to be serviced, it is necessary to decide the customers (wholesalers, retailers who buy for sale and institutions who buy for own consumption) who need calling upon and the frequency of call age. Even here, based on experience, the customers can be classified as A, B and C categories with service levels accordingly.

Basic rules on customer coverage include:

- Every customer has to be visited at least once a month.
- Every call on a customer has to be made productive.
- A customer cannot be visited by two distributors for the same products.

The owner of the distributor firm has to also visit the key customers personally apart from the visit by his salesmen.

For independent wholesalers and retailers there is no limitation on their customers. Every person who walks into their outlet is a customer.

Pricing

This is probably the most critical issue when dealing with channel partners whether they are on contract or independent. Like all businessmen, they want prices which are favorable to give them the highest margins. There is, however, a limit to the margins which can be provided as every such margin affects the end price for the product to be paid by the consumer. Most of the times, competition does decide the prices that can operate in the market.

The pricing mechanism for a consumer product works like this:

- The end consumer price is decided based on the company costs, margins expected and what the competition is doing for similar products. This is the MRP (maximum retail price) printed on the pack.
- The permitted retail margins are known and hence the price to the retailer can be worked out from the MRP.
- The retailer price also takes into account the margin to the distributor. If this permitted margin is deducted, the price to the distributor can be worked out. The company will sell the product to the distributor at this price and expects him to mark up the price to the retailer so that he can earn his margin. As mentioned earlier, the FMCG companies permit an ROI of about 30 percent for their distributors on their investments net of all expenses.
- The prices in the market with independent wholesalers and retailers also get affected by the trade promotions run by the companies. In the case of industrial products, however, the prices are negotiated and can vary between customers or even channel partners. Even for consumer durables, the discounts which companies operate can vary between dealers and so can the end consumer prices which may get influenced by competition.

Product Lines

The channel members in the market, who are independent wholesalers and retailers, decide on their own as to which product lines they want to promote. However, for contracted channel members like distributors and C&FAs, there is an unwritten rule that they will not work with competitive products once they have signed with a company for its products.

If the company has different categories of products like HUL—beverages and food products, soaps, detergents and personal products and ice creams, they would prefer to have different channel partners for each set of products. At times, it is not feasible to handle some of these products together—for example, a detergent product and branded wheat flour. Some products like ice creams need special cold storage and handling facilities, and hence need a different channel.

Rules on handling product lines through channels:

- Complimentary product lines through the same channel.
- All similar customers serviced through the same type of channel. In pharmaceutical for example, different channels may be used to cover doctors, hospitals and chemists.
- Products requiring special handling arrangements (like cold chains) to be distributed by channels capable of this.

- Separate channels may be used for special customers—like modern store formats or institutional business.

Selection of Channel Members

This has been covered in the context of wholesaling in Chapter 12. Companies have no choice in the use of channels already in the market like wholesalers, retailers, chemists, transporters, warehouse leasing companies, spare parts dealers for all equipment, hotels, and restaurants. The question of selection arises depending on the intensity of distribution and in case companies want to set up their own distribution network of C&FAs and distributors.

Companies, based on years of experience in the market place, have clearly defined parameters for selection of their channel partners. They apply these yardsticks among the prospects the salespeople shortlist in the market. For a new company starting its operations afresh, it is quite difficult to get good channel partners. They need to select from the crop available and develop them.

Termination of Channel Partners

This has been covered in the context of distributors in Chapter 12. Termination of a contracted channel partner is the most painful part of doing business with other parties. It is resorted to only when the partner is unable to meet the objectives of the company or has been caught in dishonest business practices.

Both sides discuss and decide that the relationship cannot continue. Both parties try and amicably settle the amounts due to each other as well as any statutory obligations to be completed. It has been mentioned earlier that the termination is normally handled orally by the salespeople.

Ownership of the Channel

Ownership does not just mean the investment in the business. It includes taking responsibility for developing the business of the channel principal who has contracted a channel member to work for it. It takes into account all the statutory obligations like abiding by various acts, sales tax implications, and so on.

Most of these obligations are specifically covered in a contract. However, there are unwritten rules of behavior (come into force by tradition and convention), which are also expected to be followed.

LO 5 Comprehend the way in which services use marketing channels

DISTRIBUTION MANAGEMENT FOR SERVICES

Service sector of the economy in India is twice the size of the manufacturing sector. An organization or individual offering a service will be more successful, if the services offered are exactly in line with customer demand and are presented in an appealing manner.

Services are distinguished by five characteristics. Any marketing channel used by service sector takes the following factors into consideration:

- They are intangible—they can only be felt. They cannot be easily distinguished by factors like visible features, style or performance characteristics.
- They are inseparable from their service providers—it is not possible to delegate the delivery to a third party. The services are tied to the provider of the service. Example, tailor, dentist, barber.
- They cannot be standardized—they have to be custom-made and delivered. Services are people intensive and can vary with the people providing them. They can also vary with the same person over time.
- Customers are involved in services to a great degree. They are required to define the extent of the services provided to them. Example, a client and a consultant or a doctor and his patient.
- They are perishable—they cannot be stored for delivery at a future date. Services cannot be produced and stored in anticipation of customer needs. Salvage value of an unsold service is zero.

Services are intangible. However, the service provider sometimes uses some image or object in association to make the service more tangible—LIC uses the symbol of two hands protecting a lamp with the slogan—*Yoga KshemamVahamyham*. Premium pricing or advertising can help customers visualize services in a more tangible manner. If the service is provided through a marketing channel it can be made to look more tangible (advertisements of slimming clinics).

The channel and the service provider are the same as the services are inseparable—dry cleaning, auto servicing, banks, and so on. The appearance, ambience created, atmosphere denote the quality of service provided—classy interiors of a bank may denote premium service. Even the people offering the services are trained to create the right impression. The product cannot make up for poor distribution like in the case of physical products—the service provider who is also the channel has to do a good job of delivery also.

Exhibit 14.3

Redington—A Successful Channel Partner

Redington, which is a top supply chain solution provider, is present in 24 countries with over 47000 partners. Its services support over 100 top companies in the Information Technology, Telecom, Consumer and Lifestyle products. It operates state-of-the-art automated distribution centers and has proved to be the preferred service provider for both vendors and buyers.

Broadly, the areas of expertise of Redington can be listed as:

1. Distribution of IT products
2. Distribution of non-IT products
3. Hardware support services
4. Warehousing and Logistics

5. 3rd Party Logistics Service Provider with its Automated distribution centers

A brief note on each of these 5 areas is given below:

1. Distribution of IT products—both hardware and software:
    - India operations started in 1994 and today operates 77 sales offices and 147 warehouses
    - Helps companies make their business plan along with their vendors
    - Plan inventory and credit requirements
    - Provide logistical support
    - Help in all statutory compliances
2. Distribution of non-IT products—electronics, telecom, etc.
    - Works with large format retailers, organized trade chains to help companies in their distribution
    - Focus on multi-brand outlets for telecom products
    - Focus on corporate partners for digital printing products
3. Hardware Support Services:
    - Operates 77 own and 266 with partners hardware support service centers
    - Authorized partners for companies like: HP, Toshiba, Lenovo, Fijitsu, Apple, Motorola, Huawei, Ricoh, Logitech and Konica
    - Has a 24×7 call center
    - Adopts global best practices
4. Warehousing and Logistics:
    - End to end logistics capabilities, imports, warehousing, stock movements, packing, re-packing, order processing and delivery
    - Operates 72 warehouses totalling over 1 million sq. ft.
5. 3PL Automated Distribution Centers:
    - Does forward and reverse logistics for companies
    - Industry verticals supported: IT, pharmaceuticals, FMCG, office automation, telecom, chemicals, beverages, consumer durables and electronics

Source: Company published information.

Just like in product marketing, the service provider would like to "duplicate" his good performance for a larger number of customers spread over a wide geography. If services cannot be standardized, how does he do it? Firms will attempt to achieve the maximum possible consistency. As there is a high human element involved, it requires a lot of training to achieve this.

Services require the input (involvement) of customers to perform better (barbers, fitness centres, health care). The provider has to facilitate customer involvement. The channel should be designed to maximize the sale of a service during its limited exposure to the target market (airline seats, hospital beds, concert tickets, beauty treatment). The provider has to quickly connect the service providers with all prospects (airlines use travel agents).

Some more points on service channels:

- Shorter channels than for products (doctors, dentists, lawyers, accountants).
- Franchised channels are more common (Maruti service stations, Apollo hospitals). Franchising is a formidable tool for overcoming the problem with service standardization in multiple locations.
- High degree of customization is provided (examples include: legal, health care, architects, executive search, real estate, taxi, plumbing, education, telephones, hotels and retail banking).
- The flows that carry the service through a channel are information, negotiation and promotion. Technology plays a major role in these flows.

Example from Health Services A new set of health care consultants are coming up to provide a bridge between the companies (which want their employees to enjoy the best health) and hospitals which provide a range of health services and treatment. The health care consultant is a new kind of intermediary. The consultants guide the company and its managers in keeping good health, health risk assessments and annual check-ups.

Location of the service provider is also important for accessibility and convenience (example, bank branch), use of technological innovations like (tele-banking or home shopping), and convenience (hospital).

Some common examples of service providers are:

- Direct from service provider to user: consulting, eye-care, dental, healthcare, beauty parlors, legal services, design services.
- Service provider uses an agent or broker: ticketing services, travel agents, stocks and shares, commodity trading, real estate, insurance, advertising, hotel reservations.
- The service provider can use franchisees or contractors: car rentals, courier services, dry-cleaning and fast food outlets. This alternative also gives wide market coverage and high volumes and profits.
- Service providers who want an image and selective distribution: technical services, repair and maintenance shops.
- Some service providers want an excellent image and are satisfied with limited number of valuable clients: specialized training centres, fashion design outfits.

The delivery of services can also use different media like:

- Franchisees—for product, trade name, business formats. Examples, fast food (Dominos, Pizza Hut), education (NIIT, Aptech), courier (BD, TNT), hotels and beauty parlors (Shenaz Hussain).
- Electronic channels—self-service, banking, e-mail etc.—benefits of convenience, low cost, wide distribution, customer choice, and quality control.
- Agents and Brokers—do not take possession of the merchandize and yet provide services for a fee. Services can be widely available, costs are reduced, localized marketing strategies are possible, apply special knowledge and skills for the benefit of customers and provide customized services.

LO 6 Learn about some unique distribution channels

SOME UNIQUE DISTRIBUTION EXAMPLES

In this section, we will discuss some unique distribution examples (Table 14.1). Unique and special channel systems have been developed by some industry verticals and companies keeping a clear focus on their customers, how they are dispersed and their customer service requirements. Some of these examples are narrated below.

Table 14.1 Unique Features of Some Crucial Channel Systems

Channel System	Unique Features
e-Choupal	Electronic channel
HUL Project Shakti	Empowering rural women and developing a rural distribution network
Vending machines	Non-store retailing
Eureka Forbes	Direct selling
Amway India	Multi-level marketing and direct selling
Mumbai *Dabbawalas*	A Six Sigma distribution network

E-Choupal—Electronic Channel

Indian agriculture is characterized by small fragmented farms, large number of intermediaries between the farm and the consumer and inadequate infrastructure to provide reach into or out of the rural areas. ITC started e-Choupal to overcome some of these problems. To quote directly from ITC—"the purpose of e-choupals is to inform, empower and compete".

E-Choupal has the objective of linking directly with farmers to facilitate the procurement of agricultural produce like wheat, soya beans and coffee. E-Choupal also facilitates the farmer by helping him with the latest and accurate information about the climate, rainfall/monsoon, market prices of agricultural produce, etc. so that the farmer can get better prices for his produce. In the traditional system the agricultural produce is procured from wholesale markets *(mandis)* and is dominated by middlemen who are most times unscrupulous and unfair to the farmer.

How Does e-choupal Work?

ITC sets up kiosks in villages with computers and internet connectivity in several regions in the country. Here the farmers can negotiate the sale of their produce to ITC if it is of the quality specified by the company. The PCs and internet access at these points help the farmers to:

- Obtain information of produce at the wholesale markets—help them obtain better prices
- Learn about good farming practices—improves the quality of their produce
- Learn about likely weather conditions
- Learn about inputs like seeds and fertilizers
- Operate a collaborative network of companies orchestrated by ITC with a pan-India presence.

Each kiosk with the computer and internet access is run by a trained farmer known as a "sanchalak". The kiosk can serve about 600 farmers within a radius of 5 km covering about 10 villages. The internet connection is via phone lines or a VSAT connection. The sanchalak has to bear some operating costs but is also reimbursed a small fee for all electronic transactions done through the kiosk.

For collection of the produce bought by ITC, it operates a warehouse hub run by traditional middlemen called Samyojaks. They aggregate the goods, disburse cash and arrange for transportation

Some of the noticeable benefits from the initiative are:

- Improvement in the quality of their output
- Reduction in their transaction costs
- Rise in their income from the same level of production
- Customized and appropriate information for a farmer in spite of their physical distance from the wholesale markets
- Real-time information on subjects of interest to the farmer
- Reduction in the procurement costs of produce of a specified quality for ITC.

E-Choupal is becoming a powerful two-way delivery channel efficiently carrying goods and services into and out of rural India. Presently, e-Choupal covers 10 states, 40,000 villages servicing about 4 million farmers through 6500 kiosks. This is likely to be scaled up to 20,000 kiosks in 100,000 villages in 15 states, covering 15 million farmers in the near future.

One additional and positive offshoot of the ITC e-Choupal initiative is the establishment of rural marketing hubs called Choupal Saagars by ITC. These hubs (rural malls) would be located within tractorable distance of about 30 e-Choupals. These hubs have three objectives:

- Provide a suitable place for the farmers to sell their produce to ITC at the best prices
- Act as shopping centres for farmers offering the best branded products available in urban areas
- Act as facilitation centres to farmers to deliver a range of farm related services, for example soil testing, training, product quality certification, cafeteria, medical and clinical services.

The first Choupal Saagar was set up in Sehore, Madhya Pradesh. The 7000-sq-ft mall sells consumer products as well as agricultural products.

In addition, ITC is working on the following projects to support rural development (Mission: SunehraKal)

- Watershed development for soil and moisture conservation covering 200,000 ha, benefiting 160,000 HH in 38 districts and 9 states.
- Social and farm forestry covering 200,000 ha and providing 90 million person days of employment. This helps ITC get about 60 percent of its pulpwood requirements.
- Livestock development with 256 cattle development centres in 10,550 villages
- Women's empowerment program to provide sustainable livelihood to rural women through non-agricultural activities—helping about 45,000 rural women.
- Vocational training for employment provided to about 20,000 rural youth so far.

HUL Project Shakti—Empowering Rural Women and Developing a Rural Distribution Network

"The objectives of Project Shakti are to create income-generating capabilities for underprivileged rural women by providing a small-scale enterprise opportunity, and to improve rural living standards with greater awareness of health and hygiene,"—Mr. Dalip Sehgal, then executive director of the Shakti initiative.

Project Shakti was launched in 2001. It involved working with rural self-help groups (SHGs) to educate rural women, while also making them part of the company's marketing network. The women members of the SHGs became Shakti entrepreneurs—direct to home distributors for HUL products. The venture offers high returns on low risks and supports some of the popular rural brands of the company.

A typical Shakti entrepreneur buys goods from the company and covers households in nearby villages canvassing the benefits of the company products to mostly illiterate village women and selling the products to them (for example, the Shakti lady may highlight health benefits of bathing daily and how the toilet soap Lifebuoy can help). A typical Shakti distributor sells goods worth ₹10,000–15,000 per month (about $250) and earns about ₹1000 which may not look big but is quite "substantial" for a rural lady with no income of her own till then. Some of the women have bought scooters out of the income to help them reach their "beat" better.

The Shakti initiative was started in 50 villages of Nalgonda district in Andhra Pradesh.

The Shakti Project was extended to husbands and brothers of Shakti Ammas. These men were designated as Shaktimaans and sold HUL products on bicycles in surrounding villages. There are about 48,000 Shaktimaans in operation along with the 70,000 Shaktiammas. Between all of them they cover 162,000 villages benefiting about 4 million rural HH.

Other Shakti Initiatives

1. Shakti Vani, which is a social awareness programme, was created to build social awareness on topical issues like problems of drinking, respect for the girl child, education for the girl child, hygiene at home, etc. This project was launched in 2004 and is operational in 20,000 villages in Madhya Pradesh, Andhra Pradesh, Chhattisgarh and Karnataka.
2. I-Shakti programme has been started in which desktop computers are set up in the houses of Shakti distributors. These computers are equipped with software developed by Unilever through which users can access content in categories including education, employment, agriculture, health and entertainment. They can also ask questions on any of these subjects and have them answered by experts. The programme has been developed with the help of Tata Consultancy Services.

Vending Machines: Non-Store Retailing

A vending machine has been defined as a machine which is a cash (coins or paper currency) or card operated retailing format that dispenses products (like soft drinks, beverages, magazines) or services (like train tickets, games). Vending machines can only be used for low-value frequently bought items. It has been estimated that 85 percent of the annual vending machine sales in the US is accounted for by food items and hot and cold beverages.

Advantages of vending machines are: (i) eliminates use of salespeople, (ii) provides 24 × 7 service, and (iii) placement in consumer preferred locations.

Vending machines are normally placed in locations with high consumer traffic like inside or outside stores, train stations, street corners, hotel corridors etc.

History

Hero of Alexandria is credited with building the first ever vending machine which used to dispense a fixed amount of holy water when a coin was inserted into the machine.

Vending machines became prominent only in the industrial age. The first such coin-operated vending machines dispensing post cards seemed to have been introduced in London in the 1880s. In 1888, the first vending machine selling chewing gum was set up in the US on train platforms.

Today, vending machines sell a wide range of products like beverages, candies, newspapers and magazines, tickets, snacks, etc. Now vending machines also come with bill changing facility. ATMs could be a good example of a modern-day vending machine.

Vending machines have evolved to accept bills (notes) and coins on a global basis. Such innovative efforts have been put into developing global bill acceptor models. As such, a standard known as MDB (Multi-drop Bus) has been invented. This allows for machines around the world to utilize the same bill acceptor and coin changer devices with an international specification.

Eureka Forbes—Direct Selling

Eureka Forbes was the first company in India to introduce domestic water purifiers (Aquaguard) and vacuum cleaners in India. Today it is operated in over 90 cities and employs over 6000 people. As these products were new to Indian customers and any promotional campaign to create awareness would have been quite expensive and time-consuming, the company decided to go the route of direct selling. The scores of well-dressed salesmen were the first of their kind in India and the results were a tremendous success. Today EF operates with about 5000 salesmen and adds 1500 new customers every day. The salesmen touch about 1.30 million homes directly.

Sleek, lightweight vacuum cleaners under the Eureka brand were first launched in the US in 1909 by a businessman Fred Wardell. This company adopted the direct selling route from the first day and became quite successful. Even in the early 1900s the company used to employ over 5000 salesmen operating out of 400 branches in the US.

In order to sell the concept of water purifiers and vacuum cleaners, the company adopted the direct selling route. It employs dynamic and highly motivated salesmen and calls them Eurochamps. The salespeople were to project the image of the "friendly man from Eureka Forbes".

The pioneer of direct marketing changed its policy around 1995 by moving into another channel of 2600 dealers. This additional network was used primarily for a different set of brands—Tornado vacuum cleaners and Aquaflow water purifiers which had been launched in 1995. The dealer route was initially used only for industrial customers but had grown to contribute nearly 5 percent of the company business by 1999 when this network was being used to make the company products available in consumer home appliances retail stores.

Eureka Forbes has introduced personal water purifier bottles of capacity 750 ml each.

Amway India—Pioneer in Multi-Level Marketing

Amway is a short form for American Way and coined by its founders Jay Van Andel and Richard Davos in 1959. The founders built the company on strong values and guiding principles with an intention of helping people to lead better lives. Its founding principles were based on freedom, family, hope and reward. It has over 450 products and 6000 employees worldwide.

Amway India (AI) is a wholly owned subsidiary of Amway Corporation, Michigan, USA. Amway Corporation is the one of the world's biggest direct selling companies and is present in over 80 countries world-wide. Some unique features of Amway are as follows:

- It is a company which manufactures and sells world-class consumer products.
- All its products are covered by a 100 percent money back guarantee.
- AI sources all its products from within India providing manufacturing opportunities locally.

AI started its commercial operations in 1998 and has invested over $35 million in India including a direct foreign investment of $6 million. The company's website mentions that it has provided business opportunities to about 450,000 active and independent Amway business owners—the selling and distribution arm of the company. AI is a member of the Indian Direct Selling Association.

Product Categories

AI products have been grouped into four categories—personal care, home care, nutrition and wellness, and cosmetics. There are over 130 products in all.

Distribution Network

Four regional mother depots and 55 city depots are managed through 125 offices spread all over India. The company is able to reach 3000 locations through a host of logistics service providers. The goods are sourced from seven third party manufacturers.

In March 2016, Amway India has teamed up with Microsoft for digitally enabled experience centres in India. The first such centre was set up in Bangalore and 10 more such centres are planned.

The store is meant to transform distributor and consumer experience. Each and every stage of the distributor and consumer buying pattern was studied. Using this pattern, a solution was worked out to convert each and every transaction into a memorable experience.

Mumbai Dabbawalas—A Six Sigma Distribution Network

The *dabbawalas* of Mumbai have featured in many case studies and have now got the attention as a case study in Harvard Business School. The case study of about 25 pages will trace the history of the organization, how it works, and the lessons to be learnt from them.

In essence what the 5000 *dabbawalas* do is to deliver 200,000 tiffin boxes every day without any mix up.

Mr Manish Tripathi, one of the *dabbawalas* who visits many cities and business schools, sums up the core values of the Mumbai *Dabbawalas* very well as follows:

- There is no hierarchy in the organisation—from clothes to bank balance, all the members share the same things.
- All the members are the shareholders of the organisation—holding shares worth ₹70,000.
- This is the only source of income for the members—they deliver service to customers with total commitment.
- If customers do not answer the doorbell within 10 seconds several times in a week, such a customer is given up. They do not want to spoil their service record with the rest of the customers.
- They make the process as simple as possible, teach employees multi-tasking and do not look for quick profits.

How Do They Operate?

Dabbawallas is a group of people in Mumbai whose job is to carry and deliver home-made food in lunch boxes to office workers. This service was started by Mahadeo Havaji Bachche in late 1890 who discovered that people migrating to Mumbai were finding it hard to get home-made food. Mr. Bachche decided to cater the need for home-made food by collecting the food box (tiffin) from the house of the individual (customer) and deliver it at their place of work. In the reverse logistics, the empty box is collected from the place of work and delivered back to the customer's residence.

- The *dabbawalas* collect the tiffin boxes from different residences in the territory assigned to them and bring it to the nearest railway station before 9 am.
- The boxes are sorted by destination at the station by a simple color and an alphanumeric code.
- The tiffin boxes are transported by a specific train and handed over to another person at the destination station.
- This person delivers the boxes at various offices through *dabbawalas* assigned to the specific territory before 12.30 pm.
- Exactly the same process is followed on the reverse logistics part to deliver the empty boxes at the residences from where they were collected in the morning.
- The entire process works on the principle of self-discipline and determination to achieve perfection. The customer pays just ₹300 per month (about $ 6) for this unfailing service.
- The quality of service has earned the *Dabbawalas* an ISO certification.
- In 1998 Forbes Magazine conducted a detailed study and gave them a Six Sigma rating on efficiency (strong team work and strict time management).

The system is estimated to use 25 km of public transport network, 10 km of footwork and multiple transfer points. The simple color and alphanumeric code determines not only packet routing but packet prioritising as lunch boxes are transferred from the train to bicycle to foot.

Management Practices of Dabbawalas

- Their main beliefs are: work is worship, customer is God, time is money, and unity is power.
- They have zero fuel, zero modern technology, zero investment, zero disputes, and 100 percent customer satisfaction.
- They must wear their uniform, must report on time, must respect customers and always carry identification cards.
- Decisions are made instantly without meetings and conventions.

SUMMARY

LO 1

- Channel management is in three broad phases: use of power bases, identifying and resolving channel conflicts, and channel coordination. The channel system consists of a number of players who are not all equally motivated to implement the ideal channel design as their expectations from the channel differ. It is the efficient use of the power bases that brings diverse channel partners in line for the implementation and effectiveness of the channel. The five power bases have been identified as: rewards, coercion, expertise, legitimacy and reference.
- Channel conflict is generated when the actions of any channel member come in the way of the entire channel achieving its objectives. It has been seen that channel conflicts occur basically for three reasons: goal conflict, domain conflict, and perception conflict. Channel conflict passes through the stages of latent, perceived, felt and manifest conflicts. Conflicts need to be resolved in the first two stages and not allowed to escalate into the next two stages as resolution becomes that much more difficult.
- In a coordinated channel system, all the members operate in a synchronized manner to achieve customer service objectives.
- Conflict could be the result of each channel member wanting to pursue his own goals, each wants to retain his independence, and there are limited resources which all of them want to utilize in the pursuit of their goals.
- Conflicts arise in hybrid channels primarily due to salespeople who handle key accounts giving operational instructions to the channel partners on how the key account has to be managed.

LO 2

- There are four steps to be taken to resolve conflicts: understanding the nature of the conflict and its impact, finding the source of the conflict, finding the consequences of the conflict, and identifying the solution and an action plan.
- Companies have found a number of ways to resolve conflict between channel partners. These include joint membership of associations, exchanging personnel and finally arbitration.

LO 3

- Channel management is in four steps: planning, the organization structure to deliver the customer service objectives, developing the ability to control the channel, and measuring performance for continuous improvement.

LO 4

- The major aspects of channel policies relate to: which markets to service, the customer coverage within these markets, pricing, product lines to be handled, selection of the right channel, termination of a channel membership and ownership of the channel.

LO 5

- Services (as compared to selling products) are distinguished by five characteristics: they are intangible, they are inseparable from the service providers, they cannot be standardized, customers are involved in the delivery process of a service, and they are perishable. Any marketing channel used by services sector has to take the above factors into consideration. Services can be delivered through franchisees, electronic channels or through brokers and agents.

LO 6

- The chapter highlights some of the unique distribution examples in operations like: e-Choupal using electronic channels, HUL Project Shakti which aims to empower rural women by setting them up as distributors, direct selling by Eureka Forbes, non-store selling as in vending machines, multi-level marketing as in Amway and an unique distribution network which is the Mumbai *Dabbawalas*. Each of these unique examples creates a good learning experience for the salesperson interested in developing channels.

Key Terms

Glossaries of key terms are mentioned at the end of all chapters

Accommodation
Aggression
Arbitration
Attitudinal conflict
Avoidance
Channel conflict
Channel control
Channel coordination
Channel dependence
Channel position
Coercion power
Collaboration
Compromise
Countervailing power
Customer service goals
Domain conflict
Expert power
Felt conflict
Goal conflict
Horizontal conflict
Hybrid channels conflict
Latent conflict
Legalistic power
Manifest conflict
Market domain conflict
Mediation
Perceived conflict
Perception conflict

Power
Reference power
Reward power
Source of conflict
Structural conflict
Vertical conflict
Zone of indifference

Conceptual Questions

1. What are the three main areas that give rise to channel conflicts? Explain them in brief. LO1 E
2. When is a channel said to be coordinated? What are the characteristics of a coordinated channel? LO1 E
3. What are the five sources of power used by channel members to influence each other? Explain them in brief. LO2 M
4. What is 'channel conflict'? What are the four stages in which it evolves? LO1 E
5. Enumerate the various methods used to resolve conflicts. LO3 M
6. What are the steps to be taken to resolve conflicts? Explain with examples. LO3 E
7. What are the levels of channel hierarchies where market domain conflicts can occur between channel members? Explain with examples. LO1 M
8. Five styles of conflict resolution have been recognized by experts. What are they and how do they work? LO3 M
9. Explain the terms vertical channel conflict, horizontal channel conflict and multi-channel conflict. LO1 E
10. List down some of the methods used by companies to motivate their channel partners so that channel conflicts can be avoided. LO2 M
11. Explain the four broad steps in channel management. LO3 E
12. How does distribution of services differ from distribution of products? Explain with examples. LO5 M
13. What are the factors to be considered in formulating channel policies? Explain each of them. LO4 D
14. Explain with some examples how vertical channel conflicts occur. LO1 E
15. Why do channel conflicts occur in hybrid channels? LO1 M
16. Explain the uniqueness of the distribution efforts in HUL Project Shakti. LO6 M

Note: Difficulty Level → E — Easy; M — Medium; D — Difficult

17. "e-Choupal is a concept which can be extended by many companies to improve distribution in rural areas. Discuss this topic". LO6 M
18. "Multi-level marketing companies are not successful in the Indian context". Do you agree with this statement? Please explain. LO6 D

Objective Type Questions

Select the most appropriate response out of the various options available in each of the following questions:

1. The five sources of power used by channel members to avoid conflict are legitimate, reward, coercion, __________ and __________ .
   (a) influence and expertise (b) financial and referent
   (c) expert and size (d) referent and expert LO2 E
2. Channel conflicts can occur because of conflicts of __________, domain and perceptions.
   (a) interests (b) margins (c) resources (d) goals LO1 E
3. Conflicts escalate through the stages of latent, perceived, felt and __________.
   (a) dispute (b) arguments (c) legal (d) manifest LO1 E
4. Channel members, many times are able to match each other's power through __________ power.
   (a) money (b) personnel (c) union (d) countervailing LO2 E
5. Channel conflict is a state of __________ among the organisations comprising a marketing channel.
   (a) unhappiness (b) doubt (c) suspicion (d) discord LO1 E
6. Conflict between a set of distributors of a company can be called __________ conflict.
   (a) vertical (b) multi-channel (c) coverage (d) horizontal LO1 E
7. A power derived from sheer association is called __________ power.
   (a) expert (b) influence (c) support (d) referent LO1 E
8. A specialized, valuable knowledge developed by a channel member gives it __________ power.
   (a) referent (b) leadership (c) competitive (d) expert LO1 E
9. A channel conflict can be called __________ if there is an antagonistic behavior among channel members.
   (a) unresolved (b) troublesome (c) serious (d) manifest LO1 E
10. A style of conflict resolution where both parties soften their demands is called __________.
    (a) collaboration (b) accommodative (c) supportive (d) compromise LO3 E
11. Exchange of __________ between channel partners is one of the ways of conflict resolution.
    (a) ideas (b) responsibilities (c) information (d) personnel LO3 E

12. Salvage value of an unsold service is zero as services are __________ .
(a) intangible (b) inseparable (c) limited (d) perishable LO5 M

13. A conflict arising between channel members at the same level is known as a __________ conflict.
(a) horizontal (b) vertical (c) common (d) routine LO1 E

14. In order to reduce the conflict due to channel margins, companies should focus on the ________ being earned by the channel partner.
(a) ROI (b) profit (c) revenue (d) discounts LO3 M

Application Questions

1. Medicare Pharmaceuticals is facing a revolt from six of its Mumbai distributors. Medicare is relatively new on the pharma front and is just ten years old but has well established products regularly prescribed by majority of the doctors and hospitals. When Medicare started operations in Mumbai, they had difficulty getting good distributors and hence offered 8 percent margin to the distributors. The company supported the products and the distributors quite a lot to reach the present comfortable stage. The distributors also stood by it. Now the company wants to cut down the margin to the distributors to 6 percent as their sales volumes are quite high. The distributors do not agree. They know that Medicare cannot get distributors like them. What do you think Medicare should do to sustain their business? LO2 D

2. Sam Automobiles are makers of very popular two wheelers. They started operations by combining sales and service with their dealers doing both the jobs. As long as volumes of business were reasonable, the dealers of Sam did a good job of maintaining the service for the vehicles sold by them. They could also attend to repairs quickly as they used to stock sufficient spares. In the last six months, Sam has been receiving a lot of complaints from customers that the dealers do not attend to repair and maintenance promptly and many times force the customers to buy spares at extra cost from the market. This is causing serious worries for Sam. The top management recently decided that as a test case in Bengaluru, they would take away the servicing job from the dealers and appoint separate franchised authorized service centres. This news has upset the dealers who feel that on the advice of the company they have invested a lot in the service facilities. They are willing to assure Sam of better service in the future, but Sam is not convinced. What action can Sam take starting from Bengaluru? LO2 D

3. Alankar Drycleaners is a popular dry-cleaning company in Hyderabad with three outlets. It has been in business of dry-cleaning and darning for over 20 years in one part of the city. The owner's son Prashanth has just come back to his home town after completing his management course in the US. He is highly energetic and has a number of ideas. One of the ideas he is planning to implement is to open a large number of Alankar dry-cleaning outlets all over Hyderabad considering that most of the city residents know about the cleaners. He has spoken to his bankers and they are willing to lend him finance on good terms. He is also aware that the younger population of the city would respond very well to these outlets. No other cleaning outfit has more than one outlet.

Prashanth is not, however, sure if the outlets should be owned by Alankar or franchised by them. Real estate companies assure him that it is not difficult to rent suitable premises in different localities. Prashanth's father strongly feels that all outlets should be owned by them to keep the high standards of service already established. What do you think? How should Prashanth go about realizing his dreams? LO4 M

4. *Norton India Ltd. developing "commitment" for the business in dealers*—NIL is based in a major city and makes high-end gensets with a Japanese collaboration. It has superior technology and believes in premium pricing. NIL has a set of well-established dealers (dealers have a 20 percent mark-up from which even if they give away 5 percent as discounts, they can still make an ROI of 40 percent). NIL also has an *excellent set of sales engineers*. They are confident, committed, proud of the company and work almost 24 × 7 and in the process they earn the respect of customers. Salespeople expect that the dealers should develop the same "commitment" as them.

Dealers

The dealers have the primary tasks of supporting the salespeople efforts by executing orders, installation and commissioning of the equipment. The dealers also finance the "credit" extended to customers.

Sales engineers

Their primary task is to "sell" the gensets and bring in the business. They are in touch with prospects and customers all the time. They also support after-sales efforts in ensuring that the gensets give trouble-free service to the customers.

Salespeople complete the operating tasks relating to today's biz and also make efforts on tomorrow's biz development. They would like dealers to handle more of the routine functions giving salespeople more time for planning the future. At the same time salespeople are worried that dealers may get too close to customers and may "cut them off".

What are the methods NIL can use to increase the 'commitment' to the business in dealers? LO4 M

5. *Sam Diagnostics: getting dealers to pay attention to all businesses*—Sam Diagnostics has two business divisions: Division 1: medical diagnostic equipment to hospitals and nursing homes (75 percent sales contribution to the business, slow growth) and Division 2: chemicals, re-agents and pharma products to labs and chemists (25 percent of sales contribution to the business but fast growth). SD wants Division 2 to contribute same sales percentage as Division 1 in 3 years.

The two Division Sales Heads report to a common Marketing Director. The objective of the company is to be the top performer both in medical diagnostic equipment and the chemicals, re-agents and pharma products. For the company, profit margins in the equipment division (Division 1) are much higher than the ones in the "consumables" division (Division 2). Both the divisions have common distributors but separate salespeople.

Division 2 salespeople want distributors to put disproportionate efforts on their part of the business.

One of the distributors of SD is Excel Distributors which operates in a metro city. For Excel, the salient numbers are as follows:

- Division 1 contribution 80 percent of sales and a growth rate of 8 percent p.a.
- Division 2 contribution 20 percent of sales but a growth rate of 40 percent p.a.
- SD contributes 67 percent of Excel total business.

- Excel has 30 accounts from Division 1 and 150 accounts in Division 2.
- Sales Manager of Division 2 wants Excel to grow Division 2 sales equal to Division 1 in 3 years

Excel is not clear as to how this is to be achieved and wants the Sales Manager of Division 2 to guide him on this.

Is the Sales Manager of Division 2 reasonable in his expectations? How will he motivate the distributors to work on this objective?

6. *Mercury Electronics: Need for ensuring steady sales during the month through channel partners*—Mercury is the sole distributor for one of the biggest international electronic brands in the Middle East. Mercury's business was in consumer durables, electronic products like music players, play stations, video players/recorders, camcorders, etc. The customer segments for Mercury were the various corporates, hotels, restaurants, resorts and all electronic and consumer durables dealers.

   Mercury used a variety of channel partners to reach the different customer segments—retailers, dealers, mass merchandisers, wholesalers and direct to corporate customers. At the year-end review of results, Joseph, the GM of Mercury, was analysing some of the operational issues which had affected Mercury from achieving better results. These issues seemed to be common among the different channels used. Joseph was keen that some of these issues should get resolved in order to achieve better performance in the next year and for the future. The issues were:
   - Major month end sales skew—30–35 percent sales happened in the last week of the month
   - Sales in the first week of the month was almost nil
   - There was no identifiable consistent daily average sales
   - Sales seemed to be heavily dependent on a few major customers
   - Collecting Accounts Receivables was becoming more difficult

   Joseph informally checked up with other prominent white goods distributors and he found a similar pattern of sales.

   Should Joseph just ignore the issues as just a market phenomenon or should he take any action to correct this? What do you think?

ASSIGNMENTS FOR STUDENTS

1. Meet any contracted dealer of an automobile company. Understand from him the parameters on which his performance is evaluated by the principal company and at what frequency. What are some of the problems/issues (conflicts) the dealer has had with the principal in the last one year and how were these resolved?
2. Meet a grocery retailer/kirana shop owner in the market. Find out the number of FMCG companies he deals with. In his opinion, which is the best company of the lot? Why? Which is the company he does not like much and why?

3. Wholesalers depend on companies/company channel partners to extend credit to them as their margins are low and volumes are high. A visit to a wholesaler and discussion should help you get a fair idea of the credit policies of various companies' goods the wholesaler is dealing with. Make a comparison.
4. Visit a nearby village. Meet a HUL Project Shaktiamma. If possible, follow her on her work beat for one full day. List down all the activities she does for HUL that day. Understand how her efforts benefit HUL in strengthening its presence and brands.
5. Find out and visit a village which has an ITC e-Choupal. Observe and record the proceedings which happen in the unit on the day of your visit. Talk to the farmers visiting the unit. Understand from them the purpose of the e-Choupal unit in their village and how they have benefited from it.

Reference Notes

1. Bert Rosenbloom, *Marketing Channels: A Management View*, Chapter 5, pp. 178–210; Chapter 9, pp. 308–341, 344–373, 375–399 and 402–430, The Dryden Press.
2. DJ Bowersox and MB Cooper, *Strategic Management: Channel Management*, Chapter 10, McGraw-Hill Education, pp. 306–377.
3. Maureen Guirdhom, *Marketing: The Management of Distribution Channels*, Chapter 8, pp. 118–128; Chapter 9, pp. 129–148; and Chapter 10, pp. 149–159, Pergamon Press.
4. C Glenn Walters, *Marketing Channels*, Chapter 7, pp. 170–195; Chapter 17, pp. 468–489, Goodyear Publishing.
5. S M Jha and L P Singh, *Marketing Management in Indian Perspective*, Chapter 34, Himalaya Publishing, pp. 1083–1126.
6. E J McCarthy and W D Perrault, *Basic Marketing*, Chapter 11, Irwin McGraw Hill, pp. 296–319.
7. W F Schoell, Allyn and Bacon Inc, *Marketing*, Chapter 12, pp. 331–358.
8. Kenneth W Thomas, Conflict and Conflict Management in M D Dunnette (Ed), *Handbook of Industrial & Organisational Psychology*, Consulting Psychologists Press, 1976.
9. William Davidson, *Changes in Distributive Institutions*, Journal of Marketing, 1970.
10. L P Bucklin, *A Theory of Channel Control*, Journal of Marketing, 1973.
11. J R P French & B Raven, The Bases of Social Power in *Studies in Social Power*, University of Michigan Press, 1959.
12. AJ Narus and J C Anderson, *Strengthening Distributor Performance through Channel Positioning*, Sloan Management Review, 1988.

13. G L Frazier and R C Rody, *The Use of Influence Strategies in Inter-Firm Relationships in Industrial Product Channels*, Journal of Marketing, 1984.
14. Conflict in Distribution Channels: An Exploration in Distribution Channels: Behavioural dimensions—Stern & Gorman.
15. Adam J Fein & Sandy D Jap, *Manage Consolidation in the Distribution Channel*, Sloan Management Review, Fall 1999, p. 61.
16. Geyskens, Jan Bendict. EM Sternkamp & Nirmalya Kumar, *A Meta-Analysis of Satisfaction in Marketing Channel Relationships*, Journal of Marketing Research, May 1999, pp. 223–238.
17. JR Brown, RF Lusch and LP Smith, *Conflict and Satisfaction in an Industrial Channel of Distribution*, International Journal of Physical Distribution & Logistics Management, 1991, pp. 15–26.
18. Christine B Bucklin, Pamela A Thomas, Graham and Elizabeth A Webster, *Channel Conflict: When is it Dangerous?*, McKinsly Quarterly, 1997, pp. 36–43.
19. Jan B Heick and George John, *Do Norms Matter in Marketing Relationships?*, Journal of Marketing, April 1992, p. 32.
20. Zhan G Li and Rajiv D Pant, *Effects of Manufacturer's Strategies on Channel Relationships*, Industrial Marketing Management, 1999, pp. 131–143.
21. *Mumbai Dabbawalas*. Talk by Mr Manish Tripathi.
22. Websites of companies: HUL, ITC and Amway.

CASE 14.1

Popular Foods Ltd. (PFL)

Popular Foods is a company which makes staple branded food products like wheat flour, suji and maida flour and also ready-to-eat foods, all under the brand name, Popular. Popular is very strong in one region of the country.

It is a family-owned company but strongly believes in professional management. However, it still clings on to traditional methods of management as the top management feels these methods have been time tested and proven. PFL has its headquarter in one of the secondary towns and not in a metro or a major city. It also has one of its three plants in this location. The other two plants are also located in the region where PFL is strong.

PFL has a good network of dealers in the region and many of these dealers have been with the company for many years and support the products of the company with a good distribution effort in the marketplace.

PFL is run by a CEO and a COO. It has general managers (GMs) heading production, marketing, finance, supply chain, IT, purchase, and R&D. Some of these GMs are MBAs also.

PFL does not pay high salaries as compared to the industry but is able to so far retain its people because the top management is quite benevolent and treats its people well. In recent times, a number of local big players and even MNCs are entering the industry and offering astronomical salaries to good people. In particular, sales and marketing people of PFL are very well recognized in the industry as an excellent resource for strengthening and keeping a high distribution presence for the products entrusted to them.

One of the major competitors of PFL with an all India presence, was also rapidly expanding its sales and marketing network and started looking for good sales and marketing people in the industry. Obviously PFL was the first place they started looking at. Recently, this major competitor (let us call him KLM) took away the GM-Marketing of PFL with a difficult to refuse package. Once the earlier GM-Marketing of PFL joined KLM, he started the process of "poaching" good salespeople from PFL to build his sales team.

PFL quickly promoted a veteran sales manager, with a lot of experience and good performance to his credit, as the GM-Marketing for PFL.

PFL has a serious dilemma on its hands:

- It is losing all its good sales and marketing people to KLM, which is offering huge salary packages which PFL cannot match. PFL does not seem to have enough attractions to hold back these people.
- Even though PFL allows its people at Head Office to commute from one or two major cities nearby (for education and medical facilities, the managers have to keep their families in these cities), the location of PFL does not attract the top talent in the industry.
- PFL cannot easily recruit new, experienced salespeople from the outside as many of its competitors have increased the salary levels, which again, PFL cannot match.
- PFL is worried that it may be left with salespeople who do not have a ready market in the industry.

Meanwhile, the business has to go on. PFL has also got to demonstrate to its 500 odd dealers in the region that it is still a market leader and can take care of its manpower issues effectively. The industry is also watching the moves which PFL makes.

Discussion Questions

If you are the new GM-Marketing of PFL, what action:

1. Will you take as the GM-Marketing to protect and build your valuable team?
2. Will you recommend to the top management to ensure that attrition levels are always kept at a manageable level?
3. Will you take to keep your dealers highly motivated and performing in spite of changes in sales management?

Reproduced with permission from Network 7 Management Consultants.

CASE 14.2

Gem Soaps and Detergents

Gem Soaps and Detergents Ltd (GSDL) is a major player in the industry and has been in the business for over 30 years. Some of its soap and detergent brands are brand leaders in specific geographies. GSDL has two detergent brands (one premium and one in popular category) and has six soap brands. Detergents are both in powders and tablet forms.

In recent months, one of the problems of GSDL which cropped up in a major city in India was becoming quite difficult to handle. GSDL had two powerful distributors (A and B) in this city and they were both selling soaps and detergents in clearly defined territories in this city. The salespeople had made careful analysis of the city territories and ensured that both A and B had almost equal sales revenues every month from their own territories. Both distributors had signed agreements with the company clearly agreeing to the terms and conditions of distributorship and the rules of operation.

Both A and B are located in the main wholesale *mandi* (market) of the city. Years back, when they were both appointed, the sales volumes were small and the location of the distributors did not matter. Now that the business has grown multi-fold, the location of the two distributors in the main *mandi* within 100 yards of each other is making a difference. The distributors are aware that they are instrumental in growing the business of GSDL and the company recognizes them as the two biggest channel partners in the region. Both A and B have resisted overtures from other big soaps and detergent companies to work for them and have stuck solidly behind GSDL.

The main *mandi* market is in the beat plan of distributor A.

The problem in distribution in the city started recently. Most wholesalers and retailers in the city (like any other city in India) visit the main *mandi* to buy all their requirements particularly unbranded goods like food grains, grocery products etc. It is naturally to be expected that since both A and B also have wholesale shops in the main *mandi*, a number of the city and outskirts retailers and semi-wholesalers would visit them also.

Distributor A started offering additional discounts (in his wholesale outlet) on Gem products to retailers coming to him from the territory covered by B. When B visited his territory to sell GSDL goods, he found that some of his retailers had already brought the goods from A. B started retaliating by phoning some of the wholesalers and retailers in the main *mandi* and offering them better terms on GSDL products than A. At times while going out to their territories, salesmen of B would call on A's customers in the main *mandi* and sell to them.

Both A and B were violating all norms of distribution laid down by the company but still started complaining against each other to the ASM, Murli. Murli counseled both of them separately and together to desist from selling to each other's customers. In addition, the distributors had started neglecting the coverage of the weaker markets in their own beat plans. In their efforts to try and teach a lesson to each other, they had reduced the credit percentage (percentage of outlets getting the benefit of credit from a distributor) in their beat plans but giving the credit in the main *mandi* market to lure each other's customers. Retailers and semi-wholesalers were taking advantage of this situation by playing the distributors against each other to get more benefits. New extensions and localities in the city were not being covered by either distributor. These were added on the beat plans of both A and B but were still not getting covered. Competitors were already taking advantage of this situation and nibbling into the lion's market share of GSDL in the city.

A and B also started complaining to the company that they were no longer getting decent margins from GSDL products and were getting tempted to look at competition. From the numbers available with GSDL, it was seen that both distributors had an ROI in excess of 50 percent! Neither distributor was willing to admit that the problems were of their own creation.

All efforts to reign in the two distributors A and B were to no avail. The company's dependence on both the distributors was also very high. There was a lot of debate in the company on the need to appoint a third distributor in the city by carving out the territories from those of A and B and pooling in all new extensions and localities and re-organising the beat plans of all three distributors. The objective was to get better direct coverage of all markets in the entire city. Their thinking was that with a third distributor they would have taught a lesson to A and B and also reduced their dependence on A and B. GSDL knew that the existing distributors would resist any break-up of their territory. The company was waiting for an opportunity to appoint this third distributor.

The opportunity came when GSDL decided to introduce a range of shampoos developed after a lot of research efforts. The shampoos had scored high in all test marketing efforts. GSDL decided to appoint a new distributor C to distribute shampoos in the whole of the city and not give shampoos at all to either A or B. This was opposed by both A and B who argued that they will not accept a third distributor in "their" city. On this issue both of them united. They would want shampoos also to distribute, for after all, they were the ones to have built GSDL in the city (forgetting all the marketing efforts put in by GSDL over the years to build the brands and the business).

Shampoo was a new product category for GSDL and though C was eager to be a part of the GSDL network, C was not content with just shampoo. He wanted to distribute soaps and detergent brands also. GSDL desperately wanted C to become part of the network. C had already established himself as a good distributor for some lesser known products not competing with GSDL. If they gave him soaps and detergents also, he could not be given the entire territory of the city and had to be given only a part of it. To give him one part of the city, some territories had to be taken out from A and B. If C was given only a part of the city, what was to be done about the distribution of shampoos in the territories of A and B?

Finally, succumbing to all the pressures, GSDL agreed to have three distributors A, B and C in the city. A and B reluctantly gave up some territories and also agreed once again not to sell in each other's territory on the condition that they would get to distribute shampoos also in their own territories. C was given a territory built from new areas and those taken away from A and B.

This decision was fraught with the following risks:

- The new shampoo brands may not get the desired width and depth of distribution from any of the distributors. For the first two years shampoos would contribute only 10 percent to the total revenue. (GSDL agreed to give an additional mark-up of 1 percent on shampoos for one year from the date of introduction) but required at least 25 percent of the effort on distribution.
- Selling in each other's territory may not still stop. Oral assurances from A and B have not meant anything in the past.
- A and B may make sure by their aggressive selling efforts with other customers, not to let C succeed. How would GSDL tackle this problem when it arises?
- A, B or C could start a distribution company in some other name and accept competitor products.

Discussion Questions

1. What do you think is the future for GSDL distribution in the city?
2. What should GSDL do to resolve the channel conflicts and also ensure the successful marketing of shampoos?
3. Could have the problem been resolved without appointing distributor "C"?

Reproduced with permission from Network 7 Management Consultants.

CASE 14.3

Apple Food Products (AFP)

Apple Food Products is a well-known company with a wide product range comprising soft drinks, ice creams and ready-to-eat (RTE) food products. Its brands are leaders in their respective categories. The company AFP belongs to a big group, and is a reputed organization.

A summary of the product groups of AFP is given below:

	Soft Drinks	Ice Creams	RTE Foods
No. of product variants	9	13 flavors	6
No. of brands	1	1	4
No. of SKUs	35	40	75
Product Groups	• 250 mL • 500/1 L pet bottles	• Bulk • On premises packs	• Modern retail • Retail and catering

Over the years, AFP has developed an excellent distribution system which is a combination of its own sales force and distributors. As far as possible, company salesmen and the distributors for each of the five product groups are different. Modern retail does not have distributors and is managed by the company salesmen.

While the customer segments for each of the product categories could be different, there are a large number of retailers who keep all the products and pack-sizes of AFP. Most of the products of AFP need a cold chain for distribution. Some of the RTE foods also need cold storage facilities. The investment level of distributors is quite high.

Some salient numbers on the distribution network are given below:

	Soft Drinks	Ice Creams	RTE foods
No. of distributors	Big packs—100 250 mL packs—175	Bulk—50 On premises—100	Modern retail—NIL Other retail and catering—100
No. of company salesmen	Big packs—90 250 mL—175	Bulk—70 On premises—100	Other retail and catering—140 Modern retail—20
No. of vans in operation	Big—235 250 mL—280	Bulk—150 On premises—230	Other retail and catering—120
Bottle coolers/ deep freezers	Big—6650 250 mL—5800	Bulk—7000 On premises—12000	Deep freezers—1200

The bottle coolers and deep freezers are given to the major retail points by the company and owned by it. AFP has 3P maintenance contractors on agreement to maintain these cold storage units in the market. The vans in operation are owned by the distributors and operated by them.

The company has been fortunate to find a large number of independent distributors for each of its business units and product categories. The distributors are primarily financiers for the business and their re-distribution abilities are not of top quality. Hence there is a need for AFP to have so many of its own salesmen to generate secondary sales. A look at the span of control of the salesmen will confirm this:

Number of distributors managed by a salesman

Product Group	Span of Control
Soft drinks—Big packs	1.1
SD—250 mL packs	1.0
Ice cream bulk	0.7
Ice cream—on premises	1.0
RTE foods	0.7

The company salesmen have to make 35 to 45 calls in a day.

Some of the concerns about this distribution network, which top management wants answers to, are:

- Is the role of a distributor primarily that of a financier? Is he not supposed to take care of the re-distribution of the products to all the outlets in his territory?
- What should be the role of company salesmen? Should they be used only to generate secondary sales and get new orders from the distributors? Should not the secondary sales be generated by the distributors' own salesmen?
- How will the company salesmen manage the large number of vans in operation? How does a company like AFP decide the permanent journey plan for its salesmen?
- What should be the span of control of an average salesman? Is it correct, too high or too low for AFP?
- The company has put in a large number of cold storage units in the market place. AFP has noticed that salesmen of one product group do not pay attention to the cold storage unit of another product group in the same outlet. Many times these other units may be getting misused to store competitive products. Is not ensuring the proper use of cold storage units part of the merchandizing task of the salesmen and distributors?
- The division by product groups has created exclusive "turfs" for each set of salesmen. Every distributor or salesman visiting the outlet is bothered about his product group only and there is no "company" pride.
- How would the retailer react if five distributors and company salesmen visit him every week? How would he "ration" the money available for buying AFP products among the five distributors? Would not some of their calls be un-productive? It is likely that two salesmen and distributors of AFP visit the retailer within hours of each other. Is this the meaning of intensive distribution?
- Bottle coolers and deep freezers were not maintained well in many outlets. Who is responsible for their upkeep and maintenance? Do the salespeople and distributors have any role to play in this?
- With so much specialization, is it possible to rotate salesmen between product groups? How would one design trade and consumer promotions?
- How would one design any incentive scheme for salesmen in such a multi-product, multi-distribution channel system to be equitable for all salesmen?

Discussion Questions

1. If you were given the task of reviewing the above operational points of the sales and distribution network and re-organizing the entire network, how would you go about this task?
2. Can you clearly define the roles and responsibilities of the company salespeople and the distributors?

Reproduced with permission from Network 7 Management Consultants.

CASE 14.4

Kinetic Engineering Company (KEC)

The Problem

KEC promises its dealer Star a percentage commission on the order for spares he is able to get from a major customer. The dealer also puts forth a requirement that the value benefit from any price negotiated in excess of the quote from KEC would be to the account of the dealer—KEC does not give a clear answer to this request. The dealer Star manages to get a higher price and now the company KEC wants a 50 percent share of this excess. The dealer does not agree—a conflict has arisen.

The dealer is quite influential with the major client and can affect future orders. If, however, his contention is now accepted, he could resort to fresher demands every time a new order comes up.

The Company, KEC

KEC was established in India by a technocrat about 25 years back. Mr. Krishna had just returned to India after a successful stint in the US working with leading engineering majors. He established KEC to make and sell world-class compressors, dryers and filters for air, water, gas and liquid applications in industry. KEC started a collaboration with a leading European company but after 10 years of this partnership became independent.

Over the 25 years of its existence KEC became a recognized name in several industry verticals and currently had over 1000 customers on its list many of whom were the leading players in their respective industries. The current turnover of KEC was about $10 million. It was still a small company extremely well managed by the founder Mr. Krishna.

The Project

There was a major refinery project coming up in one of the larger states in India for which a US based EPC (engineering project consultants) was working closely with the Government. This EPC was scouting for good project companies and gave the contract for the entire engineering of the project to one of the biggest engineering companies LT (Latest Technologies) in India. The project execution by LT also had a major component of compressors, dryers and filters of the kind which KEC was a well-known manufacturer.

The Contact

Star Engineers was a dealer of KEC though not exclusive. It had been set up a few years back by an influential retired government officer. Through his good contacts, Star was able to get full details of the requirements of LT in compressors, dryers and filters for this project. KEC entered into an oral agreement with Star that if he were to use his influence to get the orders for the compressors, dryers and filters on the project (totally worth about $2 million), KEC would give a commission of 5 percent of the order value (50 percent on getting the order and balance 50 percent on completion of the supplies and receipt of the payment from LT).

The Contract

The technical quote and the credentials of KEC finally helped it to get the order for the supply of equipment for the project worth $2 million to be executed in 6 months' time. Star was paid 50 percent of the agreed commission. Apart from hoping to execute the project on time, KEC was also eager to be the preferred vendor for the supply of spares on the equipment worth about $100,000 every 6 months.

Successful Completion

KEC successfully completed its part of the project in supplying the equipment covered by the order. The LT engineers inspected the equipment in the KEC works before they were dispatched to the refinery site for installation and commissioning. KEC engineers were present in the site when LT did the installation and commissioning. For KEC it was a major assignment and Mr. Krishna was proud that his team had successfully completed it on time. The payments were also received in due course and the balance commission was also paid to Star. Now KEC was looking forward to the next order on spares.

Spares Order

After 7 months, LT floated the requirement for maintenance spares for many of the equipment including those supplied by KEC. The value of KEC components of the spares was estimated at $100,000 as expected. Star was trying to get the order for himself. The Sales Manager Mr. Amrit came to know about this and persuaded Star to rightfully get the order in the name of KEC. The dealer Star suddenly started driving a hard bargain. He agreed to get the order in the name of KEC on the following conditions:

- KEC should give him 8 percent commission on the value of the order
- In case Star was able to get a price higher than the expected $100,000 any amount in excess of $100,000 would be taken by Star.

Amrit spoke to his CEO Mr. Krishna and finally agreed to the 8 percent commission. On the excess amount over expectation, the answer was quite vague like "we will see about it when it happens".

Star managed to use his influence and get the order value increased to $110,000. He told KEC that he had to be paid his commission of 8 percent ($8000) and he would also keep the excess $10,000. KEC found that the dealer was making a much higher margin on this transaction than KEC itself. KEC told the dealer Star as follows:

- We will pay you 8 percent of $100,000, which is the value accruing to us.
- You will have to share with KEC 50 percent of the excess realisation in price of $10,000.

Conflict Develops

The dealer Star refused to accept this formula. He felt that it was entirely his effort that he was able to negotiate a price higher than what KEC was content with. Why should he share this with KEC? Mr Krishna felt that it was KEC spares which were getting sold at this higher price which the customer feels they are worth. Hence he should share the excess value. The sales manager Amrit was in favor of the dealer stand but he also had to keep the company welfare in mind.

Star went one step further to tell KEC that in case his request was not agreed to, he would get all future spares orders in his own name and get it supplied by other vendors who he could easily develop.

Discussion Questions

1. How do you think that this crisis can be resolved?
2. In the described situation, what is the final payment to be made to Star and why?
3. What steps should Kinetic take to ensure a harmonious relationship with Star for the future?

Reproduced with permission from Network 7 Management Consultants.

CASE 14.5

Advanced Measuring Devices (AMD)-1

Issue

RSG, who was the Head of Sales and Marketing of AMD was discussing an issue of serious concern to the business of the company. AMD was used to successfully resolving domain and responsibility conflicts with their channel partners. However, one specific problem arising out of the enormous faith reposed in one channel partner and involving a key account was worrying AMD. The problem had reached a stage where unless it was resolved quickly, it would seriously affect the company results.

The Company, AMD

AMD is an MNC operating in many countries. It is an internationally leading laboratory and process technology provider covering the segments of biotechnology and measurement.

The AMD Measurement division manufactures equipment and systems featuring weighing, measurement and automation technology for industrial and laboratory applications.

AMD Biotech is a leading provider of cutting edge equipment and services for the development, quality assurance and production processes of the bio-pharma industry.

Key customers of AMD are from the pharmaceutical, chemicals, food and beverage industries as well as numerous research and educational institutions. AMD has production facilities in America, Europe and Asia. It has sales units and agencies in over 100 countries.

Managing a Channel Partner

AMD had its usual share of channel-related problems some of which are listed below, and these were being taken care of as and when they arose.

- Channel partners visit customers outside their own territories.
- The direct sales team visits customers who are not part of the key customers list handed over to the channel partners.
- While channel partners claim that they have to face severe competition, they also rely on heavy discounts for sales. They maximize their profits while negotiating prices and this cuts down company margins.

However, one major problem arose with a key account where AMD found that they had put full faith in their channel partner but this, in turn, resulted in a difficult situation.

Specific problem of channel control is detailed as follows

The players involved were the GM S&M, the Service Manager of AMD, and a channel partner, Solution Sam. The client was a leading pharma company—Star Pharma located in Goa. Solution Sam sold industrial weighing scales to the pharma company in Goa as the channel partner of AMD.

In a recent instance, Star asked for an Annual Maintenance Contract (AMC) from AMD for their complete range of products—process weighing instruments, platform scales, weighbridges, lab balances, moisture analysers etc.—all products supplied by AMD as well as their competitors. The order value was worth $200,000. AMD decided to execute the order (AMC) through Solution Sam as it was based in Goa and could support the client quickly. The Head of Service at AMD and the GM S&M (Sales and Marketing) asked Solution Sam to quote for the AMC.

Solution Sam

Solution Sam was a firm started by Mr. Philip who was earlier working with a competitor of AMD known as Hercules. When he started working on his own, AMD made his firm Solution Sam as a channel partner as he was fully knowledgeable about the competitor products also. SS has been selling the complete range of AMD products for a few years now.

AMC Order from Star Pharma

The order was worth over $200,000 and covered 120 weighing machines at the Star Goa plant. The job was to provide periodical maintenance for all these machines and related systems twice a year and attend emergency break-down calls when needed. In case any spares or accessories were needed at the time of servicing, the customer would pay separately for these. On receipt of the payment from the customer (Star Pharma), Sam was to divert 25 percent of the payment value as finders' fees to AMD.

Problem

Star Pharma was a supplier of bulk drugs to many US customers and was, therefore, bound by the regulations of the US Food and Drug Administration (FDA) rules and guidelines. The USFDA had the right to visit and inspect the Star plant at Goa as and when they desired. There was a recent visit of the USFDA team to Star Pharma Goa for a process audit, which is an important matter for any pharma company. The inspectors of the USFDA normally come in a group of 8 to

10 scientists and engineers and check every process of manufacturing, QC, R&D, packaging and inbound and outbound materials management.

One serious observation made by the USFDA team was that the laboratory weighing balances at Star did not have proper records of usage and maintenance. They seemed to be getting used for above or below the specified weighing range as per the USFDA norms and most of the balances failed to meet the maintenance qualification requirement of the USFDA.

AMD now discovered that Sam Solutions was not even aware of the requirements of the pharma industry QC needs and was quite clueless of the USFDA rules governing such pharma companies.

The Head of Services of AMD flew to Goa the next morning and checked the balances at the QC lab of Star at Goa. He found that all the instruments were working satisfactorily.

However, the USFDA had issued an NCR (Non Compliance Report) against all the balances in the QC lab of Star at Goa. The NCR was for all the maintenance qualification and repair qualification norms prescribed by the USFDA. There was a negative remark on the QC process of Star Pharma by the USFDA and till the "defects"' were rectified, all supplies of bulk drugs to the US from this plant were to be stopped. Even after "rectification" the despatches could not be resumed till a further inspection and "passing" by the USFDA was done. The ball was now entirely in the court of AMD. The customer, Star Pharma was obviously very furious as their business to the US had suddenly stopped. AMD had to very quickly sort out the issue.

Here are some questions which RSG raised to his GM (S&M) and Service Head:

1. How seriously did AMD take the AMC contract with Star Pharma? Could they have taken more care and if so how?
2. What were the qualifications of Sam Solution to be given the full responsibility of the WMC contract execution? Did AMD check this before giving them the responsibility? What should they have checked and how could they have prepared the channel partner better to handle this major contract with a key account?
3. If you are the GM S&M of AMD, what action will you now take to correct this serious situation?
4. What are some of the guidelines to be issued to channel partners for the future on such projects?

This case has been prepared by V M Cavale with the assistance of Rupak Sengupta, Debajyoti Sen and Samarjit Bhowmick, students of TAPMI—CEE for class discussion only.

CASE 14.6

Advanced Measuring Devices (AMD)-2

The Company, AMD

AMD is an MNC operating in many countries. It is an internationally leading laboratory and process technology provider covering the segments of biotechnology and measurement.

The AMD Measurement division manufactures equipment and systems featuring weighing, measurement and automation technology for industrial and laboratory applications.

AMD Biotech is a leading provider of cutting edge equipment and services for the development, quality assurance and production processes of the bio-pharma industry.

Key customers of AMD are from the pharmaceutical, chemicals, food and beverage industries as well as numerous research and educational institutions. AMD has production facilities in America, Europe and Asia. It has sales units and agencies in over 100 countries.

Issue

RSG, the S&M (Sales and Marketing) Head of Advanced Measuring Devices was trying to get his sales team and the dealers/distributors to work more closely as a team to exploit the exciting marketing opportunities before AMD in a market where AMD was already a recognized leader. The sales and distribution progress of one of the Strategic Business Units—AMD Biotech was under review. In AMD-B, there seemed to be some unease between the salespeople and their channel partners.

AMD Biotech

The Biotech division had two kinds of products: Capital Equipment and Consumables. Consumables have three product categories—filtration, purification and filter papers all meant for laboratories.

- Capital equipment is sold to customers either directly or through dealers.
- For consumables, the sale is through dealers to end customers and each product category has a separate distributor who may sell the product directly or through a dealer appointed by him.

Problem in Consumables Distribution

The players involved are the members of the AMD sales team, the distributors and the dealers. For each product category there is one national distributor. Some features of a distributor are as follows:

- He has national responsibility
- He handles over 500 stock keeping units (SKUs)
- He imports the products directly from the parent company in Germany
- Order value of the products varies from \$100 to \$1000 each
- The reason for using a distributor for the entire distribution was to minimize inventory, avoid payment collection and collection of sales tax concession forms

At this point of review, the business from all the national distributors for AMD Biotech was below expectations.

Sales and Marketing Viewpoint

The sales and marketing function which deals with the distributors has got certain issues with the distributors which are summarized as follows:

- Distributors do not keep adequate inventory of the products and this affects the deliveries in the process business and in order to keep relationships intact for other businesses of the company, the company has to supply directly to the customer.
- Distributors want to do business directly with the customer and at times avoid the dealer. The company has to intervene and make supplies to the dealer directly.
- Distributors do not have adequate salespeople to cover their territories.
- At times, local dealer information is not shared by the distributor with the AMD-B sales team.

- Some customers do not like to deal with either the distributor or the dealer and want to do business directly with the company. They believe that this will give them a price advantage.
- S&M is not fully aware of the secondary sales and do not know how to support secondary sales if information is not complete.

Distributors' Viewpoint

When the distributors were confronted with the above issues, they had some point of their own which they wanted the company to take note of and take corrective action:

- The AMD-B sales team does not support the distributor sales team.
- The company violates the agreements by selling directly to customers.
- Company salespeople never visit customers with the distributor salespeople.
- Company product prices are high.
- The company does opportunistic sales—whenever the order value is high, the company does direct selling.
- The distributor makes the pre-sale efforts like giving product samples etc., but when the order matures, the company takes the direct sale route.

Dealer's Viewpoint

The dealer has been appointed by the distributor and has to work closely with him. Dealers also had their own issues which they raised with the company:

- The distributor delays delivery of the products and affects dealers' customer service.
- The distributor favors certain dealers at the cost of others.
- The distributor does not extend credit whereas the dealer has to give credit to the customer.
- The dealer does not get support from either the distributor sales team or the company sales team.
- Dealers find it easier to deal directly with the company than with the distributor.

At the time of reviewing the sales performance for the first 6 months of the year, the S&M Head came across the above issues. He now wants to find a solution to the problems so that the company salespeople, the distributors and the dealers work in close harmony and achieve good customer service resulting in good sales performance.

Can you help the S&M Head with some action points so that he can resolve the issues and achieve his objectives.

This case has been prepared by V M Cavale with the assistance of Rupak Sengupta, Debajyoti Sen and Samarjit Bhowmick, students of TAPMI—CEE for class discussion only.

CASE 14.7

Vidyut Products Ltd. (VPL)

The Company—VPL

VPL is an electrical equipment company making varieties of switches, wires, Circuit Breakers, etc. It is well established for over 15 years in 2 states of South India. Its products are well accepted by both builders (for residential and office buildings) and corporate clients (for their factories and offices). Over this period, Vidyut has made a name for its quality and reliability. Its products do have the ISI certification.

Distribution Network

VPL has a distribution network of stockists who have almost become like exclusive stockists as they have come to rely on the quality of the products and the excellent customer service provided by VPL. They are proud to be a part of the VPL distribution network. The stockists are managed by the company salesmen. The span of control of the company salesmen is about 15 to 20 stockists but seems easily manageable as results till date show. Many of the company salesmen have been with the company for 10 years and above. The company factory is located in the capital of one of the states in which VPL operates.

The production and logistics facilities are just adequate to properly service customers in these two states and VPL is not contemplating any geographic expansion into other states even in S India. Stockists work on a 8 percent margin and this has been well accepted. They also get a 10 day credit from VPL based on certain levels of purchase at a time.

Pricing Pattern

Occasionally, VPL operates trade promotions for retailers but to be passed on to them by the stockists under the strict supervision of the company salespeople. These trade promotions also include a Quantity Purchase scheme where the discounts would be higher on buying specific higher quantities.

For corporate clients and projects, the stockist and the concerned salesman would negotiate specific discounts which would be higher than the market discounts. These were some of the norms set up by the electrical equipment industry and VPL was just following these market practices.

Problem

In this particular city, VPL had 4 stockists with the most prominent and biggest stockist Maharaja Traders (MT) located in the main market of the city. All the stockists would properly cater to the requirements of the retailers in the geography assigned to them.

The stockists also used to handle the project sales after getting the approval of the ASM for higher discounts.

MT would mention names of the projects he was getting and would get permission from the ASM for higher discounts on specific quantities. MT would use only part of the quantity for the project and sell the rest of the goods to retailers all over the city using the higher discounts.

This action of MT resulted in two problems in the market:

1. The remaining 3 stockists were upset as their customers were getting the goods from MT on a higher discount which they could not give.
2. Multiple prices to retailers in the market started affecting the company image.

ASM, Mr. Ranjit spoke to MT and counselled him to curb this wrong practice but no resulting action on the part of MT seemed to have been taken.

Discussion Questions

1. What are the steps you would take to resolve this channel conflict before it escalates and affects VPL business in that city?
2. Is there any punitive action which VPL can take against MT and how?

Reproduced with permission from Network 7 Management Consultants.

Chapter 15

Channel Information Systems

LEARNING OBJECTIVES

After studying this chapter, you will be able to:

- **LO 1** Understand the importance of information systems for management of channels
- **LO 2** Describe the elements of information system related to channels
- **LO 3** Recognize some performance measures for channels
- **LO 4** Discuss the principles of channel implementation
- **LO 5** Explain the important aspects of IT systems for channels
- **LO 6** Analyze the use of handheld devices for collecting channel data

Varun was in deep thought on the way forward to solve the problem being faced by Sterling Products Company, of getting adequate field information in order to take meaningful actions. Varun was the National Sales Manager of Sterling and in the recent meeting with the CEO, had been given a one month time to solve the problem with a long-term action plan.

About Sterling Products (SPC)

SPC is a personal products company in business for over 27 years with a reasonably good presence all over India. It has 5 brands and 12 stock keeping units (SKUs). These brands are well accepted by consumers. SPC operates with 25 C&FAs, 512 distributors (who between them have about 1200 salesmen), 45 company salesmen and 17 ASMs.

Data/Information Systems

In the year 2012, SPC introduced some new systems to help gather data from the field:

- Distributor salesmen would fill up retailer cards every day to capture the sales by brand/pack made to each outlet—used for sales analysis
- Recording of the total secondary sales by brand/pack every day. A weekly sheet giving the daily information would be sent by the distributor to his ASM—used for sales analysis
- Week-end brand/pack stock level (inventory) at each distributor point also sent to the ASM—used for despatch planning from the C&FA to the distributors
- Forecast by brand/pack at distributor level sent once a month to the ASM—for the planning of all the departments
- Despatches by C&FAs to distributors each week—C&FA would send the brand/pack details to the ASM—a record of primary sales
- As part of the systems implemented, SPC defined clear stock norms at the different points in the distribution network: at the C&FA—10 days of average sales and at the distributor point—15 days of average sales.

Secondary Sales

Apart from the data received from the distributors, the ASMs could also calculate the secondary sales if there were some defaults in data receipts.

The ASMs used the simple formula at the distributor level by brand/pack: opening stock + despatches—closing stock.

Review March 2016

Having completed over three years in the new system, the CEO was concerned with some of the gaps in the planning process for which the data/information being received from the field salespeople and the distributors were being blamed. The gaps were being seen in the following operations:

- Irregular receipts of forecasts. Not always accurate. Upset the entire planning process—materials planning, production and despatches
- Secondary sales data always incomplete. Constant follow-up required with the company salesmen and the ASMs. Consistent defaulters in the field.
- Stock level information not given regularly. Despatch planning suffers.

Way Forward

Varun was thinking of ways of reducing the manual interventions in the systems which resulted in the gaps. He was getting to the stage where he firmly believed that the entire reporting system from the field needs to be IT enabled. The following questions needed answers:

- What are the options available for IT enabling the reporting of the field data?
- What option should be adopted and why? At this stage the cost of the system was not being considered.

The purpose of a channel information system is to collect and analyze data about the operations of marketing channels in order to assess performance and take timely corrective action to continuously improve performance. Channel information systems are of primary use to the sales managers and through their analysis to the company as a whole.

The information system uses methods and resources to collect, process, store and use the pertinent information for decision-making relating to the channel.

The types of information needed from the distribution channels could be all operations data (facts and figures), assumptions, anticipated occurrences (forecasts) relating to the channel system.

The steps for development of a CIS are: (i) decide what information is required, (ii) the information has to be organized in a manner suitable for interpretation and action and (iii) decide who and when will use the information for what purpose.

LO 1 Understand the importance of information systems for management of channels

IMPORTANCE OF INFORMATION SYSTEMS FOR MANAGEMENT OF CHANNELS

As the name suggests, the purpose of "channel information systems" is to collect and analyze data about the operations of channels in order to assess the performance and take timely and corrective action to continuously improve performance. Channel information systems are of primary use to the sales managers and through their analysis to the company as a whole. After all, sales management and the channels used by them are the windows to the outside world where the company actually earns its revenues and profits.

The advantages of having information are obvious, as described below:

- It helps in marketing planning by making available reliable and timely information both on the external environment and internal situation.
- It helps in tapping market opportunities.
- It keeps the marketing people alert against threats of competition.
- By providing market information, it helps spot trends—favourable or otherwise.
- It helps develop action plans for growth.
- It keeps the marketing function aware of consumers' needs to enable them to fine-tune marketing/distribution programs.
- Quality of marketing decisions depends on the quality of the information available.

The advantages of information systems in channels are as follows:

- Drastically changed the way in which information is collected, stored and transmitted between channel members
- Help channel members integrate all their functions
- They also have an influence on the channel networks which can be shortened
- Streamlines operations and improves channel flow

- Changes the order in which different channel operations are performed
- Influences the physical distribution of the products
- Improve channel relationships—balance of power between channel partners, reduce chances of conflict, better co-operation and co-ordination between channel members.

Information can be classified based on the use to which a marketer will put it to (planning, operations, decision-making or control) or it could be based on different subjects (consumers, products, competition, channels, promotions, pricing, sales volume and value).

One definition of a channel information system (CIS) reads as follows:

> *"The orderly flow of pertinent operational data, both internally and between channel members, for use as the basis for decision-making in specified responsibility areas of channel management."*

The information system, therefore, uses methods and resources to collect, process and use the pertinent information for decision-making relating to the channel. The process involves four steps:

1. *Collection*—It means acquiring and placing the raw data. For example, the monthly sales by each territory.
2. *Processing*—It means analyzing of data to get meaning out of it. Processing involves arranging, modifying and interpreting the data by the user. Comparison of sales between products or territories could be an example of processing.
3. *Storage*—Keeping the information intact till it is needed.
4. *Use*—It is the application of the information for management's decision-making. For example, the sales data of the past six months may help forecast the sales for the next month.

The types of information needed could be all operations data (facts and figures), assumptions, anticipated occurrences (forecast) relating to the channel system.

Why an Information System is Required?

The information should be through a system for the obvious reason that with the huge quantity of data available, if it is not systematic, it will be almost impossible to handle.

- The system is what makes raw data into usable information.
- In a system, the information can be used many times for different purposes.
- A system not only processes data, but stores it in easily retrievable formats.

The system, if in place, helps collection, processing, storing and retrieval of information possible as shown in Figure 15.1.

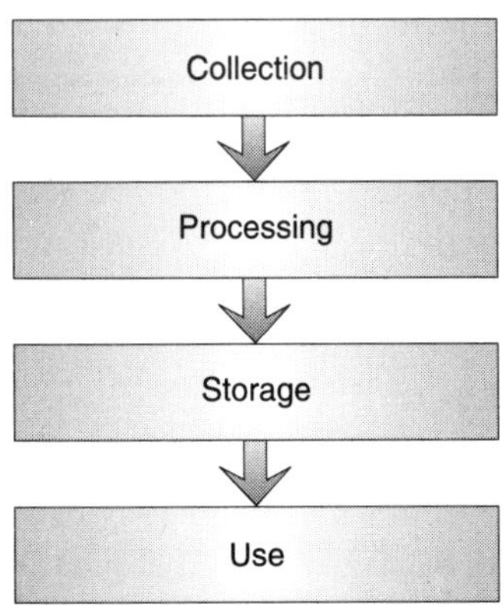

Fig. 15.1 Stages in a Channel Information System (CIS)

Components of CIS:

- Database of information
- Hardware and networks to collect, process and transmit

Infrastructure required varies between:

- B2B and B2C applications
- Retail applications
- Applications for customer/consumer interactions

Developing a Channel Information System—Channel MIS

Figure 15.2 explains the steps to develop a channel information system.

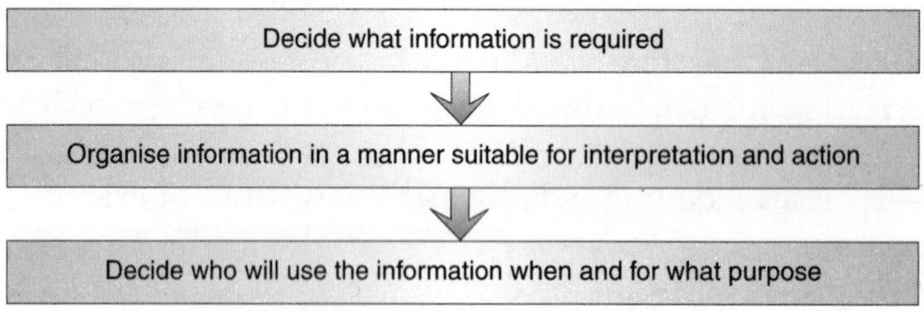

Fig. 15.2 Development of a CIS

The information may be used for planning (sales forecast or distributor indents) or control (expenses against budgets) purposes. There is a cost of collecting and analyzing information—this also should be kept in mind while deciding what information is required, how often and when. The channel information system works at the sales operational level. It has very little of strategic intent.

The source of the data could be reports (oral and written) and records of channel members and salespeople, letters, statements, market research and any information collected by the sales and channel people from the market.

At times, it may be necessary to gather data from external sources like published data, magazines, newspapers, and also trade journals. It is obvious that the data has to be adequate but not in excess or short of requirements. The salespeople who use most of the data from the channel system will, by experience, be able to narrow down the collection to the right kind and quantity of data.

In any company with a dedicated channel system, the collection of data, the formats, the frequency and the analysis are all streamlined and transparent to all the channel partners. With majority of companies using information technology methods to process data into actionable information, the process has become simpler.

Purpose of Information Systems

Obviously, the purpose is to provide timely information for decision-making. The objectives get modified based on the type of use of the data, the level at which it is used and the impact of the data on the channel system.

Operational data is used for planning of the channel and evaluation of the performance. It is further explained as under:

- Operational planning is forward looking and includes the forecasting and providing the resource support to achieve the forecast.
- Evaluation is backward looking to review the results achieved.

The level of use relates to who in the sales and marketing channel organization is looking at the data for taking action. The salesman who manages the distributors can look at the data and take limited action. The area manager, in charge of a number of such salesmen, is able to act in a lot more ways with the data as he has the authority to do so.

The impact of the use relates to whether the data helps take decisions for short term (next month planning) or longer term (launch of a new product). The channel leader has more use for the information than the channel members. Independent channel members like wholesalers and retailers collect limited data suitable for their use and hence their information systems are simple and adequate for their use only.

Volume and Value Information

In any system relating to channels, the data is always collected in two streams—one is in units (like kilogram, litres, boxes, cases) and the other is in currency terms (rupees, dollars, yen). Both volume and value data are equally relevant.

Channel information starts as raw data, which on proper analysis becomes usable information. Only when the information is in an actionable form can it be a part of the "decision support system".

If the data has to be analyzed into actionable information, it has to have a purpose defined first. There should be a defined use for the data after proper analysis and interpretation. It should be used to take action for improving the channel performance.

A Good CIS

Like any good MIS, even the channel information system should have some basic characteristics. A good channel CIS will:

- Be an integrated system to handle all regular data,
- Be a useful decision support system,
- Reflect the style of the marketing organization,
- Have to be user friendly and user oriented,
- Be convincing to the providers of the information as to why they should keep providing the accurate information in time,
- Be cost-effective,
- Not need of verification from other sources, and
- Be fast and totally reliable.

It is also clear that the information system will be as reliable as the data put into it. As the CIS is useful for sales operations improvement, it has to be accurate, complete, reliable, consistent, timely and objective.

List of some channel information systems in wide use:

- Electronic data interchange (EDI)
- Quick response system (QRS)
- Transaction-based information system (TBIS)
- Continuous replenishment program (CRP)
- Point of sale systems (POS)
- Efficient consumer response system (ECR)

Published information on some data systems developed by companies in the US:

- United Airlines—Apollo
- American Airlines—Sabre
- Johnson & Johnson—Co-operative Action Plus
- Abbott—Quiklink
- Systems developed by IBM for some companies—PrecisionCode, DataDesigns, Archer's retail database management systems, product information management system.

LO 2 Describe the elements of information system related to channels

ELEMENTS OF A CHANNEL INFORMATION SYSTEM

We will discuss the various elements of a channel information system and for each of these elements, try and understand the purpose, source of data, action possible and the impact on service delivery. First, a list of the elements of information that will interest sales managers dealing with marketing channels:

- Market information
- Competition tracking
- Distributor profiles and database
- Primary sales
- Secondary sales
- Pricing trends
- Promotions history
- Promotions evaluation
- Freight and storage costs—primary and secondary
- Distribution cost
- Distributor ROI
- Retailer cards
- Statutory information and reporting—like sales tax and vat
- Distributor's payment record

We will now discuss each of these elements briefly.

Market Information

This is the most critical part of the information for an operating sales manager irrespective of whether he is selling industrial products, FMCG products, pharmaceutical products, or automobiles. This information has to be regular, accurate, and updated continuously. The data can relate to the market potential, the different players in the market, activities of competition, activities of other channel players, actions of other non-competing but complimentary products and so on. For the channel members like distributors the information is required to be collected and reviewed every day and for the sales manager it may be required once a week unless there is a major event like a competitive product launch when the data is to be collected every day.

Purpose	To plan day-to-day activities
Source	Trade, channel partners and salespeople
Action possible	Change emphasis on products and packs to be promoted, change pricing and so on
Impact on service	Timely action to protect consumer franchise

Distributor Profile and Database

We have discussed this in detail in Chapter 12. The distributor profile compilation is a one-time exercise but the information has to be updated at least once a year. It will contain all the details of the distributor including name, address, location, name of the partners, number of years in business, number of years with the company, name of contact person, financial strengths, name of the banker, market standing, immovable properties, investment in the company business, other business interests, last three years sales performance, markets being covered, number of outlets being serviced, manpower, and other infrastructure provided.

The database on distributors will also contain details in terms of A, B, and C categories of the distributors. The salespeople have to put in a lot of effort to collect this the first time. Updating it later on, every year, would only mean adding or changing certain information.

Purpose	To plan all major promotional activities like a new product launch
Source	Salespeople collect it from the distributors
Action possible	Action major events and promotions in line with the capability of the distributor. Provide additional company support where necessary
Impact on service	The markets will be serviced at the same high standard irrespective of the category of the distributor

Competition Tracking

This is a more specific and focused extension of collecting market information. For mass based consumer products like FMCG and pharma, the activities of competition many times change the course of operating plans. The specific information to be collected includes current pricing on products, trade and consumer promotions being run, effectiveness of market coverage including productive calls, new product or pack launches, changes in distribution patterns, special events being organized and so on. The information is to be collected and analyzed almost daily and most of it is verbal communication along with periodical reports.

Purpose	To plan day-to-day corrective action to protect market shares and shelf space
Source	Trade, channel partners and salespeople

Action possible	Most of the times action has to be on the spot while in the market and taken by channel partners or salespeople
Impact on service	Timely action to provide better support to trade and retain their goodwill

Primary Sales

This is the sales done by the company to the distributors. This is the easiest information to compile. All dispatches from the company warehouses or the C&FA to the distributors form the primary sales and can be captured every day if the company has a computerized set up at the dispatch locations. The information is readily available by product, brand, and pack, both in units and in rupees (net of any deductions).

Purpose	To plan future dispatches in line with the quotas
Source	The dispatch section of own warehouse or a C&FA
Action possible	Salespeople can put pressure on the distributors to purchase more of brands needing emphasis or even to maintain inventory norms
Impact on service	Ensure that there is no stock-out of any line with the distributor so that the market does not suffer

Secondary Sales

This is the reflection of the true consumer off-take and the market shares of the company products and is critical to be measured. This is the sales done by the distributor to his customers—wholesalers, retailers and institutions in his territory.

This can be compiled in two ways:

(i) From retailer cards if these are being maintained and filled up daily,

(ii) By deduction at the end of any period: opening stocks + stock receipts during the period—closing stocks at the end of the period = secondary sales. It has to be compiled by pack size only.

Purpose	To study off-takes and plan promotions to improve off-takes. Also reflects the distributor efforts at selling
Source	Salespeople and distributors
Action possible	Focus on slow movers. For fast movers, push more primary sales
Impact on service	The pulse of the consumer and helps decide what is required and needs support

Retailer Cards

This is relevant only for FMCG and pharmaceutical kind of businesses where the number of outlets to be covered every day by the channel member is large. The retailer card has got information on the outlets like: name of the outlet and address, owner/contact person, the buying record by pack size on each call, stock level by pack size at the time of the call, approximate total value of competitor average purchases, and value of purchases during each visit. At the end of a month or a quarter, the cumulative sales in units by pack-size and value can be worked out to know the relative size of the outlet compared to the others. The data can later be used to classify all outlets into A, B, and C categories of outlets so that the focus on each category can be accordingly adjusted. The total sales from all the retailer cards for any day, is the secondary sales for the day.

Purpose	To keep a record of the purchase and stock holding patterns of retailers
Source	Data filled up by the company or distributor salesman every time he visits an outlet
Action possible	Increase sales by potential outlets. Classify outlets for deciding focus of sales promotion activities
Impact on service	Build stock pressure at retail outlets so that there is no stock-out when a consumer visits the outlet

Pricing Trends

As a routine for most consumer products, pharmaceuticals, engineering goods, automobile spares, salespeople and dealers/distributors/agents are required to collect competitors' price information. These are used for any immediate corrections required or to track the pricing trends. The data collection becomes serious and on a daily basis if one is dealing with highly price volatile products like edible oils, cotton yarn or precious metals. The prices to be collected are normally the company's price to dealer/distributor, and the price to wholesaler/retailer. The price to consumers in most mass based products are printed on the packs as MRP (maximum retail price). Price trend tracking is also relevant if the company has recently operated a major trade promotion—salespeople have got a responsibility to ensure that there is no under-selling (selling below company prices) in the market.

Purpose	To make sure that the company products are not at a price disadvantage
Source	Trade and distributors—collected by salespeople
Action possible	Corrective action to keep prices competitive
Impact on service	Ensure that the consumer gets value for money

Promotions History

Companies operate trade and consumer promotions regularly. Trade promotions are more frequent than consumer promotions. Promotions are meant for increasing stock pressure in the market (it gives that much less opportunity to competition to stock up), induce trials and force retailers to sell more to the consumers. The promotions history information includes promotions operated by product/pack-size during the year, the objectives set and the actual sales achieved, the cost of the promotion and the reaction of the competitors. The data should help in two ways: (i) scheduling of promotions and (ii) the effectiveness of the promotions and whether it can be operated in another market or repeated at a later date.

Purpose	Use past data to plan future promotions better
Source	Salespeople, trade and channel partners
Action possible	Plan same promotion better next time, extend to other areas or change targets
Impact on service	Run the promotions to provide consumers best value for money

Promotions Evaluation

Consumer promotions are designed by people from marketing (like product managers) in consultation with salespeople and operated by salespeople. Trade promotions are designed and implemented by salespeople. Both sets of people work against strict financial budgets to run their promotions and hence want that every promotion achieve the stiff targets set for them. It is mandatory for salespeople to evaluate each promotion within four weeks after the end of the promotion. The evaluation has to be done formally.

Information to be collected on trade promotions include objectives, targets compared to normal averages, territory covered, product, brand and pack-size, period of operation, results achieved by territory (secondary sales) against targets set, call productivity, cost of the promotion, spending against budget, reaction of competitors and qualitative evaluation of the promotion.

Information to be collected on consumer promotions includes objectives, targets compared to normal averages, territory covered, period of operation, brand and pack-size on which operated, results achieved by territory (secondary sales) against targets set, call productivity, cost of the promotion, spending against budget, reaction of competitors and qualitative evaluation of the promotion. It is also necessary to measure the secondary sales for four weeks after the promotion is over to check if the consumer promotion has resulted in a step jump in the average off-take.

Purpose	Study the effectiveness of consumer and trade promotions operated
Source	Distributors records/reports, trade and salespeople
Action possible	Plan same promotion better next time, extend to other areas or change targets
Impact on service	Run the promotions to provide consumers best value for money

Secondary Freight

The secondary freight is the transport cost for sending the finished goods from the company depots or C&FAs to the distributors. As the distributor's orders are managed by the salespeople, they should also keep track of how much it is costing to arrange stocks at the distribution points. Well managed companies believe that secondary freight should be the responsibility of field sales. Secondary freight works against a strict financial budget and does not give flexibility in sending less than full-vehicle loads or sending special loads outside regular dispatch schedules.

It is to be noted here that primary freight which is the transport cost for sending the finished goods from the factory to the depots or C&FAs is usually the responsibility of the production function and is not being commented on here.

Purpose	Keep track of freight cost to ensure full availability against budgeted costs only
Source	Depot staff, C&FAs and salespeople
Action possible	Use inventory and freight budget effectively to send stocks to faster moving territories
Impact on service	Optimum use of selling opportunities by placing stocks at distribution points in time and in full

Inventory Control

Inventory forms the biggest component of the working capital and has to be effectively used to maximize sales (both primary and secondary). Most of the inventory in the field (depots, C&FAs, distributors, dealers, wholesalers and retailers) is the direct responsibility of the salespeople. For mass based products, like FMCG, and pharma where there are a large number of stock keeping units (SKUs), inventory norms can be fixed for each of the distribution points. The stock norm is in terms of number of days' sales. Common finished goods stock norms in number of days' sales at different stock points are indicated as follows:

- Factory or plant: 7 days
- Depot or C&FA in same state as the plant: 10 days
- Depot or C&FA in a different state than the plant: 14 days
- Distributor or dealer or stockist: 14 days (assuming weekly deliveries)
- Wholesaler or retailer: 10 days (assuming weekly deliveries)

Purpose	Keep track of inventory levels of finished goods to ensure nil stock-outs and stocks within norms
Source	Distributors, depot staff, C&FAs and salespeople. Distributors and salespeople also keep track of stock levels in the market outlets
Action possible	Correct imbalances against norms, dispose-off unsaleable stocks quickly to avoid deterioration
Impact on service	Use stocks within norms to maximize sales

Orders/Indents from Channel Partners

It is necessary for the C&FA or depot to keep documented proof of all orders/indents received from distributors/dealers/stockists. Even when the orders are received by phone, they need to be entered into the system. This is necessary as: (i) the channel partner cannot later on say that he did not order some items, (ii) service level can be tracked by comparing the dispatch made against the order, and (iii) the distributor can be advised if an item is not available and if any other item can be sent instead (such substitutions can be tracked later if necessary to work out loss of sales opportunities). A history of orders/indents placed by the distributor during a three-month period can be tracked to inform the distributor about his primary sales record.

Purpose	Keep track of orders placed by the channel partner for comparison against his quota
Source	Depot staff, C&FAs and salespeople
Action possible	Get distributors to place orders regularly to match their targets
Impact on service	Keep the channel partners fully loaded with stocks to help achieve secondary sales targets

Distribution Costs

The performance of the sales function is also judged by the distribution cost of the marketing channel used by the salespeople to achieve the sales results. It is therefore necessary to keep track of the distribution cost against the financial budget provided for this. The cost of operation of the company depot is borne by the company. The C&FA meets all costs from the commission paid to him.

Distribution cost includes the following elements:

- Cost of operation of company-owned depots or a C&FA. This includes the cost of secondary freight (depot/C&FA) to distributors, storage cost (warehousing) and the administrative costs.
- The margin paid to the distributors—if this is a mark-up, it does not reflect in cash outflow, but has still got to be tracked as it adds to the consumer price. The distributor has to meet all his operating expenses out of this margin/mark-up.

- Any subsidies given to the distributors for covering difficult territories or rural areas.
- Cost of any credit extended to the channel partners or credit extended to any institutions.
- Cost of all damages, shortages and losses in the channel.

Cost of trade (including display contests and quantity purchase discounts) and consumer promotions is part of the product costs and is not considered a part of the distribution cost. Similarly, the cost of holding distributor meets for launching products or special events are not debited to the distribution costs. The data on distribution costs can be compared between territories to improve territory productivity. The margins given to the trade is built into the consumer MRP and is not usually treated as part of the distribution costs.

Purpose	Optimize the cost of distribution
Source	Salespeople spend and keep track
Action possible	Maximize productivity of the channel network by comparing territories
Impact on service	Provide adequate resources and returns to channel members to ensure good distribution

Distributor Return on Investment (ROI)

This is a critical parameter to be measured to keep distributors motivated to work effectively for a company. This subject has been discussed in detail in Chapter 12. Depending on the industry and the products the company can assure a certain ROI to the distributors on its business. For consumer products, an ROI of about 30 percent is considered quite good. It is necessary to measure the ROI at least once in six months for all distributors and the compiled information kept as a record. If the ROI is more than budgeted, the distributor can be assigned additional distribution tasks. If the ROI is not adequate, action is required to support the distributor with more business or his costs have to be better managed.

Purpose	Ensure adequate returns from the business to keep the channel partner motivated
Source	Data obtained from distributors and ROI compiled by sales staff
Action possible	Action to improve ROI or assign additional tasks if the ROI is more than budgeted
Impact on service	Only motivated channel partners can provide excellent service

Statutory Information and Reporting

There is a lot of data and records to be maintained in the depot/C&FA and the distributor point to meet legal and statutory requirements. These can be inspected at any time by the government authorities like sales tax/VAT officials, Shops and Establishment Act, Prevention of Food Adulteration Act and so on. This data is enormous and built up every day and month. Some of this data is to be kept in registers, the format of which is also defined by the concerned government department. Some of the data is also converted into regular reports and given to company salespeople for action.

In addition, the stocking points are expected to display some certificates issued by the government for indulging in the business they are doing. For example, every depot or distributor stock point has to display a sales tax registration certificate prominently. The sales office of the company managing that stock point has to have all copies of such certificates and also a summary record for all such stock points under its control.

Purpose	Keep data and documents as required by the law of the land
Source	All stock keeping points of the company. Responsibility rests with the concerned salespeople
Action possible	Penal action is possible if the data, record is not available or updated
Impact on service	These are control systems put in place by the government to ensure that the business is being done in a fair manner. This is a kind of consumer protection

Distributor Payments Record

Company appointed distributors or stockists or dealers normally pay for the goods bought by them from the company by demand drafts or pre-signed blank cheques. It is necessary to keep complete and updated information on the payments received against each invoice billed on them. The payment record shows the consistency of the distributor in making payments in full and on time. It will also have a record of any default (if his cheque bounced at any time and the distributor had to pay for the next three purchases by demand draft) so that salespeople have prior information about it. Where companies provide credit to the distributors, the data on the credit record has to be updated so that every time he places a fresh order the depot or C&FA can refer to the credit record before deciding if the latest order is to be shipped or not.

Purpose	To look at the history of the distributor in terms of prompt payments
Source	Depot/C&FA and sales staff
Action possible	Delay in dispatches if payment/credit record is not good. Insist on payments by demand drafts
Impact on service	Make sure that the distributor is financially strong to keep the service to the market uninterrupted

Storage and Processing of Information

Most of the operational data and information listed above is enormous and is not possible to collect and process it manually. It is obvious that information processing today, even relating to the channel system, has to be information technology (IT) enabled. The IT system to support channel information systems could be:

- An IT system developed and maintained by the company.
- There are a number of software companies who can develop simple IT systems which are customized for the collection of data and processing/analyzing it.
- It could be an off-the-shelf decision support system.
- Most of the ERPs, in their sales and distribution (S&D) modules support channel information systems.

Some noticeable operational improvements experienced with the use of CIS:

- Manage minimum order sizes
- Ensure required retail assortment
- Improves speed of delivery
- Optimize retail inventory levels
- Manage retail promotions and measure performance

LO 3 Recognize some performance measures for channels

CHANNEL PERFORMANCE EVALUATION

Expert opinion says that the purpose of distribution is to get company products within arm's reach of desire. Any channel evaluation system has to keep this in mind and find out how well the distribution channel is serving this primary purpose.

The frequency of channel member evaluation is based on a number of factors like:

- The degree of control the manufacturer has on the channel members. It is obvious that the evaluation can only be done on the channel members who are in contract with the company, like C&FAs, and distributors. There is no way that freelance or independent channel members like wholesalers will accept any evaluation from the company.
- The importance of the channel member in the performance of the company itself. A distributor in a major metro city like Delhi would be very critical of the performance of an FMCG company and his performance needs to be closely monitored as it can directly affect the performance of the firm.
- The nature of the product is also important in the evaluation frequency decision. FMCG or pharmaceutical products with a mass distribution base require evaluation more often than engineering products which have less number of products and customers.
- The number of channel members—more the number, the evaluation has to be more often to ensure that at least the majority of them are performing well.
- The category of the channel member—is he a C&FA, a distributor, a stockist or an agent for institutional business?
- The agreement or contract in operation with the channel partner.

Channel Performance Evaluation Criteria

The primary purpose of any channel member is to make the products available and visible to the consumer at a place and time where he wants it. The performance of a channel member has, therefore, got to be judged or evaluated in the context of these two primary tasks. Some of the criteria for evaluation include sales target achievement, coverage, merchandizing, and supporting all promotional activities.

In Chapter 12, we have seen other examples of performance evaluation of distributors by FMCG companies. The frequency of evaluation is the monthly sales cycle. The channel partner is to perform well on all the criteria every month. It is the responsibility of the salespeople in charge of the channel partner to ensure this and take corrective action where the results are not as expected.

Criteria for Evaluation

The criteria for evaluation of the channel members vary with their categories. The channel members to be evaluated are the company depot or C&FA, the distributor/dealer/stockist and the wholesalers and retailers. In the case of industrial products and automobiles, the authorized service centers have also got to be evaluated.

For the most common of the channel members, namely the distributor, the criteria for evaluation of performance could be some of the following as explained in Table 15.1; (please note that these criteria can be changed depending on the nature of the product).

Table 15.1 Criteria for Evaluation

Criteria for Evaluation	Popular Performance Measure
Sales target achievement	• Primary sales • Secondary sales (for FMCG) • Achievement of sales target • Sales growth by period • Market share achieved
Inventory management	• Average level of inventory maintained • Inventory turnover (inventory to sales ratio) • Inventory of slow moving packs • Storage quality
Selling resources	• Number of salespeople • Target achievement by each salesperson
Market coverage	• Calls per day • Productive calls per day • Extension of credit • Support to new product launches • Support to promotions
Back office support	• Use of PCs • Trained manpower • Reports, records

Each of the primary criteria can be given a weightage and the performance scores can be calculated as follows (it is to be noted that there is an element of subjectivity in giving the scores on some of these parameters (Table 15.2). It is assumed that the salespeople doing the evaluation will be fair to all distributors in giving the scores. However, this is the simplest way of evaluation followed by many companies.

Table 15.2 Calculation of Performance Scores

Criteria	Weightage (%)–(X)	Criteria Score–1 to 10 (Y)	Wtd Score (X)*(Y)
Sales target achievement	50	7	3.50
Inventory management	15	8	1.20
Selling resources	15	7	1.05
Market coverage	10	8	0.80
Back office support	10	6	0.60
		Overall performance rating	7.15

A similar rating can be given for each of the individual criterion (performance parameters). An example for sales target achievement is explained in Table 15.3.

Table 15.3 **Performance Rating Criteria**

Criteria	Weightage (%)–(X)	Criteria score–1 to 10 (Y)	Wtd Score (X)*(Y)
Primary sales	15	8	1.20
Secondary sales	50	7	3.50
Achievement of secondary sales target	20	7	1.40
Sales growth by period	10	8	0.80
Market share achieved	5	6	0.30
Sales target achievement	100	Performance rating	7.20

The overall performance rating can be calculated by adding the ratings of individual criteria based on their weightage.

Once the overall performance rating has been arrived at for each of the channel members being evaluated, we could then rank the channel members by these numbers to measure their relative performance to identify the good performers and the laggards. The ranking could be simple listing as mentioned in Table 15.4.

Table 15.4 **Overall Performance Score**

Channel Member	Overall Performance Score	Ranking
A	7.39	1
B	7.20	2
C	7.15	3
D	6.89	4
E	6.56	5
F	5.60	6

The bottom 20 percent on the list may need to be warned to improve their performance.

A company could also group together distributors in a range of overall performance scores and support the distributors differently. For example, the top scorers in the range have the potential to give more business to the company. The lowest ones in the range would have to be put on notice. This action is possible even without such a grouping.

In some of the other chapters, we have seen examples of the performance evaluation of other members of the channel system. These are not being repeated here, but only a summary is given ahead.

Evaluation of Channel Partner	Chapter
Retail performance measures—gross margin on inventory investment, Full-time equivalent employee, per sq. ft. of floor space	11
Transporter performance rating system—local and up-country	16
Evaluation of a prospective distributor, evaluation of distributor Infrastructure, performance evaluation of distributors	12

It has been mentioned earlier that it is not possible to formally evaluate the performance of independent channel members like wholesalers and retailers. However, there are certain observations that the field salespeople can make when visiting their own distributors (without the need for a formal evaluation) and wholesalers and retailers that can give them an idea of the "worth" of these channel members to the company. Sample checklists for such visit observations are discussed in this section.

Checklist for Field Force Visiting a Distributor

While there are methods for measuring the performance of a distributor, there are certain routines, checks, which the salespeople have to conduct every time they visit the distributor. A checklist indicating if the distributor or his salespeople are doing the following:

- The distributor has to open his office at least 30 minutes before the market opens up.
- The distributor or his sales/back-office people check the stocks available for the day's market work. It is assumed that the distributor holds between 2 to 3 weeks inventory level of saleable stocks by pack.
- All damaged and unsaleable stocks are segregated and accounted for.
- They plan the sales for the day. It is assumed that the previous day's sales reports and accounts have been completed the previous evening itself.
- All records are to be updated before starting the day's work. A physical check of the stocks with the book stock is to be done at the end of every week.
- Understand the promotion for the day properly and plan to maximize sales on the promotion products/brands/packs.
- Special emphasis is required on the recently launched product/brand/pack. The distributor or his salesman has to carry a sample of the new pack and start the sales talk in each outlet with the new launch.
- Ensure that FIFO is followed on all the stocks.
- The distributor or his salespeople should strictly follow the beat plan given by the company both for markets to be covered and the outlets to be called upon.
- All trade and consumer promotions should be conveyed properly to the trade customers and utilized properly.
- Status on filling up Retailer Cards.
- Check the point-of-purchase materials available and take them into the market regularly for use in the outlets they are meant for.

Checklist while Visiting a Wholesaler or Retailer

Wholesalers and retailers are independent businessmen and cannot be controlled by the company salespeople. Their performance cannot be measured formally. However, salespeople can judge the performance of the retailer by looking at some of these things when they visit the outlet:

- Stock level of the company products in the outlet (it is assumed that the retailer will always keep at least 10 days stocks).
- Stock level of competitors' products in the outlet. Obviously this has to be less than that of the company whose salesperson is visiting the outlet.

- How much of the stock is on display shelves and how much is in the back-store? The stock level on the shelves should at least be in proportion to the market share of the company products in that market.
- The total potential of the outlet on business would be evident from its size, space, the variety, assortment and quantity of stocks of all products in the shop.
- Quality of displays and effective use of point-of-purchase materials. This has to be checked both for company-owned products and that of competitors.
- If a company has managed to get a good shelf space display and POP use, this can be emulated.
- The importance given by the outlet to newly launched products.
- The distributor or his salesman has to first sell the slow moving and normal stocks to the retailer before mentioning any brands/packs with promotions on them. This is to get maximum mileage from each outlet.
- The distributor or his salesman should not leave an outlet without selling something. The objective is of course to increase the width and depth of distribution in each outlet.
- Action to be taken on disposal of damaged stock. Anyway such stock should never be left on display.

LO 4 Discuss the principles of channel implementation

CHANNEL IMPLEMENTATION

In Chapter 13, we studied about channel design considerations and in Chapter 14, we have looked at channel management issues including handling the difficult part of managing channel conflicts.

We will now try and understand some of the aspects of implementation of marketing channels. Some aspects of this exercise in relation to distributors in the FMCG environment have been dealt with in Chapter 12.

Channel implementation is more relevant when the channel principal has a channel which is bound by agreements and contracts and all the channel partners are part of the channel system.

Using independent channel members like wholesalers and retailers does not require much in terms of implementation effort except to distribute the products to them. These independent channels already exist and do not need to be set up. The marketer has only got to decide how many of these existing outlets he will allow his products to be present in—the "intensity" of his distribution effort.

In Chapter 9, we discussed about the intensity of distribution. The channel implementation issues vary with the intensity of distribution.

Before we discuss channel implementation further, let us look at some of the factors which influence the implementation:

- Intensive distribution allows the consumer the opportunity to shop anywhere he pleases to look for the product of his choice. Easy buyer access is possible with intensive distribution. We started the discussion in Chapter 9 by stating that the primary purpose of distribution is providing time and place utility to consumers and intensive distribution is the best way of achieving this.

- The more widely distributed products give the impression that the product or brand is the leader in its category. Studies have shown that intensive distribution in fact increases sales. Experience of good FMCG companies clearly shows that higher degree on intensity in distribution, increases sales. Companies like HUL, Colgate, Nestle, Coca-Cola, and P&G insist on their distribution partners to make sure that every outlet capable of selling their products should have their products. A lot of effort is put by these companies on "retail" distribution intensity so that the consumer looking for their products always finds it in his store of choice.
- Conversely, selective or exclusive distribution may result in loss of sales opportunities.
- At times channel members feel that a widely distributed product must be a fast seller and this is true to a large extent. However, any company will have a basket of products and brands all of which may not be fast sellers. The distribution network is expected to make equitable efforts in selling all the products and brands and packs.
- Intensive distribution is more expensive and requires more supervision. Conversely, selective distribution is easier to control. Manufacturers have to create a fine balance between the degree of control they want over the channel system or providing their products to consumers within an arm's reach of desire. Obviously manufacturers would want both in some degree. Of course, too much of control amounts to "interference" in the business of the channel partner and is not desired.
- In the case of consumer electronics or consumer durables with intensive distribution, there could be "free-riding" situations. The consumer may get all the knowledge about the product from one store and go and buy from another which gives a better bargain (as consumers we all have done it). One store bears the costs of selling efforts and the other gets the benefits. This cannot be avoided.
- The channel members prefer that the company distributes its products to the least number of other channel members so that they can have the benefit of higher volumes. Distributors are almost exclusive for companies and do not deal in competitive products.
- Even independent channel members like wholesalers and retailers in the market prefer that the leading brands are sold exclusively in their outlets. A company cannot, however, get into this tight situation as it may get "blackmailed" because of the exclusivity at some time.
- On the other hand, if a brand has a strong consumer franchise, none of the channel members can afford not to stock and sell the brands. In fact they would all want to sell the brand and in the process create an intensive distribution.
- The channel partner or the reseller (the term used in industrial goods) also has a choice in the manner in which he wants to operate his business and the products and brands he is willing to stock and sell. The implementation plan has to keep this also in mind.
- Both for the manufacturer and his channel partners, selectivity is a difficult option if the product category is important and the competition is severe.

If channel implementation has to take care of all these factors, how does one go about implementation?

- *Low value goods:* tea, cigarettes, soaps, shampoos, etc.—intensive distribution. Intensive distribution seems suitable for routine, low investment but mass based purchases—like FMCG goods. Here, better coverage makes it easier for the buyer to find the brand in an outlet of his choice. Even OTC drugs fall in this category (no wonder OTC drugs are now likely to be made available in grocery shops also). Stock-out of the brand in one outlet will compel the consumer to buy an alternative.
- *High value goods:* electronic goods or consumer durables where buyers will make comparisons across outlets—selective distribution is suitable. If a consumer wants to buy a color TV for example, he would visit 4 or 5 outlets, look at different brands and models, compare and then buy. This process happens even after a friend has recommended a brand/model before-hand.
- *Specialty goods:* Like a Mont Blanc pen or a Tag Heuer wrist watch—not an easy process of selection and the outlet has to also be extremely reputable—exclusive distribution. Here it is important for the manufacturer also to select the right outlet to stock and display his goods. It is easier for the manufacturer to sell a Mont Blanc or a Tag Heuer through a Rodeo Drive, The Leela or William Penn than any other stationery or watch outlet.

As we have seen in Chapter 8, the intensity of distribution itself depends on certain factors which are briefly recollected below:

- The influence of the channel principal on the channel members decreases with the intensity of distribution. Unless the principal has larger numbers of supervisory staff, it will not be possible to control the larger numbers of channel members.
- Intensive distribution means that the channel member's competitors also have the same brands. If Marico follows an intensive distribution policy, both Food World and Nilgiris and hundreds of smaller retailers, all, will stock and sell Parachute.
- The intensity of distribution also depends on the quality positioning of the product. For products with a high quality positioning, selective distribution seems more relevant.
- Intensity of distribution also depends on the target market. Producers of brands targeting a narrow band of consumers would prefer to have selective outlets to sell from. These set of consumers have similar buying habits.
    - A retail shop selling products meant for infants and babies is a good example of a focused target.
    - Jealous 21 jeans meant for ladies/girls have such exclusive outlets.
- The intensity of the distribution takes into account the importance of the market and the competition in the product category. For a small market, selectivity may still work. For a larger market, limiting coverage may be detrimental to the business. For a village with two big and four small outlets, the distributor may just cover the two big outlets and move on to other markets. This way, he can cover more rural markets on the same day and get his products into every village on the day's beat plan.

- Similarly, in a market with intense competition, the manufacturer will not be willing to restrict the distribution. Being selective in this case would immediately give a chance for competition to be more intensive and gain market share.

Selective distribution has certain advantages, which include:

- Selectivity in distribution is believed to cuts costs.
- However, selective distribution may also mean inadequate distribution. While selective distribution is appreciated by the channel members, the producer has a tough task in ensuring a strong support for his brand from his channel partners. He may derive this support by: (i) getting the channel members to accept stretched performance driven targets, (ii) eliminating members not willing to support the brand to achieve these targets, and (iii) support the promotion costs incurred by the channel partner on the brand.
- There is better influence over channel members with selective distribution. Lesser number of channel partners to handle means better supervision and control. To get a similar control in an intensive distribution environment, the company may need more salespeople.

  Costs may be lower because:
  - Selling expenses are less with lesser trading partners
  - Can afford to give higher levels of support to a smaller number
  - Less training and servicing is required for new channel partners
  - Larger transactions, lower processing and inventory holding costs
  - More accurate forecasting of demand because of fewer and larger orders.
- The margins of channel members may be better in a selective distribution situation.
- The manufacturer attracts more aspirants to become channel partners. Selecting the right partner becomes easier.
- Selective distribution may be particularly useful for a new product or a new market for testing the waters.

Let us now see how manufacturers support different levels of distribution.

Intensive Distribution

- Contract/signed agreements with channel members to operate in a certain manner—distributors, dealers or stockists.
- Build strong brands and force the channel partners to stock and sell the product. Lifebuoy or Nescafe or Vicks has so much brand pull that the channel member has to necessarily stock these brands.
- Limit the distribution within the intensity decided. In earlier years, Brooke Bond used to have a brand known as Special Hotel Blend Tea which was meant only for tea shops, restaurants and hotels. Salesmen were prohibited from selling this brand to the trade. There was tremendous pressure on company salesmen, from the trade, to sell this brand to them also.
- Companies advice channel members on the price at which they can sell the product so that they do not undersell. This is only possible by oral advice. At times, companies stop

supplies to wholesalers who undersell. This will only antagonize the wholesaler who will either buy the same product from another channel member or start selling competition or even spurious products with a vengeance.

Selective Distribution

Some of the methods companies may use to support such a distribution effort could include product specific training (industrial products), service support (industrial products), and support with special handling facilities (like cold rooms for pharmaceutical products) or hosting promotions jointly with the channel partner (most consumer durables companies in India do this).

Companies also would like to get the benefits of both intensive distribution and limited coverage. Some of the methods they use are building strong brands (HUL or Nestle), build brand variants by market, develop new products with inputs from channel partners or help in business development for industrial products.

Most of the channel implementation steps are decided at the time of the channel design itself. In the actual implementation, the intensity gets all the focus. Intensity of distribution is not written on stone. Companies can use it as appropriate. Let us end this chapter looking at a real example of fixing the coverage for a distribution channel and what it means in terms of the sales to be generated.

Example of Coverage and Break-even Sales

Some simple rules for deciding sales to be generated to meet distribution costs are given below. Let us make the following assumptions for a company:

Basic Data

Cost of a company salesman: ₹3,00,000 per annum
Calls per day: 35
Number of working days per year: 300
Number of calls per annum: 300 × 35 = 10,500
Salesman cost per call: 3,00,000/10,500 = ₹29
Total distribution expenses to sales (assumed as) 5 percent

Sales to be generated by salesman for cost break-even

Break-even sales to be generated by each salesman per year: 3,00,000 × 100/5 = ₹60 lakh.

Outlet revenue to be generated for cost break-even:

Assume each outlet is covered once every week.

Business to be generated by the outlet per year if it has to be covered every week: 29 × 100 × 52/5 = ₹30,160 (each visit to the outlet should generate a business of ₹580 per visit to break-even on distribution cost).

Town revenue to be generated for cost break-even:

This assumes that all outlets will be covered every week and each town gets 25-day coverage every month.

Business to be generated by the town per year to break-even on distribution costs: 35 × 25 × 29 × 100/5 = ₹61 lakh.

LO 5 Explain the important aspects of IT systems for channels

IT SYSTEMS FOR CHANNELS

So far, this chapter has dealt with the manner in which an effective and action-oriented information system can be created by the salespeople to manage their channels better. We will briefly talk about some of the IT systems which are available to help sales managers to manage their channels more effectively. For additional information on the subject, the reader is also directed to the section on "use of IT in managing supply chain" in Chapter 16.

IT solutions to business problems in managing channels primarily relate to some of the areas mentioned below:

- Ability to deliver customer orders faster
- Information in the system should be accurate and totally reliable
- The selling system should be able to manage results with the lowest inventory levels possible
- Closer integration with the other partners in the supply chain (beyond the channel system)
- Reduced freight costs (for example, better forecasting may be able to reduce month-end sales skews which can result in saving additional freight costs)
- A strong IT-enabled system also integrates the other business functions in particular sales, marketing and commercial
- Reduction in and faster resolution of customer complaints
- Customer service standards to keep improving to protect and grow market shares.

IT systems serve the twin advantages of improving operational results and also creating a competitive advantage. Some areas where this competitive advantage is obvious are:

- Creating a strategic difference in costs, speed of communication, shortening of lead times and where possible customized products.
- IT systems have proved effective in both reducing costs and improving productivity. For example, handheld computers given to a company or distributor salesmen help increase the call rates and call productivity as the time taken on non-sales activity reduces and the salesman can spend this saved time in the selling effort.
- IT systems also help the company and its channels target a wider segment of customers in the market place.
- Keeping customers informed constantly on the status of their orders.

It is not just enough to say that IT systems can create all these advantages. It is necessary for the systems to live up to the expectations and 'deliver'. Some of the Key Result Areas (KRAs) which sales managers keep track of are indicated below:

- The information being processed and used should be optimum—neither excess nor inadequate. This optimum level can only be arrived at after some experience.
- Does the system help sales and marketing to introduce new or substitute products faster into the marketplace?
- How does the support of IT for reducing costs and improving productivity reflect in profitability and market share gains?

- What is the useful life of the system which is in operation? How soon is it to be upgraded or replaced?
- Level of user (as in sales management and their channel partners) commitment to the use of and ownership (they are committed to use it fully) of the systems.

IT systems are primarily in the areas of salesforce automation (including the salesforce employed by the channel partners), integration with all other areas of the business and having robust decision-support systems. Some of the popular IT systems are listed below:

- Efficient Consumer Response (see Chapter 16): Product replenishment on shelves is based on product categories. This system is similar to the continuous replenishment programmes used in the retail industry.
- Salesforce automation systems: These help in reducing manual working in sales to speed up transactions and give more time to the salespeople for "personal selling" activities. (Siebel* systems is a good example.)
- Quick response systems: These are more relevant as a supply chain support system. As channels are a part of the supply chain, they tend to benefit also.
- Extranets: Producers can use these to share information with their channel partners. Obviously, this information is useful to the producer and the channel partner to improve customer service. (RSNet of HUL quoted in Chapter 10 is a good example.)
- In the retail industry, there are two well-known systems in use. These are:
    - Electronic shelf labels—to indicate the prices where there are a large number of SKUs and there are frequent price changes
    - Marking on shipping containers—uses scanned labels on shipping containers for quick identification
    - Electronic data interchange—the data is transferred between companies and their suppliers normally. This can be extended to finished goods also to include distributors.

SAP—Sales and Distribution Module

The objectives of the S&D module in SAP are:

- Helps manage the customer relations from raising a quotation to sales order, billing and shipping of a product or service
- Handles all the processes from a sales order to delivery
- Help execute business processes in selling, billing and shipping of products
- Handles all the activities of sales and distribution
- This module integrates in SAP with the modules of materials management and SAP production planning

---

* Siebel is considered one of the versatile solutions for managing customers across industry verticals like consumer goods, automotive, communications, apparel and footwear, healthcare, insurance, finance etc. It can be integrated with ERP solutions like SAP and Oracle. For example, in consumer goods, it provides customer relationship solutions for the entire demand chain from the end consumer through the retailer and wholesaler/distributor to the producer. Organizations use Siebel to identify consumer buying behaviors and plan new trade promotions or product offerings.

The components of the module include: master customer data, support to sales, sales information management, sales, managing contracts with key accounts, credit management, foreign trade (if any), billing and transportation.

The S&D module takes care of these specific tasks: handling inquiries and price quotes, managing sales orders, handling sales returns, handling consignments, scheduling dispatches, credit and debit memos, rush orders handling, back orders and deliveries.

Two simple flow charts give a summary of the process:

1. Sales process for trading goods:

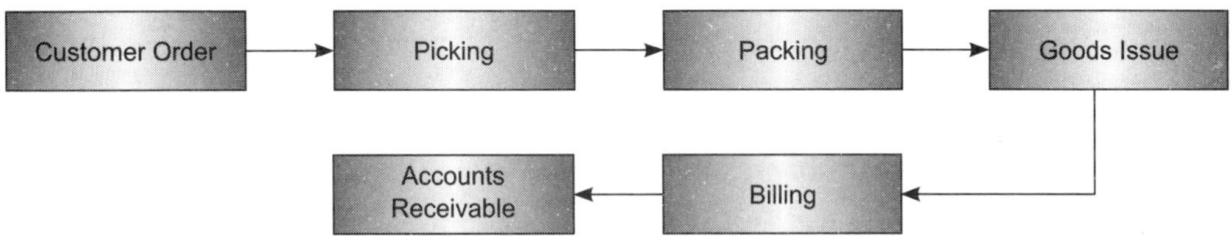

2. SAP SD process:

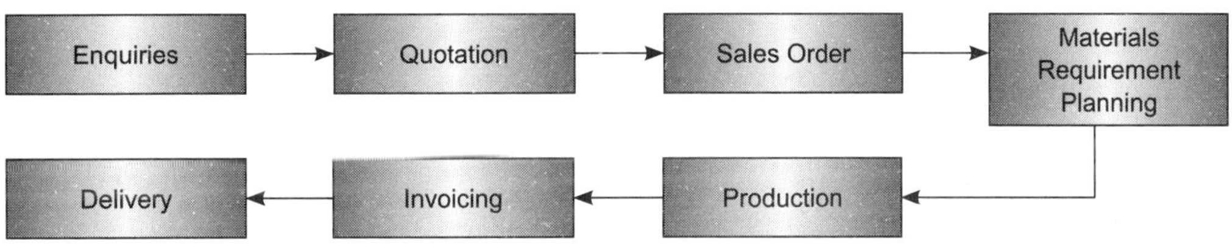

Center Steps up Efforts to Digitize Post Offices

Measures like core banking facilities, biometric devices for postmen, etc., booking a delivery of Speed Post, registered mail, sale of stamps, postal stationery and MOs to be done through these devices. As per *Economics Times*, over 1000 ATMs being set up in December 2015.

By March 2017, 1.30 lakh handheld devices were planned in rural branches.

The Postal Department set up 57 integrated state of the art parcel centers for booking, processing and delivery of e-com parcels.

The data in a CIS originates from the field—the salespeople and the channel members. Most of this data is for a regular frequency (for example, secondary sales) or at times occasional (like information on promotion sales). The earlier practice was quite tedious and time consuming as it was manual collection of data.

Thanks to the introduction of information technology software and hardware, this process of collecting data has been simplified and made faster. Most companies which rely on extensive data collection from the field have introduced handheld devices for use by the people (salespeople or channel members and their salespeople). We will understand more on this in the next section.

LO 6 Analyze the use of handheld devices for collecting channel data

USE OF HANDHELD DEVICES

Data Collection System Improvements

Data from field salespeople is required for a number of planning activities of all functions in the company including for marketing promotions. Some of the data collection, all of them at the brand/pack level includes:

- Sales forecasts at the channel partner level—to be given by company salespeople or the channel partners/their salesmen
- Primary sales data—despatches made from the C&FA/distribution center to each of the channel partners—for planning future despatches
- Inventory levels at the distribution centers/C&FAs and the channel partner points
- Secondary sales at each channel partner point—by various means

For a long time, the data collection of secondary sales in the field was being done through manual reports at specified frequencies mostly once a week.

Now the data collection from the field has benefited from the developments in the information technology area. Data collection has been simplified and speeded up by the use of handheld devices—mostly Android smart phones.

Leading companies in India are already using the power of IT enabled mobiles to collect actionable field information. These companies gather secondary sales and other field reports every day from the markets covered by their salesmen/distributor salesmen. These handheld devices (as they are called) can help do a lot more analysis than just capture data (convert data into actionable information).

Some of the data/information which these handheld devices provide from the field for companies with large number of channel partners and a widespread distribution network are summarized below:

- Route planning
- Category/sub-category/brand/pack size of goods handled
- Order booking/secondary sales information by brand/SKU
- Any authorized stock returns from the market
- Tracking daily and month to date target achievement
- Productivity numbers—number of calls made, number of productive calls
- Photographs of shelf displays when required
- Promotional sales details—both trade and consumer
- Payment collection details and any credit analysis required
- Channel partner performance analysis

- Any other specific data requirements which can be customized

Hand-Held Devices in Use

Handheld devices could also be called Personal Digital Assistants (PDAs) are being used by a number of leading companies like: HUL, P&G, Nestle, Cadburys, ITC, Abbott Pharma etc., all of which have a focus on intensive distribution.

In order to keep a distinct identity of their field information collection systems using handheld devices, these companies have given some names to their systems like Smart Dust, Quantum, On-track, Blaze, and Vajra. Most of these companies seem to be using Samsung smartphones with Android features.

SUMMARY

LO 1

- As the name suggests, the purpose of a channel information systems is to collect and analyze data about the operations of channels in order to assess performance and take timely corrective action to continuously improve performance. Channel information systems are of primary use to the sales managers and through their analysis to the company as a whole.
- The information system, therefore, uses methods and resources to collect, process, store and use the pertinent information for decision-making relating to the channel.
- The types of information needed could be all operations data (facts and figures), assumptions, anticipated occurrences (forecasts) relating to the channel system.
- The steps for development of a CIS are: (i) decide what information is required, (ii) the information has to be organized in a manner suitable for interpretation and action and (iii) decide who and when will use the information for what purpose.

LO 2

- The elements of a channel information system could include data and information on the markets, competition, pricing, primary and secondary sales, distribution costs, details of promotions conducted and statutory information, etc.
- It is obvious that information processing today, even relating to the channel system has to be information technology (IT) enabled.

LO 3

- Expert opinion says that the purpose of distribution is to get company products within arm's reach of desire. Any channel evaluation system has to keep this in mind and find out how well the distribution channel is serving this primary purpose.

LO 4

- Channel implementation is more relevant when the channel principal has a channel which is bound by agreements and contracts and all the channel partners are part of the channel system.

- Using independent channel members like wholesalers and retailers does not require much in terms of implementation effort except to distribute the products to them. These independent channels already exist and do not need to be set up.
- Channel implementation is influenced by the intensity of distribution. While there are a lot of benefits of having an intensive distribution in place, selectivity and exclusivity have advantages in specific circumstances.

LO 5

- The focus of using IT systems in channel management is obviously better customer service. Apart from delivering goods and services faster, the system should help this delivery at the lowest possible cost. IT systems serve the twin advantages of improving operational results and also creating a competitive advantage.
- IT systems in channel management are used primarily in the areas of salesforce automation, integration with the other systems in the company and developing robust decision-support systems.
- Some of the popular IT systems in use are: (i) efficient consumer response, (ii) sales force automation systems, (iii) quick response systems, (iv) extranets, (v) EDI, and (vi) CRM.

LO 6

- In order to collect field data in channel systems having large number of channel partners, products SKUs and customers, companies have started using the developments in information technology and telecommunication to provide handheld devices to all their salesmen (both company own and channel partner salesmen) to collect field data and convey the details promptly to salespeople who can process this data into actionable information for improving customer service levels.

Key Terms

Glossaries of key terms are mentioned at the end of all chapters

Channel information system
Collection
Efficient consumer response
Electronic data interchange
Evaluation
Exclusive distribution
Extranets
High value goods
Intensive distribution
Low value goods
Operational planning
Primary sales
Processing
Sales force automation
Secondary freight
Secondary sales
Selective distribution
Specialty goods
Storage
Use

Conceptual Questions

1. List the advantages of having orderly information available to support a marketing channel system. LO1 E
2. Explain briefly the stages in the collection and use of data. LO1 M
3. What are the steps in developing a channel information system? LO1 M
4. What are the characteristics of a good channel information system? LO1 E
5. List and explain briefly at least seven of the elements of a channel information system. LO2 E
6. What are the factors which determine the frequency of performance evaluation of channel members? LO3 E
7. List the performance evaluation criteria for a consumer products distributor. LO3 M
8. Explain how the channel implementation is impacted by the intensity of distribution desired. LO3 M
9. Develop a checklist of observations needed from a salesperson visiting a distributor. LO3 M
10. Develop a checklist of observations needed from a salesperson visiting a large retailer. LO3 M
11. Explain some of the advantages which salespeople can derive by the use of IT systems. LO5 M
12. How does the use of IT systems help create a competitive advantage? LO5 D
13. What are some of the key result areas which sales managers define for the performance appraisal of the IT systems they are using? LO5 D
14. Explain at least two IT systems used in sales and channel management. LO5 D
15. Explain briefly how handheld devices can be used by field salespeople to improve the customer service levels. LO6 M

Objective Type Questions

Select the most appropriate response out of the various options available in each of the following questions:

1. Channel information systems (CIS) manage an orderly flow of ________ and financial data.
   (a) marketing (b) sales (c) distribution (d) operational LO1 E
2. The information system follows the four steps of data collection, ________, storage and use.
   (a) processing (b) analysis (c) sorting (d) interpretation LO1 E

Note: Difficulty Level ⟶ E — Easy; M — Medium; D — Difficult

3. Developing a channel information system follows the steps of identifying information required, organization of information, and deciding the ______ and purpose.
(a) frequency (b) content (c) users (d) opportunity **LO1 E**

4. A CIS supports ___________ planning and performance evaluation.
(a) marketing (b) operations (c) distribution (d) sales **LO1 E**

5. The __________________ module in an ERP can help in managing channel information systematically.
(a) sales and marketing (b) production and materials
(c) finance and accounts (d) sales and distribution **LO1 M**

6. The criteria for evaluation of the performance of a channel system, depends on the channel member being evaluated and the _________.
(a) products (b) markets (c) objectives (d) frequency **LO3 E**

7. Implementation of channels is strongly influenced by the _________ of distribution desired.
(a) intensity (b) depth (c) width (d) extent **LO4 E**

8. Convenience goods require ___________ distribution.
(a) selective (b) intensive (c) exclusive (d) wide **LO4 M**

9. For a small market, _________ distribution may work.
(a) intensive (b) regular (c) selective (d) exclusive **LO4 M**

10. A reseller offers the manufacturer _________ in the product category.
(a) protection (b) sales (c) exclusivity (d) distribution **LO4 M**

11. IT systems enable the company and its channel partners to also manage the business with the lowest ___________ possible.
(a) inventory (b) cost (c) investment (d) disturbance **LO5 E**

12. IT systems improve ___________ results and create a competitive advantage.
(a) operational (b) sales (c) profit (d) monthly **LO5 E**

13. In any system, the information being processed and used has to be ____________.
(a) optimum (b) minimum (c) maximum (d) accurate **LO1 M**

14. Electronic shelf labels in retail are meant to facilitate consumers by indicating product ________.
(a) prices (b) location (c) value (d) weight **LO5 M**

Application Questions

1. Hi-Mileage Tyres (HMT) is a ₹500 crore company with national distribution of truck and car tyres and tubes. It specializes in radial car tyres. It has 200 dealers all India managed by four Regions, 20 ASMs and 20 company operated depots. It is a profitable company growing at over 15 percent in volumes year on year. The depots and ASMs convey their sales and stock figures

to the HO and Niraj, the National Sales Manager, once every month by e-mail and hard copies of standard reports. All the information processing for top management reports every month is done using the current legacy IT system. Finance has been frequently pointing out the discrepancies in the sales and stock figures and the promotional expenses. In the recent top management monthly meeting, the CEO announced the implementation of an ERP in the company shortly and he has asked all department heads including Niraj to give their information requirements from the ERP. Please help Niraj draw up a list of data, information and reports required from the ERP and the frequency of this information so that Niraj can benefit fully from the implementation of the ERP. Please note that if something is missed out now, the ERP implementer may not agree to make the changes in the system to provide this information later on. Hence this exercise is critical. LO5 M

2. For the last three years, the detergent company Safedi Detergents, which has over 600 distributors all India, has introduced a yearly performance appraisal system for all its distributors. The results of the annual performance review is summarized in the yearly distributor annual conference held every year in third week of April in the Head Office in Delhi. Akash Distributors of Chandigarh is disturbed by the poor evaluation done for them in April 2006. The owner, Omprakash, has figures of primary purchases which show that he has achieved his volume targets for the year. He has also earned a lot of commissions on the primary sales. Safedi wants him to prove this with secondary sales. Omprakash refuses to give secondary sales details. The sales management is aware that Omprakash has been supplying a lot of stocks to his brother Manoj's wholesale shop in Ambala. The Ambala distributor has confirmed this to the company. He has proved how his own secondary sales is suffering. If you are the sales manager of Safedi in Delhi, how would you convince the distributors that performance evaluation has to be on secondary sales only and how would you correct Akash? LO2 M

3. Aromatic Tea Company is based out of Nagpur with a packing unit in Buti-Bori. They are in the business of packaged tea for the last three years and have grown into a ₹32 crore business in Vidarbha. They have been selling their tea packs only to wholesalers and major retailers through their own 14 salesmen. They feel that they need to have a more intense distribution to increase sales volumes to at least ₹100 crore in the next three years by covering Chhattisgarh also. They have the production capacity to do this. They have two schools of thought within the company. One thought is that intense distribution, even in extended areas, can only be possible through company own salesmen. Another group feels that they should go in for distributors who can be given the task of this intensive distribution and can do it more effectively. This group feels that the current 14 salesmen can easily manage at least 170 distributors in the two states. If you are Girish, the Sales Director of Aromatic (you are also the nephew of the owner), what action on channel implementation will you take and why? LO4 D

4. National Electronics (NE): Increasing channel productivity—NE is a leading importer and distributor of the latest electronic goods. NE operates two kinds of distribution channels:
   - Direct from company to corporate customers
   - For consumers, the company reaches them through dealers, value-added resellers and retailers. Dealers sell both to other businesses like retailers and to consumers through their own outlets.

Some of the issues which the sales management of NE is currently grappling with are given as follows:

- Should the pricing of products for both corporate and consumer channels be the same? How does the company justify if there is a difference?
- There is a conflict between the dealers and the resellers in terms of availability of goods and the pricing. Resellers feel that the company favours the dealers in terms of business.
- At times, the company salespeople help the dealers to sell off the stocks bought by them. Is this a right policy? Is it not a secondary sales the job of dealers only?
- The market channels do not seem to be making specific efforts to increase the share of company products in multi-brand outlets. What needs to be done to achieve this?
- The company is not happy with the credit extended by the dealers to the retailers. The company feels that this could be increased to gain market shares. The dealers do not support this view. What is the action possible?

NE believes that the productivity of channels can be measured by the sales generated by them and the share of the NE business in a particular channel.

NE is currently looking at ways to strengthen the channel network and productivity. Can we help them in this process by suggesting a course of action? LO3 M

5. Leader Electric: Getting higher commitment from channel partners in establishing a brand—Leader is an electrical engineering products company and is one of the oldest and most well-known companies. During the course of its growth, it has taken over many smaller companies. One such company it took over is known as Everyday Electric. After taking over Everyday, Leader was trying to migrate the brand to Leader in the countries where both companies existed before the merger.

   This problem relates to a country called K where Everyday was a better known brand than Leader. The focus of the company after the merger was on the total company business and salespeople were pressurized to get the Leader brand well established.

   However, the distributors were focusing on the more "familiar" brand which happened to be Everyday. This was not in line with the company requirement and resulted in an obvious perception conflict. The company used to closely monitor the distributor sales and stock replenishment levels. The problem was compounded by the fact that the supply chain of Leader was better than that of Everyday.

   How to increase the commitment of the channel partners on establishing and selling the Leader brand. Do you have any suggestions? LO3 M

6. Century Software Ltd: Handling customer service through channels—Century has been in the business of distribution and reselling of software for leading software companies—it is a partner with these companies.

   There are three tiers in software selling for some software companies like Century: (i) the principal who is a software maker and vendor; (ii) the distributor who imports, licenses and also handles the shipping and customs; the distributor can also act as a reseller; (iii) the reseller who interacts with customers, handles customer orders, pricing, installation and troubleshooting.

   Most of the principal software companies with whom Century was a partner, generally did not give any credit terms to the reseller but gave 30 days credit to the distributors.

Customers were experiencing a delay in the receipt of the software as it used to move from the vendor (company) to the distributor, to the reseller and then to the customer. The whole process would take about 3–4 weeks.

Century recently faced two problems of delivery which are highlighted hereunder:

(i) For a particular product, there was no distributor. The company delivered the product electronically. The supporting media was however delayed. The customer refused to pay in advance. In the meantime, import duty of 12 percent was introduced. Who is to pay this?

(ii) Century tied up with a vendor to promote their new software. A customer wanted that the installation of the software had to be done either by the company directly or its distributor. At this point the company did not have any technical resources and hence the distributor agreed to do the installation. The installation was delayed and the customer wanted to return the software. What action is now possible? LO4 M

7. Jupiter Soaps and Detergents: How do we decide if a distributor is profitable for himself?—JSD is the No. 2 company in the market and growing at a healthy pace. It has an excellent network of distributors—many of whom have been over 20 years with the company. Distributor margins which were initially at 8 percent are down to 5 percent now. The distributors grumbled at the reduction but accepted it as the business was growing at a healthy pace.

   The company introduced the **concept of ROI for distributors**. They felt that instead of talking about margins, the company should ensure a fair ROI to their distributors. It was felt that 25–30 percent ROI was reasonable. The company would initiate corrective action if a distributor ROI was either more or less than this figure.

   One of the distributors of JSD is Classic Distributors in a major city. Classic has been with Jupiter for over 12 years. Last year Classic had an ROI of 47 percent much more than 25–30 percent which the company felt was reasonable. Classic was asked to cover additional rural markets around the territory.

   Classic politely declined this advice but made a request to the company to increase his margin from current 5 to 7 percent. Current year numbers: Turnover ₹93.9 lakh, Investment ₹6.5 lakh, Income ₹4.65 lakh and expenses ₹1.7 lakh.

   What is the ROI of Classic Distributors and what action is suggested? LO3 E

ASSIGNMENTS FOR STUDENTS

1. Meet a distributor or dealer of any prominent company. Talk to him. List all the data he (or his salesman) has to collect every day and every week. Also find out: (i) how they collect the data—manually or using any devices, (ii) how they transmit the data to their company and to whom, (iii) what is their understanding of how the company uses the data and for what purpose.

2. Get in touch with a contracted channel partner of any company: (i) marketing two-wheelers (ii) marketing consumer durables and (iii) marketing mobile telephones. Ask them if they know their ROI and how this number has been derived. Can you collect enough information from them to calculate their ROI if they are not aware of it?
3. All effort has to be made to observe a handheld device in use by a field salesperson using a PDA every day from the distributor/dealer point to every outlet he covers during the entire day of field work. Observe and record all the items of data/information he collects and the time taken. Also understand what the salesperson does with all this data at the end of the day.
4. You will need to get in touch with any company which has implemented a formal Channel Information System (CIS). Get to know from them all the "elements" of their CIS and how the collection of data on each of these elements is used to have a positive impact on their customer service.

Reference Notes

1. Bert Rosenbloom, *Marketing Channels: A Management View*, Chapter 14, pp. 460–481.
2. D J Bowersox & M B Cooper, *Strategic Marketing: Channel Management*, Chapter 11, pp. 340–362.
3. C G Walters, *Marketing Channels*, Chapter 14, pp. 376–407.
4. Gary L Frazier & Walfried M Lassar, "Determinants of Distribution Intensity", *Journal of Marketing* (1996): 39–50.
5. "The Future of Distribution Alliances", *Modern Distribution Management*, (September 1998).
6. Michael Garry, "ABC in Action", *Progressive Grocer*, (February)1996): 71.
7. "Duty Free Shops", *Business India*, (November 06, 2005).
8. "Reliance Petroleum Retail Coverage", *Business India*, (November 06, 2005).
9. "In All the Right Places", *Business India*, (April 23, 2006).
10. "In a Maze", *Business India*, (July 17, 2005).
11. *Sales and Distribution Management*, ICFAI Press.

CASE 15.1

Indian Engineering Ltd (IEL)

It was late on a Tuesday evening in March. Ramesh, the CEO of IEL, was sitting with his bright young executive assistant Amit in his office for a final review of the presentation Amit and he had put together to be put before the Board of IEL where the heads of sales and marketing (S&M) and the four regional managers would also be present.

It all started three months back when Ramesh joined IEL as its CEO. The chairman had briefed him and told him clearly that in six months' time he had to put the sagging sales and market share of IEL back on track. In the last three months Ramesh had studied the entire company in great detail and spent a lot of time with the S&M people. Ramesh had understood the issues and come to conclusions on the way forward. He was to present his recommendations tomorrow.

Brief note on IEL

IEL is an over 40 years old company in the engineering industry in India. It has been a market leader for many years in the products it offers. Its turnover last year was in excess of ₹700 crore.

In the last six to seven years, with intense competition from domestic and MNC players, it has been losing market shares and dropping margins drastically. This was the situation when Ramesh knowingly joined IEL. He had a background of having turned around the earlier electrical goods manufacturer he had worked with for seven years.

- IEL has four business divisions (SBUs) with different product groups serving separate end-user segments.
- Channels of distribution in each division is based on product characteristics (decided on 16 parameters by IEL) and the service support required (on 8 parameters). It is obvious that the channel system for each division is customized to the requirements of the SBU.
- Sales of products and spare parts and service are done either directly by IEL or through the channel partners. Institutional business is a major component of IEL sales and revenue.
- A similar strategy is followed by their competition.
- The S&M organization has a support group in HO with four regional managers and 20 branch managers (one in each state). Under the BMs are sales managers, ASMs, sales engineers, service engineers, dealers and authorized service centers all over India.
- Each SBU has a marketing wing in HO.
- There is commercial support at each branch/region.
- The field people feel that the roles of the players in the S&M function are clearly defined. Not everyone in IEL supports this view.
- IEL pays its people reasonably well in relation to the industry. Recent entrants to the industry are weaning away some good people with highly lucrative offers.
- S&M people are not exposed to any training and development except on the product and its servicing.
- The S&M function needs to interact closely with Purchase, Production, and Finance to ensure support for its efforts.

Key Business Drivers

In the intense study, which Ramesh has done of the business, he has clearly defined the factors which drive the business in the industry. These are:

- Consistency in product quality
- Customer satisfaction
- Cost effectiveness
- Brand image development
- Long-term strategic thinking
- Development of new product applications
- Clearly defined marketing policy

In a quick informal survey done with the S&M people and some dealers, customers etc., Ramesh realized that IEL figured 3rd or 4th in ranking against its major competitors on all these parameters. IEL under the leadership of Ramesh wanted to "perform" far better in the industry. Very clearly he had to recommend a lot of strategic change to the Board tomorrow.

More than the strategic recommendations, Ramesh was more concerned with the suggestions he had for the S&M function the next day. He was sure that these would not be taken kindly by most of the members.

Customer-Driven S&M

To get back its rightful share in the industry, Ramesh has got a five-point mantra for the S&M function to start all over again:

- Knowing their markets
- Knowing their customers
- Knowing their competition
- Be pro-active to meet customer needs
- Develop a strong commercial outlook—do not believe in selling cheap

Ramesh has observed the following areas where he feels that the S&M function has to radically change the way they work if they have to gain their market dominance—he is going to ask the head of S&M tomorrow to give him a time—bound plan to tackle these issues:

Sales Operations

- Salespeople hardly make regular visits to the market.
- They spend a lot of time in the office making calls and following up with production for dispatch of goods.
- Salespeople visit dealers for collecting orders or payments—never for visiting end customers
- No formal/regular beat plans have been laid for the salespeople.
- Salespeople do not submit formal reports on their daily activity.

Channel Support

- Dealers in IEL are hardly under any pressure—it does not matter if their targets are not beaten
- Service engineers are fire-fighting all the time attending to customer complaints as quality of IEL products is not consistent. They do not find enough time to meet all customer complaints satisfactorily.

- IEL products are not contemporary—for example, they still have mechanical controls whereas others have already moved on to digital/electronic controls.
- Frequently the salespeople get the approvals of the HO for discounts on products giving the explanation of the importance of the order/customer and the threat of losing to competition. They seem to have lost the ability to sell under pressure.

S&M Viewpoint

- Selling IEL products in the face of better technology/consistent quality of competition is not easy. Discounts are the only means IEL sales team has of getting sales.
- Production does not support the efforts of sales—hence the need to follow-up over phone and spend time in the office. Otherwise orders will not get executed.
- IEL is not able to support the sales/service people by being top class on the seven key business drivers.
- Getting orders and payments from dealers take away most of the time—there is hardly any time for customer visits.
- There is a lot of paper work and reports to be done—there in no computer support—hence the need to spend a lot of time in the office.

Discussion Questions

1. You know what the CEO Ramesh thinks of the S&M function. You have also heard from the S&M people their side of the story. What do you think? What should be the action plan for IEL to start gaining lost ground?
2. Do you believe there is role for improving the logistics and distribution system in IEL? What would be expected of the system? Please discuss and make out your recommendations.

Reproduced with permission from Network 7 Management Consultants.

CASE 15.2

Teekha Spices Ltd.

Teekha Spices Ltd (TSL) is in the business of marketing branded spices both straights (chilli, turmeric, *dhania,* etc.) and blended spices (*garam masala, sambar powder, rasam powder, chaat masala,* etc.) in all North Indian markets. Teekha, as a brand name in spices, is a household name for over 50 years and is the market leader in most markets in which it operates.

TSL has an excellent distribution network of over 1000 stockists in all categories of markets. It sells straight and blended spices in consumer pack sizes of 25 g to 500 g. It also has low unit packs in sachets of ₹2 (straights) and ₹5 (blended). For institutional customers like hotels, restaurants, *halwaiis,* tea shops, and bakeries, it also sells in 1 kg, 2 kg and 5 kg packs. TSL brands have an Agmark rating of purity.

TSL has done extremely well in its business and has a supportive distribution network. It is looking for additional business opportunities.

One of the marketing consultants appointed by it to explore new business opportunities gave the idea to the company to go in for branded consumer packs of rice. This seemed to be a good idea even for north India where rice consumption compared to wheat is much less.

The company decided to enter the branded and packed rice business in north India. It is now two years since the company has been in the domestic branded (the brand name is Khushbu) rice business and when a review was done recently, the following facts about the TSL branded rice business came to light:

- After two years of being in the business, the current volumes are only 100 tonnes per month. This low volume does not seem to have "disturbed" the top management.
- The total branded rice market in India is estimated at ₹1500 crore (1500 tonnes per day or 45,000 tonnes per month).
- KRBL—India Gate brand seems to be the biggest player in India with an annual turnover of ₹200 crore (6000 tons per month). The numbers in 2 and 3 were only estimates made by TSL and were not verified.
- Even after two years of introduction, TSL has not set up a good quality control system for checking the quality of the incoming raw rice to its packing plant. TSL has been informed by experts that rice quality can be checked on about 16 parameters. Now the only means of checking the raw rice is the visual inspection of samples by the buyers. Quality and consistency are the biggest problems in the rice business for TSL. In spices TSL considers its quality and consistency as its core strengths.
- Consumers all over India buy rice only if it is old. The purchase people of TSL buy new rice because it is cheaper and force the salespeople to sell it. This is an uphill task.
- TSL rice prices do not seem to be in line with its quality and definitely not in line with the market for similar quality. TSL is out-priced. In spices, TSL can command a premium pricing as the consumers rely on its quality and are willing to pay for it. TSL thought that they should also have premium prices in rice and this does not seem to be working.
- The salespeople of TSL in spices are not willing to sell rice as it requires a lot of effort in each outlet. When pressurized, they forcefully dump the markets with stocks which get returned later on. The sales force seems to have lost the ability to painstakingly introduce a new product in retail outlets and make it a success. TSL has also not made any efforts to train the salesmen about the characteristics of the rice business and how to make it a success.
- There has been not much effort to establish the Khushbu brand name of rice and hence off-takes from retailer shelves are very poor. Except for the brand name Teekha and the product coming out of the TSL stables, there is no USP on the product. Teekha is well known but not Khushbu. There are not many promotions to support the brand. It has to be sold only under pressure.
- TSL speaks proudly of its stockist network. The test of this network should be in its ability to launch and make success of new products like rice. Most of the stockists of TSL in A and B category towns and multiple stockist towns refuse to keep TSL rice. If they do not want to support a new product of TSL (even in major TSL markets), where is the loyalty to the company and what is the value of relationships built over decades? TSL is

not able to get exclusive distributors for rice in class A and B towns.

- The only people who have supported TSL rice so far are the stockists in the C and D category towns. These stockists sell about 200 to 300 kg in a month. However, an average retailer in any of these towns would be selling the same quantity of any of the major brands.
- In the last two years, TSL has introduced a number of varieties under the brand name Khushbu. The number of varieties at present is about three with ten pack sizes in all.
- There is also a working capital issue in rice procurement. If TSL has to sell old rice, it has to buy at least six month's raw rice and store it. On current volumes alone this is about 600 tonnes and has a value of ₹100 lakh. TSL is not willing to tie up so much working capital on rice.

Discussion Questions

1. What are the lessons you can learn from TSL on the distribution of a new product with enormous potential?
2. How can TSL make a success of rice using its distribution network?
3. Should TSL exit the Rice business? Will this not mean that the current distribution network built over many years is not effective?

Reproduced with permission from Network 7 Management Consultants

CASE 15.3

Ashwin Healthcare Ltd (AHL)

Ashwin Healthcare Ltd is a pharmaceutical company which has been in business for over one decade. It has a combination of prescription drugs, OTC products and some diagnostic reagents for laboratories. Many of its products are market leaders in their respective categories. AHL has grown exponentially in the last three years.

AHL has over 600 distributors all India and these are managed by a sales team of a GSM, 4 regional managers, 15 ASMs and over 150 professional service representatives (PSRs). All the PSRs have a combination of hospitals, nursing homes, chemists, laboratories and general stores as their customers. The distributors are common for all the products of the company.

The distributors have a clear, well laid out beat plan which they and their own salesmen are to follow strictly. The PSRs also have a permanent journey plan approved every month giving the details of the daily coverage of different customers expected of them.

In a recent review of the performance of the salesforce done by the CEO, it was noticed that the productivity of PSRs was falling and this was of serious concern to the top management. The number of calls made by the PSRs was falling short of the targets and so was the productivity of the calls. A detailed analysis revealed the obvious fact that the pattern of calling and converting different kinds of customers was different.

Hospitals and nursing homes took a lot of time to complete the calls. There was a lot of waiting time and procedure to meet the purchase people and on their advice, to meet some of the doctors. This amount of time had to be spent at the outlet as these customers were critical and big.

Diagnostic laboratories were similar to hospitals but were easier to call on in terms of time spent.

Calling on doctors who had their own private practice could only be done in the evenings after the clinic is opened. Most of these doctors also used to be on duty with different hospitals and nursing homes during the day and could not be met during the day. The appointments and meeting time in the evenings many times stretched to even 10 p.m. Even when a busy doctor gave a fixed time, he could not be met at that time as he would have a lot of patients who would get priority and there would also be a lot of other company PSRs waiting to see him.

Chemists followed the timings dictated by the markets in which they were located. Chemists would not want PSRs to call on them the first thing in the morning before they had done some business. Any time after 11 a.m. was convenient to meet them. Some of them were not available between 2 and 4 p.m.

The PSRs had to also call on general stores for some of their OTC products. These were similar to chemists and had similar habits and working hours.

Common tasks to be performed in all kinds of customer outlets:

- Checking physical stocks of medicines carried (not with doctors)
- Collection of outstanding payments (not with doctors)
- Obtaining fresh orders (not with doctors)
- Getting prescriptions recommending AHL products (with doctors)
- Cross-checking with chemists if doctors are prescribing AHL products
- Arranging with distributors, to take back date expired stocks from all types of customers.

Calling on a combination of these different kinds of customers and spending quality time with them was upsetting the schedules and working patterns of the PS₹The PSRs used to commute between customers on their own two wheelers.

Out of the 150 PSR of AHL, 100 of them were operating in the cities of Delhi, Mumbai, Chennai, Kolkata, Hyderabad, Bangalore, Pune, and Chandigarh. The rest of the PSRs were scattered in the various important towns of the country.

The CEO and the General Manager Sales decided to change the customer mix of the 100 PSRs in the major cities. The PSRs were spilt into three groups:

1. One set of PSRs to call on hospitals, nursing homes and laboratories only.
2. The second set of PSRs to call on doctors only.
3. The third set of PSRs to call on chemists and general stores only.

It was believed that this action would result in better call productivity and each customer would get adequate time from the company front-line salespeople and business would improve.

Discussion Questions

1. Is this a good proposal for improving distribution effectiveness? What do you think?

2. Would this not mean that each distributor would have to deal with a combination of three types of PSRs? A distributor would give priority for action to the advice of which of the three PSRs?
3. How can a PSR calling on doctors verify with chemists if the doctors have prescribed AHL products if the chemists are on the beat of another PSR?
4. Would not this split in responsibility mean a lot more time would be spent on travelling?
5. If this proposal is not right, what is the solution to the problem of falling productivity?

Reproduced with permission from Network 7 Management Consultants.

CASE 15.4

Gem Soaps and Detergents

Gem Soaps and Detergents Ltd (GSDL) is a major player in the industry and has been in business for over 30 years. Some of its soap, detergent and shampoo brands are brand leaders in specific geographies. GSDL has two detergent brands (one premium and one popular), six soap brands and two shampoo brands.

Over the years, GSDL has developed a very strong distributor network of 1250 distributors all India. These distributors are managed by 140 company salesmen. The distributors also have nearly 2800 salesmen of their own. Each of the distributor salesmen have a clear beat plan for each day of the week giving the sequence in which they are required to cover the outlets for that day. The distributor salesmen report their secondary sales using simple retailer cards.

Recording Secondary Sales

Presently the distributor salesmen reported outlet-wise daily sales through retailer sales cards which they physically filled up in each outlet. This was a tedious and time consuming process and GSDL wanted to use technology and save time.

How do Others do It?

GSDL asked a leading marketing consultant to do a quick study to find out how other well known and multi-national companies were using technology to gather secondary sales and other field reports every day from the markets covered by their salesmen/distributor salesmen.

Findings of the Survey

The marketing consultant completed the study quickly and gave some useful insights into the use of handheld devices by salesmen of many of these companies to record secondary sales. GSDL was pleasantly surprised to note that these devices could help them do a lot more analysis than just capture of data.

Some of the Salient Findings of the Survey as Given by the Consultants are Summarized Below

- The survey was conducted among a number of FMCG and pharma companies like HUL, P&G, Nestle, Cadbury, ITC, Abbott, etc.

- These companies were selected as they had a large number of channel partners and salespeople in the market at any point of time.
- The application using handheld devices had been given specific proprietary names by these companies to help their field people in instant recognition.
- Almost all the companies seemed to be using Samsung smartphones with Android features for these operations.
- The most common use of and market data collected by all these applications were as follows:
    a. Order booking information
    b. Route planning
    c. Category/sub-category of goods handled
    d. Any stock returns
    e. Tracking daily target achievement
    f. Month to date target achievement
    g. Any other specific performance metric like number of calls, number of productive calls, etc.
    h. Photographs of shelf displays

Some of the companies were also tracking some special information which is not done by the others. These are:

a. Use devices with built-in bar code scanners
b. Payment collection details
c. Credit analysis
d. Channel partner performance analysis
e. Feedback on current commercials
f. Any specific surveys like performance of promotions, sales contests etc.

Action proposed

After getting these details the sales management of GSDL were quite excited about the prospect of using similar handheld devices to enhance the performance and productivity of their field staff. While the usefulness of the devices was quite clear, it was not clear as to the cost of using these devices and any support infrastructure in their IT backbone which may be required.

The top management of GSDL agreed in principle to implement these suggestion of the use of HH devices but asked the National Sales Manager to submit a proposal with a clear cost-benefit analysis.

Discussion Question

1. Can you help the NSM create this cost-benefit analysis? Please draw up an action plan for implementation of the suggestion.

Chapter 16

Market Logistics and Supply Chain Management

LEARNING OBJECTIVES

After studying this chapter, you will be able to:

LO 1 List the principles of materials management, logistics and supply chain management

LO 2 Explain how the strategy for logistics is derived

LO 3 Understand the principles and systems of inventory management, warehousing management and transportation management

LO 4 Discuss how IT enables logistics function and learn about the use of technology in logistics function

LO 5 Review the performance measurement of logistics function

LO 6 Determine the principle for logistics in rural markets

It was the second Monday of April 2017. A brief review meeting of the performance of the year just ended (March 31, 2017) had been scheduled at the HO of Alpha Engineering, a well-known maker and market leader of fans of all varieties for household and corporate use. The meeting had been convened by Subhash, the marketing director and the only invitee was Richard, the GSM of Alpha.

Subhash congratulated Richard and his sales team on achieving the revenue, profitability and growth targets of the year. The next item on the agenda was how well the logistics part of the business had fared during the year and it was on this that Subhash had certain concerns which he wanted to emphasize with Richard so that a solution could be found for a better performance on logistics the current year onwards. These concerns were:

- The supply chain cost for the year was 17 percent of sales. The industry norm was 12–13 percent of sales.
- There were serious issues on inventory management—partly the month end sales skews seem to contribute to this—this impacted the working capital costs of the company.
- The company operated with 20 C&FAs and over 300 contracted dealers. It had 3 manufacturing plants which despatched goods to the 20 C&FAs based on indents placed by the sales people. The total freight cost was in excess of the year's budget.
- Service level to sales varied between C&FAs and ranged from as low as 62 percent to the highest which was still only at 84 percent. This was a measure of percentage of indents by SKU met by factory.

Subhash and Richard were looking to suggest a solution for these issues and present it at the next Managing Committee meeting of Alpha scheduled later in the month.

Some salient points on the planning process in Alpha are highlighted here:

- Alpha had implemented a simple ERP solution in the entire company in 2015–16. This had resulted in data integration, clean data and fast data.
- Sales people generate brand-wise pack-wise forecasts every month by C&FA.
- These forecasts are converted by sales people into brand-wise monthly indents by C&FA on the designated factories after taking into account the inventory levels in the C&FA.
- The designated factory arranges for transport and despatches the goods by full truckloads to the respective C&FA based on the indents received. Factories do not give to sales any clear commitments on despatch dates.
- Factories department in HO decides the inter-factory movement of products/ SKUs not made by any factory to meet the despatch needs of that factory.

Marketing channels provide the "reach" for a product or service to its customers/consumers. This reach has to be ably supported by the "physical" distribution efforts which are handled by the Logistics/Supply Chain functions.

Logistics and Supply Chain Management (SCM) provide support to the time (speed) and space (location) utilities of the marketing channel system. This they do by effectively managing the inventory, warehousing and transportation tasks for the company producing and marketing the goods and services.

Like every other function, Logistics and SCM also get their performance and cost effectiveness measured by specific methods on customer service delivery.

Information technology has added value to the Logistics and SCM functions by providing tools to analyze information and enhance customer service capabilities of the functions.

LO 1 List the principles of materials management, logistics and supply chain management

ORIGIN OF LOGISTICS

The origins of logistics and supply chain management are from materials management. Materials management is the function in a company responsible for the co-ordination of planning, moving, storing, and controlling materials in an optimum manner so as to provide a pre-decided service to the customer at a minimum cost.

As materials forms the largest single item in most companies, any significant contribution made by the materials manager in reducing the materials cost would directly impact the bottom line.

The materials cost as a percentage of the total cost varies between industries. It could be as low as 40 to 50 percent of total costs in industries like steel, fertilizers, and pharmaceuticals and go above 60 to 65 percent of total costs in industries like textiles, sugar, and commercial vehicles. In any case, it forms a major part of the total costs of the products and is critical to manage well.

The materials management function includes: (i) Materials planning and control, (ii) Purchasing, and (iii) Stores and inventory control.

Handling these functions independently could create a conflict of interest. Hence an integrated approach was required.

Besides this, with intense competition and the customer having a wide variety of choices in everything he wants to buy – be it products or services, customer service became the focus. This in turn led to logistics concepts to start with and more recently supply chain management.

A brief look at the time frames is as follows:

- *Before 1970s*: the functions were fragmented as transport, warehouse management, materials management and inventory control, parts and service support, and return goods handling
- *During 1970s*: Logistics came into practice in two broad areas of materials management and physical distribution
- *During 1980s:* logistics started getting integrated into inbound, conversions, and outbound

Only in the 1990s was the concept of supply chain management and integrating operations with suppliers and customers started getting focus.

Customer Service

Mahatma Gandhi said:

"A Customer is the most important person ever in this premises. A customer is not dependent on us. We are dependent on him. A customer is not an interruption of our work – he is the purpose of it. We are not doing a favour by serving him – he is doing us a favour by giving us the opportunity to do so."

Today's customer is :

- hard to please
- smarter, more value conscious
- more demanding and less forgiving
- approached by more competitors with equal or better offers.

All this is taken as given. In spite of these factors, the challenge is to produce loyal and long-term customers.

Customer acquisition has three elements to it: (i) Lead generation, (ii) Lead qualification, and (iii) Account conversion.

1. **Lead Generation**—reaching the prospects who can become customers. If a company is selling a branded shampoo, it has to get in touch with the wholesalers and retailers who are capable of stocking and selling personal care products.
2. **Lead Qualification**—to meet and judge the financial strengths and decide on the capability of the prospect to become a customer. The company selling shampoos quoted above will target all the right retailers who are well established and can sell branded personal products like shampoo.
3. **Account Conversion**—to make offers, answer objections and negotiate final terms of the sale. The personal products company has to persuade the retailers to stock and sell the branded shampoo.

The more difficult part of the task starts only after getting the customer – that of retaining him for the longer term. This is possible only if the customer is "satisfied" with the company product or service.

A satisfied customer:

- Stays loyal longer with the company and its products and services
- Has chances of buying more products and services from the same company and upgrades from existing products
- Always talks favourably about the company and its products or services
- Is also expected to offer product or service ideas to the company
- His transactions with the company become so regular that he or she costs the company less to service.
- To illustrate, a customer who has bought a Maruti Alto car and has been driving it for over a year and is fully happy with his car, can be guaranteed to talk good about the Maruti Alto to his friends and relatives and even persuade some of them to buy the same brand and model.

Customer service performance is a measure of how well the Logistics system functions in creating "time" and "place" utility for the company's customers. The customer service elements include:

- *Pre-transaction elements*—including the company policies on how to deal with customers.
- *Transaction elements*—the physical distribution of the products and services and reflects in the "ease" of doing business with the company for its average customer.

- *Post-transaction elements*—includes things like warranty, spare parts and service. In this context one readily recalls the Maruti advertisement which effectively communicates that a Maruti service station is available even in a place which may not even have a place to get decent food to eat for a weary motorist.

A company wanting to provide the highest level of customer service has to attempt the impossible as mentioned in this statement:

"You can please some of the people all the time and all of the people some of the time. You cannot please all of the people all of the time." The logistics or supply chain function in a company has to attempt this impossible task.

A leading automobile manufacturer in India has created spare parts hubs in Chennai, Delhi, and Mumbai to provide access to smaller markets also. The company also operates smaller warehouses from a select number of prominent dealers. The objective is to provide quick, JIT service to customers.

Definition of Logistics

"Logistics" means having the right thing at the right place at the right time. A rider has been added to this definition nowadays – that this has to be achieved at the right cost also. Some more definitions are as follows:

"The procurement, maintenance, distribution and replacement of personnel and materials."

—Webster's Dictionary

(The reference to "personnel" is obviously from the armed forces where the term logistics seems to have been first used). This definition also includes procurement or the purchasing function which in reality is kept separate from the logistics/supply chain function.

1. The science of planning, organizing and managing activities that provide goods or services.

   —Logistics World 1997

2. A business planning framework for the management of materials, service, information and capital flows. It includes the increasingly complex information, communication and control systems required in today's business environment.

   —Logistix Partners, Helsinki

3. The process of planning, implementing and controlling the efficient, effective flow of goods, services and related information from the point of origin to the point of consumption for the purpose of conforming to customer requirements.

   —Council of Logistics Management

The last definition is more apt for supply chain management rather than just logistics. The key words in the definitions need to be highlighted:

- *Planning* indicates a carefully thought out process that has critical implications on the operations of the company. This word also indicates that the function of Logistics is dependent and works with other functions in the organization. The plan may get generated by Logistics but has the input and support of other functions like purchase, marketing, production and commercial.

- The focus is on the flow of materials, services and information. Obviously a running operation is not "static" but is "moving" and logistics has a major role in this "movement".
- *Implementing* clearly indicates that it is a "happening" exercise and not just a "concept". Logistics is clearly "action oriented". The function does not just generate plans but has to get them implemented so that the customer service objectives of the company are achieved.
- *Controlling* would mean that all the actions, and operation has to be done within certain feasible business parameters. These parameters could include speed, reliability, consistency, efficiency and effectiveness. Even customer service has a "limit" to it and cannot ever be "at any cost".
- Communication is another key component of logistics function and all players involved need to be kept "informed" about what is happening so that they can in turn plan their activities better. These players could be suppliers, production staff or even customers.

All the activities have only one objective – meeting customer requirements. The focus is the "customer". The customer should feel and confirm that he is happy with the service and not any internal department of the company.

We shall now consider logistics operations as under:

- *Functions*: include planning, procurement, transportation, supply, and maintenance. These are strictly operational details and have to be undertaken daily. Once the company is clear on its marketing and customer service strategy, the operating managers ensure that all these details are taken care of to achieve the objectives.
- *Processes*: include determination of the requirement, acquisition, distribution and conservation. This aspect includes all the co-ordination requirements of logistics with the functions of purchase, production and marketing. Again as part of running the operations, there is a serious element of interaction with other functions to help the logistics function achieve its goals.
- *Business*: is the science of planning, design and support of business operations of procurement, purchasing, inventory management, warehousing, distribution, transportation, customer support, financial and human resources. Looks at the overall support of logistics to the business.

SCOPE OF LOGISTICS

Logistics is relevant to a wide range of manufacturing and service organizations, any of whom believes in maximizing customer service. It is equally important to manufacturing operations, government departments, educational, medical, and hospitality institutions, service organizations like retailers, traders, etc., and financial service organizations. Scope of logistics could also include:

- A company choosing the markets in which it wants to operate

- Deciding on the plant location and layout. Also decisions on whether to have own production facilities or outsource them
- All aspects of inventory management including costs and service levels
- Customer service policies
- Extent of distribution network to be built up
- Location and management of storage facilities
- Choices of mode of transport, selection and management of carriers
- Any packaging decisions that directly impact storage and transportation

Key Logistics Activities

Logistics manages the above scope through some regular activities which are highlighted below.

- *Customer service* consistent provision of "time" and "place" utility. Like it was mentioned earlier, the customer is the ultimate judge of how well he thinks his needs are being taken care of. This is the primary focus of marketing. Logistics is only required to provide the time and place utility. It has to ensure that the product or service being offered by the company is available to the final consumer or end user when he or she wants it (time utility) and where he or she wants it (place utility).
- *Demand forecasting* decisions on how much to order from suppliers and when and how much to produce for customers. This activity normally starts with the sales forecasts given by marketing and sales function. This is normally the function of sales to develop the forecast at agreed frequencies for agreed geographies. The forecast then becomes the starting point of the planning function which is the responsibility of logistics.
- *Distribution communications* need for information on distribution, which could be complex, automated and fast. This may include status of orders (from suppliers to the company and the company to its first tier customers who could be distributors), shipment dates and likely delivery dates. Logistics is concerned with the contact with the suppliers on the "inbound" side and the channel members and customers on the "outbound" side. For inbound logistics which provides "service" to the manufacturing function, there is a need to follow-up with vendors to get the raw materials and packing materials on time to support the production. On the outbound logistics, communication relates to keeping customers informed about the status of their orders. Overall, Logistics communicates with the entire organization in providing reports and records to help determine the level of customer service being provided.
- *Inventory control* this is a trade-off between the level of inventory to be maintained and the expected service levels to be provided to the customers. More on this will be discussed later in the chapter.
- *Materials handling* movement and storage of raw and packaging materials, work-in-process and finished goods. This is the physical handling of the goods within the firm and in the case of finished goods till they reach the customer.
- *Order processing* getting orders in time from customers, checking the status of execution and delivery. The salespeople get the orders and usually pass it on to the logistics function for processing and dispatch.

- *After sales parts and service support* this is very critical for all technical products, engineering goods and consumer durables. The responsibility of the company does not stop at the sale but extends till the warranty period and many times till the working life of the equipment.
- *Plant and warehouse site location* at optimized cost to the company. There are linear programming models which can help arrive at the ideal location, but this has to be "tempered" for local operating conditions.
- *Procurement* purchase of materials and service from outside organizations to support the firm's operations including selection of vendors, price negotiations, terms and supplier quality assessment. Normally the purchase function in organizations is not a part of logistics but is separate. Logistics has the task of following up with vendors on delivery schedules after purchase has negotiated the terms and placed the orders on the vendors. However, as Logistics is also a service provider to production, they do get involved in vendor rating exercises.
- *Packaging* primary purpose is that it is a form of advertising and marketing support. Logistics is concerned with providing protection for the product in transit and storage. Logistics is therefore involved in the outer packaging.
- *Returned goods handling* in case of a problem with the product or the customer. Returned goods may also be required to support production like empty bottles in the soft drink industry. Returned goods could also be date expired stocks like in the pharmaceutical industry.
- *Reverse logistics* getting back materials for disposal, reuse, reprocessing or recycling purposes. This is the logistics part of the returned goods mentioned above.
- *Salvage and scrap disposal* of all materials not usable in its original form or for its original purpose.
- *Traffic and transportation* adds place utility to the product. This is a very important activity of the logistics function. They have the responsibility of reaching the products to the C&FAs/distribution centers (primary transportation) and C&FAs/DCs to the distributors/institutions (secondary transportation).
- *Warehousing and storage* to support the time and place utility. These warehouses could be owned by the company or leased by it. An example of company owned warehouses would be the finished goods storage within the factory premises or the duty paid warehouses just outside the plant.

MATERIALS HANDLING

Materials handling is one of the functions of managing inventory along with storage and transfer of information. The activities under materials handling are as follows:

- Receiving, storing, and dispatching the goods: it could be receipt of raw materials and packing materials from vendors, storage of raw materials or finished goods and dispatch of finished goods to the distribution channels. Unless the raw materials are being received under vendor quality certification, incoming raw materials are quality checked before taking into the factory stores. Similarly, finished goods are dispatched only after the quality has been checked.

- Order picking and packing: based on customer orders, the warehouse personnel prepare a "picking" list for the workers to physically locate the goods in the warehouse and pick it up. Picking may be manual or using materials handling equipment like fork lift trucks. Packing refers to aggregating all the materials under one customer order.
- Order picking could also relate to items or components issued by the stores for meeting indents from the production shop floor.
- Sorting of goods: whenever a full truck load of assorted goods are received, there is a sorting done before storing them in appropriate pre-designated locations in the store.
- Additional processing may mean repacking where there are damages to the original packing. The goods get dispatched only after this "repair".
- Arranging transport and loading the goods on to the truck or whatever mode is required for dispatch of the goods to the selling points.

Materials handling functions today are mostly done using handling equipment as this method is more efficient and faster than using manpower for doing the handling work.

Order Processing

Order processing is part of the logistics or the supply chain function in the company and is the primary contact between the company (supplier) and its customer. The order processing function gets the order, prepares the invoice, arranges for the goods to be picked and packed, and then dispatches. It keeps track of the goods till they are delivered to the customer. The customer demand, order or indent is the starting point of this process.

The cost and efficiency of the logistics function and the company are dependent on the quality, speed and accuracy of the order processing function. These qualities will ultimately facilitate better customer service and serve as a competitive advantage.

Order management is the responsibility of marketing or salespeople who keep track of customers, get their order and pass it on to the logistics function for processing and delivery.

For processing any order which has been received, the logistics function depends on records or files some of which are listed below (this can be true in an IT-enabled environment or otherwise):

- Customer Master—it has all the information about the customer to help complete the order
- Item Master—it has all details of the items in the inventory which are ready for dispatch to the customers
- Price Master—it has all the details of the price of the items ready for dispatch
- Database—the database could also have files on customer quotations, open sales orders (orders yet to be dispatched) and customer sales history (to decide on the terms to be agreed in the invoice).

Once the logistics function has decided that the order can be processed for dispatch, the steps to be taken are as follows:

- Receipt of the order and "entry" into the system (irrespective of whether the order has been received from sales people, by phone, mail, or even on the Internet)

- If the ordered material is not readily available in stock, the order is sent to production planning department to plan.
- The payment terms of the order are checked by accounts/finance department to understand the credit worthiness of the customer.
- Inventory allocation, picking and packing—physical putting together of the order quantities
- Order invoicing and shipment—bills of lading, shipping papers and loading of the goods.

The benefits that a company can derive from a "sound" order processing system could be:

- Order cycle lead times to be continuously reduced
- 100 percent order accuracy—this is easier now with IT-enabled systems
- Eliminate costs associated with order review and follow-up
- Timely invoicing and accounting—with IT systems, this is always updated
- Improved customer service.

Types of Logistics Activities

Logistics activities are divided into inbound and outbound. Inbound or upstream logistics includes:

- Receiving, storing and issuing inputs and taking care of:
    - Materials handling
    - Inventory control
    - Inbound quality inspection along with the quality control function
    - Scheduling of production to manage "issues"
    - Return of unacceptable materials back to suppliers

Inbound logistics is the interface with the company suppliers, vendors and other service providers.

Outbound or downstream logistics includes:

- Collecting, storing, dispatching, and physically distributing the finished goods to the buyers/distribution channels/consumers and includes:
    - Order processing of all orders received through the sales system
    - Materials handling of finished goods
    - Warehousing both in the plant and in the field
    - Delivery vehicle operations and scheduling
    - Shipping and related documentation

Outbound Logistics is the Interface with the Company's Customers Any operating company is connected on the supply side with the supplier and through him the supplier's supplier (inbound or up-stream logistics). On the demand side, the company is connected with the customer and the customer's customer (outbound or downstream logistics). These links create three kinds of flows:

(i) Materials flow from the supplier end into the firm and finished goods flow till the customer.

(ii) Finance flows from the customer (payment for finished goods) into the company and out to the suppliers (payments for raw materials, packing materials, etc.).

(iii) Information flow both ways.

E-commerce players who operate on the marketplace model by recruiting hundreds of sellers on their portal can get the benefit of 100 percent FDI, says *Business India* in its edition dated April 24, 2015. This will help any sellers from villages/rural India to sell their products globally once the portal certifies their products—opens up new avenues for these humble sellers.

DIPP Allows 100 Percent FDI in Marketplace E-Commerce

This is not permitted to the inventory based model of e-commerce. New players can emerge as e-commerce gives sellers from villages an equal opportunity to showcase their products to the world at large.

EXTENSION INTO SUPPLY CHAIN MANAGEMENT

The Council of Logistics Management defines Supply Chain Management as:

> *"The process of planning, implementing and controlling the efficient, cost-effective flow and storage of raw materials, finished goods and related information from the point-of-origin to the point-of-consumption for the purpose of conforming to customer requirements."*

We have already understood, under logistics, the terms on planning, implementing and controlling. All the flows/movements have to be cost effective or at optimised costs. Companies have realized that there is a limit to cost cutting on the product and it is only more efficient supply chains which can create a clear competitive advantage.

All supply chain activities have only one objective of satisfying customers so that they keep coming back to the company and its products. A typical supply chain extends from the company suppliers (point of origin) to its customers (point of consumption) and involves three flows: (i) physical, (ii) information, and (iii) financial.

- *Physical flows* of materials in one direction from the supplier to the customers. Materials start as raw materials, packing materials, get worked upon in the company and move out as finished goods. It could also include service flow from the company to its customers.
- *Information flows* in both directions. Information is all the reports, records which get generated to let all concerned know about the status of the materials as they "move".
- *Financial flows* in one direction from the customers to the vendors. It could be payments made to the vendors for the supplies made by them or payments received by the company from its customers for the finished goods supplied to them.

Like logistics, supply chains are expected to deliver the right product at the right place at the right time and at the right price and profit to the company.

Supply Chain Management Focus

Supply chain management (SCM) focuses on the processes linking the generation of demand to the fulfilment of that demand. Obviously the starting point is the customer and what he wants and all the activities are centered around this.

- SCM creates the processes to fulfil customer service needs.

- SCM is seriously concerned with the physical infrastructure required to support these operations like plants, warehouses and transport.
- SCM manages this infrastructure to maximize service level to customers.

In many companies, considering the size and complexity of the operations and the frequency of the transactions, managing the supply chain can only happen effectively with the support of information technology tools. It is the function of SCM to set up and manage these tools.

Companies have realized the seriousness of managing their supply chains well and are now focusing on SCM as a distinct function in their organizations.

Need for a Supply Chain Review

There are some visible symptoms in business that indicate the need for a review and revamp or redesign of the supply chain processes. Some of these symptoms could be:

- Slowed down response to changes in the market. If competition launches a promotion on a popular brand/pack, the firm concerned is not able to react in time.
- Large write-offs, since what the firm is producing, does not seem to be what the customers are looking for.
- In order to meet customer service needs and demands of customers which seem to be imposing stringent conditions of delivery, the company would be taking up the easy way out by building up inventories.
- The firm is unable to commit on finished goods delivery dates. If the firm gets a major export order, it is not even able to commit a firm date for delivery.
- There could be frequent stock-outs and lost revenues as the planning seems to be not keeping pace with the market needs. The forecasting seems to upset the planning effort resulting in either excess stocks or no stocks when required.
- The various partners in the supply chain blame each other for below optimum performance and escalating costs. This kind of a "silo" approach is the most common symptom. The company would be losing out valuable opportunities in the market, but internally departments keep pointing fingers at each other.
- Meeting customer requirements means significant trade-offs in operations affecting the profitability. A major auto manufacturer used to rush car windscreens by air to meet customer requirements in another end of the country instead of planning spares inventories carefully.

Companies with a well-designed supply chain, and an effective planning process, manage these symptoms by always giving to their customers the most appropriate service offering at present, and with the growing needs of the business. They have a system to ensure proper trade-off between the manufacturing locations, flexibility, distribution cost and warehousing. They always seem to have excellent supplier and customer relations.

The physical network has been optimally designed and the system is IT enabled to ensure timely and correct flow of information in the entire supply chain network. A good example of such a system is the personal products business of Hindustan Unilever Ltd which is known for its negative working capital operations.

Reality Bite

Integrated Supply Chain Solutions Provider

Arshiya International Ltd (AIL) is a supply chain and logistics service provider which specializes in containerized rail business. It operates custom built rakes and plans to have 30 rakes by 2011. It has signed a contract with the Indian Railways to run containerized rakes for the next 20 years as reported in *Business India* (dated January 10, 2010). AIL has also set up a free trade warehousing zone in Navi Mumbai. The second such project is in Khurja near Delhi.

Influencing Factors on Supply Chain

Globalization of the market place is forcing companies to have world class delivery systems to survive the competition. Advances in technology in computing, communication and transportation have further made the situation more complicated. An increasingly demanding customer base is forcing companies to do things differently to keep customers happy. All purchase decisions are only on the dimensions of quality, price and time.

An innovative supply chain, therefore:

- Is able to meet all customer driven challenges in terms of the best price, excellent quality and delivery as specified by the customer.
- Helps reduce costs of operation. It is a well-known saying that "companies do not any longer compete with each other. It is the supply chains of companies which compete with each other".
- Improves service levels by maximizing time, place and possession utilities.
- Enhances the speed. Companies can not only commit and meet delivery dates, but can also take care of emergency requirements.
- Planning and execution are synchronized in a manner as to provide consistent excellent service to the customer.

All this goes to prove that good supply chain management is a win-win proposition for all players.

Supply Chain Integration

Richard Williams, Director, Safeway says, "While there will still be numerous opportunities to improve our own processes, the greater prizes will be achieved by working together to optimize the total supply chain across organizational boundaries".

Optimizing the supply chain requires supplier and customer involvement to integrate processes, policies, systems, database and strategies between diverse trading partners. While this may sound simple, in practice this is quite difficult to implement as it requires a large amount of transparency and trust in sharing information, which companies even today are reluctant to do. Even the entire planning exercise has to be done in consultation with the partners who could be the vendors or the customers or both.

Exhibit 16.1

A Successful Logistics Service Provider

Hyderabad based Gati has earned a name among corporate clients as a reliable logistics service provider. It counts among its wide range of clients the following: Dominos' Pizza, Piramal Healthcare, Eicher Motors. Gati has established itself as a single window logistics solutions provider in the Asia-Pacific region. In order to improve profitability even during the global downturn, Gati took some initiatives: cost cutting measures, redesigning its routes, faster vehicle turn-around and use of railways for one-way freight. As per *Business India* (January 10, 2010) Gati is probably the only multi-modal logistics company in India as it uses trucks, rail, ship and air.

Gati offers warehousing facilities also and is planning on setting up a cold chain. It already runs 100 temperature-controlled vans in North India.

Other well-known logistics service providers:

- Blue Dart—servicing 21,479 locations in the country using seven air freighters
- Deccan 360—land based surface transport and air

Supply chain integration, however, has some clear benefits which have been experienced by number of companies worldwide which have done the integration. These are:

- Reliable demand management—the forecasts are more accurate
- High customer service levels—an efficient "pull" system works
- Reduced lead times—shared planning efforts helps in this
- Optimum working capital costs—for example there is no need to keep additional inventories in anticipation of demand
- Optimum supply chain costs—Note that the supply chain costs need not necessarily be the lowest, they have to be optimum

Difference between Logistics and Supply Chain Management

There is no clear differentiation made by experts on logistics and supply chain management. In practice, managers tend to use these terms interchangeably. However, some efforts made on differentiating the meaning of these two terms have been made. These are indicated below along with the authors' viewpoint.

First Viewpoint: Pete Crosby – SCM Consultant

Logistics includes physical distribution, warehousing, transportation (inbound and outbound from manufacturing plants), and in some industries customer service also (sales order processing, inventory planning and production planning).

Supply chain (for a manufacturer) includes the logistics business functions mentioned above, and also includes purchasing, sourcing, procurement, buying, manufacturing operations, production scheduling, inventory control and materials management, facilities location planning, the information technology to coordinate between suppliers, the company, and customers (wholesalers, retailers and end-users).

Second Viewpoint (From another Logistics Consultant)

Logistics and supply chain functions can overlap. Different companies define them in their own ways. Logistics is generally concerned with strategy and coordination of flows between marketing and production (i.e. transportation and distribution).

A supply chain tends to focus on purchasing and procurement, but not necessarily so. It can include materials, inventory and production planning. There is also demand management which focuses on forecasting, but is sometimes included in either logistics or supply chain functions.

Third Viewpoint: Council of Logistics Management

❍ **Definition of Logistics** Logistics management is that part of the supply chain management process that plans, implements and controls the efficient, effective forward and reverse flow and storage of goods, services, and related information between the point of origin and the point of consumption in order to meet customers' requirements.

These are the boundaries and relationships of Logistics Management adopted by the Council of Logistics Management: "Logistics Management activities typically include inbound and outbound transportation management, fleet management, warehousing, materials handling, order fulfilment, logistics network design, inventory management of third party logistics services providers. To varying degrees, the logistics function also includes sourcing and procurement, production planning and scheduling, packaging and assembly, and customer service. It is involved in all levels of planning and execution—strategic, operational and tactical. Logistics Management is an integrating function, which coordinates and optimizes all logistics activities, as well as integrates logistics activities with other functions including marketing, sales, manufacturing, finance and information technology".

❍ **Definition of Supply Chain Management** Supply chain management encompasses the planning and management of all activities involved in sourcing and procurement, conversion, and all Logistics Management activities. Importantly, it also includes coordination and collaboration with channel partners, which can be suppliers, intermediaries, third-party service providers, and customers. In essence, Supply Chain Management integrates supply and demand management within and across companies.

These are the boundaries and relationships of supply chain management adopted by the Council of Logistics Management—"Supply chain management is an integrating function with primary responsibility for linking major business functions and business processes within and across companies into a cohesive and high-performing operation".

A Fourth Viewpoint: Jeff Ashcroft

Some use the two interchangeably, others feel there are differences, the combination of which leads to what has become somewhat of a grey area.

It does, however, seem that in the common usage, SCM seems to be becoming more prevalent in use with many new industry associations using "supply chain" in their names.

To my mind they are so inextricably related as to be almost synonymous. However in the case of logistics, it depends on the context of use.

Suffice it to say that if one had to differentiate between the two it would be to say that Supply chain management is looking at active management of the whole enchilada, while logistics can relate to part or parts within the supply chain. Unless an individual wishes to assume it, to make logistics literally synonymous probably requires the use of additional words like "total logistics management" or "integrated logistics management" to definitively mean the same thing.

Conclusion

Logistics relates to all activities within the company, namely—(i) materials procurement, (ii) production scheduling, (iii) finished goods dispatch planning, (iv) inventory management and warehousing, and (v) transportation planning. It also includes the network design of plants and distribution warehouses.

Supply chain management extends beyond the boundaries of the company to involve the suppliers and the customers/distributors in the planning process of materials procurement, production planning and scheduling and finished goods despatches to the distribution warehouses.

Logistics integrates various activities within the company in order to achieve its objectives, whereas SCM integrates the activities by going beyond the company up to the supplier's suppliers and the customer's (distributor's) customers to achieve its objectives.

There is obviously no authentic definition of the difference between Logistics and SCM. Each of the people quoted above have tried to give their own interpretation and in a confusing manner on top of it. One thing is quite clear—Logistics or SCM should NOT include purchase while it may include procurement (as in drawing off materials from vendors decided by purchase). In our opinion, Logistics is all activities within the company to ensure customer service levels and includes procurement, production scheduling, despatches handling, inventory management, transportation etc all of interest to the company only. A supply chain extends this exercise to integrate the "suppliers/vendors" and the "customers/channel partners" into the process.

LOGISTICS AND OTHER FUNCTIONS—INTERFACE

Logistics is the internal service provider for both production and sales and marketing. For production, it provides the raw materials, packaging materials and consumables required to keep the production running. For sales and marketing it provides the finished goods to help the revenues come into the company. Many times the requirements of production and S&M could be conflicting and logistics has to provide the right balance. In addition, logistics has to provide all these services in time and at the lowest cost possible.

The interfaces include:

- *With marketing:* Logistics activities include getting demand forecasts, arranging for dispatches, providing field warehousing, inventory management, packaging and transportation.
- *With production:* Logistics has to interact with the vendors, get the raw materials and packaging materials on time, help in production scheduling, arrange in plant storage and transportation.
- *With finance and accounting:* Create budgets, allocation of resources and cost management.
- *With purchase:* The purchase function negotiates terms with the suppliers and places the

orders. It is for the SC function to follow up on the delivery of the orders by suppliers so that production is not disrupted.

- *With quality control:* Even after the materials have been delivered at the plant, the SC function will not take it into the stores or issue it to production, till the quality has been checked by the QC function and approved by it. Similarly, only after the finished goods quality has been checked and approved by QC, will the SC function dispatch the goods to the field.

Marketing would like frequent batch runs for all products even at short notice. Production would like longer runs to reduce production costs and save on set-up times. The logistics manager, with an integrated approach is a good monitor and safeguard of the interests of all departments and has to balance "priorities" within agreed financial budgets and operating norms.

Major Areas of Interaction—Logistics and Marketing

For marketing, logistics or supply chain is an internal service provider to help them reach the product or service to the end user or customer. Marketing has to therefore interact closely with the logistics function in order to ensure the promised customer service deliverables. Some of the areas of this interaction between marketing and logistics are as follows.

- *Product design:* This has a direct impact on the warehouse space and transportation utilization and related costs.
- *Pricing:* The company has to decide on the optimum service levels which the customers can expect. The level of servicing the customers' demand directly affects the product costs and also decides the pricing policies.
- *Market and demand forecast:* These are critical in detailing the level of logistics resources that are needed to service the customers.
- *Customer service policies:* If marketing opts to provide a very high level of service to its customers, logistics resources like facilities (warehouse space, labour, transport arrangements) have to be considered. Marketing has to work closely with logistics to decide the service levels. There is the example of an Indian pharma company which has categorized all customers into two categories—A class and others. Their service levels to the critical A class customers is of a high level—close to 100 percent always.
- *Number and location of warehouses:* This is major area of contention between marketing and logistics. Marketing would naturally prefer a larger number of warehouses closer to its main markets. More warehouses mean more effort in servicing these with stocks and higher inventory levels. Again, here the policy has to be developed jointly by marketing and logistics. Linear programming software can also be used for the optimization.
- *Inventory policies:* A careful balancing has to be done by marketing and logistics together, between the agreed level of customer service to be provided and the costs of holding inventory.
- *Order processing:* This is the source of daily interaction between marketing/sales and logistics. A field salesperson is responsible for providing the daily orders from the customers, which logistics has to process and dispatch.

The logistics resources change with the delivery policy of the company—if it is direct to the customers or it is to channel members. Normally companies have a combination of deliveries direct to institutions and channel members. Examples in the Indian FMCG companies also abound where the dispatch planning is done as per a schedule based on the monthly forecast without the need for orders. Alternatively companies also insist on their distributors to give monthly orders in advance, broken down into weeks to facilitate dispatches.

Managing month-end sales skews is a major issue in order processing. In order processing, it is necessary to define responsibility on who receives the customer orders and thereafter the speed and efficiency of processing. This directly impacts operating costs and customer's perception of service levels. This is an important element of the customer service function in any company.

While every company was finding it easy to match the product or service offerings of their competition, it was necessary to find the element of competitive edge and order processing was one of the ways companies started to distinguish themselves from competition. They decided that in terms of the order management cycle, they would provide the customer with an unique experience. The order management cycle includes the order transmittal, receipt, order entry and the execution and this was observed to take more than 50 percent of the order cycle time. Companies, which could reduce this time, were considered superior.

Order processing includes the tasks of:

- order acquisition—by salespeople, over telephone, by mail or any other means.
- order entry in the company—normally done in the planning department or the dispatch point. If the company has managed to work with its customer to get the orders online, this would save a lot of time and errors would get eliminated.
- every order execution requires some documents to be generated like the invoice, and gate pass. The preparation of the documents is the third task in order processing. In addition, this stage could also involve generating picking lists for the persons to pick the items from the finished goods store and putting it together in one place for packing and dispatch. This physical effort also takes a considerable time.
- the final task is keeping the customer informed of the status of his order.

Delays in order processing can add to the costs of the company in terms of additional inventory to be carried or the need to use faster transport to save the time lost on order processing. This can impact the profitability.

A major manufacturer of steel (AB) has a plant in Gurgaon, which was servicing its biggest customer based in Chennai. The dispatches were made by train and the transit time was normally four days. AB handed over the outbound logistics to a logistics service provider. The LSP tracks the train at major junctions and follows up with the Railways. They could reduce the transit time to just 20 hours. This is a good example of planning.

To Summarize

As already highlighted, Logistics/SC function has to interact with various other functions within the organization in order to get materials (raw materials, packing materials, etc.) from the suppliers, convert these into finished products for delivery to the customers.

Inbound logistics interacts with production operations and engineering. Outbound logistics interacts with marketing.

The interaction with these functions helps create an integrated logistics system. Through these interactions, logistics performs the primary activities like asset utilization, inventory management, materials handling, storage and communication.

The interface also helps optimize the capacity utilization, reduce waiting time for the customers and ensure timely and complete deliveries.

Channels of Distribution

Marketing and logistics have to jointly decide the channel decisions including direct dispatches to institutions and indirect to other customers through the channel members.

Logistics Impact on Financial Health

The effectiveness of the logistics function in a company is very critical for its financial results. Logistics affects the return on investment (ROI) and it can influence the numbers on the balance sheet.

- Logistics impacts both the numbers which generate the ROI, namely the profitability and the capital employed.
- Return on investment is a function of the profits generated on the capital employed. Profitability is a function of the revenue and the costs.
- Logistics can help maximize customer service and hence increase sales revenues. Logistics efficiency helps costs. The net effect of these two actions is the increased profitability (the numerator in our calculation of ROI).

Let us now see how better logistics management helps optimize the productivity of the capital employed. Sound logistics management ensures optimum asset utilization and deployment. The assets which can be more productively utilized (more output for a given level of input) are inventory, accounts receivables (credit extended by the firm), cash collections and fixed assets (the denominator in our calculation of ROI).

It is obvious that if the numerator goes up and the denominator goes down, the ROI improves, and all this has been made possible by better logistics management.

There are a number of logistics variables which can impact both the assets and liabilities sides of a company balance sheet. Let us try and understand how this is possible.

First, we look at the assets side:

- Logistics is directly responsible for inventory management and control. Inventory policy and service levels are decided by Logistics and marketing.
- Logistics helps utilize assets like distribution facilities, materials handling equipment and transport facilities efficiently.
- Logistics uses the tools of accurate invoicing, reduced order cycle times and full order completion to reduce the accounts receivable and faster cash receipts.

In other words, logistics has helped better and more productive asset utilization. Let us now look at the liabilities side:

- Logistics helps the purchase function to finalize the purchase policies so that the company gets the maximum benefit out of the accounts payables.
- Logistics helps the Finance function use capital (a combination of debt and equity) in various options for funding inventory (working capital) and the equipment.
- Logistics has therefore helped better financing of the liabilities.

LO 2 Explain how the strategy for logistics is derived

DEVELOPING A STRATEGY FOR LOGISTICS

The logistics strategy has to be derived from the marketing strategy of the company. The marketing strategy is derived from the corporate or business strategy.

- The corporate strategy defines what business the company wants to be in.
- The marketing strategy decides the products and markets the company would like to focus on to reach the business objectives.
- The distribution strategy will define how the company would "reach" its products to its chosen markets/customers.
- The distribution strategy would have two components to it: the physical distribution or market logistics function and the channel management which is more of a sales function.

The primary focus of the logistics strategy has to be to develop a "competitive" advantage. This could be achieved by faster reach to the markets or customers and/or achieving the reach at the lowest possible cost.

The logistics strategy can be based on different directions as can be seen from the possibilities below:

- *Market based*: In this the company manages a limited number of logistics activities across different strategic business units—one example could be of sharing sales, order processing and fulfilment operations.
- *Process based*: The company runs an integrated and efficient logistics function.
- *Based on the channels of distribution*: The channel partners participate in the logistics activities to ensure superior customer service.

The steps in the logistics operations based on the defined strategy could be summarized as follows:

- Understanding the corporate business objectives and strategies
- Defining marketing strategies
- Deriving the company logistics strategy including service levels to be delivered
- Defining the objectives of the logistics function (service levels) to drive the strategy
- Specifying the required levels of performance from the logistics function—for example the expected "service levels"
- Deciding the operational design of the processes required to achieve the performance and their execution plans
- Putting in place a measurement and reporting system
- Measuring the actual performance to find any variances
- Refining and improving the operations based on benchmarks

Customer Service Elements

This list is the result of the efforts of various surveys done on customer satisfaction. The marketing function decides the elements of the customer service policy of the company. However, it is seen that a lot of activity related to logistics ultimately impacts the customer service as can be seen from the list given below:

- Frequency of delivery—the more often the better.
- Time from order to delivery—order cycle time. The customer is not willing to wait, and hence this has to be low.
- Consistency and reliability of delivery—every order has to be executed with the same efficiency.
- Emergency deliveries when required—after all, every order cannot always be properly planned.
- Stock availability and continuity of supply—there should be no excess stocks or stock-outs.
- Orders filled completely—no SKU is missed out.
- Order size constraints—some companies specify a minimum quantity of the order for execution and this may upset customers.
- Order status information—simple and quick communication of when deliveries will be made.
- Advice on non-availability—this is one of the most common grouses of buyers against vendors. The buyers are not told that stocks are not available and there could be a delay in supply.
- Convenience of placing orders—how easy or difficult it is for the customers to do business with the company.
- Acknowledgement of order—that it has been received and is being processed.
- Invoicing procedures and accuracy of invoices—as this is mostly IT enabled, this problem should not arise.
- Quality of sales presentation—not to promise what cannot be delivered.
- In-store merchandizing support—expected out of FMCG companies.
- Credit terms offered—of course this needs to be honoured by the buyer in terms of prompt payment on the scheduled date.
- Regular calls by sales representatives—most companies have a clear beat plan for their salespeople to call on all customers at a certain frequency.
- Manufacturer monitoring of retail stock levels—again in the FMCG industry and also automobile spares.
- Customer query handling—being prompt and giving correct information.
- Quality of outer packaging—so that the contents do not get damaged in transit.
- Well stacked pallets—relates to outer packaging.
- Claims procedure—it should be easy for a customer to deal with the company even if he has a complaint of any nature.
- Condition of goods when received by the customers—the goods have to be received in the best condition and should be ready for use or consumption.

- Easy-to-use by dates on outer packaging—if the company is dealing in pharmaceutical products or food products.
- Quality on inner packaging for in-store handling and display.
- Consultation on new product or package development—the best companies do this regularly.
- Regular reviews of the product range—to keep abreast of customer needs.
- Co-ordination between production, marketing and distribution—though this is an internal company matter, any problems of co-ordination would become obvious to the customer in the manner in which his orders are handled and executed.

Supply Chain Relationships

ABC is a retail fashion stores group. As per *MM Review*, January 2016, p.12, in over 1000 of its stores, it tracks consumer preferences using POS data. It places orders on its suppliers around the world using a satellite link. Hong Kong is used as a consolidation center for all incoming materials. There are 4 chartered flights a week from Hong Kong to its distribution center in Columbus. At the distribution center, goods are price marked and re-sorted for shipment by truck and air to its retail stores. The whole cycle from the order to in-store display takes just 6 weeks.

Supply Chain Process Flow

The process flows follow the following sequence of cycles:

1. Supplier end for procurement to support manufacturing
2. Manufacturing results in the finished goods to support the distribution channel network
3. The customer order cycle follows where the replenishment happens with the retailer to support the customers

All this should result in the supply chain value add, which is the customer value minus the supply chain cost.

Service Driven Logistics Systems

The starting point is obviously the customer requirements, which then drives all the planning and execution.

- Identify customer service needs
- Define customer service objectives
- Design the logistics system

These are the similar steps we narrated in designing a distribution channel system.

This has been further explained in terms of the type of service level relevant to four different kinds of products. All products can easily be classified into these four categories:

- High volume and high profitability—the availability has to be high so that no opportunity is missed out
- Low volume but high profitability—deliveries to be Just In Time (JIT)

- High volume but low profitability—important contributors to the top line. The bottom-line or the profitability has to be strengthened by cost reduction efforts
- Low volume and low profitability—need a review if the product or line has to be retained

A similar classification based on products and customers can be made:

- High value products and high volume customers—key products and accounts—need to be protected for growth
- High value products and low volume customers—customers need to be developed into doing more business with the company
- Low value products and high volume customers—need to be maintained so as not to lose out to competitors
- Low value products and low volume customers—need a review

Based on the criticality and importance of the customers, Marketing does an ABC listing. Logistics can then plan the customer service level along with marketing for each of these categories of customers.

The service level delivered by logistics or the supply chain is measured as a combination of timely deliveries and full deliveries. There are a number of parameters associated with these two basic requirements. Some of these parameters are: (i) order fill rate, (ii) on time delivery, (iii) order accuracy, (iv) invoice accuracy, (v) customer rejections. A company can give different weightings to each of these parameters and measure the performance percentage for each to arrive at a composite service index.

Obviously the order fill rate (has to be as close to 100 percent as possible) and the on time deliveries (has to be 100 percent of the orders or as close to it as possible) would get the maximum weightings.

Once the composite service index has been calculated for a channel member like a C&FA once, this number needs to be constantly improved upon. The logistics manager knows that the parameters which have scores much lower than 100 percent need more attention depending on their criticality.

Reality Bite

SC strategies create competitive advantage:

There are some parts of the supply chain strategy which result in a long-term competitive advantage. Some examples are given below:

- With better integration of the SC processes, costs can be minimized and resulting prices should be competitive.
- Efficiency and effectiveness of the SC will improve with better managed upstream and downstream logistics.
- With better level and quality of information sharing, the delivery schedules can improve.

Source: MM Review, November 2015

Exhibit 16.2

Similar Issues faced by Marketing and Supply Chain Functions

Marketing considers the supply chain function as its service provider within the company. Marketing keeps voicing concerns about inadequate production capacity, long time taken for production and distribution, running short of finished goods, missing required product assortment, high supply chain and service costs, inability to provide customized products which are required to increase competitive advantage.

For supply chain function, marketing is the first customer but within the company. Supply chain function has grievances which include: forecasts given by marketing are never accurate, too much finished goods in the system, too large is the range of products demanded that it results in uneconomical production runs adding to production costs, defined requirements of customer service are not feasible, unnecessary request for product design changes and customization.

The above clashes of interests are normally resolved in regular meetings between the marketing and supply chain functions in most organizations.

LO 3 **Understand the principles and systems of inventory management, warehousing management and transportation management**

FOCUS AREAS OF LOGISTICS AND SCM

In the next few sections, the three main focus areas of Logistics and SCM will be discussed: (i) Inventory management, (ii) Storage and Warehousing, and (iii) Transportation.

Inventory Management

Businesses manage their routine operations of manufacturing and marketing with the help of inventory. This could take the forms of raw materials, packing materials (to support production), and work-in-process on the production shop floor and finished goods (to support marketing). The objectives of inventory include:

- To maximize customer service—inventory holdings ensure availability of stocks when and where required. Inventory is a protection against any kind of uncertainty. For example, if a competitor is not able to service the market with his products for any reason, the company should have enough inventories to fill the gap in the market.
- Help minimize the cost of plant operations—production can happen in economic batches. If production has to get these economies, it has to pack lot sizes of different SKUs as per a schedule and build up stocks.

- Minimum investment to deliver the agreed customer service.

Inventory, therefore, supports production, operational and customer service requirements, acts as a hedge against market place uncertainty and assists purchase in getting order quantity discounts.

For instance, Volkswagen and its suppliers have such a close link that they share information on production plans and schedules so that production can be well co-ordinated and inventory levels managed well at both ends.

Functions of Inventory

Inventory acts as a buffer between:

- Supply and demand—both in terms of quantities and the timing.
- Customer demand and finished goods—again in terms of quantities and the timing of the demand.
- Requirements for an operation and the output from the previous operation—on the shop floor.
- Parts and materials to begin an operation and the suppliers of the materials.

It is rightly said that Inventory is the "shock-absorber" of a business. However, maintaining inventory means high carrying costs, reduced profit and even loss in market shares. In today's competitive world, wasteful inventory management practices are not permitted or tolerated.

Inventory is driven by the following factors:

- Target service level parameters—if 100 percent service level is required, it may mean a large inventory as not a single stock out situation is acceptable.
- Lot sizing practices—vendors at times dictate the minimum lot size to be purchased at a given price—this may increase the stock level.
- Safety stock and safety time conventions—arrived at with experience to handle uncertainty and disruptions.
- Volume discounts and purchase arrangements.
- Seasonal build up needs—as all raw materials may not be available all through the year—examples of tea, edible oils.

Categories of Inventory

Inventory could be of the following categories:

- *Anticipation*: This has been built in anticipation of future requirements. Examples could be of inventory meant for peak season demand, build up expecting a strike or inventory meant for a sales promotion.
- *Safety or fluctuation:* This part of the inventory is meant to cover random, occasional, unpredictable fluctuations in supply and demand and lead time. Examples could be of inventory meant to prevent disruption in operations, delivery problems, and so on.
- *Lot-size:* The need for this inventory is normally driven by the vendors who insist on a certain price or discounts only on fixed quantities, which may not be immediately required for production. The inventory could be to get discounts, reduce shipping, set up and ordering costs.

- *Transportation:* This is mostly inventory which needs to be "in transit" as it normally takes a certain time to move inventory from one point to another. This is also known as 'pipeline' or 'movement inventories'. An example could be factory to a distribution center or C&FA.
- *Hedge:* There are a number of materials which are "commodity" based where the prices fluctuate every day—like edible oils, precious metals like gold. Companies that do business in these materials would prefer to buy more when the prices are more favourable and stock for a "rainy" day—when prices are not so favourable. This is "hedge" inventory.
- *Maintenance, repair and operating supplies:* The term "consumables" is also used to describe these kinds of materials in stock. As the name indicates, these materials are meant to support operations or maintenance. They are not inputs into the production system but facilitate production. Examples could be cutting tools, spare parts, consumables and lubricants.

All the above categories of inventory are kept as raw materials, work-in-process, finished goods, MRO and in-transit/pipeline stocks.

Reasons for Carrying Inventory

Reasons for carrying some of these categories of inventories could vary between different operating situations. The quantities held may also vary. Some of these reasons could be highlighted as follows:

- *WIP or pipeline (in plant) stocks*: production rates, which depend on men and machines, are finite and well defined. Production also requires a number of steps to be completed and each stage may take varying amounts of time. Hence the need for this inventory.
- *Cycle stock*: this is again on the production line to minimize set-up costs and times which are fixed. For example, a toothpaste manufacturing line would like to complete 2 days of continuous production of the 200 g pack before shifting to a 100 g pack for the next 3 days and 50 g on the last day of the working week.
- *Seasonal stock*: the reason is obvious. The resources for production like machines, manpower is fixed but the demand can be seasonal. There is a need to build up finished goods stocks. A company selling room heaters in winter has to produce the units in other months also to meet the peak demand in the season.
- *Safety stock*: as demand is a random variable and uncertainties of supply cannot always be foreseen, some level of safety stock is always maintained. Safety stock takes care of the fluctuations in demand.
- Stocks could also be held for other reasons like price fluctuations, and market shortages.

Whatever may be the reasons for carrying inventory, the argument always arises whether inventory holding is good or bad for business. Inventory appears in the assets column of the balance sheet of a company and more of "assets" should be good. Moreover, the cost of inventory never gets directly reflected in the profit and loss statement. The argument is that if inventory is an asset and its cost is not reflected in the P&L account, is having too much of it such a bad thing?

However, it has now been well recognized in business worldwide that inventory is a working capital/supply chain cost driver.

Wrong Reasons for Carrying Inventory

While there are several good reasons for carrying inventory, which is in the interest of the organization, some companies tend to carry inventory for all the wrong reasons. Many of these reasons slowly creep in and get noticed when it may be too late. Let us examine what some of these "wrong" reasons could be:

- *Poor quality of materials and the yield*: This could happen due to supplier quality which keeps varying or the accepted level of defects as contracted is not tight enough. Even when the quality is accepted as per specs, when running the materials on the machines, the yield varies. To avoid these problems, companies keep "additional" safety stocks.
- *Unreliable supplier deliveries*:
  - The supplier does not conform to schedule. The company increases safety stock levels
  - Poor supplier production systems
  - Discrepancies in deliveries and logistical problems
  - Short notice orders or frequently changing requirements
- *Extended order cycle times*: the time between the recognition of a requirement and the physical receipt of the goods is irregular.
- *Inaccurate/uncertain demand forecast*: Companies which produce products to stock expecting demand suffer from this problem. Moreover, many of them also have the problem of month end sales skews. As a result of not so correct forecast, and last minute heavy orders, they tend to keep high inventories to protect against market stock-outs.
- *Custom items used for standard applications*: There is always a clash between purchase and production. Purchase would like to buy industry standard parts as customized requirements are more expensive as the supplier has to create special tooling. Smaller batches also increase price per unit. But production, in order to suit its processes, would still like to have customized parts thereby increasing the stock levels.

Even after implementing JIT, a major auto-maker (PQR) used to have large inventories due to logistic problems. At one time they had 300 vendors in different states with lot sizes which were sometimes 1000 units even when requirement used to be 100 units. Due to differential sales tax laws between states, the same truck could not pick up parts from two suppliers even in adjoining states. PQR appointed a consultant to conduct a study on the vendor operations.

After the study, PQR appointed XYZ–a 3P service provider. XYZ did the following:

- Combining all ancillary vendors in a state into clusters
- All components from these clusters would be consolidated for dispatch to the PQR plant
- Worked closely with a tax expert to ensure no additional tax burdens

PQR did the following:

- Rationalized the number of vendors
- Categorized suppliers into three tiers with different lot sizes and delivery schedules
- Developed an IT network to connect all the vendors.

(*Contd.*)

The net result was excellent growth year after year with a substantial reduction in inventory levels.

- Extended material pipelines. This happens mostly in the case of long distance between the supplier and the user company. Sometimes increase in inventory is also provided to take care of in-transit losses.
- Inefficient manufacturing processes:
- ◆ Process yield is poor and uses up more materials
- ◆ Large amounts of WIP on the shop floor indicating poor scheduling.

Inventory Performance Measures

In order to measure the performance of inventory held by companies at whatever stage simple measures have been used and become very popular. Two such measures are given below:

1. *Inventory turns* is the measure of the value of business which the inventory holding has helped the company to generate.
   Inventory turns = Annual cost of goods sold/average inventory in value. This could also be calculated based on volume of business like kilos, tons, litres. Obviously the higher the number, the better managed is the inventory.
2. *Number of days of supply* is another simple measure. This denotes the number of days of production (in case of raw or packing materials) or days' sales (in the case of finished goods) which the inventory holding can service.
   Days of supply = Inventory on hand/average daily usage. All figures are in kilos, tons, litres, etc.

Inventory Management and Control

As mentioned earlier, inventory is a working capital/supply chain cost driver. It has to be controlled or managed in such a way that it is always supportive to the business. In industries like automobiles, pharmaceuticals or FMCG, there could be hundreds of items in inventory. It is not physically possible or easy to manage such a large number of items. Practising managers have found a way out of this by resorting to classification of inventory in different categories and applying various methods to manage these items. Some details on the most popular classification of inventory – ABC – Always Better Control, is as follows:

❍ **ABC Classification** This is based on Pareto's Law which says that in any business situation generally,

- 20 percent of items contribute to 80 percent of the revenues or account for 80 percent of the value—these could be the "A" items.
- About 30 percent of the items contribute to 15 percent of the revenues or account for 15 percent of the value—these could be the "B" items.
- The balance 50 percent of the items contribute to 5 percent of the revenues or account for 5 percent of the value of usage—these are the "C" items.

Most operating companies have hundreds of items in stock and many SKUs to sell. It is not possible to bestow the same attention in managing the inventory of all these items every working day. ABC (or any similar classification) provides a simple but effective way of managing the inventory of the large number of items. ABC classification gives a focus to inventory management so that the most critical items get the maximum attention.

ABC inventory analysis uses the Pareto principle to classify and manage inventory:

- Influence of the item on results of inventory management
- Classify items based on the above criteria
- Apply degree of control in proportion to the importance of the group.

The procedure for classification into A, B and C is outlined here:

- For each item in an inventory, the value of annual usage is determined. It could be for the last year or for the last three years if data is available.
- All the items are listed in descending order of the value of annual usage. The highest usage item (in value) will be listed first and the lowest at the last.
- The cumulative annual usage with the cumulative percentage of items is calculated.
- Once the cumulative annual usage and the percentages are known, it is possible to classify into A, B and C based on usage and the percentage of items.
- Action after classification is around the principle of having plenty of low-value items and using the money and control effort saved to reduce the inventory of higher value items.

For each of the three categories certain rules are then followed:

- *A items—high priority*: The method of managing these "critical" items is to ensure tight control. The stock records for these items have to be always updated and accurate. These items need frequent and regular review by management. It is expected that salespeople take utmost care in giving correct forecast for these items. In relation to the vendors, the purchase/logistics function maintains a close follow-up and expediting process is in place to reduce lead times.
- *B items—medium priority*: These form the second set of important items. Normal controls are exercised and good records are maintained. This gets the regular attention of management and order processing with vendors is also normal.
- *C items—lowest priority*: These are a large number of low items and management should not waste too much time keeping a control of these. Simple controls (may be once a month checking) and simple records need to be maintained. The periodic review and two-bin system of inventory management can be followed. It is permitted to order large quantities and carry extra safety stock.

Inventory Handling

In spite of proper classification and exercising regular controls, in any industrial situation, there is always the possibility that some stocks get built up and do not move fast enough. The MSD (moving, slow moving and dead) system of stock classification helps in deciding action on slow moving stocks.

- All stocks regularly being consumed and in stock for less than 6 months could be considered as moving.
- Slow moving stocks are those which are in stock for more than 6 months but less than 2 years. Purchases of these would have been cut down of course, but in addition, the user

department has to take a call if these items can be totally eliminated.

- All items where the stock levels are more than 2 years old can be considered as "dead" stock and have to be removed from inventory quickly before they deteriorate further in value. These items will never again be procured.

  Some action points for slow moving and dead stock are:
  - To further classify into "critical" and "non-critical"
  - Purchase orders on non-critical are stopped straightaway.
  - Dead stock is checked for technical quality and specs before disposal to get a fair idea of the probable realisation in value if disposed.

Inventory Control

As mentioned earlier, inventory adds to the cost of operations and has to be minimized without sacrificing the efficiency of the operations. Some of the steps taken for this control exercise include:

(i) continuous review of the excess and obsolete inventory (excess can be known if the permitted inventory norms are already clearly defined),
(ii) part simplification and re-design—to use industry standard parts wherever possible,
(iii) review safety stocks and forecasting techniques, and
(iv) on-site supplier managed inventory—VMI.

Example: Demand Management

SKF is a bearing company in Sweden. They have a Europe wide network and have a global forecasting and supply system. Customers place orders by EDI on the nearest SKF office. System checks stocks across distribution centers or schedules production in the five major sites. Customer orders are accepted and delivery date confirmed. Information system also concurrently schedules transport.

Some inventory control methods in use are listed below:

- *Two bin system*—used on the shop floor for C type of items. At the start there are two bins which are full of the items. Every time one bin gets empty, it is filled up. In the meantime production uses the items in the other bin.
- *Perpetual inventory record system*—to count the physical stocks against the book stocks almost on a daily basis.
- *Periodic review system*—a stock check at pre-agreed intervals. Defining target level inventory or stock norms which are based on consumption rates, lead times for receipts, safety stocks and lot order quantities.

Inventory turn-over ratio—mentioned earlier—sales generated as a multiple of average inventory held.

Number of days' inventory—also mentioned earlier—average inventory as a multiple of one day's average sales (finished goods) or one day's average production (raw materials).

Inventory management and the methods used have become common in all companies. Some of these systems have been highlighted above. However, some simple rules can be followed to ensure that inventory is managed well:

- To encourage and work with suppliers to reduce lead times.
- Suppliers' warehouses to be located close to customer plants.
- Find out trends of materials usage so that there are no surprises on unwanted inventories.
- Stock records, either manual or computerized, need to be kept updated at all times.
- Improve visibility of all stocks in inventory.
- Always FIFO to be followed.
- Suppliers and customers to be involved in inventory planning.
- The production layout has to be carefully studied to make it efficient and reduce WIP.
- Storage space to be optimally utilized at all locations.
- Proper co-ordination between sales and dispatch stores.
- Quick disposal of unwanted stocks.
- Regular reconciliation of stores records with accounting records and physical stocks with book stocks.
- Quick disposal of scrap, empties, and so on.
- Regular training for sales personnel.
- Periodic review of stock norms.
- Use of Information technology wherever possible.

Inventory Costs

The cost of inventory is basically the interest cost of the inventory held, the storage costs and any losses on account of damages or deterioration in quality.

Additional costs, which are normally difficult to measure, are the costs resulting from stock-outs, capacity associated costs and quality costs. A list of costs related to inventory is given below:

- Item or unit cost—basic value of item carried
- Carrying costs—capital, storage, risks which could be damage, deterioration, pilferage, obsolescence

Reality Bite

ABC analysis and inventory optimization

ABC analysis of inventory (using the Pareto's principle) broadly states that:

A category – 10 percent of items represent 75 percent of the money value

B category – 20 percent of items represent 20 percent of the money

C category – the remaining items represent 5 percent of the money value

This should help meet the objectives of inventory management which includes ensuring adequate levels of raw materials and spares so as not to disrupt production, making adequate levels of inventory available to meet market needs, minimizing work-in-process inventory and reduce inventory holding costs. This should also result in a high inventory turnover ratio.

Source: MM Review, January 2014

- Ordering costs of materials—mostly relating to follow-up with vendors but could also include generating and sending a material release, transport or any other acquisition costs
- Stock-out costs—back-order costs, lost sales or lost customers
- Quality costs associated with non-conforming goods
- Other costs could include duties, tooling, and exchange rate differences

Inventory Strategy

A strategy for managing inventory has the focus of providing the agreed service levels at the lowest possible inventory cost. The strategy cannot be the same for companies in different industries nor for companies in the same industry as in each case the service levels and the cost the company is willing to lock up in inventory varies. However, there are some common factors which companies look at while deciding their inventory strategy:

- The first factor is the delivery lead time and service levels desired by the market and how much of this is the company willing to satisfy in terms of fill rates, order fill rates and percentage backlog of orders they are willing to carry and service.
- The second factor is the means the company has chosen to service the market. This means could take the forms of make to order, ship from ready stock, use distributors or even agree to give customized products. Each of these alternatives alters the level of inventory required.
- The third factor is the position of the company in the market. If the company is a market leader for the products it sells, it can follow a certain path on inventory. If the company is trying to significantly change market shares, it will follow a different approach. In other words, the competitive situation is a factor.
- The fourth factor is the effectiveness and accuracy of the sales forecast generated by the company salespeople. Can the company forecast market trends accurately? Is the industry dealing with volatile items? Is there seasonality in the demand? These are some questions that need answers before finalizing the inventory strategy.
- The fifth factor relates to the strategy possible in terms of inventory and its relation to the demand. Whether this is in lag, lead or at the same level. Even for the same company these could vary between different products.
- The sixth factor takes into account the company ability to take care of short-term demand changes. This kind of a surge in demand may be taken care of by overtime production, additional safety stocks or outsourcing.
- The last factor relates to the stage in the "product life cycle" at which the company products are presently. For each stage the treatment of inventory will vary.

Warehousing

Storage or warehousing provides the place utility part of logistics for any business and along with transportation is a critical component of customer service standards. The purpose of warehousing is to provide the desired level of customer service where it has been promised at the lowest possible total cost. The warehousing is that part of the company's logistics framework that stores items (raw materials, packing materials, tools, work-in-process or finished goods) at and between the point of origin and the point of consumption and also provides information to management on the status and condition of the items being stored. Distribution warehousing relates mainly to finished goods.

Reasons for Warehousing

Warehousing, as mentioned above, supports both Production and Marketing. The reasons for warehousing could be summarized as to:

- Support the company's customer service policy. If the service policy says that items would be delivered to the major customers twice a week, the stocks have to be kept in a warehouse close to the customer location.
- Maintain a source of supply without interruptions. Safety stocks have to be stored closer to the market.
- Achieve production economies in terms of set-up times. As production runs in batches and inventory gets built up, it has to be stored.
- Achieve transportation economies—for example, full truck loads are dispatched to the distribution centers and stored there.
- Take advantage of quantity purchase discounts offered by vendors or forward buying when prices are favourable. Such stocks have to be stored.
- Support changing market conditions and sudden changes in demand.
- Ensure least logistics cost for a desired level of customer service.
- Overcome time and space differentials—it is not possible to have production units close to every major market.
- Support any JIT programs agreed with suppliers or even customers—most relevant in the automobile industry.
- Provide customers with the right mix of products at all times and all locations—aggregate products made at different production units close to the consumption points.
- Provide temporary storage for materials that need to be disposed of or recycled.

Warehouses, therefore, aggregate, break-bulk, mix products from multiple facilities for shipment to a single customer and are used more as a flow-through point than as a point for hoarding.

Operating a warehouse system requires a careful balancing of total cost versus service level. There is always a clash of marketing and logistics objectives in this. Marketing wants allocation of resources to maximize long-term profitability. Logistics would like to minimize the total cost of order processing and information, lot quantities, inventory carrying, warehousing and transportation. The secret is to ensure that the ratio of value added cost to value added time is constantly improved.

Companies in the computer hardware industry have started creating regional hubs or warehouses where the products are stored in semi-knocked down (SKD) condition; the kits are assembled and delivered on receipt of orders.

Distribution Warehousing

The objective is to set up a network of warehouses closest to the customer locations to service markets better at minimum cost. The warehouses could be company owned distribution centers, depots or C&FAs (Carrying & Forwarding Agents). The warehouse location strategies could be:

- Market positioned—warehouses are located nearest to the final customer (who may not be the end user of the product). The factors influencing this location are:
  - Order cycle time—time elapsed between the customer placing the order and the receipt of the goods by him.
  - Transportation costs—the freight cost from the nearest warehouse to the customer location.
  - Sensitivity of the product—perishable products for example, cannot be stored for too long and have to be delivered quickly.
  - Order sizes—may not always be full truck loads.
  - Levels of customer service offered—for example, the frequency of delivery which has been promised to the customer.
- Production positioned—warehouses are located close to the production facilities or supply sources. Here the level of customer service may be lesser than the first alternative. This warehouse could also serve as a point of aggregation/collection for products made in a number of plants but located closest to the biggest of them. The factors influencing this location are:
  - Perishability of the raw materials.
  - Number of products in the product mix.
  - Assortments ordered by the customers from the product mix.
  - Transportation consolidation rates—example full truck loads.
- Intermediately positioned—mid-point locations between the final customer and the producer. Here high service levels are possible even if the products are made in a number of units.

Other approaches to warehouse location look at cost minimization or cost and demand elements to maximize profitability. One such popular method of location is called the "center of gravity" approach which locates a distribution warehouse or distribution center at a point which minimizes the transportation costs between the plant and its markets.

Distribution Warehouse Site Selection Factors

There are some well-known factors that need to be kept in mind to locate the distribution warehouses. These are listed below:

- Location of the major markets
- Nature of the products being distributed
- Quality and variety of carriers serving the proposed site. For example, there are certain locations where the truckers belong to a union and this may not be the ideal location.
- Quality and quantity of labour available. Most of the loading and unloading of the vehicles at the warehouse will be done by casual labour and this is, therefore, an important consideration.

- The labour rates and stability of rates.
- Cost of industrial land—mostly for lease and sometimes for buying.
- Potential for expansion—the warehouse should have the capacity to handle the business for at least the next five years.
- Local tax structures—octroi, sales tax, and so on.
- Building codes in operation.
- Costs of construction or lease rates.
- Cost and availability of utilities like electricity and water.
- Any local government tax concessions and incentives which may be available.

Warehouse Size

The factors determining the size of any distribution warehouse include customer service levels to be provided and hence the stock norms, throughout rates, size of the markets served, production lead times, size of product portfolio, economies of scale, materials handling systems to be used, stock layout, office space, aisle sizes and level and pattern of demand.

Transportation

This is an equally important part of the logistics function. Movement of the products across space or distance adds value to the products as it gets them nearer to the points of consumption and the distribution network or end users. Transportation really provides the "time" and "place" utility, which is the primary function of the physical distribution system.

Transportation or freight is one of the largest elements in the logistics costs and can significantly influence the final selling price of the product and its profitability. Operating managers have a special responsibility in managing freight without sacrificing timeliness of deliveries.

Factors influencing the transportation costs could be product or market related. The five prominent modes of transport available to any business are: road, rail, air, water, and pipeline. Another lesser used mode is that of ropeways. The mode of transport to be used is primarily dictated by the product to be moved and the location of the market to which it has to be moved. Transport or freight costs, are therefore, either product related or market related.

Product related transport costs are dictated by density of the product, ease or difficulty of stackability/storability, ease or difficulty of handling and liability on loss or damage.

Market related transport costs could be dictated by:

- Location of the markets as it decides the distance.
- Balance of freight into and out of the market concerned. Obviously, the rates in will be more favourable if the transporter is able to get return loads easily.
- Seasonality of product movements. During mango season or orange season or wheat harvest in North India trucks are difficult to get and road freight costs go up.
- Impact on customer service—frequency, load size, and so on.
- Degree of intra-mode and inter-mode competition.
- Any government regulations for transporters like permits required by road transporters in many states.

Customer Service

The customer service levels are defined by the company and accordingly the mode of transport and the frequency of deliveries are decided. The customer service factors which are then kept track of include:

- Consistency and dependability of the transporter in delivering on time every time and with the goods in the same condition as they were dispatched.
- Transit time from point of origin to the destination—very important and normally clearly defined for every "route".
- Coverage—for example door-to-door delivery.
- Flexibility in handling a range of products.
- Loss and damage performance. If losses and damages are nil, the situation is ideal.
- Additional services provided like for example, special requirements of temperature and humidity.

Advantages of Transportation

While transportation provides time and place utility for the customer, it also supports the company operations. Some of the advantages of having a good transportation system by any company are:

- It provides greater economies in the scale of production. It helps better utilization of capacity and the production units can be located in sites more suited for production. Whatever is produced, is moved out of the shop floor to a central plant FG warehouse or the distribution centers.
- By providing opportunities for business, it increases the competition among transporters and this reduces costs associated with transport, inventory and packaging. Most companies operate with 3 to 4 contracted transporters.
- Provides better customer service. Transportation creates the place and time utility as required either on scheduled dates or even in emergencies.

Transportation Selection Criteria

As seen earlier, there are a variety of modes of transport available. It is necessary not only to choose the right one from these modes, but also the right transporter from within the modes chosen. Obviously, the choice is based on the best customer service in terms of pick-up and delivery and the cost of freight. In addition, the transporter has to provide this service level consistently every time. Broadly the selection criteria can be grouped under the four heads:

- Transport rate related variables—assuming that the movement is from door-to-door (company premises to its client premises) and the willingness of the transporter to negotiate rates on open facts.
- Customer service capabilities in terms of door-to-door transit time and reliability and consistency of pick-up and delivery. In the case of road transport there should be no trans-shipment of the goods.
- It is assumed that the transporter delivers the items to the end point without any damages or losses. Even if there is some damage or loss in transit, there is a provision

made for claiming the value from the transporter. The procedure for raising the claims and recovering it from the transporter should be simple and fool-proof. It should not lead the parties into protracted litigation. Estimate of the loss and damage should be transparent. The transporter should provide the client the ability to track the shipments. Once the claim is made, it should be processed quickly and settled so that both parties can go on with the regular business.

- For some products like heavy equipment movement or products needing refrigerated movement, the transporter should be in a position to provide the right handling equipment. The transporter should not only have the right equipment, but also the trained personnel to operate it without damaging the goods.

In the next section, we will briefly discuss the modalities of the various modes of transport available.

> BhS UK is a clothing and apparel stores major. The head office determines replenishment requirements by stores based on daily information from POS data. The information is then transmitted to suppliers who package individual store requirements into bar coded parcels. The parcels are collected by a logistics service provider and sent to a trans-shipment center. The parcels are sorted for individual store delivery and sent to the stores. The exercise minimizes stocks and transport costs.

❍ **Rail Transport** In India, the rail transport system is state run and believes in the two principles of value of service on the demand side and cost of service on the supply side. The freight rates do not have a linear relationship with tonnage or distance but keep in mind social obligations and financial viability. For example, the railways may transport essential commodities like food grains over long distances any time in large quantities at highly subsidised freight rate considerations.

Rail freight considerations include:

- Speed of delivery desired—the freight on faster trains is higher.
- Distance covered—freight rates do increase with distance but telescopic rates also work.
- Ability to pay principle—as mentioned earlier, differential rates between essential commodities and commercial ones exist for the same trains and the same distances.
- One of the main considerations, like in any other form of transport, is the nature of the commodity being transported. Some of the rate related points on this are:
  - Concessions will be given on bulk bookings done in advance.
  - The freight on damage prone commodities is higher.
  - Special freight rates have to be paid on hazardous goods liable to inflammation, explosion and corrosion.
  - The size and packing of goods is also specified. Packing conditions are stipulated for different kinds of goods before the railways accept the consignment, and the freight rates also differ with the packages.

- The freight rates also depend on the extent to which the consignor is willing to share the risk in transit. The freight is higher if the consignment is sent at Railways Risk (RR) than if it is at Owner's Risk (OR).
- Depending on the demand and supply of wagons and the frequency of service required by the customer, the railways charges different rates.
- For special wagons like those which are closed or refrigerated or shock-absorbing, the rates are also higher.

The rates are classified as class rates (categories of products specified by the railways), wagonload rates, smalls (less than wagon loads), risk rates (depending on the perishability of the goods or the damage the goods can cause to other goods), trainload rates, station to station rates and special rates (to be negotiated—for moving heavy equipment, for example).

Once the railways have accepted the consignment for dispatch, they issue a clean railway receipt (RR) confirming that they have satisfied themselves on the nature of the consignment and given an unequivocal description of open or unpacked goods or goods packed in their presence. A qualified RR is issued for packed goods with a prefix of "said to contain". RRs can be sent to consignees through banks. Consignee surrenders the RR at the destination station by discharging it and takes the delivery of the goods.

When the external appearance is suspected, the consignee can ask for taking "open" delivery by getting the packages opened in the presence of the station master. The recording and vouching for the contents is witnessed by all present. Based on an Assessment Memo after open delivery, an insurance claim for the shortages can be made if the consignment has been insured.

The advantages of rail transport are that it is economical over long distances and it is reliable in all weather conditions. However, rail transport is uneconomical for small shipments over short distances. Nor is it suitable for remote locations or highly perishable goods. The terminal handling facilities are costly and the time schedules of the railways are not flexible.

❍ **Road Transport** This is the most popular and commonly used form of transport of goods in India. It is possible to hire vehicles for any destination and the trucker will ensure safe transit and responsibility of the goods when in his possession. The freight payment could be—prepaid, to pay, or to be billed later. For most companies who have road transporters on a contract, the billing is always done after safe delivery at the destination. The shipments could be full truck loads (FTL)—the standard load being 9 metric tons or smalls or less than truck load (LTL). Road transport could also be used and is extensively used for local cartage like truckloads or smalls from a plant to its local warehouse or distribution center (same town location) or local customers or interlinking with other modes like rail, air or sea.

When contracts are in operation, the trucker can have dedicated trucks for specific customers or even trucks with special equipment—refrigerated trucks, trucks with hydraulic tail gates, booms, trailers, and so on.

The road transport network and the business is so well developed in India that there is very little need for any company to have its own fleet. Own fleet has the advantages of timely deliveries, flexible and responsive service, and better care of consignments. The disadvantage is that return loads are not available and the operation could prove more expensive in the long run.

In terms of booking consignments by road transport and taking deliveries, most of the principles as in rail transport apply without the rigid formalities of the public sector railways. When the consignment is taken from the consignor, a goods consignment note (GCN) or lorry receipt (LR) is issued. The LR can be sent to the consignee for clearance or even routed through a bank.

The advantages of road transport are as under:

- There is a through movement of the goods from the consignor to the consignee without any trans-shipment.
- The company has the flexibility of deciding the drop points, the routes and these can be changed to suit changes in off-takes. Normal transport contracts ensure that these are kept flexible.
- The operation can be 24×7. It is a known fact that long distance trucks run in the night.
- As most of the truck transport is on contract, the risk of industrial action is minimized. The labour is employed by the contractor who has to take care of them.
- Insurance, claims on truckers are in practice and are quite streamlined.
- For schedules in operation for quite some time, the truck turn-around is fast. Fast turn-around is beneficial to the company and its transporter.

However, in spite of the best protection, there is exposure to weather and road conditions. Road transport is not suitable for very heavy loads where rail fares better. Even for long distances, road transport may become more expensive than telescopic rail rates.

❍ **Air Transport** This is the most expensive but the fastest of the transport modes. Air transport is most suitable for high value small volume goods that need to be transported quickly. This mode is used for getting the benefits of fast delivery in spite of the additional cost. This is used for (i) high value products—however requires less packaging and in-transit inventory costs, (ii) perishable products—like strawberries, tulips, cherries, (iii) emergency products—life saving medicines or critical machinery spare parts, (iv) live animals like race and show horses, and (v) short shelf life items like fashion items.

The consignor gets a receipt for the goods in the form of a Air Way Bill (AWB) or Air Consignment Note (ACN). This receipt can be used by the consignee to take the delivery of the goods at the destination.

Air cargo tariff is based on the volume and the economies of the route. Domestic air cargo rates are based on available capacity, market requirements and the operational economies. International air cargo tariff is based on different pricing concepts within the tariff structure, rationalization in terms of routes, competition and any bilateral trade agreements between countries.

The advantages of air transport are as under:

- Fastest mode of transport—domestic deliveries can be done the same day and international deliveries can be made in 48 to 72 hours.
- Inventory cost can be controlled.

- The service range is quite broad.
- The capacity is being built both in domestic and international sectors.

The disadvantages of air transport are as follows:

- High cost adds to the final price or affects margins in case of emergency dispatches by air.
- Weather can affect flight conditions and delay consignments.
- Limitations on bulk and heavy consignments.

❍ **Water Transport** Domestic water transport is limited to coastal areas only. For example, cement is transported from Gujarat plants to Kerala. In the case of international transport, the value of water transport is immense. Water transportation is normally used for low value to weight ratio items like timber, iron ore, coal, chemicals and cement. Commodities, which are bulky but low value where the items are not required in a hurry, are most suitable for water transport. However, in the case of international trade, any item can be transported by sea. The mode is slower but inexpensive—low cost per ton kilometre.

Note: All freight costs by any mode are measured in rupees per ton kilometre.

For international water transport (sea) there are two kinds of shipping services available. Liner Conferences is one alternative and the other is tramp steamers.

- *Liner conference*: This is a group of carriers operating two or more vessels in international waters. Obviously, they provide international sea freight services on particular routes within the geographies they have defined for themselves. All of them operate on uniform or common freight rates to help customers. The conditions defined by them have to be mutually agreed between the shipper and the consignor. Liner conferences operate through a regular organization and various committees. It is estimated that there are over 350 liner conferences in the world.
- *Tramp services*: This is more like the unorganized service in shipping. They operate very similar to taxis and can be hired between two points of interest to the customer. They normally do not have fixed routes or rates, but this has to be negotiated for each consignment. They are far less reliable than liner conferences.

The C&FA forwards the goods to the dock in case of Cargo booking by sea. The C&FA may even prepare the shipping document which is the customs document for paying any specified export duty. After getting the carting order from the shipping company, the C&FA has to shift the goods from the customer plant to the docks.

At the dock, the goods are delivered to the stevedores of the ship designated to transport the goods. The shipper gives a mate's receipt after paying the port charges. The C&FA submits the mate's receipt to the shipping company and obtains a Bill of Lading (BOL). The shipment has to be done within 7 days of the BOL to avoid any demurrage. The BOL becomes the authorized document for delivery of the goods to the consignee.

The advantages of sea transport are as under:

- Movement of bulk quantities are possible.
- Lowest freight cost in rupees per ton-kilometre.
- Long distance movement of low-value commodities.

The disadvantages of sea freight are as follows:

- This is not suitable for quick transit.
- Suits certain types of commodities only except when the goods are containerized in which case any number of commodities can be sent by sea.

❍ **Pipeline Movement** The entire pipeline will be owned by the company using it and is suitable for the products of the company running the pipeline. Pipeline movement is only suitable for transporting continuously large quantities of liquids and gases over long distances. This mode is normally used for petroleum products, gases, slurry (coal, iron ore, limestone, copper) and crude. Indian examples include Gauhati–Barauni, Ankleswar–Baroda and Mathura–Viramgam pipelines.

The advantages of pipeline movement are as under:

- It is a reliable, continuous and all weather transport.
- Low cost and the energy consumption is low.
- Low maintenance and operating costs.
- As the pipeline can be laid underground, there is no problem of space.
- The transit losses are minimum.
- It can be used in a difficult terrain also.
- The operations are 24×7 and quite safe.
- It is estimated that the throughput can be doubled with just 25 percent to 30 percent additional capital costs.

High capital costs involved and inability to transport solids are the disadvantages of pipeline movement.

❍ **Transport Using Ropeways** Ropeways are a means of transport in the private domain only except in the case of hill stations and other such cases where ropeways could transport the public. Ropeways are meant to connect two points with a large differential altitude. In these cases, the rate of rise or the gradient is not suitable either for a road or rail route. Normally this gradient is one in two. Transporters using ropeways can move materials over short distances in hilly regions. In many mines, it is a common sight to see some kind of ropeways in operation.

The advantages of ropeways are as under:

- The only mode of transport suitable for transportation of solids like ore in hilly or inaccessible areas.
- Can work in long and circuitous routes with streams and deep valleys in between.
- Suitable for all commodities that can be moved in ropeway buckets.
- Haulages are normally less than 50 kilometres.
- Has been found suitable where other modes are uneconomical or not feasible.

However, it lags behind in heavy investments and limitations on size, nature and quantity of the haul.

Selection of the Right Transport Mode

The modes of transport available for freight have been listed above along with the advantages and demerits of each. Some of the factors to be taken into account for deciding the mode of the transport in any given situation are discussed below. The obvious factors are the nature of the materials being transported, the quantities involved, the value of the commodities and the distances to be covered. The other factors are:

- Nature of the goods, the policy of the company and its customers which are all operational details.
- Comparison with the alternative modes available.
- The company and its customer's expectations on speed of delivery required, quality of the service and all this at an acceptable cost.
- Ability to track the consignment.
- Simplicity of the documentation other than the statutory requirements.
- Handling of complaints and the processing of claims.

Comparison of the different modes can be done on speed, versatility in handling various kinds of goods, reliability of delivery, availability, continuity of service and total distribution cost. The ranking of the modes (based on scores on a 10-point scale) is given in Table 16.1.

Table 16.1 Ranking of Modes

Parameter	Weightage	Rail	Road	Air	Water	Pipe line	Rope Way
Speed	30	5	6	8	4	3	3
Versatility	10	6	8	5	6	3	2
Reliability	20	6	8	5	5	7	4
Availability	10	7	8	5	6	3	2
Continuity of service	10	6	7	5	5	8	3
Distribution cost	20	4	5	2	6	7	8
Total score	10	5.4	6.7	5.3	5.1	5.1	4.0
Overall ranking	10	2	1	3	4	5	6

For suppliers who deliver seat assemblies to the Nissan plant, they are required to do the prior sequencing of the components before delivery to save time on the production line and provide a strict control on the WIP.

Transporter Rating System

For all transport done by rail, and water, which are in the public domain, it is difficult to rate the freight carrier as the alternative choices are limited. However, for road transport, which is the most common of the carriers for companies particularly in the domestic market, companies have evolved different methods of measuring the performance of the transporters to help them improve their performance and help the company.

The performance measurement could be different for a local transporter who has to take delivery from a company plant or C&FA and deliver at the distributor points in the same city and an up-country transporter who takes delivery from the same plant or C&FA, but delivers it to customers outside that city. The performance rating system (PRS) for each category is shown in Tables 16.2 and 16.3.

Table 16.2 PRS for Local Transporter

Parameter to be Measured	Weightage in Total	Rating Percentage	Score
Prompt pick-up from the plant or warehouse on the designated date and time	10		
On-time delivery at the customer point	70		
Quality of delivery – intact packaging, no damages in transit	20		
Total score for the month			

Table 16.3 PRS for Up-country Transporter

Parameter to be Measured	Weightage in Total	Rating Percentage	Score
Prompt pick-up at the plant or warehouse on the designated date and time	10		
Delivery to the customer within the agreed lead time	60		
Quality of delivery – intact packages, no damages	10		
Reporting of delivery completion to the dispatch point	10		
No trans-shipments or delays in transit	10		
Total score for the month			

However, there are some points to be noted:

- The above is only an example. The parameters and weightage against 100 can be decided by the company as it suits it.
- The rating is based on actual performance and can be both objective and judgmental.
- The score is the product of the weightage and the rating. It is expected that the score has to be as close to 100 as possible to denote excellent performance.

The monthly scores can be used to do an appraisal of the performance of the transporters and also use it at the time of rate negotiations and for improving on certain parameters.

Depending on the score achieved by the transporter, the performance can be decided as follows:

More than 90 percent—very good

Between 75 to 90 percent—satisfactory

Less than 75 percent—cause for concern

Third Party Logistics Service Providers

More and more companies are realising that order fulfilment and delivery can be better handled by people for whom this job is their core competence. This has created the system of 3P logistics service providers who are willing to undertake all the activities from taking delivery of the goods from the plant of the client and delivering them safely to their customers. Apart from all the documentation they are even willing to collect the remittances from the customers and reaching it to the client or banking it into his account. Some examples of 3P logistics service providers operating in India are:

- Transport companies which have upgraded into providing a large number of logistics services: TCI, GATI.
- Some C&F agents have taken on the additional tasks: Sembawang, Dynamic.
- Even courier companies are into providing a wide range of logistics services: Blue Dart, AFL, Safexpress.
- Multinational logistics companies have also set up operations in India: Bax Global, Geologistics, UPS.
- There are also a large number of companies in the unorganized sector who operate like 3P logistics service providers.

Example: 3P Service

This is about tie-up between the Rover Group, UK, and the courier company TNT. Suppliers and TNT deliver consolidated quantities to a specially designed trans-shipment center owned and run by TNT near the factory. Components and assemblies are moved direct to the point of use on the assembly line as scheduled. There is a smooth flow of inbound materials. There is also no congestion of delivery vehicles at the plant.

Reality Bite

E-commerce companies in India like Flipkart, Amazon and Snapdeal promise fast deliveries of goods ordered online to their customers. To facilitate this, they have encouraged the development of a number of delivery companies who specialize in providing this last mile connectivity to e-commerce companies. Some of these companies include – Delhivery, GoJavas, e-com Express, Aramex delivery unlimited, UPS, Blue Dart / DHL, Gati – e-connect, First Flight apart from Fedex.

ADVANCES IN SUPPLY CHAIN MANAGEMENT

Even though the concept of supply chain management is about two decades old, there have been a number of recent advances in the manner in which companies have made the supply chains a source of competitive advantage. We will discuss some of these concepts briefly here.

Efficient Consumer Response

Major FMCG companies in India are attempting to implement this concept that took roots in the grocery industry in the US. The idea was to supply to the final user/consumer only what he or she wanted in the most efficient manner. This was done by using scanners at the point of sale to inform the supplier of the demand for the product lifted from the retail shelf. The supplier was able to quickly fill back the shelves with the product which had moved out. This excellent understanding of the off-takes and quick replenishment also helps streamline processes relating to pricing and promotions. The advantage for the company is that it ensures that the brand/pack of the same company is replaced without giving a chance to competition to fill the gaps. For the modern retailer, he does not have to hold excess stocks in the back-store as he knows that the company will quickly replenish sold quantities. The consumers have the benefit of getting what they want, when they want it and in their favourite retail outlet.

Category Management

We have already discussed this in Chapter 10. Managing categories (groups of products which are complementary from the consumer viewpoint) of products makes the task of logistics relatively easier. Even while calling-off products based on the merchandiser negotiations, logistics can handle suppliers more efficiently. Co-ordination between retailers and their vendors has become better.

Continuous Replenishment

This resulted from tracking the online consumption of the products at the point of sale. This was pioneered in the US by Walmart and P&G. The principle is to replace stocks on the retail shelves based on the updated knowledge of consumer off-takes. Logistics helps in filling up the retail shelves based on updated marketing information.

Example: Partnership

This is the partnership of P&G and Walmart in the US. P&G gets sales data directly from the POS check-out counters at WM. P&G plans production and scheduled deliveries to WM on a replenishment basis. WM experiences much lesser inventories and stock-outs. For P&G, this means better economies in production and logistics and increased sales.

Quick Response Logistics

Here the consumer decides what he wants when and where. The logistics system has to respond fast to the needs highlighted. This is a good example of a "pull" system as the action happens based on consumer requirements. In many cases, the need may be based on a triggered impulse but still has to be met fast. The point of sale data is collected and analyzed to keep manufacturing flexible to meet the demand.

Handling Functional and Innovative Products

A functional product meets the basic needs of a consumer—like a bar of soap or a tube of toothpaste. It requires that the supply chain address the issues of time and place utility efficiently. Such a supply chain is known as a physically efficient supply chain.

On the other hand, there are innovative products like fashion accessories which are difficult to forecast and also the demand is not certain. Some of these products may even have a short life. In such cases, one is looking for a supply chain which is quick in response to the market needs. This kind of a supply chain is known as a market responsive supply chain.

Benchmarking

As the name implies, benchmarking is comparing performance of a company's logistics or supply chain systems with that of its competitors or with successful companies in other industries.

- In the case of the supply chain, processes at the supply end, the internal processes and the processes at the distribution end can all be benchmarked.
- At the supplier's end, benchmarking is possible with the quality, the lead times and the on-time delivery performance and ready availability of stocks when the company sends its purchase orders.
- Between the supplier and the company, comparisons can be made about the communication process, the planning scheduling and the performance on making sub-assemblies.
- Internally, we could measure throughout times, on-time performance of the production function and finished goods availability.
- Between the company and its distribution network, communication, effective requirements planning and working on plans for promotions together can be benchmarked.
- For the distribution network, we could measure the delivery performance, customer service levels, and any value added services can all be benchmarked.

The purpose of benchmarking is obviously to emulate/adopt any good practices of others.

Quikr Promises to Deliver Faster

Quikr is investing in warehousing space and a fleet of trucks to speed up the pick-up and delivery of second-hand goods for its customers, says *Economic Times* (April 21, 2016). Quikr is planning to start this process in 25 cities.

Alibaba uses start-ups to expand into the Indian Market

Chinese e-commerce giant, Alibaba, has attracted the attention of logistics service companies GoJavas, Delhivery and Ecom Express to provide support of delivery of packages. *Economic Times* (May 12, 2016) has reported that Alibaba has tied up for cross border shipment with a company called All Cargo Logistics. Alibaba has also invested in Snapdeal and Paytm.

LO 4 Discuss how IT enables logistics function and learn about the use of technology in logistics function

IT ENABLING THE LOGISTICS FUNCTION

Companies have realized that, speed being the essence of the customer service function, they can react faster to customer needs if they are able to utilize the strength of information technology processes. It has been established that distribution challenges can be proactively managed with real-time knowledge of business events.

E-logistics upgrades a company's supply chain function to collaborate with its suppliers and customers to make full use of the business opportunities via the Internet. This substantially alters the traditional functions of inventory management, replenishment and shipping.

Logistics information systems have the components of a data base, planning function, control function, co-ordination function and customer service.

- The data base could contain external data, customer orders, inbound logistics, internal data on production and inventory.
- The planning function includes strategy planning, demand forecasting, stock management and planning production by location, product and customer requirements.
- Control function means customer service levels, vendor performance ratings, transporter performance rating and the system performance.
- Co-ordination is for production scheduling, and sales and marketing planning.
- Customer service includes communication, customer order status, stock availability by product and location.

Use of IT in Managing Supply Chains

The purpose is to handle enormous amounts of data and enable fast decision-making which should result in getting the product or service faster to the customer. IT enabling also helps in better planning of the supply chain activities, managing inventory, measuring and cutting supply chain costs, reducing lead times etc.

There are four recognized drivers of a supply chain: (i) facilities, (ii) inventory, (iii) transportation, and (iv) information technology (IT). Of these four, IT is the most important driver. It helps co-ordinate the activities of the other three drivers. It helps the supply chain processes execute transactions and the supply chain manager to take decisions. It is said that information technology provides "visibility" for the supply chain. It has all the features highlighted in Chapter 15: (i) accuracy, (ii) timely and quick access, (iii) relevant and simple/easy to use.

IT has an enormous influence on the performance of the supply chain. It is used in the management of supply chains to:

- Collect or gather the primary data
- Process data into information
- Analyze the information
- Use the information to take decisions to improve the performance of the supply chain.

Some of the decisions on the other three drivers which information helps formulate are:

- Facilities (as in plants and warehouses, etc.)—location, capacities, schedules for usage
- Inventory (the shock absorber between supply and demand)—demand patterns, cost of carrying, cost of ordering, cost of stock-outs etc.
- Transportation (movement of inventory between points)—routing, frequencies, modes

There are basically three focus areas of IT in the supply chain—the supply end, the conversion in the company and the demand end. The IT related to these focus areas runs on the transaction management system in the company:

- Managing the inbound logistics—supplier relationships—supplier relationship management (SRM), sourcing, negotiations, buying, collaboration in product design
- Managing the "internal" supply chain of the company (ISCM), planning of supply, demand planning and fulfilment, support to field sales
- Managing the outbound logistics—customer relationships—customer relationship management (CRM), marketing, selling, order management

Use of IT Systems in Logistics

Some of the common and popular IT systems getting used in the logistics industry are: (i) Warehouse Management Systems (WMS), (ii) Freight Management Systems (FMS), and (iii) Track and Trace systems. GATI, a 3P Logistics Service Provider, uses a web-based WMS to provide the support and flexibility for its customers. The system provides consolidated real-time information to customers. The 3P logistics business in India was estimated at about $100 million by 2012.

The IT system for the supply chain has to ensure the following:

- It has to be functional to create a competitive advantage to the company.
- The SCM IT system should be integrated well with the other systems in the company so that the benefits can be realized faster.
- The implementation should be done in a manner to enhance customer service.

Some of the IT vendors in the supply chain domain are listed below:

- SAP
- Oracle
- JDA software
- Manhattan Associates
- Epicor
- IBM
- Descartes Systems
- Infor
- Highjump Software
- GT Nexus

They provide solutions in supply chain optimization, warehouse management systems, transport management systems, and materials management and materials requirement planning systems.

TECHNOLOGY IN LOGISTICS – EDI, BAR CODING, AND RFID

We are aware that "information" is a key driver of supply chains. Information also happens to be the only "intangible" driver. In a multi-product company with many production units and hundreds of customers, the information to be processed everyday is huge and can only be possible with a strong IT-enabled operation. The principles mentioned in Chapter 15 on the channel information systems, are equally applicable to information handling in the supply chain.

To illustrate with a simple example, a multi-product, multi-brand, multi-SKUs company starts its planning process by getting the SKU-wise forecasts from its salespeople in the field may be every month. The data is processed in the IT-enabled supply chain system to generate:

- A materials (raw materials, packing materials, and consumables) buying plan to be used by the purchase people
- A production and production scheduling plan by SKU to be followed by the production people
- A dispatch plan by SKU to be followed by the production people for finished goods despatches to the various selling units from where the forecasts/indents have been received.

All these operations are possible only with the help of an IT-enabled supply chain. The supply chain uses the processed data in the form of information to take decisions on facilities, transport, and inventory.

The IT system improves the quality of decision-making by being accurate, fast, cost-effective, visible, providing quick access, productive and with a high customer focus. Some of the technologies available are described briefly below.

Supplier Relationship Management (SRM)

This includes the processes for the flow of materials, etc., between the suppliers and a firm. The processes include:

- Design collaboration between the firm and its suppliers—joint product development efforts
- Sourcing—selection of the appropriate suppliers—factors kept in mind are quality, lead times, reliability and prices
- Buying—managing the purchasing process to reduce time and cost
- Negotiation—at all stages from the time of the receipt of the quotes from the suppliers and obviously relates to prices, delivery times and other terms and conditions of the transaction
- Collaboration with suppliers—to improve their performance in better forecasting, good production planning and managing optimum inventory levels.

Customer Relationship Management (CRM)

The objective of CRM is a customer-focused business strategy to optimize revenue, profitability by superior customer service and hence supportive customer response. CRM includes all processes from the firm to its customers. CRM concentrates on selling, marketing and servicing functions at all points of interaction with customers. It provides an overall view of the customer to the company irrespective of where the information or the customer interface occurs. Some of the salient features of the CRM process are as follows:

- Sales force automation—call/contact management, managing leads, analysis of quotations, forecasting, sales administration, establishing customer needs/preferences, customer buying habits and tracking sales force performance.

- Customer service—handling requests, complaints, and product returns etc.; simple interactive methods used are the help desk and the customer call center.
- Automation of marketing efforts—tracking environmental variables, tracking competition and industry trends—favourable or otherwise; the objective of getting this information is to improve the effectiveness of customer communication.
- Customer analysis—helps in customer segmentation and throws up cross-selling opportunities.
- Collaborative CRM—working with customers, getting their feedback to improve products, services, deliveries and enhance customer value delivery to customers.

Supply Chain Management (SCM)

This part focuses on the processes within the firm to enhance customer service. It takes care of all processes right from planning to fulfilling a customer's order. Some of these processes are:

- Strategic planning—like network design—location of production facilities, distribution warehouses, etc., all of which impact the performance of the supply chain.
- Demand planning—includes forecasting customer demand; it also helps in promotions planning.
- Planning supplies—developing an optimal plan to get materials to fulfil demand – ordering frequencies, quantities and inventory planning.
- Fulfilment of orders—linked to the dispatch planning.
- After sales support—managing spares, service engineers' time, and schedules, etc.

Electronic Data Interchange (EDI)

The Ministry of Finance, Government of India, defines EDI as: "The exchange of business information through standard interfaces by using computers." This defines the exchange of data in a structured form between the firm and its suppliers—can be part of the SRM described above. This method replaces oral and written communication with electronic communication.

EDI has the obvious benefits of reduced paperwork, far better accuracy, faster, improved information availability which is almost online, lower handling and processing costs and saving in inventory and time. EDI uses various kinds of data acquisition equipment like bar codes, optical character recognition (OCR), radio frequency identification (RFID), etc. These are described here briefly.

This method of communication is becoming quite common between the company and its suppliers and can be extended to customers also. It is defined as the electronic, computer to computer transfer of standard business documents, data and information. Examples of documents are purchase orders, material releases, invoices and fund transfers. Some of the benefits of EDI are:

- Reduced paperwork
- Reduction in manual processing improves accuracy
- Improved speed of data transmission and order receipts
- Reduced effort in data entry and filing

- Proactive contribution by purchase is possible
- The cost of order placement, processing and handling can get reduced
- Information availability is almost instantaneous
- Improved accuracy and reduced order cycle time also has a positive effect on the inventory levels

Bar Codes (Also called Universal Product Code)

This is the most common, popular and cost-effective way of tracking items. Bar codes are observed everywhere on packaging as a series of vertical lines which can be scanned by a bar code "reader" to identify the item. Bar codes can be linear (one dimension) or even two dimensional.

Bar code is an item identifier and is made up of a series of bars and spaces which can represent an alphanumeric identification of the desired parameters. The series of lines in a bar code are unique from each other in terms of thickness. These black coloured lines store data about the item on them. This data can be retrieved by scanning with a special device (the device is an optical character recognition device). Some of the uses of the bar codes in a supply chain are:

- Receipt of incoming materials in a plant—the bar code labels identify the item, purchase order number, supplier, lot number, date of delivery
- Tracking of inventory in the stores—for better materials management using part numbers, storage location number and help reduce transaction times
- Picking of inventory in a store—location check by SKU
- Use on the production lines—for identifying products made in different shifts
- Better and faster quality control of selected items.

Importers in the US and developed countries will not import any item from any country if it is not bar coded.

Radio Frequency Identification (RFID)

This is a very useful but as yet expensive technology for automatic data capture. RFID is an improvement over bar coding. RFID has the ability to track items, people, equipment, etc., in real time without the need for contact or "line-of-sight". The RFID tag is a "transponder" containing data like the serial number of an item or component. It transmits information carried on it wirelessly when placed in the "radio" transmission field of a reader. The reader is a radio transmitter that continuously keeps sending out an electromagnetic pulse. When an RFID tag moves into the range of the reader, the information contained on the tag is automatically read and registered.

Two types of tags are used in RFID: (i) passive and active and (ii) read only and write.

RFID technology can be used to keep track of thousands of components in a store, books in a library, work-in-process items on the shop floor or even finished goods in a retail store. It can also track the tasks being performed by employees to make them more responsive to customer needs.

RFID Used Effectively in the Dairy Industry

One of the oldest dairies in Western India introduced RFID tags over 10 years ago to keep track of their cattle. This helps the dairy to track the cattle closely, their feeding habits can be analyzed, and their health problems can be known so that their feeding pattern and nutrition needs can be taken care of to improve milk yields. The milk yield of these dairy cattle is 3 to 4 times that of the national average. The RFID tags have a 4 kb memory capacity.

Reality Bite

QR Codes

QR code is a machine readable code (similar to bar codes) using an array of black and white squares. The squares store URLs or other information and can be read by a camera on a smartphone.

QR code was invented in 1994 by Denso Wave. QR codes were first designed for the automobile industry in Japan.

Compared to bar codes, QR codes can store more data and can be read faster. Some of the applications in which QR codes are in use: item identification, product tracking, time tracking and document management. It is obvious that these applications are of special interest to marketing and logistics functions. One would notice that QR codes are extensively used in advertising.

Optical Character Recognition (OCR)

This technology is similar to bar codes but less accurate. Normally, this technology is used by companies like couriers, etc., to track or sort mails or documents.

Data Warehousing*

In data warehousing the technology works like this:

- Collects data from multiple, heterogeneous sources
- Uses tools to convert the data into information and store it, the data is stored in a step-by-step manner
- The stored integrated information can then be used for queries, analysis, and decision-making; this is a part of the Decision Support System.
- Makes the optimization of the supply chain possible through consolidation, conversion, transformation and integration of operational data.

Data Mining is an information analysis tool that automatically discovers patterns and relationships in a data warehouse.

Custom Foot is a footwear marketing retail store group in the US. Its stores carry no inventory but only samples of footwear styles, leather types and colours. Customers visiting these unique stores can make their choice of design, leather type and colour and get their feet measured exactly by a scanner for a perfect fit. Custom Foot sends electronic orders to its suppliers in Italy. The finished product to the exact specifications of the customer is delivered to him/her in three weeks. All this happens at a competitive price to the customer.

Electronic Payment Transfers

This again is the difficult part of doing the business. Most suppliers prefer only cash on delivery. Customers may be reluctant to pay through their credit cards and not all of them may have credit cards. At the time of delivery if the customer is asked for payment, there could be some problems like:

- The person present and receiving the goods may not be the one placing the order and may ask that the courier should come later to collect the cash.
- The person placing the order may not accept all the goods fully.
- It could happen that the order may not be accepted as the customer has changed his mind or bought the product elsewhere in the meantime.
- The delivery agent would have to manage the issues of accepting payments in different formats and delivering it back to the retailer.
- The delivery agent may also have to tackle the issue of goods returned by the customer if he does not want them.
- In the case of B2B transactions, the amounts are so high that it cannot be handled by cash transactions. The payments have to be by cheques or demand drafts.

Electronic banking technologies have advanced so much that they reduce the cost of making payments as they reduce a lot of paperwork while transferring funds from one entity to another (buyer to supplier). Electronic means for secure payment has speeded up the growth of e-commerce.

Payment Options

Once the customer is required to pay for the finished goods despatched to him, he has several options to pay for the goods. Some of these traditional methods include demand drafts, cheques, etc., now it is also possible to use two electronic payment methods which are described in brief:

National Electronic Funds Transfer (NEFT)

It is a nationwide payment system facilitating one-to-one funds transfer. Even individuals can electronically transfer funds from their account and bank branch to any individual or company having an account with the branch of any other bank in India. Distributors use this facility to make payments for purchases to companies.

Real Time Gross Settlement (RTGS)

This is meant for transfer of money or securities from one bank to another in real time and on gross basis. There is no waiting period for the transaction to get completed. Gross settlement indicates that no charges are deducted. Once the payment is processed, it is irrevocable.

The payments from B2C transactions are still small compared to the B2B transactions. This has brought in specialist transaction service providers who handle different payment methods like the ones described below:

- *Credit and debit cards*: Most common method of payment preferred by the suppliers. Credit card companies are taking the initiative to provide all support to sellers wanting to use the Internet for their transactions.

- *Internet service provider's invoice*: Some ISPs offer online invoicing for payments. At the end of the month the ISP invoices (bills) the customer for all purchases made during the month and this can be paid through bank accounts.
- *Demand drafts, cash on delivery*: The preferred method of payment for transactions particularly in India.

In the Western context, there are transaction service providers who collect payments from customers for the supplier.

LOGISTICS/SUPPLY CHAIN: COST OF SERVICE

The total cost of service involves all the move-store activities of the product and includes:

- Inventory costs—unit costs, storage and working capital lock-up
- Warehousing costs
- Production or supply costs
- Distribution channel costs
- Communication and data processing costs
- Transportation of finished goods
- Materials handling costs
- Packaging related to logistics
- Customer service based on policies on customer service levels committed
- Cost of lost sales as a result of stock-outs
- Any allocated administrative or overhead costs

Reality Bite

IT enabling the supply chain

IT Tool	What it does
Collaborative planning, forecasting and replenishment model (CPFR)	To minimize demand and supply uncertainties
Enterprise resource planning (ERP)	Transactional tracking and visibility of actionable information
Supplier relationship management (SRM)	Planning and operations with suppliers
Customer relationship management (CRM)	Working closely with customers for better customer services
Electronic supply chain	Processing of information in the supply chain for faster decision-making and optimizing cost
Integrated supply chain network	Collaborative working with the vendors and customers to maximize service and optimize costs
Radio Frequency Identification Device	Using radio frequencies to track items

Source: MM Review, October 2015

However, not all these costs are accounted for by the supply chain. The supply chain costs are confined to:

- Inventory costs
- Warehousing
- Transportation
- Special packaging
- Cost of lost sales if it can be worked out
- Cost of losses and damages
- Insurance costs

In some companies, the cost of accounts receivable is attributed to the supply chain. In such cases the supply chain will get credit for any accounts payable on account of payments due to suppliers.

LO 5 Review the performance measurement of logistics function

LOGISTICS/SUPPLY CHAIN: PERFORMANCE MEASUREMENT

The performance of the logistics or supply chain function can be measured both on internal and external parameters.

The purpose of the measurement is to find out how the supply chain or logistics function delivers customer service fast at an optimal cost. For this, the measurement is related to customer service provided by the inventory holdings, warehousing support, and the transportation capabilities. Companies measure the supply chain cost as a percentage of sales to keep track of the cost to ensure that it is optimum and comparable to industry standards.

A brief view on performance measurement is given here:

Internal Measurements

- The cost incurred to accomplish the objectives of customer service.
- The customer service status seen as a combination of sales achieved, order numbers received and executed, rate of stock returns, stock-outs, orders cancelled, damage claims settled and the order cycle time.
- Customer service delivered in terms of satisfying customers and could include:
    - Fill rates—ability to supply the full order in time—also referred as OTIF—on time, in full.
    - Orders shipped complete—ability to supply the full order every time.
    - Speed of response—order cycle time.
    - Consistency—delivery every time as per expectations.
    - Stock-out frequency—number of times demand exceeded availability.
    - Reliability—ability to meet customer perception of service.
- Productivity measures which show the relationship between input (effort, time, cost) and output (service provided).
- Asset utilization—equipment, transport facilities and inventory.

- Concept of the perfect order—quality of the fulfilled order in terms of customer specifications, service goals, error free invoicing and zero defect performance.

External Measurements

- Customer perception—obtained through regular feedback or surveys.
- Normally rank customer service parameters in relation to competition—parameters like order cycle time, feedback on order status, after sales service and support systems.
- Best practice benchmarking—to search for the best overall practice outside the company and adopt it. The system is normally broken down into variables affecting it and then compared—cost, quality, order processing effectiveness, transportation and warehousing efficiencies.

Lean Thinking in Supply Chain

A lean SC is the one that produces just what and how much is needed and where it is needed. Keeping the customers' needs in mind, companies try to produce more with minimal resources.

Some of the lean principles include defining customer expectations of value, deciding steps to create value, developing processes to create the right flow and continuous improvements to eliminate waste. Most of these have been clearly written by Bruce Tompkins leading consultant.

Some waste reduction practices include quality assurance to reduce defects, combining processes, eliminating excess materials, handling and associated costs, removing non-value adding processes and ensuring timely delivery of items.

Components of a lean supply chain include developing lean systems in suppliers, procurement process, and warehousing and transportation practices. Lean systems have the benefits of speed in responding to customer needs, reduced inventories and costs and improved customer satisfaction.

Source: MM Review, January 2014

6 Sigma and Supply Chain Management

Sigma is a Greek symbol used in statistics for measuring standard deviation. When evaluating quality, 6 sigma quality level is equal to 3.4 defects per million opportunities (DPMO). Yield will be 99.9997 percent. Some of the operational issues which need to be addressed to ensure a 6 Sigma supply chain are listed as follows:

- Minimizing late deliveries from suppliers
- Eliminating long waiting times for processing WIP goods
- Ensuring adequate inventory in warehouses to meet the demand
- Forecasting has to be accurate
- On-time-in-full (OTIF) deliveries of customer orders

How does 6 Sigma benefit the supply chain?

It improves the effectiveness of the supply chain as seen in:

- Good inventory management—reduced costs, timely deliveries, correct dispatches, reduced storage efforts and cost, reduced damages, and improved service levels.
- Results in savings in administrative costs on order management
- Improved customer service levels—OTIF

Source: MM Review, April 2016, p. 31

Logistics/Supply Chain Performance: Popular Measurement Ratios

- Inventory in number of days' sales (FG) or production (raw materials or packing materials).
- Inventory levels against agreed norms. For example, a target may be set for finished goods levels as seven days' sales in the plant and three weeks stocks in the C&FA or distribution center.
- Customer service levels in orders fulfilled—OTIF—on time, in full. Each order which is filled with 100 percent of the ordered SKUs and on the delivery date promised is considered as complete in all respects and gets ONE mark. Any order which is not executed OTIF gets a ZERO.
- Warehouse capacity utilization—utilization of space for the tonnage handled is the measurement.
- Warehouse labour utilization—the number of loads handled per day.
- Warehouse cost per ton handled.
- Freight cost per ton kilometre against budget.

Reality Bite

Achieving agility in the supply chain

Some of the factors in achieving agility in the supply chain include: (i) creating a culture of learning and change, (ii) closely collaborating with the supply chain partners, (iii) making agility a strategic goal of the supply chain, (iv) using technology as relevant, (v) increasing competence of the employees, and (vi) continuous monitoring of the supply chain. These factors have also been brought out well in the Materials Management Review of IIMM in its November 2015 issue.

How Does One Recognize Logistics Excellence?

There are some principles which identify an excellent logistics system. These are listed below:

- The logistics strategy has been derived from the corporate strategy.
- The logistics function has been organized comprehensively.
- The system is fully information technology enabled.
- There is still the emphasis on utilization of human resource.
- Where necessary, strategic alliances are formed with others having better core competence.
- The focus has to be on financial performance—cost effectiveness of operations.
- The system has to look at minute details.
- Economies of scale are to be fully exploited.
- At every stage performance has to be measured against set objectives.

Reality Bite

Problems to be resolved for improving supply chain performance

- High supply chain costs
- Not enough investments in IT support
- Inadequate support of public infrastructure like roads, etc.

The solutions are obvious: (i) clearly aligning the supply chain strategy with the business strategy, (ii) fully exploiting the capabilities of a robust IT system, and (iii) involvement of vendors and customers in product development activities.

LO 6 Determine the principle for logistics in rural markets

LOGISTICS FOR RURAL MARKETS

This section briefly touches upon some of the concerns of business managers in reaching their products to rural markets or for farmers to sell their produce to the rest of the country.

Physical distribution for rural is still a major concern as "access" to rural is either limited or of not such a good standard. India's vast railway network, as well as its relatively well-developed road network, is still not useful for nearly 40 percent of the villages. It is a fact that even many of the national companies use bullock carts or mobile traders on bicycles to reach the rural markets. Even the state run warehousing corporations do not have storage space/warehouses beyond the district towns.

Some numbers—a majority of the consumers in 638,000 villages in India still buy most of their requirements from about 2300 feeder towns. Companies are quite happy if their goods reach and are available in these feeder towns. Distributors in these feeder towns provide the further reach into the villages.

Some of the factors which the business manager should keep in mind while developing suitable logistics plans for rural are mentioned as follows:

- The potential for business (both inbound and outbound) is large but the collection points are many.
- Both the producers (of agricultural produce) and the users (consumers for brands) are dispersed in difficult to access village markets.
- Transporters are not willing to take the trip into the rural markets as return loads are not available.
- Agricultural produce (outbound logistics) is bulky, perishable and not of standard sizes.
- Many villages are accessible only by bullock carts. Many villages are not even accessible during the monsoons.
- For logistics of agricultural produce, it is only a seasonal business. One has to keep the assets idle in other seasons.

- Intermediaries, brokers, agents are the major element of the cost.
- Most of the storage of the agricultural produce is at the farms and liable to deteriorate in quality.

In spite of these difficulties, there are exemplary examples of many companies which have almost mastered the art of rural logistics. Some of these examples are mentioned in Chapter 9.

Vakrangee will show Amazon around rural India

Vakrangee is a Mumbai based firm with about 12,000 centers all India and expected to expand to over 50,000 outlets soon.

They have tied up with Amazon to provide the services of marketing, sales and pick-up from their centers. They are also working with Jan Dhan Yojana accounts to facilitate online payments. They also operate ATMs, insurance and e-governance kiosks as per *Business India* (August 05, 2015).

Supply Chain Efforts to Reduce Agricultural Losses

It is estimated that losses in storage of agricultural goods result in losses of about 10 percent of the produce, like food grains. Efforts are on to introduce scientific processes of storage and these are expected to dramatically bring down the losses to about 0.5 percent resulting in a savings of over ₹80,000 crore every year, as per MM Review, June 2015, p.27.

In perishables, like fruits and vegetables, the losses in the supply chain could be as high as 30–40 percent in post-harvest storage and transportation. It is estimated that only about 3 percent of fruits and vegetables get processed. India has a serious shortage of cold storage capacity—it is just adequate to take care of 10 percent of the fruits and vegetables produce. This is a major opportunity in the supply chain for farm produce. Cold storage and warehousing capacity opportunities are in the range of over 40 million tons as per expert estimates.

Important Note on Goods and Services Tax (GST)

The Government of India has introduced GST from July 1, 2017. This will have a major impact on some of the supply chain and logistics issues like:

- It will reduce the need for a large number of C&FAs and distribution centers which were setup primarily to avoid multiple taxation across states on the same set of goods.
- The GST will eliminate the need for hundreds of check-posts at state borders. This will result in avoiding goods trucks having to wait for hours at the check-posts in state borders.
- It will speed up deliveries of goods and hence the transit time will get reduced substantially.

Some salient features of GST are summarized as follows:

- Central taxes like excise duty, additional excise duties, service tax, additional customs duty, special additional duty of customs (SAD), etc. would be subsumed by GST.

- State level taxes like VAT/sales tax, central sales tax, entertainment tax, octroi and entry tax, purchase tax, luxury tax, etc. would be subsumed by GST.
- Centre will compensate states for loss of revenue for five years on a tapering basis—100 percent first three years, 75 percent fourth year and 50 percent in fifth year.
- All goods and services, except liquor for human consumption, will be covered by GST.
- Petroleum products are also exempted for the time being. Current taxes will continue.
- GST is a destination based tax. All GST on the final product will be 50 percent to the center and 50 percent to the state.
- Services mean anything other than goods.
- GST has been finalized on the slabs of 0 percent, 5 percent, 12 percent, 18 percent and 28 percent and goods under each of the slabs have been clearly defined.
- All business establishments are required to be registered under GST.

In order to facilitate an easy process of implementation of GST, the Government of India has provided the following support:

- All GST related queries can be addressed to: @askGST_GoI
- For getting more details about the various slabs applicable on different products and services, a website is created: hhtp://www.cbec.gov.in/resources//htdocs-cbec/gst/tweet-faq.pdf

All the above details have been extensively published in all leading newspapers in India. In addition, to ensure easy registration and implementation of GST, the GoI has also created facilitation centers, GST practitioners, GST Suvidha providers, offline facility for return filing and application interfaces.

In addition, the following websites are also meant to help:

- *GST Help Desk:* cbecmitra.helpdesk@icegate.gov.in
- *GSTN Help Desk:* helpdesk@gst.gov.in
- *Twitter handles:* @askGST_GOI and @askGSTech

SUMMARY

LO 1

- The support of the logistics function to an organization and its marketing efforts has evolved from a system of just managing materials to logistics and today to supply chain management which extends its activities beyond the organization boundaries.
- Logistics is a critical function in providing the time, place and possession utilities to the products and services of the company. Its customers are production (for raw materials, packing materials, consumables and production scheduling) and marketing (finished goods). Logistics has got a major role to play in providing customer service.
- The most common and regular interface of logistics is with production and marketing. However logistics has a direct impact on the financial performance of the company—it directly affects the return on investment and the balance sheet while also helping improve profitability if managed effectively.

LO 2

- Logistics strategy gets derived from the corporate and marketing strategies. The primary focus of the logistics strategy has to be to develop a "competitive" advantage. This could be achieved by faster reach to the markets or customers and/or achieving the reach at the lowest possible cost. Logistics strategy could be based on markets, processes or the channels of distribution.

LO 3

- Three important functions of logistics are inventory management, warehousing, and transportation management.
  - Inventory is money and has to be managed very skilfully. Too much means additional costs and too little means missed sales and profit opportunities. Experience has taught us many good principles and practices of managing inventory well.
  - Warehousing provides the place utility for the product. It provides the balance between production requirements of utilizing capacity and meeting customer requirements regularly. Distribution warehousing has special meaning to the marketing person as it is directly concerned with finished goods.
  - Transportation management has developed as a useful supplement to the logistics function, in ensuring materials are available at short notice. Various modes of transport like rail, road, air, and water are available with advantages and cost considerations. The logistics manager can use the most suitable mode in every case while keeping costs in check but ensuring customer service.

LO 4

- With the number of products and customers to be handled in a wide geography, the complexity of operations has increased and can be handled effectively only with the support of information technology. This is being exploited well by organizations. Companies, which have implemented enterprise resource planning systems (ERPs), find these solutions now supporting their supply chain and logistics efforts also.
- Modern day supply chains integrate the operations of a firm, its suppliers and its customers and involve all of them in the planning process for providing products and services to delight the customers. Efficient consumer response and quick response logistics are two new methods which are catching up as better supply chain practices.
- Some of the technologies used in logistics are Electronic data interchange (EDI), bar coding, Radio Frequency Identification (RFID), supplier relationship management and customer relationship management.
- The purpose of using information technology in supply chain management is to handle enormous amounts of data and enable fast decision-making which should result in getting the product or service faster to the customer.
- Order processing is part of the logistics or the supply chain function in the company and is the primary contact between the company (supplier) and its customer. Materials handling is one of the functions of managing inventory along with storage and transfer of information.

LO 5

- Good practices have been developed to understand the cost of providing customer service through the logistics systems. After all there is a limit to the cost a firm can incur on providing customer service. As the proof of the pudding is in the eating, the logistics function also has to be evaluated regularly. Performance measurement systems have been made simple but quite comprehensive. Benchmarking provides the industry standard for further improvements. Finally, excellence in logistics does mean a stronger marketing effort and more delighted customers.
- Many experts have tried to clarify the difference between logistics and supply chain management – their focus seems to be that all activities within a company would broadly signify as logistics and when customers and suppliers are also involved in the planning of customer service delivery it could be called supply chain management.
- Logistics integrates various activities within the company in order to achieve its objectives, whereas SCM integrates the activities by going beyond the company up to the supplier's suppliers and the customer's (distributor's) customers to achieve its objectives.

LO 6

- Developing a logistics network for reaching goods and services to the rural markets in India is a major challenge and there are excellent examples of how the difficulties have been overcome and networks set up.

Key Terms

Glossaries of key terms are mentioned at the end of all chapters

Air Consignment Note (ACN)
Anticipation inventory
Bar codes
Benchmarking
Bill of Lading (BOL)
Communication
Controlling
Customer relationship management
Customer service
Distribution warehouse
Efficient Consumer Response (ECR)
Electronic Data Interchange (EDI)
Full Truck Load (FTL)
Hedge inventory
Inbound logistics
Inventory norm
Inventory turns
Liner conference
Logistics
Logistics management
Lot size inventory
Materials handling
Number of days' supply
On-time, In-full (OTIF)
Order cycle time
Order processing
Order processing
Orders filled completely
Outbound logistics
Owner's risk

Planning
Quick Response Logistics (QRL)
Railway's risk
Reverse logistics
RFID
Safety stock
Supplier relationship management
Supply chain integration
Supply Chain Management (SCM)
Target service level
Tramp services

Conceptual Questions

1. What is the difference between logistics and physical distribution? LO1 M
2. What is the role of inventory management in the overall distribution task? Does it vary between products being sold? LO3 M
3. What are the relative advantages and disadvantages of various transportation modes? How would you evaluate the best transport mode in a given situation? LO3 D
4. What do you understand by logistics management? Define its scope and objectives and discuss the key decision areas. LO1 E
5. What is meant by logistics strategy? How is a logistics strategy linked to the marketing function? LO2 M
6. What are the components of a logistics plan? How are a logistics plan and a marketing plan related? LO2 D
7. What are the major functions of a warehouse? How is warehousing related to inventory decisions? LO2 E
8. Think of ways in which the inventory carrying costs can be reduced in a logistics system and discuss how each of these methods will affect the customer service levels. LO3 M
9. List the points defining logistics excellence. LO5 E
10. What are the factors to be considered for locating a distribution warehouse? LO3 M
11. In your opinion, what is the greatest obstacle to implementing the principles and practices of supply chain management? LO2 M
12. Explain briefly the difference between logistics and supply chain management. LO1 E
13. What are the steps in the development of a logistics strategy? LO2 M
14. What are the logistics operational steps once the strategy has been clearly defined? LO2 M
15. Enumerate the benefits of using technology in supply chain management. LO4 M

Note: Difficulty Level → E — Easy; M — Medium; D — Difficult

16. Briefly describe how bar coding works. LO4 E
17. Briefly describe how RFID works in managing a supply chain better. LO4 E
18. Does customer relationship management technology really help logistics? How? LO4 E
19. What is the influence of information technology on the other three supply chain drivers? LO4 D

Objective Type Questions

Select the most appropriate response out of the various options available in each of the following questions:

1. Customer acquisition has three parts to it: lead generation, lead _________, and account conversion.
(a) qualification (b) negotiation (c) approval (d) addition LO1 E
2. Logistics function includes planning, procurement, _________, supply, and maintenance.
(a) receipt (b) transportation (c) control (d) distribution LO1 E
3. Logistics is the internal service provider for both production and _________ .
(a) purchase (b) marketing (c) commercial (d) distribution LO1 E
4. Order processing includes the tasks of order acquisition, entry documentation, _________, and keeping the customer informed of the status of his order.
(a) transportation(b) billing (c) payment (d) dispatch LO1 M
5. Order cycle time is the elapsed time between placing of the order by the customer and the _________ of the goods.
(a) receipt (b) dispatch (c) payment (d) packing LO1 E
6. Order size constraint is the specification of the _________ quantity of the order for execution.
(a) maximum (b) minimum (c) average (d) full LO1 E
7. Designing a logistics system is done in the three steps of identifying customer needs, defining customer _________ objectives, and the actual structure of the system.
(a) retention (b) satisfaction (c) service (d) acquisition LO2 E
8. The three inventory systems in use are production, production-distribution, and _________.
(a) distribution (b) optimization (c) specialization (d) pure LO3 E
9. Distribution warehouses located closest to the markets to be serviced are known as _________ positioned.
(a) market (b) customer (c) service (d) near LO3 E
10. _________ positioned distribution warehouses are located between production units and customers.
(a) customer (b) intermediate (c) production (d) market LO3 E

11. Rail freight rates operate on the two principles of value of service and the __________ of service.
(a) timing (b) distance (c) cost (d) frequency LO3 E

12. Transport using ropeways operates in a gradient of __________ .
(a) two in one (b) one in four (c) two in four (d) one in two LO3 E

13. Distribution strategy defines how the company will __________ its products to its customers and markets.
(a) reach (b) sell (c) display (d) provide LO2 E

14. Logistics strategy could be based on markets, channels or __________.
(a) processes (b) products (c) competitors (d) customers LO2 E

15. Information is a key but __________ driver of supply chains.
(a) intangible (b) useful (c) critical (d) quick LO4 E

16. Use of an IT system in supply chain management improves the __________ of decision-making.
(a) quality (b) speed (c) accuracy (d) ability LO4 E

17. A supplier relationship management system also helps to __________ with suppliers.
(a) collaborate (b) negotiate (c) communicate (d) work LO4 E

18. Bar codes represent a ______________ identification of goods.
(a) alpha-numeric (b) quick (c) accurate (d) easy LO4 E

19. In RFID, a ________ contains data like the serial number of an item or component.
(a) tag (b) label (c) attachment (d) enclosure LO4 E

20. Data warehousing technology collects data from multiple, __________ sources.
(a) heterogeneous (b) homogenous
(c) dispersed (d) different LO4 M

Application Questions

1. The logistics manager of Hercules, a capital goods manufacturer, is trying to review their inventory strategy. Hercules has about 50 tier-1 suppliers. The manager is trying to understand the relationship between ordering cost and inventory carrying cost. Can you help him draw out a plan of how this relationship can be used to best advantage of his company? LO3 M
2. What modes of transportation would you use for a company manufacturing washing machines? Also give justifications for your recommendation. LO3 E
3. What are the factors you would consider for planning a warehouse for fruits and vegetables? LO3 M
4. Grow More Fertilizer Company wants to maximize its customer service to its 78 distributors in south India. Explain to them the way in which the logistics interface with various functions in the company works to help deliver customer service. LO1 M

5. How is the benchmarking of supply chain done? You are a consultant who is required to help Glow-more, a lighting products company, to benchmark its supply chain. Glow-more has 3 plants, 28 C&FAs and 576 distributors in India and is ranked number 4 in market share in the industry. How would you go about this benchmarking exercise? LO5 M

6. Fast Forward Logistics: providing additional services to support customer loyalty (FFL) was a leading logistics services provider company with a reasonable size of the business. They were present in clearing imports, helping companies send export goods and domestic logistics. Their market shares were around 7 percent which, in a fragmented market, was quite good. There were a large number of small players in the market and competition was quite severe. A brief study of competition done by the GM revealed that most competitors were trying to gain business on the basis of price but most of these companies were not quite reliable.

   Sunil, the GM of FFL was reviewing the results of the last year and trying to budget the likely business for the next year. He was worried that the growth of the company business was slowing down. Some features of the freight forward business presently were:
   - Competition was quite severe—price competition, in particular.
   - Customers expected time bound and faster deliveries. Speed and reliability in delivery seemed to be the primary concerns of customers.
   - Consistent good past performance gave tremendous credibility to companies like FFL.

   In spite of these market features, till now FFL was managing to have an excellent set of loyal customers.

   The issue in front of Sunil was: how to keep providing additional services to retain the loyalty of these customers and also develop similar new accounts? LO2 D

7. Reliable Engineering: meeting customer expectations through effective logistics. Reliable is a well-known company making engineering products with a world-wide footprint. The GM of Reliable, Mr. Sam, was trying to solve a logistics problem for their compressor division. The company was making its compressors in China for sales in many countries including in Africa. Reliable had established channel partners in many of these countries which were local dealers. The issue was making the compressor spares available in time at the customer end and at the best quality. These were the options that Sam was reviewing:
   - Airfreight from China to Africa—expensive, not feasible.
   - Sending by sea to Dubai and from there to Africa—this had resulted in inadequate documentation or quality complaints in the past.
   - Routing the materials to Africa through Pakistan, Afghanistan was also tried. As the parts were small and loose (not full container loads), there had been complaints of losses en-route.
   - Compressors are not accepted as air cargo and sending by sea was time-consuming.

   Do you have any suggestions for Sam on meeting customer expectations through effective logistics? LO3 M

8. Computer Hardware Company: Speeding up deliveries without holding additional inventory—CHC is a hardware distributor which imports computer hardware from ABC, the leader in the market and distributes it in the country of operation. It secures the hardware based on customer orders only. The main competition for ABC is from Dell and IBM.

CHC found that holding inventory was not feasible and orders could be delivered within 4 to 6 weeks. The following changes were happening in the marketplace:

- Competition from IBM and Dell was very stiff and lead times for deliveries were dropping.
- Customers were expecting faster deliveries and 4 to 6 weeks wait was not acceptable.
- Product obsolescence in the hardware industry was well known. For example, server models kept changing every 6 months.
- High-value corporate deals had long sales cycles. However deliveries were expected almost instantly.

CHC was thinking of ways of improving the speed of response to customer orders. Should they keep additional inventory?

Is it possible for CHC to speed up deliveries without holding inventory? **LO2 D**

9. Ace Lubricants Marketing Company: Optimizing stock availability to increase customer satisfaction (ACE) had a large portfolio of lubricant products both for the automotive and industrial sectors in convenient pack sizes for both categories of customers. Its products had made a name for themselves in the lubricant industry.

   ACE had a well-established channel network to reach its customers based on different segments:
   - Big industrial customers were serviced by the company directly from its plant or through the C&FAs.
   - Smaller customers were serviced through the distributors.
   - The bazaar trade (denoting walk-in customers) was also reached through distributors.
   - Vehicle repairing workshops were also serviced through the C&FAs.

   Manish, one of the Regional Managers of ACE presented his view of a developing problem to his General Sales Manager as follows:
   - The company is not being able to meet the growing demand in the automotive sector as there are always inadequate stocks at the C&FAs.
   - As the market is growing, initial losses from this segment have not been noticed. Of late, ACE is losing business to competition.
   - Ambitious targets set have not been achieved. Sales people are getting demoralized. Some good sales people have left ACE recently.

   When the GSM got into more details of the outlined problem, he was surprised to see a "blame game" in operation. Sales team pointed at the "inefficient logistics function". Logistics blames production. Manufacturing attributes poor sales forecasts from the salespeople for the debacle. The GSM set up a study group to understand the problem correctly and find a solution. Some of the findings of the study group are given below:
   - In an exercise undertaken earlier to reduce costs and improve profitability, the company had taken an arbitrary decision to reduce the inventory level at the factory + C&FA from 45 days to 15 days. The 15 days inventory had 50 percent of C items and slow movers.
   - This seriously affected A and B category items while increasing the percentage of C type items.
   - Specialized products inventory for industrial customers also went up as customers were lost.

   Please suggest an action plan to ACE to optimize stock availability and increase customer satisfaction. **LO3 M**

ASSIGNMENTS FOR STUDENTS

1. Visit the C&FA of a prominent company. Understand the functions of this C&FA as expected the company. Get to know the difficulties, concerns, issues of the C&FA in managing operations – list them down. List down all the operational costs. Find out the margins earned.
2. Surf the internet to track the entire outbound logistics for each of these companies: (i) a company selling cars, (ii) a company selling cement, and (iii) a company selling packaged edible oil. Who are all the players involved in these outbound logistics tasks? What is the role of each of them in the logistics responsibility?
3. Select any company of your choice. Find out all the elements of the supply chain cost end to end for this company. Arrive at the total supply chain cost as a percentage of sales.
4. Do some field research by meeting and talking to various channel partners like C&FAs, distributors, dealers, wholesalers and retailers. Find as to what inventory norms they normally operate with and why? How do these norms vary between different product categories and why?
5. Meet any prominent transporter in the market. Find if he operates on a contract for any company. List down the terms and conditions of such a contract. Comment on the ease or difficulty of operating each of the terms and conditions.
6. Surf the internet and access as much information as you can about the Canteen Stores Department (CSD) which provides household goods to the armed forces/services. Track the complete cycle of order booking, execution and physical delivery of goods to the hundreds of CSD canteens spread all over the country. You can take any FMCG product of your choice to track this entire supply chain.

Reference Notes

1. William F Schoell, *Marketing: Contemporary Practices and Concepts*, Allyn & Bacon.
2. Bert Rosenbloom, *Marketing Channels: A Management View*, The Dryden Press.
3. DJ Bowersox, MB Cooper, *Strategic Management : Channel Management*, Tata McGraw-Hill.
4. Maureen Guirdhom, *Marketing: The Management of Distribution Channels*, Pergamon Press.
5. Martin Christopher, "Reducing Cost and Improving Service", *Logistics & Supply Chain Management*, Pitman.
6. DR Bloomberg, S LeMay and JB Hanna, *Logistics*, PHI.
7. Christopher Gopal and Harold Cypress, *Integrated Distribution Management*, Irwin.

8. Sunil Chopra and Peter Miendl, *SCM Strategy: Planning and Operation*, Pearson Education.
9. J Tony Arnold, *Introduction to Materials Management*, F Hall.
10. T E Vollmann, WL Berry, DC Whybark & FR Jacobs, *Manufacturing Planning and Control for SCM*, Tata McGraw-Hill.
11. EE Adams and RJ Ebert, *Production & Operations Management*, PHI.
12. David F Ross, *Distribution Planning & Control*, Chapman & Hall.
13. C. Glenn Walters, *Marketing Channels*, Good Year Publishing.
14. SK Kapoor and P Kansal, *Basics of Distribution Management*, PHI.
15. *Logistic Management*, ICFAI Publication.
16. *Materials Management Review*, Indian Institute of Materials Management, several issues
17. *Inventory Management*, Indian Institute of Materials Management Publication.
18. Sarika Kulkarni and Ashok Sharma, *Supply Chain Management*, Tata McGraw-Hill.
19. *Logistics: Foundation for Transport*, Business India, 20 November 2005.
20. *KPMG*, MDI Survey of Supply Chain Practices in Indian Industry, 2000.
21. *Sales & Distribution Management*, ICFAI Center for Management Research.
22. David S Levi, Philip Kaminsky, Edith S Levi, Ravi Shankar, *Designing & Managing the Supply Chain*, Tata McGraw-Hill.
23. N Rangaraj, G Raghuram and M M Srinivasan, *SCM for Competitive Advantage*, Tata McGraw-Hill.

CASE 16.1

Snow White Paper Company (1)

Snow White Paper Company is located in an agricultural belt about 300 kilometres from a metro city. It makes writing and printing paper. Its primary raw material is wheat straw. Last year, the company had a turnover of ₹134 crore on a volume of 45,000 tonnes of paper. While preparing the business plan for the current year, the top management was concerned with the following logistics issue which they want "you" to help resolve:

Problem: Inbound Materials

SW buys about 68,000 tons of wheat straw in a year. Wheat straw is left over after the farmers harvest the wheat at the end of the season. Therefore, wheat straw is produced only for about 2 months in a year after the harvest.

However, the Snow White Paper plant needs this raw material all through the year to keep the production going. Some salient points on wheat straw procurement are mentioned below:

- Total requirement of wheat straw of 68,000 tons for the year is in almost equal quantities every day.

- Wheat straw is produced by hundreds of farmers and has to be procured from them. The company uses about 160 agents (of which about 70 are "active") to procure the WS and deliver it to the plant. All the agents are freelance operators who have direct contact with the farmers.
- The company cannot store more than about 3 days' requirement of WS at the plant (about 550 ton).
- The average price paid for the WS is ₹1200 per tonne. The price of WS paid by SW varies from ₹900 per ton at the start of the season (just at the end of the harvest) to ₹1600 per ton at the end of the season.
- The production cost for the farmer for the WS is estimated at about ₹700 to ₹800 per ton. After the harvest, the farmer stores the WS on his farm.
- The margins made by the farmer and the agent on the sale of WS are estimated at ₹100 to 150 per ton and ₹150 to ₹200 per ton respectively.
- The primary use of the wheat straw by the farmer is for cattle fodder.
- The farmer/agent can sell the WS to other paper plants within a radius of 35 kilometres of the plant or to the *Mandi* (agricultural wholesale market) located at about 80 kilometres from the SW plant.
- It is also estimated that about 15 percent of the wheat straw is burnt as the farmer has no place to store it.
- There is always an uncertainty and tension about the regular availability and a "fair" price for the wheat straw which Snow White buys.

Discussion Questions

1. If you are the purchase manager of SW, how will you ensure regular availability of WS at a fair price?
2. Do you agree with the system of using agents or is there any other method to ensure regular availability to wheat straw for SW?

Abbreviations used in the case: SW for Snow White; WS for Wheat Straw

CASE 16.2

Snow White Paper Company (3)

Snow White Paper Company is located in an agricultural belt about 300 kilometres from a metro city. It makes writing and printing paper. Its primary raw material is wheat straw. Last year the company had a turnover of ₹134 crore on a volume of 45,000 tons of paper. While preparing the business plan for the current year, the top management was concerned with the following "logistics" issue which they want "you" to help resolve:

Problem: Outbound Transport

Snow White sells its paper in about seven states with about three of them accounting for 60 percent of its business. The paper has to be transported from its plant to the geographic territories.

The transport rates for the paper depend, naturally, on the distance of the "market" from the plant/mill. SW has a market share of about 15 percent in its entire selling area but it is still a small plant compared to some of the giants in the industry.

There is a problem on the outbound transport, which is evident from the points mentioned below:

- Total transport cost of the paper for the year is ₹9 crore approximately.
- There is a transporter's Union in the town where the SW paper mill is located. SW has to distribute all its finished goods only through the transport union trucks. They cannot even get the trucks from the truck market.
- Rates for the trucks for every location are decided by the union and are not always favourable to SW.
- The union allots the loads from SW to its members through a roster system—SW cannot be sure of the truck which will carry its goods to the same location every time.
- In case the allotted truck does not have the required destination state permit, SW has to delay the dispatch till the next truck on the roster with the correct permit comes. Trucks need state permits to enter or pass through any state in the country.
- SW accounts for about 36 percent of the union's transport business from this location.
- The union president also happens to be a politically influential person of the area.

The "constraints" under which SW has to plan its transportation has been explained above.

Discussion Questions

1. How can you ensure for SW, regular availability of transport for its FG at more competitive rates?
2. What are the alternatives available to SW?

Abbreviations used in the case: SW for Snow White; WS for Wheat Straw; FG for finished goods

Reproduced with permission from Network 7 Management Consultants

CASE 16.3

Norton India Ltd.

Norton India Ltd (NIL) is a subsidiary of Norton International and has been in operation in India for the last 7 years. It is in the business of consumer products and faces intense competition from formidable companies.

NIL's mission is to be at least the second preferred brand in each category in which it operates over the next three years. Presently NIL is in the 4th position in market shares. The company brands are the leaders in the countries in which they operate.

NIL presently has 3 products, 12 brands, 47 SKUs, 2 factories, 103rd party packers, 30 C&FAs and depots and over 1600 distributors all India.

The top management comprises the CEO and VPs in Technical, Finance, IT, HR and Sales & Marketing. There are two factory managers and four Regional Sales Managers and ten Area Sales Managers.

Sales Planning

Top down yearly targets broken down monthly for the regions. Every month the RM sends a monthly plan/forecast by C&FA or depot by pack size based on which the stocks are arranged to the depots/C&FAs. The plan is always higher than the monthly target as the field people are expected to cover deficits against targets of previous months. However, in view of the severe competition, sales keeps falling behind the plans adding to the inventory levels.

Other Salient Points of NIL

- Sales to distributors are only on receipt of demand drafts with the orders. Distributors tend to delay the purchases till the end of the month so that they can sell off their stocks and then purchase fresh stocks. This results in an enormous sales skew with 55 percent of the primary sales happening in the final week and 35 percent of the month sales on the last day of the month.
- NIL sales last year was ₹514 crore with advertising support of ₹68 crore and trade inputs and promotions totalling ₹53 crore. Trade inputs are given to the distributors who are expected to pass this on to the retailers. Sales insists that this happens but finance always accepts this with a pinch of salt.
- S&M function feels that they have a tough job in the market and other departments do not understand/support their efforts. Other functions feel that S&M never reach their targets or keep their promises and need no sympathy.
- NIL is in the process of revamping its information systems (may even implement an ERP) and has appointed a leading IT consultant to advise it on the way forward. Presently the sales and stock (inventory) figures are not always timely or accurate.

In a recent review with the top management, the CEO has raised a number of questions, which you need to help find answers for. As you can see most of the questions relate to distribution and the supply chain.

Sales Planning

- Forecasts and plans are more than targets but sales is less than targets. Who should be held responsible for the additional inventory build-up? How can the sales planning be improved?
- There is a growing refrain that "as we are a growing organization, we need flexibility in planning working capital" – is this acceptable even after 10 years?
- What is the impact of month end sales skews on planning, inventory and service levels? Who is responsible to set this right and how will they do it?
- How much will the proposed IT initiative help support the planning function better? What should be the focus of this IT initiative?

Channel Management

- Distributors have to place orders along with demand drafts. This makes their purchases unpredictable and impacts planning, inventory and service levels. (Competitors operate with pre-signed blank cheques.) What should be the remedy?

- Distributor margins are 6 percent of sales (the average in FMCG is 4 to 5 percent) and in addition there are subsidies. Should NIL discontinue subsidies? Will this not create problems with the distributors?
- What is the impact of trade promotions on working capital? How should the trade promotions be operated and their effectiveness evaluated?

Distribution and Supply Chain

- Inventory in the C&FAs/depots is meant to service field sales. Should not the field sales managers be responsible to manage this inventory?
- There is no route planning for stocks sent from the C&FAs/depots to the distributors. Who is responsible for controlling secondary freight?
- Logistics function presently reports to VP S&M. Should they report to VP Technical or VP Finance?
- Who is responsible for the company supply chain costs – S&M, Finance, Technical or the CEO? Advice with reasons.

Recently the finance function calculated the supply chain cost for NIL as follows:

(all figures are in ₹ lakh)

Cost Item	₹ lakh
Primary transport – factory to depot/C&FA	612
Secondary transport – depot/C&FA to distributors	937
C&FA/depot operating expenses	523
Distributor margins (6 percent)	3080
Distributor subsidies (1 percent)	515
Inventory carrying costs (interest at 12 percent)	800
Sundry debtors interest cost (interest at 12 percent)	165
Total supply chain costs (12.9 percent of sales)	6632

Discussion Questions

1. Do you agree with the calculation of the supply chain cost? The CEO has read published data that the SC costs for FMCG companies is about 6–8 percent of the sales. He wants NIL to reduce the SC cost to half in one year. Do you think it is possible? How?
2. What should be the performance metrics for SC costs? Should it be built into the performance evaluation of the people concerned?
3. Should there be inventory norms at all stock points in a growing company like NIL? Should these norms be strictly enforced?
4. Raw and Packing materials procurement is disturbed if the sales plans are not achieved. NIL cannot make firm commitments on off-take to the 3P packers. What is the remedy?
5. How much will the IT initiative help NIL in managing its supply chain and the costs better?

CASE 16.4

Atlas India Ltd.

James Patterson, Senior Manager from the parent company of Atlas India Ltd. had been given a clear operational mandate by the Board. He had been given a time frame of 3 months and specific targets to take care of three major areas of concern to AIL: (i) increasing service level to sales to over 90 percent from the current 63 percent, (ii) reducing the working capital to sales percentage from the current 25 percent to 15 percent or less, and (iii) reducing the current freight cost of ₹21 crore ($5 million) by at least 20 percent. James was thinking as to how to go about this project which would have a major impact on the operations and profitability of Atlas India Ltd.

Atlas India Ltd (AIL) is the subsidiary of Atlas International, a world leader in consumer products. AIL has been in India for over eight decades and is a market leader in the three product groups which it makes and sells in India.

Some Salient Numbers

AIL boasts of a product, brand and pack for every consumer in the country. It has a well spread-out network of producing units.

- 25 brands, over 100 SKUs, 15 percent in sachets.
- 8 own factories and 14 satellite 3P units.
- 6 branches, 30 Area Sales Offices, 30 C&FAs and 1600 distributors.

Operations Details

AIL has been growing every year and has been profitable every year of its operation. Recently there has been a pressure on the margins.

- Working capital in the year under review: 26 percent of sales—main area of concern for the top management.
- No credit extended to distributors. Only about 8 percent of sales supported by credit—institutional sales.
- Sales: about ₹1000 crore ($200 million)
- Transport cost: ₹21 crore ($5 million)
- Service level to sales: 63 percent as measured recently (service level is the percentage of stocks indented, which are made available to sales).

Operating Style

The company has a streamlined planning cycle which has stood the test of time. The sales team is well conversant with the planning cycle and the need to achieve targets consistently. Forecasting of sales has been in practice for the past about two years.

- Weekly planning cycle.
- Month could be of 4 or 5 week periods. Each quarter pattern: 4 weeks–4 weeks–5 weeks.
- Yearly sales targets are set as a combination of both top-down and bottom-up methods. Top-down is based on industry forecasts, top management expectations on growth in volume, market shares and profitability. Bottom-up is field salespeople estimates on growth for their own territories.

- Quarterly sales targets are decided each quarter after discussions with the sales function.
- Salespeople are also required to submit monthly sales forecasts—one month firm and two months tentative. Monthly sales forecasts are broken down into weekly figures to help in the planning exercise.
- The company had not yet implemented an ERP solution.
- The average month-end sales skew: 40percent in final week.

Players Involved in the Planning Exercise

The sales team and their channel partners are key to the planning process as they generate the sales forecasts. The factories are required to produce packed goods and dispatch to the field sales based on these forecasts. However the planning process has not been working fully up to expectations.

- Weekly/fortnightly distributor indents are received by the salespeople. Distributor storage space limited to one or two weeks' sales.
- Monthly sales forecasts given by field sales in line with the targets set for them.
- Production planning is done by the respective Factory Managers for their factory and their satellite 3P units (production outsourced to independent producers on contract).
- Production Planning and Control (PPC) at HO places materials requirements on Purchase. PPC and purchase both report to VP Technical.

Planning Process

The process follows the simple system of purchase—buying the commodities (raw materials) and packing materials—and production—making the goods and dispatching to sales to meet the market requirements.

- Packing Materials – buying plan is made by Purchase
- Raw Materials (Commodity)—buying plan is made by the commodities function which reports to a VP Commodity.
- Not all factories produce all products—Production Planning and Control (PPC) advice inter factory transfer of SKUs to meet sales needs.
- Transport function is under the Commercial function—arrange trucks based on despatch plan given by factories.

Issues, Concerns, Worries

In a recent review made by the top management, some issues were noticed in the entire planning and execution.

- Each department was trying to independently optimize its own operations – the SILO effect
- Salespeople were making their forecasts and not really worried about the achievement in relation to their forecasts.
- Commodities would buy raw materials which had a price advantage irrespective of whether the resulting finished goods would meet market requirements.
- Purchase department could not properly plan buying of other materials—should it be based on sales forecasts or production plans?
- Production would produce only such products/ brands/SKUs which would help it to maximize capacity utilization. For example, they would make a lot of big size packs whereas sales would need a proper "mix" of big and small packs.

- The company is losing out—high working capital, low service level, high freight costs and inconsistent planning – demand peaks at the month end due to sales skews.
- Targets, forecasts, indents— no pattern
- Targets to measure performance/earn incentives
- Indents to meet market needs—Regional Manager and Factory Manager in touch (high indents on low stocks)
- Forecasts used for buying commodities and packing materials.
- Transport planning not possible—a factory despatching 60 FTL per week gets 120 FTL indents in final week (FTL is a full-truck-load).
- Transporters are on contract—they do not have own trucks and hence have to secure extra trucks at exorbitant cost to meet month end sales skews.
- Month end pressure on loading at the factory—needs extra "labour" on contract to be engaged.
- To achieve production targets, factory produces bigger packs while sales needs smaller packs.
- Forecasts are used for commodity and materials buying and production planning but actual sales is quite different—affects inventory at all levels.
- Marketing runs sales contests/promotions in many areas simultaneously which adds to the pressure on finished goods requirements.
- Frequent price changes require putting new MRP stickers on packs.
- Sales loses out on opportunities if stocks not adequate—inflates indents, as indiscipline pays.
- Sales offices closer to factories benefit—relationships between sales people and factory management matter.
- Commodities function buys commodities based on favourable buying prices—not necessarily what is required for production.
- Buys in quantities to get price benefit—no norms.
- Purchase unable to keep material buying in line with production—run out of bigger packs faster and land up with excess materials for smaller packs.
- No strict stock norms anywhere in the system.

There was a widespread blame game in the company when AIL asked the VP of New Business, Mr James Patterson to find a solution to the above problems. Mr Patterson was an expat senior manager from the parent company working with AIL.

As James, you are required to find answers and solutions to the questions given below:

Discussion Questions

1. Develop an integrated supply chain system which will ensure that all operational functions in the company together contribute to better customer service. An improvement of service level to sales to above 90 percent by SKU is expected.
2. How can the company reduce the working capital to sales percentage to 15 percent from current levels?
3. How can the company reduce the freight cost by at least 20 percent over current levels?

Even though the company does not have an ERP, they have a very robust legacy IT system which has been advised to fully support James Patterson in his efforts. James has been given a time limit of 3 months for this project.

CASE 16.5

Healthcare Equipment Company (HEC)

Introduction

HEC is a major MNC in the business of Health Care Equipment. One of the strategic business units of the company is in the business of importing used but serviceable healthcare equipment from the more advanced countries, refurbishing it fully and selling it to end user hospitals, etc., which cannot afford the exorbitant prices of the original equipment.

The problem arises out of delays in clearance of the consignment at the arrival airports, thereby upsetting production plans, costing heavy demurrage and a lot of time spent in tracking and follow-up to clear consignments. Mr Harish, the manager in charge of the business is trying to solve these issues.

The Company and the Business

HEC is in the business of importing used healthcare equipment and restoring it for full regular use again. It has major hospitals and nursing homes as customers. There is a good demand for such restored equipment as the original equipment is far more expensive to acquire. HEC manufactures and sells healthcare equipment like MR scanners, CT scanners, mammographs, etc. This is one of the Strategic Business Units of the company.

Silverline Operations

HEC buys old machines from its existing customers when they buy new equipment. Such equipment is "refurbished" separately in the factory after changing mandatory parts and conducting full trials/ tests. The refurbished equipment is then ready for sale and with prices much lower and affordable than the original equipment. The refurbished pre-owned HEC equipment has gone through a quality check on over hundred parameters – "it is as good as new".

The refurbished equipment is sold in the market as Silverline certified at lower prices than the original equipment. The certification programme is based on over 150 quality checks.

New original equipment of the same type is expected to cost at least 4 times that of a refurbished one. The customer can get a payback on the refurbished equipment within 12 to 18 months of purchase. Such equipment would last at least five years.

The Process

This system of importing used but serviceable costly equipment, refurbishing and selling it to needy customers is quite unique. However, the government does not appreciate this process as they consider it as "dumping" unwanted equipment on the Indian customers. The government has also imposed a large customs duty on such used, imported equipment. At the time of paying the import duties at the airport, a valuation of the equipment has to be done first.

The Problem

The custom officers will deploy a charter engineer to estimate the value of the shipment, and this is the starting point of the problem.

When a hospital sells its old equipment, it will at times put some additional items with the main machine (at times, even used chairs/tables, mats and fans, lights, etc., will come with the shipment) whereas the custom invoice will have only medical equipment mentioned on it. This will delay the clearance of the consignment which means:

- Mismatch of invoice vs. actual parts
- The Chartered engineers nominated by customers are not clear about value of some parts
- Difficulty in predicting in how many days it will be cleared
- Huge amount incurred in paying demurrage
- Manufacturing capacity lost due to unpredictability of equipment reaching the refurbishing unit.

Related Issues

The manufacturing team was not able to get the equipment due to delay in clearance at the airport. It will lose capacity and the planning process at the manufacturing shop gets affected.

The finance team was affected; in fact the business was affected due to paying huge demurrage.

Supply chain team was affected due to lot of manual tracking and follow-up.

The top management asked Harish, who is in charge of the business, to find a solution to these problems and make the business more productive. What do you think are the action points for Mr. Harish?

Discussion Questions

1. Suggest a system by which the imported used equipment can be cleared quickly through the customs to help the production team and cut out the demurrage charges.
2. Analyze the bottlenecks in the supply chain and highlight the ways in which the "total cost" of logistics can be minimized.
3. Can the company implement a simple IT enabled system for tracking and follow-up on the shipments? What should this system be?

Chapter 17

International Sales and Distribution Management

LEARNING OBJECTIVES

After studying this chapter, you will be able to:

LO 1 Appreciate the differences between domestic and international markets

LO 2 Learn how to gather information about target markets and how to choose the markets

LO 3 Explain the economic, legal, and cultural aspects of international marketing environment and formulate the entry strategies for international markets

LO 4 Understand the risks involved in doing international business

LO 5 Comprehend pricing, financial terms, and payment methods used in international markets

LO 6 Distinguish between domestic and international distribution channels, and understand the factors that influence the choice of distribution channels in overseas market

Harsha Rao was a retailer of stationery items in Bangalore. His company was well recognized by businesses and also by the suppliers in the industry. The business was growing well, was profitable, and he was now looking for an opportunity to diversify owing to growing competition. On a recent holiday overseas, he realized that there appeared to be a good opportunity in exporting products. The bug to export now bit him. The question was where to begin? How to organize the operation? Which markets and products he should attempt first? How to handle pricing and payments? And also, understanding the risks involved in the business.

The past decade has seen a number of changes in the global situation. Chief among these are the opening up of Russia, India, the Eastern European countries and China as major markets. The signing of the WTO has opened up many new areas such as agriculture, textiles, and services to freer trade.

What this means for most companies is enhanced opportunities, while at the same time increased competition and risk. In this chapter we will try and understand the implications of these momentous changes.

LO 1 Appreciate the differences between domestic and international markets

THE NATURE OF INTERNATIONAL MARKETS

International markets vary in terms of their level of development—at one end you have affluent and highly developed markets such as the US and the western countries, and on the other there are markets that are very poor and undeveloped such as few countries in Africa. Each of these offer opportunities for different reasons—the highly developed markets due to their high levels of consumption and also because of their high cost of manufacture, and the poor undeveloped countries due to their lack of industries and infrastructure. The types of products, which will be sold in each of these markets, will differ depending on the level of development.

Today, countries like the US, Japan, and Korea outsource the manufacturing of products to countries like India due to the lower cost of production. India is today a global manufacturing base for many automobile companies like Hyundai, Suzuki, and Ford, which are marketing their products, made in India, all around the world. Many manufacturers like GM, Volvo and others are sourcing components for their global operations from India. Large international pharmaceutical companies are using India as a source for many of their drugs. India is also a global source for many leading garment brands.

The main feature to note is that global manufacturers and traders will move to outsource products to areas where there is a definite cost advantage without the loss of quality. This trend has accelerated in recent years, resulting in a boom in countries like China, India, and countries of South East Asia.

Many small- and medium-sized companies are unable to take advantage of this boom as they do not have an understanding of selling in international markets. This chapter aims to provide an understanding of this aspect of business.

International markets also differ in terms of their preference for branded and packaged goods. In large parts of India, Africa, and Middle East, products such as grains, edible oils, salt, sugar, and many others are sold loose—unbranded and not packaged. Also, consumers in developed markets are very particular of the look and packaging of the product and are willing to pay a higher price for this. Since a large part of the buying is done in supermarkets on a self-help basis, there is very little sales support at the retail end in the western markets. The packaging and presentation tries to make up for these.

Due to pressure of time, consumers are looking for convenience products—such as ready to eat dinners, etc. These are not common in the less developed countries.

LO 2 **Learn how to gather information about target markets and how to choose the markets**

CHOOSING THE MARKET

Choosing the right market is a very important element when entering the field of international marketing. Some of the factors to be borne in mind are:

- The size of the market
- The language and culture of the market
- The competition in the market
- Proximity of the market, and
- Political and financial stability of the country.

While the size of the market is an obvious attraction, the manufacturer must bear in mind that all large markets will inevitably become more competitive as every manufacturer wants to get a slice of the market. The US and, more recently, India are good examples of large markets that are very competitive. Small manufacturers may find it difficult to service the large markets and would be comfortable in choosing smaller markets.

Language and cultural affinity is very important in international markets. Indian companies will find it easier to do business in the neighboring markets like Sri Lanka, Bangladesh, Nepal, and the Middle East, due to easy communication and similarity in cultures. For the US companies, it is easier to do business in Canada or Mexico than in India, due to the proximity and similarity in cultures.

For India, doing business with neighbors like Sri Lanka, Bangladesh, Nepal, and the Middle East is preferred also due to the low cost of freight, travel, and communication. One could travel to Bangladesh by bus from Kolkata and the fare from Bangalore or Chennai to Colombo is approximately the same as that to Delhi.

Political and financial stability of target countries is a very important factor to be considered while choosing the markets. In today's context, doing business in Iraq or Afghanistan is probably very risky as the countries are very unstable both politically and financially. The same would hold true though to a lesser extent for Pakistan.

MARKET INTELLIGENCE AND RESEARCH

Market intelligence and research is a very crucial activity for any exporter. Collecting primary market data is very expensive and hence not feasible for most companies. Secondary data is available from a number of sources which can be collated to get a clear understanding of the market. Some of the sources of secondary data are:

- Embassies/Consulates of the importing country
- Indian missions in the host country

- Trade and Industry organizations like CII, FICCI, Assocham, EEPC, AEPC, CAPEXCIL and many others
- Chambers of commerce and industry in the importing country
- Commercial Banks
- EXIM bank
- ECGC
- Trade journals and publications
- Internet websites

In addition, many of the chambers of trade and industry frequently host business delegations from various countries and also sponsor delegations of Indian businessmen to those countries. Such meets can be very useful in gathering a lot of information apart from establishing contacts with prospective businessmen in those countries.

An aspect of market research, which needs attention, is the buyer behavior. This will obviously vary from country to country and also will influence the sales and marketing strategy. The motivation to buy a product, the frequency of purchase and usage, the price the premium customers are willing to pay for certain benefits, attitude towards brands especially foreign brands, etc., will determine the strategy for sales. Some of this can be observed, and others by commissioning research into these aspects.

There are various agencies, including some market research agencies that have ready reports on various products/markets, which can be purchased for a fee. An Internet search for "Market Research Reports for Clothing Accessories" will provide a long list of agencies which can provide such reports at a price. The reports could be for the global markets or for a specific country. A recent report on the automobile market in India suggests that car sales in India could in a few years double from around the current 2.5 million units per year, prompting manufacturers like Peugeot, Kia, and Volvo to start manufacturing in India. The reports would also forecast the likely sizes and types of vehicles which could be sold.

LO 3 **Explain the economic, legal, and cultural aspects of international marketing environment and formulate the entry strategies for international markets**

CULTURE AND INTERNATIONAL BUSINESS

Culture is a very important factor in international markets. Culture encompasses everything from the way of thinking and doing business to the consumption patterns of the population. Understanding of the culture is important as it gives vital clues on how to do business in these countries in the best possible way.

In some countries, there is a natural hostility towards foreigners and foreign business. Although we are open to foreigners doing business in India, we can still be hostile towards them, as we have seen in the case of McDonald's and more recently to the METRO cash & carry stores. It is important to understand this when doing business overseas. Pakistan, though next door to India, maintains a hostile political and business attitude and hence although both countries can gain substantially through trade and commerce, Indian companies do not do direct business across the border. Compare this with Bangladesh and Sri Lanka where Indian companies do sizeable business.

Culture also dictates the mode of business dealings—for example, in the US and other western countries, they are forthright in communicating their inability to accept the products, whereas in the eastern countries they are more circumspect. Aspects such as keeping time, the formalities, and courtesies in doing the business, the negotiation process and even dressing vary from culture to culture, and are needed to be understood to succeed. In the eastern countries people are not very punctual and this can be an irritant to many westerners. There have been instances where software engineers, sent for on-site work, have been sent back due to their inability to observe the basic dress regulations in the client's office.

In business negotiations, people from the Far East tend to be slower and long drawn, and patience is a great virtue here.

Language is a very important aspect of international business. In many countries, knowledge of the local language is a must for doing business. It is important to bear in mind that meaning of terms and words vary with the language and culture. This is crucial in communication, including mass communication like advertisements and promotions, and brand names. When TATA was selling trucks in Africa, most people were very fond of the name as it meant "grandfather" in many local languages, and hence was easily recalled.

Also important is the way in which culture influences consumption. In the western markets, there is a tendency to use and throw most items, whereas in less developed countries, the tendency is to make a product last longer by repairing when it is broken. The Indian market tends to be very cost conscious—people tend to weld and repair broken parts of automobiles, which in the west would have been scrapped. Also, due to the lower income levels, people in less developed countries tend to buy in smaller lots or smaller packages at lower price points.

In India, we prefer to purchase fruits and vegetables which are fresh, rather than canned or frozen. This is also due to the fact that the distribution of these products is such that they are conveniently available, sometimes at our doorstep.

Culture also influences the usage of a product—a motorcycle or a bicycle in the west is a recreational product while in India it is a means of transport. This naturally will influence the way the product has to be positioned and marketed.

An international manufacturer of cars had learnt that while in the western markets, cars are usually self-driven; in India they tend to be largely chauffeur driven. As a result, cars had to rethink their designs which traditionally provided greater comfort and legroom for the front seats and less so for the rear.

LEGAL ASPECTS OF DOING INTERNATIONAL BUSINESS

Whenever business is transacted between two companies in different countries, one important aspect that comes up is the knowledge of law that prevails in case of a dispute. Generally, these are clearly spelt out in the contract document, but even so, it can be messy and expensive at times.

Some countries insist that in any dispute their local laws and courts will have the final say. Sometimes the contracts may also be written in the local language and are translated into English or some other language. In such cases too, the contract may specify that the version in the local language will be treated as original and authentic. TATAs faced a similar situation when they signed a contract for the supply of buses with a French-speaking North West African country. Considerable amount of time and money had to be spent to hire international lawyers familiar with French and local laws.

An important aspect of business these days is the protection of intellectual property rights. Many countries including Thailand, India, and China have laws that are either lax or are not well enforced, resulting in infringement of copyrights and losses for the original manufacturer. The Indian Patent Act is being amended and will soon protect product patents rather than process patents, which it protected so far. This will be welcomed by the large MNC drug manufacturers who claim that they have suffered greatly due to the lack of this facility. Designs, trademarks, and copyrights are all protected under international laws, and infringements can invite heavy penalties. Selling copycat products and passing them off as originals will no longer be viable.

Yet, another legal aspect of doing business internationally is the method of doing business in the destination country—a company could choose to have a representative, a branch office, or a subsidiary depending on the benefits. A local presence always offers a level of comfort to the buyer—Sundaram Fasteners have their own office and warehouse in Detroit from where they supply their products to General Motors. Others may choose to have only a representative or even a subsidiary depending on considerations such as the level of service required in the market, tax, and so on. Generally, a branch office's income is added to the parent company' income and is taxed in the company's home country. A subsidiary is technically an independent local entity and is subject to all local laws and taxes.

The recent case involving an employee of Infosys Technologies in a lawsuit pertaining to sexual harassment shows the liability of a vendor in foreign countries.

The US in particular has very stringent regulations for safety, pollution, and other aspects. Violation of these can result in very heavy penalties. The laws in the US require that every component should be traced back to the manufacturer and the raw material supplier, including the date of manufacture, and batch number, and may require all components from that manufacturer or the particular batch to be recalled in case of any incident involving safety or health. There have been many instances of product recalls on these counts involving automobiles, drugs, baby food, and other such products.

Product liability insurance is available and is expensive and requires the manufacturer to be certified by an approved quality certification agency like Underwriters Laboratory. The cost of such insurance must be built into the cost of the product when it is sold.

The TATAs had considered the possibility of exporting trucks to the US and even had discussions with some manufacturers, but eventually gave up the idea due to the risks involved due to these laws.

SELLING IN INTERNATIONAL MARKETS

Trade between countries occurs because of the following reasons:

- A particular product (especially natural raw materials) is unavailable in one country, for example, oil, iron ore, coal, and so on.
- There are cost advantages by buying the product instead of manufacturing locally—outsourcing occurs due to this consideration.
- The imported product offered is differentiated from the local product—countries make, buy and sell a product, for example, India manufacturers, exports, and imports automobiles.

A company may decide to sell its products in international markets due to one or more of the following reasons:

- Although it has a good market domestically, the growth is limited.
- International markets offer large and profitable opportunities.
- The company has excess capacity, which the domestic market cannot absorb.
- The company has a considerable cost advantage over its international competitors.
- The company foresees increased competition in the domestic market and seeks to mitigate the risk by diversifying.

Entry Strategies for International Markets

An important element of international marketing is to determine the entry strategy. Having chosen the market to enter, and determined the potential in the market, it is always safer to start business by trading to verify the acceptability of the product in the market. Usually for many small companies, a break into an international market is by chance—a meeting with a friend or a relative who lives in the destination country occurs, and he feels the product compares well with those in the market and can be sold. They can at times even provide some basic facts like the competitors price, likely importers, and so on.

A good way to at least assess the potential at low cost and risk is to exhibit in international fairs or Indian trade shows. Many of these shows are industry or product specific. BangaloreIT.com is a computer software show; the COMDEX Nevada computer show is an annual event with participation from the global leaders of computer hardware and software industry. The India Engineering Trade Fair in New Delhi is an engineering and automotive show. Such shows attract large number of people who have interest in the industry, and also contacts can be developed in one place. Similarly a show in Singapore or London attracts not only locals but also people from neighboring countries and even some from countries far away. The Trade Fair Authority of India frequently holds India Trade Shows in various countries—especially in developing countries. The contacts developed at these shows can then be followed up and commercial relationships can be built up.

Initially, business could be started by appointing an indenting agent to solicit customers and business. Once some volume of business is achieved, a distributor could be appointed. In case the market potential is seen to be very huge, the company could set up its own warehouse and stock products for sale locally. As mentioned earlier, Sundaram Fasteners and TTK have set up their own warehouses in the US, to stock and supply distributors and/or OEMs (original equipment manufacturers). Such facilities lend credibility to the supplier.

The other strategy is to become a supplier to a larger company which is interested in outsourcing the supplies/components. To be able to achieve this, one needs to be persistent and needs to follow the best practices in manufacturing and maintaining supreme quality. One of the major considerations of buyers overseas in choosing suppliers is the ability of a supplier to deliver the quantity and quality required at a short notice, at competitive prices, and on time. One of the major drawbacks of Indian suppliers is their inability to offer short lead times compared to Chinese and South East Asian suppliers. A number of companies are now addressing these issues by re-engineering their operations and through better management of supply chains in order to achieve lower costs and faster deliveries.

Sometimes a tie-up with a local company is preferred when entering a new market, because of the local company's knowledge of the market, ready availability of a distribution network, and a reputation in the market. Ford entered the Indian market in a joint venture with Mahindra & Mahindra. This offered them the access to a ready network of dealers and made the product acceptance easier. Daewoo, Honda, Toyota followed similar strategies for entering the Indian market. More recently, TATA Motors has tied up with MG Rover of UK for marketing TATA Indica, branded as the "Rover CityRover", across the UK and in mainland Europe.

In some markets, the law mandates a local partner to do business—for example, in Saudi Arabia or the Emirates. Care must be taken to choose the right partners because if differences arise, breakups can be very costly and painful.

Licensing and franchising are newer strategies used in products like garments, and hotels where the brand name/design is permitted to be used for payment of royalty. This model works best when a product with an internationally accepted brand image is franchised, such as Radisson Hotels, McDonald's restaurants, Pierre Cardin merchandise, Disney characters, and so on.

Each product and market is unique and must be individually studied before strategies are crafted. Whatever strategy is adopted, it must be calibrated so that the company becomes comfortable with all aspects of business and does not undertake any high risk transactions.

Organizing for International Selling

The type of organization a company adopts for international sales depends on the size and nature of its international business. Initially, most companies prefer to get a feel of the selected market by exporting their products from the home manufacturing base. If volumes are very small, they may prefer to use an agent or a local importer/distributor for doing the business. Sales personnel from the home base would then travel regularly to the destination countries to supervise the import and sale of the products and collect feedback from the buyers in the market. Once the business is steady, the company may then consider basing their own personnel in the export market to assist the agent/importer in expanding the sales.

The next step would be when the company decides to set up its own warehouse and stocks the products for local distribution and in the process reduces the delivery time. At this stage, the company may choose to have a number of local salespersons on their payroll, supervised by a sales head from the parent company.

As the volume of business grows, companies may have to choose partial or total manufacture locally. The organization could then choose to either set up a joint venture or a wholly owned subsidiary depending on the local laws. This would require commitment of a long-term nature and adequate finances will need to be made available. The staffing of the organization would then be predominantly local, except for a few expatriate staff.

PROFILE OF AN INTERNATIONAL SALESPERSON

An international salesperson needs to have the following additional qualities besides possessing all the traits expected of a good salesperson; they are:

- The ability to speak in one or more international languages.
- The ability to adapt to foreign cultures—especially food, drink, and the like.
- The ability to act independently and decisively.
- A pleasant and amiable personality.
- The ability to understand not only the product and pricing, but also financing of the sales, the instruments of payment, and foreign exchange risks.

A company may choose to appoint local persons as sales executives or representative depending on the suitability of the candidate and the peculiarities of the country. It is often found that particular ethnic groups dominate certain businesses and it may be helpful for a company if it uses the services of a salesperson from that group.

The choice of sending or appointing women in sales jobs must be decided based on the culture of the country in which the business is to be done.

LEGAL AND SOCIAL ASPECTS

Laws pertaining to distribution and retail in trade vary between countries. While the western countries are very liberal in terms of allowing foreign companies/nationals to set up trading operations, the laws in countries, which are less developed, tend to be more restrictive. In India, foreign investment in retail trade is prohibited, although the government is considering allowing some relaxation in this area by permitting large chains like Walmart and Carrefour. However, it is expected that these permissions will initially be given with conditions on the types of products that may be sold, location, and number of stores. There may also be restrictions in terms of timings of the stores in accordance with the local laws.

In Japan, the distribution channels are very closely linked to the large business groups and they tend to be largely closed to overseas products. In recent years, due to continuous pressure from the western countries, the Japanese government and industry had to to some extent relax these conditions especially in areas like automobile dealerships, auto parts distribution, and the like.

PACKING AND SHIPPING

Packing goods for export is a very important element of marketing. The packaging should be light and strong and must be appealing to the end customers. Usually buyers tend to specify the type of packing required. For example, some importers of shirts may wish them to be hanger packed so that they can be readily put up at the retailer's store on arrival. They may further wish to have them delivered in cartons of certain numbers each so that they may allocate them to various stores. They may even specify the size mix per carton, color mix, and weight of the carton for easy handling.

A Canadian importer had once demanded that ceramic floor tiles be packed no more than 10 per box and each box should not weigh more than 10 kg, so that an individual tile layer could handle the entire job himself. Likewise, in the case of fasteners, it was specified that no more than 10 kg should be packed per box for easy handling. These requirements vary with buyers and the country to which the goods are destined. In other cases, the buyers wanted packages of specific sizes to fit the store shelves.

It is also mandatory that the packing should show the contents and specify the origin, weight, and quantity of the item inside. Canada insists the labeling should be in both English and French.

In case of the long sea voyage and handling, the packaging must be waterproof and suitable rust and fungus prevention measures must be taken. Since most of the goods are mechanically handled, especially in the western countries, they must be palletized for handling by lift trucks in warehouses and stores.

Most shipments these days are done in containers, which are safer and easier to handle. Many inland container depots (ICDs) have been set up in India such as Bangalore, and Guwahati where the cargo can be cleared by customs prior to shipment. Similarly import cargo can also be cleared at the inland ports.

A vital aspect to be kept in mind is that due to the pressures of competition, most industrial buyers would like the goods to be delivered just in time so that their inventory is minimized. A supplier would therefore have to integrate his production schedules to those of the buyer's supply chain and ensure adequate stocks are maintained in the destination country to enable prompt delivery. While deciding stock levels, the long shipping time will also have to be factored in.

LO 4 Understand the risks involved in doing international business

RISKS INVOLVED IN DOING BUSINESS INTERNATIONALLY

The two main risks involved in doing business internationally are political risks, and commercial and financial risks. Political risks are those risks that involve disruption of contracts or payments due to sudden political developments such as coups, and wars. As a consequence, contracts may be cancelled, payments can be withheld, businesses expropriated, and so on. There have been situations where after having supplied goods as per contract, payments were delayed due to coups. In some instances, the goods supplied were looted in the political upheaval, but due to documentary evidence available and some persuasion, the payments were released. A number of Indian companies, which had contracts with Iraq before the Gulf War in the 1990s, had to abandon the contracts halfway through due to the outbreak of the war. The Government of India, through the ECGC (Export Credit Guarantee Corporation), subsequently compensated them.

Financial risks involve the failure of the buyer company to pay as per contract due to bankruptcy. Commercial risks involve the sudden change in the situation in the buyers' country like a sudden shortage of foreign currency to pay the invoices, although the equivalent local currency may be available.

A trader/importer in an African country faced a situation wherein he was unable to pay for his imports and release of the goods from customs due to the sudden failure of the BCCI (Bank of Credit and Commerce International) in the 1980s. The importer had his account with the BCCI and the documents from the seller were sent to the bank, which had suddenly closed. The money in his account was also frozen. While such situations may not be common, these risks are higher when dealing with foreign countries where one may not have all the information about various developments.

In another instance involving some exports to Uganda, an Indian exporter could not be paid despite the importer having deposited the local equivalent in the bank, due to the central banks' restrictions on release of foreign exchange for transactions. In many countries, such occurrences have happened with letters of credit issued by local banks—recent examples being Nigeria and Iran. In such cases, it is safer for the importer to ask the buyer to open a letter of credit confirmed by a prime international/European bank, so that the liability for payment is with the international/European bank.

During the Asian financial crisis in the 1990s, the Indonesian Rupiah which was trading at around IR 2000 = US$1, overnight crashed to around IR 20,000 = US$1. One can imagine the plight of the importer. He would have to pay 10 times the contracted amount in local currency. This would also make his product price uncompetitive and unaffordable in the market. Many importers had to abandon their consignments and also declare bankruptcy.

Many risks are covered by agencies like the ECGC which has offices in all the main cities and state capitals in India. The willingness to cover such risks will depend on the value of the transaction and the credit exposure to the country/company as well as the country's credit rating, which is frequently reviewed and updated.

LO 5 **Comprehend pricing, financial terms, and payment methods used in international markets**

PRICING AND PAYMENT TERMS IN INTERNATIONAL TRADE

Pricing of products for international markets can be done on various terms. Some of the commonly used terms are:

- **Ex Works** This refers to the price of the product at the manufacturer's factory gates.

- **FOT—Free on Truck** This refers to the price of the product, packed, palletized and containerized (where applicable) and loaded on a truck at the manufacturers factory gates (including the loading charges).
- **FAS—Free alongside** This is a trade term that requires the seller to deliver the goods at the quay beside the ship including the port charges and not including the loading charges.
- **FOB—Free on Board** This refers to the price of the product, packed, palletized and containerized (where specified) and loaded on the ship (including all the shipment port charges, and loading charges)
- **C&F—Cost and Freight** This refers to the FOB price of the product plus the cost of the freight to the destination (it could be a port or an inland warehouse/factory premises), but not including the charges at the discharge port and import duties and local taxes which may be applicable.
- **CIF—Cost, Insurance and Freight** This refers to the C&F price plus the insurance charges from the manufacturer's factory to the final destination (either a port or the importers warehouse inland) including marine insurance.

Many a times, importers who have an establishment in the exporting country may choose to buy on FOT/FAS or FOB terms, as this can give them the leverage to negotiate the freight charges with known shipping companies and also to consolidate the cargo from various suppliers into larger consignments. The risk for the manufacturers is that the buyers may delay the pickup of the consignment depending on the other supplies and availability of shipping space.

Some countries have regulations that require import consignments to be either shipped on their flag vessels or be insured with their local insurance companies only. This is to facilitate easier and faster processing of any claims that may arise.

Freight rates vary with the loading port and destination, and availability of services between the ports and the time of the year. Usually freight brokers can help negotiate better freight and insurance rates. There are many companies which can handle the entire logistics involving picking up of the cargo from the manufacturers' warehouse to delivery at the importers' warehouse including storage in the destination country if required.

Certain high-value products (jewelry, leather garments, electronic components) are also shipped by air as it is safer and the delivery is faster, which ultimately works out to be economical when considering all the costs.

Payment by cash in advance is the preferred mode. But importers will rarely agree to this as it will mean locking up their funds and exposing them to risks of manufacturers'/suppliers' defaulting. Payment against documents sent through the bank is another method of payment—here the supplier sends the documents to the buyers' bank with a demand draft payable at sight. The risk here is the importer may refuse to pay because the local market conditions have changed.

Documents against acceptance is another method used for payments—here the importer accepts the documents sent to his bank by the exporter's bank and the bank releases the documents for clearing the consignment from customs. The danger here is if the importer collects the consignments and does not pay as agreed.

Usually these two methods are used when relationships between the importer and exporter are well established and there is mutual trust. These methods enable saving considerable sums in bank charges—especially when the business is regular and considerable in size.

The Letter of Credit (LC) is the most preferred method of payment as it ensures safety and comfort to both the exporter and the importer.

The LC is a document, which is sent by the buyers' bank to the sellers' bank promising payment of the agreed amount on submission of the documents evidencing shipment of the goods being traded. The terms could be payment at sight (immediately on presenting the shipping documents) or usuance (at an agreed time after presenting documents, say like 60 days or 120 days). Various terms can be specified in the LC, including the last date for shipment and the last date for receiving the documents. This ensures that the seller maintains his commitments.

Banks usually offer "Pre-shipment credit" against letters of credit—this is like a working capital advance for the manufacturer of export goods and is usually at a rate lower than the normal borrowing rate, as an incentive to the exporters.

Some products of capital nature, like equipment that are of high unit value and contracts of large value, may require longer term financing, extending up to 7 years. In such cases, agencies such as the Export Import Bank (EXIM bank) offer financing with payments in regular installments. They may extend the finance to the seller who in turn extends it to the buyer and assumes the risk of collection from the buyer or may directly finance the buyer against suitable guarantees. In the former case, it is referred to as suppliers' credit, and in the latter case as buyers' credit. The terms will vary depending on the credit rating of the buyer, the destination country, and the guarantees available.

EXIM bank and the Government of India often extend credits to foreign banks and governments respectively for import of Indian products. These credits are in turn passed on to local buyers against firm offers and contracts from suppliers. This is a safe arrangement for the sellers as the EXIM bank and the Government of India assumes the responsibility of collection of the payments.

Currency of Pricing

Exports are normally priced in hard currency, the most common being the US dollar. Exports can also be priced in euros or Japanese yen or even Indian rupees. One of the risks involved in international business is the fluctuation of the value of the currency of pricing with respect to the local currency. A depreciation of the local currency benefits the exporters as they realize more for their export, but hurts importers. Since the main business of traders is not currency speculation, it is best to seek professional advice from either bankers or foreign exchange dealers on the future trends of the exchange rates and building suitable safeguards in the pricing. It must be borne in mind that the time required from making the offer to the conclusion of order can take anywhere up to 3 months and thereafter execution of the order could take up to 6 months—a total of 9 months or more from the time of soliciting the business. Exchange rates can vary widely in this time period and cause considerable distress to the exporters in case they are not hedged.

Banks offer various instruments like forward contracts and options on future transactions to hedge the risks of adverse movements of foreign exchange rates. In addition, when the exporters need cash immediately, banks offer "forfaiting" facilities where they effectively discount the receivables and take the risk of collection on themselves. This, however, could be an expensive proposition varying from time to time, and details can vary with the country of import, importer's credit rating.

LO 6 **Distinguish between domestic and international distribution channels, and understand the factors that influence the choice of distribution channels in overseas market**

DISTRIBUTION

Distribution plays a vital role in the success of the sales effort, by ensuring the availability of the product in the right quantities, at the right time, and at the right place. In international markets, the role of distribution becomes more important due to the fact that these markets are usually at a distance from the manufacturing base and it takes a considerable amount of time to transport the products to the market and involves crossing national boundaries and completion of a number of procedures and formalities. Added to this is the fact that due to cost pressures, large buyers—manufacturers or retailers—insist on just-in-time inventories.

Distribution channels vary in breadth and depth from country to country, and hence there can be no universal strategy. Also, markets vary in size and importance for a company and hence the channels used may differ from country to country.

In the western markets we find large chains such as Walmart, Costco, Tesco PLC, Loblaws, etc., dominating most of the retail business. There are very few small shops like the *kirana* stores which are the family controlled grocery stores in India. The large stores are usually located in the suburbs, involving long drives to purchase the goods. Because of their size and buying volumes, they are able to extract advantages in pricing and supplies, which small stores cannot. In India too, organized retail like Big Bazaar, Star Bazaar and other such supermarkets and hypermarkets are slowly establishing themselves. They contribute to approximately 7 percent of the retail sales as compared with over 70 percent in the western countries.

Developed markets have well-established distribution structures in place and also the markups and margins at each level. In developing markets, these will have to be established by companies as they develop. In many African countries, the distribution channels are still evolving.

A new entrant into the arena is the e-commerce portals which offer the convenience of shopping from home. In the west, these have caught on well and even in India they are catching on in urban centers as well as tier-two and tier-three cities.

Types of Distribution Channels

In international markets, a company can choose from a variety of options depending on the product being marketed and the size and level of development of the market.

In the initial stages, a company can enter a market using a commission agent who, by virtue of his knowledge of the product and/or the buyers, could assist in getting business. Such an agent would not buy the product, but would solicit business from buyers and arrange payments to be made directly to the exporting company.

Once the business grows in volume and number of buyers, it may be necessary to appoint a distributor who would import, stock, and sell the product to end buyers/users. Alternatively, a company may stock products in the destination country on its own account and using an agent, distribute the products to the end users. Many international logistics companies can offer services of storage and delivery in foreign countries.

As business develops, a company may choose to establish its own office with a resident representative who would undertake the job of developing customers and ensuring their requirements are met.

Once the volume of the business reaches a certain size, the company may be forced to consider investing in the market with a longer-term perspective. This could take the form of a joint venture for distribution or manufacturing or may involve the company opting for a wholly owned subsidiary for distribution and manufacturing.

The type of distribution channel chosen would also depend on the nature of the product and its positioning. Certain products, which would be considered utility products in some markets, may be considered recreational products in others—as is the case with bicycles, motorcycles/ scooters, and boats. Appropriate channels of distribution will, therefore, depend on the market where the product is being sold.

Depending on the product positioning, again the distribution channels will have to be different. It is an acknowledged fact that the image of the product gets enhanced or diminished depending on the image of the distribution channel. Upmarket stores will enhance the image of a product.

Another factor to be borne in mind is that in many countries, outlets for consumer durables and similar products tend to be specialized stores that stock and sell multiple brands. An exclusive store for a brand is almost certainly unavailable, unless it is a very high-end and high-value product.

In most countries, due to pricing pressures and economies of scale, the retail formats lead to large supermarkets and hypermarkets. Servicing such retail outlets would be akin to supplying to large industrial buyers as it would involve just-in-time inventories, large volumes of merchandise, and use of technology in line with those of the outlet. Technologies which the suppliers will be required to use include bar codes, RFID (radio frequency identification devices) or other product identification methods, technology for tracking inventories and sales by outlet and advanced communication technologies.

Role of Logistics Companies

Logistics plays a very important part in international distribution. Since distributing products to many countries involve multiple modes of transport and trade across national boundaries which involve complex documentation and payment procedures, considerable attention has to be paid to this aspect.

Many large logistics companies offer shipping, transport, custom clearance, and warehousing services under one roof. They even undertake to deliver the products to the buyer's/distributor's locations on the instructions of the seller for charges which may be considerably lower than a company undertaking these activities in-house.

With current technologies, it is possible to monitor the activities of these logistics service providers from remote locations and carry out billing and collection electronically.

SUMMARY

LO 1

- International marketing of industrial products involves many factors that need to be taken into consideration, which do not apply to domestic markets. These factors include the political and economic relationships between the two countries, the standards applicable in the destination country, the distance, language, culture, and legal system of the destination country.
- Global markets differ in many ways, like availability of resources, personnel, skills, infrastructure, marketing channels, culture, legal systems, etc. It is important to understand this before venturing into these markets.

LO 2

- Choosing the right markets is the first step in doing business globally. Secondary data from various sources could help decide whether or not a market is suited for the company. Political stability, economic conditions, cultural and legal systems, size of the market, logistics facilities, and ease and purchasing power of the citizens are all factors to be considered when choosing to enter a market.
- Entry into a new market may be done initially through an indenting or sales agent and once the market demand grows, distributors could be appointed. In some markets it may be advantageous to have one's own office and warehouse to supply goods to buyers at short notice.

LO 3

- Distribution is a very important aspect of success of a product in a market. Choosing the right channels depending on the structure of the market and buying is crucial. Offering products in the right packet sizes and at the right price points depending on the market is critical for success. Understanding the legal aspects of distribution in a country is vital. Logistics providers offer a wide range of services including stocking and delivering products and invoicing and collecting payments. Culture influences consumption patterns. Legal systems put constraints on marketing mix choices—such as choice of brands, packaging, advertising, distribution channels, ownership of businesses, and choice of personnel for working in these markets.

LO 4

- Care must be taken when pricing the products in foreign currencies as any variations in the exchange rate can favorably or adversely affect the profitability of the deals. Pricing for exports is usually done in any hard currency, the US dollar being the most common. The terms of the supply can also vary depending on the buyer—it could range from ex-works in India to delivered at the buyer's warehouse inland in the country of destination.
- Risks of doing business across countries are much more than doing business nationally. This could include risks which are political in nature, or they could be social or commercial in nature. It is important to be aware of these risks and take suitable measures to minimize them and the consequent losses.

LO 5

- Packaging and shipping are important elements of cost in the final price and these must be optimally negotiated. The payment method must be agreed upon so that there are no undue risks to either the buyer or the seller. Credits where necessary will have to be suitably insured to reduce the risk of default. Pricing products right is the key to success in a market.
- Prices in international markets are usually quoted in currencies like US dollar, euro, Japanese yen, and British pound, etc. Since currencies fluctuate, it can be a major risk for businesses given the long lead-time between quoting for a contract and execution. Payment terms and mechanisms acceptable will vary with countries depending on the country risk.

LO 6

- Distribution and logistics play a very important role in the success in international markets, since they could constitute a fairly large portion of the end price of a product. The channels available vary with the level of development of the countries and this must be examined before venturing into a country.

Key Terms

Glossaries of key terms are mentioned at the end of all chapters

Copyright
Culture
Forfaiting
Franchise
Hedging
Intellectual Property Rights
License
Outsourcing
Patent
Trademark

Conceptual Questions

1. Compare with examples the merits of using local brands vs. international brands in India. LO3 D
2. Explain what impact the entry of large format stores will have on distribution in India? LO6 D
3. How does the availability of the Internet impact international sales? LO2 M
4. Explain the impact on Indian companies, who have appointed expatriate CEOs/ sales heads, in areas like airlines, hospitality, software, automobiles and consumer goods. LO3 M
5. A number of Indian manufacturing companies are now establishing their presence overseas either directly or by way of joint ventures. Discuss why? LO3 D
6. Many multinational companies establishing their Indian operations seem to prefer 100 percent subsidiaries of their parent company. Discuss the reasons, and pros and cons of this trend. LO3 D
7. Indian software companies are now trying to become multinational by acquiring local companies in various countries. What are the advantages and disadvantages of this strategy? LO3 M
8. India is seen by many overseas customers to be a location for cheap and low quality products. Discuss how this can be remedied? LO5 & 6 D

Objective Type Questions

Select the most appropriate response out of the various options available in each of the following questions:

1. What are the factors that affect advertising themes
   (a) product (b) cost (c) market size (d) culture LO3 M
2. Brands preferred in an overseas market are
   (a) local, (b) regional (c) national (d) international LO3 M
3. Consumption patterns depend on the
   (a) product (b) cost (c) demographics (d) culture LO3 M
4. The distribution network depends on the
   (a) Market size (b) population density
   (c) Type of the product (d) product positioning LO6 D

Note: Difficulty Level ⟶ E — Easy; M — Medium; D — Difficult

5. The distribution structure for products depends on
   (a) the value of the product (b) frequency of purchase
   (c) cost of distribution (d) infrastructure available
   (e) all of the above (f) none of the above LO6 D

6. The profile of the salesperson depends on
   (a) market size (b) language spoken (c) culture (d) religion LO3 M

Application Questions

1. The US Congress recently rejected the takeover of the management of many ports in the US by a Dubai based company. The Dubai Company had taken over P&O Ports—an Australian organization that was hitherto managing the ports. The reason given for the rejection was that some of the hijackers involved in the 9/11 incident were from the region and hence the takeover posed a security threat to the US. Analyze the situation. LO3 & 4 M
2. The takeover offer for Arcelor, a steel company that is predominant in France, by Mittal Steel Company, a global steel company with headquarters in London and Amsterdam, has created ripples and concerns amongst European parliamentarians. Their main concern was that Lakshmi Mittal—an Indian by origin, controls Mittal Steel Company and there would be cultural problems. Examine the various concerns. LO3 & 4 M
3. If you were heading an Indian manufacturing company explain what your strategy will be to establish your company's brand name in overseas markets like Europe, and South East Asia. LO3 M
4. Would your choice of personnel for deputation to head your office in Saudi Arabia be different from one to head your office in USA and Japan? Explain in what way and why? LO3 M
5. Arbitrage is common in many markets—leading to a gray market for products. Explain how you will counter this threat? LO5 M
6. Discuss a distribution strategy for: LO6 D
   (a) Auto components in Japan (b) Pharmaceuticals in USA/Europe
   (c) Garments in Europe (d) Kitchenware in South East Asia

ASSIGNMENTS FOR STUDENTS

1. Conduct a secondary data market research for a manufacturer of formal shoes (both ladies' and gents') in markets like Canada and USA. Based on the findings, make a complete sales and distribution plan for the shoes.

2. Study the sales and distribution strategy of Lupin Limited, a leading pharmaceutical manufacturer in India. Critically evaluate their strategy and state how you would do it differently.
3. A leading manufacturer of glass bottles used in the pharmaceutical industry wishes to enter the market for high-end bottles used by manufacturers of premium cosmetics and manufacturers of liquor in Europe. Evaluate the opportunity and identify the key success factors.
4. Study the facilities offered by the EXIM Bank of India and ECGC for exporters in India for different countries and product categories.

Caselet 1

Sunfast is a leading manufacturer radiator caps and petrol tank caps in India and the sole supplier to the largest automobile manufacturers in the USA. These parts are rarely required in the replacement market and hence the business is mainly with the OEM industry. Also, these components are of little value, they are critical to the automobile, and deliveries have to be timely, necessitating maintenance of inventories close to many OEMs' plants.

Questions

1. Should the company have their own sales office in the USA and have a sales manager based there?
2. Should they have a local person as the sales manager or send a person from India?
3. Should they have their own warehouse and stock parts locally or outsource the activity to a C&FA agent?
4. Discuss what the company's distribution options are and the criteria for choosing the way to go.

Caselet 2

Cookers India is a large Indian manufacturer of pressure cookers and a leading exporter worldwide. In the US market, these cookers are sold through leading chain stores, which have outlets across the country. The chain stores require the manufacturer to replenish inventories as soon as they exhaust so that the stores do not keep excess inventory. Also, the chain store states that the products should carry their brand name. The company can tie up with a C&FA agency to stock and distribute their products. Alternatively, the company can maintain its own warehouse and supply to distributors in the various states who in turn will supply to the chain stores on demand.

Questions

1. Discuss the merits of the various options for the setup for distribution and sales, including the profile of the sales persons required.
2. Consider the costs vs. the service that can be delivered.
3. How should they organize themselves in order to sell their products in other geographies like the Middle East, South East Asia, and Africa?

Caselet 3

Hifa Garments is a leading manufacturer of readymade garments in India. They supply exclusively to leading brands, which in turn retail them through their own chain of stores in Europe and USA. The brand owners, who have their sourcing offices in India in order to manufacture garments as per their designs, fabric and color schemes, quantity and sizes, approach Hifa. Hifa first offers design samples with prices, which once approved results in large orders that have to be delivered by the dates given by the sourcing office. Since garments are a seasonal business, timely deliveries are extremely important—the new season's garments must be in the stores by the scheduled dates.

Questions

1. Should Hifa Garments establish their offices in the destination countries and meet with the end customers directly?
2. Should they have selling agents in these countries to sell their products to end customers? Discuss the options for the sales and distribution set up for Hifa Garments.
3. How can Hifa use the Internet and social media to promote their products in overseas markets?

CASE-CHAPTER MATRIX FOR INTEGRATED CASES

CASE	CASE TITLE	CHAPTER NUMBERS																
Nos		*1*	*2*	*3*	*4*	*5*	*6*	*7*	*8*	*9*	*10*	*11*	*12*	*13*	*14*	*15*	*16*	*17*
1	Computers (India) Ltd.					✓	✓				✓							
2	Diamond Industries Ltd. (DIL)				✓	✓	✓	✓	✓		✓			✓	✓			
3	SM Technologies Ltd.			✓		✓			✓		✓							
4	Kshema Insurance Pvt. Ltd.					✓	✓	✓			✓							
5	AP Technologies Ltd.		✓			✓												
6	Hindustan Engineering and Automotive Products Ltd.					✓					✓							✓
7	SKJ Company Ltd.	✓			✓	✓		✓								✓	✓	
8	Metal Products India Ltd.			✓						✓	✓							
9	Syndiant Ltd.		✓	✓		✓			✓									
10	Electrical Equipment Ltd.		✓			✓												
11	Sunshine Luminaires Pvt. Ltd.					✓				✓								✓
12	Taurus Analytical Solutions Ltd.		✓	✓														✓
13	GlobeSec Ltd.									✓					✓			

Case I

Computers (India) Ltd.*

ANALYZING STAFFING AND TRAINING PROCESSES

"Why were 8 out of 20 sales trainees asked to leave the job?" asked Sunil Mittal, Director (Sales and Marketing) to Ashok Sharma, General Manager (Sales), Computers (India) Ltd.

"May I respond to this question next week? As I have joined the company recently, I need time to study this problem," responded Ashok Sharma. "Okay, next week you see me with your analysis and suggestions, but why can't you be proactive, in identifying and analyzing the problem, instead of reactive!" admonished Sunil Mittal.

COMPANY BACKGROUND

The company, which was incorporated in the USA, started its sales and marketing operations in India in the year 2000. It did not have a manufacturing base for personal computers (PCs) in India. The PC plants were located in China. The company had other products and services, such as notebooks, servers, printers, software and peripherals, and so on.

The company was one of the leading sellers of PCs in the world and one of the top 5 PC suppliers in India. It had mastered the distribution strategy of selling online as well as through its own sales force. Initially, the company adopted the same global distribution model in India.

STAFFING PROCESS

The sales force staffing process followed by the company had four stages—planning, recruiting, selecting, and hiring. Area sales managers for each of the 12 geographical areas were asked to calculate the number of salespeople needed for their respective geographical market. Ashok Sharma informed the area sales managers to use sales potential method for calculating the size of the salespeople needed by them. He asked them to consider the productivity of ₹12 million per year of an average salesperson. After getting the information on the number of salespeople

---

*This case was developed by Prof. Krishna K Havaldar for classroom discussion, based on the case data provided by Debleena Roy Chowdhary, an MBA student of Alliance Business Academy, Bengaluru.

needed by each of the 12 area sales managers, Ashok Sharma totaled the figures to find the optimum sales force size of 58. He then subtracted the existing 40 salespeople and added 2 possible terminations of salespeople from the existing 40 to come up with a total number of 20 new salespersons needed.

Ashok thought that the company should review the job specifications or profile of the sales trainees before going to the recruitment, selection and hiring stages. He asked the HR executive to help him by conducting the job analysis, then preparing the job description and thereafter, developing the job specifications for the sales trainees. The HR executive concluded after completing the process that the sales trainees should be engineering graduates with specialization in information technology (IT) or computers, with traits of empathy, as well as good communication skills. For identifying the prospective candidates, Ashok asked the administration manager to advertise in national newspapers in order to cover all the geographical areas where the company's sales and service offices were located. In addition, he asked the administration manager to use the company's website to approach the applicants for sales trainee position.

The screening of applications was done by the HR executive by comparing the applications with the job specifications. The candidates, who qualified after the initial screening, were called for personal interviews. Ashok Sharma went around different sales and service offices to conduct the personal interviews of the candidates along with the respective area sales managers. The selected applicants were asked to appear for the medical check-up with the company appointed doctors.

The regional administration manager issued the appointment letters in consultation with Ashok Sharma. It was the responsibility of the HR executive to get the acceptance of the candidates for the job offers and to ensure that the new recruits reported on a specific date for the training program.

TRAINING THE SALES TRAINEES

The initial training provided to the sales trainees was comprehensive. This training was considered by the company as a part of the socialization process, and was conducted in the company's conference hall for a period of 15 days. The main objective of the training was to teach the sales trainees all the aspects of the sales job and give adequate information about the company and its policies. The content of the training program included company information, product knowledge, market information, company's sales and marketing policies and strategies, selling skills, communication and negotiation skills, time and territory management, and customer relationship management. The methods used by the trainers consisted of lectures, role-plays, group-discussions and group-presentations, product demonstrations, case discussions, multi-media presentations, and audio-video cassettes.

Besides the in-house trainers, the company invited specialist trainers from outside to conduct negotiation and communication workshops. Senior company executives were involved as internal trainers so that the company-related information in terms of the company's, mission, objectives, organization structure and key people, shared values, personnel and sales policies, and so on can be properly communicated to the trainees. The evaluation of the sales trainees was done at the end of the training program by giving them a written test on product knowledge, market knowledge, and company knowledge. The sales trainees were also asked to give a feedback, on a structured questionnaire, about the usefulness of the various training sessions, the content and the methods of training, and suggestions for improvements.

In addition to the classroom training, the company provided on-the-job training for one and half months, where each sales trainee was attached to a senior salesperson. As per the company policy, at the end of two months of training, the sales trainees were given a sales target and asked to report to a senior sales executive, who was not only the trainee's boss, but also a coach. The senior sales executives were given an additional responsibility of coaching the sales trainees, particularly those trainees who were not performing well enough to achieve the sales targets. On an average, two sales trainees reported to a senior sales executive and about 40 to 50 percent trainees needed the help of the coach to achieve their sales goals. Typically the coaching period was 90 days. At the end of 90 days, if the performance was still below expectations, such trainees were given a last chance for performance improvement for a period of 30 days. If the performance did not improve, the sales trainee was asked to leave the organization.

Ashok Sharma, after reviewing the staffing and training processes, realized that 40 percent of sales trainees in the batch of 20 were not found up to the expectations. This affected the overall sales performance. He also thought that there may be some serious problems in the staffing and training processes or in the company policy of performance evaluation of the sales trainees. He decided to review the same, so that he could make specific suggestions for improvement.

CASE QUESTIONS

1. Explain whether staffing and training processes followed by the company were proper?
2. What improvements do you suggest in order to minimize the number of sales trainees leaving the company?

Case 2

Diamond Industries Ltd. (DIL)*

Raghu, the National Sales Manager (NSM) of Diamond Industries Ltd. (DIL) had just concluded a meeting with his 4 regional sales managers (RSM) on finding long-term solutions to two of the issues worrying the sales and marketing function of DIL. These issues were: (i) attrition of experienced and talented salespeople by losing them to major competitors, and (ii) handling conflict with important channel partners.

Diamond Industries Ltd. (DIL) has been operating in the highly fragmented Indian innerwear/hosiery industry for over the last 20 years. It is one of the leading players both in terms of market share and wide geographical presence in almost all states of North India. It has set up a sales team in all the states in which it is present and supported it by a network of dealers. The dealers are also proud to be working with DIL.

It has four manufacturing units located strategically in India.

INDIAN INNERWEAR MARKET

The total innerwear market in India (for men and women) is expected to be worth around ₹18,000 crore (₹180 billion). Most of the players are regional small players. There are only about 5 branded players with a wider network like DIL. These companies seem to account for only about 25 percent of the total market. The industry estimates that it is growing at 15 to 20 percent per annum. About 10 percent of the production of the major players is also being exported.

Some of the major players have also made efforts at backward integration as follows:

- Setting up their own spinning mills
- Setting up processing factories for dyeing of grey fabric
- Setting up knitting machines for converting yarn to grey fabric

*The Case was prepared under the guidance of V M Cavale with the inputs from the students of NMIMS, Bengaluru—Gaurav Gupta, Vinit Balani, and Yashraj Deshmukh.

On the promotion front, some of the leading brand companies have roped in celebrities to promote their brands. These companies also focus on innovation in their products to meet consumer tastes. These companies have built a strong distribution network to reach their products into millions of outlets. DIL also supports all these initiatives.

DIL SALES ORGANIZATION

The sales organization of DIL is led by the National Sales Manager (NSM) Raghu. He is supported by 4 regional sales managers (RSMs) for north, south, east and west. The RSMs manage the area sales managers (ASMs) in each state. The ASMs run the sales operations through a set of territory sales officers (TSOs). DIL has one NSM, 4 RSMs, 24 ASMs and 65 TSOs in all—data by state not made available.

DIL has broadly defined the responsibilities of the people in the sales organization as follows:

- **NSM** They are responsible for national sales, and do the forecasting based on market potential. Their special responsibilities also include: (i) supporting the head office marketing department in identifying and developing new products, (ii) planning pricing and schemes support, (iii) implementation of policies agreed with the CEO. NSM sets the annual or monthly targets for the RSMs in consultation with them. NSM also decides the human resource policies like performance reviews, incentives, promotions, etc., along with the HR function of DIL. The NSM spends about 7 to 10 days in a month in the field working with the sales and channel people and meeting customers.

- **RSM** The RSMs focus on regional target achievement. They collect detailed market information from field salespeople for use by the NSM and marketing, and keep track of the working of all the field sales managers and their channel support. The RSM is given a target each month which he is responsible for distributing to his ASMs, and plan or help them achieve them. The RSM sorts out any problems in the field that his ASMs may not be able to solve on their own. The RSM spends about 15 days in a month working in the markets along with his team members.

- **ASM** They achieve targets for the state assigned to them. The ASM is the head of field operations and is responsible for the day-to-day operations of his team members. The field salespeople and at times the dealers also keep in touch with the ASM for his help or advice. The ASM is responsible for controlling the sales expenses as per the budget agreed upon for the state. The ASM manages both trade and consumer promotions. The consumer promotions are decided based on the marketing function, along with the NSM, and is implemented in the field. The trade promotions are planned and executed by the ASM for the state. The ASM manages the field sales personnel and the dealers, and resolve all issues in the state relating to DIL.

- **TSO** They work closely with the dealers to sell the products into retail, achieve targets, and ensure all promotions are run successfully. The TSO is responsible for generating both primary (sales to dealers) and secondary sales (sales to retailers). They generate all field reports including secondary sales and sales expenses along with market reports including competitor activities. The TSO works closely with the state Agent for getting primary sales. Agents operate with their own salespeople for getting orders on primary sales from the dealers allotted to them. The Agent's salespeople and the Agent take the help of the TSOs.

CHANNEL NETWORK

One Agent operates in each state. The Agent invests in an office and performs the following tasks:

- Appoint dealers in each state and collect orders from the dealers for execution by DIL.
- Fix targets as per company norms for each of the dealers. The company gives the target to the Agent for his state. The company's salespeople help the dealers and the Agents to achieve their targets.
- The Agent collects the payments from the dealers.
- The Agent operates like a C&FA without storing the company's goods.

The dealer is the bridge between the Agent and the retailers in the markets. The dealer has the following responsibilities:

- Service the retailers as per a clear beat plan given by the company's salespeople—sell the goods of DIL and collect the payments. The dealer decides in case he wants to give credit terms to big potential retailers.
- Buy goods from the company by placing orders with the Agent of the state. It is on the Agent to get the goods delivered.
- The dealers are supported by the company's salespeople to manage the business.

The Agent and the dealers get a percentage of sales as commission. DIL was not willing to reveal these numbers. DIL was very clear that these commission rates generated adequate ROI for these channel partners.

PROBLEM

The hosiery or innerwear industry has been seeing the frequent migration of salespeople and sales managers between the major players in the market. In March 2016, NSM Raghu was suddenly faced with a serious issue. One of his best performing RSMs, the RSM East, Vijay was poached by competition. He was considered a very good manager with an excellent knowledge of the company and competition.

When the NSM was reviewing this issue, he also discovered a bigger problem. In the last 6 months 3 ASMs and 14 TSOs had left the company. This was a serious issue and needed immediate attention to reduce attrition of trained and talented field people.

Raghu started a discussion with the head office's human resources function on the ways to reduce such attrition in the future. He pointed out that loss of such valuable salespeople would not only prove to be a setback to the selling effort but also will result in loss of knowledge about the company and its policies to competition. Moreover, recruiting a new person would take time for him to get trained and start delivering results.

Some of suggestions given by the RSMs to the NSM to reduce attrition are listed here. They are as follows:

- Increase in fixed component of salespeople's remuneration
- Make efforts to train and develop the salespeople—this also had a downside to it
- Arrange for frequent sales contests for salespeople, keeping their interest levels in the company high

While trying to solve the issue of salespeople attrition, NSM Raghu was also struggling with a channel conflict situation which he was trying to resolve.

DIL was quite satisfied with a unique distribution network they had established and which was serving them quite well over the years. They identified trustworthy strong businessmen in each state capital and appointed one such as an "'Agent" of DIL for the state. The Agent was required to set up a small office exclusively to serve DIL and undertake the following tasks:

- Appoint dealers across the state for DIL
- Collect orders at regular intervals from the dealers and pass it on to the company for dispatch
- Fix targets for the dealers based on company norms
- Help the dealers achieve their targets
- Collect payments from the dealers
- Work closely with the company's salespeople to perform these tasks

For this responsibility, the Agent would get a fixed percentage of sales as commission. DIL would not reveal this percentage commission.

DIL had also defined the following role for the dealers:

- Call on all retailers and service them for DIL goods
- Buy goods from the company by placing orders with the Agents
- Support company salespeople in market working, handling promotions, collections, merchandising efforts

The dealers are guaranteed a fair margin and ROI

PROBLEM

In one of the major states in North India, there was a reliable Agent, Shantilal and Co., operating for DIL for over 20 years. This Agent started working with DIL with a partnership firm which they later converted to a proprietorship firm. With the help and guidance of DIL, Shantilal was able to generate annual revenues of over ₹22 crore for DIL from his state. By early 2016, this Agent started believing that the success of DIL was mostly due to him and ignored the efforts made by the company over the last several years to build its brand equity.

Some of the issues on which the Agent Shantilal was found wanting and which came to the notice of Raghu, the NSM, were:

- Some of the smaller town dealers were being neglected and not serviced regularly. Every time it was the company salespeople were required to service these dealers.

- Orders from the dealers were being collected in an erratic manner.
- Collections from dealers for goods dispatched were getting delayed—creating working capital issues, and dealers were deliberately delaying payments.
- The company targets and messages meant for the channel partners—the dealers—were not being communicated in time. This had resulted in sub-optimal results on sales promotions in some cases.

The concerned ASMs in the state and the RSM had made serious efforts to counsel Shantilal many times. Apart from reassurances that he would not give cause for such complaints in future, the situation was not improving and the matter got escalated to the NSM, Raghu.

Please help Raghu find answers to the following questions.

CASE QUESTIONS

1. How to work closely with HR to ensure that attrition of valuable salespeople is managed better?
2. Agents are an important and critical part of the channel network and represent the company's interests in an entire state. How to ensure that they operate at the peak of their potential consistently and always sustain this performance?

Case 3

SM Technologies Ltd.*

DEVELOPING SALES STRATEGIES

Arun Kumar, Head, Pune branch office of SM Technologies, was wondering what sales strategies he should use to achieve the ambitious target of 40 percent growth in sales set for the company's Pune branch office for the year 2015–16. In the past 3 years, Pune branch achieved the sales growth of 15 to 30 percent.

COMPANY BACKGROUND

SM Technologies was a fully owned subsidiary of a UK based group, which had operations in 20 countries across 5 continents. The company had built state-of-the-art optic-fiber telecom networks in India. It offered broadband-enabled Internet services, such as voice, data, and video service, across 10 major cities Mumbai, Bengaluru, Delhi, Hyderabad, Chennai, Pune, Surat, Ahmedabad, Vadodara, and Vishakhapatnam, with plans to roll out to other cities in future.

The company's registered office was located in Mumbai. Satish Mehta, CEO for Indian operations, launched its services in India in 2001 and within a short span of time, it had become one of the fastest growing broadband players.

SERVICES OFFERED

SM Technologies offered broadband-enabled services to corporate (or business) and home (or domestic) users. For corporate users the company offered the following business services:

- Data connectivity services
- Voice connectivity services
- Managed services
- International bandwidth services

*This case was prepared by Prof. Krishna K Havaldar for classroom discussion, based on the case data provided by MBA students of Alliance Business Academy, Bengaluru—Brajesh Kumar and Brijesh Nair.

For home users, the Internet services offered by the company included world-class broadband network, which would facilitate fantastic surfing and downloading speed, live audio and video, Internet-telephone, chat, and gaming. However, till the broadband network was not set up in a residential area, the company offered dial-up Internet packs. In particular, the company's Internet-telephone service was a great cost saver for those users who wanted to make international calls to their near and dear ones.

COMPETITION

Some of the major competitors of SM Technologies were:

- Reliance Communications
- Bharti Airtel
- Tata Teleservices
- Bharat Sanchar Nigam Limited (BSNL)
- Vodafone
- Idea Cellular

SALES ORGANIZATION

Each of the 10 branch offices in India, including Pune branch, had a branch head to take care of overall sales and marketing operations. A typical sales organization structure is shown in Exhibit 1.

Exhibit 1

Sales Organization Structure at the Branch Office

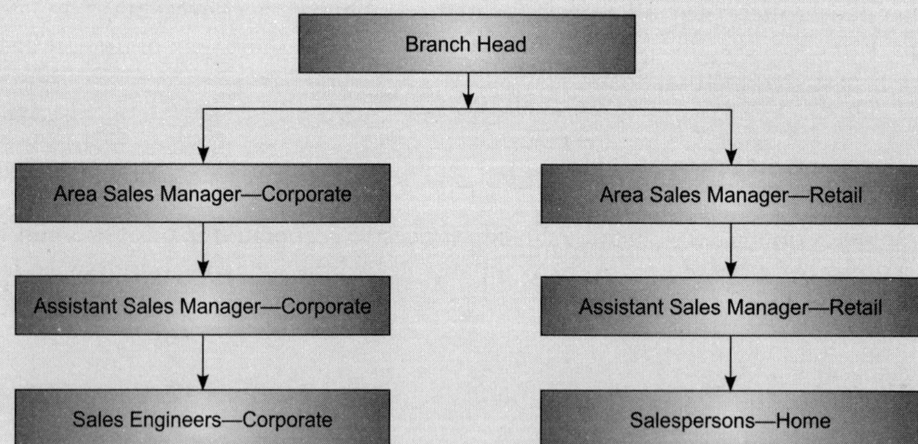

The company had a unique composition of the sales force. For corporate clients, each branch sales office had three or four sales engineers who were called direct employees and were paid a fixed salary and commission based on their performance against sales targets or quotas. For home (or domestic) users, the company employed salespersons (graduates, other than engineering) on contract basis and these salespeople were compensated by straight commission method. The salespeople were given yearly, quarterly, and monthly sales targets (or sales quotas), which were further divided into weekly sales targets. Salespersons were asked to submit daily reports to the respective assistant sales managers in a standard format. The daily sales call reports gave information about the salesperson's client visits, outcome of the visits, competitors' prices, strengths, weaknesses, and so on. A close control on salespeople had ensured that salespersons had no chance of doing any manipulations, such as over promising customers to achieve sales targets.

SALES STRATEGY

The company classified corporate or business customers into three different customer groups, as follows:

- Class "A" : High sales and profit potential customers
- Class "B" : Medium sales and profit potential customers
- Class "C" : Low sales and profit potential customers

For Class "A" customers, the company's strategy was to build long-term collaborative relationships by planning and organizing joint problem solving teams, multiple level contacts, and team selling. For class "B" customers, the strategy was to understand the customer needs clearly and offer better solutions, or meet those needs better than competitors. For class "C" customers, the relationship was transactional and short-term. The salespersons were told to visit class "A" customers four times a month, class "B" customers twice a month, and class "C" customers once a month.

Salespeople were required to have a high level of technical and commercial knowledge as well as communication, negotiation, and selling skills. To ensure this, the company had a tie-up with a leading sales training institute at all its branch sales offices. Selling technical service was a challenging task, and therefore, the company's strategy was to give due importance to training salespeople not only on technical matters but also on commercial issues such as payment terms, risk purchase clause, and bank guarantees.

In spite of an effective training program, some salespersons could not achieve their monthly sales targets. The area sales manager talked to these salespeople, used mock sales presentations including video recording in order to identify the causes of performance decline, and then suggested the areas of corrections.

CHANNEL STRATEGY

The company used direct channels of selling through the company salespeople, online selling through its website, and telemarketing. The company, in order to ensure long-term business relationships with its business customers, used its corporate sales engineers; and for household and individual customers, the company used its domestic salespersons. The Internet and telemarketing channels were mainly used for prospecting and qualifying. If the prospective customers, corporate and domestic, needed visits of the company salespersons, the same was arranged to understand the customer needs, make proposals and sales presentations, negotiations, and close the sale. The company had a separate team of engineers and technicians for installation and after-sales service.

PROMOTION

SM Technologies participated in the national and international relevant trade shows and exhibitions. These trade shows generated sales leads, prospects, and new customers. The company advertised regularly in the telecom journals and on the Internet. In addition, the company was one of the sponsors of the ICC Cricket World Cup and Indian Premier League (IPL) cricket matches. Third party references were used by the company to promote its services to potential clients. These promotional tools helped salespeople, as they created awareness and brand image for the services offered by the company.

Arun Kumar was not sure whether the present sales strategies would be adequate to achieve the ambitious growth targets. No doubt the broadband market had an immense potential to grow. But the competition was also intense. Arun Kumar wondered what new sales strategies and sales force management methods can be used to ensure the target of 40 percent growth in sales is achieved.

CASE QUESTIONS

1. Would you like to suggest any new strategies and sales force management tools for which Arun need not take permission from his senior managers for implementation?
2. With the help of decisions from senior management, which other strategies or practices should be changed or added by the company in order to achieve the ambitious target?

Case 4

Kshema Insurance Pvt. Ltd.*

SALES FORCE ATTRITION AND BEHAVIOR

Rahul Sharma, Area Sales Manager of Arakere area of Bengaluru city, is concerned about the high attrition and unacceptable behavior of salespeople reporting to him. Rahul was hired about 6 months ago by Kshema Insurance Company as an Area Sales Manager. Rahul earlier worked for a travel agency, where the attrition rate of salespeople was less than 10 percent. Rahul, therefore, found the attrition rate of about 40 percent in Kshema Insurance as very high. In addition, he thought that his salespeople were uncooperative and arrogant. They also lacked discipline, because many times the sales people did not carry out the customer visit norms set by the company's management and even for the internal meetings, called by him, they have not been always punctual.

ABOUT THE COMPANY

Kshema Insurance Pvt. Ltd. was formed in the year 2000 by the former senior executives of Life Insurance Corporation of India, a Government of India undertaking. They implemented the strategies of low premium cost to customers and remaining close to customers by opening the company offices at many locations. These strategies helped the company to grow faster than their competitors. It also resulted in having many layers of sales management in the organization structure as shown in Exhibit 1. Due to manifold hierarchy of sales managers, the decision-making has become slower. The key result areas (KRAs) for sales executives include achievement of their individual sales targets as well as recruitment of agents. They are not restricted by any geographic areas for contacting the prospective customers and agents. The compensation plan for sales executives includes a fixed salary, which starts at a minimum of ₹12,000 per month plus commission that varies from 3 to 15 percent. The branch manager has the authority to plan, recruit, and select the sales executive in consultation with HR manager. The minimum educational qualification for an applicant for a sales executive position is "Pre-University" (P.U.). The selection criteria are communication skill, general knowledge, and good physique.

---

*This case was prepared by Prof. Krishna K. Havaldar for classroom discussion based on the case data provided by Mr. Sameer Gupta, Director, Sales, SS Able Advisory Private Ltd., Bengaluru.

Exhibit 1

Sales Organization Structure

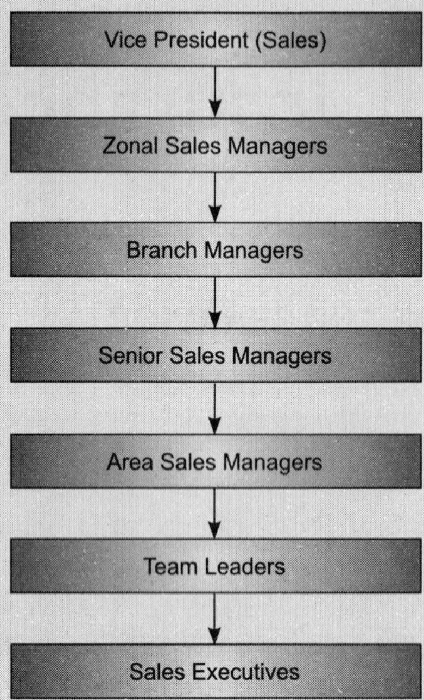

The responsibility for training is given to a trainer, who conducts classroom-based training for 14 days for fresh recruits using lectures, role-playing, and group discussion methods. This is followed by two weeks of on-the-job training with a team leader. After one month of training, the new sales executive is asked to go to the market to achieve a sales target. The zonal sales managers for each state are given the responsibility of training the existing experienced sales executives for 1 or 2 days through classroom-based training, which includes topics like the company information, sales strategy, and soft skills such as communication and negotiation. It is a standardized training program, without any consideration for training needs of individual sales executives.

The company's motivational tools for sales executives consist of financial incentive or commission of 3 to 15 percent as mentioned earlier, formal recognition programs with awards for superior sales performance, and promotion to sales management position. The performance reviews of sales executives are conducted by the area sales managers every month, in which reasons for inferior performance, if any, and corrective actions are discussed.

INSURANCE INDUSTRY

In India, insurance has a deep-rooted history. Insurance in various forms was mentioned in the writings of *Manusmriti*, *Dharmashastra*, and Kautilya's *Arthashastra*. The fundamental basis of insurance is pooling of resources that could be redistributed in the times of calamities, such as floods, fire, and earthquake. Insurance in current form has its history dating back to 1818 when Oriental Life Insurance Company was started in Kolkata. By 2012, Indian insurance was a US $ 72 billion industry.

However, only 0.2 percent of the total population was covered under the mediclaim policy. Life insurance market in India is projected to touch US $ 350 to 400 billion by 2020. There are 53 insurance companies in India, including 24 in life insurance and 29 in non-life insurance business. The Government of India, in the Union Budget 2017–18, has made provisions for subsidies in the premiums of "Pradhan Mantri Fasal Bima Yojana", i.e. crop insurance and an insurance pool under Civil Liability for Nuclear Damage (CLND) Act. India's life insurance sector is the biggest in the world with about 360 million policies which are expected to increase at a "Compound Annual Growth Rate" (CAGR) of 12 to 15 percent in the next 5 years (i.e., from 2016–17 to 2021–22). The general insurance business in India is currently (i.e., in 2016–17) at ₹78,000 crores (i.e., US $ 11.44 billion) premium per annum and is growing at a healthy rate of 17 percent. Overall, one can say that the Indian insurance market is a huge business opportunity waiting to be harnessed. However, the Indian insurance industry is currently facing the following challenges, as per a report of Confederation of Indian Industry (CII) and Ernest & Young:

- Under-penetrated market
- Very little customer pull
- Rising costs
- High-level of attrition

These above-mentioned challenges can be met in the following ways:

- Insurance industry should focus on product innovation, matching the risk profile of the policy holders.
- Make sales and marketing more responsible and answerable.
- Use multi-distribution channels, including new channels like the Internet, direct marketing, telemarketing, and non-government organizations (NGOs).
- Insurance Regulatory and Development Authority of India (IRDAI), which was established in 1999 under the government regulation, should drive transparency and simplification of products and services.

The insurance market in India has a large latent potential. Also, the Indian economy is expected to do well in the coming decades, leading to increase in per capita incomes and awareness.

PROBLEM ANALYSIS

On a Monday afternoon, Rahul had received yet another call from a customer who complained about the arrogant behavior of one of his sales executives. Rahul wondered how to correct the unreasonable behavior of his sales executives. He felt doubtful about the process of recruitment, selection, and training followed by the company. That may be the reason why he has about 6 out of 10 sales executives whose behavior with customers and office staff is unacceptable. Rahul thought whether he should talk to his immediate boss, the senior sales manager, about his views on the behavior of the sales executives and the need to hire better quality of sales executives. However, he thought his views might not be liked by the senior sales managers, particularly because he has been in this company for hardly 6 months. Instead, he felt, why not try different motivational methods, which he could use to improve the behavior as well as attrition rate of sales executives.

CASE QUESTIONS

1. What changes are needed in the process of recruitment, selection, training and motivation of sales executives?
2. If you were Rahul what would you do to resolve the problems of attrition and behavior of sales executives?

Case 5

AP Technologies Ltd.*

IMPROVING CUSTOMER DELIVERY SERVICE

"Am I the only person responsible for the costs and schedule overrun?" asked the Project Manager of AP Technologies, L Balaji, to his Vice President. "Yes, it is your responsibility to make sure that the project schedule and costs are within 20 percent of the planned schedule and costs. If this is not done, then the company's bottom line would get badly affected," responded the Vice President.

The top management of AP Technologies was concerned to find that only 25 percent of the software services projects were completed within 20 percent of the planned costs and schedule. The company was seriously considering what steps were needed to improve the situation in a highly competitive market.

ABOUT OF THE COMPANY

AP Technologies Ltd. was a global technology services company with over 20 years of experience in the information technology sector. The company delivered seamless solutions that gave tangible value to the customers. The company had over 400 clients out of which about 30 percent were Fortune 500 companies. The company secured 50 percent sales through repeat business from existing customers.

The Chairman and Managing Director (CMD) of the company informed the employees in one of the internal review meetings that if the repeat business from existing customers could be increased from 50 percent to 80 percent, the profitability of the company would go up substantially.

SERVICES OFFERED

Some of the services offered by the company were:

- Business outcome services
- System integration

*This case was prepared by Prof. Krishna K. Havaldar for classroom discussion. It does not indicate an effective or ineffective handling of business situation.

- Analytics
- Business process
- Cloud
- Enterprise security
- Digital
- Application development and maintenance

The people who had expertise in the above mentioned services were known as solution experts or technology experts. These experts were a part of the horizontals, and were drawn by the sales (or business development) executives to understand the customer problems or needs and to find solutions.

CUSTOMER FOCUSED MARKET SEGMENTS

The company had developed the domain expertise in the following market segments:

- Aerospace
- Consumer Goods
- Retailing
- Telecommunication
- Insurance
- Automobile
- Manufacturing
- Energy and Utilities
- Banking
- Travel and Transportation

The company executives who had developed domain knowledge and expertise in the above mentioned market segments were a part of the verticals in the organization structure.

SELLING PROCESS

The selling process started with prospecting, i.e. searching and identifying potential customers for the services offered by the company. The methods used by the company for prospecting included the internet, telephone, direct mail, and trade shows. The prospecting process generated sales leads or leads, i.e., the names and addresses of business firms who were probable prospects. The probable prospects or leads were then qualified to prospects by contacting them by phone or e-mails. Only "hot prospects", who were interested in the company's services and had financial capacity to buy, were handed over to business development (or sales) executives.

The first call on a prospective customer was made by a business development executive in one of the 20 sales offices located in the main business centers all over the world. Depending on the customer's requirement of the services, the business development executive would take the assistance from solutions expert (one of the horizontals), and if need be, the domain expert (one of the verticals), for further discussions (pre-sales service) with the customer to understand clearly the customer's needs and to prepare a proposal. The proposal or the offer given to the customer would include the cost, broad outline of the solution, the scope of work, the delivery schedule, and the payment schedule. The customer would have received the proposals from other suppliers also and hence, negotiations might take place subsequently with all the short-listed suppliers. The company which won the contract after negotiations would first get the letter of intent to start the work and subsequently the purchase order. After the receipt of the order, the project is assigned to one of the project managers for execution.

PROJECT EXECUTION PROCESS

The company had a project execution process to help the project manager and his team to deliver the commitments to the customer. In the project execution process, the project plan document was created through the ERP (Enterprise Resource Planning) system. The project plan was then approved by a senior executive and given to the project manager, for regular monitoring and reporting the progress once a month. The project plan included all the activities that were required for the project execution. Some of the important activities that were included in the project plan were management of people, customer requirements, quality, schedule, and risk. Balaji thought that if he followed the project execution process, nothing could go wrong.

DELAYED DELIVERY SCHEDULE

Despite regular monitoring, after 6 months of the project execution, Balaji found to his utter dismay the delay in the completion of the project. He, therefore, called a meeting of his project team members to discuss the reasons for the delay in the completion of the project, to revise the delivery schedules, and to discuss how to communicate the same to the client without affecting the client relationship. He informed the team members about the dissatisfaction of the management about the delay in completing the project. Thereafter, the team worked out the revised delivery schedule for conveying the same to the client. He also wanted to know from his team members the reasons for the delay in delivery, as the management had called a meeting of all concerned executives for taking appropriate corrective actions.

When the client was informed about the delay of the project by about two months, the reaction was, "Why you did not inform us earlier this bad news? You have upset our schedule, which depended on completion of your schedule." Balaji had to give some excuses like changes in the client specifications, resignation of a key team member, and over-optimistic approach of the company executives who accepted almost impossible delivery schedules. The client got more annoyed with Balaji's explanation of the delays and said, "We don't appreciate your reasons. You solve your problems first, before claiming to solve our problems! We would like your senior executives to talk to us."

Balaji immediately conveyed the conversation to his Vice President, who decided to call a meeting of all the project managers and business development managers to discuss and decide corrective steps.

CASE QUESTIONS

1. If you were Balaji, how would you convey the delay in delivery to the client?
2. What corrective steps would you suggest to improve the customer delivery service substantially?

Case 6

Hindustan Engineering and Automotive Products Ltd.*

MANAGING INTERNATIONAL SALES AND DISTRIBUTION

Hindustan Engineering & Automotive Products Ltd. (HEAP) was established in the early 1950s in a joint venture (JV) with a leading European company to manufacture engineering and automotive components for the growing Indian market. By the mid 1980s, the company had established three plants in eastern, western and southern India to cater to the growing demand. The company was managed by Jayant Kumar, a long-time company employee, as Managing Director.

During this period, the company absorbed considerable technology from the JV partner and was able to commence exporting its products to various markets in Africa, Middle East, and South East Asia under its own brand in direct competition with the partner. This led to a situation where the partner had to review its relationship, and eventually the partner withdrew from the company in the mid 1990s. It was, however, agreed as a part of this process that the partner would be free to establish its own operations and market its products in India under the liberalized conditions prevailing.

Foreseeing increased local competition, HEAP was now considering exporting its products to the developed markets in Europe, Japan, and the USA. Guru Prasad was recruited from an MNC to head the international operations and was asked by the top management to work out a strategy for growing the exports rapidly.

Meanwhile, a top management strategy planning group identified the lack of expertise in design and certain manufacturing technologies as the key constraint of this company wanting to enter a highly competitive and large market for engineering and auto components in Europe, America, and Japan. The prevailing market situation was such that no major competitor was willing to offer their designs or technology to avoid potential competition.

On the marketing front, Guru Prasad carried out a study and recommended that HEAP establish its own representative offices in these countries, and direct customer contact to

---

*B.S. Sachidanand prepared this case for classroom discussion. Any resemblance to any characters living or dead is purely coincidental.

gradually build a local distribution network. Each market had its own peculiar channels of distribution and to create confidence it became necessary to have a company representative office in these countries which could attend to any problems. He also recommended that the company should focus on the replacement market rather than on the OE (original equipment) segment. Traditionally, the OE market offered large volumes, but at very low margins. The replacement markets in these countries were dominated by large chains of distributors with their own brands. These chains usually bought components from companies who were Tier-two OE suppliers and often marketed the products under their own brand names.

Due to varying market conditions, HEAP had to price its products differently in different markets—leading to a situation where the same products could be bought from a distributor in one country and transported and sold in another profitably. Also since HEAP had established its products in these markets, many copycat products manufactured by some of the smaller non-OE players with similar brand names and packaging, but of lower quality and significantly lower prices, entered the markets. The dealers of HEAP complained to the management about their eroding market and margins by unauthorized players and threatened to quit if not resolved. Guru Prasad was asked to look into the problem and find a solution quickly.

The company had a good R&D team headed by Krishna Rao who was well qualified and had a PhD from a leading British university. Krishna Rao advised the management to seek a collaborative relationship with some leading Italian design bureaus which had considerable expertise and were acknowledged leaders in the field, as a medium-term measure. In the long-term it was necessary to build in-house expertise, he opined.

In the new millennium, new challenges emerged for the company. A large number of international automotive manufacturers established their manufacturing operations in India, tempted by the strong growing market. Their established component suppliers were encouraged to setup operations in India also. Thus, the major advantage HEAP had in terms of manufacturing cost advantage was now available to their competitors. Also, with the advent of Internet and social media, access to information by prospective channel partners and end buyers was easy. Due to the extremely competitive market conditions, large international buyers and importers insisted on just-in-time deliveries. This meant that HEAP would have to establish their own warehouses with stocks in geographies where they had buyers, to ensure quick deliveries. Added to this, the downturn in the western markets were forcing protectionist policies against imports.

The management of HEAP was concerned about the issues mentioned in the following section. Discuss and offer your solutions to the management on these issues with reasons.

CASE QUESTIONS

1. What strategy it should follow for the short-term and long-term so that at least 30 percent of HEAP's revenues come from exports?
2. Whether it should agree to sell its products under the distributors' brand and what impact this could have in the long run?
3. What channels of distribution they should use? Should they be the same in all markets?

4. How it should tackle the menace of low-priced competition from spurious manufacturers?
5. What would be the most effective organization structure for export marketing? Should they employ local individuals for manning their offices or should they send their own employees from India?
6. Whether it should outsource its design and R&D?
7. Whether HEAP should stock up their products in the destination countries? Whether they should do it in-house or have an external organization such as a C&FA?
8. What should be their Internet communication strategy?
9. How should/can HEAP build competitive advantage in the international markets?
10. How to meet the challenge of rising protectionist tendencies in the western markets?

Case 7

SKJ Company Ltd.*

ACHIEVING SALES TARGETS FOR FMCG

Anant Kumar, Sales Executive of SKJ Company was a worried person. He could not achieve the sales targets for the previous three months from April to June 2008. He wondered if he could retain his job. What reasons could he give to his boss, Amir Khan, the Area Sales Manager of Pune branch when he was to meet him the following week for the performance review? Was it because of the unfavorable economic situation like slowing down of the demand for FMCG (fast moving consumer goods) or was it that his efforts were inadequate? Anant was confused and was not sure why he could not achieve the sales goals for the first quarter of the year 2008–09.

ABOUT THE COMPANY

SKJ Company was a multinational company with its headquarters in UK. The company had a range of non-durable (FMCG) products like detergents, soaps, hair oil, cold cream, shaving cream, and shampoo. The company's products and brands had good reputation in Indian and international markets. The company's manufacturing plants were located at Ahmadabad (Gujarat), Kolkata (West Bengal) and Mumbai (Maharashtra). The physical distribution of the company's products was carried out, as shown in Exhibit 1.

Exhibit 1

Physical Distribution of the Products

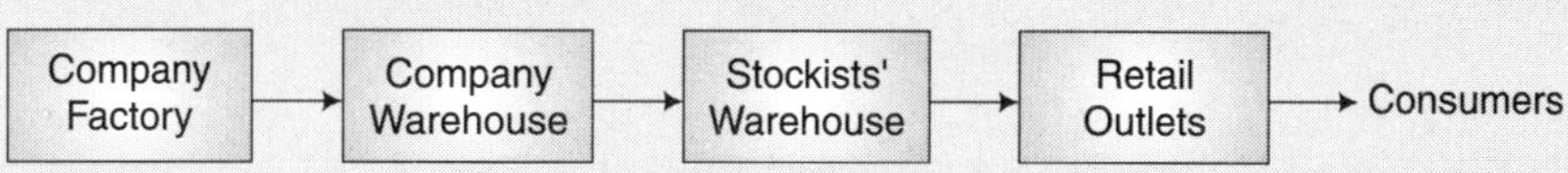

*This case was prepared under the guidance of Prof. Krishna K. Havaldar by Sudheendra Joshi, alumnus of Alliance Business Academy, Bengaluru, for classroom discussion.

The stockists were selected by SKJ Company for different geographical areas and were responsible for covering all retail outlets in specified geographical areas. Each stockist had employed a group of salespersons who were responsible to book orders from the retail outlets. The stockist's salesperson was assigned a number of retail outlets which he was required to visit once a week. The retail outlets (also called the retail environment) consisted of retail shops, such as *kirana* stores (also called convenience or provision stores), general stores, departmental stores and even *pan*-shops. The stockists had agreements (or contracts) with SKJ Company' to exclusively redistribute the company products and not to deal with competitors' products.

Products manufactured at various factories of SKJ Company were dispatched to the centrally located regional warehouses of the company. From the company's warehouses the goods were shipped to the warehouses of various stockists, based on the orders obtained by the company's sales executives.

SALES ORGANIZATION

The company had a typical geographic sales organization, as shown in Exhibit 2. The sales function was headed by Vice President (VP) Sales. Regional sales managers who handled different states reported to VP (Sales). Area sales managers who looked after different districts within a state reported to regional sales managers, while sales executives who were assigned different cities reported to the area sales manager. The sales target set for VP (Sales) was divided into different states, districts, and cities in a top-down approach in a goal setting meeting which was normally held in January of every year. Each person in the sales structure was responsible for achieving his target. Sales executives were directly responsible for field selling activities, and looked after a set of stockists in assigned cities or towns.

Exhibit 2

SKJ Company's Sales Organisation Structure

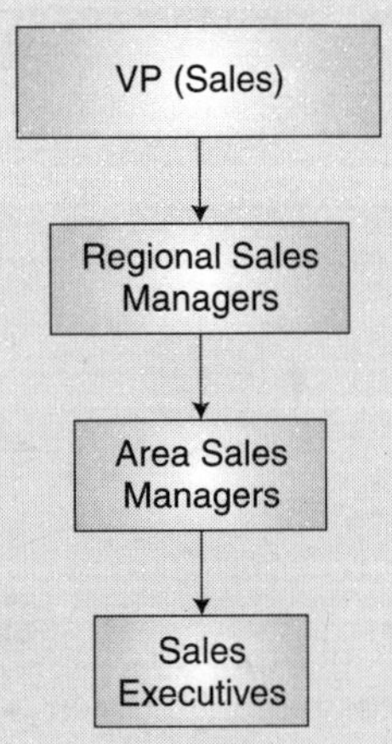

RESPONSIBILITIES OF SALES EXECUTIVES

The major responsibilities of sales executives were as follows:

- **Task Responsibility:** The task responsibility was achieving the quarterly and yearly targets, which included among the other parameters product-wise sales volumes and total sales value. The performance evaluation of the sales executive was done based on the yearly targets and the incentives were paid depending upon the quarterly performance in relation to quarterly goals. Promotion and increment decisions of sales executives were determined by their yearly performance against qualitative and quantitative goals.
- **Salesmen Training and Development:** Some other responsibilities of the sales executives consisted of training stockists' salespersons in selling skills, routing plan (to reduce travel time and increase selling time), and rearranging the shelves of retailers to improve visibility of the company's product categories. "If the salespeople do postman like calls on retailers then achieving the company's set targets would become a nightmare," said Anant Kumar, while stressing the importance of salesmen training and development.
- **Mandated Assortment:** It meant placing the right product category in the right retail shop based on market importance and demand. This would ensure that retailers' money was not blocked by holding stocks of unsold product categories. It also included ensuring "market hygiene", i.e., taking back damaged or time-expired goods from retail stores.
- **Field Promotions:** The sales executive should also ensure that the stockists implemented sales promotions and "visibility elements" in an effective manner. The visibility elements included posters, billboards (or hoardings), and hangers that were put up at the retail outlets, for which the company paid to those retailers who supported field sales promotions.

Anant Kumar thought that he performed all the above tasks in the past 3 months, ever since he completed the initial training program. SKJ Company conducted the initial training program for all sales executives who were recruited from leading management institutes. Anant was satisfied with the 3 months' training program which included classroom and on-the-job training. The company had announced quarterly incentive scheme that was linked to the sales executive's performance on achievement of sales targets and responsibilities. Senior sales and marketing executives of the company had explained to the sales trainees about the leadership position of many of the company's brands in the market.

During the past two monthly meetings of sales executives with the area sales manager, it was noticed that only 1 (out of 6 sales executives) had achieved the sales goals. Various issues like field promotions, mandated assortment, and salesmen training were discussed in the meetings. Anant Kumar was not sure what corrective steps were needed to improve his performance.

CASE QUESTIONS

1. What might be the reasons for unsatisfactory performance of Anant Kumar?
2. If you were the area sales manager, what would you do to improve the sales performance of the sales executives?

Case 8

Metal Products India Ltd.*

LOSING SALES TO NEW ENTRANTS

"Shekhar, it is high time we did something to arrest the losses in our business volume in Karnataka," urged Bhatia, President of Metal Products India Ltd. (MPIL).

"Yes Sir, I do appreciate your concern and shall certainly do something before it is too late," was the pensive reply from Marketing Manager, Shekhar.

COMPANY HISTORY AND BACKGROUND

MPIL was one of the leading manufacturers of mild steel (MS) metal sections widely used in construction, furniture, rolling shutters, and industrial sheds. The factory was located at Whitefield, on the outskirts of Bengaluru.

The market for metal sections was highly fragmented. In and around Bangalore, there were four manufacturers of metal sections. MPIL was setup in 2004 by its parent company, Madhya Bharath Metal Sections Ltd. (MBMS), Bhilai, mainly to serve the southern markets. Before this unit was set up, material was being supplied to dealers/customers in South India directly from Bhilai. The advantages perceived by the promoters in setting up MPIL were substantial savings in freight coupled with better availability of material from the dealers' perspective. Prior to 2004, there was only one manufacture of metal sections at Bengaluru, viz., Karnataka Metal Sections (KMS). Between 2007 and 2010, two more manufacturers set up their units at Bengaluru, viz., Adarsh Metals (AM) and Mahavir Metals Sections (MMS).

The total size of the market for metal sections in South India in 2012 was estimated at 70,000 metric tonnes (MT) with an annual growth rate of around 6 percent. Karnataka accounted for about 20 percent of this.

---

*This case is prepared by Dr. Shailendra Dasari, Executive Director, Sathavahana Ispat Limited, for only classroom discussion.

DISTRIBUTION CHANNEL

MPIL had tied up with the existing dealers of MBMS for distributing their products. MBMS had dealers at all the important locations in the south. However, in Karnataka they had only one dealer—Bangalore Metal Traders (BMT)—based at Bengaluru.

Apart from making use of the existing distribution channel of MBMS, MPIL also appointed new dealers at other emerging centers such as Vijayawada, Calicut, and Erode. Most of the dealers supplied metal sections in smaller lots to customers, who were mostly fabricators and small-scale industries. Apart from this, some of the dealers also operated through sub-dealers. Prices applicable to dealers were decided by manufacturers and the dealers usually marked up the prices by 7 percent to 8 percent. The prices at which dealers operated were not controlled by manufacturers and were decided solely at the discretion of the dealers. Depending on the off-take, dealers were offered volume discounts by manufacturers varying from 3 percent to 7 percent. The current ex-factory price of metal sections was ₹44,000/MT on an average, on which volume and cash discounts were offered by manufacturers.

In addition to distributing the products through dealer network, MPIL also sold their products directly to OEMS (Original Equipment Manufacturers) and government customers. However, this added up to only 20 to 25 percent of their total sales, as was the case with other manufacturers.

To support the dealers, MPIL had opened depots (i.e., warehouses) at Chennai, Coimbatore, Ernakulam, and Hyderabad.

MARKET STRUCTURE

Bangalore Metal Trader (BMT) was the largest dealer of metal sections in South India with an off-take of 4500 MT per annum, which was about 30 percent of MPIL's production. By virtue of their off-take, they enjoyed the highest slab of volume discount offered by the company. As per the understanding with BMT, MPIL was not expected to appoint dealers at other centers in Karnataka. However, there was no formal written agreement which debarred the company from appointing dealers at other stations.

Prior to the entry of Adarsh Metals (AM) and Mahavir Metal Sections (MMS), BMT enjoyed almost 50 percent share of the market in Karnataka. In view of the informal agreement with the company to not appoint dealers at other stations in Karnataka, BMT did not patronize other manufacturers and dealt exclusively with the products of MPIL. KMS had a dealer at Bengaluru named Kavery Agencies, which had branches at other major centers in Karnataka. Prior to the entry of AM and MMS, the combined market share of MPIL and KMS in Karnataka was about 75 percent.

STRATEGY OF NEW ENTRANTS

AM and MMS found it difficult to compete with BMT and Kavery Agencies, which were well-established in the market and had exclusive arrangements with their principals. To penetrate the market, AM and MMS adopted a different strategy, by offering materials directly to customers in Bangalore, though it was not as cost effective as selling through dealers, and the risk involved was also larger. In the upcountry markets, they identified prominent local traders of steel, hardware, and allied products and offered the same discounts as offered by MPIL and KMS to their major dealers. The new entrants succeeded in attracting the hardware dealers at locations like Mysure, Hubballi, Ballari, and Belagavi.

Most of the upcountry hardware dealers were the erstwhile sub-dealers of BMT. Out of the volume discount of 7 percent offered by the company, BMT used to keep 3 percent for themselves and pass on the balance 4 percent to the sub-dealers. To break the stronghold of BMT and Kavery Agencies, the new entrants started offering discounts of 6 to 7 percent to upcountry sub-dealers who found it more comfortable to deal directly with the manufactures instead of being sub-dealers of BMT.

PRESENT PROBLEM

The aggressive marketing strategy adopted by the new entrants resulted in the loss of business volume for MPIL on account of reduced off-take by BMT. As compared to 4450 MT lifted by BMT in 2011–12, during the first six months of the year 2012–13, their off-take was only 1900 MT. Though the drop in sales volume was noticed by Bhatia during the first quarter itself, in the quarterly review meeting, Shekhar attributed this to the recessionary trends prevalent in the market and the poor performance of the economy as a whole. However, this did not satisfy Bhatia on whose insistence Shekhar undertook an extensive tour of Karnataka along with the representative of BMT, and found to his dismay that in Hubli and Belgaum, two of the major markets in North Karnataka, they did not enjoy even 30 percent of the market share, whereas the new entrants had captured more than 50 percent of the market. North Karnataka accounted for about 20 percent of the total sales of metal sections in Karnataka. Most of the hardware dealers who were erstwhile sub-dealers of BMT, had been appointed as the authorized dealers of AM and MMS. However, they had not altogether stopped dealing with BMT, though the dealings were largely confined to ordering those sizes that were not readily available with AM and MMS. When this was pointed out to Bhatia, he advised Shekhar to come out with a suitable strategy to recapture the market in north Karnataka. Attempts by Shekhar and representatives of BMT to get the sub-dealers back to their fold by emphasizing on the superior quality of their product compared to the competitors and offering special incentives subject to certain guaranteed off-take did not yield the desired results, leaving Shekhar, who had been given the ultimatum by Bhatia, a frustrated man.

Case 9

Syndiant Ltd.*

GETTING BUSINESS FOR IT SERVICES

Dheeraj Shah, Vice President, Syndiant Ltd., was concerned to find 20 percent decline in the order booking in the first and second quarters as compared to the company's order booking target. He wondered where the company had gone wrong in the process of getting business from the clients located mainly in the US and Europe. He wanted to know if the business model for IT (information technology) Marketing and Sales (ITMS), which was developed by the company earlier (shown in Exhibit 1), was still valid, or it needed any changes. In any case, Dheeraj thought that something should be done to ensure that target of 30 percent growth in order booking and sales would be achieved in the third and fourth quarters.

COMPANY BACKGROUND

Syndiant Ltd. was a global information technology (IT) solutions and services firm with offices in India, USA, and Europe. The company had 40 salespeople in the US and Europe and 40 more sales and marketing people in India.

SERVICES OFFERED

Some of the services offered by the company were:

- Application management.
- Testing
- Digital
- Business Process
- Analytics
- Infrastructure management.

The people who had expertise in the above mentioned services were known as solution experts or technology experts, and were a part of horizontals. They were located in India.

---

*This case was prepared by Prof. Krishna K. Havaldar for classroom discussion based on the case data provided by Umakant Narkhede, MBA student of Alliance Business School, Bengaluru.

Exhibit 1

I.T. Marketing and Sales (ITMS) Model

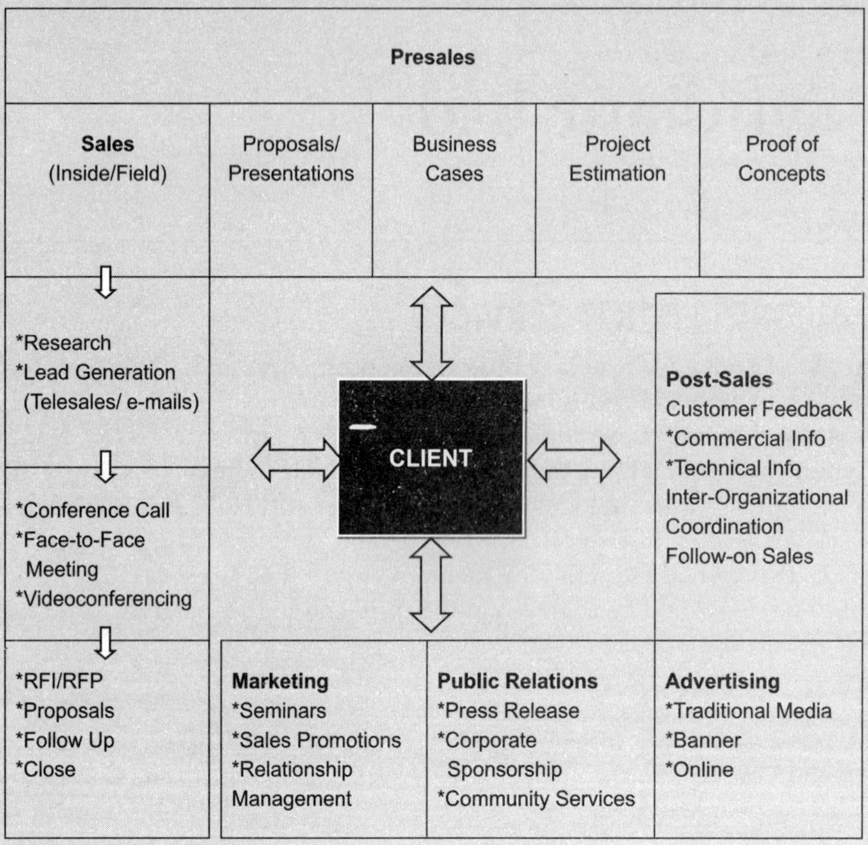

TARGET MARKET SEGMENTS

The senior management team carried out a study on market segmentation, based on which the company focused on the following target market segments:

- Finance and Insurance
- Telecommunication
- Retailing
- Pharmaceutical and Healthcare
- Manufacturing and Logistics

SALES TEAM

The sales team in Syndiant Ltd. consisted of two groups. One group, called inside (or offshore), including salespeople, were located in India. The second group consisted of field (or onshore) salespeople, who were located at the US, and Europe. Inside sales group generated sales leads by using telephones (i.e., telemarketing) and e-mails. These sales leads were passed onto the second group i.e. field (or onshore) salespeople, who contacted the leads (also called probable prospects) on phone, conference calls, or face-to-face meetings. The field salespeople in the US and Europe would first qualify the leads to the prospects or potential customers based on the level of their interest in the services being sold and their financial capacity.

About 4 to 5 percent of sales leads were interested to go to the next level, which included request for information (RFI), and/or request for proposal (RFP). The prospect evaluated the vendor by seeking a detailed information (RFI) about the vendor's infrastructure, technologies, expertise, products, services, and so on. RFP was made when the prospect evaluated the vendor for a particular need of IT outsourcing, such as Business process or Analytics. The prospect typically obtained proposals or offers from a number of vendors and finalized the project on one vendor after evaluation and negotiations. Dheeraj looked up the company statistics, and was concerned to find that the conversion ratio of the projects obtained to the proposals submitted was around 10 percent in 2015–16, as compared to about 15 to 20 percent in the previous years. He wondered whether this was due to the increase in competition.

COMPETITION

Large IT firms like IBM and H.P., who were competitors to Syndiant Ltd., had invested in offshore presence in India, China, and Brazil to become cost competitive with local IT firms. At one time, Indian IT firms like Syndiant had cost advantage, which helped them to secure more projects and to have higher conversion ratio. Besides the global and large IT firms spent more money on promotion to build their brand image. Their large investment on promotion included advertisements in online and offline journals, magazines, and newspapers and participation in trade shows and exhibitions. This gave them an edge over many Indian IT firms.

MARKETING TEAM

In Syndiant Ltd., the marketing team gave support to the sales team by carrying out certain activities like company advertising, seminars, sales promotions, brochures, public relations, and relationship management. These were mainly the promotional activities, which not only helped in brand building but also in generation of leads. Dheeraj Shah noticed that the lead generation had also declined. He thought whether the company was performing adequately in lead generation as well as converting the leads to the proposals and from the proposals to the orders (or projects). He was not sure whether the IT MS model needed any changes.

Dheeraj decided to call a meeting of the heads of the various teams like sales, marketing, presales, and post-sales to discuss and decide future course of actions.

CASE QUESTIONS

1. What should the company do to increase lead generation?
2. What are the corrective actions needed to improve the conversion ratio of the orders received to the proposals submitted?
3. Do you suggest any changes in the IT MS model?

Case 10

Electrical Equipment Ltd.*

NEGOTIATING WITH A KEY ACCOUNT

In February 2015, Bholanath Dutta, Regional Marketing Manager—Eastern Region (RMM—E) of Electrical Equipment Ltd. (EEL) was reviewing the company's offer with his Sales Engineer, Pradeep Dasgupta, before meeting the General Manager (Materials) of Voltas Ltd. EEL had earlier submitted a quotation for the supply of 10 numbers of flame-proof motors to the Kolkata branch of Voltas Ltd. Voltas had obtained an order for supplying and installing 10 numbers of pump-sets from Eastern Coalfields, against a tender at a competitive price. Voltas had also agreed for a penalty clause in case of a delay in supply and installation of pump-sets beyond May 31, 2015, at the rate of 0.5 percent per week of the undelivered portion of the order value, with a ceiling of 10 percent.

PREPARATION FOR THE MEETING

Pradeep informed Bholanath that the General Manager—Materials (GM—M) of Voltas was known as a tough negotiator. Bholanath realized that apart from a competitive price, faster delivery, and good past performance, supplier–buyer relationship would play an important role in bagging the order worth ₹10,00,000. Pradeep had established a good relationship with purchase, finance, and project people working at the Kolkata office of Voltas, considering the fact that Voltas was an important (key) OEM (original equipment manufacturer) customer to EEL for electrical motors, with a sales potential of ₹15 million per year. Pradeep had met Murli Bhasin, GM (Materials) of Voltas only once earlier as Mr. Bhasin was transferred to Kolkata from Delhi office of Voltas in January 2015.

Pradeep informed Bholanath that against EEL's offer of 10-weeks' delivery, Voltas may insist on eight weeks. Regarding the specifications of flame-proof motors and the past performance, all the short-listed suppliers were almost on par. The competing firms were Siemens, ABB, and Kirloskar, all of whom had a good reputation on quality and performance of motors.

EEL had quoted a competitive price for a 40 HP, 1,400 rpm, flame-proof motor, to work in underground coal mines, coupled with the centrifugal pump of Voltas, to make it as a pump-

*This case was prepared by Prof. Krishna K Havaldar for classroom discussion.

set. The pump-sets were to be installed latest by May 31, 2015, before the onset of rains, for removing the accumulated water in the underground mines. The designs of flame-proof motors were custom-made to avoid any explosion that might take place if the inflammable gases came in contact with a spark in the motor. These motors were to be designed and manufactured as per relevant Indian standards. The market for flame-proof or explosion-proof motors was served by the reputed manufacturers such EEL, Siemens, ABB, and Kirolskar. There was hardly any competition from small-scale motor manufacturers.

EEL had given a volume discount of 20 percent on the basic price, in the quotation, to Voltas. In addition, Bholanath was allowed a discretionary discount of up to 5 percent for negotiation by the Marketing Manager located at Mumbai. The Marketing Manager agreed to give further 7 percent discount to Bholanath and assured to improve on delivery from 10 weeks to 8 weeks despite the application of the penalty clause.

NEGOTIATION

Armed with the necessary authorization from the head office, Bholanath and Pradeep arrived at the Voltas office five minutes before the appointed time for the meeting with the GM (Materials). Bholanath sent in his visiting card, and after receiving the nod from Murli Bhasin's secretary, he entered the meeting room along with Pradeep. With a smile on his face, he said "Good afternoon, Gentlemen, I am Bholanath Dutta from Electrical Equipment Ltd. and this is my colleague, Pradeep Dasgupta." Murli Bhasin extended his hand to welcome Bholanath and Pradeep and introduced himself and his Project Manager and Purchase Executive. "Well, you have been one of our key suppliers of electrical equipment, and we value the long-term relationship between our organizations. This is the reason we have called you first amongst the various suppliers of flame-proof motors. We have received the order for the supply and installation of 10 numbers of pump-sets from Eastern Coalfields, despite a stiff competition on price and delivery. I would like to know what best can you offer for your motors, which should be better than your quoted price and delivery," said Murli Bhasin coming straight to the point. There was a pause after which Bholanath responded, "Thank you for considering EEL as one of your key suppliers. We too value our long-term relationship and we assure you to work together to resolve your problems, not only for this order, but also for all the future orders, so that both the organizations are benefited. Now, coming to the present issue of Eastern Coalfields order, I would like to know what are your expectations on price and delivery. However, before we come to the important issue on the price, may I suggest that we discuss other matters related to delivery, freight, transit insurance, installation, warranty, and after-sales service?"

Murli Bhasin looked at his Project Manager and after getting his nod, remarked, "OK, let us first discuss other issues and then come to the pricing matter. We want the delivery to commence in four weeks from the date of the order at the rate of two or three motors per week, and completion in eight weeks, failing which penalty will be applicable at the rate of 0.5 percent per week. The freight is to be borne by you from your Mumbai factory to our factory at Kolkata, and transit insurance will be covered under our open policy. Is this acceptable to you?" Bholanath responded, "Well, we shall meet your delivery completion date of eight weeks and also penalty clause of 0.5 percent per week with a ceiling of 10 percent on the undelivered value of the order. Delivery will commence in six to seven weeks and we will deliver all the 10 motors in one or two full truck-load to avoid any damage or delays that may take place if we dispatched part truck-load consisting of 2 or 3 motors only. I hope you appreciate the problem of part truck-load and the long distance between Mumbai and Kolkata. As regards bearing the freight cost, we would have to incur an additional cost that would be about 3 to 4 percent of the sales revenue. We agree to your proposal of bearing the freight cost, but keeping in mind its impact on the price. I hope, you understand our point of view."

"Yes, yes, we understand and appreciate your points, but at the same time you should also appreciate that we have bagged this order in the face of tough competition at a very low price and low margins. Now, tell us about warranty period, after-sales service, and installation service arrangement for the motors," said Murli Bhasin. Bholanath observed the body language of the GM, paused for a moment, and responded slowly, "Well, we are aware that your margins are low and we would like to assure you that we will also keep our margins thin, so that both of us make some profits in this order. We shall give you 12 months' warranty from the date of installation or 18 months' warranty from the date of dispatch of motors, whichever is earlier. If you need any help in installation, we shall give it free of charge, although we have quoted for only supply of motors. During the warranty period our service will be free, but later on, Eastern Coalfields will have to pay for any services or repairs. I hope this is okay."

"Yes, it is acceptable to us," said Murli Bhasin, "and now let us discuss how much discount you can give us. You have already given us 20 percent discount on the basic price. We need further 15 percent discount to make your prices competitive. If you agree to our proposal, I will finalize the order now with you. If not, I shall negotiate with other reputed motor manufacturers and then take an appropriate decision." Bholanath looked at Pradeep and then requested the Voltas team to give a break for about 15 minutes to discuss the matter before conveying their decision. The Voltas team agreed.

Bholanath asked Pradeep's opinion on the discount particularly because he had the approval of his boss to give a maximum of 12 percent discount, whereas Voltas had asked for 15 percent. Pradeep said he was not sure whether the GM (Materials) was telling the truth. However, Pradeep was keen to get this order in view of long-term relationship with this important OEM. After the break, Bholanath informed the Voltas team that EEL could give further a maximum of 12 percent discount if the entire order for 10 number motors was placed on them. Murli Bhasin remarked, "Well, you are forcing us to negotiate with others. We shall inform you about our decision in about 3 to 4 days. Thank you for coming over and the meaningful discussion." Bholanath and Pradeep shook hands and thanked all the negotiating members of the Voltas team.

While driving back to their office, Bholanath wondered whether they would get the order, and remarked to Pradeep whether they could have employed any other options while dealing with a key account like Voltas.

CASE QUESTIONS

1. Are you satisfied with the way Bholanath had conducted the negotiations with Voltas? Justify your answer.
2. If you were the regional marketing manager of EEL how differently would you have handled the key account like Voltas for getting this order?

Case 11

Sunshine Lumieres Pvt. Ltd.*

RESTRUCTURING SALES AND DISTRIBUTION ORGANIZATION

Sunshine Lumieres was established in 1992 in Bengaluru, India, to manufacture lamps mainly for household use. The company was established by Dr. Srinath Kashyap who had extensive experience in the lamp industry with the major multinational manufacturers in India and overseas.

Sunshine was involved till now in manufacturing and supplying lamps for consumer and household use under various brands for the leading lamp companies. Dr. Kashyap was involved in looking after the manufacturing and marketing functions while his wife looked after the Finance and the HR functions. The company had a total of 50 employees and grossed revenue of ₹9 crore (₹90 million) in 2005.

The market in India was large and growing due to the increasing affluence and the massive rural electrification programs of the government. Post the liberalization in 1992, the market dynamics slowly started changing due to increased competition from leading brands looking to capture larger market shares. Dr. Kashyap felt it was time to diversify this business and get into newer product segments.

The lamp industry can be classified into various segments like:

- Consumer household Lamps
- Industrial and commercial lamps
- Specialty lamps like high-intensity lamps used in medical and office equipment
- Automotive lamps
- Miniature lamps
- Energy efficient lamps like CFL lamps, LED lamps, etc.

While the large MNCs were present in all segments, most local manufacturers were involved in consumer and household lighting. Typically, household lamps were sold at around US$ 0.25 per piece at the retail level while the industrial and commercial lamps were sold at prices upwards of US$ 25 per piece retail.

*This case has been prepared by B. S. Sachidanand for classroom discussions. Any real-life resemblance to the characters in the case is purely accidental.

Sunshine Lumieres hired Dr. Mohan Das, a bright Engineer from IIT and a MBA from a leading business school. After working in some leading companies, Mohan felt it was time for him to exploit his innovative skills and create world class products. In a very short span of time after joining Sunshine, Dr. Das was able to produce some very interesting and technologically advanced products.

Early in 2004, Sunshine was approached by leading global players interested in sourcing products from Sunshine for the European and American markets. These markets were large, but almost saturated, with demand coming mainly for replacements. Although this would guarantee large and assured business, Sunshine would have to compromise on margins. Also, the products would have to be offered under the sourcing companies' brands and these companies were sticklers for deliveries.

Around this time, Mohan met his old friend Sachin Sharma, also a fellow alumnus from his business school. Sachin had spent many years in Africa and Europe with India's largest companies and had an excellent understanding of the international markets and had a large number of contacts. Sachin had just returned to India after his overseas assignments and was looking for a suitable opportunity. He suggested to Mohan that he could help Sunshine export their products to Africa, where he had some good contacts. He was willing to work on a commission basis on the business he delivered.

The African markets were small, but were mainly for household lighting only. This market was highly price sensitive as the products from China dominated the market. The distribution was done through family-owned electrical stores. The market for industrial lighting was minimal as there were very few industries. Street lighting was the purview of the municipalities who procured by tenders only. Some local agents virtually controlled this market. Although the MNCs dominated these markets too, using a good agent, it would be possible to enter this market. Sachin's contacts in this area could be of great help. Sunshine could sell their products under their own brand in these markets.

Dr. Kashyap felt that over time, in low-value products like lamps, the large MNCs would be forced to give way to players from developing countries like China and India, who would eventually establish the products under their own brands. Establishing the Sunshine brand in due course was therefore vital for the future.

Meanwhile, Mohan had designed a slew of new and innovative products—comparable with the best in their class in the world, in the energy efficient and industrial lamp categories. Given suitable financial investments, these could take the company's revenues to over ₹100 crore (₹1000 million) by 2008 between the domestic and export markets.

As he looked out of his office window, enjoying the light drizzle and cool breeze of Bengaluru, Dr. Kashyap realized that he was at a point of inflection. If the current opportunities were exploited fully, it could lead to great fortunes for himself and his family. He could even take the company public and unlock the value of his holdings. However, it would also mean that Sunshine would have to evolve into a professionally managed company and have a larger number of employees. He wondered how he should go about structuring his Sales and Distribution organization so as to grow manifold both domestically and overseas within the next three years before taking the company public.

With the rapid growth of the Internet and easy and affordable communications, access to information and or suppliers or buyers globally was quick and at very low cost. With India's profile becoming more visible after the IT boom, a large number of overseas buyers were considering sourcing from India. Also, with wages rising in China, it was no longer as competitive as they were earlier, and Indian companies could match the Chinese in terms of quality and price. This offered an unprecedented opportunity for Sunshine to grow. However, Dr. Kashyap's children who were married and settled in good jobs did not show interest in joining the business. This put Dr. Srinath in a quandary as to what he should do now.

Dr. Kashyap was convinced that he needed to seek professional advice. He invited Dr. Vasant Rao, an old friend and a leading management expert in Bengaluru to visit his office for a discussion on a broad game plan.

CASE QUESTIONS

1. How Dr. Kashyap should go about professionalizing and restructuring his organization?
2. Should Sunshine opt to sell out to a larger company or at least sell a substantial stake in the company to an established player in the industry?
3. How should Sunshine exploit the advantage of the Internet?
4. Which areas should Dr. Kashyap focus on first?
5. Should Dr. Kashyap have separate departments/personnel for each category of products?
6. Should the sales be organized on geographic or product basis?
7. Should the distribution be common for all products?
8. Should Dr. Kashyap have his own Sales and Distribution organizations in some countries?
9. Should domestic and export organizations be separate?
10. Should Dr. Kashyap prepare an exit strategy since he has no successors? What options should he explore?

Case 12

Taurus Analytical Solutions Ltd.*

It was first week of March 2009, when the CEO of the Taurus Analytical Solutions Ltd., Phillip Kutty, called for a meeting of the marketing manager, the human resource manager, the finance manager and the business development manager to critically analyze the problems faced by the company and to find a way forward. Sales of the company were bleak and the pipeline of projects for the next financial year, 2009–10, seemed almost dry, with only 4 long-term projects from key accounts. The company had witnessed 50 percent dip in the sales and its profit figure showed just US $5 million when compared to the previous year's profit of US $10 million. The Marketing Manager, Arun Mehta, met with varied prospective clients over the last 6 months especially in the US, but even after persuasive selling there were no fresh projects coming in for the current year primarily because of unfavorable economic conditions in the US. The company had created key account teams with separate and dedicated working units for the four key clients with which it had contracts for the long-term projects. Except for the key accounts, other clients who had promised to provide new projects backed out stating certain economic and political reasons. Arpana Sharma, the Human Resource Manager, had pursued the manpower planning, taking into consideration the expected projects and thus recruited domain people from various research and management institutes. As the company had already provided them the offer letters and mentioned the joining dates, it was not in a position to back out from its promises. This new batch was to join by the mid of March 2009 and further it had to be trained for the next 3 months. Given the above environment, the CEO was concerned about how would the company be able to increase its sales and justify its expenditure, the failure of which would push the company into considerable loss.

COMPANY

Taurus Analytical Solutions Ltd. provided services of sales and marketing analytics, and business consulting for the pharmaceutical and healthcare industries. Since its inception in the year 2004, it had worked in 290 therapeutic disease areas and had around 700 employees. Although

*This case was prepared under the guidance of Prof. Krishna K. Havaldar by Srujana H.M. and Soumya Patil, MBA students of Alliance Business Academy, Bengaluru, for classroom discussion.

headquartered in Bengaluru, it had client offices in the US and European countries. All of its clients were from the western world, primarily from the US. The company provided the core analytical services such as competitive intelligence, sales forecasting, predictive modeling, suggesting suitable marketing mix, branding and positioning strategies, and developing suitable patient monitoring and data collecting tools for the top 50 pharmaceutical companies. The company's services addressed decision-making, strategic planning and the routine business needs of the customers, across geographies, both at headquarters and affiliate levels.

Taurus Analytical Solutions provided holistic services in population-based epidemiological study analysis, pharmaco-epidemiological study analysis, feasibility studies for clinical trials, and epidemiology database applications. The company supported epidemiology, marketing research, and outcomes research groups in plugging the epidemiological data gaps they might have with reference to patient-based models, especially in the emerging markets. Taurus identified cost-effective sources of secondary data and the research publications that provided estimates, and wherever feasible, validate those against other sources and its physician network to deliver evidence-based disease estimates.

Exhibit 1

Services offered by Taurus Analytical Solutions

Sl. No.	Services Provided	Applications	Niche Market
1	Marketing Analytics	Marketing research, marketing mix, STP with reference to patient based models.	US
2	Sales Analytics	Sales forecasting, sales automation, and sales effectiveness.	US, UK
3	Forecasting	Business development and product forecasts for planning and development.	US
4	Modeling	Predictive and analytical models based on the historical client data.	UK, US
5	Software tool development	Knowledge management, CRM databases.	US

PRICING STRATEGY

Even though Taurus was based in a developing country, India, it was unable to generate business from this market and primarily relied on western markets, i.e., the US and certain European countries. Their services were high priced and were suitable for premium customers. Arun was of the opinion that Indian pharmaceutical companies did not require the kind of services that Taurus provided because of the following reasons:

- The pharmaceutical sector in India was still in a nascent stage and thus these pharmaceutical companies were not in need of sophisticated and niche services provided by Taurus.
- Indian pharma companies cannot afford and may not be willing to pay the premium service charges of Taurus.

As the pipeline had almost gone dry now the company was introspecting on its segmentation strategy to boost its sales.

EXTERNAL ENVIRONMENT

Since the major business of the company is generated from the US, the prospects of the company were considerably influenced by the policy and economic framework of health care sector in the US. United States historically had given a huge emphasis on the development of health care sector. It had numerous, conducive public policies like medical expenditure reimbursement and insurance policy coverage to the general public. The reimbursement was up to 100 percent for the chronic diseases. This gave a huge boost to healthcare and pharmaceutical industries in the US. Thus, all the pharmaceutical companies including the pharmaceutical-analytical companies showed an impressive growth and profits till 2008. However in 2008, due to economic downturn or recession, the US economy was worst hit with its repercussions being felt in pharmaceutical-analytical companies like Taurus Analytical Solutions. In addition to this, the US Government wanted to reduce its health care burden, which was increased due to non-conducive demographics, i.e., decrease in the population of working class and increase in the population of old aged and dependent infants. In this regard the US Government decided to reduce the government medical reimbursement to only 75 percent; this non-conducive political development had considerable negative impact on the healthcare and consequently on analytical industry, which was deeply felt by Taurus.

COMPETITION

Taurus Analytical Solutions faced considerable competition from players across the globe, with two major competitors located and operating in the same geographical region in which this company operated. As the company was midsized and comparatively new, the competitors enjoyed a greater market share. The developed economies posed a good market for the pharmaceutical analytical companies, and hence all the competitors focused on increasing the market share in the specified geographical locations like UK and the US, thereby increasing the competition.

DIVERSIFICATION STRATEGY

The company thought of diversifying into other markets like Japan and China, but its efforts were not successful primarily because Japan, being highly conservative nation, posed the entry barrier and China specifically posed the language barrier.

Traditionally regulated market such as European Union was backing generics and bio-similars (i.e., biologic mimics of off-patent biologic drugs) with conducive policies. On the contrary, the US was undergoing intense negotiations with varied stakeholders for the standardization of the bio-similars and generic policies. This had considerable negative impact on the sales and revenues of pharmaceutical industry and consequently influenced the pharmaceutical analytical industry.

Now the marketing manager was in a dilemma as to what should be the sales and marketing strategies for the next year, so as to boost the sales. He wondered whether the company should increase sales efforts in the rapidly growing markets or build effective strategies for marketing the services in the domestic market in view of existing macro environmental issues.

CASE QUESTIONS

1. Analyze the economic environment in the financial year 2008–09, and its impact on the pharmaceutical and healthcare industries as well as on Taurus Analytical Solutions.
2. What should be the sales and marketing strategies of the marketing manager to boost the sales of the company in the recessionary economy?

Case 13

GlobeSec Ltd.*

Khurshid Patell, VP-Marketing of GlobeSec Ltd. Looked at the letter in his hand again. It was from his old friend, Ganesh Pillai, owner of Ganesh Pillai & Sons (GPS), Trivandrum.

GPS was an 80 year old firm in Trivandrum. It was set up by the grandfather of the present owner. They were dealers in hardware and security systems and had exclusive stores, salesmen and vans for Globesec products in the districts of Trivanrum, Kollam and Pathanamthitta. They were the biggest contributors to Globesec's sales in Kerala supplying to other retailers and institutional buyers like builders and interior decorators. GPS was able to ride the growing construction wave early and had a high share of the market for locks and security systems in Kerala for Globesec's range.

Lately, there has been a spate of cheap imports from China. Dealers were clamouring for cheaper prices from GlobeSec but Globesec has been insisting on their quality and stepped up their promotional campaigns and participation in building material exhibitions. Patell was confident that their new 'GSLite' range, as a price warrior, will withstand the Chinese threat. Due to lower margins on this range, GlobeSec was offering a lower commission to the dealers. Before launch, Patell was even contemplating selling this range directly to key accounts like large builders.

It is at this stage that Nakul Kumar of Nakul Constructions (NCC) approached him with the idea of direct purchase of locks for his new multistory projects in Trivandrum and other cities. When he assured a minimum off take GlobeSec products in spite of attractive offers from direct Chinese exporters, Patell agreed. At least two orders were executed in the last 4 weeks.

Patell was expecting reactions from the Kerala dealers and the letter from , Ganesan Pillai was the first salvo. Ganesan Pillai had accused him of betraying the dealers, especially GPS who had done a lot of ground work introducing GlobeSec products in Kerala 22 years ago. He was particularly annoyed because NCC had held back ₹1,20,000 to GPS for locks supplied in the last 5 years on some ground or the other. There was veiled threat in the letter that all the dealers may boycott GlobeSec products and may opt to stock competitors' products.

Patell once again read the letter before putting it into his pocket. He decided to discuss this with his consultant Chandra when he meets him at the Presidency Golf course the next day.

If you were Chandra what would you advise Khurshid Patell?

---

* Case prepared by Prof. V. Harihara Subramanian based on real life experiences modified for class room teaching of management concepts and practices.

Glossary of Key Terms

- **360-degree feedback** It is one of the increasingly popular performance assessment techniques wherein the company gets evaluative feedback from an employee, his or her peers, subordinates, superiors, and customers (applicable for salespeople).
- **Absorption training** This includes supplying product manuals, books, articles, and CDs to salespeople, who read (or absorb) these materials without immediate questioning or feedback.
- **Accommodation** This refers to the style of conflict resolution indicating abject surrender by one party to the dispute.
- **Accordion theory** The theory of evolution of retail outlets from general to specific to general to meet customer needs.
- **Activity quotas** These are goals set for job-related activities of salespeople that are useful for achieving their performance targets.
- **Administered VMS** One channel leader in the channel network influences and controls the other channel partners.
- **Aggression** It is the style of conflict resolution where one channel member is concerned with his own goals without any concern for the goals of other channel partners—a selfish approach.
- **Agility** The ability of the channel to handle changing demand patterns without additional effort or cost.
- **Air consignment note (ACN)** It is the receipt for transport of goods by air.
- **Anticipation inventory** Inventory built up to take care of future requirements.
- **Application blank** It is a convenient and systematic method of collecting relevant information from the applicant in a form. It is also called **formal application form** or **personal-history record**.
- **Approach** It is one of the steps or stages of the selling process in which the salesperson meets the prospective buyer for the first time.
- **Arbitration** This refers to using a third party to resolve the conflict between the two channel partners.
- **Assessment center** It is a centralized unit of a company that evaluates job applicants and employees in a uniform and comprehensive manner, by asking candidates to perform simulated exercises like role-play, case analysis, business games, and individual presentation.

❍ **Assimilation** It is the second stage of socialization process, which begins when the applicant accepts the job offer made by the company. It is the process through which the new salesperson learns values and norms of the company as well as how to perform various activities of the sales job.

❍ **Assortment** This refers to the range of choices offered in terms of brands, styles, models, colors, sizes, etc. (Also see **Merchandise depth**).

❍ **Attention, interest, desire, action (AIDA) formula** It is a sales presentation method, which uses a structured and well-known formula or steps, called AIDA, meaning attention, interest, desire, and action. A salesperson takes the buyer through these mental states in the buying process.

❍ **Attitudinal conflict** This refers to the disagreement on role, expectations, or perceptions between channel partners.

❍ **Avoidance** This refers to the style of conflict resolution where both channel members ignore or postpone decisions on the problem.

❍ **Bar codes** These are pre-printed bars on packages with unique identification to track goods in the supply chain.

❍ **Behaviorally anchored rating scales (BARS)** It is one of the methods used for evaluation of salespeople, in which salespersons' behavior is linked with specific results, which allows sales managers to arrive at more consistent and objective evaluations.

❍ **Benchmarking** Comparing performance of supply chain systems between companies to help adopt best practices.

❍ **Bill of lading (BOL)** It is the receipt for transport of goods by sea.

❍ **Bonus pack** A special package that provides extra quantity of a product to consumers at no extra charge over the regular price.

❍ **Bonus** It is a lump sum payment (a one-time payment) for an outstanding performance. It is also called performance bonus. Bonuses may be offered in the form of cash, merchandise, or free travel.

❍ **Bottom-up (or Build-up) approach** In this approach, the sales forecast is built from the grass-root level of salespersons and then these sales forecasts are combined at territory level and thereafter, from the territory level to the company level. In this approach, the sales forecasting methods used are, for example, the survey of buyers' intentions, and sales force composite.

❍ **Bounce-back coupons** These coupons are placed inside packages so that customers can redeem them later for repeat purchase of the brand.

❍ **Break bulk** This refers to converting large-quantity products to small lot sizes to make it suitable for buying by consumers.

❍ **Breakdown method** This method is used to decide the basic territories by equalizing the sales potential of territories by companies who have decided to have intensive distribution strategy, mostly for selling consumer products.

❍ **Brokers and agents** They do not take title to the goods but perform a limited range of functions of a wholesaler.

❍ **Browsing** This refers to looking at the various alternative products in an electronic retailing format.

❍ **Build-up method** This is another method used to decide the basic territories by equalizing the workload of the salespeople, and is commonly used by manufacturers of industrial products and services or by companies that want a selective distribution strategy.

❍ **Business games** These games are pre-programmed computer packages, which help in learning the impact of decision-making by allowing the sales trainees to make decisions on sales forecasting, pricing, advertising, and the like. Thereafter, the trainees are given a feedback regarding the outcomes of their decisions.

- **Business selling** Selling to a business customer, such as a government or a private sector organization.
- **Canned sales presentation** It is one of the methods of sales presentation, in which the salesperson makes a prepared or memorized presentation. It is also referred to as **stimulus response method**.
- **Capability gap** When a salesperson does not have the required knowledge, skills, or capabilities to become successful in the job, it is called a capability gap or deficiency in the salesperson.
- **Capacity** This refers to the continued successful performance given even at higher volumes of business.
- **Cash and carry wholesale** A channel member who sells to the trade on cash.
- **Catalog marketing** A company uses printed catalogs giving details of the product to sell directly to its customers.
- **Category** A distinct and manageable grouping of products that customers perceive as interrelated and interchangeable.
- **Channel conflict** Channel conflict is generated when actions of any channel member come in the way of the entire channel achieving its objective.
- **Channel control** This refers to the measurement of progress towards achieving the channel system objectives.
- **Channel coordination** Channel members work together to advance the goals of the channel rather than own, independent goals.
- **Channel dependence** It is a mix of the benefits derived by the channel members (utility) against the background of absence of alternatives (indispensability).
- **Channel formats** These are the various types of channel designs available for a set of goods or services.
- **Channel information system** This refers to the orderly flow of operational data within the firm and with its channel members for tracking results and improving performance of the channel system.
- **Channel position** This is the reputation a manufacturer acquires among the channel members.
- **Channel system** This refers to the bridge between the manufacturer and the end customer of the products or services offered by the company.
- **Clearing & forwarding agent (C&FA)** The channel partner who stocks goods and distributes to downstream channel partners.
- **Closing** It is one of the steps of the selling process, in which the salesperson helps the buyer to make a buying decision. It is also called **concluding the sale**, or **getting the purchase order** (or the order) from the customer.
- **Coercion power** It refers to the hint of punishment for the channel member who does not fall in line with the requirements of the system.
- **Collaboration** It refers to the style of conflict resolution where both parties jointly work to resolve the conflict to a win-win situation.
- **Collection** It is the process of acquiring and placing raw data.
- **Combination quotas** These are the goals set by companies to control the performance of the salespeople on key selling and non-selling activities by using points as a common measure.
- **Communication** This refers to keeping all players involved in working with logistics informed about the status of action.

❍ **Compensation mix** The method by which salespeople are paid is called a compensation mix, which includes elements like salaries, commission, bonus, and fringe benefits.

❍ **Competition power** This is the power that creates a healthy competition among channel members so that they try and out-perform each other.

❍ **Compromise** It refers to the style of conflict resolution where both parties to the dispute forego some points to arrive at an amicable solution.

❍ **Consistency** This term describes the channel network which delivers the same targeted level of service always without fail.

❍ **Consultative selling** It is one of the sales presentation methods in which salespeople or sales teams help customers solve their problems or fulfill their needs. The sales team works in collaborative relationship with the customer to achieve the strategic goals of the customer.

❍ **Contest** A type of consumer sales promotion in which consumers compete for prizes on the basis of skills or ability, and winners are determined by judging the entries based on certain criteria. A proof of purchase is usually required for the contest entry.

❍ **Continuous replenishment program (CRP)** This refers to the use of electronic scanners on retail shelves to inform the suppliers about the movement of their products off the shelves, so that they can replenish the stocks on the shelves.

❍ **Contractual VMS** This refers to the convenient arrangements made between channel members to exploit favorable opportunities and economies of scale.

❍ **Contribution approach** It is one of the methods used for profitability analysis of a marketing unit, in which only direct expenses are allocated to the marketing unit. Indirect expenses are not included. Profit contribution is equal to sales minus cost of goods sold minus direct selling expenses.

❍ **Control unit** It is a geographical unit, such as a metropolitan area, city, district or town that is used for territory analysis and design.

❍ **Controlling** It refers to ensuring that all operations are carried out within agreed, feasible parameters.

❍ **Convenience store** These are small stores normally located in residential areas offering a limited variety of fast moving goods.

❍ **Cooperative advertising** It is a trade-oriented sales promotion (or advertising program) in which a manufacturer pays a certain percentage (usually 50 percent) of the costs a retailer or distributor incurs for advertising the manufacturer's products in a local market area.

❍ **Copyright** Another form of intellectual property protection used for products like books, music, and software.

❍ **Corporate VMS** These are successive stages in production and distribution handled by one entity.

❍ **Countervailing power** Channel members are dependent on each other. For every power which one channel member uses on another, there could be a power which the target also can use.

❍ **Coupons** These are price-reduction certificates, offered by manufacturers and retailers to consumers on specific products, which can be redeemed (i.e. exchanged for a price-off or a discount) on a subsequent purchase.

❍ **Creative selling** It includes selling the company's product or service to existing and potential customers by providing a better solution to the customer's problem than that by a competitor.

❍ **Cross-ruff coupons** A coupon offer for one product that is placed in a package and redeemed by the purchase of another product. Both products should fit together and be used or consumed at the same time.

❍ **Culture** A set of common beliefs and shared values, customs, language, religion, music, and art.

- **Customer loyalty program** Programs organized by a store to increase the "stickiness" in its customers.
- **Customer relationship management (CRM)** It refers to software solutions that help companies manage customer information. It allows for effective management of the buyer-seller relationship.
- **Customer service goals** The service levels which a company may specify for key customers in particular.
- **Customer service** This refers to all activities required to make the transfer process of goods from producer to consumer more convenient and pleasurable.
- **Customer value** It is a sum of product value, service value, and image value for any retailer.
- **Dealer** They sell company products like a distributor but have no restrictions on territory or selling competitive products.
- **Decomposition** This is one of the methods of sales forecasting in which the company's previous periods of sales data are broken-down (or decomposed) into major components, such as trend, cycle, seasonal, and erratic events. These components are then recombined to forecast the sales for the future period.
- **Delphi method** In this method of forecasting, opinions (or forecasts) of the experts are taken by a coordinator separately, which are summarized and informed to the experts, who again give their opinions on the same matter. This process is continued till there is a near consensus.
- **Department store** A store that carries several product lines in different departments based on the category of the product.
- **Determining needs** These are the add-ons which a store provides to the customer and which become a distinct mark of the store.
- **Digital Payment methods** Electronic/mobile phone payment systems by which the customer or buyer can pay for the goods or services.
- **Direct selling** The company sells directly to its customers without the aid of any intermediaries.
- **Discount store** A store that has standard merchandise sold at low prices and at low margins.
- **Distribution channel** This refers to sets of independent organizations involved in the process of making a product or service available to customers for consumption.
- **Distribution depth** This refers to the quantity of each brand or pack sold into an outlet by the distributor.
- **Distribution management** This refers to the broad range of activities concerned with the efficient movement of finished goods from the end of the production line to the consumer.
- **Distribution objectives** This refers to the goals to meet the expectations of the customers in the most convenient manner to them.
- **Distribution warehouse** A network of warehouses located closest to the customer's location to service markets better at a minimum cost.
- **Distribution width** This refers to the number of brands or packs of a company sold into an outlet by the distributor.
- **Distributor** They are the channel members who buy goods from the company for redistribution to wholesalers, retailers, or institutions.
- **Domain conflict** The channel members understand responsibilities and authorities differently.
- **Econometric analysis** This is another method of forecasting sales in which many regression equations are built to forecast industry sales, general economic conditions, or future events, with the help of computer hardware and software.
- **Effectiveness** It is the analysis of how well the channel system meets its objectives consistently.

❍ **Efficiency** It is the effort required to achieve a desired service output level using minimum resources.

❍ **Efficient consumer response (ECR)** The system of correctly identifying the customer's demand in time, and meeting it promptly.

❍ **Electronic channels** The use of the Internet to sell products or services to the consumer.

❍ **Electronic data interchange (EDI)** Electronically connecting suppliers, production units, field distribution centers, and key customers for exchanging data and information.

❍ **Electronic retailing** This refers to shopping on the Internet without having to visit a physical store.

❍ **Employee referral program or scheme** It is one of the methods of locating sales recruits and includes the company employees referring or recommending known persons for hiring for sales positions. The program or scheme states the extent of monetary rewards given to the employees whose referred persons are hired and also indicates the initial performance goals to be achieved by the new recruits.

❍ **EPSS (Electronic Performance Support System)** This system improves on the traditional computer-based training, by making a large amount of information available to the salesperson immediately and in a personalized manner.

❍ **Equitable distribution** When a set of goods is in short supply, this system ensures that all customers get a supply at least in proportion to their normal purchases.

❍ **E-selling** Selling products and services through the Internet.

❍ **Ethics or Business ethics** Ethics is defined as the moral principles and values that govern the behavior of a person or group with respect to what is right or wrong. Business ethics deal largely with the relationship between business practices and the moral concept of right and wrong.

❍ **Evaluation** It is the review of the results achieved after any operational activity.

❍ **Event marketing** A type of consumer promotion where a company or brand supports an event (a sports or social activity) for promoting a product or service, and creating experiences for consumers.

❍ **Event sponsorship** A type of consumer promotion whereby a company develops sponsorship relations with a specific event like a sport or a musical concert.

❍ **Exclusive distribution** Making a product available in one or two outlets only. Exclusive for one company brands only. This is done especially in cases of specialty goods.

❍ **Executive opinion** In this method of forecasting, the views of the senior executives of the company are obtained for forecasting the sales.

❍ **Expectancy theory** This theory from Vroom is based on the assumption that Salespeople have expectations about what they should receive from their employers as a result of their work efforts.

❍ **Expense plan** A system that reimburses salespeople for their food, lodging, travel, entertainment and any other legitimate expenses incurred while on the job.

❍ **Expense quotas** These are the targets or goals aimed at controlling selling expenses of marketing (or sales) units like sales territories and salespeople. Often expense quotas are stated as percentages of sales, so as to bring them in-line with sales volume.

❍ **Expert power** It is the special knowledge possessed by one channel member, which can be beneficial to the others in the channel system.

❍ **Exponential smoothing** This is a forecasting method in which the forecaster can allow sales in certain periods to influence the sales forecast more than the sales in other periods, by using a smoothing constant (L) in the equation: sales forecast for next period = (L) (actual sales of this period) + (I-L) (this period's sales forecast).

- **Extranets** Producers use these systems to share information with channel partners.
- **Felt conflict** Also known as **affective conflict** as the discord starts hurting the channel system results.
- **Financial flow** The investment in the goods made by the channel till it reaches the final consumer or end-user.
- **Financial support** This refers to help by providing monetary support to complete the transaction process to send the product to the end users.
- **Footfalls** The number of people who visit a store on any given day.
- **Foreign direct investment (FDI)** Investment permitted to foreign retailers to invest in retail business in India.
- **Forfaiting** Means of minimizing payment risk by selling the receivable to a bank or a financial intermediary for an agreed discount, usually on a non-recourse basis.
- **Formula method** It is one of the methods of sales presentation in which the salesperson uses a structured formula, like AIDA. It is also referred to as **formulated approach** or **mental states selling approach**.
- **Forward buying** A practice whereby retailers and wholesalers buy more quantity and stock up on a product that is offered by a manufacturer at a lower price during the sales promotion period and resell it to consumers after the manufacturer's promotional period has ended.
- **Franchise arrangement** A contractual arrangement between a producer and a retailer to sell the producer's products exclusively.
- **Franchise** A form of license where the user company (franchisee) uses the name of the franchisor to provide services—hotels, food industry.
- **Frequency program** A frequency program, also called **loyalty or continuity program**, that rewards customers for repeat purchases of the same brand of a product or service over a period of time.
- **Full service wholesaler** They carry stock, manage a sales force, offer credit, make deliveries, and provide management assistance.
- **Full truck load (FTL)** A complete truck load of goods, which is normally about 9 tons, sent by road.
- **Full-cost approach** Also called as **net profit approach,** it allocates all marketing costs (both direct and indirect), in addition to the cost of goods sold (production costs), to the marketing unit, such as a sales territory, a product or a market segment, which is, under study of profitability analysis.
- **Functional aspects** The aspects of a store design that take care of the convenience of the shopper including easy access, placement, information, and displays of the products.
- **Goal conflict** It refers to the difference between the objectives of the channel members.
- **Goods and Services Tax (GST)** One indirect tax on goods and services across India subsuming many indirect taxes like excise, sales tax, value added tax, entry tax etc. Has come into effect from July 01, 2017.
- **Gross margin return on inventory** The multiple of the gross margin and the ratio of sales to inventory.
- **Hedge inventory** The inventory built up of a volatile price commodity when prices are most favorable.
- **Hedging** Means of minimizing risks by taking an opposite position; usually used in foreign exchange.
- **Hertzberg's dual-factor theory** In this theory, sources of dissatisfaction are called hygiene factors and the sources of satisfaction are called motivational factors. For a salesperson to feel motivated, factors like recognition, responsibility, and opportunity for growth (work related factors) must be present. Absence of hygiene factors (such as working conditions, supervision, company policies and interpersonal relationships that are related to working conditions) can cause dissatisfaction.

- **High-value goods** Goods where the possible gain from making comparisons is large compared to the time, effort and mental discomfort involved.
- **Hiring** In this stage, the company makes a job offer to the applicant. It concludes with the acceptance of the job offer by the applicant.
- **Horizontal conflict** The conflict that arises between channels at the same level as in between distributors.
- **Horizontal marketing system** These refer to two or more unrelated companies working together using the marketing channel to benefit both.
- **Hybrid channels conflict** Two different channels working with the same set of customers can get into this kind of conflict.
- **Hybrid channels** It refers to the use of multiple channels to reach different customer segments.
- **Inbound logistics** It is the receiving, storage, and issue of inputs to the production system.
- **Incremental method** For calculating the optimum (most favorable) size of the sales force, incremental method is used in which additions are made to salespersons until incremental revenue from the last salesperson is equal to or more than the salesperson's incremental cost.
- **Information flow** This refers to a two-way data or information flow between a set of channel partners and the firm they are working with.
- **Ingredient sponsored cooperative advertising** This advertising is supported by manufacturers of raw materials and/or components whose objective is to help their customers to promote or establish the end products that include the ingredients (i.e., parts or raw materials) supplied by the manufacturers. For example, "Intel inside" cooperative advertising fund is offered by Intel to all personal computer (PC) makers.
- **Inside salespeople** To reduce time demands on outside salespeople, many companies are using inside salespeople, such as sales assistants, technical support people, and telemarketers, who perform certain tasks by remaining within the company.
- **Instrumentality** It shows the degree to which a salesperson believes that higher performance will lead to some kind of reward.
- **Integrated marketing communications (IMC)** It is the strategic integration of various marketing communications tools, such as advertising, sales promotion, personal selling, public relations, publicity, and direct marketing. The objectives of IMC are cost effectiveness, strong message with clarity, consistency, maximum impact, and achievement of the desired communications goals.
- **Integrity** Channel does business in a fair and honest manner.
- **Intellectual Property Rights** The right which enables the creator of a unique product or process to benefit by allowing the person exclusive rights to manufacture the product or use the process. They could be licensed to others on agreed terms. Examples—designs, software, music, and so on.
- **Intensive distribution** This refers to making the product available in as many outlets as possible.
- **Intermediaries** They are all middlemen or channel partners between producers and consumers.
- **Inventory norm** It is the targeted level of inventory to be held in any material.
- **Inventory turns** It is the value of business which the inventory holding helps generate.
- **Job analysis** A formal study conducted by a company to identify job duties and responsibilities, and also the important activities to be performed by a salesperson.
- **Job description** A formal written statement describing the detailed account of the job, including job title, responsibilities, location, and requirements.

- **Job qualifications or specifications** The company sets certain qualifications or specifications that are necessary in an applicant for the successful performance of the job.
- **Key accounts** These are important customers having large sales and profit potential. They are also referred to as major accounts, national accounts, corporate accounts, house accounts, and global accounts.
- **Latent conflict** Some amount of discord exists between channel members but does not affect working relationships or results.
- **Leadership** It is the ability to influence other people towards the achievement of specific objectives and goals. Leadership ability can be learnt.
- **Lean thinking** The concept in the supply chain which ensures goods are produced in quantities just in line with customer needs.
- **Legalistic power** The power or influence derived from contracts or written agreements.
- **Legitimate power** This is enforcing any task expected of the intermediary as per the agreement or contract signed with the company.
- **Leisure shopper** A shopper who visits the store for leisure or entertainment, without any purchase in mind.
- **License** Permission given by a company to another company to use its trademark, process or product design for use in specific markets on payment of an agreed fee.
- **Limited service wholesaler** They offer a limited range of services.
- **Line position or line authority** It means any person in the management position has a formal power or authority to direct and control immediate subordinates.
- **Liner conference** This is a group of carriers operating two or more vessels in international waters.
- **Logistics management** This refers to the planning, implementation, and controlling of materials and information flows within the company.
- **Logistics** A business planning framework for the management of materials, service, information, and capital flows.
- **Lot size inventory** Inventory built up to avail the price discounts on fixed quantities as specified by vendors.
- **Lot size** This refers to the most convenient size of the product which the customer can buy at a time.
- **Low-value goods** Goods where the possible gain from making comparisons is small compared to the time, effort, and mental discomfort involved.
- **Mail order wholesalers** They sell to small retailers and industrial users through catalogues.
- **Management by objectives (MBO)** An evaluation method in which the sales manager and the salesperson discuss and agree on the salesperson's specific objectives, goals, and an action plan. They evaluate or review the actual performance against the objectives periodically and take corrective actions, if needed.
- **Manifest conflict** It refers to the conflict between channel members which has escalated to a stage of open confrontation or blocking of each other's efforts.
- **Manufacturer's agents** They are independent wholesaling salesmen or manufacturer's representatives selling on commission basis for several manufacturers of related but non-competing products. For example, all plumbing accessories.
- **Market domain conflict** This refers to the conflict that arises out of doubts on which channel member is to cover which markets.
- **Market forecast** It is the expected market demand or industry sales forecast of a given product or service at one specific level of industry marketing expenditure, in a given market, for a specific period of time.

❍ **Market potential** It is the best possible (or maximum) estimated demand for a given product or service for the entire industry, in a given market, for a specific period of time.

❍ **Marketing audit** It is a comprehensive, periodic, and systematic examination of a company's marketing plan and environment, objectives, strategies, tactics, performance, organizational structure, and people with a view to find out opportunities and problems, and recommend an action plan to improve the company's marketing performance.

❍ **Marketing channels** This refers to networks through which a producer's goods reach the end-user.

❍ **Marketing cost analysis** It is the study of a company's marketing costs. The purpose of marketing cost analysis is to determine profitability of marketing units like market segments, sales territories, and products.

❍ **Maslow's hierarchy of needs** Maslow proposed five levels of needs that every individual seeks to satisfy. These needs form a hierarchy. As per this theory, unless lower order needs (like physiological needs of food, clothing, and shelter) are satisfied, the higher order needs (like esteem needs of status and recognition) will not be aroused.

❍ **Materials handling** This refers to the function of managing inventory along with storage and transfer of information.

❍ **Mediation** This refers to the use of parties friendly to both channel members in a dispute to help resolve the problem.

❍ **Merchandise depth** This refers to the number of brands, models or styles carried by a retailer for each product category. (Also see **Assortment**).

❍ **Merchandise width** This refers to the number of non-competing products offered by a retailer for sale.

❍ **Merchandising** These refer to the efforts put by the salesperson for display of the products in each outlet, maximizing shelf space, and skillful use of point-of-purchase materials.

❍ **Missionary salespeople** They provide product information and promote goodwill about the product and the company. They do not ask for orders. Medical representatives from pharmaceutical industry are good example of missionary salespeople.

❍ **Motivation** Desire to spend effort to satisfy a need is motivation. In a sales job, motivation is the effort a salesperson makes to complete various activities of the job.

❍ **Motivational mix** It consists of various motivational tools or methods used by sales managers to motivate salespeople. These are financial rewards and non-financial rewards.

❍ **Moving averages method** In this method of sales forecasting, the moving averages of the company sales of the previous periods are calculated for forecasting the sales of the future periods. When a sales forecast is developed for the next period, the sales in the oldest period is dropped from the averages and is replaced by sales in the newest period and hence the name "moving averages".

❍ **Multi-channel marketing system** A firm uses two or more channels to reach different segments of its market.

❍ **Naive or Ratio method** It is a sales forecasting method, which is based on the assumption that what happened in the immediate past will continue to happen in the immediate future. The formula is:

$$\text{Sales forecast for next year} = \frac{\text{Actual sales of this year} \times \text{Actual sales of this year}}{\text{Actual sales of last year}}$$

❍ **Non-verbal communication** It is driven by our subconscious and consists of posture, gesture, eye-contact, facial expressions, and overall grooming.

- **Number of days' supplies** The number of days' production or sales which a particular level of inventory holding can service.
- **Objective and task method** This method is used for allocating the expenditure budget to the various items or categories of selling expenses. The procedure includes deciding the sales volume objective, and the tasks or activities to be carried out to achieve the objective. Then, the costs of carrying out the tasks are estimated. The sales manager reviews sales revenue, costs, and profits figures until he is satisfied with the sales and profit objectives, tasks and budgeted costs or expenditures.
- **On-time, in-full (OTIF)** The ability to dispatch orders in full and on-time—one of the measures of the performance of a supply chain.
- **Operational planning** It is concerned with forecasting and putting in the resources to achieve the forecasts.
- **Operations management** It focuses on day-to-day activities or issues, such as revenue, costs, and profits through various activities or functions like sales, marketing, production and human resources.
- **Order cycle time** The time elapsed between a customer placing an order and when he receives the goods as per the order.
- **Order processing** Part of the logistics or the supply chain function in the company which facilitates dispatch of a customer order
- **Orders filled completely** No Stock Keeping Units in the glossary of the order is missed out but all are dispatched in full.
- **Outbound logistics** It refers to collecting, storing, dispatching, and physically distributing finished goods to the marketing channels
- **Outsourcing** When a company decides to let an external agency take over and handle a function or a process—marketing, HR, and advertising.
- **Owner's Risk** Goods dispatched by rail, where the railways do not accept liability for any damage or loss to the goods. The owner of the goods is solely responsible for any losses.
- **Partnering (or Collaborative) relationship** A type of relationship marketing in which a selling organization works continuously with its high-sales and profit-potential customer to improve the customer performance in terms of operations, sales, and profits.
- **Patent** A form of intellectual property protection—usually used for designs or formulations.
- **Payment flow** The consideration paid for taking the title of the goods. This is normally the price of the goods and services and all applicable taxes.
- **Payment gateway** This refers to the provision for paying for goods bought on the Internet.
- **Perceived conflict** Channel members become aware of the opposition but go about their tasks in a business-like manner.
- **Perception conflict** Channel members' understanding of the environment and actions are different.
- **Personal Digital Assistants** Hand held mobile devices which can be used by company or channel salespeople to complete the sales transactions at the retail points.
- **Physical flow** This deals with the storage and transportation of the goods.
- **Place utility** This refers to making the product available to the consumer where he wants it.
- **Planning** This refers to the designing the activities in the right sequence.
- **Plateau salesperson** The salesperson who has almost stopped improving and developing, following a period of progress.

- **Point-of-purchase (POP) promotion** A display or demonstration of products or brands that takes place at the point of purchase or sale in a retail store.
- **Positioning** The manner in which the retailer wants to "present" himself to his customers.
- **Possession utility** This refers to facilitating transfer of ownership of the product from the producer to the end user.
- **Power** The ability of one channel member to influence another.
- **Pre-approach** This is one of the steps in the selling process in which the salesperson collects information about the prospect and plans the sales call on the prospect. It is also called **pre-call planning**.
- **Premium** A gift or incentive offered to consumers by a manufacturer after purchasing a particular product or brand.
- **Primary sales** The sales made from a company to its distributors.
- **Processing** The process of analyzing the data to get meaning out of it.
- **Productive call** These refer to every call where a sale takes place.
- **Productivity analysis** Productivity is usually measured by ratios between outputs and inputs, like sales per salesperson. One main benefit of productivity analysis is that productivity ratios can be compared directly across the sales organization levels within the company (for example, branch offices) and also with other sales organizations.
- **Profit contribution quotas** These are goals or targets that are worked out by subtracting the costs of sales or costs of goods sold (that is equivalent to the cost of manufacturing the product) and salespersons' direct selling expenses (such as salaries, travelling, lodging, boarding, and customer entertainment) from sales volume (or sales revenue).
- **Profitability** It is a measure of financial efficiency that is determined by subtracting costs from sales revenue of a company.
- **Promotion flow** This refers to the advertising and other support given by the firm to help the channel reach the product to its end-user.
- **Prospecting** It is the process of identifying potential customers for the company's products and services.
- **Qualifying needs** These are the basic needs of the customer which the store is expected to fulfill.
- **Qualifying** The probable prospect, the suspect or the sales lead is qualified as a prospect or potential customer if the person or the firm has a need for the company's product or service, the authority to make the buying decision, and the financial resources to buy.
- **Quick Response Logistics (QRL)** This refers to the planning of the entire logistics activity based on point-of-sale (POS) data.
- **Rack jobbers** They "display" and sell products not normally carried by retailers. They sell by visiting retailers and studying their shelves.
- **Radio frequency identification (RFID)** Radio frequency waves to track items, people, equipment, etc., in real time without the need for contact or "line-of-sight".
- **Railway's Risk** Goods dispatched by rail where the railways accept liability for any damage or loss to the goods.
- **Rebate** A consumer sales promotion in which a manufacturer refunds or gives back a part of the purchase price to the consumer after the receipt of the proof of purchase from the consumer. The term rebate and refund are used as synonyms.

- **Recruitment** It includes activities and processes to get individuals who will apply for the job. The purpose of recruitment is to provide a pool of job applicants from where the company selects the right persons.
- **Redistribution** This refers to buying of goods from the manufacturer by a distributor for further distribution to retail or consumption points.
- **Reference check** References are the names of persons from whom information can be obtained regarding an applicant's ability and character. Reference check means the checking done by the company from the references provided by the applicant about the applicant's ability and character by an e-mail, telephone, or a personal visit.
- **Reference power** Power derived from association with a highly reputed channel partner.
- **Referent power** This emanates out of the eminent position that the company holds in the industry.
- **Refresher training** It includes continuous training of experienced salespeople to overcome deficiencies, and also retraining of salespersons whose job requirements have changed due to promotion or other reasons.
- **Regression analysis** It is a statistical method of sales forecasting that derives an equation based on relationship between the company sales (dependent variable, x) and independent variables, or predictors (y_1, y_2, etc.) which influence the sales. If there is one independent variable, it is called simple (or linear) regression analysis and if there are two or more independent variables, it is called multiple regression analysis.
- **Relationship marketing or Relationship selling** This refers to the process by which a firm builds a long-term relationship with its customer for mutual benefits, in order to create a customer loyalty. In relationship selling, which is a part of relationship marketing, salespeople concentrate their team selling efforts on building trust and superior service on a few carefully selected customers (or key accounts) over a long period of time with the aim of becoming the preferred or sole supplier.
- **Reliability** The company can make promises about delivery to customers knowing that the promise will be definitely met by the channel system.
- **Response selling or Stimulus response selling** A method of selling in which the salesperson tries to get favorable responses from the customer by providing stimuli or clues such as statements, questions, actions, audiovisual presentations, and demonstrations. The salesperson continues the process until he gets a positive purchase decision.
- **Retailer** The last link in the distribution chain. He interacts directly with the end user.
- **Retailing** All activities involved in selling or renting goods or services to ultimate consumers for personal consumption.
- **Return on assets managed (ROAM)** Assets managed for a sales unit include inventory, accounts receivables, or any other assets at each sales organizational level (like a branch, district, or regional office).

$$\text{Return on assets managed} = \left(\frac{\text{Profit contribution}}{\text{sales}}\right) \times \left(\frac{\text{Sales}}{\text{Assets managed}}\right)$$

- **Reverse logistics** Getting back materials for reuse, disposal, recycling, or reprocessing purposes.
- **Reward power** Benefit derived by a channel member for conforming to behavior in line with the channel system.
- **Risk bearing** The wholesaler invests in the goods he is selling, and hence takes the risk associated with any price change.

- **Routing** It is a travel route taken by a salesperson for making customer calls in a territory.
- **Safety stock** This refers to the minimum stock level to be maintained to take care of all uncertainties.
- **Sales analysis** It is a detailed inspection of a company's sales data, which includes collecting, classifying, comparing, and drawing conclusions. It is used by sales managers to evaluate performance, take corrective actions, and do future planning.
- **Sales audit** It is a comprehensive, systematic, diagnostic, and prescriptive tool that is used to assess whether a firm's sales management process is adequate, and to give direction for improvement of sales performance and to recommend the needed changes.
- **Sales contest** A sales competition among the company salespeople or retailers' salespeople. Those who achieve or exceed their sales targets (or quotas) win cash or other prizes.
- **Sales force automation** This reduces manual working, speeds up systems and releases more time for salespeople on actual selling efforts.
- **Sales force composite method** In this sales forecasting method, each salesperson estimates sales of the company's products and services for the forecast period. The sales estimates are made by the salesperson based on how much quantity or value each existing and prospective customer will buy of each of the company's products and services in his or her territory. The company's sales forecast is made up (or composite) of all the salespersons' sales forecasts.
- **Sales forecast or the Company sales forecast** It is the estimated company sales of a given product or service, under a proposed marketing plan, in a given market, for a specified time period.
- **Sales management** It is defined as the management of personal selling part of a company's marketing plan or the management of the company's sales force.
- **Sales potential or the Company's sales potential** It is the best possible (or maximum) estimated sales or demand for a given product or service of a company, in a given geographic area, for a specific period of time. It is also defined as the maximum share (or percentage) of the market potential that is expected to be achieved by a company.
- **Sales professionalism** A customer-oriented approach that uses truthful and straight-forward ways to satisfy the long-term needs of both the customer and the selling firm.
- **Sales promotion** It is one of the components of communication-mix or promotional-mix, which includes various tools, mostly short-term, to encourage quicker or greater purchase of particular products or services by consumers or intermediaries through the offer of incentives such as samples, coupons, prizes, sweepstakes, rebates, and so on.
- **Sales quotas or Quotas** These are the sales goals or performance standards set by a company for its sales units like salespersons, sales territories, and sales regions.
- **Sales territory** It consists of a group of present and potential customers in a geographic area assigned to a salesperson. The territory may or may not have a geographic boundary. However, generally, a salesperson is assigned to a geographical area consisting of present and potential customers.
- **Sales volume budget** It is the detailed estimate of expected sales volume and selling expenses for the company's products and services, for the budget period. The sales volume budget is generally set slightly lower than the sales forecast to avoid excessive risk.
- **Sales volume quotas** These are the sales goals or targets, expressed in rupees (or dollars) and product units (like numbers or tons), that are set for marketing units (such as salespersons, distributors, geographical territories, and products) for a specific period of time.

- **Samples or Sampling** Sampling (or a sample) is a new product given free or for a nominal price to consumers to encourage trials. Satisfied consumers may become regular buyers.
- **Scheduling** It is planning a salesperson's specific time of visits to customers.
- **Secondary freight** The freight cost incurred for dispatching finished goods from a company depot or C&FA to its distributors.
- **Secondary sales** These sales are made by the distributors to their customers. This is a true indicator of the off-take of the products.
- **Security deposit** These are deposits given by the distributor to the company to protect the company against any defaults by the distributor.
- **Segmentation** This refers to the kind of consumers the retailer wants to service.
- **Selection process** It consists of a number of tools or steps which are used by a manager to help in selecting the applicants that are best suited for a position.
- **Selective distribution** This refers to making the product available in a few selective outlets only. (Also see **Exclusive distribution**).
- **Self-liquidating premium** A premium that requires consumers to pay some or all of the cost of the premium plus handling and mailing costs.
- **Selling agents** They handle the entire marketing tasks for their principles. They may operate nationally with a range of competing products.
- **Service deliverables** This refers to the level of service demanded by target customers from a channel system for a given product category.
- **Shopping basket** These are all the items which form the average buying of a shopper in a retail store.
- **Situational leadership** It means the sales manager who has the ability to use the leadership style (transformational or transactional) that fits the situation in hand and the salesperson.
- **Social aspects** These aspects of a store design relate to image, ambience and attractiveness
- **Social responsibility** It is the obligation of management to make decisions and take actions that will help in the welfare and interest of the society and the company.
- **Socialization** It is the process through which the new salespersons learn values, norms, and behavior of people who are already working in the organization.
- **Solution vendor** A sales position in which a salesperson has expertise in solving a customer's problems with the company's products and services.
- **Source of conflict** The reason or situation that generates the conflict.
- **Span of control** It means the number of individuals reporting to a manager.
- **Spatial convenience** Facilitating the customer to buy his desired product from an outlet of his choice.
- **Spatial discrepancy** This refers to bridging the distance gap between the production point of a product or service and its consumption point.
- **Speciality store** These stores carry a narrow product line with a deep assortment.
- **Speciality wholesaler** They handle only one chosen set of goods like fruits and vegetables.
- **Specialty advertising or Promotional novelties** Promotional gifts like pens, calendars, T-shirts, and so on that have the advertiser's name, logo, and/or message imprinted. These are given free to customers during festive seasons to strengthen business relationships.
- **Specialty goods** These refer to high value unique goods where the comparisons between different brands is almost mandatory before making purchases.

- **Staff position or staff authority** It is the position with staff authority, which allows a person to advise, recommend or counsel in his area of expertise.
- **Staffing** It is a process consisting of five stages, i.e., planning, recruiting, selecting, hiring and socialization of salespeople within a company.
- **Standard Industrial Classification system (SIC)** It is the United Nations' system for classifying economic data, in which it first categorizes the economy into different divisions (denoted by a letter code), then each division is divided into major-industry groups (denoted by two-digit code), each major-industry group is further subdivided into industry groups (denoted by three-digit code) and each industry group is further subdivided into elementary activities or product categories (four-digit code). Each four-digit SIC code provides information about organizations that are subclassified by location, annual sales, number of employees and net worth. The SIC system is used for identifying prospective customers in each market.
- **Stickiness** This aspect of a store popularity is measured by the number of customers who keep coming back to the store for their purchases.
- **Stimulus response method** The assumption made in this method is that if a salesperson makes the right stimuli (i.e., sales presentation), he can get a favorable response from the prospect. It is also called **canned approach**, or a **memorized sales talk**.
- **Stock turnover ratio** This is the value of revenue generated divided by the average inventory held by the store.
- **Stockist** They may work with one company in a designated territory but do not redistribute goods.
- **Storage** Keeping the data intact till it is needed.
- **Store ambience** This refers to the pleasing shopping atmosphere created by a store.
- **Strategic business unit (SBU)** A large and multi-business company divides its businesses into parts to make strategic analysis and planning easy. These parts are called "business units" or "strategic business units" (SBUs). Each SBU meets the market needs with its product(s) and service(s) and is managed by a person responsible for strategic planning and profit performance.
- **Strategic planning** It consists of making decisions on the company's long-term objectives and strategies. Strategic planning demands action in three key areas: (i) managing the company's businesses as an investment portfolio, (ii) assessing the strengths and weaknesses of each business unit or SBU, (iii) developing strategies for achieving the long-term objectives.
- **Structural conflict** Discord between channel members based on tangible and well-articulated causes.
- **Supermarket** These are large, low-cost, low-margin, high-volume, self-service operation with a wide offering.
- **Supervision** It is directing of the day-to-day activities of salespeople. The objective of supervision is to improve job performances of salespeople.
- **Supplier–relationship management** This refers to the processes of the flow of materials and information between the company and its suppliers.
- **Supply chain integration** The process of optimizing the supply chain by supplier and customer involvement to integrate processes, policies, systems, database and strategies between diverse trading partners.
- **Supply chain management (SCM)** The process of planning, implementing, controlling the efficient and cost effective flow and storage of raw materials, finished goods and related information from the point of origin to the point of consumption for the purpose of conforming to customer requirements.
- **Support power** The company provides financial or other support to the better performing channel partners to induce the others to do better.
- **Survey of buyer's intentions** It is a method of sales forecasting. It is also called as marketing research or survey method. In this method, the existing and potential customers are asked about their

likely purchases of the company's products and services, during the forecast period. This information can be obtained by means of personal interviews, telephone surveys, e-mail surveys or other methods.

- **Suspect** A person or a business firm that is a sales lead or a probable prospect is also called a "suspect"; they become the prospect, if the individual or the business firm needs the product or service, has an ability to make a decision, and the financial capacity to buy.
- **Sweepstakes** A consumer sales promotion in which consumers submit their names for selection of prizes and winners are determined by chance. A proof of purchase as a condition for entry is not required here.
- **T-account close** This method or technique is used by some salespeople to close the sales by drawing a large T on a piece of paper and writing the benefits and the drawbacks on the left and right sides respectively.
- **Target service level** The customer service goals of a logistics system.
- **Task focused shopper** A shopper who visits the store after planning his purchases
- **Team selling approach** Companies often use multiple-person sales teams to deal with multiple-person buying centers (or purchase committees) of their customers. The multiple individuals in the sales team are from different functional areas, such as marketing, sales, manufacturing, design and physical distribution.
- **Technical selling (or Technical support salespeople)** Technical specialist, sometimes, a part of sales team or a type of inside salespeople, to provide technical information and answers to customer's questions. They may assist in design, specification preparation, installation, training customer's employees and technical service.
- **Temporal discrepancy** This refers to bridging the time gap between the production point of a product or service and its consumption point.
- **Territory** These refer to the designated areas for the distributor to focus on coverage and distribution.
- **Test marketing** This is a forecasting method that measures consumer acceptance of a new product. This is done by estimating the sales or demand for a new product or service in a small representative market, which is extrapolated over the total market to estimate the total demand for the product. It helps a company to become aware of how much is the market demand and also how customers and intermediaries respond to using, handling, and repurchasing of the new product or service. The major methods used for consumer-product market testing are: (i) full-blown test markets, (ii) controlled test marketing, and (iii) simulated test marketing. For industrial products, the methods used are: (i) alpha testing (i.e., testing within the company) and (ii) beta testing (i.e., testing with outside customers).
- **Theory of natural selection** This refers to the influence of environmental factors based on which the retail organizes itself.
- **Time utility** This refers to making the product available to the consumer when he wants it.
- **Title flow** It can also be called as ownership flow. This is when the ownership of title of the goods passes from one entity to the other.
- **Top-down or Break-down approach** In this approach, the company sales forecast is developed at the business unit level by using suitable forecasting methods. Thereafter, the head of sales and marketing breakdowns the company's sales forecast into the sales goals for each region, district, territory, salesperson, and customer. The different sales forecasting methods used are executive opinion, moving averages, exponential smoothing, and regression analysis.
- **Trade promotions** Trade-oriented sales promotions that are directed at the traders (i.e., resellers like distributors, wholesalers, dealers, and retailers) to carry stock, promote and sell (or push) a product to the customers.
- **Trademark** A symbol, or logo, or name, or tagline which distinguishes a company's products and is to be used exclusively by the company.

- **Trading area** The "catchment" area of a store from where most of its customers come.
- **Trading or retail format** The total physical and service factors of the store which give it its image or personality
- **Tramp services** This refers to the unorganized shipping services.
- **Transactional leadership** Describes those supervisory activities that relate to the day-to-day operations and control of the salespeople. Sales managers who are transactional leaders provide verbal feedback in terms of appreciation and criticism to their salespersons.
- **Transactional selling** A type of selling in which salespeople make one-time sale to price-oriented customers, who are not contacted again.
- **Transformational leadership** These leaders transform or change the basic values, beliefs, and attitudes of their followers such that the followers are willing to perform at levels above and beyond expectations. Such leaders are also referred to as "charismatic leaders". They make worthwhile difference in the performance of their followers.
- **Trial close** It is one of the steps in the sales process in which the salesperson checks the opinion of the prospect about the product or service by asking certain questions. If the response is favorable, the salesperson closes the sale.
- **Truck wholesalers** They operate from rolling warehouses and sell from them a limited line of products. A distributor visiting rural markets with ready stocks would be a good example.
- **Use** This refers to the application of the information for management's decision making.
- **Valence** It is the value placed on a particular reward by a salesperson.
- **Value (or Customer value)** This refers to benefits minus cost or benefits divided by costs. In other words, it is the worth of a market offering which may include economic, technical, serviceable, social, and emotional benefits that is received by a customer in exchange for the price (or costs) the customer pays (or incurs) for the market offering.
- **Variety** The different kinds of goods or services offered by a retailer. (Also see **Merchandise width**).
- **Vendor managed inventory (VMI)** This refers to the arrangement by which a supplier maintains inventory on behalf of his customers.
- **Vertical conflict** Channels at two different levels get into this kind of conflict. Frequently it is a domain or perception conflict.
- **Vertical integration** One organization does all the work relating to production of goods, marketing and distribution.
- **Vertical marketing system (VMS)** Channel entities band together to deliver services to the customers.
- **Waiting time** Time elapsed between the desire in the customer to buy the product and the time when he can actually buy it.
- **Wheel of retailing** Traces the manner in which retail firms change during their life time.
- **Wholesaler** A person or firm that buys merchandise and resells it either to retailers for subsequent resale to the consumer or to a business firm for industrial and business use.
- **Workload method** To calculate the size of the sales force, one of the methods used is workload method, in which an assumption is made that all salespeople will have equal quantity of workload.
- **Zero channel level** This channel system is a direct distribution system where the firm directly sends the product or service to the end-user without any intermediary.
- **Zone of indifference** Channel members accept orders from other channel members without becoming conscious of the authority.

Index